FIFTH EDITION

LESLY'S
HANDBOOK

of *Public Relations*
and *Communications*

Other Books by Philip Lesly

Public Relations: Principles and Procedures (with T. R. Sills)

Public Relations in Action

Everything and the Kitchen Sink

The People Factor: Managing the Human Climate

How We Discommunicate

Selections from Managing the Human Climate

Ahead of Time

Overcoming Opposition: A Survival Manual for Executives

Bonanzas and Fool's Gold

FIFTH EDITION

LESLY'S
HANDBOOK
of Public Relations
and Communications

PHILIP LESLY, EDITOR

CB
CONTEMPORARY BOOKS

Library of Congress Cataloging-in-Publication Data

Lesly's handbook of public relations and communications / edited by
   Philip Lesly. — 5th ed.
       p.   cm.
   Includes index.
   ISBN 0-8442-3257-2 (alk. paper)
    1. Public relations—Handbooks, manuals, etc. I. Lesly, Philip,
1918–   .
HM263.L472   1997
659.2—dc21   96-40864
                                     CIP

Interior design by Terry Stone

Published by NTC Business Books
An imprint of NTC/Contemporary Publishing Company
Copyright © 1998 by NTC/Contemporary Publishing Company
4255 West Touhy Avenue, Lincolnwood (Chicago), Illinois 60646-1975 U.S.A.
Manufactured in the United States of America
International Standard Book Number: 0-8442-3257-2

18   17   16   15   14   13   12   11   10   9   8   7   6   5   4   3   2   1

CONTENTS

Section 3
ANALYSIS, RESEARCH, AND
PLANNING   275

Section 6
THE PRACTICE OF PUBLIC RELATIONS   683

Advisory Board

Ann H. Barkelew

John F. Budd

Thomas E. Burke

J. Kenneth Clark

Dr. Ray E. Hiebert

Stephen J. Kaye

Michael M. Klepper

Robert L. Lauer

Dr. Otto Lerbinger

Craig Lesly

Mary Ann Pires

Steven R. Polcyn, Jr.

Dr. Albert Walker

Dr. Frank W. Wylie

Contributors

Richard A. Armstrong
Past President of the Public Affairs Council

John N. Bailey
Past Executive Director of the International Association of Business Communicators

J. Carroll Bateman
Past President of the Insurance Information Institute

Don Bates
Sumner Rider & Associates

Herbert M. Baus
Public Relations Counsel

Herb B. Berkowitz
Vice President, Public Relations, for Heritage Foundation, Inc.

Richard Bevan
Towers, Perrin, Forster & Crosby, Inc.

Mace Broide
Past Executive Director of the Committee on the Budget of the U.S. House of Representatives

Dr. Robert O. Carlson
Associate Professor at Adelphi University

Richard R. Conarroe
Founder of Walden Public Relations

Ronald R. Conarroe
Formerly Senior Member of the Professional Staff at Newsome & Company

William W. Cook
Director of Public Communications Services for United States Steel Corporation (Retired)

Martin M. Cooper
President of Cooper Communications, Inc.

John W. Felton
University of Florida

Alec Gallup
Gallup Organization

George Gallup, Jr.
Co-Chairman of Gallup Organization

D. Parke Gibson
Formerly President of D. Parke Gibson Associates, Inc.

Patricia P. Gibson
Formerly head of D. Parke Gibson Associates

Ronald I. Gow
Director of Sales Promotion for Whirlpool Corporation (Retired)

William I. Greener, Jr.
Fleishman-Hillard

Robert W. Hefty
Director of Creative Services for the Detroit Edison Company (Retired)

Raymond L. Hoewing
President of the Public Affairs Council

JAMES L. HORTON
Robert Marston Associates

LOREN J. KALLSEN
Owner of Vibrant Film & Videos, Inc.

JOHN D. KRAFT
Formerly President of John F. Kraft, Inc.

ROBERT S. LEAF
Burson-Marsteller, Ltd.

PHILIP LESLY
The Philip Lesly Company

TERRY MAYER
Terry Mayer Associates

DERMOT MCKEONE
Infopress Group

JAMES F. MINEHAN
Manager of Public Information for New York State Electric & Gas Corporation (Retired)

EUGENE MILLER
Executive Vice President of USG Corporation (Retired)

P. DANIEL MILLER
Whirlpool Corporation

PAUL R. NELSON
Board Chairman of Flagler & Nelson, Inc. (Retired)

HUGH C. NEWTON
President of Hugh C. Newton Associates, Inc.

WILBUR J. PEAK
Formerly Assistant Vice President in Public Relations for Illinois Bell

HOWARD A. PRAEGER
Assistant to the President of New York State Electric & Gas Corporation (Retired)

CHARLES E. PROUT
Vice President Communications of Eaton Corporation (Retired)

MICHAEL RADOCK
Advisor to the President of the Charles Stewart Mott Foundation

MARVIN L. RAGLOR
Whirlpool Corporation

RONALD E. RHODY
Public Relations Counsel

JUDITH RICH
Executive Vice President and Executive Creative Director–USA for Ketchum Public Relations

MORRIS V. ROSENBLOOM
President of American Surveys International

LENARD F. SCHWEITZER
Director of Communication of the Marketing Group for Whirlpool Corporation

PHILIP W. TAGGART
The Philip Taggart Company

GEORGE J. TANBER

DR. FRANK WALSH
Walsh Public Relations

MARVIN C. WILBUR
Past Assistant Vice President of the United Presbyterian Foundation

ERNEST WITTENBERG
Public relations counsel

FOREWORD

GAYLORD FREEMAN
HONORARY CHAIRMAN
THE FIRST NATIONAL BANK OF CHICAGO

These are uneasy times for anyone who manages an organization. A good manager inherently seeks to make the task manageable—to set out the elements of the operation so they can be seen and evaluated and directed. He or she wants to base decisions on tables of figures that can be assessed, reports on the facts to be weighed, timetables for needed facilities, personnel, and budgets. The emergence of management technology that was so widely heralded in the first part of the century and that has since been adopted almost everywhere has certainly helped transform the face of our world and turned the pyramid of poverty-and-wealth around in advanced countries.

But even while the miracles of our advanced web of institutions have increased, recent trends make it clear that the real problems facing managers—and all of society—are no longer in the tangible areas of management technology, but are in the attitudes of people.

We are in the midst of a revolution of attitudes. Throughout history humankind has faced shortages in the essentials of life. Our outlook and our institutions developed to provide security against want, predators, and untreatable disease. Now, in the Western world, we begin to see that our greatest dangers stem from abundance. The mechanisms and techniques that man's genius has developed have begun to outrun themselves. The approaches used in converting a hostile wilderness may no longer appeal to people who believe they face a hostile man-made cosmos.

All the benefits and concepts that shaped our civilization since people first began to write are now being questioned or assaulted. Which will evolve and survive, and which will be replaced or reshaped? What kind of human society will come out of this cauldron of ideas?

In the individual organization, these questions take on day-to-day importance. Planning the utilities to function vigorously and to meet public needs depends as much on the attitudes of people about land use, pollution, and transportation as on their technical or financial capabilities. Plans of banks to serve the public without being inundated by paper or throttled by inert regulation depend on the attitudes of people and their congressmen. The ability of our schools to function depends on the community's attitudes as much as on the skills of teachers.

What we do next in every aspect of our society does not depend primarily on advanced techniques of production or finance. It depends on reconciling the drives of millions of persons with the orderly development of very complex systems needed to keep society viable. What industry can do, what banks can do, what education and medicine and government can do depends on whether people understand and will cooperate with the plans that are developed.

We now live in the most powerful, most complex system ever known. It is made up of countless interacting institutions and organizations. Will this conglomeration of elements drift ever faster without guidance, or will some sort of new consensus evolve?

That depends on how managers of our organizations see the patterns evolving, how they shape their policies to serve these patterns, and how well they communicate to achieve understanding and support.

These three facts are the elements of public relations. Recognition of their importance is behind the rapid growth of public relations and public affairs in the consideration of managers. This book—which for more than 45 years has set the pattern for this burgeoning field—is most timely. It embodies concepts and guidelines for meeting the new challenges at all levels.

These challenges call for integrating all functions and communications of an organization to optimize the operation of every element. This book deals with how to achieve this integration.

Lesly's Handbook of Public Relations and Communications should be a valuable aid to managers and practitioners in the field, a compendium of ideas and tools whose time is here.

PREFACE TO THE FIFTH EDITION

All of human society today pivots on communication. Public relations deals with understanding and using mass communication. So this book—encompassing all the principles and practices of public relations—deals with many of the basics of how human society functions today.

The vast and rapid changes of recent years have made an even greater impact on human affairs than on science and technology. A few years ago social changes tended to come singly and slowly; now they occur in all areas simultaneously and in rapid sequence. All institutions and elements of society are interlinked; as each changes, it wreaks changes on others. The whole human spectrum is, therefore, an ever-changing shape.

Understanding human institutions and the attitudes of their members has emerged as one of the greatest needs of our time. This understanding, plus knowledge of how to cope with these attitudes and direct them, comprises the rationale of public relations. It is axiomatic; consequently, that kaleidoscopic change has brought significant changes in the public relations field.

The gap between theory and the multifaceted, constantly changing operations in the field has grown tremendously. This is true in all aspects of the art: sensing trends and the climate of attitudes; developing policy; planning; programming; execution of activities; and feedback and evaluation. This book bridges that gap.

Breadth of Experience and Expertise

No classic survey or academic approach by one or a few people can be complete or up-to-date in the face of multiplying disciplines and intensifying complexity. It must encompass the latest and most-expert knowledge of many proved practitioners, combined into a diverse but unified composite.

That is what *Lesly's Handbook of Public Relations and Communications* does. This volume had its ancestry in three editions of *Public Relations Handbook* edited by me—a work that in 1950 promptly became the pre-eminent authority on its fist publications among practitioners throughout the world. In recognition of this primacy and to identify it as a new work based on this heritage, a later, vastly changed edition appeared in 1976, entitled *Lesly's Public Relations Handbook*. This Fifth Edition of the new volume—restructured, retitled, and significantly revised—carries on the constant evolution of the treatment necessary to meet the field's needs. It includes many additions and changed treatments of other aspects of the field.

Organization of the Information

Because this is a reference work intended for repeated use and multiple purposes, the essential information to be sought on a specific major subject has been combined in a single chapter. Although somewhat similar information on a few overlapping subjects may appear in two or more chapters, unnecessary duplication has been avoided. However, because a complete section on the techniques of communication has been included, these are touched on in other chapters only as they apply specifically to their subjects.

Many of the illustrations and references that appear in individual chapters are applicable to others. For instance, some illustrations in the chapter on nonprofit organizations are just as meaningful for corporations, government, or other organizations. Accordingly, going though the whole book to gain the essence of these illustrative materials adds to what the reader can gain from any one chapter. Cross references are indicated where more information appears in another chapter. In these ways the resources of the whole volume are applied to the subject of each chapter without requiring full and close study of the whole at one time. Integration is achieved at the same time individual subjects are treated specifically.

Most lists and various sources of information are assembled in the Appendixes, rather than being scattered within individual chapters.

This handbook is a guide, a sourcebook, a reminder, and a stimulator that will enable anyone with imagination and intelligence to chart a course, knowing he or she is proceeding along sound lines.

It is hoped that this new *Handbook* will continue to raise and define the standards and practices of public relations as it continuously fills burgeoning needs throughout the world. In addition, by giving guidance to those who establish public relations programs, as well as by giving direction to those who have public relations responsibilities, *Lesly's Handbook of Public Relations and Communications* will help bring the conciliatory principles and practices of public relations into universal practice among groups of people.

Philip Lesly

Acknowledgments

For helping make this *Handbook* complete, acknowledgment is due to all organizations whose material is used to illustrate points made in the text or whose activities are cited as examples

Special acknowledgment is due to Carolyn Matheson for her assistance and corrections, and to other members of the Philip Lesly Company staff who have helped on various editions.

Virginia Lesly helped immeasurably with her insights and support. Craig Lesly has provided research help. Besides members of the Advisory Board, others who provided special help include Richard G. Claeys, Bruce Anderson, Arthur (Terry) Newmyer III, Ronald Kostka, Chester Lasell, Steve Fisher, Karyn Lewis, and Lawrence Ragan. And scores of colleagues, associates, friends, and professionals have helped in many ways. No book of this scope would be possible without the cooperation of many people.

FIFTH EDITION

LESLY'S
HANDBOOK

of Public Relations
and Communications

Section 1

WHAT PUBLIC RELATIONS IS AND DOES

1

THE NATURE AND ROLE OF PUBLIC RELATIONS

PHILIP LESLY

Philip Lesly, president of The Philip Lesly Company, Chicago, until his death in 1997, was a leading authority on public relations and a leading practitioner.

Before going to college, having attracted attention as organizer and editor of the country's only daily high school newspaper, he joined the editorial staff of the Chicago Herald and Examiner. *Two years later, at eighteen, he was awarded a scholarship to Northwestern University, from which he was graduated magna cum laude and possessor of a Phi Beta Kappa key.*

He entered professional public relations work immediately after college and two years later became vice-president of one of the country's larger counseling firms. He has planned, directed, and carried out public relations programs for scores of corporations, trade associations, and nonprofit organizations. He has received the Gold Anvil award of the Public Relations Society of America. In an international poll by P R Reporter *he was voted the leading active practitioner. His firm now concentrates on counsel and major creative contributions to major clients. It formerly was one of the largest full-service firms, with multiple offices in the United States and abroad.*

His first book, which was a milestone in the field, was Public Relations: Principles and Procedures. *Next he published* Public Relations in Action, *a volume of case studies. His* Public Relations Handbook, *this volume's predecessor, quickly became the most widely used volume on the subject throughout the world. He lectured widely, wrote for many publications, and authored the bi-monthly* Managing the Human Climate. *His books* The People Factor *(Dow Jones-Irwin, 1974)*, How We Discommunicate *(AMACOM, 1979)*, Overcoming Opposition *(Prentice-Hall, 1984)*, and Bonanzas and Fool's Gold *(Acclaim, 1987) have been widely quoted.*

The Continuing Evolution of Public Relations

Public relations has changed considerably since its early days, when it consisted solely of publicity—which today comprises but one facet of this comprehensive field. This new "science of attitude" came about due to the growing difficulty people of differing backgrounds had in learning about and understanding each other. Publicity provided an organization with a systematic way to tell others about itself. Since then, the field has expanded tremendously to include hundreds of activities employed by virtually every group to achieve multiple objectives. Public relations has come to mean a great deal more than informing others about someone or some group. It also tells the group what others think of it, helps the group determine what it must do to gain the goodwill of others, plans the ways and means by which to do it, and then implements the activities to achieve goodwill. This entire process known as public relations encompasses a great many functions, concepts, and techniques—including the range of activities in "public affairs" that help an organization come into confluence with the social forces affecting it. All are integrated into a *gestalt* of coordinated ideas and functions.

Public relations is a phenomenon and a necessity of our times. It has been created by the forces that increased the tempo of the world, casting people into many diversified groups, all seeking different objectives, yet sharing a common need to work together toward common advantages and progress. The growing complexity of civilization has created problems undreamed of when social, economic, political, and religious classifications were simple and distinct.

Change has been magnified by the combined forces of technology, education, mobility, and especially, communications. Widespread literacy is less than five hundred years old, and until early in the twentieth century the only media of communications were speech and print. Then, in quick succession, came the motion picture, recordings, radio, television, computers, and other electronic media. The explosion of communications led to an implosion of the once vast and remote world. Suddenly, it is all there to see, to experience, and to judge—multiplying a person's scope of awareness and judgment thousands of times. Diverse, instant communication has changed the world of humankind much more than humans have changed their institutions for living in that world.

These forces that have changed the world in just a century have been leveling forces. They have greatly exalted the position and importance of the masses, while greatly reducing the power and control of those who are leaders. Today as never before in history, people are led by their own consent. They are their own masters, guided solely by their own opinions as expressed through the mores and demands of the groups to which they belong—such as "farmers," "wage earners," "Catholics," "youth," and so on. The command of a king or a tycoon is no longer the word of law, automatically obeyed. It is now necessary to first obtain the acceptance, if not the support, of those being ordered, even in repressive countries, such as North Korea and China.

This change has occurred very quickly. In the same way, the science or business or profession of public relations (its true status has not yet been established) has evolved rapidly and is today a very significant actuality in all the important associations among diverse groups of our civilization.

Invention dominated the first third of the twentieth century. Administration dominated the second third. The last third of the century is being dominated by the human climate—the attitudes of people that determine how all segments of society function. It is the distinct role of public relations to deal with the human climate—to sense its turns, to adjust to it, to help direct it.

These functions, concepts, and techniques comprise the subject of this book. Its purpose is to put down what they are for the benefit of everyone. In so doing, this book expedites the efforts of different groups to get along better. It informs anyone with any public relations responsibility or function—and this, in the broad sense, includes everyone—of the ways to protect and develop acceptance. It also helps the public relations profession to develop in an orderly manner for the benefit of all those who practice it, as well as those it serves.

Many definitions of public relations exist, as can be expected for a field that includes so many aspects and reaches into almost every facet of human society. However, for simplicity as well as for completeness, *public relations* can be defined as *helping an organization and its publics adapt mutually to each other.*

This definition conveys the vital fact that the essence is mutual accommodation, rather than one-sided imposition of a viewpoint. It recognizes that a key factor facing every organization is the insistence of each individual in modern free societies on having a say about every organization and institution that affects his or her life.

The Dual Role of Public Relations

The distinctive role of public relations is explained in Part II of the report of the Advance Planning Committee of the Public Relations Society of America.[1]

> Increasingly, the stability of our society depends on bringing into reasonable equilibrium the many social, political, and cultural forces—all

[1]Written by Philip Lesly.

of which are determined by group attitudes. Group attitudes are the special milieu of public relations. . . . Top public relations people have special contributions to make, involving these forces, that cannot be made by others.

> Public relations people have the role of being always in the middle—pivoted between their clients/employers and their publics. They must be attuned to the thinking and needs of the organizations they serve or they cannot serve well. They must be attuned to the dynamics and needs of the publics so they can interpret the publics to the clients, as well as interpret the clients to the publics.

> This role "in the middle" does not apply to any other group that deals with the climate of attitudes. Experts in other fields—journalists, sociologists, psychologists, politicians, etc.—are oriented in the direction of their specialties.

> The role of the public relations professional is to apply this unique and increasingly crucial orientation—plus our special skills—to reading the trends in attitudes; assessing what the trends will mean for society and for various organizations; and recommending what to do to accommodate to these conditions and trends.

> Our society is increasingly one of competing demands for limited tangible and psychic resources. . . . Increasingly, concern among leaders and citizens is focused on achieving accommodations that will forestall crises.

> The need and the opportunity converge. There is a gap in the makeup of the forces that are shaping society. Other inputs are distorted by the specialized position and background of their sources. Public relations by its nature is broad-gauged and is engaged in accommodating various viewpoints and inputs.

Terms and Scope

Despite the worldwide use of the term *public relations*, there has been continuous confusion about the field's scope and terminology. To resolve this, a Committee on Terminology of the Public Relations Society of America studied the question and issued a definitive report, written by this author as chairman. Its key findings can be summarized as follows:

- The field has matured to encompass an extensive scope of functions. Consequently, using the "umbrella" term *public relations* to represent this wide range of functions ensures widespread understanding among people. All other terms that have been introduced refer primarily to one or a few of the many elements comprising public relations today.

- No other term has gained any appreciable acceptance.

- The prominence of the public relations function has made it a common topic in all aspects of public life—the media, government, business, various institutions.

- Literature dealing with the subject almost universally uses the term *public relations*— whether describing the role of consultants in proxy fights, referring to government information efforts, discussing employment opportunities, or other matters. The term *corporate communication* is typically used in corporate-sponsored reports. *Public affairs* is confusedly used to describe what happens in government and policy making more often than when dealing with organizations' relations with government and public groups. *Communication* is prominently used to discuss such matters as telephone and computer systems.

- The function's prominence grows steadily, and new public relations trends are constantly introduced. *Public relations* is increasingly entrenched in the general language.

- *Corporate communications* and *corporate relations* are clearly limited to the corporate sphere. These terms are denigrating, because they focus on only limited two-way functions rather than on policy and strategy. *Public affairs* seems to have settled as a term for dealing with government and external groups. *Communication* labels the

practitioner as a functionary in a limited area. Other related terms are function-specific: *investor relations, issues management, publicity*.

- Using a term that deals with a function labels its practitioners as technicians and not as professionals.

- The broadness and nonspecificity of *public relations* prevents it from becoming associated with any one type of function. Because it is a general word, it remains suitable as an umbrella term covering many types of function. However, some practitioners assign the term to what is really just publicity.

Recommended terminology

We recommend that all people in the field, who are professionals in the careful use of language, use all terms applying to this field with clear and precise meanings. We recommend that these terms be used in the following ways.

Public relations. Helping an organization and its publics adapt mutually to each other. The overall term for the scope of functions detailed in this handbook and not for any of the following specialized areas.

Publicity. Dissemination of purposefully planned and executed messages through selected media to further the particular interest of an organization or person without specific payment to media.

Communication (in relation to public relations). Interchange of information; also conveying thought from one party or group to another.

Public affairs. Working with governments and groups who help determine public policies and legislation.

Issues management. Systematic identification and action regarding public policy matters of concern to an organization.

The Responsibilities of Public Relations Professionals

Every executive within an organization—indeed, every member of the organization—holds responsibilities for public relations functions. Public relations responsibilities cannot be assigned to a specialist or even to a group of specialists and then forgotten, leaving them to be taken care of solely by those individuals. For this reason, the contents of this handbook are the concern and part of the requisite working tools of every executive.

For direction and carrying out of the functions, however, organizations call on men and women who, through training, are equipped to serve as public relations specialists. So far, two primary types of practitioner have specialized in this field.[4]

The first type is the person who serves as an employee of the organization, being part of its internal structure and subject to its controls. His title is often "director of public relations," and often he has a staff to assist him. He may be a vice-president, and his portfolio may include public affairs, advertising, investor relations, and other functions. He is likely to report to a top executive of the organization.

The second type is the public relations counsel, who is retained by the organization and works closely with it, but does not become part of its internal structure. She provides an objective approach to the public relations of the organization, serving in the same manner as professional attorneys, engineers, and accountants. Usually the counsel has a staff.

How staff and counsel work together

The director of public relations and the public relations counsel may function together for an organization, or either of them may be found separately performing all the functions involved.

Where they are both involved, there are two common arrangements: the staff of the organization conducts many of the activities and serves as the coordinating force within the organization, while the counsel provides guidance, the benefit of experience, creativity, contacts, and various services for which he and his staff have experience, skill, and resources. Usually in this arrangement, the counsel advises the organization's management officials as well as the Director of Public Relations.

Alternatively, the director of public relations serves as liaison within the organization, while the counsel and his staff perform most of the required functions.

The trend seems to be moving toward both of these arrangements. The type of dual arrangement varies with the nature of the organization, the problems involved, and other factors.

Developing effective workers

Since the profession has developed so rapidly without a formal framework within which to train workers, there continues to be a severe shortage of capable public relations people who are qualified to perform all of the functions of the true counsel and practitioner. The educational system (which often lags behind the requirements of the rest of society) is awakening to this need and now offers training. More than three hundred colleges and many community colleges in the United States now offer one or more courses in public relations. The demand among students indicates

---

[4]For a discussion of the procedures in a public relations structure, see Chapters 46 and 47.

the widespread recognition of the profession's future.

The continuing development in our society of problems requiring the mutual understanding of many groups and the acceleration of the social processes hold great promise that the use of public relations principles and techniques will continue to grow until every organization follows its precepts. Today, it is such an important factor in the operation of any enterprise that it is a matter of interest and significance to every executive.

How Public Relations Builds Goodwill

The strength of an organization's public relations efforts depends on the type of organization and on its situation at a given time. But broad outlines of the factors that influence public relations may be set according to basic classifications of types of organization. The factors to be considered in other categories are treated by specialists in later chapters. This analysis concentrates on the business corporation.

Perhaps the most important force affecting all organizations and governments today is the opinion of people. Business people realize this when they talk of "goodwill." Business goodwill today means not only the attitude of the consumer toward the company's products, but also the attitudes of its employees, the community and government, stockholders, dealers and distributors, suppliers, and others. All must be integrated in understanding and acceptance of the organization and its purposes. Since all of these groups are vital to the success of a company, obtaining the goodwill of every one of them is indispensable. This holds equally true for all other types of organization.

The value of goodwill is most evident when it is absent. Employee productivity may be lower than in competitors' plants; morale may be poor; turnover and absenteeism may be abnormally high—resulting in higher costs, lower production, and the inability to compete with companies that have a higher level of goodwill among their employees. Frequently, strikes are symptoms of neglected goodwill among employees. Difficulty in getting workers, failure to attract enough good dealers, a high volume of customer complaints, fast turnover of stockholders, frequent stockholder complaints, and resentment of the community toward the company and its operations all are signs that the attitude of these groups is at an unsatisfactory level. An organization that becomes the target for attacks by activist groups protesting alleged pollution, job discrimination, or exploitation of consumers; that is singled out for review by government agencies or Congressional committees; or that is vulnerable to "takeover" efforts or financial raids may be showing signs of blindness to attitude trends and ineptness in planning. Just as a person appreciates the value of protecting her health when she becomes ill, so can an organization best recognize the necessity for fostering goodwill when it suffers from one of these problems. By the same token, it is much wiser to prevent disorders than to wait for them to appear before seeking the remedy.

For this reason, management executives today realize that, along with production, sales, accounting, finance, and engineering, their businesses must use the most expert assistance in developing and maintaining goodwill.

Fostering good public relations goes beyond winning favor among various groups by telling them what an organization does. Expert public relations recognizes that everything the organization does affects the opinion of someone—that opinion is a unification of many impressions, so those impressions must be integrated.

The Phases of Public Relations

Public relations today involves complete analysis and understanding of all the factors that influence people's attitudes toward an organization. It usually consists of eight phases:

1. **Analyzing the general climate of attitudes and the relation of the organization to its "universe."** Every institution functions within a "universe" or system, dependent on everything that happens to this totality. It is vital to gain as much understanding as possible about the trends within this system and how they may be affecting the organization. This involves feeling the "pulse" of the various publics with which an organization may have relations, in order to determine their attitudes toward the organization and toward the field it is in.

2. **Determining the attitude of any group toward the organization**. This may be the employees, the customers, the stockholders, or some other segment of the public. When the attitudes are known, it is possible to see where the organization is misunderstood and where its policies and actions are creating unfavorable opinion.

3. **Analyzing the state of opinion**. This investigation may disclose unrest among a group of employees—unrest that may well break out into very serious uprisings. It may reveal that the stockholders desire to know more about the company and its products, or that an activist group is launching an attack on the organization. It may indicate that consumers do not identify products with the manufacturer. Analysis will aid in making plans to improve the opinion of the various groups about which the company is concerned.

4. **Anticipating potential problems, needs, or opportunities**. By using analysis and surveys it is sometimes possible to detect what changes may be developing in the attitudes of various groups. Then plans or actions can be recommended to respond to those attitude changes at the most advantageous time and under favorable circumstances.

5. **Formulating policy**. Analysis may indicate that certain company policies should be modified to improve the attitude held by certain groups. Often the change involves eliminating causes of misunderstanding and misinterpretation.

6. **Planning means of improving the attitude of a group**. With an understanding of what people think of the organization and a clarification of the organization's policies on matters that affect public opinion, groundwork has been laid. Next comes the programming of activities that will explain the company and its products, overcome misunderstandings, and promote goodwill.

7. **Carrying out the planned activities**. The tools of public relations—publicity, institutional advertising, printed materials, employee activities, stockholder reports, events, company publications, films, video, and other things—are then employed to do the job. With proper preliminary planning and guidance, these become the most tangible phase of a company's public relations activity.

8. **Feedback, evaluation, and adjustment**. Conditions change constantly. Public relations functions both contribute to change and are affected by it. So it is important to constantly get readings from the publics being approached. These readings help to assess the results and developments, and to adjust the public relations program—and often the entire policy of the organization—accordingly. (*See* Figure 1.1.)

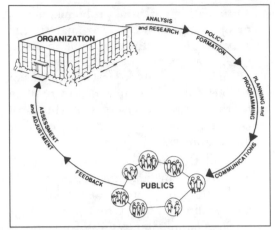

THE PUBLIC RELATIONS CIRCUIT

Figure 1.1 Schematic diagram of an optimum process in public relations. It is continuous, not oriented to single events or objectives; interacting, with each phase affecting the conception and execution of every other phase; and proportioned, with no one element (such as communications) functioning predominantly.

This scientific approach to an organization's goodwill goes far beyond the familiar publicity releases and hit-or-miss efforts to please employees or members. It is a task for highly skilled specialization and talent. It demands high-caliber thinking by a number of experts, experience in the ways of public opinion and the techniques of influencing it, and the facilities to do everything that must be done in a well-planned program.

For this reason most substantial corporations and other organizations in North America and an increasing number in other countries rely on well-established specialists to serve as public relations counselors and directors. Thus they obtain the best brains for analysis and planning, the benefit of experience based on a large number of other programs, the staff of specialists necessary to achieve peak results in every bit of activity, and the extensive facilities required to carry out all the necessary functions.

The Public Relations Universe

Confusion has been caused both by the broad scope of what public relations encompasses and by the use of a variety of terms as substitutes or euphemisms—such as *corporate affairs*, *communications*, *external affairs*, and *public affairs*.

For clarification, Figure 1.2 depicts what the "universe" of public relations embodies.

In this book the elements of public relations that fall into the category of public affairs are covered in Chapters 4–9 and 16— all integral to the total scope of public relations.

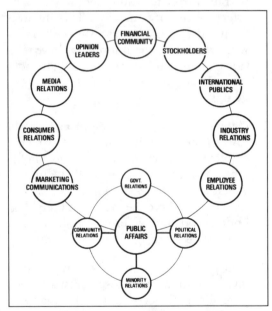

THE PUBLIC RELATIONS UNIVERSE

Figure 1.2 This diagram represents the various functions and publics that make up the "universe" of public relations. The large circles represent "planets"–including "public affairs"–and the small circles are satellites of "public affairs," which is one of the planets. The satellites are related to public affairs, but are also part of the total integrated public relations cosmos.

The Results of Public Relations

Many objectives can be achieved through expert public relations activity. Any one of them, any group of them, or all of them may form the basis for an organization's public relations program. Professional public relations directs every activity toward reaching a selected objective. Extraneous efforts are avoided—merely collecting a volume of press clippings is meaningless.

Objectives that may be sought include the following:

1. Gain prestige or "favorable image" and its benefits
2. Promote products or services
3. Detect and deal with issues and opportunities
4. Determine the organization's posture in dealing with its publics
5. Foster goodwill of the employees or members
6. Prevent and solve labor problems
7. Foster the goodwill of communities in which the organization has units
8. Foster the goodwill of the stockholders or constituents
9. Overcome misconceptions and prejudices
10. Forestall attacks
11. Foster the goodwill of suppliers
12. Foster the goodwill of the government
13. Foster the goodwill of the rest of the industry
14. Foster the goodwill of dealers and attract other dealers
15. Enhance the ability to attract the best personnel
16. Educate the public about the use of a product or service
17. Educate the public on a point of view
18. Foster the goodwill of customers or supporters
19. Investigate the attitude of various groups toward the company
20. Formulate and guide policies
21. Foster the viability of the society in which the organization functions
22. Direct the course of change

The Benefits of Public Relations

Prestige or "image"

The familiarity and reputation of its name are among the greatest assets of any organization—whether it deals directly with the public or not. Everyone is influenced by reputation in choosing everything he or she buys and in every association he or she makes. The prominence of a name is taken as a sign of success, because reputation in industry can rarely be won without true accomplishment. Whether a company makes chewing gum or emery wheels, prestige will help to sell its goods, attract dealers, back up sales efforts, attract the best employees, please the stockholders, provide a bulwark against price-cutting competitors, and clear the way for introduction of new products. Phrase-makers from time to time promote other terms to define prestige: *corporate image*, *public personality*, and others. A company's prestige determines the "climate" of receptivity toward all its messages—making them more or less effective than their intrinsic merit would warrant. A survey by Opinion Research Corporation found that 89 percent of adults said the reputation of a company often determines which products they buy. Seventy-one percent reported that the more they know about a company, the more favorable they feel toward it. (Exceptions occur when a company has been the object of recent heavy unfavorable attention.)

Promotion of products or services

Telling people about products and interesting them in purchasing requires more than advertising and sales efforts. People's tastes and desires are developed by the influences around them—the things they read, radio and television, what they see in the movies, what they hear others talk about. These influences make an immeasurable impact on the public's desire to buy. They create a desire for the product or service. They support the direct-selling activities of advertising and merchandising, giving them an added dimension. They associate product names with the prestige of the company. The many ways in which public relations people can create desires are indispensable to the modern sales program.

Detecting and dealing with issues and opportunities

Monitoring social trends, devising strategies to deal with them, and conducting programs to help direct those trends are among the most crucial functions in public relations. They are dealt with in depth in Chapter 2.

Position of the organization with its publics

Increasing sophistication has modified how organizations approach their relations with various groups. Three major tactics exist for accomplishing this:

1. **Master the publics.** Direct what they should think and do, according to the desires of the organization involved. This action approach perceives the publics as targets of the organization's self-interest. It was a prominent aspect of public relations' rise during the era of unquestioned dominance of society by its institutions.

It is occasionally the necessary course when an organization faces an adversary whose demands are untenable or destructive. In such cases, firmness in support of the organization's principles or purposes is judicious.

2. **Block and parry.** React to developments and problems and respond to events or the initiatives of others by blunting them. This "low profile" approach was a prominent aspect of public relations' rise during the era when all organizations were considered private entities, responsible only to their managements and stockholders or members. There are occasions when a low profile is judicious to avoid turning an issue or an adversary's maneuvers into sensation.

3. **Achieve mutual adaptation.** Develop relationships of mutual benefit to all parties involved, such as customers and producers, exuders of wastes and environmentalists, or employers and the working staff.

Either of the first two approaches may achieve an organization's immediate goals or survival. However, in the present human climate, the third approach has become the most widely taken course. This era is marked by the individual's demands for independence, and a voice and role within every organization that purports to speak for him or her. It is an era in which the management principle of participation by individuals ascends over the authoritarian approach.

Gain and sustain goodwill of employees or members

Satisfied workers are those who feel they are important parts of a worthwhile activity, who identify themselves with the creation of good things for others, and who understand the workings of their company. Giving them a sense of identification and satisfaction provides the means toward employee goodwill.

This involves expert analysis of the employee situation, preparation of plans to create goodwill, and the development of activities to carry out these plans. The tools to choose from are many: employee media; employee councils; industrial recreational activities; presentation of awards for service and achievement; identifying symbols for all workers; plant community publicity of all kinds; developing the support of local clergy, teachers, and club people; and educational material for the employees, such as inserts in pay envelopes, printed material on the nature of business, and periodical reports on earnings.

Prevent and resolve labor problems

Public relations can help stabilize labor conditions through the type of employee relations activity just mentioned. It can also help by implementing special educational activities based on the conditions in the plant, the industry, and the union involved; by creating goodwill in the community, so that an atmosphere entirely favorable to the company is created that provides a barrier to the destructive efforts of agitators; by working closely with the industrial relations officer, providing aids that help him in his dealings with the union; and by telling the company's story to the people and workers when a dispute threatens or breaks out.

The use of public relations as a labor-stabilizing aid is preventive as well as curative. It is most beneficial when carried on continuously rather than only when strike clouds appear.

Foster the goodwill of local communities

The attitude of the community frequently determines the attitude of the workers toward the company. Workers closely identify with the community and unconsciously absorb the tenor of the locality's attitude. Not only does high standing in the community provide a bulwark of morale against unsettling influences, but it also attracts the better workers from the area when they join the labor force. High regard of the community also is invaluable when environmental questions arise, when special assessments are being considered, when special privileges such as parking permits and zoning regulations are desired, when tax rates are being set, and in all other dealings the company has with the local authorities.

Ensure the goodwill of stockholders or constituents

When the investors in a company understand and appreciate its operations, they are more likely to retain their stocks for a long period, giving the corporation's securities a desirable stability. Stockholder confidence also is felt by other segments of the public, particularly when the stock is widely held. This confidence usually is reflected in higher market values for the company's stock—important in negotiating mergers as well as in seeking additional capital.

Professional attention to annual reports and periodic communications to the stockholders, as well as sound relations with the financial community and careful placement of news about the company in the financial sections of newspapers and in business publications, go a long way toward winning loyalty among stockholders.

Overcome misconceptions and prejudices

Investigation sometimes reveals that unfounded opinions about an organization are injuring its efforts to win goodwill or actually hampering its operations. Prejudices that may exist due to the spread of misinformation also threaten the success of a business.

Analysis of the situation, plans for meeting it, and the dissemination of correct information can clear up these difficulties.

Forestall attacks

Most people in the Western world today have been conditioned by television, where instant action applied to any "problem" brings a quick "solution"—in dramatic shows, in countless commercials, even in news and documentary programs. In this climate, activism has become an alluring means of seeking quick fulfillment of expectations. Resorting to "action" meets the participants' view of how things get done and feeds the hunger of media for "movement" and controversy. All types of groups, including congressional committees and regulatory agencies, use the tactics of activism against all types of organizations. Forestalling these attacks and blunting their effects is increasingly a function of analysis, planning, and effective public relations.

Maintain the goodwill of suppliers

The importance of being on good terms with sources of supply is demonstrated during major strikes, when materials are scarce. Suppliers always have an important influence on the attitudes of others toward a company—prospective employees, customers, financial leaders, and so on. Formulating policies that build a reputation for good dealing and creating an opinion that the company will be an increasingly good customer because of its growing success are effective means of gaining the favorable attention of suppliers.

Maintain the goodwill of government

In most cases, the attitudes of government officials and public servants are based on what they know and hear about a company. In North America the government is moved by the opinions and attitudes of the public. The soundness of a company's public relations usually determines its relations with public officials. If they are kept informed and feel that an organization operates in the public interest, government executives are less likely to make unreasonable demands or to issue unfair restrictions. Establishing the goodwill of the government requires two factors: goodwill of the public and a sincere effort to keep government agencies informed about the company.

Maintain the goodwill of the industry at large

The respect of competitors is a great tribute to an organization and greatly influences the attitudes of others. It also leads to helpful cooperation, gives the company a role when another firm encounters a Bhopal or a *Valdez* disaster, and strengthens a company's position in its dealing with trade associations and other industrial organizations.

Maintain the goodwill of dealers and attract other dealers

Keeping dealers informed is a necessary function of every business that does not sell directly to the customer. Retailers and wholesalers are eager to know what the manufacturer is doing or planning, so they can make plans with a degree of assurance. Providing public relations aids for dealers, such as publicity material they can use locally, helps to win goodwill. It is through the dealers that a company can perform its most effective work in building goodwill among consumers. Dealers must be educated to identify products with the manufacturer—and the prestige of the manufacturer must be made as great as possible. Frequently, the public relations executive works closely with the sales staff in coordinating all dealings with dealers and wholesalers.

Attract the best personnel

No organization's future is any better than the caliber of future executives it is able to attract. Research tends to confirm what many experts have long believed: young people whose abilities and promise give them a choice of employers tend to choose those whose standing with the business world and the public are the highest. Making a company or organization known and respected is necessary to ensure its healthful development.

Educate the public in the use of a product

When promoting an entirely new and unheralded product or service, it is necessary to capture the imagination of the public to make the item attain steady sales. There are numerous examples of products that have won a regular place on the American purchasing list through effective campaigns of educating the public to their use. Such things as oranges, sunglasses, musical instruments, bicycles, automatic washing machines, electric razors, vcrs, and men's toiletries indicate how effective these campaigns can be. When a company brings out a new type of product, public relations must support advertising and the sales staff in capturing the public's imagination.

Educate the public to a point of view

When an organization seeks to win support for its method of operation, its principles, the system that supports it, or any other viewpoint, its most effective means are those channels of reaching the public constantly used by public relations people. A utility, for instance, can systematically tell the people why private

ownership benefits them; a store may wish to make the people understand its "no credit" policy; an automobile manufacturer may explain why it must recall cars to check possible defects. The guidance and assistance of the public relations organization assure the effectiveness, favorable reactions, and low cost of such educational efforts.

Maintain the goodwill of customers or supporters

Establishing means of good relationships at the point where the purchaser meets the company or its product is one of the most important steps in building a company's goodwill. The manner in which the purchaser is treated, the services and information made available to him, and the handling of his complaints are crucial to his or her satisfaction with the product. Such considerations are part of the full-scale public relations program.

Determine the attitude of various groups toward the organization

Taking the pulse of various groups' attitudes plays an important role in the public relations program. During planning it is important to know what employees think, how people regard the company in relation to its competitors, and what they think are the company's weaknesses and strengths. Opinion research often reveals unsuspected opportunities for developing neglected potentialities. This research is aside from the market analysis carried on by the sales and advertising departments.

Formulate and guide policies

Everything done by an organization that influences any group—employees, consumers, stockholders, the community, the general public—should be examined in advance for its possible effects on opinions and attitudes.

The guidance and counsel of a public relations person who is constantly in touch with public reactions is as important to proper policy forming as is the attorney or the financial expert. Prevention of errors is a most important phase of good public relations.

Deal effectively with emergencies

This activity consists of three phases. The first phase involves monitoring whatever may cause unexpected difficulties for the organization, from explosions to charges leveled by a government agency. The second phase includes preparing for meeting the full range of such emergencies—for example, with prepared factual material, preconditioning the media with authoritative information ("filling the pipelines," as the author was quoted in *Canadian Business*), training executives in responding when an emergency strikes, and establishing facilities for emergency communications. The third phase is the actual handling of matters when an emergency occurs. This includes fast and full disclosure, availability of executives to the media, and for-the-duration handling of inquiries and funneling information. It includes providing objectivity and judgment during a stressful situation. As the author was quoted in *Time*: "Everybody involved is emotionally charged."

Support the society in which the organization functions

As an element of the community (which includes the nation and, indeed, the world), the organization is an institutional citizen, with a citizen's responsibilities to the community. Its ability to function will depend on the state of the community. Ability to attract personnel to any area is strongly influenced by the conditions there. Accordingly, most corporations find that the best public relations functions benefit the cosmos in which they operate, benefit their own ability to function and grow, and project a favorable impression to their publics.

Manage change

At its best, public relations is a bridge to change. It is a means to adjust to new attitudes that have been caused by change. It is a means of stimulating attitudes in order to create change. It seeks to help an organization see the whole of society together, rather than from one intensified viewpoint. It provides judgment, creativity, and skills in accommodating changing groups to each other.

Each of these objectives can be a basis for a program of its own, and increasing specialization is leading to segmented attention being given to each aspect of many organizations. Yet *the reputation of every organization is indivisible*. It must be conceived and attended to in total before the proper perspective can be given to any elements of the total public relations spectrum. The activities and subsequent outcomes of any one of these phases can and usually do have an early effect on many other phases. Each of these phases fits into the total of the organization's public relations considerations. Each of them or any narrow group of them is subordinate to the complete complex of factors that make up the organization's rapport with the human ecology with which it deals.

This picture of the widely diversified factors in expert public relations reveals that today public relations is a highly skilled field, requiring people, techniques, and facilities able to meet all the conditions involved.

In the chapters that follow, men and women who are experts in their fields outline the techniques and facilities necessary for successful development of good public relations in the major areas of human activity.

2

POLICY, ISSUES, CRISES, AND OPPORTUNITIES

PHILIP LESLY

In the year 1513, Niccolo Machiavelli provided history's most famous management advice when he said that:

> knowing afar (which is only given a prudent man to do) the evils that are brewing, they are easily cured. But when, for want of such knowledge, they are allowed to grow until everyone can recognize them, there is no longer any remedy to be found.

That sage advice rings even more true today than it did 484 years ago when Machiavelli offered it to his prince. Then, events moved slowly, and society changed a little at a time. In our modern world, changes can be as fast as the electronic signals that often drive it, and the changes in our social and economic structures are sudden and startling. For example, the 1994 election of a conservative Congress arrested a seemingly relentless shift toward statism in the United States. Another example is the abandonment of the term *generation gap*. Just a few years ago this condition seemed to forecast the future pattern of American life, propelling the new generations in opposite directions from their parents. Today the term is rarely used, and the concerns of various groups now tend to coincide.

The reshaping of the world's economy further illustrates the speed with which even massive changes can occur. Servan-Schreiber's book, *The American Challenge*, published in 1967, depicted the takeover of the global economy by American business. Less than ten years later, the alarm sounded over the rapid decline of the United States's ability to compete globally and domestically. In 1997 the American economy was again flourishing. Numerous incidents throughout recent history demonstrate how the fate of vast industries can suddenly transform. In the mid-1960s Texas natives Lyndon Johnson and Sam Rayburn were president and Speaker of the House, respectively; some of the most powerful senators were oil men. Then in 1975, after the composition of power in the government had changed, a bill that would have dismantled the major oil companies failed in the Senate by just a few votes.

By the same token in 1978, the American automobile industry enjoyed universal acceptance as the most dominant and powerful industry in the world. Then, the only real criticism aimed at the auto industry was that it was so powerful it administered prices and forced people to buy what it wanted to sell. However by early 1980, much of the public refused to buy American cars or to pay high prices for them, throwing the U.S. auto industry into disarray and resulting in its largest accumulative deficit in history for that year. General Motors, the industry's leader, epitomized the "profit-is-our-reason-for-being" philosophy throughout its history; yet in 1980, GM Chairman Thomas B. Murphy stated in the company's Public Interest Report:

If business people have learned one overriding lesson from the '70s, it is that economic success alone is not enough. Important as they are, superior products are not enough; nor are innovations in manufacturing, marketing or service. And certainly, returning a profit on our stockholders' investment, although absolutely necessary, is no longer sufficient by itself to ensure a firm's acceptance. . . . Because today's public relies heavily upon the broad marketplace of ideas to form its opinion, any business which chooses not to enter this arena does so only at its own risk.

The Increasing Importance of External Forces

The recognition of a new arena vital to the survival of organizations has been perhaps the most pronounced phenomenon of the past two decades in the world of management. Emergence of the "broad marketplace of ideas" has been more than just another new challenge, however. For more than a century, the field of organizational development has added new areas that require management. To concern for products, materials, manpower, money, and transport have been added instant communication, multiple forms of transportation, international considerations, computerization, automation, unionization, sophisticated management techniques such as management-by-objectives, and other aspects of administration. But virtually all of these have been subjected to assessment through management techniques within the enterprise. The new challenges have been monumental not only in scope but also in type. The majority fall outside the scope of the enterprise—interest groups, activists, minorities, women's groups, government, courts, intellectuals, media. They are intangible—not subject to charting and quantifying with managerial discipline; they appear to

be irrational and unpredictable; and they seem to respond to none of the skills that masterful managers have developed.

In fact, perhaps the most significant fact about the new challenge is this: the greatest force in building our vast and complex economic and social system has been the development of managerial science, while the greatest force behind the threats to our economic and social system is *exactly the opposite of how scientific managers are trained to function.*

Building and operating the complex organizations of today has demanded discipline-minded managers who can cut through masses of inchoate information and get to the facts so they can make proper judgments. That kind of masterful manager is tough-minded and direct. He or she demands accountability and measurability, because those skills are necessary to bring profits and orderly growth out of the multitude of elements the business must deal with. The computer has become the indispensable tool of professional management because it makes it possible to sort out a multitude of facts and bring them down to a "bottom line." The greatest mark of the masterful manager is his ability to cut away the fuzzy, intangible, immeasurable digressions that cannot be analyzed and quantified with such computerized discipline.

The factors changing the ground rules for the sophisticated organization, however, consist precisely of elements that are fuzzy, intangible, and immeasurable—the attitudes of groups of people. Nearly all of the forces causing management of all kinds of organizations their greatest troubles comprise public attitudes—the human climate. Government incursions, including tax policies and opposition to bigness, are all "political," which is a synonym for public attitudes. Environmentalism, conservationism, minority demands, women's claims, union policies, community positions, a sense of entitlement, litigiousness—all these and others reflect external attitudes. The lingering attitude from the 1890s that railroads must be saddled with restrictions to control their rapaciousness indicates how pervasive and entrenched an attitude can be.

The human climate has become as vital in determining the operation of business as the natural climate is for the farmer. Just as weather patterns bring storms that can destroy all the farmer's best work, so, too, can failure to detect and deal with emerging human climate patterns devastate the best management of an organization.

Recognition of this fact has led to gradual development of approaches to managing the human climate. It appears under various labels and in many forms, but it can be summarized as incorporating consideration of public issues and opportunities in all the deliberations of management.

At American Telephone & Telegraph Company, analysis of the "future business environment" now precedes the budgeting and operational planning.

Robert Cushman, chief executive officer of the Norton Company, expressed the new situation facing management as follows:

> If you were to ask the heads of the nation's top 300 companies what factors would have the greatest influence on the future of their businesses in the coming decades, I suggest the vast majority would say *government and the force of public opinion on public policy*. All our skills at managing—financial, manufacturing, marketing, research and development, and the like— all these put together will not influence our destiny as much as what happens in political and economic arenas.

As a consequence, managers of big institutions—whether they be presidents of corporations, foundations, or government agencies— must spend more time trying to understand and influence external affairs than they spend on the more traditional job of internal management.

While for a century American business has spent its time looking for *customers*, today we are looking desperately for *constituents*.

The Growing Opposition to Corporate Interests

The search for constituents is necessary to counteract the self-proclaimed public interest organizations that oppose corporations.

Millions of people have been given the time and opportunity to contest established organizations. The rapid spread of education and the increased freedom of time and movement have led these people to believe themselves entitled to direct the course of events. As a result, there has been a burgeoning of activist groups. The Foundation for Public Affairs registers an overall tally of about one thousand public interest groups, ranging from The Abalone Alliance and Accountants for the Public Interest to Zero Population Growth and Zoological Action Committee. Even without such a constituency, the groups proliferate. Jeffrey M. Berry, a political scientist at Tufts University, published a study of public interest lobbies that found 30 percent of the groups had no members at all. T. R. Reid of the *Washington Post* estimated that half the groups in existence at any given time have no members.

Like a fish's eggs, from such a large mass a few are certain to hatch into causes. A cause that captures media attention or academic support then often matures into a movement. Movements often grow into pressure groups that interfere with a business's operations (such as pressures on operating in Cuba or mandatory hiring policies), or they grow into proposed legislation or regulatory rules.

It usually is only when a movement has led to a proposed governmental action that an affected business becomes aware of it. As the Conference Board points out:

> Once an issue is the subject of prospective legislation, a company has relatively few options. Usually the choices are to support, oppose or seek to amend a bill. As for laws and regulations, all a company can do is try to influence their administration so as to minimize their adverse impacts and capitalize on their favorable consequences.

Distinguishing Among Issues, Crises, Emergencies

In recent years two areas of concern have emerged: "issues management" and "crisis management." Issues management arose first. Then, when it became popular for organizations to concern themselves with crises, the line between issues management and crisis management tended to blur, and the two concerns became intertwined. Yet neither adequately addresses most of the nonstandard developments that arise during "emergency management."

- An *issue* is a matter in dispute; an *emerging issue* is a matter that shows signs of developing into a dispute. Disputes generally involve differing points of view between adversaries about what should or should not be done, or how some matter of mutual concern should be handled.

- A *crisis* is a stage at which all future events affecting a person or an organization will be determined. It is a major turning point resulting in permanent drastic change. It is far more crucial than most issues or emergencies. Crises are of great importance, but they are rare.

- An *emergency* is a sudden, usually unexpected occurrence that requires prompt action. Crises fit that definition, but so do a great many more events. While demand-

ing serious attention, emergencies do not indicate a major turning point in the person's or organization's existence. Issues become emergencies when they develop into challenges requiring action.

Confusing the distinctions between issues, crises, and emergencies can lead to serious errors in four ways.

1. Identifying a problem in the wrong category can lead to making unsound plans and conducting ineffective programs. This is akin to declaring a state of war because a group of zealots have taken over a local armory.

2. Alarm and upset can spread unnecessarily among important groups—employees, stockholders, and communities. If the issue of unitary taxation, for instance, is approached with the mindset of dealing with a crisis, many people will be needlessly upset and much company effort will be expended fruitlessly.

3. Fuzzing the lines between these conditions leads to overstressing their impact. "Crisis management," particularly, tends to group together all potential problems, from layoffs needed because an obsolete product is discontinued to sabotage of the company's products on store shelves. Discovery of a product defect, which will have transitory effects on the company's profits, is equated with a takeover attack, which will determine whether it survives.

4. That approach can lead to a siege mentality, raising the company's defenses and storm warnings so singlemindedly that the whole organization is frozen into a defensive mindset. When management focus is on defensiveness, everyone down the line inevitably will develop a defensive outlook. Rather than focusing on initiative and venturesomeness—the essence of a thriving and dynamic organization—they tend to focus on how to avoid loss, how to reduce

vulnerability. In the parlance of sports, they "play not to lose" instead of playing to win. Many new products have been sidetracked because a defensive climate dictated caution rather than aggressiveness. Many plans for growth have been shelved or cut back because the management concentrated too much on forestalling damage from external sources.

For every issue that calls for monitoring and dossiers of plans, for every crisis that, if not defused, can destroy an organization, there are scores of emergencies of many kinds. Management of emergencies embraces issues and crises plus all other unexpected developments that can disrupt or derail an organization. (*See* Figure 2.1, pages 24–25.)

Dealing with unexpected events requires first taking specific actions *before* any sign of emergency appears, as follows:

1. Establish beyond doubt among everyone in the organization that management will put first the interests of all people concerned—employees, their families, neighbors, communities, customers, personnel of sales outlets, investors.

2. Clarify to all that the organization will be as open about what is happening as the facts and conditions permit.

3. Give priority to resolving the emergency and protecting the interests of the people affected until it is completely resolved. Dealing with a business emergency can no more be a sideline activity than dealing with a heart attack.

4. Emphasize that, despite stress and danger to the company, it will be fair to all—including, to the extent possible, critics or opponents who may have instigated the problem.

If such policies are spelled out in an ethics code, and the code is clearly enunciated to all employees, federal guidelines allow an organization to limit monetary damages in case of a lawsuit by a "whistle blower."

Preparations should involve two levels of personnel:

1. Those who are responsible for *management decisions* that will be affected in the event of an emergency.

2. All those who might be *involved* during an emergency—of whatever type. Alternates should be designated for every function, in case the first assignee is unable to perform. This system fulfills four vital functions.
   - Gives participants a sense of personal involvement not only in the planning but in whatever may activate an emergency plan later.
   - Provides valuable inputs from their combined experience and intelligence.
   - Helps make them aware of the emergency plans and what is required of them when a need arises.
   - Reduces recriminations when damage occurs, because they were also involved in the planning and assignment of responsibility.

It is necessary to set up a framework for anticipatory and preparatory activities. There is a great difference between an explosion and a months-long boycott by activists, or between a government-demanded product recall and the kidnapping of a company executive.

Accordingly, it is essential to break down the range of possibilities into more coherent categories. There are four main distinct categories to consider.

1. Internal versus external, or both? For example, a disaster such as a fire or an earthquake produces strong effects on both the company's people and on many outside groups, such as customers, dealers, investors, and the plant community.

1. Monitoring and Issues Identification

Objectives:

To monitor, interpret, identify and label corporate public issues, e.g. socio-political situations, actual or potential, susceptible of having an impact on corporate interests.

Desired outcomes:

• Timely identification and labelling of trends and issues.

• Comprehensiveness of issues identification process.

2. Characterization & prioritization

Process:

• Identify focal point.

• Focal point characterizes the issues using the Issue Evaluation form (impact; volatility; maturity; leverage; probability; etc.).

• Public Issues Dept. prioritizes using salience index (NOTE: see attachment for explanation).

• Cluster related issues

• Public Issues Dept. profiles priority issues.

Process output:

• Clearly defined corporate public issues.

• Priority listing of public issues (subject to validation by PP&IT).

• Issue profiles describing context and situation for priority issues (used for issues management plannning and communication purposes).

• For priority issues, an overview of current issues management activities and tactical status.

SAMPLE ISSUES MANAGEMENT STATEMENT

Figure 2.1 This chart outlines the structure of Dow Canada's sophisticated issues management program. (PP&IT stands for Public Policy & Issues Team.)

2. A sudden emergency or a developing one? For example, the sabotage of a company's products on retailers' shelves differs considerably from cumulatively increased demand that a plant either reduce its toxic waste emissions or close.

3. One-shot or lasting? A planted but undetonated bomb can create panic and havoc; however, its effect typically decreases in a day or two. A companywide strike may last one day or threaten to go on for months.

4. Human or nonhuman? Ugly rumors about the company or its products plumb the nuances of mass psychology. Typically, the breakdown of a power plant is disruptive, but its repair is primarily mechanical.

3. Issues Management Strategic Planning and Oversight

Goals:

• Define objectives

• Develop and assess issue management options.

• Select a strategy for recommendation to Operating Board.

• Deploy resources; oversee plans and activities.

• Evaluate

Desired outcomes:

• Integration of corporate issues management with business/functional/corporate strategic planning.

• Clearly defined and well understood positions and objectives.

• Maximize opportunities for Dow to influence public debate.

• Marshall resources towards issues management objectives.

4. Communications and Issues Management Training

Objectives:

• Disseminate public issues intelligence among key stakeholders; facilitate networking among them.

• Provide interpretative advice and information.

• Define opportunities for, and sponsor issues management training sessions.

Desired outcomes:

• Organizational focus, buy-in, commitment, and effectiveness.

Figure 2.1 *continued*

Fully Examining Grievances

An issue arises when one or more of an organization's publics develops a grievance or a fear. Before submitting to the natural reaction and rushing to the defense, it is wise to explore how the grievance or fear arose, then develop plans for dealing with it. This investigation should include the following actions:

1. Analyze the reasons for the grievance. Is there something wrong with the activities of the organization—a problem of quality, of explanation, of service? Is there something wrong with the role of suppliers, dealers, service organizations, employees, or members? Is there a gap in com-

munication, poor exposition, or faulty presentation?

2. Analyze the source of the grievance and the nature of the people who have made it.

3. Study all the facts about the subject of the grievance. Review all reports and documentation. Discuss the matter with experts within the organization.

4. Review outside reports and sources: government; other comparable organizations, associations, or coalitions; libraries; and suppliers.

5. Make an objective analysis of present attitudes about the grievance: in government, among competitors or other comparable organizations, among critics, in public media, and in specialized journals.

6. If the climate is unclear, conduct opinion surveys to provide further clues—among groups affected by the grievance, among various activist groups that may become involved, among employees, among stockholders or members.

7. Determine what is being done by others affected by this grievance. Avoid duplication; coordinate, form coalitions, assign responsibilities.

It is a mistake to assume that all those who oppose an institution are alike and should be dealt with in the same way. In general, opponents can be grouped into at least five classifications of personality.

1. *Advocates* are people who propose something they believe in, such as a reduction in the emission of carbon dioxide.

2. *Dissidents* are against something—and sometimes are against many things, because it is their character to be sour on things.

3. *Activists* want something done or something changed.

4. *Zealots* may harbor some traits of the others, but they are distinguished by an overriding singlemindedness.

5. *Fanatics* are zealots with their stabilizers removed.

Clearly, the means used to deal with an advocate will be futile with a zealot. On the other hand, to treat an advocate in the same way one treats a zealot results in creating enmity where none existed. The basis for dealing with reasonable people is reason. The way to overcome zealots is to wither away the support they depend on.

Priority Publics

Priority publics are those groups on whom an organization should focus its attention when dealing with any issue. It is essential to develop plans with which to interface and communicate with all the priority publics that may be involved—with approaches and messages suited to each specific group. The roster of key publics includes the following:

- Employees and their families
- Potential allies
- Potential critics
- Probable neutrals
- The government/regulatory interface
- Fanatics, zealots, activists, dissidents, advocates
- The media—assessed individually
- Third-party experts; academia
- Mutual aid coalitions, existing and potential—regional, local, national, international
- The plant community
- Unofficial opinion leaders
- Stockholders
- The financial community
- Customers and outlets

Gaining Public Favor

In an issues management context, persuasion constitutes a two-way, interactive process—not just something one party does to another. If the groups being addressed don't feel that the organization's actions are in their best interests, they'll turn off—and may turn on the organization itself.

The following principles must be applied when dealing with groups of stakeholders:

1. Participate with all interested parties to reach agreements together. Treat them as equals and listen before speaking. The reason the issue is being dealt with is because of the public's interest in it—so what they have to say serves as the starting point for discussion.

2. When talking to a group, first confirm understanding of what is on their minds—whether or not the organization is in agreement with their mindset. This establishes rapport. Building rapport is the first action toward eliminating mistrust so audiences will listen attentively and empathetically. In turn, the organization must respond with sensitivity to groups' concerns.

3. Make them feel it's *their* process—and not that the organization is making concessions or condescending by taking up the issue. When the public "owns" the process, they feel not only appreciated but motivated to develop an acceptable solution and to then make it work.

4. Don't expect communicating *at* them to do the job. They are not targets; they are people with a strong sense of self-worth and a degree of zest for their point of view and self-interest. Communicate *with* them. Show eagerness to share goals and to participate in reaching them.

5. Integrate all functions and communications to assure consistency, cohesiveness, and clarity. Uncoordinated channels can breed confusion and distrust.

Responding to Public Opposition[1]

As this circumstance has become evident, managements of many organizations have moved to broaden their options. They have been establishing various programs to manage public issues and opportunities, based on (a) detecting them early; (b) analyzing their implications; (c) tracking them as they develop; (d) developing programs—including lobbying, participation in the formulation process, and mass communications; and (e) evaluating the results.

As this process has evolved, sophistication has increased. Both passivity and combativeness are giving way to processes for steering the course of the human climate—from the time a cause emerges until the time it matures. (*See* Figure 2.2, page 28.)

This approach is presented by James E. Post, School of Management, Boston University, in *Public Affairs Review*:

> Rather than waiting for new public goals to fully evolve in the public policy process and then reacting, or attempting to manipulate the political system to thwart change, a number of firms have devised a third approach aimed at continually narrowing the gap between emerging public goals and emerging corporate goals. This is the *interactive* approach. Sometimes action is taken to influence public opinion; at other times, to change corporate behavior. The two prerequisites for successfully using the interactive approach are a management commitment to anticipating external change and a willingness to adjust the corporation's normal operations to minimize the gap between performance and expectations. *When consistently applied over time, an interactive approach tends to produce goals that the company and the public can accept.*

---

[1]*Overcoming Opposition*, by Philip Lesly, pp. 75–76.

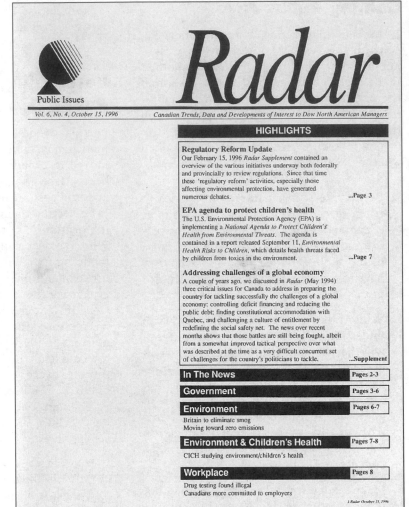

SAMPLE PAGE FROM A QUARTERLY NEWSLETTER

Figure 2.2 This quarterly publication reports and analyzes developments that affect issues of concern to Dow Canada. It is distributed to Dow managers and consultants. *Reprinted with permission from Dow Chemical Canada Inc.*

Therefore, the elements of a sophisticated program for dealing with public issues and opportunities are likely to include the following:

1. Identifying issues or opportunities and trends

2. Evaluating their impact and setting priorities

3. Establishing a company position

4. Designing company action and response (e.g., communications, lobbying, lawsuits, advertising, etc.)

5. Implementing the plans

6. Feedback and evaluation

The Media's Important Role

Increasingly, it is the orientation and procedures of the media that set the conditions under which organizations must deal with issues or pursue opportunities. (*See* Chapter 21.) For instance, the instant coverage of news by television dictates that organizations respond quickly to events or charges, plan their responses with the immediacy and superficiality of TV in mind, and focus on visual drama rather than on detailing facts. Print media, on the other hand, cover a very wide range of subjects—so their writers tend to be expert in few. The same reporter rarely covers any one source for long. These conditions are compounded by the fact that erroneous information, once published, becomes a matter of record and self-perpetuating.

For these reasons, expertise in sensing the procedures of the media and in dealing with them is necessary.

It is also necessary to be constantly alert for *opportunities* to create a more favorable human climate, as well as to combat threats or "issues." Furthermore, it is important to estimate the impact of cross effects among various departments and activities. That calls for joint participation in the program by various departments and for keeping each other informed at all times.

Because they are necessarily preoccupied with other things, senior executives should be drawn into issues and opportunities programs only at vital points—to consider, resolve, or otherwise dispose of a top-priority matter. The Conference Board recommends that a steering committee or task force to deal with issues and opportunities should, taken as a whole:

- Be diversified by function
- Comprise persons of sufficient stature to act as spokepeople for their peers
- include at least one highly qualified person from outside the organization
- Consist of "restless minds"
- Include members from all key operating segments of the enterprise

Program Management and Implementation

Developing an effective program calls for approaching the structure from several lev-

els. One process involves organizing by topic the issues and opportunities considered germane to the organization. For example:

- Natural environment (ecology, conservation, waste disposal, pollution, etc.)
- Social and cultural environment (minorities, women, activist groups, etc.)
- Technological environment (effects of fiber optics, microprocessing, genetic engineering, etc.)
- Political environment (single-issue groups, makeup of legislative bodies, climate of regulatory agencies, etc.)
- Economic environment (general and competitive)

Another process involves categorizing the issues and opportunities by time frame: strategic, emerging, or current. A third process involves weighting the items according to *importance* and *probability*. Then the products of these weights are used to arrive at a ranking of issues and opportunities that at least will generate meaningful discussion among management.

A further analysis calls for assessing the type of response the organization will make in each case: reactive (opposing or postponing change), adaptive (open to change), or dynamic or proactive (working to influence or direct change).

Determining which of these postures to take requires realistic assessment of the entire climate surrounding the issue. This ensures that inwardness of thinking and the personal stake of individuals do not lead to wishful decisions or failure to recognize all the influences involved.

Reactive and adaptive responses are well known, but a sophisticated proactive approach involves thinking ahead and organized functioning. In dealing with any issue, treatment by the media is likely to be crucial. An organization can do a number of things to optimize the treatment it receives.

1. Assess the media that will be involved with the organization and the issues likely to face it. This must be done medium by medium, rather than as a group. Although much lockstep coverage by media exists, it is unsafe to generalize.

   In each case, assess how the medium has treated the organization in the past: its essential fairness or susceptibility to being seduced by extremists when approaching new subjects; the background and maturity of its editorial staff; its concern for its reputation for accuracy and fairness; and its own stake in the welfare of the organization.

2. When a new issue is emerging, assess how each medium is likely to treat it. Does its staff have a stake in what activist groups will bring up? What is its record in handling similar matters?

3. Establish accessibility *in advance* to the key gatekeepers at each medium. Get acquainted with the pertinent editors—business, environment, city, or others. Establish understanding about the organization's functions, its concerns about the community and the public, its concern with the objectiveness of its coverage of any issue, and its readiness to answer questions and provide information. Establish your reliability as a source by answering all inquiries fully and promptly even on matters of little importance or unrelated to the organization's interests.

4. Humanize the organization. Leaders of the organization should become known, seen, heard, and respected.

5. Seed the flow of information on the emerging issue in advance. Develop authoritative, sound, fair material on the subject that is better than anyone else can produce. Make it available in personal contacts and by delivery to key people at every medium on your list. Encourage inquiries, requests for materials, and discussions.

   Ensure that no objective person or organization can draw up a proposal on what concerns you without including what you have to offer.

6. Become the key reliable source on the subject. Make sure that whenever any medium covers the subject, it's likely to think of you first or at least contact you.

7. Establish visibility. Do things about the subject in question that command respectful attention. Preempt the front of the stage on that subject.

8. Hold media people responsible. When media were unassailable, it often was fruitless to protest shabby treatment. Now the extensive scrutiny focused on media people makes them sensitive to what can damage their esteem. That esteem is augmented when major stories are achieved but diminished when their methods are shown to be shabby. This concern for the respect of their peers is your best channel for preventing shabby treatment.

Use fair and objective means to show that the organization will fight such treatment. Protest first to the journalist and request redress. If that fails, protest to his or her boss. If that's unsuccessful, then consider "going public." If you do, develop a scrupulously accurate, thoroughly documented demonstration that the treatment was irresponsible—not just routinely inaccurate. The offense must be glaring to gain a sympathetic hearing for a rebuttal. Don't aim to embarrass anyone. Just set the record straight and make it clear you will respond to other off-base attacks.

Several functions should be undertaken before it becomes clearly apparent that a problem has emerged:

1. Prepare an authoritative document on the issue that can be the key source for everyone who is concerned with it. It should emphasize the key points and highlights, with the bulk of supporting information

used as backup documentation. Make the material as inviting as possible. (*See* Chapter 3.)

2. Either distribute it or be prepared to distribute it through personal contact, e-mail, or Internet to affected government officials and personnel, colleges, journals, public media, other interested organizations, associations and societies, and libraries.

3. Designate which officials of the organization are to be constantly briefed on this issue or opportunity. Establish the lines of authority to be followed and the communications channels to be used.

4. Prepare those officials for tough questioning by the media, in confrontations with activists, in testifying to committees, and in conducting meetings.

5. Prepare fact cards on the issue and the designated officials of the organization (with their home phone numbers), for distribution to the media.

    Other functions may have to be carried out if the issue surfaces enough to call for concerted action. As much as possible, preparations should be completed in advance. Then they should be selected and carried out expeditiously and professionally.

6. Prepare testimony to be delivered before governmental bodies.

7. Set up an emergency plan for each local unit of the organization and on each potential issue. It should include the line of authority, designated personnel to deal with each likely function, and facilities for the media at the site where action may occur.

8. Statements should be prepared as responses to charges made by opponents or in response to potential questions. They should be concise, punchy, clear, and quotable.

9. Plans and facilities for press conferences and television coverage should be set in advance.

10. Readiness for preparation of press releases should include having all factual materials available at every possible site, word processors or computer terminals, facilities for reproducing releases and photos, and fax machines or mail facilities.

11. Fact sheets and illustrations should be prepared in advance for distribution to the media if needed.

12. Videotaping facilities and provision for making copies of videotapes should be set up or a fast source identified in each location. Videotapes should be used for recording events, as material for TV stations and for the organization's own dissemination, and as a deterrent to media distortion by providing a record of actual occurrences and statements.

13. Brochures and other literature should be written and dummied up, ready for final revision and printing.

14. Bulletins or letters should be prepared to reach employees immediately with explanations of the issue and the organization's position.

15. Inclusion of this type of material in all employee publications, e-mail, the intranet, and video news programs should be planned.

16. Notices should be prepared for bulletin boards.

17. Advertisements that present the facts—in a direct and noncombative tone—should be prepared in preliminary form. They might include insertions in major newspapers, newspapers in localities where the organization is active, publications of opinion leaders concerned with the issue, and publications reaching members of the opposition group.

TV and radio commercials should be prepared for possible placement with local stations that accept editorial-type commercials.

18. Letters and literature addressed to key customers or supporters should be roughed out.

19. Letters to stockholders or members should be prepared in preliminary form.

20. A list should be readied of the various public platforms that may be available for spokespersons of the organization, and speeches should be drafted for delivery by designated officials.

Throughout this process of action and readiness, schedules should be set up with priorities, time requirements for completion of each function, and the time needed for clearance and approval of various materials.

Flexibility must be maintained to allow for unexpected developments and changed emphases. This means that all schedules, assignments, and budgets should not be made firm. Some things may become unnecessary, and others may arise at any time. Parameters for expenditures can be set at the start, with limits that cannot be exceeded without specific authorization.

It is important not to assume the attitude of siege or war, but there is much similarity between a campaign on an activist issue and a battle. Alertness, fluidity, readiness to change position, constant review of tactics, thrust and counterthrust, knowing how many resources to commit without overcommitting, integrating, and coordinating—all of these are necessary.

General Electric's approach

General Electric, which has been working on processes for "managing uncertainty" since the 1960s, cites the conditions that are needed to make a program fully effective:

- It should be **holistic** in its approach to the business environment. It should view trends—social, political, economic, technological—in total, not piecemeal.

- It should be prepared to deal with **alternative** futures. In an uncertain environment, it is not possible to predict "the" future; however, it is possible to speculate about alternative possibilities.

- It should be oriented toward **contingency** planning. Many of the most important needs will result from surprises.

- It should be **continuous**, not one-shot.

- It should be **integrated with the decision-making system** of the corporation.

GE also sets these guidelines:

- Assess the long-term trends for **opportunities**, as well as for problems.

- Develop a **constructive** rationale for action (internal and external), matching options to the long-term trends.

- Build **flexibility** into the corporate strategy.

- Search out opportunities for **alliances** (with other companies, with labor, with government, etc.).

- Apply normal **managerial tools** (goals, objectives, measurements).

Taking the Right Approach

Each organization's own scope, nature of operations, competitive position, and other factors can determine how it approaches the need. Two illustrative examples follow.

At a large insurance company, the planning process involves the following:

1. Strategy meeting of senior officers in January, leading to CEO's planning a guidance statement in February.

2. Divisional preliminary plans in spring; approved by CEO in June.

3. Final detailed plans developed in fall and approved in December.

4. Performance reviews conducted at three, seven, and twelve months during implementation year.

A corporate issues inventory, in the form of a looseleaf notebook, is prepared and updated at quarterly meetings of the CEO and division heads. Each issue includes a brief definition statement followed by key background information, a statement of the company's position, an outline of the strategy and work plan, and the designation of officers with lead responsibility for the issue.

It is notable that this process seems to leave no provision for meeting unexpected developments that might call for immediate response or action, and that little attention seems to be given to flexibility within the timetable. Since the most severe demands tend to come from unexpected developments—disaster, an attack by an activist group, a proposed new regulation or restriction—these absences seem to contradict the apparent foresightedness of the company's approach.

The first example focused on procedures. The second shows a structure that has evolved in a large oil company. It comprises a Committee on Public Affairs and a working group that reports to it.

The committee consists of the following members:

- Senior Vice-President for Public Relations and Advertising (Chairperson)
- Senior Vice-President (responsible for government relations)
- Vice-President and Assistant to CEO
- Vice-President–Finance
- Vice-President–Planning
- Vice-President–Public Relations and Advertising
- General Counsel

- Vice-President–Washington Office
- Working Group Chairperson

The working group is composed of a manager from each department represented on the committee.

The fact that all members are employees of the company with the same orientation and background reflects the inwardness that has been a major cause of oil companies' estrangement from the human climate.

The Price of Neglect

The damage incurred by companies that fail to follow a conscious plan of detecting issues early and dealing with them forthrightly is illustrated in the case histories that follow:

Intel could have minimized a minor problem with its Pentium chip if it had immediately recognized that *no* problem is considered minor by people spending heavily for computers. By trying to brush it off, the company created a storm, and its stock value plunged.

Exxon could have reduced the furor over the *Valdez* oil spill in Alaska had its chairman immediately shown great concern.

Benetton used startling ads to command attention and to create an aura of being anti-establishment—appealing to teenagers and young adults. They included photos of homosexuals caressing and Catholic nuns kissing. When protests arose from angry citizens and the Catholic Church, Benetton at first acted as though the critics were benighted. Only after business was affected did the company offer signs of contrition.

Audi met widely publicized tests showing safety lapses by merely denying them. Sales plummeted. It took several years for the impact to abate and sales are still well below previous levels.

Nestlé Company was confronted by a worldwide boycott of its products after it apparently was late to detect—and underestimated—a barrage of public sentiment against practices used in the company's marketing of its infant formula in underdeveloped countries.

A producer of utilities equipment lost $400 million in orders because it didn't know in advance that the Sierra Club had gotten grants from the Ford Foundation to study air pollution in the area where a customer proposed to build four coal-fired, electricity-generating plants in southwest Utah. The restrictions that were attached killed the project.

The Value of Preparation

Advance planning and preparation can do much to protect and sustain an organization's status with its publics, as demonstrated by the following examples.

A manufacturer identified an opportunity to lower its interest costs. It then worked in conjunction with other organizations to garner an amendment to a tax law that greatly lessened the number of loans subject to state interest rate ceilings. That led to first-year savings of $6 million.

Johnson & Johnson achieved notable success in dealing with the alarm caused by the poisoning of Tylenol. United Airlines was applauded for the effective way it responded to a crash in Sioux City, Iowa.

Atlantic Richfield detected growing criticism of oil companies as shortages grew and public irritation with long lines at service stations built up during an OPEC-created shortage. Instead of running ads arguing its need for profits, it ran a campaign soliciting suggestions on how to meet the energy shortage.

A large food company discerned that it would probably get strong opposition to running its commercials on TV shows with strong violence or sexual content. It established a policy that, whenever possible, it would not let a commercial appear on such a show. It has received far fewer negative reactions from organized parents and teachers than some of its competitors.

Corning Glass recalled 18,500 "Electromatic" coffee pots as soon as it received reports of a few accidents. It sent out press releases, ran a series of ads, and contacted Action Line editors. The effort was so successful, it not only avoided negative publicity for Corning but evoked commendations from government agencies and consumer organizations.

Aetna Life and Casualty detected a swelling resentment against insurance companies that resulted, among other things, in a tendency of juries to make huge awards to accident victims. It has sought to defuse the lack of information that is partly responsible for the resentment. It has repeatedly encouraged public discussion on critical insurance industry issues, such as fundamental problems in the health care and health insurance system, provision of product liability coverage to small and high-risk manufacturers, availability and cost of automobile insurance, and variables to be considered in calculating automobile insurance and life insurance rates. This pattern has contributed to Aetna's image as one of the most responsible of the large multiple-line insurers. (However, Aetna aroused the ire of plaintiffs' lawyers with an ad decrying the boosting of insurance claims and had to apologize.)

An essential aspect of preparation involves readiness to effectively communicate the company's point of view. Reginald H. Jones, former CEO of General Electric, says:

> We must raise these issues with our employees, our customers, our shareowners and others who have a direct, personal stake in the success of American business. . . . Their potential as a base of support for sound policy is enormous. But we are not going to have their support unless we work for it—earning their trust, discussing the issues, demonstrating how they are personally affected, and asking them, directly and persuasively, for their wholehearted support.

Several guidelines should be kept in mind when planning an issues and opportunities program.

1. It is a mistake to follow diagrams and blueprints; every organization is different. Conditions within each organization change constantly, making flexibility vital. The organization's particular position and objectives greatly affect its needs and programs.

2. Placing emphasis on issues leads to a negative or siege mentality. Equal attention to issues *and opportunities* is called for.

3. It is a mistake to set up firm programs on a long-term basis (and in today's climate, one year may be long term), because that tends to prevent alertness to nuances of change, taking advantage of opportunities, and vigorous response to unexpected developments.

4. It is important to fill the pipelines of information about any potential issue before opinion jells on the basis of others' input.

5. Flexibility must be maintained. For instance, an executive designated as the spokesperson in case of emergency may be affected and so unable to perform. An alternate should be named in advance.

6. Diversity of mind and experience are essential. A group composed of executives trained to focus on tangibles and who are all employees of the same organization is likely to amplify its myopia and prejudices.

Issues and Opportunities Checklist

The following checklist is a guide, not a blueprint. Every organization should modify it after careful, perceptive analysis, and it is subject to constant review or change.

I. Structure
  1. Public Issues and Opportunities Task Force
     • Corporate Planning
     • Operations
     • Finance
     • Marketing
     • Production
     • Law
     • Government Relations
     • Public Relations
     • Human Resources
     • Outside Counsel

II. Preparation for Each Issue or Opportunity
  1. Research what is known about the issue or opportunity
     1.1 Analyze causes
        • Technical factors
        • Supplier fault
        • Company's procedures
        • External problems (blockages, weather, etc.)
        • Snag in employee communication
        • Snag in communications with customers
        • Snag in communication with stockholders
        • Snag in communication with government agencies
        • Snag in communication with legislators
        • Snag in relations with external organizations (environmentalists, minorities, etc.)
     1.2 Study facts, reports, experts within company
     1.3 Review outside sources
        • Government
        • Other industry
        • Associations
        • Libraries

- Suppliers
- Publications

1.4 Analyze the present climate
- Government
- Competitors
- Other industry
- Critics' groups
- Media
- Journals

1.5 Conduct opinion surveys
- Among groups affected by issue
- Activists
- Employees
- Stockholders

1.6 Determine what others are doing on this issue (avoid duplication, coordinate, counteract)

2. Establish company's position on the issue
   2.1 Write policy as guide for all in company
   2.2 Distribute on need-to-know basis

III. Publics to Be Dealt With
1. Employees
   1.1 All
   1.2 Select groups
   - Executives
   - Operating staff
   - Subsidiaries' staff
   - Local plant and office level
2. Government
   2.1 Federal elected officials
   2.2 Federal appointed officials
   2.3 State elected officials
   2.4 State appointed officials
   2.5 Local elected officials
   2.6 Local appointed officials
3. Financial community
4. Stockholders
5. Customers and prospective customers

6. Unions
7. Suppliers
8. Plant and office communities
9. Academia
10. Other opinion leaders—churches, civic groups
11. News media
    11.1 Press
    11.2 TV and radio
12. Other media
    12.1 Books and reference works
    12.2 Business publications
    12.3 Trade publications
    12.4 Alternative press
    12.5 The Internet

IV. Activities
1. Prepare authoritative document on the issue or opportunity that can serve as the key source for all concerned with it
   - Distribute to affected government officials and personnel, colleges, journals, public media, other industry members, and associations
2. Assign company representatives on this issue or opportunity and establish lines of authority for communicating on it. Also designate alternates and make alternative plans in case of major disruptions
3. Prepare executives for questioning by media, testifying to committees, and conducting meetings
4. Prepare testimony before Congress, government agencies, etc.
5. Prepare fact cards or backgrounders on the issue and company sources (with home phone numbers) for distribution to media

6. Set up emergency plan
   - Line of authority
   - Facilities for the media on the site
7. Prepare in advance statements responding to charges or questions
8. Press conference
9. Press releases
10. Fact sheets and photos for the media
11. Prepare to use e-mail and Internet
12. Videotape
    - Record events
    - Provide proof of developments and deter media distortion
    - Prepare news footage for TV
13. Literature
14. Employee bulletins or letters
15. Employee publications
16. Advertising
17. Scripts for radio broadcast
18. Customer information—letters and literature
19. Letters to stockholders
20. Bulletin boards
21. Community meetings
22. Speeches
    - Key executives
    - Others at local levels

V. Set Timetable (with built-in flexibility)

VI. Establish Budget

VII. Review and Evaluation
   1. Conduct survey as a measure against analysis of problem or opportunity at the start
   2. Analyze cost of manpower utilization in terms of alleviation of the problem or progress in fulfilling opportunity

3

THE NATURE OF EFFECTIVE COMMUNICATIONS

PHILIP LESLY

The unique way we communicate is a fundamental part of the human experience, distinguishing humankind from the rest of creation. An individual's ability to relate with another person through the exchange of ideas marks the first stride toward differentiating human beings from other creatures. Our ability to record thoughts and information for others to respond to—immediately or later—forms the basis of the cumulative dissemination and exchange of all experience and knowledge. And the ability of a single individual or a group to communicate in order to associate with and influence other groups is integral to the entire social nature of the human species.

Accordingly, there is no subject more basic to understanding human processes and to facilitating human endeavors than communication. Yet it is only recently that any semblance of scientific inquiry into this field has been made, and we are still in the early stages of defining its basic principles.

However, the power of effective communication has long been realized, going back to antiquity. Plato clearly defined its essence when he wrote in his *Dialogues*:

> Gorgias. What is there greater than the word which persuades the judges in the courts, or the Senators in the Council, or the citizens in the assembly, or at any other political meeting? If you have the power of uttering this word, you will have the physician your slave, and the trainer your slave, and the money maker of whom you

talk will be found to gather treasures, not for himself, but for you who are able to speak and to persuade the multitude.

Communication is basic to the everyday existence of every modern individual and of every organization of any size. Even at the most primitive levels, people need to know the weather forecast, the expected food supply, the movings of nearby tribes and herds, and many other things. Every organization needs to know what is going on among all the groups that impinge on it and how to reach the various publics it deals with. A society's degree of complexity can be measured in terms of how much information, opinion, and speculative knowledge are needed to keep it operating with reasonable consistency.

Although Chapter 1 shows that public relations encompasses much more than communication, the essence of public relations embodies the broad definition of the term *communications*. Public relations, as a comprehensive form of communications, involve the following:

- Sensing the status of the organization's rapport—or the lack of it—with the involved publics

- Interpreting that status in terms of the organization and its objectives

- Assimilating the implications of this interpretation, then adjusting the posture and thrust of the organization accordingly

- Developing the thoughts and messages representing what the organization wants to project to the public
- Transmitting those thoughts
- Assessing the effects
- Adjusting messages and procedures accordingly

Communication Methods

Since communication encompasses so much of the spectrum of human activity, full treatment of it (even in its present partially developed state) fills libraries. For simplification, we can identify six major forms of human communication:

1. Oral
2. Written
3. Signs and symbols
4. Gestures, such as finger movements, facial expressions, etc.
5. Nonverbal sound, such as music, drum signals, etc.
6. Combinations of any of these, such as oral language, music, and visual happenings on television; or oral language and gestures in conversation

Communication as it involves the public relations person encompasses all of these forms. However, it predominantly involves *mass* communication rather than exchanges between individuals.

Effective Versus Ineffective Communication

Largely because most comments about the communications process have been prepared by communicators, such as Plato, the potency of the communications *process* has been over-

rated through the centuries. While it's true that deliberate communications processes often bring about monumental developments and changes, it is also true that a great deal of communications effort either fails or negatively impacts the source. The researches and conjectures about communication have been derived from the constant search to understand what makes communication effective or ineffective. Whether the communication actually occurs—whether the conceptualized ideas and information originating with the sender are received in similar form by the intended recipient—depends on a number of conditions and circumstances. These include the following:

1. The *predisposition* of the intended recipient. This consists of a composite of his heritage, his outlook on life, his opinion on the subject of the communication that has accumulated through his lifetime, his fears, training, group memberships, and so on.

2. The innate propensity to believe what comforts one's psyche or that shields it from guilt or fear.

3. The basic needs of the individual, such as individual worth, group acceptance, self-admiration, security, skill, knowledge, and power.

4. The basic need for harmony between the individual's needs and desires, and the social demands and pressures on him, including conscience and other forces. The person inherently moves toward acceptance of what enhances harmony and shields himself from what might create dissonance within him.

5. What Stuart Chase referred to as the fidelity of the message. Does it reach the recipient in the shape in which it was sent? This involves the physics of transmission— sound waves, light waves, and so on; the clarity of both transmission and reception,

including such matters as whether accents are recognizable or colors are clear; and the semantics involved: do sender and auditor give the same precise meanings to words and symbols?

6. The skill and experience of the communicator—*the overriding factor in all communications efforts.* Masterly skills can work wonders; ineptness or amateurishness can create directly opposite results. Is she sharply attuned to "getting inside the skin" of the recipient, understanding how he will receive and respond to any messages? Is she a master at formulating and projecting messages so they will reach the recipient under optimum circumstances and be readily decoded into the desired form?

It can thus be seen that in many instances the barriers against a communications transfer exceed the influences favoring it.

As pointed out by J. A. C. Brown: "The will to believe is more potent than any mere experience and emotion is stronger than reason in the vast majority of people." Berelson and Steiner in their summation of findings from many studies reached this conclusion in *Human Behavior*:

> People tend to misperceive or misinterpret persuasive communications in accordance with their own predispositions, by evading the message or by distorting it in a favorable direction.
>
> For example, anti-Semites tend to misread the tolerance propaganda put out by Jewish groups; political partisans misinterpret the position of their candidate to bring it more nearly into line with their own position on the issues; partisans on both sides tend to judge neutral speeches as favoring their own point of view; partisans are more likely than others to accept as "fact" those news reports supporting their own position.

The propensity for screening incoming communications to shape them to one's own predilection was found in early studies by Douglas Waples of what people get out of their reading: "What reading does to people is not nearly so important as what people do to reading."

Impact of group identification

One element of predisposition is the individual's affiliation and identification with a specific group or groups. As Berelson and Steiner concluded: "On matters involving group norms, the more attached people are to the group or the more active within it, the more their membership determines their response to communications."

W. Phillips Davison points out:

> As a result of . . . cultural and individual selective mechanisms, each person gives his attention to different portions of the stream of communication. If, for example, a group made up of people with varying interests and from a number of countries is given fifteen minutes to examine a newspaper and each individual is then asked to write down the headlines of the stories he remembers, it is usually found that every person recalls a different list. Each will be likely to remember items dealing with his own country, and most will recall items dealing with their own professional or nonprofessional interests.

This predisposition, to a large extent, not only determines how the recipient interprets the communication, but also the degree to which he exposes himself to an idea. Berelson and Steiner found that "people are more likely to talk about controversial matters with like-minded people than with those who do not share their views."

People who are already interested in a subject and inclined toward it are the ones most open to receive new communications about it. "Those who read about a topic also tend to listen, and those who pay attention at one time also tend to pay attention at another."

J. A. C. Brown spoke of this pattern as "the Law of Primacy . . . that the earlier an experience, the more potent its effect since it influences how later experiences will be interpreted."

Varying receptivity

There also exists a wide range of what might be called *susceptibility* to being moved by communications. Berelson and Steiner said, "People with low self-esteem (i.e., those persons high in measures of social inadequacy, inhibition of aggression, and depressive tendencies) are more likely to be influenced by persuasive communications than are those with high self-esteem; but those with acute neurotic symptoms (i.e., neurotic anxiety or obsessional reactions) are more likely to be resistant. Those low in self-esteem are easily persuadable by others because they lack character of their own; the neurotic are too disturbed, too self-concerned, or too negativistic to pay attention or to care."[1]

Although the recent predominance of television as an influential force in shaping the communications habits of the populace may be changing this, Berelson and Steiner found that "the higher the education, the greater the reliance on print; the lower the education, the greater the reliance on aural and picture media."[2]

Among the most important variable factors determining which communications are effective is the rapport between the source and the intended recipient.

> The more trustworthy, credible or prestigious the communicator is perceived to be, the less manipulative his intent is considered to be and the greater the immediate tendency to accept his conclusions. However, within reasonable limits, the credibility of the source has little or no influence on the transmission of *factual* information.
>
> When the audience has little or no prior knowledge of the communicator's trustworthiness, it tends to decide a question on the basis of the content itself—i.e., the conformity of the content to predispositions. When the audience does expect or attribute manipulative intent . . . it develops resistance to acceptance of the message.[3]

Accordingly, Berelson and Steiner concluded, "The effect of communication programs that try to convert opinions on controversial issues is usually slight. If the issue matters to the audience, predispositions block the conversion. If the issue does not matter, it gets little attention."[4]

Joseph Klapper said, "Communications research strongly indicates that persuasive mass communication is in general more likely to reinforce the existing opinions of its audience than it is to change such opinions."

Edward R. Murrow, the late television commentator and head of the United States Information Agency, pointed out that she who seeks to influence opinion can accelerate a trend in public opinion, but cannot reverse it. Brown came to the conclusion that "there is every reason to believe (that) well-meant but incompetently conceived propaganda . . . can . . . have positively undesirable (results) or even . . . lead to effects diametrically opposed to those desired."

Research in this field has advanced to the point, therefore, where observers now realize how much more difficult it is to communicate than was commonly believed. Much communications activity appears to communicate but actually fails to reach, to be observed by, and to motivate the intended audience; and it often backfires completely. It is vital, therefore, for any user of communication, which means everyone, to recognize the complexities and pitfalls involved and to narrow the range of error before proceeding.

---

[1]Berelson and Steiner, *Human Behavior*, p. 548.
[2]Ibid., p. 533.
[3]Ibid., pp. 537–38.
[4]Ibid., p. 542.

Communication: A Complex Field

For many years, the essence of mass persuasion was thought to entail exposing the targeted audience to an idea, a name, or a product. The success of these endeavors was measured by the number of people reached and the number of times exposure took place. The inadequacy of this exposure theory has since been demonstrated through the knowledge gained of how the human mind responds to efforts to reach it.

Some of the major factors determining the effectiveness of any communications effort, aside from exposure, are now known to include the following:

1. Within the intended audience a very wide range of mental capacities exists, even if it is a specified group or classification of people. For simplification, however, we may generalize that most people tend to think in either "abstract" or "concrete" terms. The abstract thinker is the writer, the artist, the idea person, who lives with intangibles, is excited by unseen prospects, and seeks the unknown and the new. The concrete thinker is the production person, the accountant, the lawyer—the practical person who generally must feel or see something before he or she recognizes its existence; who is trained to resist as untrustworthy anything that cannot be measured or calculated.

    Both of these types are essential to the proper working of society and indeed to the success of any substantial organization. Yet when a suggestion for a course of action is presented to a mixed group of both types, the task of the communicator is most difficult. When any idea, concept, product, or service is exposed to a group made up of both types, the range of acceptance by the individuals can vary from complete to entirely negative.

    Wherever possible and practical, it is the task of the communicator to determine the mental posture of the various elements within the public he seeks to reach, to separate the "abstracts" from the "concretes," and to frame his communications in the appropriate form for each group. With the "concretes" he may utilize charts, tabulations, diagrams, photographs, mock-ups and models, and any other devices that tend to make his message tangible. For the "abstracts" he needs to stimulate the imagination, inspire the enthusiasm, and whet the appetite.

2. Increased education, greater participation in running things, and other liberating factors have elevated the sophistication of the American people, who have assumed an attitude of skepticism toward communications seeking to influence them. As pointed out in *Business Week*: "People are suspicious of hogwash. They are pausing to evaluate. They feel they have been fooled and don't want to be fooled again." This author has stated:

    The individuals to be reached. . . are far more complex beings. . . . They have within them much more knowledge and experience. They . . . believe they are distinct and independent beings, each with the right to question everything and be skeptical of everyone.[5]

    As a result, patently insincere communications not only are ineffective but build resistance that will prevent acceptance of future efforts.

3. With sophisticated audiences skeptical of efforts to influence them, with the great diversity of mental "bents" that must be accounted for, and with the vast number of would-be communications directed toward each individual every day, the function of public relations is to inject ideas

---

[5]Lesly, Philip, *How We Discommunicate*, AMACOM, 1979, pp. 14–15.

and information into that broad stream of communication. There they will coalesce with all the other ideas and information, be affected by them, and course their way into the screening processes of the audience. The skill of the public relations person comes in selecting the means and the context of the information put into the stream of communication, in making it appeal to the recipient in his own frame of reference, in timing, in integrating all the other things for his interest. The effectiveness of the public relations function depends on how well the information and ideas it communicates are adopted by the individual, so that they become part of his own body of thought from which he draws his attitudes. Because of its need for these talents, public relations demands the abilities and skills of true scientists of public opinion, rather than information producers, ballyhoo artists, or other narrowly specialized technicians.

4. For some time, a theory has maintained that the flow of communications is a two-step process, in which influence comes from "opinion leaders." This concept was first clearly expressed by Lazarsfeld, Berelson, and Gaudet when they suggested that "ideas often flow *from* radio and print *to* the opinion leaders and *from* them to the less active sections of the population."[6] (The theory of the flow of influence is diagrammed in Figure 3.1.)

As Klapper pointed out in discussing this study:

The "opinion leaders" who exercise such influence were found to be widely dispersed through all social classes, and to be much like the persons they influenced. "Compared with the rest of the population, (however,) opinion leaders were found to be considerably more exposed to the radio, to the newspapers, and to magazines; that is, to the formal media of communication."

These specific others, or "opinion leaders," or "influentials" may serve a following of one, of three or four, or of somewhat more, but they typically do so in reference to only one topic; the fashion leader, for example, is not likely to be a marketing leader, nor is the physician who influences others to adopt a new drug more likely than his colleagues to influence their view on public issues. . . . The leader, however, is typically found to be more exposed than are his followers to the media appropriate to his sphere of influence. . . . After the follower has been influenced by the opinion leader, mass communication may provide material which the follower selectively attends or perceives to buttress his newly adopted opinion.

While the concept of the "opinion leaders" is revealing, the problems involved in locating them are generally insurmountable. Because they are not clearly identifiable by position or otherwise, on the basis of this theory it remains necessary to con-

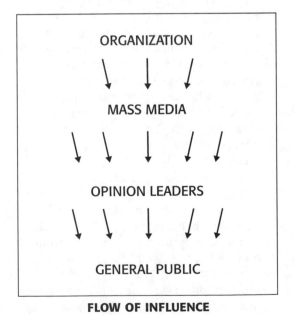

FLOW OF INFLUENCE

Figure 3.1 The traditional concept of the flow of influence.

---

[6]Lazarsfeld, Berelson, and Gaudet, *The People's Choice*, New York: Columbia University Press, 1948.

centrate on the mass media from which the opinion leaders tend to derive the fuel for the development of the opinions they pass on to others. A mass medium need not, however, be a national magazine, a newspaper, or a television show, for a specialized publication read by a few thousand specialists in a given profession, a group of women's club members, or a group of church leaders may provide the avenue whereby the ideas are brought to the attention of the opinion leaders among the readers.

However, evidence indicates that some media are far more suited than others to imparting information and ideas to opinion leaders in the areas they cover. This provides the public relations person with the area of selectivity for communications.

5. Now seeming to counterbalance the two-step process is the rise of instant visibility of events and issues. Television brings "reality" and "meaning" directly into the lives of the mass audience. Sensing this, presidents since Kennedy have geared their approach to reaching people directly through TV appearances.

The impact of television, as well as a great increase in educational levels, affluence, and free time, has transformed the way influence is generated. It is now clear that there are at least three separate groups in the "leader" category and that most of them are increasingly removed from close contact with the general public. They are as follows:

- *Vocal Activists*, who devote themselves to propounding a cause
- *Opinion Leaders*, who are members of the mass media and key educators
- *Power Leaders*, the legislators, government officials, judges, and regulators who have the power to take actions that affect organizations and society

The focal group increasingly becomes the Power Leaders. They can actually make things happen, and they increasingly feel empowered to initiate actions that affect private organizations and individuals rather than moving only when public demands or needs are felt. The Vocal Activists, Opinion Leaders, and the general public provide input to the Power Leaders but hold little power themselves.

However, the input that gets to the Power Leaders is much greater from the Vocal Activists and the Opinion Leaders than from the public and most private organizations. (The present pattern of the flow of influence is diagrammed in Figure 3.2.)

As a result of this new pattern, the Power Leaders—responding to the far heavier input from Vocal Activists and Opinion Leaders than from the private sector or general public—often greatly over-

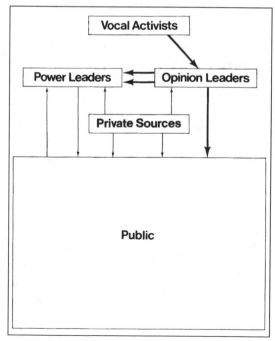

FLOW OF COMMUNICATIONS ON ISSUES

Figure 3.2 Present flow of influence.

rate the actual dissatisfaction among the public on any given issue. They tend to assume that the disproportionate impressions they receive from the small articulate groups reflect what the public at large feels. Often, in responding to these strong inputs with alarm and proposals for new government controls, they stimulate greater public dissatisfaction than would otherwise exist.

6. As the proportion of people who have grown up with television as the primary influence increases, the whole pattern of how ideas are established has changed. People who are oriented to instant visual involvement tend to be impatient with complicated interplay between elements of society. They have less patience with "working things out." They see all problems resolved in a thirty-minute drama and all commercials assuring answers to desires. This tends to create a euphoric certainty that all things are attainable readily and quickly, resulting in frustration when answers don't come easily, but, instead, problems grow. Communicating with these people requires graphic, action orientation.

7. The primacy of visibility determines the level of importance given to any subject. When activism against the Vietnam War was high in late 1969, America was losing about eighty-five men a week. At the same time, more than one thousand people a week were lost in automobile accidents. But the war was highly visible and had been made into an emotional issue. Automobile accidents are seldom shown on TV; a camera is rarely focused on bereaved relatives; a mother is not shown receiving a folded flag from the casket of a son who died in a smashed car. The toll in Vietnam was terrible, but it was its visibility that made it a flaming issue on the streets while the slaughter on the highways got minor attention.

In the TV age, visibility is clearly of great importance. But it is too simplistic to define "visual" as only what can be shown. Music that motivates emotion creates mental images—as the Beatles and Woodstock proved. Messages that stir emotions resulting in action become visual—as Hitler and Churchill showed.

So the principle is: When something can be made to capture the imagination by becoming a real force in people's minds—actions, emotion-stirring music or speeches, films, dramatizations, events, observances, displays, or symbols—it can also capture public support.

8. It must be remembered that in most cases the person selects the media to which he really exposes himself. Appearance of a message in a medium to which he has elected to expose himself predetermines a likely disposition toward at least recognizing and considering that message.

This is increasingly a vital factor in weighing the comparative value of *discretionary* media exposure (editorial material in newspapers and magazines, broadcast content of TV and radio, theatrical motion pictures, books) and *imposed* media exposure (advertisements, TV and radio commercials, literature not requested by the recipient, commercial motion pictures, propaganda speeches). Without willing exposure by selection of the medium, many people cannot be reached by many messages, regardless of how much is spent or how massive the efforts to impose the message on them.

However, when the message is not critical to the person's psychic assurance, as pointed out by Herbert E. Krugman, under certain circumstances with massive communications efforts, it is possible to get a specific concept to take hold.

9. As pointed out by Elihu Katz, there is great variation in how diffusible various messages will be. Some matters involve much more risk or danger to the respondent's psychic equilibrium, and some demand more extensive and pervasive changes than others. It is not possible to judge precisely what a person may assimilate by studying what she has previously assimilated, because no two messages involve the same degree of effect on her psyche.

10. There exists what is called the "source effect" in communications. As pointed out in a milestone study by Theodore Levitt of Harvard: "a company's generalized reputation has an important bearing on how its sales prospects make buying decisions." As noted in Chapter 1, it is probable that this effect of reputation—the net effect of the total public relations of the organization—influences the attitudes of prospective shareholders and employees, government officials, civic leaders, and all other publics.

11. For communication to take place, the audience must be in what might be called a "posture of receptivity." As we have seen, the adoption of a message by its object results from a complex combination of preconditioning influences. Aside from those that make up the character of the recipient, there are the many previous exposures to the source of any given message. This is of extreme importance in public relations; it's becoming recognized that the favorable inclination of an individual toward all messages from a given source is the result of the individual's total experience with that source. The character of the organization as exemplified by its actions, the sincerity and trustworthiness of its previous statements, the value provided in its products or services, and other influences set the

stage for the enthusiasm or rejection with which the organization's communication is met.

This means, of course, that when effective public relations have been practiced for an organization—when its actions and its statements have developed a positive image and a degree of goodwill—not only is a reservoir of support developed, but every other message from that source will receive much more acceptability. In practice, for instance, this results in very expensive advertising investments returning far greater benefits per dollar when the "posture of receptivity" has been developed through good public relations practice. The welcome a company's salespeople receive when they call on prospective customers, the interest of a prize college senior in talking with the company's personnel recruiters, the eagerness with which the investment public greets a new offering of securities—all become far more favorable as a result of the modest costs of the sound public relations program.

12. As shown in Chapter 30, we now know it is very unlikely that ideas can be sold through direct, overt messages similar to the hard-sell advertising that is effective in selling products if there is no previous "posture of receptivity" to the idea. Where a negative opinion or indifference exists, obvious efforts to inject one's opinions into the minds of others is, at best, ineffective and at worst increases resistance.

13. There is a *threshold of consciousness* that must be reached and passed before an idea becomes a factor in the attitude of an individual or a group. With millions of subjects attempting to intrude upon the consciousness of each individual, the process through which a concept passes from complete obscurity through the var-

ious stages of awareness in one's mind, until at last it "is there" and an influence, is an underexplored area of psychology. There is no doubt, however, that every idea that comes to have an influence passes through the screen of resistance that the individual must erect to block out the great majority of clamoring ideas seeking his attention, to become a part of his mental reality and resources. Whether it is one of thousands of attractive young women who somehow becomes what the public knows as Madonna or a concept of social change requiring a broadening of one's horizons to encompass formerly foreign interests, it is only through a multitude of impressions coming from many directions that the threshold is crossed and the concept embeds itself.

14. From this we can discern that establishing an idea in the public mind calls for a "multiple-channel approach." If the idea of owning a boat is expressed a dozen times by one's teenage son, for instance, it is quite different from having twelve different respected people, in a dozen different situations and circumstances, talk enthusiastically about the fun and excitement of boating. When a multiple combination of impressions impinges on one's attention, the impression is created that the idea is all-pervading, that it is "the thing to do." It therefore has considerably greater influence. The same number of messages is likely to be far more effective if they are directed through many channels—newspapers, radio commentators, television programs, inclusion in motion pictures, word-of-mouth discussion, club meetings, and other channels—than repeatedly through the same means. It is no longer likely that successful communications can be confined to a company newspaper, or just advertisements in the local press, or any other one or two

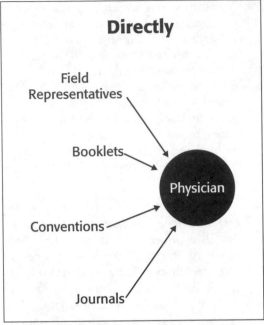

HOW INFORMATION AND INFLUENCE DIRECTLY REACH INDIVIDUAL

Figure 3.3 Information and influence reach persons from many directions. This part of a two-phase diagram indicates those that are directed specifically at the physician.

outlets. Public relations, to be effective, must be as versatile and as all-encompassing of communications channels as the available resources and talents will permit.

When Ivy Lee, Edward L. Bernays, and other early public relations practitioners were formulating their methods, the world of communication was simple and confined. In the United States three wire services, a few magazines, and a few major newspapers constituted the key channels of communication. The educated public that exposed itself to ideas or took a part in events was a small fraction of the population. Under these conditions, one staged event or one article in a magazine could alter public opinion. (*See* Figure 3.3.)

Today we are experiencing an explosion of the scope that influencing of public opinion must cover. Besides the wire services and major newspapers, there are many more magazines, plus the multiplying forces of network, cable, and satellite television; radio; motion pictures; VCRS; computers; and mass-distributed books. A majority of the population represents the public to be reached, and it is educated, diffuse, and skeptical. Except for an extremely rare occasion, such as the first landing on the moon, the attempt to assassinate President Reagan, or the assassination of Israel's Prime Minister Yitzhak Rabin, no one event achieves general recognition immediately.

People must be reached by many channels, over a period of time, in the contexts of many diverse outlooks and windows on the world. (*See* Figure 3.4.)

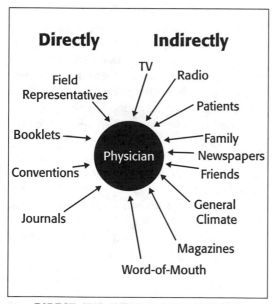

DIRECT AND INDIRECT INFLUENCES

Figure 3.4 When the many indirect avenues to the physician are added, "the multiple-channel effect" surrounds him with the subject, and his awareness greatly increases.

15. The more closely a communication is beamed to a specific audience or single recipient, the more likely it is to be received and accepted. "Communications directed to particular audiences are more effective than those directed to the 'public at large,'" concluded Berelson and Steiner.

16. The more sharply the key point of a communication focuses on the recipient, the more likely he or she is to grasp it. At the same time, it must not condescend or seem to insult his intelligence. The recipient should be led to draw the conclusion, yet not feel that his conclusions are being imposed upon him. Berelson and Steiner's research showed:

   Especially on complex matters, the explicit drawing of conclusions by the communicator is more effective in bringing about audience acceptance than relying upon the audience to draw its own conclusions from the material presented—and presumably this is the more so the less intelligent or the less educated the audience.

17. The early reaction to events may disguise their actual effects. Great publicity and furor may seem to create public opinion because of their immediacy, visibility, and force. But often there is a reaction against that furor that is more substantial and lasting. The uproar caused by the Students for a Democratic Society in 1968—especially in disrupting the Democratic convention—was aimed at grabbing public attention and radicalizing millions of young people. The tumult they created was a greatly exposed news event. Yet studies made by the University of Michigan after the election showed that more young people were moved to vote for right-wing candidates than were moved to follow the SDS.

18. The number and types of media have expanded greatly and there is a vast range

of subjects that clamor for the individual's attention. The days when a person read or at least looked at everything exposed to her are over. The individual is free to choose the communications she will expose herself to.

It is necessary to make the person's self-interest so visible, immediately, that she feels the urge to expose her psyche to the message.

Discommunication

In numerous ways efforts to communicate actually have the opposite effect and "discommunicate." They result in failure or even a counterproductive reaction. The most common forms of "discommunication" are the following:[7]

Putting art ahead of communication

The purpose of graphic materials in public relations is to aid the communication process. When artists or designers emphasize their creativity or personality at the expense of conveying the message, discommunication results. This takes various forms. Type treatments that defy legibility repel the audience instead of communicating. Multiple, repeated fast cuts in films thwart the audience's efforts to discern what is shown. Multimedia presentations often drown the audience in impressions but communicate too little. Color combinations are chosen deliberately to affront the eye but make the subject or words illegible. Stylized artwork or photos often convey no message to the reader.

Artwork is helpful if it conveys an impression in addition to its inherent meaning; but impression for the sake of impression is phony and fails.

The lure of "controlled" communication

It is tempting to try to project information and ideas to the audience exactly as one would like them, rather than through the screening of third parties such as editors. However, we have seen that imposed communication materials are far less effective than those the audience is exposed to by choice or in another context. Thus idea advertising (*see* Chapter 30), literature not requested by the recipient, and other "controlled" materials often discommunicate.

Names that communicate nothing

The name of an organization, like that of a person, serves as a primary source of the impression it makes. Efforts to devise "neutral" names disregard this vital source of impression and often cause only confusion. (*See* Chapter 49.)

The snobbery of jargon

Segments of society are being separated by the languages they create. Special terminologies that result from growing specialization make it harder for various groups to understand each other. But increasingly there is another contributing factor: snobbery. People who want to make sure others recognize they are on a different level deliberately develop jargon that sets them apart. Examples are *motivational deprivation* for laziness, *an interrelated collectivity* for group, *conceptualize* for imagine. When a jargon term becomes well known it is often changed: *dementia praecox* became *schizophrenia*, and *infantile paralysis* became *poliomyelitis*.

Euphemisms

Efforts to becloud a subject are treated by today's forthright and skeptical public as evasions. Examples are *Assigned to committee for reconsideration* for rejected, *discontinued* or *laid off* or *given early retirement* for fired, *deac-

---

[7]See Lesly, Philip, *How We Discommunicate*, ibid.

cession for unloading an unprofitable division, and *inventory shrinkage* for losses by theft.

Condescension

Communication is a form of courtship. The source is a suitor who presses his case with logic, ardor, charm, and persuasion to overcome the indifference or reticence of his intended. A suitor who is intent on demonstrating superiority over his love object and disdain for her interests is likely to be unsuccessful. Yet people who are supposed to be professional communicators seeking to beguile their audiences, often repel them. They show that the viewer is a target for their own objectives. When a communicator is eager to exhibit his own stature and superior intellect, he shows he is manipulating the audience rather than serving it. He shows condescension for her readers or viewers rather than respect. He uses big words and obtuse references and refuses to translate foreign words or phrases. That exhibits the primacy of ego over purpose. Ego is singular, likely to be massaged in solitude. Communication is plural, involving interaction with others, and makes it possible to win over multitudes. Ego is the enemy of communication.

The lost art of expression

Many recent studies have shown that the ability to express oneself both in writing and in speech has been declining steadily. While the complexities of society increase, making the need for clear expression greater than ever, the prevalence of sloppy and even semiliterate communication material has grown. Probably the most vital single attribute of the communicator is exceptional skill in expression. This goes beyond mere competence in putting together manuscripts that contain the necessary information and arguments. Some people use language merely to cover a subject; others use it to show the subject at its best.

They are the ones who sway attitudes and make things happen.

In writing for public relations, versatility and flexibility are needed. Not all music is a symphony, nor is it hard rock. Each situation and each need calls for a fresh analysis and a fresh approach.

In any approach, however, some traits are needed to be effective.

- *Simplicity.* Good writing consists of the richest thoughts put into the simplest language. The most effective is almost always stated simply.

- *Clarity.* You're not talking down to a Ph.D. if you write so a high school dropout can understand—unless you write condescendingly.

- *Brevity.* The heaviest tomes often carry the least weight with their audiences. Brevity does not mean length; it means conciseness. The right length for any manuscript depends on its purpose and audience.

- *Precision.* Ask yourself what every word *means*. Use exactly the right word. Writing that is "almost right" is like an "almost right" 23-foot leap over a 25-foot chasm.

- *Substance.* What you write must be meaningful, do the job, and merit the attention of the reader.

- *Purpose.* Do not write to express yourself or to create beautiful phrases. Ensure that what you write does what you set out to do.

- *Organization.* It's as important for each element to fall into its proper place as it is for each aspect of an attractive person to appear where it has the best effect.

- *Coherence.* Clarity, consistency, unity, and association of the beginning and the end are more important in writing than in speech, because the writer doesn't have the advantage of facial expressions, tone of voice, or other body language.

- *Effectiveness.* Churchill could have said, "It's going to be a tough fight, but if we accept sacrifices, we can win." Instead he said, "I have nothing to offer but blood, toil, tears, and sweat. . . ." And he moved a nation to win a war.

- *Facility.* Good writing may be hard work, but it must never sound labored. It must flow and march, not calling attention to itself but to what it says.

- *Felicity.* Really good writing has a flair, a character that moves the spirit as well as the mind. It makes the reader's psyche respond, as well as the brain. It has the same power to move souls that marks a great piece of music or a great work of art.

- *Credibility.* Exaggeration, unfounded claims, insincerity, hype, whitewash—all of these destroy persuasiveness.

- *Impact.* Good writing should leave the reader changed—in the way you want him or her to be changed.

- *Motivation.* This is the culmination. The readers should be moved to act as you want them to be moved. That requires a combination of information plus emotion to create motion.

The difference between a merely competent writer and a really good writer is the difference between a hamburger chef at McDonald's and the head chef at Lutece. Both will provide you with sustenance, but only one will make a memorable impression on you.

There are at least eighteen functions of writing in public relations—and several of them are often involved in one piece of writing:

- Inform
- Record
- Cover your rear
- Justify
- Soothe
- Attract supporters
- Provide the basis for people to form judgments
- Overcome another viewpoint
- Put down opponents
- Argue
- Persuade
- Agitate
- Avert criticism
- Divert attention from another subject
- Carry on a continuing discussion
- Create goodwill
- Motivate
- Be quoted—to leave an impression on the minds of the audience that will last beyond the first exposure

Unless the writer is clear *at the start* about what function the material is to perform, the reason for reading it will be unclear to the audience. With so many other barriers to reaching and influencing an audience, that almost surely means the objective will not be achieved.

Writing is a two-way transaction, like love. The writer is the suitor who seeks to win the audience; and the audience wants to be won if the conditions and the message are right.

Advice by George Orwell, author of *1984* and *Animal Farm*, from *Shooting an Elephant and Other Essays* is pertinent to all public relations persons:

A scrupulous writer, in every sentence that he writes, will ask himself at least four questions, thus: What am I trying to say? What words will express it? What image or idiom will make it clearer? Is this image fresh enough to have an effect? And he will probably ask himself two more: Could I put it more shortly? Have I said anything that is avoidably ugly?

To this should be added: Who am I trying to reach and what is that audience's orientation?

Embracing what's new but taking a step backward

Modern *sans serif* type, now widely used for printed materials, is harder to read and more tiring than *serif* type, which is more traditional.

Conviction and motivation

From the evolving principles we've discussed, we can sum up the necessary elements that lead to *conviction* and *motivation* in the mind of the object of communication. The primary elements are the following:

Acceptability

Unless the source of the information is respected and objective, communication is unlikely to take place. The statement or claim must reach the person when he is primed for acceptance—when he has opened his mind to a spokesperson he is willing to have invade the privacy of his inner convictions. An unknown or suspected spokesperson causes him to close his mind and even to resent the person who makes the effort to change his thinking. Credibility is the *earned* right to be heard.

Compatibility

The message must relate to the recipient's posture of thought and identity. People reject or distort whatever is alien to their heritage, background, and sources of self-assurance. They respond to what reinforces their conception of themselves and their view of the world.

Intensity

The degree of impact the message delivers is determined by the prominence it receives in competition with many other efforts to capture the recipient's attention. Information presented casually or in a mass of other information makes much less impact than information presented prominently and in isolation.

Visibility

The communication that is most nearly real, that involves the person by making her almost a part of it, has the greatest power to sway her. In early days it was the drama and the "revivalist" platform artist that were most activating; today it is television and the film.

Pervasiveness

When a subject appears to be all around him, a person tends to accept it and take it for granted. It becomes part of the atmosphere in which he lives. He finds himself surrounded by it and absorbs the climate of the idea itself.

Variety of impressions

Pervasiveness results from encountering a subject in a wide variety of ways. As we have seen, this multiple-channel approach to persuasion is vital.

Persuasiveness

No amount of impact, variety, or pervasiveness will influence attitudes and opinions unless the context of the communication is persuasive. It must be most deftly developed to reach into the subconscious of the person and tune to her urges, interests, and desires. Mere expression of the communicator's point of view will not succeed; it must be attuned to the mental and emotional bent of the audience.

The Cooperative Extension Service of the U.S. Department of Agriculture has studied the comparative effectiveness of various forms of communication. It postulates that effectiveness of the learning process among the audience increases as it moves from *listening* to *seeing* to *doing*; that people remember about 20 percent of what they are told, 30 percent of what they see, 50 percent of what they see and hear, 70 percent of what they say, and 90 percent of what they do. It projects an ascending scale of learning effectiveness from bottom to top as follows:

- Talks and printed matter
- Charts, graphs, posters, maps, illustrated talks
- Radio, recordings, still pictures
- Slides, filmstrips
- Movies, TV, theatricals
- Exhibits, displays
- Field trips, tours
- Demonstrations
- Discussions
- Contests, judging
- Participation in dramatics
- Working with models, games
- Actual experience, projects

This type of generalized guide is helpful but, like all aspects of communication, varies greatly according to subject, timing, nature of the audiences, and other factors.

Communicating in the New Human Climate

A number of trends have changed and expanded the methods available for communicating with the public, rendering some traditional practices and methods obsolete.

1. People are less able to read. Television, educational permissiveness, and the development of graphic textbooks and other materials have all led to lessened reading ability that persists throughout life.

2. People are less willing to read. Sales of books have not kept pace with either population or levels of education; many bestsellers are quasibooks on diet, cults, anecdotes, and formulas for living. Readership of serious magazines is small and newspaper readership has been declining gradually. Most people read about a few favorite subjects.

3. People in professional careers—an increasing proportion of the populace—face more to read than ever. Journals and studies are numerous. In self-defense, these people avoid reading unless they have strong concern about the subject involved.

4. Solid bodies of type are the antithesis of the visual communication that most people like. A manuscript or report composed of solid type, without graphics or open space, seems to many people to be an invasion of their time and inclinations.

5. People are accustomed to having problems neatly wrapped up for them. Television shows usually end with a clear-cut conclusion. Journal articles often begin with a précis and end with a summary. People now expect to find an answer that sticks out of a manuscript like a handle they can grasp.

To communicate effectively in this climate requires that one carefully avoid discommunicating because of information overload. No matter how complex or lengthy written material must be, it can be made more persuasive by using the following techniques:

1. Make the case in a summary that precedes or opens the weighty matter. It should be simple, direct, and brief.

2. Summarize the key point with pithy, concise statements, itemized and preceded by bullets (·).

3. Grasp the audience's self-interest at once by ringing a bell in its mind or driving home an urgent point.

4. Use graphics if they are available and show motion to create emotion.

5. Keep it brief, with an economy of words. If a full document is needed to support

the case, it can be in an appendix attached to a brief summary. Sometimes it will not be necessary to provide the full document, and it can be offered on request to those who really want it. That will maintain credibility provided by the full documentation but save considerable expense in producing unneeded copies.

Many factors create schisms *within* any large audience. To approach any sizable audience on the assumption that it is cohesive will lead to communication mistakes. The *makeup* of *each* audience should be analyzed.

- There are audiences with different levels of sophistication and knowledge. Speaking to one level too closely will turn off the others.

- Most audiences include people who think in *concrete* ways (the computerlogs and numbercrats) and others who live in the *abstract* (the theorists and the mystics). Aiming only at the practical will lose the dreamers; aiming at the intangible will get an impatient brush-off from the hardheaded.

- In a somewhat similar vein, some will respect facts and reality; others will lean toward Eastern philosophies, astrology, and other mystiques. Telling just the facts is not a sure way to prevail, and talking only in terms of concepts such as vibrations and the supernatural is likely to lose.

- Some members of any audience will be in a receptive mood on any given day. Others will be more indifferent or even more hostile than they might be at another time.

- Most sizable audiences will include opposing orientations on many subjects: men and women on working objectives, emphasis on competition, pro- or anti-discipline, and so on.

- Different size audiences require entirely different approaches. The psychology in which the message is couched, as well as its content, must be determined carefully. One audience may consist of just your boss. Another may comprise a small group of your superiors or your colleagues or an opposition group. A fourth may be a mass audience, such as all employees in a company.

- A highly significant schism exists between the *picture-minded* and the *word-minded* . . . TV versus print, show versus tell, demonstrations versus explanations.

Changing Public Opinion

Many people believe that changing public opinion is a rare achievement that requires a massive undertaking.[8] In many ways that is correct, but they often consider it difficult for the wrong reasons.

This feeling comes in part from associating public opinion with human nature—under the assumption that people's opinions are part of their nature, and since "you can't change human nature," it's very difficult to change opinions. The fact is that human nature changes constantly, and so do many elements of opinion.

The pattern of opinion about various questions varies, but in general what follows are the main factors (*see* Figure 3.5, page 56):

- A few extremists usually can be found on both sides of the question—perhaps 5 percent at each end. They hold their opinions zealously and nothing is likely to shake them.

- Perhaps 80 percent of the public involved is inert on the question—not caring much one way or the other and not likely to pay much attention to discussion of it.

---

[8]Philip Lesly, *Overcoming Opposition*, Prentice-Hall, 1984, p. 184.

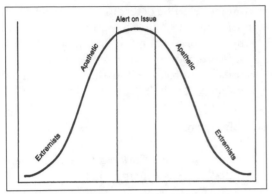

DIAGRAM OF DISTRIBUTION OF PUBLIC INTEREST

Figure 3.5 Diagram of the distribution of public interest in a hypothetical issue. Extremists cannot be affected. Apathetic people have little interest. Modifying the opinions of some of the small group of the alert and concerned can change the momentum of attitude on the issue.

- That leaves perhaps 10 percent who are pivotal—concerned but not fanatical, and interested enough to pay attention to discussion.
- A basic factor that's usually overlooked is *momentum*—which way the direction of opinion on the question is leaning. When the momentum is toward a liberal attitude, for instance, the aware 10 percent are likely to lean in that direction. In most cases, a shift of a few percent among the aware 10 percent will change the direction of the momentum. Thus, even before it changes the actual percentage of opinion, a small shift—less than 5 percent of the total public—can create the momentum for a shift and alter the state of public opinion on that question.

Accordingly, changing public opinion does not mean transforming the viewpoint of the entire public. It doesn't even mean transforming the viewpoint of a majority. It can be brought about by getting a comparatively small number of aware but passive people to

reflect on the question and form an opinion they haven't had.

It is also important to recognize that "winning" does not necessarily mean conquering the opposition or putting its cause to rout. Most people are intellectually apathetic. If there is no clear-cut "answer" on a question, they tend to lose interest and to avoid that subject. It no longer is of great concern to them. So *neutralizing public opinion on a subject that is threatening or disruptive can create the desired effect.*

Influencing Behavior

Although there clearly exist a great many barriers to motivating an audience to accept the viewpoint of the communicator, the full weight of history and everyday experience indicates that it is often achieved.

Because most shifts in opinion originate among the 10 percent who are alert and concerned with the specific issue, changing public opinion requires changing the focus of that segment.

The pattern for shifting the viewpoint of the alert groups includes the following:

1. Identify the 10 percent to be targeted, keeping in mind the segmentation that exists within all groups. This calls for identifying them by various traits.

   - **Self-interest in the subject.** Who are the ones with something clearly to gain?
   - **Intellectual level.** Which ones grasp the seriousness and nuances of the issue, can articulate it to others, and through leadership will get others to follow?
   - **Locale.** Is the issue particularly pertinent in certain areas, such as a region dependent on certain jobs or one with a prominent health concern? Are there areas where the media are already recep-

tive and their influence can lead to gaining media attention elsewhere?

- **Group membership.** Are there certain bodies, such as churches or civic organizations, in which members of the alert segment are concentrated? Are there some whose position is already the same as yours and who can be rallied into a coalition?

- **Sex**. Is the issue primarily of interest to one gender or the other?

- **Age**. Similarly, is the issue mainly important to one age group or another?

2. Efforts should concentrate on the prime groups, resisting the temptation to disperse resources by trying, at the start, to reach a broad base. When you have momentum built and your position is in the spotlight, the spectrum of coverage can be broadened with little added effort.

3. Embody your position in the context of the audience—making it part of their thinking. This can be accomplished by (a) tying all messages to what's in it for the audience, (b) getting them involved so it's their effort too, and (c) making the communications theirs by communicating with them, not at them. Don't preach, lecture, admonish, threaten, frighten, or otherwise try to impose on them what's on your mind.

4. Fill the pipelines of communication on the issue *long before it jells*. Forestall opposition arguments becoming embedded before your offsetting arguments are heard. While people are comfortable accepting an assertion or slogan as revealed truth, they are uncomfortable if there is conflicting information that must be weighed and evaluated. Then they are likely to withhold judgment and be receptive to your case.

5. Use a variety of channels and media.

6. Be consistent. No walls separate what one group of people hears from what reaches others. Blue-collar workers hear what is said to executives. Men hear messages directed at women. Seeming to make contradictory or inconsistent statements gives the impression of duplicity. That destroys the credibility essential to keeping the support of any audience.

Report changes in the relevant environment

A clearly seen change can most readily bring about a change in viewpoint. Perhaps the most striking example is the attitude of Americans toward the Japanese and German peoples, both of which were the objects of hatred during World War II. Within a few years, observations showing both groups had adopted American-like economic and social outlooks, especially with regard to their support of comparatively democratic regimes, brought about what appeared to be remarkable conversions.

Much advertising is devoted to focusing prospects' attention on new products or features intended to change the person's attitude toward that class of product.

Enhance current behavior patterns

Determining what information people want and providing it frequently provides effective means of gaining their goodwill and support. Much of American aid to underdeveloped countries has come in the way of providing information on better farming practices, improved health procedures, and other matters of clear benefit to the recipients.

Selectively reinforce prevailing attitudes

An individual may hold conflicting objectives, though they may be kept below the conscious level. For instance, she may want both better schools and lower taxes. By selectively focusing on the strong points of one of these, the communicator may enable the person to settle on that one in her mind even though she must give up the desirability of the other one.

Focus attention

The more complex society becomes, the greater the number of exposures to viewpoints that confront the individual. Often these are not in harmony with each other. By focusing on any one of them and bringing it to the fore in the individual's mind, it can take dominance over the others. For instance, often many issues in an election campaign hold some interest to a voter. A candidate who focuses on one of them to the point of making that voter strongly aware of his or her self-interest in it is able to get the vote even though the candidate may not conform to the voter's viewpoint on the other issues.

Activate existing attitudes

A person may remain a silently loyal alumnus of his college but do nothing to help it. If communications bring his loyalty to the action stage, he may be persuaded to contribute funds, to recommend the school to the prize high school students in his area, and to attend its football games.

Develop new interests and attitudes

A person may have never thought of participating in skiing. Yet, seeing a thrilling and beautiful motion picture of skiing in the Swiss Alps may motivate her to undertake the sport.

Suggest new behavior patterns

When confronted with a major change in condition, an individual develops a strong receptiveness to information that will help him adjust to it. For instance, a young man who is recruited into the Army may have given little thought to the procedures of military service and how to thrive. Finding himself about to be in uniform, he may become a prime audience for information that will help him in the new environment he faces.

Guidelines for Effective Communication

From what we know about the methods that work, two verbal/graphic aids can be applied:

1. Coercion creates conflict and Persuasion promotes pliability.

    These "sound bites" help one remember that trying to impose one's will usually fails; establishing rapport with the audience fosters readiness to accept your message.

2. The process for winning acceptance can be charted like this:

Basis of fact
↓
Credibility
↓
Identifying with audience's self-interest
↓
Visibility
↓
Awareness
↓
Audience's accommodation with personal goals
↓
Acceptance

Section 2

WHAT PUBLIC RELATIONS INCLUDES

4

DYNAMICS AND ROLE OF PUBLIC AFFAIRS

RAYMOND L. HOEWING

Raymond L. Hoewing is president of the Public Affairs Council, the nonprofit association that functions as the professional society for public affairs officers in 425 leading U.S. firms.

Hoewing, who has held a variety of positions with the council since 1962, formerly was director, public affairs, for Quaker Oats Company. His background also includes production management with Inland Steel (1955–1962).

A former mayor of Country Club Hills, Illinois, Hoewing has been involved in both state and federal political campaigns in Maryland. He holds a master's degree from the Woodrow Wilson School of Public and International Affairs at Princeton University.

Nearly fifty years after the establishment of the first formalized public affairs department in a U.S. company, public affairs remains a recognized and critical function within most leading firms. The question is not whether public affairs will continue to grow, but rather how dynamic and constant changes in the sociopolitical climate will affect its development. The evolution of the modern sociopolitical environment, which began in the late '70s, presents Corporate America—and its public affairs functions—with a complex set of opportunities and challenges.

Although public affairs has become widely recognized and utilized throughout the business sector, its definition—what constitutes *public affairs*—varies from company to company. In its broadest sense, it can be defined as the management function that interprets the corporation's noncommercial conditions and directs the company's response to those conditions. A more specific but restricted perspective of public affairs refers to a company's involvement in political actions and its government relations.

Historic Development

Many large companies operated effective lobbying programs at the state and federal levels at the beginning of the twentieth century (so much so that alleged excesses spawned a variety of federal and state regulatory efforts in the early decades). Most firms, however, eschewed direct involvement in the political process. Even less attention was given to a company's social role. Despite creation of such federal instrumentalities as the Federal Trade Commission and a variety of state regulatory bodies, business generally faced a benign governmental climate until the 1930s.

The Great Depression changed that. High unemployment and widespread economic suffering gave rise to widespread criticism of business. The "titans of business" were tempting targets for leaders of the New Deal attempting to bring the nation back from the economic brink. Unprecedented business restrictions and regulations were enacted at the federal level. Under fire from politicians and the media and suffering from a sharp inferiority complex, business drew back. It was not a time for a "high profile."

The birth of the public affairs movement can be related to two events: (a) the growing power of organized labor, and (b) the record of the first Eisenhower Administration. Abetted by legislation that facilitated union organization, "Big Labor" developed great influence in government, in sharp contrast to the receding political activity of business. In time, a number of business leaders began to discuss how business might offset the growing clout of labor. Most business firms realized the futility of polarization politics, and the movement did not long take the form of an antilabor crusade.

Many business leaders had assumed that General Eisenhower would prune government programs and budgets and restore the preeminent role of business in setting the country's economic policies. However, by the time of Ike's second campaign most business leaders were reconciled to having a new "silent partner" (as some executives dubbed the federal government).

Against that background, the Washington-based Public Affairs Council (then called the Effective Citizens Organization) was established in 1954. Though it would later become the professional association for corporate public officers, its original mission was to stimulate and train business executives to become active and effective in politics. At roughly the same time such companies as Ford, General Electric, and Johnson & Johnson established "political education" or "good citizenship" programs to activate their own executives.

By the end of the 1950s a handful of companies had established public affairs departments. Their major priorities were to formalize the firms' federal government relations and stimulate their executives to political activities. The 1960s were experimental years of growth for public affairs. The Public Affairs Council estimates that during that decade upwards of five hundred thousand business managers and executives attended formalized political education courses, often the U.S. Chamber of Commerce's "Action Course in Practical Politics."

Toward the end of the 1960s an outbreak of riots in some large cities triggered the development of "urban affairs" and "social responsibility" units in many firms. A traumatized business community undertook new philanthropic and community initiatives, frequently added to the public affairs officer's portfolio. By the mid-1970s a research report that included the responses of 356 corporations and was published by the Conference Board[1] revealed a great variety of activities, including jobs and job training for the disadvantaged, housing, transportation, law and order, health, education, and economic development. (Even as this research was being completed, however, overwhelming evidence surfaced, showing that most companies had jettisoned or downgraded many of their urban affairs and minority-oriented programs.)

The 1970s witnessed the most substantial growth. Data developed by the Public Affairs Council and the Conference Board suggest that the number of formalized public affairs programs probably doubled in that decade, the number of corporate members in the Council almost exactly doubling from 1970 to 1980. In addition, the number of professionals tripled. It is estimated that about two thousand national companies now have public affairs departments.

---

[1]*Managing Corporate External Relations: Changing Perspectives and Responses*, Phyllis S. McGrath, The Conference Board, 1976.

New Role for Business in Society

The role of business in our society has been under almost constant attack since the unrest of the late 1960s. Though negative public attitudes about business have eased from the troughs of the mid-1970s, big business today is generally more tolerated than respected. Furthermore, public opinion polls suggest that skepticism about the practices/methods and ethics of business is growing.

What has caused business to reassess its public posture? Much of the explanation traces to developments in the 1970s. For example, public concern about deterioration of the nation's environment and the public's desire that business be held responsible for both the problem and its solution forced a long-term corporate commitment. Similarly, rising concerns about product safety, reliability, and pricing propelled Ralph Nader and other public interest spokespersons into positions of political prominence. Business, its reputation tarnished and its resistance to legislative and regulatory initiatives diminished, was buffeted by still another force with the advent of the Arab oil embargo in 1973. Though the public's rage was vented mainly at the oil industry, all of business paid a political price.

Critics regarded some business responses as cosmetic. For example, a large number of programs were undertaken to "educate" the public, as well as a company's own employees, about how the economic system works and its contributions to social well-being. Some companies undertook expensive advocacy-advertising programs to carry the "business story" to the public. Still others hoped that sponsorship of high-quality television programs, increased charitable contributions, and similar "good works" could replenish public goodwill. Such efforts continue today, but most corporations recognize there is no "quick fix"—that business exists at the sufferance of the citizens and the politicians they elect.

The growth of public affairs departments signifies business' recognition that managing business-society relations is an ongoing task. Contemporary business recognizes that a company's strategy must go beyond image-building, political action, or "social responsibility." The political and social environment must be examined in a holistic way. Out of this need a term—*issues management*—began to crop up in the business press in the late 1970s. A broad review of this appears in Chapter 2.

Today's Political Climate

The election of Ronald Reagan in 1980 and a Republican Congress in 1994 reflected a variety of forces that challenged the sensitivity and innovativeness of corporate public affairs. Markers of this new environment include the following:

- Reduced role of government in public life—at all levels
- Substantial cutbacks in federal funding of social programs at the local level
- Improved incentives for business investment and growth
- Reform and relaxation of regulation of business

Cutbacks in spending and reduced regulatory activity at the federal level required companies to pay more attention to their state government relations (*see* Chapter 6). Even more challenging was growing pressure on business (much of it emanating from Presidents Reagan and Bush and Congressman Gingrich) as the federal government cut funding for a variety of social programs and urged a greater business role at the community level, ranging from job training programs to philanthropy. Critics and supporters of business called for

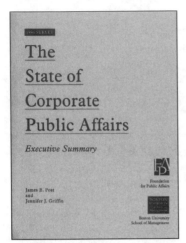

1996 Survey on The State of Corporate
Public Affairs (published by The
Foundation for Public Affairs and the
Public Affairs Research Group, School
of Management, Boston University).

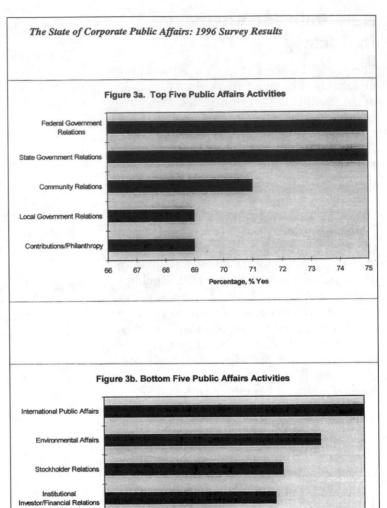

Figure 4.1 This page from the Public Affairs Council survey shows the range and relative importance of some of the areas of corporate public relations.

more initiatives from business, including employment and training, loaned executives, community development, and private-sector options for public services.

The "community relations" function has gained prominence in many companies. Traditional community relations activities— financial support of such high-visibility organizations as the United Way and a variety of "glad-handing" chores—are being expanded into more substantive areas. For example, Honeywell and Levi Strauss have developed strategic plans for external affairs that include an active community involvement program.

Public Affairs Programs

The need

There was a surge in the creation of public affairs departments in the early 1970s, a period in which consumerists and environmentalists were at their peak. Nader became a household word, oil company profits "obscene," and *multinational* a term of opprobrium.

Thus, crisis accounts for the establishment of most public affairs programs. Another factor is incrementalism—the patient, step-by-step education of top management and establishment of a fledgling public affairs effort by an executive in public relations or the legal department, for example. A third has been peer pressure: the reactions of a CEO to a colleague whose company already has a successful public affairs program, or the missionary efforts of the firm's principal trade association.

Functions and activities

What follows is an outline of a typical public affairs department:

- *Communications*
  —Publicity
  —Media Relations

- *Government Relations*
  —Federal
  —State
  —Local

- *Political Action*
  —Political Action Committees
  —Political Education
  —Grassroots Activities
  —Communications on Political Issues

- *Community Involvement/Corporate Responsibility*
  —Community Relations
  —Philanthropy
  —Social Responsibility Programs

- *International*
  —Political Risk Assessment
  —Monitoring International Sociopolitical Developments

Organization

Management style, industry type, the nature of issues faced externally, and a variety of other factors help shape the way companies organize their public affairs activities. Organization of departments varies tremendously from company to company. Nevertheless, the trend toward a single department coordinating all external relations has been rapid and constant. In many cases it is headed by the chief public relations executive. Others have separate public affairs units. (*See* Figure 4.1.)

New strategies

Several new tactics have emerged in recent years that have been implemented in the public affairs programs of a growing number of companies—including the following:

1. **Political Action Committees** (PAC). Beyond doubt, the "PAC" has in the past decade been the most important tool to many companies in pursuing their government relations objectives. So widespread is the use of the PAC to "gain access," as public affairs officers put it, that it is almost an anomaly for a larger firm not to have a PAC.

2. **Management Committees and Task Forces.** Interdepartmental groups have been established in some companies to set policy on key legislative or political issues or opportunities. These groups coordinate the company's position and orchestrate its response.

3. **Regionalized State Government Relations.** A number of companies have established regional state government relations offices. Typically, these executives are

responsible for monitoring developments in the six to eight state capitals of a major region.

4. **Integrating Public Affairs with Job Performance.** A few companies such as General Mills and several phone companies integrate public affairs responsibilities into performance standards for non–public affairs executives. Job descriptions of International Paper executives, for example, have provisions relating to developing personal relationships with key elected officials.

5. **Linking "Public Relations" and "Public Affairs."** The artificial—but all too real—demarcation between public affairs (read "government relations") and "public relations" (read all other corporate affairs and communications in most companies)—is waning. The complexity of dealing with the many external constituencies has led some companies to effectively integrate *all* communications—sometimes merging the functions into a "corporate affairs" or "external relations" department.

Involvement at the executive level

The Business Roundtable (BRT), composed solely of CEOs of about two hundred large business firms, develops its positions through "task forces" on specific issues. Buttressed by research resources of the member companies and aided by extensive face-to-face CEO lobbying with Congress, BRT has played a significant role in a number of legislative battles in Washington.

A higher profile for CEOs is evident in other ways. For example, there are state versions of BRT—in Illinois, California, and Pennsylvania, to name three.

Furthermore, CEOs have been conspicuously active in their efforts to deal with what many business people regard as the number one problem of the 1990s—a failing public

education system. CEOs of IBM, Procter & Gamble, BellSouth, and Xerox were among the many corporate chieftains deeply involved in efforts to reform education in the 1990s.

Educating corporate executives

Despite growing recognition that the most important variables affecting the "bottom line" are external factors, men and women entering business fresh out of business schools are rarely equipped to deal with public affairs. Nor will their perspectives of public affairs necessarily broaden as they climb the corporate ladder. The definition of the problem as described by a Shell Oil executive holds true:

> Little in the education and business experience of most present and many oncoming corporate executives prepares them to understand the relevance of social and political issues to successful corporate performance, much less to participate in the untidy and bruising public policy process which resolves such issues.
>
> People become executives of major corporations by virtue of almost total absorption in the traditional business affairs of their companies. As a result, many of today's high-potential managers have been developed thus far to be executives of the corporation of the 1950s.[2]

Recognizing this new dimension of management skills, most business schools have added or upgraded business-government and business-society courses to both their undergraduate and graduate programs. As yet, no graduate school offers a degree in public affairs, but as the field grows a number of business schools are offering outstanding course work—notably Boston University, University of California at Berkeley, and Ashland College (Ohio).

The need for midcareer exposure to public affairs has caused a growing number of

---

[2]"Career Development for the Public Policy Dimensions of Executive Performance," Francis W. Steckmest, *Public Affairs Review*, op cit.

companies to develop specially designed in-house seminars. A much larger number of firms systematically send senior executives to public policy seminars offered by such organizations as Brookings and American Enterprise Institute. Additionally, numerous seminars are available to sensitize and educate middle-level managers tapped by firms to participate in grassroots or legislative contact programs. Frequently held in Washington, the typical meeting consists of a two-day event featuring such speakers as senators and representatives from the states and districts in which a firm does business, plus political commentators and experts on issues of critical importance to the company.

Participation of all managers

The public affairs officer is no longer viewed as a "specialist" with the sole responsibility of handling the company's external relationships. In a number of progressive companies, public affairs has become a "part-time" responsibility of many other executives. A few examples follow:

- **Grassroots.** Many companies have initiated effective legislative contact programs wherein plant managers and other executives are expected to develop personal relationships with key state and federal legislators and to communicate their companies' positions on key legislative matters. International Paper, ARCO, and Union Carbide are examples.

- **Issues and opportunities management.** Many companies utilize task forces, or committees, composed of people from both line and staff departments that study key political and social issues, determine a company position, and orchestrate the company's response. TRW, Weyerhaeuser, and ARCO have such mechanisms.

- **Emerging issues.** Companies such as Dow Corning make extensive use of interde-

partmental committees to monitor periodicals and newspapers and to work with the public affairs department in delineating emerging issues.

- **Speakers' bureaus.** The oil industry pioneered a program in the late 1970s and early 1980s that put its executives on the hustings to discuss the companies' positions on key issues. These organized efforts have often involved professional training for the speakers, systematic efforts to obtain forums, and intensive assistance in researching and writing the speeches. While some programs continue—Dow Chemical has a well-organized program, for example—the Public Affairs Council believes the total number has decreased in recent years.

A Difficult Balance

From a political standpoint, companies today seem to see a "best-of-times/worst-of-times" future. In many ways, they are enjoying a more hospitable political climate at both the federal level and in many states because of the country's general turn away from governmental control.

On the other hand, its detractors and defenders expect business to fill an unaccustomed role. Companies are being pushed and pulled from a variety of sources to help meet the "gaps" in social programming.

Spokespeople have been quick to point out that business' first social responsibility is to be productive and profitable. But that is not a sufficient response.

Public affairs officers are helping their chief executives more precisely articulate a reasonable social role. The dilemma was well-put in a statement by the Business Roundtable:

Business enterprises are not designed to be either political or cultural institutions, but the business community will be well-served by a habit of mind that stays alert to social currents.

In considerable part, increased public confidence in business as a positive force in society will depend upon the way corporations respond to the public's new and expanded expectations regarding business.

Corporations . . . have a responsibility to themselves, to each other, and to their constituencies—including society at large—to make a reasonable and effective response.

A corporation's responsibilities include how the whole business is conducted every day. It must be a thoughtful institution which rises above the bottom line to consider the impact of its actions on all, from shareholders to the society at large. Its business activities must make social sense just as its social activities must make business sense.[3]

Ongoing Problems and Obstacles

Present challenges facing the field include the following:

- Converting public affairs from the perceived job of a "specialist" to a company-wide task for all management

- Maintaining credibility as the "window in" communicator, often of bad news

- Moving the public affairs position from a "fire fighting" to a "fire prevention" concept

- Viewing public affairs in holistic terms, well beyond political action and government relations, with interconnections to and wellsprings in social trends

- Winning the confidence of all management—superiors, peers, and subordinates—to view public affairs as a direct, bottom-line function

[3]"Statement on Corporate Responsibility," *The Business Roundtable*, 1981.

Budgetary concerns

Nothing was more representative of the U.S. business community in the 1980s and 1990s than the turbulent "restructuring" of firms in virtually every industrial segment. Driven by international competition, Wall Street pressures, and rapid technological change, companies variously closed down operations, merged with other firms, and realigned business strategies. One effect of this spasm of restructuring was frequent and often recurring cutbacks in personnel, with corporate staff often bearing the brunt of the reductions.

Naturally, public affairs departments did not escape the need to "downsize." More than a few companies (particularly those in severe economic difficulty) completely eliminated their public affairs staffs. (One of the interesting manifestations was the heretofore-unprecedented closing of Washington offices in the 1980s—perhaps as many as forty to fifty.) And if it managed to avoid demise, the typical public affairs department experienced its own type of "restructuring"—i.e., pared-down budgets and staffs. In fact, it is fair to characterize the past decade as one of "plateauing" or modest growth at best, if the gauge is the number of professional personnel. About the only exception was the state government relations field which—for reasons noted in Chapter 6—was a "growth industry" in the 1980s and 1990s.

These pressures have added momentum to a trend already developing in public affairs—the effort to evaluate, justify, and "quantify" public affairs activities. New tools (at least "new" to public affairs) were developed, such as the following:

- Benchmark studies—how does the productivity of Company X public affairs compare to that of Company Y?

- "Process audits"—for example, when Company X undertook a program to influence the state legislature, were its procedures and activities intelligent, comprehensive, and fully implemented?

- "Profit center" concept—what "return," if any, did public affairs make to the "bottom line"?

There is little reason to doubt that cost pressures on public affairs operations will continue. If so, one earmark for the profession in the coming years will be further efforts to enhance the kinds of tools noted before as public affairs executives seek to preserve and protect their budgets and staffs.

Resources

Following are some of the principal organizations and publishers providing resources for the public affairs professional.

Professional associations

Public Affairs Council
1019 19th Street, NW
Suite 200
Washington, DC 20036

The Conference Board
Public Affairs Research Division
845 Third Avenue
New York, NY 10022

Association public affairs

U.S. Chamber of Commerce
Public Affairs Department
1615 H Street, NW
Washington, DC 20062

National Association of Manufacturers
Public Affairs Division
1331 Pennsylvania Avenue, NW
Suite 1500N
Washington, DC 20004

Selected list of public policy research organizations

American Enterprise Institute for Public Policy Research (AEI)
1150 17th Street, NW
Washington, DC 20036

The Conference Board
845 Third Avenue
New York, NY 10022

Committee for Economic Development
2000 L Street, NW
Suite 700
Washington, DC 20006

Cato Institute
1000 Massachusetts Avenue, NW
Washington, DC 20001

Foundation for Public Affairs
1019 19th Street, NW
Suite 200
Washington, DC 20036

Heritage Foundation
214 Massachusetts Avenue, NE
Washington, DC 20002

Institute for Policy Studies
1601 Connecticut Avenue, NW
5th Floor
Washington, DC 20009

Brookings Institution
1775 Massachusetts Avenue, NW
Washington, DC 20036

Key periodicals and newsletters
General

Impact
Public Affairs Council
1019 19th Street, NW
Suite 200
Washington, DC 20036

Business and Society Review (Quarterly)
200 West 57th Street
New York, NY 10019

Common Cause
2030 M Street, NW
Washington, DC 20036

Managing the Human Climate
155 N. Harbor Drive
Suite 5311
Chicago, IL 60601

Federal Affairs

Congressional Monitor
1414 22nd Street, NW
Washington, DC 20037

Congressional Quarterly
1414 22nd Street, NW
Washington, DC 20037

Roll Call
900 2nd Street, NE
Washington, DC 20002-3557

State and Local Affairs

Governing
2300 N Street, NW
Suite 760
Washington, DC 20037

Political Action Committees

Campaign Practices Reports
Congressional Quarterly
1414 22nd Street, NW
Washington, DC 20037

Campaigns and Elections
1511 K Street, NW
Washington, DC 20005

Issues Management

Corporate Public Issues
207 Loudon Street, SE
Leesburg, VA 22075-3115

Community Relations

Community Relations Report
P.O. Box 924
Bartlesville, OK 74005

Community Relations Letter
The Center for Corporate Community
Relations
Boston College
McGuinn Hall
Chestnut Hill, MA 02167

5

WORKING WITH THE FEDERAL GOVERNMENT

ERNEST WITTENBERG
PHILIP LESLY

Ernest Wittenberg was vice chairman of E. Bruce Harrison Co., a counseling firm headquartered in Washington, DC. A frequent writer on communications topics from the nation's capital, he is coauthor (with Elisabeth Wittenberg) of the book, How to Win in Washington. *Previously, he headed his own firm, with national and international clients.*

A former newspaperman in Pennsylvania and Ohio, Wittenberg worked as a corporate public relations director and counselor before coming to Washington to work in the Kennedy White House. He is a graduate of New York University and a contributor to various national publications, including the New York Times, The New Yorker, *and* American Heritage.

In describing the federal government's resistance to new ideas and ways of doing things, Franklin D. Roosevelt, while assistant secretary of the Navy in the Wilson Administration, said it well when he stated, "Making a change (in the government) is like punching a feather bed." Eventually, it resumes its shape—but after many years of constant punching, pushing, tugging, and shoving by multiple interests within the American democracy, each demanding to be heard and attended to, it has assumed a very remarkable shape, indeed.

The federal government is, by far, the largest enterprise in the United States, encompassing a range of interests and activities to dazzle the mind. Yet, the U.S. government remains open, interested, polite, responsive, and a font of information for its citizenry— from the entrepreneur aiming to amass a for-

tune with molybdenum, to the housewife wishing to prepare a savory pot roast. Furthermore, it serves as a receptive public, or audience, to the public relations practitioner.

Public relations functions much the same in Washington, DC—aside from the very special audience to which it usually plays—as the profession does with other types of organizations and publics throughout the country. The required processes, as well as the skills needed to fulfill them, are identical: identify the problem; research the issue; create a logical and innovative program by which to address it; and finally, effectively implement the program. When dealing with one side or another of public issues, the Washington practitioner frequently directs programs that in one way or another inform or convince a government audience, or public. This public might include the president of the

United States, policy makers in executive government offices, members of the House of Representatives and the Senate, as well as their staff, or independent regulatory agency personnel. Conversely, the public relations plan might be an integral component of a marketing program designed to help a company sell a product to the private sector's biggest customer: the federal government.

Practitioners seeking to inform or influence the federal government direct much of their media placement, grassroots efforts, and communication materials—such as brochures, fact sheets, and multimedia presentations—toward the select public of 435 congressmen and 100 senators. (To illustrate the extent of these efforts: next to tourism, printing is traditionally the largest industry in Washington.) Sometimes entire programs with substantial budgets focus on only two or three elected representatives who serve as members of a subcommittee having jurisdiction over the issue in question.

Since the federal government's decisions extend across wide economic and social boundaries, both nationally and internationally, Washington has become a magnet for increasing numbers of virtually every industry type that represents human endeavor. The capital plays host to significant populations of business, labor, church groups, educators, nonprofit organizations, consumerists, agricultural interests, professional associations, state and local governments, and of course, the media. The magnitude of their presence in Washington ranges from fully staffed operations occupying entire buildings, such as the U.S. Chamber of Commerce and the AFL-CIO headquarters, located across from the White House on Lafayette Square, to one-person offices housing a single representative who keeps the home office informed and doubles as a lobbyist.

These various and often divergent interests share common objectives:

- To maintain a firsthand view of—and a pulse on—the government

- To create and sustain an opportunity to affect government

- To stay abreast or ahead of proposed legislation, regulations, trends, and national developments threatening the health or survival of entire industries or institutions, as well as the group itself

The latest figures from the General Accounting Office reveal that more than 116 governmental agencies and programs currently regulate business. In turn, business conducts the largest lobby—as indicated by the more than 500 U.S. companies and 3,000 national trade associations maintaining government relations offices in Washington. Furthermore, the *Wall Street Journal* has reported that corporations are upgrading their principal government relations posts to be filled by "a top corporate officer—often one earmarked for future stardom."

The *Journal* continues, "Because chief executives are currently confronting rather than avoiding Washington, the post of government affairs executive has taken on added luster. A tour through the government affairs department can be a quick route to the top. Booz-Allen & Hamilton, Incorporated, the big consulting firm, says in a recent study, that of eight skills it has identified to future top-management success, no fewer than three involve working effectively with the government."

The constant interaction between so many segments of the nation and the federal government provides a vital role for the public relations practitioner in Washington. He or she faces multiple challenges in maintaining the flow of communications between the organization and the government:

- To marshal the facts

- To package the information

- To select the proper communication channels with which to tell the story or impart information
- To gain media support
- To win assistance from grassroots organizations
- To keep all involved parties on the organization's side fully apprised of and conversant in the latest developments

In this environment, you're only as good as your latest information.

Washington Public Relations Activities

The basic body of work of Washington public relations generally includes the following parts:

1. Research (gathering information)
2. Informing management and interpreting the potential impact
3. Taking an advocacy position and building a public information program
4. Communicating management's positions and actions to government
5. Taking the story public: working with the news media

Gathering information

To the "watchers of Washington," the flow of accurate information is essential—it is their meat and potatoes, forming the basis on which they counsel their employers and construct effective communications programs. In Washington, facts arrive by the truckload, not the teaspoonful. And public relations professionals with a "need to know" about matters in Washington must scan and sort through hundreds of thousands of words in scores of publications every day.

The day begins with a review of the Washington daybook of coming events on the tickers of United Press International (UPI) or Associated Press (AP). Both wire services lease machines that give public relations offices the essence of Washington activities at the most public levels. The daybooks chronicle congressional hearings, presidential appointments, press conferences and briefings, and other special events, many of which are covered as news later in the day by AP or UPI. A source that digs still deeper into the coming day on Capitol Hill is the daily *Congressional Monitor*, a privately published newsletter.

Government information gatherers also typically review the three dominant newspapers in the field of government relations: the *Washington Post*, the *New York Times*, and the *Wall Street Journal*. The news and opinion columns of these three papers carry great weight with government officials, and overlooking them places the practitioner at peril.

Another overnight daily wonder publishes without even a small fraction of the *Post's* news staff of five hundred, but rivals its coverage: the *Congressional Record*. Every word and report of the previous day's session in Congress hits the streets with the morning mail in the *Record*, along with thousands of words in newspaper reprints, speeches, and other comments not made in debate but authorized by members of Congress. Also doing its part to help make the Government Printing Office the world's biggest publisher is the daily *Federal Register*, which prints in magazine format proposed new regulations, presidential proclamations, and executive orders, and gives proposed timetables for new actions to take effect.

The information sources mentioned thus far primarily represent the "general" press. Considering the numerous sources of information available in the city, the information gatherer must quickly narrow the sphere into the confines of the specific area of interest and work with the specialized or trade press. Substantial empires have been established in Washington by specialists in many areas who capitalize on publishing needed information on a regular basis about one single industry, making their newsletters or magazines essential. A few examples are the *Kiplinger Washington Letter*, *Broadcasting*, and *Oil Daily*.

All of the above, valuable though they are in bringing the practitioner information, are still yesterday's news. It takes personal contact and the development of a "beat" similar to a reporter's to provide up-to-the-minute news. Contacts on Capitol Hill among members and staff, within the administration, industry sources, perhaps embassy personnel, trade association officials, and reporters round out the news days and make the information gatherer feel reasonably secure in his knowledge.

Resources to help get to the right person on a new beat are the *United States Government Organization Manual*, which describes the agencies of the legislative, judicial, and executive branches and also includes useful charts of agency structure; the *Congressional Directory*, the official handbook of the organization of Congress, with names and telephone numbers of key personnel in all areas of government and the correspondents accredited to the House and Senate galleries; and the *Washington Information Directory*, which broadens out to include sources in the private sector among its five thousand listings. Those who have reason to talk to Congress and the executive departments regularly swear by the *Yellow Books* as a dependable way to uncomplicate the Washington watcher's day. (*See* Appendix.)

In a previous edition of this handbook, Howard P. Hudson commented on the maze that comprises Washington information gathering and called attention to the belt-and-suspenders method used by large organizations for assurance. "There is so much information and some obscure new regula-tion may be fraught with so much significance that they protect themselves in depth. They may subscribe to numerous services, maintain their own news ticker from the AP or UPI, receive reports from associations, maintain their own staff of information gatherers, and retain a Washington public relations firm, a lobbyist, and a Washington law firm in order to feel protected."

As the public affairs director of Borg-Warner Corporation told the *Wall Street Journal*, "Without someone in Washington, all we know is what's published in the *Federal Register*—and by then, it's too late." Borg-Warner learned this lesson the hard way when, due to an EPA ruling, the company paid $1 million more than it had anticipated for construction of a waste-water treatment plant in Virginia. "If we could have gotten in while they were writing the legislation, perhaps we could have saved that money."

An experience in 1981 with the new Reagan administration reconfirmed the importance of close monitoring of federal activities by state and local governments. Word filtered across the country that the president was proposing to eliminate tax-free industrial revenue bonds, which are used by cities and states to prop up private industrial and commercial development in decaying downtown areas. Representations were made to the administration, demonstrating the potential costs to local governments by curtailing or eliminating the incentives compared with their loss to the federal government as "tax loopholes." The proposal was dropped, at least temporarily.

Informing management and interpreting potential impact

The trained Washington practitioner treats information with the same urgency a wire service reporter applies to a breaking news story. It is kept moving. Until it is in the hands of people who can use it, the information has no value. Transmitted with dispatch, it could mean a competitive edge for the client or avoidance of some costly marketing error. It might highlight a superior investment opportunity or provide the final piece of intelligence persuading an organization to commit itself and its resources to a major public struggle.

For timeliness, picture what even minutes would have meant to a financial institution hearing about, say, President Carter freezing Iranian assets in the United States or Nixon's earlier decision to devalue the dollar. An example of public interest monitoring was the close examination of every official and semi-official act of Secretary of the Interior James Watt, whose collected views alarmed conservationists. A flood of information about the secretary's intentions channeled out of Washington by the Wilderness Society and the Sierra Club mobilized public opinion, prompting reversal of the Interior Department's positions on off-shore drilling.

Despite the need for speed, it is essential to carefully evaluate Washington information. What is the source? Is it an official act or a trial balloon? Can it be confirmed? How much background must be provided before it is intelligible? If it is a rumor, should it be passed on? Some managements, notably Japanese businesses, encourage the transmittal of rumors—if properly identified and labeled as such—because they add to the range of possible options in evaluating a still-unresolved situation.

In transmitting congressional developments, the trained Washington practitioner is already anticipating the next steps and preparing to counsel management on the potential impact. Who is behind the action? What is the background and constituency of the representative or senator introducing the bill? Is he or she doing it for hometown consumption with little real hope of affecting national policy, like urging a strongly protectionist foreign trade policy in a speech aimed at voters in a depressed factory town? Is it the start of a serious congressional movement with backing by strong coalitions? Is there a National Association of Manufacturers or U.S. Chamber of Commerce position? How likely are hearings? What committee will it be assigned to? Is there an Administration position? These are just a few of the considerations needed to sort out the Washington chaff and keep a client reliably informed.

Sources of information about some of the political questions asked above can be found in the *Almanac of American Politics*; at the Federal Election Commission, which monitors political action committees; and in the financial disclosure statements made by congressmen to their own chamber. The rest might be located in the *Congressional Quarterly*, which is published weekly; *National Journal*, a monthly magazine; *Roll Call*; and the U.S. Chamber's weekly newspaper, *Washington Report*.

Information moves out of Washington as fast as necessary, consistent with the importance of the news. Bulletins and flash news always go by telephone or computer, followed by fax transmittal of the details. Otherwise, overnight courier, express mail, and, as a last resort, regular mail is used.

Taking an advocacy position and building a public information program

When the information shows an unmistakable trend, management must act. This action may consist of taking a position for or against a bill. Or perhaps it means fighting a ruling at a regulatory agency. Its right to petition government for redress of grievances is basic to the system; it is in the First Amendment to the Constitution.

A typical next step involves a meeting or series of meetings by a "war council" gathered in Washington. The corporate executive in charge lays out the problem, then seeks strategy and support plans. Among the key players might be the house legal counsel, Washington lawyer, public affairs director, Washington public relations counsel, a consulting economist, the company's Washington representative, and an outside lobbyist. Though the lines cross and each case varies, it can be said generally that the lawyers establish the position, the economist embellishes it with facts and figures, the lobbyist and Washington representative identify the key public figures who must be convinced and the complications in convincing them, and the public relations/public affairs contingent is responsible for developing a climate of public opinion.

The programming and planning skills of the public relations people come into play when the overall objectives and principal audiences are identified. Working with the facts and figures of the case, the PR/PA team takes the assignment of marshaling opinion by telling the story as much as possible from the perspective of the public interest. Position papers are prepared and become the source for a variety of communications that may be required, depending on the complexity of the situation: letters to members of Congress and other government officials, fact sheets, brochures, booklets, issue advertising, media tours around the country, audiovisual materials, press information packets, and Internet news groups.

Many questions arise during the planning phase of the public information program: Are there natural allies for our position to give us a broader base of public interest and an opportunity to speak for a larger segment of the economy than our own sphere? When the West Coast shipping interests tried to end a crippling strike through Washington intervention, a key element in their success was an alliance with Midwestern farm interests whose produce, worth billions of dollars, was rotting because it couldn't be exported. The farmers' active desire to end the strike

brought on board entire blocs of congresspersons and senators who otherwise might not have seen a constituent issue in a labor problem along the Pacific.

Such coalitions are among the fundamentals of effective modern government relations. They provide a wider lobbying base, as well as increased prospects for contributions to the war chest. Issues frequently link seemingly irreconcilable odd couples on the same side. Business and labor saw eye-to-eye on limiting imports of Japanese cars. Consumerists joined with both when all were threatened by a bill that would change rules for lobbying.

An example of how interests coalesce to make their combined voices heard in Washington was the Alaska Lands Bill, which occupied the capital's attention for years. Commercial interests opposed to setting aside 26.5 million acres of the forty-ninth state as wilderness mounted public opinion programs. That coalition included oil companies, mining interests, labor, Alaskan citizens, the state of Alaska, hunting guides, the timber industry, and the National Rifle Association. Proponents of the bill banded together as the Alaska Coalition. They included the Sierra Club, National Audubon Society, Wilderness Society, League of Conservation Voters, and the National Wildlife Federation. Public opinion campaigns on both sides brought the fight across the country city by city.

On a smaller scale, a coalition called the National Committee to Preserve the Family Business was set up to call attention to a problem faced by family-held businesses. These businesses needed relief from huge estate taxes required to be paid on the death of the founder or principal owner. The coalition, with an active advisory board selected from districts and states of key congressmen on tax legislation, won its case in four months.

The public information program must include segments covering the handling of prospective congressional hearings on the issue and the preparation of witnesses who will present the case to the public. Sample media relations decisions might concern whether it is important enough to schedule a news conference or appropriate to bank on less grand but often more effective techniques, such as one-to-one briefings with the key press, editorial conferences, presentation of the facts to columnists, appearances on TV and radio talk shows, and speeches before important forums. An additional element that is being used more frequently is media relations activity in the home districts of legislators with important jurisdiction over an issue—grassroots programs designed to spur letters and calls from the "The District."

Communicating management's positions and actions to government

The staffs of the House and Senate committees and subcommittees are generally willing to provide a forum for all sides of an issue in hearings and special meetings, in position papers set before the senators and representatives, and in accepting invitations to briefings and presentations. Knocking at the right doors in the executive departments and even the White House will usually find at least a sympathetic ear if not an advocate. All regulatory agencies have built-in systems for accepting advocacy statements before a cut-off date. The system is remarkably open and ready to be used. The challenge lies in coordinating the effort, utilizing the appropriate arguments, and successfully bringing public opinion to bear.

The importance of informing and convincing congressional staffers in today's Congress cannot be overestimated. They are the detail men and women for the members and control the flow of information reaching them. Their briefings are often the last word before the hardening of a position on an issue by a congressman or senator, who knows that

the key staff person has studied the issue and highlighted the pros and cons with the legislator's best interests and those of the constituency always in mind. In the constantly complex legislative arena where more than ten thousand bills are introduced in a session, an offer to clarify and inform is generally welcomed by the staff.

The Washington community is virtually unanimous in believing that the most effective person to get a story to and a vote commitment from a member of Congress is a constituent. So, with precision and frequently ingenuity, constituents have become organized groups in all of the 435 congressional districts. They have been mobilized and readied for action with letters, telephone calls, faxes, and visits by all of the interest groups with a stake in the outcome of an issue.

Letters and telephone calls from constituents ranked first and second as the most important kind of communications to the Hill in a survey conducted by the Institute for Government Relations of American University. The survey, financed by the Marsteller Foundation, asked 123 congressional staff members to rate ninety-six different types of communications according to their effectiveness in influencing senators and representatives.

Impressive and sophisticated national constituent networks with the capability of swiftly swamping congressional offices with legitimate democratic expression from voters in specific areas are operated by the U.S. Chamber of Commerce and the AFL-CIO. Letters are counted and treated with due respect by the elected representatives as the voice of the people, even when they come by the truckload, as they did during a struggle over labor law reform. One of the most enterprising freelance programs to exploit public opinion was carried out by a Portland, Oregon, real estate management company that invited tenants in eighty buildings to enter a drawing for a boat cruise and dinner. To become eligible for the prize it was necessary only for the tenants to write a letter to the area's congressman urging support for President Reagan's economic program.

Public hearings held by congressional committees and subcommittees to consider the impact of prospective legislation are the most important formal Washington forum for mobilizing public opinion. The hearing collects a printed record for the committee members, including the prepared statements of all witnesses and the crossfire of questions and answers as Congress probes for facts. When hearings are announced, invitations to testify go out from the committee to government agencies and segments of the private sector most closely concerned. Industry positions are usually set out by trade associations, but significant splits in the industry front will be reflected by the appearance of individual companies or ad hoc coalitions of companies. If time does not allow scheduling of everyone who wants to be heard, written statements from those excluded are accepted for the record.

Recognizing the importance of congressional hearings to the fate of their positions, elements of the private sector exert great effort and expense in preparing testimony and rehearsing the witness who will present it. Lawyers and public relations personnel draft and redraft the prepared statement, measuring it for clarity, accuracy, convincing arguments, and nearness to the mainstream of perceived public interest. They spend hours grilling the prospective witness on possible questions that might be asked by senators and congressmen and then evaluating the answers. Press releases are prepared and distributed to coincide with the scheduled appearance. Hearings are conducted in the Washington equivalent of a goldfish bowl, open to all. Important hearings receive heavy media attendance, both pencil press and electronic.

Publicizing the story and working with the news media

Washington is the news capital of the world. Its dateline on a news story commands attention. Its press corps of five thousand reaches virtually every newspaper in the world, every magazine and trade paper, every TV and radio network. Reporters, editors, columnists, investigative journalists, and commentators abound. The big attractions, of course, are the White House and the Capitol, the seats of power and the sources of most headlines.

The public relations practitioner working on a government relations issue often presents the facts to the news media in the hope of increasing public awareness of the case and, frequently more important, bringing it directly to the attention of Washington's decision-makers at breakfast in the morning newspaper or at dinner with the evening news. Articles and editorials in major daily newspapers rank fourth and fifth in the top ten forms of communication regarded as most effective by congressional staff members.

The *Washington Post* is considered the most influential published voice affecting public affairs. Few representatives, senators, White House assistants, agency heads, correspondents, or lobbyists leave home in the morning without having scanned the *Post*.

The *New York Times* still has clout, particularly with the television news executives who read it every morning in New York and with the foreign policy community both in Washington and New York. However, in purely Washington terms, nothing compares with the *Post*.

The public relations practitioner faces the challenge of keeping the client's issue current, timely, and in the news cycle. In working toward hearings and in scheduling events such as press conferences, briefings, and one-on-one interviews, he or she competes with no less a personage than the president of the

United States. When a news story breaks in Washington it sometimes seems that all five thousand correspondents drop everything and converge on it. Big-name figures with important announcements have been known to talk to empty press conferences when the president suddenly summons the press.

The *Wall Street Journal, New York Times, Los Angeles Times*, AP, and UPI, as well as Knight-Ridder, Gannett, and other large bureaus are in hot competition with the *Post* for news. So are *Time, Newsweek*, and *U.S. News & World Report*, as well as the producers of TV network news and cable networks such as CNN. Many stories are broken on the morning news-talk shows, like *Today* and *Good Morning America*, and in segments of the network evening news. Numerous Washington radio/TV news bureaus feed stories to cities and towns across the country. These range from AP Radio, which serves approximately 620 stations, and UPI Audio, to such long-established bureaus as Cox, RKO General, and Storer.

The Washington public relations practitioner also works closely with cable TV, which has become an influential medium. Cable News Network (CNN) and C-Span operate bureaus in the capital.

The preeminent source of information in media relations is *Hudson's Washington News Media Contact Directory*, 44 W. Market Street, P.O. Box 311, Rhinebeck, NY 12572. It appears annually and is updated quarterly for subscribers.

Washington practitioners often resist requests from management for full-scale news conferences, not because of possibly competing with the president, but because they question the hardness of the news they have to offer. The alternative is to target the story to a few interested reporters and meet with them one by one.

Public relations people who represent foreign interests are required to register and report their fees and activities to the Department of Justice under the Foreign Agents Registration Act.

Other references

Helpful sources of information about or available from the federal government include the following:

Davidson, Roger H., and Walter J. Oleszak. *Congress and Its Members*. Washington: Congressional Quarterly Press, 1985.

Hess, Stephen. *The Ultimate Insiders*. Washington: Brookings Institution, 1986.

Peters, Charles. *How Washington Really Works*. Reading, MA.: Addison-Wesley, 1981.

Rolle's Directory of Washington Communication. Bethesda, MD: Rolle Communications, 1995.

Safire, William. *Safire's Political Dictionary*. New York: Ballantine Books, 1980.

Wittenberg, Ernest, and Elisabeth Wittenberg. *How to Win in Washington*. Cambridge, MA., and Oxford: Basil Blackwell, 1989.

Additional Tips on Legislative Hearings and Lobbying

The only purpose of many legislative and regulatory hearings is to create media events. Those who call the hearing are likely to use it as a springboard for gaining media attention. Senator Joe McCarthy used them in his rampage to prominence in the 1950s—and was brought down by his excesses at his hearings on alleged Communists in the army. Senator Estes Kefauver orchestrated hearings on organized crime and pharmaceuticals—playing up a "revelation" in time for each day's deadlines, scheduling witnesses so the most sensational (previously coached) got the play and responsible ones were ignored.

Such hearings meet the same purpose as Communist "show trials," where the result is foreordained and all testimony is for propaganda.

This technique can be devastating to an organization. Thwarting it calls for sophisticated planning and action. Each hearing should be sized up thoroughly as soon as it is scheduled.[1]

- Determine the motives of all involved— including officials who called the hearing, other agencies or bodies involved, scheduled witnesses, and other groups who may try to obstruct, distort, or shout down the proceedings.

- Determine what traps must be watched out for: Trick questions? Phony accusations? How might the questioner imply wrongdoing and cut off any chance to offer corrective information? What might be done to provoke your anger—just when the TV cameras and reporters are alerted?

- What might you do to neutralize would-be opponents? What evidence can you get in advance to demonstrate the weakness of their arguments or their irresponsibility?

- Size up the media situation and make thorough plans.
  —Make advance contact with the specific media most likely to be interested.
  —Determine each medium's attitude. Alert its staff to the upcoming hearings, their significance, and the nuances involved.
  —Try to affect their attitude and alert them to what the opponents are likely to attempt.
  —Encourage or discourage coverage of the hearings by providing facts on their importance or validity.

—Provide information and/or an interview subject (and an interviewee) that can set the medium's approach, save the reporters' time in covering the hearings, and help assure fair treatment for your position.
—Provide thorough and careful service to the media during the hearings.

The broad scope of lobbying

With political parties weakening and voter independence growing, the impact of constituents' opinions has grown and is more immediately felt.

Here are the steps most often called for in rallying grassroots opinion to "lobby" government officials.[2]

- **Analyze the climate.** Which way is opinion moving on the subject? It's hard to influence opinion in a direction opposite to the way it's moving, but you can accelerate a trend of attitudes that's moving in the direction you desire.

- **Identify your opponents, as well as your existing and potential allies.**

- **Identify the small group who will determine the climate of opinion** on the issue involved. Focus on the small group that is alert and concerned about this issue.

- **Form coalitions** of various groups who currently agree or will agree in exchange for your support on other matters. But don't give up your ability to organize, to take the initiative, or to get things done.

- **Set goals** to meet the patterns likely to exist **by the time your efforts can take effect**.

- **Analyze your cause and define it** so clearly that everyone can understand it immediately.

[1]*Overcoming Opposition: A Survival Manual for Executives*, Philip Lesly, Prentice-Hall, 1984, adapted from Chapter 7.

[2]*Managing the Human Climate*, January–February, 1983, No. 78.

- **Analzye the various segments of that audience.** Develop strategies and appeals geared to each.

- **Assess the media** and other channels of communication available: How informed, accessible, biased are they? What's your relationship? Who has access?

- **Develop your case** based on the best available expertise and on complete objectivity. Get that into the pipelines of consideration of this subject **early**—before policies and legislation jell. Usually the best sources on a subject are available to private organizations but their expertise isn't heard until the theorists and ideologues have framed proposals that are nearly final.

- **Maintain flexibility.** Issues, like rivers, seldom carve a straight course. Prepare for diversions and digressions.

- **Integrate** all aspects of your program to assure consistency and efficiency.

6

WORKING WITH STATE GOVERNMENT

RICHARD A. ARMSTRONG

Richard A. Armstrong is a consultant to and the former president of the Public Affairs Council, the nonprofit, bipartisan professional organization of corporate public affairs executives headquartered in Washington, DC.

Mr. Armstrong joined the Public Affairs Council (formerly The Effective Citizens Organization, Inc.) in 1957 as field director and was named executive director in 1959. Under his direction, the Public Affairs Council became the recognized professional and clearinghouse organization for more than five hundred corporate public affairs programs. His business and professional experience includes posts with the University of Minnesota, the Minneapolis Chamber of Commerce, and the Mutual Benefit Life Insurance Company.

Mr. Armstrong holds a bachelor of arts degree from the University of Minnesota and has done graduate work at the University of Birmingham in England and the American University in Washington, DC.

Two of the first ten amendments to the U.S. Constitution, which comprise the Bill of Rights, exemplify the importance of communication between the people and their state governments.

ARTICLE I

Congress shall make no law respecting an establishment of religion, or prohibiting the free exercise thereof; or abridging the freedom of speech, or of the press; or the right of the people peaceably to assemble, and to *petition the Government for a redress of grievances* (italics added).

ARTICLE X

The powers not delegated to the United States by the Constitution, nor prohibited by it to the States, *are reserved to the States respectively, or to the people* (italics added).

The Need to Influence State Governments

Until the early 1970s only a few organizations had state government relations programs worthy of the name. State governments were ignored by most businesses, associations, and other private institutions. Beginning in the 1950s dozens of companies opened Washington legislative relations offices or hired consultants or law firms for their "eyes and ears" on the national scene, but they were virtually oblivious to legislative events in such state capitals as Springfield, Sacramento, and St. Paul. The "need equation" between business and state government, which was so apparent before the turn of the century, had been pushed out of management's consciousness by the accretion of power at the national level.

Hindered by antiquated and restrictive constitutions, malapportioned legislatures, poor use of resources, and massive public distrust or disinterest generated by earlier abuses of power, state governments had become unable or unwilling to fully exercise their residual powers. The federal government responded long before the states to the complex problems of modern society, and it did so with an aggressive expansion of programs and services. Into the vacuum of state inaction gradually moved the subsidy programs and the administrative agency control of the Washington colossus. States became distribution agents for federal funds—a role that further eroded their legislative initiative through the overlay of federal decisions on state priorities. Controlled largely by rural interests, state legislatures were unresponsive to urban needs; cities logically turned to the federal government for help that, in turn, bypassed the state level in its response. The Depression, World War II, the growth of the cities, and the complexities of urban problems all encouraged public acceptance of the national government as the dominant force in political life.

Today, however, there is a resurgence of the power of state legislatures—attributable partly to the reapportionment decisions of the Supreme Court in the mid-1960s and the more recent implementations thereof, and partly due to the growing realization that the federal government is just too big and too remote to deal directly with the needs of local communities.

The year 1981 brought a significant turning point in the power swing within the federal system and in the re-emergence of a viable need equation between state government and private organizations.

The inauguration of Ronald Reagan brought to the presidency a man determined to restore the power position of the states in

relation to the federal government—to a degree that went far beyond states' rights rhetoric and the revised federalism that had been advocated by Richard Nixon.

Reagan's "New Federalism" was designed, as he put it, "to curb the size and influence of the federal establishment and to demand recognition of the distinction between the powers granted to the federal government and those reserved to the states or to the people."

During the 1970s federal grants to states and cities jumped from $30 billion to more than $91 billion annually. By 1981, states and local communities were relying on federal funds for more than one-fourth of their revenues. For the most part, however, the money flowing from Washington went directly to state and local programs targeted by federal agencies, with the recipient areas given little if any voice.

Reagan's New Federalism called for the allocation of federal block grants by the states and cities as they themselves saw best, in light of their own needs and priorities. The concept, initially welcomed by many governors and mayors, drew widespread criticism from them when it become clear that, overall, it would drastically cut funds from Washington with the private sector expected to fill many of the gaps that would be left in social and other programs around the country. This was further emphasized by the Republican Congress elected in 1994.

The implication of the move toward a New Federalism was, however, clear: the need equation between private organizations and state government had been reestablished.

The Future of State Government Relations

What does the future hold? Will the need equation be sustained and strengthened? The following observations are offered:

Continued expansion of state power

The number of state administrative agencies has soared in recent years, as has the total of state regulatory agencies—from three hundred of the latter in the early 1960s to more than twenty-five hundred today. These increases reflect the states' interest in a far broader range of issues than ever before.

Shortened lead time for responding to new issues

According to veteran state observers, until recent years one could confidently project a three- to five-year cycle from the introduction or passage of a landmark bill in the first state until it appeared on the agenda of most of the other forty-nine legislatures. Now, they say, lead time on a major issue is often very short for the following interrelated reasons: (a) the nationalization of politics and issues, (b) the rapid growth of activist groups, (c) the facilitator of both the above factors—rapid communication.

Significant rationalization and sophistication of the state government apparatus

The enhanced capability, vitality, and resources of state government will obviously affect the states' development and the elements that contribute to it.

- **The executive branch.** Extensive bureaucratic reorganization, professionalization of personnel, higher salaries, widespread constitutional revision in the direction of increasing executive power

- **The legislative branch.** Upgrading of staffing, salaries, and research; vastly increased flow of information among state legislative leaders; revitalization of legislative procedures and practices

- **The judicial branch.** Discernible trend toward unification of the court system, streamlining of judicial administration—through constitutional revision or ongoing work of the various state judicial councils

Increased discretionary powers

Legislative bodies the world over face a dilemma: As the volume, variety, and complexity of public problems increase, more and more responsibility inevitably falls to the agencies administering specific programs. Enabling legislation establishes the broad policy framework; implementation is, of necessity, left to the bureaucrats. As a result it occasionally happens that the application or interpretation of a statute can contravene or go beyond its purpose through the arrogation of power not delegated. In that case, having an exclusively legislative orientation offers an organization's government relations program no advantage. The executive branch obviously plays an administrative and rule-making role of considerable importance.

The need to integrate all levels of government relations efforts

Many organizations with Washington offices coordinate all their governmental activities from there; others achieve coordination through a vice-president or director of public affairs at headquarters. Whatever the system, multilevel coordination has proven necessary for the following reasons:

- Governmental action at one level of government tends to stimulate pressures for parallel action at other levels. When the Food and Drug Administration announced sweeping new labeling requirements for food products, within days almost half of the states were considering their own labeling regulations.

- Federal law often promulgates guidelines for national policy on a problem but delegates the implementation to the states and/or local communities (e.g., air and water pollution control programs and occupational health and safety regulations).

- Interest groups seeking passage of a bill are usually flexible, working simultaneously for action at any level—in city hall, county court house, state capitol, or halls of Congress. For example, efforts have been made at all these levels to affect policies in such key areas as hazardous waste control, tax reform, and pension funds.

- Business itself has grown more pragmatic about the most desirable level for legislative remedy. Some industries (notably the automotive, canning, and detergent industries) have openly endorsed federal preemption on some issues because of the threat of contradictory and costly variations in the laws that in effect act as internal trade barriers between the states. On the other hand, the more traditional tactic of "leave it to the states" has proven sensible for an industry hard-pressed by a tough bill in Congress.

- Implementation of the New Federalism concept may activate or strengthen regional offices of some major domestic agencies on one hand, and move control of spending into the hands of state and local elected officials on the other (such as the recent welfare reform). This creates the necessity for increased knowledge of, and access to, state and local power structures.

The pace of change in state legislative affairs

Some of the aspects are aptly described by a state lobbyist.

It's a different ball game, compared to when I first came on the scene. Things were a lot simpler then. When an offensive bill came up you knew only a few people usually counted— often only one man, the Speaker, because he could pretty much kill a bill if he really went all out. At other times you might be worried about the committee chairman, maybe the majority and minority leaders, and probably how the labor lobbyist felt. Today you get your votes one at a time—no power brokers. It's a much more fluid situation. Not only is the power more fragmented in legislatures I cover, but there are a lot more outside groups which have their say. Even when you think you've got a situation well in hand you're never quite sure until the vote is over.

Other elements include changes in the institutions and the players.

A change in the type of legislator

The new breed is younger, better educated, and varied in background. The average age of state legislators today is between thirty-five and forty; it used to be in the fifties. Hundreds of members are in their twenties. Forty years ago the "typical" member came to the "typical" legislature with a background in farming or ranching; today, he or she is most likely to come from teaching or the law. Legislatures boast more women and minorities and are more attuned to urban matters. And as Alan Rosenthal, director of the Eagleton Institute of Politics at Rutgers University, has put it, "There's no place for amateurs any more. The part-time citizen legislator is out of style. The full-time, professional legislator is imminent, if not already on the scene, in perhaps half the states."

Moans one corporate veteran: "Some of these new guys think it's wrong to be seen with a lobbyist; you can't even talk to them."

Institutional changes in the legislature

Longer and more frequent sessions, presession committee work, and continuity of responsibility, interest, and expertise through the work of the legislative councils combine to raise the quality and increase the flow of legislation.

Ad hoc political groups

The proliferation of new citizen lobbies and interest groups creates an unstable element in many legislative struggles.

Initiatives and referenda

In theory, ballot measures—initiatives and referenda—represent democracy at its purest because they are acted on directly by the people. In practice they can, and often do, complicate the public policy process. Initiatives, authorized in some two dozen states, can be used by special interest groups to circumvent the legislature by taking a question to the voters who themselves (a) are far less likely than the legislators to have studied the matter in any detail, and (b) may be more susceptible to sloganeering and emotional appeals. On the other hand, referenda, authorized in most states, allow legislators to avoid accepting voter-delegated responsibility on a touchy issue by referring the matter to the public for decision at the polls. Initiatives in particular warrant close attention from the public affairs officer. They can be extremely costly in time and money to corporations targeted by initiative-minded interest groups. An antismoking initiative in California required an expensive countereffort by the tobacco firms before it was rejected at the polls.

Grassroots public affairs

Many issues likely to surface in coming years will require public affairs programs transcending the legislative arena. For example, in recent years power companies launched sizable information campaigns to inform the public about the intricacies of air pollution; insurance companies undertook public information and advertising campaigns to generate support for their positions on disposition of gasoline tax revenues. The rationale for this kind of grassroots program is derived not only from the nature of the issue but from the methods of the opposition. To illustrate: on environmental matters every citizen is affected. Since activist groups are often community-based they can effectively seek understanding and support on this issue at the local level.

From the cumulative weight of these factors it seems apparent that the need equation between private organizations and state government can no longer be obscured by the Washington colossus. And whatever the reasons for the new look in state government, the ballooning impact of state government activity on the general business community has impelled a wider corporate awareness.

Purpose of State Government Relations

In the last twenty years hundreds of organizations have established broad programs to encourage better employee citizenship and to enable them to exercise their rights—and responsibilities—as corporate citizens. The terminology applied to these efforts varies—*good government, effective citizenship, civic action*—but most are generally thought of as *public affairs programs*. The Public Affairs Council estimates that about eight hundred of America's largest corporations currently have fairly well-developed overall programs that include at least some government relations activities. Until the 1950s no firms had formal employee and corporate citizenship programs.

The following examples show how organizations use public affairs activities to complement and reinforce state government activities:[1]

---

[1]Many of the principles and techniques that follow are applicable to relations with local governments.—Ed.

- **Encourage employee political involvement.** A clear-cut policy that encourages employees to be good citizens (register, vote, work for a candidate or party, become active in a community organization) and facilitates their involvement through liberal time-off policies, leaves of absence, and promotion-evaluation standards rewarding such activities can obviously make a favorable impact on government relations.

- **Communicate with employees on state issues and problems.** Many organizations use their publications, plant newsletters, paycheck inserts, the intranet, and other devices to inform employees about pending legislation.

- **Facilitate good state government-business relations.** Corporate efforts to this end include the following:
  —Inviting candidates for state office to the organization for plant tours, political rallies, etc.
  —Promoting company efforts to attract industry and tourism, to support needed constitutional amendments, to identify with legislative reform efforts, and to otherwise support "good government" issues
  —Encouraging company executives to serve on state commissions and advisory boards.

- **Establishment of bipartisan state political action committees.** These committees, legal in many states, permit the collection and pooling of voluntary contributions from eligible employees and the allocation of those funds to selected candidates.

These are some of the elements of a well-rounded total state program. Most professionals in state government relations, in fact, view their function as the tip of the iceberg. The depth lies in these supportive public affairs activities.

Influencing the Executive Branch

In 1917 a program for state administrative reorganization, enacted in Illinois, set in motion a series of nationwide changes that transformed the governorship to a position of increased administrative power and enhanced political prestige. These changes were due in part to declining public confidence in the state legislatures; but they also stemmed from the lessons of business experience that taught the importance of giving the chief executive control over the administrative department heads by making them directly responsible to the governor. Thus the movement toward legislative reform has paralleled that of the executive branch. Accordingly, knowledge of the current executive structure of all states in which the organization has an interest is more and more essential to an effective state government relations program.

Influencing the executive branch, however, is often as difficult as it is necessary. Not only must the lobbyist deal with the governor, his or her staff and appointees, and other elected officials, he or she must also continuously cope with an increasing number of professional career administrators whose everyday actions could significantly impact his organization. Thus, the elected and nonelected government officials constitute separate elements within the executive branch, each having quite different characteristics with regard to their access to or use of power.

Elected officials

The governor heads the ticket and is the most visible of the elected officials having executive responsibility. His or her actual powers are of course constitutionally limited and may depend as much on qualities of leadership and a good staff as on legal authority. However, the range and depth of information essential to maintaining this leadership is often sought from experienced lobbyists whose expertise can add perspective and practicality to the governor's legislative policy.

In addition to the potential for contributing to the development of a legislative program, the well-prepared corporate state lobbyist with established access to the executive offices can offer advice on appointments to advisory commissions, exercise influence on the use (or threat) of a veto on a given piece of legislation, and—in the ongoing development of rapport and respect— contribute to a favorable political/business climate.

Two specific items to note: (a) Today at least forty-three states give the governor line-item veto on appropriation bills; and (b) the New Federalism's block grant program to states is intended to give *added discretionary authority to the governor.*

Nonelected officials

Obviously, the goal of lobbying at this level of the administrate hierarchy is to achieve administrative personnel's understanding of and identification with the day-to-day problems of a particular industry or interest. Influencing the professional career administrator (or regulatory commissioner/board member) is often the most challenging aspect of the government relations executive's job. One such executive expresses this problem succinctly:

> Regulators in general are far tougher (than legislators) to lobby, because they rarely have an elective constituency on whose goodwill they are dependent.

Once an agency or position is created it tends to develop a purpose and direction of its own, with self-perpetuation its primary goal. The state relations professional frequently develops expertise in the program field that goes far beyond the original mandate as a technique for attaining indispensability. Thus the experienced lobbyist knows that the traditional function of providing information/expertise is performed with special attention to detail and a high degree of sophistication when working with career administrators. Although their self-image can sometimes exceed their performance, these individuals consider themselves to be experts, and they usually are. Respect for the bureaucratic sense of professionalism is therefore essential. It can be demonstrated by understanding the overall complexities of the problems confronting the administrator, as well as by precise knowledge of the matter at hand. The lobbyist's credibility and access are improved by carefully researched and updated material tailored to the appropriate reference.

Successful communication with non-elected officials can also arise from prior lobbying success in the legislature. For example, significant input is possible in the construction of the authorizing legislation for agencies affecting an organization's interest. Consistently providing reliable information to and working well with individual legislative committees and committee chairmen puts the lobbyist in a position to set the stage for future relationships with the agency—by influencing how the bill is written and the tone of its guidelines and criteria. Thus at the regulatory stage—when the rule-making power inherent in the interpretation of the legislation is actually implemented—the lobbyist's points of view are represented and his or her leverage is projected through the legislative oversight function of the committee chairmen whose support has been gained.

In summary, today's successful state government relations program necessarily includes an executive as well as a legislative lobbying effort because of the compelling potential for

- Multiplying effectiveness through the interaction and integration between the two branches
- Creating a favorable political/business climate through rapport with elected administration officials, including the governor

Figure 6.1 Actions taken by the Illinois Senate affect thousands of organizations in Illinois. In response, many have established broad-based state government affairs programs to monitor legislation and communicate their point of view to legislators. *Courtesy Secretary of the Senate, Springfield, Illinois.*

- Contributing to the development of the governor's legislative policy
- Offering advice on appointments and on use of the veto
- Providing essential information to non-elected government officials in implementing legislation affecting the organization's interests

Elements of State Government Relations Programs

What are the components of a successful state government relations program? Technique? Type of industry? Political climate? Attitude

of top management? What follows is a discussion of all of these and more.

Lobbying techniques

"There are less than a dozen basic techniques of lobbying," according to one expert, "whether one is trying to influence the United Nations or a village council." Accordingly, a useful way to discuss approaches to state government relations is to focus on these basic techniques. (*See* Figure 6.1.)

A few organizations use all the basic approaches. The best illustrations are often found among large one-state companies with an obvious and unavoidable vested interest in effective state relations—companies whose very existence, or at least operating conditions, are dependent on state government—for example public utilities.

The one-state company

An examination of the state government relations activities of one large utility company in an eastern state reveals these key approaches.

- The company maintains a year-round presence in the state capital. A staff of two full-time professionals monitors state legislative activities, orchestrates the company's effort to influence legislation, and assists home office personnel in their relationships with the state regulatory body and other key administrative agencies.

- Managers and executives throughout the state are expected to cultivate relationships with state legislators from their localities. The manager of each local office, for example, becomes acquainted on a first-name basis with his or her state representatives and senators and works hard at cultivating the legislators' understanding of the company and its problems.

- Occasionally the company retains a legal firm in the state capital to help the company's professional lobbyists handle a particularly difficult legislative situation. Generally this occurs when the company is confronted with an issue in which the law firm has special competence and credibility or when a close relationship with key legislators would be especially beneficial.

- The company is also an active member of the state chamber of commerce and several other state business organizations. On some issues it coordinates its efforts closely with the association's state government relations staff or relies on the association for the entire load.

- On relatively rare occasions and in the face of a very serious legislative problem, the company may turn to satellite groups for assistance. If a proposed bill, for example, would seriously inhibit the company's growth, the firm might communicate its position to suppliers, customers, the company's labor union(s), and other groups that might be affected by company adversity.

- On even more infrequent occasions, the company may take its case on a particular problem to the grass roots. This would occur when management concludes that "taking it to the people" is the only way to win on an important vote in the legislature.

This company makes its case with the help of six kinds of individuals or organizations: (a) professional lobbyists on staff, (b) line personnel, (c) consultants, (d) associations, (e) satellite groups, (f) people.

The multi-state company

Multi-state companies do the best they can to adapt and combine these techniques. Unfortunately, only a minority of the *Fortune* 500 companies have anything worthy of being called a "program" in state government relations. Instead, the most typical approach is the "home-office troubleshooter" technique. This system has worked often enough that its successes have tended to obscure the need for a longer-range view.

- The company may have a professional staff member assigned to watch the state where the company is headquartered and in one or two other states critical to the company.

- Alternatively, the company's public affairs officer (who usually has other responsibilities) has to develop some kind of mechanism to stay informed about important legislative developments in these few states.

- The company pays little attention to legislative developments in other states. In effect, it relies on trade associations or sister firms from its industry in other states to protect its legislative interests.

• Crisis: One day the company feels threatened by a proposed state law or regulation. It puts together an ad hoc operation to meet the challenge—quick contacts with trade associations, employment of high-cost legal firms or government relations consultants, a number of trips to and from the state capitol by the assembled team of experts—resulting in an accommodation perhaps just short of catastrophe. The learning value of the crisis often does not penetrate deeply, and the company may revert to its normal degree of disinterest until the next threat arises.

At least a few of the same six groups that work for a one-state company are at work. However—due to occasional success in conjunction with lack of budget, staff, and management commitment—this typically perpetuates an inefficient system.

Emerging strategies
The professional staff lobbyists

Many of the organizations with investment or marketing interests in all the states, as well as a staff of full-time professional government affairs experts, find that a regionalized structure may offer a workable system. The country is divided into contiguous regions, each of which is assigned to an executive. Typically, a region may be composed of from six to ten states. Most companies coordinate their regional offices out of the central corporate office through the director of government relations or of public affairs—although a great diversity of organizational and operating relationships does exist. The regional representative is expected to monitor the state legislatures within his or her territory, to handle most of the legislative problems, and to develop strong ties with influential legislators and their staffs.

The effectiveness of a numerically limited professional staff can be expanded and supported in a variety of ways. Here are a few:

• If necessary, the organization can establish representation in every state capital through full-time employees, consultants, or a combination, with corporate executives handling the most important states.

• The company may supplement regional executives by using consultants and law firms.

• The company may limit its coverage to the states in which it has the most intense interest. Legislative problems in other states are then handled on an ad hoc basis.

• The company may rely heavily on operating, sales, and staff personnel for much of the monitoring and contact work, with the regional executives coordinating and servicing such legislative activities.

Line personnel

Few organizations knowledgeable in state politics ignore the potential for political effectiveness within the ranks of its employees. The trend in newer state programs is to more effectively involve plant or regional-level corporate executives in the legislative program. In the words of one public affairs officer:

> We have come to recognize that the name of the game is grassroots involvement. A plant manager acquainted with his legislator, or assisting in his campaign, or writing him a personal letter on a particular issue—these things may count more than whatever I can do. After all, he's a constituent.

Some companies have systemized what has been called a "man-to-man defense," whereby executives are assigned to cultivate personal relationships with designated legislators or administrators. Other companies conduct periodic inventories of middle, as well as top, management to discover "who knows whom" in state government. A large number of companies occasionally request that managers, on a voluntary basis, communicate the company position on a pending issue to elected officials.

Corporate grassroots lobbying efforts may be divided into three broad categories:

1. **Involvement.** This means getting the plant manager, as well as those above and below him, interested in and informed about the issues relating directly to their bottom line. It calls for their personal participation in politics and political action committees—participation stimulated by political education, awareness, and motivation, as well as economic understanding.

2. **Meaningful relations with politicians at all levels.** Company representatives frequently boast of knowing this or that politician. The real question, however, is, Does the politician know—*really* know—the company representative? "Meaningful relationships" does not translate into shaking hands at the Rotary Club or saying hello at the airport. Meaningful relationships with politicians must be cultivated as assiduously and carefully as the salesperson courts the purchasing agent. They exist only when the company representative and the politician gain a mutual understanding and appreciation of each other's situation. With due respect to the professional lobbyist, often no substitute exists for the plant manager standing eyeball to eyeball with the mayor or other official.

3. **Community support.** Is the company's point of view shared by the community—the politician's constituency? If so, prove it. The endorsement of civic and business groups, perhaps supplemented by editorials in the local press, will help the politician see that your firm's position or request is not an isolated, individual (perhaps selfish) one. It's a major asset any time it can be shown that what the company wants will help the community, and by doing so aids the politician's voters. And if he goes along, let him make the announcement and let him take the credit.

Although most experienced public affairs officers recognize the importance of such grassroots involvement, problems do exist. For example, more than one company has been embarrassed by an executive's letter that overstated a problem, threatened the legislator, or was otherwise impolitic. This fact suggests that if managers are to play an effective role in the company's program, they might welcome some help with the subtleties of politics and government, some form of communication and information to keep them up to date and motivated, and some overall assistance and guidance from the public affairs department. To meet such needs, one company with a number of state government relations committees has developed the following mechanisms:

- Regular meetings of these state committees
- An information newsletter to keep members posted on legislative developments and to build support on key issues
- A "Public Affairs Manual" providing background information and guidelines for the committee members
- Annual meetings, often hosted by the company president, at which the importance of the local executive is noted and applauded
- Occasional seminars designed to build political sophistication, conducted by either the company or an outside organization.

Consultants

Almost all large companies with records of success in state government relations on occasion have used consultants. No state capital is without these experts who either have their own public affairs or government relations firms or are specialists within the public relations and legal firms having a government affairs capability.

The usual reasons a company uses a consultant include the following:

- The cost on an occasional basis may be less than the necessary expense for a continuing corporate program.
- The company doesn't know its way around politically in the particular state.
- The consultant happens to be a specialist in the particular field in question.
- The consultant has particular influence with legislators who have important control of the issue in question.
- Outside objective expertise is called for because of internal jurisdictional conflict between the government relations, legal, or public relations departments.

On the other hand, as one highly respected consultant puts it, "Consultants are a mixed bag. It's hard for the uninitiated to sort out the doers from the talkers." And obviously, by the nature of their profession, even the best of the doers cannot be identified exclusively with the organization or have thorough knowledge of its concerns—a fact that carries the possibility of dilution of effectiveness or, at worst, an unrecognized conflict of interest. A further caution: The company should implement an absolutely clear agreement that details what it expects a consultant to do, how much discretion he or she can exercise, and what the financial arrangements will be.

Associations

The role of business associations (multi-industry groupings such as state manufacturers' associations) and trade associations (single-industry groups such as a retail merchants' association) in state government relations appears to be in transition (see also Chapter 35). As a whole, these groups devote more resources to this task than ever before,

yet many active companies are uncertain about their effectiveness. Most feel they cannot rely exclusively on associations, but they are quick to suggest that associations can play a useful role as eyes and ears in the state capital, that they are often effective on general issues that cut broadly, such as business tax legislation, and that they are undoubtedly helpful in activating apathetic elements in the business community. Associations, because they represent diverse elements, must reach a compromise position on most issues—compatible with all constituents. This often does not square with the particular company's position. Accordingly, in general, trade associations are probably valued more highly than are business associations as legislative action vehicles.

No generalization about associations can be made, however. Each association in a given state must be evaluated on its own performance. A highly regarded association under dynamic leadership can develop respect both within the business community and at the capital. Most companies will approach the question on a state-by-state, issue-by-issue basis. They will compare the assets the association may bring into a particular situation with the accompanying liabilities.

Affiliation with an association can be valuable as:

- A general contributor to a better business climate.
- A source of intelligence and information on key legislative issues in that state.
- A major instrument in the company's overall program. For example, a company dominant in its industry may prefer not to appear dominant and so will work principally through associations.
- A major factor in coalescing and coordinating state legislative activity among member firms. One large association, for example, launched a comprehensive program to

"assure consistent, responsible and constructive action by the industry in regard to the legislative and administrative activities of state and local government." Elements included appointment of a coordinator for each state, creation of state government relations committees, and appointment of a national director for the overall program.

Satellite groups

At least two national companies rely principally on working through suppliers, customers, and other satellite groups. This is a technique that has been used selectively by a growing number of companies.

The public affairs manager of a company that has pioneered this technique identifies three preliminary steps:

1. **Mobilize the broadest possible group of satellites at the highest possible level**—the executives of those servicing, or serviced by, the company (banks, unions, insurance, storage, and distribution companies, for example).

2. **Develop comprehensive profiles of each satellite** (its ties to the company, sales, employment, potential political strengths, contact persons).

3. **Establish and maintain good working relationships with satellite groups on a continuing basis**, so when the crunch develops the company will be able to illustrate how the proposed statute or regulation could help (or hurt), and will be in a position to offer assistance in the form of a plan of action.

The people

It can safely be predicted, for reasons noted previously, that companies will be successful in many future legislative and regulatory struggles only if they are effective in grassroots public affairs. In essence, they will have to win the support of the public before they can prevail in the legislative arena.

This probability will hold true not only for the one-state company (which often may constitute a major portion of the state's economy or provide a major portion of its services), but for the multi-state company as well—even though such a task may seem staggering for a major national organization.

A major, though controversial, tool now used by many companies and associations to reach the public on policy issues is advocacy advertising, sometimes known as public affairs or idea advertising. Such advertising via the print and/or electronic media effectively persuades (*see* Chapter 30) key segments of the public, at the community or even the international level that an organization's policies and practices are well advised and proper—and that they merit official support. An individual company can often aid an entire industry or cause through a well-planned advocacy campaign conducted on its own, but more and more firms on occasion are joining to conduct coordinated campaigns in behalf of a common issue in a state or community.

(Advocacy advertising should not be confused with public service advertising. The latter, while it conveys worthwhile messages on such general subjects as health, safety, and education, is usually prompted simply by the company's desire to keep its name before the public in a positive context.)

Advocacy advertising can be a particularly useful device for corporate "issues and opportunities management" when a matter is up for consideration in a legislature (*see* Chapter 2). More precisely, it can be an important instrument in a company's *response* to the issue. (The term *issues management* is misleading. Though widely used, it carries implications of manipulation and arrogance and sounds monumentally self-serving. Issues cannot be managed; the corporate *responses* to them *can*.)

Objectives and Challenges

There are as many problems as there are companies and units of government, but two stand out as common to almost all companies considering the establishment of a state government relations program: (a) maintaining effective surveillance and (b) gaining management support.

Maintaining effective surveillance

Almost 250,000 bills are introduced within any two-year period in the various state legislatures. For a company with nationwide interests this volume appears to create an insurmountable obstacle. Furthermore, many bills are so complex or ambiguous that evaluating and analyzing even the most important would seem hopeless. There are no simple solutions, but what follows are ways some companies are handling the problem:

1. **Utilize private legislative information services.** While efforts have been made to establish such services, many have floundered on the immense "front end" cost of establishing an effective network with the accompanying analytical capability in the fifty state capitals. Consequently the good ones are expensive and scarce, and the time between bill introduction and notification sometimes is unacceptable. In terms of selectivity of information, the value to the client is apt to be quantitative rather than qualitative.

2. **Provide a monitoring system for all capitals where the company has serious interests.** Some companies hire consultants or stringers to do this. Others with a regional setup may rely on their staffs. A few train operating or staff executives to do the job.

3. **Rely on the company's own ad hoc system.** This typically combines several tactics, for example: participation with the industry association in some states; corporate watchdogging in the more important capitals; or using consultants, legislative reporting services, or an informal liaison in remaining locations.

Gaining management support

A long-time consultant in government relations flatly states that the single biggest failure among companies in this field is lack of management commitment. He suggests that too many companies regard public affairs and government relations as a kind of fringe activity—underfinanced, understaffed, and out of the mainstream of corporate priorities.

Significantly, he believes that the failure is not totally that of top management but rather of the government relations staff. The government affairs executive must relate his or her function to the "bottom line."

A number of corporations have estimated the costs saved by legislative efforts resulting in passage or defeat of important legislation. A survey of more than seventy corporations several years ago disclosed fifty-four such cases with computed corporate public affairs "savings" of more than $20 million (most of it in the legislative area). Such figures can be misleading, of course. Seldom can the government relations executive claim that his company's efforts alone killed or passed a bill. Some defeated "bad bills" realistically may have had no chance of passage anyway—with or without the company's involvement.

Even if the relationship of the state government relations program to the bottom line is measurable to a degree sufficient to make a case, the government relations executive is still more likely to be successful if the company already has the public acceptance generated by a strong overall public relations program.

Broad-scope public relations objectives—well communicated by word and action, initiated and sustained by a high degree of top management commitment—are essential in dispersing adversary attitudes between the private and the public sector and in developing a climate receptive to recognizing a mutuality of interests. Thus, in the final analysis, it is the chief executive who sets the tone and whose decisions will make the difference in business-government relations.

Oversimplified, in the long run top management interest and support will come as a result of a creative and integrated combination of the following:

- A well-prepared "selling and telling" job when the program is initiated—so the top executives clearly understand the rationale and have related it to overall corporate self-interest. Development of a corporate policy statement establishing the rationale and objectives of the government relations program can be useful.

- Education of and communication with management as a continuing and cumulative process.

- Use of top-level policy committees to develop corporate positions on key legislation. This can help in the growth of political understanding among those who develop the positions.

- A major public issue that threatens the company earnings, perhaps its very viability. Often only a crisis can sensitize management on the importance of government relations. The tide of environmentally related legislation, for instance, has stimulated establishment or broadening of dozens of government relations programs in the affected industries—notably paper, chemicals, oil, and steel.

- A major public issue with high visibility that clearly conflicts with another major issue that causes equivalent public concern—for example, when "environment" meets "energy shortage." Such a polarity of interest can result in a temporary problem-solving truce in which top management can be encouraged to play a constructive role with government. For by responding positively in areas where business-government cooperation is necessary to overcome a problem, business can create the opportunity to increase its effectiveness on other issues touching more vitally on corporate self-interest.

Getting Started

The following is a list of things to consider in developing a state government relations plan:

1. **Profile the company from a government relations point of view.** In how many states does it have a significant interest (such as plant/operating, product/marketing, etc.)? Identify the legislative or regulatory areas in which operations and profits are affected or potentially affected by state actions.

2. **Inventory the company's political resources.** What's the track record? How have things been handled and with what success? How strong is the overall public affairs program? What percentage of employees is active in political and community affairs? What is the company's public image? To which business or trade associations does the company belong?

3. **Determine the components of a successful program within your industry.** Gather information from the corporate sources listed in the following section. Which method worked best? What organizations were most reliable? How was surveillance maintained? How was top management support achieved?

4. **Review the political climate of the state(s) in which the company might be politically active.** Is the company likely

to be in a vulnerable position? Are there conflicting statutes in different states? What are the voting statistics? The party strengths?

In establishing a new state government relations program, these suggestions will be helpful:

• Resist an unrealistic deadline. Insist on enough time to do the necessary homework.

• Develop a hard-nosed rationale. The case must make business sense.

• Be specific. Develop anticipated costs, outline problems and obstacles, define priorities and procedures.

• Outline options, properly analyzing costs, benefits, and disadvantages.

• Use the company and satellite group structure in long-term roadmapping. Catalog such items as technical division expertise, supplier interest, plant manager, local contacts.

Your efforts should result in the creation of one or more new positions for state government relations work. Many companies promote from within to fill these new positions, perhaps tapping an executive who has been very active in politics or community affairs or the person who previously handled the infrequent contacts of the company with state government. The trend, however, is toward bringing from the outside an individual with political and legislative experience. As the manager of one of the country's most sophisticated corporate state programs puts it:

> Ideally, we need a person who knows the company through and through and is also well indoctrinated in state legislative matters. Naturally, we have few such people already as employees. Though many of my colleagues in other companies would disagree with me, I take the political experience over the company background because I think I can provide him the necessary information on the company. But I can't teach

him political instincts or the subtleties of politicians. In our company, therefore, we have obtained most of our new lobbyists in recent years from among the ranks of trade association lobbyists, ex-legislators or legislative staff members, and lobbyists working for other companies or special interests.

Corporate Program Information: Sources and Resources

To develop a program tailored to its own goals the organization getting started in state-level government relations needs some basic information on other programs to compare and evaluate, and from which to form guidelines. A list of sources follows:

Other active companies particularly within the industry

The administrators of successful programs usually will be glad to share their perspectives and brief you fully on their activities. For names and addresses write the Public Affairs Council, 1019 19th Street, NW, Suite 200, Washington, DC 20036.

The industry association

Most large associations employ trained government relations specialists who are familiar with the activities of leading companies within the industry. One excellent source is The National Association of Manufacturers, 1331 Pennsylvania Avenue, NW, Washington, DC 20004.

State and local chambers of commerce

Many are aware of strong corporate programs within their jurisdictions and can provide leads. The Chamber of Commerce of the

United States, 1615 H Street, NW, Washington, DC 20062, also keeps track. The Council of State Chambers of Commerce, 122 C Street, NW, Suite 330, Washington, DC 20001, can give addresses of its member chambers.

The Public Affairs Council

The Council's Department of Government Relations Services provides counsel on an individual basis with companies setting up state programs and acts as a broker of information on corporate government relations programs at all levels. In addition, the council conducts lobbying workshops, seminars, clinics, and conferences for executives with varying degrees of experience. The sessions are held in various cities around the country. Write the Public Affairs Council, 1019 19th Street, NW, Suite 200, Washington, DC 20036.

Consultants

A few public affairs firms specialize in advising companies on how to initiate and implement a state capability. Some companies retain a consultant on a continuing basis to furnish ongoing guidance on procedures and strategy. Specific information is available from the Public Affairs Council.

State Government Information: Sources and Resources

Once the preliminary decisions have been made about the format of the program itself, the organization must get to "know the territory" from a political standpoint—how the various state governments with which the company will be interacting are structured; the powers, duties, and responsibilities of

these governments, plus something of the history and economy that bear on attitudes of the electorate and the elected. What are the issues of prime concern? What are the positions of individual office-holders apt to be? A list of sources follows:

State government

- Most state tax commissions publish revenue and expenditure charts.
- The budget and budget message can be obtained from the governor's office.
- State election boards sometimes publish reports on election returns, votes on referenda, etc.
- The Legislative Council or its equivalent, or the "boiler room" of either House can usually supply a directory of legislators, an outline of procedures, or a summary of proceedings.
- Reference libraries and research bureaus affiliated with the three branches of government can provide copies of bills, committee reports, or other key documents.
- Regulations governing a given industry are best obtained directly from the appropriate state commission.
- Individual legislators and other government officials and their staffs usually respond readily to specific requests for information.

State organizations
Chamber of Commerce

In those states where it exists, the chamber is a good source for an overview of the economy with statistics and percentages quickly at hand. It usually will have a directory of the major state industries, the manufacturers and trade associations, and the statewide volunteer organizations and their officers.

Industry and trade associations

These organizations often monitor government activities and publish periodic bulletins on significant developments. The state chamber of commerce or the chambers of the larger metropolitan areas may do this, too.

The League of Women Voters

In most states, the state league office publishes and tries to maintain an up-to-date profile of the structure and operation of the government, often including a section on the history and economy. Brief biographical material on state office-holders, as well as their position statements on selected issues, can be made available on request since leagues usually gather this information for their pre-election voters' guides. State leagues also monitor legislation on issues they favor or oppose and some publish legislative newsletters available by subscription.

Interest groups

A variety of single-interest groups regularly monitors legislative activities in virtually every state. Their newsletters and research reports can be very useful to the state government relations executive.

National organizations

National or regional trade/business associations

On particular issues of widespread corporate impact, these organizations monitor state as well as national legislation. Write the Chamber of Commerce of the United States, 1615 H Street, NW, Washington, DC 20062, or the National Association of Manufacturers, 1331 Pennsylvania Avenue, NW, Washington, DC 20004.

State Government Affairs Council

This coalition of business firms and trade associations works with the states to improve the effectiveness of state administrative, legislative, and regulatory processes, policies, and programs. Its address is 1255 23rd Street, NW, Washington, DC 20037.

Interest groups

Hundreds of Washington-based groups, ranging from one end of the issue and ideological spectrum to the other, provide useful information on state activity important to their constituencies.

Legislative organizations

Generally speaking, the organizations on the following list devote themselves to facilitating the interchange of various types of state government information—through research and publication, training programs, forums, and the like. Publications of these organizations known to be particularly useful are listed.

Council of State Governments

Iron Works Pike, P.O. Box 11910, Lexington, KY 40578. An association with affiliates of state officials, their staffs, and the professional organizations of various types of state officials. Seeks to strengthen and improve state government through research on the various aspects of the state's political system. Publications include: *Book of the States* (biennially) and *State Government* (bimonthly).

The National Conference of State Legislatures

1500 Broadway, Denver, CO 80202. NCSL is a nonpartisan public interest group— funded by the states—that works to improve the quality and effectiveness of state legislatures, to assure states a strong, cohesive voice in federal decision-making, and to foster inter-state communication and cooperation. Publications include: *State Legislatures* (monthly) and a bimonthly fiscal letter.

Additional sources

Reporting services

Several reporting services provide timely, comprehensive reports on state government activities. Staffed by professionals who have extensive experience working with or in state governments, the major services offer computer-expedited analyses and reports on every type of state regulatory and legislative activity. They can cover individual states, groups of states, or all fifty, tailoring their reports to their clients' requirements. The Public Affairs Council can provide information on services that specialize in a particular state. Two services that cover the states are Information for Public Affairs, 2101 K Street, Sacramento, CA 95816, and Commerce Clearing House, 521 Fifth Avenue, New York, NY 10175.

U.S. Dept. of Commerce

Bureau of Census, Customer Service Branch, Data Users Services Division, Washington, DC 20233, publishes *Census Catalogue and Guide*.

National Civic League

1445 Market Street, Denver, CO 80202. Monitors trends in state government; does research in areas of electoral reform; publishes periodical, *National Civic Review*.

7

HAVING A VOICE IN POLITICS

MACE BROIDE

Mace Broide was executive director of the Committee on the Budget of the U.S. House of Representatives. From 1968 to 1978 he was a partner in DeHart and Broide, Washington public affairs counselors. For ten years prior to that he was the top assistant to then Senator Vance Hartke (D-Ind.), managed two successful campaigns for Hartke, and had important assignments in several political campaigns. In 1961–62 Broide was secretary of the National Democratic Senatorial Campaign Committee.

A newspaperman and television commentator in Indiana, Broide's forte was politics for nearly ten years.

The concert of politics and government is probably the strongest single interactive force affecting the lives of individual Americans. Every day these interactive forces shape our activities. To the extent we involve ourselves and our organizations in the political process, we can influence the direction of government. To remain aloof from politics is to minimize one's influence on government at any level.

Whatever your field, chances are there will be times when your organization will have a problem with government or a point of view to express to someone who can do something about it.

Whether it's a national, state, or local problem, you'll be better off if you know personally an elected official to whom you can talk. You will be in a better position to talk to that official, and get him to listen, if he knows you, or, better yet, if you helped him get elected. By helping him when he needs help, at election time, you get a chance to get to

know him or his staff—and he or they get to know you under favorable circumstances. It's like helping any prospective business associate or customer.

Just put yourself in the official's shoes. Who is he or she going to show more sympathy for: The fellow he has never heard of who shows up suddenly with a problem? Or the fellow who worked in his campaign who shows up with a problem?

The more government becomes involved in business, manufacturing, advertising, professions, labor relations, and all the other fields of private enterprise, the more important it becomes for representatives of all those areas to participate in politics and campaigns.

Many political beginners think they have to be making major policy in Washington to be effective in politics. That isn't true even on a national scale. The person or organization working effectively in a representative's hometown is doing a mighty important piece of work—and the representative knows it and appreciates it. Moreover, that's how most of the big-time political leaders started.

The rest of this chapter is designed to explain basic party and campaign organization and to help sort out some of the ways public relations people may be helpful and attain their organizations' voice in government.

Politics Is Civic Service— and Good Business

In a democratic society a great deal depends on voluntary actions by individual citizens. It's a civic duty to help forestall pollution and serve in the PTA.

Volunteer work in politics is also good business—or good labor, or good agriculture, or good medicine, or whatever your immediate economic or professional interest is. That's how our founding fathers designed it (see *The Federalist Papers*).

Time was when business executives shunned politics, political parties, candidates, and even holders of public office. "It's bad for business" was a common tenet.

That's not true today in any event. Many business people participate in political activity and often it helps their business by increasing their public visibility.

The president of one of America's largest appliance manufacturing firms was selected for that position after he had served a term as the politically appointed president of the Board of Safety in a medium-sized city.

A former roofing company head walked into a political headquarters one day to find out how he could help and was immediately drafted to address and stuff envelopes. A short time later, following success at the polls by his party, he was named to head an important board.

Literally hundreds of company executives, many of them in public relations, today serve as volunteers in the campaigns of representatives, senators, and governors.

Volunteer work is a big business in politics. It involves menial and prosaic work like addressing envelopes. Most often it involves donating and raising money. But professional advice and skill also are avidly sought by party executives and candidates for office. Ability to write and communicate in other ways is a skill that is sought by political organizations, committees, and candidates.

Companies and trade associations in recent years have recognized the desirability of guidance in their relations with governmental agencies at all levels and with political figures and organizations. Increasingly, companies and trade associations have sought in-house executives and outside consultants with political and governmental expertise. Often, former public officials are sought for these positions, but the politically experienced can be just as effective even if they've never held elective office.

When such a public affairs liaison person has been hired or retained, the expertise is useful for maintaining and developing political and governmental contact and for directing political action committees and coordinating political volunteers for the company or trade associations.

Voting, Politics, and Government— Related but Different

Voting itself is the most important act of participation in politics and government, an act basic and elementary.

Yet the United States rarely approaches the 70 percent mark of participation by eligible voters in state and national elections. So voting—informed voting—is the first basic step, but only that. Elections are one-day affairs. Politics and government go on 365 days a year.

At the outset, some elementary distinction must be made between politics and government. *Politics* is the process of selecting, nominating, and electing people to conduct public business. *Government* is the actual management of those affairs. As with most definitions, these are dangerously oversimplified. Politics and government are so intertwined in daily practice that they are often almost indistinguishable.

It's hard to be objective and say who is more concerned with public welfare and who with sheer politics.

The fact is that the public welfare often determines good politics. Thus government—good and bad—makes politics and political issues.

The point is that politics is a means to an end. The desired end is having influence in the shaping of government. Politics is organized group action, people working in concert toward common goals. Moreover, politics is local. All local elections are local, but so are all national elections. So success in politics usually means working with others, starting at the community level—with friends, neighbors, and people who live in the same block or in the same part of town.

The real work of politics is accomplished by organizers who work constantly at that level. The better and harder they work, the better the chance of success on election day. Since elections are the heart of politics, success on election day is the measured goal of politics.

Political Party Organization and Structure

The purpose of organized political parties is simple. Their goals are to nominate candidates and win elections. In his booklet, *The*

Role of Political Parties, U.S.A., Joseph C. Harsch describes the American political party in terms of a corporation:

> The American party is made up primarily of those persons who choose to work in that political corporation for the benefits which continued employment in it, and service to it, can offer. Those voters who tend to support one party are its stockholders. The rest of the country consists of customers who tend to shop around for services in return for their votes.
>
> This is not a bad system. On the contrary, it is a very good system. It is just as good, and as desirable, and as useful in politics as it is in the market place. It is the system which long, and painful, experience has proved to be best adapted, by and large, to the needs and interests of the American people.

You and the Political Organization, one of a series of booklets prepared by the Chamber of Commerce of the United States for its action course in practical politics, outlines the development of political parties in America this way:

> George Washington, in his Farewell Address, deplored the danger of a party system, particularly a division along geographic lines. Yet, while Washington was still President, the Federalist party began to form under the leadership of Alexander Hamilton and the Democratic [Republican] (or anti-Federalist) party took shape under Thomas Jefferson. The Federalist group wanted a strong central government. They represented most business interests and the Northeast. The Jeffersonian group favored strong state government and a limited national government. It represented agrarian interests and centered in the frontier areas and the South.
>
> Subsequent realignments of the parties took place on the basis of issues. The Federalists died as a national party following the defeat of Rufus King by James Monroe in 1816. By 1828, the Jacksonians had split off from the Democratic Republicans, principally over differences on tariff and monetary policy between propertied interest on the one hand and the agrarians and

frontiersmen on the other hand. Webster, Clay and Calhoun were the founders and leaders of a new Whig Party made up of various factions of the traditional Democratic Republicans and surviving Federalists.

In the 1850s, both the Whig and Democratic Parties splintered over the slavery question, leading to the formation of the Republican Party, Lincoln's victory in 1860, and the reduction of the Democratic Party to a southern regional party for many years.

The parties originated and reformed on the basis of issues, but . . . there have been two major parties with no realignment of forces successful enough to produce a new national political party.

The two parties no longer differ as dramatically on issues as they once did. Both parties now contain people representing a wide variety of political philosophies.

Today, whether individuals are Democrats or Republicans depends to some extent on issues, but also to some degree on what party their families have traditionally belonged to—their religion, ethnic, racial and economic groups—and also on where they live.

Party loyalty is determined only to a limited extent by the issues. Some people believe the two major parties take about the same position on the issues. Others indicate they don't know what position either party espouses.

Comparisons of issue-orientation vs. candidate-orientation seem to show that the presidential candidates are far more important in the voter's mind than the issues.

The issues tend to blur and the success or failure of the parties has come to depend more and more on the appeal of the candidates and the effectiveness of the party political organization.

On the local level—the level which ultimately decides all elections—the issues tend to be played down and candidates played up. The comparable strength and effectiveness of the party organizations are principal factors in deciding who wins.

Political party structure, which is largely shaped by the various state election laws, generally parallels government structure. That is,

Figure 7.1 Pattern of U.S. political parties.

it consists of a pyramiding of responsibilities from the basic election district, called a *precinct* in most states, to the party national committee at the top, in much the same way that local government is responsible to county government, county to state government, and state to federal government in many areas. (*See* Figure 7.1.)

State laws and traditions largely shape political party organizations.

Precinct sizes and the whole election process, including methods for nomination and election and for voter eligibility, are products, usually, of state law. In some states the way these laws are written actually helps strengthen and tighten party organizations. In others the general election laws tend to break down party organization and loyalties.

For instance, where it is possible to crossfile and enter primaries of two parties there is a tendency to break down party organization and discipline and to put a premium on individual power and personal organizations. Likewise, if state laws call for primaries closed except to those who declare for one party or another, and if election board and other positions are clearly defined for representatives of party organizations, then parties are strengthened.

In some states and areas the political clubs enjoy much of the real power of local politics. But, generally speaking, it's the formal party organization—based in the precinct—

that enjoys formal recognition and actual power.

Occasionally, in recent years, presidential campaigns have been organized from strong committees dedicated solely to the success of the candidate for the White House rather than to his party. In those instances, the real power in the presidential election has remained with these special committees. Increasingly, candidates for other offices have run independent campaigns even while wearing party labels.

Ultimately it's the individual or group that can deliver the vote on election day that enjoys the basic power. More often than not, that's in the precinct.

The Precinct: Fundamental Election Unit

While precincts differ in size, shape, and number of voters, they usually are geographically close-knit. The average precinct contains something less than one thousand voters, but there are voting districts with only a few dozen voters in sparse, rural areas or because of quirks in laws or perhaps by design of some political leaders. One state permits as many as fifteen thousand per precinct. Ideally, there are few enough to allow each to vote on election day without long lines.

Key party contact in the area is the precinct leader, who's closest to the people because he or she lives there. If he is a good committeeman, he knows the people well and marks closely the moving in and moving out of "constituents."

The precinct leader who is dedicated stays in touch with "his" voters all year long. The best of them tend their "flock" as a minister would. But, good or bad, the committeeman or -woman is very important. The better the job is done, the better the chance of success on election day.

He organizes and gets the vote out. That means he not only keeps track of his people, but he helps get them registered and voted.

Often in local government the precinct leader not only represents the neighborhood in higher party councils but is their advocate before public officials of the party.

In some tightly organized communities, the fastest way to get the street fixed or a street light replaced is to call the precinct committeeman. Often he or she is the first one to greet a new family, faster than the "Welcome Wagon" lady.

A well-organized precinct will have a file of all voters with their normal party preferences entered. On election day it will be the job of the leader and committee to get out the vote, concentrating on the people most likely to support their party and its candidates.

Often, in urban areas, the precinct leader will appoint and supervise "block captains" who will each take charge of a square block to get residents registered and voted.

Political Clubs

In New York City the sheer mass of people and strong ethnic ties have given rise to a different kind of political organization. These are political clubs. The most famous became known as Tammany Hall.

Baltimore, Chicago, and many others of the industrial cities with long political organizational traditions also follow clubhouse organization. Sometimes the clubhouse is a social center; sometimes it's a social service center, clearing requests for filling holes in the streets and dispensing Thanksgiving turkeys.

The clubs may be Young Republicans or Young Democrats or college or teen versions of these national organizations. Often, however, they're ethnic (the West Side Polish Club) or geographic.

These clubs function the year around and serve social and cultural functions as well as political. Usually they'll have specific roles during campaign and election-day activity. Sometimes the party will seek them out to suggest candidates who provide geographic or ethnic balance to the ticket. Sometimes the clubs that are well organized will bring their own influence to bear on the regular party organization, insisting on such representation on the ticket or for patronage and other "recognition" later.

During a political campaign auxiliary clubs often are organized. These allow participation by people who normally might not be able to join a regular club or who might be unwilling to join one of these or the regular party organization.

Candidates find that they can get work, funds, and ideas by helping supporters organize along professional, business, trade, or ethnic lines. Hence there are "Doctors for Davis" clubs as well as "Democrats for Bush," "Women for Smith," and "Actors for Clinton-Gore."

The U.S. Chamber of Commerce has outlined the basic functions of political clubs as follows:

1. **Keeping party workers together all year round.** Club activities keep workers from drifting away from the organization between campaigns.

2. **Enlisting new party workers.** Clubs continually recruit new members and act as a catalyst in changing politically nonactive citizens into regular party workers.

3. **Serving as a manpower pool** to supply volunteers to the party for precinct work and campaign headquarters work.

4. **Providing a political training ground** for workers and leaders. The organization and operation of a political club provide

basic training in political mechanics and management.

Some clubs serve two additional functions that, while not quite so basic as the four already mentioned, are also important:

1. **Providing members an opportunity to study—and so better understand—issues** and government organizations. Such understanding and knowledge can be used in developing campaign issues and better-informed party workers.

2. **Raising money.** Some clubs make a point of recruiting people who are political donors to the party war chest. Their membership causes them to identify themselves more closely with the party.

Nomination: A Key

The beginner often overlooks the nomination as the point in the election process where hard work is most needed and where you can win or lose long before general election day.

In many states primary election day is when all candidates for the general election are nominated and precinct leaders are chosen. Some states retain the convention for nomination of statewide candidates or for endorsements to the regular primary. Since these are specialized as well as exceptions to the rule, we'll deal here with the primary.

If you and your supporters want to influence basic party organization, you have to do it at the primary as well as by volunteering later. If you want to help choose candidates, including possible winners, you have to begin before the primary.

Out of one hundred voters in a precinct, no more than sixty or seventy are likely to turn out for a general election. In years when there is no presidential election, fifty or sixty electors will turn out.

In most elections, about half of these will back the whole ticket of the majority party. About a third will back the minority party. The rest will scatter and split their tickets.

In many places, only about one-fourth to one-half of the people who will support the ticket in the fall take the trouble to vote in a primary. So seven or eight people out of one hundred can determine the outcome in a precinct. It is this base that often really determines elections. It is not the mass you should focus on but these key "swing" voters.

Political Campaigning

Product selling and promotion of services are simple compared with the political campaign. There's no second chance; no second day to offer the merchandise. A third or fourth place product can be profitable; in politics, all but the victor show a complete loss.

The political campaign is the ultimate in relating with the public.

While no two campaigns are identical, the basic organizational and procedural form does remain and it's similar to that in other campaigns for other people.

Probably the most mistaken word used in connection with a campaign is *organization*. Most likely, it's disorganized.

While the organization of a campaign may be plotted and planned well in advance, daily tactics, maneuverings of the opposition, current events, media treatments, and availability of time and money necessitate tactical changes.

Thus, while a basic organization with a basic plan must be set up, it must be flexible enough to change as required.

The basis of the campaign "game plan" has to be building upon a foundation or base— the nucleus of the candidate's original strength. Thereafter, the plan seeks to attract support from some who are leaning to the

opposition and always convincing the "undecideds." The whole campaign is convincing, unconvincing, and confirming.

The campaign will function through both party organization and candidate organizations. The degree of cooperation between and among these will depend on issues, geography, tradition, and a lot of other things.

In the better campaigns, professionals are enrolled increasingly. Many county candidates and political organizations use professional advertising agencies. Some retain public relations counsel.

Pollsters, photographers, copy writers, media buyers, registration experts, campaign managers all can be hired today with specific political campaign background. And that list is by no means complete.

But the skill and time of others is always sought on a volunteer basis. There simply isn't enough time and money for the candidate and the regular political organizations to do these jobs themselves or hire them out.

That's where people with skills to donate— or just plain spare time—come in.

The practice by which a business loaned an employee to a campaign while continuing to pay his or her salary never was a good idea. Nowadays, in the post-Watergate spotlight on morality, it's worse. In most cases, it's probably illegal. Certainly it is so by the standards of the Federal Elections Law.

Your people can try volunteering. Most likely, they'll be accepted. They'll usually start low, but with the opportunity to move up.

We've already suggested that they might volunteer to work in a precinct or to do some writing or address and stuff envelopes. There are all sorts of jobs available.

They might make speeches. Or set up meetings. Or run a coffee klatsch or a cocktail party to raise funds or have people meet the candidate. Or just think about campaign ideas and speech subjects and pass them on. Or make calls for the candidate. Or organize baby-sitting services for election day or car pools to get your candidate's supporters to the polls.

There are literally hundreds of kinds of things volunteers can do to help political parties and candidates. But it's *vital* that they take directions from the campaign manager. Uncoordinated efforts can create havoc for which the transgressor will be remembered with distaste.

Campaign Financing

The financial end of political campaigns is delicate and complex. Here we will provide a brief primer.

The cost of running an effective political campaign today is staggering. Candidates and political parties pay high rates for media time and space. Usually they have to pay cash on the barrelhead. Because their demand for consultation, production, and other aspects of preparation are compressed into a relatively few weeks, they often have to pay a premium for these services.

It is not uncommon for expenditures on behalf of a single candidate to run twenty-five times the annual salary—if the candidate is elected. Thus all candidates for office and both political parties, at every level, are in a constant scramble for sufficient funds to wage campaigns.

Anyone with expertise in raising money can get a spot in any campaign or party organization. There are other ways to help, too. Chief among them is to donate or to help organize a mechanism by which people in your company or industry or trade association or union or neighborhood can raise money for a party or candidate or group of candidates.

As with political organization, financing is structured in several ways. First there are the major political parties. At local, state, and national levels the parties are constantly seeking financial supporters. An individual or a group can donate money to the party at any level at any time, within limits set by law. Or you can participate in specific fund-raising affairs such as dinners, shows, social events, and the many events that are designed to produce needed funds.

Second, there are specific campaigns. The campaign may be at any level of government. It can be for a primary or a general election. It may encompass a group or slate of candidates. Or it may involve only one person running for mayor or governor or Congress or the state legislature.

Federal election financing laws and those of many states have undergone drastic revision in recent years. There are well-defined limits to contributions to candidates, committees, and political action committees. It is necessary to check on the status of these laws before each campaign.

The state laws covering donations to committees and candidates are varied. The candidate or the party or your organization's lawyer can guide you. (*See* Chapters 6 and 48.)

Generally speaking, however, corporation and union checks may not be used as political contributions.

Political Action Committees

A common device employed more and more in recent years to collect and disburse money for political campaigns and candidates is the "political action committee"—the PAC. Labor unions, companies, industries, and some professions have them now. On the local, state, and national scene there are such organizations as COPE (AFL-CIO Committee on Political Education), AMPAC (American Medical Political Action Committee), and literally hundreds of lesser but similar organizations.

The United States Chamber of Commerce publishes some excellent booklets on the do's and don'ts of forming PACS.[1]

The importance of a committee of this kind—even if it's no more than a couple of dozen executives in your organization—is that together you can make meaningful contributions to the party or candidates of your choice. You can register approval or disapproval of parties and positions by your contributions.

Don't get the idea that you can buy a candidate or an official, however. Most of them can't be bought. Those who can usually aren't worth it.

Volunteer help at campaign time is the chief way you can let officials or candidates know you believe in them and what they stand for. There's nothing wrong in supporting the people, positions, and parties you agree with. And there's nothing wrong in donating your skill, your time, and your money to build friendship with candidates, officials, and parties. It's common sense and it's good business.

Some Practical Ideas on Donations

Every candidate for office has a finance committee—even if it's the regular local organization of his party.

There are also the regular party organizations (Iowa Republican State Committee, Democratic National Committee), and congressional and senatorial campaign committees of both parties.

A donation might be made directly to one committee functioning for a candidate or group of candidates. Or it might go to the "regular" organization. Or it might go

to the congressional or senatorial campaign committee.

Here are two special points to observe:

When you decide to donate to a candidate or a party, whether through direct donation or a fund-raising affair, whether individually or through your own version of a PAC, do it as early as possible. A candidate most often needs money early in the campaign. Moreover, late in the campaign a contribution can get lost in the shuffle of heavy activity.

Don't insist on making your donation directly to the candidate. He may—as many candidates do—not personally accept any funds.

More than likely, he's going to be too busy anyway, especially if he's an incumbent in high office. Get it directly to his campaign manager or someone very close to the candidate himself if you hope to have your contribution recognized.

Again, don't expect that you're buying something for your contribution, no matter how large. And don't expect anyone to be 100 percent on your side. You can expect that you or your group will be more likely to get a sympathetic hearing, if and when you need one. At the least, you should get listened to. And you may even make your point, if you have a good case.

It's not much different from helping anyone else. It's very much like doing a good turn for a customer or client.

Your Role in Politics

The field of politics and campaigns is vast. The jobs are manifold.

Anyone with intelligence, skill, energy, and common sense can find a way to contribute something in services at some level. Certainly anyone can contribute some money to someone or some groups he believes in.

If you don't know anyone specific you want to help, but you do want to get involved and

---

[1]1615 H Street, NW, Washington, DC 20062.

become associated with one side, the best person to see is the county chairperson of the party. He or she is probably well equipped to advise you and is probably the key person in the area.

Don't be surprised if you or your organization is put right to work. Don't be hurt if you are sent out to a precinct to start.

Do be prepared to learn as well as to help. Don't try to take over the party right away. Do offer constructive suggestions on how to improve anything that you think needs improving after you've been on board a while.

Go in with your eyes wide open. Don't expect material rewards. Don't get disillusioned—at least until you find out the why of what's being done.

Chances are you'll get a lot of satisfaction out of the experience. And it might help you or your organization have a greater say in the course of events.

Watergate, Abscam, Clinton's fund-raising, and other well-reported happenings may have caused a wave of cynicism, or confirmed earlier cases of cynicism. Is politics too dirty to mess with?

The simple answer is "no." Besides, every dedicated, honest, decent person who becomes involved makes it less likely that someone less honest will.

There are a lot of people coming into politics who are willing to play by the rules and to abide by the new political morality.

Young people, especially women and minorities, are sought. But so are people of all ages who have something to give—time, effort, advice, money. The more who do give, the better off we all are.

You'll probably find quickly that there are no more scoundrels proportionately in politics than there are outside politics—maybe a few less.

8

COMMUNITY RELATIONS

BILL PEAK

Wilbur J. (Bill) Peak was assistant vice-president in public relations for Illinois Bell Telephone Company, Chicago.

After graduation from Knox College, he began his Bell System career with Western Electric. Shortly thereafter he joined Illinois Bell and began his career in public relations as a supervisor.

Over the years, Mr. Peak covered the spectrum of company public relations. Emerging functions, such as Community Relations, sprang from his responsibilities at Illinois Bell. Under his supervision, the company won several national awards and public relations honors. He received the 1966 Knox College Alumni Achievement Award and the 1971 Distinguished Service Award from the Public Relations Society of America (Chicago chapter).

Community relations has undergone more change in recent years than perhaps any other area of public relations. At the same time, it has probably impacted the practice of public relations more profoundly than any other area within this field.

At one time community relations functioned as little more than a courtesy performed as an aside from the other activities done to advance the health and welfare of the business. Today, regardless of an institution's size or status, it can be undermined by a haphazard community relations effort. Both the organization and its community hold an interest and play a part in creating an atmosphere of mutual respect and understanding through a solid community relations program—forming a bridge between the company and the community.

We now live in an age in which the actions of even the smallest minority groups can seriously disturb all levels of the religious, educational, and governmental institutions that form the foundation of our society. In this environment, can any company ignore the risk of suffering similar damage or destruction, either through direct affronts to it or indirectly through affronts to its community?

This chapter primarily examines community relations from a business (corporate) standpoint. However, this does not presume that business alone carries the responsibility for building and sustaining a strong community—and the concepts presented here apply equally to other forms of organizations.

No institution is without responsibility or capability in this area. No community can expect any one segment of its society to carry on without the support of its other segments.

The world of business has learned much about its role in the community. Those outside as well as those inside the business community can draw from these pages an impetus to fulfill their vital community role.

Community Relations Today

Terms *ecology* and *environment* today are heard more than *community*. Defining these words is useful for understanding community relations and how the concept has changed.

Ecology is a science. It once restricted itself to the relationship of biological organisms to their environment. But business, in a social and economic sense, is also an "organism" operating in an environment. This relationship should be studied, understood, and appropriately responded to.

When speaking of environment, we refer to all the circumstances that surround a business (organism). Obviously, circumstances affect a business, are affected by a business, or affect and change themselves.

Finally, the term *community* has changed. It refers not only to a group of people living in the same locality, but also to the interaction of those people. Community, in this sense, is also an organism. Individuals create or join groups; groups oppose each other, unite for a common cause, or attack problems in their own ways.

In the past, the tendency was to treat a community as a rather simple entity—a collection of people, a "home town." Today we are beginning to recognize each community as a complex dynamism of diverse, constantly changing, often powerful, and always important forces. Today such forces are often skillfully organized and well-led. To learn how well organized and effective they can be, one should read handbooks on community problem-solving techniques.

Community relations, as a public relations function, is an institution's planned, active, and continuing participation with and within a community to maintain and enhance its environment to the benefit of both the institution and the community.

The Importance of Community Relations to Business

Business is an organism; so is its community. They can and do have profound effects on each other. Both affect and are affected by their mutual environment.

Complex challenges confront America's cities and suburbs today. They require the unified commitment of both the public and private sectors of society, the combined talents and energies of both individuals and organizations.

Two important differences between a community and a business are notable: (a) a community surrounds and permeates a business; and (b) a community is unfettered by the policies and organization that control and restrict the operations and performance of a business.

One can conceive of business as somewhat rigid, rational, orderly, protective, and playing to its strengths. The community, on the other hand, can be said to be more flexible, emotional, unpredictable, and seeking strength and protection outside itself.

Business marries the community it settles with. It takes on inherent responsibilities with this association. The need for community relations now might be seen as one partner (community) taking a close look at the marriage vows and discovering that the other partner (business) owes more than simple financial support (taxes). Let one partner ignore or refuse to fulfill those other marital responsibilities, and he or she has the neighbors (public opinion) and the courts (local government) to contend with.

What's at Stake for Business?

From a practical standpoint, only a business's management can specifically answer what's at stake for business. The relationship of each business, community, and environment is different. While some common considerations can be suggested here, fact-gathering by you can both dramatize your company's stake in a sound community relations program and suggest the direction and form it ought to take.

You can give yourself a quick indication of this without research (at this point). Take a sheet of paper and with a pencil draw lines dividing it into quarters.

- **1st Block:** List the things your company *provides* its community/environment aside from goods and services it is your business to provide. (Jobs? Investments? Tax support? Attractive buildings?)
- **2nd Block:** List the things your company *gets* from its community/environment. (Employees? Transportation? Land? Police and fire protection? Water?)
- **3rd Block:** List the things your company *needs* (but hasn't gotten or needs more of) from its community environment. (More employees? Lower taxes? Better reputation? Zoning changes?)
- **4th Block:** List *your* gripes about the community/environment *you* live in. (Air pollution? Poor garbage removal? Traffic snarls? Crime?)

Certain considerations should suggest themselves. First of all, the hardest list to create is probably the first one. Subconsciously, you almost have to construct it from the community's point of view.

It wouldn't be unusual for items in your second list to be the same as those of your first. For example, providing jobs in a community may well benefit it. But if the employees your company needs won't settle in the community or the community itself can't provide employees, neither your company nor the community benefits.

So the second list should not only suggest the importance of the community to your firm, but may debunk, or at least modify, the idea that business somehow puts more into a community than it takes out.

The tax support argument ("We pay for what we get") bears closer scrutiny than it's generally given. The tax argument is hardly valid until someone sits down and puts dollar values on community benefits, along with the costs to a company of duplicating those services and facilities.

If the point has been made that your business needs its community as much as the reverse, that is sufficient. The third list should show that the community can provide more benefit for your company. Your community relations can help it do so.

But what of the fourth list? It speaks to *your* gripes with good reason. What perturbs you personally about your community may be viewed otherwise by your company. But what bothers you and your fellow employees directly affects your company. This list will suggest areas in which your company could play a vital community role.

No company alone can cure a community illness (unless the company itself is the problem), but it can and should help. You have your own personal reasons for wanting that help.

As illustrated by your lists, the reason for company involvement is simple: A company cannot hope for a healthy economic climate in which to thrive if the community and environment are unhealthy.

Perhaps the most fatuous idea in business today is that community relations is a corporate philanthropic act, when in fact it's sound business practice. It's a function of corporate self-interest rather than just being a "good citizen."

Community Activism Emerges

Until a few years ago communities tended to take more passive roles toward the business world. A company coming into a community generally was considered a benefit, and the community contented itself with the same rationale businesses used. A new company meant more jobs, more tax support, and more money in the community. The community needed business to survive, still does, and is loath to jeopardize its relationships with business.

Communities today, however, find they cannot remain passive. Other survival factors arise that rival the mere presence of business.

Some communities have also learned that most businesses are sufficiently mobile to relocate from one community to another. Some communities have learned they must compete for business. All they can offer is what the community itself can provide. An area that is unattractive, problem-beset, or otherwise unhealthy can fail to attract the new business it needs and can lose the business it has.

More to the point, communities have found themselves increasingly less able to cope with the problems that have grown right along with the social, economic, and technological improvements in society generally. Community pockets of neglect become pockets of force for change, mindful of their needs and wants and not impressed with the beneficence of either community or business.

The community, unable to cope with the growing magnitude of its problems, is being forced to turn to business for help. It is reluctant to do so, and each day of delay compounds the problems business ultimately will have to face or to physically abandon.

For large urban communities both the problems and their magnitude are patently evident. Businesses in smaller communities may still hold the advantage of responding to community needs before those needs get out of hand.

A Community's Structure— Its People

As said earlier, "community" is a complex organism, a collection of diverse, changing, and potent forces. A community is much more specifically definable and must be carefully analyzed before any reasonable community relations program can be developed.

The basic unit of a community is, of course, the individual. We start with him or her[1] because he's directly responsible for the changing nature of the community.

Humanity has attained increasingly greater knowledge, affluence, and highly sophisticated means of communications and transportation. These not only provide more, but daily remind that more is available. People not only have been able to define needs and wants better, but can articulate the resulting values placed on them. (This may be one reason company presidents seem to get more and more mail from the citizenry.)

While an individual finds he can achieve certain ends by speaking out for his "rights," he also learns two other important facts. One is that if he joins with others in seeking essentially the same rights, the group voice grows louder and delivers a greater impact. The success of many "consumer groups" points up how effective such voices can become. The other is that within the community are other

---

[1]Wherever a masculine term is used, it applies equally to women.

individuals with common problems who collectively have common control or leverage in a vital function of that community.

Teachers, doctors, plumbers, maintenance personnel, cab drivers, police officers, fire fighters—these natural groupings, even when not formally unionized, become strong bargaining units in any size community. Their leverage is simply the possible withholding of their service to a community, a service the community cannot reasonably do without.

Whether a group has natural leverage or is simply formed to achieve a specific short-term goal, that group is a force in the community.

Furthermore, whatever the justification of its goals, any group can achieve at least three things: recognition, a hearing, and consideration. It can get these things with minimal effort in a free society with the means of communications the smallest community possesses.

With the first of these acquisitions—recognition—a group can gain additional sympathy and support within the community. Then the force of the group grows.

Rotary, Lions, Kiwanis, women's clubs, PTA, Masons, Knights of Columbus, chambers of commerce, League of Women Voters, and the like are common community groups. Such groups generally are so ingrained, so identified with the community, and so traditional, we take them for granted. They can present potent forces working in support of sound, company-community goals. Other groups even more likely to involve themselves with company-community goals include such minority-group organizations as Urban League, NAACP, NCCJ, and Operation PUSH.

Still other groups can be identified with much less certainty. These groups usually have names, but we tend to give them labels— minorities, dissidents, liberals, radicals, left-wing, and right-wing groups. In recent years many *new* groups have been formed to act as gadflies in such areas as public housing and discrimination. Sometimes it's hard to find out what they really want from the community. Still others are intrinsically negative— we know it—and if they have a wholesome objective, it's lost in the unwholesome approach.[2]

All the groups, plus perhaps a few social segments not yet organized, equal the community. All of them work for change in the community's environment.

Some groups actually might serve, or could serve, your company's best interests. Any of them could turn their force against your company, with or without a good reason.

In any case, the first step in a community relations program is to know the community and its components intimately.

Measuring Community Strengths and Weaknesses

Intimate knowledge of the community's components is one of three major areas of research for a sound community relations program. The second is knowledge of the community's strengths and weaknesses. (The third will involve in-house analysis of your company in terms of its own needs and welfare. Does your organization properly share responsibility for the maintenance of a good environment in which its people can live and work, as well as one that is conducive to successful functioning? Does it fulfill the responsibility not only in financial contributions and donations made to worthy causes but also in making available the experience and skills gained in the conduct of your business?)

No company can deal with all components of a community or take on all of a community's problems. Nor should a company try. Only some groups and individuals can serve

---

[2]*See Overcoming Opposition*, Philip Lesly, Prentice-Hall, 1984.

a company's needs. Only some can harm a business if ignored or handled poorly.

Community strengths and weaknesses, advantages and problems, are circumstances (environment), some of which have no effect on your business. Others can substantially alter the course of your business and its future.

But which ones?

Business, which prides itself on careful judgment and money-management, often handles community relations investments—like financial contributions—on the merest hunch they will help the community, let alone the business.

Pure philanthropy is fine, but even it requires the kind of judgment that business daily applies elsewhere. Another hospital wing for respiratory ailments, after all, is not the solution to a growing air pollution problem.

Let's look at good contribution judgment at work. The downtown area of Akron, Ohio, was deteriorating. Slum conditions festered in commercial and residential property on some four hundred acres around the B.F. Goodrich plant. City and company got together, and B.F. Goodrich gave Akron $300,000 for a feasibility study on renewal.

The result was the start of an urban renewal project in the company's area estimated at $37.5 million. To this the company donated $3.5 million, plus legal and public relations consultation.

A sound community relations program must be selective. But selection should take into consideration all the available options. These have to be assembled.

Weighing needs and capabilities

Listing all the problems of a community— crime, pollution, shortages in housing or employment, poverty, inadequate health or education facilities—is important. But so is listing community strengths, including those that account for locating your business where it is.

A community needs to maintain its strong points and enhance them. The community's adversities won't be substantially curtailed if the attractions to that community decline or if nearby communities begin to excel in your community's strengths.

For example, if your company is in the community because of its strong purchasing power, a campaign to attract more industry to town (adding to the purchasing power) may prove highly advantageous to your firm while making your community ecstatic. Promoting your community as a good place to live and work may be an important step in easing a tight labor market.

Once you know the makeup of your community and the environmental factors affecting it, a little cross-indexing can improve both research elements. Relate the wants and needs of individuals, as well as the groups' causes to the community's strengths and weaknesses. Note those areas that should be receiving attention but are not. Remember, too, that the most despicable individual or group you know still may strive for an environmental change your community really needs.

Priority Setting

It's good, at this point, to establish priorities from the standpoint of the community. What does the community need most? What does it need most to do? Establish these priorities without regard to your company's presence.

Once this is done, make the in-house analysis of your company in terms of its own needs. What community factors best serve the interests of your company?

This is the point where the four lists suggested earlier should be pursued in earnest.

Now you can relate company priorities to community priorities. Don't attempt to pare down resulting lists. Ten areas for community relations programs, based on what activities will be required, may be simpler to coordinate than two on someone else's list.

All you have, at this point, are areas, or targets, for programs.

By inspection, some of the priorities—from both the community and business standpoints—will suggest long-range programming; some others, short-range. You may want to divide your priorities in this fashion.

Milestones Reached

What have the list of priorities and the three research analyses involving community, environment, and your business given you?

1. You have determined the most appropriate target areas on which your company can and should concentrate with regard to its community.

2. You have established target areas with the soundest reasons for your company to take them on (why they are important to your business and the community).

3. You know who, if anyone, is presently working on these target areas. You can determine whether to support the work of individuals or groups in these areas or to work independently, and you know the ramifications of either approach.

4. You should have a better idea of the pertinence of the actions or lack of actions on your company by the various individuals or groups. You should know which groups are in essence helping your business and the community, and which may be causing your company trouble now or in the future.

5. You have an important list of "publics" for your communications and actions in community relations activities.

6. You have integrated your plans with all other elements of your organization affecting public attitudes.

Before getting into the creation and implementation of programs, two final points need to be made. First, you may now be aware of one or more activities engaged in by your company that may appear wanting in terms of your present perspective. They may well be worth keeping on the grounds of goodwill or philanthropy. Great care is needed when dropping or easing out of such activities. Yours is not a job of creating new community relations problems for your company.

Second, some sensitivities already may be offended by the "commercial" approach to corporate community relations advocated in these pages. Our rationale is this: your company will help the community more if (a) it can see the practical benefits, (b) it brings to bear its own business expertise on the solutions, and (c) it stops buckshotting its efforts in a variety of causes with unstudied or unevaluated worth to the community at large.

Until now, because charity and community relations work overlap, we've not attempted to separate them. Charity is and should be carried on by everyone, including companies. This chapter leaves charity *per se* to the dictates of conscience and community relations (whether or not charity is involved) to the dictates of common sense.

Applied Community Relations: Program Planning

However target areas in community relations are stated, they need considerable refinement. The object is to set reasonable goals that can be reasonably met.

Failure to spell out specific goals kills some community relations programs before they get started. In attacking problems on too broad a front, some companies pour money, time, and talent down bottomless holes.

Lump all of a community's concerns under the heading "urban crisis" and you immediately create a single, gargantuan problem and the perfect excuse for avoiding it.

Sound company relations programs should give company and community tangible results, not simply warm feelings of "doing good" by simply doing something. Certainly such programs should avoid actions that seem patronizing.

Ameritech, headquartered in Chicago, concentrates on two primary target areas to which it feels it can effectively apply its years of experience—education and employment. The reason for them: as a major employer, the company is in constant need of new employees with adequate educational levels and skills.

These two areas, even before being reduced to specifics, suggest the corporate potential to the telephone company. Programs in these areas may mean more and better qualified employees for the company. Certainly they can mean more wage earners with better, higher-paying jobs as potential customers for the company's service. The payoffs to communities, like Chicago, are self-evident . . . not to mention the values to individuals directly affected. But what was needed by Chicago in education and employment that the company could provide?

Efficient distribution of resources

To find the answer, the company not only had to select among apparent and hidden community needs, but they also had to relate these to the corporate resources available for programs. These resources—common to all business—are people (time and talent), equipment, facilities, and money (aside from the fiscal value of the other three).

The company had long provided educational aids for use at all levels of both public and private school systems. School relations people within the company continued to seek advice from and help for teachers in classroom needs.

The company increasingly recognized the need to relate the learning process to life as the students will live it, to embed through student experience the practical applications of learning. It also recognized the importance of giving students as accurate a picture of the business scene as possible so they could make better and earlier decisions about their careers and their educational needs.

To that end the company works with educators to develop economic education presentations for use in high school curricula. These focus on the information an informed consumer needs in a variety of everyday business situations, as well as lectures and simulations that help teach economic concepts.

In another program aimed at high schools the company cosponsored, together with Montgomery Ward and others, "Consumer Education Forums" for high school teachers—graduate-level courses to help educators develop innovative teaching concepts, materials, and student projects for classes in personal economics and consumer education.

At the college level, the company developed College Colloquiums, a program offering experts from company affiliates throughout Illinois to lecture or conduct dialogues with students about practical applications of the theory being learned in the classroom, covering about 120 topics in nineteen academic areas.

The company continues to develop training aids for use in the schools, but the thrust of its main education efforts focuses now on face-to-face encounters with students.

Changing employment practices

In one example relating to employment, the company uses its hiring and training skills to address the problem of so-called unemploy-ables. What problems are inherent in the test-ing and employment prerequisites for these people? New methods and new standards of testing—without lowering pertinent quality needs—have been developed. Special train-ing is provided.

A training and work center gives work to people previously considered unemployable. Such a center combines adult education with production jobs—with pay. Those perform-ing at a satisfactory level move into perma-nent jobs at regular going wages.

Educational relations is another area of community relations work that can generate a positive reaction in every level of society.

Information and publicity can combine to create an educational program of impressive scope. At Western Electric's regional head-quarters in Aurora, Colorado, the original objective of the Technical Advisor Program was to show high school students the nature of the work in various technical-support occupations.

In a few years the program grew from a once-a-week visit by two "advisors" from an affiliate to a city-wide program using twenty-three advisors from eleven companies and drew enthusiastic support from the Denver Chamber of Commerce.

Conceived to enrich the standard curricu-lum through demonstrations of new equip-ment, new films on current innovations, and individual assistance with student projects, the program continued to expand. It grew to encompass, first, a deepening commitment to the career concerns of the students, and even-tually more formal teacher-advisor develop-ment of ways to demonstrate the importance of career decisions and career planning. Expansion of the list of participating com-panies was particularly valuable, since the Technical Advisor Program involved direct contact with actual jobs through visits arranged by the advisors.

The school system was pleased that indus-try and business people became intimately involved in the education process. Business viewed the project as an opportunity to improve the community and to benefit every-body. The chamber of commerce, although it had long been in contact with top school administrators, was pleased that input at the classroom instruction level yielded such a positive and rewarding response.

Having established target areas, how do you establish specific goals or program plans? Finding the specific need may sound simple. But consider the following first.

Call or visit your community's chief polit-ical officer. Give him your target area and he'll tell you the jobs that need to be done. You'll get other sets of tasks from each civic leader, the local chamber of commerce, and other groups. (Don't forget the lists you made for the target areas.) Newspapers and broad-casters often state community goals worth considering.

What you're collecting are *opinions*. Facts begin with opinions. They're important. But how much research sits behind the mayor's view? Does he really have the whole picture? What motivates his view?

The value of input

Opinions help enlarge the field. Enough of them can give you the assurance of knowing the range of possibilities. Seeking advice has a good public relations ramification, too. It lets each community leader know your com-pany is civic-conscious, is dedicated to tak-ing an active role in the community, applies judgment and research to the task, and respects the civic leader enough to seek her advice.

Narrow your list of opinions to likely pros-pects and begin to seek expert advice. At this point you are asking about specific tasks and potential programs.

Keep careful records of who told you what in all your interviewing. Playback and recog-nition of individual contributions to the selected programs are both appropriate and wise. Unused opinions or facts at least deserve follow-up thanks to their providers. A channel of advice, once opened, needs at least this minimal maintenance toward future use.

State in writing the specific goals that seem most appropriate to your company's interests. Spell out what appears to be involved. Define the limits of the program as you see them.

Then apply the general reasoning developed for the appropriate target areas. Cite the sources that led to your recommendation.

Does the specific objective suggest what company resources will be needed? If so, note what you think these will be should the company adopt your plan.

Previous experience may permit you to outline in detail the specific requirements of a plan, including estimated costs. Use such detail, at this point, with caution. You want first to weigh the program, not the costs.

If your program is well received but costs appear prohibitive, you may wish to propose the involvement of others outside the firm to share in the accomplishment, benefit, and costs.

A final reason for care in spelling out resource usage and costs is the availability of others in company management who can find ways of cutting costs once the objective and plan are agreed on.

Organization

Pity the company president. In many companies, the extent of community involvement is regulated by the number of activities the president can chair. Somehow the idea has taken hold that a community function becomes a company function only if the top executive is directly involved. He or she may delegate work to others, but only personal presence makes it official.

Community relations properly begins at the top, but it needn't stay there. Unless the top executive needs community exposure, he may welcome projects that spread the management participation.

Another tendency is to involve only the "front people"—those whose work responsibilities directly involve the public. The theory is additional community duties may produce valuable contacts for these people and at least help them become better known.

The theory may be true, but it warrants closer examination. Companies that involve only their contact people in community relations work overlook an untapped gold mine. Managers and craftspeople working in the catacombs of a business can thrive in the sunshine of the community, enlarging the corporate capability.

General Electric is a good example of personnel resources heavily used in community relations work. GE's concentration of activity is problem-oriented. Much is directed to the problems of the disadvantaged across the country, wherever the company's plants are. Company motivation springs from both social concern and the need to fill many new jobs. The company recognizes that many people for these jobs must come from underutilized segments of the population.

These include the so-called hard-core unemployed—the illiterate, the untrained, the poorly housed youth dropped or dropping out—people ready and wanting to work but already overcome by basic needs of food, clothing, housing, or medical treatment.

Within each General Electric facility are also people with skills and talents potentially helpful in solving community problems in human relations. Most are sympathetic, and—judging from the company's experience—most can be motivated through encouragement, direction, and the experience of others.

Such motivation starts at the top. Corporate commitment begins with contributions of money, facilities, and executives' participation in joint company-community programs to attack those problems that individual efforts alone cannot handle.

Companywide involvement

At GE the responsibility for community relations moves down through every level of management, including front-line supervision. Managers may have titles like engineer, statistician, materials, controller, legal counsel. Their work stations may have labels like Power Transformer Department, Mechanical Drive Turbine Department, Insulator Department. But they join together as General Electric people trying to help.

Many GE community activities are company activities, carried on by employees as part of their assigned work. But to a greater extent, the efforts are clearly personal activities—employees throughout the company using their own abilities to meet community needs. In recognition of outstanding employee participation in this broad area, General Electric established the Gerald L. Phillippe Awards for Distinguished Public Service.

A company's community relations activities may be initiated by a community relations person or even be coordinated by him or her. However, the efforts can properly involve as broad a spectrum of company personnel as can be reasonably committed.

The community relations person's pivotal role

A community relations person can easily become a corporate scapegoat. He can be the only company person the community sees. He joins all the major clubs and is seen at all the luncheon meetings. He doesn't get too involved in club projects or committees (they conflict with many other meetings). But if you'd like anything from his company, he's the person to see (he and the president are the only employees of the firm anyone really knows).

As with other public relations activities, the community relations person can serve best from behind the scenes. Requests for support or participation in community affairs correctly should come to him. He should evaluate them and make recommendations as to company involvement.

These recommendations, particularly on matters such as contributions and company-paid memberships in community organizations, should be highly selective. Employee memberships sponsored by the company in the sense that dues, fees, and other expenses incurred by individuals are paid by the company require surveillance. The company's investment here should mean active, participatory membership.

Each employee holding such a membership becomes a potential resource center—helping keep the company, through its community relations person, apprised of circumstances in the community as gleaned from that club or organization. That person may also provide the means of getting a company message distributed and understood by the community through the civic association. Otherwise, such company-paid memberships are a useless cost.

Volunteers' role

In organizing for community relations, the role of the employee volunteer must be treated with utmost care. The distinction between a company activity and an individual's activity should be carefully defined.

If, for example, the employee is active in Girl Scout leadership on her own time and expense, the company has little cause to take bows for that employee's contributions.

It's one thing for a company to take pride in the widespread involvement of its employees' volunteer activities. But credit expressed must go to the individuals, normally with their knowledge and permission. Overt attempts to capitalize on an individual's extra-curricular activities will harm personnel relations and may do more harm than good for the company.

Company-sponsored activities in which employee volunteers participate should be distinguished by tangible evidence of the company's contribution. Even in these, work performed by volunteers should be spelled out in any promotion or discussion of the program.

The volunteer has always provided an essential ingredient in community relations. The word and concept *volunteer* deserve protection they don't get when an employee assigned to a task is publicized as a volunteer. If the old military practice of naming "volunteers" is operative in your firm, and you can't stop it, start looking for a euphemism when you actually need volunteers. A good distinction, perhaps, between a "company" position and "volunteer" participation is seen in the policy statement of General Electric that says, in part, that the company has been, is, and will be strictly nonpartisan; it neither supports nor endorses any political party or candidates. The company does contribute constructively to the *discusssion* of public issues by providing information on a continuing basis (and, when appropriate, even taking a stand on certain questions that have an impact on the business). The company encourages its employees as individuals to participate on an active and informed basis in political campaigns. Company nonpartisanship among the parties and candidates in no way abridges the right of its employees, as individual citizens, to volunteer or work in politics.

Determining assignments

Responsibility for the specific elements and activities of your organization's community relations program, then—who does what, when, and how—must be carefully determined. If the program planned can be handled solely as a company activity, the following questions should be answered:

1. Who in the company should be recommended for the task? Play to your company's strengths: Who's best qualified? What expertise is available? Who has control of needed equipment or facilities?

2. Who should have primary responsibility for chairing the program?

3. Will volunteer help be needed and/or desirable?

If the planned program requires outside participation:

1. Whose help should be sought?

2. How should that help be sought? It may be best to work through an intermediary. For example, an education program might be coordinated through the local school board.

The nature of the program should suggest the appropriate formal structure. Generally, a committee will suffice to start. Once a program is approved and key participants selected, the community relations person should help get the program underway. Even if all details have been worked out to the point where he feels his added contribution is nil, he should at least maintain *ex officio* status on the primal committee.

Under no circumstances should a community relations person turn away from a program or its committees. Even if other public relations aspects of the program are delegated, he or she remains the essential catalyst for the program's success (as the remainder of this chapter will show). In addition, he or she is responsible for ensuring that everything is integrated.

Taking Action

It's obvious that community relations, as described in these pages, is action-oriented. (*See also* Chapter 2.) That meaningful action is sometimes misunderstood is illustrated by two types of groups with whom today's community relations person is confronted. These are extremes, with many variations and degrees in between.

The first is the local community chapter of a usually well-respected, service-oriented national organization. The average age of this group seems to increase annually. It admittedly has trouble attracting new (and young) members.

Typically, this group shares its national parent's pride in accomplishment in several areas of community relations. The local itself is perplexed by its poor membership drive results and the declining attendance at meetings. The prevailing feeling is: "With all of today's community consciousness and with all the good we're doing, one would think our ranks would grow."

This group certainly considers itself, as does the community, active. But inspection often shows a paucity of real involvement in the actual needs of the community. Funds are solicited and portions of dues are committed to worthy causes. The membership raises money that moves through channels to its ultimate worthwhile goal.

The work of such groups is vital; it deserves support and encouragement. But it is, by-and-large, community action by proxy. Members give money, not themselves. They don't participate directly in the action. This group doesn't get as members those who want personal involvement, want to feel and see accomplishment. Neither the reputation nor the experience nor publicity suggests the local chapter is so committed.

At the other end of the spectrum are the activists. They demand social change—often accurately identifying community problems with inherent inequality, injustice, or indignity. This group demands and gets the full range of publicity.

"Action" for them consists of the placard, the march, the rally, angry shouts and slogans, diatribes, and sometimes physical aggression. Reasoned solutions and concrete efforts to solve anything often are nonexistent.

Surely some groups whose activities resemble these exist because their alternatives have been exhausted. This means *is* effective in building community concern for their needs. But contemporary society has spawned professional dissidents with nothing to lose. Their gain is the thrill of combating "the establishment." To these latter we refer.

Between the two extremes stands the community relations person's programs. The company's "actions" can easily resemble the results of either. On the one hand, the company's efforts can become as detached and noninvolved as some groups'—and die from lack of interest. On the other, company committees can meet, debate, and deplore community problems, loud and long, without ever getting to the point of working on the ills.

Case studies

There are numerous good examples of how to get action programs started. A few samples follow.

At its Indianapolis Operations, the Detroit Diesel Allison Division of General Motors sought broad management participation in that community's affairs. "Operation Involvement" was created.

Planning for this program began with a review of some fifty Indianapolis area civic organizations and local government agencies. The second step was to match the names of Allison supervisory personnel with each organization on a basis of knowledge and interest. Local organizations were contacted to determine their interest in obtaining Allison support. Management personnel were appointed to selected organizations.

Nearly two hundred Allison management people soon became involved in eighty-one community projects. These ranged from work on the mayor's task forces to school system advisory groups. Allison personnel served on the air pollution control board, police review board, board of public works, Urban League, and others. The company's management *actively* participated, playing to its own strengths and expertise.

RCA Corporation translated "strength and expertise" as "opportunities" for company, communities, and individuals. RCA Service Company's educational services activity led in providing educational programs designed to meet the needs of society's disadvantaged. Programs were developed and carried out at federal, state, and local governmental levels. The education and training services performed ranged from custom designing curricula and training materials to complete management and operation of large-scale residential centers that provide prevocational, vocational, academic, and social education. In communities where the programs were centered, RCA developed public and community relations liaison to acquaint residents with goals and progress of the project to enlist local participation.

RCA developed programs to help seasonal farm workers and their families in North Carolina, Choctaw Indians in Mississippi, adult prisoners and youthful offenders in Pennsylvania, handicapped youth in West Virginia, and the chronically unemployed in Chicago, Los Angeles, New York City, and Camden and Newark, New Jersey.

Criteria for activities

Action considerations are obvious and not-so-obvious. Some of the forms action (problem-solving and simply community-enhancing) can take include the following:

- Creating something needed that didn't exist before
- Eliminating something that causes a problem
- Developing means for self-determination
- Broadening use of something that exists to include "have-nots"
- Sharing equipment, facilities, professional expertise
- Tutoring, counseling, training
- Reconstituting, repairing, dressing up
- Promotion of a community outside its confines
- Activating others

Preparing the community

Shell Oil Company's Exploration and Production Organization wanted to do some exploratory drilling off the coast of California. Possible public sensitivity to drilling had been made clear by the previous forced cancellation of plans for an atomic energy power plant near the area of proposed drilling because of community objections.

A community relations program was created to inform various groups and organizations that might object to the drilling program and to win their acceptance of it, even before public announcement of the plans.

Shell anticipated the likely questions. Would oil rigs spoil the view from shore? What were the possibilities of aquatic pollution in the drilling process and subsequent production work? Would structures be left on the seafloor that would impede commercial fishing?

The company sought to reach biologists of the University of California, land owners of shore sites, users of beaches, the Sierra Club, sports and commercial fishermen, and others. The main means of reaching these groups was to talk to them face-to-face. A Shell expert carried out this assignment and subsequently outlined the drilling program to the local media.

Following this community relations program, the only objections to the drilling that remained were those of bottom-dragging commercial fishermen. Plugged and abandoned drilling sites would leave obstructions on the seafloor that would foul their nets.

Normally, remaining obstructions sit one foot above the seafloor. Engineering studies indicated protruding pipe could be cut off and plugged below the seafloor at a moderate cost. Shell agreed to the added expense and acceptance of the program was complete.

Overcoming imagined fears

With all the problems that actually beset communities, it seems incongruous that people would see problems where none in fact exist. But situations are judged not for what they are but how they appear. Fanned by rumor, and often faulty logic, imagined problems take on all the reality of their real counterparts.

For example, a company by virtue of being in the chemical industry can be linked with air pollution though it causes none. About all it takes is a mention in the media that a by-product of some chemical process is an air pollutant. This, through rumor, becomes "chemical companies pollute." Add the faulty logic: "The xyz Company is a chemical company; therefore, it pollutes." The xyz Company and its community end up with a problem they might never have dreamed of.

Denials may not be enough. But a planned action program, even though no circumstances are or should be changed, may turn such a problem into a company- and community-enhancing experience.

If people may exhibit shortcomings by imagining problems where none exist, they sometimes compensate by mistaking token gestures for meaningful action. A well-conceived plan and continued surveillance of its implementation protects against this.

This final piece of advice on action programs is rather basic: before planning for action down the street, make sure the community relations problem that needs attention isn't closer to home.

Are there problems your company itself might be the cause of? What enhancement in your company might set a worthy example for others to follows? The poet Robert Burns wished us all the gift of seeing ourselves as others see us. He concluded: "It would from many a blunder free us, and foolish notion."

Communicating

In community relations, publicity and promotion are tools in support of an action program, not substitutes for it. To test the efficacy of the written communications used in a specific program, ask: Is the program being described one that the reader/viewer can react favorably to without additional prompting? In short, does the program stand on its own feet?

Recognition for community relations work is not only desirable for a company but for the community itself. It shows that something for the community can and is being done. It may encourage others to participate. It's upbeat news; it's progress. For example, Illinois Bell (now part of Ameritech) instituted the Alexander Graham Bell Award for outstanding community service, presented annually to employees and retirees who volunteered their time and energies in community activities. For years, the Ford Motor Company honored employees—and wives or husbands of employees—who performed outstanding service in their communities. Nominations for the awards came from fellow employees, relatives, and civic leaders. There was a Good Citizen citation, an Outstanding Service plaque, and the "Citizen of the Year" Town Crier bell, the program's highest award. The program was available to each company location served by a community relations committee.

Recognizing individuals for their community relations work is laudable, but the awards were backed with widespread publicity that not only saluted award recipients but reminded the community of what Ford people did for it. The articles became "how to do it" models for other employees and the folks in the community at large.

Inland Manufacturing Division of General Motors in Dayton, Ohio, recruited more and more from that city's predominantly black west side. Inland's public relations people met with the editor of the black newspaper there and asked, "What can we do to help you?" His answer was simple, "Just let us know what you are doing for your black employees and for the west side community."

The upshot of that conversation was a change in basic policy at Inland. Until that time, the company had reported only personnel promotions in managerial levels. But this west side paper, like so many others, was interested in *all* promotions featuring west side people. It was interested in *all* activities that show community progress.

Health and safety programs

Two areas of community relations work that cross all lines to affect every level of society are health and safety. Information and publicity can combine to form a health program of impressive scope.

Allstate Insurance Company, of course, is concerned with promoting safety, and its corporate conscience has led the company into a number of health and safety activities where it feels a genuine need exists for involvement. Through the Allstate Foundation's Nursing Scholarship program thousands of scholarships have been provided. Other community health and education activities have included involvement in day care centers, housing ren-

ovation, Opportunities Industrialization Center's body shop programs, and a drug rehabilitation program.

Leadership in national campaigns for major reform in laws and safety standards that affect all people who use streets and highways is a familiar role for Allstate. An extensive advertising campaign and citizen action programs led the fight for drunk driver laws. Implied consent laws were passed in thirteen states in one year alone to help protect the driving public by greatly increasing the police's ability to determine whether a driver is legally drunk. (Drunk drivers are involved in more than half of all fatal auto accidents.)

Allstate led the effort—started in 1973—for better bumpers on today's cars. Now Allstate leads several committees devoted to researching ways to control the cost of insurance by reducing the frequency and severity of fire and theft losses, as well as those from traffic accidents.

One of the most effective ways to help the public help themselves is to get general information to the public. Allstate created many program manuals and collateral materials for community action programs to deal with auto theft, home protection, and fire and arson prevention. Each year, the company supplies millions of pamphlets and brochures to the public about auto and bicycle safety, home security, and fire safety. Also, films are available on a loan basis to schools, groups, and organizations. An extensive speakers' bureau brings important information to the consumer.

Traffic safety is of major importance to the nation's second largest auto insurer. Allstate's past and present involvements include development of driving simulation instructional materials, teacher training seminars, scholarships for driver education teachers, and active membership in local, regional, and national safety organizations.

Selecting publicity outlets

As in any other communications considerations, be imaginative and complete in selecting media within and outside the community. Cover all appropriate "publics." Avoid sameness in advertising. Meet change with change. Realize that some of your publics will judge your company by the image it projects in the media. Then, don't stop with these long-recognized considerations.

Where would the activists be if they limited themselves to the time-honored means of communications? Their secret is communication that affects all the senses; communication that itself conveys a sense of involvement.

There is little, if any, physical difference between students marching with placards to city hall in protest and the city's mayor leading a "Keep Our Town Clean" parade past the same city hall. Both may get about as much television news coverage. Whatever happens after a protest march, the parade may lead to spruced-up streets and a Clean City award. Dramatization can be inspirational, participatory, and, of course, legal.

It's a shame when a carefully planned and executed community relations program is kicked off or signed off with a couple of inches of copy and a posed photo in the local paper. It's a shame, because virtually any action program can serve to focus a community's need for concerned attention and effort.

Publicity content

Press releases should spell out the community need and the reason your organization is involved. That is how community leaders, with whom you've previously consulted, can also help. Their prestige (enhanced in the process) and their message relative to your program are news.

Whatever you can get others to say about the program, and whatever attention-getting dramatizations you use, play the actual news straight. Identify your company in the releases, along with any company references pertinent to the program, and let it go at that. It's hard for an editor to become a believer in a company's altruism when the releases contain product information or corporate puffery. Photos of "work in progress" with company advertisements obviously in the scene give editors jaundiced eyes.

On the other hand, your efforts toward keeping the mood altruistic (from the company's standpoint) can help an editor catch the spirit of your program. Your stories may run with single mentions of your firm's name. Then, editorials and media-initiated articles can compound those mentions with considerably more impact.

Timing communications, as always, is critical. Initial attempts at attracting publicity are a commitment to follow through with the program. Regardless of how small a mention such an announcement may draw, someone (including editors) will be looking for program action.

The world still looks for "goodwill toward men," but with some suspicion. It wants to see the motives and the action. Once these become evident, the initial shy attention can be largely overcome.

When outside participation is involved, make sure those with you from the start share in the initial publicity. Use the entry of others into the program as pegs for continuing coverage. Where broad participation is sought, your publicity efforts should run under full steam for as long as it can continue to attract.

If your program involves physical change, don't forget those "before" photographic shots and videos. The results of such programs are likely to depend on photographic reminders of how things were at the start.

Perhaps the most crucial timing occurs in a program with inherent special sensitivities. If your program is designed to help the community's disadvantaged to self-sufficiency, a publicity program early in your efforts may result in no recipients for your aid. The last thing the disadvantaged need is exploitation.

The general rule is, don't even inadvertently attempt to capitalize at the expense of the project. It may be months before publicity, for whatever good purpose, is advisable—and then should be undertaken only with the participants' advance approval. Again, the benefits of a community relations program should be in the program, not the publicity.

Program Evaluation

Operating a community relations program without evaluation is like exploring uncharted territories and not bothering to map them. You put serious limitations on the value of your discoveries, and you stand a good chance of getting lost.

Assume your program will be a complete success, will live up to all expectations. You'll want to know what made it work and apply what success factors you can to future programs. Other people may want to know how you did it. And, if your program is to be repeated, you'll want to know which activities turned out to be extraneous, and what program parts can be improved for even greater success.

It's more likely, however, that your program will vary considerably from your plan. You'll run into problems with which you may or may not be able to cope. Factors may cause the programs either to fail or to fall far short of your goals. At such times, the need for analyses becomes poignantly apparent. And how sad it is to discover your program's cure after your program has died.

For these reasons, fact-finding and record keeping are vital, forming the basis for analysis and evaluation.

We've previously stressed fact gathering as a prelude to program formulation. Obviously, fact gathering and fact refining must occur throughout the development and execution of a program. Programs tend to expand, taking in new considerations. These must be spotted and understood. For example, a new group joins the program. Its role, motivation, and makeup are new pieces of knowledge you should have.

Maintaining momentum

Facts change. Just keeping up with the turnover of community leaders presents a maintenance problem.

Values change. Your program efforts involve influencing others. But efforts to influence come from other directions, too. Community, even apart from environment, is in a constant state of flux.

Surveys are an important consideration and a tool of evaluation (*see* Chapter 18). Surveys conducted before and after a program help determine the nature and effectiveness of your program's influence. Interim surveys can help determine potential problems, the degree of effectiveness, and the need for addition or change to your program.

Costs in time, effort, and money will influence your use of surveys. If you use them, make them work well for you. Taking great care in assuring who and how you survey provides the most useful information. Commit yourself to accept the results you get without forcing those results into preconceived notions of what you'd like them to be.

Keep all information in a handy form, easily used and comfortable to work with. No collected fact is too minuscule to collect. But big facts can be "thrown away" simply by misfiling them so they can't be recalled when needed.

From the day planning starts, keep a log or diary to record details each step of the way. This record keeps project control in your hands. It furnishes useful ideas for publicity angles. It tips you off to otherwise missed opportunities.

A careful log of your program will keep the relationship of that program to your plans clear. Whatever the plan, whatever the program, there will be variations between them and an ongoing need for adjustment.

Evaluation, then, is interpreting the data and records you've collected and drawing lessons, conclusions, and new courses of action from them.

It's to your advantage when reviewing a completed program to identify weak spots in it and note what changes might have strengthened them. Do this while your program is still fresh in your mind. Later reviews may give broader perspective, but important considerations by then may be forgotten.

However you report results, remain objective. Identify and use qualifiers. Unless and until you've completely solved a problem once and for all, don't convey the impression that the results are in. You don't want to stultify future work in areas where there is still work to be done.

Maintaining continuity

It's an unusual community relations program that can be completed with no need for some continued maintenance. This doesn't mean that once your company takes on a program it's yours for life. But your evaluation should determine the needs for preserving the good your program has done.

This suggests at least one final action: if your company's participation must end, make sure the baton is properly passed. Find a successor, make sure he or she understands the maintenance task, and provide copies of the material that will be needed.

Entering or Departing a Community

So far our emphasis has been on the relationship of a business within a community. But good community relations are essential to a company *before* it moves into a community. And poor community relations in moving a business out of town can affect a company long after it leaves.

As more and more companies are learning, it's one thing to buy property upon which to build and quite another to get acceptance for what they want to build there. A classic example is the attempt to bring clean power to New York City by building atomic power plants in the area. The best motivations and even the best public relations efforts may block corporate plans if community opposition is determined enough.

Community relations work prior to a move into a community is designed to gain more than passive acceptance of a company. One obviously can't build a cement factory in the heart of town and expect to receive community cooperation. But a company can prevent fears of imagined problems. It can win enthusiastic acceptance and pave the way for long-lasting, grateful community relationships. (*See* Figure 8.1.)

E. I. Du Pont De Nemours & Company accomplished that in the Fayetteville, North Carolina, area. When Du Pont announced it was exercising options to purchase land for a plastics manufacturing facility, efforts had already been made to build rapport with the area's news media and opinion leaders. The appointed plant manager was introduced to the media and important members of the community. A luncheon attended by some

TO: JEFFERSON COUNTY RESIDENTS

On June 7, Texaco withdrew its original tank terminal application in order to "clear the air" and start again at a new site.

Certain parties opposing this project have vowed to "fight against it" regardless of where it's located in Jefferson County. Why should a small group of weekend residents be able to deny Jefferson County this project, with its tax base to benefit schools, increase fire and police protection and add jobs?

We invite you to come visit with us about the project at our Open House on Saturday, July 22. It will be held at the Opera House in Monticello, from 1 to 5 p.m.

There will be lots of food (catered by Cornucopia), entertainment and many door prizes (including a 19" color television set and gift certificates to local businesses). It will be fun for the whole family.

We look forward to seeing you there.

Texaco Trading and Transportation Inc.
260 W. Washington St.
Monticello, FL 32344
TEXACO

"Let's Work Together for a Better Jefferson County"

AD PROMOTING A CORPORATE FACILITY
Figure 8.1 Engaged in a battle with an activist group attempting to block a tank terminal, Texaco acted as host for the community. This ad features attractions, but the goal was a chance to show how benign the tank terminal would be. *Courtesy Texaco Trading & Transportation, Inc.*

375 people in Cumberland and Bladen counties featured state officials and favorable remarks by the lieutenant governor. Later, a steak cookout for about twenty opinion leaders was held—devoid of formal speeches and devoted to building rapport with key people.

Activities too numerous to list were begun to meet three main objectives:

1. Provide factual information promptly on appropriate events and various stages of the project.
2. Familiarize key groups and individuals with the Du Pont Company, its products, its policies and its people.
3. Continue to build relationships after plant startup.

Two activities were particularly noteworthy. One was a concerted effort to personally make known within the community key Du Pont people through face-to-face meetings, both formal and informal.

The other was the study of the health of the Cape Fear River (involved in the plant location) and other aspects of the environment control program.

Dr. Ruth Patrick of the Academy of Natural Sciences of Philadelphia not only made pertinent studies for Du Pont, but her work was covered by news media. At a dinner attended by the press, she discussed her work in water management. Along with television appearances by Dr. Patrick, a booklet was distributed on Du Pont's pollution control program.

With talks by another expert on his plant life study of the area and by Du Pont engineers on air emissions plus follow-up talks by Dr. Patrick on her biological survey, Du Pont's plant entered production with little community fear for and much knowledge about its effect on environment.

When Boston Edison was planning to erect a major new power plant at Weymouth, Massachusetts, it began early to meet with local officials and state representatives. It arranged for establishment of a local site reutilization committee and kept abreast of its reactions.

When contractors were called in to bid on the project, they also met with town officials to learn about the community's concerns.

The company made sure that everyone in the community with an interest in the project was informed in advance. A briefing session was also held for employees before the announcement. "Employees are the best resources you have," said Walter Salvi of Boston Edison, referring to their influence as a grassroots force in the community.

Concurrent with the news conference announcing the project, community relations professionals canvassed the community to tell people what was happening. The press followed, picking up reaction interviews.

Follow-ups to the announcement included a series of high-level briefings, starting in Weymouth and moving out to neighboring areas.

An open house was also held on site. Specific concerns were addressed and the company explained employment opportunities, as well as the company's role as a major employer in the area.

As a result, they experienced no organized opposition to the project, at a time when many other localities were blocking such construction projects.

Continuing familiarization

Introducing a plant continues after a plant is built. Chrysler Corporation's Toledo Machining Plant is a good example. Shortly after the contractor completed the final work, a series of plant visits were scheduled. These included a "Government Day" for local, state, and U.S. officials representing the community, as well as a "Contractor Day" for principals in the firm that built the plant. "Industry Day" welcomed the leaders of business and industry in the area, and "Education Day" brought in school superintendents and other leading educators in the community.

Each program included coffee on arrival, a brief orientation on Chrysler Corporation and the Toledo plant's role in the company, a tour of the plant, a tomato juice reception, and lunch served in the office cafeteria. After lunch came a talk by a speaker, such as the Ohio governor on "Government Day."

Each guest received a follow-up questionnaire in the mail. Chrysler not only got a high response (68 percent) but also insight on the considerable success of such plant visits, the feelings of the community, and how future plant visits might be improved.

The General Foods Corporation has become a proven expert in careful entry community relations, as demonstrated by introductions of plants in Lafayette, Indiana, and Topeka, Kansas. Thoroughness in reaching all community audiences and in using all appropriate public relations means to do so, was again the key, but other factors were also involved.

General Foods learned, as most companies are now learning, that it is almost impossible to secretly consider, let alone secretly plan possible sites for new plants. While this may mean potential trouble and additional work for companies, it also means valuable opportunities for community relations personnel.

As soon as General Foods took options on available properties, it made brief, factual announcements to local media. The company carefully emphasized it was studying possible sites in a number of locations. It earnestly worked to avoid building up false hopes in any community. (*See* Figure 8.2.)

With the announcement of such studies, community relations people have an opportunity to begin investigations that can benefit the company's planning. The early investigations can help a company select its plant location, or learn what particular conditions will have to be met to minimize problems attendant to the company's final decision. Time, that all-important public relations commodity, is extended in these situations.

Once General Foods decided on the sites, they took another important community relations step. They pointed out in press releases to the "losing" communities that the places chosen simply came closer to meeting the company's particular set of requirements. They noted other companies, with different requirements, might well have reached different decisions. They avoided entering local controversies over local industrial development programs by resisting all efforts to ascertain specific reasons why a community was not chosen.

A comprehensive study of an earlier General Foods plant relocation was the subject of

News

John Hancock

USA
OOO

OFFICIAL LIFE INSURANCE SPONSOR
1994/1996 U.S. OLYMPIC TEAMS

CONTACT:
Steve Burgay, John Hancock
(617) 572-6507

Robert O'Toole, Boston Police
(617) 343-4520

Terry Yanulavich, Northeastern University
(617) 373-5439

MEDIA ADVISORY

The Boston Police Anti-Gang Violence Unit in partnership with John Hancock and Northeastern University will unveil a unique program which enables at-risk, inner-city teenagers to spend the summer earning money while developing job, life and leadership skills.

WHO: Mayor Thomas Menino
Police Commissioner Paul Evans
John Hancock Chairman Stephen L. Brown
Northeastern University President John A. Curry
Program Participants

WHAT: Brief presentation of the program
Interview opportunities with speakers and some program participants
Opportunity to see the program in session

WHEN: Wednesday, July 20 at 1:30 p.m.

WHERE: John Hancock City View Room on the 60th floor (Observatory)
200 Clarendon St.

Parking available for media: The Kinney lot on the corner of Stuart and Clarendon St. will have free spaces reserved for media covering the event

John Hancock Mutual Life Insurance Company and affiliated companies/John Hancock Place/P.O. Box 111/Boston, Massachusetts 02117

Figure 8.2 Sample PR release/media advisory. *Courtesy John Hancock Mutual Life Insurance Company, Boston.*

1995 CRA Statement
Harris Trust & Savings Bank

Figure 8.3 Harris Bank of Chicago issues an annual report on its community relations activities. The century-old bank, recently acquired by a Canadian firm, needs to show it still serves the community in many ways. *Courtesy Harris Bank, Chicago.*

a book by Edmund S. Whitman and W. James Schmidt, published by the American Management Association. The book, *Plant Relocation, A Case History of a Move,* is not only a guide to opening a facility in a community but to shutting down outmoded plants in other communities.

In the book, General Foods noted its public relations program for leaving a community was based on the following:

- Full and early disclosure of all management decisions to employees and the public in that order

- Involvement of top management through personal contacts with community leaders

- Continuing communication through bulletins from top management to the affected employees, assisting each employee to decide what was in his or her own best interest

- Concern for the welfare of the affected community and the earnest attempt to ease the blow

The creation, implementation, and follow-through described earlier apply in community relations programs for corporate arrivals and departures. If there is a difference, it is that corporate survival is a little more obviously dependent on your success. (*See* Figure 8.3, page 135.)

As previously stated, business marries the community it settles with. The decision to move into a community requires a careful courtship. And the price for separating a business from a community primarily depends on how well the appropriateness of the break is understood and accepted.

Emerging Trends

No business or individual can physically exist in a community without having an effect on it or being affected by it. It's that simple, and the ramifications of that point are coming to be fully understood by business.

To summarize applied community relations: *act in regard to the community, think in terms of groups, and address yourself to the individual.*

9

WORKING AND COMMUNICATING WITH MINORITY GROUPS

D. PARKE GIBSON
PATRICIA P. GIBSON

D. Parke Gibson was president and senior consultant of D. Parke Gibson Associates, Inc., a New York-based, minority-owned consulting firm, providing management, marketing, and public affairs counsel and services to domestic and international firms.

He was the author of $70 Billion in the Black: America's Black Consumers, *published in 1978 by Macmillan.*

Patricia P. Gibson headed the firm founded by her late husband. She has been alternate delegate with nongovernmental status to the United Nations for the National Council of Negro Women, a member of the National Board of Girls Clubs of America, and a member of the Advisory Committee, NAACP Crisis Magazine.

American and international companies that do business in the United States spend billions of dollars annually trying to tell the public who they are, what they produce (or market), and why they are good corporate citizens. These efforts often miss their mark with America's minority populations.

Why? Because the public relations programs of both for-profit and nonprofit groups serving minority groups frequently fail to effectively communicate how their products or services benefit those communities.

The events of past and recent years clearly indicate continuing minority unrest and polarization. The consequent effects of this unrest pose significant challenges for the field of public relations, particularly with regard to communication.

Understanding Minority Perspectives

America is home to more than forty-five million people who, through their ethnicity, belong to one or more of several minority groups. African-Americans comprise the largest of these minority groups, with more than thirty-two million members. Consequently, African-Americans traditionally have been the most vocal of the various minority groups, and have had the most attention paid to them. The Spanish-speaking and Spanish surname (Hispanic) population, at fifteen million represents the second largest minority consumer market.

There are growing Asian populations—especially Chinese, Japanese, Korean, and Vietnamese—and Native Americans, though their population has dwindled, continue to be a factor. (There are media that reach each of these groups, and the concepts applying to African-American and Hispanic media generally apply to them.)

Confrontation by minority groups is likely to increase. How well public relations men and women act and react can have a bearing on the results.

The confrontation does create awareness. For many years the majority population acted as if the minority population scarcely existed in America, because it was not pictured in communications practices or the media.

The prospects of confrontation and race relations problems that exist call for serious study by public relations executives. Increasingly, they will be called upon by management to interpret what is happening in race relations and, inversely, to interpret to America's minority communities what business and industry are doing that is of particular interest to them.

How well public relations helps bridge the communications gap between business and the minority communities, as well as those nonprofit groups having an interest, can determine the course of race relations in the years ahead. How well public relations executives *understand* the problems of the minority community and *interpret* them to management will help determine the policy and the course of action to be taken.

The attitudes of African-Americans, as well as those of other identifiable minority groups, must be understood. For example, it should be known that in the black community the number one concern is employment—not

education, housing, voting rights, or social integration. This does not mean, however, that all efforts should concentrate on one priority.

In the minority communities, primarily in the black community because it is the largest, tailored public relations practices will have to be employed.

The ideal in public relations would be to create one effort that would equally influence all publics. That is not possible, of course, because publics vary. As long as we have a multicultural society in the United States, the need to communicate separately with these publics will remain.

The Growth of the Hispanic Public

It is important for those who hope to gain a bigger share of the Hispanic market to look closely at its statistics.

1. The single biggest group of Hispanics is the Chicanos, people of Mexican origin. They are concentrated primarily in the Southwest.

2. Most Spanish-origin persons live in metropolitan areas. The greatest concentration of this ethnic group is in New York State, particularly metropolitan New York.

3. The Spanish-origin population is young, having a median age of twenty-two years compared with thirty years for the rest of the nation.

4. Hispanic groups are united by language and their commitment to Roman Catholicism. However, significant differences exist among them, including age, occupation, educational and economic attainment, income, and residence.

Companies and advertisers with increased awareness of the growing potential of the burgeoning Spanish public are making a conscious effort to reach them. Some distinct characteristics have been noticed. Much like African-American consumers, Hispanics are brand conscious. "They have a strong desire for quality," notes a major advertiser, "coupled with the insecurity of the newcomer—that leads logically to a high level of brand loyalty."

Prime medium

In the national Spanish-speaking public, radio is the primary medium, based on the size of Spanish radio audiences and the number of stations reaching it. The average Hispanic person listens between twenty-six and thirty hours per week. However, the impact of TV is potent and growing rapidly.

Distribution to Hispanic media is offered by some firms listed in Chapter 20. Derus Media Service provides a translation service. *Hispanic Media Directory* (available from ADR Publishing, Newport Beach, CA) lists print and broadcast outlets. Latin Reports, 230 W. 41st Street, 17th Floor, New York, NY 10036-7207, (212) 730-6036, offers clipping and analysis of Hispanic media.

Language vehicles

More and more organizations realize the need to create targeted material and to channel their messages through Spanish-language media.

There are more than 250 radio stations and 60 television stations in the U.S. with partial or complete Spanish programming, often beaming to both sides of the Mexican border. Additionally, there are more than 50 Spanish-language newspapers, several Spanish-language magazines, and many special publications. (*See* Figure 9.1, page 140.)

Increasing numbers of messages and public announcements now appear in English and Spanish on city buses in Los Angeles and San Antonio, at bus and train stations in Miami, on subways in Philadelphia and New York City, and on billboards.

Establishing the Organization's Position

How does one begin to work and communicate with minority groups? The following are some recommended approaches that have been used with success in learning "where you are, so you can know where to go":

1. Determine what is being done in the company or organization that would be of particular interest to minority groups. (Keep in mind that what is being done for African-Americans may not be of particular interest to other minority groups, and vice versa.)

2. Ask your human resources department, if your organization has more than twenty-two employees, to share with you the firm's EEO Form 100, which details minority-group employment, as well as the company's plan to increase minority-group employment. In many cases the human resources department has an awareness of and far more contact with minority groups than does the public relations department, and can be very helpful.

3. Conduct research to determine how the company is regarded within minority communities or among minority-group leadership in headquarters, plant, or branch cities.

4. Research ethnic-oriented publications to determine what type of public relations material they carry, including that of competitive firms and organizations.

These steps will provide a background of where your company or organization cur-

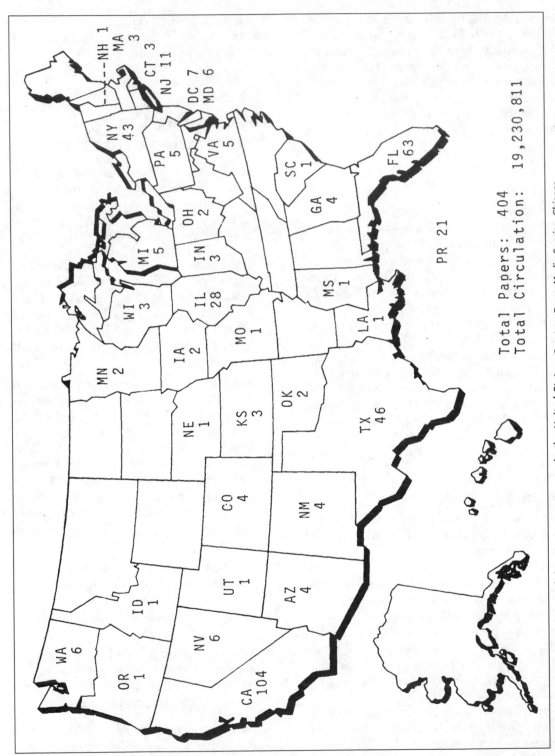

NH 1
MA 3
CT 3
NJ 11
DC 7
MD 6
NY 43
PA 5
VA 5
SC 1
FL 63
GA 4
OH 2
MI 5
IN 3
PR 21
WI 3
IL 28
MS 1
LA 1
MO 1
IA 2
MN 2
KS 3
OK 2
NE 1
TX 46
CO 4
NM 4
UT 1
AZ 4
ID 1
NV 6
WA 6
OR 1
CA 104

Total Papers: 404
Total Circulation: 19,230,811

Figure 9.1 Distribution of Spanish-language newspapers in the United States. *Courtesy Derus Media Service, Chicago.*

rently stands in regard to minority communities. Here is where the practice begins.

There are three basic ways in which public relations is practiced in the minority communities nationally—*press relations*, *community relations*, and *publicity*. Almost all successful public relations efforts in the communities have effectively used direct lines of communication to the African-American and other minority communities.

At one time, perhaps, minorities could be influenced through white-oriented mass media—including daily newspapers, magazines, radio, and television—and through spill-off of some general public relations efforts. It is doubtful whether this could be accomplished now. A medium that talks *about* a minority group and not *to* it can hardly influence that group.

Ethnic media—newspapers, magazines, broadcast, and other specialized types—serve a wide audience, and can be effectively used for communicating with the audiences they serve.

These media are important today and will be increasingly, especially in the African-American and Spanish-language communities of America. Communications to white-oriented media will also have to be directed to black-oriented and Spanish-language media for the *interpretation* necessary for those minority groups to *understand* that the messages include them, too.

It is important for public relations people to understand that tailoring communication to minority interest media is not *segregation-in-reverse,* but simply good communications practice.

Any public relations executive worth her salt knows when she has a good legitimate story to tell, as opposed to "horn-tooting." However, it is important to understand what may be routine or unimportant to whites may be of significant interest to a particular minority group. Study of media can rather quickly help determine this.

Relaying the Story

To reach minority groups there are newspapers, magazines, radio stations, neighborhood theaters, and in some Spanish-speaking communities television programming in Spanish.

The most important responsibility public relations people can have, as part of their responsibility to clients and organizations, is to understand that all media should be serviced, how they should be serviced, and why. This should include media geared to the interests of millions of Americans who are not white.

Here are sixteen suggestions, proved in practice, to keep in mind when servicing ethnic-oriented media:

1. Prepare material with the publications in mind. Most publications in the black community are weeklies and monthlies. In the case of Spanish media, have material translated. (*See* Figure 9.2, page 142.)

2. Publications are usually understaffed. The right material prepared with a publication's format in mind stands an excellent chance of being used.

3. Routine business announcements, unless they involve minority groups, have little chance of being used and should not be sent.

4. If product publicity is continually sent, the advertising department or the agency can expect to be solicited.

5. News releases and product publicity accompanied by photographs with African-American or Hispanic subjects have a better-than-average chance of being used.

6. Keep names of editors of ethnic media up-to-date. Do not send material addressed impersonally (i.e., to "Editor"). Ethnic media need more personalized attention.

7. Black- and Spanish-oriented media representatives should be invited—even if they

IMPORTANT: Washing a Single Item

● **Washing a single item**, such as a sweater, bath towel or jeans, is not recommended. As the machine tumbles the load prior to final spin, it may sense an out-of-balance load. If an out-of-balance load is sensed, the washer will stop briefly and tumble for a short time to try to balance the load. This stop-tumble action may occur several times before the end of the cycle. If the load can not be evenly balanced, items may feel wet at the end of the cycle. Adding 1 or 2 similar items will help balance the load.

● If a load becomes tangled and out-of-balance, it may be necessary to rearrange the load by hand. Stop the washer by pushing in the cycle selector knob and open the door. Remove the load, untangle the items and return load to tub. Close door and restart washer.

● **A single bulky item**, such as a bedspread, comforter or sleeping bag, can be laundered without adding extra items to the load.

IMPORTANTE: Lavando un artículo sólo

● No es recomendable **lavar un sólo artículo**, por ejemplo, un suéter, una toalla de baño o pantalones vaqueros. Como la máquina la da vueltas a la ropa antes de la rotación final, ella puede detectar una carga fuera de equilibrio. si se detecta una carga fuera de equilibrio, la máquina parará por un momento para tratar de equilibrar la carga. La operación de paro/volteo puede ocurrir varias veces antes del final del ciclo. Si la carga no puede ser equilibrada, puede que las prendas que se laven queden húmedas al final del ciclo. Si se agregan 1 o 2 prendas similares ayudará a equilibrar la carga.

● Si una carga se enreda o está fuera de equilibrio, puede que sea necesario reacondicionar la carga a mano. Pare la lavadora empujando la perilla selectora de ciclo y abra la puerta. Saque la carga de ropa, desenrede los artículos y vuelva a ponerlos en la tina. Cierre la puerta y arranque de nuevo la lavadora.

● **Un sólo artículo grande**, tal como una cubrecama,cobertor o bolsa de dormir puede ser lavado sin que sea necesario agregar artículos extra a la carga de ropa.

IMPORTANT: Laver un seul article

● Il n'est pas recommandé **de laver un seul article**, comme un chandail par exemple, une serviette de toilette ou un jean. Quand la machine fait tourner la brassée avant le dernier essorage, cela peut entraîner un déséquilibre. Si la machine sent ce déséquilibre, elle s'arrête automatiquement pendant un bref instant et se remet à tourner le linge pour essayer de rééquilibrer la brassée. Cette manoeuvre d'arrêt et de remise en marche peut arriver plusieurs fois avant la fin du cycle. Si la brassée ne peut pas être correctement équilibrée, les articles peuvent être encore un peu trempe à la fin du cycle. On peut rééquilibrer la brassée en ajoutant un ou deux articles.

● Si une brassée est emmêlée ou déséquilibrée, réarranger la brassée à la main. Pour cela, arrêter la laveuse en appuyant sur le bouton de sélection du cycle et ouvrir la porte. Retirer la brassée, démêler les articles et remettre la brassée dans le tambour. Fermer la porte et remettre la laveuse en marche.

● **Un seul article volumineux**, comme un couvre-lit par exemple, une couette ou un duvet, peut être lavé sans ajouter d'articles supplémentaires.

P/N 131632900 (9608)

Figure 9.2 Frigidaire's tumble-action washer comes with these trilingual instructions. *Courtesy Frigidaire Home Products.*

do not attend for one reason or another—to the same press functions as other media.

8. Because of weekly deadlines, often servicing the black press before a news release time does not violate good practice, can improve usage, and can lead to treatment more in keeping with the "news" angle.

9. Public relations departments should maintain subscriptions to national and local ethnic-oriented media to ensure familiarity with format, editorial philosophy, and the type of publicity material used.

10. Public relations representatives should know when corporate advertising is being considered or run in African-American–oriented or Spanish media (e.g., Brotherhood Week, new plant openings, recruitment ads) and, if desired, prepare editorial copy to support this effort.

11. Deal frankly and honestly with representatives of ethnic-oriented media. Do not patronize but be understanding.

12. Understand that most ethnic-oriented radio stations carry international, national, and local news, *and* news of particular interest to minority groups. This is often an overlooked, twenty-four-hour-a-day, direct line to these communities that can be used effectively.

13. Newspaper supplement and magazine editors' needs should be thoroughly analyzed *before* they are approached for story consideration. The story must have a distinctly ethnic angle or one that can be developed through graphics.

14. In using models for publicity purposes, *do not* select models that might be mistaken for white. Instead, choose those who are *identifiable* to the minority group and will photograph well.

15. Remember why ethnic-oriented media exist and help fill their needs for tailored information and publicity.

16. Be sure your program is integrated with all other functions and communications that affect public attitudes about the organization. (*See* Figure 9.3, page 144.)

Interaction with Groups

The second route to building goodwill, in addition to press relations, is through community-relations activities, particularly with national leadership organizations. The cultural diversity of American society is shown in certain organizations' names: many organizations with "American" in the title are white, and many with "National" in the title are black. For example, there is an American Medical Association and a National Medical Association, the latter composed primarily of black doctors; the American Bar Association and the National Bar Association; an American Dental Association and a National Dental Association.

The American Medical Association's stand on many issues, especially where race is concerned, differs from that of the National Medical Association. Part of the success of public relations in the black community is knowing what message to get to whom—and when.

National black organizations have been created by the social, political, economic, and educational horizons open to blacks in the United States during the twentieth century. Although many barriers in racial communication have been breached over the years, it is still necessary for blacks to foster closer ties among themselves—partly in recognition of the realities of a divided American society.

There are about 124 predominantly black national organizations in the United States. The background of such organizations sug-

Figure 9.3 Dow Chemical Company devoted one of the ads in its former series "Dow lets you do great things" to the support it gives to educating blacks. *Reprinted with permission from Dow Chemical Canada Inc.*

gests that they are likely to continue. Thirty-seven of one hundred major black organizations are over fifty years old, with the Prince Hall Masons, the oldest organization, formed in 1789. The national organizations reach about seventeen million members, who are also consumers and influencers.

Numerous opportunities exist for public relations efforts among these organizations, from having executives appear before audiences at national conventions to exhibits and displays at convention sites, other extensions of courtesy, and undertaking special projects with these groups. Many opportunities also exist at the local level, using chapters of national organizations as the springboards for local public relations communications and program activity.

Customizing the Message

The third channel to the national nonwhite population—publicity—encompasses the first two. Material is tailored to the African-American or Hispanic press, and then it is called to the attention of opinion makers through reprints and other means.

Publicity is a most important tool in the effort to let blacks, Hispanics, and other minority groups know and understand that they are being "included." The manner in which it is shaped and the plan to get it into the right hands are vitally important.

The material should also retain its effectiveness when it is reprinted for distribution to leadership in the minority communities. This technique has worked rather well and expands the limits of the audience served by the media themselves. (A third-party endorsement is gained from the influence and prestige of the medium, as well.)

Stories on the effective utilization of minority manpower, for example, could also be used effectively in reprint form by the human resources department in compliance reviews, as well as to document the organization's progress in diversity.

Developing Well-Targeted Material

In addition to the three main channels to the minority community, a fourth avenue is always hoped for—word of mouth.

Because of their rich culture and position in this society, African-Americans think, act, and respond as a minority almost automatically. These responses provide an almost automatic unidentifiable channel of communication among the group.

Another successful technique to reach and influence leadership has been the creation and development of company-sponsored black- and Spanish-oriented printed materials and publications.

The following examples show how some companies have created target material for the black community.

Avon products created integrated posters on good grooming, showing well-groomed black and white teenagers. They are distributed to schools throughout the United States on request. In addition, Avon regularly mails tailored materials on good grooming, featuring attractive black models, to the national ethnic press.

The American Airlines Guide to Black Conventions and Conferences profiles 124 national black organizations with more than fifteen million consumers and influencers, listing their annual conventions and meeting schedules. The annual guide affects the $3 billion black convention travel market.

Anheuser-Busch commissioned black artists to develop original art portraying Black Kings of African History. This project then grew into an advertising campaign, booth

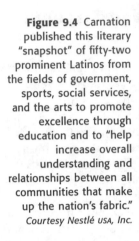

Figure 9.4 Carnation published this literary "snapshot" of fifty-two prominent Latinos from the fields of government, sports, social services, and the arts to promote excellence through education and to "help increase overall understanding and relationships between all communities that make up the nation's fabric." *Courtesy Nestlé USA, Inc.*

exhibits at black conventions, and public showings in key cities.

The Brown & Williamson Tobacco Corporation's Kool cigarettes advertising campaign theme, "There's only one way to play it—Kool," was supported by a series of Kool Jazz Festivals in twenty major markets and selected military bases across the country. The campaign was a "pan-racial" marketing and public relations concept that reached and influenced ethnic and general market audiences through the universal language of music.

Carnation Company (now Nestlé) prepared a series of booklets that were distributed nationwide to schools, organizations, and individuals. Several pamphlets prepared by Carnation in English and Spanish have had broad national distribution. "How to Get and

Keep the Right Job" is made available to schools, career centers, and agencies that operate employment programs. "Rising Voices" contains biographical sketches of fifty-two prominent Hispanics, for distribution to Hispanic organizations, schools, and interested individuals. (*See* Figure 9.4.)

The Heritage Calendar, developed by Adolph Coors Company, of Golden, Colorado, depicts contributions of early black settlers to the building of America, such as fur trappers, the Buffalo Soldiers, cowboys, and miners. Through their beer distributors' network, Coors provides the calendar to liquor stores and restaurants in targeted marketing areas.

The Greyhound Corporation sponsors scholarships at more than fifty colleges with predominantly African-American and Hispanic student bodies and supports the American Indian Science and Engineering Society, as well as the Native American Rights Fund.

The Great Black Inventors Calendar sponsored by the Miller Brewing Company shows black Americans' contributions to America and the world. It is distributed to numerous black colleges, institutions, and individuals.

Philip Morris issues directories of black and Hispanic organizations to facilitate relations between members of these minority groups.

Miller Brewing Company features achievements of blacks in calendars distributed among the black population.

Multiple purposes

The technique of company-underwritten black-oriented publications, reprints of significant articles appearing in ethnic media, and tailored programs of interest to minority groups accomplishes several objectives.

The publications are sent directly, by name, to black leadership. In addition, they appear on college campuses, in libraries, in doctors' offices, and in many other gathering places.

On college campuses they also appear in placement offices and may determine how a young man or woman feels about a particular company and whether he or she seeks employment there. The publications offer the opportunity to discuss progressive employment practices and company interest in the minority communities.

They also enable the company to associate its interest in good minority relations with its products and services.

The annual report to stockholders should also be considered for evidencing good corporate citizenship. Copies of the report should be sent to top ethnic leadership to indicate concern for minority groups.

Black history advertising and public relations programs, as well as those reflecting contemporary life (and this has similar appeal to other minority groups), can provide important vehicles for attempting to influence opinion or to sell more products and services to these segments of the consumer market. They can serve as effective means of establishing identification and can help encourage initiative by providing concrete examples of accomplishment that are little noted elsewhere.

Since this technique will continue to be important, here are some guidelines in considering black history or contemporary life among minorities in institutional advertising and public relations programs.

1. Get technical help to avoid inaccuracies or misuse of material.

2. If good, clear pictures are unavailable, use sketches or artists' conceptions.

3. If the theme of the campaign is thought to be at all insensitive to the particular minority group, research it in the community before too much investment is made.

4. Plan how and where the campaign is to be executed—such as conventions, colleges and universities, libraries, banks—and what supporting materials will be needed.

5. When applicable, alert dealers and distributors about the campaign and seek their cooperation to make it effective.

6. Do not attach a hard-sell to this campaign. The soft-sell can help the program gain a much higher degree of acceptance.

The public relations executive who can establish a position in the minority communities in terms of current practices and then relate the organization's efforts to these communities will go a long way toward winning friends and influencing people. Whether it is a corporation or a nonprofit service organization, tailored materials and efforts can pay dividends.

10

WINNING SUPPORT FOR AN IDEA OR CAUSE

HUGH C. NEWTON
HERB B. BERKOWITZ

Hugh C. Newton is president of Hugh C. Newton & Associates, a public relations firm based in Washington specializing in issue-oriented communications. He has been awarded two Silver Anvils by the Public Relations Society of America. His clients have included The Heritage Foundation, Reader's Digest, National Review, The Republic of China (Taiwan), Amway Corporation, American Council on Science and Health, Hillsdale College, National Federation of Independent Business, National Right to Work Committee, and National Right to Work Legal Defense Foundation.

Herb B. Berkowitz is vice-president of public relations for The Heritage Foundation, a major policy development organization. He is a former magazine editor. He writes and lectures on media-related topics and has been awarded a Silver Anvil by PRSA.

In October of 1989, the U.S. Congress made a rare, almost unprecedented, move when it voted to repeal a major benefits program. George Mason University Political Science Professor Hugh Heclo, a renowned authority on the federal bureaucracy, recalls only two other instances in its two hundred–year history in which Congress had taken similar action, wiping out what is now known as an "entitlement" program. The most recent occurred in the 1930s when Congress, in a fit of pique, wiped out a program for tenant farmers. Some sixty years prior, in the 1870s, Congress abolished the Freedman's Bureau, intended to assist former slaves.

Even more remarkable than the October '89 repeal itself was that it came just one year after Congress had passed the same program,

a major expansion of Medicare providing "catastrophic" health-care coverage and other benefits to the elderly.

This repeal met considerable opposition from the White House, the House's own leadership, the Department of Health and Human Services, and the powerful 31-million-member strong American Association of Retired Persons (AARP), which had led the initial fight to win approval of the program.

Virtually the only people who favored the repeal were retirees who had decided that the legislation was an expensive bad deal—and they let Congress know. Contributing greatly to this opinion was the work of a thirty-year-old analyst at the Heritage Foundation, Edmund Haislmaier, who wrote numerous widely distributed articles and studies that warned the elderly of the legislation's costs and negative consequences. This initially lone voice of contention was soon joined by that of millions of others who opposed the bill, including those of a national citizens' coalition headed by James Roosevelt, son of Franklin D. Roosevelt—the patron saint of Social Security.

Congress, hearing the message of dissent, responded.

Though this catastrophic health-care battle was extraordinary in that it did away with the manna of politics—an entitlement program—it stayed true to form in one important way: it demonstrated that winning in the public policy arena often depends on one side's ability to mobilize wide-scale public support or to at least create the appearance of such support.

This provides an important lesson for public relations practitioners because it differs significantly from other types of activity. Whether pushing for or fighting against change, an informed and aroused public affords a most powerful weapon, indeed.

To wit: Though meaningful gun control proposals first came before Congress during the mid-'60s, almost all of these bills (the Brady bill being an exception) have languished for more than thirty-five years, because the public remains insufficiently convinced that strong gun control legislation will alleviate the problem. Conversely, Superfund legislation, which requires industry to pay for cleaning up toxic waste dumps, did get enacted, because the chemical industry failed to convince the public that they were not at fault for the "Love Canals" filling the news. Yet organized labor has failed, despite numerous efforts, to significantly change federal labor law, because it has been unable to win public support for its special-interest agenda. Similarly, the Reagan Administration, despite his repute as the "great communicator," could never create a public mandate for the centerpiece of its Latin American policy—to pro-

vide military assistance to the anti-Communist "Contra" rebels in Nicaragua. And the Clintons' effort to impose a government-dictated national health plan flopped because they failed to get public support.

Widening the Circle

Rallying public support behind an idea or cause is the coinage of issues-oriented public relations. Borrowing from political scientist E. E. Schattschneider, former *New York Times* Washington Bureau Chief Hedrick Smith in his best-seller, *The Power Game*, describes the process as "widening the circle." Smith notes that "spreading information to summon political allies . . . or to rally public opinion" often is essential to success in Washington. It "is the regular stuff of the power game. Everyone does it, from presidents on down, when they want to change the balance of power on some issue . . . [or] stir up public opinion and use public pressure to influence" the debate.

While "everyone" does it, they don't all do it well. Business, especially, often seems mystified or intimidated by the thought of having to win public support on an issue, even when failure to do so will affect their bottom line as much as (or more than) a strategic product or marketing blunder. Yet the same corporations are aggressive and creative in marketing their products.

Here are two case studies in which business was outshouted, outgunned, or outmaneuvered by its opposition.

Alar

The so-called Alar information campaign orchestrated by Fenton Communications in 1989 is a classic example of effective issues-oriented public relations, except for one disqualifying flaw: it was based on a "scientific" premise that most credible scientists consider seriously flawed (if not utter nonsense). Industry's response, however, was even worse: it choked.

Alar is the trade name for an agricultural chemical, daminozide, used by a few U.S. apple growers to prolong the tree life of their fruit, thereby improving the color. In February 1989 the "Alar scare" became an almost overnight phenomenon after CBS-TV's *60 Minutes* gave credibility to a "study" by the Natural Resources Defense Council linking consumption of apples that had been treated with Alar to the development of cancerous tumors. Using distorted methods of scientific extrapolation, the NRDC concluded that continued use of Alar could result in millions of U.S. schoolchildren developing cancer later in life.

The word *cancer* is a powerful motivator. Consider some of the leading environmental scare stories of the recent past: Love Canal, Three Mile Island, radon in our homes, and "global warming." The "cancer threat" is central to three of them and involved in the fourth. When the "threat" of cancer is combined with another powerfully motivating "C" word—children—the combination is compelling.

After the *60 Minutes* segment aired, the public panicked. Grocers pulled apples from their shelves. School officials in New York City and elsewhere ordered apples and apple products removed from school lunch menus. The Environmental Protection Agency ordered a temporary (soon to be made permanent) emergency ban on the rarely used chemical. Though a few public health experts, such as Dr. Elizabeth Whelan, executive director of the American Council on Science and Health, cautioned that the threat was being vastly overstated, they were drowned out in a cacophony of fear.

Technically, in execution if not in sound policy, NRDC appears to have done all the right things. Unlike the case in most corporate or industry public relations efforts, NRDC was aided by compliant media willing to accept and amplify the organization's charges without question, because alarms attract audiences.

The apple growers retained a major corporate public relations firm to help combat the misinformation—but the damage was already done.

Though Alar is no longer used in apple growing, there still is no scientifically credible evidence that anybody was "at risk" from eating apples containing trace amounts of the chemical.

In addition to scaring many people and to gaining attention for the NRDC and possible new clients for Fenton Communications, the Alar scare had one more effect: by sharply reducing apple sales, it drove a number of growers into bankruptcy. While total losses are unknown, the Reuters news agency reported in November 1989 that the Alar scare caused an estimated $100 million to $140 million in losses to Washington state apple growers alone.

The Alar campaign was a costly lesson for business: In the war of ideas, it doesn't pay to be a pacifist. If industry finds itself under attack, it must be proactive and aggressive. In this case it did too little, too late, and had already lost the fight by the time it decided to retain Hill and Knowlton for a reported $700,000 to help it fight back.

The Superfund

Another example of the consequences of losing the battle for public support is the chemical industry's "campaign" against the environmental Superfund, which is administered by the Environmental Protection Agency. It is a pool of money intended for cleaning up toxic waste dump sites. These funds are raised by taxing companies that produce such wastes, primarily chemical companies.

The chemical industry's top public relations executives made a conscious decision early in the battle that they would backpedal rather than try to win. The lesson here is that if you don't even try to win, you probably won't.

Washington's Importance

The emphasis here is on Washington, because that is where most public policy decisions are made. The same rules and lessons apply to the state and local policy battles as well, but as Hedrick Smith notes in *The Power Game*, Washington "is where the nation's destiny is set." The same principle applies in capitals of other democratic countries.

The spreading impact of the federal government on every aspect of corporate life can be traced to the passage of the Interstate Commerce Act in 1887. Since then a succession of federal laws has given the federal government regulatory control over virtually every aspect of corporate life. Although some deregulation has occurred, top business executives can no longer concern themselves merely with "product" and "marketing." They can no longer live in isolation from the public policy debate.

A joint survey by the Public Affairs Council and *Business & Public Affairs Fortnightly* identified the kinds of issues that most concern the typical chief executive officer: tax policy; insurance liability; federal budget policy; trade policy and the organizations involved in such matters, such as the General Agreement on Tariffs and Trade; Federal Reserve Board policy on money supply and interest rates; energy policy and oil prices; toxic wastes; the value of the dollar; health-care costs and "mandated" fringe benefits; antitrust; military preparedness; plant closing legislation and industrial policy; "comparable worth"; and affirmative action. To this list the contemporary CEO also might add Third World debt, U.S.–Eastern European relations, clean air, acid rain, the future of

Hong Kong, illegal immigration, packaging and labeling standards, the security of the Panama Canal, the unification of Europe's economies, and so on. The common thread in all of these issues is that they are driven by Washington.

As the late John Adams Wettergreen noted in an important book, *The Imperial Congress*, the federal government today is very different than it was just a few decades ago. The rise of the public sector in the late 1960s and early 1970s—fueled in part by corporate America's unwillingness or inability to stop or slow the "consumerist" juggernaut that seemed to be driving policy at the time—resulted in the following: "(1) the assumption of vast new authority by the central government; (2) the establishment of regulation as the typical political activity of the United States; and (3) the assumption (*de facto* and *de jure*) by Congress of administrative functions, with a consequent increase in conflicts with the presidency." To the business community the most important change was the enormous expansion of the federal government's regulatory apparatus. From 1964 to 1974 alone, Wettergreen noted, "The size of the commercial regulatory apparatus alone more than doubled. . . . In particular, not only did the number of commercial regulatory agencies increase from fifty to seventy-two, but thirty-five of the fifty established agencies were substantially reformed," becoming "economy-wide" or even "society-wide" in purview.

Corporate executives, government officials, and others involved in public policy agree that the public should be provided the information needed to develop a reasonably informed opinion on critical issues. Meeting the demand for such information is the cause for rapid growth of political and governmental public relations.

In addition to rapid growth of corporate public relations representation in Washington and increasing involvement of professional and trade associations in issue-oriented public relations, there have arisen many "single-purpose" organizations.

For example, the National Right to Work Committee, National Tax Limitation Committee, National Coalition to Ban Handguns, National Center for Employee Ownership, National Coalition Against the Misuse of Pesticides, Americans for Energy Independence, and National Coalition Against the Death Penalty all exist to influence opinion on a single issue or set of closely related issues. Such groups can be an important factor in winning or blocking passage of special-interest legislation, stirring community action, galvanizing public opinion, or helping elect political candidates.

Winning Public Support

How does one go about winning vocal public support for an idea or cause? What ethical considerations are involved? To what extent can one influence people? Can public support, once it is won, be converted into favorable action? If so, how? In other words, what are the basic principles to follow in planning, developing, and conducting a public relations program to win support for an issue or idea?

A number of guidelines can be applied (*see* Chapter 3), including the following:

1. **Define your problem in the simplest terms.** In the case of government issues, as Hedrick Smith writes, "The distance between Washington and the rest of the country is partly a matter of language. Jargon is a vital element of the Washington game. Washington jargon is impenetrable and often deliberately so, to exclude all but the initiated." The task of the public relations executive is to translate jargon surrounding an issue into words and images

the populace can understand and embrace. First and foremost, obey the *KISS* doctrine: *Keep It Simple, Stupid!* Instead of talking about "payloads" or "throw-weights," talk about the explosive power of the bomb(s) carried by a particular missile.

2. **Focus your program on the heart of the problem.** Use every opportunity to focus public attention on the principle at stake and avoid being dragged into unproductive tangential arguments. The opponents of Superfund legislation failed because they were unsure of what they wanted. They had creative talent, a substantial budget, and some solid arguments on their side but their campaign had no focus. Rather than staking out a position, they wavered. As a result, they were forced to haggle over how much Superfund legislation would cost them rather than seeking to defeat it on its merits.

3. **Organize a staff that believes in what it is doing.** Dedication to the cause is no substitute for professional competence, but a combination of both is essential in this type of effort.

4. **Think about what you are doing before you do it.** Planning is a key to any successful effort, whether defeating an unwanted initiative by others or building a new house. Planning, for example, can help identify allies. In forming the Nitrate Safety Council, leaders of the meat industry found they could count on support from farm groups, meat packers, processors and other specialized meat producers, as well as food retailers. With such a strong coalition, the industry was able to act in unison to ensure that the $12.5 billion processed meat industry survived attacks on the use of nitrates in curing meat. The council's campaign was successful only because the industry was organized with its allies and had the ability to

reach millions of Americans who love their hot dogs and bacon.

This technique was employed by the Calorie Control Council. The leaders of the soft drink industry joined with others interested in the use of artificial sweeteners and were able to mobilize the support of millions of Americans, who at the council's urging wrote Congress not to ban saccharin, as was being urged by the sugar industry.

Planning also enables you to staff properly and to determine what type of outside counsel is needed. Planning, rather than reacting, will result in effective use of research and public opinion studies. It will also help determine on whose terms the battle will be fought. Planning does not guarantee success, but without it success is improbable.

5. **Determine where the public stands on the issue.** The *Dictionary of Mass Communications* defines public opinion as the expression of all members of a group who are giving attention in any way to a given issue. That opinion may be favorable, unfavorable, or apathetic to your cause; but before you can plan your program, it is vital to know what the public believes, and why. (*See also* Chapter 18.) In utilizing opinion-research data, keep the following factors in mind:

- Attitude change is related to the immediacy and potency of the issue to the individual.

- Events play an important part in changing attitudes and opinions. Actions do speak louder than words.

- A major role in shaping public opinion is played by opinion leaders. To recognize and gain the support of opinion leaders in key economic, social, and political groups should be a primary task of public relations.

As Philip Lesly wrote in *Public Relations Journal*, "It is almost impossible to reverse a trend of public opinion through communications efforts alone. However, once a trend has begun to swing around, we can greatly accelerate it by focusing public opinion on it. Look at the tax revolt, the demand for at least minimal education in the schools, and the new tougher attitude toward criminals."

6. **Keep your policies simple** and provide the staff with strong backing.

7. **Keep the staff "tight."** As Lesly said in an article for *Association Management*, "A small group of highly talented, knowledgeable and conscientious people will almost always outperform the largest staff of ordinary personnel."

8. **Keep the program honest.** Critics of public relations refer to its practitioners as "hidden persuaders" who are sinister in molding public opinion in favor of certain products, ideals, and institutions. On the contrary, in a battle for public opinion there is no place for "the Big Lie." While sticking to the facts and honesty don't guarantee success, deviating from the truth is an almost certain invitation to a PR failure. That does not mean you should shy away from expressing your opinion, even an unpopular one. It does mean you should be able to justify the opinion. The Natural Resources Defense Council's Alar message, for example, was relatively straightforward and to the point. NRDC did not use pernicious propaganda techniques. It did not lie. What it was promoting was the point of view of a very small minority within the scientific community—a point of view that was given full credibility by some gullible and compliant media that over the years have become unapologetic advocates for the "environmental" movement.

9. **Take your case to the people.** Arouse public opinion at the grassroots level and let it press Washington. The "grassroots," of course, includes a variety of publics: local political and opinion leaders, community activists, newspaper editorialists, business executives, and civic-minded members of the general public, to name a few. They help set the public agenda and, more important, arouse even wider public concern about a given issue. The ultimate purpose is to generate enough "heat and light" to win the political battle.

Carefully targeted direct mail communications can make a deciding difference. Throughout the country or area involved there are thousands of editors, columnists, radio, and TV talk-show hosts, and other opinion leaders who can help tell your story if you can rally them to your side.

For the public relations practitioner, it is especially important to remember that policy makers in government don't take all their signals from the major media or single vocal officials. Members of the legislature are equally or more concerned with what editors of their local newspapers and local broadcasters say about an issue. After all, it is with these people they must deal when re-election time comes, not with the big newspapers or TV channels.

Senator Patrick J. Leahy (D-Vermont) said he was far more concerned with the editorial positions of a small local newspaper like the *Weatherford Weekly* than with the media giants "because it is read by far more Vermonters . . . (and) it is far more typical of Vermont thinking."

10. **With this in mind, target your communications** to those who really count. To win public support for an idea or cause, it is unnecessary to win everyone over to your side. As Lesly has noted, "At the extremes on most issues are zealots who will not be changed no matter what we do. Say they represent 5 percent of the public at each extreme. Then we have perhaps 80 percent who are apathetic—actually, inert. They can be grouped on the two sides of the issue, but their attitude is so superficial it's not really important. That leaves about 10 percent who are aware of the issue and have a definite opinion on it. Typically, perhaps 6 percent lean one way and 4 percent the other. So changing the leaning of 3 percent of those 10 percent—3 percent among the total—can shift the direction of the momentum on that issue. If we can identify the small group that is alert to the issue and convert a small portion of those who are not firmly opposed, we can create a shift in public opinion."

11. **Keep the political decision-makers informed.** Let Congress and the president know when public opinion shifts or an important publication takes a position on an issue. Remember an "important publication" may be a small hometown daily in a key congressional district. Set up a formal information and research program. Keep your efforts low-key. Don't try to force your cause on the Congress or members of the White House staff. But do let them know what your group is doing and what others are saying about these issues.

Most successful issue-oriented public relations programs over the years have been keyed to going first to the people, then to members of the legislative and executive branches.

12. **Get to know the individual newspeople and editors you need to know** to communicate your story. Keep in mind that journalists are busy too—they are buried with news releases, background studies,

and invitations to news conferences. You must gain their attention, confidence, and respect. If you don't introduce yourself to those people who will be interested in your materials, they are unlikely to find you; there are hundreds of other sources for information. On any given day in Washington you may compete for attention with the likes of the White House, the various cabinet- and sub-cabinet-level agencies of government, 535 congressional offices, congressional committees and subcommittees, the Democratic and Republican National Committees, several influential think tanks, hundreds of trade and professional associations, the AFL-CIO and dozens of affiliate unions, and hundreds of single-purpose and special-interest groups.

The best way to gain the attention, confidence, and respect of news people is through a combination of personal contact and becoming the source of material that is intelligently prepared, timely, accurate, and useful—and presented early, before opinions jell. (*See* Chapter 3.)

Don't be misled into thinking that technology can substitute for a coherent and compelling message. In the world of public policy communication, the medium is not the message. As we told a Public Relations Society of America seminar:

In this day of breathtaking technological innovation, the world has become flooded with information and with quality materials. Some PR people are using all these new technological techniques (video news releases, fax machines, the Internet, etc.) to flood news offices and editorial staffs. What they're doing, unfortunately, is turning people off. The media are tired of "faxes" from people they've never heard of; they're tired of express packages from people they've never heard of, never saw, and probably don't want to see.

Issues-Oriented Campaign Planning

The primary rule about public opinion programs is that each one must be approached individually. The conditions, emotions, people involved, barriers, opportunities, and objectives are all different; using techniques borrowed from other programs must be done only with flexibility and experienced judgment. Combating continuing worldwide efforts to discredit transnational corporations, for instance, has little in common with efforts by the Potato Chip and Snack Foods Association to combat the notion that snack foods are bad for children.

However, some guidance can be derived from observing the techniques used in some successful programs (as well as from studying unsuccessful ones, such as the campaign to get the public to squeeze their own oranges rather than use concentrate or reconstituted juice). Two case studies follow:

Common Situs

On August 25, 1975, President Ford reversed his long-standing position and said he would sign legislation legalizing what's known as "Common Situs" picketing. (*See* Figure 10.1.) The bill would have allowed any union to picket a site where any other union was on strike. Since the bill already had been passed by the House, was actively supported by the then-secretary of labor, the AFL-CIO, and some business interests, and probably would be approved by the Senate, it appeared it would become law.

Intensive planning sessions were held by the executive staff of the National Right to Work Committee (NRWC) that showed, despite the best efforts of employers, contractors, and other opponents of monopoly union power, Common Situs would be approved unless:

Figure 10.1 United Mine Workers show support for a cause. *Courtesy United Mine Workers of America, photo by Keith Mestrich.*

1. The issue could be put into terms meaningful to most Americans.

2. Millions of Americans could be motivated and mobilized.

3. Their efforts were channeled into enough pressure on opinion leaders and politicians to either kill the bill in the Senate or to make it prudent for the president to veto the legislation.

Since opinion polls consistently show that most Americans believe union membership should be voluntary, NRWC felt it had at least a chance if it could quickly and carefully focus public attention on the fact that by granting new coercive powers to union organizers, the situs bill would further erode individual freedom-of-choice of construction workers and employers and endanger the public interest.

The Right to Work Committee realized that any pressure would have to come from the grassroots. Key ingredients—each tailored, when possible, for maximum impact with a particular audience—included the following:

- Briefings and coordination on the issue with key political supporters from both parties

- Full-page ads in forty-nine major newspapers in seven states and Washington, DC:

- Contact with special "publics," such as minority contractors and black journalists

- An educational and informational direct-mail program designed to motivate citizen action. During a four-month period, eight major mailings were sent to more than four million individual Americans. One measure of success was the fact that the White House received 646,152 letters and cards urging the president to veto Common Situs, versus only 7,379 letters and cards asking him to sign the legislation. In addition, members of the Senate and House received more than one million letters and cards. The total, according to political observers, was the most mail received on any issue up to that time since the Vietnam War

- A politically oriented direct-mail appeal from then-Senator Paul Fannin (R-Arizona) that was sent (at Right to Work Committee expense) to two hundred thousand key Republican contributors and party leaders across the country, enlisting their help

- Special efforts to focus attention on a new opinion poll that showed most Americans, including union members, opposed the bill

- Personal briefings for several dozen syndicated columnists and the editorial page editors of more than fifty major newspapers

- A variety of news bureau activities designed to gain attention and magnify media coverage

In less than four months, President Ford turned around and vetoed the bill. The *New York Times* said, "Employer spokesmen and the National Right to Work Committee marshalled their formidable resources to induce the President to veto it."

Sugar's ongoing battle

Because of its universal use and visibility, sugar has for years been a target for lay nutritionists and promoters of fad foods and diets who want to capitalize on the Baby Boom generation's concerns about personal health.

The industry faced a barrage of criticism in the media suggesting that public consumption of ever-increasing amounts of sugar was responsible for a far-ranging variety of health problems. As the volume of the criticism increased, so did concern among the industry's primary publics: the medical commu-

nity, nutritional professionals, food manufacturers and retailers, and government health officials.

The Sugar Association needed to reach its key publics with the facts about sugar and to enlist their aid in educating consumers. And it needed, over the long run, to convince the broadest possible audience that sugar is a safe food that should be a part of a balanced diet.

All association advertising was dropped, since even a nutritional message would appear to be self-serving. (Advertising on controversial issues can sometimes backfire, because it flaunts the sponsor's wealth and could be perceived as an effort to impose one's views rather than conduct a dialogue). (*See* Chapter 30.) Moreover media objectivity and balance was the prime concern, not necessarily extensive coverage. The program also involved surveying public attitudes, enlisting leading medical experts to counsel and speak for the industry, and preparing a bibliography of existing scientific data and literature.

As a result of the long-term program, gratuitous attacks on sugar in the media have diminished sharply, despite the still-increasing media focus on personal "wellness." The criticisms that do appear, meanwhile, tend to be more balanced, and much material favorable to sugar is appearing.

Timing and Delivery

To a great extent, a public relations program to promote a cause or to influence public opinion will be conducted within a timeframe determined by others. There are times, however, when you have the luxury of setting the agenda yourself. That was the case in 1984, for example, when The Heritage Foundation introduced a book-length policy report, *Mandate for Leadership*, to the Washington policy community.

In the real world of public policy, a sound book is important in the long run, but unlikely to affect the day-to-day policy decisions made in Washington. *Mandate for Leadership: Continuing the Conservative Revolution* differed. *Saturday Review* said, "If ideas really do have consequences, this may well be one of the most important books published in 1984."

Mandate II was a detailed policy blueprint intended to provide policy guidance during the second Reagan term. The book contained some thirteen hundred specific proposals for reforming the federal government and strengthening U.S. defenses. It was formally released December 7, 1984, after an intensive month-long publicity campaign. Disclosure of its contents, the *New York Times* said, "produced a spate of front-page reports and its unveiling . . . has become a major media production."

Work on the complex policy report began in early 1984, and from the beginning public relations played a key role in the overall planning. A review of previous efforts and off-the-record discussions with members of the national press corps confirmed the suspicion that publication of a "think tank" book immediately following the November 1984 federal elections would be viewed in Washington as a *political story*, not a *policy story*. *Mandate II* was a policy book, not a political book. To focus attention on the key policy recommendations required creating a program to stimulate interest in the individual proposals, holding that interest for weeks, and multiplying that interest into a media crescendo that would hit its peak just when the book was ready to be released.

The book would be issued officially on December 7, but projecting it couldn't move forward until after the early November election, since the book assumed a Reagan victory. That provided less than a month for pre-publication publicity.

Research into media coverage of similar comprehensive studies revealed that with a few exemptions the Washington press corps is overwhelmingly concerned with domestic and economic policy. Extra effort was needed to focus attention on the foreign policy and national security recommendations. Finally, the report was very complex. It dealt with every cabinet-level department of government, the Environmental Protection Agency, the federal personnel policy, the budget process, military reform, and other issues. Attention had to be focused on many separate recommendations within a very short time frame.

The program involved a layered strategy, combining the following:

1. Early efforts to "place" generic stories about the forthcoming book

2. A series of controlled placements with selected major media outlets (defined internally as the Associated Press, United Press International, the *New York Times*, *Washington Post*, *Washington Times*, and major supplemental wire services

3. A series of targeted news briefings—one for the national security media, a general briefing to formally release the book, and a third briefing that focused on foreign policy

4. Private briefings for major news organizations and individuals, including the *New York Times* editorial board, the *Wall Street Journal* editorial board, *Washington Times* news and editorial management, and conservative writers and columnists

5. Follow-up

The three formal news briefings attracted more than two hundred U.S. and foreign journalists, and the various recommendations generated hundreds of editorials and columns in major publications across the country.

The *New York Times* (February 22, 1985) in its "Washington Talk" column said, "It might be a bit of exaggeration to suggest that President Reagan, in preparing his State of the Union speech . . . used as a role model the Heritage Foundation's *Mandate for Leadership II: Continuing the Conservative Revolution* . . . but while the wording of the president's speech and the foundation's document were different, many of the proposals were strikingly similar." The book was instrumental in shaping policies, some of which were enacted.

To win public support for an idea or cause, you must first believe in the power of ideas and have faith that you can win a public debate. You must also commit whatever staff and resources are needed to accomplish the task; then define victory, not compromise, as your ultimate objective.[1]

---

[1]To consider the value of neutralizing opposition, rather than "winning," *see* Chapter 3.

11
INVESTOR RELATIONS

EUGENE MILLER

Eugene Miller was executive vice-president of United States Gypsum Company and a member of the firm's management committee. He formerly was chairman of the Department of Business and Management at Northeastern Illinois University in Chicago and had his own consulting firm.

Previously, he was senior vice-president, Marketing and Public Relations, of The New York Stock Exchange and a member of its executive Committee. He has also been senior vice-president, Corporate Relations, of CNA Financial Corporation and vice-president, Public Affairs and Communications, of McGraw-Hill. Previously he was associate managing editor of Business Week in New York. He served as a speechwriter to President Dwight Eisenhower and as consultant to Secretary of Commerce Luther Hodges. He is the author of several books and hundreds of magazine articles. For eight years he wrote a syndicated newspaper column on business and finance.

Dr. Miller has a B.S. degree from the Georgia Institute of Technology, an A.B., magna cum laude, from Bethany College, and an M.S. from the Graduate School of Journalism at Columbia University. In addition, he holds an M.B.A. from New York University and a diploma for graduate work in economics from Oxford University, England. In 1969, he received an LL.D. degree from Bethany College.

For some time investor relations quietly maintained its segregated corner in the public relations field. In recent years, however, this highly specialized field has gained vital prominence. Organizations of varying types and sizes—from major corporations to entrepreneurial start-ups—have established or expanded existing investor relations positions and departments to undertake the demand for improved relations with shareholders, security analysts, and the financial media.

At the same time, agencies specializing in investor relations have increased, in direct competition with the general public relations agencies that are also handling investor relations business.

Several catalysts are responsible for this growth, including the following:

- Increased number of corporations whose shares are held by the public and financial institutions

---

Parts of this chapter are adapted from the chapter on financial public relations by Weston Smith in predecessors of this volume. Important contributions have been made by Thomas E. Burke.

- Growing need for businesses to raise capital to meet increasing domestic and foreign competition as well as to finance growth

- High visibility of corporate mergers and acquisitions and the desire for higher stock prices to make these transactions attractive

- Other efforts to thwart takeovers

- Creation of new corporate entities through spinoffs by conglomerates and companies fighting takeovers or restructuring after a takeover

- Sophistication of security analysts and their increasing concentration on large companies

- The sharp rise in the role of institutional investors—mutual funds, pension trusts, banks, insurance companies, university endowments—and their emphasis on disclosure and full valuation of securities

- Demands for better management performance that is translated into higher stock prices

- Much tougher requirements for disclosure of information by the Securities and Exchange Commission, the stock exchanges, and the futures markets. Also, policies set forth by the Financial Accounting Standards Board have established stringent requirements for providing accounting data to stockholders in annual and other reports

- Growing realization of the need for expert guidance, particularly in view of court cases involving the work of investor relations practitioners that have laid down some specific guidelines in certain areas while posing questions still unresolved

- Expanding importance of foreign financial markets for financing American business and industry

Shifting Markets

A number of developments have markedly altered the way American business is financed and the way the financial markets function.

One such major development is increased growth in the trading of stock options. That in turn has been strongly affected by the electronic mechanization of the markets.

In the spring of 1973 the new Chicago Board Options Exchange (CBOE), created by the Chicago Board of Trade (historically the world's leading marketplace for farm commodities), started options trading. It set up a basic market in "call" options.

A call option gives the option holder the right to purchase 100 shares of the underlying security at a given price during a given period. Trading volume on the CBOE on many days has exceeded the trading volume of the American Stock Exchange, the nation's second largest market for stocks. Spurred by the success of the CBOE, a number of stock exchanges—including the American and the Pacific—now feature active option exchange trading programs. In addition to call options, many put options are traded on the option exchanges. These put options are the reverse transaction of call options. Put options give buyers the right to sell the underlying security at a fixed price during a fixed period.

The Chicago Mercantile Exchange, another large commodities marketplace, established a strong financial futures operation as a rival to the CBOE. Together they facilitated greater computerization of securities trading, which the established exchanges in New York had not pursued aggressively.

Availability of instant information and trading, plus the added dimensions of trading in futures as well as securities themselves, led to increased interest in risk arbitrage (in which trades are made to offset up and down risks) and innovations such as program trading (in which certain stock movements automatically set off instant trades). The occasional wide swings in market activity that these sometimes caused led the New York Stock Exchange and the Chicago exchanges to establish "circuit breakers" that go into effect when wide swings occur.

All of these developments accentuated the importance of expert handling of financial information and relationships.

Weak markets of the 1970s, the low price-earnings multiples on many stocks, and declining interest of many individual investors caused many companies to reevaluate their investor relations programs. Previously, it was believed that effective communications of a company's activities, financial results, and strategy would result in the marketplace providing the stock with a fair price-earnings ratio. That idea was shattered in the 1970s when even the most expert investor relations programs were rather ineffective in helping companies improve price-earnings ratios or in attracting individual investors into the marketplace. Now, many companies seek new ways to attract the interest of professional investors, stockbrokers, and individual investors.

Some of this new effort concentrated on getting the companies' stocks listed on foreign exchanges and on stepping up efforts to get foreign investors to know more about their companies. Results of these listings are currently being monitored by companies to determine whether this is a worthwhile activity. Meanwhile, a number of companies have increased their visits abroad to meet with members of foreign financial communities. It has become commonplace for executives of leading companies to regularly visit cities such as Tokyo, London, Edinburgh, Paris, Frankfurt, Geneva, Zurich, and Brussels to meet with members of the financial community. Some companies publish their annual reports in a variety of foreign languages to better communicate with foreign investors and shareholders. Still other companies have stepped up their direct communications with

registered representatives in brokerage firms in the hope of gaining the interest of the representatives who, in turn, can interest investors. These efforts take the form of special meetings of company officials with registered reps, special visits by reps to company headquarters, plants, and offices, and special written communications from the company to these representatives.

However, the stock market plunge of October 1988 and subsequent sharp swings have frightened many individual investors. Institutions, including mutual funds, have become preponderant, at least temporarily, so some companies are not actively pursuing the retail market or its brokers.

Financial Publics

The investor relations department or firm should act as the liaison between the company's top management and the following influential financial groups:

- Stock exchange member firms, customers' brokers, branch office managers
- Members of the security analyst societies and individual analysts
- Unlisted or over-the-counter dealers
- Investment bankers
- Commercial bankers (trust departments)
- Registered investment advisory services
- Insurance companies and pension funds that buy common stocks
- Mutual funds and investment trusts
- Investment counselors
- Trustees of estates and institutions
- Financial statistical organizations
- Investment magazines and financial publications (semiweekly, weekly, biweekly, semimonthly, monthly, and quarterly)
- Large individual shareholders

- Debt rating agencies (Standard and Poor's, Moody's)
- Portfolio managers
- Lender banks
- Foreign markets

Other important audiences to be kept informed include customers and prospects; vendors; insurers; government officials and regulatory agencies; civic leaders; foreign business contacts; management recruits; business media; the stock exchange specialist for the company's stock; and internal groups—the board, management, employees.

Requisites for the Investor Relations Executive

The growth in investor relations has been accompanied by a sharp increase in the demand for qualified personnel. This demand came suddenly and grew faster than general public relations practitioners were prepared for, leaving a gap that has not yet been completely filled. Part of this gap has also been created by the attitude on the part of some that financial public relations is too complex to be handled without a specialized education or a solid financial background.

While there are many areas of common knowledge between general public relations and investor relations, a number of major areas must be mastered in order to handle investor relations effectively.

Basically, the investor relations person must become an expert in these three major areas, in addition to having basic public relations skills.

1. The regulatory guidelines for publicity in the Securities and Exchange Acts of 1933 and 1934, as well as the disclosure requirements of the national stock exchanges, the

over-the-counter market, and court cases relating to them

2. The analysis and evaluation of financial statements
3. Very detailed knowledge of the business activities of the company or client

The scope of responsibilities and functions of investor relations includes the following:

- *Liaison with executive management:*
   1. Board of Directors (primarily through the board chairperson)
   2. Executive Committee
   3. Finance Committee
   4. Key officials (president, vice-presidents, chief financial officer, secretary, and controller)
   5. Certain department heads (Sales, Research, Accounting, etc.)
   6. Directors of public relations, industrial relations, employee relations
- *Working with security analysts:*
   1. Identifying key analysts interested in the company; maintaining up-to-date lists
   2. Surveying analysts to determine the extent of their knowledge of the company and their attitudes toward the company
   3. Arranging for individual analysts to meet the company's executives
   4. Visits of the chief executive officer, chief financial officer, and others with major financial institutions when in their cities
   5. Arranging for management to speak before various analysts' societies, including specialized and general groups
   6. Preparing and distributing informational materials to analysts such as statistical summaries, news reports, special surveys, videotapes, etc.
   7. Arranging tours of company plants, research facilities, and headquarters for analysts' groups

8. Maintaining continuous liaison with analysts to ensure an open channel of communications

9. Setting up special luncheons and dinners for analysts

- *"Stock watch" activity:*

  1. Maintaining constant watch on action of company's stock on markets

  2. Observing activities and stock action of competitors

  3. Monitoring rumors and other information about stock accumulation, arbitrageurs' activity, etc.

  4. Informing board and executives when anything of potential interest occurs

- *Preparation of corporation annual report and quarterly earnings statements* (explained at length in accompanying text)

- *Other stockholder publications:*

  1. Quarterly earnings statements converted into newsletters, digest booklets, and "stockholder magazines"

  2. Folders interpreting company policies, proposed changes, advertising techniques, public relations creeds, etc.

  3. Dividend "stuffers" or inserts (sent without extra postage with quarterly or semiannual dividend checks)

  4. Reprints of speeches and articles by officials of company

  5. Arranging postmeeting report to be printed and sent to absent stockholders

  6. Biographical digests of executive officers and members of board of directors

  7. Calendars, almanacs, diaries, product directories, recipe lists, etc.

  8. Information found on the company's Web site, if it has one

- *Financial and educational advertising:*

  1. Cooperation with financial executives, advertising manager, and advertising agency

  2. Financial advertising (dividend announcements, redemption notices, annual meeting call, requests for bids on new securities, etc.)

  3. Institutional advertising (annual report and quarterly statement advertisements; announcement of mergers and acquisitions; opening of new plants, departments, and sales territories; change in corporate name; etc.)

  4. The media that cover the company and its industry

- *Conducting stockholder surveys:*

  1. To determine nature of distribution of shares (geographically, average number of shares held, sexes, age levels, occupations, length of time stock is held, etc.)

  2. Readership of corporation annual reports and quarterly earnings statements (request for suggestions as to content and handling of financial statistics, criticisms, changes, additions, etc.)

  3. Other purposes (utilizing stockholder lists for opinion surveys—all names or a selected sampling—to determine majority preferences, to test new products, to select trade names, etc.)

- *Financial publicity:*

  1. Uncovering and developing news of interest to stockholders through liaison with key executives within the corporation

  2. Contacting and cultivating friendships with financial editors of press services, newspapers, magazines, trade publications, radio, TV, and cable TV

  3. Directing the preparation of financial press releases (annual and interim news releases, dividend declarations, manage-

ment changes, operating statistics, security redemptions, financing, mergers, executives' speeches and articles, proxy fights, etc.)

4. Arranging media interviews with company executives

5. Preparing and executing defense against unfair treatment by media (*See* Chapter 21.)

6. Interviewing newspaper financial reporters and feature writers for financial and business publications and TV programs to determine their needs

7. When called on to do so, supplying requested information to the media, statistical agencies, investment services, financial analysts, investment trusts, brokerage houses, investment banking firms, and others

• *Stockholder correspondence:*

1. Letters of welcome to new stockholders (signed by the company chief executive officer)

2. Answering inquiries for financial and other appropriate information

3. Proper treatment of complaints from both large and small investors

4. Letters of thanks for mailing in signed proxies

5. Special form letters covering exchanges of shares in splitups, stock dividends, and scrip certificates; explaining financing, options, and changes in dividend policy (inauguration, increases, reductions, and omissions)

6. Monitoring lists of shareholders—including making sure that E-mail and fax addresses are included when available—can be invaluable in the case of an unfriendly takeover effort

7. Foreign investors and the foreign financial community

• *Planning the annual meeting of stockholders:*

1. Organizing a program (schedule of routine and extra features)

2. Selection of place of meeting

3. Preparations for answers to questions and criticisms

4. Serving refreshments at meeting, or consideration of a luncheon or dinner in company restaurant or cafeteria or at a club or hotel

5. Dealing with representatives of the media

6. Consideration of closed-circuit TV coverage to reach stockholders in other parts of the country

7. Consideration of methods for effectively handling vocal stockholders, including a "War Book" that details various contingencies, responsibilities to be assigned, questions likely to be asked, actions to be considered, facilities needed, etc.

8. Consideration of producing and sending out video cassettes to stockholders

• *Regional meetings of stockholders:*

1. Selecting cities where company has largest numbers of shareholders

2. Making reservations at hotels in accordance with expected audiences

3. Providing for slides or motion pictures; videotapes; exhibits of products

4. Serving refreshments (a product of the company if in food or beverage industry)

5. Distributing samples, booklets, calendars, or other souvenirs

• *Special services to stockholders:*

1. Locating dealer nearest to stockholder for company's merchandise

2. Offering gift packages at special prices for Christmas

3. Distributing "dividend" of sample of new product when appropriate

4. Assisting stockholders in the sale of large blocks of shares

5. Arranging for visits to executive offices, factories, branches, etc.

(Activities in defense against proxy fights and tender offers are treated later in this chapter.)

As the extent of knowledge and professionalism required has grown, most firms have designated an executive as a specialist in investor relations, often with the status of an officer. In many cases the individual in charge of investor relations reports directly to the chief executive officer.

In 1969 the National Investor Relations Institute was formed as the professional society embracing those doing investor relations work. Its objectives were to improve corporate investor relations through a variety of functions. Its ranks include the investor relations managers or officers of many major U.S. corporations, as well as general and investor relations counseling firms.

NIRI has earned national attention by serving as a spokesman for investor relations professionals and their companies on a wide variety of topics, including proposed rules and regulations on disclosure, tender offers, and the like. NIRI representatives appear before the SEC to voice the organization's position and testify at congressional hearings. The organization holds a major fall meeting with prominent personalities in government, business, and the securities industry as speakers. It also holds other meetings, directs the NIRI Research Foundation, and publishes a regular newsletter that discusses topics of special interest to its members. NIRI is headquartered at 8045 Leesburg Pike, Vienna, VA 22182.

Unlike general public relations practice, investor relations activities are often dictated or shaped by certain legal or regulatory requirements. (*See* Chapter 48.) For instance, the Securities and Exchange Commission has specific guidelines for publicity activities during the period a company has a registration statement for the sale of its shares outstanding. In another area, companies listed on either the New York Stock Exchange, or one of the other exchanges, or NASDAQ must meet specific obligations for disseminating required information to stockholders and the general public.

Without the aid of a solid background in reading financial statements, an investor relations person would find it almost impossible to communicate with two major publics—security analysts and institutional investors. An investor relations person without some knowledge of accounting and corporate finance trying to discuss cash flow with a security analyst is somewhat similar to a blind person trying to discuss the relative merits of the color red versus green.

The Public Relations Society of America, 33 Irving Place, New York NY 10003; the American Management Association, 135 W. 50th Street, New York, NY 10020; National Investor Relations Institute, 8045 Leesburg Pike, Vienna, VA 22182; and several other professional organizations offer seminar courses in investor relations. Adult education and university courses are also available in the more technical areas, such as securities analysis, accounting, and corporate finance.

The investor relations practitioner also can easily launch a self-education program, using numerous easy-to-read articles available on the technical aspects. Some suggested readings are included in the bibliography of this book.

At a minimum, a self-education program should include a study of accounting terms and procedures, the analysis of corporate financial statements, the 1933 and 1934 Securities and Exchange Acts, a review of general corporate financial policy, and a review of stock market operations and procedures as well as a thorough study of the disclosure policies of the New York and the American Stock Exchanges.

Program Development

Before you implement your investor relations plans and programs, it is essential to first gain a thorough understanding of your target audience. The first step involves research and, whenever possible, establishing key personal contacts.

Next it is vital to know everything important about the company. Providing incorrect information or appearing vague and uncertain when asked questions undermines credibility.

The most effective means of acquiring the necessary knowledge and at the same time laying a foundation for a broad program is to build a series of profiles describing the corporation's major aspects. These profiles should be as detailed and accurate as possible, rather than a mere thumbnail sketch of the corporation. They will be valuable in dealings with analysts, since they will put all of the vital facts and statistics at your fingertips.

The most important profile would be an outline of the corporation's competitive position. This should include an analysis of the company's:

- Products and services—their features, benefits, and weaknesses
- Markets (overall, niche, vertical, etc.) and corresponding marketing strategies and methods
- Industry position—a competitive comparison with similar organizations within the industry
- Sales history
- Response to various economic conditions
- Research and development strengths and weaknesses, particularly with regard to new

products or services targeted for marketing in the near future
- Production capabilities

Some estimate should also be made of how much products add to the public's recognition of the company as an investment vehicle. Consider how the recognition of products such as Coca-Cola, Xerox machines, Polaroid cameras, IBM computers, DuPont nylon, and Campbell's soups helped these companies establish recognition as investment possibilities.

Financial profile

A profile of the company's financial position should also be constructed. Particular attention should be given to relating the company's history not only in terms of dollars and cents, assets and liabilities, or just sales and earnings, but also in terms of return on invested capital, profit margins, debt-equity ratio, inventory turnover, cost of sales, cost of production, and so forth.

This type of analysis should also reveal the reasons for the company's earnings figures, rather than just relate them. For instance, it is one thing to say that a corporation earned $2.50 a share and quite another to say that the company earned $2.50 a share and at the same time increased its profit margin per unit of sales because of production efficiencies. This becomes more significant when comparing the firm with other corporations. A company increasing its profit margin by more efficient operations is by far a more attractive investment than a similar company with the same sales or better and the same price-earnings level. Similarly, there is a considerable difference between earnings gains generated internally and those generated by acquisition.

A profile should also be made of the company's securities. An investor relations person who does not have an intimate knowledge of the market performance of the company's stock, its distribution of shareowners, including major holdings of institutions and individuals, or the performance of the stock under varying economic and market conditions is like a salesperson trying to discuss a product about which he knows nothing. Here again, the market performance of the stock should be compared with other companies in the same industry. An additional step in this initial phase of study would be to review security analysts' recommendations and attitudes concerning the stock over the most recent year.

Management profile

Most corporate annual reports cite the company's management and its employees as its most valuable assets, but in terms of describing a corporation these most valuable assets are often overlooked. True, it is difficult to quantify good management or even to describe it in some cases. However, administrators' performances, like stock prices, can be charted. For instance, an electronics corporation whose director of research has made a significant contribution to the industry, such as development of the laser, is certainly in a better competitive position from a research standpoint than others in the same field. A management profile should incorporate such vital data as experience, education, age, diversified abilities, major contributions to the corporation, and industry achievements.

A final step would be to determine the company's present image among security analysts and in the financial press. A brief survey should be made of analysts who cover the industry to get their current views of the company and to determine how well the company is getting its corporate message across. A review of press coverage would include discussions with key financial editors and a review of press clippings to determine how much attention the company has received and what aspects of its performance received the

most attention. A broader evaluation of the company's image might be gained by employing a professional public opinion sampling organization. (*See* Chapter 18.)

A review of the company's internal public relations policies should also be made to determine what procedures are followed in disseminating information, how confidential matters are handled, how SEC and NYSE or American Stock Exchange rules are policed, what guidelines must be followed in speaking with the press, who acts as the company's spokesperson, how analyst visits and interviews are handled, and so forth. If the company has never had an active investor relations program, policies may have to be revised or new guidelines developed.

Four basic groups

All publicly held companies must cultivate confidence and build prestige among these basic publics:

1. Existing registered shareholders
2. The investing public, including those with shares in brokers' names
3. The financial community, including bankers, brokers, investment advisers, trustees of estates, security analysts, mutual funds, insurance companies, pension funds, and others who influence opinion of securities
4. The general business and business-interested public whose attitudes greatly affect the acceptance of a company's securities, as well as its products

Shareholder Communications

Maintaining a good relationship with shareholders is not only sound public relations practice, but also sound financial management. A solid base of loyal shareholders is highly advantageous for any company. A number of corporations have managed to fend off takeover bids in part by appealing to this loyal shareholder base. McGraw-Hill is an example.

Stockholder communications takes a more direct approach than communications with the general public. There are many ways to communicate with stockholders—newsletters, magazines, quarterly reports, special letters, annual reports, company biographies, the Internet, and booklets describing the company's products and operations.

More imaginative communications are being employed increasingly. Some corporations have produced annual reports on CD-ROM and even in Braille. CNA Financial sends out audio recordings of its annual reports for people with impaired vision. Dayton-Hudson has published an original pop art poster suitable for framing with the quarterly report printed on the back. A number of companies issue annual reports especially written for employees.

Types of annual reports

For many years annual reports were merely historical documents, consisting of a brief statement from the president summarizing the year's events, and the financial statement that was meant to be glanced at, then filed. Today's annual reports, however, have taken on the appearance of high-quality magazines and in a growing number of cases could be classified as promotional pieces. Some are made available on computer disks and CD-ROMS.

Many of the better annual reports employ a theme that communicates the corporation's business philosophy and goals rather than just facts and figures. These reports not only explain how the corporation earns its money and how it has met its challenges in the past year, but, more importantly, the company's business philosophy, its long-range goals, how it intends to achieve these goals, and what has been done during the year to accomplish these goals. Some themes of annual reports in recent years have been productivity, quality control, inflation, cost reduction, capital spending, and corporate strategy.

Graphics are used to underscore the theme of the report and make it more attractive and easier to read. A number of international corporations distribute annual reports in several foreign languages.

There are three schools of thought on what level of sophistication an annual report should follow. One school believes that the report should be simple and to the point and not confuse people with a lot of facts and figures. Another believes the annual report should merely convey the financial results for the year with no attempt to explain their meaning. The third offers a compromise between these two extremes. The complexity of financial statements can be eased considerably by working into the text an interpretation of financial statements explaining the significance of gains and losses in the various items in the statements.

Some companies publish comprehensive booklets of financial information and make them available to stockholders who request them. Nearly all companies with a substantial number of stockholders make available on request the 10-K reports they prepare for the SEC. Some incorporate these into the annual reports that go to all stockholders.

Preparing a well-balanced annual report

While the corporation annual report is now regarded as the keystone of the investor relations program, it is also being accepted as one of the cornerstones of a well-rounded public relations plan. Before deciding on the variety of the content or the style and character of the format, it is advisable for those preparing the annual report to acquire some knowledge of the quality or intelligence level of the readership. (*See* Figure 11.1, page 172.)

The large majority of shareholders have little or no training in finance, accountancy, or bookkeeping. So all materials intended for them must be clear and readily understandable by the average reader. If sophisticated and technical material is to be provided for security analysts and others, it should go into separate documents or, at least, be contained within separate sections of shareholder reports where it will not unduly confuse the primary recipients.

A key point is that the annual report is a portrait of the character and outlook of the company's management—the portrait most people get to see. Companies that spend millions of dollars on visual identity systems, corporate advertising, and other programs all aimed at portraying the company as warm, progressive, and public-spirited often undermine these efforts in the annual report.

When developing an annual report, keep the following guidelines in mind:

1. Objectively determine the company's distinctive character. For example, if your company is an oil company, how does it differ from other oil companies?

2. Determine how the traits of that distinctive character can be projected to the audience so it will be a credible reality in people's minds.

3. Plan the annual report as an entity commensurate with the distinctive character that is established. Theme, cover, writing, artwork all should be planned together to make up a consistent whole.

4. The writing especially should reflect the company's personality. Don't make the text sound dull and stodgy.

5. Make sure the artwork and the copy carry the same tone. Often they shout different things about the company: For example, the artwork is avant garde while the writing is conservative.

6. Make sure the graphic treatment and artwork project the character of the company and not of the photographer or artist. Avoid art for art's sake. The purpose of the report is to communicate the company's information.

7. Follow the other rules of good communications, including attracting readers through their interests. Make your message interesting to them in the headlines, captions, and the way it is written.

8. It is usually best to have one person do the final rewrite. Don't have a report read as though many people were involved, each with his or her own style of writing and approach. The final result should be completed on one talented individual's keyboard to give it a feeling of cohesiveness rather than of a series of articles stitched together.

The SEC has established some requirements for the format and contents of the annual report:

1. Financial statements and footnotes should be printed in type at least ten points in size.

2. Differences in accounting principles from those used in other company documents must be explained in a footnote.

3. Audited financial statements for the past two years must be included, as well as a five-year summary of operations and a management analysis of this summary.

4. A "brief description of the business" that indicates the general nature and scope of operations must be included.

1996 ANNUAL REPORT SCHEDULE

Date	Action
Monday, June 17	Planning begins with initial brainstorming of theme
Tuesday, July 16	Designer presents initial concepts
August	Design refinement
Thursday, August 29	Sign-off by management
September–November	Photography
Mid-December	Review photography needs
Friday, December 13	Printer selected/reserve press dates/place paper order
Sunday, December 29	*Fiscal year ends*
Week of January 6	Receive templates from designer for theme section Do initial layout with photos and draft copy of theme section
Wednesday, January 15	Proofs of theme section to VPs/CEOs/GMs
Friday, January 17	Complete photography
Monday, January 20	Info for charts and graphs
Wednesday, January 22	Edits to theme section
Thursday, January 23	*Earnings released*
Friday, January 24	Copy for management letter and proof of grid to Corporate VPs
Tuesday, January 28	Revised letter copy for flow in
Wednesday, January 29	Senior management photo (drop dead date)
Thursday, January 30	Revised proofs of cover, letter, theme section, and grid to group heads
Monday, February 3	Final 4/c photography to printer
Monday, February 3	Financials due (to include typeset income statement, balance sheet, cash flows, business segments, notes, quarterly results, management and auditors' report, and shareholders' equity)
Friday, February 7	Release cover to printer Edits to letter, theme section, and grid
Tuesday, February 11	Receive final randoms for color approval Board mailing (to include typeset income statement, balance sheet, cash flows, business segments, notes, quarterly results, management and auditors' report, and shareholders' equity)
Thursday, February 13	Review color laser proofs for front of book
Friday, February 14	Receive cover proofs from printer
Monday, February 17	Release disk for 4/c front of book; return cover proofs to printer
Tuesday, February 18	*Board Meeting*
Thursday, February 20	Review color laser proofs for back of book
Friday, February 21	Receive bluelines and cromalins from printer for 4/c front of book
Monday, February 24	Release disk to printer for 2/c back of book
Tuesday, February 25	Return bluelines and cromalins to printer for cover and 4/c front of book
Thursday, February 27	Receive bluelines and cromalins for 2/c back of book
Monday, March 3	Return bluelines and cromalins to printer for 2/c back of book
Monday–Thursday, March 3–6	Annual Report on press
Wednesday, March 19	Annual Report ready for pick-up/shipment from printer

Figure 11.1 This timetable for preparing the Tribune Company's 1996 annual report itemizes all the stages necessary for producing an annual report electronically. *Courtesy* Chicago Tribune.

5. Breakdowns of sales and earnings for various lines of products or categories of business must be listed in the same form in which they appear in the 10-K report to the SEC.

6. All directors and officers must be named with their principal business affiliations and the nature of the organization for which they work.

7. The principal market for each class of the company's voting securities must be named, with the quarterly high and low prices for each of these securities for the past two years and the quarterly dividends paid in the past two years.

8. Copies of the 10-K report must be offered free to any stockholder in a prominent notice.

9. Companies are required to take affirmative action to make sure an annual report and proxy reaches each stockholder whose securities are held by a broker or other firm.

These requirements do not detract from the need to use creativity and excellent communications techniques to make the report an effective document.

When the annual report brochure is humanized to a point where it will be understood by the small investor, the management finds that the same booklet will serve the needs and requirements of its employees and of many others who have an interest in the corporation's affairs or who are important as opinion-forming groups and should be given an opportunity to read the report. Many companies now recognize that millions of homes as well as businesses have computers. They are also producing annual reports on disks and CD-ROMs, available upon request.

Some idea of the different groups to which the modernized annual report is being sent is presented in the following section.

Expanded Distribution of Annual Reports

The following contacts—in addition to stockholders and employees—should receive the annual report. A cover letter from the president should be created for each separate group and distributed with the annual report.

National Level

Associated Groups

Suppliers of Raw Materials, etc.
Agents and Representatives
Dealers and Jobbers
Distributors
Retailers (Chain Stores)
Customers
Trade Associations

Press, Television, and Radio

Big City Newspapers
  Financial Editor
  Business News Editor
  Selected Financial Writers
  Editorial Writers
Press Services
Financial Publications
Journals of Commerce
Business Magazines
Selected Trade Papers
Accountancy Journals
Advertising Publications
Washington Newsletters
Public Relations Publications
Women's Magazines (if appropriate)
Feature Writers and Columnists
News Syndicates

Radio News Rooms
Selected Radio Commentators
Television Newsrooms and Commentators
Foreign Press Services and Newspapers

Financial

Big City Commercial Banks
Big City Trust Companies
Investment Bankers
Stock Exchange Member Firms
Investment Counselors
Statistical Agencies
Financial Services
Investment Trust Executives
Insurance Companies
Credit Agencies

Governmental Officials

SEC, ICC, FTC, FCC, etc.
Department of Commerce
Department of Labor
Other Selected Cabinet Members
Library of Congress
U.S. Senators (all or selected)
Representatives (all or selected)
Governor of State Where Incorporated
Secretary of State Where Incorporated
States Where Plants Are Located

Other

Big City Public Libraries
Leading Universities and Colleges
Schools of Business Administration
Schools of Commerce and Finance
Philanthropic Institutions

On Request—Through Paid Advertising

Big City Newspapers
Financial Publications
Journals of Commerce
Business Magazines
Selected Trade Papers
Selected National Magazines
Selected Women's Publications
Labor Publications

Community Level

Associated Groups

Suppliers of Raw Materials, etc.
Union Leaders
Employment Agencies
Transportation Services
Chamber of Commerce Members
Rotary, Kiwanis, Lions Clubs

Press, Television, and Radio

Editors of Local Newspapers
Editors of County Weeklies
Suburban and Community Magazines
Local TV and Radio Stations
Chamber of Commerce Paper, etc.

Financial

Local National Banks
Local Savings Banks
Savings & Loan Associations
Brokerage Office Managers
Small Loan Associations

Opinion Leaders

Heads of Local Business Firms
Judges and Police Officers
The Clergy
Professional
  Physicians
  Dentists
  Hospital Directors
Offices of
  Fraternal Societies
  Women's Clubs
  Welfare Organizations
Parent-Teacher Associations
Principals and Teachers of
  Grade Schools
  High Schools
  Business Schools
  Trade Schools
  Colleges and Universities
Leaders of Youth Groups
  Boy and Girl Groups
  YMCA and YWCA

Junior Achievement, Inc.
Sunday Schools

Municipal or Township Officials

Mayor or Borough President
Members of Board of Supervisors
Department Heads

Other

Local Libraries
Movie Theater Operators
Barber and Beauty Shop Managers
Druggists
Gas Station Operators
Chain Store Managers

On Request—Through Paid Advertising

Local Newspapers
County Weeklies
Community Magazines
Suburban Publications
House Organs or Tabloids
Church and Fraternal
  Publications
  Programs
Local Labor Union Publications

The physical requirements, trim size, and number of pages of the annual report will depend on the following factors:

1. The type of industry represented (manufacturing, distribution, transportation, etc.)

2. The size of the corporation (sales volume, total assets, number of stockholders and employees)

3. The readership to which the annual report will be sent (whether only stockholders, or if it also will be seen by employees and others)

4. Desired life of the annual report (whether it is a year-end review to be read and discarded or a "yearbook" to be retained for

reference and sent to new stockholders and employees throughout the year)

Generally speaking, most annual reports will vary from sixteen pages and cover to forty-eight pages or more, plus cover—multiples of eight pages are the most economical to print. The most popular trim size is letter size—8½″ × 11″ or thereabouts—which will fit in the standard filing cabinet or fold in half to fit into the coat pocket.

In a typical report about 50 to 60 percent of the contents are devoted to editorial content and financial statistical tabulations. The other half of the booklet consists of charts or pictorial graphics, maps, photographs, and other appropriate decorations distributed throughout the pages to lend variety to the text without giving the impression of a catalogue.

In most cases reports should be in at least two colors, and four or more colors are frequently used. In the case of larger corporations with fifty thousand or more stockholders and employees, a generous supply of color in type and full-color reproductions of illustrations and photographs are warranted because the unit cost per booklet is small when the printing run is large. When only two colors (black and one primary color) are utilized, a three-color effect can be obtained by using tint blocks or reverse plates and various patterns of Ben Days for both main headings and subheads.

Lacking an anniversary or some distinctive aspect of the company to be projected, a keynote might be some outstanding event of the past year that can be dramatized: a new product or service; expansion of plants, properties, or distribution facilities; establishment of a new research laboratory; achievement of management or employees recognized by an outside authority; competitive position of the company in its industry; the new philosophy of the management in serving the public

USAA
Annual Progress Report
1995

The Sacrifices of Military Service

ANNUAL REPORT—USAA

Figure 11.2 A theme for an annual report emphasizes an aspect of the company that it wants to get across to investors and the financial community. The United Services Automobile Association (USAA) gave tribute to the sacrifices of military service in its annual report for 1995, the year membership eligibility for the association was extended to enlisted military personnel. *Reprinted with permission of USAA, copyright © 1996. Cover photo: AP/Wide World Photos.*

interest; introduction of a creed or code of public relations principles, and the like. In its 1995 annual report, for example, USAA celebrated the Board of Directors' decision to extend the company's products and services to enlisted military personnel. (*See* Figure 11.2.)

Outline and continuity of annual reports

The content of any corporation annual report will follow a basic pattern, but the arrangement of the material can be adjusted to suit the preferences of the management. In humanizing the report, it has been found a good policy to feature the narrative in the front portion of the booklet, which lends itself to dramatization by means of photographs, pictorial graphics, maps, and other appropriate illustrations. Key financial data are usually provided in the first two pages, with most of the statistical data appearing in the middle or latter portion of the report. Thus, the reader who will not study the comparative financial statements, because of lack of interest or inability to comprehend statistical tabulations, will gather the information sought in reading the text and perusing the illustrations and charts. Featuring key points in larger type in the margins also helps the skimmer get the main points. Subheads are also desirable where large copy blocks would give the appearance of a gray mass. All headings, as much as possible, should convey action rather than just serve as labels: "Ongoing Development of Manpower" is better than "Personnel and Labor Relations."

The following outline is suitable for companies operating in almost any industry and can be employed with applicable additions and variations.

Cover Design—Front Cover:
   Name of corporation and title "Annual Report" or "Yearbook"

Year of report if calendar year—otherwise the full fiscal year ending
Illustration, photograph, or pattern appropriate to the corporation or the industry it represents (*See* Figure 11.3, page 179.)

Frontispiece—First Right-Hand Page or First Two Pages:
   Name of corporation and statement "Annual Report" or "Yearbook"
   Addresses for executive offices, general offices, or other offices to which recipient can write for further information
   Year of the report
   Table of Contents, Foreword, or Credo
   Suitable decoration or illustration

Narrative—Each Page Illustrated Differently with Photograph or Chart:
   President's and/or Chairman's Letter (usually only two or three pages)
   Highlights—comparative round-number operating statistics
   Departmentalized Summaries:
      Financial results interpreted on per share basis
      Distribution of gross revenue or the "sales dollar"
      Trend of sales, earnings, and dividends
      Simplified balance sheet—trend of net current assets
      Prices or rates—policies or program
      Research and technology
      Advertising and public relations
      Improvement of facilities
      Employment (hours and wages)
      Management development
      Products or services (improvements, diversification, or new)
      Competitive position
      Industry situation

Taxation and cost of government
Legislation affecting the company
Government regulation
Raw materials and inventories
Utilization of productive capacity
Changes in capitalization—
  financing and refinancing
Trend in number of stockholders
Important events of the year
Discussion of future prospects
International activities

Financial Tabulations and Other Statistics and Reference Material:
Comparative consolidated balance
  sheet, indicating increase or decline
  or percentage change in each item
Profit and Loss Statement
Comparative Income Accounts
Results breakdown by division or
  product line
In conglomerate companies, results by
  segment
Tabulation of operating statistics for
  ten years or more
Tabulations of financial position and
  allied statistics
Footnotes to Accounts
Independent Auditors' Report
Study of long-term debt, if any
Statistics on number of stockholders,
  the distribution of shares
  geographically, by size of holdings,
  classes, sexes, etc.
Employment statistics—average
  number per year, total man-hours
  worked, annual payroll, average
  weekly hours and earnings
Management listing: board of directors,
  executive committee, finance
  committee, officers—each identified
  with outside connection or title of
  position with corporation
List of products, subsidiaries, branch
  offices, routes, etc.
Pension costs

Explanation of changes in inventory
  policy
Quarterly data on prices of stock and of
  inventories
Management analysis of the summary
  of operations
Impact of inflation on company's assets
Number of employees in company's
  Employee Stock Ownership Plan
Major pending litigation

Annual report graphics

There is an almost unlimited opportunity to interpret every phase of a corporation's operations and records by means of a pictorial graphic or line-and-bar chart. Caution must be exercised to maintain the simplicity of each chart by including in one chart only related data and not attempting to cover too many kinds of statistics at one time. Complicated charts often defeat their purpose by confusing the reader, creating the risk of misunderstanding when trend lines or characters are not clearly identified. All captions, subheadings, and numbers must be in type large enough for an older person to see without a magnifying glass. Care should be taken in any photo reduction not to make any of the data undecipherable.

The following statistics are suitable for graphic presentation. The list is not all inclusive, but will serve as a guide and suggest other appropriate ideas.

Financial:

Operating Results—Trend of sales; distribution of sales dollar; trend of prices or rates; trend of earnings and dividends; export or foreign trade operations; trend of production by products or various services; trend of unfilled orders; etc.

Operating Expenses—Trend of cost of raw materials; trend of wages; trend of taxes; trend of advertising expenditures; trend of equipment replacement; trend of bond

THE SHARPER IMAGE®

Growing through multiple concepts.

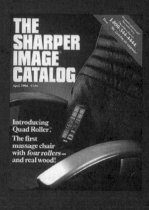

Sharper Image Corporation
Annual Report 1995

Figure 11.3 The Sharper Image emphasizes its multiple marketing concepts and profit centers by showing catalog covers and a web page on the cover of its annual report. *Courtesy The Sharper Image.*

interest; trend of dividends; trend of earnings reinvested in business; etc.

Balance Sheet Interpretation—Pictorial balance sheet in form of scales; trend of total assets; trend of working capital (net current assets); trend of inventories; trend of net worth or book value; etc.

Factual:

Products or Services—Uses; other industries served; by lines of different products; trends of distribution; per capita consumption; dates of introduction of new and improved products; etc.

Organization—Parent company in relation to subsidiaries; flow of operations in the making of primary product; flow of management authority from president through executive officers to department heads or branch managers; etc.

Employees—Trend of average number employed; trend of hourly or weekly wages by averages; accident and safety records; cost of benefits (pensions, group insurance, etc.); analysis of length of service, age groups, sexes; etc.

Stockholders—Trend of the average number; trend of average holdings by classes (individuals, fiduciaries, mutual funds, insurance companies, charitable and educational, brokers, and others); trend of holdings by number of shares; etc.

Maps—Locating plants, branches, sales offices, distributors, stores, dealers, and consumers; indicating sources of raw materials; showing routes; geographical distribution of stockholders; export and import lines; etc.

The selection of appropriate photographs is simplified by relating the picture to the paragraph it is intended to illustrate. An accumulation of both news and commercial photographs during the year will usually build up an ample supply from which to choose. Larger corporations can well afford to hire a special photographer to take a series of views of their plants, operations, and products, and thus build a morgue that can be drawn on for several years. But such pictures should not be "head-on" shots—they should be taken with some imagination, possibly from an angle or showing action.

An annual report illustrated with carefully retouched commercial photographs of plants and products provides the appearance of a sales catalogue and loses effectiveness. The buildings can be photographed at different seasons of the year or with the employees flooding in or out. Products should be shown in the actual process of manufacture or in use after they have been sold, with the worker or user in action.

Each year more annual reports illustrate the chief executive's letter with an informal photograph of the executive, often at the desk or on an inspection tour around the plant. A picture of the board of directors in session provides an excellent opportunity to identify the management and executive officers. Many reports today run a series of individual photographs of the board members and executive officers with a thumbnail biographical sketch of each. On occasion, the death of a major official will call for a photograph and obituary notice with the expression of regret by the president at the loss of this member of the official family.

In recent years many reports have included actual samples of products "tipped" in on the pages or inside covers—such as swatches of fabrics, carton board, and dress patterns. Other reports have utilized their products as the cover, including wallpaper, boxboard, and aluminum ink.

Additional Stockholder Publications

Some companies, such as Weyerhaeuser Company, issue summary annual reports that are brief and simple.

Although the annual report is the primary means of keeping the stockholder informed, corporations that publish quarterly earnings statements also can use a number of techniques to present information during the remainder of the year. Stereotyped quarterly reports can be converted into attractive bulletins, newsletters, or digest booklets edited in news style and illustrated with charts and photographs.

A number of companies produce fairly lengthy, high-quality shareowner magazines three or four times a year as a supplement to the annual report.

Corporations paying regular quarterly dividends have the opportunity to mail a "stuffer" or insert to stockholders with the dividend check as a "free ride" on the same postage. These stuffers sometimes are combined with the quarterly earnings report, but when the dates do not coincide, they serve as an extra contact with shareholders. Such inserts have been employed to introduce new products, announce executive appointments or promotions, and to provide a return coupon requesting a sample of a product. The conventional use of dividend stuffers is to provide a form for a stockholder's change of address.

A corporate "Fact Book" that is sent to security analysts and others in the financial community is used by a number of companies to consolidate into one publication many facts about the firm. Some are in the form of computer disks and CD-ROMS.

Annual Shareholder Meetings

The annual meeting of the shareholders is the one function of the corporation during the year where the investor can meet the management face to face and hear the report of stewardship from the lips of the president. This is the shareholders' forum, but they will

not or cannot attend in large numbers if the meeting requires a long and expensive journey. Hence, some managements bring the meeting to the stockholders by conducting meetings in various larger cities or where there is the largest concentration of holdings. Some companies provide free transportation to meetings held at the "corporate office" when it is located in a small town that is inconvenient to reach.

The modern stockholder meeting is no longer a stuffy affair with hard seats, poor ventilation, and bad lighting. Progressive managements usually conduct both their regular and regional meetings in the ballrooms of the better hotels and often a luncheon is provided. Features of these meetings include demonstration of a new product, showing a motion picture or slide show or videotape, and distributing samples and appropriate literature. A discussion period is provided at which any stockholder can "take the floor" and offer his or her compliments, suggestions, or criticisms. There is a genuine informality about many of these annual meetings that makes the stockholder feel at home and an integral participant in the activities of the corporation.

With the sharp increases in numbers of stockholders, geographic broadening of ownership, and such movements as investment clubs and Employee Stock Ownership Plans, some large companies have found it useful to arrange for closed-circuit telecasting of their annual meetings into large halls in major cities across the country. Showings are set up throughout the companies' facilities for the many employees who own stock due to expanding employee stock ownership plans. In this way, they permit thousands of additional stockholders to "attend" the meeting.

For a number of years there have also been regional meetings for shareholders, held on a schedule that can fit the needs of company executives. However, these are so demanding of the officials' time and often so anticlimactic, following the annual meeting at which the news and discussion were timely, that they have not proven suitable for most companies. Closed-circuit television appears to be more satisfactory for all concerned. General Electric Company has used such a service.

Vocal stockholders

Corporations have had to handle the problem of vocal stockholders since the first publicly owned company held its first annual meeting. Regardless of how well management has performed during a particular year or how comprehensive or accurate its policies are, one or another stockholder will be critical, and sometimes actually become belligerent about some point.

Since stockholders are the owners of the company, they are entitled to be critical and to review management's actions. However, they do not have the right to disrupt the orderly flow of business at a stockholders' meeting. This type of action deprives other stockholders of an equally valuable right.

Management's role in these situations should be to ensure that all stockholders receive equal treatment. By answering stockholders' questions and by either accepting their criticisms or showing that these criticisms are baseless, the chairman or president presiding at the meeting may be able to satisfy both sides, thereby avoiding unnecessary interruptions.

Each situation is different and requires different handling. However, some ground rules can be applied.

1. Be patient—allow stockholders to state their views or ask their questions.

2. Be polite—avoid abrupt, flip, or sarcastic answers.

3. Answer all questions fully and clearly. If it appears that a point has been misunderstood or completely missed, go back and repeat it.

4. Respond to all queries from the floor. Do not attempt to avoid a stockholder who is known to be openly critical by refusing to recognize him or her.

5. Anticipate the criticisms that may arise and prepare to meet them, preparing slides or film clips if necessary. Have a "War Book" prepared with answers to all questions that may be asked, plus pointers on how to meet various developments in the meeting.

6. Utilize the full executive staff in answering questions. If it is a financial matter, the chief executive officer may wish to have the vice-president of finance or the treasurer supply the answer. This may also be useful if one answer is insufficient.

7. Do not allow personalities or sarcasm from the floor to dictate the content or tone of your response.

8. As a last resort, be prepared to evict unruly people. This should be done calmly, with a minimum of force, and as quietly as possible. Explain to the audience that the action is taken in stewardship of their interests as company owners.

A number of corporate annual meetings have been disrupted by activist groups. Some attempts have been made to exclude these groups from annual meetings by restricting the meeting to stockholders only. However, it must be recognized that it is not difficult for activists to become stockholders and thereby gain entrance to the meeting. In fact, a number of groups have already been formed, such as Proxies for People and CAUSE (Coalition for Action, Unity and Social Equality). Many church groups now make appearances at meetings to raise questions concerning social issues and ethical matters.

Since legitimate stockholders cannot be excluded from annual meetings, management must be ready and able to use tact, diplomacy, and public relations skill to handle various activist demonstrations at annual meetings. The goal should be to answer the questions and criticisms raised and to prevent the dissident group from taking complete control of the meeting or forcing a confrontation, a situation in which management, no matter how justified, will probably come off looking unfavorable. The guidelines outlined earlier, while simple, can be helpful in this type of situation.

The annual meeting presents another major opportunity for stressing the company's theme. Displays, exhibits, films, slides, and speeches can all carry this common theme through to the audience. Special annual meeting literature, perhaps somewhat more promotional in nature than the annual report, can be distributed.

Some corporations have distributed sample packages of their products to stockholders at meetings. The Chessie System offers stockholders special discounts on train tickets and at the Greenbrier Hotel, which it owns.

The Post-Annual-Meeting Report

Despite geographic shifting, generally only a small fraction of shareholders are able to attend the annual meeting. Still, all shareholders have a right to know what happened at the meeting. Some companies, an estimated 10 percent of all publicly held companies, accomplish this by means of a post-meeting report.

As a minimum, the post-meeting report should include a report of the presiding officer's remarks; any new developments; results of voting for directors, auditors, and resolutions; and any pertinent questions asked from the floor, as well as the answers to the questions. In the latter area, management should try to be as candid as possible and include all

questions and answers even though these may be embarrassing. Do not identify the questioner. One of the major criticisms of post-meeting reports is that significant questions are ignored. If a stockholder reads a newspaper report of an embarrassing question asked at the meeting and this question has been omitted from the post-meeting report, he or she may wonder whether management has omitted anything else from the report.

Letters to Stockholders

One of the most effective means of cultivating the interest and confidence of new stockholders is a letter of welcome from the company's president as soon after the shares are registered as possible. A copy of the latest annual report and an interim earnings statement are sent, and the new owner is invited to ask questions and offer constructive criticisms. The following is typical of the "letter of welcome":

Dear Sir:

Our records show that you have become a stockholder of our company. We express our appreciation of the confidence you have in our organization.

As a part owner of this business you will want to know about our products (services), our people, and our policies. A quite complete review of our operations was presented in our recent annual report, and a copy is enclosed for your information, together with the announcement of the latest quarterly earnings and dividend action.

We invite your active interest in the corporation and are prepared to receive your comments and answer your questions. You will later be invited to attend the annual meeting of the stockholders, but if you are unable to attend, a report on it will be mailed.

We trust that whenever possible you will buy the products of our company and interest your friends in doing the same. Our sales department will be happy to cooperate by providing the name of the dealer nearest you.

Cordially yours,
(Signature)
President

Publicizing Financial Information

Financial publicity reaches the present and prospective shareholder and at the same time provides much of the information that must be conveyed to the professional financial community. This dissemination of information involves the following five basic areas:

1. News releases with copies of any document referred to, such as annual reports, quarterly reports, and other materials issued to stockholders

2. Releases on dividend declarations, new financing, mergers and acquisitions (in progress or announced), annual, regional, and special meetings of shareholders, labor relations, expansion of facilities, management changes, litigation, employment data, security redemptions, and statements on industry trends or the company's outlook

3. Handling inquiries from media

4. Speeches on financial matters by company officials before business groups, government bodies, societies of security analysts, and other organizations

5. Interviews with financial publications, business writers, and commentators on radio and TV

Of course, many other areas not directly involved with financial matters are of vital interest to the financial community and shareholders. These involve new products, scholarship programs, community projects, statements on the company's contributions to suppressing environmental pollution, and more.

Special financial news outlets

In addition to the media in Chapters 22 and 23 that include business and financial news among their coverage, a number of media specialize in this information and are primary outlets for financial publicity. A list is in the Appendix.

Broadcast outlets include:

- *Wall Street Week*, featuring discussions with security analysts and other experts on the financial markets, broadcast weekly on many stations on a syndicated basis. Its address is Maryland Center for Public Broadcasting, Bonita Avenue, Owings Mills, MD 21117.

- *Moneyline*, which combines daily financial news with analyses of industries and companies. Its address is CNN, 5 Penn Plaza, New York, NY 10010.

- *Business Report*, a daily program provided by the Public Broadcasting System.

- CNBC, a cable network that concentrates on business and financial news.

Dealing Effectively with the Press

Most dealings with the financial press will involve the handling of spot news stories. Spot news stories generally are top priority items for the financial pages of newspapers, financial publications, and news wire services.

The competition to break a spot news story is always keen between the wire services (Associated Press, United Press International, Dow-Jones, Bloomberg, and Reuters). The investor relations practitioner should always try to make simultaneous delivery to the services and carefully avoid favoring one over the other. A written copy of the press release is always preferable to a telephone call. However, simultaneous hand delivery is not always possible. They will accept transmission by facsimile from large organizations, but it is necessary to get approval first and to be sure no one service gets faster reception than others. The commercial newswires, such as PR Newswire and Business Wire and their counterparts in other cities, can be useful in making a simultaneous release to several points. (*See* Chapter 22.)

While concentrating on the major financial publications, many corporations overlook the value of the smaller daily publications in other areas of the country, particularly plant areas or areas that contain high concentrations of shareholders. The corporation should attempt to service as many of these publications with spot news and feature stories as possible.

The public relations person should establish rapport with reporters and editors, and key executives should make an effort to become familiar with the media. Of course, establishing personal contact with a large number of editors is time consuming and cannot be accomplished overnight.

A number of other methods can also be used to familiarize the press with the company and to meet with key executives. These include interviews, orientation tours, plant tours, demonstrations of new products, and special press trips.

Registration Period Publicity

A question that often arises is whether a company can make disclosure during the period between the time it files a registration statement with the SEC and the effective date of the registration statement. The answer is a very definite "yes"—for legitimate news.

The goal of the SEC requirements in this area is to avoid the issuance of any announcements, advertising, speeches, or statements that might tend to implant the idea of an optimistic future for the issuing corporation in the minds of the investing public, or inordinately promote the company beyond its normal flow of news.

The following are among the various types of publicity forbidden:

- Estimates or projections of sales or earnings for the industries or product lines in which the corporation is engaged, including dollar projections, percentages, or even in broad general terms
- Predictions of increased sales or earnings that may stem from new products or discoveries

The company can still issue its normal press releases, provided they contain no financial projections; announce new products or developments; announce annual and quarterly earnings; announce dividends; continue normal product advertising; and present speeches, provided they contain no financial forecasts.

Publicity Aimed at Security Analysts

Professional analysts of securities are a vital group among opinion leaders in the financial community. Employed by brokerage houses, banks, institutional investors such as universities and pension funds, insurance companies, investment advisory services such as Standard & Poor's, mutual funds, and others who buy securities or advise others, they are specialists in acquiring and evaluating information about companies. Most of them concentrate on a given group, such as oil, transportation, chemicals, or foods. In very large brokerage houses, an analyst may concentrate on only a few companies (within a single industry). Managers of large mutual funds generally concentrate on one fund.

The analyst generally issues reports to the members of his or her firm, who are then guided in their own purchases or in the advice they give to customers. Many analysts either write or contribute to the market letters that have a great influence on investors' practices. Analysts representing brokerage firms are called "sell side" analysts, and those from banks, pension funds, mutual funds, and insurance companies—"money managers"— are called "buy side" analysts.

Analysts narrow their interest to certain companies rather than trying to cover the entire universe of publicly held companies. This means that each company needs to identify and work with those who study its industry or who are otherwise specifically interested in it, rather than on all analysts as a group.

The Financial Analysts Federation, 1633 Broadway, New York, NY 10019, publishes a list of its members. The National Investor Relations Institute publishes a directory of financial analysts throughout the United States.

Public relations people communicate with these analysts in the following ways:

1. Arranging for the president or other key executive of the company to talk before one of the societies of analysts. Companies are invited to appear on the basis of their interest to the group, recency of latest appearance (generally no more often than every two years in New York), schedule availability, and the interest in the company. Generally, the company is expected to give detailed, unadorned information about its operations, plans, and outlook. Literature of direct interest to the analysts may be distributed. In most cases the media are invited, and the company may release information about the talk for pub-

lication not earlier than the time of the meeting.

2. Special reports for analysts, containing detailed and technical financial information, plans that can be revealed without violating disclosure regulations or aiding competitors, illustrations of plants and facilities, and related material.

3. Tours of the main plant and facilities, or a group of plants, for one analyst or a group of up to a dozen. They should be accompanied by key company officials and by specialists in the processes and operations being visited. Ample time for a question-and-answer discussion should be allowed.

4. Simultaneous dissemination of financial and corporate news to both analysts and the press.

5. Meeting specific requests for information received from analysts, insofar as corporate security and the rules on equal disclosure permit.

6. Personal visits with analysts at their offices or in the offices of the investor relations department or counsel.

7. Small discussion meetings with selected analysts having special interest in the company.

8. Appearances before "splinter" groups of analysts who specialize in the company's industry.

9. Presentations at the company headquarters for large groups of analysts at intervals of two to three years. Deere and Company's meetings at its famous Saarinen-designed building in Moline, Illinois, are good examples.

Analysts' needs

The investor relations person's concept of what is pertinent information may not coincide with that of the analyst. George Putnam, chairman of Putnam Management Company, a large manager of investment funds, described the analyst's interest in a talk before the New York Chapter of NIRI:

> The analyst really wants to know *how* to analyze the company—what makes it tick, what the risks are, what the unknowns are, what the leverage is, how different economic conditions will impact it; its vulnerability to recession, to interest-rate shifts, to competition, to new technical discoveries, to government controls, to material shortages, to weather, to seasonality, etc. Most analysts do not want their conclusions handed to them in "packaged form," but they want to learn enough from the company to be able to examine the environment and then make judgments as to how changes will affect the company's earnings prospects.

The analyst's functions

The function of the analyst is almost similar to that of the reporter, except that the analyst must make a value judgment on the company researched—weighing it in terms of whether it is under- or overvalued in regard to its present market price and its long-term prospects.

Just like the reporter, the analyst faces many deadline pressures and must use time to the utmost value. Therefore, the analyst should be afforded the same considerations, in terms of time-saving and assistance, as the financial reporter.

More importantly, the investor relations person should appreciate the fact that the securities analyst probably already has a great deal of general information about the company. What is needed, then, is a broad picture of the company's goals and a quick synopsis of current news events. The analyst's interest in the company will be centered more on the future, including the effect of recent events, than on the past.

Generally, the analyst will concentrate on how current news events will affect the com-

pany over the long term. Generally speaking, discussions with analysts will be considerably more penetrating than those with financial reporters. The analyst generally will search for answers to the "why" rather than the "what." This is the main reason the investor relations person must have a good technical background and an intimate knowledge of the company.

Credibility issues

The investor relations profession has come under some criticism because of its handling of corporate financial information to the public and to analysts. Much of the criticism has been based on the claim that investor relations people have been quick to boast of corporate accomplishments, often distorting the picture with misleading and sometimes inaccurate financial data, particularly in terms of earnings projections, but have been steadfast in withholding any negative data.

Obviously, such claims will affect the relationship between practitioners and analysts and ultimately the investing public. And, while it is probably true that there have been instances where investor relations people have provided misleading material, this is not true of the great majority. It is highly important that no credibility gap exist between the company and the investing public. The investor relations person should, therefore, strive for accuracy and truthfulness.

As Philip Lesly points out in *Managing the Human Climate*, "Credibility is the *earned* right to be heard."

Often, actual discussions with analysts are arranged for top corporate officers rather than with the investor relations person unless he or she is also fully familiar with all corporate financial information and is sophisticated in finance. However, the investor relations executive or counsel usually attends or is alert to such discussions, so if any information that might have a bearing on the action of the stock is revealed, an immediate full distribution of the news can be made to comply with the stringent full-disclosure rules. Investor relations people also maintain contacts with analysts to learn what they would like from the company and to provide a listening post of investment-community opinion to provide to the management.

A fully qualified company officer should be available to qualified analysts as freely as schedules permit.

Analysts' meetings

Many contacts with securities analysts will be on an individual basis, but at times the company may be asked to address large groups of analysts. Some of these meetings will involve such large groups as the Analyst Societies in New York, Boston, Philadelphia, Chicago, San Francisco, or Los Angeles, and many other cities, but may also involve smaller groups of analysts—the so-called splinter groups—who specialize in the industry group of which the company is a member.

In handling analysts' meetings, considerations include whether the president should address the group alone or whether executives with individual expertise should be used, whether the presentation should be strictly oral or should include visual aids, what material should be distributed at the meeting, and—most important—how the company will distribute any material information that might be disclosed. In many cases full text and charts used in the presentation are given to the analysts following the talk and scripts are sent to other analysts after the meeting.

A common mistake with many analysts' meetings is to rehash the volume of information already known about the company. Sending analysts a company Fact Book, if it contains well-planned information, can provide them with most of the figures they need. It is far more profitable to spend the time telling analysts those things that are not

known about the company unless, of course, the company is relatively unknown to the group.

One of the complaints often heard from analysts is that corporations spend too much time telling how they make their money and not enough time explaining why they make money. In short, they would like to know what the company's guiding philosophy is; what makes it significantly different from other companies; its goals, plans for achieving them, and obstacles faced; and, most important, what will make this company unique in the future.

Inviting the media

Another consideration is whether the media should be invited to attend analyst meetings. In some analysts' societies meetings are closed to all but members, automatically excluding the media. To some extent this forces a decision on the company. However, the New York Stock Exchange strongly urges companies to invite the media to analysts' meetings whenever possible. If the media cannot attend, Exchange regulations require that, if any new material is discussed during the course of the meeting, it must be promptly released.

Of course, there is the other side of the coin—that the analysts are not really concerned with the investing public as much as servicing their firms' clients. Their goal is to provide clients with more and higher-quality data than they can glean from the newspapers.

Obviously, both of these groups cannot be satisfied simultaneously, and a middle course must be chosen. The only compatible solution seems to be to try, whenever possible, either to have the media attend or to provide them with the same or a similar presentation. If the media is not permitted to attend, the company must fulfill its disclosure requirements with an immediate press release covering any material developments covered in the course of the meeting.

An increasingly popular solution is for the company to host the meeting for security analysts with an interest in the company. In this case invitations can be limited to analysts.

Some recent developments include conference calls between executives and analysts, or sending analysts tapes of key comments by senior officers of the company. Some corporations have an 800 "hotline" phone system so analysts and stockholders can have their questions answered.

The Directory of Securities Research, Nelson Communications, 551 Fifth Avenue, New York, NY, 10017, lists stockbroker firm analysts by industry specialties.

Additional Communications Outlets

A discussion of additional avenues to be included in many financial communications programs follows:

Investment clubs

Investment clubs consist of groups with some similar interest—such as employment in the same company, membership in the same profession, residence in the same neighborhood, or just friendship—who also are interested in investing. They form a pool by each putting specified amounts into a fund monthly. This is invested on the basis of joint decisions. Information on clubs and how to reach them is available from the National Association of Investors Corporation, 711 W. 13 Mile Road, Madison Heights, MI 48071.

Recently the NAIC has become much more active with companies and invites corporate sponsorship. Such sponsorship permits companies to participate in NAIC investment fairs and other benefits. Other new services also

provide special help in identifying interested brokers.

Public relations news wires

Some of the teletype services that distribute press releases to media (*see* Chapter 22) also distribute them to brokerage offices.

Dealing with stockbrokers

Some companies also woo stockbrokers. There are more than twenty stockbrokers' associations in major cities. They sponsor meetings in the same way as analyst societies, and often company executives appear before them. Often companies are charged a substantial fee for such meetings and must pay the luncheon or dinner costs. The value is questionable. In other cases, companies have found it useful to have the meetings at individual brokerage offices where top corporate officers discuss the company with a group of brokers, usually after the close of the market. The *Registered Representative Magazine*, 18818 Teller Avenue, #280, Irvine, CA 92715, provides distribution to fifty thousand registered representatives and affords another vehicle to reach this group.

Dealing with Proxy Fights and Tender Offers

The most stressful and crucial element of investor relations is forestalling and defending against efforts of outside interests to take over the company.

Widespread ownership of corporations and the growth of mutual funds and other institutional investors have greatly increased the potential role of the nonmanagement stockholder.

When companies were held by a few owners, often related to each other or partners in operating the enterprise, changes of management came about through "palace revolutions" but seldom involved people outside the inner circle.

The democratization of stock ownership has made corporate control attainable through additional means.

Basic differences in takeover efforts

Efforts to take over the management of a company against the wishes of its board and officers take two general forms: the proxy fight and the tender offer. Both involve appealing to the mass of stockholders, but they are quite different.

In a proxy fight the two sides seek to gain a majority vote of the voting stock outstanding. Each stockholder is expected to retain his (her) holdings. This means that for the stockholder, the issue is which of the contestants shall control the company in which *he or she will continue to have funds invested*. The issue in a proxy fight is usually the adequacy of the management.

On the other hand, a tender offer is designed to get the stockholder to dispose of the stock. The offer is made attractive enough to get the stockholder to sell and cease being concerned about who will manage the enterprise (except where the purchase involves securities in an enterprise that will control the one that is sought).

In a proxy fight, the appeals to the stockholder involve loyalty, comparative confidence in the known management as opposed to the insurgents, concern for the future of the investment, and other considerations that will be of concern in the future.

In a tender offer, money is the overriding issue. For example, a stockholder who has bought a stock at 35, finds it selling on the market at 40, and receives an offer to buy it from him at 50, is seldom inclined to consider loyalty to the management or any other factor except that he or she can make a very

substantial profit immediately, as compared with the previous experience with the stock. (Where the stockholder has held the stock for a long time and would have to pay a substantial capital gain tax on the appreciation, he or she may have doubts.)

Almost all stockholders own their securities for the financial benefits they expect. A tender offer at a price substantially above the market value—especially when there is no early expectation that the stock would reach that level under other circumstances—is extremely attractive to the great majority of stockholders. This means that, other things being equal, the group making the offer has a substantial initial advantage.

Defending against a proxy fight

In a proxy fight, the public relations of the defending company essentially focuses on informing the stockholder and the financial community about the merits of the present management's operation and plans for the company as opposed to what the insurgents represent.

To forestall takeover efforts by dissident stockholders through an effort to elect a majority of the board of directors, a number of basic tactics apply.

1. Constantly developing confidence in the management through a thorough and continuous investor and public relations program, especially in the financial areas described earlier.

2. Making additional efforts to build up confidence in the management when specific issues seem to be arising that could be the basis for a proxy fight. These are essentially the fundamental functions in a corporate public relations program, perhaps intensified.

3. Maintaining close relationships with the media, assuring they will be inclined to come to the company first when news or

rumors about it arise and that they will have a high degree of acceptance of what the company says.

4. Publicizing information that will undermine acceptance of the opposition's charges and promises. This is based on facts about the opposition group and its records, requiring as much advance research and documentation as possible.

5. Using effectively prepared and timed communications in addition to publicity, such as advertisements, letters to stockholders, and so on.

Timing is vital in both proxy fights and tender offers. In proxy fights, the most crucial time is later in the battle, just before solicitations of the stock vote for the stockholders' meeting at which the vote will be counted. Where stockholder votes and proxies are involved, *it is the last proxy received from each stockholder that is counted.* A campaign that climaxes too soon can bring in proxies that will later be superseded by proxies from the same stockholders who have been motivated by the opposition.

Dealing with tender offers

Since these are based almost entirely on the dollar attraction of the offer, most of the factors involved in defeating a proxy attack are not involved in protecting against a tender offer. The stockholder is deciding whether he or she would rather take the money or new securities and get out, or continue to hold stock in the company at probably a lower price—and hope the price will improve under the present management. (It is to meet this kind of hope that many companies have been restructuring, selling off weak units, buying their own stock, sharply reducing some expenditures, etc.)

The stockholder is thus voting with his or her bank account, not the ballot.

This attitude often presents the insurgents with a number of advantages over the management.

1. **The immediate monetary attraction of the offer is difficult to offset** with convincing evidence that the current management can do better in giving the stockholders a higher price in a short time. The stockholder tends to ask: If the management can assure a higher value for the stock, why hasn't the market price been higher?

2. **Brokers generally have the opportunity for double or even triple commissions** when they prevail on a stockholder to sell. They get a commission on the sale by the stockholder, another on the purchase by the insurgents (who immediately make known their willingness to pay such commissions), and often a third commission when the customer buys other stock with the cash received.

3. **Arbitrageurs**—who profit by taking advantage of the differences between the offering price and the selling price on securities—**often find an opportunity to pick up stock** at somewhat lower than the offering price and turn it in to the offerer.

4. **What would be considered strength of management under normal circumstances and especially in a proxy fight often become attractions to insurgents in a tender offer.** Especially attractive are companies that have a low amount of debt, a large amount of cash, and a good reputation that will make it easier to obtain finances for buying up the stock. The higher a firm's earnings, the more attractive it is for a takeover, since insurgents often have high debt ratios and can use the earnings to pay for the company they acquire.

5. **Mutual funds and other large investors sometimes find they can make a substantial profit** by buying into a company

they expect will be subjected to a tender offer, and then selling to the insurgent. If they hold a stock for other reasons they may well accept the offer as a means of making a good profit.

Much will depend on the nature of the tender offer. If it is for cash, the stockholder faces the simple decision of determining whether he or she will be better off taking that amount and then finding another investment for it or staying with holdings in the company. Since cash tender offers are not tax-free, this judgment will be affected by his or her tax position, the length of time the stock has been held, the condition of the market in terms of finding other investments, current capital law, and other considerations. If the offer is for new securities either with or without partial payment in cash, the stockholder's consideration is more complicated. He or she is faced with trying to determine the prospects for the enterprise in which new securities will be held, how marketable they will be, conversion rates, and often the comparative elements of a complex structure that may involve fractional shares, subordinated debentures, and other technical matters.

The stock's recent experience on the market will have an important influence. If the stock has been declining or failing to keep up with the trend of the market, many stockholders will welcome an opportunity to dispose of it. Also, stockholders who do not face a tax on gains are much more likely to sell than those who would have to pay a capital gain tax on the appreciation of the stock.

The nature of the company's stockholders can be important. Stockholders who have held the shares for a long time may not have done so out of loyalty, which can be readily displaced by profit, but because they are inherently conservative and slow to change. Such stockholders are less likely to jump at any attractive offer that comes along.

Some studies indicate that about half of the companies sought in takeovers are acquired by the first bidder or restructured, and another 25 percent have made mergers they otherwise would not do in order to avoid falling into the hands of insurgents. In other cases, maneuvers taken in defense—such as making acquisitions otherwise not planned—have substantially changed the target company. In total, a substantial proportion of target companies can be said to be transformed or materially changed as a result of takeover efforts.

Defensive strategies

Strategies and plans to forestall a tender offer may be classified as *strategic measures* and *public relations*. While the strategic measures are not strictly within the public relations sphere, they are of vital importance; the public relations or investor relations executive must be aware of them and, wherever possible, participate in their planning.

Because the rules and interpretations in this area have been changing steadily and are likely to continue to change, it is wise to keep up to date on SEC actions, court decisions, and state laws.

A number of tactics popularly known as "shark repellents" have been developed.

1. Where state law allows, the election of the board of directors may be staggered so that only one-third are changed each year. This means that a group gaining voting control could change no more than one-third of the board in any given year.

2. Where state law allows, the bylaws may be changed to provide that no merger action or substantial change in the control of the company may be effected with less than an 80 percent vote of the stock represented. This provides some defense against control being exerted by a group that may

be the largest stockholder but has less than 20 percent of the total.

3. Assets on the company's books should be fully valued. Often it has been considered good practice to leave real estate, for instance, recorded at the nominal acquisition price, even though it may have multiplied in value. This tends to keep the apparent value of the company too low and may underprice its stock. Undervalued assets attract raiders. Analysts give special attention to the breakup value of a company—what its various parts might attract in payment if sold separately.

4. If the insurgent company is small enough or its stock is priced low, the target company or its allies may buy the insurgent's stock. This can give it leverage in affecting the insurgent's tactics, scare it off, or in some cases lead to a change of control of the insurgent company.

5. Within prudent limits, let the company's pension fund acquire company stock. Usually it will be clearly in the best interests of the employees to prevent takeover by a distant and unproved insurgent company.

6. Encourage employees to become stockholders. Special attention might be given to the Employee Stock Ownership Plan (ESOP or a 401(k) investment plan). (Keep in mind that employee-stockholders who see a loss on the stock when the market has declined are a potential source of unrest and disaffection. They then may be most likely to accept an attractive offer.)

7. Keep a perpetual watch on the stock record lists to observe movements of holdings. A number of warning signs should be investigated, including large purchases, an unusual rate of market activity, and large blocks picked up in "street names" that permit shielding the identity of the true purchaser. Close liaison should be maintained with the specialist in the company's stock on the floor of the stock exchange, the company's stock transfer agent, and, where applicable, market makers.

8. The company's banks, investment banker, friendly brokerage houses, and others should be cultivated to ascertain how they would act or could be urged to use their influence in the event a takeover effort comes from any of a number of directions. When an active defense is undertaken, the investment banker and attorney, supported by the investor relations executive, usually manage it.

9. The transfer agent that keeps track of the changes in ownership of the company's stock can provide daily reports not only of the number of shares traded, but the names and addresses of buyers and sellers. A stockwatch proxy firm can also provide help of this sort. With computerized records, it is possible to obtain detailed information on each purchaser—dates of purchases, percentages of the total shares represented by each holder, etc. Such information can make it possible to watch the buying action of any purchaser when the name is known.

10. Keep the company's contingency plans current, activating them as soon as evidence of a takeover effort is imminent. These may include the following:

- Making acquisitions that will put stock into friendly hands.

- Making an acquisition or entering a new field of activity that would put the company into competition with the would-be insurgent and create an antitrust conflict.

- Splitting the stock (before the tender offer is publicly announced) to delay tendering through paper work involved in issuing new stock certificates.

- Restructuring, including spinning off some units.
- Launching a leveraged buyout, in which members of the management borrow funds to buy control or all of the company. This, of course, is a drastic action and requires the counsel of professionals in investment and law.

11. Suppliers who value the company as a customer may, in turn, be customers of the insurgent company. They can sometimes be motivated to express their disapproval to the insurgents and create concern among the stockholders of the insurgent company.

12. The active support of the communities in which the company operates should be developed, on the basis that in many cases after a takeover has been effected, plants have been shut down or operations reduced. In many cases the new owners remove management functions from the taken-over company's headquarters city, causing local lawyers, accountants, banks, and others to lose clients. Phillips Petroleum and Dayton-Hudson (department stores) fought off takeovers by arousing their communities against the loss of civic contributions and local management personnel.

13. Unions can sometimes be enlisted as allies of the management when they can be shown that the new owners might be a threat to the interests of the workers, to the continuation of some of the operations and therefore of many jobs, or to a good relationship between management and labor. The fear of having to deal with a hostile union can make a potential offeror back off.

14. Many states have passed legislation to hinder a takeover of a company headquartered or with operations in the state. These laws vary. In some cases a threat-ened company can call on the protection of these laws when only one of its operations is in a state with such legislation. However, some state laws have been challenged successfully in federal courts.

15. It is important to keep in touch with the senators and congressmen representing the area of the company's headquarters and other major operations. In many cases, they can be helpful in stimulating antitrust investigations, examinations by the Securities and Exchange Commission, and other governmental deterrents to the takeover.

16. If the company's finances warrant, the dividend can be increased. This is a visible stimulus to the enthusiasm of the stockholders.

17. If finances warrant, the company may want to buy its own stock for the treasury. Treasury stock cannot be voted, but since it is not actively on the market it is not available for purchase by outsiders in their efforts to gain control. The fewer the number of shares outstanding, the higher the earnings per share. Also, treasury stock is used in making acquisitions that can put that stock into voting position, generally siding with management.

18. All substantial stockholders should be cultivated consistently and kept informed about their interest in continuing to keep their investment in the company.

19. A firm confronted with a takeover by an organization its management feels will not be congenial with its interests may turn to a "white knight"—another firm it fancies more—to acquire it. When a second or third would-be acquirer enters the picture, however, the first may increase its bid and prevail. Some managements, to forestall that, have issued options to their chosen "white knights" for large blocks of the stock at a price

close to that of the first bidder, making it more difficult for the insurgent to get a controlling interest. However, this can be challenged as contrary to the best interests of the stockholders—who could benefit from a bidding war—and so may prove vulnerable in court actions or SEC reviews.

20. Some companies have adopted lucrative severance pay plans for many of their executives in the event of a takeover—known as "golden parachutes." The costs of those severances may deter a company contemplating having to meet the payments to executives it intends to cut loose if the acquisition goes through.

Public relations activities

Forestalling the tender offer takeover can involve a wide range of public relations strategies and activities. The most basic are as follows:

1. Utilize constant public relations efforts that maintain a high level of confidence in the company's stock and help assure that it sells at a good price-earnings multiple. Efforts to shore up the stock price will probably be self-defeating, but legitimate activities that attain a justifiable multiple are the responsibility of every company's management.

2. Keep the public aware of the company's plans for growth, its future prospects, the quality of its management, and its effective use of its funds.

3. When a tender offer is imminent or has developed, report quickly and incisively on events, statements of the management, and other developments.

4. Maintain mailing-address lists of stockholders, continuously updated so at least two mailings can be made very quickly. Where E-mail addresses have been ob-

tained, use them for immediate communication. Or faxes can be sent to stockholders when fax numbers are known.

5. Prepare possible letters written in advance, leaving blanks for the name of the insurgent company and the terms of its offer. These can be reviewed, revised, and processed quickly when the time comes, instead of having to compose them under stress and with inevitable delays for creativity and clearances.

6. Prepare possible advertisements in the same way. (*See* Figure 11.4, page 196.)

7. After the offer is made, immediately reserve space in the newspapers to be used. Then make advance reservations for every two or three days thereafter for at least a week.

8. Arrange for the CEO to make personal visits to the major financial institutions that have blocks of the company's securities or who influence other large holders. Some other officers and outside directors may also make calls.

9. Develop plans for immediate telephone contact with all substantial stockholders, including the tentative message to be conveyed and deployment of all persons who will be assigned to make calls. This requires getting the telephone numbers—business and home—in advance and listing them on the stockholder information sheets.

10. Plan E-mail or fax messages to go to other substantial stockholders. Make sure the office can handle the volume. Otherwise you may want to apportion the list among various offices nearest the groups of recipients.

11. Make advance arrangements for all-night services that may be needed: producing, stuffing, and mailing letters to stockholders; producing printed material (either by company personnel or com-

An Open Letter From AVON

ENOUGH IS ENOUGH

To The Shareholders of Avon:

On Friday, November 10, your company was informed that a partnership including officers and directors of Mary Kay, as well as numerous members of the families of the Fisher brothers' and Gordon Getty, has acquired more than 5 percent of Avon's stock.

There can be little doubt that this marks the beginning of yet another effort to seize control of Avon.

This crop of raiders says it has no intention of merging Avon with Mary Kay or otherwise interfering with the operations of the company. But that's double talk, because at the same time, they say they will immediately install a financial man from Mary Kay as Avon's chairman and chief executive officer.

Avon has beaten back three unsolicited takeover efforts in the last year. We were prepared to fight to keep Avon independent then—and we're prepared to fight again.

You should know that our determination to remain independent is every bit as strong now as it has been since Avon was founded 104 years ago. We, the Directors of Avon, continue to believe the long-term interests of our shareholders will best be served by letting us get on with our business plan, which is already yielding solid results for our shareholders.

Now would be the worst time to sell Avon—and the company isn't for sale.

The fact is, Avon was created for business, not for battle. We're like thousands of other businesses in New York State and hundreds of thousands in the U.S. We were created to make products and then, if they met customers' approval, to sell them. That's what we've been doing successfully for more than a century—and what we'd like to continue doing.

There's always been a special dimension to Avon, a human dimension that outsiders tend to overlook. Avon is uniquely a people business. Around the world a million-and-a-half Avon Representatives are calling on women in their homes and places of work. They are delivering and selling beauty products, of course.

Just as importantly, they are bringing a touch of beauty and brightness into peoples' lives.

Underlying this process is an essential element of trust and goodwill. Avon Representatives are literally being welcomed into their customers' homes.

This has always been the great strength of Avon and its real value as a business. These Representatives are very special human beings. They are not machines or mailing lists to be bought or sold. Money people may overlook things like that.

In fact, Avon Representatives, in overwhelming numbers, have told us they can't be sold and that they won't go to work for Mary Kay. To our Representatives, Mary Kay is the enemy.

We're not asking the Mary Kay people and their partners to take our word for this. We're inviting our Avon Representatives to write these people themselves, and say how *they* feel. The man to write is:

> Mr. M. Anthony Fisher
> General Partner
> Chartwell Associates L.P.
> 299 Park Avenue
> 42nd Floor
> New York, NY 10017

As for the Board of Avon, we unanimously support Avon's management. We think the company has been subjected to enough unproductive and disruptive take-over attempts. We think the statutes of the State of New York were written to establish the ground rules for how business is done in this State. Not how business can be continually interrupted to the detriment of everyone.

These distractions have already cut measurably into the productivity of Avon's salespeople. The attacks on Avon are undermining our business and thereby hurting you, the shareholders.

Enough is enough.

Sincerely,

James E. Preston   Ruth Block   Daniel B. Burke   Hays Clark

Stanley C. Gault   Charles S. Locke   Emil Mosbacher, Jr.   Merlin E. Nelson

Ernesta G. Procope   Joseph A. Rice   Cecily C. Selby

November 15, 1989

Figure 11.4 This ad by Avon opposing a takeover effort by Mary Kay Cosmetics aims to rally its sales representatives, dispersed across the country. It does not attack the opposition or stress the interests of shareholders. *Reprinted with permission of Avon Products, Inc.*

mercial twenty-four-hour printers); layout and preparation of ads; and manning switchboards, fax machines, and computers.

12. Publicize the negative aspects of the insurgent group, where securities are involved in the purchase package or any doubt can be cast on its ability to finance the deal or run the company—such as the disadvantages of owning securities in various types of conglomerate or diversified companies, weaknesses in the structure of the insurgent company, scandals or other vulnerabilities in its record, and so on.

13. Develop public opinion in plant communities, among suppliers and customers, and whoever else would not like to see the change. This can be aimed at bringing negative reaction to bear on the insurgent company, its customers, its bankers, and others.

It is vital to keep in mind that the *appeal* and the *warmth* of the communications are perhaps as important as the facts. Cold facts alone—especially if they sound like expostulations of the management to the stockholder—can be deadly and drive the stockholder to get out as quickly as possible. Appeals that show concern for the stockholder's interests, that address him or her with respect and in return evoke respect for the humanity of the management, can go a long way in overcoming the sheer emotion of the dollars offered.

In no other aspect of public relations is secrecy of such great importance as in the takeover area. Extreme security measures are required within the office of the public relations staff, among reproduction and mailing offices, with printers, and in every other area where some part of the information and strategy can be exposed. Would-be insurgents often include in their plans the suborning of employees inside any of these places. Sometimes employees who want to be in the good graces of the new management provide information that helps them achieve their goal. Insiders who violate privacy go to jail.

There are many legal aspects on both sides of takeover fights (*see* Chapter 48). The company's legal staff and the best available legal counsel experienced in these matters should be involved at all stages.

However, time is probably the most critical single factor. Unlike proxy fights, where the key time is at the end of the battle, in tender offers the critical period is immediately after the offer has been announced. Immediacy in decision making and in carrying out all functions is urgent. Speed can determine whether a company survives. While no violation of the law should ever be recommended, the nuances of legal interpretations often must be left for later—even at the expense of settling a lawsuit or satisfying a government agency—if it means preventing a takeover that would make all future considerations irrelevant.

Holding Special Events

Some companies encourage stockholders to visit the "home office," the plants, and the branches. One company makes it an annual policy to invite shareholders to visit the main plant during their summer vacation automobile tours. A special reception committee is on hand to conduct the visitors on an inspection around the property. Other companies have set aside weeks or days during the year when "open house" is held for all stockholders. Attractive invitations are sent to those who live within a reasonable distance of the property. Refreshments are served and souvenirs are often distributed to those taking the opportunity to attend.

Surveying Shareholders

As important as it is to determine the attitude of analysts, it is equally important to assess the attitude of shareholders. This can be done quite easily by mailing a simple questionnaire to shareholders (*see* Figure 11.5). The questionnaire should determine

1. Whether shareholders understand the financial section of the company's annual report as presented

2. Whether the shareholders understand the company's operating problems and progress

3. What shareholders think the annual report should contain

4. What shareholders think should be added to the annual report and other reports.[1]

A personal letter, perhaps from the president or chairman, should accompany the questionnaire to explain its purpose and try to elicit suggestions and criticisms.

A few corporations employ professional opinion research agencies to send out personal interviewers to a selected list of stockholders to obtain direct answers to questions regarding management policies and to obtain helpful suggestions and constructive criticism. One company "checked" only its women stockholders, because they accounted for the majority of the ownership, while another approached only the employee-stockholders. In both cases, the results of the surveys revealed a high degree of misunderstanding on the fundamental conception of the management's policies and the American enterprise system.

---

[1]In addition, some companies find it desirable to survey their shareholders to determine how many companies they own stock in, how well-informed they are on financial matters, and the level of their understanding of financial reports. Such information can be very helpful in planning the content, tone, and sophistication of communications material. *Ed.*

Additional Resources

A growing array of statistical and distribution tools have become available for investor relations directors. For example, the VISTA service provided by Computer Directions Advisors, 11501 Georgia Avenue, Silver Spring, MD 20902, develops quarterly computerized lists that show institutional holdings in company stock. The service also can indicate which financial institutions own stock in competitive companies. This service provides investor relations departments with a wealth of information, statistic trading patterns, and other data that can be used to check present ownership.

Research Magazine, 2201 Third Street, San Francisco, CA 94107-3125, provides means for getting company information and financial statistics in the hands of fifty thousand registered representatives in a format that can also be used for the representatives to send to their customers.

Technimetrics provides up-to-date lists of analysts and registered representatives that can be broken down in many ways to develop special mailing lists. The REPDEK service offered by Technimetrics permits a company to determine which registered representatives are interested in the company and to build up a special mailing list of these brokers.

Effective Disclosure

Since the Appellate Court's decision on the Texas Gulf Sulphur case in 1968 and the NYSE's revision of its disclosure requirements, hundreds of thousands of words have been written and spoken on disclosure. The amount of information disclosed and the concern about disclosure have reached unparalleled levels in the field of financial communications.

Although this concern about adequate disclosure has been beneficial, much of it re-

STOCKHOLDER'S QUESTIONNAIRE
(No Signature Requested)

I HOW DID YOU ORIGINALLY ACQUIRE YOUR COMMON STOCK? By gift . . . . . By inheritance . . . . . . By purchase . . . . . .
If by purchase, did someone recommend it to you? Yes . . . . . No . . . . .
(If yes) By Banker . . . . Broker . . . . Lawyer . . . . Friend . . . . Relative . . . . Other person . . . .
What is the principal reason you decided to buy this stock?
. . . .
. . . .

II HOW MANY SHARES OF OUR STOCK DO YOU OWN?
. . . .

III HOW IS YOUR STOCK HELD? By an individual . . . . In joint tenancy . . . . By a corporation . . . . By an institution . . . .
In an estate or trust fund . . . .

IV WHY ARE YOU HOLDING THE STOCK? Primarily for income . . . . In the hope of selling it at a higher price . . . .

V WOULD YOU BUY MORE OF OUR STOCK? Yes . . . . No . . . .
(If yes) Under what conditions? . . . .
. . . .
(If no) Why not? . . . .
. . . .
. . . .

What should the President discuss in his message? Matters pertaining to Company operations . . . . . Matters pertaining to the over-all economy . . . . . . Both . . . . . . Other . . . .
. . . .
. . . .

In general, this is what I liked about the Report . . . .
. . . .
. . . .

In general, I did not like . . . .
. . . .
. . . .

VIII DO YOU THINK THE COMPANY IS GIVING ITS STOCKHOLDERS ENOUGH INFORMATION ABOUT ITS ACTIVITIES? Yes . . . . . . No . . . . . .
If not, what kind of information would you like? . . . .
. . . .
. . . .
. . . .

IX HOW WOULD YOU EXPRESS YOUR OPINION OF THE MANAGEMENT OF YOUR COMPANY?
Very favorable . . . . Favorable . . . . Uncertain . . . . Unfavorable . . . . Very unfavorable . . . .

VI DO YOU OWN OTHER STOCKS? Yes . . . . No . . . .
Several (2 or 3) . . . . A few (3 to 10) . . . . A larger number (over 10) . . . .
(If other companies' shares owned) Do any of these companies follow practices you would recommend? Yes . . . . No . . . .
(If yes) What company? . . . .
Please describe the practice . . . .
. . . .

VII DID YOU RECEIVE THE COMPANY'S ANNUAL REPORT LAST MONTH FOR THE FISCAL YEAR?
Yes . . . . No . . . . . .
If you did, did you read it? Yes . . . . . . No . . . . . .
Was it easy to understand . . . . . Hard to understand . . . . . .
Fully informative . . . . . . Not fully informative . . . . .
Should it contain pictures or illustrations? Yes . . . . . . No . . . . .
Should it contain graphs or charts? Yes . . . . . . No . . . . . .
Should it be "dressed up" more? Yes . . . . . . No . . . . . .
Did you read the President's message in the report? Yes . . . . No . . . .
If so, what was your opinion of his message? Very favorable . . . . . Favorable . . . . . . Uncertain . . . . . Unfavorable . . . . . . Very unfavorable . . . . . . Why? . . . .
. . . .
. . . .

Why? . . . .
. . . .

X DO YOU USE ANY OF OUR PRODUCTS? Yes . . . No . . .
If so, what do you think of them? . . . .
. . . .

XI DID YOU NOTICE THE ADS ENCLOSED WITH THE LAST ANNUAL REPORT? Yes . . . . No . . . .
If so, what did you think of them? . . . .
. . . .

XII THE FOLLOWING BRIEF ANSWERS ABOUT YOURSELF WILL ALSO HELP US TO KNOW MORE ABOUT OUR STOCKHOLDERS.
Male . . . . Female . . . . Married . . . . Single . . . . Widowed or Divorced . . . . Age . . . Occupation . . . .

XIII FURTHER COMMENTS OR SUGGESTIONS:
. . . .
. . . .
. . . .
. . . .
. . . .
. . . .

Figure 11.5 A typical stockholder questionnaire.

sulted from overanxiety about fulfilling regulatory requirements. Still, it is a tribute to American business' desire to do the right thing.

Four key sources of information in this area are the Securities and Exchange Acts of 1933 and 1934; the New York Stock Exchange's (11 Wall Street, New York, NY 10005) booklets *Expanded Policy on Time Disclosure* and *The Corporate Director and The Investing Public*; and the American Stock Exchange's (86 Trinity Place, New York, NY 10006) booklet on disclosure policies.

Actually, there is little reason for public relations people to worry about disclosure requirements, provided they follow a few simple rules.

The New York Stock Exchange's disclosure requirements were developed over many years of experience in this area. A condensed abstract follows.

SEC Disclosure Guidelines

In addition to stipulating how and what a publicly held company must disclose as news, the Securities and Exchange Commission has established other disclosure requirements.

The SEC calls certain actions, such as payment of incentives to overseas officials beyond clearly established and what it considers reasonable commissions, to be information that must be disclosed to the company's shareholders. Bribes to domestic officials or others, or other matters that may fall outside the limits of the law, such as political contributions by the corporation, are also considered material and, therefore, require reporting.

In connection with tender offers, the SEC has moved to a more aggressive position regarding disclosure of information by both the offeror and the target company.

These areas are evolving and are likely to be the subject of court actions and modifications on the basis of experience. It is necessary for anyone responsible for the financial communications of a publicly held company to keep up-to-date in this area.

New York Stock Exchange Guidelines on Disclosure[2]

201.00 Introduction

A company which lists on the Exchange is expected to be guided by Exchange practices and procedures regarding disclosing and reporting material information as detailed in the Listing Agreement and in this Manual.

The Exchange's current listing agreement generally seeks to achieve the following objectives:

- Ensure timely disclosure of information that may affect security values or influence investment decisions, and in which shareholders, the public, and the Exchange have a warrantable interest.

- Ensure frequent, regular, and timely publication of financial reports prepared in accordance with generally accepted accounting principles.

- Provide the Exchange with timely information to enable it to efficiently perform its function of maintaining an orderly market for the company's securities, to enable it to maintain necessary records, and to allow it the opportunity to make comment as to certain matters before they become established facts.

- Preclude certain business practices not generally considered sound.

---

[2]Condensed from regulations of the New York Stock Exchange. The complete regulations can be obtained from the NYSE, 11 Wall Street, New York, NY 10005.

202.00 Material information

Numerous forces and events can affect the value of securities and investment decisions. All information in which shareholders, investors, the general public, and the Exchange itself have a warrantable interest should be disclosed in an accurate and timely fashion.

202.01 Internal handling of confidential corporate matters

Unusual market activity or a substantial price change occasionally occurs in a company's securities shortly before the announcement of an important corporate action or development. Such incidents cause extreme embarrassment and damage to both the company and the Exchange, since the public may quickly conclude that someone acted on the basis of inside information.

Negotiations leading to mergers and acquisitions, stock splits, the making of arrangements preparatory to an exchange or tender offer, changes in dividend rates or earnings, calls for redemption, and new contracts, products, or discoveries are the type of developments where the risk of untimely and inadvertent disclosure of corporate plans are most likely to occur. Frequently, these matters require extensive discussion and study by corporate officials before final decisions can be made. Accordingly, extreme care must be used in order to keep the information on a confidential basis.

Where it is possible to confine formal or informal discussions to a small group of the top management of the company or companies involved, and their individual confidential advisors where adequate security can be maintained, premature public announcement may properly be avoided. In this regard, the market action of a company's securities should be closely watched at a time when consideration is being given to important corporate matters. If unusual market activity should arise, the company should be prepared to make an immediate public announcement of the matter.

At some point it usually becomes necessary to involve other persons to conduct preliminary studies or to assist in other preparations for contemplated transactions, e.g., business appraisals, tentative financing arrangements, attitude of large outside holders, availability of major blocks of stock, engineering studies, and market analyses and surveys. Experience has shown that maintaining security at this point is virtually impossible. Accordingly, fairness requires that the company make an immediate public announcement as soon as disclosures relating to such important matters are made to outsiders.

The extent of the disclosures will depend upon the stage of discussions, studies, or negotiations. So far as possible, public statements should be definite as to price, ratio, timing, and/or any other pertinent information necessary to permit a reasonable evaluation of the matter. As a minimum, they should include those disclosures made to outsiders. Where an initial announcement cannot be specific or complete, it will need to be supplemented from time to time as more definitive or different terms are discussed or determined.

202.02 Relationship between company officials and others

Security analysts, institutional investors, etc.

Annual reports, quarterly reports, and interim releases cannot provide all of the financial and statistical data that should be available to the investing public. The Exchange recommends that companies observe an "open door" policy in their relations with security analysts, financial writers, shareholders, and others who have legitimate investment interest in the company's affairs.

A company should not give information to one inquirer which it would not give to

202 WHAT PUBLIC RELATIONS INCLUDES

another, nor should it reveal information it would not willingly give or has not given to the press for publication. Thus, for companies to give advance earnings, dividend, stock split, merger, or tender information to analysts would clearly violate Exchange policy. On the other hand, it should not withhold information in which analysts or other members of the investment public have a warrantable interest.

If during the course of discussion with analysts substantive material not previously published is disclosed, that material should be simultaneously released to the public.

202.03 Dealing with rumors or unusual market activity

The market activity of a company's securities should be closely watched when consideration is being given to significant corporate matters. If rumors or unusual market activity indicate that information on impending developments has leaked out, a frank and explicit announcement is clearly required. If rumors are in fact false or inaccurate, they should be promptly denied or clarified. A statement to the effect that the company knows of no corporate developments to account for the unusual market activity can have a salutary effect. Management should be checked with prior to any public comment so as to avoid any embarrassment or potential criticism. If rumors are correct or developments arise, an immediate candid statement to the public as to the state of negotiations or of development of corporate plans in the rumored area must be made directly and openly. Such statements are essential despite the business inconvenience this may cause and even though the matter may not have as yet been presented to the company's Board of Directors for consideration.

* * *

202.05 Timely disclosure of material news developments

A listed company is expected to quickly release to the public any news or information which might reasonably be expected to materially affect the market for its securities.

202.06 Procedure for public release of information

(A) Immediate Release Policy. The normal method of publication of important corporate data is by means of a press release. This may be either by telephone or in written form. Any release of information that could reasonably be expected to impact the market for a company's securities should be given to the wire services and the press *For Immediate Release.*

The spirit of the immediate release policy is not considered violated on weekends where a "Hold for Sunday or Monday A.M.'s" is used to obtain a broad public release of the news. This procedure facilitates the combination of a press release with a mailing to shareholders.

Annual and quarterly earnings, dividend announcements, mergers, acquisitions, tender offers, stock splits, major management changes, and any substantive items of unusual or non-recurrent nature are examples of news items that should be handled on an immediate release basis. News of major new products, contract awards, expansion plans, and discoveries very often fall into the same category. Unfavorable news should be reported as promptly and candidly as favorable news. Reluctance or unwillingness to release a negative story or an attempt to disguise unfavorable news endangers management's reputation for integrity. Changes in accounting methods to mask such occurrences can have a similar impact.

Any projections of financial data should be soundly based, appropriately qualified, conservative, and factual. Excessive or misleading conservatism should be avoided.

Few things are more damaging to a company's shareholder relations or to the general public's regard for a company's securities than information improperly withheld. On the other hand, a volume of press releases is not to be used, since important items can become confused with trivia.

Premature announcements of new products whose commercial application cannot yet be realistically evaluated should be avoided, as should overly optimistic forecasts, exaggerated claims, and unwarranted promises. Should subsequent developments indicate that performance will not match earlier projections, this too should be reported and explained.

Judgment must be exercised as to the timing of a public release on those corporate developments where the immediate release policy is not involved or where disclosure would endanger the company's goals or provide information helpful to a competitor. In these cases, the company should weigh the fairness to both present and potential stockholders who at any given moment may be considering buying or selling the company's stock.

(B) Telephone Alert to the Exchange. When the announcement of news of a material event or a statement dealing with a rumor call for immediate release to be made shortly before the opening or during market hours (presently 9:30 A.M. to 4:00 P.M., New York time), it is recommended that the company's Exchange representative be notified by telephone at least ten minutes prior to release of the announcement to the news media.

(C) Release to Newspapers and News Wire Services. News which ought to be the subject of immediate publicity must be released by the fastest available means. The fastest available means may vary in individual cases and according to the time of day. Ordinarily, this requires a release to the public press by telephone, telegraph, or hand delivery, or some combination of such methods. Transmittal of such a release to the press solely by mail is not considered satisfactory. Similarly, release of such news exclusively to the local press outside of New York City would not be sufficient for adequate and prompt disclosure.

To ensure adequate coverage, releases requiring immediate publicity should be given to Dow Jones & Company, Inc., and to Reuters Economic Services.

Companies are also encouraged to promptly distribute their releases to Associated Press and United Press International, as well as to newspapers in New York City and in cities where the company is headquartered or has plants or other major facilities.

A copy of any such press release should also be sent promptly to the attention of the company's Exchange representative.

The New York City addresses and telephone numbers of these national newswire services are:

Associated Press
50 Rockefeller Plaza
(212) 621-1500, 24 Hours

Bloomberg Business News
499 Park Avenue, 15th Floor
(212) 318-2300

Dow Jones & Company, Inc.
200 Liberty Street
(212) 416-2471

Reuters America Inc.
1700 Broadway
(212) 603-3300

United Press International
1400 Eye Street, NW
Washington, DC 20005
(202) 898-8000

Every news release should include the name and telephone number of a company official who will be available to confirm or clarify the release.

203.01 Annual report requirement

The Exchange requires that companies publish at least once a year and submit to shareholders an annual report containing financial statements of the company and its subsidiaries prepared in conformity with generally accepted accounting principles. The company must distribute its annual report to its shareholders not later than three months after the close of each fiscal year, but at least fifteen days in advance of the annual meeting. When the annual report is mailed to shareholders, four copies should be sent to the Exchange together with advice as to the date of mailing to shareholders.

(A) **Method of Publication.** The Exchange requires publication of the annual financial statements, as well as their submission to shareholders.

While distribution of the statements to shareholders usually results in their receiving some publicity, to ensure news coverage companies should submit the statements or a news release based thereon to newspapers of general circulation in large cities and to the national news wire services as described in the "Immediate Release Policy." (*See* Paragraph 202.06[A].) In addition, the statements, in the form in which sent to shareholders, should be sent to the securities statistical services, in whose publications they will remain available for ready public reference.

*   *   *

(D) **General Information in Annual Report.** The Exchange recommends that the following information be included in all annual reports:

• Address of principal office
• Names of directors and officers

• Identification of directors comprising the Audit Committee and other major committees of the Board of Directors
• Names and addresses of trustees, transfer agents, and registrars
• Number of employees
• Number of shareholders

(E) **Occasional Delay in Issuance of Statements.** The probability of a delay in the issuance of annual financial statements ordinarily can be foreseen. As soon as it becomes apparent that a delay is imminent the company should advise its Exchange representative of the circumstances and the probable extent of the delay.

If the statements cannot be sent to shareholders at least fifteen days in advance of the annual meeting, it may be necessary for the company to postpone the meeting or to adjourn it without transaction of business to a date which shall be fifteen days after the statements are issued. Whether or not such postponement or adjournment will be necessary can be determined only in the light of the particular circumstances. The matter should be discussed with the Exchange representative as soon as the possibility of the delay becomes apparent.

203.02 Interim earnings reporting requirement

(A) **Time of Publication.** No specific time limit for publication of interim earnings statements has been set, but it is assumed that such statements will be published as soon as available.

(B) **Method of Publication.** The Exchange requires publication of interim statements as news items in the public press. It is not required that the statements be sent to shareholders, although most companies do so. Whether or not the statements are sent to shareholders, to be sure of adequate coverage the statements should be released to newspapers and to the national news wire services as described in the "Immediate Release Policy." (*See* Paragraph 202.06[A]).) In addition, they should be sent to the securities statistical services.

(C) Form of Interim Financials. The listing agreement merely requires publication (quarterly or semi-annually, as the case may be) of a statement of earnings; it does not require that such statements be sent to shareholders. Interim earnings statements shall be on the same basis of consolidation as the company's annual financial statements and shall disclose, as a minimum, any substantial items of unusual or non-recurrent nature and either net income before and after federal income taxes or net income and the amount of federal taxes. Additional information, and particularly sales data, will, of course, be useful to shareholders.

Readers interested in learning more about details of corporate disclosure should consult the following sources:

- *New York Stock Exchange Company Manual*—loose-leaf notebook updated periodically and made available free to corporate secretaries and key executives of all listed companies.
- *American Stock Exchange Company Manual*—similarly available.
- *Nasdaq* (National Association of Securities Dealers Automated Quotations) is now monitoring movements of securities traded over-the-counter (not listed on an exchange).
- *Financial Accounting Standards* prepared by the Financial Accounting Standards Board, published by all major accounting firms as a service to clients. Public relations people can probably learn more about the communications problems caused by certain standards (No. 33—Accounting for Inflation and No. 52—Foreign Currency Trans-

lations) by examining several current corporate annual reports.

- Sec Materials: Securities Act of 1933; Securities Exchange Act of 1934; forms, rules, and regulations thereunder. Generally available free of charge from any printer specializing in legal materials. An important source of most current sec disclosure requirements is Regulation S-K which became effective May 24, 1982, and is widely available from the same sources. The sec does not provide copies of its rules to the general public.

Maintaining Long-Term Effectiveness

The investor relations person is basically a communicator of information. Through expertness in communications, he or she helps many people reach the decision to buy or hold the company's stock. Success can be measured in many ways but is best reflected in a realistic appraisal of the company and of its securities. To accomplish this, the public relations person must be professional, have a high regard for truthfulness and accuracy, and lean on the side of conservatism in discussing future developments of the company. This does not mean that the individual cannot strive to show that the company is a good investment, but he or she must at times restrain enthusiasm in favor of a realistic appraisal that in the long term will establish or maintain the company's reputation for integrity and, at the same time, lay the basis for developing a core of loyal long-term stockholders.

Although actions and words may fulfill today's needs by the press and public, the investor relations person must keep in mind that they also will be judged in light of the company's future performance.

12

EMPLOYEE COMMUNICATION

RICHARD BEVAN
JOHN BAILEY

Richard Bevan is a vice-president of TPF&C (Towers, Perrin) and leader of the firm's communication consulting practice. He has twenty-two years of experience in employee communication, including employee research, strategy and planning, implementation of communication programs, and training.

He is located in TPF&C's Seattle office. His prior assignments included periods in the UK and Australia. He has a BA in Engineering Science from Oxford University and a Diploma in Business Administration from Manchester Business School. He has served on the Executive Board and Accreditation Board of the International Association of Business Communicators.

John Bailey was Executive Director of the International Association of Business Communicators, a professional society for individuals in organization communication and public relations. Under his direction the association won awards for its publications, total communication program, books it published, membership development techniques, and conference programming.

Bailey has been a spokesman for organizational communicators throughout North America and Europe.

An organization's success is determined by its employees' skills, knowledge, and commitment. A key factor, more than ever, in employee motivation and performance is communication. This is especially true where downsizing and other personnel-cutting moves have shaken employees and decreased their loyalty and confidence in management's concern for their interests. It is through employee communication that an organization shares information, builds commitment, and manages change.

Communication is more than symbols or messages. It is the vital process by which the organization survives, adapts, and thrives.

The fundamental objectives of communication are to provide employees with the information needed to perform their individual jobs, as well as ongoing feedback on their respective job performance. Once these primary requirements have been satisfied the employee may be ready to learn about the goals and results of his or her respective work unit, that unit's functional role and impact on the organization as a whole, and the ways in which he or she can contribute.

This information can be communicated to employees orally or in writing, face-to-face or remotely, one-on-one or in groups—using visual, audio, or electronic media. People constantly communicate—with customers, external publics, their immediate work group, other groups, and managers. They talk and listen; advise and respond; generate ideas; and develop attitudes and loyalties.

Roger D'Aprix has characterized this employee communication process—and the employees' corresponding need for information—as a hierarchy or pyramid. In the model below, each level represents an issue, or employee need for specific information, expressed as a question. Initially the employee focuses on individual job responsibilities: What's my job? As the employees gain satisfactory information about each issue, they move successively to broader issues—eventually gaining enough understanding of the "big picture" to enable them to explore ways in which they can make a greater contribution to the organization: How can I help?

Question	Issue
What's my job?	Individual job responsibilities
How am I doing?	Personal performance feedback
Am I valued?	Individual needs and concerns
What are we up to?	Work unit plans and results
Where do we fit?	Work unit role and charter
How can I help?	Commitment and participation

Research on employee communication preferences clearly shows that employees prefer face-to-face communication with their immediate supervisor. That process is direct, personal, informal, and can provide imme-diate discussion and feedback. But as the volume of information increases and as time becomes scarcer, face-to-face processes cannot accomplish every communication need.

The organization needs a framework of well-planned and implemented communication programs, using a variety of media, to meet employees' basic information needs and to facilitate the upward flow of information and ideas.

Print Communications

Communicators can choose from a wide and continually expanding range of print media. The choice depends on the purpose of the message, its content, its urgency, the intended audience—and the available resources. This may consist of a simple memo to an elaborate brochure; from a newsletter prepared on a word processor to a full-scale newspaper.

Regular publications

The most prevalent medium for communicating information to a group of employees is a regular publication. (*See* the second section of this chapter for an extended treatment of this subject.) This can communicate all kinds of information in a variety of formats. It can be aimed at the general population or to special groups, such as managers.

Newsletters

Newsletters are the simplest, fastest, and least costly to produce. The page size is small and the number of pages limited. Articles tend to be brief and illustrations modest. The small scale makes the newsletter inadequate to handle the information load of a large corporation, but ideal for departments or divisions. The newsletter offers the advantage of being inexpensive to produce (increasingly, using desktop publishing) by nonprofessional communicators having modest editorial skills.

Newspapers

Newspapers are prevalent among large organizations, where a large volume of information requires a frequent and sizeable publication. They can have few pages or many, short articles or long, straight news or feature pieces, spot illustrations or photo-features. Frequency of publication ranges from daily to monthly.

Publishing an internal newspaper is a labor-intensive endeavor. It will generally require a full-time staff or a committed external resource with a broad range of skills: information gathering, writing, copy editing, photography, layout, and design. Editorial personnel must work with news sources, designers, artists, typesetters, printers, and mailers. A newspaper's great strengths are immediacy and credibility, especially if it is seen as oriented to reporting rather than to advocacy for management positions.

Magazines

Magazines can vary greatly in size, length, and design. But the format is best suited for fewer, longer, interpretive pieces and more open layouts. The high quality of paper stock lends itself to full-color treatment and the liberal use of photos and illustrations. Because of their greater expense and longer production cycle, magazines are seldom published more frequently than monthly.

A well-planned and executed magazine can convey a strong sense of quality and organizational values. The material is often suitable for reaching a variety of other publics— including customers and suppliers. Being the recipient of a magazine whose primary role is internal can give them a sense that they have some special insights into the organization on which they depend for orders or for service.

Other publications

One-time publications

These publications are produced for many programs or initiatives. They can include handbooks, brochures, pamphlets, and fliers. Other items that may have a place include paycheck inserts, posters, table tents, letters to the home, and special displays in cafeterias or other high-traffic areas.

Internal memorandums

Memorandums are the most prevalent means of written communication in many areas of the organization. But their prevalence in an age of information overload means that a memo from a senior executive may not receive the desired attention. Nonetheless, this method is fast and has the great strength of using readily available internal resources for production and distribution. Creating slight variations on the basic format (for example, using different colored paper stock) can enhance visibility and attention.

Letters

Letters to employees' homes increase the chance that the message will be shared by the employee's family. In some cases (for example, changes in the health care program), family members are as important an audience as employees. The issue is more likely to be raised, reviewed, and discussed at home. But the letter will have to compete with other mail for attention, and some people see this approach as intrusive. On balance, letters to the home can be highly effective but should be used sparingly and only when the nature of the message is appropriate.

Bulletin boards

As the name suggests, the bulletin board is a medium of brevity and immediacy. As such it is most effective in reporting time-sensitive information—events or breaking news—that cannot wait for scheduled publications. Ironically, many bulletin boards feature long-standing information (some of a necessary statutory nature). As a result, they may receive little attention. The bulletin board is also a poor vehicle for communicating detailed information or for discussing concepts or issues.

But organizations that invest in effective design and management of bulletin boards find them a highly effective and immediate information channel.

They should be placed in areas where they are easily visible and comfortably read. They must be regularly organized and updated. The impact is reduced when important messages have to compete for space with outdated or trivial ones. Some organizations deal with clutter by putting bulletin boards behind glass and limiting access to authorized people. Others set up separate boards for different kinds of material. A posted message must be read quickly and in passing, so the content should be brief—preferably on one sheet—and strictly factual.

Visual Communications

Television/Video

Television, a pervasive medium at home, is now a major feature in the workplace—not surprisingly. It is the medium with which most people are most familiar; it has high impact and entertainment value; it can convey information and ideas very effectively through a combination of sound and images. And it requires little active effort on the part of the viewer.

There are, however, some major drawbacks. Commercial television has accustomed people to receiving information in very short segments and often without real depth. The power of TV to entertain places heavy demands on the organizational communicator to create effective programs that retain employee attention and interest. Accordingly, long and detailed programs ("the book on tape") are giving way to much shorter, faster-paced programs that set a tone or to well-produced documentaries that combine narration with interviews and location shots.

Accordingly, TV is often used not to convey key messages but to establish a theme. For example, at a meeting to discuss quality issues a short videotape may be used to create an atmosphere and establish interest. But hard information about the meaning of quality and the role of the employee may be better communicated in a live presentation.

This vivid, high-impact medium is not likely to supplant printed publications as the primary source of information. Indeed, it can generate interest in supporting print media, just as broadcast TV creates demand for newspapers. But TV has clearly established itself as an important vehicle for large-scale employee communication.

Staff needs are large—producers, directors, scriptwriters, reporters, editors, camera operators, and other technicians. It is generally only larger companies that retain an in-house TV capability. Instead, most rely on a thriving network of production companies to create their programs.

Organizational video is distributed in several ways, including live teleconferencing, distribution via satellite downlinks, closed-circuit broadcast networks, distribution to employees' homes, or continuous loops run in high-traffic areas. But the most prevalent method is probably to show the program in a specially convened meeting. An introduction (from someone qualified to answer questions following the program) will focus attention. (*See also* Chapter 27.)

Overhead projector

Despite the prevalence of video, more presentations are made using overhead projector slides than any other medium. Transparencies can be made very quickly, requiring nothing more than a blank sheet and a suitable pen. More elaborate slides can be produced in one or several colors. The equipment is almost universally available and is suitable for small to medium groups (up to thirty or forty). For larger numbers the technique can still be effective, but careful planning is needed to ensure that text is readable.

35mm slides

Slides also continue to be widely used and have received new impetus from computer-assisted methods of generating text and graphics. These permit quick and easy development of presentations with impressive use of color and graphics. Revisions can be made easily and inexpensively. The equipment is also suitable for large groups with a projector equipped with a zoom lens. A slide presentation can be transferred to videotape and a sound track added. Style and impact will not generally match moving images (although a high degree of movement and animation can be achieved with multiprojector applications). But this is a useful and inexpensive technique, even if only to simplify distribution (for example, via videocassette to employees' homes).

Electronic Communications

Electronics and computer technology, often combining with long-existing methods (such as telephone), are placing exciting new tools into the hands of organizational communicators. Here are some of the more promising developments:

Desktop publishing

Desktop publishing eliminates many of the separate and costly processes commonly associated with the creation and preparation of printed publications. (*See* Chapter 33.) With the right equipment and software, a single person sitting at a workstation is able to write stories and headlines, create a layout (usually within an already-established format), and print the final product—or create camera-ready artwork.

Initially suitable for relatively simple one- or two-color applications, the technology is now applied to the design and development of high-quality full-color publications.

One risk: just as the word processor doesn't make a writer of a nonwriter, desktop publishing doesn't make everyone into a designer—although it puts a powerful tool at his or her disposal. Creating attractive and effective layouts still needs the attention of a specialist. The strength of the technology is that the designer can create a style sheet that a writer can then work with.

Electronic bulletin boards

These permit employees with access to personal computers or terminals to obtain news and information, and to exchange individual messages. They can receive much greater detail and variety than with bulletin boards or telephone hotlines, and can arrange to download or print text as needed.

This medium is most effective in an office environment with an extensive computer network, where large numbers of employees have computers on their desks.

Electronic mail

"E-mail" usually operates in parallel with electronic bulletin boards and on the same equipment. It enables employees to create and send text messages to anyone on the network, and to grouped lists of people. The system handles addressing and distribution automatically, so that once the list is established, a manager (for example) can send the same message to many individuals—instantly.

Voice mail

Phone or voice mail is growing very rapidly and offers the voice equivalent of electronic mail. It is an effective application of interactive communication technology (*see* the following). Its power and attractiveness lie in the fact that everyone has access to telephones, and that the system can be reached remotely (i.e., from a phone other than one's own). The user can record a message and use the keypad to direct it to any number of recipients. The user can listen to messages left on the system for retrieval, and can then delete them, save them, or transmit them to someone else—with or without comment.

Interactive media

The computer's power, flexibility, and ability to retrieve stored data have opened a new era in personalized communication. Interactive systems permit employees, in a user-friendly environment, to receive and provide information of their choice. The most common interactive communication device is the touch-tone telephone, programmed so individuals can choose from a menu of offerings. Personal computers also run a variety of interactive communication programs. Intranets are now widely established to make information and interchange effective. (*See* Chapter 29.)

There are many applications in employee benefit plan administration and communication, and others (such as job-posting, employee education, surveys, and suggestion systems) are growing rapidly.

Applications in the benefit plan area can provide information, permit employees to make administrative changes to items such as savings plan accounts, handle enrollment for new programs, accept claims for medical benefits, or provide models for looking at future retirement income.

Interactive vehicles can replace some face-to-face meetings (just as automated teller machines have the same role in banking) saving paper and time, and raising the accuracy of data entry.

Telephone hotlines

Like bulletin boards, telephone hotlines are effective for reporting current news. The employee dials the hotline number to get a recorded message or to reach an operator (or team) who can provide needed information. In either case, the system can be interactive, with the employee using the telephone keypad to select information options (one of which may be to reach a "live" person).

Messages need to be brief, factual, of significant interest, and regularly updated if employees are to be encouraged to call again.

Unsurpassed for speed, the hotline is the preferred vehicle for crisis reporting and fast-breaking developments. And it can be an extremely effective support mechanism when complex information is being communicated (for example, during a reorganization or during communication of changed pay or benefit programs). The hotline offers several advantages over bulletin boards. Message distribution uses existing telephone systems rather than a network of individuals in remote locations. That can save labor and assure control. Moreover, the hotline information can be accessed at any time from any location that has a telephone.

The hotline's effectiveness depends on employee initiative. Energetic promotion (through posters, publications, and managers) may be appropriate.

Teleconferencing

This process combines TV and telecommunications technologies to join groups from different locations for meetings. Teleconferencing has become an especially useful vehicle in national and multinational corporations with large, geographically dispersed employee populations.

Virtually any subject of a conventional face-to-face meeting is also suitable for teleconferencing. The senior executive has the same opportunity to communicate directly with a large employee group, and discussion and questions are also possible.

Setting up a teleconference requires careful preparation of a highly technical kind—notably setting up satellite links among the locations. But there are substantial economies in linking people who would otherwise have to spend the time, and incur the cost, of traveling to a meeting at a single location.

Employee Feedback Channels

Management needs access to and must listen to what employees have to say. The stream of employee feedback to management—or upward communication—is a critical element in the communication strategy of any organization.

Effective upward communication can accomplish the following:

- Allow employees to contribute information and ideas.

- Keep management in touch with concerns, issues, and questions.

- Contribute to development of a shared understanding of organizational goals. Employees often say that senior management seems remote from the realities of the workplace and insufficiently interested or involved in day-to-day problems and opportunities. Only positive reports and reactions filter up to the top of the organization, because of the widespread practice of "shooting the messenger"—blaming the bringer of bad news.

A survey of human resource professionals in top U.S. companies revealed that the majority of them characterized their upward communication as only "fair." In companies where upward communication is working well (supported by top management and where management is willing to act on employee ideas), the effect on morale was seen as very positive. Most organizations believe that high morale can be a major contributor to good performance.

Employees are more than ready to communicate upward. But how effectively they do this and how well the organization makes use of their ideas depends largely on the attitude of senior management. Upward communication works best in a climate wherein senior managers trust and respect their employees and recognize their value not just as workers but as thinkers and contributors.

How does the organization listen to its employees? The most important and powerful method is through regular informal interaction among employees and their supervisors. For those responsible for promoting effective communication, this process can be supported by many formal and informal programs.

Meetings

Most large group meetings include a "Q&A" segment in which the audience can comment or ask questions. The spontaneous give-and-take creates a positive atmosphere of openness, candor, and mutual sharing.

To protect employees who may be fearful of reprisals, not so much from the senior executives who might lead such a meeting but also from their own managers, questions can be sought before the event. They are then read and answered by the executive at the meeting. Some meetings end with the distribution of feedback forms.

Employees generally prefer to receive information face-to-face, and meetings, large and small, are highly popular sources of company information for employees.

Suggestion systems

One of the oldest upward communication vehicles is the suggestion box, through which written suggestions are submitted. Employees whose suggestions are adopted are often rewarded with cash or recognition or both. This vehicle works best when suggestions are studied seriously and acted on and when feedback is fast and effective.

Support for this process is not universal. Many organizations striving to continuously improve their operations believe that a fundamental responsibility of every employee is developing improvement ideas. In this context paying for suggestions seems conflicting.

Speak-up programs

Speak-up programs allow employees to pass along ideas, concerns, or questions to a coordinator. This person then passes them on—without the name of the employees concerned—to the appropriate senior executive. The response is channeled back through the coordinator.

Where appropriate, responses may also receive wider distribution through internal media. The key to success is the assurance of confidentiality and the certainty of a timely response.

Surveys

The most widely used "formal" upward communication system, employee surveys can be used to diagnose organizational strengths and weaknesses, pinpoint issues that need immediate attention, and assess employee morale. (*See* Chapter 18.) These employee research efforts can help management prepare for change by:

- Assessing employee morale and attitudes
- Identifying opportunities to improve quality or productivity
- Exploring the reasons behind high turnover
- Evaluating the effectiveness of communication and the benefit of reward systems
- Measuring the gaps between the organization's stated values and operating principles and actual management practices (the "say-do" analysis)
- Testing ideas and plans before implementing them
- Establishing benchmarks for measuring progress

Surveys can be quantitative or qualitative, broad in scope or narrowly focused, conducted via written questionnaires, personal interviews, group interviews, or the telephone (programmed interactive or with an interviewer).

Broad-based opinion surveys

These surveys assess employees' opinions on work-related issues, such as pay, benefits, working conditions, communication, and management style. They frequently use written questionnaires. In smaller organizations every employee might be invited to respond. In larger ones a sample is used.

By administering a consistent survey instrument at regular intervals, the organization can track attitudes over a period of time. As with any communication program, the organization needs a clear definition of its goals for conducting a survey and its intentions for follow-up. Specifically, surveys should be seen as tools to develop information on which management can act rather than as a research exercise in themselves. If no action results, employees will become cynical about future survey activity—and opportunities for change will have been missed.

Communication audits

These audits have a narrower focus than broad-based surveys, although they may employ a broad range of data-gathering techniques. They focus on employee perceptions of the overall communication climate and on the effectiveness of specific programs and media. They are typically used to evaluate existing programs or to develop long-range communication strategies.

Data may be gathered in a written survey, interviews with executives, focus groups (*see* the following), by studying and evaluating existing media, by observations of the communication process, and other approaches.

Readership or media surveys

These surveys evaluate the effectiveness of a particular medium. They might focus, for example, on an employee publication or a video magazine program.

Focus groups

Focus groups are a powerful method of gathering qualitative data in small group meetings. In an approach borrowed from the market research arena, a trained facilitator meets with a small group of employees (typically, eight to twelve).

In an informal atmosphere, employee opinions are explored, usually using a structured interview guide designed to ensure consistency and to make reporting of multiple groups simpler. The facilitator's role is to guide, probe, and listen; to keep the discussion focused; to assess where there is consensus and where there is not. In the communication context, one of the most useful applications of the focus group is in pre-testing communication material and identifying changes to copy, style, or substance that will make the material more effective.

The grapevine

Not a formal medium but a ubiquitous channel of upward and downward communication, the grapevine deserves mention. Employees generally rate this informal, unplanned, and unofficial information exchange with fellow employees as their primary source of information.

Where there is an information gap, guesswork and rumor will quickly fill it. Accordingly, if communication in the organization is not meeting the basic information needs of employees, activity in the grapevine will increase (and accuracy will decline).

A hotline or similar approach to rumor control can be effective, especially during times of rapid change or crisis. (*See* Chapter 2.)

"Management by walking around"

This technique encourages informal visits to the workplace in which a manager or supervisor will engage employees in informal, unplanned conversations. The person doing the walking around may be the employees' immediate supervisor or a more senior manager. The practice has many strengths. It increases management visibility; exposes managers to current ideas, concerns, and information; offers opportunities for positive feedback on performance; and reassures employees that management is aware of current issues and conditions.

Management by walking around need not be random. It can be planned as a regular part of a manager's schedule, and an informal agenda can be used. For example, managers can try to ask all employees with whom they interact in this way their opinion about some recent event or initiative. It builds trust, provides a good opportunity to exchange information, and keeps management in close touch with the workforce.

Open door

The "open door" means different things in different settings. Sometimes it simply describes a culture that is open and in which employees can feel free to approach their manager (or others) with an idea or a problem. In other settings, the policy may be more specific and refer to the fact that any employee can seek a meeting with the manager's boss. It takes a very open and supportive management style, as well as support from all levels of the company, for the open door to be successful.

Skip-level meetings

A formal implementation (and perhaps a less threatening one) of the "open door" principle is the skip-level meeting. Here, employees meet as a group, perhaps on a regular basis, with their manager's boss. Typically, therefore, employees from more than one work group will be represented. The meetings provide a good forum for direct distribution of information, for discussion and questions, and for the manager to gather opinions and ideas.

Communication Planning

A communication plan is a blueprint for action. It lays out what information needs to be communicated, to whom it should be sent, and how it should be conveyed. It does this in the context of the organization's overall mission and goals. Its purpose is to ensure that the media the organization uses and the messages they carry support the overall direction of the organization.

There are many approaches to communication planning, but most contain statements of the organization's overall mission and goals, such as the following:

- An understanding of management and employee needs: what management wants communication to achieve and the information employees need (and want)

- Several key result areas, based on these inputs, in which employee communication can have an impact

- Message strategy, consisting of a summary of major messages for each segment of the employee audience

- Detailed plans for media that will deliver those messages appropriately

- Integration with all other forms of communication

- Measurement and valuation mechanisms

Organizational goals

Not every organization has a clearly stated mission. Even then, the planner still needs to have a sense of direction to ensure that communication plans are appropriate. It is surprising (but appropriate) how often the planning process begins with an exploration of issues much broader than specific audience groups and media.

Management and employee input

The planning process should include a detailed assessment of the organization's priorities, as well as the communication needs of managers and employees.

By interviewing senior executives and reviewing both long-term and short-term operating plans, the communicator confirms or refines the organization's priorities and can then formulate specific communications objectives to support them.

Through meetings and surveys of employees and managers, the communicator determines issues of concern, perceptions about the organization, and the level of understanding of priorities and goals. Communication objectives should also reflect these factors.

Key result areas

These areas might include customer relations, quality, cost containment, competitiveness, safety—and others drawn from the mission and from management goals. The number should be limited to no more than six to eight. For each, a communication goal can be developed, describing what outcome in terms of employee action or attitude is targeted.

Outcomes of communication activity cannot always be specifically tied to that activity (many other factors may be having an influence). But the process of setting targets and measuring results still yields many useful insights.

Message strategy

In this stage the key audience segments (such as first-level supervisors, production staff, sales representatives) are identified and key messages developed for each. For example, a component of the message strategy might be that every employee should understand that quality of service is the key to the organization's success and that this will be recognized in reward and other programs.

Media plans

The messages, once defined, must then be implemented through specific communication programs tailored to the target audience segment. Publication schedules for regular publications are sketched out, and tentative content is assigned. Special program needs are identified and planned, and needed staff and financial resources are identified.

Evaluation

Finally, the effectiveness of the messages and the programs must be assessed. Some measures may be relatively objective (the number of customer complaints, the extent and timing of employee enrollments, error rates on forms, turnover), while others will be subjective (management's evaluation, readership, and other research).

A well-conceived and executed communication plan should strongly support the organization's priorities. It should also reflect the concerns and needs of employees. It can be a dynamic and coordinating force that expresses the organization's mission and culture and makes a major contribution to moving it forward.

Crisis Communications

The quality of employee communication is severely tested in times of organizational crisis: strikes, layoffs, plant shutdowns, takeovers or mergers, bankruptcy, natural disasters, or personal tragedies. (*See* Chapter 2.)

Whatever form it takes, a crisis is certain to impact employees. It will affect morale and attention to the job and is likely to have a negative impact on performance.

Moreover, the key to resolution of the problem may lie with employees. The ability to respond to a natural disaster and restore normal operations is likely to depend on the support and commitment of the workforce. And in a major organizational change, it's essential to win the continued commitment of employees.

Crises in large organizations are often public events. So employee communication efforts should be closely tied to those of the other communication functions, notably publicity, community relations, and investor relations. Close coordination assures that employees receive the same messages at the same time as the outside public. In a crisis employees like to hear from the organization before they see it on the TV news.

While a crisis is usually unexpected, contingency planning can make all the difference. For example, management can

- Identify ahead of time those responsible for managing the crisis and for handling communication

- Commit to communicating openly, honestly, and frequently throughout the crisis

- Develop communication plans that outline media and distribution networks such as local TV or radio, press releases, special briefings, hotlines, and other methods

- Study vulnerable operations or locations and develop worst-case scenarios

- Establish a crisis management team and train the key individuals

- Set up a contact plan to ensure that key people can be reached on very short notice

- Review the policy and plan on a regular basis to make sure they're still workable in light of changing business situations and personnel

Professional communicators can't control a crisis but the skill with which they interact with employees can have a profound and lasting effect on the organization.

Emerging Communications Issues

As key participants in the change process, professional communicators need to be aware of the issues that influence organizational performance, drive management thinking, and concern and interest employees.

Managing change and diversity

Survival may depend on the ability to enhance competitiveness, to commit to quality, and to effectively deal with change. To do so, the organization has to win the commitment of an increasingly diverse workforce. Changing demographics, as well as changing attitudes toward work, are altering the nature of the organization and the way it communicates.

This increasing diversity as women and minorities enter the workforce in record numbers is changing traditional ways of communicating. The new workers bring with them different values, attitudes, skills, and languages.

Building a shared understanding of organizational goals among these groups presents a major challenge—a challenge compounded by an increasingly severe shortage of skilled labor. Literacy is a key issue, with workplace programs certain to expand dramatically.

The new generation of employees has different values and expectations about work. They expect more meaningful jobs, more control, greater flexibility in working patterns, and help in balancing work and family pressures.

Globalization

The world is rapidly shrinking as competition for markets becomes global in scale. The nations of Asia are growing as a major force; the nations of Europe are becoming a unified economic entity; and the Eastern Bloc nations are emerging into the free-market economy.

To compete and prosper, U.S. companies will become increasingly multinational in their outlook and operations, their workforce, marketing approach, and internal communication. There will be more multinational communication staffs, more multicultural communication strategies, and more multilingual communication vehicles. And computer technology of all kinds is playing a much larger role.

Health-care quality and cost

Trying to achieve employee understanding of and appreciation for a costly benefits program has always been a challenge for the organizational communicator, even when the news was mostly "good." Now the need to control costs while maintaining the quality of care has made this challenge even more severe.

There is intense need for education on health-care issues. Employees and other groups need to understand the nature of the crisis. And employees need assistance to find their way through an increasingly complex set of alternatives for sources of health care. The benefits communication challenge has become one of helping employees to understand the health-care cost and quality issue, gaining employee acceptance of changes, and teaching employees to become more knowledgeable consumers of health-care services.

The trust gap

In the '80s and '90s many corporations experienced profound upheavals. Very often employees were the losers: jobs were lost, earnings fell, and pressure for performance increased. As a result, employees have grown much less confident in the stability of their organizations and less trusting in the competence and intentions of the people who lead them. Yet now survival depends on renewing the commitment to that belief—and demonstrating it. Closing the trust gap presents a formidable challenge to employee communication professionals who must reestablish an information climate of confidence, fairness, and openness in the organization.

It also presents them with a rare opportunity to exert their full potential as professionals. Senior managers are increasingly looking to them not only as implementors, but also as strategists—and full partners in the effort to gain and hold the loyalty and confidence of employees.

The Manager's Role

Several factors contribute to an effective communication program:

- An understanding of the audience (or audiences)
- A commitment to direct and honest communication
- Clearly defined goals and expectations
- The resources to present information, and to seek it, in ways that will be responsive, appealing, and understandable
- An active approach to listening to employees' input
- Consistency with the organization's overall goals
- Effective support and involvement from management at all levels

Senior management

The CEO defines and shapes the culture of the organization. As a powerful role model for all managers, the CEO's attitude and behavior in relation to employee communication will probably determine the pattern throughout the organization.

Senior managers have spoken for years about people being their "most important resource" and the importance of enlisting employee commitment and support. In meeting the challenge of managing the scarce and diverse resources of "Workforce 2000," enlisting employee support and commitment will be a key not just to success but to survival.

Recent surveys indicate that the views of senior managers about their own communication role are changing. Many believe that their communication with employees influences job satisfaction, job performance, and commitment. Yet most devote a small percentage of their time to communicating with internal audiences beyond their immediate staff and subordinates.

How should they do this? They should listen and talk. From informal breakfasts with employee groups, to site visits, management briefings, and a Q&A section in an internal publication, as well as through countless other forms of communication, senior managers can stay in touch with people while communicating a vision and direction for the organization.

First-level managers

If senior executives create the communication climate in their organizations, it is first-level managers who are the primary communicators.

Managers spend most of their time communicating: face-to-face, on the phone, and through other written formats. Management, it has often been observed, *is* communication. Managing effectively means communicating effectively.

In survey after survey employees identify their immediate supervisors as their preferred source of information. Those employees routinely depend on their bosses for direction and support. It is natural that they also turn to them for the information they want and need to do their jobs effectively.

Unfortunately, many managers are ill-equipped for the task. They lack skills or may not always be well-informed themselves. They may also not be encouraged to communicate or motivated to do so. But more organizations are devoting considerable resources to keeping managers better informed and improving their communications skills. Through special newsletters, training programs, briefings, and other meetings managers are receiving more attention, training, and information. Communication roles and responsibilities are increasingly well-defined. Communication skills are increasingly likely to be considered as part of the criteria for promotion and other rewards.

The communication manager

The often-used term *communicator* may be misleading. Given the multiple roles fulfilled by organizational communication, the responsibility for managing the process is a major one. Execution—at least in terms of face-to-face communication—is the responsibility of line managers.

The role of the communication specialist is to support the goals and objectives of the organization by planning, implementing, and facilitating communication programs and processes.

Communication is not a matter of instinct and intuition. Nor is it a matter of reacting to events and reporting news. It contains elements of management, advocacy, planning, and facilitation. Like any other organizational function, communication operates within a framework of goals, strategies, and plans. It requires a disciplined, professional, systematic yet flexible approach. Above all, perhaps, it requires initiative and innovation to help the organization solve problems and respond to opportunities.

Employee Publications

Internal communication has grown rapidly, thanks to the gradual evolution of employees toward the top of the list of important audiences. Until recently, many organizations—and their internal communicators—continued to rely on the principle: "tell 'em as little as possible, but be firm about it." They concentrated their efforts on publications when other communicators were using an array of media. They disseminated classic house organ material—babies and bowling teams—when workers hungered for substantive information about their company and its future.

Now internal communicators discuss serious issues through a number of media. The change reflects how employees are viewed by senior managers in most corporations.

Publications featuring management exhortations and chitchat are a dying breed, and accompanying them to the grave are single-medium communication programs.

Communicators now generally consider many methods of communicating a given message and, indeed, often counsel management on what that message should be. They also face the challenge of explaining to internal and external audiences alike why the organization is in business and what it believes in.

The growing stature of employees as an audience—due in part to their key position in the struggle to increase productivity—and the skyrocketing production costs involved in virtually any communication program mean that internal programs must be measurably effective. (*See* Figure 12.1, page 222.)

Employee Information Needs

The International Association of Business Communicators and the consulting firm of Towers, Perrin cosponsored an Employee Communication Effectiveness survey to find out how well organizational communication programs meet employees' information needs and what media they use to achieve their objectives. The survey queried nearly 46,000 employees in forty U.S. and Canadian organizations. The results showed the employees are most interested in information about the company itself and their own future in it.

Employees are most interested in issues affecting the organization and their jobs, and they want the information they receive to be both candid and well balanced. Regarding publications, employees felt the information they received was accurate and believable, but

not balanced. The majority felt they didn't receive the full story.

What is needed is to match the message and media to employee preferences. Clearly, a single publication cannot fulfill the needs for information employees expect.

In addition to traditional print media possibilities, the internal communicator today should be aware of—and able to take advantage of—the rapidly increasing variety of trends and technological developments treated in the first portion of this chapter.

The electronic revolution in the communication field presents two major challenges for all communicators. First it dramatically increases the media possibilities at their disposal. And it makes ongoing professional development essential as communicators with "traditional" editorial and production skills confront computer-related technology.

Establishing Objectives

Publications and other media are not isolated units operating in a vacuum. Though each should have its own reason for being—its own objectives and audiences—each should also be part of an overall organizational communication plan. The word *organizational* is important because it implies top management's discussion, approval, and probably its input. Internal communicators with a firm set of guidelines supporting the goals of the organization will have fewer problems planning publications and other elements of a communication program. In addition, the approval process probably will run more smoothly if communicators can show how individual articles, new publications, or annual programs fit into the total picture and support overall organizational goals.

General Electric's employee communication program concentrates on five major themes: satisfying customers, surpassing com-

Figure 12.1 Sample employee publications. The Tribune Company uses a variety of formats to communicate with its employees. *Photo by Glenn Kaupert,* Chicago Tribune.

petition, minimizing costs, responding to change, and relating to employees specifically to communicate management's concern for their best interests and explain how they share the company's success through various compensation plans. The program emphasizes the importance of communicating these themes by reporting and interpreting specific events that illustrate them: orders won, orders lost; the names of competitors and how they are doing in worldwide competition. In the area of employee concerns, the program calls for reporting the way employee benefits go to work in specific people situations, etc.

GE's long-range, continuing communication plan's main purposes are as follows:

• Seek employee "effort and cooperation in achieving specific goals and overcoming specific business problems."

• Build an appreciation of management's efforts to treat them fairly, so that they will be willing to listen to what management has to say, even when they disagree.

By concentrating on building employee understanding, the plan also lays a groundwork of employee support in the event of a change or crisis. "In the emotional atmosphere of crisis situations," according to one summary of the program, "employees often misunderstand and reject facts that, if presented in the calmer atmosphere of day-to-day operations, they would have readily understood."

General Electric's short-term communication efforts concentrate on those "needs that at that period are of particular importance to the success of the business—matters on which management is concentrating its efforts and for which it needs the full cooperation of certain employee groups." These needs include achieving production or cost reduction goals, improving productivity with new machines or methods, explaining new employee relations practices, and so on.

Short-term goals are also considered from the standpoint of both "business needs" and "employee concerns." Full information is provided on the immediate goals and related problems involved, steps being taken by management, and how and why employees should help. Employees are kept informed on continuing progress toward meeting the goals. At the same time, employees' needs and wants must be considered.

Selecting Media

Once overall goals have been established, the communicator can begin selecting media to reach those goals. First, he or she must identify the target audience (or audiences) and determine the objectives of each publication or other program element in order to choose the medium that most effectively will convey the message to the audience. A vital consideration, of course, is budget.

In small organizations most channels of communication often can be aimed at the entire employee group, with departmental meetings satisfying more specific needs. Or a general employee publication might be supplemented with a newsletter for managers or departments. But the major trend is toward a multiplicity of specific publications aimed at specific audiences, particularly in organizations that have a large number of internal groups requiring specialized communications. Hospitals, for example, often have separate publications for doctors, nurses, paramedics, volunteers, clerical and support staff, and the community at large, including donors, board members, business leaders, and the local press. Other possible audiences include re-

tirees, dealers or agents, branch office staffs, company communicators, and shareholders.

Although audiovisual media are rapidly gaining ground, the print medium remains the most commonly used method for reaching all audiences, external as well as internal. However, the use of intranets as computerized employee communications channels is growing. (*See* Chapter 29.)

The most popular print formats are magazines, newspapers, and magapapers (tabloids that fold to an 8½″ × 11″ size and have a magazinelike cover). Each offers its own advantages and each demonstrates versatility in actual use.

The magazine is the most sophisticated of the print formats used in employee communication and until recently was the most common. (*See* Figure 12.2.) Today magazines and newspapers are used about equally. Magazines are most effective in situations where the objective is in-depth news and feature reporting. Most are printed in an 8½″ × 11″ format that will fit easily in standard file drawers and mailing envelopes. A variation in size, therefore, will help give a magazine a look of its own but may cause problems in distribution or filing.

Production quality varies with budget, but many are characterized by skillfully executed photographs and original artwork, often in four-color, and fine design work. The corporate magazine is usually a company's prestige publication, distributed to community, business, shareholder, and political audiences, as well as to employees.

JD Journal, the award-winning quarterly of Deere & Company, Moline, Illinois, is an example of excellence in corporate magazines. The four-color publication is the flagship of the company's employee communication program.

The newspaper format is best suited to shorter news articles, though a mixture of brief articles and features is common. Photographic technical reproduction quality is

Figure 12.2 Canada Post issues its employee magazine in both English and French because it has postal workers in French-speaking Quebec as well as in all Canada's English-speaking provinces and territories. *Copyright © 1996 Canada Post Corporation.*

frequently less than that found in magazines. Newspaper photos, for the most part, record or interpret an event, while the photographs in *JD Journal* and other top-level corporate magazines function as art elements. The newspaper versus magazine question, however, often rests on budget. Newspapers are much less expensive to produce, though the use of two- to four-color printing and high-grade paper stock can increase production costs while adding a feeling of quality.

Magapapers have grown in popularity because they, like newspapers, are relatively inexpensive to produce yet offer some of the magazine's design versatility. The standard magapaper format is an 11″ × 17″ tabloid that folds to 8½″ × 11″ for distribution. When folded the back cover of the "newspaper" becomes the front and back covers of the "magazine," which usually features large, magazinelike photographs in a style that uses more white space than the average newspaper style.

Planning the Publication Schedule

Individual publications, like overall organizational communication programs, need specific objectives, but with these, long-term planning wins the prize. Working out an editorial plan for a year or more gives the communicator an opportunity to balance editorial objectives with the goals of the overall program. It provides more time to research and write articles, solicit material from outside sources, gain approvals, and locate existing photographs or arrange for new photography. It minimizes the risk of the missed deadline. For publications with advertising, it enables the editor to promote ad placement well in advance of themed issues.

Some editors of publications reaching outsiders begin soliciting material a year in advance. Officers and marketing representatives from various departments and member companies are surveyed annually for story ideas. The general criterion for suggestions is to provide targeted communication to support marketing efforts in a unique, efficient, and high-quality manner. The strategies listed for each issue can be as specific as that objective is general. They include the following:

- Featuring customers, potential customers, and specific industries in three stories of interest to other senior business executives
- Promoting the company's field of interest with prominent cover stories that highlight it
- Describing in detail various products or services offered in one story per issue

Publication content

In addition to conforming to general and specific communication goals, contents of internal publications should match information needs of employees. Employees are most interested in information relating to the organization's plans, personnel policies and practices, productivity improvement, and their jobs, including advancement opportunities and effects of external events on the job. Topics of moderate interest include: the organization's competitive position, news of other divisions, the organization's use of profits, its stand on current issues, and community involvement. At the bottom of the list are personnel news and stories about other employees.

They want information about the company as it relates to them and their jobs, and they want that information to be accurate and well balanced. That is important to remember if publications and other formal channels of employee communication are to supplant the office grapevine. They are vital tools in integrating all information about the organization.

Fortunately, the trend is toward candor with all segments of the public—consumer, shareholder, and employee. Publications like *ArcoSpark* from Atlantic Richfield Company and *Ford World* from Ford Motor Company make special efforts to be first with news—good or bad—that will affect or interest the employee and to interpret the material in a meaningful way. The emphasis of the monthly *Ford World*, for example, is on company business.

Editors of internal publications should call on the same writing versatility that characterizes the best journalistic efforts, including conventional news stories and features, question-and-answer columns—even fiction. Other features popular in the general press—humor, crossword puzzles, cartoons, contests, directories—also will help draw readership.

Publication design

Design is as crucial as editorial content in determining publication readership. Columns of unbroken gray type make even the most interesting material seem dull and uninviting. Thoughtful use of graphics and photographs, typefaces in a variety of sizes, generous white spaces and—if the budget permits—color add eye appeal.

The look of a particular publication depends on its purpose, audience, and often the nature of the sponsoring organization. An internal newsletter for bank managers, for example, might be dignified in appearance, while a general-interest internal magazine might be breezy and informal. The same goals that guide editorial policy will help formulate design.

Whatever the individual situation, however, the editor without formal design training or without a graphic artist on staff should seek professional help in the initial designing of a publication. The designer will provide a nameplate or "flag," choose typefaces and sizes, and suggest ways for laying out short news items, long features, photographs, and graphics. The result should be a general set of design guidelines—or a grid—that editors can follow in subsequent issues. The cost of outside design help may seem high but should be regarded as a necessary one-time expense, amortized over the production cost of successive issues.

Supplemental Media

One major goal of any internal communication program is dissemination of organizational news. If the general employee publication is a weekly newspaper, dealing with all but the direst emergency is no problem. If it's a monthly or a quarterly, however, interim measures also are necessary. Many of the possibilities can serve other communication needs as well.

Newsletters

After newspapers, magapapers, and magazines, newsletters are the most frequently used print medium for internal communication. They supplement more formal publications, reach special-interest groups from managers to retired employees, and, especially in smaller organizations, serve as the main communication vehicle.

Like newspapers and magazines, newsletters come in many shapes, sizes, and formats, including multipage editions with photographs, some even in four-color process. They can also be effective when simply and inexpensively produced, including one-page sheets using typewritten rather than typeset copy. For visual appeal, use of an attractive logo, uncluttered design, colored ink and/or paper stock are favored. Copy should be presented in short, snappy, easy-to-read news items.

Bulletin boards

According to the Employee Communication Effectiveness survey, bulletin boards rank fourth as a major source of organizational information, preceded only by the immediate supervisor, the grapevine, and employee handbooks. Employees more often look to bulletin boards for company information than to the regular employee publication.

Bulletin boards range from elaborate, one-time displays tied to a theme—energy conservation, for example, or the company's history—to ongoing programs featuring regular newsletters, special daily news bulletins, employee benefits information, and so on. To be most effective, they should be placed in well-lighted, well-traveled areas. They should be attractive and frequently updated. Enclosure in a glass case will protect the contents and give the communicator control over the program. A prominent section can be headed "Company News" to set it off from legally required notices and other material.

Employee annual reports

Some companies merely recycle the financial information from the shareholders' report into an employee package, but others make a special effort to interpret the material in terms of the employees' interests. Some minimize financial data, choosing to concentrate instead on issues, such as productivity, or employee concerns, such as effects of computerization in the company. In most instances the emphasis is on people—the importance of the employee to the organization. One economical option is featuring the report in a special issue of the regular employee publication.

Telephone hotlines

These hotlines are particularly suited to providing news updates between regularly scheduled publications. The employee calls an internal number to hear a recorded message. Its major advantage is that the hotline can be updated throughout the day, as needed. Like newsletter material, hotline items should be kept short and to the point.

The technique can also be used for upward communication. Questions left by employees on a telephone answering machine are forwarded to the appropriate manager or executive by a monitor. They evoke written answers. If anonymity is desired, the monitor can act as go-between without revealing the name of the employee who submitted the question. The hotline can be connected to the organization's existing phone system and, unlike publications, represents a one-time-only installation expense.

The Multimedia Revolution

Although print media still dominate, video has had great impact, spurred by audience demand and a continuous parade of new techniques and technologies. Magazines and newspapers give audiences an opportunity to reread or file important articles. A video program might introduce and help explain a new employee benefits program, for example, but it's the benefits handbook the employee will refer to if he or she has a later question.

A major problem with building an in-house video department is the initial cost of the equipment. The communication department might be able to cut the costs somewhat by sharing the purchase price with other departments that will benefit from using it. In some cases, the video operation is part of the training department and the main productions are training, management development, and merchandising tapes.

Another rapidly growing video trend is teleconferencing, whereby a meeting held in one location is transmitted by satellite or telephone line to various locations around the country or world. (*See* Chapter 28.) Most teleconferences feature one-way video and two-way audio, though two-way video also is possible.

Word processing and desktop publishing

The major benefits of desktop publishing technology (*see* Chapter 33)—increased productivity and lowered costs—make widespread adoption inevitable. Similarly, the rapid growth of communication by computer makes this medium a vital part of the total mix of employee communication.

Feedback Programs

Upward communication programs can give top management continuing feedback on what employees think of company policies and practices, as well as provide an ideal source for suggestions on improving productivity, saving energy, increasing safety, etc. These programs also can identify levels of knowledge and understanding among employees prior to the establishment of, for example, programs on public issues and opportunities or economic awareness. For the communicator they can identify those problems and concerns that should be addressed in internal communication efforts and serve as a tool for determining whether those efforts have been successful.

Feedback mechanisms include small group question-and-answer sessions, formal or informal surveys with questionnaires distributed on the job or mailed to the home, hotlines, suggestion boxes, the intranet, and employee response columns in publications. Whichever method is used, the response should be fast, confidential, and candid; otherwise, employee participation and interest will decline.

Sometimes an anonymous employee attitude survey can have startling results. The National Standards Company, Niles, Michigan, surveyed the 505 employees in three plants to discover their perceptions of the company before instituting a quality circle program. The results sent shock waves through the company: 81 percent of the employees gave poor marks to the company's upward communication process, 72 percent responded negatively to management communication downward, and 64 percent faulted company leadership. "They do a lot of things without any explanation at all, and this gets rumors started and workers mad," one employee said.

The company delayed the quality circle program until an effective employee communication program could be put in place. Program elements included *The Shop Rag*, a candid monthly tabloid; a daily news bulletin for posting in the plants; and a series of regular meetings for management, union leaders, and employees. The first issue of *The Shop Rag* took an honest look at the survey results under the headline "Communication Stinks!" In addition to reporting the results, the issue outlined the steps being taken to rectify the problems. A follow-up survey was later scheduled to check the effectiveness of the new communication program.

Occasional readership surveys, included in a publication or mailed to the homes of randomly selected employees with a copy of the publication, can help guide editorial policy by pinpointing how much of the publication is being read and identifying the kind of subject matter in which most employees are interested.

Internal and Outside Help

The makeup of employee communication staffs varies widely, from a one- or two-person editorial team to a multinational editorial network.

Depending on the size of the organization and the scope of its communication activities, the internal communicator also may be involved with external communications or even advertising, graphic arts, audiovisuals, and training. A large organization will have all or some of these functions represented in one interrelated area, often with a single generalist manager overseeing the contributions of many specialists. Smaller organizations are more likely to have public relations/editorial generalists on staff and go to outside consultants for less frequently used, specialized services.

Whether internal or external sources are used, the generalist in organizational communication today is likely to need an increasingly broad assortment of skills, particularly reporting, editing, basic design, writing, and production techniques for both print and audiovisual media. At the managerial level, considerable business acumen frequently is required as well.

In the "average" communication staff, the top post usually carries the title of manager or director, supported by associate or assistant editors. The ideal communicator has a working knowledge of the business with which he or she is involved, but it's the editorial and writing skills that are the most important.

In all but the largest organizations, having people on staff to fill every communication need is a budgetary impossibility. One-time or occasional projects, such as annual reports and audiovisual or training programs, therefore, are often assigned to outside consultants. Some services, such as typesetting and printing, usually are hired outside. The International Association of Business Communicators (IABC) survey results show that, in the course of a year, 41 percent of the association's members buy outside audiovisual production services. Other outside services purchased include printing, 86 percent; typesetting, 69 percent; meeting services, 33 percent; and public relations counseling, 23 percent.

For organizations with an ongoing internal communication program, an in-house staff large enough to handle the workload is usually more cost effective than using outside consultants. An in-house staff also provides better job continuity, more control, and a comprehensive knowledge of the organization and its problems. In an often crisis-ridden field, having someone on hand to fight fires as they arise is an important consideration. Outside consultants, by comparison, offer other advantages, including a fresh approach, an unbiased outside viewpoint, and top creative talent in a number of diverse fields.

Overview of Internal Communication

Originally the specialist in employee communication was defined as an editor of the house organ. Now even the term *house organ* has fallen into disfavor because of its association with the kind of publication that was too often a management mouthpiece, telling employees only what management wanted them to know.

The field has grown into a major area of specialization for which success requires the same elements essential to effective external communication planning: excellent general communication skills, comprehensive knowledge of the organization and its goals, the ability to reach a diverse audience effectively, and the tools to measure and interpret the results of communication planning.

Indeed, in many organizations internal and external communication are important functions of the same department and logically so. Employee attitudes about an organization have a considerable impact on the perceptions of people outside that organization. One objective of internal communication should be providing employees with the information needed to build positive attitudes in communicating with friends, relatives, and associates within the community.

This is the "Age of Communication" and the challenges are formidable, but so are the opportunities. The problem is that the field is evolving so rapidly that it may pass many communicators by. Only through continuing education and ongoing professional development—in the workplace, in colleges or universities, or through professional associations—can they cope with the flood of change.

Professional organizations

The International Association of Business Communicators, One Hallidie Plaza, Suite 600, San Francisco, CA 94102, is the professional organization for communication managers, writers, editors, and audiovisual specialists worldwide. Services include the magazine *Communication World*; an annual international conference; seminars geared to different areas of interest and levels of experience; an accreditation program; a publica-

tion critique service; and "Idea Files," a comprehensive lending library reference service. Iabc has chapters in the United States, Canada, and the United Kingdom, and affiliates around the world.

The Public Relations Society of America, 33 Irving Place, New York, NY 10003, is the professional organization for public relations professionals. Prsa's integrated professional development program includes the monthly *Public Relations Tactics*, the quarterly *The Strategist*, seminars and conferences, an accreditation program, local chapter services, and professional interest sections.

Women in Communications, 3717 Columbia Pike, Arlington, VA 22204, is a national organization for professionals and students in print and broadcast journalism, communications education, public relations, advertising, publishing, and photojournalism. Wici offers *The Professional Communicator*, published five times a year; professional chapters and student chapters around the United States; local career development programs; local and national job placement services; and an annual national conference.

13

PUBLIC RELATIONS AND LABOR MATTERS

ROBERT W. HEFTY

Robert W. Hefty is a Detroit public relations consultant. He retired in 1985 as Director of Creative Services for Detroit Edison Company, and in 1982 as the director of the International and Diversified Products Public Relations Office, Ford Motor Company, after more than thirty years in industrial and public relations with that firm. As director of public information on Ford Motor Company's Public Relations staff, he was responsible for all corporate publicity and press relations, including coverage of Ford's triennial contract negotiations with the powerful United Auto Workers union.

Except for Army service in World War II and the Korean War, Mr. Hefty was with United Press Associations, lastly as Northwest news manager headquartered in Minneapolis. Prior to that he was assistant manager of the Detroit bureau where he covered the automotive, labor, and general news beats.

At Ford he became corporate press relations manager in 1959, News Department manager in 1960, Ford Division public relations manager in 1963, and director of public relations for Ford North American Automotive Operations in 1976.

For simplification, this chapter will deal with a manufacturing company and how its public relations staff handles labor matters. However, the term *company* is intended to be generic. It is expected that the points covered will be applicable to most other organizations also, including the labor unions with whom industry often is in an adversarial position.

In the public relations of labor relations, there are two primary targets, or audiences: the customer who buys a company's products, and the employee who helps make them. They in turn—and especially the customer—are part of a larger and more amorphous amalgam called "the public."

There are special audiences, of course—stockholders, dealers, distributors, suppliers, the government, and so on. But they are incidental compared with the two main audiences—and besides they help comprise the larger consumer-public target that places them at least peripherally in one of the major spotlights.

The two principal audiences are of transcendent importance because they hold the power of life and death over the enterprise—the customer by buying or not buying, the employee by building or not building.

It therefore is necessary to communicate with both of them regularly, honestly, and openly, to establish a rapport built on mutual confidence, understanding, and respect that will see the company through whatever emergencies may arise.

With the employee, the need to communicate begins when he walks in the door and continues until he walks out. Actually, with the special type of employee who must be recruited, it begins well *before* he walks in the door.

Employee communications are particularly vital in times of crisis, though perhaps the most effective and believable communicating is done in times of calm—when the crisis often can be averted.

The public relations practitioner concerned with labor relations should understand from the outset that the employee—and particularly the unionized employee—is not the enemy. He is the heart of the organization— probably the one element without which the company cannot function.

The average employee is essentially honest—willing and usually eager to give a fair day's work for a fair day's pay. But his or her expectations grow with the growth of the enterprise, and his or her desires reflect the enormous transformation that has overtaken the land. American business—and indeed world business—is coming more and more to realize that money and security have lost some of their fascination for the modern-day worker—especially the *young* worker, who wants more than good pay and a comfortable retirement. He or she wants better working conditions and a more challenging job. Employees want the company to contribute to a better life and to be known for its good works. If these things are not forthcoming, employees often rebel—by quitting or striking or just taking the day off. Absenteeism, turnover, and the incidence of disciplinary cases in U.S. industry has grown substantially, mirroring the unrest and indiscipline still manifest in many aspects of modern life.

Restless Employees: A Significant Challenge

Meeting the challenge of the restless, demanding employee is a major assignment of present-day industrial public relations. Not only must the company public relations man or woman help communicate intelligently with the employee, he or she also must help persuade management to make the changes necessary to provide an on-the-job environment that motivates its workforce and gives every person on the payroll—from the chairman to the janitor—a reason for pride.

Employee expectations are not always reasonable. Labor unions usually enter contract negotiations demanding more than they expect to get, eliciting predictable resistance from management. The sparring that ensues provides a continuing test of the talents and mettle of the public relations specialist assigned to labor relations.

One of the corporate communicator's primary assignments is to avoid management-employee confrontations whenever possible. A good starting point is an informed workforce.

The first step in communicating with employees, particularly new employees, is to tell them where they stand—what the company is prepared to do for them and what's expected of them in return. This usually is done in early interviews, but it should be implemented with written statements of personnel policies covering wages; holidays and vacations; sick, personal, and military leave; cost-of-living, separation, and transfer allowances; layoff benefits; promotional, training, and extended education opportunities; personal and employment counseling; hospital-surgical-medical protection; recreational activities, and other benefits. Separate information booklets for hourly rated and salaried employees usually are desirable, and of course they should be kept up-to-date as conditions change.

Once the employees have been initially informed of their rights, benefits, and responsibilities, every means should be taken to keep them posted on everything in the company orbit that affects their welfare—from capital investments to changes in leave time for jury duty. They should be given the bad news along with the good; it is better they hear the former from management than from a source claiming management is trying to "cover up." This goes back to the premise that believability and honesty are essential ingredients of an employee communications program.

The media available for communicating with employees will vary with the means and philosophies of the employers, but generally they include company magazines, company and plant newspapers, individual and mass meetings, newsletters, bulletin boards, suggestion programs, closed-circuit television and videotape messages, motion pictures, public-address systems, information racks, pay enclosures, open houses and plant tours for employees and their families, and direct mail. (*See* Chapters 12 and 31.) The last-named—usually consisting of letters to employees from their supervisors or top corporate management—are most effective when directed to the employees' home so they have time to read them at leisure and can show them to other members of their families. (In many companies, employee communications actually fall within the responsibility of the industrial relations or personnel department rather than public relations, but the principles remain the same.)

The Importance of Timing

Employee communication requires careful timing. Employees like to hear things about their company before neighbors and the public do. Hence, the most appreciated communication is one that arrives at least simulta-

neously with a public announcement and preferably somewhat before. Where precise timing of the public disclosure is important (*see* Chapter 11), a general communication to employees considerably in advance of the public announcement would make it difficult to keep the information from "leaking" to news media and other outsiders.

As indicated, the labor relations function of public relations comes into play most forcefully in times of emergency, crisis, or other unusual activity—contract negotiations, strikes, plant closings, temporary layoffs and shutdowns, union organizing campaigns, representation elections, votes on employee concessions, and the like. It is in times like these that the company's and management's long-term reputation for fair dealing and honest communication stands it in good stead and faces its severest test.

Most major industrial labor contracts are for periods of two to three years, with interim negotiation permitted on reopenable issues in some cases. Generally a company can expect relative labor calm between the signing and ratification of a labor agreement and the reopening of negotiations on a new contract several years hence. Still, the interim period can be marked by authorized or unauthorized strikes, slowdowns, lockouts or threatened lockouts, and demands for contract reopenings or modifications on either the national or local level.

Whether new-contract negotiations are approaching or just concluded, therefore, the public relations job is never done. It intensifies, however, six months to a year before the scheduled start of formal company-union talks.

Preparing for Negotiations

A logical first step in preparing for a new round of contract negotiations is formation of a communications task force consisting of key public relations, labor relations, personnel, and government-affairs representatives. (The last-named is required because government continues its close surveillance of the private collective-bargaining system and wants to be kept informed of major labor-relations developments in key industries.)

The task force's first assignment is to agree on what the company hopes to accomplish with information programs directed to its two principal audiences—the employees and the public. There's nothing very mysterious about this. Generally, any organization preparing to enter contract negotiations with its principal union or unions hopes to achieve the following:

1. **Reach a settlement** that is in the economic interest of the company, the employees, the stockholders, and the customers

2. **Eliminate or minimize the risks of a strike** prior to conclusion of an agreement

3. **Keep employees and the public** (plus, of course, other special audiences, such as dealers, distributors, stockholders, suppliers, and so on) **informed** of major developments, and solicit their support for—or at least understanding of—management's positions on basic issues

4. **Discourage government involvement** in the bargaining process.

It is important that both the communications goals and the media used to attain them include built-in flexibility that enables management to move quickly in the constantly changing atmosphere that characterizes modern-day labor-management relations. One unexpected union move could require a whole new set of guidelines for the company's negotiators and their communications specialists.

Once the goals are set, the public relations person assigned to labor relations must move quickly to help realize them. This means acquainting himself or herself thoroughly with every facet of the negotiations picture. It means "living" with labor relations for the duration—attending briefings on the major issues (wages, cost-of-living, pensions, profit-sharing, vacations, and so on). It means gleaning every scrap of information available on the union's likely demands and objectives—from union statements, speeches, news releases, press conferences, interviews, speculative news stories and columns, and conversational exchanges with colleagues in the corporate public relations–labor relations fields. It means keeping detailed, codified records on information gathered from these sources, for ready use by both public relations and labor relations personnel. It means maintaining friendly but strictly professional and ethical relations with counterparts in the public relations departments of competitive companies and the trade unions to the advantage of the parties most properly concerned—management, labor, and the news media.

Safeguarding Proprietary Information

It is important to remember that if the public relations professional maintains an appropriate relationship with labor relations colleagues, he or she will be entrusted with much more information than he or she is expected to divulge to outside sources. Protection of proprietary data that are not available—for good business reasons—to either the union or the company's competitors is requisite to proper working of the private collective-bargaining system. The public relations specialist therefore is the protector of some of the company's most vital operating secrets and must screen the release of the information accordingly.

Once the public relations specialist has done his or her labor relations homework and has established a specific set of objectives as determined by the communications task force, he or she is ready to start communicating with major audiences.

Informing employees

Before and during the negotiations, the corporate communicator will make systematic use of the media already mentioned—company newspapers and magazines, letters, films, videorecordings, booklets, PA systems, and so on—to keep the workforce informed about the company's plans, positions, and activities. News material will recapitulate and dramatize the company's already generous employee pay and benefit programs, announce the negotiating timetable and makeup of the company's bargaining team, and explain the company's economic position as it enters the negotiations. To the extent that they can be revealed without undermining management's bargaining strategy or violating company-union agreements to refrain from public discussion of issues and positions, communications to employees further detail company offers as they are presented to the union negotiators and spell out company answers to specific union requests or demands. Some companies set up "hotline" recorded telephone messages, updated daily or as often as developments warrant, that employees can hear by dialing designated numbers.

There are legal limitations to what can and cannot be included in company communications to employees. Section 8(c) of the Taft-Hartley Law states that the company can express an opinion or put forth its point of view in written, graphic, or visual form, so long as the material "contains no threat of reprisal or force or promise of benefit." This clearly authorizes the company to take its case directly to the employee, but the message should be drafted with extreme care. To the careful communicator it mandates that communications to employees be reviewed by attorneys familiar with both the letter and the various interpretations of the laws dealing with such communications. (*See* Chapter 47.)

The public

Communicating with the public often goes in tandem with employee communications, because in many cases management can best tell its story by providing the news media with copies of letters and other materials sent to employees. However, there are numerous other means—both direct and indirect—of telling the company's story through the public media.

The most obvious *direct* routes are through written news releases, radio tapes, videotapes and film clips for television, motion pictures, and advertising. They provide the advantage of presenting the company story in precisely the form management wants it told. In other words, they offer the greatest degree of immediate control, although of course in the case of the news release there is no way to predict the final form in which its content will appear.

Less controllable but still direct means of telling the management story include on-the-record interviews, news conferences, and plant tours.

The Value of "Briefing" the Media

Perhaps the best *indirect* method of presenting the company's positions on actual or potential bargaining issues is off-the-record "backgrounding" of newspeople by key labor relations personnel at both the corporate and local-plant levels. Months before the actual contract negotiations are set to begin, reporters, columnists, editorial writers, and radio and television commentators can be brought in to gather material from company labor relations experts that is not to be attributed to them but can be used to add perspective to the reporters' own speculative stories about the forthcoming negotiations. This is a perfectly legitimate technique in labor reporting and often is preferred by the reporter, who then can write or speak knowledgeably about his or her subject in print or on the air and at the same time speculate with the assurance that he or she is not "off base" on an important issue or position. Further, the backgrounding provides the savvy reporter with an added dimension that can be used to gauge the impact of future developments on both the management and labor sides of a dispute.

One important point: a public relations specialist should *always* sit in on the backgrounding session. Not only does he or she provide a needed "backstop" for both the reporter and labor relations source in the event of disagreements over interpretation, attribution, and so on, but the PR person gains, in the course of the interview, additional experience and knowledge that—discreetly used—will make him or her an even more effective communicator for the company.

While we will not attempt to list specific subjects for either on-the-record or background interviews, a word of caution is offered on discussing management's ability to cope with the economic liabilities inherent in union demands. Enlisting public sympathy for such things as the corporate "profit squeeze" is difficult at best, and it is a hazardous exercise anyway, since it may lead to union demands to "open the books." And a company usually does not bargain with the union on the basis of costs or ability to pay. However, this does not preclude encouraging business and labor writers from discussing, on their own, the relationship of increased labor costs to product prices and the total economy.

The question of "opening the books" sometimes is subject to negotiation. During recession periods there are times when employers have to ask employees to make concessions on wages and benefits in order for the company to remain competitive—primarily with lower-cost importers. In such cases, general or selective cost information has to be shared with unions representing the employees in order to document the need for concessions. However, in such cases the unions usually are willing to cooperate with the employers in safeguarding the confidentiality of such information.

The question usually arises in any prenegotiations period whether it is worthwhile to try to debate issues in the public press, or whether they are best left to the bargainers in their private sessions. At least in the past, management too often has been willing to let union charges go unanswered on the theory that anything said would be twisted out of context by the union and used against the company. Labor thus was constantly on the offensive and management constantly on the defensive. With millions of readers and listeners hearing only the union side of the story, management was "guilty until proved innocent."

It is to be hoped that this time is all but past. Enlightened management now recognizes that it has an obligation to itself, to its stockholders and customers, and indeed to the very employees represented by the union it is rebutting, to present an honest and detailed account of how it stands on the issues. This again, of course, is subject to the constraints of bargaining strategy, but the fact is that more often than not, American business management now is disposed to acknowledge, explain, and when necessary refute union claims and demands. It is the trained public relations practitioner who helps determine the success or failure of this effort.

Primary Responsibilities

Both prior to and during the contract negotiations, public relations has three principal assignments:

1. Serve management
2. Keep employees and the public informed
3. Help the news media do their job

In serving management, the public relations labor specialist has the following responsibilities:

- Seek forums for effective enunciation of company positions—in speeches, interviews, news conferences, letters, public statements, and the like.

- Research, write, and clear the necessary documents—releases, speech texts, scripts, letters, advertisements, and so on—needed to gain optimum advantage from these forums.

- Help keep management minutely informed on union developments, by attending (and when possible tape-recording) union conventions and news conferences, reviewing and clipping union publications, obtaining the union's news releases, and passing along views expressed by labor reporters, union public relations people, and other experienced observers.

- With labor and government-relations specialists, maintain an instantaneous reporting service for management on business, labor, and government developments that might have even a slight bearing on the negotiations and the company's positions therein. This includes monitoring business and labor columns, editorials, radio and TV commentaries, wire service copy, and so on.

- Maintain scrupulous records on all written materials pertaining to the negotiations—newspaper and magazine clippings, company and union news releases, union publications, employee communications, advertisements, company-union or union-employee correspondence, company and union speech texts, and so on.

- Prepare or help prepare background memoranda or "white papers" on specific problems at issue in the negotiations (wages, profit-sharing, cost-of-living, fringe benefits, automation, foreign outsourcing of products and/or parts, union in-plant representation); on comments by business, government, and labor leaders on the state of the economy, the dangers of inflation, competition from imported products, and settlements in other key union-company negotiations that might indicate "patterns" for the negotiations at hand.

- Prepare quick-reference question-and-answer sheets for use in answering news media inquiries—trying to anticipate questions likely to be asked by newspersons, and preparing carefully documented answers for quick use when the questions arise. This can be overdone, however. Rather than try to anticipate every conceivable question (which is a futile exercise anyway) the public relations labor specialist would do better to cultivate his labor relations sources for prompt, fresh, and authoritative responses to unexpected inquiries.

Public relations' role in *serving the employee* by keeping him or her informed already has been covered, and its role in *serving the public* coincides with *helping the news media* do the best possible job of covering the negotiations and developments leading up to them. Prompt, accurate, balanced reporting is in the company's interest, as well as the news media's and the public's.

Helping Newspeople

Newspeople can and should be assisted before and during contract negotiations in these ways:

- News releases—written stories, recorded and filmed statements.

- On-the-record interviews and news conferences.

- Background briefings (covered previously).

- Answers to spot questions.

- Guidance on questions that cannot be answered directly or for attribution. Discreet "steering" of a reporter groping for information with which to speculate can prevent embarrassment for both him or her and the company.

- A "fact book," distributed in advance of negotiations, containing historical information on past negotiations and strikes; company data on plants, employment, payrolls, products, and so on; and a list of key labor relations personnel involved in the bargaining.

- Data cards with home and office telephone numbers of public relations personnel assigned to labor relations and available to media representatives around the clock.

- A press room equipped with typewriters, telephones, fax machines, computer transmitters, work tables and chairs, copy paper, copier, and other materials. Because news coverage of contract negotiations usually involves long hours of waiting and "sweating it out," provision also should be made for lounge chairs and sofas, television and radio sets, card tables, food and soft drinks (but never alcoholic beverages), and current magazines and newspapers. There should be tables for copies of corporate *and union* news releases, fact books, annual reports and other reference materials, chronological files on key newspaper and magazine stories reporting the negotiations, and, where appropriate, transcripts of company news conferences held prior to or earlier in the negotiations. A whiteboard and bulletin board should be placed for easy posting of announcements and messages. The press room should be kept neat and clean at all times. When located on company property, it should be convenient to the negotiating room and union and company caucus rooms (which are off-limits to the press), but far enough away to ensure a reasonable measure of privacy for the bargainers. Union public relations representatives should be made to feel welcome in the company press room, and in fact should be encouraged to be present to answer reporters' questions and in another location to work with corporate public relations people on joint statements, news conferences, and announcements. Similarly, as a service to reporters, spokespersons for the bargaining teams should be encouraged to drop into the press room from time to time—preferably daily—even when they have no progress to report or must spend most of their time declining comment.

- An interview area outside the main bargaining room, for newsmen and -women to question the chief negotiators for both sides as they enter and leave the sessions. The area should be large enough to accommodate reporters from print media, radio and television crews, and company and union observers (including public relations staffers), but small and isolated enough to discourage unwanted kibitzers. It should provide sufficient power for television and videotape lights and cameras; ideally, a company electrician should be on hand to assist with power and lighting requirements. Drapes and carpeting should be provided to improve acoustics, and a mixer system should be available for tape recorders. Space should be provided off the main interview area for a radio-TV sound control room and equipment storage.

- Where possible, advance notices on both company and union statements and news conferences, both to reporters in the negotiations press room and to other media representatives obviously interested in covering the events but not presently staffing.

This "backstopping" of reporters and photographers not able to cover the negotiations on a continuing basis is essential to good media relations; it helps give smaller but still important news outlets an even break with the more prosperous media that can afford to staff, when desirable, on a round-the-clock basis.

• Parking space near the press room for the news "regulars."

Organizing to Meet the Challenge

Throughout the negotiations and prenegotiations periods, the function of top public relations management is to work with the principal officers of the company to help shape bargaining strategy, to select the timing of various public and employee announcements, and to weigh the likely public and employee reaction to the proposed settlement and other developments. Actual staffing of the negotiations and their attendant press coverage is left to trained specialists down the line.

The ideal public relations staffing arrangement involves an "inside" person and an "outside" teammate. The "inside" staffer really is an ex-officio member of the corporate negotiating team who attends the bargaining sessions as an observer, maintains a constant liaison for the public relations staff with key company negotiators, is the principal company contact with the union public relations staff, and accompanies the chief spokesperson for the corporate negotiators at all times in his or her contacts with reporters and union strategists. He or she writes the basic news releases and policy statements, supervises preparation of "sidebar" and background materials, and maintains the official negotiations log or diary for public relations. His or her main function, in short, is to serve the management and specifically the company negotiating team.

The "outside" specialist complements the work of the inside anchor person by following through on clearance and reproduction of releases, contacts with key labor reporters, supervising the press room, and relaying information from the "inside" staffer on the start and end of bargaining sessions, scheduled news conferences, and availability of key company negotiators for interviews, clearance of public relations materials, and other purposes.

As the negotiations approach their climax, more public relations personnel—including public relations management—will help with the day-to-day news effort. Public relations executives, of course, will have worked behind the scenes, mainly on policy matters, from the beginning, but in the final days their assistance will be needed on the scene and their own interest in the proceedings ensures their presence.

Local activities

In companies with operations in a number of states, it is essential that regional public relations and employee or labor relations representatives be kept abreast of all developments from the home office on the one hand, as well as feed information on local negotiations *to* the home office on the other. This continuing two-way exchange is vital to the maintenance of a consistent corporate posture wherever the company does business.

As indicated, it is important that company public relations personnel maintain an effective relationship with their counterparts in the union, again on a regional as well as on a central basis. This ensures a proper exchange of information on news releases and other public announcements, news conferences, and scheduled participation by the company and union principals in key bargaining activities.

It also helps the news media, as well as both parties to the negotiations, that the company and union publicists act in concert whenever such action is appropriate. From the company's standpoint, it is important that the union's concurrence be obtained in the handling of joint statements, announcements, and press arrangements.

Cooperation can be overdone, of course. Whenever possible, company public relations strategists will want to time important corporate releases so as to avoid undesired "split play," in which the union has enough lead time to issue counter-statements that will share billing with—and perhaps eclipse—the company's pronouncements. The union, of course, will strive for the same kind of preferential timing for its key announcements.

One element that enters into media coverage of many key negotiations is the so-called news blackout. This has become almost traditional, for example, in the auto industry. When the bargaining between the United Auto Workers and the so-called target company enters a critical stage, where one inadvertent statement by either side might impair the progress of negotiations, the two sides may agree on cessation of public comment for either a specific or indefinite period and newspersons are advised of the fact. Either party can end the blackout after serving an agreed-on notice, but in the meantime the negotiators' lips are sealed and reporters must rely on their ingenuity to keep the pot boiling. Usually they do very well.

Reporting the Results

Contract negotiations end with a settlement that may or may not be preceded by a strike. Public relations coverage of the results is governed pretty much by the same principles and techniques that apply to coverage of the negotiations themselves.

In the case of a peaceful settlement, both the company and union want to be first to give the details—after a joint announcement that agreement has been reached. Being first requires four things:

1. Good feedback from "inside" public relations representatives of details on issues as they are agreed on

2. Swift preparation of written releases

3. A well-oiled clearance machinery for necessary reviews by financial, legal, and labor relations experts, as well as by top management as required

4. A first-class publicity reproduction and distribution system

Not only does superior performance in these areas enable a company to report settlement details first in its own language, it also endears the company to the eager newspersons and company employees who are panting for the details and are duly grateful to the party that delivers first.

One word of caution, however: it is better to be late than to sacrifice accuracy, thoroughness, and responsiveness in a document of such vital importance to the audiences concerned.

Also it is generally the practice to withhold details of the settlement until union members have voted either to ratify or reject it. Because the union controls the ratification process, it obviously has an advantage over the company in reporting details promptly.

The announcement of a settlement usually takes two forms—a news release and a news conference with the heads of the bargaining teams. Again, it is desirable to be first in talking to reporters, because it gives the company spokesperson an opportunity to lead with his or her interpretation of the settlement and also to avoid argumentative questions based on points made by the union spokesperson in an earlier news conference.

Depending on the judgments of the nego-tiating parties as to probable interpretation by news media of the settlement terms, a "gentlemen's agreement" is often reached that one or the other of the chief spokespersons will appear first to "meet the press." Such an agreement rarely if ever applies to written reports on the settlement details, however, and therein lies the competition for the ear and gratitude of the eager employee and the restless reporter.

There are times—though not usually in connection with formal contract negotia-tions—when company and union spokesper-sons agree to meet the news media simulta-neously. For example, when Ford Motor Company and the United Auto Workers union sent a joint study team to Japan, top Ford and UAW executives held joint news conferences both on the spot in Tokyo and later at Ford's World Headquarters in Dearborn, Michigan.

Dealing with Strikes

There are two principal types of strikes. An *authorized* strike is one that is permitted under the company-union contract, has been approved by the union membership, and has been endorsed by the parent labor organiza-tion. It can be a "national" strike, in which all union employees of a large, multiplant company walk out at once, or a "local" strike involving a single plant. An *unauthorized* or "wildcat" strike is one staged in violation of the contract, often by a dissident minority in a local chapter of the union and usually on short notice.

The company-wide strike is of primary concern to public relations, although it should be noted that a local strike at a plant that makes parts for other plants in the company system can result in a swift shutdown of the company's total manufacturing operation.

Careful public relations planning is possi-ble with authorized strikes, because such stoppages often are preceded by prolonged negotiations and always—under contractual mandate—by a strike "notice" and the set-ting of a specific strike "deadline."

Once a strike is imminent or has started, the same public relations outlets and tech-niques are used as in the case of negotia-tions—public statements of management's position through selected channels (news releases, interviews, news conferences, adver-tisements); letters to employees, stockhold-ers, suppliers, dealers, distributors, and so on; statements and stories in company publica-tions; and company communications to the union that are made public. Media fact books are needed on plants, employees, and prod-ucts affected; wages and supplier outlays lost each day of the stoppage; previous strikes; and chronological events leading to the cur-rent walkout.

For a company with plants located in a number of states or communities, a strong field public relations network becomes even more essential than during the negotiations. Management and reporters alike will need daily reports on local strike reaction, possi-ble picketline incidents, and in-plant negoti-ations to settle local issues.

Once the strike is under way, negotiations to end it are covered closely by the news media, both because of immediate interest in the strike and because of the likely settlement "pattern" that will be established for other companies in the same industry (assuming the struck company is a major factor in the industry). The actual or potential effect on companies supplying the struck manufacturer also will be of interest.

Public relations' handling of the strike and strike settlement generally tracks that of nego-tiations that manage to end without a walk-out. Speed in relaying accurate, detailed accounts of the settlement, again, is para-mount for both employees and reporters.

A prime objective in communicating the results of a settlement—with or without a strike—must be to minimize the likelihood of a bad "aftertaste" in the mouths of the employees, the community, or the public. This requires a delicate, subtle representation of the settlement terms, emphasizing the balanced nature of an agreement that serves the interest of both parties and the public. Above all, there must be no "winner" or "loser."

A disturbing element in American labor is a tendency of union members to refuse to ratify even the most favorable-appearing settlement terms—often in defiance of contrary recommendations by their union leaders. This is a problem for labor as well as management, because it reflects a growing unrest and militancy, especially among younger workers. Helping persuade employees to approve economically sound settlements poses another demanding test of the public relations person's communications skills.

It should be noted that this trend is not restricted to the United States. Indeed, it is considerably more pronounced in other countries—notably Great Britain and Australia. It poses a particular problem for multinational companies with operations in a variety of work environments worldwide.

Complicating the situation for these companies is continuing pressure by international trade union organizations to impose controls on the behavior of multinational enterprises. This is usually done by seeking access to parent-company management, either to pursue support for union positions in local labor disputers or to participate in basic investment and sourcing decisions affecting employees of the subsidiary companies. Frustrated in most of their efforts to obtain a voice in such decisions, these international unions have taken two courses:

1. Accelerating efforts to coalesce the unions representing employees of the various subsidiaries of multinational companies

2. Pressuring for the adoption of mandatory codes governing management's conduct of labor relations

It follows that the public relations practitioner assigned to multinational labor relations must monitor and understand international trade union objectives and activities. He or she must also help management explain its positions on efforts by international unions to insert themselves into areas in which the company believes they would impinge on its management prerogatives.

Space will not permit specific recommendations on handling—nationally or internationally—other labor-related matters such as plant closings, layoffs and temporary shutdowns, lockouts, union elections, and union organizing campaigns. However, a few general rules apply to coverage of strikes and contract negotiations, and they apply anywhere in the world.

1. Tell the company's story forcefully and honestly.

2. Inform employees of impending developments at least as soon as the public is advised, and preferably somewhat beforehand.

3. Keep employees and the public informed for the duration of the event.

4. Help newspersons cover the event quickly, accurately, and impartially—in the interests of your company, its employees, and the public.

5. Keep management informed of all developments affecting the current situation and likely to influence the outcome.

6. Organize and staff properly. Establish goals, select information outlets and targets, assign competent personnel, and ensure prompt and thorough feedback

from local and field public relations sources.

7. Do your labor relations homework. Know your subject intimately, but know also which information should be made public and which should not.

Handling Other Conflicts

Recently some unions, faced with constant loss of influence and membership, have taken aggressive actions. One of these actions is the "corporate campaign," in which unions solicit support from other groups—consumerists, environmentalists, activist minority groups, and others—to bolster their thrusts against companies they feel suppress unions' efforts to proselytize and solicit members.

As a countermove, some companies have filed lawsuits under the federal Racketeer Influenced and Corrupt Organizations (RICO) statute, claiming unions have conspired to drive them out of business.

This is a new front of the company-union conflict. As it unfolds, there may be changes in how companies position themselves, and in how unions feel about their tactics.

14
PUBLIC RELATIONS AND MARKETING

JUDITH RICH

Judith Rich is executive vice-president and executive creative director, USA of Ketchum Public Relations, the seventh largest public relations firm in the United States and the tenth worldwide. Ms. Rich also directs the National Consumer Branded Product Marketing Task Force at Ketchum.

Previously she was executive vice-president and national creative director of Daniel J. Edelman, Inc.

She has specialized in consumer product and package goods public relations on behalf of many large producers of consumer goods.

She gives speeches and workshops on creativity across the country.

A graduate of the University of Illinois, she is listed in Who's Who in America, Who's Who in American Women, *and the* International Biographical Directory.

Imagine, if you will, that you are witnessing a meeting of a group of business decision-makers who are discussing how and when to spend their marketing budget dollars. They consider: Should funds be used for publicity? For a promotion? Or should a campaign be devised that mixes both of these elements with advertising?

The term *marketing* actually encompasses all of these disciplines—yet each remains distinct. Though they work integrally with one another, they blend not as in a melting pot but like a salad. All the ingredients go well together, but the lettuce can be distinguished from the tomatoes—the public relations unique from but integrated with the advertising. The skilled "marketer" understands these differences and is adept at applying them appropriately.

Assuming that, collectively, our fictional group of business people is smart, they will carefully weigh the benefits of each marketing element and make their decision based on the strengths and weaknesses of each.

Marketing came to the forefront of American society during the 1980s. People who once associated the term with purchasing produce at the grocery store began to use it as a catchphrase for everything that concerned the act of selling.

Charities and colleges typify the breadth and scope of today's widespread application of marketing.

Charitable organizations, once passive in their efforts to raise money for their causes, have adopted marketing jargon to describe their activities. Rather than engaging in mere fund-raising, they "segmented" their donors and "positioned" their cause as a "product" to be sold with skill, using "demographic" and "psychographic" factors.

Our most respected institutions of higher learning, faced with a declining pool of young people, turned to marketing strategies to fill their classrooms. Administrators identified their curricula as a series of carefully defined products. They learned to position the college with consumers they identified as likely "customers"—potential students with whom they could communicate with minimal cost and effort.

However, long before charities and colleges learned marketing-speak and began to use marketing techniques, they used *public relations* to achieve these same objectives. As institutions relying on public support, they have long realized the value of a sound public reputation, as well as the importance of protecting it. Unfortunately, these same institutions too often fail to transfer their appreciation of the benefits derived from solid public relations to their curricula.

The typical six-hundred-page college marketing textbook probably contains little more than a few pages on public relations. In most cases, public relations is treated as a subset of promotion—and promotion is considered one of the four subsets of marketing, the four Ps: product, price, place (distribution), and promotion. With marketing textbooks and instructors giving public relations so little emphasis, most marketing students rarely get enough exposure to public relations to become interested, let alone adequately knowledgeable, in it. As a result, even graduates of the country's finest marketing schools often graduate knowing little or nothing about public relations and publicity, consequently neglecting their possibilities.

When these graduates then become tomorrow's decision-makers—if they consider public relations as a career at all—they frequently view it simply as a means to get their company some news coverage. If they do consider public relations, they often see it as only publicity—providing the media with material about the company's product or service—and fail to utilize it as the broad-scope, multidimensional function portrayed in this handbook.

Decision-makers' limited understanding and appreciation for public relations can and often does translate to a lack of respect and inadequate funding for public relations programs. Then, if the majority of the marketing budget is directed toward advertising, for example, and public relations gets only leftover dollars, it is likely to diminish the impact of the public relations effort.

Fortunately, many organizations have experienced or at least observed the value of public relations and subsequently use it effectively to build their sales and to enhance their public image. Conversely, those who fail to recognize the value of public relations, or recognize it too late, have not reaped the benefits.

This chapter examines a variety of public relations applications (and absences).

Publicity: The Active Arm of PR

Public relations is a complex task best performed by skilled professionals.

In this discussion, the framework of public relations is presented in its broad scope, but most of the *activity* in marketing public relations consists of *publicity*, with some *promotion*. Although many people in the field tend to use the term *public relations* constantly, what they are usually referring to is publicity functions. (*See* Chapter 1 for clarification of terms.)

Publicity and promotion are highly creative fields. No limitations should be set on practitioners' innovativeness, other than ethical ones. It has *not* all been done before. The work of creative, skilled people *will* stand out. The best attention getter is targeted quality work.

Professionals know that the most creative work is effective only if it is on-line with the organization's strategy and integrated with all functions and policies. Bright ideas that don't communicate the organization's message to the proper target audience are best left on the cutting room floor.

An element of risk makes public relations an exciting business—not risking the organization's money or reputation, but the risk of trying and accomplishing something that no one else has ever done before.

True public relations professionals do it all—analyzing, guiding, advising, planning, writing, budgeting, supervising suppliers and artists, providing client services for agency professionals, and management interface for corporate professionals.

Advertising Versus Publicity

Publicity professionals must communicate to decision-makers the specific and distinct role their discipline plays that differentiates it from advertising.

With advertising, you can choose your message and your medium. But your message, when delivered, may face the skepticism the public sometimes holds for a paid message. Readers and viewers look for the news, not the advertising. With publicity, you can be part of the news.

When the audience reads or views a product as news, it implies "third-party endorsement." The manufacturer and the public are the first two parties; the news people are the third party. The public expects the news media to be critical, so they are more likely to believe a news story that says good things about a product.

Publicity delivers the message and selects the medium but, unlike advertising, must filter its message through a reporter or a spokesperson. That means things can some-

times go awry. A reporter may accept your information, ask clarifying questions, and then get the facts completely wrong or dispute or refute everything you say. But a skilled publicity practitioner who presents clear information and is available for follow-up will usually communicate his or her message well enough so little is changed by the "filter." In fact, preparing it so it can't be used without credit to the source is one of the best skills of a publicity practitioner.

A company spokesperson, unless carefully trained and rehearsed, may abandon your agenda and go off into subjects totally unrelated to your key points. Spokespersons are made, not born. Solid media training by skilled public relations practitioners can prepare the spokesperson to divert bad questions, to deliver good answers to tough questions, and to bring the conversation around to the company's agenda. The skilled spokesperson can help market a product or a concept at the same time he or she builds the organization's image.

Spokespersons, whether corporate executives or outside experts hired for the roles, are the "face" the organization shows to the public. To the reader, listener, or viewer, the spokesperson *is* the organization.

Advertising delivers a precise message, but at higher cost and often with lower credibility than publicity. Skilled publicity can also effectively deliver a message and at less cost, with higher credibility.

Dual role

In its strictest sense, publicity performs two tasks within the organization:

First, it helps sell products and services by communicating their benefits to carefully targeted audiences, by means of media, programs, and events carefully selected for the purpose.

Second, it speaks for the organization, acting as its conscience. It can serve as the guardian of the organization's image.

Even if an organization has not identified someone to perform publicity functions, the need for a corporate spokesperson and conscience still exists.

Publicity *will occur* whether you want it to or not. Likewise, it can be negative or positive; the more it can be "directed," the more likely it will work to the organization's benefit.

An organization "naturally" interacts with its customers; local, state, and federal officials; its stockholders; special-interest groups; the news media; the so-called general public; and certainly its employees. An organization can examine the interests of each group, evaluate how each group perceives the organization relative to their personal interests, then take steps to communicate with those groups the organization feels need more or different information. Or the organization can ignore all that and accept whatever happens. Well-planned, well-executed publicity makes good marketing sense.

Publicity's Role as Salesperson

People buy products that are well marketed. A better mousetrap will sell only if the marketer designs a mousetrap with benefits the consumer feels he or she needs and wants (product or service). The mousetrap must sell at a cost the consumer considers reasonable (price). It must be available at a retail facility convenient to the consumer or through the mail (place). The reasons the consumer should purchase it must be communicated to the consumer (publicity and promotion).

Publicity and new products

New products and publicity form natural partners. The word that traditionally gets the most consumer attention is *new*. Some products are big news. Bill Gates seemed to make history, not just news, every time he introduced a new Microsoft product. But every new product represents an opportunity to the skilled publicist.

Heinz U.S.A. turned to publicity to introduce a newly developed full-line alternative to strained baby food in jars—a complete line of instant baby food. The new product was shelf-stable and, with its plastic resealable cap, as much or as little as desired could be used at any time. To reconstitute the product, the user need only add water and mix.

As with any new product, a key objective was to interest consumers in product trial and purchase. In this case, the prime audience was mothers of children under one year of age. Home economists and the medical community—especially pediatricians and nutritionists—were also important audiences because of their influence on the mothers.

Heinz nutritionist Dr. Ida Laquatra became the spokesperson for the new product. After extensive media training, she traveled to sixty markets across the country and conducted more than 260 interviews, selected with target audience viewing, listening, and reading habits in mind.

Canisters of Heinz Instant Baby Food (complete with utensils for mixing it), along with facts on infant nutrition and baby feeding, as well as information about the new product, were distributed to health, food, and feature news media across the United States.

Heinz and Ketchum produced a two-part video news release as well as a series of nationally syndicated radio features and weekly newspaper articles. Heinz offered free consumer information and a brochure on infant nutrition through an 800 hotline.

Heinz Instant Baby Food made business news in many major media.

Dr. Laquatra's cross-country media appearances, the video news feature, and syndicated newspaper features reached the product's key audiences in large numbers. Heinz received thousands of requests for consumer information and the free booklet offered.

The product passed a particularly crucial test for Heinz—it not only did well on its own, but it did so without taking sales away from the company's other baby food products. Heinz regular baby food sales *increased* even as the instant product was introduced successfully.

A double obstacle faced the Hyundai Excel. Not only was Hyundai a new company in the U.S. market, it was one of the first Korean products ever marketed here.

Hyundai and its agency, Ogilvy and Mather, started their campaign with visits to key opinion leaders. The corporation chairman personally visited the publishers and editors of *The Wall Street Journal, Time,* and the *New York Times.* The chairman discussed not only the automobile, but also the development of Korea and its place in the world economy. That transformed the product's supposed handicap as the only major Korean product in the United States into a strength. Hyundai was seen as a vanguard product from an emerging country—a newsworthy concept. Related articles appeared in *Business Week, Forbes,* and *Fortune.* The automotive press picked up on the product, also meeting with Hyundai executives, and test-drives were offered to automotive reporters in every major American city.

The result—in its first year in the U.S. market, Hyundai temporarily became the fourth-highest-selling imported car.

Publicizing Mature Products

Publicity can breathe new life into old-line products that the public may perceive as no longer exciting. Velveeta processed cheese spread had been around for sixty years when Kraft asked Ketchum to help rebuild consumer excitement for the brand.

The agency-client team decided to reposition the product's image, concurrent with the sixtieth anniversary. The anniversary came in an era of dual-wage-earning families who had limited time for meal preparation. That provided a platform for the repositioning.

The decision was made to contemporize the product. The team created a new kitchen personality, the Velveeta Shortcut Chef. He was trained to demonstrate how the traditional product adapted to modern kitchens, with microwave cooking an obvious way to demonstrate Velveeta's meltability.

A short-statured chef was suited for the role and was introduced to national media at a sixtieth anniversary party in New York. The event began with a cocktail reception where guests looked at old Velveeta television commercials, print ads, memorabilia, and packaging, while sampling Velveeta hors d'oeuvres. The chef demonstrated three new recipes in ten minutes, one of which was the basis for lunch. Velveeta kitchen timers were presented as gifts to underscore the quick preparation time. To go further with the "shortcut" theme, mini-sized media kits and recipe brochures were distributed.

Several press guests wrote or aired stories about the anniversary and the chef. Velveeta, long a traditional product, was repositioned in the minds of many a modern consumer as a product that adapts well to current trends.

Publicizing Products in Decline

Sometimes publicity can help sell a product whose prime has come and gone.

General Health Care Corporation (GHCC) of Piscataway, New Jersey, found advertising was not able to stave off a twenty-year decline for its cotton diaper service company. Modern parents considered cotton diapers a relic and looked at disposable diapers as a time-saving, convenient innovation.

In 1988, GHCC hired Geston & Gordon Associates. Since there were questions about the environmental impact of disposable diapers, the agency researched the subject and surveyed current and former disposable diaper customers to measure attitudes and awareness of the problem. Lists were compiled of environmental, consumer, and business editors, and of legislators. People on these lists were sent information discovered through the research and surveys. Concurrently, they also received the message that an alternative to disposable diapers, the diaper service, still existed.

The agency-client team created a character, "Crusader Baby," as a symbol of environmental conscience. Crusader Baby's image was used in all campaign print materials and made public appearances in the form of a ventriloquist's dummy. It appeared at malls and other key locations.

Brochures presenting the case that disposable diapers harm the environment were developed, including information on GHCC's cotton diaper service. These went to current customers, childbirth educators, health food stores, and environmental and civic organizations. Comprehensive environmental packets with cover letters were distributed to legislators, pediatricians, obstetricians, childbirth educators, environmental and consumer organizations.

As a result, GHCC's sales went up significantly for the first time in twenty years.

Publicity in Support of Advertising

Publicity can be used to extend the reach and impact of advertising.

Marketers at Ralston Purina wanted to develop new customers for the company's Butcher's Blend dry dog food, so they reformulated the product with a fresh-cooked bacon aroma. Traditionally, pet foods are known for having less-than-appealing aromas, so the new Butcher's Blend would be the first dog food ever marketed on the basis of its smell.

It was decided to introduce the new product to consumers by using a new type of advertising for pet food—bacon-scented Scratch 'n' Sniff newspaper ads. To draw attention to the innovative ads and stimulate trial purchases, Ralston Purina's publicity firm developed a media pitch "warning" dog owners that Fido might run off with Sunday's newspaper if he smelled the bacon-scented ad. Dr. Larry Myers of Auburn University, an expert on canine olfactories, served as a credible and objective spokesperson.

To herald the first freestanding insert, the agency nationally distributed media kits, including information on the scratch 'n' sniff advertisement, interesting facts for dog owners about a dog's sense of smell, and a copy of the ad. For a second ad run, they produced a video news release (VNR) entitled "The Nose Knows." It discussed a dog's superior sense of smell and warned that dogs may run off with Sunday's paper. The VNR was distributed via satellite to create a "hard news" impression. Each media announcement was released the Monday before the respective ad insert was to run.

During the week before the insert, the agency followed up actively with the news media.

Publicity efforts reached a combined print and broadcast audience of more than 61 million consumers.

The publicity magnified the impact of this freestanding insert (FSI) that might otherwise have been lost in the clutter.

Extending Advertising Awareness with Publicity

Even well-budgeted national advertising campaigns can't run endlessly. However, creative publicity programs can extend their impact efficiently and effectively.

The California Raisin Advisory Board had stirred up interest and sales with its television spots of Claymation raisins dancing to "I Heard It Through the Grapevine." Because their budget limited advertising to a concentration in the fall months, Ketchum developed a campaign to help extend awareness throughout the year.

The agency-client team created live costumed Dancing California Raisins. The costumed characters made key appearances in the Macy's Thanksgiving Day parade and at White House functions, were the centerpiece for a national contest to name each character, toured across America on "vacation" to greet fans, attended CALRAB events, were covered by *Good Morning America*, *Entertainment Tonight*, and various other national print and broadcast media.

The Dancing Raisins more than maintained the momentum of the advertising in nonadvertising periods. In their first year, even though the commercials were virtually off the air nine out of twelve months, the California Dancing Raisin campaign remained the third most-recalled commercial campaign. Over a three-year campaign period, raisin sales increased by 20 percent.

As in the case of the California Raisins, sometimes a product's advertising becomes a rich source for publicity activities. Publicity can not only bring advertising characters to life, it can associate them more closely with the brand they represent and the audiences they're trying to reach.

Advertising impact made Morris the Cat, 9-Lives cat food's long-time spokescat, seem to be a real-life cat to whom cat owners and cat lovers could relate. The agency took him out to meet his public via a Morris look-alike contest, a Win-a-Date-with-Morris contest, two nonfiction best-sellers, and even a "campaign" for the U.S. presidency.

Publicity in Support of Promotions

Edward Lowe Industries used publicity to support its national promotion, the Tidy Cat 3 Cat Box Filler Photo Contest.

The contest, designed to select "America's most photogenic felines" for Lowe's cat calendar, began with a nationally distributed Sunday newspaper freestanding insert that contained contest entry information and product coupons. Supported by follow-up news releases encouraging participation, the contest caught fire. More than twenty thousand feline photos were entered.

Twelve winners were selected (one per calendar month) and flown with their owners to Chicago for the "finals," which were held during National Pet Week. News releases advised the news media in each winner's hometown of their selection.

The selection of a grand prize winner (and three runners up) was turned into a media event, with a panel of four journalists and a celebrity judging. A UPI wire photo of the grand prize winner resulted, as did local Chicago media coverage. Each of the twelve winning cat owners was interviewed, and news releases and video footage were distributed to their home markets. Publication of the cat calendar was an opportunity for follow-up publicity in each local market.

The Tidy Cat 3 Photo Contest was a multidimensional program, combining sales promotion, advertising, couponing, customer relations, and publicity.

Creating a Market

KPMG Peat Marwick, a large accounting and management consultant, had developed an unusual service. It was so unusual that its potential customers had no idea they would even need such a service.

Peat Marwick developed Runaway Systems Management (RSM), a service designed to stop what the company called "runaway computers." Companies of all sizes, Peat Marwick said, sometimes got off track when developing their computer systems and discovered they had built a costly system that did not meet their needs. Research of its current clients estimated that 30–35 percent of American start-up computer systems were "runaways."

The agency used this information to develop a profile of a runaway and to identify runaway victims. Both were used to communicate to chief executives and chief financial officers a problem they never knew they had.

First, the agency focused on James Willbern, founder of RSM, calling him the "Red Adair" (world famous oil fire tamer) of computer consulting because of his ability to put out "fires." To reinforce the image, a brochure with an oil rig blowout was developed.

The program's keystone was a Sunday *New York Times* business section story about "runaways." It described Willbern as the "Red Adair" of the computer industry. The *Times* even published Willbern's office telephone numbers, leading directly to $4 million in business.

Business, trade, and local publications published articles on "runaways" and cited Willbern as an expert. Within one year, the RSM practice grew from an idea to a $15 million per year business and from a regional service to a national one.

Influencing Consumers Using Nonconsumer Groups

Marketing managers instinctively put primary focus on the ultimate consumer. Publicity can address other key publics that may influence an organization's bottom line.

For example, Kellogg advertised "All Bran" by utilizing the National Cancer Institute Guidelines recommending a high-fiber, low-fat diet. Market research indicated that consumers made the switch to such a diet only when there was a recommendation by a health professional or if there had been an incidence of cancer in a close friend or relative. After reviewing the research with its agency, Kellogg reasoned that one way to market All-Bran was to communicate with health professionals who influenced consumers about their diets.

Kellogg's agency created a comprehensive fiber information program and called it "Good News!" to underscore the good news about what Americans can do to maintain healthy lifestyles. The release of all material was timed during April—Cancer Control Month.

The program began with an information kit sent to 45,000 physicians and dieticians. It included a scientific white paper on dietary fiber; a colorful "Spoon It On" poster that communicated fiber is not just for breakfast but can be spooned on salads and vegetables as well; a *Step-By-Step Guide to a High Fiber Diet* booklet; a "Quick and Easy Tips to a High-Fiber Diet" leaflet that was offered in large quantities for distribution to patients; and a response card to measure results and order additional supplies. The response rate was exceptional: 15,000 response cards were received, a rate of more than 33 percent. Of those returned, 7,600 requested further information.

To supplement efforts directed toward health professionals, the campaign also targeted the media. The kit was reformulated into a media information kit with the addition of press releases and photos. It was then sent to food, health, medical, and science editors at newspapers and magazines nationwide.

Kellogg continued to spread the Good News! by hiring a well-known physician and author of cancer prevention books to become the spokesperson for a selected market media tour. They also distributed mat releases with fiber-rich recipes to weekly and suburban newspapers and radio scripts to government extension home economists.

The program was expanded the following year and called, "Good News! Bran News! . . . It's As Easy As ABC" (All-Bran Cereal). A survey of frequent travelers was conducted at major airports, where respondents were quizzed on their knowledge of fiber and their ability to maintain a high-fiber diet while traveling. Results of the survey were sent to health reporters.

An All-Bran Breakfast Bar was held in New York City and became the subject of a *Today* show remote with weatherman Willard Scott. The bar was set up in Penn Station, and fiber breakfasts were sold to benefit the American Cancer Society.

The campaign worked on two levels concurrently—with health professionals who influenced consumers and with consumers themselves.

Competing for Awareness and Support

If publicity is so effective in support of marketing, why is it not used more often and more extensively? There are several reasons.

All public relations, by its nature, does not call attention to itself. When done properly, public relations is unrecognizable and often uncredited as such by an organization's man-

agement. Nobody gets up, as at the Academy Awards, and thanks all the people behind the scenes. Public relations practitioners get used to being invisible. This can be the price of third-party credibility; but if you're invisible, management may forget you.

Publicity may not appear to be a driving force. When it is used to sell products, the organization often considers publicity a "helper" for advertising. Top management does not think of "helpers" first.

Publicity sometimes faces a lack of understanding because the marketer is unfamiliar with it. Large amounts of money are rarely risked on the unfamiliar.

Publicity needs to justify its outcomes with hard numbers and facts. To compete for attention and funding, practitioners must measure and research their recommendations definitively.

Measuring success

The day of the "hunch" or "warm feeling" system of measurement is behind us. When management asks, "What has public relations done for me lately?" the publicity professional can't simply show a stack of news clips as evidence. (*See* Chapter 49.)

To be effective, publicity must be targeted to the right audience, not just a random hit. For example, a privately held toy company with no intention of going public would gain little from a *Barron's* article about its latest innovation. That message should go primarily to mothers, fathers, and other toy buyers and would be much more meaningful in *Parents*. Business media can be helpful, though, in reaching toy retailers. Likewise, the message has to deliver the correct copy points. A story that mentions the toy and doesn't explain its merits, pricing, availability, etc., does little to further its sales.

So the broadest possible coverage should not be confused with a strategic approach. A good measurement system links resources (dollars, hours, people) with results. Advertisers, for example, look at such measurements as cost per thousand (CPM) impressions to evaluate their efficiency.

A better system links planning to execution and execution to results. That is, a plan is first evaluated on which aspects of the plan were actually accomplished. Did the press release go out on time? Was the brochure prepared? Did the video news release (VNR) reach all the recommended stations? Then these elements are further evaluated as to results. Was the press release successfully picked up? (What constitutes success should be determined in advance.) Did the copy points hold up in the published and broadcast reports? How many brochures were requested and distributed? How many stations played the VNR? How did they use the VNR? How effective were the stations in reaching priority audiences? And, of course, were these exposures effective in motivating the audiences?

Planners should determine performance objectives before launching a publicity program. A good measurement system can provide a solid basis for evaluation when results are in.

The best way to target media efforts is to aim at the audience, not the print or broadcast vehicle. Popular major media and trendy shows may be captivating, but they may not reach the right audiences.

Effective, strategic publicity considers which audiences are most influential as consumers, investors, or public interest groups. It then matches these audiences with the media most influential with them. (See Figure 14.1.)

Computer systems are widely used for planning and tracking publicity. For example, Ketchum's Publicity Planning and Tracking System is programmed with statistics on national media, segmented by various audience demographics.

Communications managers can use information from this database to customize national publicity plans. Media can be selected according to the targeted audiences. It's important to consider not only total audience but also target audience and priority market reach.

It is also important to measure the overall quality of messages that are being communicated. Reaching the right audience is vital. Communicating the right message to that audience is equally critical. "Points" can be allotted to the impact of each message communicated to each audience.

After considering target audience and message quality, the system can compare the publicity plan with achieved placements as a measure of effectiveness. The concept is simple: develop your plan, determine your measurement of success, then evaluate what you accomplished in relation to that plan.

Armed with clear, measurable results, the publicity practitioner can show the organization's management what publicity does to advance its interests. Managers appreciate numbers. Faced with a choice between unsupported and supported programs, the supported programs will be preferred.

The Spokesperson as the Company's Conscience

The bulk of this chapter, thus far, has been devoted to the sales role of public relations. Another role, the role of the organization's spokesperson and conscience, can make it the equal of both the marketing department and the legal department. In the role of the organization's "mother," public relations practitioners help the organization do the right thing.

As mother, the public relations person warns and encourages. Fair warning: you're

—Richard Kuntz, President, General Business Forms

"My parents started this company.

I learned to spell

by setting type on

their old printing press."

"My mother would check it when I was done. I can't remember a time when I didn't have some little job around here.

"When my mother died, the family lawyer said we should declare bankruptcy. We owed more than the company was worth. But my brother and I wanted to make a go of it. That was 50 years ago.

"My daughter is the treasurer now, and we want to buy some new equipment, so she went to the bank the other day and borrowed six million dollars. "I wish my mother could have seen that."

It's your life's work. Does your bank understand that?

American National
the **bank** *for* **business**

Chicago, suburbs, Rockford and Milwaukee

CREATING POSITIVE AWARENESS

Figure 14.1 Testimonial from a satisfied customer helps build awareness of American National as a bank for business. *Courtesy American National Bank and Trust Company of Chicago.*

not always liked when you remind people to button their coats.

Sometimes everyone else in the room applauds a new TV commercial, but the sound PR person must stand up to say it's potentially offensive to minorities, or church people, or others. Some may agree with you, but others will see you as someone who spoiled their good idea.

Sometimes PR must advise that an organization face the media when everyone else wants to hide.

Boston's largest bank pleaded guilty to accepting over a billion dollars in cash from overseas sources without notifying the IRS, as required. The Bank of Boston's president said the offense was an administrative foul-up and paid the maximum fine.

When the *Boston Globe* reported that the bank may have unwittingly been laundering money for drug dealers, the president called a press conference. Unfortunately, he did not apologize. Instead, he tried to minimize, which, of course, raised media and public curiosity.

The *Globe* dug up facts proving that a branch of the bank had accepted cash *and* issued cashier's checks in return—effectively laundering the money. Most of the cash came from the alleged head of organized crime in New England. The bank president blamed it on "teller error."

The *New York Times* posed the paradox: "The bank pleads guilty to willfully and knowingly committing a felony, but contends it was merely negligent."

Failure to show remorse harmed the bank. Its stock dropped from $47 to $42. Congress and state banking committees scheduled hearings.

A strong public relations "mother" would have advised candor. If the public thinks you're hiding something, you'll end up revealing more than you ever thought possible. People can understand administrative errors. They see them every day. They also under-

stand repentance and straight answers. Anything less and you get yourself in trouble.

Leona Helmsley's lack of repentance may have done more than harm her image. She built and cultivated an elitist, disdainful image that she did not moderate, even during her trial for income tax evasion. She showed up at the trial in expensive clothes and maintained an attitude that landed her on the cover of *Newsweek*, over the caption, "Rhymes with Rich."

Helmsley's attributed statement that "only little people pay taxes" and her attitude may have affected the verdict and sentencing. Juries are, after all, a small specific target audience.

Neither the Bank of Boston incident not Leona Helmsley's demeanor was involved with the businesses' marketing—but the effects had massive marketing impact. Good public relations on behalf of these institutions—going far beyond the publicity aspects of a "marketing mix"—could have done more good than millions of dollars spent on advertising and other marketing activities.

Impossible mission

Public relations can be very effective, but it can't succeed when called on to rescue a bad marketing decision.

Before the early seventies Schlitz was the strong number two beer in market share. A consumer's selection and purchase of a brand of beer are not done scientifically. Image is basic.

In the early seventies, Schlitz management made a fateful decision to become a low-cost producer of beer. They used lower-cost ingredients. Schlitz didn't hide these changes, but they didn't promote them to their consumers either. They did bring the changes to Wall Street's attention, however, in seeking to raise the price of Schlitz stock.

Then they switched to a fermentation process that cut aging time up to 40 percent.

Lower production costs did raise profits . . . at first. The stock did rise. But the word got out to beer drinkers: It's not the old Schlitz any more.

Schlitz had to defend its shortcuts. Sales plummeted. In an attempt to reverse the decline the company eliminated the shortcuts and went back to brewing a quality beer. Unfortunately, perception always lags behind performance. Customers had given up on Schlitz. Schlitz breweries were eventually purchased and the brand's sales shrank to almost nothing.

What can a public relations person do in such a situation? The answer is chronological. If a skilled public relations practitioner is consulted early, he or she has the opportunity to influence a decision. If he or she is brought in at a point where management has just realized it has made a mistake, the public relations practitioner can advise management to publicly admit they did wrong and to take corrective action. If the PR practitioner is consulted after the product has established a steady decline because of a mistake, it is usually too late to save the product.

Underestimating the public

Coca-Cola polled many people regarding the taste of their new Coke formula—but they didn't tell the people polled that they planned to retire the old Coke. Consequently, survey results made the company believe that the public would prefer the new Coke.

So Coca-Cola was surprised when the public rejected their plan to replace the old Coca-Cola formula. Coke should have known that tampering with an American institution would attract enormous publicity. They committed the error of underestimating their own importance in the mind of the American public.

Coke's director of corporate communications was not consulted until the decision to replace Coke had already been made. He was asked to develop ways to communicate the soundness of the decision, rather than being brought in early enough to advise management whether the decision should be made.

The story was so big, it took on a life of its own. Polls were taken of outraged consumers. Protest songs were written. Old Coke was hoarded. The company made the wrong kind of news by swearing by their limited research.

This was another case where the public relations professional should have been consulted at a point where his advice could have influenced the outcome.

Averting marketing disasters

The Procter & Gamble false rumor problem and the Tylenol poisoning case—both treated in Chapter 2—were examples of marketing disasters averted through sound public relations judgment and practice. Standard marketing procedures in these and other cases would probably have been disastrously ineffective.

Showing conscience

Pioneer Hi-Bred International, Inc., of Des Moines, Iowa, the largest producer of commercial seed corn, feels a natural bond to rural America. As such, Pioneer established its "Search for Solutions" program, a series of employee and community relations conferences designed to provide residents of rural America with many of the "tools" needed to improve their quality of life.

Conference participants are employees and sales representatives of Pioneer from across the country, bringing with them their community leaders representing the areas that most critically affect the well-being of rural America—health care, economic development, and education. The conferences are designed to inform and challenge the participants and better equip them to become agents of change in their local communities.

As another example of organizations supporting their markets in time of need, San Francisco companies went to the aid of their customers in a direct fashion after the Bay Area earthquake of 1989. Safeway trucked in food and water for the victims. Bechtel volunteered engineers. Six companies donated $1 million or more to disaster relief.

Public Relations' Vital Role

Public relations must be one of management's frequently considered choices. Too often it's a leftover when it should be a main course. Continuing the metaphor, effective marketing is like a healthy diet. It needs all its basic groups. Public relations is a basic component of successful marketing. Marketing, like public relations, should be part of a totally integrated battery of communications intended to influence the organization's publics.

Public relations can help marketing better when the respect from its spokesperson/conscience role carries over. Practitioners can help themselves by justifying their programs with results-oriented measurement.

Public relations can help ensure that a product is not rejected for reasons that have nothing to do with the product. Public relations can help the organization take smart risks and avoid the bad ones.

15

BUILDING EFFECTIVE DEALER RELATIONS

RONALD I. GOW
LENARD F. SCHWEITZER

Ronald I. Gow was director of sales promotion and Lenard F. Schweitzer was director of communications, Marketing Group for Whirlpool Corporation, Benton Harbor, Michigan.

Also contributing to this chapter are P. Daniel Miller, vice-president, Sales and Distribution, and Marvin L. Raglon, director, Distribution Education, Whirlpool Appliance Group.

Dealer relations comprises the combined total efforts that a supplier employs to build and to sustain a favorable image with its network of dealers.

The marketing executives maintain primary responsibility for dealer relations. However, many other supporting activities—finance, service, publicity—also make an important impact on dealer relations. In fact, virtually every department within a typical company affects dealer relations.

The Impact of Dealer Relations

Suppliers of consumer products who depend on independent, multiline retail dealers to sell their merchandise to the ultimate consumer

---

Major factors affecting dealer relations, such as the consumerism movement, safety, and government regulation of products and distribution policies, are treated also in Chapters 4 and 16.—*Ed.*

must garner the loyalty and support of those dealers to succeed in the marketplace. How the dealer feels about a company, its representatives, and its products will ultimately provide the measure of that company's success. Never has this been more true than now. Consequently, never has the art of building and maintaining good dealer relations been more vital.

In most industries today such traditional marketing advantages as superior product performance, styling, service, and price have all waned, due to the generally high degree of similarity between competing products of like type and quality. As a result, these benefits are being replaced by various support programs designed to help and encourage dealers to sell one brand of product over another. Product quality, styling, service, and price remain important, but suppliers must now also compete in supporting dealers' efforts to sell to the ultimate consumer.

In the final analysis, a loyal dealer is one who makes a profit selling a specific brand of product; when profitability ceases his loyalty shifts to another brand. This is as it should be in the free enterprise system.

Communications' Role

Every dealer needs to know the kind of help a manufacturer provides—a job calling for the skills of the public relations practitioner. This involves building dealer loyalty and respect, making each dealer feel an important part of the team, and supplying special information on new products and programs. Unless dealers are completely familiar with the supplier and feel important, they usually will not do the best job for the supplier.

Channels available for communicating with dealers include field sales representatives, conventions, service representatives, training programs, and the like. The types of mass communications techniques commonly found among public relations skills are extremely effective for those channels. They include the application of accepted public relations techniques, such as graphics, copy, printing, and the rapid dissemination of information, to communicate with a specific audience or public. The information transmitted is likely to be received exactly as sent out. Also, they are generally the most economical methods of dealer communications available.

The prime vehicle is the printed word and picture. Since this type of communication provides no way to induce absorption of the message by the recipient, it is essential that the vital presentation be attractive and that the content be interesting and *useful* to the recipient. Though one of its merits is economy, skimping on quality in this area can prove costly.

In addition, effective dealer communications programs encourage dealer response and provide channels through which it can be accomplished.

Audience Research

In developing a dealer communications program, start by understanding the audience to which the communication is directed. The communicator must know what makes the dealers tick, their problems, the nature of the markets in which they operate, their customers, their vernacular, and the common characteristics that set them apart from other types of dealers. It is also important to identify the different types of dealers comprising the dealer organization: large or small, rural or urban, sophisticated or not. Most manufacturers of consumer goods include a mix of these types. A question of particular importance is, What do the dealers think of the supplier? Many other questions also need to be answered, but the important point is that it is virtually impossible to communicate effectively unless the audience is characterized.

To get answers to these questions, the public relations practitioner may wish to conduct a survey. (*See* Chapter 18.) A survey performed and properly interpreted by experts will not only provide the information needed to communicate effectively, but will also often yield additional insights into dealer attitudes that will aid the supplier's entire marketing efforts.

For example, a survey can be an efficient means of monitoring the effectiveness of new merchandising programs or the acceptability of new products.

The public relations specialist can also learn a great deal about the dealer organization through association with other members of the company—particularly those who have regular and direct contact with retailers. The most effective method of all is direct, face-to-face contact with dealers. This can be done during trips for other purposes, as well as at sales meetings and trade shows. Most suppliers conduct or participate in numerous dealer meetings, seminars, and conventions during the year, both in the field and at the home office.

Trade publications provide yet another source of information. Constantly monitoring them enables one to learn a great deal about the industry and its leaders. Active participation in industry associations is also an effective way of acquiring useful knowledge about dealers and their functions.

Knowing the organization

It is essential for the public relations practitioner to know the organization before effective dealer communications is possible. Products, policies, sales and service capabilities, and programs relating to such areas as finance, distribution, marketing, advertising, sales promotion, sales training, dealer education, and personnel must be clearly understood. The major goal is to help sell the company and its products to dealers—an impossible task if the communicator is not thoroughly familiar with both. Dealer relations are part of the total integrated function of the company.

Getting to know one's own company (or the client of a public relations firm) and staying on top of what's going on is a demanding task. It requires establishing viable working relationships with all departments within the company, since each makes important contributions to the total dealer relations program. The public relations practitioner must gain their respect and cooperation to be effective.

Forms of Dealer Communications Media

Though many media are available, the public relations specialist usually finds that the options are determined by prudent use of budgets provided for dealer communication. While such communications devices as motion pictures, closed-circuit television, recorded messages, and slide or video presentations can be very effective and definitely have their place, the major medium used to communicate with dealers will generally be the printed word and graphics, using various delivery systems—mail, express package services, fax, and others.

External house publications

Perhaps the most widely used and effective printed dealer communications medium is the external house publication. Prepared in a wide assortment of formats and sizes, varying widely in quality of content and appearance, the external house publication has become "standard equipment" for thousands of U.S. companies engaged in dealer communications. The state of the art is improving rapidly, with more and more good publications reaching dealers' stores every year. Some even rival the better consumer magazines in both appearance and editorial content.

These publications, often referred to as dealer newsletters or magazines, offer some distinct advantages that make them by far the most practical mass medium available for dealer communications. (*See* Figure 15.1.)

Flexibility

A dealer publication can let you offer something for everybody—large dealers and small—small town and large—high volume and low. Just as most product lines offer a wide variety of models to meet specific market requirements, a dealer magazine can vary its content to meet specific audience requirements.

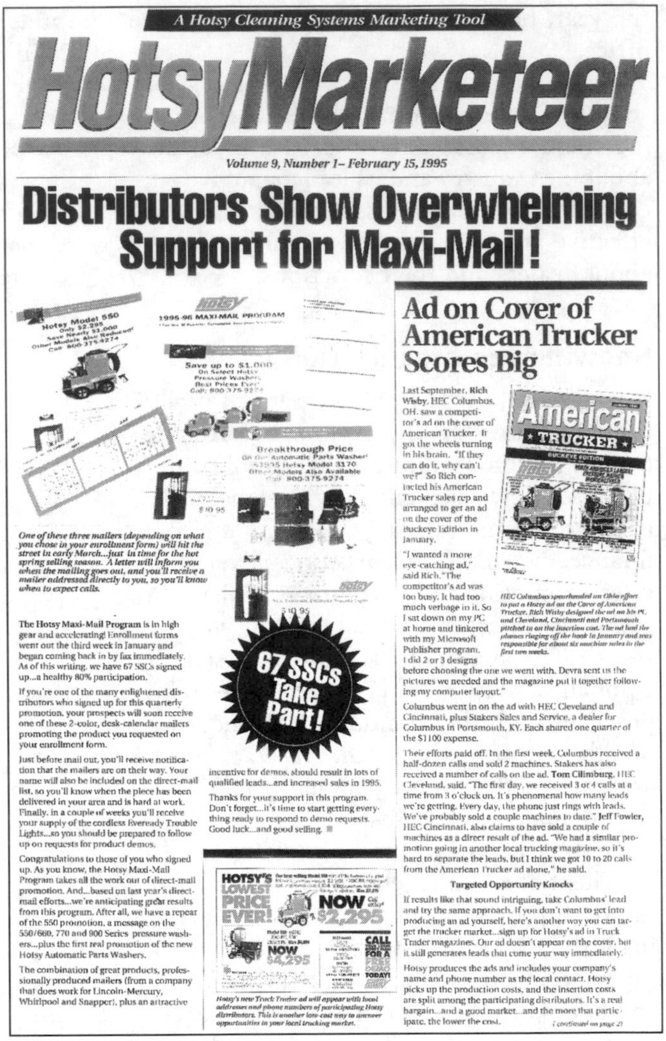

A Hotsy Cleaning Systems Marketing Tool

HotsyMarketeer

Volume 9, Number 1– February 15, 1995

Distributors Show Overwhelming Support for Maxi-Mail!

One of these three mailers (depending on what you chose in your enrollment form) will hit the street in early March...just in time for the hot spring selling season. A letter will inform you when the mailing goes out, and you'll receive a mailer addressed directly to you, so you'll know when to expect calls.

67 SSCs Take Part!

The Hotsy Maxi-Mail Program is in high gear and accelerating! Enrollment forms went out the third week in January and began coming back in by fax immediately. As of this writing, we have 67 SSCs signed up...a healthy 80% participation.

If you're one of the many enlightened distributors who signed up for this quarterly promotion, your prospects will soon receive one of these 2-color, desk-calendar mailers promoting the product you requested on your enrollment form.

Just before mail out, you'll receive notification that the mailers are on their way. Your name will also be included on the direct-mail list, so you'll know when the piece has been delivered in your area and is hard at work. Finally, in a couple of weeks you'll receive your supply of the cordless Eveready Trouble Lights...so you should be prepared to follow up on requests for product demos.

Congratulations to those of you who signed up. As you know, the Hotsy Maxi-Mail Program takes all the work out of direct-mail promotion. And...based on last year's direct-mail efforts...we're anticipating great results from this program. After all, we have a repeat of the 550 promotion, a message on the 550/660, 770 and 900 Series pressure washers...plus the first real promotion of the new Hotsy Automatic Parts Washers.

The combination of great products, professionally produced mailers (from a company that does work for Lincoln-Mercury, Whirlpool and Snapper), plus an attractive incentive for demos, should result in lots of qualified leads...and increased sales in 1995.

Thanks for your support in this program. Don't forget...it's time to start getting everything ready to respond to demo requests. Good luck...and good selling.

HOTSY'S LOWEST PRICE EVER! NOW $2,295 NOW $4,295 CALL FOR A FREE DEMO TODAY!

Hotsy's new Truck Trader ad will appear with local addresses and phone numbers of participating Hotsy distributors. This is another low-cost way to uncover opportunities in your local trucking market.

Ad on Cover of American Trucker Scores Big

Last September, **Rich Wisby**, HEC Columbus, OH, saw a competitor's ad on the cover of American Trucker. It got the wheels turning in his brain. "If they can do it, why can't we?" So Rich contacted his American Trucker sales rep and arranged to get an ad on the cover of the Buckeye Edition in January.

"I wanted a more eye-catching ad," said Rich. "The competitor's ad was too busy. It had too much verbage in it. So I sat down on my PC at home and tinkered with my Microsoft Publisher program. I did 2 or 3 designs before choosing the one we went with. Devra sent us the pictures we needed and the magazine put it together following my computer layout."

HEC Columbus spearheaded an Ohio effort to put a Hotsy ad on the Cover of American Trucker. Rich Wisby designed the ad on his PC, and Cleveland, Cincinnati and Portsmouth pitched in on the insertion cost. The ad had the phones ringing off the hook in January and was responsible for about six machine sales in the first two weeks.

Columbus went in on the ad with HEC Cleveland and Cincinnati, plus Stakers Sales and Service, a dealer for Columbus in Portsmouth, KY. Each shared one quarter of the $1100 expense.

Their efforts paid off. In the first week, Columbus received a half-dozen calls and sold 2 machines. Stakers has also received a number of calls on the ad. **Tom Cilimburg**, HEC Cleveland, said, "The first day, we received 3 or 4 calls at a time from 3 o'clock on. It's phenomenal how many leads we're getting. Every day, the phone just rings with leads. We've probably sold a couple machines to date." **Jeff Fowler**, HEC Cincinnati, also claims to have sold a couple of machines as a direct result of the ad. "We had a similar promotion going in another local trucking magazine, so it's hard to separate the leads, but I think we got 10 to 20 calls from the American Trucker ad alone," he said.

Targeted Opportunity Knocks

If results like that sound intriguing, take Columbus' lead and try the same approach. If you don't want to get into producing an ad yourself, here's another way you can target the trucker market...sign up for Hotsy's ad in Truck Trader magazines. Our ad doesn't appear on the cover, but it still generates leads that come your way immediately.

Hotsy produces the ads and includes your company's name and phone number as the local contact. Hotsy picks up the production costs, and the insertion costs are split among the participating distributors. It's a real bargain...and a good market...and the more that participate, the lower the cost.

(continued on page 2)

Figure 15.1 The cornerstone of a dealer communications program, the dealer newsletter builds support by highlighting programs that generate prospects and sales. *Courtesy Maximail Inc., Chicago.*

Frequency and regularity

It is extremely important to ensure that dealer communication takes place often and with regularity. Not only does this confirm the company's interest, but it also serves as a regular reminder of your products and services versus those of your competition.

Education

Today's dealer is hard pressed to make a profit for a variety of reasons. A well-prepared publication is an ideal way to provide dealers with solutions to their marketing problems. This is an area where knowing your dealers is extremely important because generally the key to one dealer's success is the solution to a problem plaguing many others—and the information can be relayed through the magazine. Ideally, the dealer communication function serves as an information clearinghouse, no matter which media are used, and the dealer magazine is particularly well suited to the task.

Economy

With modern equipment and techniques now available it is possible to produce good-quality dealer publications at a reasonable cost, particularly for a large dealer organization. It generally holds true that a fairly high volume is required to bring the per-unit cost down appreciably; but when compared to the cost of a salesperson or personal call, even an expensive magazine can represent a good value.

Visual impact

The combination of good graphics and meaningful copy, using color whenever possible, is an effective way to tell a story.

Some rules to remember when planning a dealer magazine (and virtually any other type of dealer communication) include the following:

• Make sure your material is timely and meaningful to your audience. If your dealers can't use it, don't print it.

• Don't use it to toot the company's horn. Unless the activity under discussion will directly benefit your dealers, it will not interest them and they will stop reading the publication.

• Don't skimp on production any more than necessary. The publication is a reflection of the company. Four good issues a year are generally better than eight poor ones. If your budget won't permit a good-quality production, consider using less-expensive mailers or newsletters.

• Use as many good illustrations and as much color as the budget allows. These are well-established tools for increasing readership.

• Set a schedule and keep it. Continuity and frequency are essential.

• Maintain the mailing list. Know who's receiving the publication at all times. Remember that most dealer organizations are constantly changing.

• Include something for everybody and make sure material is helpful and timely. Remember: DEALERS WANT FACTS, NOT THEORY—AND MOST CAN TELL ONE FROM THE OTHER.

Other printed media

Circumstances such as lack of time or cost will often dictate the use of other forms of printed media. The following is a partial list to consider:

Monthly, quarterly, or weekly newsletters. Low in cost and easily prepared, informative and relevant newsletters can be an expedient dealer communication device.

Special mailers. Useful for special events and as fill-ins between regular publications, but don't overdo them. Dealers already get too much mail; don't compound the problem. (*See* Figure 15.2.)

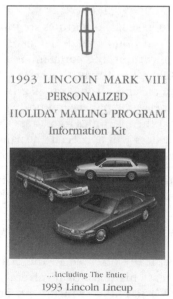

Figure 15.2 A folder announcing a holiday mailing program for Lincoln Mercury dealers. Lincoln Mercury sent personalized holiday greetings and an invitation to a test drive event to prospects of dealers who participated in the program. *Courtesy Maximail Inc., Chicago.*

Figure 15.3 Promotional posters are another component of an effective dealer communications program. *Courtesy Maximail Inc., Chicago.*

1993 LINCOLN MARK VIII

RESERVED – ROY KING

News releases. Sometimes regular news releases can double as dealer mailers. If an event concerning the company is newsworthy to the press, it may also be of interest to the dealers, and all it costs is a little more press time, some paper, and postage or wire charges. When it comes to matters that affect them, dealers will appreciate hearing it first, before reading it in the press.

Brochures, annual reports, executive speech reprints. Quite often, material prepared specifically for other activities within the company can be used as a valuable adjunct to a dealer communications program. Though not specifically oriented to the dealer, they can increase his sense of involvement in the company's activities, which is an important factor in building dealer loyalty. Since the major costs of preparing such materials are generally borne by other departments or budgets within the organization, using them in dealer communications can be a real budget saver.

Feature articles in trade and consumer publications. Trade and consumer publications have an insatiable appetite for good editorial material. They are generally delighted to receive and use *good* feature stories that will appeal to their readers, even when they are proprietary in nature. The time and effort required to prepare feature stories—or to assist the publication in preparing them—are well spent, for they represent an extremely effective method of communicating not only with the present dealers and the public, but with prospective dealers as well. It's also important to remember that outside sponsorship will tend to add credibility and therefore value to the story. Finally, don't assume that dealers will read the magazines using your material; have reprints made and mailed to them.

This is by no means a complete list, but it will serve as a thought starter. The important things to consider when selecting material are: Is it timely, interesting, relevant, and/or useful to the recipient?

Special situations

Though the average public relations department will, for budgetary reasons, have to rely on print materials, there are times when circumstances will call for extraordinary measures to communicate a specific message to dealers as swiftly and dramatically as possible.

For example, a merger or the acquisition of another company, a major government action affecting distribution of the product, a major internal reorganization, an attack on the industry or the company by an outside group, or a change in distribution might require rapid communication to minimize confusion and disruption within the dealer organization.

On the other hand, the introduction of a new line of products or the initiation of a major quality improvement program might well call for dramatic treatment to maximize impact. (*See* Figure 15.3.)

In such cases, more time-consuming and costly methods of communication—such as personal contact, telephone, faxes, E-mail, dealer conventions, videotapes and records, motion pictures, closed-circuit television, or trade advertising—are not only justified but essential to achieve the desired results. The structure of the organization will determine the public relations function in these more costly methods of communication. The cost in time and money must be weighed against the desired result in determining the best communications method to employ in a given situation. The public relations specialist should be knowledgeable about the method— its advantages as well as its disadvantages.

Dealer Communications Content

Content is another factor to be considered in dealer communications. The possibilities are almost endless, but a partial list includes the following:

- Government activity
- Policies on warranties, repair services, etc.
- New products and features
- Industry statistics
- Research projects
- Finance programs
- Meeting schedules
- News of the industry
- Advertising schedules
- Ad reprints
- Promotion plans
- Sales training tools
- Forecasts of future business
- New markets for product
- New sales material
- Company's progress
- Company's future plan
- Case studies of dealers' solutions to problems, successful ideas, etc.
- New consumer programs
- After-sale services

Whatever media are used, they should, of course, be integrated.

Providing Dealers with Training and Customer Service Help

The manufacturer is in an ideal position to advise dealers in every phase of product retailing and to employ highly skilled training specialists for assistance. Making this training available to the dealer and dealer personnel is, of course, an activity of great mutual benefit.

This is especially true in those areas that affect customer satisfaction—the condition of the product when it is delivered and after it is in use.

Training programs for dealer personnel, then, become a vital phase of any manufacturer's effort to forestall consumer and government complaints. As products become more complex, the training of retail personnel becomes an unceasing requirement. Some manufacturers insist that dealer service personnel attend periodic training courses offered by the manufacturer to ensure product expertise.

Satisfying consumers

To the manufacturer, any dissatisfied product user is not only a source of ill will and damaging word-of-mouth, but part of a potential ground swell of consumerist pressures. So though a given dealer may not be responsible for an individual consumer's disgruntlement because the product was bought elsewhere, everyone suffers from the resulting negative attitude toward the brand.

Accordingly, in addition to supporting the retailers' sales and service operations, manufacturers are responding directly to consumer questions and complaints. In 1967 Whirlpool Corporation initiated the toll-free Cool-Line® Service to allow Whirlpool appliance owners with problems or questions to call factory specialists for help from anywhere in the continental United States, twenty-four hours a day, seven days a week. About 95 percent of all Cool-Line callers seek information that trained specialists can provide immediately. The others are handled in the field by Whirlpool consumer service representatives. The goodwill generated and the reduction in the number of frustrated customers have proved valuable.

16

CONSUMER AFFAIRS AND CONSUMERISM

JOHN W. FELTON

John W. Felton is on the faculty of the University of Florida. He was vice-president of corporate communications for McCormick & Company, the world's largest spice, flavor, and seasoning firm, from 1977 to 1994. Prior to joining McCormick in 1975, he was director of public relations and public affairs for Interstate Brands Corporation, Kansas City, Missouri.

A native of Roanoke, Virginia, "Jack" graduated from the University of Michigan in 1951 and received a Master's there in 1952. He served as a first lieutenant with the U.S.A.F. Strategic Air Command during the Korean war.

He joined Interstate in 1969, after assignments in the Public Relations Department of United States Steel Corporation in San Francisco, Salt Lake City, Chicago, Los Angeles, and Pittsburgh.

He has served on the Vocations Committee of the White House Conference on Children and Youth; is former chairman of the Public Relations Council of the National Association of Manufacturers, former chairman of the National Consumerism Committee of the Public Relations Society of America, and former trustee of the Foundation for Public Relations Research and Education. He is a member of the Board of Directors of the Independent College Fund of Maryland, the advisory council of the National Press Foundation, the council of the International Public Relations Association, the council for the President's Citation Program for Private Sector Initiatives, the American Spice Trade Association, and the Arthur W. Page Society. He was elected national president of the Public Relations Society of America in 1986 and 1987.

His professional writing includes eight plays published by Baker's Plays, Boston, and an award-winning film, The Bread Winners. *In 1974 he was awarded the George Washington medal from the Freedoms Foundation for a play,* Segments in Stained Glass. *One of his plays,* Peace Is an Olive Color, *was produced for public television to celebrate the sesquicentennial of the state of Michigan.*

According to language experts, the most confusing thing about Americans' careless use of the English language is that whenever we don't have a word that fits what we want to say, we simply make one up. One such word, *consumerism*—a word not even in dictionaries until just a few years ago—not only symbolizes but is symptomatic of our times. It is both causative and a cause.

The word *consumerism* still strikes fear into the hearts of much business because it arose out of protest, conflict, and crisis. A catalyst for change, it quickly swept away many of the prevailing attitudes and opinions that most Americans grew up with. We were taught and believed we were the biggest and that U.S. products were the best.

But all things change, including our feeling about consumerism. Now that we have learned to live with it, consumerism is less frightening. Ironically, an advertising agency originally coined the term *consumerism* to help soften consumer protests. The strategy was this: Come up with a word the American public would associate and confuse with another word; consumerism was chosen because it sounds similar to communism. This strategy obviously failed. Consumerism grew and flourished, evolving into a cause to advance the rights and interests of consumers.

Since then, it has matured from the conflict and crisis of yesterday into the concern and commitment of business and other organizations. And as consumerism has changed, so too have the public relations strategies required to deal with it.

Consequently, the Public Relations Society of America formed a task force on consumer relations and later a special committee to deal with emerging consumer issues. Much of the information covered in this chapter comes from the experience of that dedicated group of public relations professionals, each representing a different view, company, or institution. In addition, this text also encompasses concepts put forth by early consumer affairs pioneers, such as Elaine Pitts, Joanna Maitland, Edie Fraser, and Hal Warner.

The Birth of Consumerism

Consumerism did not begin simply with the creation of a new word during the 1960s. Streets filled with pickets, mailboxes filled with letters of protest, and offices filled with sit-ins gave the concept momentum. Americans were tired of bad news about automobiles, food safety, and a long list of other products and services in their daily lives.

Historical perspective can help us understand the strong frustration that engulfed consumers and business in the 1960s.

In truth, most technology, nearly all products and services—even government—had actually improved over the years. The decade of the sixties was one of the best times in history to be a consumer.

The rise of consumerism did not begin with Ralph Nader, although he played an important part. Nor was it triggered by business greed, insensitivity, shoddy products, or poor services—although the public could certainly point to examples of these. Nor was public frustration of the sixties brought on by some instant enlightenment that rang an alarm and suddenly woke up millions of consumers who had been asleep at the checkstand all those years.

To a major extent, consumer attitudes were born out of public frustration during a period of social turmoil, unrest over civil rights issues, and a divisive war in Southeast Asia that no one liked.

Suddenly Americans witnessed strobe-light changes. With every blink, blink, blink of flashing light on a television screen society changed a little more. A president was assassinated, then viewers saw in their own living rooms the gang-like murder of his accused killer. The horrible realities of the Vietnam War were acted out on the six o'clock news.

In short, the storms of the 1960s blew away many of the signposts that had helped the public find its way in the easier, more predictable decades that came before. In the middle of this turmoil and flashing changes, several other things happened.

First, Americans in vast numbers began to satisfy their own material wants and needs. Average workers found themselves able to afford things they never thought they could own. New expectations began to take over. We advanced from a nation of "have not" citizens to a nation of "have" citizens and with each new purchase the level of expectations increased.

A second reason for public frustration began when business found its advertising techniques were starting to backfire. The TV-type persuasion that sold *Monday Night Football* and consumer products created a vast difference between what was real and what was expected. That created an expectation gap. What happened on the television screen did not happen at home to consumers. The viewer did not change into a *Vogue* fashion model or movie star overnight. Seeing was not believing.

The complexity of the marketplace and its multitude of products led to even more confusion that worsened the gap between what people expected and what they got. Legislation proved to be no cure-all either. Often new laws or regulations caused more problems than they corrected. Tris, a substance regulators demanded manufacturers use to protect children's sleepwear from flammability, turned out to cause cancer. Demands to cure one ill created another—sometimes worse.

A third factor that helped to frustrate Americans was a rise in "investigative" journalism. That brought increased communication and better information. These journalistic exposés were both a cause and an effect in the growing tide of dissatisfaction.

Effect of the media

Each new and shocking exposé caused further dissatisfaction, further stimulating journalists to find more that seemed to need correction. Some reporters didn't care if they ruined the reputation of a company or public official. In effect, they considered everyone and every company guilty unless later found innocent.

So long as they got a headline story some didn't care if they got the facts right. Under the excuse of "investigative" reporting, they even went through Henry Kissinger's garbage and faked auto accidents. Some reporters became television stars themselves or authors of best-sellers, which increased the tempo and encouraged others to follow their example and dig for more dirt.

These factors—social turmoil, unfulfilled expectations, and exposés—lit the fuse of a rebellion in consumer attitudes. The explosion they caused was given the general name "consumerism." Like any explosion, this one has taken its toll on all American institutions and all consumers.

Government's increased role

Studies show that one person out of every five feels he or she has been cheated on purchases. As a fact, this is probably not true, but public relations practitioners know perceptions and feelings usually do more to shape attitudes than the facts do.

As a result, fully two-thirds of the American public supported new laws to get full value for its money. Three-fourths favored more government regulations to ensure product safety. More than 60 percent of the American public lost faith in all institutions—the church, the schools, and especially business and government.

These attitudes triggered a trail of legislation and regulation affecting virtually every aspect of the marketplace. Historically, consumer legislation has always been a by-product of social turmoil. The tragedy is that some in business treated it not as a symptom of the times, but as an independent force to be fought.

To be able to evaluate this period of public frustration, to look at consumer affairs today, or to forecast what lies ahead, we have to look at what came before.

Historical perspective

Because the primary consumer products have always been food, early consumer protection centered on the preparation and selling of food. Egyptians established laws to control the handling of meat and oils. The Greeks and Romans had laws to determine the quality of bread and to prevent diluting wine with water. Laws against those who tampered with the food they sold were severe indeed. The death penalty for consumer fraud was not uncommon.

The first consumer protection in the United States was a food law passed in Philadelphia in 1784, just eight years after the Declaration of Independence. Today's sanitary meat marketing bears no resemblance to the unsanitary conditions of the meat industry that Upton Sinclair, Ida Tarbell, and other journalists decried early in this century. But consumerism reached new levels in the 1960s. Vance Packard, Ralph Nader, Rachel Carson, and others led off the sixties with books on consumer safety, manipulation, waste of natural resources, and the danger of pesticides in our food supply.

In 1962 President John F. Kennedy identified consumers as the only important group not effectively organized. He framed the "Consumer's Bill of Rights," which set forth the following rights:

- Right of product safety
- Right to be informed and protected
- Right to choose from a variety of products
- Right to be heard by government

To look after the four rights, President Kennedy appointed ten private citizens to a Consumer Advisory Council. Succeeding presidents have had consumer advisors on their staffs. Esther Peterson, Betty Furness, and Virginia Knauer were the best known of these advisors.

President Ford added a fifth right, the right to consumer education.

Prior to the consumerism decade of the 1960s, protective legislation attacked problems one industry at a time—railroads, foods, and drugs. Then came antitrust measures and regulation of practices in the financial community.

By the 1960s and 1970s, consumer advocates were tackling virtually the entire spectrum of buyer-seller relationships. A few of the 1960s enactments included the following:

- Truth-in-Packaging (1961)
- Fair Packaging and Labeling Act (1966), and the National Traffic and Motor Vehicle Safety Act (1966)
- Truth-in-Lending (1968)
- Occupational Safety and Health Act, with great significance for employers and employees (1970)
- Consumer Product Safety Act (1972)

Since then there has been an outpouring of regulations on such matters as toxic substances, food inspection, product warranties, safety of cosmetics, utility rates, cable TV rates, leasing with option to buy, deceptive mail solicitations, safety of child products, bailouts of savings and loans, nutrition labeling, and product liability. Advocates have created mini-consumer-affairs departments in nearly every agency of federal and state governments.

Consumerism has grown into a maturity recognized by most organizations and their consumers. It has become a way of life in which the buyer is aware and has ways to let it be known that the seller had better beware.

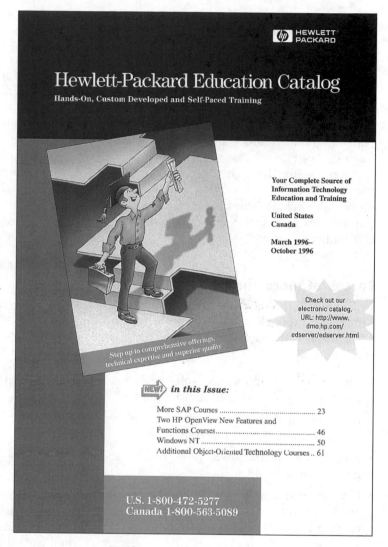

Figure 16.1 Hewlett-Packard's Education Catalog. Teaching customers how to use its products increases customer satisfaction. *Reproduced with permission of Hewlett-Packard Company.*

Results and costs

Virtually every major goal of the consumers wave of the sixties and seventies was achieved. Products are safer. Product recalls have become automatic when dangers are found. Food is labeled with specific contents. Perishables are marked with clear dates. Warranties and credit contacts are loaded with so much disclosure that larger forms were designed. Accuracy of checkout scanners is monitored.

Agencies now exist to monitor virtually all that goes on in business, and there are bureaus for handling complaints when things go wrong. Host organizations have 800 numbers or "hotlines" to handle consumer problems. Many have departments devoted entirely to consumer affairs. (*See* Figure 16.1.)

The cost of this progress has been great. By the 1980s, there were more than 1,000 federal programs, some 41 regulatory agencies, and an estimated 100,000 federal employees whose main job was to administer the "Thou

Shalts" and "Thou Shalt Nots" of consumer affairs. The annual cost of protecting consumers rose to $130 billion, or roughly $2,000 per family. Of what consumers pay for a new home, an average of $2,000 is there because of regulatory requirements. The cost of a new car is more than $600 higher because of federally mandated safety and environmental features.

After racing through the turbulent and rocky sixties and seventies, we reached more stable relationships between advocates, buyers, and sellers. But that does not mean tranquility.

Forces of more change

Undoubtedly the years ahead hold many significant changes that will have an effect on consumerism. These forces of change include the following:

- The move toward business self-regulation and away from government regulation

- More direct dialogue between consumer activists and business representatives

- More sophisticated coverage of consumer issues by the media

- Greater awareness on the part of the "average" consumer of the power that can be exerted through collective action

- Move delegation of regulation to the states rather than federal government

In the past, the consumer was happy when expectations were met. The consumer asked for a certain quality and certain level of service and usually got more than was asked. But the buyer and seller have begun to realize that there is a price to pay for most of these consumer demands.

The challenge for today's consumer affairs specialist is to focus these expectations and clarify what is wanted and acceptable, as well as the prices consumers are willing to pay for them.

For a price, Americans can produce almost any product or service. The challenge is to balance quality, safety, and realistic needs with the added costs consumers are willing to pay. That includes the need to decide which regulations are necessary for better control and what choices consumers want left to themselves.

As usual, the choice is up to the consumer. It is the role of the consumer affairs specialist to help tailor those choices and expectations to the mutual benefit and understanding of the buyer and seller.

Communication challenges

As with many public issues, consumerism has three primary communications challenges: perception, prevention, and performance.

Consumer history has many examples of organizations that ignored early warning signals until it was too late. The ability to perceive potential problem areas, to head them off, or to make corrections early has saved many products and services. If unheeded, a rumble can become a roar. As with a fire, it's easier to respond to the first sparks of a problem than to try to control a flaming public controversy. It is usually much cheaper, too.

For this reason, it is imperative that the consumer affairs professional have an "ear" tuned outside the windows of the organization. Not all sparks require the same amount of attention, but it is important to know where and how they are being ignited. Then management can be kept properly informed and quick corrective actions taken if needed. (*See* Chapter 2.)

It is also important for consumer affairs specialists to remember that just as all organizations are not honest, consumers are known to cheat too. They wear clothing and jewelry and return them for credit. They misuse products, then make outlandish or false claims. A major bakery firm thought it had a serious quality problem until a computer check discovered the same elderly lady was making nearly all of the complaints using different names but the same address. Just as consumers need to beware of sellers, sellers also need to be alert to consumer fraud.

In addition to being an ombudsman for those who use the organization's products or services, the consumer affairs professional must be an enthusiastic advocate for quality performance throughout the organization. Reputations are carefully built one step at a time, but often lost by a single misstep. Programs that encourage employees to "do it right the first time—every time" not only prevent problems but usually increase profits.

A proactive, "get ahead of the issue" consumer affairs program enables an organization to build and keep a credible reputation, anticipate problems, improve quality control, increase volume, and obtain repeated sales. It also prevent attacks by activists, the media, and governmental agencies. Thus a creative consumer affairs program becomes a competitive tool in the marketplace. The basics of consumer affairs are: be aware, be honest, be responsive, be quick, and be fair!

Program Elements

Organizations differ and so do their constituencies. While no outline is appropriate for all organizations, a model consumer affairs program should contain these basic elements:

- A strong published statement of consumer philosophy and fair policies by top management.
- Printed literature, frequent public statements, and speeches reinforcing management's commitment to consumers and their concerns.
- Internal awareness programs to encourage employee sensitivity and responsiveness to consumers.
- An ongoing audit of public perceptions of the organization's performance, products,

and/or services. How well are they understood, used, or misused by consumers?

- Close and frequent communications by consumer affairs with top management, legal, marketing and sales, product development, production, in-store merchandisers, public relations, and the user public.
- A detailed communication plan for reaching consumers, employees, news media, shareholders, and potential customers.
- Consumer considerations included as an ingredient in the organization's long-range planning and programming.
- Prompt reporting of all consumer complaints so types and patterns can be analyzed and corrections made.
- Provisions for monitoring emerging consumer issues among the general public, influentials, and the media.
- A product recall committee and detailed procedures for handling product emergencies, including a crisis plan.
- A complaint-handling policy and manual with procedures and sample letters or responses.
- Frequent dialogue with industry associations, trade groups, government, and professional consumer groups.
- A "hotline" or 800 number to receive consumer inquiries and to offer information and help.
- Prompt redress procedures for those grievances requiring legal action or settlement.
- An actively encouraged consumer idea-suggestion program with recognition or rewards for participants.
- Point-of-purchase information and how-to-use educational materials including warranties, credit terms, service centers, return policies, etc.
- Consumer advisory committees made up of community thought leaders, teachers, and grassroots consumers.

Section 3

ANALYSIS, RESEARCH, AND PLANNING

17

ANALYSIS, PLANNING, AND PROGRAMMING

PHILIP LESLY

Most public relations participants—just as with participants in statecraft, politics, and military affairs—deal with the daily execution of *techniques*. A smaller portion control the *tactics* that set the pattern for the techniques. An even smaller portion, a few broad-gauged individuals, analyze the big picture and develop the *strategy* that gives meaning and direction to it all. Then these select few determine whether these efforts will accomplish anything meaningful.

In rare cases and with limited goals, carrying out specific activities without an overall strategy can bring values. This may occur when product publicity is desired to augment the other exposures of the product and its uses. It may be helpful to a politician or an entertainer who needs to become known to the public. It offers some degree of value to a company whose stock is offered to the public or that needs to be known to prospective employees.

In most cases, however, the entire value of the public relations operation will depend on the quality and thoroughness of the analysis, as well as the forethought preceding the implementation of techniques.

Characteristics Required

Providing this caliber of intelligence calls for the following:

- Breadth of scope capable of seeing the whole of the organization's "universe" and understanding how the various elements affect each other

- Judgment capable of evaluating the significance of various symptoms and the soundness of suggestions for action or inaction in any given situation

- Diversity of experience and education, with as much training as possible in all the tactics and techniques of public relations

- Creativity, both in bringing forth ideas and recommendations, and in expressing them so they will persuade others

- Objectivity—being far enough removed from the intricacies of the organization to see it as others do, and forthright enough to express the viewpoint of these outsiders to the management

This is a formidable combination of attributes. It is at this critical level, therefore, that the highest caliber of counsel or internal executive makes the great difference between various organizations' public relations efforts. Where the internal executive does not have all of these traits, he and his stature benefit from combining with a counsel who augments him.

Laying the Groundwork

Before any notes are made on possible programs or activities, the following aspects should be thought through:

What are the objectives? Are there a few clear, vital goals for the public relations function to achieve or contribute to, or has there been just an accumulation of mostly unrelated tasks? Following is a paraphrased excerpt from a confidential analysis made for a large association:

> Events and trends in this field and in our social system have rushed on, while the members and the Association have been absorbed in keeping up with their own affairs on the basis of training received a generation ago. Trends and circumstances have thus outrun the member's usual pattern of concentrating on here-and-now affairs and developments. As a result, there is too little relationship between the climate of attitudes that now engulfs the field and the priorities of the Association in dealing with this climate. It appears that to a considerable extent, functions in the Association have *accumulated*, rather than been planned. Much of this accumulation has been through projects and functions that have been imposed by individuals, committees, or others, rather than been planned as an integral and coordinated part of a whole.

What are the present climate of attitudes and the underlying forces that affect whatever the organization will do or say? This calls for assessing the entire cosmos in which the organization functions: internal conditions and plans; the industry it is in; local, national, and international social trends; the attitudes and practices of the media to be dealt with; and so on.

Often this will call for opinion research (*see* Chapter 18) and analysis of literature and other sources (*see* Chapter 19).

In an analysis and program made for a large fraternal organization, the following factors were pinpointed as having a bearing on the group's planning and its public relations requirements:

- The rapidly increasing level of education, which greatly broadens people's sophistication and independence of thought.

- Urbanization and suburbanization, which break down the importance of fraternal organizations in men's lives.

- The multiplication of interests for people to pursue. When there was little to do outside working hours, the lodge was very attractive. It now must compete with travel, books, music, education, television, sports, hobbies, boating, and art.

- An increased number of organizations and functions that attract potential members' interests, including many urged on them by their employers.

- Growing interest of educated younger people in various movements and issues that differ from the traditions and purposes of the lodge.

- Independent interests of young men, with many assuming major responsibilities early.

- The "anti-Establishment" attitude of many young men, in which fraternal organizations are identified with the Establishment.

- The problem of momentum. It is extremely difficult to reverse a down trend in interest, such as has faced this group in recent years.

The planning and program were devised in keeping with these factors, and periodic evaluations of the program were related to the changes in these patterns.

This analysis of the human climate should include judgment on where the trends are leading and what the climate will be when the organization's efforts have had time to take effect. A large proportion of public opinion programs attack problems as they existed two years ago.

Has an objective analysis been made of the organization? It is especially important to define how it is different from all other organizations. No organization can succeed in trying to be all things to everyone, and few organizations can succeed in modeling themselves after some other organization they would like to duplicate.

Have the targeted audiences been carefully defined and described? No matter how compact an organization, today it must think in terms of multiple audiences. On almost any subject, whatever an organization does is certain to be unpopular with some segments of its publics. There are many antithetical groups, even within what would normally be considered a given public. For instance, "women" include millions of dedicated homemakers and mothers, as well as millions of women who consider a career and complete autonomy to be the essentials of a fulfilled life.

Great variations exist in sophistication among segments of every organization's audiences, as well as in the extent of knowledge and the degree of suspicion. The sources of influence on them vary greatly. They are likely to be geographically dispersed. They hold varying degrees of receptivity, and they look to completely different sources for their leadership.

What are the specific obstacles? Is there a political barrier, such as solid entrenchment of opposition in a strong bloc of Congress? Is there a prejudice against the organization that logic and information will not dispel? Planning may encompass working around these, rather than attempting to beat them down.

What are the special opportunities? When the American Music Conference was formed in 1946, it was pointed out that postwar America was fed up with austerity, people were hungry for individuality and self-expression, and parents and educators were concerned about creative outlets for children's energies. These and other factors in the social climate were played on to create the boom in music making that marked the next twenty-odd years.

What are present activities and how do they measure up against these criteria and conditions?

What are others doing: allies, opponents, others not directly related but whose functions will compete for attention or affect what may happen?

Is emphasis being placed on leading the target—on establishing the climate of attitudes in the future, rather than responding to what has happened to date? Hundreds of companies began to communicate about their efforts in curbing pollution and improving their products after massive attacks on them had been launched. Inoculation against the virulence of criticism is much more healthful than attempting to cure the rampant disease after it has struck. In general, the climate of opinion about issues should be worked on two years or more before it is likely that an audible criticism will be felt.

Is there an overview of the entire system that logically considers the chain reaction of various activities? As in chess, an amateur considers one move at a time; a master considers the chain of consequences many moves ahead.

Have allowances been made for the specific personalities, politics, and peculiarities of the situation? For instance, a professional society such as the American Dental Association is not only an association in which control is diffuse and diverse, but a political organization in which the leaders are elected and must be responsive to the nuances of the grassroots. Plans and activities that do not account for the politics in such a situation are likely to fail. In one company the chief executive may be outgoing, articulate, eager for respect; in another he may inherently resent anything that puts him into the limelight.

Has your case been carefully developed? Have the ideas and facts that need to be conveyed been selected and identified? Have the most effective appeals been worked out, in terms of the interests of the audiences? A remarkable number of organizations never take these essential steps. They have no tightly reasoned case, their concepts are not highly refined, and the basis for seeking the interest of the audience is vague.

Have the media and other channels of available communication been assessed? What is their present posture in regard to the organization and the field it is in? How accessible are they? What is the organization's stature and credibility with each of them? What are their prejudices that must be recognized and dealt with? What are their relationships with the publics that the organization has identified as the universe it must work with?

Are plans integrated with all other functions and communications?

What resources are available—budgets, manpower, allies? If new needs are demonstrated, can new resources be obtained? If not, can priorities be shifted to eliminate some "sacred cows"?

Clarifying these factors is often the most crucial aspect of all. As Donald W. MacKinnon of the Institute of Personality Assessment and Research at the University of California, Berkeley, has said:

> When a problem is properly conceived, the very statement of the problem carries within it hints or suggestions as to how it is to be solved. . . . The first task . . . is to make a sufficient analysis of the situation, narrowing down and simplifying the complex situation until the crucial difficulty in the task is isolated.

Planning Elements

Every analysis will be different. So will every plan. It is tempting for the experienced executive or the public relations firm to draw on experience to the extent of building on familiar frameworks. Some firms even use a "basic presentation" that is changed just enough for each prospect or client to make it look original. But the primary value of good public relations judgment is its capacity for studying the uniqueness of each situation and coming up with original thinking, even while drawing on reservoirs of experience.

With this need in mind to avoid predetermined outlines, the following are some general functions that are likely to be involved in any plan:

- Spell out objectives incisively. Don't have more than a few major ones so they will definitely be focused on.

- Determine the functions, again being selective so the vital ones will get enough attention.

- Establish the budgets.

- Recruit, train, and assign the personnel—and block in how the principals of the organization will be involved.

- Retain the needed outside help—counsel, a range of services, specialists such as artists and photographers, and so on. Except where necessary, do not be confined to internal specialists in any area, who then must be used for that function whether or not they are suitable for each task that comes along. One artist may be excellent for an annual report but impossible for a cartoon book or a display for an open house. One photographer may be good for industrial shots but mediocre on portraits or action events. The best available choice can be made in every case when all talents in the field are available—and the specialists are not on the payroll all year long, finding things to do (with expenses) to keep busy.

- Set up a flow chart of the functions, with lead time, relationships, responsibilities clearly defined.

- Set up feedback and research points to measure progress or assess trends.
- Arrange for periodic review of plans and functions, to assure flexibility. It is usually best not to do this at twelve-month intervals; the very regularity of such a period is out of keeping with how things happen, and therefore deceptively artificial. Sometimes a new look might be wise in a few months; some things should not be expected to be assessed in less than two to three years. While organizations may require annual budget approvals, this should not require that the period for fresh looking be the same.
- Build in procedures for keeping the principals informed and involved, and integrating with other functions.

In more limited planning for campaigns and specific programs, the procedures in Chapter 20 will provide a more specific and detailed guide.

For planning activities related to issues and opportunities, the procedures in Chapter 2 will be helpful. Combining the thought processes called for there with those in this chapter will provide good discipline for the analysis, planning, and programming of almost any organization.

Following is a representative outline of priorities for a hypothetical corporation.

Sample Corporate Priority Schedule

Basic Functions—Initiative
  Financial
    Stockholder publications, including the annual report
    Financial announcements
    Security analyst communications
    Feedback from financial community
    Annual meeting

Corporate
  Developing and proposing programs for meeting problems and developing goodwill
  Providing information and assessments on public attitudes and trends, for the knowledge and consideration of management
  Contacting and cultivating the media—business publications, newspapers, broadcasters, key trade publications
  Special events—new plant openings, ground breakings
  Corporate announcements—new officers and directors, etc.
  Producing external and internal publications
  Issues planning and organization (*See* Chapter 2)
Employee Recruitment
  Literature
  Career conference
Product Publicity
  New-product introductions
  Continuous publicity on products on basis of budget allocations
  Handling media requests for loans and purchases at a discount
Government Relations
  Liaison with Congress
  Liaison with federal regulatory agencies
  Liaison with state and municipal government bodies

Basic Functions—Passive
  Financial
    Handling inquiries from media
    Handling inquiries from security analysts
    Screening and assessing correspondence from stockholders
    Maintaining lists for mailing of reports, etc.

Periodic studies of stockholder and
analyst attitudes
Corporate
Handling inquiries from
media
Keeping biographies, photos, facts
up-to-date
Preparing backgrounders and fact
sheets on divisions and
operations
Representing the company in
various associations, on boards
and committees, etc.
Participation in intracompany
groups—Policy Committee, inter-
plant liaison and communication,
etc.
Bulletin board and reading rack
programs
Community Relations
Contributions program
Periodic research on corporate
"image," public attitudes

Possible Unanticipated Needs
Financial
Merger or acquisition—strategy
discussion, announcements
Corporate
Change in name and identification
program
Emergencies—disaster, attack by
militants, problem with a
product in the market, etc.
Government Relations
Appearance before congressional
committee
Dispute with regulatory agency

Secondary or Optional
Financial
Seeking and arranging additional
security analyst meetings
Setting up circulation of displays
for brokerage offices and bank
windows
Corporate
Plant open houses
Scholarship programs
Communications seminar for
junior executives and trainees

Obviously, this is not complete for any company, and the pattern for any firm will vary
greatly.

Allocations of effort

It is important that sufficient flexibility be
built into such a priority outline. Many of the
most important needs for public relations help
will be unpredictable; the proportion of time
and resources left uncommitted should be
great enough to assure ample attention to
them. Giving in to the temptation to provide
a tight, neatly packaged program months or
a year in advance can result in a sterile, routine operation that will be unprepared for the
great challenges and opportunities that cannot be anticipated.

In the above hypothetical outline, the
Basic—Initiative portion might be allocated
about 45 percent of the effort, the Basic—
Passive about 25 percent, Possible Unanticipated Needs 25 percent, and Secondary or
Optional (and therefore expendable if something has to give) 5 percent.

18
OPINION RESEARCH AND PUBLIC RELATIONS

ROBERT O. CARLSON
GEORGE GALLUP JR.

Robert O. Carlson is associate professor and former dean of the School of Business Administration at Adelphi University. Previously he served for eighteen years as an executive with Standard Oil Company of New Jersey (now Exxon) working on management problems of the parent company in the United States and those of its operating affiliates in the Middle East, Africa, the Far East, Australia, and Europe.

He received his A.B. from the University of Pittsburgh and his Ph.D. in social psychology from Columbia University. He has served as president of both the Public Relations Society of America and the American Association for Public Opinion Research, as well as having been the executive officer of the American Sociological Society. For many years he was chairman of the editorial board of the Public Opinion Quarterly.

George Gallup Jr. is co-chairman of the Gallup Organization, Princeton, New Jersey, with which he has been associated since graduating from Princeton University in 1953. He has also studied at Oxford University in England.

He has made thorough studies of the voting behavior of various groups in the population and has published reports on voting patterns among farmers, young voters, intellectuals, African-Americans, and members of labor unions.

The assistance of **Alec Gallup** of the Gallup Organization is gratefully acknowledged.

Purposes and Types

Public relations research typically serves three basic functions: to *confirm* assumptions, to *clarify* unclear or insufficient evidence, and to *reorient*, or reframe, the interpretation of data.

Most frequently, public relations research merely *confirms* the organization's existing assumptions and "gut feelings" about the public's opinion on an issue, a product, or a company. Although hardly world-shaking, this kind of feedback is highly useful. In many ways, it can be likened to the quality control systems used in the manufacturing side of the business.

Public relations research can also be used to *clarify* data that do not sufficiently answer the company's specific questions—because only limited information is available, or the data seem contradictory, or both. Research can help sort out what people really mean when they say they like or dislike an organization or product by determining the reasons they cite for these feelings and even the origin of their preferences. Research can help determine whether expressed attitudes relate to actual behavior—in the supermarket, the voting booth, or a fund-raising campaign.

Finally, research occasionally *reorients* our thinking and conceptualization regarding a specific public relations issue. Most likely that was the case when the banking industry discovered it was scaring away potential small customers with its austere, no-nonsense image. That certainly would explain the profound change that has occurred in the public posture of the banks. Nowadays, it would not be surprising to see a bank advertisement inviting community members to stop by their friendly neighborhood bank for a social drink with one of its vice-presidents.

Conducting research brings with it an unintended bonus. The process of designing the research project and assigning areas to investigate forces various individuals and departments within the organization to explicitly express their beliefs about which publics and which problems are priorities. This type of exercise frequently generates an internal dialogue that uncovers surprising differences in opinion regarding the exact nature and degree of importance that different people and functions attach to various issues.

Available Techniques

Those who have had little first-hand exposure to formal research cannot fully appreciate the variety of available techniques and study designs. A very old and still useful method is to carry out a *content analysis* of how a topic, an organization, or a problem is treated in the press, textbooks, radio, or television. Such research gives a pretty fair measure of the saliency of the problem and often useful hints as to which aspects of it seem to be arousing greatest public interest. Several caveats must be observed with respect to content analysis studies—what weights, if any, should be assigned to the length of coverage, position on the page, the page number itself, and so on. Used with intelligence and a clear recognition of its limitations as a research instrument, content analysis can be a useful tool.

Public relations programs for which the chief objective is to raise money for some cause or to help get some candidate elected to public office can derive much benefit from *secondary analysis* of past giving records or previous voting profiles. Census data providing information on age, sex, income level, and education on a district-by-district basis then can be compared with past giving or voting records.

For many people, the term *research* is synonymous with *public opinion surveys* and their various survey techniques, each of which has its merits and its limitations. Properly used, these different techniques can complement one another and produce a mosaic of data giving new insights into long-standing problems.

If an organization is embarking on a public relations program for the first time or if some new or relatively unknown factor becomes relevant for an ongoing program, the *profile survey* can be useful. It is a one-time snapshot (or perhaps X-ray) of public reactions to a particular company, issue, or program. Correctly used, it can help identify subgroups who are most favorable or most hostile with respect to the issue in question. It can give a general idea of the saliency of an issue; the extent to which people are getting information about the issue from the several media or from their friends, family, or fellow workers; and the context in which they view it. The danger of using a profile type survey is that it is static. Its findings may become perishable or biased by reason of some unique political or economic event. Properly employed, it can provide valuable analytical labels for describing subgroups in the public at a given moment in time.

When a profile survey is repeated, retaining the basic sample design and interview guide but employing a new sample of respondents, a *trend survey* is taking shape. Trend surveys are a double-edged sword, particularly if they are employed as *effectiveness studies* of an information program. Properly used, they can provide critically important clues as to which facets of a message are getting through to the audience and which are not. But when misused and wrongly interpreted, they can create no end of mischief. Some first-class programs have actually been sabotaged, because poorly designed and poorly interpreted effectiveness surveys have suggested that the message was not getting through.

Before-and-after reading

By definition, effectiveness surveys must have a before-and-after reading in which data are typically gathered on matters such as how informed people are about a topic or a particular company and whether their feelings are generally favorable, unfavorable, or apathetic. The general public, it should be noted, has very limited information or interest in the major business corporations of the country. They have difficulty correctly identifying a product with the company that manufactures it. They have only the dimmest ideas of who constitutes the management of these companies and what the "corporate philosophy" of these firms may be. Under these circumstances, it is not surprising that surveys turn up a great deal of "no opinion" or "don't know" responses. In recent years, perhaps out of frustration at finding a low level of public awareness and interest in the institutional message of large companies, opinion researchers have developed elaborate scales that are said to discern delicate shifts in the public feelings toward our major corporations. While the aim of these fancy scales is laudable, the research results are of questionable validity and use. Slight movements in a more favorable direction on these rating scales are seized upon with delight by overanxious practitioners concerned about justifying a large outlay of money. In many cases these "favorable research findings" result from the sampling procedures and, in other instances, they are the artifact of the random answers to questions that have a low level of interest or relevance to the respondent.

It is both amusing and dismaying to observe the excitement generated by "findings" from an effectiveness survey that shows an increase in favorable attitude of three, four, or even five percentage points. By themselves, such data mean very little, especially if they do not look for the canceling-out effect that takes place in public opinions. For example, a survey may show little or no change in the general public's attitudes on civil rights. Closer analysis, however, would show that during the period under study, upper-class, professional people were becoming more sympathetic to this cause, but that this shift was being canceled out on an overall basis by the fact that middle-class, white-collar workers were growing less sympathetic to the civil rights movement. Even when a survey spots this canceling phenomenon, it usually can provide only limited information as to its causes.

Only when the time, trouble, and expense are taken to permit the same respondents to be reinterviewed on another occasion can these trend surveys be converted into a *panel survey*. These panel surveys permit the dynamics of opinion change to be more fully studied. By reinterviewing the same respondents on one or more occasions, it is possible to identify the context for individual shifts in attitudes from one time period to another and to probe for specific reasons that might account for these changes.

Other tools for public relations

Two other forms of opinion research provide useful tools for the public relations profession. One is the *depth survey*, which is nothing more than an effort to let the public tell the researcher, in its own words, how it views a company, a public issue, or a particular individual. In these surveys the researcher carefully avoids imposing her point of view on the respondent. Rather, she encourages the person being interviewed to freely associate and ramble on in his own words to describe his perception of the matter under study. Depth studies are useful in the early stages of a program in giving clues to the perimeters of a problem. They also can provide some really valuable themes that copy writers and creative departments may incorporate into a campaign.

Finally, a stepchild of the research field is the *pretest*. While pretests are rather extensively used in product advertising campaigns, they tend to be less used in developing storyboard treatment of films or in sharpening a print advertisement campaign or testing reader interest in proposed pamphlets and executive speeches. This is a pity, for while effectiveness studies can tell us whether a program struck out or not, this information is a bit academic inasmuch as money has already been spent on films and advertisements. Apparently, pretests are viewed with alarm by some creative people who see in them a threat to their prerogatives. This is unfortunate, for properly used they can give powerful support to creative people in developing better, more effective copy.

How to use the tools

It is not realistic to expect formal research studies to be part and parcel of the everyday routine in a department or counseling firm. There is simply not enough money to support such studies, nor enough wisdom latent in the archives of the social sciences or our profession to recommend them as a constant diet. But they can be helpful tools when employed at the right time by practitioners who make reasonable demands on them.

Research in public relations is not primarily a product to be bought or sold as our whims or anxieties may dictate. It is preeminently a point of view, a way of looking at problems, a predisposition for organizing past and present experiences. In this sense, research is not detached from the ongoing activities of a public relations program, but is at the heart of it. Research is the educated counsel and experience that are brought to bear on the design of a new program based on the cumulative experience of all the public relations people who discuss, dissect, and define it. It is the knowledge of the successes and the failures of others in the past who dealt with similar problems. It is the feeling in the air of professional meetings and luncheons and the prevalence of small talk with colleagues that alert us to some innovative new concept or development in our field.

Good research takes time; management often needs answers in a hurry. Management frequently feels it must have research results immediately if they are to be of any value in planning action programs. This sense of urgency runs smack into the irksome fact that good research requires a reasonable time to organize, pretest, execute, analyze, and write up.

Good research, unlike good wine, need not age and, in fact, usually goes sour with time. There are few problems on which at least some significant preliminary data cannot be collected within a few weeks. Subsequent analysis and refinement of these data will actually benefit from the early comments and questions management addresses to these initial findings.

There is no need to doggedly pursue to the bitter end every research study simply because it seemed like a good idea at the time it was approved and money has been authorized for it. Public relations problems are frequently elusive and may occasionally defy systematic research study. That still leaves plenty of room for the educated, intuitive guess for situations in which events move fast and critical variables influence these events.

Still other problems are so general and all-inclusive as to almost certainly result in banal research findings that contribute nothing to the planning of an action program.

Determining the Value of Research

There are no clearcut criteria by which management may evaluate the worth of a public relations research study. In actual life, the most widely accepted criterion of the success or failure of a study is whether or not our boss likes the finished job. But a first reaction has only limited validity and longevity. The boss cannot know whether a particular study

meets the needs until there has been a chance to translate some of the findings into action. In fact, initial reactions to a research study may change—growing more or less favorable as the relevance of the findings is tested out in day-to-day operations.

Under the heading of bad or useless research one must certainly place those studies that are commissioned solely in the hope they will support a particular point of view that may be under challenge by others in the organization. Research cannot afford to be the tool of special pleading by any person or faction in an organization.

Unfortunately, research is often regarded as a kind of report card on the performance of an individual, a department, an advertising or consulting agency, or on a particular program. This view is unfortunate for it does not take into account the many variables that have an important bearing on performance at any given time. These variables include changing political and economic conditions or competing events that may detract from or give heightened attention to the program or problem under study. Very likely, practitioners themselves are ambivalent regarding the desirability of research. While they might gain a better understanding from research data, they fear these data may also measure their performance unfavorably.

Evaluation of a research study is a complicated business. It would be very wrong to assume that top management has the training or resources for translating research findings into public relations programs. It is likely that more than one boss has decided that a particular piece of research was bad when, in fact, the real problem was that the boss did not have the staff or the personal ability to translate research findings into successful programs.

Public relations research often deals with those frail and invisible entities—attitudes and information. Such data are by their very nature intangible and far more elusive than, for example, findings from advertising research studies whose data can be validated by comparison with subsequent sales figures, share of market data, and so on, or employee relations research findings that can be measured at some later date against manpower turnover figures, rates of absenteeism, rates of productivity, and other factors.

The Changing Public Relations Landscape

In the past, corporate public relations programs concentrated their time and money on reaching certain predictable audiences thought to be of greatest importance to the corporation—shareholders, employees and their families, customers, key government officials, the financial community, and other opinion leaders. In turn, these subgroups were the subjects studied in corporate public relations research programs. It is easy to understand why management elected to use this method of classifying its publics. The system has the merit of being neat and quickly understood by top corporate executives. Moreover, delivery systems for reaching these static publics are relatively simple. Mailing lists can be compiled for each of these groups, speeches directed to them, and print advertisements and television commercials tailored to their special interests.

But emerging political and social forces have changed this simple and safe way of categorizing the corporation's critical publics; and these forces, in turn, have redefined the focus of public relations research. Three massive social and political movements had profound impact on the corporate world and appeared for the first time on the agendas in board rooms where policy is shaped. These three issues were:

1. A concern with protecting and improving our physical environment

2. Consumerism (including concern about protecting investors)

3. Demands to upgrade the career opportunities for women and disadvantaged ethnic and racial groups

These political and social movements, and the resulting legislation they generated, caused corporate public relations programs to become more "issue"-oriented and less "public"-oriented.

Today, public relations researchers recognize that criteria previously thought to be sound for studying their publics—place of residence, level of education and income, sex, and race—are no longer reliable indicators of an individual's lifestyle and his or her social and political, intellectual, and emotional orientation. The design of a public relations research study cannot make any firm assumptions about the attitudes of a particular sample based solely on their census characteristics. For example, in the area of attitudes on environmental issues, the long-haired activist on a college campus may well be a co-worker with a conservative suburban housewife in campaigns to protect the environment and to prevent companies from building new plants and facilities in a particular community. The conservative small-town banker may find himself joining with the politically more liberal professors of economics in bringing pressure to ensure that financial reporting by major corporations is more explicit and reliable. In still another area of public concern, black middle-class urban dwellers may be as outraged as their white suburban counterparts when abuses are found in urban relief, unemployment, and welfare programs.

The labels *politically conservative* or *liberal* no longer apply to particular subgroups in our population. This enormously complicates the job of the public relations researcher in trying to identify key target groups whose attitudes might affect the well-being of his or her organization. Corporate institutional advertising is increasingly being directed at particular issues rather than to specialized publics. Better research techniques are needed for measuring the effectiveness of these new "issue"-oriented corporate messages carried in the "op ed" pages of leading newspapers or in magazines and professional journals favored by politically militant groups.

Perhaps the single greatest challenge facing public relations researchers today is devising better early-warning networks for their management. These networks help identify the still small and inarticulate public interest movements that may one day impact the company's future well-being. Some companies employ an in-house early-warning network to gather data on public attitudes toward them. They are looking to the observations and experiences of key employees as a source of their information. These employees often provide timely early warnings regarding new problems on public relations issues that are only beginning to yeast in the public's mind.

A program for systematically debriefing these employees several times a year represents a form of public relations research that is inexpensive yet holds significant findings. Among employees who are likely candidates for such debriefing sessions are salespeople, retailers, those working in human resources departments interviewing applicants for jobs, and those who recruit professional staff personnel on college campuses.

Conclusion

The importance of sound and significant public relations research to management of all organizations is greater today than it has been in the past. Top executives in the petroleum, automobile, chemical, paper, and drug industries (to cite a few examples) are spending many hours each week worrying about how public attitudes toward their industries may translate into unfavorable legislation affecting their future operations.

The focus of public relations research has been changing from the study of traditional publics to greater attention to the study of "issues" and how best to modify public attitudes on them. (*See* Chapter 2.) The development of public relations research models, based on the sophisticated use of electronic data processing techniques, is bringing timely and actionable data into the hands of decision-makers in a matter of days, rather than weeks or months.

Guidelines and Techniques[1]

With survey research fast becoming an indispensable part of public relations programs, persons engaged in the field of public relations need at least a general knowledge of research techniques and capabilities.

Preliminary steps

The public relations person must first decide what the survey objectives are. A survey that starts without well-defined objectives often produces a mass of extraneous data.

Next, identify the target groups—that is, the specific groups whose attitudes and beliefs are of significance with respect to the problems. These groups might consist of consumers of a given product, dealers, purchasing agents, business leaders, financial analysts, bankers, employees—or the general public.

He or she then must determine what degree of accuracy is required for his purposes. Is only a general overview needed? If so, perhaps a five-hundred-case sample or less is suitable.

On the other hand, if he is interested in determining the division of opinion with a high degree of accuracy, or "reliability," or

[1]By George and Alec Gallup.

wants to analyze the findings by subgroups within the sample, he should consider samples of one thousand cases or more.

In interpreting survey results, it should be borne in mind that all sample surveys are subject to sampling error—that is, the extent to which the results may differ from what would be obtained if the whole population surveyed had been interviewed. The degree of such sampling errors depends largely on the number of interviews.

Accuracy in all sampling operations tends to increase with the addition of cases. However, it is important to keep in mind that the addition of many thousands of persons has very little effect on the survey result after the first few hundred.

Survey Essentials

An effective survey includes four essential elements:

1. **Sample**—expertly designed to represent the population being studied
2. **Questionnaire**—carefully tested to ensure that it will obtain the required information
3. **Interviewers**—trained and experienced in the art of asking questions
4. **Analysis**—carefully conducted so as to provide a reliable basis for decision making

The sample

Once the survey takers have identified the large group called the "universe" that the sample is to represent, the sample method can be selected and the sample drawn. The sample can be carried out using one of two methods: quota sampling and probability sampling.

Quota sampling

This technique divides the population into subgroups and assigns each subgroup a proportion in the final sample. Normally, the subgroups are selected on the basis of (a) geographic location, (b) community size, (c) economic level, (d) sex, and (e) age. The final sample in a survey of the total adult population must include the right proportion of persons who live in large cities, suburbs, small towns, and rural areas. It must have the right proportion of men and women, and of older and younger adults. The resulting sample will be representative in terms of these five controls, but the sample may not be representative in other important respects. This is the problem with all quota samples.

Probability sampling

This technique overcomes this defect in the quota method by selecting the sample so that all units of the population have a known probability of being selected. If the sample is drawn in this manner, all subgroups in the population will be represented in approximately correct proportions, provided the sample is large enough and the completion rate is sufficiently high.

The questionnaire

Before the questionnaire is formulated, an important first step is for the researcher and the public relations person to talk informally to the types of people the survey is designed to reach. These conversations will provide important insights into the thinking of the target groups.

A wealth of information can emerge from discussion groups in which an unstructured questioning technique is used in the preliminary stages of a survey. Respondents can be encouraged to express frankly and openly their views about a company, a product, an institution—or a major social or political issue.

The next step is to formulate the questionnaire, paying particular attention to the wording of the questions.

Designing the questionnaire

Formulating the questions is a delicate task. The questions must be worded so that everyone in the sample can understand exactly what is being asked. They should contain no unfamiliar words or words with ambiguous meanings.

The questions should be unbiased, using no pejorative or emotionally charged words. They should seek one answer at a time.

The form of the question is as important as its wording and depends on the nature of the subject, how widely it has been discussed, how clear the issues may be, and other factors. Some questions ask simply for a "yes" or "no" answer. In others, the person is asked to pick from several statements the one that comes closest to expressing his or her own view. Or the person may be asked for a general opinion in an open or free-answer question.

Dealing with complex issues

In any given survey, the researcher inevitably must deal with complicated issues for which it is difficult to state both sides clearly and fairly.

In such cases, it is often wise to use what is termed an open-end or free-response question, such as, "What do you think of this plan?"

On some issues it is important to separate informed persons from the uninformed and to measure opinion in more than one dimension. This can be done by a simple question design devised by the Gallup Poll. It is a series of questions that begins, "Have you heard or read about 'X' issue?" The respondent can answer "yes" or "no."

If the answer is "yes," the respondent is asked, "In your own words, what do you consider the chief issue to be?" This question determines the extent or level of knowledge possessed on the subject. The interviewer then records the respondent's exact words.

The next question asks, "How do you think this issue should be resolved?" or, depending on the nature of the controversy, a variation of this question. The respondent is permitted to explain his or her views with as many qualifications as wished.

The fourth in this series of questions poses specific issues that can be answered "yes" or "no." Often it is possible to explain the issues in a few sentences; in effect, to inform the person being interviewed, then to record his or her opinions. Individuals who said they had not heard or read about the issue are eligible at this point to answer both this and the last question.

The fifth and last question attempts to establish the "intensity" with which the respondent holds her views. How strongly does she feel that she is right? What steps would she be willing to take to implement her opinions?

Intensity of opinion

Measurement of the intensity of opinion is obviously of key importance. Whether people feel keenly about an issue can make a difference in what they do about it. Similarly, it is important to those who have the responsibility of interpreting the views of the group interviewed.

One key development in public opinion research has been the invention of rating scales to measure the intensity of opinion in a form suitable for use in typical interviewing situations. Two such scales were devised by Jan Stapel of the Netherlands Institute of Public Opinion and by the late Dr. Hadley Cantril, former chairman of the Institute for International Social Research and former chairman of the psychology department of Princeton University.

The Stapel Scalometer was the first of its type. Basically, it is a column of 10 answer boxes. The top five boxes are white, the bottom five, black. The boxes usually are numbered from "minus five" at the bottom to "plus five" at the top.

The interviewer hands the respondent a reproduction of the scale and explains its use in these or similar words: "You will notice that the boxes on this card go from the highest position of plus five—for something you like very much—all the way down to the lowest position of minus five—for something you dislike very much. Now how far up or down the scale would you rate the following?"

The interviewer then asks the respondent to rate the person, company, or proposal with which he is concerned. The scale can be used to measure intensity of feeling by asking the person interviewed how strongly he or she feels about the issue, how certain the individual is that he or she is right, how much the person hopes that his or her view will prevail and how hard he or she is willing to work to see that his or her view is adopted, and so on.

Researchers have found the extreme positions on the scale are the most indicative and the most sensitive to change. These are the positions "plus five" and "plus four" on the favorable side, and "minus five" and "minus four" on the unfavorable or negative end of the scale. Frequently in reporting, these two positions are combined to produce a "highly favorable" or a "highly unfavorable" rating.

Getting at the "why"

Persons who are asked to give their opinions in a survey usually are asked to tell why they hold the opinion they do. But often the "why" behind the opinion comes out more clearly from a careful analysis of the findings by different groups in the population and by cross-tabulations with other questions these persons have been asked.

Every survey result can be analyzed from the viewpoint of the education of the respondents, their religion, age, sex, economic status, section of the country in which they reside, and occupation. From such analyses

it is possible to shed light on the "why" behind the public's views.

Motivation research

Employing psychological techniques to gain insights into behavior and attitudes can be an important part of a research program. However, unless this research (typically undertaken with a small number of people) is coupled with quantitative research (a full sample), the findings should not be projected to the universe being sampled.

Interviewing

Two basic methods are used to obtain interviews—by *independent samples*, where different respondents are interviewed each time, or by *panels*, where the same people are interviewed a number of times.

In independent samples, interviewing is normally conducted in four ways: (a) with personal interviews; (b) with telephone interviews; (c) with mail interviews; and (d) with personal drop-off.

Personal interviewing

This method is generally considered the most reliable. It has obvious advantages, because it is possible to obtain a more representative sample than by other methods and because greater *in-depth* interviewing is permitted.

Telephone interviewing

This approach is less expensive, but there are disadvantages in this method. One is that the refusal rate is normally higher than with personal interviewing. Another disadvantage is that there is a bias in favor of upper income people, since those who do not have telephones are found chiefly in the lower income levels.

Mail interviewing

Although it also is relatively inexpensive, the great disadvantage of mail interviewing is the problem of return. Low-income and poorly educated persons are less likely to return the questionnaire than are others in the sample.

One way to minimize this problem is to send out a second request to persons not replying to the initial contact, urging their participation in the survey. The characteristics of this latter group can then be compared with the group that initially responded. If there is little or no difference, the assumption may be made that you have a reasonably good sample. Another approach is to sample the nonrespondents either by telephone or in personal interviews, and weigh the results accordingly.

Personal drop-off

This is a combination of personal and mail interviewing and has advantages of both methods. First of all, response rate is high because the interviewer who "drops off" the questionnaire at a particular household has already established rapport with the respondent (often through a personal interview). Second, the dropped-off questionnaire (or portion of it) is self-administered (filled in by the respondent himself), thus providing fuller and franker responses than can sometimes be obtained in personal interviews. The dropped-off questionnaire is either mailed to the headquarters of the survey research organization or picked up by an interviewer for this organization, usually the one who made the initial contact.

Panels

These are used less frequently than independent samples for public opinion research, although they are used extensively in marketing research. Panels have the advantage of enabling the researcher to measure changes in attitudes exactly, since the same person is interviewed on successive occasions. The disadvantage, particularly in the case of surveys measuring awareness of knowledge, is that the panel being interviewed tends to become super-informed and thus atypical.

Research Expertise

The problems discussed in the preceding paragraphs demonstrate the need for public relations practitioners to have at least some background or experience in survey research. The need for research know-how is apparent when decisions must be made about survey methods and costs.

In addition, the research-oriented public relations person should work closely with the researcher in each phase of a survey—in defining the objectives of the survey, in question formulation, and in interpretation and analysis.

The researcher is in a good position to give valuable advice on how to translate the survey results into an effective public relations program. He or she has lived closely with the survey and is likely to have insights that might escape the public relations person who is not experienced in analyzing survey data. He or she is also typically more familiar with the limitations of the sampling procedure.

It is often in the sponsor's interest to have the survey conducted by an independent organization, since otherwise findings may be viewed with suspicion.[2]

Survey Cost Guidelines

A well-directed and properly conducted survey will usually yield valuable returns for a relatively small financial investment.

The cost of survey research depends on many factors, including the size of the sample, length of interview, the type of questions, and whether the survey is "syndicated"—that

[2]Discerning editors and others are learning to identify those organizations and research firms that issue "surveys" that are slanted to produce desired "facts." Misuse of research by such groups is a constant threat to the credibility of all research and public relations people. Selecting a research firm whose reputation for sound and unbiased studies is impeccable is increasingly a "must" for professionals.—*Ed.*

is, shared by other clients, or specifically designed for one client.

To provide a general idea of costs, it may help to bear in mind that many research companies set a total price for a survey that is roughly four to six times the total cost of the interviewing—typically the single most costly item in the survey.

A high-priced quotation for a survey is not necessarily an indication of a competent job. Some research organizations must ask for high prices because they have high operating costs. On the other hand, if the price quoted is extremely low, it may be an indication of shoddy work, of cutting corners.

Survey research has reached a high level of sophistication. Aided by the computer, it is destined to play an even greater role in our lives. Not the least benefitted will be the public relations person.

Other Considerations*

In the past few years research has been accentuated as a means of meeting the growing demand of management for demonstration of effectiveness. By producing numbers that appear to be solid "proof," surveys and other studies are tempting tools for the public relations person. However, as seen in consideration of measures to evaluate public relations in Chapter 49, relying too heavily on numbers and such "proof" is dangerous and can be counterproductive.

First, it tends to rule out functions that will not be subject to later measurement, such as advice that prevents making mistakes or introduction of ideas and methods that have never been used before—among the most valuable functions of public relations.

Research studies are most valuable as guidelines and tests of limits, not as blueprints

---

*Section written by Philip Lesly.

or photographs that supposedly print an actual state of affairs.

Additional techniques

Public relations people are increasingly using methods developed by researchers in marketing and politics. They include the following:

Focus groups

These are groups of perhaps six to ten representative members of a selected public. They gather under the direction of a skilled presenter to discuss the topic of the study. The interchange stimulates thinking and leads to more penetrating expressions of opinions and attitudes than can usually be obtained by questionnaires or interviews.

Advisory committees

A group of particularly knowledgeable people is asked to keep an eye on matters of interest to the organization and to offer comments and suggestions, either individually or as a group. They may be called on for their opinions and inputs on specific questions, issues, or proposed actions.

Toll-free 800 telephone lines

The organization's entire public or a selected segment is asked to phone in their reactions to a move or to a proposed policy.

Analysis of mail and telephone

These are screened for a specified period to determine how correspondents and phoners respond or express their opinions.

Added elements of sampling

Also adapted from marketing and political research are *demographics* and *psychographics*. Demographics analyzes in detail the makeup of a given public by its physical traits—age, sex, education, location, and so on. Psychographics analyzes a group by its attitudes and psychological makeup. These considerations then may enable the communicator to precisely focus messages. This area includes techniques such as VALS (Value and Lifestyle Opinion Research), developed by Ketchum Public Relations.

Abuses

Falsified studies to foster a viewpoint (such as "proving" that Americans really don't want school choice) are common and are often picked up by media. These can be combated by having objective experts analyze the questionnaires and polling techniques to show how the results were skewed.

Similarly, some users of research use only those parts of a survey that establish their viewpoint. Others fail to mention when a survey was conducted, hiding the fact that conditions may have changed and opinions with them.

Many stories in the media about surveys are placed by people who have done no research at all. If an organization's name sounds like it's worthy, some editors accept what the organization reports without asking to see the survey.

Recently a pernicious technique has arisen in political polling, influencing the choice of officials who may determine important forces on people's lives. This is the "push poll," in which questioners supposedly are conducting a poll but actually they are planting negative information about a candidate they oppose.

Public relations people, especially, should be aware of such abuses and be prepared to challenge them.

Resources

Often it is unnecessary to repeat research that has already been done. For instance, the Roper Public Opinion Research Center at Williams College, Williamstown, Massachusetts, has on file more than fifteen thousand opinion surveys (going back to the 1930s).

19

FACT-FINDING FOR PUBLIC RELATIONS

WILLIAM W. COOK

William W. Cook, retired director–public communications services, United States Steel Corporation, has been a public relations man, newspaperman, and magazine editor.

He joined United States Steel in 1959 after six years as a partner in the New York City public relations counseling firm of Pendray & Cook. Before that he was an account executive in Cincinnati and New York for Hill and Knowlton, a copy editor on the New York Times, *and executive editor of* Motor Magazine.

He received a B.A. from the University of Michigan and an M.S. from the Graduate School of Journalism, Columbia University.

Mr. Cook served two terms as national treasurer and a member of the board of directors of the Public Relations Society of America and was president of the society's New York Chapter. He is a trustee and past president of the Foundation (now Institute) for Public Relations Research and Education, and a member of the Public Relations Advisory Committees of Pace College, New York, and Fairfield University, Fairfield, Connecticut.

Facts and their implications are the bricks and mortar of public relations. These essential materials—the facts about the organization—determine the success, or failure, of the PR practiioner's efforts, regardless of how skilled he or she may be with the tools of the trade. Only secondarily does success depend on the PR person's mastery of public relations tools and techniques—publicity, films, speeches, and other communication methods designed to build public support for and understanding of the organization.

Few outsiders fully appreciate the degree to which the practice of public relations depends on painstakingly documented facts.

To the distress of many practiioners, the harshest criticism leveled at them stems from the laymen's mistaken conception that public relations is based not so much on the assimilation, documentation, and presentation of facts as it is on their distortion or suppression. Though the conscientious public relations professional often may wish for more palatable facts with which to work, he or she does his best with what is available, then stands or falls by the results. An axiom of good public relations (as with good business practice generally, the two are usually synonymous) holds that people like to do business with companies they trust. Consequently, when preparing a news release or a speech, the public relations person is acutely aware that the accuracy of the communication will directly impact the organization's reputation.

To effectively present the organization's case in the court of public opinion the experienced public relations person recognizes the importance of marshaling all the pertinent facts—both pleasant and unpleasant—with the diligence a skilled lawyer employs to investigate an issue being tried in a court of law. The PR practitioner, like the attorney, serves as an advocate for the company or client. He or she must remain constantly alert to protect against the pressures of advocacy clouding one's judgment and to guard against assessment of the situation being based on incorrect or inadequate information or colored by preconceptions. The fleeting comforts of self-deception cannot be afforded, because the PR professional's usefulness is directly proportional to his or her ability to ascertain the truth, correctly analyze it, and lay the results on the line.

Even under the most serene conditions, public relations is never static. People and their opinions change constantly. In today's strong current of rapid change, new opportunities and crisis situations arise at a breathtaking rate. Rarely can the public relations personnel of most organizations relax for even a moment with any more reassurance than a fleeting feeling of allayed apprehension. It is essential, therefore, for the public relations person to possess the abilities to stay abreast of changing situations and to keep myriad changing facts in perspective.

Minimizing the Element of Chance

The service that fact-finding performs in public relations has been likened to the function of radar in guarding air and sea lanes by warning of approaching hazards. The more information we can gather to assess the nature and scope of a public relations problem, the better able we are to approach it with some assurance that we have minimized uncertainty.

The burden this places on research is clear. Those responsible for an organization's public relations find that they must be skilled fact-finders in an awesome variety of disciplines. Obviously, the well-rounded practitioner today must have a thorough knowledge of the organization and the field in which it operates. Increasingly, however, he or she is expected to also have an up-to-date knowledge of fast-changing conditions in business and finance generally, the political arena, education, international affairs, and the social sciences, with growing emphasis on subdisciplines such as socioeconomics and ethnology, let alone such arcane natural sciences as ecology and agrobiology.

Much of the information a public relations person needs lends itself to systematized storage and retrieval—for example, literature such as reports, news clippings, and statistics. But some of the most useful information does not lend itself to a mechanical or electronic retrieval system. How, for example, can one store in a filing cabinet or on tape the knowledge of how to deal with sensitive racial issues accumulated from a lifetime of study, discussion, and personal experience?

While the busy public relations executive can never delegate all the functions of what is generally regarded as research, he or she increasingly needs to call on others to help with various aspects of it. To see what parts of the job can be delegated, let us examine what we mean by "public relations research."

The term *research* itself presents a semantic problem, since it tends to conjure up visions of owlish Ph.D.s in white smocks hunched over vaporous beakers. In fact, research for public relations, while always an exacting and often an arduous job, is simple enough in concept. The term *public relations research* is commonly used to mean: (a) *public opinion* research for public relations purposes; and (b) the series of functions involved in the following:

1. Keeping close watch on the social, political, and economic scene in a "radar scanning" operation to detect early signs of problems and developing trends that are likely to affect an organization's public relations.

2. Deciding which research activities, including public opinion research (*see* Chapter 18), are needed to determine the nature and scope of developing problems or trends and obtain the information required to deal with them.

3. Gathering the information.

4. Analyzing the data in terms of the organization's public relations needs and the specialized interests of individuals and departments.

5. Getting the appropriate information into the right hands.

6. Filing the information for ready retrieval.

7. Retrieving information bearing on a particular subject or project as needed.

8. Analyzing this information, as well as data from other sources, in terms of a specific public relations problem and using it in a public relations project or program.

9. Evaluating the results by means such as public opinion research, analysis of press and radio-TV news coverage and commentaries, and field reports from all available sources. At this point our series comes full circle, and we find ourselves back watching our radar screen for signs of significant trends and shifts in opinions and attitudes.

Since public opinion research is dealt with in Chapter 18, we shall focus our attention here on the other aspects of finding and using facts for public relations purposes.

Qualitative Skills Needed in Fact-Finding

First, we should recognize certain qualitative distinctions among various steps in the series.

Step 1, scanning the horizon to detect signs of public relations problems and trends, calls for broad knowledge of the current scene outside the organization, as well as a thorough grounding in the organization's history, structure, policies, products and people, its operations and its aspirations, and an awareness of its public relations objectives and activities.

Steps 2–5, deciding which research activities are needed, gathering information, analyzing it in terms of public relations needs, and getting it into the right hands, call not only for knowledge of the organization and the social, political, and economic scene, but also for the special skills of a researcher who is familiar with the tools and techniques of fact-finding and versed in the behavioral sciences.

Steps 6 and 7, filing the information and retrieving it as needed, call for experience found in a variety of specialists, including file clerks, secretaries, librarians, research librarians, and, increasingly, computer operators and programmers.

Step 8, analyzing the information in terms of an organization's public relations needs and using it in a public relations project or program, calls for an architect of ideas. It is best handled by someone who can recognize the scattered bits and pieces that apply to a particular situation and adapt them to it. The idea architect should have the experience and vision to see how an article in *Fortune* can be used to address a situation developing in a plant community; how a statement by an eighteenth-century prime minister clarifies a point the chairman wants to make in a speech to stockholders; how the failure of a public relations project attempted a decade ago by another company points the way to success today.

Step 9, the final step, evaluating the results, again calls for the researcher skilled in the methods and techniques of fact-finding, versed in the social sciences, and keenly attuned to subtle changes in opinions and attitudes.

While the distinctions among the various steps seem clear enough when we consider the differing skills they require, they are distinctions that sometimes escape not only top management, but an occasional public relations director as well. At times the person who is skilled at storing and retrieving facts is expected to perform as an idea architect too. This often leads to the disillusioning discovery that the qualities that make her or him excel at processing information are not necessarily the ones needed to interpret the information wisely in terms of public relations need.

The point, then, is that while all these functions are essential to get maximum mileage out of the fact-finding operation, the talents needed to handle them are not always found in the same individual. Thus, such questions as who will do the fact-finding and analyzing, who will file and retrieve facts, and who will apply them to the practice of public relations, are by no means academic in setting up the mechanism to handle these functions.

Often these questions answer themselves in simple terms of manpower. In public relations' earlier days, the practioner usually did his own research, often aided by his secretary. This still holds true in smaller departments and firms where personnel limitations make versatility not just a virtue, but a necessity. However, as public relations firms have expanded, and corporations, banks, associations, and other organizations have come to rely more and more on inside and outside assistance, there has been a growing tendency to set up some special facility to handle the functions involved in gathering and processing facts.

Such standard repositories as filing cabinets, desk drawers, and library shelves and stacks are customarily used for information storage and retrieval. Increasingly, however, computers are being called on to take over the chores of storing, retrieving, transmitting, and to a limited extent, analyzing information used in public relations work.

Terminals that provide access to a central time-sharing computer enable different units of the same company, such as district public relations offices, to share a single data bank. Each terminal may be used to feed into the bank data such as names, dates, and statistics, and documents such as news releases, executive speeches, and policy statements, and to retrieve these and similar materials fed in from other terminals. A system of this sort enables a company to transmit news releases or other copy without delay from one terminal to any others on the network, and simultaneously to store it in the data bank where it is on call at a moment's notice from all points. It also makes possible the analysis of press coverage of an important news story across the country from data supplied from all terminals. As in other cases in which a latter-day Aladdin summons an electronic genie to help him, though, it is well to keep in mind the dictum, "Garbage in, garbage out."

Information on gaining access via computer to sources of information outside the organization appears in Chapter 29.

Resource Knowledge Is Essential

No matter who—or what—handles various parts of the fact-processing operations, certain sources of information are uniform for virtually any public relations operations. A working knowledge of these sources, together with a handy reference shelf in one's own office, eliminates the need for a great deal of original investigation. It helps prevent us from "inventing the wheel" all over again when we undertake a new project. Anyone engaged in public relations should become thoroughly familiar with these sources.

Certain standard works are so useful to public relations practitioners in every field that they are virtual "musts" for the office bookshelf. These include staples such as a dictionary (preferably two: a desk edition within arm's reach and an unabridged close by); *Roget's Thesaurus*; *World Almanac*; *Information Please Almanac*; a good world atlas with adequate maps of the United States and individual states as well as all other parts of the world; the *Congressional Directory*; statistical and fact books of special interest to the organization; and public relations reference works and case studies. Other volumes, such as the *Statistical Abstract of the United States* and *United States Government Organization Manual*, may be used often enough to warrant keeping them close at hand.

The procedures for gathering and arranging facts so they can be applied to the solution of public relations problems are fairly uniform. The late Dr. Karl E. Ettinger, a New York public relations and research counselor who contributed the chapter on fact-finding for previous editions of this handbook and to whom the present writer is indebted for much of the material that follows, set forth certain requirements for a basic fact file for each project or client. Dr. Ettinger visualized this file as a ready source of facts and figures to inform both the practitioner and the public. Such a file must be constantly updated, in a continuing intelligence activity that helps adjust policies and actions to the changing scene and recognizes trends likely to affect an organization and its plans. What follows are some of the things recommended for such a file:

1. Statistical figures concerning the organization

2. Charters and bylaws of the organization

3. The organization's publications, news releases, advertisements, speeches, background statements, and the like

4. Color and black-and-white photographs of plants and other facilities, products, activities

5. Biographies and pictures of key personnel

6. Pertinent clippings from newspapers, magazines, trade publications

7. Radio and television monitoring reports

8. Basic reference books dealing with the activities and problems of the organization

9. Trade association and trade union literature of organizations concerned with your own or similar problems

10. Lists of key individuals interested in your organization and its problems (board of directors, trade association officers and members, public officials, opinion leaders, others)

11. Lists of related or interested organizations

12. Mailing lists of selected groups

13. Lists of all government agencies and officials (federal, state, county, municipal, international) concerned with the organization

14. Pertinent legislation and pending bills; important legal decisions

15. Access to computer data banks and Internet

16. Reports on government and legislative hearings

17. Findings of public opinion studies concerning the organization or matters related to its interests

18. Lists of editors, reporters, and commentators in all media covering the organization's news

19. Literature of competitors and antagonists

20. Information about individuals and institutions from which an adverse influence on public opinion may be expected

21. Biographical data on individuals with whom contacts are desirable

22. Calendar and timetable indicating occasions for publicity (anniversaries, memorial days, plant dedications, conventions, national weeks and days) and occasions when publicity or events should not be planned because of holidays, conflicting or competing events

23. Lists of possible publicity tie-ins with other organizations, products, or events

24. Files of videotapes and computer disks prepared for the organization or pertaining to it

By subscribing to the services of clipping bureaus and radio-TV monitoring services, (*see also* Chapter 20 and Appendix) some of the material needed for continuous compilation of the file may be obtained. Most of the remaining material will accumulate from a systematic reading of literature that normally flows across the practitioner's desk.

Computerized searches for reference materials are available from Burrelle's Business Research Center, (800) 631-1160; Facts on File, (212) 683-2244; Fact Set Data Systems,

(212) 444-2772; Facts That Matter, (212) 935-0221; and KR Source One, http://www.krinfo.com/Krsource one.

Many free materials available

It is useful to make sure that those who are responsible for gathering facts are placed on lists to receive the many free materials available from industry, government, and other sources as research tools. These include speeches, annual reports, fact booklets, news releases, company publications, and research reports of similar organizations, as well as a variety of government publications that are available free or at a nominal charge. Another source not to be overlooked, of course, is regular contacts with people performing similar functions in other organizations who can provide leads on research techniques, reports, and surveys, and offer guidance on contemplated projects.

Gathering information about a company or client and seeing that maximum use is made of it is important. Equally useful, at times, is collecting adverse criticism and analyzing it objectively to keep a running account of where the organization stands in public opinion. The public relations person is paid to know what is going on and to counsel management on what to do about it. Anytime he or she finds he is being paid to tell management what it wants to hear, rather than what he thinks management should know, he is well advised to take his talents elsewhere.

In approaching a public relations problem, the following procedure is useful:

• **Determine in writing what the problem is.** Formulating it in this manner is advisable even where you are conducting the study alone, for it helps to clarify your thinking and supplies your organization with a record. Where more than one person works on a problem, a written record

SOURCES OF INFORMATION

Printed Material	*People*	*Others*
Reference books and reference periodicals	Own organization and staff	Data banks
Other books and periodicals	Own observations	Electronic libraries
Newspapers and clippings	Customers	The Internet
Government publications	Government officers	Public registers
Company and association literature	Governmental information departments	Correspondence
Competitors' publications	Librarian, public library	Pictures
Newsletters	Librarians, special libraries	Foreign sources
Directories	Newspaper and trade paper editors	U.S. Patent Office
Newspaper morgues	Association executives	Monitorings and recordings of radio and TV broadcasts
Library catalogs	Technical and other experts	Documentary and other motion pictures
Trade lists	Legislators	Detective services
Who's Who	Lawyers	Experiments
Chronologies	Witnesses	Price lists
Maps	Other public relations people	Samples
Census reports and other statistics	Public opinion researchers	

Figure 19.1 Sample roster of sources.

is indispensable to avoid misunderstanding and duplication of effort.

- **Write down the questions you want to answer by collecting pertinent facts, figures, and opinions.** Public relations problems tend to be complex, and a single fact rarely supplies all the information needed to solve one.

- **Look for precedents.** Compare your organization's situation with those of others in similar circumstances. You need to learn as much as you can about the technical conditions and social forces that have played a role in comparable situations in the past.

- **Make a list of all available sources you intend to use.** Preparing such a list at the beginning of a fact-finding operation helps you organize it quickly and efficiently. The list will include a bibliography, and the names, addresses, and phone and fax numbers of all potential sources of useful information. In preparing the bibliography, con-

sult the catalogs of libraries, reference books, a volume such as *Guide to Reference Books* (American Library Association) and the bibliography services offered by the Library of Congress. For sources other than printed ones, list all persons with experience in the field in which you are interested. These may include association executives, government employees, and trade journal writers and editors. Your roster of sources may then look like Figure 19.1.

- **Examine the sources that look most promising.** You will soon find which ones are likely to provide the most useful information and be able to judge the relative weight and bias of the material available. Often it will be unnecessary to consult all the sources listed, since you will arrive at a satisfactory answer after studying the most productive ones. In assembling facts and figures, a standard form of collecting such materials is useful. Short notes may be written or typed on file cards. More voluminous material may be copied, computerized, or microfilmed for future use and reference. A tape recorder or other recording device may be helpful. Whatever method you use in collecting your material, the following requirements should be met:

1. Indicate the sources of every fact so it can be checked.

2. Make a record that is readily understandable to others who may work with you or carry on the project.

3. Date your notes so you can reconstruct the sequence of the study.

4. When you quote others, use quotation marks to separate your statements and conclusions from theirs.

5. Order reproductions in the standard 8½" × 11" size so they will fit into your reports, and indicate sources of photocopies and pictures.

6. File your material in accordance with a standard system so you and others can locate portions of it as needed.

- **Prepare progress reports at intervals**, giving your findings and indicating sources that have been consulted without results. In some situations, negative findings are as useful as positive ones.

- At the end of your investigation, **prepare a comprehensive report of your findings**. This may include summaries of progress reports drawn up in the course of the project, as well as updated findings and conclusions from previous studies in the same area.

- As a final step, **prepare and submit your recommendations for public relations actions based on your findings**.

The Appendix includes lists of information sources and other resources.

Section 4

THE TECHNIQUES OF COMMUNICATION

20

PREPARATIONS FOR COMMUNICATING

HERBERT M. BAUS
PHILIP LESLY

The communications function comprises just one part of the total spectrum that constitutes public relations. Yet it often serves as the point at which the whole operation brings about a desired result. It appears at the end of the spectrum—after research and analysis, policy formation, planning, and programming. The communications component is typically followed by an assessment of the public relations efforts and their results, as well as feedback regarding the public's reactions to the organization. Though other activities take place before and after it, communications is the most visible part of the public relations spectrum—the area in which the organization's officials can see tangible evidence of public relations efforts and in which the effect on the publics can be observed.

Consequently, the communications elements of public relations, which contributed greatly to the field's rise, remain its most prominent aspects. While the concept that public relations consists only of communications is fading, the communications role continues to employ most of the field's personnel, consumes most of the budgets, and gets most of the attention.

A thorough knowledge of and an ability to judge these communications functions is vital to the public relations executive's ability to

advise the principals, plan the operations, employ and direct staff, and assess accomplishments. However, some public relations executives lack these abilities, having only rare dealings with these functions.

This section contains fourteen chapters that deal with the techniques and principles of communicating. Seven of these chapters deal with the various aspects of publicity, while the other seven deal with other communications techniques.

Role Varies in Other Countries

Of the multiple facets of public relations, communications probably varies the most from one country to another. Publicity in North America is dominant because of the diversity of media, their openness to all sources of information, and the receptivity of the people to all the information media.

In many other countries, even among democracies, the media are restricted either by political affiliation or traditional suspicions between the press and other aspects of society. Many newspapers and magazines expect payment for editorial coverage, either directly or in advertising. In many countries, television and radio are limited to govern-

---

Herbert M. Baus is a public relations counsel and author.

ment-operated outlets and to either no others or limited private sources. In these areas there is a natural emphasis on communications that the source can control, such as printed materials, meetings, posters, and sponsored films.

Publicity Program Planning

The job of publicity is to tell the story.

In a broad sense, all techniques employed by an organization to convey its messages are facets of publicity.

Almost everything printed in a newspaper or a magazine, or broadcast by television or radio, is publicity for some person or some thing. It is the job of the publicity person to find the news, interesting information, and ideas in the organization, or to develop it and to present it in a form that will qualify it for publication, broadcast, or other dissemination.

Promotion is a word that covers the field between publicity and advertising, and in application includes them both. It connotes tie-ins, special events, and stunts to get attention, whereas publicity is more often regarded in the sense of getting something printed or broadcast. Publicity is slanted more from the straight news side; promotion more from the advertising and commercial side.

Publicity work boils down to analyzing the vast store of human interest and news material that is inherent in any organization of human beings, selecting a portion of it, dressing it up properly, and making it available to media of information. In other words: it requires a nose for news, a technique for production, and the energy to do the work.

News as Publicity

News is something that interests many people today. From the point of view of the *New York Times,* that means many people in New York and many of the national readers of the *Times*. From the point of view of the *Oakland Post,* it means many African-Americans. To the editor of a house magazine, news is something that interests many employees of the plant served.

Every medium has a news standard of its own, and that is the criterion the publicist goes by in attempting to address publicity to the public through that medium.

The basic factors of publicity are people, time, and place. What are the people doing, and how does what they are doing affect other people? At what time are they doing it? Something a group of people does for publicity interest may command liberal newspaper attention on Tuesday, but on Wednesday it may be shaded if not obliterated by a flood, a murder, or an outbreak of war. What is news in Port Angeles, Washington, may be of no interest in Miami Beach, Florida.

From the publicity person's point of view there are three classifications of news: *spot news,* or any news not planned or developed by the publicist; *feature news,* which has broader interest and usually less critical timing than spot news; and *created news,* which he or she controls and/or helps to create.

Spot news

Spot news usually consists of a spontaneous outburst of nature or of mankind, such as a flood, earthquake, typhoon, war, revolution, fire, or accident. It may be an attack on an organization by an activist group.

Spot news concerning his or her organization is often negative, although proper handling of it can to a major degree relieve the harmful impact. For example, a railroad accident is unfavorable news to the railroad. The railroad's publicity director can win sympathetic news handling by making himself or herself and staff of maximum assistance in reporting all the facts quickly, accurately, and fully.

Suppose the railroad publicist is notified at three o'clock in the morning that a calamitous accident on the desert has wrecked one of the company's trains. He or she immediately notifies the news media and rushes reporters and photographers to the scene of the accident. The media appreciate this courtesy in helping to cover a necessary story. The story treatment is more likely to be sympathetic to the railroad. It emphasizes the railroad's efficiency in clearing the wreckage, accentuates the heroism of the train crews, indicates that the railroad was not at fault, desensationalizes the details, and gives the railroad the benefit of every doubt. The publicity is temperate, because the newspapers have confidence they are getting all the facts and the railroad is doing its best.

On the contrary, suppose the publicist attempts to censor news of the accident by trying to belittle the scope of the disaster and striving to keep the newspeople from locating and reaching the scene. This forces the media to undergo considerable expense to ferret out the details of the catastrophe. Perhaps they charter a special plane, scour the desert, and eventually locate the wreckage. By this time their tempers are up at the unnecessary suppression, and they are pressed for time on their deadlines. The tone of the stories castigates the company for its effort to cover up. The newspeople are suspicious that the noncooperation indicates unsavory circumstances that the railroad is attempting to hide from the public. To justify their expenditures in getting the story, the editors spread the subject sensationally and make all they can of it. Bad public relations in handling of spot news has severely penalized the company.

Ways to make news

Here are some of the most effective, legitimate ways to create news. There are many ways, but what follows are the basic ones:

- Tie in with the news events of the day
- Tie in with another publicity person
- Tie in with newspaper or other medium on a mutual project
- Conduct a poll or survey
- Issue a report
- Arrange an interview with a celebrity
- Take part in a controversy
- Arrange for a testimonial
- Make an analysis or a prediction
- Arrange for, write, project, cover a speech
- Form and announce the names of a committee
- Hold an election
- Announce an appointment
- Celebrate an anniversary
- Issue a summary of facts
- Tie in with a holiday
- Adopt a program of work
- Make a statement on a subject of interest
- Take a trip
- Bring a celebrity from elsewhere
- Make an award
- Hold a contest
- Pass a resolution
- Appear before public bodies
- Stage a special event
- Write a letter
- Release a letter you have received
- Adapt national reports and surveys locally
- Entertain
- Stage a debate
- Organize a trade promotion
- Tie into a well-known "week" or "day"
- Fete an institution, such as the Bill of Rights
- Inspect a project
- Organize a tour
- Develop a community calendar or program
- Issue a protest

- Issue praise
- Issue and diagnose statistics
- Stage a demonstration
- Stage a "gag"
- Make a picture (this may accompany many of the foregoing)

When is it news?

It is news when it contains one or more of the major ingredients of human interest, namely:

- When it is news; e.g., launching a man into space
- When it is novel; e.g., identical twins suffer identical injuries
- When it relates to famous person; e.g., any entertainment column
- When it is directly important to great numbers of people; e.g., information about the income tax
- When it involves conflict; e.g., battles, divorces, athletic contests
- When it involves mystery; e.g., many crimes
- When it is considered confidential; e.g., the revelations of columnists
- When it pertains to the future; e.g., plans for improving a city
- When it is funny; e.g., a group of Young Pathfinders get lost on a hike
- When it is romantic or sexy; e.g., check what catches the eye scrutinizing the "cheesecake" of any newspaper or magazine

Strategic Publicity

Publicity is not merely a process of getting stories and pictures into the newspapers. It is a large-scale operation requiring planned and ordered execution of thousands of small details. Effective publicity is being achieved when the citizen sees the subject being publicized in the morning paper, in some technical publication, in two trade journals, in the neighborhood free-circulation newspaper, in a national magazine, on a ticket, on a couple of direct-mail pieces, in a church leaflet, on labels and lapel buttons, on automobile bumper strips, on outdoor billboards; when he or she hears about it on radio and sees it on TV; or when he gets a telephone call about it and discusses it with friends at lunch. This is the kind of planned publicity that brings in a volume of sales, or votes, or results of whatever kind may be sought.

All of this costs money, requires manpower and experience, and consumes time and resources. It can be done in an ordered manner like a well-planned military campaign geared to encounter every problem of enemy ingenuity, adverse weather, and sudden circumstance, or it can be done in a slipshod manner with hit-or-miss efforts that may or may not muddle through.

The steps in planning a publicity operation that get results follow.

Research

Analyze the history and existing facts of the subject to be publicized. Examine the records and fine-comb the scrapbooks. Check the computer data bank. Meet the key people and as many as possible of the little people, obtaining the benefit of their ideas and experience and giving them the psychological lift of feeling that they are called upon to make contributions to the publicity. (*See also* Chapter 18.)

Pry into the basic statistics and facts. Study the profit-and-loss record. Analyze past and present policies. Go over the calendar and pick out the anniversaries, historic dates, elections, and traditional special events. Make a complete file of the names and pedigrees of the officers. Make a record of such statistics as the number of members, employees, and stockholders. Make an inventory of resources. Some publicity offices maintain a complete library or "morgue," including all this information with such details as pictures and complete biographies of all principals for immediate reference in case of death, promotion, or other sudden news developments.

Set the objective

The publicist may desire to sell products for a company. Does she aim at a local, regional, national, or international market? The Pasadena Tournament of Roses has a double objective—to attract hundreds of thousands of people to see one of America's most colorful winter pageants and to create national news that will publicize the fact that Southern California's climate is so balmy as to attract 1.5 million people to come out in their shirtsleeves to see dozens of floats spectacularly bedecked with flowers. A big trade show might have one or all of these objectives: attract a large paying audience, publicize widely the concentration of products and a market in the given area, and win perennial confidence of exhibitors so they will purchase display space in future years. A small community may present a festival with the dual objective of attracting cash customers and informing people in forty-nine other states and one hundred nations of the charms and advantages of the community.

The Republican Party has a broad national objective and a number of more limited local objectives. A Lions Club may wish no more than a notice to its own members to get them out to the Thursday luncheon.

Most events and indeed, most news, magazine, and broadcast features, are planned with an objective. The publicist must analyze the subject, because the scope of effort will influence the tools, the direction, and the money spent. Every bit of effort plunged into national publicity, for example, may detract from the intensity of local publicity.

Local publicity aims at local newspapers, radio stations, television stations, house magazines, trade publications, and direct mail.

Sectional publicity, aimed at a part of the state, expands on the local technique with an additional effort to send copy and illustrations to a wide number of community newspapers. *Regional publicity*, going statewide or to several states, introduces news and photo syndicates. If an intensive effort is contemplated, it requires a greater staff to produce localized news for aiming at specific publications in local areas. *National publicity* brings into heavy play the news and photo syndicates, plus national magazines and network television. (For international publicity, *see* Chapter 45.)

Direct coverage is likely to be limited to a mailing list of one hundred to two hundred major newspapers and perhaps additional pinpoint efforts such as, "Mr. John Citizen of Our Organization, who graduated from high school in Walla Walla, Washington, today did thus and so. . . ."

Plan work with individual media

While considerable emphasis is placed here on mass distributions and lists, often the most important publicity is the result of work with individual publications or broadcasters. In fact, mass distribution is less desirable than carefully selected placements with major media. For instance, placement of a story with Associated Press, United Press International, or one of the major press syndicates will reach many newspapers under the aegis of a service they subscribe to and respect. This is clearly more effective—and much less expensive—than mass mailing the story to many newspapers from a source they consider to be an outsider. "Over the transom" mail and electronic submissions are heavy in all publications' offices, and each piece has an uphill fight to get attention and acceptance. On the other hand, the wire service or press service story gets priority attention and prime acceptance. (*See* Figure 20.1.)

In the same way, placement of an exclusive article in an important national magazine will

| 286 | Oklahoma – continued | Daily Newspapers |

Circ: (eS)6,410; **Coverage:** Bryan County; **Owner:** Donrey Media Group; **Wires:** AP; **Ad Rate:** $6.50
Management/News Executives:
Publisher. . . . . David Crouch
Editor. . . . . Richard Chase
Editorial Page Editor. . . . . David Crouch
News Editor. . . . . Richard Chase
News Assistant Editor. Stephen Cole
Photo Reporter. . . . . Patrick Barrett
Advertising Director. . . . . Paula Howell
Circulation Manager. . . . . Chris Howell
Editors/Reporters/Columnists:
Business Editor. . . . . Richard Chase
Computers/High Tech Editor. . . . . Richard Chase
Entertainment/Arts Editor. . . . . Lisa Reed
Farm Editor. . . . . Richard Chase
Food Editor. . . . . Lyn Fene
Home Editor. . . . . Lyn Fene
Lifestyle Editor. . . . . Lyn Fene
Radio/Television/Cable Editor. . . . . Lisa Reed
Sports:
  Editor. . . . . Harold Harmon
  Outdoor Writer. . . . . Harold Harmon
Travel Editor. . . . . David Crouch
Women's Editor. . . . . Lyn Fene

Edmond – 52,315; County: Oklahoma;
  DMA: Oklahoma City, OK; (43)

EDMOND EVENING SUN (OK-D150)
123 S. Broadway   **(405) 341-2121**
Edmond, OK 73034-3899   FAX: (405) 340-7363
Circ: (eS)9,727; **Coverage:** Oklahoma County; **Owner:** Livermore Newspapers; **Wires:** AP, NY Times; **Ad Rate:** $9.00
Management/News Executives:
Publisher. . . . . Ed Livermore Jr.
Managing Editor. . . . . Carol Hartzog
Editor. . . . . Ed Livermore Jr.
Editorial Page Editor. . . . . Carol Hartzog
City Editor. . . . . Steve Gust
Metro Editor. . . . . Carol Smaglinski
Advertising Manager. Jack Hovorka
Editors/Reporters/Columnists:
Automotive Editor. . . . . Carol Hartzog
Book Review Editor. . . . . Jeana Nolen
Business Editor. . . . . Steve Gust
Computers/High Tech Editor. . . . . Steve Gust
Education Writer. . . . . Jonathon Leal
Entertainment/Arts Editor. . . . . Jeana Nolen
Environmental Editor. . . . . Carol Hartzog
Farm Editor. . . . . Carol Hartzog
Features Editor. . . . . Carol Smaglinski
Food Editor. . . . . Carol Smaglinski
Home Editor. . . . . Carol Smaglinski
Medical/Health Editor. . . . . Curtis Kilman
Political Editor. . . . . Curtis Kilman
Radio/Television/Cable Editor. . . . . Jeana Nolen
Real Estate Editor. . . . . Carol Hartzog
Sports:
  Editor. . . . . Terry Tush
  Outdoor Writer. . . . . Carol Hartzog
Travel Editor. . . . . Carol Smaglinski
Women's Editor. . . . . Carol Smaglinski

El Reno – 15,414; County: Canadian;
  DMA: Oklahoma City, OK; (43)

EL RENO TRIBUNE (OK-D160)
201 N. Rock Island   **(405) 262-5180**
El Reno, OK 73036-2758
Circ: (e)4,755, (S)4,947; **Coverage:** Canadian County; **Owner:** The Tribune Corporation; **Wires:** AP; **Ad Rate:** $4.20
Management/News Executives:
Publisher. . . . . Ray T. Dyer
Publisher. . . . . Sean Dyer
Managing Editor. . . . . Ray T. Dyer
Advertising Director. Jamie Watson
Circulation Manager. . . . . Mark Lyle
Editors/Reporters/Columnists:
Business Editor. . . . . Ray T. Dyer
Entertainment/Arts Editor. . . . . Brett Barrett
Food Editor. . . . . Ivy Coffey
Lifestyle Editor. . . . . Pat Hammert
Sports Reporter. . . . . Glen Miller
General Columnist. . . . . Ray T. Dyer
General Columnist. . . . . Pat Dyer

Elk City – 10,428; County: Beckham;
  DMA: Oklahoma City, OK; (43)

ELK CITY NEWS (OK-D170)
P.O. Box 1037   **(405) 225-3000**
Elk City, OK 73648
Circ: (e)6,000, (S)10,500; **Coverage:** Beckham County; **Owner:** Family Corporation; **Wires:** AP; **Ad Rate:** $5.04
Management/News Executives:
Publisher. . . . . Larry Wade
Managing Editor. . . . . Bob Fisher
Editor. . . . . Larry Wade
Editorial Page Editor. Larry Wade
City Editor. . . . . John Lyon
Photo Editor. . . . . John Lyon
Advertising Manager. . . . . Sharon Denney
Editors/Reporters/Columnists:
Automotive Editor. Sharon Denney
Book Review Editor. Owene Scott
Business Editor. . . . . Larry Wade
Education Writer. . . . . Bob Fisher
Entertainment/Arts Editor. . . . . Owene Scott
Environmental Editor. Bob Fisher
Farm Editor. . . . . Bob Fisher
Food Editor. . . . . Owene Scott
Home Editor. . . . . Owene Scott
Lifestyle Editor. . . . . Owene Scott
Medical/Health Editor. . . . . Helen Burnett
Political Editor. . . . . Larry Wade
Radio/Television/Cable Editor. . . . . Sharon Denney
Sports:
  Editor. . . . . Brent Lansden
  Outdoor Writer. . . . . Brent Lansden
Travel Editor. . . . . Helen Burnett
Women's Editor. . . . . Owene Scott

Enid – 45,309; County: Garfield; DMA: Oklahoma City, OK; (43)

ENID NEWS AND EAGLE (OK-D180)
227 W. Broadway   **(405) 233-6600**
Enid, OK 73701   FAX: (405) 233-7645
      News Phone: (405) 237-6397
Circ: (m)23,655, (S)24,581; **Coverage:** Garfield County; **Owner:** Thomson Newspapers; **Wires:** AP, Thomson; **Ad Rate:** $16.28
Management/News Executives:
Publisher. . . . . Ed Hauck
Editor. . . . . Jerry Pittman
City Editor. . . . . Jeff Mullin
Photo Editor. . . . . Bill Edson
Advertising Manager. Tom Bradley
Editors/Reporters/Columnists:
Book Review Editor. . . . . Kathryn McNutt
Farm Editor. . . . . Beth Lilley
Features Editor. . . . . Kathryn McNutt
Food Editor. . . . . Holly Long
Lifestyle Editor. . . . . Kathryn McNutt
Radio/Television/Cable Editor. . . . . Kathryn McNutt
Sports:
  Editor. . . . . Mark Rountree
  Outdoor Writer. . . . . Mark Rountree
Travel Editor. . . . . Kathryn McNutt

Frederick – 5,221; County: Tillman;
  DMA: Wichita Falls, TX Lawton, OK; (139)

FREDERICK DAILY LEADER (OK-D190)
P.O. Box 190   **(405) 335-2188**
Frederick, OK 73542   FAX: (405) 335-2047
Circ: (eS)3,200; **Coverage:** Tillman County; **Owner:** Donrey Media Group; **Wires:** LA Times; **Ad Rate:** $4.57
Management/News Executives:
Editor. . . . . Terri Erickson
Assistant Editor. . . . . John Banks
Editorial Page Editor. . . . . Terri Erickson
Advertising Manager. . . . . Sherri Hopkins
Circulation Director. . . . . Tammy Cox
Editors/Reporters/Columnists:
Business Editor. . . . . Terri Erickson
Features Editor. . . . . Terri Erickson
Sports Editor. . . . . John Banks

Guthrie – 10,518; County: Logan; DMA: Oklahoma City, OK; (43)

GUTHRIE LEADER (OK-D200)
107 W. Harrison   **(405) 282-2222**
Guthrie, OK 73044-4741   FAX: (405) 282-7378
Circ: (e)3,500, (S)4,200; **Coverage:** Logan County; **Owner:** Donrey Media Group; **Ad Rate:** $5.68

Figure 20.1 Sample page from *Bacon's Newspaper Directory*. It can be used to make one's own mailings or to designate editors and papers to be serviced by Bacon's distribution service. *Courtesy Bacon's Information, Inc., Chicago.*

Education Editor. . . . . Victor Dwyer (416) 596-5399
Entertainment/Arts Editor. . . . . Patricia Hluchy (416) 596-5358
Technical Editor. . . . . Mark Nichols (416) 596-6052

NEWS CANADA (34C-210)   C ✦
366 Adelaide Street W., #606   **(416) 599-9900**
Toronto, Ontario M5V 1R9 Canada   Fax: (416) 599-9700
Circ: 1,300; **Freq:** Monthly; **Uses:** Ind News, Personnel, Events, By-line,
Staff, No Photos; **Sub Rate:** 120.00.
Profile: Feature clipbook for newspapers and carries weekly columns
and seasonal sections on a variety of general interest subjects.
News Executives/Editors:
Publisher. . . . . Rod Morris
Editor. . . . . Linda Kroboth

NEWSWEEK (34C-220)   C
251 W. 57th St.   **(212) 445-4000**
New York, NY 10019-6999   Fax: (212) 445-5068
                                          E-Mail: new150a@prodigy.com
Circ: 3,100,000; **Freq:** Weekly–Mon.; **Pub:** Newsweek, Inc.; **Uses:** New
Prod, Ind News, Events, By-line, Staff, Letters, Books, Entertain, Color
Photos; **Online:** Prodigy; **Ad Rate:** $81,475; **Sub Rate:** 41.87.
Profile: Focus is on reporting and analysis of the world and the nation
through news, commentary and analysis. News is divided into national
affairs, international, business, lifestyle, society, health, science, technol-
ogy, and the arts. Opinion columns also deal with trends in politics, the
economy, current affairs and the Washington scene.
News Executives/Editors:
Publisher. . . . . Harold Shain (212) 445-4754
Associate Publisher. . . . . Gregory Osberg (212) 445-4802
Editor In Chief. . . . . Richard M. Smith (212) 445-4469
Editor. . . . . Maynard Parker (212) 445-4470
Senior Editor. . . . . Ann McDaniel (212) 445-4363
Managing Editor. . . . . Kenneth Auchincloss (212) 445-4468
Assistant Managing Editor. . . . . Alexis Gelber (212) 445-4451
Assistant Managing Editor. . . . . Sarah Crichton (212) 445-5088
Assistant Managing Editor. . . . . Mark Whitaker (212) 445-4497
Assistant Managing Editor. . . . . Evan Thomas (212) 445-4727
News Associate Editor. . . . . Paul Keating (212) 445-4242
National News Senior Editor. . . . . Jon Meacham (212) 445-4584
National News Senior Editor. . . . . Melinda Beck (212) 445-4359
National News Senior Writer. . . . . . . Tom Morganthau (212) 445-4459
International News Managing Editor . . . .
                              Kenneth Auchincloss (212) 445-4468
International News Assistant Managing Editor. . . . .
                                       Mark Whitaker (212) 445-4497
International News Senior Editor. . . . . Nancy Cooper (212) 445-4355
International News Senior Editor. . . . . Russell Watson (212) 445-4437
International News Senior Writer. . . . . Tom Masland (212) 445-4553
International News Associate Editor. . Steven Shabad (212) 445-4445
International News Associate Editor Constance Wiley (212) 445-4460
International News Writer. . . . . Tom Post (212) 445-4438
International News Writer. . . . . Mark Frankel (212) 445-5140
City News Reporter. . . . . Gregory Beals (212) 445-4453
Photography Editor. . . . . Guy Cooper (212) 445-4626
Photography Deputy Editor. . . . . Lisa Burroughs (212) 445-4705
Advertising Sales Vice President. . . . Gregory Osberg (212) 445-4802
Book Review:
  Editor. Malcolm Jones Jr. (212) 445-5110
  Senior Writer. . . . . David Gates (212) 445-4426
  Senior Writer. . . . . Laura Shapiro (212) 445-4424
Business:
  Advertising/Marketing News Senior Writer. . . . .
                                      Annetta Miller (212) 445-4583
  Banking Associate Editor. . . . . Marc Levinson (212) 445-4588
  Business Assistant Managing Editor Mark Whitaker (212) 445-4497
  Corporate Management Associate Editor. . . . .
                               Leslie Kaufman-Rosen (212) 445-4155
  Economy Senior Writer. . . . . Michael Hirsh (212) 445-4178
  Investments Contributing Editor. . . . Ellyn Spragins (212) 445-4130
  Personal Finance Associate Editor. . Dody Tsiantar (212) 445-4617
  Stock Market Senior Editor. . . . . Allan Sloan (212) 445-5567
  Calendar/Events Associate Editor. . . . . . Paul Keating (212) 445-4242
Computers/High Tech:
  Senior Editor. . . . . George Hackett (212) 445-4455
  Senior Writer. . . . . Michael Rogers (415) 658-8720
  Contributing Editor. . . . . Katie Hafner (212) 445-5509
  Contributing Editor. . . . . Steven Levy (212) 445-5503
Education:
  Senior Editor. . . . . Aric Press (212) 445-4376
  Assistant Editor. . . . . Connie Leslie (212) 445-4405
  Writer. LynNel Hancock (212) 445-4569
Entertainment/Arts:
  Senior Editor. . . . . Cathleen McGuigan (212) 445-4413
  Assistant Managing Editor. . . . . Sarah Crichton (212) 445-5088
  Theatre Critic. . . . . Jack Kroll (212) 445-4410

Classical Music Senior Writer. . . . . . . Katrine Ames (212) 445-4408
Popular Music:
  Editor. . . . . Jeff Giles (212) 445-4398
  Senior Writer. . . . . Karen Schoemer (212) 445-4285
  Senior Writer. . . . . David Gates (212) 445-4426
Fine Art Critic. . . . . Peter Plagens (212) 445-4423
Television Editor. . . . . Rick Marin (212) 445-4270
Environmental Senior Writer. . . . . Sharon Begley (212) 445-4379
Food:
  Senior Writer. . . . . Laura Shapiro (212) 445-4424
  Wine Senior Writer. . . . . Laura Shapiro (212) 445-4424
Home Building/Architecture Senior Editor . . . .
                                  Cathleen McGuigan (212) 445-4413
Legal/Legislation:
  Senior Writer. . . . . David Kaplan (212) 445-4479
  Senior Writer. . . . . Aric Press (212) 445-4376
Letters Associate Editor. . . . . Abigail Kuflik (212) 445-4409
Lifestyle:
  Assistant Managing Editor. . . . . Sarah Crichton (212) 445-5088
  Senior Editor. . . . . John Capouya (212) 445-4723
  Senior Editor. . . . . Jerry Adler (212) 445-4388
  Senior Writer. . . . . Michel Marriott (212) 445-4168
  Senior Writer. . . . . John Leland (212) 445-4401
  Family/Parenting Writer. . . . . Michele Ingrassia (212) 445-4928
  Religion Senior Writer. . . . . . . Kenneth Woodward (212) 445-4362
Medical/Health Senior Writer. . . . . . . Geoffrey Cowley (212) 445-4360
New Products Editor. . . . . Richard Ernsberger (212) 445-4209
People Associate Editor. . . . . Kendall Hamilton (212) 445-4466
Political:
  Senior Editor. Joe Klein (212) 445-4402
  Senior Editor. . . . . Jonathan Alter (212) 445-4364
  Editor. . . . . Jon Meacham (212) 445-4584
  Contributing Editor. . . . . John Sedgwick (212) 445-4000
Radio/Television/Cable Editor. . . . . Rick Marin (212) 445-4270
Real Estate Senior Writer. . . . . Annetta Miller (212) 445-4583
Science Senior Writer. . . . . Sharon Begley (212) 445-4379
Women's:
  Society:
    Assistant Managing Editor. . . . . . . Alexis Gelber (212) 445-4451
    Editor. . . . . Jean Seligmann (212) 445-4365
    Senior Editor. . . . . Aric Press (212) 445-4376
  Sports:
    Editor. . . . . Mark Starr (617) 350-0300
    Contributing Editor. . . . . Curry Kirkpatrick (212) 445-5300
Transportation Senior Editor. . . . . Hank Gilman (212) 445-4579
Travel Senior Editor. . . . . John Capouya (212) 445-4723
Washington Assistant Managing Editor Evan Thomas (202) 626-2000
General Columnist:
  "Periscope". . . . . George Hackett (212) 445-4455
  "Between the Lines". . . . . Jonathan Alter (212) 445-4364
  "Public Lives". . . . . Joe Klein (212) 445-4402
  "Cyberscope". . . . . George Hackett (212) 445-4455
  "My Turn". . . . . George Hackett (212) 445-4455

Selected Editorial Offices/Bureaus

NEWSWEEK (34C-220F)
11835 West Olympic, #870   **(310) 444-5250**
Los Angeles, CA 90064-5009   Fax: (310) 444-5287
Bureau Manager. . . . . Susan Zelman (310) 444-5290
West Coast Editor. . . . . Stryker McGuire (310) 444-5251
Photography Editor. . . . . Susan Zelman (310) 444-5290
Business Correspondent. . . . . Donna Foote (310) 444-5266
Films/Video Reviews Critic. . . . . David Ansen (310) 444-5226
Correspondent. . . . . Mark Miller (310) 444-5248
Correspondent. . . . . Andy Murr (310) 444-5257
Correspondent. . . . . Donna Foote (310) 444-5266

NEWSWEEK (34C-220H)
388 Market Street #1650   **(415) 788-2651**
San Francisco, CA 94111-5317   Fax: (415) 788-4437
Bureau Chief. . . . . Patricia King
Computers/High Tech Senior Writer. . . . . Michael Rogers

NEWSWEEK (34C-220I)
1750 Pennsylvania Ave. N.W., #1220   **(202) 626-2000**
Washington, DC 20006-4578   Fax: (202) 626-2011
Bureau Chief. . . . . Evan Thomas (202) 626-2048
Deputy Bureau Chief. . . . . Howard Fineman (202) 626-2058
Assistant Managing Editor. . . . . Evan Thomas (202) 626-2048
Bureau Manager. . . . . Gail Tacconelli (202) 626-2014
Business Correspondent. . . . . Steve Waldman (202) 626-2024
Economics Correspondent. . . . . Rich Thomas (202) 626-2028
Legal/Legislation Correspondent. . . . . Melinda Liu (202) 626-2034
Political Correspondent. . . . . Howard Fineman (202) 626-2058

Figure 20.2 Sample page from *Bacon's Magazine Directory*, which features trade publications and magazines. Information is provided to facilitate selecting distribution for each mailing. *Courtesy Bacon's Information, Inc., Chicago.*

reach many people in the area where a locally placed story would appear. Being in a national publication tends to give it greater stature in the mind of the reader. (*See* Figure 20.2.)

A network television program or widespread showing of a film or videotape show also multiplies the impact of the television showing both numerically and in influence.

Working to arrange individual placements requires the time of capable people and is the source of many complications, such as arranging to see the proper editor, waiting for a response to the inquiry, meeting further requests for added information and service, and the like. For this reason, many publicity people prefer to take the easier route of mass mailing releases, photos, films, and tapes. Once they have the material prepared, it can be turned over to the mailing department and be done with.

It is far more profitable for the publicist to spend the client's money on production and mailing than staff time on working with editors. For this reason, the organization should review the wisdom of a program in which the preponderance of effort and expense budget is devoted to mass distributions. Also, a volume of mailings *looks* like more work is done than the invisible work with editors and producers, so officials often mistake the volume for effectiveness. Local programs or others with special circumstances may justify the mass approach, and there are often merits in individual mailings when mass impact placements are not attainable. But this should not be assumed to be the case.

(Factors involved in working individually with the various media are covered in Chapters 21–26.)

Publicity alerting services

Publications that provide advance tips on which media and writers are working on stories and can use publicists' material include the following:

Bacon's Media Calendar Directory
Bacon's Publishing Company
332 S. Michigan Avenue
Chicago, IL 60604

Bull Dog Reporter
1250 45th Street
Suite 200
Emeryville, CA 94608-2924

Issues & Policy
1250 45th Street
Suite 200
Emeryville, CA 94608-2924

Party Line
35 Sutton Place
New York, NY 10022

Media Distribution Services
307 W. 36th Street
New York, NY 10018-6496

Providing spokespersons

Media often want to interview people who are authorities on a subject and who are articulate. Offering well-qualified persons in advance can often get them put on lists to be referred to when a story is breaking. A service that enables the publicist to put such persons before more than three thousand editors and broadcasters is *The Yearbook of Experts, Authorities and Spokespersons*, Broadcast Interview Source, 2233 Wisconsin Avenue, Washington, DC 20007-4104.

Lists and distribution

Lists to govern distribution of news material may require irksome detail work. Difficult enough to get at the outset, they invariably react to frequent changes in media and staff by becoming dated before one can finish them. However distressing, these annoying compilations constitute perhaps the most vital single detail of successful publicity.

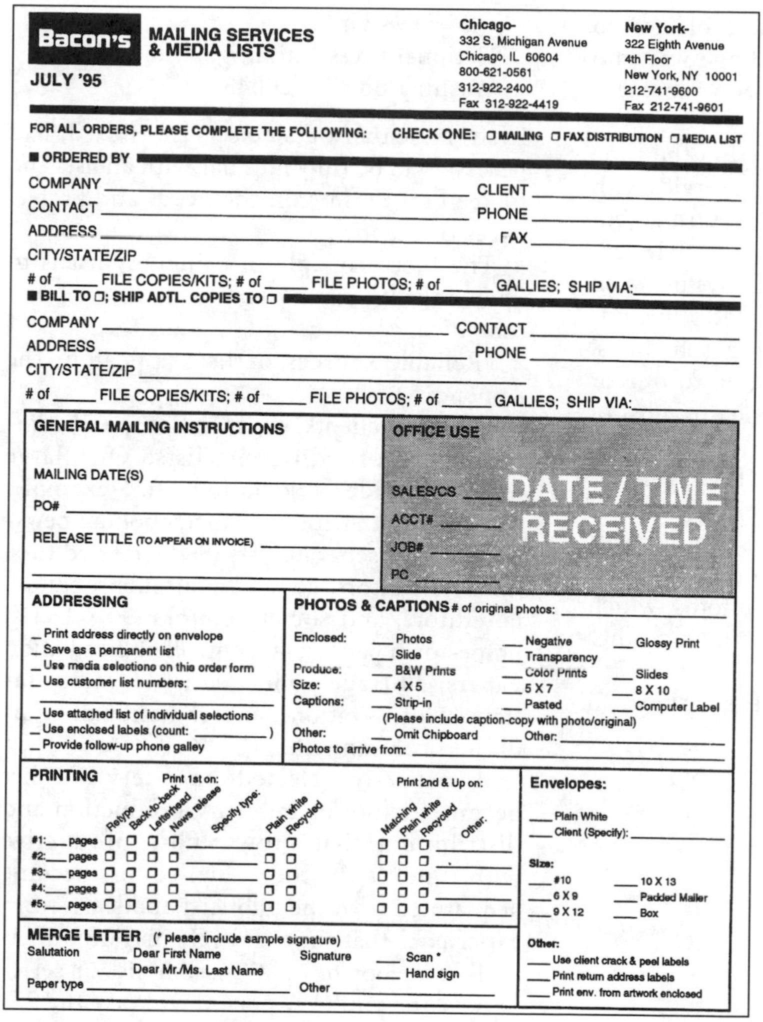

Bacon's MAILING SERVICES & MEDIA LISTS

JULY '95

Chicago-
332 S. Michigan Avenue
Chicago, IL 60604
800-621-0561
312-922-2400
Fax 312-922-4419

New York-
322 Eighth Avenue
4th Floor
New York, NY 10001
212-741-9600
Fax 212-741-9601

FOR ALL ORDERS, PLEASE COMPLETE THE FOLLOWING: CHECK ONE: ☐ MAILING ☐ FAX DISTRIBUTION ☐ MEDIA LIST

■ ORDERED BY

COMPANY ______ CLIENT ______
CONTACT ______ PHONE ______
ADDRESS ______ FAX ______
CITY/STATE/ZIP ______
# of ______ FILE COPIES/KITS; # of ______ FILE PHOTOS; # of ______ GALLIES; SHIP VIA: ______

■ BILL TO ☐; SHIP ADTL. COPIES TO ☐

COMPANY ______ CONTACT ______
ADDRESS ______ PHONE ______
CITY/STATE/ZIP ______
# of ______ FILE COPIES/KITS; # of ______ FILE PHOTOS; # of ______ GALLIES; SHIP VIA: ______

GENERAL MAILING INSTRUCTIONS

MAILING DATE(S) ______
PO# ______
RELEASE TITLE (TO APPEAR ON INVOICE) ______

OFFICE USE

SALES/CS ______
ACCT# ______
JOB# ______
PC ______

DATE / TIME RECEIVED

ADDRESSING

_ Print address directly on envelope
_ Save as a permanent list
_ Use media selections on this order form
_ Use customer list numbers: ______
_ Use attached list of individual selections
_ Use enclosed labels (count: ______)
_ Provide follow-up phone galley

PHOTOS & CAPTIONS # of original photos: ______

Enclosed: ___ Photos ___ Slide ___ Negative ___ Transparency ___ Glossy Print
Produce: ___ B&W Prints ___ Color Prints ___ Slides
Size: ___ 4 X 5 ___ 5 X 7 ___ 8 X 10
Captions: ___ Strip-in ___ Pasted ___ Computer Label
(Please include caption-copy with photo/original)
Other: ___ Omit Chipboard ___ Other: ______
Photos to arrive from: ______

PRINTING

Print 1st on: Retype, Back-to-back, Letterhead, News release, Specify type:, Plain white, Recycled
Print 2nd & Up on: Matching, Plain white, Recycled, Other:

#1: ___ pages ☐ ☐ ☐ ☐ ______ ☐ ☐ ☐ ☐ ☐ ______
#2: ___ pages ☐ ☐ ☐ ☐ ______ ☐ ☐ ☐ ☐ ☐ ______
#3: ___ pages ☐ ☐ ☐ ☐ ______ ☐ ☐ ☐ ☐ ☐ ______
#4: ___ pages ☐ ☐ ☐ ☐ ______ ☐ ☐ ☐ ☐ ☐ ______
#5: ___ pages ☐ ☐ ☐ ☐ ______ ☐ ☐ ☐ ☐ ☐ ______

Envelopes:

___ Plain White
___ Client (Specify): ______

Size:
___ #10 ___ 10 X 13
___ 6 X 9 ___ Padded Mailer
___ 9 X 12 ___ Box

Other:
___ Use client crack & peel labels
___ Print return address labels
___ Print env. from artwork enclosed

MERGE LETTER (* please include sample signature)
Salutation ___ Dear First Name ___ Dear Mr./Ms. Last Name
Signature ___ Scan * ___ Hand sign
Paper type ______ Other ______

Figure 20.3 First page of a distribution order based on *Bacon's Magazine Directory.* *Courtesy Bacon's Information, Inc., Chicago.*

There is not only a great diversity of media to be considered, but a wide range of services available to reach many of the media or to help with the production tasks. Since changes occur rapidly in this field, it is wise to check the facts about any service before using it or to recheck if it has not been used for a few weeks. Prices should be obtained for each project or assignment, or ordering should be done with purchase orders indicating that the charge is authorized.

A number of organizations have set up services to meet many of the publicist's needs. Among these are firms that maintain mailing lists and will produce and distribute releases on order. (*See* Figure 20.3.) By spreading the task and cost of maintaining lists, production equipment, and staffs among many customers, they are in a position to do the job more expeditiously, more inexpensively, and more quickly than many individual publicity offices. It is important, however, to evaluate the quality of the service, the speed, and the costs in comparison with what would be involved internally.

Also, safeguards must be set up to assure

secrecy, since personnel in these offices do work for many publicists, including some who compete with each other or who represent competitive clients.

Another factor to be weighed is the time required to reach the distribution service with the material to be processed. If it must go out of town, the unpredictability of mail service—from one day to several days between any two points in the United States, including intracity—can foil mailing schedules. Express service reduces this time to one or two days. Copy can be sent by fax to most of these services.

Each service should be individually investigated and cost quotations received. Many of the services provide forms that can be readily checked to indicate which media are to be serviced, which are to receive photos, which are to be delivered or sent by fax, and other determinations.

The following are among the services in this field are:

Associated Release Service
2 N. Riverside Plaza
Chicago, IL 60606

Bacon's Mailing Services
332 S. Michigan Avenue
Chicago, IL 60604
322 Eighth Avenue
New York, NY 10001

Derus Media Service
500 N. Dearborn Street
Chicago, IL 60610

Media Distribution Services (MDS)
307 W. 36th Street
New York, NY 10018

Metro Publicity Services
33 W. 34th Street
New York, NY 10001

PROffice's PRpro (computer access to 100,000 media contacts)
4325 E. Forbes Boulevard
Lanham, MD 20706

U.S. Newswire
National Press Building, Suite 1272
Washington, DC 20045

Even if such an outside service is used, it is necessary to be fully familiar with all lists and to keep up-to-date on the needs and preferences of the media.

The first principle in using any list is to *update the list every time it is to be used in a campaign.*

(Reliable sources of lists appear in the Appendix.)

Different clients, organizations, and campaigns require different lists. One large regional trade association, for example, requires a list including 5 metropolitan newspapers with separate lists of the city editors, financial editors, general columnists, editorial editors, and society editors; 90 selected home-town papers; 40 controlled-circulation papers; 30 trade publications; 16 radio stations; 11 TV stations; and 15 nationally syndicated columnists.

A properly selected and serviced list becomes a tool of publicity production and distribution that grows more productive with time, as the individual editors become acquainted with the publicist and learn from experience that they may rely on him or her.

To develop the best possible list or series of lists, the publicity person will take the following steps:

- Obtain the basic lists.
- Seek, compare, and analyze all available existing lists.
- Select from the classified section of the telephone directory all classifications to be included.
- Obtain as many lists as possible from such sources as large corporations, railroads, advertising agencies, trade associations, and other organizations that may have them.
- If you do not have access to a computer for lists and mailings and do not use one of the computerized mailing services, note each

of the media and names on a 3″ × 5″ card, including the medium's name, address, telephone number, fax number if any, date and frequency of publication or show broadcast, publisher's or producer's name, editor's name, name of any other key people for publicity purposes, deadline date and time, subjects covered, circulation or audience, and classification (for example, consumer interest, architecture, medicine, association, special group). Use of 3″ × 5″ cards in master lists overcomes duplication and facilitates assembly of special lists. "Working" lists can be transferred from the cards to paper with a photocopier, after which the individual cards are returned to their position in the master file. Where computer facilities are available the list can be programmed and readily corrected and updated. That can replace the 3″ × 5″ card file, because a printout can be had of the up-to-date list or any category in it whenever it is needed.

- The distribution services mentioned earlier maintain many lists. They use computers, whose efficiency is made available to each client.

- With important lists it is a wise precaution if the time is available to verify each item by telephone. Publications and other media come and go; editors and addresses change.

It is *imperative* to revise each list at least once a year and to revise it before using it in a new campaign.

Other Services

- *Directory of News Sources* lists organizations for use by journalists seeking information. National Press Building, 529 14th Street, NW, Washington, DC 20045.

- *Media Net* funnels reporters' inquiries to organizations and other sources. P.O. Box 1087, Carlisle, PA 17013.

- *Business Wire* provides electronic distribution of photos. It is at 1185 Avenue of the Americas, New York, NY 10022.

- A similar service is offered by *PR Newswire*, 810 Seventh Avenue, New York, NY 10019; *Feature Photo Service*, 62 W. 45th Street, New York, NY 10036; and *U.S. Newswire*, National Press Building, 529 14th Street, NW, Washington, DC 20045.

- Feature articles, full pages, and sections are prepared and distributed to newspapers by *Metro Publicity Services*, 33 W. 34th Street, New York, NY, 10001. Nineteen themed sections are offered annually, in which feature stories may be placed.

- *North American Precis Services*, 210 E. 42nd Street, New York, NY 10017, distributes packaged releases and illustrations to metropolitan, suburban, and rural newspapers.

Make the budget

A basic problem in any publicity campaign, or in planning a permanent publicity program, is formulating the budget. Ideally, the publicist should determine the objective, the geographical limits, the media to be used, and set the budget accordingly. Often, however, he or she will be arbitrarily limited at the outset by a maximum figure and be required to adjust efforts to the limitations of that figure.

The following elements figure in a well-balanced publicity budget:

Fee

In the case of a publicist who is the employee of an organization on a permanent basis, the salary can be anything from $500 a week to more than $150,000 a year. There is also a wide range in fees for serving an organization on a client or campaign basis. In general, it is a more satisfactory basis to stipulate a fee as the contractor's personal reimbursement and charge all expenses in addition. A package arrangement, in which a contractor undertakes to meet the expenses within an overall fee, will make the fee seem much larger than it actually is to a client and tends to lead to suspicions by the client that the contractor is skimping on expenses. (*See* Chapter 47.)

The simplest way to arrive at an equitable fee is for the publicist to figure how much he or she wishes to make for an hour of work, figure how many hours the particular contract will require, multiply the two figures, add overhead and a small margin of safety, and set the fee at the total.

There are expenses, in addition to fee, that will be encountered in publicity work.

Photographs

Photographs will usually cost not less than $20 a negative plus $1.75 or more for each 8″ × 10″ black-and-white print in addition to the first one. Many photographers quote by the day rather than by the negative. Typical rates are quoted for a half-day (often the minimum time available) or by the job (plus extra for prints). Prices in New York are considerably higher than in other parts of the country. The publicist should make arrangements with a photographer on the basis of how many pictures are to be produced and stipulate the total amount on the budget. Some photographers are willing to work on a basis of a set fee for their time plus all expenses, including travel and supplies.

For a local campaign, one different picture will be needed for each local daily with about two extra to allow for a choice by every editor. For a national campaign, one different negative will be required for each photo syndicate plus some extras to allow for choice.

Suppose the photographer charges $20 per negative plus $2 per extra print. The publicist desires to produce six picture stories. A picture story may include six versions of a single subject, each one sufficiently different to justify simultaneous publication by different editors. Six stories times six pictures is thirty-six, which multiplied by $20 would entail a total cost of $720. However, at this volume, a quantity rate often can be arranged. Allowing for emergency calls for other pictures, extra prints to take care of trade publications and contingencies, a budget figure of $900 would be in order.

A list of photographers available to publicists appears in the annual *Feature Writer and Syndicate Directory*, a part of the *Working Press of the Nation* series, 121 Chanlon Road, New Providence, NJ 07974. Names, addresses, and phone numbers of qualified photographers in various areas are available from the commercial divisions of Associated Press and United Press International.

Film footage

Television stations sometimes will accept film or videotape from a publicist to use on news programs or in local documentaries. This filming should be done in color by a professional motion-picture or television camera operator. Prices should be obtained for each assignment. (*See* Chapters 25 and 27.)

Mats and glossies

Smaller newspapers will not undergo the expense of engraving most publicity pictures, but many of the community papers like interesting photographs if sent to them in mat form. Many newspapers now use glossy proofs for offset printing. The same photographs that are produced for the metropolitan dailies offer a selection from which a photo can be chosen for reproduction into a mat or glossy proof.

Basic prices for mats and glossy proofs vary in different places. Price quotations should be obtained, including the halftone, composition, and proofs to accompany mats and to show editors what the picture looks like. With this information, the publicist can figure budgetary requirements on the basis of how many small papers are to be served, how many releases are to be distributed, and what size mats and proofs will be used. The total represents the budgetary figure for mats and proofs.

Distribution to smaller newspapers

The press associations of several states offer added service in the form of publicity release mailing service. Often, for a nominal fee, the association handles all the details of reproduction, making mats of glossy proofs, and mailing. The story and art copy with instructions as to what coverage is desired are all the publicity representative needs to supply. (For sample press releases, see Figures 20.4, page 320, and 20.5, page 321.)

If, as is necessary in some cases, the mats or glossy proofs are made by someone outside the regular service offered by the association, the only additional cost is a slight handling fee and the additional postage costs.

This system has many advantages to the publicity representative. The material is mailed to an up-to-date list on stationery from the newspaper's own organization and is therefore given priority attention almost without exception.

In addition to the state newspaper publishers' associations, other organizations are set up to perform a similar service. (*See* Chapter 22.) The publicist should contact the available service, get its rates, figure out the volume of the work, and analyze the budget figure accordingly.

Mailing

If a volume of mailing is to be done, the publicist should get in touch with the nearest postal station and inquire about pertinent details from the superintendent or the assistant in charge. It is advisable when inquiring about rates for printed matter to submit a copy to the post office rather than to ask for a telephone ruling.

The publicist should watch carefully all rules of proper addressing and packaging. He or she should be careful of colors used so they will show up well and not fade out.

Because postal rates and regulations are changed frequently, it is wise to query the post office before any large or unusual mailing, and to keep in touch with regulations.

Many services will handle large mailings of stuffers and literature for flat rates, including folding, stuffing, addressing, and actual mailing. Postage, of course, is extra. When the campaign, such as a political campaign, requires a heavy volume of such mailing, it may be advisable to engage such a service.

Production of copy

Large volumes of copy can be produced by photocopying, multigraphing, offset, letterpress printing, or other processes. (*See* Chapter 33.) Many different organizations offer these services, but each job presents an entirely separate problem. General rates are almost impossible to quote, each contract depending on such facts as which process will be used, size and grade of paper, fold, manner of stamping, current labor rates, and other factors.

Important new technology makes it possible to increase the use of material sent to newspapers that set their type by computer, whose numbers are increasing. They use "scanner-ready" copy, whereby material is transposed directly from the copy to type ready for publication. This has the added advantage of often reducing the amount of changing done by the editors.

Messenger

Messenger service is important to deliver and pick up items in a hurry, deliver copy and illustrations to city desks and broadcast stations, and many other spontaneous duties in a publicity campaign. Rates vary in different cities.

Mileage

Most publicity campaigns involve a certain amount of driving. Costs should be figured

N E W S R E L E A S E

FOR IMMEDIATE RELEASE   CONTACT: Maureen Musker
                                                                 (312) 540-4553

Bobby Sherman takes a fond look back at his life, his loves, and his sensational career in a new autobiography

Almost thirty years since he first became a generation's teen heartthrob, Bobby Sherman shares the captivating story of his life and of a remarkable era in American popular culture in his autobiography, *Bobby Sherman: Still Remembering You* (October 1996) written with journalist Dena Hill. From his television debut on "Shindig" through the phenomenal "Bobbymania" years of hit records, sold-out concerts, and a starring role in the popular television series "Here Come the Brides," Bobby Sherman details his life in the limelight: how he made it to the big time and how he kept his sanity once he got there.

A refreshing glimpse into the world of superstardom without the cynicism we've come to expect in show business, this memoir reveals the Bobby Sherman his fans hoped he was and friends always knew he was. As Bob Claver, executive producer of "Here Come the Brides" says, "Bobby's just a very good soul. There aren't a lot of people like Bobby in the entertainment business–or any other business." Even today, instead of resting on his teen idol laurels or dwelling on his "glory days," Sherman volunteers his time as an instructor of emergency medics for the LAPD. And the path that led from belting out "Hey Little Woman" for adoring fans to saving lives as an emergency medical technician is fully recounted in this fascinating autobiography.

This entertaining memoir also includes interviews with family, friends, coworkers, fans and fellow teen idols of the '60s and '70s, as well as reproductions of rare memorabilia including Bobby's *Tiger Beat* covers and articles. Packed with nearly 200 photos–many never before seen–as well as Bobby's story in his own words, this book will delight the legions of Bobby Sherman fans who may have stopped screaming but haven't stopped dreaming.

ABOUT THE COAUTHOR
Dena Hill has worked as a reporter, feature writer, and actor. She currently specializes in film and theater reviews and entertainment writing.

October / Bobby Sherman and Dena Hill / 0-8092-3206-5 / $16.95 / 8 x 10 / 240 pp (paper) / 180 b&w photos

C O N T E M P O R A R Y B O O K S

TWO PRUDENTIAL PLAZA, SUITE 1200, CHICAGO, ILLINOIS 60601-6790
(312)540-4500 FAX(312)540-4657

Figure 20.4 A press release announcing the publication of a book by a teen heartthrob of the 1970s. *Courtesy NTC/Contemporary Publishing Company.*

SALT RIVER PROJECT
P. O. Box 52025
Phoenix, AZ 85072-2025
(602) 236-5900

Richard H. Silverman
General Manager,
Salt River Project

Richard Silverman was named general manager of the Salt River Project on January 20, 1994. SRP, based in Tempe, Arizona, is one of the nation's largest public water and electric utilities, with annual operating revenues of $1.3 billion.

Since joining SRP in 1966, Silverman has served in various legal and managerial capacities, most recently, associate general manager of Law and Administrative Services.

Silverman earned his baccalaureate degree in business from the University of Arizona in 1962. He received his Juris Doctorate in 1965 from the University of Arizona.

Silverman is affiliated with the Arizona Bar Association, the Federal Bar Association, the 9th U.S. Circuit Court of Appeals, the U.S. Supreme Court and the Steering/Audit Committee of the Utility Air Regulatory Group.

Silverman is a member of the board of trustees of the Heard Museum, the Herberger Theater Center and the Barrow Neurological Institute. He is a member of the Arizona Academy. He also serves on the boards of the National Conference of Christians and Jews and the University of Arizona Foundation.

He is a board member of the American Public Power Association, the Large Public Power Committee, Western Energy Supply & Transmission (WEST Associates), Western Electric Power Institute and the Electric Power Research Institute.

Born in Chicago, Illinois, in 1940, Silverman and his wife Susan have two children: Amy and Jennifer.

Figure 20.5 This press release announcing an appointment summarizes the career of the new general manager of a utility company. *Courtesy Salt River Project.*

on a mileage basis, with allowance for likely increases in costs.

Entertainment

Many publicity campaigns involve and justify a certain amount for purchasing dinners and luncheons, and other entertainment expenses. In some instances, this item may include one or more planned dinners or cocktails parties with many persons to be present. This item can be figured out for a certain allowance and budgeted accordingly.

Models

In some publicity campaigns, it will be preferable to engage photographic models rather than to rely on volunteer models to contribute their time. In such a case, it is desirable for the publicist to inquire as to fees and make the indicated provisions. In cities where there are no model agencies, college women and women appearing in local night club shows may take freelance modeling assignments.

Clipping service

Clipping services' charges vary. The publicist can figure how many months to carry the service and allow an override for the big volume of clippings that may be expected to come in at the end. In a publicity campaign of any size, it is impossible to compute how big the bill might grow to be for the clipping service. The advisable thing to do, if this cost must be limited, is to make a flat sum arrangement with the clipping service, ordering all clippings that can be purchased up to the sum stipulated. (*See* "Press Clipping," page 331.)

In various campaigns, other charges may be involved. Sometimes the publicity director will handle an advertising campaign; the amount should be figured and broken down appropriately between the media to be used. Perhaps if a broadcast is to be arranged for a special event, several hundred dollars to more than $3,000 dollars may be required to pay the charges of installing wires, microphone,

engineers' charges, light rentals, transportation, and other items. The campaign may involve such items as automobile bumper strips, posters, outdoor advertising sheets of various sizes, display materials, props for pictures, such as costumes and special lighting, and many other details.

The *steps* in planning a budget will include the following:

1. Determine the overall figure to be allowed, or monthly allotment, if it can be set.
2. If the figure has not been set, determine the desirable figure on the basis of total budget of the enterprise, estimating objectively the work to be done.
3. List the *items* to be used in the program, including those analyzed above and any others to be employed.
4. Telephone or contact the suppliers in *each* instance to get the exact up-to-the-minute rates, including local taxes and other details.
5. Weigh the relative value of the different items in light of the total figure and with respect to their potential weight in solving the particular problem involved.
6. Total each item on the basis of the volume of it to be used.
7. Total the entire amount.
8. Allow a sum of at least 10 percent of the expense budget for miscellaneous and contingency, because in every program there will be unforeseen requirements, changes, sudden charges for important new ideas, price increases, and similar factors.

In *billing* the client, properly support each item with bills or receipts substantiating the amount claimed. Be precise and detailed. This eliminates misunderstanding.

Miscellaneous

It is well to have a fixed amount budgeted for miscellaneous expenditures, which can include such items as odd postage, supplies, petty cash items, long-distance telephone, electronic transmission of copy and releases, cab fare, purchase of and subscriptions to publications, making copies of clippings or documents, and others.

Schedule the activity

In a regular, year-round publicity assignment, the schedule will fit into the calendar of the organization. Publicity will be timed with the annual election, annual banquet, new products, special events of the organization, appointments and personnel changes, annual report, new construction, and subsidiary campaigns when called for by activities of the organization.

In scheduling a specific short-term campaign, either as part of a continuing program or an isolated one, the first step is to research the situation and accumulate as many ideas as possible. Sit down in solitude and make an unrestrained list of ideas, stories, pictures, supporting events, personalities, special media promotions, and tie-ins. Let the list cool off for a few days. Redigest it. Weed it out. Revise. Review it with a photographer, a friend, an assistant. Trim it. Eliminate ideas, add others. Then begin reorganizing the pieces, adapting them to other factors such as budget, list of media, timing, objectives.

Three separate lists are then in order. If the event is to be a pageant of national importance, for instance, the highlight event of the advance buildup may be presenting an honor award. The selection of the recipient may be the nucleus of an *event list* something like the following:

* Announcement of the contest
* Selection of district candidates
* Narrowing of the contest to forty or so candidates
* Close-up stories of the different contenders

* Choice of the seven or so finalists
* Picking the winner, putting the other six in backup roles
* Stories on the winner's activities, private life, aspirations
* Several events for the winner's appearance and participation
* Advance preparations for the presentation
* The event where the award is given

Now will come a *list of stories*. Each event on the event list is the possible nucleus of several stories. Suppose the elimination of candidates to seven finalists takes place on the beautiful lawn of a prominent local luminary. Advance stories of this semifinal elimination go to all the local papers. One day it is presented as a straight story in the general news section. Another day it is formed into material for the lifestyle pages.

Little items are offered to the columnists. Then comes The Day. The queen is named with fanfare. Cameras are clicking. The big story goes out to the papers, with negatives to place with the syndicates. Possibly some radio or TV station will dignify the event with a spot broadcast or a taping for rebroadcast that night. Maybe a TV station or local show will have a star present to confer a crown of flowers on the lucky queen, in which event their publicists and cameras will be present. The story list has anticipated this barrage of individual "breaks" built around one feature on the event list.

Closely geared in with the list of stories will be a *list of visuals*. The three lists are threaded into a master list, a "script" or "shooting schedule," which includes the timetable and assignment sheet. During the campaign, the plan may be revised daily, with substantial chunks of it torn out to make room for better ideas. Progress of a campaign and effect of outside ideas may frequently stimulate new ideas and new opportunities.

Some publicity planners overlook no detail in their advance calculations and listings. They make a cross list of publicity materials (events, copy, visuals) and days. They set down each ingredient of publicity to be used. Under each head are listed the steps to be taken, in chronological order. Under each step are listed the items necessary to complete it, and opposite each item appears the date by which it should be accomplished. After counterchecking, a datebook or flow chart is then filled in, with the details to be disposed of on each date enumerated under that day on the calendar. After such a blueprint has been perfected, execution is the only remaining required step in the campaign. (*See* Figure 39.2 in Chapter 39.)

Many new things will come up, but the more smoothly the campaign is planned, the more smoothly things will run. A big backlog of material is stabilized and ready. No matter what emergencies develop, the fundamentals are organized and the machinery is purring. Crises, last-minute switches, protests of activists, or disruptions of nature and human temperament do not often retard an organized publicity machine.

It is better to overplan than to underplan. The more of a "stockpile" of pictures and stories the publicist can build up in advance, the surer he or she is of impact and volume in the closing rush. It is better to throw away some of this material than to miss major opportunities because needed materials are not available.

Obtaining Approvals

All materials prepared in a communications program should receive the approval of an authorized executive of the organization on whose behalf they are to be issued. The process for obtaining approval varies greatly between organizations and depends on the nature of the material.

Material originating within the organization is usually submitted for approval and verification to the executive in charge of the function involved. For instance, a press release about a company's quarterly earnings is likely to be approved by the treasurer, who may also submit it to the chief executive officer or other executive. Photographs and captions on a new product are likely to be approved by the head of marketing for the division responsible for that product, who may also call for the approval of the division's top executive.

Approval involves making certain that the facts, quotations, and other content are accurate and have the support of the management. It also alerts those who see the material to what is to be released so they can handle inquiries from the media properly.

Material originating with an outside firm is usually submitted for approval to the public relations liaison person within the client organization. He or she then approves it or submits it to the executives who would receive it if it had been prepared internally.

In most organizations the approver is asked to initial the copy he or she has seen and return it. This is a way to make certain any changes are made as the approver has indicated, and that the initialed record of the approval process is in the file in case any question should arise.

When the final version of the material—press release, photographs and captions, literature, speeches—is produced, copies are sent to those who approved it and to others in the organization who need to know what is involved. In the case of films, videotapes, and other materials requiring special handling, the executives are usually invited to a screening or told that the material is available for their review on request.

File Organization

Materials to be filed tend to become voluminous. For efficiency in keeping track of information and activities, as well as to assure accurate records for verification and reports, files should be set up carefully. The following are included in a basic filing system:

1. Background information on the organization and its activities, source materials, reference materials, information on opposition groups and competitors, and so on.

2. All manuscripts prepared in the program —press releases, backgrounders, speeches, TV and film scripts, and others. Each should include at least one copy of the final manuscript, corrected copies of the manuscript as received from approvers, source materials used, references to sources contacted, and a copy of the distribution order.

3. Photographs and other illustrative material. (*See* Chapter 21.)

4. Correspondence, memos, and other materials exchanged with executives, sources, or others.

5. Legal records, such as model releases, lawyers' approvals, and documents to and from government agencies.

6. Copies of reports about the program.

7. Copies of finished materials—copies of booklets and financial reports, newspaper and magazine clippings, transcripts or reports on television and radio coverage achieved.

8. Bills, purchase orders, and other records of payments and expenses.

Event Coordination

Special events are acts of *news development*. The ingredients are time, place, people, activities, drama, and showmanship. One special event may have many subsidiary events, such as luncheons, banquets, contests, speeches, and many others, as part of the buildup.

The special event is the *coup de maitre* of publicity, propaganda, and public relations. From the launching of a man into space to prove a nation's prowess in science to the yearly Oscar Awards presentation in California, from a state band competition in Chicago to a scout jamboree in Maine, the special event is a publicity splash. Done on a major scale, it includes and involves all the tools and techniques of publicity.

A special event involves a mass of details skillfully blueprinted, presented, dramatized, and reported.

An entire book is not big enough to include a fully detailed checklist for special events. They follow certain elements of a formula. The prime rule is to check details with precedent, with each other, and with the world about, in order to avoid conflict, to assure acceptability, and to synchronize so that the end product is integrated and will function.

The elements of a special event are the basic "news questions" with which all journalists are familiar.

- **What?** Name of event, its scope, necessary buildup, budget, elements of program
- **Why?** Purpose and objective
- **When?** Full schedule of timing, with deadlines for each preliminary, all worked out as to dates and hours
- **Where?** Geographic locale, facilities, including ample facilities for every detail necessary to complete functioning
- **Who?** Who will engineer, star, be invited, attend, follow up?
- **How?** How will all these things be done?

Publicity arrangements for an event include the following:

- Advance planning for full coverage
- Announcements by press, TV, radio, magazines, direct mail, outdoor advertising, and other media
- Stockpile of stories, pictures, features

- Mechanical arrangements for coverage— press room, typewriters, computers, telephones, fax, accommodations for press, provisions for photography, wiring for radio and TV, quiet room for interviews

- Information arrangements—advance copies of speeches and reports, programs, interviews, press conferences

- Checking coverage—staffer to check details, photographer to get pictures for distribution afterward to publications not taking their own pictures

- Follow-up—thank-you notes, scrapbook, final report

The most important detail of publicity and special events is staffing. People with the know-how and sense of responsibility to follow through are the keys to any planned human activity.

Special events of every description—even summit meetings of presidents and premiers—are created to tell a public relations story and influence public opinion. They serve as media in themselves and as focal points for other media. A major special event will merit coverage by press, radio, television, and magazines to further the impact beyond the actual on-the-spot audience.

Major forms of special events are

- **Shows, displays, and exhibits** ranging in magnitude from world fairs to local trade shows limited to commercial audiences.

- **Road shows** packed and put on the road for reshowing in numerous locations.

- **Fairs,** of which more than 2,200 are annually presented in the United States before combined audiences of some 90 million.

- **Parades, pageants, and processions**, such as the Tournament of Roses.

- **Mass demonstrations** and entertainment events, such as demonstrations against segregation.

- **Athletic competition** with sideline effects of showmanship.

- **Commercial displays** in store windows, inside of stores, and on thoroughfares. These may be tied in with fiestas as is done in Southern California communities to commemorate the region's early Spanish traditions. Christmas decoration of a commercial center constitutes another example.

- **Stunts**, such as miniature parades, gags like marching an elephant down the street, and such devices as massed flights of airplanes and a massed review of ships.

- **Banquets and luncheons**, attracting a large number of people and providing a sounding board for the expression of certain ideas by certain leaders.

- **Meetings**, both with and without food and drink, ranging from small and confidential affairs not designed for publicity to elaborate convocations that every medium in town will want to cover.

- **Conferences and conventions** usually offer productive publicity possibilities because of the large number of people attracted from distances, and the substantial number of leaders who come to address such an audience. "An expert is a man away from home," it has been said. A fellow who may be quite ordinary or at best only human at home in Chicago or New York or Seattle is sometimes made into a one-day minor prophet by performances and utterances while traveling in a distant section.

With proper coverage, the convention is a sure springboard of man-made news covering as many localities as may be represented by delegates. The formula for covering a convention, properly adapted, is an effective blueprint for covering most special events.

Press room

Set up near headquarters with plenty of telephones, computers and printers, copiers, tables, and supplies. At big conventions, a fax machine may be most helpful. Remember to have special wiring that may be needed for TV lighting, a tape recorder or two, a bulletin board to post messages for reporters, a display of speech manuscripts, releases, photos, and other materials for the visitors to choose from. Often neglected is a quiet room where TV and radio interviews can be held without background noises interfering. Often there is also need for another small room where an official and one reporter can have a private discussion.

Personnel

This press room should be manned at all times by at least one informed person capable of answering questions, rendering service, and getting information. Frequently a local business college or school of journalism will furnish such helpers—who sometimes are glad to serve for the experience.

Advance copies

More than anything else, reporters will welcome and appreciate advance copies of speeches and reports. Advance copies are the hardest of props to obtain, because many speakers prefer to speak from notes or extemporaneously and will not undertake to make copies; and other speakers do not get the copies in on time. Such copies will greatly facilitate the work of both reporters and publicists and will probably multiply the results obtained. Advance film footage helps TV coverage.

Press memos

Daily or even more frequent last-minute round-up memos of what will happen during the day to come assist in the coverage. When possible, it is well to furnish city desks, syndicates, and broadcasting news rooms before the convention opens with a complete agenda of the proceedings, and copies of printed programs, if any.

Badges and tickets

Plenty of badges and tickets for every session, luncheon, banquet, and party will be appreciated by news representatives.

Committee helpers

Local members "in the know" can be helpful by cooperating in helping reporters make connections. A major convention is bound to be too big for a single reporter or publicist to handle, and indeed some of them have squadrons of publicists and several details of reporters and photographers from major metropolitan dailies and news services.

Messengers

It is a helpful service to make messengers available to deliver telephone messages from city desks of the newspapers to working reporters, to deliver rush stories and art from reporters and photographers to their editors, and to perform other duties that require quick action.

Liaison

The publicity department may serve the media by remaining in constant touch with all departments of the convention so that any sudden newsworthy event or last-minute change will be reported reliably and rapidly to the media. Frequently spot news, elections, resolutions, and similar features will require instant action.

Celebrities

Provision should be made for setting up press interviews with celebrities, speakers, and other dignitaries who may attend the convention.

Convention newspaper

Publishing a daily paper during the convention can not only increase interest among attendees. It can help focus media attention on the most significant news possibilities.

Publishing a newspaper requires early arrangements for printing and distribution at the site, plus staff and equipment. Large conventions may assign the job to outside specialists, such as Atwood Convention Publishing, Overland Park, Kansas.

Special events

In addition to the type of event described above, many publicists build stories or features around special "days" and "weeks," such as Law Day or Music Week.

A primary benefit of such observances is getting people who are directly concerned with the activity involved and aware. In addition, publicity possibilities often make an impact on outside publics.

Such a "day" or "week" is made the climax for numerous subsidiary events. Committees develop phases of the observance. Meetings, luncheons, banquets, speeches, queens, picture ideas, and special "propaganda" stories are part of the technique.

These special "days" and "weeks" can be springboards for the so-called *propaganda* type of publicity—legitimate publicity planned to instill an idea with the public for general observance throughout the year.

The formula for this publicity is the established general publicity formula: create news. Develop events that attract names and manufacture news ipso facto.

Another form of special event is the *observance*, such as laying cornerstones for new buildings, placing tablets on completed buildings, presenting awards, and unveiling statues and plazas. Observances are constantly built into events for stimulating popular interest and publicity coverage.

Observances of this type are symbolic events betokening accomplished facts. The technique is to build a program around the symbolic event, to assemble prominent personages, and to have one or more speeches delivered to convey thoughts appropriate to the occasion. The necessary element of drama is provided by the prominence of the leading participants and by showmanship in the decorations and music.

Typical observances, with important effect in their respective locales, are America's thousands of graduation ceremonies.

A peculiar and colorful form of special event is the *stunt* created strictly as a feature vehicle of sufficient human interest to qualify picture and story material for widespread publication and broadcast.

Special events tell the story of the sponsoring organization and/or area while they furnish a setting for the presentation of features by many individual sponsors who join the overall events as a medium for telling their individual stories. For example, a major industrial exposition may be sponsored by several cooperating trade associations. Each sponsoring organization will benefit from this opportunity to dramatize its story to the public. Hundreds of exhibitors will benefit from the opportunity of presenting their particular story and product. All of the sponsors and exhibitors will pool their efforts and money to produce an overall show and an overall publicity campaign that attracts strong public interest.

The public relations effect is extended not only by news coverage through established media, but through tie-ins of all kinds, such as travel advertising to bring in people from elsewhere, inserts in mailings, marking on auto license plates, stickers, bumper strips, soap wrappers, and many other devices for projecting the story to more people. A network TV program may be imported in its entirety to the show for a run of several days, providing substantial exploitation benefits to the event, TV network, and sponsor. Half-price tickets to the show may be distributed to hundreds of thousands of people, enclosed with monthly statements through arrangement with a major utility or department store.

The special event may be a tour, such as the numerous tours of editors and writers conducted by the National Aeronautics and Space Agency as pilgrimages to its facilities at Houston. Many tours are sponsored by hotels interested in publicizing new resort sites.

Publicizing Products

Most publicity activity on behalf of a firm's products or services generally follows the patterns of publicity. (*See* Chapter 14.) There are a few principles, however, that are distinct to product publicity.

When planning product publicity, it is most important to base the approach on the status of the product, as determined by one of these three basic conditions:

1. The product starts a whole new field; it performs a function not performed by anything else. In this case, the primary objectives should be (a) to preempt the concept of that product for the manufacturer and (b) to stir potential purchasers' desire for what it will do.

2. If the product is an advance in an established field, the publicity should focus sharply on the new features.

3. If the product features nothing particularly new or unique—if it is mature and established—associate it with characteristics the public is interested in. Ceramic tile for years was publicized in stories about keeping bathrooms and kitchens clean to protect health or enabling the homemaker to do the cleaning with a minimum of work. Maytag developed plans for many types of "model laundry rooms" because it found few homes had sensible provision for this second-most-demanding task. Of course, cosmetics, deodorants, fashions,

and jewelry base their publicity on desire for social acceptability.

Samples and giveaways

There is a fine line between graciousness to the media and implied attempts at bribery. When a new product is being introduced to the press, samples are usually in order when they are modest in value and especially when using them for a while is important in evaluating the product. Thus it may be appropriate in introducing a new hair spray to give a container of it to each editor or writer contacted. But it would be inappropriate to give out samples of a new television set.

There are pitfalls in product sampling, as well as ethical questions. When Milton Reynolds introduced the first ballpoint pens in the United States at a retail price of $15, he gave them out to media people all over the country as if they cost a few cents to make (which they did). This helped generate a vast amount of publicity—partly because the new writing instruments intrigued hundreds of people who wrote for a living, but also because a large proportion of the pens failed to write.

Giving away products in return for publicity is another technique with both ethical and practical considerations. Working with television and radio giveaway shows is a special field (*see* Chapter 25) with established rules and avenues to pursue. Some newspapers and individual broadcasting stations occasionally will run "auctions" in which they turn over the proceeds to charities or their own public service projects. They auction off products they obtain free from manufacturers who seek both product publicity and a slight aura of service from cooperating. So long as these arrangements are open and generally known, no onus attaches to them. They can be judged on their merits as publicity vehicles.

Some professionals feel that having a product frequently identified as a giveaway demeans the product in public esteem. Something that is so often seen being given away may not seem attractive enough to pay substantial amounts for.

Media of Publicity

Media are the tools by which an organization tells its story to the public. Just as different weapons are needed to fight a war, different media are needed to solve different problems—to fight a political campaign, support a sales program, win a community's goodwill, or explain the client's viewpoint in a dispute.

As the weapons of war have advanced from the spears and swords of the old days to the missiles and H-bombs of today, so have media advanced from letters and signs and speeches to include radio, television, computers, fax, and the Internet.

But just as the slogging foot soldier carrying a sharp dagger is still important in our army, speeches, pronouncements, and signs are still fundamentals of modern public relations. New media will command attention and offer variations of attack, but the old and basic media of word-of-mouth and person-to-person communication remain necessary to attain the objective.

Detailed reviews of the various publicity media are given in following chapters.

Rumor Control

Any organization or individual that gains public attention is likely to encounter rumors that can be at least annoying and at worst severely damaging. Coping with them is the most nebulous aspect of the communications operation.

Rumors can arise from seemingly frivolous causes. Members of the British Parliament began to receive letters charging that McDonald's, the hamburger chain, was supporting the Irish Republican Army (IRA), which was attacking British soldiers and civilians. A search discovered that the Cable News Network (CNN) in the United States had carried a story on IRAS, Individual Retirement Accounts. McDonald's was mentioned as a firm especially generous in contributing to its employees' IRAS. Some British viewers had picked up that CNN story by satellite. McDonald's was able to scotch that rumor before it became damaging.

Procter & Gamble was not so fortunate. For many years its logotype included a profile of the man in the moon plus a group of stars. Religious fundamentalists started the rumor that this was P&G's way of denoting that it supported devil worship. It took several years and a lot of money—plus modification of its logo—before the company was able to dispel the rumor.

Particularly when a publicity program is about to increase an organization's visibility, or when it is about to enter a controversial area, it is wise to take precautionary steps to cope with rumors.

1. **Establish a rumor center.** Someone should be assigned to this responsibility on a constant basis. All members or staff people should be alerted to report any rumors they hear, and to enlist their friends to call their attention to reports that may be true or false.

2. **Send out the facts.** When a rumor develops that is erroneous, even if it may not be harmful in its original form, consider disseminating correct information without referring to the substance of the rumor. Be sure this will not give more exposure to the rumor itself. That may

forestall the spreading and cumulative distorting of the rumor.

3. **Consider holding a news conference.** If the rumor is important and the consequences are serious, it may justify calling the media together to get the facts, ask questions, and clear up the situation. The exposure of reporters to this exposition of the information will also help forestall the circulation of other rumors of a similar type.

4. **Get a third-party spokesperson to comment.** If the rumor deals with a matter that puts the organization's own credibility in doubt, ask a respected person who is not directly associated with the organization to scotch the rumor.

5. **Give the facts and demonstrate the truth.** Don't just issue a denial or repeat previous statements. Present the facts fully. If possible, show that the reports are false. Many a politician has disproved rumors about estrangement from his wife by having her prominently with him on a long trip or vacation.

Professor Frederick Koenig of Tulane University, a specialist in dealing with rumors, advises: "Ride it out. Trace its origins. Treat it locally. Rebut it with facts—but don't deny a rumor before the public hears about it."

Press Clipping

The most helpful tool in arranging a report of publicity results is the press clipping bureau, which will furnish clippings from newspapers and publications over a given area, whether international, national, or local, for fees based on the nature of the service contracted. (*See* Figure 20.6, page 332.)

Clipping bureaus may be divided into four classes: national, sectional, state, and specialized. In the United States, there are about fifty such companies. (A list of clipping bureaus is in the Appendix.)

Uses of clippings

There are literally hundreds of uses that can be made of a clipping service. It can provide any information appearing in the press, and it can be adapted to almost any need.

A director of public relations of a business or enterprise that is subject to legislative attacks or that, for any reason, must be sensitive to public opinion, will find the clipping service an invaluable tool to watch for all rumors that may lead to the type of action against which he or she is entrusted to safeguard. A clipping service acts as a watchdog in detecting the sources of such rumor, or the beginnings of such agitation. For example, a clipping of a report of a resolution passed at a local club meeting may reveal a move that has serious possibilities and may be adjusted to or stopped in the beginning by prompt and diplomatic action.

Publicity should be carefully planned to accomplish a specific objective. Clippings and broadcast reports are a measure of the degree of its success. If the objective is to reach a given public or constituency, the clippings will show whether the stories have been published in the papers of the area where the constituents reside, as well as in the papers they read. For example, a West Coast industry that has numerous heavy stockholders in the New England states may desire, through financial news in the papers of that area, to keep the stockholders informed about their investments. Clippings indicate the extent to which the released material is reaching the desired audience.

If the subject featured is controversial and of wide interest, clippings of editorial comment and letters to the editors provide an index of public opinion, as well as indicate the points of misunderstanding. This infor-

Figure 20.6 Sample of a display of clippings included in a report. This one, with samples of publicity received by Sanford Corporation, features a wide variety of subjects and publications. *Courtesy Sanford Corporation.*

mation will help determine the nature of future releases.

Publicity that endeavors to keep a certain name before the public in the best light and as constantly as possible should, obviously, be directed toward the greatest circulation. The success of publicity cannot be gauged entirely by the number of clippings. The summary must include the types and circulation figures of the papers from which the clippings are taken. Some clipping services show circulation figures on the tab that identifies each clipping. (The final and vital determinant of what effect the publicity has on the readers depends on still further factors. These require assessment of the psychological response. *See* Chapters 3, 18, and 49.)

If publicity is designed to create interest in a coming event, a required volume of stories and pictures about the event may be scheduled well in advance of the opening date. An actual ratio is sometimes established between the volume of good publicity attained at a given point on the calendar and the volume in gate receipts when the event opens. For example, a large annual event such as a county fair may, after maintaining clipping records for a number of years, determine the volume of publicity necessary a month prior to the opening to assure the desired volume in gate receipts.

Assuming that a clipping service is reasonably complete, even the absence of clippings on a given story can be a means to a worthwhile saving. The results may indicate that the story is not properly written and that considerable time, materials, and postage are being wasted in sending out such stories. Careful study may show that a different slant, more brevity, better photography, or other improvements get better results.

Anyone contemplating use of a clipping service must be cautioned that, at best, they are seldom more than 35 percent efficient. On national coverage, they frequently find no more than 25 percent of all stories appearing on a given subject. For this reason, if the budget permits, it is wise to employ two or more services. The duplication of clippings probably will not be great.

An aid in using clippings is a computer service that scans, indexes, and stores clippings. It is offered by SpinWARE (305) 254-5664. By entering information on the project or client and specifying criteria, an immediate report can be printed out.

PROffice offers CLIPpro, which permits scanning clippings, importing others on-line, and archiving them. Call (800) 345-5572.

Broadcast and Composite Reports

Broadcasts, unlike press material, leave no ready record to be gathered in. The broadcast signal goes out into the air and is lost forever unless special effort is made to retain it—either in the form of a tape or videotape of the original, or in an audited report from a listener or viewer.

When the publicist knows in advance that a broadcast will use material, he or she can often arrange to order a tape, film, or videotape.

Videotape reports of most programming on news, public affairs, and talk shows in major cities are available from Video Monitoring Services of America, 330 W. 42nd Street, New York, NY 10036, (212) 736-2010, an affiliate of Burrelle's Clipping Services. It maintains offices in major cities across the United States. Another is Radio-TV Reports, 317 Madison Avenue, New York, NY 10017, (212) 309-1400. It also has branch offices. Monitoring is also done by Nielsen News Media Research—SIGMA, 375 Patricia Avenue, Dunedin, FL 34698, (813) 734-5473; and Broadcast Information Services, 340 S. Potomac Way, Suite E, Aurora, CO 80012, (800) 359-1205.

Periodic or terminal reports on a publicity operation are important. Creation of a scrapbook, a report, or a summary of results, plus recommendations for the future help assure clear understanding of the program by management, and serve as guides for continued efforts. Things to do may include the following:

1. Prepare a scrapbook of all clippings, TV reports, radio scripts, tapes, and photos of exhibits, displays, and signs.

2. Prepare a written report of results and accomplishments. The results should be neither interpreted nor reported in terms of column inches, total pages, and other quantity standards. The results of publicity and its quality, what it says and not how much, are what count. Above all, reference should never be made to whatever dollar volume in advertising the publicity might be thought to approximate. This represents a conception of publicity as "free advertising," which is completely false. Publicity is news of interest to many people and should be so regarded. A report that "so-and-so many inches were obtained, or an equivalent of so-and-so many dollars in paid advertising" is meaningless and misleading. Money could not buy the coverage under any circumstances. Most publicity coverage is more effective in influencing opinion or behavior than advertising.

3. Organize and winnow the "morgue" of information, notes, and papers for future guidance.

4. Organize and winnow the "morgue" of photographs, many of which will be useful in the future.

5. Draw an outlined plan and schedule for future activities, including suggestions of things to be avoided and suggestions for new approaches or themes to be adopted.

21
RELATIONS WITH PUBLICITY MEDIA

PHILIP LESLY

As the liaison between the organization that employs him or her and the media, the publicist's long-term effectiveness depends on his or her ability to satisfactorily represent the employer while meeting the needs of the various media. Accordingly, the publicist serves as a catalyst that influences both parties with which it deals without being unduly influenced by either.

In terms of dealing with the client, the publicist must use sound journalistic integrity—including (a) strongly advocating the fullest disclosure feasible, (b) securing the availability of company officials, and (c) responding promptly to the media. It also requires being fair, frank, accommodating, and conscientious with the media.

This balanced role can be accomplished only through employing sound judgment and absolute integrity with all concerned parties, and with experience. The publicist who compromises these principles is likely to find herself without media alliances—or an employer.

An effective publicist, or publicity staff, embodies these combined characteristics:

- Sound editorial judgment—with the diversity and versatility to apply to a great variety of media.

- Creativity—with the capability to identify and define the interesting, the unique, or the significant in any subject that arises.

- Communication skills—with strong writing ability, a sense for graphics, and an ear for oral communication.

- High productivity and motivation.

- Thorough knowledge of all types of communications media covered in this book—including how they work, as well as their needs, specialties, and standards.

- Initiative in working within the organization and in approaching the media.

- Media acceptance—earned on the basis of respect and confidence. The closer the relationship, the better; however, social acquaintance is no substitute for skill and integrity.

- Adequate physical resources and budget to do the job—directories, lists, access to sources and services, handbooks, equipment, telephone and fax service, funds for necessary travel, etc.

The Media's Autonomy

In the United States and virtually any free society no other entity, no faction of society, wields more sovereignty than does the independent communications medium. Presidents rail against their impotence with Congress, bureaucracies, and the media. Industrial tycoons deal with restrictions imposed by multiple government agencies, the

335

courts, the media, and labor unions. Such is not the case for an individual newspaper, magazine, broadcasting station, and trade publication—which often can, and do, operate with Olympian independence. Even if their actions do cost them a subscriber or an advertiser or two, most media—especially those with little or no direct competition—barely feel the loss.

As a result, as well as because of the media's inherent power, they sometimes seem almost exempt from the give-and-take accommodations placed on most individuals and institutions in our country.

Consequently, it stands to reason that the relationship between a source of information and the medium is not an equal two-way pattern. In most cases, the medium has absolute control over what material it uses, and when and how it uses it. The only substantial determinants are the medium's editorial judgment and attitudes, however they may differ from those of the organization.

Although all responsible media operate on a policy of accuracy and fairness, and will often correct (inconspicuously, usually) proven errors, the organization has little other recourse to counter the media's negative judgment or treatment toward them. Both the publicist and the employer must recognize this sovereignty held by the media—and that no one can argue with a printing press or a broadcast tower.

Though this presents problems it is integral to a free press. The media must remain as independent as possible from all sources of pressure; inevitably, this independence sometimes translates into what would otherwise be considered arrogance.

Media that operate in an honorable manner far outweigh those occasional few exceptions that distort the context, whether by omission or commission, or that bow to the pressures of major advertisers. People have a keen sense for who they can most respect and typically help make these individuals or organizations more successful. Therefore, much diversity and competition among the media are needed to ensure that all organizations have access to multiple and varying information choices, as well as to ensure against any medium becoming entirely sanguine in its omnipotence.

Methods for Working with Media

Three basic patterns exist for working with the media, which are as follows:

1. Responding to the requests of the communications media. This passive, service function calls for having organized information and sources, then conscientiously responding to the initiatives of those to be served.

2. Arranging for media coverage and dissemination of information on events and the routine output of the organization. This calls for constant awareness of the news-making functions within the organization and of routine channels of contact with the media, but it is essentially a passive function.

3. Using initiative to stimulate the media to carry the organization's information and viewpoint. This calls for creative development of ideas and concepts, maintaining and nurturing respected liaison with hundreds of media people and writers, and using constant initiative to make them receptive to the organization's ideas and materials.

Although all of these are important, only a minority of publicity staffs do an effective job on all three. Standard use of the third method in particular usually marks the exceptionally effective operation.

Media people have the same basic motivations as other people. The surest way to gain their coverage is to relate a subject to their self-interest. For instance, the general attitude of the media toward crime was that it attracted an audience and was the fault of society—until media people became victims. Not until editor Peg Murphy and Patricia Hearst were kidnapped and reporter Don Bolles was blown up in his car while working on an exposé did the media begin to demand that crime be reduced and the culprits be severely punished. Similarly, it was not until editors found they could not find applicants who could write well that the media began to expose the decline of the nation's schools.

Disseminating Information

There are many ways to disseminate information—the most prevalent being news conferences, media briefings, and press showings.

News conferences

The most recognized publicity activity is to call together various media representatives—a technique well known to the public due to its heavy use by heads of state and the media's extensive reporting of it. When they have something to report, executives and publicity people often immediately turn to this method; consequently, it is overused.

The media meeting should be considered from the viewpoint of media people first. To call a news conference or briefing that ten or more media people will attend means a composite of many hours of expensive staff time, transportation, and shifting of schedules.

Accordingly, the first rule with regard to *news conferences* is to call a media meeting only if it will be of real service to the media and provide them with something they could not get in simpler ways. They should find it

beneficial by getting more information or illustrations than they could get in releases and advance photos, by being able to probe an important subject by getting substantive answers to their questions, by meeting really important people who are likely to be newsworthy in the future, by being able to explore important plans, or by seeing a new building or product that must be seen to be fully understood.

A second rule is that a news conference should be called in the case of a major news event, such as a violent disruption, a major accident, the sudden death of a top official, or some other emergency. It should help forestall rumors and confusion by presenting the facts, affording an opportunity to answer questions, and clarifying rumors.

Third, in general the location should be wherever it is best for the media people. The organization's office—boardroom, conference room, auditorium—is good if it is convenient to those who are invited or necessary because of availability of materials that cannot readily be moved. Otherwise it is best to hold it in a central place. The city in which the organization is located is generally best, because the local media are the most concerned and most likely to deal with it. However, New York, Chicago, Washington, DC, or another metropolitan center with heavy media representation may be desirable if the news is of major importance and the home city is not suitable for the media who will want to cover it. (Always be sure the evaluation of the news is *objective* and not colored by internal wishes or hopes.)

Sometimes it is wise to consider simultaneous news conferences in two or more places. For instance, some organizations will have some executives meet the local media in their hometown while national media meet other executives in New York.

This has been carried further by using closed-circuit television to hold simultaneous meetings in several cities. Firms that arrange for such events include the following:

Beach Associates
200 N. Glebe Road, Suite 720
Arlington, VA 22203

Chanticleer Communications
8760A Research Boulevard, Suite 510
Austin, TX 78758

J-Nex Television
5455 Wilshire Boulevard, Suite 2010
Los Angeles, CA 90036

Medialink
708 Third Avenue
New York, NY 10017

A good hotel with quiet meeting rooms and good service is a logical choice if the meeting is to be held away from headquarters. A club is suitable if it has no rules against women or minority-group members, who now make up a substantial portion of media staffs.

Fourth, facilities should be planned to meet the needs of both print and broadcast media. It may be desirable to have two separate rooms, so the broadcast people can have quiet surroundings and access to authorized spokespeople while the print people listen to others. Or, if urgency is not overriding, there should be two sessions, with the print media usually first. In either case, these arrangements should be explained in the invitations and at the start of the conference.

There should be ample seating to ensure that all who come have seats within good hearing and seeing range. Coffee, tea, and soft drinks should be available, with rolls if the conference is in the morning. It is usually best not to serve lunch at a news conference, unless it is something of a socializing event, or the urgency of it coincides with lunchtime. In that case, it will probably be best to have a variety of sandwiches and salads, rather than a leisurely meal.

Cocktails should be served, usually, only if socializing is part of the occasion or (as explained later) the event is a briefing or introduction.

A convenient coatroom should be near the entrance and well staffed so the guests will have a minimum wait either arriving or leaving. Ensure that no tipping is permitted and that a large sign to that effect is clearly visible.

If transportation is needed by any of the guests, arrange to have it available and explain it in the invitation. For instance, out-of-town press people sometimes will not have ready transportation available to and from the airport. If the organization's office is in a suburb or a small town, transportation may be needed from the nearby transportation center.

An ample number of telephones should be nearby, and the switchboard should be prepared for a sudden heavy load.

If possible, fax service should be available to those who want to transmit their stories to their offices.

It is often desirable to make a tape recording or videotape of the session. It can be referred to later by media people who want to check exact quotations or statements; it can provide a record of what the management said for review when memories are fuzzy or commitments are being checked. It also affords a record in case the Securities and Exchange Commission, the Anti-Trust Division, the National Labor Relations Board, a court, or other government body questions what occurred.

Fifth, developing the invitation list calls for balancing various judgments and considerations. Invite everyone who regularly reports on the organization or who has a regular interest in the subject of the conference. That will include specialists in the organization's field, local media, trade press in fields the organization serves, and so on. No one should be omitted because of hard feelings, personal quirks, or arbitrary numbers.

If the news is strong enough to go beyond this group, all categories of media should be sifted: newsmagazines, other magazines of various types, television and radio news departments, foreign-language, and other minority media. A list should be made up especially for the occasion, since each news event has its own characteristics.

In the case of newspapers in the area, the invitation should go to the city editor. A backup invitation may go to a staff person who regularly covers the organization, indicating that the city desk has also received an invitation. Out-of-town newspaper outlets and magazines should be addressed to the managing editor, with backup invitations to specific individuals where desirable.

Sixth, invitations may be sent in various ways, depending on the time needed, the extent of the list, and other factors:

- A **letter** from the president of the organization or the public relations director. It should contain all information about the meeting and give enough information about what will be covered to enable the recipient to judge its importance. The letter calls for individual typing and personal signature.

- A **memo** to editors that may be mass-produced and consists of at least the essential information.

- A **fax** should be faster and receive greater attention from the recipient. (When sending material by fax or E-mail it's wise to ask the recipient for permission in advance.)

- **Public relations newswires** (*see* Chapter 22) can reach most of the media in major cities in a short time. Those not on the wires' lists can then be covered in separate fax or telephone contacts.

- If time is vital, if manpower is available to disperse the number of calls, if the content

of the invitation can be covered easily without laboriously spelling out details, and if most media people can be reached at convenient times, **telephone** is the surest means. E-mail can greatly ease the workload.

The invitations to the print and broadcast media should set different times if two sessions are to be held.

If it is important to know approximately how many will attend, it is permissible to ask for a reply. A return postcard or form may be enclosed with mailed invitations.

A prudent and gentle follow-up by telephone the day before the event to those not yet heard from is usually acceptable.

Invitations that try to be cute or to command attention through novelty are like humor in other forms: helpful if very good but chilling if they are not.

Seventh, timing the news conference involves a number of considerations. If spot news is involved, it should be called immediately—even in the evening in the case of a real emergency. Otherwise, there is some advantage to alternating news conferences between morning—about 10 A.M.—and afternoon—about 3 P.M. This follows the traditional concern about afternoon and morning newspapers, going back to the days when newspapers and press services were the only news media of importance. It is now unwise to follow this practice rigidly when television, radio, newsmagazines, and other publications are involved.

In general, the morning tends to be better for news coverage by the press services, television and radio, magazines, and trade publications. This allows time for the writer to get back to the office, prepare the story, and process it the same day.

Tuesday, Wednesday, and Thursday are generally the best days of the week, with Monday slightly behind. Friday is a less-desirable day, because the weekend media generally have less room for news.

However, it is important to consider what competition there will be for news. If others are likely to schedule events or announcements for these prime times, it is likely that news in the other periods will do better than if in a head-on competition.

That means that one of the first things to be done when any press event or release is planned—except spot news—is to check on what other news it may be competing with on the contemplated day. That can be done by checking chambers of commerce, hotels and clubs, some of the media most likely to be invited, and so on.

Eighth, the news conference should be geared to conveying the essential information and meeting the needs of the media. That means it should follow a tight format with no frills.

The highest available official should be the focal point. Support him or her with specialists who can provide expert knowledge in answering questions. The principal should be at the head table, with the others preferably in an informal arrangement nearby rather than as a phalanx facing the press. If the crowd will be large, microphones should be provided for all who will participate and for those who will ask questions.

The meeting should start promptly—no more than five minutes after the time designated, in the case of hard news, or ten minutes if there is less urgency.

The public relations person may introduce the principal, then let him or her conduct the session. If desired, the public relations person rather than the principal can direct the questions to the proper authority, but should say as little as possible. That avoids any impression that it is a public relations meeting rather than a session for the benefit of the media.

It should be explained how the print media and the broadcast media will be served—

either in separate rooms or in succeeding meetings.

Photographers and TV camerapeople should be permitted, with the understanding that they will not flash lights directly into the faces of the speakers or get in the way of others.

The principal should make a concise statement of the news or the position of the organization on the issue involved. He or she should explain what materials are available, so reporters will not take needless notes. Then the meeting should be thrown open to questions from the visitors.

Ninth, whenever possible, the executives who will participate in the conference should go through a briefing session in advance. This should attempt to anticipate the trend of the conference, with special emphasis on the toughest questions and even "nasty" ones. While few media people will deliberately try to embarrass someone, some use this technique as part of their reportorial approach. Often inadvertent information or reactions resulting from probing questions will provide more meaningful material than other materials. It is important that the executives expect this and maintain their poise.

Participants should be cautioned to say, "I'm sorry, but I can't comment on that," if a question would call for information that is highly confidential, improper because of pending lawsuits, or otherwise unanswerable. They should *not* ask that anything be "off the record." The media people were invited to get material for their use, not to hear what they cannot use. It is further assumed that nothing can be truly secret if a substantial number of people have been called together to hear it.

Tenth, prepared materials might include the following:

• A background article on the subject

• Printed materials that are directly pertinent

- Pictures of the subject and, for requests only, of the principal spokesperson
- A news release, if it can be prepared in time
- Visual materials for television on-camera use, if suitable materials are available.

Eleventh, follow-up activities involve those who are not able to attend the conference, as well as those who do.

The news release and other pertinent materials should be sent to those invited who could not attend. Those who took the trouble to come should not be penalized; but they will have had the news soonest, will have had the opportunity to ask questions and to hear the answers to questions asked by others, and will have had a broader backgrounding. With limited staffs and many news events, media cannot cover all the things they would be interested in reporting.

Requests by guests for specific materials or photos should be met as expeditiously as possible. If a private interview is requested, it should be arranged if the spokesperson is available and if the number of requests is not excessive.

Media briefings

Sessions intended to provide background to interested media people, rather than hard news, can be more relaxed and informal. They may involve a lunch or dinner, or be held at the cocktail hour with drinks, tea, soft drinks, and canapes served.

Invitations should point out that the meeting will be a briefing and will not involve hard news. That will make certain that no one who comes will feel misled, and that no one will be afraid of missing something essential if he or she does not come.

A press kit (*see* Chapter 22) may be prepared for distribution.

Briefings may be held for such purposes as a year-end review of the organization's oper-

ations or outlook, a discussion of forthcoming labor negotiations, an airing of a dispute with a dissident group, or a periodic updating of the media because considerable time has elapsed since the last one.

Except for the physical requirements, the rules are generally the same as for the news conference.

Press showings

When a new product is to be introduced, a striking new building announced, or some other news involves showing or demonstrating something, the characteristics of the news conference and the briefing may be combined. (*See* Figure 21.1.) If no urgency is involved, the occasion may be more social than a news conference. For instance, a model of a new building may be unveiled at a lunch or dinner at which the mayor is a guest.

If the product is small and inexpensive, samples may be made available to the media people.

Greater attention is usually given to photos, and a press kit may be called for.

Granting an Exclusive Story

Determining whether a story should be given exclusively to one medium or offered to all who might be interested calls for as much judgment as any area of publicity. Individual conditions will have important bearing—the nature of the organization, the locale and its media pattern, the nature of the story, the responsibilities to law or specific groups such as stockholders, previous relations with the media involved, and others.

Some basic guides in reaching decisions follow.

First, a reporter is generally entitled to an exclusive on a story he or she discovers or develops. For instance, if he calls to say he is

Panasonic
Personal Computer Company
Two Panasonic Way Panazip 7D-6
Secaucus, N.J. 07094

PANASONIC
MEDIA ALERT

Figure 21.1 A media alert to an editor inviting coverage of an event—in this case, showing a new product. Though individualized, it is sent to a list of potentially interested editors. *Courtesy Creamer Dickson Basford Public Relations.*

To*: Tin Albano, PC Magazine*
From: Dawn Holstein, Creamer Dickson Basford
Date: 7/11/95

- Panasonic Personal Computer Co. will soon announce the launch of its newly enhanced CD-ROM integrated multimedia notebook PC and an MPEG full-motion video pack.

- The unit is commercially available August 1 and represents a new generation of the multimedia Panasonic V41 launched in late 1994.

- John Harris, national marketing manager for Panasonic Personal Computer Co., will be in your area July 31 and would like to give you a demonstration of the great new features of the unit and how it works with the MPEG full-motion video pack.

- We will call you shortly to schedule an appointment. In the meantime, feel free to call me at 212-887-8154 with any questions.

###

doing a feature story about an organization's work with underprivileged children, he is entitled to protection in keeping his secret until his story runs. That is true even if the organization was in the process of developing publicity on that subject. It is also true if the story is likely to be unfavorable, unless there is strong reason to feel that it will be biased (*actually* biased and not just seeming so in the partisan eyes of the organization).

However, if a reporter calls about a story with broad legal or other requirements—such as a major new product not yet announced by a company whose stock is publicly traded—other factors must be considered. In this example, it would be wise to consult the stock exchange where the company's shares are traded, to avoid possible accusation of failing to make full disclosure. (*See* Chapter 11.)

If the news is of great importance not only to the organization but also to the community, as in the case of decisions regarding a strike or plant relocation, the judgment must be made whether the medium involved would provide sufficiently broad announcement. If it is AP, Reuters, Dow Jones, UPI, Bloomberg, or one of the broadcasting networks, its exclusive treatment would usually mean wide dissemination. If it's a trade paper or one modest-sized local medium, however, the consequences might be more serious.

Even in the rare case in which an exclusive cannot be permitted, however, the reporter who originated the story must never be beaten on it. He or she should be told that the circumstances demand that the organization make its announcement to coincide with publication or broadcast.

Second, when a major feature (not news of general importance) is being placed, it is usually necessary to offer it exclusively to one medium in each classification or even to only one, regardless of classification. An editor is unlikely to accept a feature article if he or she feels one much like it may appear in a competitive outlet.

If a story is offered on an exclusive basis, it must not be offered elsewhere until a decision has been reached by the first outlet not to use it. That entails problems when the editor is slow or fails to respond. If time drags on and it becomes necessary to try elsewhere, the first editor should be informed that because time has run out the offer of the story has to be withdrawn. That is preferable to the severe irritation of having two media, both thinking they had exclusives offered, coming out with the same story.

In some cases it is feasible to develop one for newspapers, a variation for magazines, a third for TV, and a fourth for a trade paper. This requires strong story judgment and a sense of the medium's individual viewpoint. If in doubt, fewer versions should be attempted.

General news or matters of strong public or financial importance should never be offered on an exclusive basis. This is the material that all interested media consider themselves entitled to receive and that the people affected have a right to expect to find in whatever suitable media they read or view.

Third, some publicity materials are of limited interest and might not be run by any medium if the editor feels that all have received it. Yet as a modest offbeat story, it may appeal to one if the editor knows he or she has exclusive use of it. This is true, for example, of the "human interest" story, such as discovery that a grandniece of a former vice-president of the United States is working as a computer programmer in xyz Company's inventory department.

Fourth, the confidences of any reporter must be honored at all times. For instance, if a writer should call to get information for a general roundup story, which may or may not mention the publicist's organization at all, it is a gross violation to tell any other medium that such a story is being developed. Publicists' reputation for trustworthiness or lack of it spreads widely and rapidly.

Handling Media Inquiries

A publicity staff may spend more than half of its time and energies on matters it does not initiate or plan.

It is a mark of a successful publicity program when writers, editors, broadcasters, and others come to the staff with requests for information, opportunities to interview officials, or suggestions for broadcasts. The more effectively the total publicity job is done, the greater the appetites of the media for such service. Often two organizations in the same field—such as two life insurance companies—may have a vast difference in the frequency of their inquiries from the media. In this type of situation, the organization contacted most can expect to have far more publicity than the other.

It is desirable, then, to create a climate in which media people will think of the organization whenever it might be part of a story.

Some of the things that create this climate include the following:

1. The verities of publicity practice—absolute reliability, accuracy, promptness, fairness, objectivity.

2. A good batting average in meeting the difficult or unattractive requests, such as interviews with an official when a controversy or unfavorable story is developing, providing background information on matters that may have no apparent publicity value to the organization, and verifying or correcting controversial material or rumors.

   · The publicist is in the middle—with the client or employer on one side and the media on the other. In satisfying both, a good part of the time the publicist will not seem entirely accommodating to either. He or she must press his advocacy of good media relations with the client to prevail over its objections as often as possible, at the same time pressing his or her representation of the client with the media to modify their expectations or demands.

3. Establishing the best and most readily available source for a body of information can make the publicity staff a focal point for the media. For many years the American Music Conference's public relations firm was the storehouse of information and photos on amateur musical activity in the United States. Media editors and broadcasters knew that this was the one place to turn whenever they were dealing with that subject. At times fully half of the publicity about musical activity was the result of media coming to the firm for help on stories and broadcasts they thought of. In most cases, the resulting article or program carried some of the flavor of what the AMC was interested in conveying to the public.

4. Helping the media reach information sources is a valuable means of building acceptance. This means more than prompt, courteous, reliable response to contacts made at the office. The after-hours and emergency contact is most appreciated. Many publicity offices provide large lists of media with file cards listing the names of members of the staff, their special fields of expertness, and their home and vacation telephone numbers. These should be replaced with updated cards whenever changes occur.

   Often a publicist can build goodwill by helping a medium locate or identify an authority or source not associated with her own organization.

5. Convenience of the media is most marked in connection with locale. Being human, reporters tend—other things being equal—to contact someone close by whenever they seek information. As a result, since most media people are in New York, they most often contact those organizations, or the organizations' publicity firms, located in New York. A consequence is the often-discussed myopia of much press and broadcast coverage, reflecting conditions and attitudes within five miles of Rockefeller Center rather than in the rest of the world.

   Aside from being located as close as possible to the media offices or having a publicity firm there, the following things can be done to heighten accessibility:

   • Make it just as easy for a reporter to reach the publicity office by phone as if it were four blocks away. If the organization has an 800 number, let the media know that their calls will be accepted on the recipient's line without cost. If not or if the line is busy, acceptance of all collect calls from media can be authorized. Let the media know what arrangements are available for their calls, including direct call numbers for each person in the publicity office, enabling the caller to bypass the organization's voice mail system. Similar arrangements for receiving collect calls and direct-dial calls should be made for the home phones of all staff members.

- Make a suitable spokesperson available for an interview by phone or a fast trip to New York, Chicago, or elsewhere. Except in emergencies, it is seldom possible for a writer to arrange an interview with a New York executive on less than a day or two's notice. An executive can fly in from Beloit or Knoxville just as promptly. This calls for the publicity office having up-to-date travel schedules for all officials at all times, so the regularly scheduled trips can be utilized to set dates or a person can be rerouted for the purpose.

6. Press kits and background articles or "white papers" serve the added purpose of providing file material for the media. When the material is referred to later, it reminds the editor of its source and stimulates calling to get new information.

7. Occasionally media personnel dealing with advertising sales will contact the publicist. This may or may not be an effort to use implied influence with the editor to have the medium considered as an advertising outlet. That is rarely the case with important media. Such calls should always be referred to either the advertising department or the advertising agency. Every effort should be made to keep editorial and advertising relations entirely separate. Editorial people resent any indication that their own advertising staff or any publicist feels they can be bought through advertising pressure.

Maximizing Media Treatment

An organization can do numerous things to optimize the treatment it receives:[1]

---

[1]From *Overcoming Opposition*, Philip Lesly, pp. 90–93.

1. Assess the media that will be involved with your organization and issues likely to face it. This assessment must be done medium by medium, rather than as a group. Although there is much lockstep coverage by various media, it is not safe to generalize.

   In each case, assess how the medium has treated the organization in the past, its essential fairness or susceptibility to being seduced by extremists when approaching new subjects, the background and maturity of its editorial staff people, its concern for its reputation for accuracy and fairness; and what its own stake is in the welfare of the organization.

   What is your organization's status and credibility with each medium? What are the medium's prejudices? What is its relationship with leaders of any opposition or competitive groups you may be confronting?

2. When a new subject or issue seems to be emerging, assess each medium in terms of how it is likely to treat it. Do its staff people have a stake in what opposing groups will bring up? What is its record in handling similar matters recently?

3. Establish accessibility *in advance* to the key gatekeepers of news coverage at each medium. Get acquainted with the pertinent editors—business, environment, city, or others. Establish an understanding about the organization's functions, its concerns about the community and the public, its readiness to answer questions and provide information, and so on. Establish your reliability as a source by answering all inquiries fully and promptly even on matters of little importance or unrelated to the organization's interests.

4. Humanize your organization. Let the media get to know and respect *people*, rather than trying to have them deal with an institution. Leaders of the organization

should become known, seen, heard, and respected.

5. Seed the flow of information on the emerging subject or issue in advance. Develop authoritative, sound, fair material on the subject that is better than anyone else can produce. Make it available in personal contacts and by delivery to key people at every medium on the list you have developed. Encourage inquiries, requests for materials, discussions. Make sure that no objective person or organization can draw up a proposal on what concerns you without incorporating what you have to offer.

6. Become a key reliable source on the subject. Be sure that whenever any medium covers the subject it's likely to think of you first, or at least hesitate to complete its coverage without contacting you.

7. Establish visibility. Do things about the subject in question that command respectful attention. Preempt the front of the stage on that subject.

8. Hold media people responsible. When media were unassailable it often was fruitless to protest shabby treatment. That has changed. The multiple forms of scrutiny now being focused on media people make them sensitive to what can damage their esteem.

Aside from money, probably the most precious asset of the journalist is the esteem of his or her peers. That esteem is augmented when major stories are achieved but diminished when the methods used are shown to be shabby. This concern for the respect of peers provides the most available channel for preventing shabby treatment.

Use fair and objective means to show your organization will fight such treatment. Protest first to the journalist and request redress. If that fails, protest to his or her boss. If that's unsuccessful, then consider "going public."

If that decision is made, develop a scrupulously accurate, thoroughly documented demonstration that the treatment was irresponsible—not just routinely inaccurate. The offense must be glaring to gain a sympathetic hearing for a rebuttal. Don't aim to embarrass anyone. Just set the record straight and make it clear that you will respond to any other such off-base attacks. Become known among media people as a porcupine rather than a rabbit.

Conducting Sensitive Interviews

A number of guidelines apply for dealing with media in possibly unfriendly situations.

1. In interviews, establish at the beginning that you recognize the importance of a clear and responsible exchange. Both parties should come to it openly and frankly. Accordingly, indicate that you will make a record of the interview so everything can be checked: use a tape recorder or have someone take notes; if it's for TV, make a videotape of the entire interview.

2. Ask the reporter how the facts will be checked. Make it part of the record that you expect facts to be verified and that the reporter indicated he or she would go to responsible sources.

3. If any of the sources the reporter mentions he or she will check do not have your facts or position, make sure the sources receive them immediately—not in order to thwart the reporter, but rather to ensure that the source can benefit from your input.

4. Write up the notes on the interview immediately. Get information to fill any blank

spots at once. Stay ahead of the reporter. But keep that separate from the transcript of what was actually said in the interview, so the record of the interview is unblemished in case of a disagreement on what was said.

A major benefit of this procedure is to apply discipline to the reporter by establishing that there will be a basis for accountability.

In interviews or telephone discussions with media people, it is important to use terms with precision. Several standard terms and responses are defined in the list that follows, indicating the meaning the media will probably infer when used by interview subjects or news conferences. However, you should discuss the meaning with the individual reporter to verify that they share your interpretation.

- *Background only.* Usually this means that what is provided is not to be attributed to the source.
- *Off the record.* May not be published or broadcast. But some media refuse to accept this restriction. Check it first.
- *Not for attribution.* The information may be used, but without revealing the source. Get agreement on whether this will include the organization as well as the spokesperson, and how the attribution used will be worded.
- *Check this with us before using.* When the proposed material is checked back you can correct errors or misunderstandings but cannot withdraw what was provided or said.
- *Read it to us before using.* There is no promise to make any changes or even corrections of fact.
- *I don't know* or *no.* Indicates the question will not be answered—a safe out when a reply could be in error, misconstrued, or mishandled.

- *We'll get back to you on that.* To be sure information is accurate and up-to-date, taking a little time is better than gambling on an immediate answer. Make certain you get back to the inquirer as soon as possible.

Handling Emergencies

Relations with the media are most critical in stressful, unexpected situations. (*See also* Chapters 2, 20, 22, and 37.) It is the purpose of the media to get the most spectacular news, which a disaster or crisis usually represents. At the same time, the organization involved is disrupted by the unexpected event, and its personnel have a natural tendency to protect it that can become a barrier to the media.

In dealing with the media in the course of an emergency, the way it is handled will determine not only how the organization is made to appear to the public in the news report, but the coolness or warmth of its rapport with the media for years ahead.

Robert L. Barbour, the late editor of *PR Reporter*, cited the two major types of critical situations that have faced organizations:

1. Noncatastrophic situations that are usually of local concern. For example, a hospital is suddenly deprived of water when a main breaks. Or an area-wide commuter train delay occurs that may last for hours due to flood conditions or a power outage.

2. Sudden catastrophes of national, regional, or local concern, involving heavy and increasing pressures exerted by the news media and the public, with such initially unknown factors as the originating cause, the extent of loss, and legal entailments. For example, an explosion traps miners underground; a chemical plant explodes with a number of casualties; or a plane crashes.

To these types of emergency there now must be added a third:

3. The attack. A militant group disrupts a convention, a bomb destroys the company's offices, or a mob turns over and sets fire to the company's trucks.

Guidelines for emergencies and disasters

In the case of the localized emergency, Barbour pointed out, the greatest need is likely to be communicating with relatives and friends in the community to avert panic and assure them that things soon will be restored to normal. Much of this is internal: telephone calls to staff people who can inform all employees and occupants of the building; in the case of a hospital or school, calling relatives. Releases might be needed for the local radio and TV stations and the newspapers. Inquiries from the media should be answered promptly and with a frank explanation.

In the event of an occurrence such as a fire or a serious accident, the fundamental principle in dealing with the media is to recognize that it is a legitimate news event on which they and their public are entitled to have the facts.

Additionally, since widespread attention to the disaster is inevitable, the public relations staff's effectiveness is based on its ability to attain coverage that is as factual and unemotional as possible with the least amount of criticism toward the organization. If the facts are freely available quickly to the media, it lessens the chances of their exaggerating the seriousness of the event or of criticizing the organization for efforts to cover up or mislead.

Making up an advance "disaster plan," then, starts with the assumption that the role of public relations will be to expedite the orderly and accurate handling of information in cooperation with the media, excepting only such matters as classified government contracts and research operations.

For disaster plans, the following guidelines are cited by Barbour:

1. Make a list of all the things that conceivably could happen to your organization (explosion, collapse, fire, riot, plague, food or chemical poisoning, flood, mass electrocution, crash or collision, hurricane, power outage, water cutoff). Don't rely on just your imagination in compiling the list; talk with those who know what could happen. Try to divide the list into emergency and disaster situations as explained in Chapter 2. Remember that your concern is with on-premises, unforeseen physical events of an emergency nature affecting *groups* of people rather than an individual.

2. Try to develop plans that include techniques and procedures applicable to all your potential emergency or disaster situations. But don't try to cover every detail of every situation under every conceivable circumstance, or you'll never get your plans off the ground. Include instructions to improvise, where indicated, as common sense and imagination dictate.

3. Spell out exactly—by name, title, extension, and home telephone number—the sequence of notification to be followed the moment an emergency or disaster occurs. This is generally a chain procedure (each person notified notifies others) that usually starts with calls to the chief operating office, the director of public relations, and the head of the department involved, if any. Make it clear who starts the ball rolling. Allow for the fact that, in some cases, a person in the chain of responsibility may be incapacitated or unavailable. Designate alternates and backups, preferably people at different sites so one event can't eliminate several.

4. Remember that in time of crisis, instant internal and external communication channels *must* be kept open and clear. Unless you make arrangements for the necessary physical equipment and personnel ahead of time, an emergency will clog your lines of communication and frustration will heighten confusion all around. So use the following checklist to determine what arrangements you can make *now*:

- **Press room.** Needed instantly in disasters and graver emergencies. Determine where it shall be (easily accessible to news people, preferably near public relations department); plenty of telephones, desks, chairs quickly available; typewriters, faxes, copy paper, pens to be brought in; supply coffee (urn available?) and sandwiches (if long duration is probable).

- **Telephone switchboard.** Discuss with head operator—and with telephone company, if indicated—how best to assure that the extra load of in and out calls and faxes will be handled without delay (extra or specially assigned trunk lines? call-back on purely business calls? minimum conversation request? embargo on personal calls not emergency-connected?). Arrange for switchboard operators to be on call, and for switchboard to stay open on your request with full complement of regular or special operators.

- **Short-wave radio or cell phone.** If telephone lines are knocked out, a means of calling the police and fire department—and possibly also a friendly company headquarters or plant nearby—will keep you in two-way touch with the outside world.

- **Electronic bullhorns.** Keep at least one in your office (you'll find them useful during special events, too). If a communication emergency occurs, your voice will carry up to around fifteen hundred feet. But practice using it, first.

- **Personal check-in.** Have a member of the Public Relations Department check with you at regular intervals for errands and assignments and report to you when completed (in person or by portable phone). You'll need to know what's happening in areas you can't reach in any other way.

5. After outlining your Public Relations Emergency and Disaster Plans and making the necessary arrangements to assure free-flowing crisis communication, include the assignment of specific responsibilities. For example:

- Stay in your office!—if your staff is large enough to cover all critical fronts. As public relations director, you're the key person in linking your organization to the outside world. There'll be 1,001 matters of information, coordination, and judgment you'll have to handle personally, and no time must be wasted finding you. If you cannot remain at your post, have your secretary cover the telephone and keep her or him informed every time you move from one location to another (or tell the switchboard operator).

- Keep press, visitors, and victims apart. Station someone—anyone—at the building entrance to direct newsmen to the press room and relatives and friends to the boardroom or some other quiet segregated area. All questions by newsmen and visitors should be referred to the person in charge of each room.

- Assign your assistant or press relations head to the press room. Give him or her authority to answer questions fully and frankly within predetermined limitations and to make on-the-spot decisions and arrangements necessary to proper news coverage. Also post a competent, calm PR man or woman in the room to which visitors have been directed, with instructions to answer questions briefly, as positively as possible, and with discretion. Supply coffee.

- Assign a "floater" from public relations to tour all public relations posts and other vital areas on the property rotationally, to check on how things are being handled and report to you regularly with comments and suggestions.

- Make your office the press room—if you operate a one-person public relations department. Carry a cell phone or portable phone with plenty of range. Brief your secretary on how to handle press and telephone inquiries, then give authority to do so if you're on another line or out of reach. Set up a room for relatives and friends of victims nearby, and post a corporate officer's secretary there with instructions (see above). Do your own "floating," but as you make the rounds, recruit whomever you can for errands, assignments, and liaison. Go over all suggestions in steps one and two of this outline to determine how you can best adapt them to the limitations of your one-man office.

Guidelines for handling attacks

The activist assault on an organization creates a number of additional challenges not present in either the emergency or the disaster. In these cases, there is no intent to make the organization look bad; there is no opposing intelligence mapping strategy that must be anticipated and coped with; and there is no possible predilection on the part of the media to side with the source of the trouble. As unpredictable and stressful as handling media

coverage of a disaster may be, these additional complicating factors make the handling of an attack much more difficult and potentially more damaging to the organization.

A number of factors must be included in planning and coping with this type of problem.

1. Stay alert to all of the organizations and groups that are likely to become activist in your area or in connection with the industry you are in. Study each group's nature, tactics, and especially the objective it might seek to attain in attacking your organization. Management should be prepared to deal with the legitimate requests or complaints. But the plan should be drawn up to prevent the attacking group from attaining its other objectives by using your organization as a symbol, to gain widespread publicity for itself, or otherwise to exploit the situation.

2. Assess objectively what the response of the media is likely to be. Have they shown a penchant for featuring the spectacle of any attack rather than the merits of the situation? Are they likely to make every effort to make the organization look good, or might they take advantage of the opportunity to make the militants look good? In many cases, the organization that has been attacked and whose buildings have been bombed or burned down has seemed the villain in the media treatment.

3. It is important to recognize that in the arena of present "attitude management," not the facts but the *impression* people get of a situation is the true reality.

   What the public thinks—not the merits or the actual conditions—will probably determine the result.

   You cannot be sure that if the facts are on your side you will prevail. In countless cases, the dramatic visibility of a contrived situation has prevailed.

What really happens at a demonstration or a confrontation is not crucial; what gets out to the public is.

4. In this climate companies, institutions, industries, and individuals are all "inbounds" to activist critics. The right to privacy is being eroded for individuals but blasted away for organizations. Few functions now retain true confidentiality. The new posture of activism is a "smart bomb" that seeks out any organization it seeks to attack.

5. It is important to note that impersonal organizations are most vulnerable to attack, because their size makes them visible and they seem to be inhuman monoliths instead of human institutions. Every effort should be made to personalize and humanize the organization.

6. It is also important to consider that a "low profile" indicates secretiveness. In today's human climate the impression of secretiveness breeds distrust.

7. It is vital to recognize that communication in our society is in revolution. The standard processes whereby information and ideas seep through the populace, from the top down or horizontally, cannot compete with the visible, dramatic, easy-to-sensationalize communication that results from activism. (*See* Chapter 3.) Accordingly, the standard word-oriented transmission-process communication is no match for the spectacular imagery of the activist attacks.

8. It must also be recognized that dissidents have little to lose and can afford to be irresponsible. They can act as wildly as necessary to capture attention; they can focus the attention of the media and the public on untrue assertions; they can create the movement and the action that are the raw material of communications media today. That means, of course, that responsible institutions operate at a disadvantage, and strategy for coping with such events must take that into account.

9. Objectively assess the climate your institution has among the media and the public. In the event of a breakout of hostility, would they be likely to give you the benefit of the doubt?

10. Assess the climate of the dissidents. Do they have the advantage of the underdog role? Have they been wearing patience thin with an accumulation of abrasive actions or irresponsible accusations?

11. Assess the timing and the current circumstances. When the air controllers' union struck in 1981 and were fired by President Reagan, the tempers of the media and the public were entirely different from that of a year earlier when almost any labor action was viewed favorably.

12. Weigh the political realities within your organization. Are there limitations resulting from the makeup of your stockholder group or membership that have to be weighed along with the other factors that determine what you do, what you say, who your spokesman is, and so on?

13. Weigh any other factors that may be involved. Do you have legislation pending or ongoing negotiations with civic organizations or labor unions that could be materially affected by what happens in the confrontation? However, concern about immediate consequences should not obviate consideration of overall long-range matters.

14. Determine what can be done to reconcile the situation related to the activism. An activist thrust may represent those who feel the need for change and have been unable or unwilling to wait for "normal processes." Many institutions have lost their independence because they held

firmly to their "principles" (based on the old and the entrenched) against efforts to get them to accommodate to the new.

15. Determine what visible action can be taken. Don't settle for a statement, appointment of a study group, or other nondramatic steps. What can your institution *do* in connection with what the dissidents are driving at? How can you make a *visible impact*?

16. Include an objective, broadly experienced participant in all your organization's considerations. In no situation is the outside, questioning, widely experienced viewpoint more essential than it is here. A group, no matter how capable, who all see things from the same axis point are unlikely to make a proper reading of either the dissidents or the public.

17. Make sure you have a clear understanding of the actual workings of all communications media involved—especially how activist groups time their actions to make certain TV shows and press deadlines, to create the headlines with the greatest impact, and to create situations embarrassing to you.

18. Anticipate and prepare in advance. Set up "war games" plans on the basis of each foreseeable circumstance. Have all the facts ready and in clear form. Prepare statements and have them in readiness. Have the spokesmen and other officials ready and briefed. Know where they can be reached at all times. Put them through the kind of grilling they will get in a confrontation, in a hostile press conference, before a congressional committee, or whatever other circumstances might be involved. Have your staff briefed and constantly available, literally on a twenty-four-hour-a-day basis so they all can be on hand when needed. Be sure you have access to copying and photo departments, and have arrangements lined up with

all-night outside services. Set up plans to deploy all of your people to make phone calls to those they know, so that everyone important can be contacted as quickly as possible, preferably by someone he or she knows and trusts.

19. Consider the attitudes and possible reactions of the nonmilitant crowds on the periphery of the action. Curiosity seekers and others may be neutral or sympathetic to the organization, but become panicked or "radicalized" by the impression they get of what occurs or through lack of calm explanation. Plans for an outdoor public address system or a powerful bullhorn to be manned by an executive who will be fully posted on the situation should be an integral part of the preparations.

20. Brief all personnel who might become involved. Panic by factory workers, office staff, or others can have serious consequences on the public reaction. This should be done in a matter-of-fact way, indicating that no such development is expected but that the organization feels everyone should be prepared for any eventuality. At the same time, it should not be so detailed that a leak would tip off would-be activists to what the organization's responses would be.

21. If it's possible to anticipate which group might attack and what its accusations will be, advertisements should be prepared in advance and ready for immediate placement in the newspapers and, possibly, on radio and television. These should succinctly and factually explain the entire situation, putting it into proper and unhysterical context.

22. Keep your constituents fully and immediately informed of the issue and your position. This includes employees, stockholders or members, suppliers, and others. Properly informed and sympathetic,

they can serve as a backstop against automatic acceptance of what the dissidents may charge or do. This will also ensure that your functions will be integrated with others in the organization.

Other Critical Concerns

A lot of hocus-pocus has been made about "contacts" and "knowing the right people." It is much more important to produce sound material and service for the media than it is to have a big entertainment budget and know a lot of media people by their first names.

Other things being equal, a publicist can do a better job if he or she knows a given editor or reporter or photographer. A friend in the news media can give the publicist the benefit of the doubt, tip him or her off on stories, and sometimes advise on advance planning. These friendships almost always result from being dependable, effective, expeditious aides to the media. Friendships based on other factors are ephemeral when experiences turn sour or when inevitable shifts in jobs replace a friend with a new person in the position.

Media have antennae that will bring in information. They are psychologically more disposed to play up concealed information than information revealed with frank reasons for not releasing it at the time. This author rarely has had a professional journalist violate a confidence.

Foolishness can reach extremes in the matter of gifts to media people. A *gift* is given in a spirit of generosity with nothing expected in return. A publicist who considers his or her effectiveness to be measured in any way by gifts is a living insult to the media.

A dangerous tendency of some publicity people is to develop a patronizing attitude toward journalists. They should not try to control everything the reporters find out about their clients. What is planned for the media should be guided by policy and effectiveness. On the other hand, when the client talks with the media, he or she should not be so restricted that he loses the integrity of his own personality.

Keys to media relationships

The sound public relations professional follows several points in media relationships.

News editors and reporters

- Lose no opportunity to give them service.
- Answer all questions fully, honestly, and promptly.
- Treat a newsperson the same as a customer.
- Know the organization, its details, and its spellings.
- Never be a barrier or obstruction; the public relations person is *not* a "suppress" agent.
- Honor a legitimate "exclusive," however much temptation there is to balloon it into a more general break.
- Be impartial between one medium and another.
- Do not bluff, misrepresent, exaggerate, or pad.
- Make every effort to provide a story for a newsperson who desires one.
- However much provoked, don't be abrupt with a newsperson.
- Be as energetic in helping the media cover an *adverse* story as any other kind.

The Cameraman or photographer

The person with a camera has the toughest job in journalism. The reporter usually can get a story without being in the spotlight, but a photographer is identified and slowed down by a camera and is sometimes considered fair game by ruffians who want to obstruct the work of the media.

- The skilled publicist exerts extra effort to help the news photographer or TV cameraperson.

- He or she knows what constitutes good graphic material and helps the photographer line up pictures, set up props, pose subjects, and write captions.

- He or she lets cameramen photograph what they are assigned to "shoot," whether or not the client desires the picture to be used. It is a major error to hamper a photographer at work.

- He or she always makes accommodations—tickets, meals, a place to "shoot" from—for photographers, and treats a photographer in the same way as a managing editor.

The experienced publicity person makes it a point, whenever possible, to deal with the editor who actually will handle the type of copy being moved.

Most important is to observe all deadlines. The early publicist gets the play, because all editors need time to process their material and what can be done unhurriedly and scheduled early will get preference.

The thoughtful publicist avoids taking too much of an editor's time. She or he does not persistently check up on the fate of a story once it has been delivered.

The good publicist is careful to avoid "double planting"—placing two or more stories on the same subject with two shows on a TV station or in different sections of a newspaper of the same edition. If duplicates of a release are sent to more than one department, each is marked to show who is receiving copies.

22

PUBLICITY IN NEWSPAPERS

HERBERT M. BAUS
PHILIP LESLY

Though broadcast media have become the most predominant and influential form of communication in our society, the newspaper has retained a powerful position. To the majority of the population, publicity means getting coverage in the newspapers—and justifiably so.

This popular belief is based on good psychological and logistical reasoning. The primary psychological reason is that most families in the Western world have one or more newspapers they consider "their" newspaper. They praise and defend it. They turn to it for information that directly influences them, helping to articulate and shape opinions—perhaps more than any other medium. Often, it carries the power to motivate its readers to action.

Much of the newspaper's psychological power derives from its nature as a medium. Most literate North Americans read, as a matter of habit, at least one newspaper a day and typically become addicted to certain features. Because the newspaper is produced locally, it serves as a lifeline between the citizens and the outside world surrounding them. Television—having abdicated its opportunity to provide this lifeline by focusing on money-making entertainment programming rather than on meaningful material geared to its viewers' daily lives—has allowed this critical position to be filled by newspapers alone.

Another inherent advantage of newspapers is that they can be read whenever the reader desires. The printed word waits for a convenient time, whereas the electronic message is tyrannically demanding, forcing the reader to grasp it only while it is being broadcast.

As a "periodical"—published regularly at specified intervals, usually daily—the newspaper lends itself to cumulative buildup. The reader can save it and easily refer to it later or repeatedly over time. When perusing the newspaper, the reader is alert and actively involved in the process; conversely, the reader is in a relatively more passive and relaxed mode when listening to the radio, watching television, or driving by a billboard. This elevates the importance of the message, because it enables the reader to integrate the message within the kaleidoscope of life revealed by the newspaper.

Another advantage is that readers presume that the news columns of most newspapers reflect an impartial viewpoint. However, a notable trend toward "interpretive" reporting has surfaced in recent years. In these cases, both news and feature coverage may reflect background detail provided by the publicist, for example. On one hand, this trend broadens the potential motivating power. On the other hand, it brings into question the paper's impartiality, which may weaken its credibility.

Of course, newspapers do have their drawbacks. Each issue's time period of effectiveness is short. Advertisements placed in newspapers usually cannot be as attractive and spectacular as in slick paper magazines that, with their fine engraving and lavish colors, set the stage for drama in print. Finally, newspapers do not bring the living, pulsing, vital essence conveyed by radio, television, and film.

Daily and Sunday Newspapers

According to the *Editor & Publisher Yearbook*, the circulation of daily newspapers is nearly 63 million. *Bacon's Newspaper Directory* reports that 1,565 daily newspapers and 779 Sunday newspapers are published in the United States—in addition to 8,856 weekly, semiweekly, and triweekly newspapers. In the *Newspaper as an Advertising Medium*, published by the American Newspaper Publishers Association, it is estimated that each copy of a newspaper reaches 2.5 adult readers, or approximately 157 million readers of daily newspapers alone.

The able public relations person understands the many separate departments of a daily newspaper and knows the techniques of preparing and processing news for use in the different sections.

Most publicity matter is designed for the *city desk*, which supervises the general news. This serves as the clearinghouse for the great volume of general news about events on the state and local scene, and for many newspapers, on international and national matters as well. Any publicity material not directly suitable for one of the other departments, each of which is designed to cover a limited field, may be best presented to the city side. If there is a question as to this, the recommended procedure is to discuss the designation of the story material with the departmental editor, who will be glad to advise and to use the material if it is appropriate to his columns.

Because the *editorial page* content is determined by the policy of the paper, it is usu-

ally well to present material for this department in the form of a letter to the publisher or managing editor, a procedure that the chief of the editorial page is likely to follow in any event. There are cases in which the editorial page chief has a large measure of leeway in deciding what will be published and other cases in which, for personal reasons, the publicist may prefer to deal directly with the editor or publisher.

Producing editorials is a matter of persuading editorial editors to write in favor of or against a given event or subject.

The easiest and most direct way is to send all editorial editors a letter detailing the information to be editorialized. Who will sign such letters, the publicist or an appropriate official, depends on the press relationships and other factors involved.

Another method is to make a personal call on the editors to discuss the subject. Sometimes it pays for officials of the cause being publicized to contact the editors or make arrangements with publishers.

If editorialists are put on general lists to receive news releases, they will sometimes pick up items to write about.

Some organizations include editorials in their clipsheets (see later treatment) or their periodic mailings to newspapers. Others employ the services of a sophisticated distribution firm, such as North American Precis Syndicate, 201 E. 42nd Street, New York, NY 10017; branch offices in Chicago and Washington, DC. Naps not only produces and distributes columns, cartoons, and editorials, but will write editorials for the client if requested. Fees are based on the services, size of the material, distribution volume, and postage.

Remember that editorials reflect the policy of a newspaper. If the paper's policy is opposed to the cause being publicized, favorable editorials will not result. If the paper's policy is on the fence, it may be appropriate to make efforts to persuade the newspaper publishers involved to back the policy at issue.

The *cartoon* of most newspapers is an editorial page feature and is subject to the same control as the choice of editorial matter. In suggesting editorial treatment, the publicist will generally find it beneficial to include cartoon suggestions in the same package. Because there is usually only one cartoon a day, it is generally devoted to international and national events, although in certain local connections such as Community Chest drives the cartoonist will often be invited by the paper's management to make a local subject.

Letters to the Editor has an appeal to the discriminating newspaper reader who may seek in this column an index to public opinion. On certain days some newspapers largely devote the editorial page to this form of public forum. When a matter of serious public interest is at stake, it will frequently justify a publicist's efforts to encourage a client or a private individual to express a view in a letter to the editor. In most metropolitan newspapers, a better effect will be obtained if the letter comes from a private citizen rather than from a publicity person, because it is generally an editorial policy to judge letters on their merits as interesting documents treating vital public issues, rather than allowing the identity of the letter writer to influence them.

Many newspapers now have *op-ed pages* on which they carry material written by people not on the paper's or a press service's staff.

If the public relations person serves an organization that has activities of interest in the world of sports, society, women's activities, science, agriculture, and other such fields, specific treatment can be applied to qualify the material for one of these departments. Frequently, applied creative imagination will make possible expansion of an activity into some of these.

For example, a special preview of an entertainment event for a social or charitable purpose can secure publicity on the lifestyle page, as well as on the entertainment page. Combining a new line of sports equipment with new sports clothes is one way to produce a lifestyle page or sports page feature. The story of a furniture maker can be expanded into a feature story for a decorating or home-building editor.

In dealing with these specialized sections of a metropolitan daily newspaper, the following principles apply:

1. The subject matter and the people involved must be pertinent. For example, women's page material must be about women's activities, women's clubs and organizations, and women's leaders. Some newspapers have limited space. Others, such as the Milwaukee *Journal*, St. Louis *Post-Dispatch*, and *Chicago Tribune*, devote considerable coverage to women's interests, now often titled "family interest" or "lifestyle."

2. On many occasions, stories and art must be arranged for weeks or months ahead of time. In few cases does the material have the time and news urgency that prevails in the general news section. Many stories and pictures offered with a time element are nevertheless held and published at a later time, suiting the exigencies of make-up and editorial discretion.

3. Pictures are judged less from the point of view of news impact than the pertinence and importance of the persons in the photographs. In spite of this, almost all editors lean toward pictures of attractive people because such pictures make up a more effective newspaper page.

4. Usually the specialized sections have specific policies of their own on what is news, what may and may not be mentioned, timing, and other specifics. Intensive publicity work on a specialized subject justifies great pains to learn these points and to apply them.

Columnists constantly seek material and are grateful for exclusive bits that fit the style of their columns. Some publicity people, particularly in the New York theatrical and Hollywood TV and movie firmaments, make a living entirely by feeding items to columnists. Many New York show publicists seek items of no particular concern to their own clients but of interest to the entertainment columnists. They hope only to be repaid by a concession now and then in the form of a plug for one of their clients.

Every columnist has his or her own unique field and individual style. It behooves the interested publicist to provide appropriate items and to make them exclusive, for it is part of the stock in trade of the columnists to present precious bits offered by none of his competitors. The material can be offered by telephone, by letter, or in person.

It is advisable to put columnists on distribution lists to receive general publications, brochures, programs, and releases. Sometimes from this material the columnist may find an "angle" or become motivated to follow through and develop an aspect of the subject.

State page or *state edition* covers the news of the state outside the paper's own metropolitan area. Often papers will maintain "stringers," or correspondents, paid by the column inch. In some important towns salaried bureaus are maintained. The state page or edition will be interested in news of a small community festival, fair, pageant, or show, and will desire coverage when something newsworthy happens to a client or a client's official in an outlying town.

Comics sometimes constitute a publicity medium when a subject of broad general interest is treated in them. For example, some cooperate with the Boy Scouts of America during national Boy Scout Week. Gift-giving holidays, environment, other causes, sports, science, motion pictures, and many other topics are featured in the comics.

Every metropolitan daily has a number of "beats," such as *court, police, political,* and *hotel.*

Beats are segments of the city's life that require special coverage, which is obtained from staff members assigned to get the news they have to offer. Sometimes the beat is a sort of branch office. For example, the police beat is in the press room at police headquarters. The hotel beat is an office with typewriters and telephones in some central hotel, from which reporters dash about town to other hotels.

Many publicists constitute "beats" for newspapers. An airline publicity person covers the line as a beat. She or he reports important arrivals, covers the details of accidents, and reports new equipment and many other specific facts of news value to the papers and of publicity value to the line. The publicity person for an association covers the organization as a beat and keeps the city desks posted on all happenings of news interest. Publicity people for all other organizations likewise become regular sources of news for the papers.

The relations of publicists with newspaper beats are a special problem in each instance. The publicist who does not know the particular beat person and is in doubt should work through the city desk. The publicist who has regular dealings with a beat is urged to consult beat reporters and operate through them. They prefer this and are properly indignant when routine matters appear to be routed past them. They will promptly refer a matter to the city desk if that's where it belongs.

Any reporter who generates a good story not assigned by the editor enhances his or her position. The publicist who gives a good story directly to any beat reporter is helping increase acceptance. The reporter welcomes such material and is grateful for it.

Political beats

Political beat reporters cover the city hall, county courthouse, and state capitol. Today most large newspapers have a Washington, DC, correspondent or staff. Political beat people usually are assigned to cover, edit, and in many cases make decisions regarding political campaigns and issues. Hence any public relations person whose work includes political action in any form will find it imperative to know and work with the political editors and writers of the metropolitan daily newspapers.

Public interest writers

Many newspapers now assign staff people as specialists on environment, minority interests, women's interests, and other movements. They are especially interested in activities, studies, protest meetings, and other news-producing matters.

Court beats

Court reporters cover federal, state, county, and city courts. They have power of decision on whether to use or ignore a particular attorney's name, whether to pose him or her in a picture, and whether to mention the name to advantage or omit it.

Other beats

Newspapers tend to develop special beats to cover specific interests in their area. For example, most maritime cities have a marine department. The waterfront reporters cover arrivals and departures of ships, waterfront labor problems, naval news, and interesting cargoes.

Towns in agricultural areas have farmers' sections. Mining towns, factory towns, river towns, and lumber towns develop beats to cover their industries. Many papers have labor experts.

Rising newspaper specialists in new fields are eager for any news they can get. For instance, many papers have added science and medical editors, and papers in some centers of aircraft manufacture have developed aviation editors.

General Sunday section

The big Sunday edition of a metropolitan daily newspaper includes many sections, usually compiled under the direction of a Sunday editor. On other Sunday papers, each section editor is responsible directly to the managing editor.

General Sunday papers often include television, book, entertainment, travel, and magazine sections and enlarged departments for such daily features as sports, books, and comics.

Often newspapers with no Sunday issue bring out these special sections on other days.

The general news section usually has a special Sunday makeup editor who begins assembling Sunday copy on Tuesday or Wednesday afternoon. Most of the Sunday paper is compiled and sent to press on Thursday or Friday, with many of the early editions mailed to suburbs and resorts for Sunday sale. The flow of spot news slows down on Saturday, with the courts and other sources of news closed. Since it is usually also larger, the Sunday paper is more open to publicity than the daily editions.

Publicists have debated the relative effectiveness of material in the Sunday paper. Those favoring it cite its greater circulation, its more leisurely reading, and the tendency of the entire family to absorb it. Those preferring the daily edition say the Sunday paper is so full that any one item is likely to be lost. However, surveys of readership indicate Sunday papers are well read, and the large volume of advertising they carry demonstrates that advertisers also have found this to be true.

The intelligent course is to route material to the papers as it comes up, being careful mainly to avoid days on which the papers are either especially thin or overcrowded.

Religion publicity

Papers often give religion a page on Saturday, with past-tense stories on Monday. Daily papers that also have Sunday editions tend to run religious copy Saturday, Sunday, and Monday.

The religion editor will be interested in festivals with religious implications or in civic or charity projects of interest to church people. Occasionally the publicist may circularize a list of ministers with the suggestion that they mention a certain subject. This has interest for the religion editor.

Financial page

Of particular importance to the public relations worker for a business or industry is the financial section, much more widely read and understood today than a few years ago. Business news has gained so much interest that some material formerly appearing on the financial pages now frequently appears in the general news section.

In a check with some of the leading financial writers of New York City, *Editor and Publisher* found such improvements in handling of financial releases as the following:

1. Elimination of numerous items that interest only financial experts

2. More interpretive writing for the mass of new investors

3. A broadening of the base of the financial page to provide economic interpretation of day-to-day finance in the average home, and to aid in transactions such as buying a house or planning for retirement

Television-radio sections

Newspaper TV-radio sections have value to publicists of the broadcasting companies and of entertainers and programs. They also benefit publicists using television and radio publicity media who desire to mention that fact in the newspaper TV-radio section in order to increase listenership and overall publicity effectiveness.

Drama and movie sections

Appearing prominently in every day's issue of the metropolitan newspapers, this section carries news about performers, motion picture theaters, legitimate theaters, outdoors pageants, and various shows and festivals.

Home and garden sections

Sometimes this department is integrated with the real estate section. Sometimes it comprises a special magazine in the Sunday paper. It is primarily an advertising medium for contractors, seed companies, fence builders, furniture manufacturers, and other makers and distributors of materials that improve the home.

A publicist for a garden club or a civic organization's cleanup campaign can often prepare material for the home and garden section.

Automobile sections

In addition to automobile publicity and advertising, the automobile page covers accessory industries such as the tire, gas, and oil industries.

Travel sections

Travel sections of newspapers usually comprise canned stories and stock pictures about the glories of certain localities, but many now carry exclusive stories on trips, locales, or transportation. They are a valuable medium for the travel and community publicist drumming up travel.

Real estate sections

The real estate section appeals chiefly to realtors and home builders and their associations. It is used as a clearinghouse for their news and advertising.

Many real estate sections include home and garden material. Some are expanded into business and industrial fields and constitute a weekly summary of the entire business picture.

Books

Limited to book reviews, news about books, and advertisements, this section is of increasing general interest.

Special editions

Special editions of metropolitan newspapers furnish an excellent publicity medium for organizations that carry advertising space and for community organizations and associations.

Annual editions

Many large papers publish these on New Year's Day, Labor Day, and other holidays or anniversaries.

Periodic editions

These are issued when a city has a world's fair, a Mardi Gras or other pageant, or a huge convention.

Educational editions

Before each school term, educational sections usually come out with stories about local institutions' needs and problems, and preparing children.

Special business editions

Some papers put out special financial editions around New Year's Day. Many put out special automobile show editions with the beginning of a new automobile year. Often when a new store or business institution opens, a small business edition is published.

A masterpiece of special-edition work occurs when the publicist can sufficiently build his or her subject so that special editions are wrapped around it. Such an achievement provides a whole section, supports the client with advertisements paid for by many others, and bends the publicity efforts and budgets of numerous copy writers, photographers, and photo suppliers to the advantage of the special edition and the subject it honors. Many such sections, however, are contingent on providing a specified volume of supporting advertising.

Local Press

America has more than 8,600 weekly, semiweekly, and triweekly newspapers.

Whereas the metropolitan mammoth reaches tens and hundreds of thousands of readers, the small-town paper reaches thousands or only hundreds. But it *reaches* them. It reaches their hearts.

A majority of the readers of a small-town paper know its editor or some staff member. The hometown paper is a member of the family, hence it *can* tell the reader. Because it carries the names of many people the reader knows, it is read thoroughly. When a publicist has a story in a small-town paper, a good audience is assured. For this reason, aiming material at the small-town newspaper is more important than the circulation of the paper might indicate.

For years publicity people have dumped avalanches of general mass-produced articles in the mails. Estimates are that editors of small-town papers have dumped as much as 95 percent into wastebaskets.

The formula for success with the hometown press is simple, but the application is difficult because there are so many community newspapers. Local news plus local contacts will do the job.

If an organization has a local branch, representative, official, dealer, or other person who can deliver the story material by hand, its chances for publication greatly increase. If the trouble is taken to mention a local name or place or some local "angle," it will probably mean the difference between the editor's using and discarding the story.

The armed forces make particular use of a device often employed by hotels, schools, and other organizations. They send specific stories to hometown papers about the activities of servicemen from those towns. If Mr. John Doe from Dearborn, Indiana, becomes engaged in some activity elsewhere—gets promoted, gets married, wins an award, is graduated, or whatever—it will make a good story for any small-town newspaper serving Dearborn, Indiana.

The local contact method of national coverage involves effort by a central headquarters to organize the contacts. The most efficient method is a form of publicity kit, copies of which are made available to each local publicity person, chairman, or contact. The kits include general instructions for efficient publicity in the community. Usually, there is a calendar with suggestions for stories at various times of the year. There are a number of prepared stories with blanks for filling in local names. In many cases a new kit is sent out each month. Vital elements of news are *names* and *locations*. The central office cannot furnish these through mass mailings. But a kit furnishes the skeleton, conforming with a national policy. The local contact can fill in the all-important local news facts, names, and angles, then deliver the completed story to local editors.

Motion picture publicity often approaches the community newspaper through the local theaters, not directly from the studio. The local theater advertises in its own name, not in the name of the studio that produced the

picture. The manager eats at the club with the newspaper editor. The copy is local copy. Of course the substance was generated in Hollywood, but it was planted with a local angle supplied by the local theater manager.

One publicist for a big city company with many small branches made it a point personally to cover the rural front. He knew the newspaper people by their first names and occasionally took them to lunch. One of the editors told him, "If the President of the United States was assassinated just at press time, I'd still say, 'Let the presses roll.' But if Jim Jones of the local high school got an attack of appendicitis, I'd say, 'Hold the presses and include the story.'"

Increasingly, computerized lists and systems are being used to simplify and speed localized releases. They make it more practical to make large mailings of localized releases from a central point. *Publicists* offered the following tips that are especially helpful in localizing mailings when computerized systems are used:

- Include the name and telephone number of a local or regional contact in the heading if one is available. These are merely two more blank spaces to be filled in by the computer.

- Write a model release text, leaving blank spaces for local information.

- Prepare an itemization of the material to be inserted into the various versions of the release. Label each with a part key, such as AA, AB, AC, etc.

- List the geographic localities to which releases are to go. Each locality should be keyed to an entry in the list of fill-ins.

- Select the types of media for which the releases are suitable.

Computerized mailing services will select all media of the types indicated that serve the localities listed. They will produce the number of releases required for each locality by filling the local information into the model text. Each release will appear to be individually typed, with no evidence of fill-ins. The localized releases will be inserted mechanically into the appropriate envelopes and mailed out. Among these services are the following:

Media Distribution Services
307 W. 36th Street
New York, NY 10008

Media Distribution Services has full-service plants in Atlanta, Boston, Chicago, Detroit, Los Angeles, Minneapolis, Philadelphia, Pittsburgh, San Francisco, and Washington, DC.

PR Data Systems
15 Oakwood Avenue
Norwalk, CT 06850

The cost of making computerized mailings of localized releases will usually run between 50 percent and 100 percent more than the cost for the same number of releases that are not individualized. (Lists of weekly newspapers in directories are mentioned in the Appendix.)

The hometown press is a soapbox or cracker barrel for business. Because the editors, like farmers, are free enterprisers themselves, they are natural champions of private initiative in business. Because these newspapers are small and intimate, they exert more influence with their readers than do metropolitan daily newspapers. Of course, the publicity person can make a bigger splash in the *New York Times*, but often the person-to-person effort to put a message across in the hometown press will accomplish sufficient results to justify the difficult task involved.

Special Newspapers

Publicity workers will find the many foreign-language dailies and hundreds of weeklies worthwhile media for reaching specific racial and national groups, especially on controversial matters, such as politics and discrimination. Sometimes these papers are rather thin and verge on being advertising rackets; they should be studied and understood before they are used.

Financial and business newspapers, such as *The Wall Street Journal*, *Investor's Daily*, and the *Journal of Commerce New York*, are excellent media for all kinds of business, professional, technical, and financial news.

A new form of business newspaper is the local or regional publication. This differs from other local business publications, usually published monthly or biweekly, that are magazines rather than news publications. (A list is in the Appendix.)

Labor papers generally carry news about social as well as economic problems, gossip, and news on amusements, industry news, legislation, and negotiations affecting wages and working conditions.

In most cases, labor papers are mailed to the homes of union members.

There are about 235 foreign-language or immigrant-interest newspapers in the United States, both daily and weekly. Many of these have a strong influence on their readership. Their interest is predominantly in ethnic and neighborhood matters of direct concern to their readers. For effective treatment, material should be provided in the language of the newspaper, whenever possible. Lists are available in the *Editor & Publisher Yearbook*.

There are about 750 newspapers primarily for an African-American audience. Most of these carry only material of direct concern to their readers, though some function as the primary newspapers of their audiences. It is important to know the viewpoint of each paper, since some are oriented to helping their readers succeed in American society while others are strongly militant.

Using News Syndicates

For spreading news over a wide area from regional to international in scope, the publicity worker will find that syndicates of various kinds bring much better results than direct servicing by mail. The material must be especially good to be accepted and distributed by a syndicate, but if a syndicate picks it up large circulation is obtained with no further trouble and expense to the publicist.

The major U.S. news networks or "wire services" are the following:

Associated Press
50 Rockefeller Plaza
New York, NY 10020

Reuters
1700 Broadway
New York, NY 10019

United Press International
1400 I Street, NW
Washington, DC 20005

Each has local offices in important cities.

These news syndicates welcome news from publicity sources. Often they pick up news of a publicity origin from newspapers and other local media. Where a publicist's material has potential interest to these networks, a copy of the story should go to the wire services at the same time it goes to the newspapers and broadcasting news rooms. This not only speeds coverage and gives the story full attention, but also makes it easy for the syndicate editors to telephone the source and further develop the story.

If national publicity is a prime objective, the publicist should prepare special stories for these services in the specific styles they prefer, and so mark them. Frequently the services will work with a publicist to develop a story.

Special attention is required for timing, specifications of the syndicates, the pattern of regional services and relay points that limit geographical coverage of story material, deadlines, and other details. Every publicist will build a different pattern, depending on the requirements of clients. If he or she serves more than one client, a different pattern of syndication for each client should be developed.

Many types of syndicates can help public relations organizations in specific ways. For example, the National Catholic News Service, 1312 Massachusetts Avenue, NW, Washington, DC 20005, is an excellent medium for reaching the Catholic readers of America because it directly serves the diocesan press. Reuters and the Department of State, as well as AP and UPI, are among services for distributing news internationally. The Associated Press, Reuters, Bloomberg Business News, based at 499 Paric Avenue, New York, NY 10022, and UPI financial wires and the Dow Jones News Service, headquartered at 200 Liberty Street, New York, NY 10281, handle business news. In some metropolitan areas a local "city news service" is subsidized either by a group of local papers or by a national news service to service local news to many client papers within the metropolitan region. (A list of news syndicates is in the Appendix.)

Syndicated Features

Some 350 feature associations of varying sizes buy, promote, and distribute comic strips, preprint releases, news features, columns, cartoons, and other services.

(The leading feature syndicates are listed in the Appendix.)

Syndicated Photographs

One of the most important national publicity outlets of the publicity worker is the photo syndicate. When a photo syndicate accepts a picture, prints are mailed or wire-photoed to newspapers and magazines constituting the service's clientele. Because so many publications use syndicate photos, the results when a photo syndicate distributes a picture are great.

Photo services constitute one of the most formidable challenges of publicity. For a combination of reasons, photo syndicate people and TV camera operators are the most exacting craftspeople in the news profession. Their standards necessarily are high, because the photograph is a permanent record and a form of art, although often made under difficult, fast-moving circumstances. Photographers must coordinate composition, angles, lighting, and shutter speed with the action they are photographing.

These challenges of their trade make photo syndicate personnel fast and sharp. They dislike amateurism and are annoyed by the many examples of it shown by publicity photographs submitted to them.

Here are a few principles to remember when serving the national photo syndicate:

1. Whenever possible, submit a negative rather than a print.

2. The picture must stand alone. In local publicity the picture often accompanies a story that amplifies and helps carry it. In national syndicate publicity, the picture and caption must measure up without a story. Hence:

3. The picture must tell a story. It must be so framed that with its caption it will be completely self-explanatory.

4. The picture must have universal interest. What is universal interest in a picture?

   - Beauty of scene or limb
   - Imagination and contrast, like the New Year's publicity gag showing Father Time coming out of the sea accompanied by four nymphs in bathing suits, to convey the idea that it's warm in dead of winter in the specified resort area
   - The ingenuity of mankind, as shown, for example, in a picture of dozens of newly manufactured airplanes symmetrically poised to take off
   - Colorful events, like a parade of floats with flowers and beautiful girls

"Universal interest" in a picture will command the attention of any reader anywhere.

5. The picture must be mechanically right. The composition must be good. The background must be suitable. No unnecessary objects may be shown. Everything in the picture must have a reason and explain itself or logically work into the caption. The focus must be exact, with lighting, exposure, and techniques combining. Good mechanics also implies economy in size. The more compact the picture, the more easily the editors can use it. The best picture is so flexible that an editor can run it in full for a three- or four-column cut, or can crop it to a one- or two-column cut without damaging it.

Photo syndicates have thousands of pictures submitted daily and select only a few in a stringent competition.

6. The picture must be well captioned. Captions have "sold" many pictures to editors and readers. The publicist must inject the client's message and explain everything not manifest in the picture in a very few words. All persons must be named. The place and occasion must be described.

7. A series of negatives should be made. Shoot four identically similar negatives on each setup, one for each major syndicate. Newspapers do not like to get the identical pictures supplied to their rivals, but syndicates do not object. They frequently cover towns not supplied by their rivals.

The major picture syndicates and their addresses are as follows:

Associated Press News Photo
50 Rockefeller Plaza
New York, NY 10020

Black Star Publishing co.
116 E. 27th Street
New York, NY 10016

Globe Photos, Inc.
275 Seventh Avenue
New York, NY 10001

UPI Newspictures
1400 I Street, NW
Washington, DC 20005

Wagner-International Photos
62 W. 45th Street
New York, NY 10017

Wide World Photos, Inc.
50 Rockefeller Plaza
New York, NY 10020

Some of these organizations have offices in other major cities. If they are not stationed in a given area, negatives may be sent to their nearest editors. Photo services are always looking for good pictures and will gladly consider them.

When moving negatives to the syndicates, the publicist can often simultaneously offer prints to the local papers and get the always desirable local break in addition to national coverage.

U.S. Newswire, National Press Building 2, Washington, DC 20045, (202) 347-2770, sends press releases and photos to about fifty newspapers that agree to consider them, for a fee paid by the publicist.

Feature Photo Service, 62 W. 45th Street, New York, NY 10036, (212) 661-6120, sends sheets of publicity photos to more than 500 newspapers. Editors select those they want.

Distribution Firms

Certain national and regional copy, editorial, photo feature, and cartoon services distribute publicity material commercially as a service to public relations people. In many cases such a service is more effective and economical than direct distribution. (*See* Figure 22.1.)

To distribute publicity material to hundreds or thousands of newspapers, the element of expense frequently requires that copy be produced in numbers. Major newspapers prefer to make their own engravings, but smaller papers cannot afford this process and usually will not use art unless it is supplied in the form of matrices, glossy proofs, or reproduction proofs. Mats are more effective if accompanied by proofs showing what they look like. If the caption is cast with the cut in the mat, it guarantees against loss of caption and ensures the desired credits. Some syndicates and services get out full pages or sections in boilerplate or mat form, or glossy proofs for offset printing.

Some of the publicity distribution services feature one or more of the above processes. Some of them offer a choice of processes.

These services keep their lists up to date. Many of them have especially good standing with editors because they handle only material of acceptable quality. The cost is moderate. (A list appears in Chapter 20.)

In general, color is used for food, decorating, or travel pages or for special sections or Sunday magazine sections of the paper. Publicity budgets favor food on an all-year basis. To cover the cost of photography and distribution, use by many papers should be assured if the project is to be worthwhile. A color service provides lists of U.S. and Canadian dailies with color facilities, handles mailings, and analyzes returns on the numbers of papers using the supplied material in various forms.

```
DERUS MEDIA SERVICE, INC.                    February  3, 1995
500 N. DEARBORN STREET
CHICAGO, ILLINOIS  60610



John & Jane Doe                  Clips        :       152
Doe Incorporated                 Circulation  :  2,122,049
1 Main Street
Productville, US


EJR-63      SAMPLE PRINT REPORT
```

PUBLICATION	CITY	STATE	CIRC	DATEUSED	BUREAU	DATESENT
The Delta Paper	Delta Junction	AK	1,200	07/30/92	B	09/14/92
Beacon & Alabama Citizen	Mobile	AL	7,000	07/25/92	LBA	09/14/92
Journal-Independent	Piedmont	AL	3,450	03/23/94	L	05/10/94
The Star Progress	Berryville	AR	2,300	08/05/92	LBA	09/14/92
Times-Echo	Eureka Springs	AR	2,500	08/06/92	LBA	09/14/92
Tribune	Green Forest	AR	2,700	08/05/92	LA	09/14/92
Inyo Register/Review-Herald	Bishop	CA	12,300	04/14/93	BAL	05/27/93
Bulletin	Carson	CA	18,000	04/14/93	L	05/27/93
Bulletin	Compton	CA	22,000	04/14/93	L	05/27/93
Inglewood Tribune	Compton	CA	10,000	04/14/93	L	05/27/93
Lynwood Journal	Compton	CA	15,000	04/14/93	L	05/27/93
Mobile Home News	Garden Grove	CA	2,500	08/26/92	D	10/14/92
Observer	Sacramento	CA	46,200	07/29/92	L	09/14/92
Observer	Sacramento	CA	46,200	10/14/92	L	12/07/92
Observer	Sacramento	CA	46,200	10/28/92	L	12/07/92
Observer	Sacramento	CA	46,200	01/28/93	L	03/11/93
Observer	Sacramento	CA	46,200	04/27/94	L	06/16/94
Precinct Reporter	San Bernardino	CA	55,000	07/09/92	LB	08/06/92
La Oferta Review	San José	CA	40,000	08/01/92	LDA	09/14/92
La Oferta Review	San Jose	CA	40,000	10/14/92	ADL	11/06/92
Leisure World Golden Rain Ne	Seal Beach	CA	9,000	07/23/92	D	09/14/92
Midway Driller	Taft	CA	4,500	07/09/92	BLA	08/06/92
Beacon	Wilmington	CA	10,000	04/14/93	L	05/27/93
Herald	Haxtun	CO	1,500	07/15/92	B	09/14/92
De Soto Sun Herald	Arcadia	FL	9,500	07/29/92	L	09/14/92
Weekly Journal	Bristol	FL	3,800	07/08/92	A	09/14/92
Levy County Journal	Bronson	FL	1,100	07/30/92	BA	09/14/92
Capital Outlook	Tallahassee	FL	11,333	07/16/92	L	09/14/92
Daily World	Atlanta	GA	40,000	07/02/92	BL	08/06/92
Enterprise	Douglas	GA	6,200	07/15/92	L	09/14/92
Herald-Journal	Greensboro	GA	4,300	07/10/92	B	09/14/92
Journal	Armstrong	IA	836	08/05/92	LA	09/14/92
Sentinel	Aurelia	IA	1,200	07/08/92	B	08/06/92
News	Bettendorf	IA	4,500	07/09/92	B	08/06/92
N. Warren Town & Country New	Norwalk	IA	1,176	08/20/92	BA	10/14/92
Marion County News	Pleasantville	IA	1,322	07/30/92	BA	09/14/92
Freeman-Journal	Webster City	IA	5,000	08/28/92	LBA	10/14/92
Chicago South End Citizen	Chicago	IL	25,375	07/06/92	DB	08/06/92
Chicago Chatham Citizen	Chicago	IL	28,630	07/06/92	D	08/06/92

Figure 22.1 Sample report of placements from a publicity release distributed by a media services company. *Courtesy Derus Media Service, Chicago.*

Often a color placement is offered exclusively to one editor in a city in the major cities where papers have facilities to run color.

Public Relations Newswire Services

Public relations newswires now operate in many major cities of the United States and Canada. These frequently make available direct connections with the offices of public relations firms and other subscribers to the service. They accept news stories by wire, fax, phone, or mail and retransmit them into the news rooms of daily newspapers, magazines, radio and television stations, and some brokerage and financial firms.

Speed and simultaneous coverage are the obvious advantages of this service. For example, an action taken by a company's board of directors that may affect stockholders, employees, and customers can be relayed to all interested media within a few minutes. A story can be transmitted simultaneously to the public relations newswires in all the cities that have them and can also be relayed to similar public relations newswires serving the major cities of Canada, England, Japan, and some other countries.

Several of the U.S. operations are also set up to handle fast distribution of photographs and speeches or background material that is too lengthy for wire transmission.

The U.S. and Canadian public relations newswire services include:

U.S.—National

PR Newswire
810 Seventh Avenue
New York, NY 10019
(212) 596-1500

PR Newswire has branches in Atlanta, Boston, Charlotte, Cleveland, Denver, Detroit, Los Angeles, Miami, Minneapolis, Orange County (CA), Orlando, Philadelphia, Pittsburgh, Salt Lake City, San Diego, San Francisco, San Jose, Seattle, Washington DC.

PRN
150 E. 58th Street
New York, NY
(212) 832-9400

An affiliate, Universal News Service, serves the United Kingdom.

Business Wire
44 Montgomery Street
San Francisco, CA
(415) 986-4422

Business Wire has branches in Atlanta, Boston, Charlotte, Cleveland, Denver, Los Angeles, Miami, Minneapolis, Nashville, Orange County (CA), Philadelphia, Phoenix, San Diego, Santa Clara (CA), and Seattle.

U.S.—Regional

Empire Information Services
640 Franklin Street
Suite 302
Schenectady, NY 12305
(318) 372-0785

Iowa/Missouri Link
406 Stevens Street
Iowa Falls, IA 50126
(515) 648-4639

Oklahoma Newswire
305 Mid-Continent Tower
Tulsa, OK 74103
(918) 582-6011

PR News Service
35 E. Wacker Drive
Suite 792
Chicago, IL 60601
(312) 782-8100

Mid-Atlantic Newspaper Services, Inc.
2717 North Front Street
Harrisburg, PA 17110
(717) 234-4067

Southwest Newswire
2301 N. Akard Street
Suite 300
Dallas, TX 75201
(214) 871-2940

Wire News Network
200 N. Broadway
Suite 1800
St. Louis, MO 63102
(314) 231-2104

Canada

Canada Corporate News
One Financial Place
25 Adelaide Street East
Suite 500
Toronto, Ontario M5C 3A1
(416) 362-0885

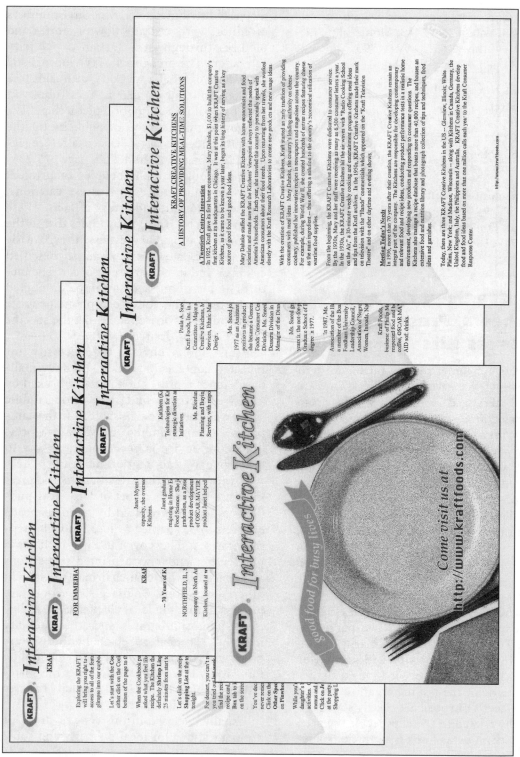

Figure 22.2 A press kit contains such items as news releases and articles for publication, background information directed to various types of media, a fact sheet, and a portfolio of illustrations. The cover has pockets inside for grouping the materials. *Kraft is a registered trademark of Kraft Foods, Inc. Photo used with permission.*

Canada Corporate News has branch offices in Calgary, (403) 266-2443; Montreal, (514) 861-7801; Ottawa, (613) 722-4793; Vancouver, (604) 683-1066.

Canadian Newswire Ltd.
10 Bay Street
Suite 914
Toronto, Ontario M5J 2R8
(416) 863-9350

Telbec
1111 rue Saint-Urbain
Suite 1-11
Montreal, Quebec H2Z 1Y6
(514) 871-1161

Effective Use of Clipsheets, Press Books, and Press Kits

Clipsheets are sometimes a valuable form of mail coverage for national publicity. They are material, arranged in column widths, from which selections of news can be made by the editor. With a clipsheet the editor can see how the story will actually appear and what size space it will fill.

The editor has a choice of several stories of various lengths and on various phases of the sender's subject. Some clipsheets include a selection of photos and cartoons for which mats or glossy prints may be obtained on request. Editors often hold them for use when a hole of a certain size is available in a page about to go to press.

Clipsheets are an admirable conveyance for "filler copy," little one- and two-paragraph squibs. They now are used primarily by editors of small newspapers for quick insertion into blank spaces that occur in makeup.

The name of the issuing organization and the clipsheet's purpose are clearly stated.

Closely related to the clipsheet is the press book or kit. A press book is a mine of source material distributed to provide large numbers of editors with a steady flow of stories and pictures throughout a sustained publicity campaign. The press book is the journalistic equivalent of what a speakers' manual is to a speakers' bureau campaign. Press books fit such campaigns as a motion picture's publicity campaigns, a season of publicity for the United Fund, or a world science fair. (*See* Figures 22.2, page 369, and 22.3, page 372.)

Press books are photocopied or printed. They contain stories, pictures, cartoons, graphs, editorials, and arrays of facts. These features can be arranged by topics that fit the campaign's subsidiary events; they can be arranged by dates; or they can be presented *en masse* and in no particular order. The pictures and cartoons shown can be numbered so the individual editor can phone or write to the publicity office requesting the specific photos or mats desired.

Press books obviate the necessity for repeated contacts or weekly and daily mailings. Hence a press book must be backed by a stiff advertising budget or strong public interest in the campaign subject. If the campaign is strong enough to warrant a press book, the device is an economical way to develop a large amount of publicity.

A variation of the press book is the press kit. One version is a sort of loose-leaf publicity blueprint prepared by national headquarters to be adapted by local publicity representatives. The cover usually includes a publicity calendar with printed suggestions and space for the local chairman to write in other suggestions. Boldface suggestions are printed urging the local chapter to save clippings, photos, programs, and other publicity material. National or regional addresses are given with the request that local material be forwarded. The national office uses this material as the basis for national publicity releases and as part of its record.

Usually enclosed in this type of press kit are suggestions for local publicity and some publicity stories with blanks for insertion of local names, places, and dates. Local chairmen are urged to convert this canned copy by injecting all local names and facts, then to place the material personally with local newspapers and other media.

Such press or publicity kits may include such enclosures as the following:

- "Publicity code" or formula for acquiring local publicity
- Brief on rules and mechanics of publicity
- Brief on press relations
- National matter for pickup and local "planting"
- Prompting for local participation in national moves, such as anniversaries, national conventions, contests, and others
- Photos and mats for local "planting"
- Features
- Clipsheets
- Canned editorials
- Shorts and fillers
- Stimuli for each local unit to contribute its resources and information to the national headquarters and to other local units
- Calendar to be followed locally
- National features, announcements, events, and other details for local adoption
- Guidance for local participation in and extension of national events
- Cartoons for local use
- Monthly suggestions to keep the speakers' bureau active
- Monthly suggestions to stimulate local committees to new activity
- Suggestions for stimulating local activity by generating competition with other local units

Press kits are also developed for national use or for a local program, rather than to be used as source material by a grassroots unit. A bank about to move into an impressive new building, for instance, might have a press kit containing releases, feature stories, photos, historical and statistical background, and so on. Press kits are also often developed for introductions of new products (*see* Chapters 14 and 20).

Press Publicity Mechanics

Copy is the backbone of publicity production. Copy is the text of a story, a picture, a broadcast, a letter, or a publication. The basic rule of copy is to include all that is needed to tell the story, in the right order, in the most direct and simple language possible—that, and no more. As a general rule, conform as closely as possible to the style requirements of the particular medium for which placement is planned.

The following are rules to be followed in preparing copy:

1. When using names, the first name, middle initial, and last name should be given, and the person's title, if any. In stories to out-of-town papers using a name to establish a local angle, the person's home address should be given, both for its local interest and to facilitate matters if the newspaper desires to contact the person or family for additional information.

2. Good newspaper copy is written in a simple, straightforward, objective style with sentences neither too long nor too short. It is important to avoid editorial comment, personal opinions, colored words, or conclusions. Where material of this kind seems desirable, it must be presented as the direct quotation of an important individual whose name is used to "carry" the story.

3. The most acceptable copy paper is 8½" × 11" in size and good clear stock. To facil-

NEWS   U.S. SMALL BUSINESS ADMINISTRATION

Contact: R.P. Griffin, 312/886-0705

SMALL BUSINESS ADMINISTRATION'S CHICAGO DISTRICT OFFICE HONORS OUTSTANDING MINORITY BUSINESSES AND ADVOCATES

Illinois Minority Small Business Person, 8(a) Graduate and Majority Private Sector Firm of the Year Named Today

Chicago, September 19, 1995 -- The U.S. Small Business Administration's (SBA) Chicago District Office today named Pedro Cevallos-Candau, Partner, Primera Engineers as the Illinois Minority Small Business Person of the Year.

Also receiving awards today as part of the SBA's 13th annual celebration of Minority Enterprise Development Week (MED Week) are Illinois 8(a) Graduate of the Year Raymond Mota, president, Mota Construction Co., Inc., and Illinois Majority Private Sector Firm of the Year Harris Trust and Savings Bank for its efforts in supporting minority small businesses.

"MED Week is celebrated annually to honor the contributions and achievements of minority businesses and advocates throughout the U.S.," said John L. Smith, the SBA's Chicago District Director. "The success of Primera Engineers, Mota Construction and Harris Bank confirms the American dream can be realized by all. Diversity today is accepted and valued. As a result, the contributions of all cultures -- whether in arts, politics or business -- have become recognizably more significant."

As Minority Small Business Person of the Year, Cevallos-Candau and Primera Engineers have developed a reputation as one of Chicago's rising stars in the consulting engineering field. The eight-year-old company has grown at an impressive rate and has established itself as consistent performer in its field. The company was named Architectural and Engineering Firm of the Year both this year and in 1993 by the Hispanic American Construction Industry Association.   (more)

Figure 22.3 A good example of a news release. *Courtesy Harris Bank, Chicago.*

SBA MEDWEEK/2

The 8(a) Graduate of the Year, Raymond Mota, leads one of the largest Hispanic-owned construction companies in the Chicagoland area. Established in 1977, the company has more than 40 professionals working on projects throughout the greater Chicago area. The company is one of three minority-owned firms leading the construction of Harris Bank's branch expansion program. The SBA's 8(a) Business Development Program is one of several SBA programs designed to assist minority small business owners.

The Illinois Majority Private Sector Firm of the Year, Harris Bank, is receiving this honor for a second time. Harris was also the 1993 winner. Harris Bank has demonstrated its commitment to the small business community, including minority-owned businesses, through creative approaches to lending, developing below-prime borrowing opportunities for small businesses and a willingness to use SBA products tailored to providing increased capital to small businesses. The bank worked with the SBA to develop a loan program for minority and women subcontractors working on the McCormick Place expansion project and to design the SBA's Women Prequalification Program. Additionally, the bank's five-year-old Women in Business Banking Team continues to finance and educate women business owners, and the bank is actively using minority- and women-owned firms on the construction of two dozen new branches.

MED Week will be held next week, September 24. This year's theme is "Minority Business: Building America's Future Through Economic Growth and Job Creation."

# # #

Note: Award winners will be honored at a reception today at 4:30 p.m. at Harris Bank, 115 S. LaSalle, 37th Floor Guest Dining Room.

Figure 22.3 *continued*

itate any urge by the editor to check details or seek more story material, source of the story is usually given in the upper left-hand corner. Information desired includes name of the client and name, address, and telephone and fax numbers of the publicist. If the source is an agency handling several accounts, including the name of the client not only identifies the object of the story at a glance but preserves mention of the client's name in the story.

4. Release instructions should go in the upper right-hand corner. If the news is to be released when issued, the instruction should read "FOR IMMEDIATE RELEASE." If the copy is issued somewhat in advance of release date, release instructions should read "for Thursday *Times*" or "release Saturday, June 22, 2 P.M." By setting the release date ahead, the item can be handled by the editors and set into type during slack time. A release date or time should be used only when it is required or justified, as in the case of an actually scheduled meeting or announcement.

5. If the release is more than one page long, pages should be numbered and the word "more" should be at the end of each page except the last. The story should be closed by an end mark such as "30" or "###" or "*****." Whenever possible each page should end on the end of a paragraph.

6. The staff of an afternoon paper is at work before 7:30 A.M. Copy should be placed in the editor's hands during the middle of the preceding afternoon if possible. In few instances will a story get full attention if submitted later than 11 A.M. of the same day. Morning papers should receive publicity releases between 10 A.M. and noon of the preceding day. Stories submitted before 3 P.M. are likely to make all editions, and important stories usually can be placed with morning papers as late as 10 P.M.

7. Sunday copy should reach the city desk before Friday noon, or before Thursday noon if the paper has advance "bulldog" editions for country circulation. Spot news can be submitted as late as 4 P.M. Saturday.

8. When a story is short, skip a third of the page to allow room for copy-desk marking. Type all stories with double or triple spacing. Leave ample margins on both sides. Type on one side of the paper only. Sometimes a well-written headline three spaces across the top of the "lead" or in the upper right-hand corner helps to "sell" a story to the editorial desk.

9. Always have the date on a release. It can be in the dateline (Des Moines, Feb. 7, —) or at the beginning or end of the story. Editors want to know whether the material is timely when they get it. Also, when copy is filed and then referred to later, there is no way of telling when it originated unless it is dated.

10. The newspaper lead—that is, the opening—answers these questions: Who? What? When? Where? Why? How? The expertly written news or publicity story can be cut from the bottom up and still be complete. It is severely accurate. Where possible, copy conforms to the style of the publication to which it is issued. The name of the client or the publicity point of the story is woven into the lead or as high into the story as possible in such a way that it cannot easily be deleted without destroying the core of the story.

11. Every editor's interpretation of news is different.

Whether or not a story is news depends primarily on three points:

- The actual, universal news interest involved
- The individual newspaper's policy
- The local angle—local names, organizations, interests

An important publicity challenge, sometimes requiring simultaneously the judgment of a Solomon and the tact of a Talleyrand, is concerned with exclusives, special breaks, whether to offer a story to morning or to evening papers, and rotation of such breaks. (*See* Chapter 21.)

When a release is broken in the morning papers, it should be reslanted or given a new lead in the P.M. papers if possible.

Only the rarest publicity stories will involve a high ingredient of universal news interest. Inadequacy of news interest and neglect of policy and local angle account for estimates that more than 90 percent of the publicity written and distributed goes into the wastebasket.

Graphics

Photographs have many advantages to the publicist. A good photo may be syndicated to hundreds of newspapers and magazines. Although hurried or lazy readers may not see a news story, they can hardly miss the pictures. Seeing a picture, they will absorb the message at a glance. A big advantage of the photo is that it seldom can be altered by editing. It is either used or it isn't; if it is, it tells the story, providing it was properly conceived.

The photographic program begins with planning the pictures, synchronizing them with the story schedule. The photographer is carefully briefed on what the publicist desires to achieve.

Good publicity pictures are framed to fill as small a space as possible, because an editor who can't use a large picture may have space for a small one; if he likes the small one, he can always blow it up. The best pictures are those that can be either used in full or cropped—with part of the picture cut off without hurting the remainder.

A news picture in itself tells the story. It may be good enough to tell the story without even a caption, but it will never be printed if submitted without a caption.

The best pictures convey action or a candid view. Models who look directly into the lens usually "look" the picture right out of the newspapers. "Poster" or "billboard" pictures in which models are displayed holding signs that tell the story lack originality and creativeness and usually get no farther than the editor's wastebasket.

The caption identifies all persons in the picture with full name and initials, in order left to right, with sufficient background information so there is no question in the editor's mind. It is better to tell too much than too little. The caption is best pasted under the print or stripped into the print so the editor can look at picture and caption without shifting. It is never wise to write on the reverse side of the print.

Most publicity art is printed on glossy 8″ × 10″ paper. With some newspapers, matte (dull finish) will do. If the photo is exceptionally good, it may pay to present it in the more spectacular 11″ × 14″ or 20″ × 24″ sizes. Portraits may be 5″ × 7″.

In working with Sunday magazine sections, color may be used. A transparency is preferable to a print. For the most part in placing color publicity on a widespread basis, it is preferable to work through a service set up to make national contacts (as previously discussed).

When mailing or dispatching photo copy, a manila envelope with cardboard or plastic inserts to prevent cracking is suitable. The image side is best pointed toward the back of the envelope so the post office stamp won't damage the print. It is advisable to plainly mark: "Photographs, Do Not Bend."

Reaching a cost understanding with the photographer in advance provides good budget insurance. The photographer can be paid on a so-much-a print basis or on a time-plus-expenses basis. Best results are obtained if the photographer is hired for excellence, not economy; no savings are realized in pictures that editors will not use.

It usually pays to send out a publicity person to help the photographer. Often two people may be needed to arrange props, handle lights, record names for captions, and take care of other details.

The publicist's job is to make all arrangements, line up the place, see to it that the models and others involved are there on time, and have all necessary props on hand. Most publicists make suggestions to the photographer but find it profitable to heed the photographer's judgment.

For legal safety, it is wise to have everyone appearing in a picture sign a simple form to the effect:

> Permission to use my name and/or photograph for publicity purposes is hereby given.
>
> ————————————————— (signed).

(A more complete legal release form is shown in Figure 48.1, page 722.)

There are several types of publicity pictures:

1. Straight news shots are photos of news events such as train wrecks, or combat shots of troops and/or equipment in action.

2. "Mug art" is the trade name for straight portrait pictures. These are easy to produce, economical, and attractive to editors because such shots require only one column by 3″ of space or can even be run in the same column beside type.

3. "Leg art," known in the trade as "cheesecake," will be popular as long as beautiful women hold their places in the minds, hearts, and imaginations of men.

4. Action shots show the subject doing something, such as a mechanic working on an engine or an athlete performing.

5. Pattern shots—or inanimate object shots—show views of objects usually arranged in patterns to attain a striking arrangement, symmetry, and perspective. These are excellent for industrial publicity.

6. Product shots are designed primarily to show off a product.

Good taste is paramount in photographs. Because the editor may have an eye for a pretty woman is no cause to overdo cheesecake. Corny gags may make the papers, but create laughs *at* the client instead of *with* him. Better no picture than one that reflects negatively on the subject. "I don't care what you say about me just so you use my name" is an axiom of the pre-public relations era of publicity. It is unsound today.

For many purposes, stock or special photographs may be needed. Most cities have shops that can provide such pictures for local use. For national use, good sources include the following:

Advertising Age
740 N. Rush Street
Chicago, IL 60611

Corbis/Bettmann Archive
902 Broadway
New York, NY 10022

Comstock
30 Irving Place
New York, NY 10003

Culver Pictures
150 W. 22nd Street
New York, NY 10001

Ewing Galloway
Rockville Center, NY 11570

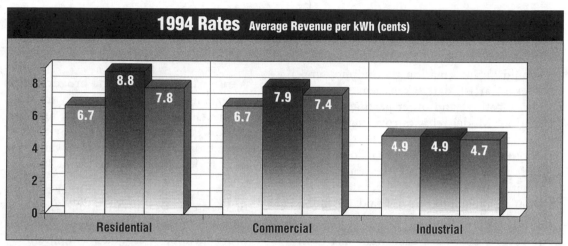

1994 Rates Average Revenue per kWh (cents)

Residential: 6.7, 8.8, 7.8
Commercial: 6.7, 7.9, 7.4
Industrial: 4.9, 4.9, 4.7

Figure 22.4 A bar chart distributed by the American Public Power Association compares the cost per kilowatt-hour to customers of publicly owned, investor-owned, and cooperative electric utilities in 1994. *Courtesy American Public Power Association, Washington, DC.*

Globe Photos
275 Seventh Avenue
New York, NY 10001

Historical Pictures Service
921 W. Van Buren
Chicago, IL 60607

Photo Researchers, Inc.
60 E. 56th Street
New York, NY 10022

H. Armstrong Roberts
4203 Locust Street
Philadelphia, PA 19104

United Press International
1400 I Street, NW
Washington, DC 20005

World Wide Photos (Associated Press)
50 Rockfeller Plaza
New York, NY 10020

The picture syndicates, listed previously in this chapter, are excellent sources from which to purchase pictures on a variety of subjects.

Stock photograph sources also are listed in the classified pages of telephone directories in many major cities.

Other types of illustrations include cartoons, maps, drawings, graphs, architects' plans, and architects' drawings. (*See* Figure 22.4.) If the subject has enough news interest, frequently a newspaper's artist will cooperate in preparing an illustration sufficiently different from the usual photographs to be a good attention-getter.

The most frequently used types of non-photo graphics used by newspapers are maps (46 percent of uses) and bar charts (17 percent). Though more and more papers are using color, the majority are still black-and-white and a relatively small but growing percentage are in four-color.

Illustration Files

It is essential to maintain systematic and complete files of all illustrative materials. There are a number of filing systems, but all good ones should include the following:

1. A central file containing a file copy of each photo or piece of art in whatever form it may have been taken—black-and-white, color transparency, color print,

slide, drawing, chart, or overhead projector transparency. This copy should be marked "DO NOT REMOVE." With it should be information on the photographer, or artist, date taken, negative number, location, and other pertinent information. Model releases covering persons shown either should be filed with the photo or a note should be enclosed indicating where the model release is filed. If the item has been purchased, information should be filed on the price paid, to whom, and for what rights.

2. A record of where each item has been submitted. It is especially important to indicate when it has been offered exclusively to one medium, with what story, and for what period. If an item has been mass produced and distributed widely, either a summary of the distribution or a copy of the distribution order should be kept with a copy of that item.

3. A record of publication, broadcast, or other use of the item. This is to avoid future embarrassment in using an illustration that has been previously seen, if the editor or broadcast outlet wants one not previously exposed to public view.

4. Cross references indicating other versions of the item. For instance, one shot may have been used for newspaper publicity, in a slidefilm, in a booklet, in an annual report, and in an advertisement. Both color and black-and-white versions may exist. It is essential that whoever encounters it in any file knows that other versions exist and should be checked.

23

PUBLICITY IN MAGAZINES

HERBERT M. BAUS

Magazines feature the combined aspects of newspapers (designed to be read on the run) and books (designed to be read at leisure). The magazine serves to elaborate and to interpret matters of current interest.

Since magazine stories often allow the writer a degree of personal opinion, many magazines provide excellent vehicles for explaining an organization's policy. An effective article also tends to make a strong impression on the reader and can be especially useful in reprint form for direct mail and other secondary forms of distribution.

Though magazines are good for single spectacular publicity "breaks," it is likely these breaks will stand alone like a monolith in a desert of silence. Newspapers and broadcast publicity media, on the other hand, provide advantages in their more constant and frequent intimacy with the individual, as well as their local perspective. Newspapers, radio, and television also lend themselves to the kind of day-in/day-out persistent treatment of subject matter crucial to shaping public opinion.

However, utilizing magazine articles as a secondary line of publicity coverage has become increasingly common. In addition to the standard print versions, some magazines are now offered on computer disks, cassettes, the Internet, and CD-ROM. Some magazine material is later recycled to create other types of materials, such as yearbooks, how-to manuals, and so on.

Approximately 430 monthly consumer magazines are currently published in the United States. Scores of weekly and several thousand trade magazines as well as numerous company publications also exist. The best general references of magazines and similar periodicals are *Bacon's Magazine Directory*,[1] *The Standard Periodical Directory*,[2] *Burrelle's Media Directories*,[3] *Standard Rate and Data Service*,[4] *Working Press of the Nation*,[5] and *Writer's Market*.[6] All of these directories classify magazines by types and specify what they publish. (The Appendix includes lists of major magazines of various types that are applicable to public relations professionals.)

Consumer magazines fall into three major categories: general-interest magazines, news and illustrated magazines, and specialized magazines. Each of these three broad types follows a different approach, impacts its readers in a different way, and must be approached using different publicity techniques.

Unlike newspapers, magazines tend to be quite distinctive from one another not only by their type, or category, but also by their individual style and scope within the general categories. Therefore, it is advisable to first study two or three consecutive recent issues of a specific publication before submitting story ideas or material to its editor.

---

[1]332 S. Michigan Avenue, Chicago, IL 60604.
[2]150 Fifth Avenue, New York, NY 10011.
[3]75 E. Northfield, Livingston, NJ 07039.
[4]3004 Glenview Road, Wilmette, IL 60091.
[5]121 Chanlon Road, New Providence, NJ 07974.
[6]9933 Alliance Road, Cincinnati, OH 45242.

Figure 23.1 First page of a memorandum to editors alerting them to an event and offering services for media covering it. *Courtesy Creamer Dickson Basford Public Relations.*

CREAMER DICKSON BASFORD
EUROCOM CORPORATE & PR

MEDIA ALERT
(THIS WEEK!)

Olympic fever isn't the only thing sweeping Atlanta -- according to a recent survey, 80% of Atlantans are also suffering from **chicken fatigue**. Common symptoms of chicken fatigue:

• You eat it more than three times a week

• You've exhausted all of your chicken recipe possibilities

• Your children and your spouse greet you with "oh no, not chicken again!"

Relief is on the way... During the week of August 28 (Tuesday, Wednesday or Thursday), Kraft Creative Kitchens will stage a "Chicken Makeover" with a local family to show Atlantans new ways to shop for, prepare and present chicken. In fact, we have a family in the area who's agreed to open up their kitchen to our Home Economist and your news staff.

The Makeover will consist of several parts:

1. The Kraft home economist will take stock of the family's pantry and of its current recipe repertoire; opportunity to interview all family members on menu likes and dislikes

2. The home economist will lead the family through a local supermarket to offer tips on how to shop most efficiently, effectively and creatively

3. Back at home, the home economist and family cook will prepare a quick, easy and tasty chicken dinner using tips from the dietitian and a variety of products.

Dealing Effectively with Magazine Editors

Major national magazines—as rated in terms of circulation and staff strength—prepare or buy their own material. They rarely, if ever, use publicist-written text intact. They do, however, use the services of publicists. This requires from the publicist news judgment, intuitive or lucky timing, sure feature sense, reliable research, and a sense for good illustrations—in short, editorial ability.

While top-circulation general magazines have long been averse to using trade names or credits in editorial material, recent changes in format help the publicist. In general, publicity on a product treated generically is much more acceptable than material about one brand of product. However, product credits are also attainable under certain circumstances.

For example, a publicist for the diamond industry may readily place a number of feature ideas dealing with the great gems of the world, favorite gems of well-dressed women, and so on, in all cases offering research and anecdotal material, and aiding the editor in crystallizing a feature about the appeal of gems. In the same way, a publicist who represents an association—say, florists or fishing tackle manufacturers—can place a feature favorable to all by supplying factual material, suggesting interview possibilities, helping set up photo arrangements, and performing similar functions to meet the editor's needs.

The large magazine is bombarded with thousands of publicity releases a day, scores of visitors bent on publicity missions, and constantly ringing phones. How then do you reach an editor?

Almost every editor relies on a list of known experts when information is required,

September 19, 1996

Dear Editor,

Our goal is to feed an additional 1,000,000 hungry and housebound Americans in 1997. Your readers can help!

Reynolds Metals, a long-time supporter of the National Association of Meal Programs, is joining forces again with Meals On Wheels to help feed the housebound people throughout the nation. Joe Regalbuto, the actor who plays Frank Fontana on CBS's Murphy Brown, and his wife Rosemary, the director of the Santa Monica/Malibu Meals On Wheels program are lending their support to help achieve Reynolds' goals.

1997 marks the 50th anniversary of the introduction of an American favorite, Reynolds Wrap® Aluminum Foil.   To celebrate, Reynolds is launching a nationwide search for 50,000 new Meals On Wheels volunteers, and donating 50 new vans to Meals On Wheels programs across the nation. In addition, Reynolds has created, 1-888-MEAL-HELP, a toll free number to call to volunteer for local Meals On Wheels programs.

Enclosed, for consideration in your February issue, is a slide and caption which feature Joe and Rosemary Regalbuto volunteering their time to Meals On Wheels by loading up a new van donated by Reynolds Metals. We believe your readers would also like to become involved and lend their time to this important organization and help Reynolds achieve their goal. I will call you next week to follow up and be sure you received these materials. If you would like further information please feel free to call me at 212/887-8076.

Thank you for your time and your assistance in helping your readers keep volunteerism alive.

Sincerely,

Kristin Francini
Account Executive

Figure 23.2 First page of a short memo to an editor offering a suggestion for an article, and indicating the nature of material that can be provided. *Courtesy Creamer Dickson Basford Public Relations.*

keeps a file of those who are well placed and well known as suppliers of usable news and ideas, and avoids those who "follow up" too frequently to check on the status of their offering.

Rewarding primary contacts with an editor are made in a number of ways and can lead to productive cooperation over the years.

There are several effective ways to approach these important national media.

Visits to the editor

The editor who knows and respects the publicist may extend herself by letting the publicist submit a story about a client, by assigning an ace staff writer to the subject, or by accepting a batch of material and having it rewritten for the magazine. She will be more receptive to personal letters than will an editor who does not know the writer of the let-

ter. Major magazines are targets of bales of letters, manuscripts, and communications of all kinds. It goes without saying that an approach from someone known to the editor and who has earned his or her confidence will have better results than the random shot. However, the welcome of the editors can easily be outworn by overuse. Request an appointment. Don't drop in unexpectedly.

Writing to the editor

Often a well-written letter or memorandum will spark the interest of an editor and lead to a request for more material to determine whether a story will be wanted. (*See* Figures 23.1 and 23.2.)

Queries

When a feature idea requires extensive research, it is best to query the editor in advance with a brief outline. If he feels it may be a good possibility, he will suggest you develop it for serious consideration.

Contacting local magazine outlets

Many national magazines have local editors and correspondents in many areas to serve the local freelance writers and to assure full national coverage of story possibilities. These local magazine representatives are looking for good ideas. Proper contact with them will sometimes enlist them as energetic proponents of the proposed article. Some publicists find it worthwhile to keep a large file of pictures for these local magazine writers and representatives, while others circularize them regularly. One large chamber of commerce, charged with publicizing its area, sponsors and helps finance a "Professional Writers' Association" and presents periodic dinners to maintain the contacts and stimulate the activity.

Press conferences or showings

Meeting with the organization's officials or dramatic displays of new products can be a meeting ground for the publicist and for many magazine editors. It is important that the new product justify the editors' time. Frequently a breakfast, luncheon, or other entertainment is associated with the press conference. Editors prefer clear invitations and timetables. An invitation that specifies *Cocktails: 12:30; Luncheon: 1:00* saves the time of a teetotaling or heavily booked editor. A press conference not associated with entertainment also can be held effectively when the occasion warrants—at a company plant, in a hotel ballroom, at an exhibit hall, or elsewhere. Any press conference should begin on time, be concisely planned, and allow for early exit. (*See* Chapter 21.)

Hospitality suites

In connection with a convention, a trade show, a symposium, a junket, or similar event, hospitality suites can be maintained for the working press, including newspaper and magazine editors. A suite in a leading hotel or on the premises—at a housewares show, builders' show, furniture show, or elsewhere—can be opened to provide comfort and sociability and can be staffed by the publicist. Some hospitality suites offer morning coffee, extra typewriters or computers, carrying cases for trade literature, coat checking, or champagne. Depending on the occasion and the facilities, the publicist serves as would any host or hostess. Press kits are made available for visitors, and company officials are encouraged to be on hand for informal introductions and interviews. Notice of the hospitality suite is provided well in advance to editors.

Product demonstrations and special entertainments

The chance to use a new product or see it demonstrated is often most persuasive in forming editors' judgments. New cars may be demonstrated and tried out by automotive or other news editors. Snowmobile rides can be arranged in a public park (usually by securing a city permit in advance) for sports editors and other guests. Meals planned around a new food product may be sampled by food editors at a company luncheon. A separate showing of an industrial "musical" can entertain the media and allow subsequent sampling of new products, such as foods or sports equipment. The use of consumer panelists on stage may encourage editors to ask questions and secure typical case histories of product use. Filmed presentations can add a dramatic backdrop to product introductions. The techniques can be as unlimited as the publicist's creativity. Often events of this type offer a welcome change of pace. Some events are scheduled annually, such as award lunches, trendsetting fashion shows, and manufacturers' presentations.

Tours

Editors may be invited to view an interesting site—vineyard, spa, factory, research center, recreation area, resort hotel, striking new building, planned community, design center. A tour of this kind adds to the editor's background data and strengthens the professional relationship with the publicist and organization.

Releases and photographs

Often the dissemination of news is confined to the standard release and captioned photograph. These are the year-in/year-out foundation for keeping editors informed. Too often incoming publicity material is discarded because of journalistic lapses. For instance, all material should include the date—undated material is a bane of editors; and all material should be factually complete—full names and titles, specifics on quantities and locations.

Major magazines will generally take their own photographs or use press service pictures unless there is a truly distinctive and excellent photo available on an exclusive basis.

Work with established writers

Sometimes a writer whose material is often used by a magazine can be interested in doing a story. If he or she queries the editor in effective style and with the assurance that it will get a receptive review by the editor, the chances of its being accepted are greater than from a direct query by the publicist. The writer must be free to treat the story as his or her judgment indicates, of course. He need not check it with the publicist or have any obligation to treat it as the publicist desires.

Also, the writer should let the editor know he is working with the source. Payment should be by the magazine or by the publicist with the editor's full knowledge—so she can be aware of the self-interest that may underlie it—not from both.

A partial list of freelance writers and the types of things they write appears in the annual *Feature Writer and Syndicate Directory of the Working Press of the Nation*. (*See* Chapter 20 and Appendix.) An additional list can be found in the *International Freelance Writers' Directory*, 1450 S. Havana Street, Aurora, CO 80012.

Try a freelance article

The biggest magazines will buy articles from unknowns—if they make a hit. If the subject has possibilities, it may pay to try this. These articles should be submitted free to the magazines, since it is not ethical to be paid both by the magazine and by the client. The research necessary to write the story undoubtedly will have other useful applications. A book that may be useful in writing material for magazines is *Magazine Writing Today*, by Jerome E. Kelley.

Few editors consider it part of their work to supply clippings or progress reports. The publicist should follow each issue of a publication or—more economical from a time standpoint—rely on a clipping bureau. (Clipping bureaus are discussed in Chapter 20.) The clipping bureau should be supplied with a copy of material sent to the magazine or should be alerted to watch for specific mentions.

Coordinating with Magazines' Calendars

Many of the large-circulation national monthlies work three or four months ahead or more. An April feature is completed and is in proof in January. Christmas features are well wrapped up for the printer by August or September.

Although department editors plan their own pages, regular staff meetings are scheduled to balance the "book" as a whole. The monthly magazine editor thus needs a good running start to germinate an idea, get it scheduled for a specific issue, produce text and photographs, and provide the printer with final material months ahead of the newsstand distribution date. The publicist should thus plan contacts a couple of months before the magazine's deadline or about six months before publication.

News magazines, weekly magazines, illustrated magazines, and trade magazines work on shorter deadlines. A news weekly, as the name implies, calls for rapid production of material and requires the publicist to make advanced preparation to supply statistics, stock photographs, or other material immediately.

Trade magazines are more relaxed in their requirements than consumer monthlies and often close the main editorial section a month before distribution date.

It is naturally helpful to know which magazines may be planning to do stories on given subjects. Though there is considerable secrecy within editorial offices on most stories, they often must contact what they consider good sources for material they need. So being recognized as a good source—for instance, for having excellent files on musical activity in the United States, or boating, or research being done on mental health—is an excellent way to increase the volume of magazine coverage.

Sometimes editors or writers will let it be known they are seeking certain types of material. For instance, *Bulldog Reporter*, 1250 45th Street, Emeryville, CA 94608, conveys notes of this type and changes in staffs.

Magazine Classifications

While the directories mentioned contain full lists and information, it is helpful to cite key publications in the major categories that will be of interest to publicists as well as guides on working with them. (Lists appear in the Appendix.)

Weekend newspaper magazines

A variation of the general magazine is the newspaper magazine, edited and produced nationally and distributed as a weekend feature of a number of different newspapers. The major nationally distributed newspaper magazine is *Parade*, 711 Third Avenue, New York, NY 10017.

Many Sunday newspapers publish their own magazines as separate sections. They should be checked separately because type of content and style of material vary greatly.

Each has its own type of material. As with all magazines, it is always wise to be familiar with the style and content of each publication before seeking to place any article.

News and Illustrated Magazines

Outgrowths of modern journalism, news magazines attempt to summarize the news highlights of the entire world. They confront the publicist with a unique problem. Chances of getting a story into them by individual effort are more limited than with newspapers, although it is done frequently. News magazines boil down volumes of news material into a limited space.

These magazines get their material from four sources:

1. Wire, photo, and feature syndicates
2. Field editors and "stringers"

3. Clippings from newspapers and other publications
4. Reliable sources such as publicists who provide them with leads and source materials

Efforts to place material in news magazines should be directed first to building up material in syndicates, an important source of news to the news magazine; second, to cultivating field editors and "stringers" who may establish a good story from the publicist's locality; third, to achieving heavy results with regular newspapers and trade magazines, because news magazines frequently pick up material from these sources; fourth, to approaching directly the appropriate department editor, who is always seeking good material.

Stringers come in all types. Some are competent people whose judgment is respected at headquarters; others are less able. The paid bureau managers are trusted and capable, but sometimes too busy to respond. If the local person is busy, ask him to let you work up some material and send it in to the main office with a note, "Correspondent suggested I send this to you." Also send a copy to the correspondent.

Specialized magazines

In recent years the trend has been toward growth of special-interest magazines and a decrease in the number and comparative dominance of magazines reaching vast audiences. This is due to the ascendancy of television as the medium that has the greatest appeal to large audiences; the advanced educational levels and other factors that have made millions of people seek individual interests that set them off from the crowd; and increased affluence and leisure time that give millions the means and opportunity to pursue their special interests.

Accordingly, more of the publicist's work in the magazine field is being devoted to specialized magazines. Often this type of "rifle shot" placement is more effective than a comparable article in a mass magazine, since the audience may be precisely the one that will take a strong interest. For instance, an article about an idea in *Harper's*—reaching opinion leaders in government, education, and the media—may have more consequence in fostering it than an article of the same size in *Reader's Digest*.

Approach to the "special" magazines—those reaching specialized groups but not trade publications—depends on several things. When they are national the same processes can be applied as those used in reaching the large general magazines. When they are local, the technique is much the same as it would be in the case of a local newspaper.

The special magazines—there are many types—are frequently available by indirect penetration through an influential member of the group to which the magazine circulates. The "class" magazines might be effectively reached through the intervention of a respected socialite. A sports figure might be a better advance runner than the publicist for a sports magazine. Institutional magazines are often more accessible by the indirect method of using an important figure in the institution.

It is sometimes effective for the intermediary who acts as the liaison with the particular publication to place the story and/or to use a byline, although the story may actually be ghostwritten by the publicist. This kind of personal handling will usually please the editor and frequently make the story of greater value to the publication and of greater interest to its readers.

Developing the campaign

To cover special magazines on a significant scale will require extra manpower. To do a magazine publicity campaign, first draw up a list of the publications to be used. Because many magazines and magazine editors come and go rapidly, diligently keep the list up to date. Check the magazines carefully and list them in a chart, including the name of the magazine, the editor, the address, and telephone and fax numbers. Leave blank spaces for other information to be filled in after a personal approach has been made.

Approach each editor, preferably in person or by telephone. Discuss the suggested subject. Sell the editor on using the story you have in mind. Learn how long a story will be acceptable, what the deadline is, how much of what kind of art will be accepted, and any angles that should be stressed.

After the preliminary survey, a complete work chart will include a column of deadlines that tells the dates by which the material is due. Another column notifies at a glance how many and what kind of pictures are desired. The job then is to research for information and write the copy to fill the specifications. After mailing the copy and pictures to the editors or sending them by messenger, it sometimes pays to follow up with a discreet telephone call to ascertain whether the material satisfies the editor's standards.

Several other techniques are used to reach many magazines simultaneously. In some cases mass copies of a memo or study will get good results with a large group of trade or technical publications interested in the general subject being covered. Editors may use the releases as they are or revise and slant them to fit the particular publication's requirements and interests. Frequently such releases lead to negotiations resulting in special stories.

Another technique for servicing a large group of magazines simultaneously is to arrange a group tour for editors and writers. Some tours may consist of a planned afternoon in a plant. Others may be a long trip covering a big installation or series of installations.

Class magazines

The "upper bracket" periodicals deal chiefly with expensive recreations, quality clothes, fashions, styles, and elegant living. They are potential media chiefly to publicists whose clients deal in such things.

Women's and home magazines

Excellent media to reach women, because they are so thoroughly read by them, this group of magazines also deals with the planning, building, furnishing, and landscaping of the home; with clothes and fashions; with marriage and sex; with children; with the needs of career women; and with other subjects specifically important to women.

Juvenile magazines

Dealing largely with matters of appeal to children, the juvenile magazines are of interest chiefly to publicists with long-range programs designed to reach today's youth with the objective of influencing the adults of tomorrow, or with products or services for children.

Intellectual magazines

This chiefly unillustrated group is valuable mostly for disseminating ideas. They reach those who lead the thought and often the actions of others.

Digests

Reader's Digest is the dean, in point of age and size, of the digests that reprint most of their material from other magazines, newspapers, books, and various publications. Their material is in the main of general interest. Because so much of their material is reprinted, they offer a less susceptible field for a direct approach than most publications. Some do use original material.

Newsletters

Not magazines in the strict sense of the word, newsletters are usually four-page leaflets approximately 8½" × 11" in size, purporting to present news and information of a confidential or semiconfidential nature about a given subject. Like the digest, the newsletter has become a large family of imitators with a small nucleus of well-established successes enjoying substantial circulation. The newsletter is a worthwhile medium for a publicist covering a subject in its particular field, because it is likely to enjoy an intense, concentrated audience.

Many newsletters are listed in *Newsletters in Print*, 835 Penobscot Building, Gale Research Co, Detroit, MI 48226.

Sport and hobby magazines

Some sports magazines cover specific sports like football, baseball, golf, and bowling; others cover the whole realm of sports. They are excellent media for sports publicists and for publicists plugging geographic localities through seasonal sports.

Institutional magazines

An institutional magazine is the official organ of some specific organization of people united in their interests, occupations, ideas, religion, or social life. Institutional magazines include religious, fraternal, university, lodge, and organization publications.

An official organ is must reading for the devoted members of a movement, and it is usually skimmed by the casual members. With material in an institutional publication, the publicist is certain of an attentive readership in a specific stratum of society; here he or she can slant material to register definite ideas to fit a known pattern of thought.

Many institutional magazines also fall into other classifications. *Boys' Life*, for example, is both a juvenile magazine and the official organ of the Boy Scout movement.

Local Magazines

A field that is becoming important and that offers many opportunities for publicity programs in their areas are the magazines dealing with interests of individual cities, states, and geographic regions.

Business Periodicals

Business publications range from nationally known outlets, such as *Fortune* and *Business Week*, to local business reviews with a limited circulation. General business magazines are news and feature publications covering the immense field of business for the business executive.

Fortune devotes detailed articles to major business organizations and developments. *Business Week* covers the field of business as comprehensively as a news magazine covers general news. It has field editors in sectional business capitals such as San Francisco, Chicago, Detroit, and Washington. Backing up this organization is an array of "stringers" who, on a commission basis, cover other important business centers by correspondence. Any of these field editors or stringers are glad to receive acceptable business news from publicists in their territories.

Forbes is distinctive but includes traits of *Fortune* and *Business Week*.

Agricultural magazines

A number of important magazines circulate exclusively or chiefly to farmers and constitute effective media for conveying a message to them.

Trade publications

Trade publications are craft- or industry-specific magazines circulating among specific industrial groups or trades and members of trade organizations. For example, *Iron Age* is a trade publication that reports on the metal industry to business people interested in the metal trades. *Editor and Publisher* is a trade publication that circulates news about the newspaper business to editors, publishers, publicists, and advertisers.

For publicity purposes this category may include technical and professional magazines and, sometimes, agricultural publications—although the latter category is sufficiently distinctive to justify a separate classification.

Designed for doctors, lawyers, architects, and other professionals, the technical and professional publications are limited in their appeal. Their content, usually highly technical, is restricted to their particular group's professional mysteries. Only when the publicist has a subject of obvious interest to a professional group will its journals be eligible vehicles for publicity messages.

Usually the public relations worker will find it desirable to build a list of trade publications to fit the particular organization, client, or campaign being served. For example, to publicize the annual Home Show of Southern California, a list of more than 100 publications was built up from such sources as the fifteen sponsoring trade associations, publicity people in the construction field, classified telephone directories, *Bacon's Magazine Directory*, and *Standard Rate and Data*. As a campaign develops, editors not on the list will hear about it and ask to be included, which adds to the scope of the coverage.

Included among trade publications are those limited to a specific trade, such as bakers, and those limited to a certain organiza-

tion, such as the journals of the American Medical Association and similar organizations, national and local.

Also included are more general scientific and technical magazines, such as *Popular Science*, *Scientific American*, and *Popular Mechanics*, which are of interest to a great many trades. Another type is a publication such as *Television*, which in general covers an entire industry. These magazines are frequently outlets for product publicity and other business publicity.

In almost every category there are dozens of trade and specialty magazines. Here, too, a list will crisscross many categories.

For example, in directing publicity for a major manufacturer of heavy machinery there are more than 60 metal trade publications, 65 petroleum publications, 170 municipal and county publications, 54 civil engineering and construction publications, 100 aviation and aerospace publications, 161 building publications, 686 business and commercial publications, 158 electrical and electronics publications, more than 450 computer publications, and many others to consider. Among these, the publicist may prefer, on a given story, to work exclusively with one magazine in each field, or use a saturation approach as in the case of an announcement for an important new product.

In working with the trade and professional press, the publicist can often rely heavily on the standard news release and the captioned photograph. Frequently the material will be used approximately as presented, provided it meets all the usual journalistic standards. Sometimes it will be edited or rewritten or included partially in round-up stories and survey articles. Trade names and other product data including model numbers are included in many trade releases.

Trade editors are as eager for fresh material as their consumer counterparts, and will often work receptively with a publicist on an exclusive feature of benefit to their readers.

In developing and using lists of trade publications, constant reference to *IMS*, *Standard Rate and Data*, *Bacon's Magazine Directory*, or *The Working Press of the Nation* is essential. (*See* Chapter 20 and Appendix.) The number, variety, and scope of these publications demand careful analysis and selection in each case.

Internal house magazines

These publications, sometimes called employee or company publications, are published for and about employees by business organizations. They constitute one of the most effective resources of modern public relations. For most outside publicity subjects, house magazines are generally inaccessible. Their subject matter is confined in the main to treatment of the company that publishes it and its people.

Some extraneous matter of interest to all employees is sometimes admitted, such as publicity about the Community Chest, public welfare activities, and general public information. If the company is participating in an outside event—for example, a sponsor of the Miss America Contest—the activity may be publicized in the company publication. Some sophisticated employee magazines, such as Deere & Company's *J.D. Journal*, use professional articles of general interest.

Company publications sometimes furnish excellent outlets for publicists representing firms that use the company's products. Such publicity, explaining the end use of the products, by helping to educate employees of contracting firms constitutes good supplier relations and tends to expedite production.

Although there were a few house magazines as far back as the 1880s, today the *Internal Publications Directory*, 121 Chanlon Road, New Providence, NJ 07974, lists more than thirty-five hundred company publications of all types. Their readership probably exceeds fifty million.

External company publications

Of greater value to the publicist than a company's internal publication is its external publication. Generally, this magazine is mailed free to stockholders and customers (present or potential), as well as to community leaders and business executives whom the company would like to familiarize with its story.

Original artwork, graphic design, and informative articles that sell "softly" if they sell at all characterize the best of external house magazines. Many of these publications compare favorably with general consumer magazines in terms of circulation, writing, artistic talent, and originality of ideas.

Most external house publications utilize a magazine-type format and carry articles on a wide variety of subjects in each issue. Travel, fashion, art, international problems, social problems, and space exploration are typical external magazine fare.

Publicists wanting to use the medium of company publications—either internal or external—may most quickly develop a list pertinent to the need by using the *Internal Publications Directory*.

24

BOOKS AND OTHER PUBLICATIONS

HERBERT M. BAUS
PHILIP LESLY

Books are being used more often and in several ways as public relations media.

One way is to garner the placement of appropriate information in books published by others, particularly textbooks. In the past, American textbooks tended to stress the "robber baron" side of business, rather than business' contributions as the foundation of our standard of living and our nation's comparative international strength. This tendency stems, in part, from the neglect of business itself, which has often failed to provide its story and facts to the scholars who write textbooks. Consequently, these authors have primarily relied on other information sources that are often based on documents such as records of legislative investigations and other atypical situations.

In recent years businesses and their trade associations have made an increased effort to convey the constructive story of business in textbooks.

Books, in themselves, can serve as public relations vehicles. Some have constituted tremendous propaganda campaigns, such as *Das Kapital* by Karl Marx, *Mein Kampf* by Adolf Hilter, the works of Voltaire, Harriet Beecher Stowe's *Uncle Tom's Cabin*, Wendell Wilkie's *One World*, and Gunnar Myrdal's *An American Dilemma*.

By the same token, the autobiographies (written with professional writers) of Lee Iacocca, formerly of Chrysler, Armand Hammer of Occidental Petroleum, and Donald Trump not only became best-sellers, but also effectively promoted the authors and their companies.

Other types of for-profit books written by professional authors may bring a publicity value to certain sources, such as the travel guide series published by Mobil Corporation. The publication of some books of this type may be initiated or subsidized by a publisher, rather than by the company alone.

Some organizations do develop their own books—for example, a company history or a reference book for the industry at large. As public relations vehicles these books are more powerful, personal, and permanent than print or broadcast advertising—but they are also more limited in range. A clothbound (hardback) book provides one major advantage: it is seldom merely thrown away. However, in many cases it also goes unread. Sound judgment is required to ensure the book is of vital interest or use to the audience and does not merely espouse the viewpoint of the sponsor.

Constructive books about business portray the spirit and personality of an organization, particularly when it performs a useful function for the recipient.

A clothbound book is a handsome gift that induces appreciation and carries with it an implied obligation to read and preserve it. It makes the recipient feel singled out for a distinction. The drawbacks to books as media are the comparatively high cost of the individual unit, the difficulties of widespread distribution, and the uncertainty that the entire message will be read.

Arranging for publication

A sponsored book may be privately printed and issued by the sponsor. However, in order to hold true merit as a book and to ensure the likelihood of its being read, it is probably best for it to be issued by an established publishing house as part of its standard book list.

Publication arrangements can be made with any one of a number of well-known publishers using the most appropriate of these three common methods:

1. **Underwriting.** The sponsor agrees to cover any costs (plus a reasonable margin of profit) not recovered by the publisher from sale of the book. Costs to the sponsor can ultimately range from nothing to virtually 100 percent of the cost of editing, printing, binding, handling, and distributing the work.

2. **Purchase of copies.** The sponsor agrees to buy for its use and distribution a quantity of copies at an agreed-on price. The total is usually enough to ensure the publisher a profit, no matter how few copies may be sold through regular channels.

3. **Subsidy.** The sponsor makes an outright payment to the publisher, sufficient to ensure profitability of the venture.

In all cases, of course, the publisher insists that the book meet standards of quality and integrity in keeping with its reputation in the publishing business. Even after sponsorship has been agreed on, the publisher may refuse to put its imprint on it if it is likely to be criticized by respected critics for puffery, distortion, or other abuses. The more honored and valued the colophon of the publisher, the better the book must be—and the more effective it is likely to be as a spokesman for its sponsor.

Some excellent books have been issued through sponsorship. *Everything and the Kitchen Sink*, sponsored as a service to industry by Crane Co. during its centennial, was widely lauded by critics, government officials, educators, and businessmen. More than five thousand copies were distributed by the U.S. Department of State to its libraries all over the world as an excellent means of clearly and simply depicting the human benefits resulting from American industrial enterprise.

A three-volume history of the Ford Motor Company by Allan Nevins and Frank E. Hill was written by those distinguished historians with the full cooperation, but not the review, of the company. It was widely praised by reviewers, historians, and educators for its thoroughly objective treatment. Though it contains material the present members of the Ford family probably would prefer be forgotten, it has raised the general esteem of the company among opinion leaders.

Some other books that have been subsidized or written with the "supervision" of the subjects, however, have drawn scorn from the intended audiences. They have been prose versions of the romantically flattering portrait that is admired only by the subject or his descendants and usually can hang with honor nowhere but in the company's boardroom.

A few "vanity" publishers are in the business of primarily issuing books for payment by the authors. These rarely receive any attention, but copies are as useful as books printed for the sponsor with no colophon.

Using Books to Foster Your Ideas

Books are usually considered a mass medium, and slow in their influence. But they may be the most overlooked medium in a program to shape opinion.

Most people think of books as being bought one at a time. But many of the most influential ones were distributed in clusters and spread like seed on a lawn. Rachel Carson's *The Sea Around Us*, George Gilder's *Wealth and Poverty*, and Tom Peters' *In Search of Excellence* were bought in large quantities and distributed to select groups.

A book can command attention when a brochure, an ad, or a sponsored film cannot. When it is received with the enthusiastic endorsement of someone we respect, it carries authenticity and prestige.

Follow these guidelines for effectively using books to shape opinion:

1. Determine the book's objective in advance, based on these two effective applications:

   • To open doors for the organization's ideas on the subject covered by the book. This paves the way for personal discussion, attendance at meetings, participation on committees, attending film showings, reading other literature.

   • To seed thinking on what's in the book. President Reagan's distribution of *Wealth and Poverty* led to opinion jelling in Congress on cutting taxes and increasing incentives. A substantial portion of the sales of *Overcoming Opposition* by Philip Lesly has been in quantity orders.

2. Distribute books that have been published by recognized publishers and are marketed through normal channels: bookstores, catalogues, direct mail, and book clubs.

3. Mark key passages—the ones that make the germane points and are persuasive. They should be few and brief. The key passages of *In Search of Excellence* would add up to a dozen pages.

4. Draft an abstract that contains some of the key points. Include the page numbers of the book on which those are expounded, so the recipient can find them—and

can read only those if so inclined. That will greatly reduce the percentage who never read it at all.

5. Attach the abstract with the book and a cover letter to the recipients. Urge them to read the book (or at least the key points) and tell them why.

6. Direct your flow of influence—motivate recipients to spread the message or stress that the message is esoteric and not suitable for indiscriminate circulation. Often creating an "in" feeling can add substance to the message's impact.

Paperbacks and Minibooks

The paperback book became a medium of public relations a few years after the burst of popularity of these low-cost volumes in the 1940s. Their use has been accelerated by the rise in price of newsstand paperbacks from their original 25¢ to a range between $3.95 and $19.95. The cost of the books when ordered in large quantities by a commercial sponsor makes it possible to sell them at an attractive rate and thereby liquidate their cost. The Maytag Company recouped the full cost of producing its *Encyclopedia of Home Laundry* in less than three years. It has put hundreds of thousands of copies into use among home economics teachers, public utility home economists, dealers, and consumers. In addition, thousands of copies have been sold through regular book outlets.

What follows are three basic arrangements for publication of a paperback by a commercial organization:

1. Commitment for a specified number of copies to be produced by a regular publisher of paperbacks. This calls for a volume that the publisher agrees meets desired standards for its imprint and sales. In this arrangement, the sponsor gains the prestige and acceptance of the publisher's imprint among the public, and some sales

through normal book channels, handled by the publisher for whatever return it will bring. It is rare, however, for a sponsored book to get much display space, and therefore sales are well below what would be required to make an unsponsored publication worthwhile to the publisher.

2. Having the book produced for the sponsor's distribution only. This may or may not carry the imprint of the publisher. This procedure permits being more direct in fostering the sponsor, and can be targeted to a precise audience.

3. A sponsor may contract for a quantity of a book published for general distribution, arranging to have a special cover bearing its name. That usually requires an order for at least fifteen thousand copies and payment of a production fee.

Examples of the first type, in addition to the *Maytag Encyclopedia*, include the *Home Comfort Handbook* (sponsored by the National Fuel Oil Institute); the *Weyerhauser Building and Remodeling Book* and *Home Decorating Made Easy*; *Top Form Book of Horse Care* (Merck & Company); and *Westinghouse Cook Book*.

Examples of the second type include *Feel of the Road* (Ford); *Elementary Fishing* (Garcia Corporation); and *Vision—The Story of Boeing*. An example of the third type is the purchase by Canada Dry of two hundred thousand copies of a guide to entertaining guests, *The Entertainers*, published by Bantam Books.

Another growing practice is syndication of books. The Benjamin Company produced *How to Manage Your Money* and arranged for production with different covers for various banks in the United States. *Consumer's Buying Guide* was produced for various Better Business Bureaus, then sold for public relations use to various manufacturers, utilities, and savings institutions. A shorter version

may be produced of a book developed for another sponsor, where a nonexclusive arrangement has been made by Benjamin.

Among firms active in the paperback book field is Snibbe Books, 1115 Ponce de Leon Boulevard, Clearwater, FL 34616.

Costs will vary depending on the number of pages, the number of illustrations, quality of paper, and how much color is used. For art and production—exclusive of editorial costs and internal illustrations—an order of ten thousand copies will average 55¢ a copy, depending on specifications.

A later development is the minibook. While the typical paperback measures about 3¼″ × 7¼″ and contains 150 to 200 pages, the minibook measures 3½″ × 5″ inches and contains about 64 pages.

While most minibooks are produced for use as premiums and in sales promotion, some serve public relations purposes. Examples include *Questions and Answers About Contact Lenses* produced for Barnes-Hinds Ophthalmic Products, and *A Complete House Plant Guide* for Plantabbs Corporation.

Publicizing via Cartoon Booklets

The cartoon booklet medium, once considered for children alone, is now doing a man-size public relations and promotion job. No longer are cartoon books pure entertainment. They are being used to subtly sell products, win votes, raise money, organize workers, educate, and instill messages. Some of the better ones are directed at a well-educated audience.

Principal commercial users of cartoon booklets are large corporations and trade associations that employ them as public relations or sales-promotion tools, most notably the electric and gas utilities.

Several branches of the U.S. government, too, have made widespread use of such booklets. Church, labor, and political movements also use this medium, as do more than two thousand schools that supplement classroom teaching in specific courses of study with cartoon books.

Some users employ made-to-order cartoon books. Others find that stock commercial cartoon books for imprinting serve their purpose. In many cases, sponsors of cartoon booklets are able to check results carefully.

Consumers Power Company, Jackson, Michigan, first offered two cartoon books in its catalogue on resources available for teaching use. Modest requests were received. When a third booklet was published samples were mailed to teachers. Large orders came in for the new one as well as for the first two. In the first nine months of this procedure more than 128,000 booklets were provided for school use in the company's service area.

The company began to use cartoon books with reservation because it felt teachers might have a negative reaction to this form of literature. According to Romney Wheeler, former Director of Public Relations:

> We suspected teachers might tend to associate any cartoon books with noneducational publications like *Batman* and *Superman*. Yet, cartoons have been used to convey information ever since the first cave drawings. Michelangelo used cartoons as the preliminary drawings on which he based his masterpieces. Hogarth used cartoons for savage satire. Indeed, it has been only in the last fifty years that cartoons have become identified with comic books and comic strips.

When the teaching value of this form of material was pointed out to the teachers, they agreed. Content of the booklets is heavily informative and nonpropagandistic.

A popular variation is the cartoon book that also includes puzzles, quizzes, and other educational techniques. A leading producer of these is Culver Company, 400 Main Street, Stamford, CT 06901, (203) 348-9808. It produces booklets both for school distribution and for businesses such as the electric and gas utilities.

Prices of cartoon books vary. A made-to-order booklet will involve preparation of a script, artwork, engravings, and printing in color on newsprint stock.

Some publishers of comic books handle every phase of the commercial job, from story line to printing and drop shipment. Some use creative studios that handle the entire job, subcontracting for the printing. Some specialize in miniature books used for package inserts, premiums, and giveaways. Some specialize in books with coloring pictures, quizzes, and games.

Specialty Publications

The literature of an organization—the reports, histories, surveys, pamphlets, brochures, directories, books—can range from unpretentious photocopied leaflets to expensive tomes done in velour with plastic covers.

Of vital importance is skilled technical assistance on art, layout, typography, and composition. Frequently a public relations person who is not a specialist on such publications will find it wise to consult with a specialist who will supervise the production. In such an event it is standard practice to allow the specialist a fixed fee in advance to produce a complete dummy for approval before final arrangements are made. That will make possible a cost analysis of the overall job and will present a clear picture to the client of what kind of a publication is being developed.

The publication should be planned on the basis of budget, objective, length, amount of art, amount of type, sectional breakdown, and general style.

The experienced public relations person will guard against too elaborate a production to avoid seeming extravagant. At the same time, he will guard against falling below proper quality standards. In public relations work, this rule is a sound one: DO IT WELL OR NOT AT ALL.

Some organizations issue magazines that are prepared by publishers of established consumer or business magazines. They are treated in Chapter 31.

(For information about types and production of printed materials see Chapter 33.)

Display Rack Booklets

Many factories and offices offer small booklets on helpful subjects that are displayed in racks. Employees are encouraged to take them. The companies that produce these and sell them to the employers sometimes accept suggestions for topics and material to be used in them. Copies of these booklets may be purchased in quantity for secondary distribution to an organization's members or to supporters, employees, stockholders, or others.

25

PUBLICITY IN TV AND RADIO

PHILIP LESLY

Of all mass communication media, television currently ranks as the most pervasive and influential. With its combined powers of sight, sound, and immediacy, television carries myriad impressions and a plethora of information into virtually all homes in developed countries and to multitudes in less-developed countries. In fact, millions of people today actually consider the selected segments of programming displayed on their picture tubes to be more "real" than other aspects of their lives.

Similarly, radio continues to exert considerable and immediate impact on millions of people. In developed countries, it provides a major source of news and music; in less-developed countries where TV has not yet reached predominance, radio forms an invisible cord of communication that binds together communities or spreads dissension. In the United States and Canada talk radio has become a major political and social force.

Yet, neither TV nor radio is without its limitations. Whereas humanity has had thousands of years to assimilate speech, thousands of years to incorporate written language, and five hundred years to accommodate printing—society has had less than three generations to absorb the broadcast media. Millions of living, active people today grew up before even radios were common in homes.

The veritable infancy of these media presents a number of challenges to the publicist.

Much of the population continues to look toward the print media for information, ideas, and motivations. By the same token a large percentage is predominantly influenced by film and the broadcast media. Consequently, no publicity program that exclusively utilizes only one form is likely to reach the full audience effectively—and no publicist who primarily focuses on one form is likely to achieve maximum results.

This "media gap" is among the realities that public relations people must address when planning and implementing a publicity program.

Another challenge facing today's publicity staff is that the broadcast media continue to evolve at a rapid and constant rate. In addition, these media are structured and operated quite differently from one country to another. Even the Canadian system—for which the government-operated Canadian Broadcasting Company is predominant—differs markedly from the U.S. system.

Because of the limited number of broadcast channels that can be used without causing chaos, U.S. broadcasting systems—unlike print media—are licensed by the federal government. The Federal Communications Commission (FCC) administers broadcast licensing authority. These licenses must be periodically renewed; however, for years this renewal was automatic, and today the license often can be sold for millions of dollars.

In recent years, changing social patterns, such as the desire among minority groups for greater representation in the media, have elevated broadcast station licensing to a public issue.

Other developments that have a bearing on the pattern of broadcasting include the following:

- **Cable TV** transmits many types of programs into homes, offices, and schools by cables that do not affect the limited span of the broadcasting band. This has multiplied the number of stations, the variety of programming, and the sources of financing. Besides providing many new outlets for films, news, and interviews in competition with broadcast TV, cable is capable of helping the viewer shop by exhibiting available products, showing stock tickers, electronically transmitting newspapers, sending mail, carrying police and fire communications, connecting each outlet with centralized libraries and databanks, delivering telegrams, and providing two-way banking transactions and information. Publicists can provide complete shows or long messages for some channels. Other cable channels and the various cable networks function much as the standard networks do.

- **Pay-per-view TV**, involving the individual's selection of programs seen at a specified charge.

- **Space satellites** that not only transmit live programs immediately over vast distances but may bypass the network and perhaps even the local station, and that also carry programs directly to the receiving set from almost anywhere in the world. Satellites are being used by publicists to send prepared materials to TV stations for their use. In the future they may be able to bypass the stations and reach viewers directly.

- **Videotapes** and **videodiscs** that capsule programs, much like home movies, to be shown at any time on any properly equipped receiver. These permit delayed viewing of regular telecasts or selection from a vast variety of recorded cartridges or discs with educational, hobby, cultural, or other programming.

- **Low-powered TV stations** with a narrow coverage area, added to the present stronger stations, greatly increasing the number of broadcasting units.

- Utilization of the TV receiver in conjunction with **information banks**, **computers**, and **facsimile systems**. This enables the individual to call on the resources of the central bank for any information, news, feature material, entertainment, or other material—and in many cases, to make a paper copy of what is wanted.

In a field where developments have been so rapid, it is vital that the publicist keep ahead of changes in order to know what the facilities are and how to use them. (*See* Chapter 28.)

Broadcast Media Relations

The electronic media differ from print media for the publicist in the following key ways:

1. Broadcasting puts predominant emphasis on entertainment—music, humor, adventure, drama. There is comparatively little room for information and persuasion.

2. The broadcast signal is ephemeral. While video cassette recorders permit recording shows for later viewing, most shows reach tuned-in audiences only.

3. The broadcasts are much less susceptible to promotional use than magazine and newspaper articles that can easily be reprinted and distributed.

The publicist should consider the distinct features of the two major types of broadcast media: television and radio.

Television

The major characteristics of television that are important to the publicist are the following:

- The immediacy and personal identification with personalities and ideas that television brings directly into the home.

- The effectiveness of television as a means of persuasion—combining sight, sound, motion, and immediacy with personal involvement of the audience.

- The great flexibility in showing timely events whenever the audience is available, aided by the development of videotape.

- The opportunities, through VCRs and closed-circuit television, to inform large audiences at a single showing about new products and services, events at a meeting of shareholders, new techniques in surgery, and many other subjects for widely scattered but specialized audiences.

- The growth of public information programming. Numbers of large corporations now sponsor or initiate public service features. Safety quizzes, panel shows, and debates are all used for public information purposes.

Radio

The principal characteristics of radio that follow are important to the publicity person:

- The strong listener identification created by enlisting the listener's imagination to complete an impression.

- Radio's ability to reach people outside the home—while driving on expressways, sunbathing at the beach, etc.

- People can pursue other activities—eating, housework, do-it-yourself projects—and listen to radio simultaneously.

- The around-the-clock news coverage provided by many stations has accustomed people to rely on radio for news and weather reports. More of the total broadcast schedule is based on conveying information and comment on radio than on television.

- The "open mike" or audience telephone programs give listeners a sense of participation and active interest in the events under discussion.

- Because many radio outlets are independent of networks and other controlling structures they have much more freedom to express nonestablishment viewpoints. That leads to some tasteless programming, but it also makes possible potent commentaries and discussions.

- The excellent sound reproduction available on good stereo and FM receivers attracts many discerning and well-educated people who now spend little time with commercial TV or AM radio.

Activism in Broadcast Media

Sensing both the impact of television and the penchant of broadcasters to feature action and excitement, various groups of activists have shaped their entire existence to get TV coverage. Often issues are selected and events are planned solely with television in mind. If the TV stations cover it, it is considered successful. If TV ignores it, no matter what the merits of the "issue" or the "event," the activist group knows it has failed.

The organization subjected to such activist efforts is placed at a great disadvantage in this situation. It usually cannot know where or how the attack will come, and it is restrained by a need to be responsible that often is not felt by the attackers.

The impact of action and controversy as exhibited on television screens is so great, every organization must try to overcome these disadvantages.

This calls for the following functions:

1. Constant alertness to which groups may be singling out the organization for attacks, what their issues may be, and how they generally operate.

2. "Inoculating" the broadcasting news staffs against unquestioned acceptance of the legitimacy of what may be attempted or charged, by providing them in advance with background on the matters involved. They should also be provided with film footage, stills, names and contact points of spokespeople, and other materials that will help them get balanced coverage should something occur.

3. Briefing officials on how to handle themselves in various types of situations—demonstrations, riots, shouted insulting accusations, provocative questioning by reporters, and so forth.

4. Informing the print media in advance and giving full cooperation in anticipation of various events. Balanced treatment in one type of medium helps deter other media from going overboard for a sensationalized effort to manipulate the news. All media are increasingly sensitive to being proved unsound in their treatment.

Understanding Broadcast Media Organization

The origin of programs varies greatly. Network shows usually come from New York or Los Angeles. Networks also pick up "remotes" from member stations, relaying the shows in turn to other outlets. A national network broadcasts to as many as 300 stations.

Independent stations originate their own programming. Other stations are either owned by a network or affiliated with a network. If network-owned and -operated, the station normally carries much of the programming originated by the network. If affiliated, a station exercises a wider choice in its programming. Stations associated primarily with one network sometimes broadcast programs from other networks. In one-outlet cities, a station may carry programming originated by all four major networks.

Increasingly, larger local stations are originating their own worldwide news coverage through the use of satellites. This is especially common when an event elsewhere can be given local tie-ins, such as interest of local people with German roots in the breaching of the Berlin Wall.

Prepackaged features are produced for local stations to fill out their news material by the services listed in Chapter 21 and others.

Syndicates produce and distribute programs to both local stations and networks, selling the right to use programs they produce. These independent contractors are also known as packagers.

For audience-participation shows that give merchandise prizes, some independent contractors serve as brokers in obtaining the products to be awarded. Many such programs are completely produced by independent packagers.

Other syndicators distribute news feature and institutional films, but most syndicated material is in the quasi-entertainment category.

Programming

Programs on radio and television fall into two basic categories: *information* or *entertainment*.

Information includes news, special events, and public information shows.

Entertainment includes audience-participation programs, panel or game shows, interviews, all show business formats, dramatic programs of all kinds, variety programs, and the like.

Personnel

The following people are responsible for radio and television programs:

- *Program managers* supervise all progamming at an individual station.
- *News managers* supervise all news-type programs, directing camera operators and reporters.
- *Producers* are in charge of overall presentation and supervision of a program: timing, content, casting, and technical requirements. Producers are often responsible for originating show ideas. At individual stations, the producer may write material and act as interviewer or star, as well.
- *Writers* research and write a comprehensive script, ready for broadcast.
- *Directors* put the various elements of a show together and develop it into a smooth unit.
- *Announcers* read or present copy prepared by writers.

Broadcasting personnel and programs change frequently. When the size of the audience falls or fails to meet expectations, program personnel are sometimes replaced. New personnel are added as shows expand or modify formats.

The publicist must keep up-to-date on changes in both programming and personnel.

Publicity Placement

In working with various levels of broadcasting, the publicist finds many similarities. Networks, syndicates, and individual stations all produce news, public service, and entertainment programs.

In general, *information* and *public-service* shows offer the greatest potential outlets for publicity materials. However, *entertainment* programs are also receptive to good ideas and content.

Information programs

Information shows—which include news, public service, documentary, think programs, and special events programs—offer a wide range of opportunities.

1. *News shows* are a common type of program on radio and television, national or local.

   Gaining acceptance on a network news show is a challenging assignment. The story must have major significance and the publicist must adhere to good journalistic standards: copy must be accurate, objective, factual, concise.

   Radio and television newsrooms almost always subscribe to one or more of the newswire services. A large percentage of broadcast news comes from these sources. Therefore, material accepted by news services often gets on the air.

   Along with a news release aimed at television, pertinent motion-picture or video-tape footage is welcome.

   Newsroom staffs are small. News directors welcome imaginative and professional outside material. Once the publicity person proves to be a reliable source, he or she can hope to get consistent coverage.

2. *Public service shows.* By Federal Communications Commission policies, a percentage of broadcast hours should be educational or cultural. The public service program helps meet this requirement.

   This includes shows that interpret and explain historical significance of news, explain worthy causes, offer practical advice, or explain scientific and technical developments.

3. The publicist often finds an effective vehicle in the *documentary*, a program designed to interpret history and current events or to explore economic, philosophic, religious, or cultural subjects.

   Documentary techniques on radio and television are basically journalistic. The material also could be used to write a series of feature stories in a magazine or newspaper. The producer works from interviews and other information to form an overall profile.

   A radio documentary is composed of taped interviews, commentary, and sound impressions. Television adds the picture, movement, and color.

   Facts and statistics, suggested locations for filming, possibilities for interviews, suggestions for subjects—all are welcomed by documentary researchers, writers, and producers. Material covering vital social, economic, political, and governmental issues is particularly well received.

4. Producers of special commentary, discussion, and so-called *think programs* will consider suggestions on topics and authoritative guests. Interview shows, such as *Nightline*, need authorities on many types of subjects or persons with special knowledge about a current controversy, such as censoring of government aid to the arts. The publicist sometimes suggests a team of guests who present parts of an overall theme, one of whom is the publicist's spokesperson. In some cases, producers demand controversy. In this event, the publicist would be wise to point out the controversial aspect of the subject and perhaps suggest a guest who would take the opposing viewpoint.

   Suggestions are submitted to producers of public affairs programs at the network. Since many documentaries are produced by news divisions, contact with the news staff is also appropriate.

   Public affairs shows at individual stations are similar to the network formats, with the appeal more localized.

   At a local station, the newsroom is usually the hub of public service activities. Material can be directed to the program director, as well. Local issues frequently suggest documentary themes: how one state lowered its highway death rate with a sound sign program; how one community organized an amateur symphony orchestra.

   Panel discussions or authoritative interviews on local issues are often welcome.

5. *Special-events shows* include roundtable and panel discussions, individual interviews apart from regular programs, talks, monologues, and scientific or other demonstrations. Programs may comprise several elements—for instance, a monologue followed by an interview; a debate followed by a demonstration.

   Also included are live or taped coverage of sports events, religious and educational services and ceremonies, presentations, groundbreaking ceremonies, open houses, ribbon cuttings, dedications, activist rallies, political speeches, parades, and other events not covered on regular programs.

   A special event often does not exist until someone suggests it. Therefore, the publicist is free to conceive of an entire program.

Entertainment programs

There are five basic types of entertainment programs:

1. *Audience-participation shows* in which products or services are often given away as prizes to winners. Prominent and favorable on-the-air exposure of the product is

given in exchange for prizes donated. Game shows, both local and national in origin, are primarily featured on television. The publicist makes arrangements with the syndicator or station producing the show.

2. *Magazine-format programs* may include a variety of elements—music, interviews, monologues, exhibitions, filmed features. Usually an established host serves as master of ceremonies.

Magazine programs on local stations are especially receptive to suggested materials. At an individual station, contact with the program director or station manager is called for.

Magazine programs, although included in the *entertainment* grouping, are often partially informational. This is particularly true of women's interest and farm-interest shows.

In many areas, farm and women's commentators are influential personalities in the community. Inclusion on one of their shows, implying endorsement, often offers valuable exposure of a subject.

3. *Talk programs*, whether the conversation variety on television or the "open-mike" type on radio, fit into both the *informational* and the *entertainment* categories. Producers of these shows are very receptive to suggestions from the publicist, whether the suggestions be topics for discussion or possible guests.

The radio audience-participation program, in which listeners are invited to telephone the station to participate in a discussion or to ask questions of a guest, is a common type of radio program.

Some of the television conversation programs, telecast by local stations, also invite audience participation via telephone to give opinions, ask questions, etc.

4. *Discussion programs*, such as the Ricki Lake show, thrive on controversial and lurid topics, using guests most likely to stir up outrage or sensation. The wisdom of placing someone on such shows is often debatable.

5. *Show business formats—variety and dramatic programs*—offer the least opportunity for the publicist. One approach is lending products as props for television programs. Another is arranging for a product or service to be included in the action of a dramatic script. (*See* Chapter 27.)

However, these techniques are comparatively unpredictable and time-consuming, and usually comparatively expensive.

Approaching Broadcasting People

Professionals are conscious of the following day-to-day techniques for dealing with broadcasting people:

- In the first conversation or letter, clearly state what client, firm, or service is represented. Specify your suggested idea, story, guest, or prop. Instead of asking a producer how an idea might fit into the show, show through your suggestion that you understand what the program uses.

- Contact the person responsible for making the decision. On network programs, associate producers often handle the various aspects of the same program. Only one is assigned to your interest. Find him or her. Others may be willing to listen but are unable to make a decision.

- The broadcasting publicity specialist is meticulous about detail. Guests are rehearsed well in advance of interviews. The producer is briefed about the guest. Product photographs and artwork for television flipcards are assembled. Biographies of guests are submitted, along with discussion questions.

- Broadcasters usually prefer a brief memo or letter following the telephone call, outlining the program ideas. Detail what has been agreed and confirm a scheduled recording, broadcast, or rehearsal.

Ensuring the Effectiveness of TV Interviews

Perhaps the most common opportunities for an organization to reach a television audience are through interviews of its spokespersons, or their participation in panels. This distinctive type of communication differs from all others the individual may have experienced. The following tips for the interviewee help to assure the effectiveness of the interview, as well as to forestall negative effects:

1. Remember that television is show business. Everything from heart disease to a distant war is treated in terms of dramatic effect. Broadcasters know from experience that their best efforts to really educate the audience by providing substantial background and detail result in poor ratings.

2. As much as possible, give answers and dramatize dangers; do not just explain. Television dramas, documentaries, and commercials always neatly wrap up the subject. The audience has been trained to expect pithy points and tied-up ends, and so do television interviewers.

3. Visualize yourself in the average person's living room, not with your peers at the University Club. But do not talk down. The audience is not sophisticated or knowledgeable, but it is not stupid.

4. Don't express an opinion if you can cite a fact. But if you are an expert in the field being discussed, you may cite your views as being based on the study that has made you an expert.

5. Study the style of the interviewer in advance. Does he or she help the interviewee by leading his comments, or does he try to show up the guest? Does he talk much or leave most of the exposition to the interviewee?

6. Prepare in advance three or four cogent, concise sentences that make your key points. These are most likely to survive editing and to get on the air; and they are the hardest to edit into conveying another meaning. Watch for the chance to use these, even if you have to answer a question only obliquely. Then you need not rely on the interviewer to ask the questions that will enable you to make your points. (*See also* Chapter 21.) Have something to say beyond what you think you will be questioned about. If the interviewer runs long, he or she might offer you time to say whatever you want.

7. Use your hands as well as your mouth to express yourself. That may prevent the camera from closing in too much. Close-ups are not only unflattering; they may intimidate the audience.

8. Don't use jargon. Use examples or metaphors to help people visualize what you're talking about.

9. Keep your answers about 20 to 30 seconds long. That will help the audience grasp your points and prevent distortion of what you say through editing.

Satellite media tours

According to Nielsen Media Research, about 85 percent of American TV stations now carry "tours" of spokespeople that are transmitted by satellite. The person is interviewed in a studio and the message goes to those stations that request it as a result of an electronic offering.

The average number of stations carrying such an interview when produced by a highly qualified studio is ten to twenty-five. The average number of viewers ranges between one million and four million. The average time needed to arrange a tour is one to two weeks. The average time required for producing the interview is two to four hours.

A handbook on satellite media tours is available from Medialink, which has offices in New York, Chicago, Los Angeles, Dallas, London, and Washington, DC.

Public Broadcasting Opportunities and Challenges

This field is undergoing significant changes and must be followed closely by the publicist before it is approached. Changes in government funding and in sources of private support are changing the ability of the stations and the Public Broadcasting Service to provide various types of programming. Though the PBS stations have shown greater receptivity toward commercial interests, many PBS supporters continue to express concern about commercialization.

As with private broadcasting, opportunities for the publicist exist at both the national and local levels. All of the more than four hundred public and college TV stations are free to develop programs of their own.

Since they attempt to fill a full schedule with a variety of material, and their budgets are highly restrictive, they need much input from local organizations. Experts can be placed on discussion shows, films of significant regional activities may be welcome if they are balanced and noncommercial, and public service programs can be used.

Some of the stronger stations—notably those in Boston, Chicago, New York, Washington, DC, Pittsburgh, and Los Angeles—produce shows that are syndicated to other public stations. Opportunities to underwrite national programming are available through these producing stations.

Public Broadcasting Service

PBS is the national organization of public television stations. It selects, schedules, promotes, and distributes a national repertoire of programs, coordinates services for the stations, and represents the stations' interests nationally. PBS is located at 475 L'Enfant Plaza, SW, Washington, DC 20024, (202) 458-5000.

It is through underwriting of programs offered by PBS or individual stations that private organizations most often deal with public TV. In many instances PBS contracts with program packagers or producers for a show or series, such as *Masterpiece Theater, National Geographic,* or *The Civil War*. It then contracts with one or more underwriters—as differentiated from sponsors on commercial TV—to cover part or all of the costs of the production, promotion, and distribution. For the underwriting costs the organization gets the right to have its identity at the beginning and end of the program (but often no product or other self-interest matter) and may promote viewership of the show in ads and other means. Some stations now permit brief references to the underwriter's interests. The stations are now also carrying low-key commercials. (*See* Figure 25.1, page 406.)

Public radio

National Public Radio, 635 Massachusetts Avenue, NW, Washington DC 20001, (202) 414-2000, provides network programming to more than two hundred public radio stations covering almost all of the United States and Puerto Rico. Funding to underwrite some programs is accepted from foundations, associations, and corporations.

Figure 25.1 In exchange for underwriting a website and documentary series on the West, General Motors was mentioned before and after each installment, as well as in promotional ads like this one. *Created by N. W. Ayer & Partners for General Motors to promote "New Perspectives on the West," a companion educational website to documentary filmmaker Ken Burns's latest television epic "The West," a General Motors Mark of Excellence Presentation.*

There are about thirty-five AM and nine hundred FM stations that are either sponsored by educational institutions or function as public broadcasters. They are located in most urban areas. Because their programming and policies vary greatly, it is necessary to study each one to ascertain what will be of interest. Program directors must be contacted individually with suggestions on program materials.

Self-Produced Program Syndication

A study by Nielsen Research found that 83 percent of all TV stations were using taped news and program material from outside sources. Self-produced syndicated programming is growing rapidly.

West Glen found that 95 percent of stations prefer videocasettes to satellite transmission, with somewhat fewer preferring them on spot news stories.

Material prepared for TV use must meet the quality standards of material produced by the stations themselves. Since much of what is broadcast originates with the networks and top production studios, those standards are high. For that reason, most such materials are produced by specialists, rather than in-house (*see* Chapter 27).

Some of the production firms in this field are:

Beach Associates
200 N. Glebe Road
Arlington, VA 22203

Broadcast News Associates (BNA)
770 Lexington Avenue
New York, NY 10021

Chanticleer Communications
8760A Research Building
Austin, TX 78758

Dwj Television
1 Robinson Lane
Ridgewood, NJ 07450

Impressive Images
1360 Peachtree Street, NE
Atlanta, GA 30309

J-Nex Television
5455 Wilshire Bouldvard
Los Angeles, CA 90036

Media Strategy
343 W. Erie Street
Chicago, IL 60610

Medialink
708 Third Avenue
New York, NY 10017

MG Productions
216 E. 45th Street
New York, NY 10017

National Satellite/Production Media
    Services
8075 West Third Street
Los Angeles, CA 90048

Ntv Studio Productions
50 Rockefeller Plaza
New York, NY 10020

On the Scene Productions
5900 Wilshire Boulevard
Los Angeles, CA 90036

Orbis Broadcast Group
100 S. Sangamon Street
Chicago, IL 60607

Reuters Corporate Television
    Productions
1700 Broadway
New York, NY 10019

Translink Communications
301 E. 57th Street
New York, NY 10022

Washington Independent Productions
400 N. Capitol Street, NW
Washington, DC 20001

West Glen Communications
1430 Broadway
New York, NY 10018

North American Precis Syndicate
201 E. 42nd Street
New York, NY 10017

Distributes slides and scripts to TV stations and scripts to radio stations.

Most of these firms provide distribution services, often including satellite transmission.

Gaining Optimum Value from Broadcast Coverage

Favorable exposure on radio or television is a worthwhile accomplishment in itself. However, to get full benefit from the broadcast, the publicist must do the following:

- Report the event completely and clearly to the personnel of the organization or client
- Promote interest in the program through other media
- Examine the broadcast material for secondary uses

Reporting results

Newspaper and magazine coverage can be reported through clippings and tear sheets from the publication, or through reproductions. Similarly, moderate-priced equipment is available for making off-the-air videotapes of programs. The videotape recorders are in use in many public relations offices. Videotape made this way may not be rebroadcast because of copyright regulations.

Ideally, of course, the publicist will alert concerned officials before the show is broadcast so they can tune in the actual program. However, broadcasting is unpredictable, so caution should be voiced that while a show is *scheduled* at such-and-such a time, last-minute changes may interfere.

Furthermore, alerting everyone is not always advisable or economical. Therefore, publicity people generally seek other reporting methods. A number of ways are available when videotapes cannot be made off the air because the broadcast time is unknown or because the equipment is unavailable.

1. **Scripts** reporting verbatim on the show. If the publicity aspect of the show is short, it can be recorded by personal monitoring.
2. **Videotapes** can sometimes be purchased from the television network or station.
3. **Still photographs** of a guest at a broadcasting studio—sometimes with the show's master of ceremonies—illustrate coverage effectively. Pictures are worthwhile adjuncts to tapes or scripts.

The following services monitor TV shows and provide videotapes or audiocassettes:

Broadcast Information Services
390 S. Potomac Way
Aurora, CO 80012

Also in St. Louis, Chicago, New York, and Philadelphia

Newsclip
363 W. Erie
Chicago, IL 60601

Nielsen New Media Research—SIGMA
375 Patricia Avenue
Dunedin, FL 34698

Radio/TV Reports
41 E. 42nd Street
New York, NY 10017

VMS
330 W. 42nd Street
New York, NY 10036

VMS has other offices in many cities.

```
                              - 4 -


    ANNOUNCER:          If a group wanted to stage such a program in their own
                        community, what would they do?

    MRS. MOORHEAD:      Information and materials for such a program can be
                        obtained by writing to the National Safety Council in
                        Chicago.

    ANNOUNCER:          And how about the free reflective tape?

    MRS. MOORHEAD:      These you can get from your own local Veterans of
                        Foreign Wars post, or you can write to the VFW
                        Headquarters in Kansas City, Missouri.  This
                        distributing of tape is a part of the Veterans of
                        Foreign Wars' "Lite-A-Bike" program.  This is a national
                        safety campaign in which they have given away enough
                        free tape for 10 million bicycles.

    ANNOUNCER:          That's a lot of tape.  Just why is this tape a safety
                        plus, as you call it?

    MRS. MOORHEAD:      It's the same material used in reflective license plates
                        and traffic signs. It makes a bicycle visible in the
                        headlights of a car at distances of 1,500 feet or even
                        more.

    ANNOUNCER:          So it's a safety aid for after-dark cycling.  Is that a
                        problem area for school cyclists?


                              - more-
```

Figure 25.2 A page from a script for a radio interview show. The interviewer directs the course of the discussion with questions but leaves most of the commentary to the guest, who is usually an expert in the field.

Publicizing the broadcast

When a person or product is featured on a broadcast, this event itself can be handled as news. Alert publicists get additional benefit from radio and television coverage through magazines, newspapers, and trade publications.

An announcement story preceding the broadcast is often appropriate. This offers another opportunity to talk about the organization, service, product, or idea. Publicity about a show also helps increase its audience.

Advance stories timed for release to coincide with the broadcast are particularly appropriate when a speech or discussion can be reported as news, quoting the program as the source.

After the broadcast, stories can be distributed to newspapers, business, and specialized publications. Pictures taken at the studio are often well received, particularly by trade publications in the field of the organization involved. Publicity about the show should follow news standards, quoting the guest or broadcaster briefly and significantly.

Publicity staffs at networks and larger stations are often helpful. By supplying the station's publicity people with advance material about a guest or product, the publicist may get additional coverage at little cost.

Secondary uses of broadcast material

After arranging broadcast coverage and promoting it internally and externally, the publicity person should examine the broadcast material for other uses.

Scripts, broadcast reports, tapes, and films —at one time or another—can be pressed into additional service. (*See* Figure 25.2, page 409.)

- Reports and scripts make effective mailing pieces to dealers and field representatives.

- Tapes and films are valuable aids for sales meetings, showing coverage that backs up the efforts of the selling force.

- Pictures and reports can be used as editorial material for the organization's publications.

- Live audiences—stockholders, schools, clubs, civic groups—are frequently eager to view films produced for television.

- Rebroadcasts are often possible. When a film or tape has been used in one city, the publicist can often arrange additional broadcasts on other stations. Broadcast film clips are often held and resubmitted for use in a documentary program.

26

PUBLICITY IN THE MOVIES

MARTIN M. COOPER

Martin M. Cooper formed Cooper Communications, Encino, California, in 1982. He represents, among others, a number of clients in motion pictures and entertainment. He formerly was senior vice-president/ corporate communications and marketing director for Playboy Enterprises. Previously he was senior vice-president of Harshe-Rotman & Druck Public Relations, where he supervised programs for major corporate, association, and leisure-time industry clients; public relations manager for the Recreation Division of Universal City Studios and its parent company, MCA, Inc.; and Disneyland's advertising and promotion manager, in charge of its advertising, promotion, graphics, and market research.

Cooper earned his undergraduate degree in 1963 at UCLA, where he was editor of the Daily Bruin. *He has also attended Cambridge University in Great Britain.*

Two of the most powerful tools available to any communicator today are film and video media—whether the images are projected on a wide screen in a darkened movie theater or on a twenty-seven-inch television.

The world's movers and shakers have long recognized and taken advantage of the motion picture's ability to sway people's beliefs and behaviors—including political leaders, from Hitler to Clinton; product-promoting companies, from Procter & Gamble to General Motors; and issues-driven organizations, from Greenpeace to the United Negro College Fund.

Few would dispute the fact that motion pictures greatly influence the general public. When Clark Gable revealed his muscular torso beneath his shirt—sans undershirt—in the film *It Happened One Night*, the film's release precipitated a steep decline in undershirt industry sales. On the other hand, the

hot colors that were the trademark of the popular *Miami Vice* television series and the shaggy haircuts worn on the more recent popular TV sitcom *Friends* each started whole new fashion trends.

However, this kind of unanticipated, trendsetting response to TV and film is the exception, not the rule. More typically, the product or location depictions that impact, or potentially impact, the public result from the deliberate effort, hard work, and close cooperation of the organization's public relations staff and the firm's production and/or marketing people.

Within the past decade three major factors have effectively changed the way film and television are used to promote products and ideas:

1. The growing sophistication and competitive nature of the marketers of films

2. The advent of cable television, home video, and other delivery systems

3. The evolution of product placement as an organized marketing strategy

A Brief Historic Overview

A historical perspective is required to understand the significance of the aforementioned changes.

In the early 1950s public relations professionals realized that there was a vast audience—of more than fifty million people weekly—viewing theatrical motion pictures, ready to be influenced by the on-screen depiction of their products or services.

For the next two decades products were given to film executives to influence their choices. The same model automobile that raced across the scene occupied the producer's garage; the same brand of dishwashing detergent appearing in a domestic scene was found on the sink of the property master's kitchen; and the star's wardrobe would end up in his or her personal closet when the production was completed.

An actor would take a drink from a readily identifiable bottle of Scotch . . . and would receive a case of liquor each month for years. Legend still has it that one well-known film comedian has a warehouse filled with "gifts" from firms whose products he mentioned or displayed in his films.

While some of this still exists, the product placement business has supplanted this haphazard approach to onscreen promotion.

Another promotional vehicle that proved to be mutually beneficial was the postproduction advertising joint promotion. Whether initiated by a manufacturer or the studio publicity department, the results were the same. The star of the film would pose with the product—such as a refrigerator—for full-page advertisements in major women's magazines.

The advertising would also mention that the star was now appearing in such-and-such a film.

Cigarette, liquor, and automotive advertisers used this approach most widely.

These activities, which did not depend on the use of the product in the film, would stretch the advertising exposure the film received without adding to the studio's budget, while gaining the manufacturer a glamorous star to help sell the product.

But the breakdown of the studio system in which the star could be told what to do, along with the advent of highly paid, highly independent actors led to a sharp decline in this type of advertising.

Today, the star has supplanted the film as the focal point. Instead of a movie star promoting a product with plugs for a film, the individual is highly paid, and there may or may not be a film related to the advertising campaign: James Stewart for Campbell's soups, Michael Jackson for Pepsi-Cola, and Elizabeth Taylor for perfume—and not a mention of a film in sight.

Motion pictures have changed greatly in recent years and so has the potential for using them as a publicity vehicle. The emphasis now is on film marketing tie-ins, rather than on in-film use of products. There are a number of reasons:

1. **Television is the single largest factor.** When TV first appeared, Hollywood's leaders scoffed at the "little box." Their scorn turned to panic, however, as theatergoers by the millions discovered they could enjoy film entertainment in the comfort of their own living rooms . . . and for free. The star system faded, huge studio overhead could no longer be supported, and Hollywood appeared destined for ghost-town status.

   Television programming executives soon realized, however, that the highest ratings were to be snared by using Hollywood films that had been stored in film vaults, and by providing movies made for television.

So television became the savior of the industry it almost destroyed. But it altered the motion picture business so greatly that no longer could three or four major studios control most of the total production. Today studios supply as much film product, or more, to television as they do to theaters, and many films made for American television are released theatrically abroad. Conversely, many films distributed theatrically do not turn a profit until sold to a network or a television syndicator a year or two after initial release.

Television also has usurped movies' role as the major vehicle for promotion because advertising agency executives realize how many more people can be influenced by a popular TV series than by a film that may be in release only three or four months.

The author of this chapter at one time was in charge of public relations for a major passenger cruise line. Through a contact at a studio, the opportunity arose to film several scenes for a film on one of the firm's ships. Afraid of the potential disruption to the ship's routine, the owner rejected the opportunity. A few years later, under new ownership, the same line not only allowed its ship to be used as the locale for a TV series, but based its entire marketing campaign on the series. The company: Princess Cruises. The TV series: *The Love Boat*. The result: publicity that money could never buy.

2. **Television, whether pay cable or free over-the-air, has also complicated the situation** because of product interchangeability. A film made for theatrical release might later be sold to television. Federal Communications Commission guidelines prohibit "plugs" within editorial programming. Also, potential sponsors of a

television program will not buy into a film that has a competitor's product displayed prominently within it.

3. **The "studio system" is reduced.** At one time the film industry supported five or six major studios and several secondary ones; now production companies produce the bulk of American film product. Many production companies work out of tasteful Beverly Hills offices rather than on sprawling movie lots. They hire technical, artistic, and theatrical people only as they need them. Today a publicist must work with dozens of propmen, assistant producers, and writers, not just a handful as in the past.

4. **Exhibitors came to resent what they considered to be overcommercialism** on the big screen. One studio publicity director recalls that in a few cases blatant film plugs caused theater owners to object so strenuously that initial prints had to be withdrawn and deletions made.

5. **Fewer pictures are being made today** than in past years. From the inception of motion pictures to the early 1950s, going to the movies was a major outlet for the nation's leisure time. It was a family event, usually occurring one night a week, and on Saturdays for the children. The studios had to turn out hundreds of films a year to satisfy a seemingly insatiable demand. A major studio that once made sixty pictures annually now produces fewer than twenty. The fewer movies released, the fewer opportunities there are for publicity in films or promotion related to them. Conversely, television, including the blossoming cable TV and home video markets, exhibits an appetite for film product unequaled since the beginning of the motion picture process a century ago.

6. **Not only the number but the type of films being made has changed.** The "small film," once the staple of Hollywood, has

become the made-for-TV movie. Today's theatrical trend is toward the "big picture"—big in scope, big in budget, big in promotion.

7. **The cost of attending a first-run movie has escalated.** Tickets have jumped from the long-ago $4.50 for a double-feature bill to $7.00 for a single-feature first-run film. Although these increases have not been out of line with other general inflationary costs, they are competing with free television programs, $3.00 home video rental charges, and a monthly fee for a pay cable service that starts at around $30.00.

As these factors have reshaped the movie business, they have altered the opportunities for the publicist. While most of the following points relate to theatrical motion pictures, the basic concepts are almost equally applicable to television dramatic programs.

Current Publicity Opportunities

Excellent opportunities exist for the creative publicist to use motion pictures as a promotional medium. With the increase in cable television opportunities and the lessening of the FCC stranglehold on commercial TV, publicity on the small screen is growing. Although the scope and type of such use varies greatly, publicity in the movies can be divided into three major areas: use of locations, in-film promotion, and tie-ins.

Locations

One of the most basic elements of any film is the location. Historically, Western films have been shot in undeveloped areas of the West, films shot in urban locations have been photographed on city streets, and interiors have been recreated within giant Hollywood sound stages. Since the advent of talkies in the late twenties, sound stages have provided the setting for most films. Interruptions caused by airplanes, passing motorists, and other distractions are eliminated, and the cinematographer need not plan the shooting around the weather.

But today's films are making greater use of specialized locations, and a publicist can take advantage of that trend. Such locales as amusement parks, airports, cruise ships, and skyscrapers are hard to fit into a sound stage. Publicity personnel should be aware of the possibilities of motion picture filming in, on, or around locations they represent.

By maintaining close relations with the major producing companies and reading the Hollywood trade papers, one can learn which scripts have been sold to which producers. A telephone call or letter offering your location can often bring an interested response. One firm that operates several amusement parks carries on an active program of having movies and television shows emanate from their properties.

On a broader scale, cities, states, and even foreign nations are aware that movies or television programs can be a positive force. Nearly every state actively seeks to have films produced within its borders, and many have "film councils" whose job it is to attract production companies.

Municipalities such as New York City and Chicago are also well aware of the dual advantage of filming within their city limits: tourists and those with investment projects are reminded of the advantages of such a location, and the economic benefit realized by the expenditures of the production company for products and services are valuable to the local economy. They realize that location shooting benefits both the television industry and the tax coffers of their areas.

In-film promotion

Even with decreased opportunities for depicting products in films, this does have potential. Each film presents its own problems for the property master. Hundreds of household items, automobiles, and all the trappings necessary to create an environment are needed for each film. While much of the material is either stored by the studio or constructed specifically for the film, many opportunities for providing products do exist. Today's directors are seeking realism, and realism means using real products.

There is no guarantee, of course, that the director or cinematographer will use a provided product to the degree the publicist might wish, unless a major promotion timed to around the film's release has been prearranged. Keeping an eye on the Hollywood trade papers for announced film projects that logically have need for a specific product or offering your product to a prop master can be helpful.

Perhaps the most successful case of a product's use in a film was the trail of Reese's Pieces that the title character followed in *E.T. The Extra-Terrestrial*. Sales of the candy soared 66 percent within three months of the release of that box office champion.

Similarly, soon after Paul Newman and Tom Cruise appeared in *The Color of Money*, sales of billiard equipment rose 30 percent.

There are even awards given for the most effective product placement.

Some placements are obvious overkill, however. *Boxoffice Magazine* scored the dancing Pepsi-Cola can in Eddie Murphy's *The Golden Child* as the "most blatant product plug." And Bill Cosby's box office bomb, *Leonard Part 6*, featured repeated, unobstructed views of Coca-Cola cans to the degree that the soft drink company had to defend the in-film use as "synergistic marketing."

Success in product placement led to the emergence of product placement specialists, usually small entrepreneurial firms which, for a fee, place products in films. Those fees can range from $2,500 to $25,000, depending on the film, how long the product is on-screen, whether dialogue is related to the product, whether the star holds or refers to the product, and whether there are opportunities for post-production promotions or tie-ins.

Recently studios have realized that such fees might as well go to them, so they have retained personnel or even created small departments to seek out product placement opportunities.

Cigarette companies seem to be particularly aggressive in arranging tie-ins. Eve cigarettes is reputed to have paid $30,000 to appear in *Supergirl*, while Marlboro reportedly paid $42,000 to appear in *Superman II*.

Clearly, product placement, whether through one of the fee-based firms dealing in the field, an advertising or public relations agency with good entertainment industry contacts, or directly through the studio or production company, is here to stay.

The most likely to continue to grow is the trade for what can't otherwise be obtained free. For example, film crews are expensive to transport, but perhaps a producer can build in a shot of an American Airlines jet in return for free travel. If the film is built around automobiles, why not go to the Ford Motor Company and offer free exposure for use of their cars in the film or TV show?

With the increased "shelf life" a theatrical film has today, given the ever-increasing product needs of cable television and home video, good product placement of all types becomes an ever-more-valuable tool.

Release-related tie-ins

Even more than in-picture product placements, producers look for tie-ins that will help market their product—the movie.

While promotional tie-ins have been used for years, the variety of outlets is more diverse than ever. A few examples follow:

- *Back to the Future II* was backed with a national promotion with Pizza Hut, offering sunglasses for $1.99 with a purchase, and another with Texaco built around free toy car giveaways with an eight-gallon minimum purchase.

- A Chicago confectionery company distributed its regular summer supply of two billion gumballs, imprinted with the words "Gumball Rally," at no cost to the film's producer.

- A major dairy chain in the Northeast based a three-picture (*The Bad News Bears, Won Ton, the Dog Who Saved Hollywood*, and *The Big Bus*) tie-in with Paramount Pictures, based on milk carton panels with artwork from the films.

T-shirts, bumper stickers, paperback books based on the screenplay, posters, sound track music albums, and many other items—some traditional and some zany—have been used to promote box office sales. At the same time, the popularity of a film can be used to sell the publicist's product.

Most promotional tie-ins last for the theater life of the picture, ranging from a few weeks to a year or more.

Maximizing Publicity Opportunities

The best way for the publicist to take advantage of the continuing stream of motion pictures is to create ideas that will help sell both his or her product and the picture, and to convince the appropriate people at the studios of the mutual benefit to be gained.

The basic rules for success in using motion pictures as publicity vehicles are similar to other areas of publicity:

1. **Know the product.** The publicist should have a rudimentary knowledge of motion pictures and how they are produced, distributed, and promoted.

   The number of books on film production, distribution, and marketing grows daily. There is less literature on television. Perhaps even more important, however, is a close reading of the key industry periodicals, including *Daily Variety, Hollywood Reporter*, and others.

2. **Know the potential.** Obviously, some films lend themselves better to publicity opportunities than do others. The motion picture trade journals provide good information on which producer has announced what project, which studio (or production company) will film it, who will write the screenplay, etc. These publications provide the best "early warning system" regarding upcoming films and are a source of ideas. One of the trade publications, *Boxoffice*, runs a "Showmandiser" section that details promotions being arranged and reports on the results of previous efforts.

3. **Know the people.** The successful publicist establishes good relationships with professionals in the field. Producers, wardrobe masters, property masters, screenwriters, advertising and publicity directors, and others are able to make decisions related to the use of products, places, situations, and marketing activities.

4. **Know the timing.** One grocery chain executive approached the location finder of a studio with an offer to allow the production company free use of one of his supermarkets—two weeks after the scene had been filmed! Make sure to contact the right people—at the right time.

5. **Learn from film promoters.** Few industries have as many skilled promotion and publicity people as are employed in motion pictures. Being aware of—and learning from—their campaigns can provide many lessons. The promotional tie-in and publicity campaigns for *Batman, Who Framed Roger Rabbit, Star Wars, Superman,* and *Raiders of the Lost Ark,* while not solely responsible for the success of the films, played major roles in making them all box office hits.

Perhaps no other industry values the creative publicity stunt, the innovative marketing idea, the fresh approach to a tired subject more than does the film and television industry.

27

SPONSORED FILMS, VIDEOS, AND OTHER AUDIOVISUAL MEDIA

LOREN J. KALLSEN

Loren J. Kallsen is president of Vibrant Films and Videos, Inc., a Minneapolis-based producer of sponsored motion pictures. His company has made public relations, marketing, and motivational films and videos for clients such as AT&T, 3M Company, ITT, Burlington Northern, The Minneapolis Grain Exchange, and the U.S. Fish and Wildlife Service. He has produced, written, and directed throughout the United States and Western Europe, in the Caribbean, and in South America.

His productions have won numerous Gold Awards at such leading competitions as the annual CINE Festival in Washington, DC, and the International Film & TV Festival of New York.

Prior to forming Vibrant in 1973, Mr. Kallsen was for eight years executive producer for films and broadcasting on the headquarters corporate relations and advertising staff of ITT Corporation in New York City. In that capacity he had responsibility for the creation, production, and administration of ITT's public relations films worldwide. He also handled public relations contact with the TV networks and major stations.

Before his assignment at ITT, Mr. Kallsen was a freelance filmwriter in New York City and for five years a reporter, writer, and producer at WCCO radio and KSTP-TV in Minneapolis.

Audiovisual communications—the medium that combines sight and sound—achieves the greatest impact and the highest rate of retention as a mass communications vehicle.

Of course, this assumes that (a) the audience is duly sight- and sound-oriented (as are most people born since the universal acceptance of television), and (b) the subject matter lends itself to audiovisual application.

Due to the potency of appropriately applied audiovisual techniques, they are increasingly used in various ways to communicate via television and/or theaters with publics ranging from small meetings to audiences composed of millions of people. (*See* Chapters 25 and 26.)

Motion Picture Sponsorship*

The motion picture, whether produced on film or videotape or shown via direct projection or TV, is the most effective audiovisual medium. To the elements of sight and sound it adds the crucial dimension of motion, with all the excitement, drama, and impact that motion imparts. It attains a high degree of audience involvement.

Public relations people use sponsored motion pictures because they present most stories more quickly, accurately, and memorably than speech or the printed word alone. These productions include not only public relations films/videos but also those used for marketing to and education of the sponsors' many internal and external audiences.

In making motion pictures there are at least as many exceptions as rules for both the buyer and seller of the film/video. But it is possible to set down certain guidelines that will help assure the effectiveness of the final product . . . that will help keep all concerned out of The Graveyard of Floundered Projects.

It is essential that everyone involved realize that making a successful public relations film/video is a complex aesthetic, technical, and political undertaking. It follows that the basis of any serious project is *professionalism* on the part of both the sponsor (or agency) and the producer of the picture.

Getting started

The first step is for the sponsor to analyze and write down the objectives and audiences

---

*For the purposes of this chapter, videotape is included in the broad "motion picture" category. Unless otherwise indicated, either specifically or by context, the terms "motion picture," "film," "picture," "video," "tape," and "videotape" are used interchangeably.

for the potential film. These may change as the project is further defined, but for the time being all will at least have a common reference point.

Before going further, the first-time sponsor may wish to gain some general background by reading one of the books on film/video published by Hastings House, New York City.

Selecting the producer

The next step is to bring in a fully professional producer. How do you find him? Word of mouth may be the best way; talk to some satisfied clients. The Yellow Pages phone directory can provide leads. A number of production directories can give you pointers: not all the producers listed are good, and not all the good ones are listed; but it's a place to start.

One of the more useful is the CINE *Golden Eagle Awards*, published annually by the Council on International Nontheatrical Events, 1001 Connecticut Avenue, NW, Washington, DC 20036. This brochure lists only award-winning producers whose films/videos have survived multiple judgings.

Regardless of how you locate your producer, it is important to learn his or her capabilities and reputation firsthand. Screen recent work. Talk straightforwardly and insist that he or she do the same to you. (Do not, however, demand a firm quotation during your initial conversation; usually the producer can respond meaningfully only after tighter specifications have been developed.) Match the producer to the job. This does not mean that he has to be an expert in your subject or that he must have already made a film just like the one you think you want; that may or may not be helpful. Rather, it means that you should be able to infer from the work he has shown you and from his long-term record that you can expect to get the desired result.

Contracting, budgeting, paying

Having made your commitment to the motion picture medium and selecting the producer, the next step is to set up a mutually useful working relationship. For a project of any complexity, this relationship should be carried out under a formal client-producer contract that clearly spells out the obligations of each party. Properly drawn, this document is to everyone's advantage. It will save a lot of misunderstanding as the project progresses.

Normally there are separate contracts for the script and for the production. This practice has two virtues: (a) The script, which is a separate cost, provides meaningful specifications on which to base the production contract and price. (b) If the script fails to meet the client's requirements, he or she can escape from the project without further obligation except to pay the script fee.

Typically, whether it is a script or a production, payment is made on a step basis. Though arrangements may vary, there normally is a substantial advance payment upon signing of the contract: anywhere from 33 percent to 50 percent, depending on circumstances. There will be one or two progress payments at specified points and a final payment on delivery.

What is an appropriate budget for a motion picture? There is no blanket answer. A film/video can properly cost only a few thousand dollars or it can cost hundreds of thousands, depending on many variables: where it is shot, over what period of time, the number of locations, the size of sets, types of costumes, the quality, the style, the amount and kind of animation and opticals, the kind of music, the kind of cast, and so on.

Length is, of course, an element of cost, but it is generally not a meaningful index. Cost per minute is a seductive way of evaluating the price of a picture (it's neat, like buying a pound of this or a foot of that), but it is usually misleading. The true indices of cost are the variables that go into each minute.

The sum of this, perhaps, is that there is no such thing as a cheap picture; there are only those that do the job for you or fail to do the job. Good pictures can be made on lean budgets, but they cannot be made on inadequate budgets. A $35,000 film/video that fails to give value is far more expensive than a $70,000 picture that does what it is intended to do.

The client's best protection is to "learn the territory" and deal with a trustworthy competent producer, whether that producer is from a client's in-house unit or is a commercial independent.

Developing the script

With the working relationship defined, the next step is to develop the script, which is the basis for all that follows. If you don't have a good script, the rest of the project may degenerate into nothing more than a salvage operation.

Research is part of the creative process and precedes serious writing. It is important that the client open necessary doors and supply essential information; that the producer or the producer's writer be given any reasonable assistance.

Once subject research has been completed, the script usually is developed in either two or three stages, depending on the complexity of the project, the exigencies of schedule, the client's internal approval procedures, and so on.

First comes a brief *concept*, which should deal with the broad story line and the production approach. Will professional actors be used? Shot on location or on a stage? Original or library score? On-screen or off-screen narrator? Animation, and what kind? 16mm or 35mm film? Videotape? Which format? (As a practical matter, a tentative oral concept frequently precedes research, thereby helping guide the research and keeping the researcher from constantly going over old ground.)

Next is the *treatment*, a longer document that is not yet a script but that will give the reader a good idea of what the picture will look and sound like. It will not have complete description of action and sound. (If the concept has been quite detailed, or if time presses, the treatment in some cases may be bypassed.)

Finally comes the *script*, which will contain scene-by-scene action and sound descriptions as well as the approved narration and/or dialogue.

The client has the right of approval throughout. Before giving approval at any particular stage of scripting he or she should be sure that wants are met. Changing specifications later may be costly.

Production

Under the word *production* we include the three aspects of picture making that follow scripting: preproduction, production itself, and postproduction.

Preproduction covers the plans made and actions taken after script approval but before shooting begins. Preproduction includes such things as defining the production contract, location scouting and clearances, casting, selection and assigning of production personnel, scheduling, and the hundreds of details that must be handled before the cameras turn. While the burden of preproduction falls on the producer, the client also needs to contribute. On a corporate image film/video, for example, he or she will have to make any necessary arrangements within the company. Many times the client will be asked to gain the cooperation of, say, other businesses or government agencies. The client will also be responsible for setting up approval

procedures and making sure that designated representatives actually have the authority to make decisions as they are needed. Like scripting, preproduction requires close collaboration between producer and client. Good preproduction leads toward an effective conclusion. Its absence leads to chaos.

Production is the actual shooting of the picture and the recording of all synchronous and nonsynchronous sound connected with the shooting. The client should be present during the shooting of those scenes that require on-the-spot technical or political approvals. His or her presence during the rest of shooting is a matter of the extent of interest and the strength of legs. Many people quickly discover that watching a film crew at work can become a boring and exhausting experience.

Once production is under way it is wise to follow the producer's recommendations in film-making matters. To meet his or her obligations requires maintaining consistency of creative viewpoint and technical procedure. Surprises forced by the client will tend to deteriorate the quality of the picture and raise its cost.

Postproduction covers the many steps necessary to complete the film. It includes picture and sound editing, recording studio sound, creation of music and sound effects, opticals and titles, final script polish, and laboratory work. (*See* Figure 27.1.)

During postproduction, the client evaluates the picture and gives approval at least three times: at (a) rough edit, (b) fine edit, (c) completion.

The role of careful planning and control throughout the project will be reaffirmed to both client and producer during postproduction. If major changes must be made because, as it turns out, the approved script is inadequate or because the client has new ideas not in the script, the picture will be more expensive to the client. If major changes

Figure 27.1 The crew in the Hawthorne Communications on-line editing suite combines all audio elements, such as voice, sound effects, and music during this sweetening session. *Courtesy Hawthorne Communications*

must be made because the producer did not fulfill the specifications of the script, he or she will incur additional expense. If no serious changes must be made, both parties are winners.

Distribution

Distribution is frequently the most overlooked aspect of the public relations use of motion pictures. (*See* list in Appendix.) A film or videotape is of no use unless it is seen by its target audience. Yet that is the fate of many productions; they sit on the shelf for lack of foresight in planning or funding.

A distribution strategy should be developed and its costs foreseen during the conception of the project. Sometimes the sponsor may wish to handle its own distribution, but the planning and funding must nonetheless be provided. Under some circumstances the producer may be set up to distribute. Generally, if it is intended to reach a large and dispersed audience, a picture receives its most effective handling through a full-scale distributor.

Distributors are prepared to build audiences according to the type of message and the sponsor's objective. They will promote the picture; schedule, ship, and maintain the prints; and prepare collateral material. They will turn in accurate reports of showings, including such information as number and makeup of audience, date, location, name of organization, or call letters of the TV station. If the picture appears on public service TV, the report will give the station call letters and affiliation, estimated number of viewers, time slot, and a figure on what would have been the air cost of the telecast had it been purchased rather than shown on free time.

A leading distributor of sponsored films/ videos, with offices and film exchanges in major cities, is DWJ Television, 1 Robinson Lane, Ridgewood, NY 07450. Sponsored pictures can be distributed to service clubs, professional meetings, civil and social organizations, consumer groups, trade fairs, resorts, and other bodies and audiences of many kinds.

Schools welcome good films/tapes that are factual without being too commercial. They must be open and fair and clearly indicate the sponsor. For best effect they should be colorful and entertaining as well as educational. Those are traits of all good sponsored films.

As with production, it is meaningless to generalize much about the cost of distribution. There are too many variables in terms of saturation, schedule, objectives, and acceptable ratios of cost effectiveness. (Talk with the distributors; the reputable ones all have price lists and descriptive literature they will supply without obligation.) It can be said that with good planning and a large long-term distribution program the right kind of public relations film/video can reach millions of people at a cost per viewer that compares favorably with the cost of advertising exposure through national TV or national magazines.

The life span of a public relations picture varies with the subject and its handling, the sponsor's commitment to the medium, and the dating factors in the story. For most films/videos, an excellent run might be four to seven years, at which time a judicious updating might provide rebirth. One of the earliest industrial films made in color, *Steel—Man's Servant*, was used for twenty-two years before it was retired. At more than 104,000 screenings, it had been viewed by nearly ten million persons, mainly school children.

Effective Use of TV Releases

The growth of television, with its daily coverage of the news, led to the demise of newsreels in theaters. (*See also* Chapter 25.)

From the public relations viewpoint, the newsreel has been translated into the TV news tape release. This is a video of, generally, one to two minutes in length that is distributed free of charge—and without obligation—to the news or public service departments of individual stations and networks. To be considered for airing, handouts must look and sound like news tape and must have, within the standards of the evaluating organization, bona fide news or public service interest. As a practical matter they also contain information or a viewpoint that benefits the sponsor. Their commercial content should be minimal or they will not be used.

Handout TV news tape usually falls within one or two broad categories: hard spot news, which is produced against a deadline and must hit the air quickly to be valid, and the feature "evergreen" story, which is not tied tightly to a specific event or date and is airable any time for weeks or even months after it is produced. Sometimes "evergreens" masquerade as public service announcements (PSAs).

From a technical viewpoint, news tape can be turned out by any competent producer. However, the client is likely to be better served if, for this somewhat specialized medium, he or she engages a producer with working TV news experience. Generally he or she will have the better grasp of news format and content, and will be able to contribute an intangible judgment that will enhance the acceptability of the handout.

The great disadvantage of handout news tape is that the sponsor cannot absolutely control the message; the news organization may rewrite or edit the picture in such a way that the message is deleted. On the other hand, if the sponsor's viewpoint gains the air, the handout news tape takes on credibility that a TV commercial can never have; the message has squared with the considered news judgment of the broadcaster.

Most TV stations, groups, and networks in the United States (and throughout the world, for that matter) utilize handout news tape at one time or another. So does the government's

International Communications Agency in the tape it ships or satellites overseas. At each place there usually is a single best person to receive a tape. This may be the news director, or the assignment editor, or a producer, or a syndication editor. It is important that the distributor of the tape—whether the client, or the producer, or the commercial distributor—knows to whom to send it. Again, past experience in the TV news business is valuable. In the absence of personal acquaintance with key individuals at key stations, *Broadcasting Yearbook* is a good place to start to build a mailing list; it identifies the news directors at stations throughout the country. *Broadcasting Yearbook* also lists many, though not all, commercial producers who have news tape expertise.

Slide Presentations

Although normally less impressive and dramatic than motion pictures, slides can be successful communications vehicles. When the budget cannot stand the cost of a motion picture, or when the subject requires audiovisual treatment but would not be enhanced by motion per se, the answer may be a slide show.

A slide show may be presented with or without a recorded sound track. When recorded sound is not used, the cost of production is cut. Also, the human element is injected into the presentation by the person making it, and he or she can expand or minimize any particular information at will. The disadvantage of using a live presenter is that the message may not be conveyed equally well at each showing, not to mention the likelihood of flubs: the human element works both ways.

A recorded sound track, which can be as simple or elaborate as desired, is necessary when exact reproduction of the message is needed.

Usually slide shows cost from one-fourth to one-half as much as motion pictures, though it is dangerous to generalize because they can become extremely complex, with costs that equal or exceed those of a motion picture.

For example, large multi-image shows of the kind that became popular in the late 1960s (and remain popular today) are expensive. They are essentially slide shows, but the standard single screen has been increased from two to six or more screens, and the projectors have been increased from one to anywhere from two to twenty, and their control is complicated. In addition, the sound track contains not just one unadorned narrative voice but a whole cast of voices with original music. When this happens, generalizations about relatively lower costs break down. Such a "slide show" can be an excellent value if there is a need for a showstopper in a setting that calls for multi-image: at expositions, theme parks, one-shot extravaganzas, etc.

Volumes of material are available on the various types and uses of slides. But the only true way to explore these possibilities is through experience. Thus, as with motion pictures, it is wise in the search for the proper audiovisual medium to be guided by a professional.

Visual and/or Audio Aids

Tests made on oral communications by the University of Minnesota have shown that, on average, 75 percent of the things we say escape the listener's mind. With only 25 percent being retained, it is important to consider the use of visuals with an oral presentation.

Overhead and *front projectors* permit projecting onto a screen the contents of a transparency, which can be made from a printed page, a chart, a photograph, etc. A pointer can pick out specific items while the image is on the screen, and erasable ink markings with a water-base marker can be written on the transparency by the speaker. Some overhead projectors will accept lighted crystal display (LCD) panels that enable the user to project images directly from a computer to a projection screen.

Rear projectors are a convenience that permits material at a lecture or in a display booth to be projected from in back of a screen while it is read from the front.

Using *opaque projectors* materials in their solid form—rocks, pieces of machinery, a page from a bound book, etc.—can be shown on a large screen. This is often effective at a quick press conference when a new device or mineral find is being shown to a large group and other ways of showing it might be confusing or time-consuming. Also it is useful when materials that should be handled only by experts, such as very delicate crockery or sections of tissue, are to be shown.

Charts are by far the most-used visual aid. A chart may be painted, printed, or drawn. It must be large enough and simple enough to be seen and comprehended in the presentation setting.

Flannel boards consist of board covered with felt. Sticky-backed visuals are placed on the surface, allowing a speaker to put some movement and flexibility into an otherwise static presentation.

Magnetic boards are much like flannel boards except that magnets permit the use of heavier three-dimensional visuals.

Dry-erase whiteboards and markers permit changing or erasing messages easily, without dust.

Audiocassettes are useful in overcoming some of the difficulties of working with a diffuse and loose-knit organization. They assure that all concerned get exactly the same message with the desired emphasis. For example, monthly voice memoranda from the director of public relations at a company's headquarters may go out to plant and branch personnel, commenting on surveys, new programs, problems being explored, ideas submitted from the field, and other matters. Field people may respond in the same medium. Generally, these audiocassette communications, though carefully prepared, are modest in their techniques. They intentionally do not have the ambitions—or costs—associated with full-scale audio productions. (*See* Chapter 28.)

The *tele-lecture* is a useful technique for making an audiovisual presentation at a distance. With the help of the telephone or satellite company there is a hookup from a speaker's office to a meeting or classroom where visuals can be shown while the speaker is heard. Members of the audience can ask questions through a two-way hookup. This permits the speaker to "appear" at many locations without the time or expense of going to each, and it permits remote groups to engage speakers they otherwise would not attract.

Facsimile sends between distant cities, via telephone, exact copies of blueprints, layouts, and other printed materials. It is now used increasingly to transmit copy between the offices of an agency and its client or between an organization and a communications medium.

28

CONTROLLED ELECTRONIC COMMUNICATIONS

JAMES L. HORTON
DERMOT McKEONE

James L. Horton, senior manager, Robert Marston Associates, has exten-sive experience in investor relations, corporate communications, and marketing. He concentrates on public relations processes/business prac-tices and the strategic use of public relations and technology.

Horton's clients have included computer and high-tech companies such as Wang and Control Data Corporation, and financial services firms ranging from banks and brokerages to large accounting firms.

Horton holds an M.B.A. in marketing and finance from Northwest-ern University, as well as M.A. degrees from the University of Missouri School of Journalism and from UCLA in English.

Dermot McKeone is the director in the Infopress Group, London, respon-sible for a wide range of technical and computer-related accounts. Author of a popular business textbook on computers, he was the founding chair-man of the UK-based Public Relations Consultants Association's Indus-try and Technology Group and spent two years as the chairman of PRCA's Education and Training Committee. He served on the PRCA's Board of Management for four years.

He graduated from Aston University in 1968. He joined Infopress in 1974 and was elected deputy chairman of the consultancy ten years later.

The accelerated evolution of electronic com-munications—and the equally dramatic changes in social, political, and economic behavior caused by these technologies—pose significant challenges for today's public rela-tions professionals.

These developments include the following:

• The deluge of televised images has led some commentators to believe that words have been forever eschewed in favor of "live" pic-tures that emote, provide few facts, and only loosely correspond with hard-edged reality.

• Electronic networks have flattened orga-nization structure—thereby tying more closely together employees, stockholders, public interest groups, political organiza-tions, dealers, suppliers, and customers.

• Computerized information management systems allow the CEO to sit in an office and track the minute-by-minute sales of a water pistol in two hundred stores, or in one store, or even on one specific cash register of one store. This capability has enabled U.S. toy retailer Toys "Я" Us to pinpoint the start and end of fads faster than its competitors. Initially developed and used by various types of U.S. companies as a means to control inventory, this has become a sophisticated and widely used sensor for determining the interests, or pulse, of the American public.

- The toll-free 800 number links corporations to customers. In 1988 total "800" calls rose to 7.03 billion from just 1.9 billion in 1983. As a result, American Express Company and American Telephone and Telegraph (AT&T) joined forces, forming a partnership to expand interactive phone marketing.

- The growing use of 900 numbers—for example, as a fund-raising device for educational television, a voting booth for TV viewers, and a vendor of aural pornography. One California law firm launched a $2-per-minute legal service by phone, using a 900 number.

- The Internet opens access to many sources of information and provides a way to make information available to its subscribers anywhere, at any time.

- Cellular subscribers totaled about 92,000 in 1984 and grew to more than 37 million by the mid-1990s. Growth has been so rapid that many users today complain of "cellular fatigue"—the inability to get away from phone calls.

- Technology enables "demassification"—the division of the public into more segments having fewer numbers per group and greater cultural, demographic, and attitudinal diversity.

Of course, not all of the new and emerging technologies will survive or "catch on" as readily as expected. Some face barriers. The videophone, for instance, was introduced decades ago, but is still not a reality for most Americans.

In addition, some technologies fit more comfortably into some cultures than into others. France's Minitel videotext system that permits the viewer to order via television, has become a way of life in that country—offering more than eight thousand services, a twenty-five-million-entry electronic phone book, and a "pink Minitel" network of erotic and other messages offering illegal acts. Despite numerous attempts, videotext has failed to take hold in the United States.

So-called high touch technologies—that is, those that accommodate established human behavior—tend to fare significantly better than those that do not. People tend to be conservative. Electronic communications must adapt to the public's patterns of receiving, processing, and responding to communications—not vice versa.

This chapter first examines internal electronic communications techniques, then extends outward to external groups—moving from individuals to departments, the organization itself, the immediate external publics, larger and broader audiences, and finally to international cultural concerns. Several electronic technologies cross all boundaries.

Three issues are covered here:

1. Existing electronic technologies—foregoing speculative items and focusing on known tools and services at the time of the writing

2. Why electronic communication is important to public relations practitioners

3. How public relations people should employ these technologies and techniques

Figure 28.1 An office communication system permits combining telephone, paper-based mail, facsimile, and electronic mail with input of handwritten or voice messages. *Courtesy International Business Machines Corporation. Unauthorized use not permitted.*

Electronic Communications and the Public Relations Practitioner

For the modern office, electronic tools to communicate or facilitate media production abound. A brief inventory includes the following:

- Hardware: Personal computers or terminals, fax machines and computer-based fax boards, smart phones, voice mail, electronic mail, local area networking, electronic printers—laser, dot matrix, ink jet, thermal, pen plotter—mouse and trackball controllers, floppy and hard disk data storage, optical read-write and Write Once Read Many Times storage, modems for telephone line communications, and more

- Software: Word processing, desktop publishing, electronic spreadsheets, database programs, computer graphics and computer-aided design, personal and group calendars, personal note takers, phone books with auto telephone dialers, external data-

base research, file managers, digital to-do lists, alarms and clock programs, computer-based calculators, phone message centers, and more

New and old technology have merged. Computers blend phones and terminals. Some terminals have phone sets built into them: you answer and dial through the terminal screen. Computers blend image and data. You can fax from a computer as easily as from a fax machine. You can receive video directly on your computer screen—the local television station, a video conference call from a colleague. You can call up photos from computer storage as easily as reaching into your file drawer. (*See* Figure 28.1.)

With electronic "pixel-painting" you can crop photos, remove hills, insert trees and lakes, and change the sky from morning to midday. This has hurt the credibility of photographs because no one can know now whether a picture has been modified.

These technologies offer communicators ways of making messages more effective and more efficient while enhancing personal productivity. But how does one use them? The best way is through personal learning.

Years ago the authors learned to write on typewriters—a nineteenth-century invention. Moving to late twentieth-century word processing opened huge productivity opportunities in spelling and grammar checking, typesetting, formatting, rewriting, and more. Well-planned moves to other technologies can accomplish similar gains.

- Fax machines and computer-based fax boards speed document transmission at lower overall cost.

- Smart phones allow call forwarding, caller identification, conference calling, speed dialing, call tracking, intercom paging, message interrupt, custom messages, and auto answering.

- Voice mail has reduced or eliminated receptionists. One can leave personal or group messages in several phone mailboxes or in the computer terminal hooked to the phone that will show the message on the screen in text when the person called returns.

- Electronic mail is reducing the use of memos. E-mail lets you drop a note from your computer to your colleague across the hall to read when he or she returns from vacation or to your counterpart in Hong Kong to see in the morning. You can digitally copy messages to one, ten, or a thousand people.

However, individual electronic communications and tools need study, planning, training, and careful implementation. The public relations professional cannot expect to learn new tools by osmosis. An attitude is required that accepts rather than rejects opportunities offered. It demands patience to stay with the new technology until one is comfortable. The result is ability to accomplish far more at greater quality in less time.

Electronic Communications Within Departments

All the tools mentioned, linked in digital networks, let you restructure the public relations function and more closely monitor the effectiveness of communications efforts.

This is a matter of process and deals with two questions—why and what if. For example:

- Why are we doing weekly newsletters to top management? What if we used E-mail? My newsletter editor could do what she has always done but deliver daily. Why do a newsletter at all? What if my newsletter editor did a series of flash reports by E-mail using certified E-mail that tells whether a manager has opened the box? Why not send two flash reports a day—one at 9 A.M. and one at noon? That would eliminate design, printing, and distribution. That reduces the newsletter budget by 50 percent.

- Why use an outside typesetting shop for brochures? What if I used desktop publishing for simple brochures with a 400 to 600 dots per inch laser printer or in-house typesetter? When I finish writing, I would send the article on the network to the editor. The editor would send it on the network to the designer. The designer would format. It would look just as good. It would be three days faster than the old way. It would reduce my departmental typesetting budget by 25 percent and the time travelling between desks by 50 percent. It would let my in-house designer spend more time designing than coordinating.

- Why are we still compiling clipping sheets without analysis? What if we used a content analysis program to provide top management with trends indicators on major issues? We can buy a PC-based program to do it. We can track audiences as well as issues. We can track reporters, their interests, attitudes, and understanding. We can use it as the centerpiece of our media strategy. We can send weekly reports over the network to key managers to help planning and management.

• Why suffer during annual budgeting in trying to explain to top management what the public relations department does? What if I put in a time accounting system and track job requests from the business units? I could then show who uses the department and how much. I could show how important we are to line units. Each person in my department would log time into the network system and my controller would have it weekly, or even daily.

The cost of running a public relations department can drop dramatically, or conversely the same budget can achieve greater impact through reduction of wasted effort and redundant support services. But if used poorly computers actually decrease efficiency.

Electronic Communications Across the Organization

Information has become strategic at major organizations. We see the following today:

• Local area networks tying together departments, floors, and buildings.
• Wide-area networks linking plants and offices in cities using optical fiber, satellites, and microwave transmission. In 1986 one corporation, Williams Companies, a petroleum pipeline firm, threaded fiber-optic cable through one thousand miles of unused pipe crossing the country and suddenly was on the leading edge of telecommunications, selling data transmission services nationwide. ABC television experimented with moving television transmissions from satellite to fiber-optic cable in a network that

tied together the east and west coasts. Fiber is interference-free, can be accessed without moving a dish into place, and can transmit and receive simultaneously between the master station and affiliates.

• Private and virtually private networks in which the company sets up and runs its communications entirely outside of a regulated phone utility, or uses a system managed but not owned by the telephone utility. American Airlines has purchased fifty thousand personal computers for use by employees and travel agencies on its Sabre Travel Information Network. Metropolitan Life Insurance Company that same year replaced its private voice network with a virtually private network from AT&T to move more data and save 10 percent on its $2.5 million annual phone bill. (Intranets—internal computer communications systems— are discussed in Chapter 29.)
• Vendor-supplied networks in which data moves on regulated and unregulated phone utilities. There has been a proliferation of commercial E-mail services in which one can leave a computer message for a colleague, client, vendor, or supplier in an AT&T, MCI, or other-branded mailbox.

The networks move data, text, voice, and image. They tie to key vendors for ordering parts, sending invoices, and paying bills. They tie to banks to move cash in and out of the organization. They tie to customers to provide goods and services. There is a multiplicity of wires weaving through the organization—each with a different purpose.

Networks link an organization's primary internal and directly interested publics intimately together. What the networks transmit influences opinion about the company and its reputation. They replace millions of paper forms, phone calls, and personal visits.

The public relations person should look at networks as fundamental public relations communications media. Though millions of network messages are mundane, the mundane shapes a company's reputation.

The question is how to use the network to an organization's advantage. Answers come through analysis of what each element of a network does. For example:

- A network allows the equivalent of the bill stuffer in the customer invoice. For example, it can be used to broadcast company changes—meet the new CEO or make the United Way target.

- Networks actively serve as electronic bulletin boards if managed well—not used for advertising used cars or apartments for rent.

- From the beginning networks have served as an employee grapevine. As the *Los Angeles Times* has noted, managers form "watercooler gossip groups" on the network out of top management's sight. Network gossip can be more vicious than in person. Public relations people who want to learn the feelings and insights of internal publics should look into network grapevines.

- Networks are fundamental to crisis communications. They are a fast way to find out when a crisis is developing and to broadcast to employees, vendors, and others. A Houston firm offered an emergency warning system that can call more than one hundred phones a minute with a thirty-second message with just four minutes' advance notice.

- Many organizations use in-house networks for employee information programs. These include 800 call-in numbers to hear company news, designated mail boxes to leave questions, comments, or complaints, and standby operators to answer personnel questions.

- Organizations have installed video and radio networks to reach internal audiences regularly as part of training, company news, and product demonstration. (*See* Chapter 12.)

- Networks help make sure all communications are integrated so everyone is "on the same page."

As useful as networks are, they pose problems. Networks can bog an organization as much as speed it up. Users should be aware of "network merry-go-round" in which E-mail memos go from one manager to another in an eternal circle of opinion and comment. Badly planned and poorly implemented uses of networks have resulted in costly public relations failures—especially in-house video in which equipment "obsolesced" rapidly, viewership remained small, and production budgets were high.

Practitioners should segment network users as much as audiences are segmented in traditional media. This requires analysis of shaping media and messages. One place to learn what to do is through cultivation of the network manager. Tapping into system lore will tell one a lot of how it can be used.

Electronic Communications with External Publics

This includes communicating with and through news media to shareholders, to regulators and politicians, to special-interest groups and communities, and to all the external stakeholders who have a self-interest in an organization's mission, strategy, and actions.

Many of the electronic tools already discussed reach these audiences in different formats. Examples are discussed in the following sections.

Research

The rise of electronic news and information databases has changed how the public relations person works. (*See also* Chapter 29.) It is a snap to get at your desk the last ten articles on use of Internet for use in writing a press kit. Hundreds of databases exist with stories from the *New York Times, Washington Post, Business Week, Fortune, Forbes*, and *Time*, obscure medical journals, hobbyist collector magazines, defense procurement newsletters, and more. One CD-ROM optical storage disk carries whole encyclopedias, dictionaries, and other reference works.

Public relations people can communicate with greater accuracy than ever before, especially to the news media. Almost all recorded knowledge can be accessed from one's desk. Information can move from a narrow recitation of facts to larger linkage with community, industry, and world events to make information more persuasive and meaningful.

Knowing members of the news media is easier. It is simple, especially with hypercard databasing, to store not just a reporter's name, address, and phone number but also personal data, a bio, and interests and dislikes. Hypercard software allows one to hide "buttons" behind words and icons on any one card that links to another one. For example, clicking on a reporter's name might reveal his education and place of birth. Clicking on the television station she works for might reveal her previous beats. Clicking on her title might give a listing of previous titles.

Hypermedia now combines text, data, sound, and voice into a single database. Designed principally for education, hypermedia allows one to study a Beethoven symphony by hearing the music, seeing the music unfold as it is played, and providing chapters from a book on Beethoven's life, and a short movie to go with it. This breakthrough combines computers, videodiscs, and terminals into an entirely new way of experiencing information. This can be used to track major news programs, for example, with actual samples of stories and reporters.

Allied to this on a simpler plane is the computer novel. Here, as in hypercard technology, one can click on any paragraph or key word in a paragraph and watch a story unfold in dozens of different ways. Custom textbooks are now being produced in which professors preselect chapters and have the book published the way they want.

Corporate reports can be custom produced. Interactive company brochures already exist.

Some data vendors already have moved beyond names and addresses in media categories to in-depth discussions of publications including capsules, overviews, demographics, editorial profiles, editorial calendars, and discussions of each major editor. There is little excuse any more for the one mistake that infuriates news media—not knowing a publication or show, its editors and producers, or its audiences.

Media measurement is possible in many forms. Electronic measurement systems are available on personal computers advertised in public relations industry journals or as service bureau offerings. Articles can be measured for content, position, percentage of the organization's message included, positive or negative slant, and other categories.

Contact

Many organizations commit a financial earnings release to paper only after it has appeared on the Dow Jones, Bloomberg, or Reuters wire, or in the UK after it has been sent to the stock exchange by modem link. Approved copy is sent from computer to computer where it is edited and transmitted. Only then is the release replicated on paper for audiences with less-urgent needs, or who could gain advantage by trading illegally before company news hits the screens.

Videotapes, video news releases, network and cable television programming, interactive video, ad hoc satellite, and optical fiber transmission form a gigantic well-developed industry on the verge of major leaps forward to high definition television and re-emerging video disks. The Japanese started regular broadcasting of high definition television in June 1989, ironically with scenes of the Statue of Liberty and New York Harbor.

Image has overshadowed words in informing the American public—particularly in political campaigns. Political strategists use television to make points on issues and candidates. As one said, the words reporters speak behind images mean little any more. Strong criticism is lost in well-crafted, camera-pleasing events that pass through reporters and editors directly to viewers' eyes and attitudes. Public affairs counselors have moved ahead of the rest of public relations in exploiting television to influence behavior.

Great events take place on camera as they happen—fires, floods, earthquakes, hurricanes, or changes in political dynamics in China and Eastern Europe, rockets exploding on takeoff, and impeachment of presidents. Information is instant even though meaning is not.

Public relations people should be studying the grammar of images as well as the grammar of words.

The telephone system—a nineteenth-century invention—is driving many changes. Even before the breakup of the regulated monopoly, the move to digital electronic communications was on. AT&T finished wiring the nation in optical fiber more than ten years ahead of original plans. At this writing more than twenty experiments of linking fiber optics directly to the home are in progress.

So many technologies are erupting from the telephone that public relations people face issues of rights and privacy. One at the time of writing—number identification service—was a subject of lawsuits and hosannas. Caller ID lets one know at the moment a phone rings the number and name of the person calling.

JC Penney, the retailer, calls a customer's account on screen even before picking up the line. A real estate agent greets customers by name when answering calls before they have a chance to introduce themselves.

On the other hand, social workers dealing with disturbed patients are terrified that the patients can trace them through their unlisted phone numbers and abused spouses fear they can be found by violent mates. Meanwhile, hundreds of businesses store the phone listings of anyone who calls their 800 or 900 telephone numbers, then sell them to vendors of similar products.

Electronic Communications and Global Public Relations

More than one commentator has said that the greatest source of change in Eastern Europe other than President Mikhail Gorbachev of the Soviet Union was radio and television from Austria, West Germany, and other countries bordering the infamous Iron Curtain.

The squashed uprising in China was called a fax revolution because dissidents were using the machines to communicate worldwide. Tens of thousands of calls were made daily just from the United States. The Federal Communications Commission said calls to China averaged three thousand a day before the Beijing demonstrations. A Stanford University graduate student set up a computer message service called ChinaNet to provide instant news worldwide. The network sent about one hundred messages a day to Chinese students across the United States who were worried about family and friends at home. When the Chinese army attacked Tiananmen Square, much of the on-site reporting was done by cellular phone.

Fiber-optic cable links to Europe and Japan from the United States have been built. In

Southern California, where eight hundred Japanese firms have offices, calls from the United States to Japan rose from 20 million minutes a year in 1978 to 180 million minutes a year by 1987. Forty percent of all transmissions are by fax.

The E-mail networks that connect Michigan to Missouri can now just as easily link London to San Francisco. A public relations network of firms—PRX International—regularly uses E-mail to swap messages and media lists.

The prevalence of electronic communications globally has caused as many misperceptions among publics as positive changes. Many communicators fail to understand that beneath pervasive images and messages are deeply rooted behavioral patterns that are not changing nearly as fast as one might expect. Communicating with a Japanese is vastly different from communicating with Californians, Canadians, British citizens, Parisians, and Frankfurters. Each audience has subtle differences in attitudes, perceptions, cultural behavior patterns, nuances of language, and learning that cause messages not only to fall flat but sometimes offend deeply. One E-mail message does not fit all, nor does one videotape or brochure.

Public relations people must cross cultural boundaries and understand how to communicate with publics in countries other than the United States. Cultural imperialism projects the same comic-book image of America that hundreds of television series have portrayed to the world.

Scaling the Mountain of Electronic Communications

It is tempting to give up in the face of the rapid changes wrought by electronic communications. It is easier to say, "as a public relations person I will specialize in a few technical areas, such as writing or media placement." Unfortunately, that also means one will reach limited public segments and become over time the communications "buggy whip" of the late twentieth and early twenty-first centuries. Most importantly, it bypasses what the highest practice of public relations is all about—protecting and enhancing the relationships between organizations and their publics, using communication in all its various forms.

The electronic communications revolution is nothing to fear. It provides great opportunities to public relations that are being exploited already by visionaries. Results are not immediate or easy, but the new media provide new ways to look at organizational relationships internally and externally.

We believe public relations people will change from narrow specialists to generalists with specialized skills. Understanding, using, and managing a range of communications skills are essential.

Consequently re-education is as important to the public relations person as it is for doctors, engineers, lawyers, auditors, and other professionals who have found that the flood of information outdates their skills in as little as five years.

29

THE INFORMATION SUPERHIGHWAY AND PUBLIC RELATIONS

PHILIP LESLY

With the rapid growth of computers has come a boom in systems and equipment for using them to receive and convey information. Changes occur rapidly and in various directions, so the public relations practitioner must make sure the resources and information are up-to-date.

What follows are nine basic areas in which electronic services are used in public relations:

1. Obtaining information and illustrations

2. Monitoring events

3. Monitoring media and other coverage

4. Offering constant information to media and others

5. Offering spot news to media and others

6. Attracting responses or input from various publics; interactive exchanges

7. Sending and receiving mail electronically (E-mail) from clients, staff, sources, and others

8. Establishing internal communications systems—"intranets"—that make accessible to employees or dealers masses of filed material and instant news or reports

9. Mobilizing support of various groups or the public at large

The services most helpful in these functions are the following:

- E-mail

- The Internet—the interconnected network of computer networks

- Web sites—organizations' places on the Internet

- CD-ROMs—disks containing information, graphs, illustrations, etc.

- Fax-on-demand—a means of sending information by fax when requested by a medium or other inquirer

- Broadcast fax—sending information to many recipients simultaneously

The Internet

The use of the Internet is both receptive—obtaining information—and active—disseminating information.

Receiving involves using an on-line service that offers stored data or tapping into the "webs" stored by clients who want to make their information or services available.

Major on-line services include the following:

America Online (Vienna, VA)
(800) 827-6364

CompuServe (Columbus, OH)
(800) 848-8990

Dow Jones Personal Journal (Princeton, NJ)
(609) 520-4000

Desktop Data Personal Journal (Waltham, MA)
(800) 255-3343

Lexis®-Nexis® (Dayton, OH)
(800) 227-9597

NetCruiser
(800) 501-8649

Prodigy (White Plains, NY)
(800) 776-3449

Services that provide information for retrieval include the following:

CDP Online: A service of CDP Technologies, featuring about 160 databases with a focus on biomedical data
(800) 289-4277

Dialog: A Knight-Ridder service that provides more than 45 databases with 2,500 magazines, journals, and newsletters; 100,000 international magazines and other publications
(800) 3-DIALOG

Dow Jones News/Retrieval: Exclusive access to the *Wall Street Journal* articles, plus 70 databases
(800) 334-2564

Lexis®-Nexis®: LEXIS® law library and NEXIS® news service covering newspapers, magazines, trade publications, newsletters, wire services, and other sources
(800) 227-4907

Orbital Online Service: Science and technology
(800) 456-7248

The Internet is accessed by a computer through a modem and a telephone line. All major commercial services such as CompuServe and America Online provide links to all elements in the Internet and "browsers," with interchanges available. Browsers provide efficient means of searching the Internet at less cost. They include the following:

Netscape Navigator 3.0
http://home.netscape.com

Microsoft Internet Explorer 3.0
http://www.microsoft.com/ie/

In general, colleges, universities, and research centers use the Internet without charges. Most others are charged a fee or a monthly charge by the commercial firm used to access it. Monthly charges are usually $15 to $20 for forty hours of prime time, according to Ron Solberg of EasyCom.

The most advanced address or connection to the Internet is a page on the World Wide Web. The "page" may be set up through one of many service providers, who charge fees for storage of information, connection, and address. (*See* Figure 29.1.)

PR Web is a commercial site that offers news and hypertext links to many firms and organizations. Its WWW address is: http://www.sme.com:80/prweb.

News release services for use by publicity people include the following:

PR Newswire
http://www.prnewswire.com

Business Wire
http://www.quote.com/info/bwire.html

Without a place or "page" a computer owner can access the Internet by using the previously listed services.

An on-line information service planned especially for use by journalists seeking information is offered by MediaSource, 130 E. 59th Street, New York, NY 10022, (212) 308-0800.

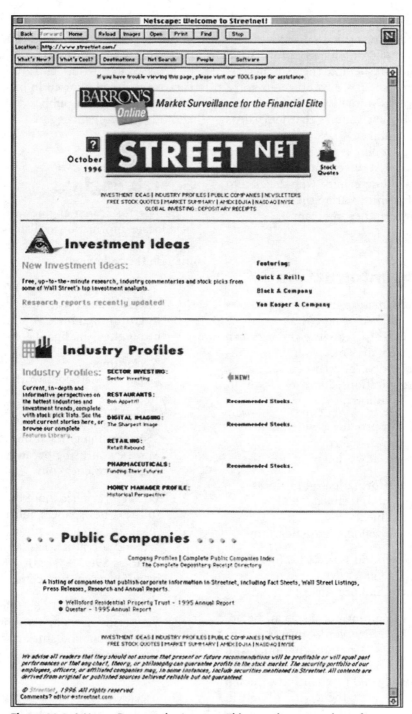

Figure 29.1 A Home Page on the Internet. This one shows a variety of financial information available from a division of Buyside. *Compliments of Buyside, Ltd.*

It can access "pages" or be reached by organizations offering information directly.

Journalists may download information received on the Internet into their storage systems for later use. It's advantageous for a source to have its information in these files along with all other sources that journalists use on a given subject.

Northern Telecom, Nashville, Tennessee, offers Rapport, a service that enables agencies and clients to determine who dialed into a Web site, what information they were looking for, and where they are from.

Obtaining Information

Archives of information from many publications can be searched at no cost.

By using keyword searches, the user can link up with Web sites of universities, companies, associations, government agencies, and private organizations. Some sources available include the following:

Fed World can provide a wide range of information or referrals: http://www.fedworld.gov

Dialog has information on business, environmental, technical, and scientific subjects: http://www.dialog.com/dialog/html

Annual reports and financial information are available at http://town.hall.org.edgar

An electronic "clipping service" can be accessed by using a key word—just as a clipping service does—to track national and international media. This can provide references immediately and inexpensively, though it will require time at the keyboard and in using the printer. It will check only media on the Internet that have few or specialized publications.

Clippro permits scanning of clippings and importing of others on-line, (800) 345-5572.

A wide variety of illustrative material can be browsed to provide "clip art"—stock illustrations that can be used in brochures, publications for various publics, annual reports, and other documents.

Search Engines

A number of search engines are available to help locate information available on the Internet. All but Electric Library are free. They include the following:

Alta Vista has a very large Web index, offers detailed searches; requires time to go through huge volume. http://altavista.digital.com

ATT Worldnet. http://www.att.com/worldnet

C/net's search.com permits launching a wide variety of searches by combining 250 search engines at one gateway. May be confusing because of scope. http://www.cnet.com

Electric Library has more than 1,000 full-text newspapers, journals, and magazines; reference books; images; art; and literature. Fast and accurate. Charges $9.95 a month. http://www.elibrary.com

Excite has access to 11.5 million pages. Very fast. Offers news, sports information, and stock quotes. Produces many irrelevant hits. http://excite.com

Infoseek Guide provides relevant matches, related topics to search, and news and expert views. Can search entire Web or selected categories. Has

fewer categories than others.
http://guide.infoseek.com

Lycos has a large database that covers text, graphics, sound, and video. So many hits can be achieved that much time may be needed to process them. http://www.lycos.com

Magellan offers a wide variety of searches across entire Web and by category. Rates many sites by popularity to help searchers know what others find useful. Long list of categories may be daunting. http://www.mckinley.com

Mci. http://www.internetmci.com

Msn (Microsoft Network) provides Internet access and on-line information service. http://www.msn.com

Netcom includes ClariNet news service. http://www.netcom.com

WebCrawler focuses on the 25 most visited sites on the Web so it is fast. Limited if searcher wants to cover a broad range. http://webcrawler.com

Yahoo! permits both browsing and searching categories. Easy to browse, but content may be limited due to selectiveness of Yahoo! staff. http://www.yahoo.com

Setting Up a Web Site

Establishing a site on the Internet calls for acquiring a Web Home Page that identifies the source of information. It should be one that no one is using (which may take some ingenuity as the number of entries burgeons), clearly differentiates the source, and is as brief as feasible.

The communications features of a Web site are cited by Ron Solberg of EasyCom:

1. It can post text, pictures, graphics, moving video, and sound on a Web page.
2. It provides "hyperlinks." Keywords or graphics on an individual page can be marked or highlighted by a mouse to move the searcher to another page of the Internet within seconds.
3. A page is immediately accessible to a global audience that was forty million in mid-1996 and growing rapidly.
4. Pages are interactive. A person who accesses them can issue commands to individualize responses.

To set up a Web site, unless an expert is available in-house, it's wise to consult an expert such as EasyCom or E-Fax.

Those who have set up World Wide Web pages report total costs between $20,000 and $60,000 in 1995 dollars. There are important limitations to consider.

- The burden is on the recipient to do the work of searching out and recording the information. That is the opposite of traditional procedures whereby the provider is the one who is eager to have its information used and takes the initiative.

  People tend to be lazy. Bob Hacker of Target Marketing describes the Internet as "a huge library with 2,500 branches (in 1995) and no Dewey Decimal System. If 98 percent don't respond to a direct mail piece placed directly in their hands, what percentage will drop out of cyberspace with all the . . . irrelevance?" The response is likely to improve when seekers access the Internet, because they want information. It is a mistake to take it for granted that the Net will assure wide dissemination.

- This means that the service must be promoted. Otherwise, the Web space will be like a reference book in a library—used mostly by someone seeking some specific information.

- To stand out from the vast array of other entries, yours must attract attention through good writing and design. These are the qualities that have always marked the better communications.

- The Internet is not ideal for simultaneous distribution of information to many recipients. E-mail delays can cause problems for information such as financial announcements, for which simultaneous reception is essential.

- Information on the Internet is not secure. It can be breached by users to spy on what others are researching; or material can be altered so it provides misleading or harmful information to whomever requests material. It is unsafe to conduct confidential interchanges. Special care is needed to avoid sending anything that can be changed into incriminating or libelous form.

Services are available that advise and help set up Internet programs. You can contact:

EasyCom, Inc. (headed by Internet guru Ron Solberg), (630) 969-1441
76703.575@compuserve.com (Web site)
510-836-6000; http://www.efaxinc.com
(E-Fax communications)

Other steps are recommended by Ron Solberg:

- Refresh the content of your page at least monthly. Indicate when you last revised it.

- When an E-mail response mechanism is included, make sure to read and to respond to queries promptly.

- Get the page listed on Internet directories. These include Yahoo!: http://yahoo.com; Lycos: http://www.lycos.com; WebCrawler: http://www.webcrawler.com; and elNet Galaxy: http://www.elnet.com.

- Check indexes that specialize in subject areas related to yours.

- Contribute your page address and description to publishers for listing.

Cyberspace clipping services provide reports on uses of a provider's information. Such services include the following:

Edelman PR Worldwide
(212) 768-0550; (312) 240-3000

eWire Cyberspace Clipping Service
(Joint with PR Newswire)
(914) 288-0000

In the storm of excitement created by the explosion of computer communications, there has been a tendency to consider them the answer to all communication needs. Actually, they are only new tools—and like all tools can be misused or expected to do too much.

Rapid growth has led to frequent crowding of the system. Sometimes Web site services return thousands of responses to a simple query, and yet these constitute only a portion of the Web. As the *Wall Street Journal* points out, search engines (as of December 1996) won't find articles that appeared on the sites of the *Journal*, the *New York Times*, and many scientific and other specialized publications.

Also, because they scan a database compiled in advance, most search engines are weeks or even months behind in logging changes and additions to Web pages, as well as indexing new sites. As the number of Web pages surges each day, the ability to find something becomes ever more problematic.

To get around these limitations, some surfers prefer to use Web-reference services that offer indexes of Web sites compiled by humans, not computers. These sites, including Yahoo! and Magellan, serve as a sort of table of contents, with brief descriptions of hundreds or thousands of sites and often ratings for usefulness. But they have their own drawbacks: They encompass only a fraction of what's on the Web, and the ratings are subjective.

Additionally, crowded lines can sometimes mean long waits and extensive sifting.

It's important to recognize these limitations and not become too reliant on cyberspace. Other methods should also be cultivated.

The factor that determines the success of communication is still the message. *Computers merely deliver information. Only content communicates.*

A service that provides information from one hundred newswires and other services can be used to match a client's customized search list of potential raiders, activist groups, government regulatory agencies, and other potential problems. It immediately signals when "hits" are found and informs the client's computer. It is offered by Desktop Data of Waltham, Massachusetts.

Intranets

These use the electronic communication system for internal communication—with employees, suppliers, dealers, stockholders, and other groups. Silicon Graphics lists the most common uses as:

- Corporate news and distribution of information
- Database searches
- Sales tools
- Work group productivity
- Internal support
- Employee training

PR Marketing Forum

This worldwide service permits people interested in public relations to provide or exchange information, communicate with E-mail, and debate various topics.

It tends to attract those with mid-level or lower positions who find it useful in broadening their viewpoints and contacts. More senior people tend to focus on major issues and on promoting their careers or businesses.

Its Web site is http://www.prsig.com.

CD-ROMs

These store information for retrieval on computers. They contain 650 megabytes of information—equivalent to 451 floppy disks. They also provide seventy-two minutes of sound and twenty of video, plus text and simple graphics.

CD-ROMs may be offered to media on matters of long-lasting interest or on such news events as a merger, a major expansion, or a major dispute with government.

Fax-on-Demand

When a reporter dials an 800 number, interactive voice response takes her through a series of custom-designed prompts. The journalist can focus on the information needed or request a menu of everything available. Fax-on-demand then provides the specific information or menu immediately. A file of fact sheets or white papers can be stored to meet such requests at any time of day or night, holidays or Sundays, without human intercession.

Books to help in understanding and using the electronic services:

Communication and Technology: The Complete Guide to Using Technology for Organizational Communication, Shel Holtz. Ragan Communications, Chicago, 1995.

The Internet Guide for New Users, Daniel P. Dern. McGraw-Hill, New York, 1994.

The Internet Media Directory, Ragan Communications, Chicago.

Internet Navigator, 2nd edition, Paul A. Glister, John Wiley & Sons, New York, 1994.

Keys to the Internet, Stephen Ross, Weka Publishing, New York, 1994. Includes disk of information equal to 500 pages.

Navigating the Internet, Mark Giggs and Richard Smith, Sams Publishing, Indianapolis, IN, 1994.

The PR Pro's Guide to the Internet, Shel Holtz, Ragan Communications, Chicago, 1995.

The Whole Internet User's Guide & Catalog, 2nd edition, Mike Loukides, O'Reilly & Associates, New York, 1994.

Software for Media Contacts

A wide assortment of software is available to help with phases of media relations. They should be checked to find what most nearly meets the need of the user. Sources include:

MediaMap, (671) 374-9300

Adobe, (800) 521-1976

SpinWARE, (305) 254-5664

Right Brain, (612) 229-6299

Cetex Corporation, (609) 953-1406

Desktop Solutions, (717) 938-4270

Symantec Corporation, (408) 253-9600

Infocom Group, (510) 596-9300

Modatech Systems, (800) 804-6299

Turnkey Computer Systems, (718) 761-0732

Polaris, (800) 722-5728

30

USING ADVERTISING FOR PUBLIC RELATIONS COMMUNICATION

PHILIP LESLY

Americans have long considered advertising the predominant method by which business and other organizations communicate with their publics. It is only one of numerous techniques used to reach a targeted audience and is itself composed of various categories, such as print advertisements, radio commercials, television commercials, billboards, and others. Yet advertising overshadows the other, more indirect means of communication because it

1. became an important communications vehicle long before most other forms had matured;

2. provides a means of financial support for so many communication media, making it intrinsically important to both the media carrying the advertising and the public exposed to it;

3. is always immediately recognizable as a direct form of communication used by a party seeking to reach the public—thereby achieving a level of conscious prominence absent from indirect communications techniques;

4. is essential to the sale of vast quantities of goods produced by our advanced manufacturing industry—and as a result derives

many times the amount of investment as do other communication forms;

5. is always clearly visible and often measurable to the sponsor, so it readily gains understanding and support from the practical executive.

This has resulted in widespread misunderstanding about advertising's role and the extent of its use in the organization's projection of its image, inclusion in its overall communications practices, and planning of its public relations functions.

Advertising's Unique Communication Properties

Since public relations encompasses all functions that project to large groups the character of an organization and its messages, it is apparent that advertising is one of the techniques involved in public relations. However, the basic function of the great majority of advertising is to sell a company's product or service. This is a highly specialized form of communication and one that usually requires intensive impact, controlled forms of communication, controlled choice of medium, selection of timing, and other factors.

The nature of the selling message is sufficiently different from other forms of communication that many of the principles applied to publicity, literature, films, meetings, and other techniques do not directly apply. A company can, of course, create enemies and a bad image through product advertising that insults the intelligence of its audience, depicts the company as a group of sharpies attempting to put things over on people, and annoys the sensibilities with brash and repetitive exhortations. However, bold and direct pleading of the company's selling purpose in a sound and tasteful way is clearly acceptable in advertising, whereas such aggressiveness could not be acceptable in other techniques. (*See* Figure 30.1.)

Accordingly, there is a great difference between the types of mentality and abilities needed in directing effective advertising for a company's products and in conducting an effective opinion-developing program involving other means. Advertising to sell products or services is a selling function and therefore a subordinate phase of the marketing operation of the company. Consideration of its other effects on public attitudes involves public relations judgment, but effectiveness as advertising calls for the direction of hard-hitting sales-minded people. On the other hand, persuasive communication through indirect means calls for sensitivity to public attitudes, sensibilities, and tastes; restraint in beating the drums for the product, the cause, or the organization; and judgment covering the whole range of human psychology and attitudes.

For these reasons, there are few instances of an effective advertising person or organization who is equally capable of performing in the broad public relations field. And, for the same reasons, the fully effective public relations person or organization is seldom capable of performing at full effectiveness in the product advertising area. The fields are as different as a carpenter and a jewel cutter: both deal with hammers, but the force and deftness with which they use them are at opposite poles.

Yet a knowledge of advertising and how to employ it is vital to the public relations practitioner, who will be involved in its effects on the organization's *total* posture, and who may use it for specific needs in communicating.

In fact, public relations is most effective when it directs the integration of all communications and is involved in the organization's total policies.

John Orr Young, a cofounder of the Young & Rubicam advertising agency and later a consultant to management on public relations, said that

> the public relations practitioner . . . must, at some time or other, use every known medium of communication and enlightenment to execute programs that will achieve the desired results. . . . A public relations practitioner who does not understand the history, the uses, the techniques, and the value of advertising is simply not equipped to perform all of his job. Technically, advertising used for public relations purposes must be good advertising; but to be *good* public relations, it also must be the *right* advertising. Advertising so used does not lose its identity, but its voice and the message it speaks become the legitimate child of public relations. It is a clear-cut case of advertising helping public relations to help management.

Effectively Using Advertising in a PR Program

As a result of the more prominent knowledge of advertising than of public relations techniques, broad confusion has continued regarding the utilization of advertising as a public relations technique per se, aside from the sale of products or services. There have been many instances in which organizations, seek-

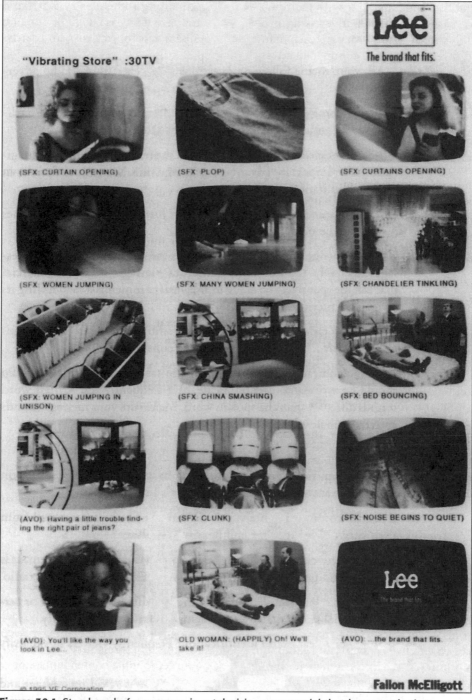

Figure 30.1 Storyboard of sequences in a television commercial that humorously ties together the various elements of the product and the corporate name. *Courtesy Fallon McElligott and Lee Apparel Company.*

ing to establish understanding with their publics, have turned to broad advertising programs in the belief that the way to reach many people in this country is to conduct an advertising program that "gets the story across." Being duly impressed with what advertising has done in helping to establish the mass production and mass distribution systems in America, the assumption has been made that it can just as readily "sell" ideas.

An analysis of what advertising can and cannot be expected to accomplish in a public relations program is preliminary to planning any broad communications effort that might include the purchase of space in publications, broadcast time, and other forms of advertising.

Functions it can be expected to accomplish if properly planned and executed include, first, *conveying information*. For example:

1. Announcing to a community that a company is planning to establish a plant there, what its purposes will be, the personnel it will be interested in employing, the economic and social effects of having the company's plant as a new neighbor.

2. Notifying personnel of changes in work schedules, layoffs, or recalls, and similar information that must reach employees when they are not in touch with company facilities.

3. Explaining the reasons for interruptions in service and what the public should do—such as a power-line failure of an electric utility, or the effects of a wreck on a railroad's services.

4. Reporting on changes in the company name and the reasons for them. For instance, an extensive advertising campaign was conducted by Exxon when its name was changed from Standard Oil Company of New Jersey and by Sara Lee Corporation when its name was changed from Consolidated Foods.

5. Explaining the issues in a strike or work stoppage *if* care is taken to present the facts impassively, objectively, and fairly.

6. Reporting on the company's activities. Some companies run an ad when a major new product is introduced, or when a space achievement is aided by one of their components. Some run ads from time to time to report on progress—a year-end look at growth, an acquisition, entry into a promising new technological field—to assure publication of the complete story when and where they seek to reach the desired publics.

7. Contributing to the image of the organization in the public mind, along with the product ads, when the advertisement is oriented from the viewpoint of the audience and not from that of the company. For example, ads that say in effect: "This is what we want you to know about X Company" are efforts to impose themselves on the reader, rather than to provide information or service to the reader. Such ads are interpreted as saying, "Please spend five minutes of your time listening to what I have to say about myself, because I've spent good money on it." On the other hand, the advertisement for one of the companies making a contribution to recent advances in health care, relating what its role has been, is interesting and significant to the reader and conveys the image of the company as a by-product. (*See* Figure 30.2.)

8. Affecting the climate of opinion in advance of a liability lawsuit. The tendency of plaintiffs' attorneys to publicize the alleged damage done by companies in preparation for going before a jury has recently led to counteraction by defendants. For example, shortly before a case against the Dow Chemical Company charging a half-owned subsidiary, Dow Corning, with causing illnesses through breast implants, Dow

One day we may help save your life.

Maybe you've heard of us.

We're Baxter. And even if you don't know us by name, chances are you've used our products.

We're in the operating room. The emergency room. The hospital pharmacy. We're I.V. solutions. Diagnostic products. And critical-care devices. In fact, we can provide two-thirds of everything a hospital needs.

Our innovations have made kidney dialysis and open-heart surgery lifesaving realities. We developed the first products for treating hemophilia. And we perfected ways to collect and store blood so it's there whenever and wherever it's needed.

These are just a few of the health-care products and technologies that we've pioneered. And we will continue to work with leading medical experts to discover new ways to preserve and improve the quality of life.

Baxter. We mean a lot of things to a lot of people. Someday, we could mean a lot to you. For an annual report or additional information, call Jeanne Ayers at 312.948.4128, or write her at Baxter International Inc., One Baxter Parkway, Deerfield, Illinois 60015.

Baxter

Figure 30.2 Focusing on the reader's interest, this ad attracts attention to the story of Baxter that would probably be ignored if it were featured in the headline. *Courtesy Baxter Healthcare Corporation.*

started an ad campaign. It didn't refer directly to the strong evidence that implants do not cause health problems. Instead, it presented the many benefits of silicon and gave evidence of its harmlessness in human applications.

A second function advertising can accomplish is *performing a needed public service* and establishing the interest of the advertiser in the welfare of the community. As examples:

1. The New Year's Eve advertisements by a whiskey company urging that "the one for the road" be coffee, for safety.

2. Ads informing the public about the importance of local causes or projects, such as the Community Fund or the local job-training program.

A third is *alerting the public to an issue* it may not be aware of, where the interest of the company and of the public may be closely allied. Ads by various utilities about the need to develop coal resources, solar power, and other sources of energy are this type. Ads urging support for the fund-raising efforts of colleges are others.

Public Relations Uses of Broadcast Media

With the dominance of television as the medium that reaches most people, many organizations have developed means of using television for public relations advertising.

This is aside from the use of TV as an advertising medium to sell products or services, as an unpaid outlet for publicity material, or for the sponsorship of noncommercial TV shows as a public service (*see* Chapter 25).

There are three basic forms of public relations utilization of commercial TV.

1. Sponsorship of programs that perform a public service, with commercials absent or confined to the beginning and end, or strictly institutional in character. This projects the company's name and character with no apparent commercial axe to grind. A notable example was sponsorship by a division of what is now Exxon of a series of British-produced plays of Shakespeare. The series was about to be abandoned when the company came to the rescue, gaining not only the usual goodwill but a great deal of extra attention and public commendation. Though the series originated on a noncommercial station, it was carried on commercial channels in some cities.

2. Sponsorship of an informative program on such matters as science, education, or natural resources—with the tone and nature of the commercials adapted to the character of the show. Though the commercials deal with products, they are more subtle than usual, and often have a relationship to the program's theme.

   In one notable example, the 3M Company devoted a commercial on its documentary shows to its policy of allowing research people to pursue their own ideas. (*See* Figure 30.3.) It told how one researcher found a liquid that wouldn't do anything to anything—and how that "useless" substance gave rise to many possible product applications. Mail was heavy both from industries wanting samples of the inert liquid to try out applications, and from young people—especially in college and high school—expressing interest in 3M as a place to work. Though the sequence was a paid portion of a commercial TV show, it had significant public relations benefits.

3. Paid announcements, utilizing television in the same way announcement ads have been utilized in newspapers for many years.

Local radio is also employed in these ways. Radio affords a means of reaching desired

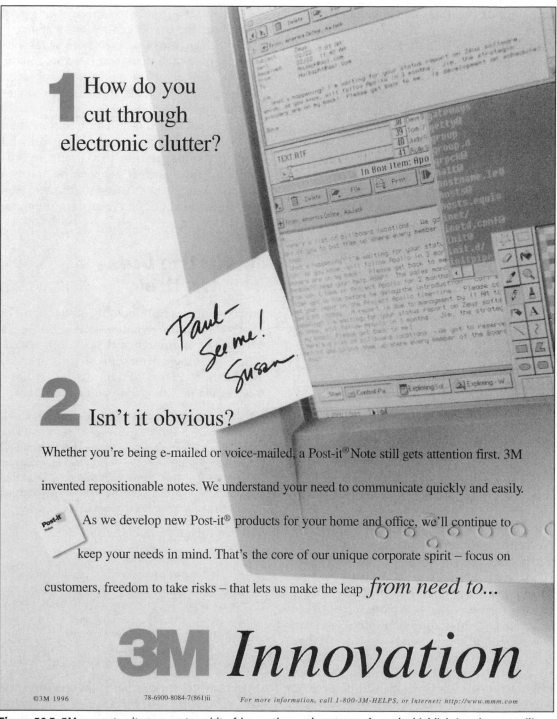

Figure 30.3 3M promotes its corporate spirit of innovation and customer focus by highlighting the versatility of its Post-it® Notes. *Advertisement courtesy 3M.*

segments of the total audience, at a much lower cost than buying time on an area-wide TV station. Illinois Tool Works, for instance, has bought spots in a daily morning newscast on a major Chicago station, timed to reach many businesspeople who drive to their offices. The commercials have been geared to the theme: "You're never more than a few feet away from a product of ITW," to convey the firm's broad diversification, rather than to promote individual products.

The question of whether an advertiser can buy "idea" commercials on regular television and radio stations has been hotly contested for a number of years. Until the early 1970s, the Federal Communications Commission took the position that broadcast stations, as government licensees, could take no stand on controversial issues and could not make their wavelengths available to others to take stands. That policy was modified to permit broadcasters to editorialize so long as they made time available for rebuttals by dissenters. However, the broadcasters for the most part continued to deny others access on over-the-air stations (as contrasted with closed-channel stations) even when the intended advertiser offered to pay for the time of the opposition.

Many local stations, including those affiliated with the networks, have been accepting idea ads that the networks refused.

In a memorable case, Kaiser Aluminum was refused the right to buy commercial time on the ABC TV network after an ABC show, *20/20*, had carried what Kaiser felt was an unfounded attack on its electrical wire. Kaiser refused to accept that rejection. It fought the issue in the courts and in an intensive opinion campaign against what it called "Trial by Television"—the tendency of broadcasters to act as accusers, witnesses, judge, and jury when attacking an organization or person. Finally, after many assertions that it would never give Kaiser a chance to respond, ABC established "Viewpoint" as a show that af-

forded others a chance to express their views. Kaiser was the first organization to appear.

Public demands that the media be responsible to more than their own interests and the growth of many other outlets for expression of viewpoints may make the networks' stonewalling approach untenable.

It is likely that this situation will be fluid and will vary from network to network and from individual station to station. Accordingly, public relations people who want to consider using broadcasting to express viewpoints should check on the current situation.

Ineffective Uses of Advertising

Advertising has been notably unsuccessful in most efforts to overcome a prejudice or an attitude of indifference that is deep-seated. The psychological reasons for this are well established. Pierre Martineau in his book *Motivation in Advertising* pointed out that

> almost all adults . . . resent direct suggestion. All of us have had the experience of seeing an idea of ours violently rejected by another only to find that some time later the person had adopted our idea as if it had come from his own thinking. When he can feel that the idea came from his own thinking, he is far more likely to follow it.

Dr. Rex F. Harlow in his *Social Science in Public Relations* observed:

> People distrust a person or an organization with an obvious ax to grind. They resist messages that smack of selfish propaganda. . . . In most situations an indirect content and an indirect approach tend to win more acceptance and support of an idea or a cause than a hard-hitting content and a direct-attack approach.

Many advertising campaign failures illustrate this. The effort of several years and several million dollars by the Men's and Boy's Wear Institute to shame the American male into spending more money for clothes by telling him to "Dress Right—You Can't Afford Not To," followed by the signature indicating that the money for this exhortation came from the people who sell clothes; the extensive efforts to convince people that the benefits of whole oranges are substantial enough to overcome the extreme conveniences of frozen and prepared orange juice; the series of advertising campaigns by the Better Home Furnishings Council of Greater Chicago to shame the householder into refurnishing the home rather than spending money on other things; and the many ineffective campaigns directed toward the labor movement, tax levels, and other social and economic concepts, in each case exhibiting the self-interest of the sponsor and thereby notifying the reader that someone with a selfish interest is paying substantial money to try to force him to change his viewpoint.

Early in 1989 the AFL-CIO launched a major TV ad campaign with the theme "Unions, YES!" Since then the proportion of workers who are unionized has steadily declined.

On the other hand, when the interests of the *readers* are being fostered, advertising has been effective. The Savings and Loan Foundation ran ads calling for tax breaks for savers. The new tax law passed that year included such breaks. However, it was the action by the savers in writing to their representatives in Congress—stimulated by the ads—that was effective rather than the ads themselves.

Efforts to force the image of a company on an uninterested public are at best very ineffective in relation to their cost. The type of ad referred to earlier in which a company seeks to command attention to a description of itself is typical.

Pleading a selfish cause when the reason is apparent is equally ineffective. The company that signs advertisements urging that new tax revenue be raised through a sales tax rather than an increase in corporation taxes is likely to solidify the resentment of its original opponents and to sway the undecided person toward the opposite viewpoint.

Also dubious is the practice of running ads in publications reaching those already convinced of the advertiser's viewpoint, such as an exposition of the merits of free enterprise in the *Harvard Business Review*.

Frequently a complex case for a viewpoint cannot be made through advertising unless it is simplified to create one key opinion in the public's mind. For example, an extensive series of ads was run by the steel industry during a strike. They attempted to cover so much ground in such a complex way that later studies indicated readership was largely confined to people who already strongly sympathized with the steel companies.

Advertising is an exceptionally alluring medium because it enables the advertiser to say exactly what it wants, exactly when it wants, to exactly the audience it seeks to reach. For these very reasons it is probably often the most ineffective and wasteful form of mass communications for public relations purposes. The fact that it permits the advertiser to control the conditions and direct the messages at the audience makes it a one-sided form of communication. It is likely to be ignored, to be discounted, or even to create a resentful backlash because it is a visible effort to impose others' ideas on the audience.

Offsetting negative images

Some companies use advertising to seek a "do gooder" image because they are in industries that are under attack. Budweiser plumps for temperance at the same time it promotes beer drinking. Smirnoff vodka ran ads to foster literacy programs both because the product has a Russian connotation and public criticism of promotion of hard liquors had been rising.

Burger King was both praised and criticized for running ads offering to put 25¢ into a fund for helping earthquake victims from the sale of every Whopper. The goal was clearly not only to help the victims but to sell more hamburgers.

Philip Morris ran an expensive campaign in praise of the Bill of Rights—ostensibly to mark that document's two-hundredth anniversary. At that time, however, it was beset by strong efforts to severely restrict advertising of cigarettes and by campaigns to restrict smoking—which Philip Morris fought on the basis that smoking is a right.

Such approaches risk making knowledgeable people—the influentials who can mean much to a company's stature and acceptance—skeptical about everything a company does. Mobil has carefully kept separate its two types of idea advertising—that promoting listenership for broadcasts of the Metropolitan Opera, which Mobil sponsors, and op-ed page ads pleading for or against a cause or issue.

Helping worthy causes

A recent form of advertising that projects a favorable impression of a company is "cause-related marketing." Companies advertise or run promotions in support of a charity or cause rather than for products.

Johnson & Johnson advertises that it makes a contribution to Shelter Aid, a network of shelters for battered women, for each package of sanitary napkins sold.

Scott paper products urge schools to collect seals from packages of toilet paper to be redeemed for school aids such as children's books and computers.

Children's Miracle Network, which supports 165 children's hospitals, is supported by Breyers ice cream, Maxwell House coffee, and Hershey's chocolate. The manufacturers run newspaper insert ads and use retail displays.

This approach may lose some effectiveness if it becomes so common that people become inured to it. In the meantime everyone seems to benefit: the advertiser, the consumer, the cause, and the public.

Accordingly, the use of idea advertising requires even greater sensitivity to the viewpoint and self-interest of the audiences than other public relations functions. Unless it is conceived and carried out with exceptional finesse, it may be an expensive means of aggravating the advertiser's relationship with the public.

Finally, a barrage of advertising is unlikely to overcome many years of neglect of proper public relations. Efforts by the railroads to gain public support for releasing them from government supervision and the problems of "featherbedding" in employment met great resistance because for many years the railroads had been ignoring the importance of public goodwill. Airlines and truckers were deregulated before the railroads. Similarly, the heavy barrage of advertising run by the oil industry after it was blamed for the effects of the Arab oil embargo had far less beneficial effect than the companies expected. Their long-term neglect of the principles of sound public relations made the sudden loud pleas for understanding—especially since many were oriented to the advertisers rather than to the interest of the audience—seem opportunistic. Since opportunism was one of the charges made against them, the effect was to some extent counterproductive.

Special Inserts

A growing form of advertising used to convey ideas is the special section. A series of several pages is run in a publication—usually, a news magazine or business publication. Articles are written to seem like editorial material, although the section is clearly marked as an advertising supplement.

To further differentiate the section from the publication's own content, the body copy is likely to be set in sans serif type.

This type of advertising is attractive to sponsors for the following four reasons:

1. It creates an impressive body of material in the publication that says exactly what the sponsor wants.

2. Costs often can be offset by selling space to interested parties, such as a bank located in the state or city featured in the section.

3. It can be reprinted and used as a brochure for distribution by members or supporters to their customers and prospects.

4. Members and those who sign the articles in the section feel good about seeing themselves treated in a prestigious publication.

There are also disadvantages:

1. Readership for these inserts is far lower than for the non-paid portions of the publications.

2. The use of sans serif type further reduces the likelihood that the information will be read and absorbed (*see* Chapter 33).

3. It is obvious that the material is the self-serving presentation of the sponsors, so acceptance is less than that of the publication's editorial material.

31

DIRECT COMMUNICATIONS METHODS

HERBERT M. BAUS
PHILIP LESLY

Public Speaking

The speakers' bureau provides one of the most challenging of the public relations techniques in terms of effectively communicating with a sufficient number of people. It requires a lot of detail work to line up the speakers, to arrange the meetings, to prepare the speakers to relay the right story, and to orient them sufficiently to handle questions as well as to avoid potentially damaging errors and omissions. In addition, the public relations person faces uncontrollable dangers, such as the speaker being late or missing the appointment.

Yet speakers are very valuable as a medium of communication. They project the public relations story before live audiences that concentrate their attention on the subject during the speech. This is an effective mass publicity method if the speech and its delivery have the power of motivation.

The speakers' bureau can take advantage of the numerous meetings, forums, lectures, panels, symposiums, roundtable discussions, and similar occasions that are held by all kinds of organizations.

A number of large corporations and associations—the American Medical Association, for example—prepare speech kit material for members, enabling them to make polished public appearances. The typical kit outlines the basic structure of a good speech and advises on persuasive ways to gain and hold attention.

Each such speech has the attendant publicity value of prior announcements and subsequent coverage in the press, publications of the audience organization, and direct mail.

The speakers' bureau is a sensitive device of public relations in that after the speaker is chosen and dispatched everything is up to him or her and the public relations director has lost control of the planning, objectives, and presentation of ideas.

The technique of building a speaker's bureau includes the following steps:

1. Develop a file of research data, perhaps a "speaker's manual" summarizing the information about the subject being publicized.

2. Prepare material in advance to send out with speakers for distribution at meetings.

3. Develop a list of speakers and subjects. Choose men and women who speak well, are well received, know the subject. List all pertinent data about speakers, including information necessary for proper authority and publicity.

4. Set up training programs for speakers who have not had such instruction. Cover subject matter, styles of delivery, how to handle question-and-answer periods. A

457

number of professional training services are available.

5. Select a few titles—preferably active and catchy, aimed at the interest of the audience. "Where Has All Your Money Gone?" is better than "The Problem of Deficits."

6. Make sure that what is conveyed in speeches is integrated with all other communications.

7. Formulate a list of organizations to which speakers will be offered. Contact them by direct mail or other means. Promptly fill all requests.

8. Follow through with advance and spot coverage publicity to all local newspapers and broadcast stations, "house" papers or trade publications, and so on.

9. Get maximum publicity from the speech itself. Often the impact will be greater from the stories about what is said, appearing in mass-circulation newspapers or other media, than from the effect on the audience. Though a speech should not be written "around" the audience, it should have as much newsworthiness and as many sharp quotations as possible to catch the media's interest as well as that of those present.

10. Follow through afterward for audience reaction, dropping poor speakers and moving the good ones up on the list for more frequent use.

A public relations person will often be called on to talk. He or she will be required to direct committees. Without necessarily being an orator, the skilled public relations worker knows how to say enough and not too much in simple language. If he or she cannot get up and leave a message squarely in the laps of the audience, he or she may be well advised to take speech courses and learn how to do so.

Speeches that make a difference

Thousands of speeches are delivered each year. Less than one-half of 1 percent receive any significant attention beyond their immediate audience. And only a few affect the climate of attitudes surrounding their subjects.

The same is true for the multitude of statements in organizations' publications, videotapes, and literature. They fail to make and sustain the message part of the mainstream of ideas.

> In addition to other reasons, the main cause of this widespread failure is the *absence of memorable and quotable expressions.*

In the tidal wave of communications today, unless what one says stands out and is sharply identifiable, it is almost certain to go awash.

All of the great molders of opinion have known that secret: Jesus, Jefferson, Lincoln, Churchill, De Gaulle, Franklin Roosevelt, John Kennedy. Even Ronald Reagan, though known as the "Great Communicator," had little notable effect on the human climate, other than the movement he represented, because his facile statements rarely included a memorable and quotable phrase.

It's not surprising that in the battles for the public's support, superficial but facile phrasemakers have been prevailing over responsible but unquotable leaders of our organizations. This can be called "the sound-bite effect."

Other clues to making a difference with communications include the following:

• Get attention—but only in the desired way. We learn early the preference for patting a child's cheek to slapping it. The type of motion and the target area are the same, but the kind of response is certain to be different. The purpose of attitude-forming communication is to arouse emotion, but only of the desired type. What we say must be stirring but not upsetting.

• Make it visible. Use the age-old devices: examples, parables, anecdotes, slogans. A speech or presentation need not be a slide presentation to be visible. In fact, few statements prepared with such graphics have lasting impact on public opinion. But "visibility" can be achieved by helping the audience create images in its mind.

- Combine the key fact or idea with "motion" —the impetus of what action is desired— to create emotion that stirs the audience. The quotable or memorable items should *move toward the objective of the statement*, not just sound good.

Although it is much better to speak spontaneously or to use notes, if a speaker must read the talk, either because of limited ability as a speaker or because of the danger of being misquoted on a delicate subject, the following points will make the reading better received:

1. Mark the manuscript in advance with places where there should be breaks, pauses, or emphases.

2. Do not apologize for reading.

3. Read slowly and loudly, avoiding monotone, and pause from time to time for variation.

4. Look up from time to time, seeking the eyes of different people in different parts of the audience.

5. Sometimes relief devices are helpful, such as looking away from the speech and repeating an important point in spontaneous words or asking a question as if the audience were expected to answer.

The point is to inject vitality into the talk, not to make it a perfunctory reading.

If possible a video prompter should be used. It enables the speaker to read without seeming to. When a video prompter is not available, use large type. (*See* Figure 31.1.) Video-Cue, 330 W. 58th Street, New York, NY 10018, makes them.

It is symptomatic of our confusion that so many people say, "If we can put a man on the moon, we can solve our problems on earth by putting our minds to it and committing the necessary funds." But the moon is a fixed target. Our scientists could predict exactly in 1960 where it would be on July 20, 1969. No other circumstances would change the nature or the scope of the challenge.

Unfortunately, each of the problem areas on earth is constantly changing. Other circumstances develop that alter every social target we set. Secondly, the moon program was a triumph for the very "systems approach" we neglect here at home. All conceivable elements were considered together, and the interplay between them was accounted for in calculations, in planning, and in patient trial before the historic Apollo event.

Figure 31.1 Page from a speech manuscript typed with large print. Actual type is about three times this size. Large typeface makes delivery easier without undue attention to the manuscript. Each page always ends on a complete sentence.

When playing host to a speaker, pay him or her every courtesy. What are the speaker's travel preferences, ticket and reservation needs? Have arrangements been made to escort the speaker to the hotel room? Is someone following up with a letter thanking the speaker? Have precautions been taken to avoid cluttering up the program with overlong announcements, committee reports, and trivial speeches, and to avoid the equally disagreeable bad timing of introducing the after-dinner speaker so soon that he must compete with waiters' juggling of dishes?

Speeches are often sent to a press distribution list, with highlights marked or verbatim. A major speech can receive extensive exposure.

The Telecommunications Component of Public Relations

A telephone call is more effective than a letter or fax as a last-minute reminder or an incitement to action. The telephone is good for getting a person to do something he or she should do although preferring not to, such as attending a meeting. A letter can be dodged more easily than the personal commitment of a telephone conversation. But for a technical or monetary commitment both parties will find it advisable to put it in writing to seal the telephone agreement.

The secret of success in a large-scale telephone campaign is to obtain reliable telephoners—people with pleasing telephone personalities and strong voices, and the persistence to keep after each number. They are far more effective than impersonal mass calling programs.

Maximum effectiveness is obtained in a telephone drive when every prospect is reached over the phone by a personal acquaintance.

During all election campaigns, workers for all parties make extensive use of the telephone to line up votes for their candidates.

Telephone companies have published booklets about telephone courtesy that will be helpful to anyone using the phone as a contact device. The telephone being an instrument of human contact, courtesy and tact in its use are important in winning the understanding and goodwill of the person on the receiving end. The telephone personality of an organization and its employees is a vital aspect of its relations with the entire community, with many different publics, and with every individual contacted by phone.

Employees can be trained to answer promptly and clearly and arrange for the phone to be answered in the absence of the party who usually responds. Thoughtful employees will leave word of approximately when they will return. If they are out for a great deal of the time, they will check in as often as feasible to pick up and return their calls.

It is courteous to let the other party hang up first.

Telephone transfers are irritating. It is good policy to avoid them if the party originally called can possibly take care of the caller.

People in business can win goodwill by answering their own telephones if possible. It is poor telephone manners to have a secretary ask every caller, "Who's this?" "Who are you with?" "What is the call about?" "Couldn't I have someone else help you?" Use of voice mail to avoid answering the phone is irritating and even turns friends into critics.

The story is told of a trade association executive whose salary was raised because of the spectacular success of his public relations program. The boost sufficiently impressed the executive that he instructed his secretary to be a barrier to people trying to reach him over the telephone. One of the nation's most important trade associations decided to hire a permanent president and named a committee that tried for some time to get by the executive's secretary. She refused to let them reach her boss without explaining their business. Because they declined to explain to her that they were offering him $150,000 to take a new job, they searched elsewhere to make their appointment.

A glaring telephone discourtesy is to have a secretary put a call through and then hold up the party being telephoned because the caller has become tied up with something else. It is better for people in business to make their own calls.

The president of a major corporation fired his public relations man because the president was made to wait while being telephoned. The president said, "He obviously is a poor public relations man if he treats *anybody* that way on the telephone."

Activism as a Communications Tool

Activism as a means of gaining public interest probably antedates widespread literacy. Activist tactics were a force behind the rise of Christianity, and the split in Christianity was accelerated by such activism as Luther's nailing his ninety-five theses to the church door.

However, the rise of television as a primary force led to a strong movement toward visualization and action. This, in turn, magnified the role of activism in various ways:

- By showing activism vividly in full motion, sound, and color, affording "instant involvement"

- By feeding the appetite of the media for sensation and controversy

- By multiplying the number of activist forces exerting pressures at the same time

- By accelerating their growth and aggravating their impact

- By motivating others to agitate for their causes

In the late 1960s, the tide of activism in the United States seemed to be superseding all other aspects of mass communication. Demonstrations, occupation of college buildings and public parks, provocation of the police, and heckling of public figures all gained widespread attention. However, it became apparent that using these techniques was increasingly dangerous. It was often like letting loose a force that could as readily turn on the originator as achieve his ends.

In 1968, for instance, the activism of the forces for Senator Eugene McCarthy attained extreme visibility and public attention. But studies after the presidential election by the University of Michigan showed that more votes had been swung to the Nixon position than to the extreme position of immediate withdrawal from Vietnam that McCarthy had espoused. The results reflect the resentment and fear of the multiple activist groups felt by millions of voters who responded to Nixon's appeal to "lower our voices." They rejected those who aggressively sought to force drastic change.

To understand the tendency of the public to be influenced and predict how it will respond to any form of communication, its heritage and character must be assessed. Throughout its history the U.S. social and political system has been a flexible one, able to absorb many variations, but thereby almost always diverting all extremes into the midstream that represents the great majority.

Activism is often an extreme form of press agentry—a form that is often embraced by media that would scorn other types of press agentry. But like press agentry of other types, it may succeed in getting attention while failing to achieve its purpose, or even backfiring against its source.

In general, public attitudes often follow laws of physics: the greater the potential potency of a given influence, the greater the potential reaction against it. Careful, low-key, gradual communications may take a long time and be drowned out, but they are not likely to create a negative backlash. Aggressive methods may bring fast, dramatic results, but the chance they will lead to setbacks is great.[1]

Withstanding activism

Organizations that are the targets of activists must understand their opponents and know how to forestall their disruptive efforts.

There are at least four classifications of opponents, and the way to deal with each is different.

1. **Advocates** propose something they believe in, much as a businessman proposes that lower taxes would help the economy.

2. **Dissidents** are against something—and sometimes are against many things because it is their character to be sour on things as they are.

3. **Activists** want to get something done or something changed.

4. **Zealots** may have traits of the others, but they are distinguished by an overriding singlemindedness. They are likely to be absorbed with one issue and to feel their mission in life is to achieve that purpose by aggressive means. Zealots are activists with their governors removed.

In proper form, reason can be used to deal with advocates; logic and selected emotions with dissidents; logic and strategic actions with activists. But you cannot change a zealot with any direct approach. Coping with the zealot calls for creating a climate of opinion and understanding among the public around him or her that will isolate the zealot and wither his zeal.

---

[1]*Overcoming Opposition*, Philip Lesly, Prentice-Hall, 1984.

The means of dealing with an advocate can be futile with a zealot; and to treat the advocate as if he or she were a zealot results in creating hatred where none existed. Analysis, strategy, plans, and activities must all be tailored to the nature of the opposing group.

Thwarting disruptive opponents

Many activist groups, schooled on Saul Alinsky's *Rules for Radicals*, use extreme or outrageous tactics to disrupt an organization or society. There are a number of "Sagacities for Stability" that can nullify those efforts.

1. **Don't give ammunition to your enemies.** Whatever they're up to—especially when it seems most outrageous or unfounded—ask yourself what they're really after . . . and don't give it to them. If they want to create an incident that they can exploit with charges of brutality, ignore them, ridicule them, divert them, but don't give them the action they're trying to provoke.

2. **Your opponents need conflict.** They keep the support of their group by stirring it up. Getting you into conflict proves that they have an enemy and must rally.

3. **They need victories.** Few movements can sustain the passion needed to withstand the boredom of dull debates or waiting for decisions. Activists don't achieve a victory and disappear; they go on seeking more and more. So give them no small victories and you're less likely to have to give them big ones.

4. **Don't let them focus on a single segment of the total situation.** Activists focus on one isolated aspect of the problem that they can dramatize. They grab the elephant by the tail and say that's the problem and you're responsible for it. So keep the big picture in focus at all times.

5. **Nature abhors vacuums but activists love them.** If they can be the overwhelming

source of "information" on a subject they can scare or anger people and get action. Alinsky said: "Men will act when they are convinced their cause is 100 percent on the side of the angels and that the opposition are 100 percent on the side of the devil." When information on a subject is reasonably balanced, unless it's of critical concern to someone, he or she is likely to shrug it off as not worth the trouble of deciding which side is right. So fill information vacuums.

6. **Add emotion to logic.** Activists needn't be responsible—the media and "thought leaders" are likely to respond to assertions even if they're unfounded. You stand for stability, so you can't be irresponsible. Tons of facts have little weight if they don't get through to the emotions of people that fertilize ideas into sturdy attitudes. Make what you say emote, move, stir—not just argue. Often emotion alone or fact alone is like sodium or chlorine unmixed—lethal. Properly joined they are the salt of persuasion.

7. **The root of persuasion is the need of the human mind to visualize things.** Activists have mastered the visual event and stirring pictorialization. Use the ways to make things form images in people's minds—examples, parables, analogies, and comparisons as well as pictures, diagrams, and graphics.

8. **People who become activists have declared themselves to be "aginners" on at least one subject.** They demonstrate they are dissatisfied. They are likely to become dissatisfied with any movement they join. That's why all major movements split into rival groups. Give them reasons to divide; help them split.

9. **Don't let them create your semantics.** Activists take on impeccable terms and assign derogatory names to established groups. Don't fall into the habit of using their terms.

10. **Confound their strengths; compound their weaknesses.** A strength of activists is skill in using emotional messages and tactics. They tend to be weak on facts to support their assertions; and since they consider information only a tool to achieve their Only Truth, they distort or fabricate information. Exposing their falsifications and deceit can often puncture their balloons—if excellent communications techniques are used.

11. **Focus on creating doubt in the minds of the 10 percent of the population who are alert on your issue.** Since the radicals want to force change, you usually don't need action by that crucial coterie; you need only to prevent it from wanting the opponents' action.

The power of the grapevine

Word of mouth can spread like a prairie fire. If the subject and content are right, it can burst into spontaneous combustion as an entire forest may suddenly be overrun by a conflagration. Through word of mouth, rumor and innuendo may spread with extreme speed and spontaneity if the subject is close to the emotions of people. Feelings and not thoughts most quickly take wing on word of mouth. In stimulating a word-of-mouth campaign, the important thing is to present subject matter of such interest as to cause people to repeat it to others.

Word of mouth is perhaps the most subtle of publicity tools. It is the hardest to control. At times it is the most negative and destructive, taking the form of gossip and slander. Its use is not subject to cut-and-dried mechanics, as are many publicity media and instruments. The following things contribute to word-of-mouth circulation:

1. A spectacular and successful event or product
2. A spectacular publicity or advertising campaign
3. A good catchword or slogan
4. Capitalizing on a mass trend or catchword

When Daniel P. Moynihan first ran for the Senate from New York, his greatest handicap was that word of mouth about him was negative among the large black electorate. He had advised, a few years earlier, that a policy of "benign neglect" be pursued in regard to blacks and one of his best-known studies reported on the dispersal of black families. He overcame the problem by disseminating literature and stimulating word-of-mouth communication on how strongly he supported having the rest of the country help New York City and New York State out of their financial crises. He emphasized that his opponent, Senator James Buckley, advocated fiscal responsibility for New York governments, which would mean temporary reductions in welfare and other payments.

When he sought the presidency in 1976, Jimmy Carter faced the problems of being little known and having an undistinguished record in his one term as governor of Georgia. His campaign used word of mouth and other means to exploit the public's dissatisfaction with the government establishment.

In both cases, they countered the negative word of mouth and fed the stream with what they wanted.

Direct-Mail Letters

Letters, which enable one person to reach out to another without the limitations of time that cut down on personal visits and telephoning, are among the most ancient and still important media of communications. It has been said that letters are the only selling medium that, if taken away, would disrupt the entire modern business structure. Less than 15 percent of mail is personal correspondence. All else is commercial.

The well-written letter has a major advantage over other written media—it is directed *personally* to an individual. If it is designed to please and flatter him or her rather than to irritate as an invasion of privacy, it commands attention for a little while—perhaps just long enough to motivate the recipient to do what the writer wants.

One trouble with letters is that there are so many of them. There is too much competition. It is true that people like to receive mail. But mail is a personal thing. The citizen likes to get a letter written *for* him or her. He likes it to express regard for him, offer him a better job, make a promise, or contain a check. When a publicist sends out a letter written for the client's benefit instead of for the recipient's, the recipient's privacy is being presumed upon. The recipient may resent it. He may throw the letter away without reading it, or read it only to turn against the writer.

One survey showed that 58 percent of those in advertising and related fields think that less than 15 percent of the direct-mail pieces are effective. Only 5 percent think that more than half of the direct-mail pieces are effective.

If direct mail is too *cheap*, it can be the most expensive publicity available. On the other hand, when well done it has extensive possibilities. Both quality and selectivity of mailing are factors to be weighed. A maker of automatic controls picked up $2 million in orders as a result of a mailing to 110 key executives.

Direct mail at its best is direct mail that is or appears to be *direct* mail, namely shooting with a rifle and not shooting with a shotgun.

The following elements will help attain the maximum in results.

Lists

Lists constitute the aiming of direct mail. Their importance cannot be overemphasized. A misspelled name or a slovenly address means the cost of processing a good direct-mail letter has been wasted. Lists can be grouped according to interests. Ways to get direct-mail lists include: members of organizations, house-to-house canvass, precinct lists, telephone books, "coupon" advertisements, list brokers, directories, publication subscription lists. Lists can best be kept up to date with computers but in their absence the lists can be kept effectively by filing on 3″ × 5″ cards and by noting address changes as they come in. Lists are available from many brokers. A central source of information is the Direct Marketing Association, 6 E. 43rd Street, New York, NY, 10017.

Approach

Letters can be personalized in physical appearance and content. Most tests show that first-class mail more than pays for the extra cost in increased results over second-class. Fill-in letters are more effective when the name, address, and salutation are indistinguishable from body type. Electronic methods of letter preparation make it possible to repeat the family name or make other individual references in the body of the letter to personalize a mass-produced presentation. These are available through large mailing houses and through service offices of firms that sell computers and word processors.

It is important who signs the letter. It is well for the signature to be by the person with most influence on the addressee, and signed personally rather than processed, if possible.

Contents

Appeal, specific application, and instructions for action are vital ingredients. The "hook" can be made concrete, sincere, persuasive, and vivid. It is worth the trouble to make the contents timely and based on confluence of interest between the writer and the addressee. A simple writing style that seems in character with the writer is recommended. Attention, interest, desire, action, in that order, have been found to furnish the most effective sequence.

Outward form and appearance

Paper, letterhead, envelope may be planned to be of appealing color, style, size, and quality. Typography is advocated that looks distinctive as well as dignified. Readership is increased if each envelope is individually addressed or addressed to look almost exactly like original handling. It is cut down by a printed postage permit used in place of the stamp. Even the style of folding is important. The standard twice-horizontal folding is best in most cases.

Faxing eliminates the envelope and stamp but in many cases it loses the desired impact of personal attention conveyed by a good letter.

Enclosures

Copy and layout can be designed to attract attention and tell the story effectively. The use of too many different enclosures annoys and bewilders the recipient.

Continuity

It has been estimated by a trade spokesperson that continuity in mailing is next in importance to a correct mailing list:

> On the basis of 100 percent for the success of a direct mail campaign, one mailing will be worth about 5 percent; two mailings 15 percent; three mailings 40 percent; four mailings 60 percent; five mailings 75 percent, and six to eight mailings 100 percent.

With repeated mailings, intervals not exceeding two weeks best sustain the effect of preceding mail. In a series, earlier letters may best concentrate on information, later ones more on appeal to action.

Timing

Letters mailed Monday usually hit the target in midweek, the best time. Letters mailed late in the week hit the offices on Monday, when the desk is piled with the weekend accumulation.

Testing

Especially in a large mailing, it may be good insurance to try out a letter on a random portion of a group. A test of reasonable size can usually be depended on to indicate the percentage of return to be expected from a mailing to the entire group.

Etiquette of letters

Concise letters, written with sincerity and restraint, will make the writer's voice heard by elected legislative and executive officials of the national or state government. The proper manner of addressing these officials is as follows:

To the President of the United States:
The President
The White House
or
The President
Washington, DC 20500
Salutation is:
Sir:
or
To the President:
or
My dear Mr. President:
Complimentary close is:
Respectfully submitted—
or

Yours respectfully—
or
Faithfully yours (informal)

To a Cabinet Member:
The Honorable _____
Secretary of State
The Department of State
Washington, DC 20520

To a Senator:
The Honorable _____
The United States Senate
Washington, DC 20510
Salutation is:
Dear Sir or Madam:
or
My dear Senator:
or
My dear _____ (informal)
Complimentary close is:
Very truly yours

To a representative:
The Honorable _____
The House of Representatives
Washington, DC 20515
Salutation is:
Sir or Madam:
or
Dear Sir or Madam:
or
My dear Mr., Mrs., Ms. ____ (informal)
Complimentary close is:
Very truly yours

Style in writing to state and local officials will follow these models.

There are elements of courtesy by mail that pay off in cumulative dividends. It is well to answer personal mail within twenty-four hours. When that is impossible, an aide can write a polite explanation, promising a full reply at the earliest opportunity.

To put as much individuality as possible into every letter, an executive will find it best to sign his or her own mail. Use of a form letter to answer a personally addressed letter is an insult and will be so interpreted by the recipient. It is well to salute and sign with first names if the degree of acquaintance warrants. A personal jotted addition stresses the individual attention given.

In any business matter where there is the slightest possibility of subsequent misunderstanding, it is advisable to put the matter on record with a letter to avoid future misunderstandings and to supplement the memories of all concerned.

Every letter an organization mails is a little public relations worker. Its work will be good or bad, according to the quality of the worker. An organization that mails thousands of letters daily has, in that fact, a public relations opportunity. Recognizing this, many firms make letter-writing courses available to their employees.

Postcard Mailings

Postcards—quick and easy to prepare, quick and easy for the recipient to absorb, economical to mail—constitute an effective adaptation of direct mail to reach large numbers of people with a message that can be punched home in a paragraph.

In many campaigns, large numbers of individuals can be stimulated to sign and then send postcards to their own friends and contacts. This personal touch has more influence with the recipient than would a communique from a stranger.

The picture postcard on one side publicizes an attraction and on the other provides space for mailing and a personal message. Many restaurants, hotels, and resorts provide free mailings to encourage the dispatch of more of these cards. A real advantage of postcards is that, because they are so easy to prepare, they are a convenient method to enlist patrons to do personal advertising for an organization—giving it a personal touch with their individual endorsements.

Newsletters

Another form of direct-mail communication that is increasing in use is the *newsletter*. Despite the term, many of these do not deal with news and they are not letters. Any publication of a few pages, usually written in concise form and generally appearing at regular intervals, is called a newsletter.

The newsletter originated as a commercial publication, providing hard-to-get and up-to-date information on a specific subject for an annual subscription price. *The Kiplinger Washington Letter*, for instance, reports weekly on developments and expectations in the capital that may be useful or interesting to the subscribers. Many others deal with limited subjects, such as the petroleum market, demand for gold, or grain trading.

The public relations newsletter is usually provided free to a selected list of customers or clients, prospects, media, and others who can be helpful to the issuer. In some cases, the subscription method and free distribution are combined. Philip Lesly's *Managing the Human Climate*, for instance, goes to clients, prospective clients, and media without charge; it is sent on a paid subscription basis to others, and it is provided as a supplement of *PR Reporter*. This publication, like many others, does not deal with news but with other material that is expected to be helpful or impressive to the recipients. (*See* Figure 31.2.)

Many newsletters are highly graphic and are printed in more than one color. Others are usually all-type and in one color.

The decision to start a newsletter constitutes a long-term commitment, so advance planning is critical to its success over time. Before undertaking a newsletter a number of points should be considered.

Managing the Human Climate

Guidelines on Public Relations and Public Affairs

by Philip Lesly

No. 153
July-August, 1995

Identifying a New Mission: A Credible Mission Statement

At the same time managements have been hacking inefficiency and makework, countless hours (some billable) are spent writing "mission statements" (a.k.a., credos, principles, values, vision statements, etc.)

They should ask hundreds of thousands of employees who were axed only to cut costs about their former employers' mission statements.

> The past few years have shown that it's not possible to live up to highflown wishes when reality requires exceptions and variations.

The hard truth is that mission statements are wish lists -- and so are usually wishful thinking.

Most mission statements are as passé as the stone missions of the Old West.

Here's how "Chris Howard," a Canadian economist, put it:

> "Most mandates, missions, visions, values, philosophies -- the whole constellation of high-flown statements -- aren't worth the paper they're printed on and almost everyone in the organization knows it. In fact, I'd go so far as to say that if I were an investor in a previously successful firm that announced it was working on a mission statement, I'd be strongly tempted to sell."

But, it's objected, an organization must have an articulate expression of what it stands for. So if someone feels a need, it should be credible and attainable, perhaps like this:

LISTED IN "WHO'S WHO IN THE WORLD" (MARQUIS)

Figure 31.2 First page of a newsletter featuring helpful information and commentary. Other newsletters emphasize concise news.

1. Does the organization have something to offer in a newsletter that meets an unmet need and that will make the desired impression for the issuer? It is unwise to issue a newsletter just because others do or if it will be one of a number on the same subject, without distinctive value.

2. Will it convey to the audience what is unique about the organization or why the recipients should give special attention to the source?

3. Is a distribution list readily available or can it be assembled and maintained with reasonable effort and cost?

4. Is there someone available with the knowledge, skill, time, and access to sources that are necessary to do an excellent job with every issue? Many newsletters are poor and damage the reputation of the issuer.

5. How often should it be issued? Is immediate news a major factor, so weekly or even more frequent dissemination may be called for? What can the budget provide for? In any case, it should be issued no less than once every two months. It is unlikely that recognition can be maintained if the intervals are longer.

6. What should the format be: four pages, more, or variable with each issue depending on how much material there is? Should enclosures be made from time to time, such as reprints of speeches or articles? Should it be black-and-white or multicolored? Should it regularly contain illustrations or be essentially all type?

7. With all these considerations and others peculiar to the organization, are you sure this is the best means to accomplish the objective? Other media may not require so much staff time or such a long-term commitment. Is it worth the cost when budgets are prepared with a liberal allowance for increases in postage rates and other growing costs?

With the advent of desktop publishing, many offices can now produce newsletters internally at lower costs than before (*see* Chapter 33).

A source of information is *Newsletter on Newsletters*, 44 W. Market Street, Rhinebeck, NY 12572.

External Magazines

Magazines designed to reach specific audiences the organization may wish to reach generally fall into one of two categories:

1. Those published by the organization and distributed free to its list of recipients

2. Those for which the organization is the single advertiser, that may be offered for sale on newsstands, and for which distribution may be controlled by the sponsor

The Furrow, published in a number of editions for various types of farmers, is Deere & Company's medium for getting intensive attention from its customers and prospects. It may have the largest circulation of any farm publication in the world.

Meredith Corporation, Des Moines, Iowa, produces magazines for outside companies, as well as custom books and booklets.

Some publications are directed at both external and internal audiences. Exxon publishes *The Lamp* primarily for stockholders, but also sends it to opinion leaders and other influential people.

Recently many company-sponsored magazines have appeared that are actually produced by major magazine publishers. They use either material from general magazines or articles written and illustrated by those magazines' editorial staffs.

Some clearly identify the sponsors in their titles, such as *Target the Family* for Target Stores and *Mercedes Momentum*. Others carry their efforts to make readers think they are reading objective information further by using generic titles, such as *Today's Focus* for Key Corp. banks and *Unlimited* for Marlboro cigarettes.

As with infomercials on TV, editorial-style ads, and other efforts to beguile an audience into absorbing nonobjective information in disguise, the effectiveness of these magazines is in dispute. In reporting on their rise, *Business Week* (whose staff produces just such a sponsored magazine for the Professional Golfers Association) says:

> . . . some marketing experts suspect that the costly custom publications are going from the mailbox straight into the trash.

Communicating Through Extension Home Economists

There are about three thousand offices of extension home economists (EHES) scattered throughout the United States. They are operated by federal, state, and local governments to educate consumers on matters such as food, money management, health care, home remodeling and repair, education, home decoration, safety, clothing, toys, gardening, housekeeping, and community problems.

Some of the EHES write regular newspaper columns. Others have television and radio shows, or write monthly newsletters, or speak before various audiences.

As a group, the EHES represent an influential audience that in turn reaches many individuals. Lists of the offices and services for reaching them are available from Media Distribution Services, 330 W. 34th Street, New York, NY 10001 and 2 N. Riverside Plaza, Chicago, IL 60606.

Other Forms of Direct Media

Other forms of direct media include the following:

1. E-mail commands attention but at a loss of some individuality embodied in letters. It reaches people quickly and almost simultaneously.

2. An economical reminder is to use stickers glued on letters, postcards, envelopes, newsletters, bills, windshields, windows, doors, and other convenient places.

3. Inserts are frequently designed to accompany letters, bills, and other mailings. Pocket calendars are handy to have around and often are kept for use, whereas the ordinary insert is usually thrown away, sometimes without more than a cursory glance.

4. Many organizations use their regular bank checks to carry messages. Several national associations have promoted this plan by sending sample checks to members illustrating the use that can be made of this medium. The technical space of the check is reduced to provide a greater margin, which usually carries a sketch in color to put across a message.

5. Lapel buttons make emissaries out of human beings, label a person as a supporter, stir up questions and curiosity. When many adherents wear them, it creates a feeling of power and mass endorsement.

6. Thousands of persons can be reached at little or no extra cost by stamping mass mailings with postage meters using for special messages the boxed space ordinarily taken by post office canceling machines. The problem is to prevail on organizations using postage meter machines to use a cut putting over the message being publicized. For drives in the public interest, such as

for Red Cross, Community Fund, Easter Seals, and the like, a postage meter manufacturer[2] will usually make available a list to clients. For example, the Red Cross may work up a letter to go to all clients, address Red Cross envelopes from the postage meter company's list, and send out the letters. The letters urge the individual client to buy from the postage meter machine company a cut publicizing the Red Cross. For mass use of this medium in such drives, the desirable first step is to contact the postage meter company, which will outline the steps to be followed.

7. A rubber stamp can be created, carrying a message sometimes including a drawing, and used to stamp the message by the thousands on envelopes or letterheads.

8. Jokes are themselves a medium. They can be devised or revised, and adapted, for directing favorable attention to a subject when related before meetings, printed in publications, embodied in comic strips, or broadcast.

9. Often a catchy slogan, adopted for a campaign or an organization, can be worked into posters and signs, referred to in talks, and made a catchline for editorials and story mentions.

   Slogans and catchwords have decisive impact in political publicity. "He kept us out of war" helped elect Wilson for his second term. McKinley rode in on the slogan, "The full dinner-pail." Bush said, "Read my lips—no new taxes."

   The form of the slogan can be, among others:

   • Statement of character—"We're More Than Paper"

   • Imperative—"Find Your Own Road"

   • Admonition—"Don't look if you can't stand the sight of courage."

   • Claim of superiority—"Better Sound Through Research"

   • Reason why—"Because Life Is Not a Spectator Sport."

   • Play on words—"Does she . . . or doesn't she?"

   • Summary of benefits—"Everything You'd Never Expect"

   • Prediction—"Good things begin to happen when you start a meal with soup."

   • Prestige—"How the Big Shots Take Snapshots"

   • Suggestion—"Enjoy life more with music."

10. Symbols—objects that carry instantaneous meaning—are effective tools in mass impulse and propaganda. A flag, a national anthem, a great man are all symbols. The caduceus is a symbol of the healing professions. The swastika was the symbol of the German Nazis; the hammer and sickle was the symbol of the Communists. John Bull for England and Uncle Sam for the United States are symbols. These accepted tokens convey immediate meaning. They are eloquent tools of expression and are used repeatedly as shafts of publicity and propaganda.

11. Bumper stickers are another publicity medium, often used by advocates of a public policy, a political candidate, or a fund-raising organization. Preferably these should be presented to the car owners, rather than applied without permission, to maintain goodwill. Many people will refuse to mark their cars with public stands on issues or a memento of a resort, even though they support them.

[2]Pitney-Bowes, Inc., 1 Elmcroft Road, Stamford, CT 06926.

12. Literature of various types is covered in Chapters 12 and 33.

For use in literature it is often necessary to have a source for stock illustrations. The following provide books of drawings on many subjects that can be pasted into layouts to make the material more attractive or to set the tone of the message:

Creative Art Productions
22552 King Richard Court
Birmingham, MI 48010

Dynamic Graphics, Inc.
6000 N. Forest Park Drive
Peoria, IL 61614

The Educational
Communications Center
P.O. Box 657
Camp Hill, PA 17011

Signs, Bulletin Boards, and Posters

Probably the oldest advertising medium in history, outdoor advertising dates at least as far back as ancient Egypt and even now is a large, successful business in areas like China where other media of modern advertising are largely undeveloped. Pasted posters on building walls are part of the decor of Rome.

Outdoor advertising features the following types of posters:

1. **Poster panels**, in which the poster is pasted up for a given period of time

2. **Painted bulletins** that go up on walls or specially erected **signboards**, a more elaborate and expensive form

3. **Electric "spectacular displays"** and semielectric painted bulletins, the most dramatic—and expensive—of all types, jointly accounting for a small proportion of the total outdoor advertising revenue

4. **Mobile billboards**, mounted on truck chassis

In addition, store signs are a basic form of outdoor publicity.

Reputable outdoor advertising concerns make every effort to maintain attractive signs, landscaped and decorated to contribute to rather than to deteriorate the surrounding area. By their endeavor to protect scenic sections of rural roadside from inappropriate commercial use and to preserve areas with recreational or historical value, outdoor advertising companies have followed a public relations policy that makes their medium of greater value to their clients.

For public relations purposes, outdoor advertising has a strong reminder value. It helps spur to direct action. To get the best results, it is necessary to present outdoor advertising in few words and distinct outlines so the story will be told at a glance, because the passing motorist or pedestrian for whom it is prepared will have only a passing instant to absorb the message.

A variation of sign media is the bulletin board, used by organizations for display of posters and messages in meeting places. Bulletin boards have a strong "habit value" when located at places where employees or other constant audiences gather regularly. They are a good medium for reminders, special messages, and official announcements.

Posters of all kinds for display from counters, in store windows, in meeting halls, in schools and offices, in lobbies, and in many other places constitute a sign medium widely used in special promotions.

Advertising signs suspended from or dragged from behind by airplanes and blimps can be effective, particularly at night when colored lights are shown. This kind of publicity is often used by the entertainment industry at crowded places. These signs are sometimes accompanied by sound effects to intensify their impact. A variation on this medium is the illuminated mobile blimp.

Fairs and Exhibits

One of the most spectacular special events and at the same time most tangible media of publicity takes form in the fairs and exhibits that enrich the life of America with dynamic showmanship plus salesmanship.

Every year the United States has approximately 2,200 fairs. And, beginning with our first overseas venture in Bangkok, Thailand, in 1954, American exhibits have been seen by millions of people throughout the world. Hundreds of millions of dollars are invested in various fair properties. Some individual establishments are worth more than $50 million. Considerably more than ten thousand people are employed yearly by these fairs, with wages running into uncomputed millions.

Fairs constitute both a merchandising medium and a publicity medium. As a merchandising instrument they can have good effect if exhibitors plan their displays cleverly.

Except when the publicity is tied in with direct merchandising of specific products, as in the case of store displays in the windows of stores, exhibits at fairs, conventions, trade shows, and elsewhere sometimes tend to cost more money and trouble than they are worth for publicity alone.

The function of the fair has changed with broadening of communications and attractions for the public. Whereas fairs used to offer many wonders that were not otherwise available to the public, now television, full-color magazines and books, foreign travel, audiovisual techniques in education, and other factors bring wonders within easier reach of the population. It is no longer necessary for people to travel hundreds of miles, go to great expense, and walk for miles to see any exhibit except the extraordinary.

Special-interest fairs, such as trade exhibits and agricultural fairs, continue to have a strong attraction because they serve functions not otherwise met.

A variation is the display a company may sponsor in museums such as the Museum of Science and Industry in Chicago, or theme centers such as Epcot Center in Orlando, Florida.

When considering publicizing a client with a fair exhibit or museum, weigh all the angles: timeliness, dramatic possibilities of the display, competition from other displays, publicity possibilities, tie-ins available, etc.

Displays

Important considerations with respect to acquiring, planning, and arranging window displays to influence the public were outlined in a booklet entitled *Displays*, published by the public relations department of the American Red Cross:

> The merchant's window is his most valuable stock in trade, and he there features the merchandise by which he wishes to be judged.
>
> The window display is set up to motivate the onlooker to action—to come in and buy.
>
> Window displays are gauged to focus public attention sharply on a certain point, and each display should be used to drive home a single idea.
>
> Window displays should be carefully timed, and launched simultaneously to capitalize on press and broadcast work to incite to action.
>
> A sufficient number of window displays creates an atmosphere of urgency abetted by the feeling that the entire community is behind the project.
>
> A window display should not be crowded with details, should offer a simple idea that can be grasped at a glance.

The best displays lure the eye with a device that helps to tell the story and has the unity of a good poster. Its purpose is the same as a poster's, to excite, not to instruct.

The display should fit the character of other displays in the same store.

Color harmony is important, and a safe rule is to combine one predominant with two off-setting colors.

Preparing a window display schedule requires knowledge of how many stores of each type exist in a community. The more that is known about stores in relation to economic and social areas and traffic movements, the more efficiently a publicist can place his displays properly to accomplish a specific purpose.

Displays should be planned and arranged well in advance, because stores tend to tie them up with merchandising drives far ahead of time.

Types of stores include drug, grocery, barber and beauty shops, hotels, banks, jewelry stores, women's and men's clothiers, variety stores, utility offices, and department stores. Usually department stores prepare their own exhibits, but the publicist must be prepared in the other cases to furnish all or much of the exhibit material . . . Leading types of display are these:

1. The simplest window display is a poster. The most desirable window location for a poster alone is adjoining the doorway.

2. Photographic prints, 11″ × 14″ or larger blowups, make eye-catching displays, alone or with other materials.

3. Displays of models, cutouts, figures, and materials with captions and perhaps with posters furnish dramatic exhibits.

4. The outdoor display has the same problem as the outdoor advertisement—to catch the eye of a public on the move. "Tell it. Tell it simply. Tell it briefly," is the formula. The types of outdoor display are:

   • The fixed display, which must have familiarity of symbol to register quickly, unexpectedness to catch the eye, impact to hold the attention and leave an impression.

   • The moving display, an affair of floats and costumed figures.

   • The exhibit, which must possess lure, originality, color combined in forms and figures that will halt the steps of the roving spectator. The exhibit should be manned by personnel able to meet the public, explain the booth, and sell the merchandise. The exhibit must combine showmanship with salesmanship.

Public Address Systems

Public address systems at meetings, shows, gatherings of employees, or mass audiences of any kind make it possible mechanically to project the human voice before large numbers of people.

Mounted on a truck, the PA system can be transported from place to place, presenting speakers and programs as it goes, and reaching a widely distributed audience. Sound trucks can also be rigged up at stationary locations, providing facilities for meetings and special programs in lieu of a permanently installed PA system. In Texas, six sound trucks were used to reach three million people in an election campaign. Portable bullhorns afford great mobility wherever amplified sound is needed. It is bad public relations to use sound amplifiers where the noise will annoy local residents.

Recordings make it possible to "capture" a speech or radio program and replay it by radio, before an audience, or over a PA system anywhere. Some recordings are made on the spot at special events. In other cases, special programs are deliberately produced at a recording studio.

32

WORKING WITH INFLUENTIAL GROUPS

HERBERT M. BAUS

Opinion Makers

Influential groups may comprise simply the "thought leaders" of the community. A single individual, or any one or combination of organizations, large and small, may serve in this capacity.

These thought leaders do not necessarily hold titles in organizations, though the community's titleholders typically are among the thought leaders. A person becomes a thought leader not out of authoritative status alone but rather by reason of vitality, personality, intellect, communication skills, gregariousness, or any of a range of characteristics and interests. Therefore, the thought leaders of a community may include an articulate barber, a concerned citizen, or a person who belongs to many groups but serves as an officer of none.

Any service club, women's group, trade association, political party, labor union, religious unit, civic organization, welfare body, veteran's group—or any type of organization—can constitute an influential group.

Each group represents a segment of the community. Each carries over to other groups within the community through its members' association with other groups, relatives, friends, coworkers, and other people with whom they interface. Consequently, the stance or actions of any given group influences that of other groups, and the attitudes of that group's members, in turn, carries over to other groups, and so on. Every time a new group is won over, the victory contributes to the larger goal of winning public opinion as a whole.

When these influential groups endorse or align themselves with a cause—or product, or organization—they provide a valuable media source. Their power is tremendous. (*See* Figure 32.1, page 476.)

One need only look as far as our political system to see the power of these groups. As a system that, by design, reflects the popular will through representative rule, it virtually functions like a government of organized minorities. Influential groups often control large blocs of Congress and state legislatures; accordingly, they often define the policies and personnel of government. For this reason these groups are sometimes referred to as "The Third House" of Congress or "The Invisible Government."

Many forms of communication are effective for reaching these and other influential groups: direct mail, speaking to their membership, interviewing their leaders, telephoning, publicizing in their publications, among other forms.

A sound public relations strategy, particularly when dealing with openly controversial matters, such as political campaigns with an underdog start, is to attack the problem with a "divide-and-conquer" tactic. This procedure is designed to win over one group or one clus-

50 East Huron Street
Chicago, Illinois 60611-2795
USA

Telephone 312 944 6780
Fax 312 440 9374
Toll Free 800 545 2433
TDD 312 944 7298
E-mail:ala@ala.org
http://www.ala.org

AmericanLibraryAssociation

For Immediate Release
March 13, 1997

Contact: Joyce Kelly or Linda Wallace
312-280-5043/5042

M E D I A   A D V I S O R Y
Supreme Court to hear CDA challenge March 19;
Case tests freedom of speech in cyberspace

The United States Supreme Court will hear oral arguments in the challenge to the Communications Decency Act (CDA) next Wednesday, March 19, at 10 a.m. The historic case is the first to consider how freedom of speech rights guaranteed by the First Amendment apply to the Internet.

"Under this law, many materials that are perfectly legal on bookstores and library shelves would become illegal in cyberspace," says Elizabeth Martinez, executive director of the American Library Association (ALA). "We are optimistic that the Supreme Court justices will affirm the decisions of the lower courts and act to uphold freedom of speech on the Internet."

Judith F. Krug, director of the ALA Office for Intellectual Freedom, notes that the vast amount of helpful information available online far outweighs the risk of children being exposed to inappropriate material. "We believe the best way to protect children is for parents to supervise their children and to teach them to make good choices."

Under the Act, passed last year as part of the Telecommunications Act, any person who knowingly sends or displays materials over the Internet to minors that could be interpreted as "indecent" or "patently offensive by contemporary community standards" could be imprisoned for up to two years and fined up to $250,000.

The Supreme Court case, titled Reno v. ACLU, combines a suit filed by the Citizens Internet Empowerment Coalition, which includes the American Library Association as lead plaintiff and the Freedom To Read Foundation, with a suit filed by the American Civil Liberties Union (ACLU). Two federal district courts have declared the Act unconstitutional. The rulings are being appealed by the U. S. Department of Justice.

Bruce J. Ennis, counsel to the ALA and the Freedom to Read Foundation, will present the case on behalf of the Citizens Internet Empowerment Coalition and the ACLU. The Solicitor General of the United States will argue the government's case. A decision is expected in early summer.

For more information, contact the ALA Office for Intellectual Freedom, 50 E. Huron St., Chicago, IL 60611. Telephone: 312-280-4224 or see the ALA Web page at http://www.ala.org

####

To arrange to interview ALA spokespeople on March 19, please call the ALA Washington Office at 202-628-8410 or Pro-Media Public Relations at 212-245-0510.

Figure 32.1 The American Library Association was a leading plaintiff in opposing the Communications Decency Act, which was ruled unconstitutional on June 26, 1977, by a unanimous vote. *Courtesy American Library Association.*

ter of groups at a time—taking on small, easy-to-handle groups in succession. As each group is won over, the cause gains strength, advocates, and allies.

Indeed, a basic in public campaigns is to create a group with an attractive name, as a "Greater New York Committee" might be set up to support a campaign to pass bonds for the improvement of the City of New York. The "Committee for Tolerance" was set up to fight a misnamed "Fair Employment Practices Act" in California and was a strong factor in defeating a measure represented by its backers as a provision for the economic betterment of minorities.

When such an organization is set up as a campaign weapon, the first step will be to name prominent citizens—"thought leaders"—as members of the committee. The very presence of their names on the committee's letterhead wins powerful support for the cause. Because many of these figurehead committees are not what they seem—for example, American Youth for Democracy, a pretty name for what was formerly more honestly labeled the Young Communist League— prominent citizens are well advised to study carefully every such organization and make sure of its *real* backers and its *real* motives before lending it the use of their names. In establishing such a group it is important to have all facts open and available for study.

Women's groups

The "women's movement" has focused attention on the anomaly of women as potent forces in our society: On one hand women's groups are powerful organizations; on the other hand, women increasingly dislike being treated as a separate "public."

While the women's rights movement flourishes, the interests of women as women are important considerations; and the women's club is a readily identifiable focal point of women's interests.

Winifred Jordan said that "to ignore the importance of women's clubs and their tremendous influence in swaying public sentiment is sheer folly." She further stated that some industries—namely, the food, airline, motion picture, broadcasting, and life insurance industries—have done a good job with this, the biggest of all special groups.

Realizing that people can best be influenced through the organizations to which they belong, many groups now address the "women's club market." The market contains a heavy proportion of those leaders who influence other women.

With purchased mailing lists likely to be few and incomplete, and with state and national federations jealously guarding their lists for fear of exploitation, the women's group has been hard to reach.

Illustrating the technique by which a group may be reached, some manufacturers have hired speakers and listed them with speakers' bureaus. (Refer to Chapter 31 for information on arranging speaking engagements.) Others buy advertising space in magazines published by state and national federations of women's clubs. Still others retain skilled specialists who will prepare a program package, mail it to a list of clubs, and handle requests for other clubs that hear about the literature and want it. The "program package" appeals to leaders of women's clubs who must not only plan a year's schedule of meetings for their groups, but must also help member-speakers to stage their respective programs.

A list of leading national women's organizations that may be of interest to public relations workers appears in the Appendix.

Farm groups

Although their numbers are declining steadily, farmers remain a major influence group, especially in heavy agricultural states, such as Iowa and the Dakotas, and in mostly urban states with extensive farm areas, such as Minnesota.

A list of major organizations of farmers is in the Appendix.

Veterans' organizations

Another major influential group consists of war veterans. They express themselves through powerful organizations such as the American Legion, Veterans of Foreign Wars, and others, listed in the Appendix with their national headquarters. Also listed are related patriotic organizations.

Church groups

The thousands of churches of America and their millions of followers constitute another major influential group of the United States. (*See* Chapter 40.) They can be approached through denominational magazines and newspapers, national headquarters, and local ministerial associations as well as by means of direct mail and personally approaching the individual minister. The publicist representing a cause that enjoys or can obtain church approval can project a story with the help of church groups by the following techniques:

1. Sending direct mail to ministers

2. Obtaining endorsement of ministerial associations and clerical organizations

3. Disseminating the story through church press and publications

4. Sending speakers to special events, forums, meetings, and other church events that will receive outside speakers on appropriate subjects.

5. Aligning with issues and causes that have church backing.

6. Making prominent church personages officials of or participants in the organization, association, or cause being publicized.

7. Working through church-affiliated groups such as the Knights of Columbus

8. Developing special events jointly sponsored by church groups

Leading religious publications and news services of America are given in the Appendix. Other religious publications of local or regional character can be obtained from the IMS directory, mentioned previously.

Other influential groups

Lists of organizations representing business, education, fraternal and service organizations, labor, minority groups and their allies, and welfare groups are in the Appendix.

These lists are useful for national campaigns and nationwide public relations work. For local or regional campaigns, corresponding lists of more localized organizations, or regional and local headquarters of the national groups, may be obtained from the usual sources such as chambers of commerce, classified telephone directories, associations, and other public service groups.

The members of an individual's fraternity or service club form a specific group. Women form an independent public. Children form another public. Each age group of children constitutes an independent public of its own. Labor is a public. White-collar workers are a public. Farmers constitute a public. Every minority group is a public. Every religious sect is a public. Opinion leaders are a public, ranging from an estimated few thousand to 20 percent of the adult population and including editors, ministers, writers, financiers, teachers, heads of associations, and other people in a position to shape the public opinion in their communities. Each of these publics is a potential group of considerable influence.

An early step in any public relations operation is to make a list of all the publics important in achieving the goal and to map a campaign to produce the desired impact on each of these publics and, cumulatively, on the total public.

Interlocking effect

While the best results might be obtained from dealing with individuals as such, there is seldom enough time or resources for such an exhaustive task. Handling the problem on the basis of the general public without effort to concentrate on specific publics would usually be the easiest way but is too often tantamount to spreading ammunition shotgun fashion. Effective campaigns aimed at specific publics will contribute to the impact on the general public. The important thing is to choose the most important specific groups or publics as targets, and do the best possible job with them. (*See* Chapter 3.)

The employees of a company constitute one public. Many of them will be members of other publics that affect the company's destiny. As citizens they may bring pressure for or against the company in the sphere of its government relations. The creditors, suppliers, stockholders, dealers, or any other public of a company will include many persons who may be influential in causing some other public to which they belong to go either for or against a company.

A basic public relations problem of a company or other organization is to make these publics allies rather than enemies. They can be enemies even though the company does business with them. For example, many employees of a company dependent on energy generated by nuclear plants may be active opponents of nuclear power plants. If an entire public, or most of it, feels animosity toward a company this unfavorable opinion will automatically, through the processes of human relations, be contagious and spread into other publics. Goodwill is similarly contagious.

A vast campaign ground for publicity workers is the national capital, or any state capital. A flood of communication pours out daily from federal, state, and local government bureaus; federal, state, and local legislatures; propaganda agencies, both domestic and foreign; and from trade associations, the armed services, and private newsletters such as Kiplinger.

All of these are potential media of expression for a public relations operation. They are concentrated in the national capital because the nation's strongest concentration of influential groups' headquarters is in Washington. Others are in state capitals. Many operatives are stationed in Washington and lesser political centers to be close to them. The government sources in particular have a profound influence on people and frequently offer direct access to the first-line media. (*See* Chapters 5 and 6.)

One of the quickest ways to get national publicity is by arranging to have the client's messages conveyed through one of these political channels. To stage an event in Washington that will put the message to be publicized into the news by causing it to be projected from the floor of Congress or from a federal investigation of some kind, is to enlist the powerful and numerous Washington press gallery in publicizing the particular subject. Many publicists send a batch of copies of their releases to the National Press Club, National Press Building, Washington, to reach the Washington representatives of hundreds of newspapers. (*See* Chapter 5.)

Schools as a Communication Medium

As a particularly good long-range medium adaptable to programs having a five-, ten-, or twenty-year point of view, the schools are strategic. Schools include an immense network of present and future purchasers and voters including students, teachers, and administrators. More than fifty million students are enrolled in 93,000 elementary and secondary schools in the United States.

Approaching these students from a public relations standpoint differs from the barrage of sales and advertising messages aimed at them. It is estimated that twelve thousand companies and associations now try to reach schools through direct mail, telephone marketing, and other sales and promotion efforts. Those include ads on scoreboards and vending machines provided to the schools, computers placed at little or no cost, sponsorship of sports events, advertising in yearbooks and school newspapers, products at cost for fundraisers, and book clubs and fairs.

There are many ways to work effectively with schools when the material is presented in an educational and generic way rather than as ads or promotions. A film, for example—*How a Newspaper Is Published*, or *How Shoes Are Made*—will often be acceptable for assembly programs. Booklets—*How to Use the Telephone*, or *How to Read a Map*—will be usable by teachers on the elementary school level. Demonstration charts—"How to Cook Frozen Vegetables"—are suitable for the high school home economics teacher.

Educators Progress Service of Randolph, Wisconsin, produces catalogues listing pamphlets, booklets, filmstrips, and videotapes, including *The Story of Cotton*, produced by the National Cotton Council and *Choosing the Right Detergent* from the Maytag Company.

The value of school materials depends on their educational value and the subtlety with which the sponsor is identified. Bic pens provides a teaching kit, "Quality Comes in Writing," that includes work sheets on how to write a letter, a ballad, a diary, an ad, a rebus, and a newspaper story. Its logo appears on each sheet and an accompanying wall poster.

Many visual devices can be adapted for educational purposes. Frequently, local teachers, principals, and Parent-Teacher Associations will provide opinion on acceptability or usefulness for various levels.

Materials may be publicized through personal visits to administrators, educational magazines, booths at teachers' conventions, or informative mailings to school facilities.

The importance of tours in arranging programs with schools should not be overlooked. Field trips may be arranged with some teachers to visit industrial or cultural sites—a trip to a major baking plant, for example, or a tour of a new building will attract student groups.

Forums and presentations

Forums or other presentations can often be arranged at department stores or banks with auditorium facilities or at local halls and community organizations with meeting areas. Exhibits, safety discussions, good-grooming demonstrations, and other presentations with a public service aspect can often be presented in this way when school assembly halls are unavailable or otherwise engaged.

Cooperation with school Career Days often yields excellent results. Speakers from the company or industry, brochures about the business, films, visual aids, posters, and other tools aid the guidance counselor who is instructing students in preparation for various fields.

Projects for schools—to be launched only after getting acceptance of the plan from qualified educators or consultants—include art competitions, sewing contests, essay awards, athletic prizes, or other tokens of merit that inspire student effort and cooperation.

Examples of organizations providing effective materials for schools include Johnson & Johnson (offering first aid materials, course materials in baby care for home economics students, dental care instructional material, and other study aids); Eli Lilly and Company (offering educational material about the proper use of drugs); Parke Davis & Company (providing material on poison prevention); Aetna Life & Casualty (issuing material on home safety); and Bausch & Lomb (supplying material on recommended eye care).

One major corporation publishes a number of illustrated science booklets for free distribution to schools. The corporation also makes available elaborate scientific charts and posters. It provides motion pictures and gives away a number of small scholarships. The company's policy is that the educational program is primarily a constructive contribution to the community and the country, with the added advantage that it results in favorable publicity among members of a group—school students—who will for many years spread the resulting goodwill.

Companies have provided such educational aids as a handbook on *How to Organize a Teen-age Night Club*, a calendar featuring the work of leading artists, and books on family income management and "better buymanship."

Westinghouse Electric has conducted a Science Talent Search since 1942. The Search annually evaluates the science potential of about fifteen hundred high school seniors. This group is sifted down to forty finalists. These youngsters are awarded trips to the Science Talent Institute in Washington, where they compete for $205,000 in scholarships. Ten receive scholarships of $10,000 to $40,000. The others get $1,000 each.

Films

Filmed material to reach schools is often effective, but costs dissuade some sponsoring organizations. In some cases a portion of the cost of a film for school use can be recouped through sale of prints, when the film is considered by schools to be truly educational.

Among the firms sponsoring such school films have been a bank (on credit), a container company (on lunchroom etiquette), and a cosmetic company (on grooming).

It is often advisable to set up a panel of educational consultants or a special board of advisors made up of nationally known persons in the educational field when launching a special project or educational resource program.

Basic principles of dealing with schools as a publicity medium require that the publicizing organization adhere to the following guidelines:

1. Refrain from being too commercial.

2. Hold the educational needs and interests of students as the paramount consideration.

3. Avoid activities that may interfere with studies or unbalance the daily schedule.

4. Remember that schools must never be used to promote any activities except those conducted for public benefit.

5. Remember that school activities and materials must always conform to standards of educational value, factual accuracy, and good taste.

College students can be reached with information of direct interest to them through college newspapers and magazines. Nearly ten thousand such publications are listed in the *Directory of College Student Press in America*, Oxbridge Communications, 150 Fifth Avenue, New York, NY 10011.

33

HOW TO USE GRAPHICS AND PRINTING

PAUL R. NELSON

Paul R. Nelson, retired board chairman of Flagler & Nelson, Inc., Buffalo, New York, had broad experience in public relations and in graphic arts for more than forty-three years. A former vice-president and director of public relations for The Birge Company of Buffalo, he was also account executive with Selvage & Lee, public relations counsel. He is a past chairman of the Advertising Agency Council of the Buffalo Area Chamber of Commerce.

A graduate of the University of Illinois School of Journalism, he has been a typography salesman, printing estimator, and assistant sales manager of a printing plant. He was a member of the editorial staff of the St. Louis Post-Dispatch *and has edited a number of internal and external company publications.*

Printing's Crucial Uses in Public Relations

Despite the virtual explosion of communication technologies—from solid state, to satellites, interfaces, floppy disks, lasers, multiple terminals, computers, and networking systems—don't expect graphics and printed matter to go the way of the buggy whip.

Today, through satellite systems, national newspapers simultaneously print on the east and west coasts. Similarly, major metropolitan newspapers in many areas operate satellite printing plants in the suburbs so newspapers can reach readers more quickly with the latest news. Computerized word processing and "publishing" systems can be used to set hundreds of different typefaces and to lay out entire pages of type with photographs sized, cropped, and in position. These computer-generated pages are then transferred to a disk or tape and sent to a printer, or they can be electronically transferred over a network to the printer. The printer utilizes these electronic text and graphic files to print the newspapers. Today many printers use laser-enhanced equipment that reproduces faster than most other forms of printing units and often with equivalent or better quality.

The need to distribute printed matter to various interest groups continues unabated. In recent years the number of magazines targeted at small groups with special interests has vastly increased. Though newspapers have contended with the bugs of electronic transmission to control information normally distributed by the graphic arts community, the public relations profession must continue to inform a multitude of interest groups directly by using its own printed matter. Now, more than ever, the public relations practitioner must have a command of the basics of printing to properly instruct those preparing printed matter—thereby preventing delays and costly errors.

There are many types of printing and printers, and each has its use for someone in public relations. In printing, as in almost any trade or business, you usually get what you pay for. Since labor costs in a given locality are about the same and material costs usually are identical, price differences almost always reflect differences in quality. Most printers can give constructive counsel in the preparation of printed matter. The more a public relations person tells the printer, the more he or she understands the printer's problems, the better results will be from cost, quality, and service standpoints. Therefore, it is desirable for the public relations person to know the basics about printing, and it is particularly important to become familiar with the following fundamentals:

- The principles of layout and graphic design
- Types and uses of printed material in public relations
- Methods of distributing public relations printed matter
- Printing processes and techniques
- Preparing copy for printing
- Typography

Types and Uses of Printed Media

Basically, there are three forms of printed matter:

1. The flat piece called a *sheet* or *leaf*
2. The *folded sheet*, or folder
3. The *book* made up of a collection of leaves

These basic forms, used in varying sizes and shapes, are utilized frequently by the public relations person in his or her work.

Announcements

In addition to news releases, there are many occasions when public relations people will be called on to prepare formal announcements of consolidations, purchases, new products, new offices, changes in offices, changes in officers or directors.

Annual report

The yearly summation of a firm's financial activities for the information of stockholders and employees is presented in the annual report. (*See* Chapter 11.)

Answer set

Response to inquiries stimulated by product publicity should be carefully planned. Too often this phase is overlooked or left to someone not concerned with a company's public image. Materials included in such an answer, such as a form letter, brochures, and samples, are called "Answer Sets." Answer Sets should go out as soon after receipt of an inquiry as possible. Answer Sets will vary with the reader audiences, which may be the general public, dealers, or industrial or commercial users.

Award

Sometimes takes the form of a hand-lettered and framed citation or a printed certificate, much like a diploma. The art of hand lettering or caligraphy is fast disappearing but may still be found in major metropolitan areas. Script and cursive faces, now available in digigal typesetting, are used increasingly.

Book

In addition to annual reports, on other occasions public relations people may use the book form for a special testimonial when a highly esteemed person retires from active business, for textbooks used in employee training, and, rarely, for a biography or historical sketch, where the life of an individual or organization is particularly interesting to the public. (*See* Chapter 24.)

When publications of such proportions are planned it is generally advisable to obtain the counsel of experienced book designers.

Booklet

A stitched pamphlet of eight or more pages, usually with a cover, the booklet ordinarily is small enough to be carried in a pocket. This form frequently is used for employee manuals, union agreements, group insurance, and profit-sharing or pension programs.

Broadside

A single sheet of paper with at least two folds, a broadside usually opens up to a large display (*see* "Bulletin" and "Clipsheet"). It is economical because it requires no binding. Sometimes it is used as a self-mailer.

Brochure

Larger, more impressive booklets, such as anniversary books or histories, are called brochures. Generally, they are distinguished from books and catalogs by their binding, which usually is saddlewire stitching.

Bulletin

The bulletin may be an official notice posted on a company's bulletin boards, a factual report sent to technical people in an industry, or informative material sent to salespeople, distributors, or dealers. Bulletins are issued at irregular intervals when information becomes available. They may be used, for example, to encourage employee participation in a suggestion program or to advise distributors or dealers of opportunities to capitalize on something newsworthy.

Circular

An announcement of an activity, event, or product prepared in any of the three printing forms. A circular may be used, for example, to announce the opening of a store, to describe an organization launching a fund-raising campaign, to announce a contest, or to describe a new product.

Clipsheet

A sheet or bulletin containing a variety of stories, filler material, illustrations, and charts prepared in newspaper style and mailed to editors is called a clipsheet. Clipsheets may be accompanied by mats or glossy proofs of certain material, particularly illustrations and charts, to encourage use by publications that otherwise might find reproduction costs prohibitive. Clipsheets enable overworked editors to see at a glance how the stories would appear in their publications.

Comic book

An effective means of mass dissemination of a message in pictorial form.

Company publication

A periodical publication in booklet form, designed either as a magazine or newspaper, which explains the philosophy of a firm's management to customers, dealers, or employees, and promotes goodwill. (*See* Chapter 12.)

Computer letters

It is now common to individualize form letters printed by computer, inserting names and addresses in the body of the letter.

Employee manual

This is an informative handbook or guide explaining company policies, shop practices, employee benefits, obligations, and privileges—an excellent opportunity to build goodwill among employees. It is usually prepared in booklet or loose-leaf form.

Fact sheet

Detailed background information and data that may be included in a press kit with a news release, captioned photographs, and samples.

Flip cards

Generally reproduced in small quantities, frequently by silk screen process, flip cards are effective aids in oral presentations of corporate messages to community, family groups, customers, and stockholders.

Illustrated letter

This is usually a four-page folder 8½″ × 11″ with the front page resembling a letterhead and designed to carry a typed, signed message. The other pages may carry pertinent illustrations and printed matter.

Insert

A folder or leaflet enclosed in pay envelopes or accompanying correspondence with dealers or customers is called an insert.

Instruction book

The instruction book is a booklet or manual, occasionally a book, used to teach the proper usage of equipment or materials.

Invitations

Invitations to press parties, open houses, and other important functions vary from the severely simple, formal invitations to very colorful printed pieces, which may include specially designed envelopes, to attract attention and to pique the interest of editors and writers regularly bombarded with requests to attend press parties or special affairs.

Leaflet

A thin printed booklet. Often a single sheet folded once. Used for carrying a specific message, for wide distribution, envelope enclosure, and so on.

Memorandum

Usually a booklet, a memorandum is used to inform legislators of an organization's views on a matter of public interest such as pending legislation.

Newsletter

A publication usually 8½″ × 11″ that goes periodically to a specific audience to convey news, opinion, or other information. It usually consists of four pages, but can be more or only two. (*See* also Chapter 31.)

News release

Release forms are sheets bearing the name, address, fax number, and phone number of the organization issuing the release. (*See* Chapter 20.)

Pamphlet

Similar to a leaflet, though often containing more pages.

Paperbacks

Associations and corporations call on the producers of paperback books to tell their industry or corporation stories to the public. Generally the industry or corporation will find that in addition to the books purchased for distribution through industry or corporation channels, paperback producers will place quantities of such books on sale at bookstands through their regular book distribution channels. (*See* Chapter 24.)

Posters

There will be times when posters, single leaves of paper or card, should be posted in public places to announce a public meeting, an open house, or some other event of general interest. Poster messages should be brief and exceptionally legible.

Press kit

Package of material generally containing one or more news releases, photographs, fact sheets, and, occasionally, samples provided for those attending a press party or conference.

Questionnaire

Usually questionnaires are sheets or folders containing questions with space provided for answers. They should be designed for ease in answering, returning, and collating the gathered information.

Reports

Reports of special findings or surveys that require wide dissemination may be printed in book form. Many firms make special reports of progress to their employees on their business at the time financial or annual reports are made to stockholders. They may be in booklet or newspaper style.

Return card

A return card is enclosed in a mailing, often postage-free, for the convenience of readers.

Self-mailer

This is a direct-mail folder, booklet, or book that can be mailed without an envelope or wrapper.

Welcome booklet

An informative booklet on a company and its products for distribution to visitors at a firm's reception desk. It is an excellent means of making a visitor's lasting first impression of an organization a good one.

White paper

See "Memorandum."

Distributing Printed Matter

Time and *appropriateness* are of primary importance in distributing public relations literature. Postage economy is of secondary importance, but it is inappropriate for a public relations person to use postage needlessly.

Items of a very timely nature, such as releases, annual reports, clipsheets, and questionnaires, generally are mailed at first-class rates to assure prompt delivery. Often, to overcome a natural tendency by recipients to discount the importance of printed matter dispatched by third- or fourth-class mail, the public relations person will send other printed matter such as booklets, bulletins, circulars, and illustrated letters at first-class rates.

Occasionally company publications may be mailed first class. More often, they will be mailed at lower rates.

Ask the post office about current postal rates and regulations. By consulting on mailings you will facilitate the handling of your printed matter and avoid costly errors and delays.

Printing Methods and Technologies

The printing industry has been undergoing immense change. Today the computer, video screen, and laser are taking over many functions.

Offset lithography

This has become the method used most frequently for printing materials—including public relations material.

Offset printing permits many economies. Word processors and laser imagesetters permit imprinting directly from typing, and the "hard copy" can be reproduced readily.

Offset permits soft gradations in color tones, enhancing the appearance of printed color solids, tints, screens, and both black and white or color photographs.

Silk screen

One of the oldest forms of printing, silk screen printing until recently was too slow and too costly for public relations people to use except on rare occasions. Now that screens can be prepared photographically rather than hand cut and screening is mechanical rather than by hand, the use of this process is expected to increase.

One of the most commonly recognized uses of silk screen is for materials that glow in the dark. Silk screen is excellent for posters.

Silk screen printing uses a transfer of ink through the mesh of a silk (or other material) screen stencil by use of a squeegee. The ink is pressed directly onto the paper, cloth, or other surface. The inks, either opaque or transparent, usually are deposited in layers.

Copiers

Advances in copying systems are so frequent it is difficult to keep pace with them. With so much to choose from, the public relations executive must constantly bear in mind the end product desired—the copy. Cost per copy, quantities desired, quality, speed and ease of operation, and space required should be considered when planning lease or purchase.

Copying devices now turn out copies at rates as high as five thousand an hour on ordinary bond paper—and the companies in this field are investing heavily in research that will bring about continuing advances.

Desktop publishing

This method has expanded the use of computers for printing. Employing a word processing program, specially designed software, and a laser printer, a personal computer user can write, lay out, typeset, and print a piece—without leaving the office.

The growth of desktop publishing can be attributed to ongoing advancements in the technology. Better software packages and laser printers have helped spread desktop publishing to small as well as large firms. Professional desktop publishers can produce material with ranges up to four colors at very little cost.

To begin desktop publishing, hardware and software must be chosen. The decision on which hardware (computer components) and software (computer programs) to select is based on the needs of the user—present and future. A consultant can assess those needs to help avoid making costly mistakes.

Text Preparation for Printing

Typesetters, desktop publishers, and printers are skilled in handling copy and exert every effort to turn out work that will reflect to their credit. Unfortunately, they are not mind-readers.

Clean copy properly marked, correctly cropped and scaled artwork, and an accurate and detailed layout are your best assurances of a good job. Don't expect printers to think for you. Their responsibility is to follow copy.

Copy tips

- Copy should be typewritten with the lines double- or triple-spaced.

- At least one inch should be allowed for margins on all sides.
- Place the word *more* at the bottom of a page if copy continues to the next page.
- Type on only one side of a sheet of paper.
- Number pages and place an identifying word or phrase at the top of each page.
- Clearly indicate end of copy.
- Mark copy to show where copy is to go in layout, such as "Copy A" or "Caption 1," duplicating such markings in the layout.

Artwork

Photographs, drawings, tint blocks, and other decorative matter should be marked for size and position in the finished job.

Never mark on the back or face of a photograph with a hard pencil or pen, for it is very likely the impression will be picked up in reproduction.

Your advertising department or advertising agency probably deals with art studios and freelance artists having special talents. One may be a retoucher, another may do excellent line art, another wash drawings, and one may be a cartoonist. When in need of specific art talent, get a specialist to do the work for you. It will save you time and money and will result in a better job.

With today's technology much of the above is becoming obsolete. A professional desktop publisher can handle your entire job and, working with your printer, can produce the project on disk for quick and efficient turnaround.

Layout

In determining the layout or format of a printed piece—the binding or folding, colors, illustrations, paper, shape, and size—it is advisable to consult someone fully experienced in printing matters until you become

familiar enough with printing processes to avoid costly mistakes.

The design of printed matter is an art comparable to architecture; in fact, many of the basic concepts of printing design are based on architectural symmetry. As in architecture, printing avoids the use of the perfect square in illustrations, blocks of copy, and sheet dimensions as being monotonous. Preferable dimensions approximate the "Golden Oblong" of architecture, a three-to-five or five-to-eight proportion.

When placing illustrations in a layout, attention should be given to balancing one illustration with another or with a block of copy. The balance of a page revolves around the optical center, which is equidistant from left- to right-hand sides and slightly above the center of the page from top to bottom.

A solid page of text is dull and repelling, except in books of fiction where readers have become accustomed to accepting such a format. Even in books of fiction, an attempt is made to break up solid masses of type with frequent paragraphing.

Another important rule is to use type with serifs in body copy. Sans serif faces tire the eye and quickly repel the reader when they are used for more than a few words. It is considered by some people to be old-fashioned to use the easy-to-read faces that have been standard in book publishing for many years, but in this case the new is not the best.

In selecting type variations for a layout, select type that will reflect the message you wish to convey. Select type variations that will harmonize, and avoid too many type variations.

For the beginner, the simplest and safest means of obtaining an attractive printed piece is to confine selections to the variations within one type family—variations such as boldface, condensed, italic, all capital letters, capitals and small capital letters—and changes in type sizes.

When making layouts in which illustrations are to bleed (run all the way to the edge), make certain to indicate the bleed plainly, both on the illustration and the layout, providing at least one-eighth of an inch additional area to assure a clean trim.

When possible, the head and foot of a page should be squared off. It is bad to end a page or start a new one with a "widow"—a short line of reading matter.

Pictures should face into the copy they illustrate, or in the direction the designer wishes the reader's eye to follow, wherever possible.

Long blocks of copy should be broken with subheads to relieve the monotony and encourage the reader to continue.

Use of color

Color adds greatly to the impact of printed materials. The extent of its effects varies with subject matter—whether the material deals with sober information or less-demanding subject matter, as well as other factors. A study of the effects of color made by Kinko's, the copying service company, resulted in these suggestions:

• Use color sparingly. Concentrate it in a few large areas on pages rather than scattering it throughout a document. Be careful with colored headlines. They may grab attention and cause readers to skip adjacent text.

• Avoid too many different colors. The human brain seeks a sense of order. It cannot process chaos. Too many colors confuse and cause the reader to reject the image. Black plus one or two accent colors is best. An effective use of one accent color is to have it at full value in some areas and screened in a lighter tint in others.

• Use color to communicate, not to decorate. A color scheme should be easy to understand so it enhances and simplifies a document. Apply color consistently and use it to link elements together logically.

• Don't sacrifice legibility. Limit color in body copy and make sure it contrasts strongly with adjacent colors. Colored or reversed type may need to be larger and bolder. Be very careful with backgrounds. Black text on white background is easiest to read. Otherwise you may sacrifice legibility.

• Select colors to convey an image. Make sure the colors work well in both presentation and printed pieces. Be consistent.

Material in different colors should *never* be overprinted if legibility would suffer. The objective is to communicate, not to impress the reader with one's "creativity."

Typography Techniques

Today's "composing room" is electronic, using laser technology. They create impressions that can be used directly in the printing process.

Automation is rapidly changing all stages of printing so it is difficult to keep up with the advances. The public relations professional who may not be in constant touch with the printing industry would be well-advised to use the services of a professional for most printing needs.

Teletypesetting

This method whereby the same copy may be set in type simultaneously in widely separated printing establishments is of importance to public relations people, principally in dealing with newspaper chains using such facilities. It emphasizes the importance of sending information to the main office. The increase of multiplant commercial printing operations would indicate that this method of composition might prove helpful in handling the dissemination of large-scale, bulky printing.

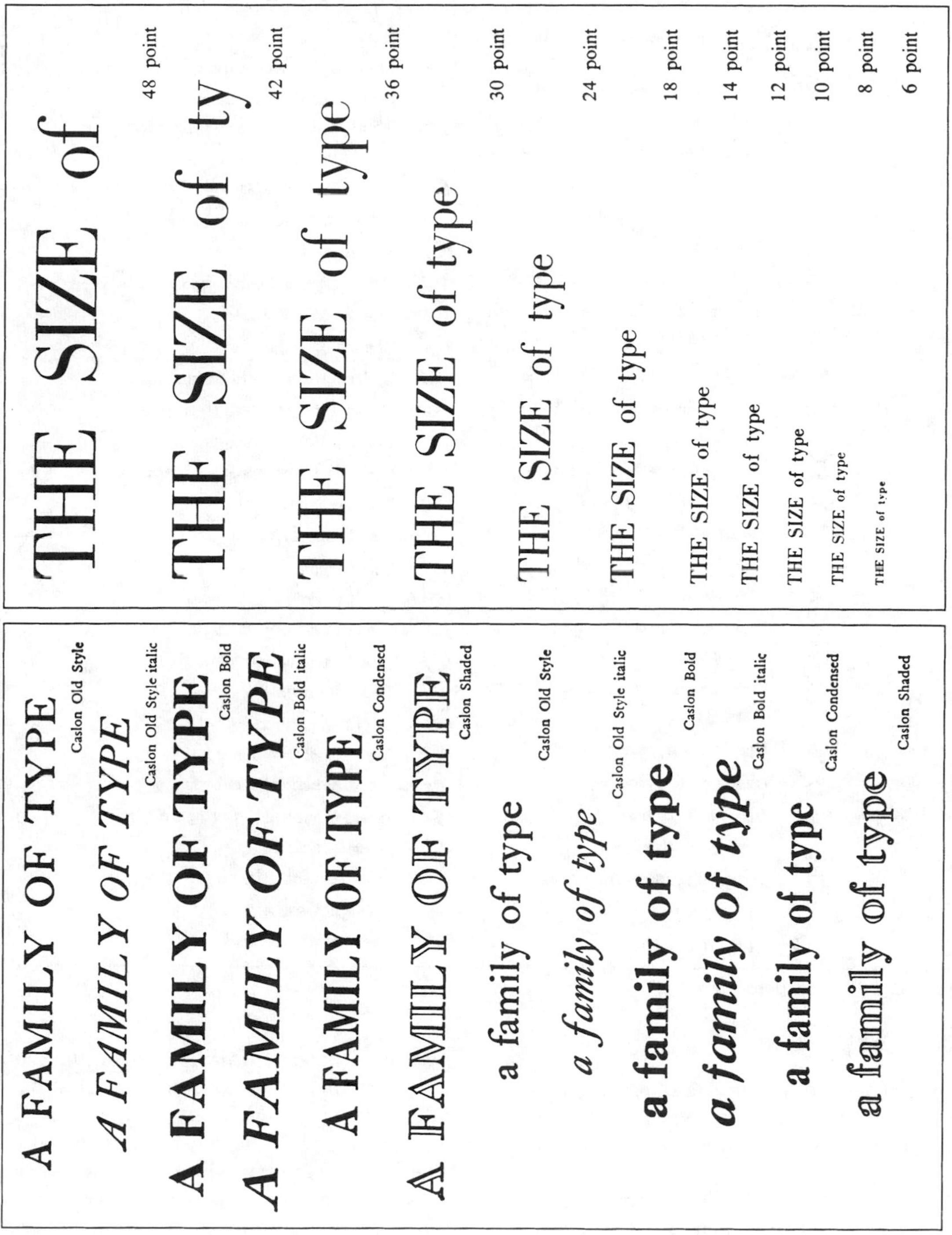

THE SIZE of — 48 point

THE SIZE of ty — 42 point

THE SIZE of type — 36 point

THE SIZE of type — 30 point

THE SIZE of type — 24 point

THE SIZE of type — 18 point

THE SIZE of type — 14 point

THE SIZE of type — 12 point

THE SIZE of type — 10 point

THE SIZE of type — 8 point

THE SIZE of type — 6 point

A FAMILY OF TYPE — Caslon Old Style

A FAMILY OF TYPE — Caslon Old Style italic

A FAMILY OF TYPE — Caslon Bold

A FAMILY OF TYPE — Caslon Bold italic

A FAMILY OF TYPE — Caslon Condensed

A FAMILY OF TYPE — Caslon Shaded

a family of type — Caslon Old Style

a family of type — Caslon Old Style italic

a family of type — Caslon Bold

a family of type — Caslon Bold italic

a family of type — Caslon Condensed

a family of type — Caslon Shaded

Figure 33.1 At left, font variations of one roman-style family (Caslon) and at right, common type sizes (Bodoni Book).

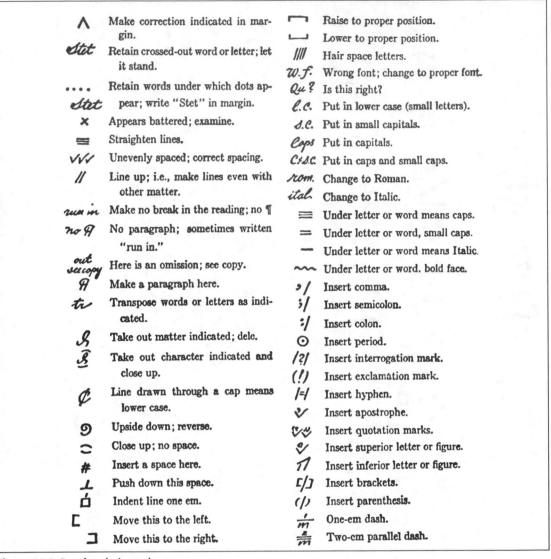

∧	Make correction indicated in margin.	⌐	Raise to proper position.
Stet	Retain crossed-out word or letter; let it stand.	⌐	Lower to proper position.
....	Retain words under which dots appear; write "Stet" in margin.	////	Hair space letters.
Stet		*w.f.*	Wrong font; change to proper font.
×	Appears battered; examine.	*Qu?*	Is this right?
⸗	Straighten lines.	*l.c.*	Put in lower case (small letters).
⋁⋀⋁	Unevenly spaced; correct spacing.	*s.c.*	Put in small capitals.
//	Line up; i.e., make lines even with other matter.	*Caps*	Put in capitals.
run in	Make no break in the reading; no ¶	*C+s.c.*	Put in caps and small caps.
no ¶	No paragraph; sometimes written "run in."	*rom.*	Change to Roman.
out see copy	Here is an omission; see copy.	*ital.*	Change to Italic.
¶	Make a paragraph here.	⸗	Under letter or word means caps.
tr	Transpose words or letters as indicated.	=	Under letter or word, small caps.
ℐ	Take out matter indicated; dele.	—	Under letter or word means Italic.
ℐ	Take out character indicated and close up.	∼	Under letter or word. bold face.
¢	Line drawn through a cap means lower case.	,/	Insert comma.
⑨	Upside down; reverse.	;/	Insert semicolon.
⌒	Close up; no space.	:/	Insert colon.
#	Insert a space here.	⊙	Insert period.
⊥	Push down this space.	/?/	Insert interrogation mark.
□	Indent line one em.	(!)	Insert exclamation mark.
[	Move this to the left.	/=/	Insert hyphen.
]	Move this to the right.	᾿⌄	Insert apostrophe.
		⌄⌄	Insert quotation marks.
		⌄/	Insert superior letter or figure.
		⋀	Insert inferior letter or figure.
		[/]	Insert brackets.
		(/)	Insert parenthesis.
		$\frac{1}{m}$	One-em dash.
		$\frac{2}{m}$	Two-em parallel dash.

Figure 33.2 Proofreader's marks.

Font Styles

Sans serif describes a number of typefaces that have no serifs and are recognized as "modern." These typefaces work well when used as headlines.

Italic type originally was designed as a spacesaver. The principal uses for italic today are to *emphasize* words or phrases; indicate *foreign words or phrases*; show the *title of a* *book, play,* or *periodical*; indicate an *individual letter* when referred to in copy; and provide *variety in headlines*.

Roman type is the most commonly used type in this country. There are many variations of roman type, but all roman types have one thing in common—serifs—and it is the variations in the serifs that largely account for the differences in roman type.

Type families

A type family includes all of the sizes and variations of a typeface such as italic, boldface, boldface italic, condensed, expanded, extra condensed, inline, outline, extended, and so on. (*See* Figure 33.1, page 491.)

Type is measured in "points," each of which equals ¹⁄₇₂ of an inch. "Body type"—the typeset material of the main portion of books, magazines, newspapers, leaflets, and other printed material—is generally set in sizes ranging from 7 point to 12 point, and heads and subheads are generally set in the main text size or larger.

Selecting a typeface

There is a seemingly endless number of type faces and their variations. When selecting

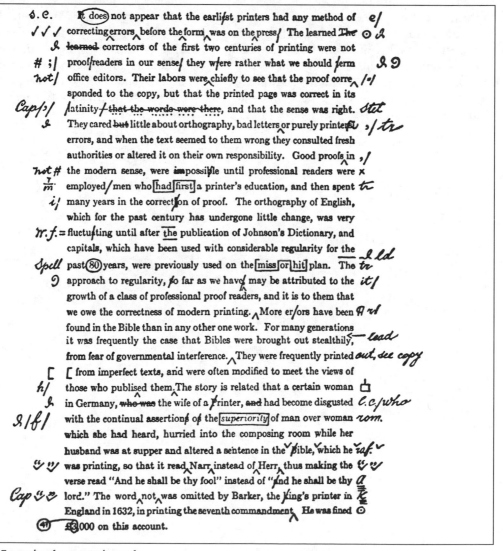

Figure 33.3 Example of corrected proof.

typefaces, it is well to know which families are available to you through your supplier.

In most typefaces, the public relations person may obtain additional interesting contrasts in the same face and size by using capitals, capitals and small capitals, small capitals, boldface, and so on.

Leading

Once type sizes and faces have been selected, the amount of space between the lines of type must be decided. A tiny amount of space is "built in" to each type font, but additional space is generally added in one-point increments. A minimum of two points extra space, called *leading*, is considered best for readability but can be sacrificed in cases of very

tight fit. Copy is said to be set "solid" when no leading has been added.

Proofreading

There are two systems for marking proofs, the *book* system and the *guideline* system. The guideline system simply circles the section in the text that needs correcting and draws a line to the nearest margin where the proper proof marks are made. The guideline is used primarily on newspapers.

The book system is the better system for public relations people to use, for there is less likelihood of confusion, particularly when it is necessary to make many corrections. Figures 33.2 and 33.3 (on pages 492 and 493) show the standard proofreader's marks and their application.

Section 5

HOW AN ORGANIZATION UTILIZES PUBLIC RELATIONS

34

THE UTILITY AND ITS PUBLICS

HOWARD A. PRAEGER
JAMES F. MINEHAN

Howard A. Praeger, before his retirement, was assistant to the president of New York State Electric & Gas Corp., a utility serving one-third of the area of New York State.

He was associated with public utilities for more than twenty-five years, primarily in the field of public relations and advertising. He was a reporter on daily newspapers and had editorial and business experience in book publishing.

James F. Minehan was manager of public information for New York State Electric & Gas Corp. He joined the public relations and advertising department in 1958 as a copywriter, specializing in employee communications and press relations. He was named head of the department in 1971.

Mr. Minehan is former chairman of the Public Relations Committee of the New York Power Pool and former president of the Public Relations Society of the Southern Tier (NY). He has served as a national officer of the American Association of Industrial Editors.

Practicing good public relations is vitally important to utilities—for whom the word *public* is virtually synonymous with the word *customers.* Conversely, however, utilities are prone to the changing winds of public opinion that blow across the country and especially through their individual service areas.

An effective public relations program for a utility fundamentally includes customer-oriented objectives, sound management, and the ability not only to give customers quality service at a fair price but also to communicate favorably with them in every way. One of the most difficult concepts for customers to understand is that the utility must provide investors with a fair and reasonable return so they can provide customers with the quality service they need and demand.

Today most people take for granted their ability to access the services provided by utilities. They often think of the utility in simplistic terms, rather than as the complex operation it is. For, in a very real sense, a utility is a corporation that must manufacture its own consumer product (electricity) or buy from national pipeline suppliers (natural gas). It must engage in all the marketing development and servicing generally found in many different business organizations marketing consumer goods.

The public relations executive within the company, often assisted by outside counsel, must be on the policy-making level. Through recommendations, leadership, and participation in policy decisions, he or she must ensure that good public relations is the concern of everyone in the company. Just as Socrates was the gadfly to the conscience of the State, the public relations practitioner needs, on occasion, to act as a gadfly to the conscience of a corporation.

Thus the executive responsible for public relations in a utility and his or her key assistants keep the two-way channels of communication open between the company and the public and within the corporate organization itself. These techniques of communication may well be called the tactical side of the operation. The strategic side of public relations is understanding changing public opinion and keeping the policies of the company harmonious with the desires of the public— and in many instances showing real leadership in the communities served. On the tactical level alone, the person with assigned public relations responsibilities is merely carrying out policy that has been formulated by the organization's executive management. On the strategic level, he or she enters the policy-forming councils of the company and in a large measure helps to set policy. And it is only when the public relations person begins to think as a manager and understands all aspects of the business that he or she can help the company live in harmony with society.

A Unique Environment

The utility business is different in concept and operations from other investor-owned, business-managed corporations. This chapter examines both the concerns and opportunities that utilities have in an era of heightened social awareness and competition. Young people who are interested in public relations careers will find employment in the utility field both stimulating and rewarding. Of primary concern is the operation of the investor-owned electric and gas utilities, but the concerns and opportunities that call for constant public relations judgments are often similar for airlines, railroads, and the telephone industry as well. The telephone utilities especially have community concerns that are quite comparable to electric and gas utilities; we will note these in commenting on some of the special considerations they must meet.

Public utilities today vary greatly in size, in character of the areas served, and in gross revenues received from customers. These variations naturally influence public relations programs. Utilities serving great urban centers cannot possibly have as close person-to-person relationships as those serving smaller cities and villages or predominantly rural areas.

However, utilities exist by virtue of franchises to serve specific areas and, from the point of view of public relations, utilities should perform as if they were re-earning the franchise to do business every day. The public utility, being "affected with a public interest," must serve all the public without discrimination as to rates, service, and employment policies. This is a proper responsibility, but one that requires constant attention and review.

An overriding obligation of utilities is meeting the growth in the use of energy. That growth may be broadly equated with the standard of living and working in America . . . or worldwide with that of civilization. Since the Arab oil embargo of 1973–74, growth rates of electric consumption have diminished but have not leveled off. Interaction of a broad range of social factors, difficult to predict with certainty, determines long-range rates of energy growth. But data clearly indicate new facilities must be built to meet future needs.

The public relations challenge is compounded by the long lead times necessary to build economical and reliable production facilities. Ten or more years are needed for electric generating stations, three or more for natural gas sources. Consumers, accustomed to dealing with much shorter time spans, cannot easily reconcile their perceptions of change with the need of utility managers to press on with construction programs despite a drop in overall usage rates and a rapidly changing pattern of competition. While consumers mistrust utility efforts to build new facilities, utilities dare not accept short-term trends, since to do so could lead to the crippling of the public's economic and social well-being.

Because of the nature of utility service and changing perceptions by consumers of their self-interest, clashes about how best to serve the overall public interest are increasingly common. One of the challenge areas involves *consumerism.* Another involves *environmental considerations.* A third is competition and market forces. All of these issues have economic and social impacts on consumers and the overall economic and social systems that people accept without thought. (*See* Figure 34.1, page 500.)

The resulting dialogue often escalates to widespread levels, as in the case of voting about the value of constructing nuclear electric generating stations and long-distance gas pipelines across Alaskan wilderness. Strong spokespersons of superior talent are needed to assure that the public will have enough information to make wise choices.

Relations with many publics

Although utilities do have a specific public—customers within the franchise area—they actually have many publics and through the proper consideration of all these publics, a successful public relations effort benefits from a synergistic effect.

However desirable it may seem to the orderly mind, one cannot place each person in only one of the publics (as in a pigeonhole) and deal only with one approach to an individual. Although it is true that there are special interests and associations, there are also overlapping interests. The public relations function should embrace all of the relations between an organization and its publics because all affect a company's reputation.

Customers who are, of course, the primary public that receives the company's service are classified as residential, industrial, commercial, and prospective customers of certain categories, as well as municipalities. But there are other vitally important publics, too; for example, governmental publics, the financial community, communities served, trade allies, utility industry peers, industry associations such as the Edison Electric Institute and the American Gas Association, the educational community, and the media. Employees, too, are often regarded as special members of the public as well as company workers.

Customers

In addition to quality service at a fair price, many other functions can be provided to customers. Services that can enhance the character of the utility include information on how to get the best performance from appliances, economies that will benefit the customer, improved operations for commercial and industrial enterprises, better lighting for communities, and information regarding safe practices in the use of electricity and gas. In addition, the people must understand the reasons for safe practices in regard to transmission lines and substations.

Today there is growing customer interest in residential and commercial electric heat and that interest provides a good opportunity for public relations. Utility specialists

American Public Power Association

News

2301 M St. N.W.
Washington, D.C. 20037-1484
202/467-2900
FAX 202/467-2910

For information: Madalyn Cafruny 202/467-2952
James J. Nipper 202/467-2931

PRIVATE COMPANY 'POWER GRAB' ENDANGERS CONSUMER INTEREST
AS CONGRESS MARKS UP BILLS TO SELL FEDERAL RESOURCES

WASHINGTON, D.C., Sept. 18, 1995 – Tomorrow will be a day of
reckoning for American consumers as three Congressional committees begin
to mark up bills that could send all consumers' electric rates soaring, according
to Alan H. Richardson, executive director, American Public Power
Association.

"The issue is this: Will the nation's waterways continue to belong to the
American people, or will they be sold to private companies with deep pockets
and the desire to own and control our natural resources?", Richardson said.

The House Commerce Committee, House Resources Committee, and
Senate Energy and Natural Resources Committee will each consider separate
but similar proposals to sell federal resources to private power companies.

At stake are three of the federal power marketing administrations
(PMAs). The House Commerce and Senate bills propose to sell Southeastern
Power Administration that provides electricity to citizens in 11 states and
Southwestern Power Administration that provides power in seven states. The
House Resources Committee proposes to sell Southeastern Power
Administration and study sale of Southwestern Power Administration. The
House bills also put on the table studies to sell the Western Area Power
Administration, serving 15 states.

"Privatization 'fever' coupled with its desire for quick cash has prompted
Congress to consider a grave abrogation of its responsibility to the American
people," Richardson warned. "The Congress is placing the corporate interest
before the public interest by proposing to sell these valuable assets to the highest
bidder. The immediate result will be much higher electric rates, disruption of
local economies, and loss of public control of the nation's waterways."

-more-

The American Public Power Association is the national service organization representing the nation's more
than 2,000 local publicly owned electric utilities.

Figure 34.1 Press release from American Public Power Association opposing proposed privatization of three federal power marketing administrations (PMAS), publicly owned hydroelectric facilities. *Courtesy American Public Power Association, Washington, DC.*

can advise customers on the best utilization for their specific needs and make sure contractors understand proper installation procedures.

Regulatory agencies

The regulatory climate related to the utility's operations is extremely important. Utilities must ensure that they maintain effective communications with these agencies on both a state and federal level. Actually, the interests of regulators and customers are complementary and managements of utilities will not be successful in meeting their financial requirements if they ignore that fact. Regulation must simultaneously protect the interest of the consumer while providing the investor in utility securities with a fair and reasonable return so the utility can raise the capital necessary to assure adequate and dependable supplies of energy for the growing requirements of its service area.

Considerable expertise is required from the public relations executive and counsel in preparing the informative program for a rate increase. Public acceptance is vital in regard to rate submissions. Assessment of public opinion prior to submission of a new rate schedule should be a primary responsibility of public relations. This assessment is helped by opinion surveys, by counseling with the company's managers in various communities, and by a general appraisal of economic and social conditions. Regulatory bodies, too, feel that full informative programs for the public must be carried out with every rate submission.

Financial community

This community includes company stockholders, investors and potential investors, investment banking firms, institutional investors, commercial banks, security analysts, national financial press, and state and national leaders of business and industry whose interest in the particular utility might be primar-

ily financial. Included as well are stock exchanges and the Securities and Exchange Commission. Company relationships in this area call for considerable financial sophistication that many public relations people do not have. Consequently, these relationships are usually carried on by senior management and the company's general legal counsel through a virtually day-by-day association. The rules of full disclosure must be observed, and the public relations executive should be fully cognizant of the full disclosure requirements. (*See* Chapter 11.)

Although the public relations executive and staff may not be financial experts, they can contribute to financial relations in a significant way through preparation of financial news releases, assistance with the annual and quarterly reports to stockholders, and sound publicity exposure for company matters on the business pages of daily papers, in financial journals, and on radio and TV news programs.

The public relations executive may participate in procuring opinion surveys conducted by professional firms with security analysts and in evaluating those surveys. In the public utility field, these surveys should include a heavy sampling of opinion from the most influential analysts. Security analysts in our largest metropolitan areas have strong influence with investors in utilities.

Communities served

Deeper community involvement than in the past in socioeconomic programs of the company's service area can give the utility the kind of identity it needs. It can offset the idea many people have that the government should be the only participant in achieving new social and economic goals. We will examine some of these opportunities later.

Trade allies

Development and growth for utilities are closely associated with trade allies. These are manufacturers of household appliances and commercial and industrial equipment, distributors, contractors, and the various professional associations these allies are identified with in their business. In recent years the concept of trade allies has been broadened to include insulation manufacturers and retailers, proponents of energy-saving devices, architects, and others interested in energy conservation and preservation of resources.

Employee relations

It is a cardinal principle of public relations that good relations must begin with the particular organization. Employees can be the best goodwill ambassadors in the community or they can downgrade a company faster than disgruntled customers. Management, of course, must have an enlightened approach to employee relations or there is no bedrock on which to build community relations through employees. (*See* Chapter 12.) Like most other people, employees of a public utility think in terms of self-interest. However, because they are in a public service organization, they take pride in the character of their work as a public good.

What the employees think and say about the company on a people-to-people basis will carry more weight than any other single type of publicity. They all know many people in the territory served. The smaller the communities, the more effective the employee group will be. Although this need for employee enthusiasm and commitment is vitally important, many companies overlook the real asset they have in their own people. Because utilities generally offer security to employees, this advantage is a strong factor in maintaining employee stability. But a good program makes certain that security in the job does not create an unproductive employee and that the company does not allow long service and familiarity to stand in the way of employee advancement. The ways in which employees

can interpret and build the company's character will be considered in more detail later in this chapter (see "Communicating with Specific Groups").

Areas of Primary Concern

Consumerism

As indicated earlier, the public has a strong interest in consumerism. Perhaps the utility is less vulnerable to criticism from consumers than are manufacturers of goods and service enterprises. That is, the utility should be less vulnerable if it provides good service at a fair price and has sympathetic understanding from its public about the costs of doing business.

However, the utility that is operating in the interest of the consumer in every way the company can, may nevertheless stumble into pitfalls. This situation could be brought about through poor communications with its public, through inept handling of customer complaints, through a "we are always right" attitude. Although management may be trying hard to please customers, utility employees who develop bureaucratic attitudes may, on the face-to-face customer level or over the telephone, negate company policy.

The preservation of good customer relations requires constant vigilance. Is the point of view of the customer considered sympathetically? Can you admit that the company may be wrong in regard to a bill? If a shutoff notice is sent to the wrong person or hung on the doorknob, is there a recognizable signature on that notice that gives the customer someone to call immediately? Does the company have a list of qualified electricians, appliance service organizations, plumbers, and contractors that can be given to the customer who is new in the community or doesn't know where to get competent service?

Consumerism also includes being aware of the interests of such research groups as "Nader's Raiders," the groups of activist investigators who probe into many fields. Regulatory commissions must consider consumerism in all commission decisions. They are committed to the protection of the consumer and their rate and service decisions will be scrutinized closely by consumer groups.

The electric light and power industry continues to be more favorably regarded than a number of other major industries. However, reflecting a burst of cost increases in oil, 44 percent of people in a national survey felt the cost of electricity was rising faster than other costs; 70 percent felt rates were high or very high. While 23 percent were concerned about dependence on foreign oil and about 14 percent worried about shortages, 15 percent feared nuclear plants, and 21 percent worried about the effect of utilities on the environment. Surveys have demonstrated that those who are favorable toward the industry on a variety of questions are much more likely to consider rate increases justifiable. The value of good, lasting communications on basic issues is clearly demonstrated by the response.

Despite continued attacks by dedicated opponents, support for increased construction of nuclear power plants continued. In a survey by Market Facts in July 1989, 81 percent said nuclear energy should play an important role in U.S. energy strategy. Polls by Cambridge Reports and Gallup found that more than 75 percent of the public expect the United States will have to build more nuclear energy plants. However, questions of safety and the disposal of nuclear wastes continue to be major factors in dampening support.

Environment

Although ecologists, environmentalists, and undoubtedly philosophers have long recognized that everything on this earth has an effect on everything else, the concern with regard to environmental considerations had been limited until recently. Now it seems everyone has discovered the "environment." Everyone wants to save it, but specific ecological knowledge on how to do it has been limited.

Once the sweeping environmental reform movement became active, the electric utility industry committed manpower and money to achieve notable results. Costs of meeting environmental regulations were an estimated $55.1 billion between 1980 and 1990, increasing capital expenditures of the industry by 10.8 percent. Other costs of meeting regulations, estimated at $13.4 billion, increased annual operating expenses by 19 percent. Costs have continued to increase since.

A great public relations and management challenge has emerged as a result of the disparity between people's attitudes about the need for environmental protection and their distaste for higher rates. Costs associated with environmental protection are not easily identified, particularly when they are not associated with "add on" features but rather with a state of mind that influences basic planning and simply rules out some design choices as environmentally unacceptable.

Furthermore, years can pass before environmental expenditures find their way into utility rates. The long lag between action and rate change makes it hard to keep consumer awareness focused on the cost of environmental protection. When the costs show up on utility bills it is too late to retract the order. The utility, not the public call for environmental protection, may seem to be the problem. (*See* Figure 34.2, page 504.)

To date neither utility managements nor consumers have found mechanisms for determining how much money should be spent for various purposes. Environmental protection is not the only one. Others include providing poor and low-level fixed income persons with minimum amounts of energy for household purposes at rates they can afford;

Figure 34.2 A utility's concern for the environment and public opinion can be demonstrated effectively in the design of new facilities. Virginia Power's residential substation near Arlington, Virginia, is an outstanding example of utility engineering being applied to please the aesthetic interest of the community served.

how major facilities, such as power stations and high voltage transmission lines, should be located, assuming that power lines do not emit harmful radiation; and how utility rates should be designed to best serve complex social and economic needs of consumers and investors.

A host of considerations confront the utilities in relation to environment. Most utility managements have standing committees on environment or full-time technical experts with ecological experience. There is, in addition, the prominent role of the federal government. Most states have established environmental departments.

Don C. Underwood, public relations counselor who worked closely with electric utilities, suggested that the electric industry adopt the following position:

The electric utility industry asks the rest of society to recognize that both the industry and society are beset with a dilemma. The dilemma arises from the legitimacy of two social goals: one is the continuing development of future supplies of adequate, reliable electric power; the second is the preservation and improvement of our natural environment. These social goals are not and should not be allowed to become mutually exclusive. What this means is that we must take a "balanced approach" to these two goals. This balanced approach will have to be mapped out by all the sectors in our society which have a legitimate interest, working in close cooperation and taking into account all the factors involved. The industry is ready, willing and able to take this approach, but it requires the understanding and cooperation of society to do so.

Most people recognize that for every benefit there is a cost. Utilities are allocating substantial budgets to water resource studies aimed at pure-water objectives. They are adopting designs for transmission towers and substations that are aesthetically pleasing and safe. Utility managements adopted antipollution controls for their motor vehicle fleets in advance of any legal requirements. Many years ago most utility planning was characterized by a strictly engineering approach to projects—e.g., a straight line is the shortest distance between two points—but fortunately that attitude is no longer a dominant factor in the business. Technological research will undoubtedly show how to develop further operating procedures that will enhance the environment.

That environment costs must be met must be recognized not only by regulatory bodies, but by the public at large, which must pay for this protection in the price of the product. Communicating that fact effectively is the responsibility of those engaged in public relations. Attaining new social goals will cost money, and this fact will revise priorities in regard to how people budget expenditures.

Environmental considerations will be all-encompassing for utilities for many years. (*See* Chapter 2.) Expertise in this field will be a must for the utilities public relations officer.

The successful utility communicator will need to adopt imaginative approaches to the public, convince customers that the company has a commitment to preserving the environment, and point out the ways, for example, that the use of electricity for automobiles and in industrial and commercial enterprises

will reduce pollutants. He or she will need to work with management in developing a socially acceptable approach to choosing sites for new generating stations and transmission lines. He or she will need a thorough knowledge of the use of nuclear energy in generating electricity and in nuclear technology related to the development of natural gas resources.

Once a positive attitude toward environmental matters permeates management, it will act as a catalytic agent throughout the company. Members of employee speakers' groups can do much to acquaint the public with the environmental program. Actual commitment of expenditures with accompanying publicity will put the company on record as moving in the right direction. Plant tours for the public can acquaint them with newly installed equipment that controls air quality and thermal discharges to rivers and bodies of water.

Garnering Community Support

Utilities, because of their experience in business management and because their economic well-being depends on the economic and social health of their communities, should consider the many ways they can participate in advancing their service areas.

Industrial development

Traditionally, utilities have worked with community, regional, and state industrial development groups in encouraging industries already located in the area that are expanding to build their new facilities in the service area. Utility industrial development departments also work with other agencies to attract new industries to the area. Not only do they advertise nationally and provide pertinent site and economic information to industries, they can also, through news releases and service-area advertising, let the public know about their efforts to develop a healthy economy for the area.

Assistance for low- and middle-income families

The necessity of utility service for lighting, heating, and cooking is well recognized. The utility industry has adopted programs that involve education, budget assistance, and cooperation with public and private agencies.

Goals of specific programs change with time as social and economic conditions shift. During the 1960s several utilities earned considerable respect for programs to develop greatly needed housing and apartment projects. Of course, these had to meet various legal and regulatory standards.

During the 1970s, the need shifted to issues related to pocketbook problems. Consumers found household budgets getting strained by inflation. Utilities, which are particularly vulnerable to inflation, found it necessary to institute a series of rate increases. Gaining public acceptance of the reasons for price changes is not enough. Farsighted managements and public relations practitioners are also seeking ways for consumer to help themselves.

Many utilities have conducted programs involving energy conservation. Insulation is an inexpensive and convenient device for producing quick results. Booklets ranging from how to purchase and install insulation to how to decide the most cost-effective areas to insulate, for example, walls versus ceilings, are now widely available. Nearly all are distributed without charge. Most are written on behalf of local utilities and are therefore excellent guides based on local weather conditions, energy-use patterns, and energy costs. Some utilities have programs that provide their customers with financing assistance in buying insulation.

Also complex but promising are ways to help customers make conscious choices about when energy should be devoted to particular tasks. These take two basic forms: (a) controlling appliances so they operate only at specific times, or (b) charging different rates for energy consumption at various times. The goal is to encourage energy consumption when existing utility equipment can best meet the needs. This reduces the need to construct new facilities and avoids higher rates due to costs of financing construction and added interest on debt.

The implications of such programs are far-reaching. But it is obvious they present public relations issues of compelling proportions. Those practitioners who will do well in this area will have a thorough knowledge of utility financing, rate making, and the needs and aspirations of consumers.

Essential to the longest-range goal of better understanding is education of young people about the relationships between energy use, environmental protection, and economic stability at household, regional, and national levels. Teachers in many states now have access to instructional aids for all levels from elementary through college that deal with various aspects of energy issues. Those that have been most quickly adopted have been designed to fit into existing teaching syllabi. Restraint and acceptance by educators require that commercial messages not be included in material for classroom use.

Minority group hiring and training

Another plus for the utility in forwarding socioeconomic goals is through minority hiring and participation in essential training programs for the disadvantaged. Much progress is being made in this regard. Acceptance of this community responsibility enhances the character of the utility.

Community health, welfare, educational, and cultural interests

For many years utilities have supported the social agencies of their communities through contributions, service on boards of directors, and employee participation in the work of these agencies. Many employees have been engaged in volunteer work with youth groups, many serve on boards of education, and in rural areas a great many are in volunteer fire departments.

Utility managements have supported both private and public colleges through contributions, and they are contributing now to community cultural programs and foundations. In many states these contributions cannot be charged against operation; consequently they must come from earnings, the equity the shareholder has in the business.

A community is an intricate collection of groups, organizations, political, economic, and religious interests and affiliations, and although all industries need to be concerned with community involvement, it is particularly rewarding for the public utility. Members of a community, especially those who are concerned about its general welfare, are quick to recognize participation in the many worthwhile programs that make a community a better place. (*See* Chapter 8.)

Communicating with Specific Groups

Employee relations

As indicated earlier, in a utility employees form the basic foundation for developing good community relations. They are a direct link with the customer either through the requirements of their work or through community activities or with friends and neighbors. The astute practitioner will review the status of employee relations regularly. He or she will check the efficacy of the information program for employees and will be concerned with the company's training program for those employees who are in direct contact through their jobs with customers.

Effective communication with employees and good communication between all levels of supervision within today's corporation is one of the most difficult achievements in corporate relations. Supervisors find it difficult to communicate with those who report to them and often find it difficult to communicate with their own superiors.

Good communications within the corporation may well be more difficult to develop than good communications with the public. There is no easy road for the practitioner, who will need to try different programs and innovations and to rely to some extent on periodic employee opinion surveys.

Some guidelines will help, but none will guarantee success. We have indicated that utility employees, like others, think in terms of self-interest; they may read statements from executive management, but they are not "turned on" unless the matter touches on their self-interest.

A more detailed approach to employee communications in general is covered in Chapter 12, but we should briefly consider the methods one can use for communication within a utility.

For the new employee there is an orientation program and a handbook on opportunities, benefits, and obligations. Perhaps he or she has been reached originally through a recruiting booklet that has been prepared by a collaborative effort of the public and human resources departments. As an employee, he or she receives a company magazine or newspaper on a regular basis. Often this periodical goes to all the media within the service area as well.

Many utilities keep supervisors and key salaried employees acquainted with company affairs through a special management newsletter. Also, information programs prepared by the public relations department are often carried out through discussion sessions that a supervisor conducts with the group reporting to him or her. Electronic systems also have some distinct advantages because of the speed of transmittals. Desk-to-desk dialing systems, public address systems, fax, and closed-circuit television are used with increasing frequency.

Because of the ever-increasing tempo of American business, the ideal communications program can be organized to do four things:

1. Send important messages within seconds.

2. Send more detailed information to the entire employee force within hours.

3. Send regular, lengthy, and complete reports on major items of interest, trends, and long-range developments to the entire employee organization. Those lengthy communications may vary in form, content, and purpose, depending on what part of the employee force they are designed to reach. For example, research and development people do not have the same interests as supervisors, yet both groups need reliable information.

4. Allow easy and swift upward communication from all levels of the organization to the top.

One of the most effective ways informed employees can promote company public relations is through speakers' clubs. (*See* Chapter 31.) Only a limited number of talks need to be on company subjects. Let the employees of a utility choose their own material, be sure the presentation is sound, help with speech techniques through training courses, and see that top management keeps in touch with the program. If a company speaker has an interesting informative talk or an entertaining one, she will be well received. The very fact that he or she has come to speak to a group and is identified as an employee of a utility will benefit the utility's community relations.

Business and social peers

Active memberships in service clubs and other community clubs and organizations are important to utility community relations. Through these clubs a company can keep in touch with influential business and government people. Company policies can be explained in a friendly atmosphere; in critical situations community leaders can be reached quickly and can hear the company's side of a controversial issue.

Government agencies and officials

Because a utility exists by reason of franchise and is a regulated corporation "affected by a public interest," it is imperative that relations with this special public on every level of government be excellent. (*See* Chapter 6.)

These relationships are the responsibility of both senior management and company managers in each community. In addition to the company's own relationships, public relations and public affairs officers should be in touch with overall industry relations with government. They must study proposed legislation and regulation at all levels of government and the effect such legislation may have on utility operation.

Media relations

Good media relations are extremely important to utilities. Recommended press relations policies covered in Chapter 21 and elsewhere in Section 4 are pertinent to utilities. However, here again the peculiar nature of the utility business means that its operations are under daily scrutiny by all media.

Viewed as a public (rather than as media), the press is influential as an opinion molder among all the other publics. Even a newspaper's selection of letters to the editor can have an effect on the character of the utility. The attitude of columnists toward a company is also extremely important.

It is especially important that editorial department news people have the names of company people to call in case of emergency or just to make queries. A good idea is to see that a map of the utility's territory is also at hand. An ideal method is to prepare a brief press background kit that can be kept up-to-date and would be quickly available to news media. In addition to the information the media have, everyone in the utility company who has relations with the press should have a brief handbook on company press policy. It is virtually impossible for the central public relations department to report on regional storms and outages, for instance. Information of that type must be handled quickly by company people in the affected area.

Media relations through advertising

Although utilities are usually not major advertisers in their area, they may develop promotional advertising programs in support of dealers and contractors. The public relations executive has a policy responsibility in regard to this type of advertising because it reflects the character of a company.

The institutional advertising program is the special province of the public relations department. This program can be as varied as the ingenuity of the department can devise. Institutional advertising can expound the policies of a company and promote its services and special projects. Such advertising may be particularly helpful in rate submissions because it can present the company's position exactly, whereas the news releases may be subject to the vagaries of the particular reporter who will rewrite the story in his own style and the style of the newspaper—often with disastrous results.

In many states self-styled consumer advocates have challenged the right of utilities to charge some or all advertising costs to rate payers as a legitimate business expense. These efforts are in addition to long-standing involvement by regulatory agencies in determining what type of advertising expenses are acceptable for inclusion in rates. The practitioner must remain familiar with these efforts and work closely with legal counsel and senior management to protect consumer and business interests.

Considerations Specific to Telephone Utilities

As indicated earlier, the general business character of telephone utilities is comparable to a high degree with electric and gas utilities.

The telephone industry has been committed to extensive research programs for many years. That commitment has enabled it to achieve remarkable technological development. Meeting the accelerating demand has, of course, created some real problems. These have been primarily regional, and improvement of service in areas affected by extremely rapid growth in use is a prime concern.

One does not usually think of a great utility as being competitive but the telephone companies face increasing competition with respect to their services since the breakup of the Bell System created seven large regional companies and opened the way for scores of other manufacturers and service companies to compete in this industry. All of these companies face public relations problems and needs. They affect the use by millions of customers of not only basic telephone service but the transmission of data, computer communications, television transmission, teletype, facsimile, microwave relays, videoconferencing, and other services.

Expansion by cable TV and other communications systems not only presents multiple new problems, but it may lead to a complete restructuring of the entire communications spectrum.

Where there was once a quiet mostly noncompetitive climate in which telephone companies operated, they now face aggressive competition and rapid technological change. Former elements of the Bell System are invading each other's territories. Mergers create new diverse giants. The future of the entire industry and of all the organizations in it are likely to be determined as much by the attitudes of many groups—consumers, stockholders, unions, employees, business users, competitors, international communications agencies, government agencies, Congress, and many others—as by any other factor.

The rising thrust of consumerism is a very potent force for telephone companies to deal with, just as it is with other utilities. Here again quality service at a fair price is basic policy.

Commitment to communities served through involvement with the needs of the community is a policy that is receiving increasing emphasis. The telephone industry serves the great metropolitan areas, and the welfare of large cities is extremely important to the successful operation of that system. Participation in training programs, especially for the disadvantaged of the cities, is now a policy principle.

Just as with other utilities, there has been a drift away from the customer. The dehumanization of companies through technological advances must be counteracted by programs that rebuild employee-customer friendly relations. Employee turnover means constant attention to training.

special public relations and advertising programs are open to individual utility participation. The Edison Electric Institute[1] runs a broad program covering every aspect of electric utility interest. The Institute's Public Relations Committee has developed a comprehensive handbook on utility public relations and is deeply involved in setting annual goals for institute staff. Staff carries out a broad range of functions, including publication of a magazine, press contacts, seminar planning, and distribution of educational materials for teachers. The American Gas Associations[2] sponsors excellent workshops on public relations, both national and regional. Many utilities are also members of the Nuclear Energy Institute.[3]

Both the Edison Electric Institute and the American Gas Association sponsor national advertising programs that stress themes such as conditions that force prices up, the value of energy conservation, and long-range energy requirements.

Other advertisements promote the use of nuclear energy and long-range benefits for the public in the generation of electricity. Media used in the program are television and magazines.

The Utility Communicators International[4] is one of the oldest advertising societies in the United States. The association is primarily a forum for the exchange of ideas in utility advertising.

Although it is not a trade association, many electric utilities subscribe to the services provided by Reddy Communications.

Relations Within the Industry

Although no one voice can speak for the electric and gas utilities, trade associations and

[1]Edison Electric Institute, 701 Pennsylvania Avenue, NW, Washington, DC 20004.
[2]1515 Wilson Boulevard, Arlington, VA 22209.
[3]1776 I Street, NW, Washington, DC 20006.
[4]5316 E. Kings Avenue, Scottsdale, AZ 85254.

Aligning Growth with Supply

Not many years ago utilities were promoting the "all you want when you want it" theme in regard to the supply of energy. Now meeting growing demand will be an accomplishment of major proportions, both for electricity and gas.

Somnolent socialists will undoubtedly awaken to challenge private operation of utilities. Their song has long been "anything you can do, government can do better." These political opportunists generally ignore the tax differential in the operating costs for private utilities and the regulatory controls that govern investor-owned utilities.

Meeting projected growth is clearly one of the major tasks for utilities. Despite a break in the rapid rate of increasing energy consumption, the nation's energy needs are still growing. There is unease within the utility industry about whether demand for electricity will stabilize within the more modest growth rates now used in planning.

As the Edison Electric Institute has pointed out in national advertising, today we are in the midst of a great transitional storm between the two energy epochs—the fossil fuel age and a future energy era, as yet not fully defined. To many, it appears that conversion of basic energy sources to electricity may increase as the transition continues. Since it takes ten or more years to build generating stations, some doubt that all needs could be met if increased consumer demand were to accelerate.

The nature of the public relations challenge is highlighted by the public's widespread acceptance of generalities but its failure to accept the personal responsibilities required. The disparity between views on conservation and actual consumption levels is a case in point.

The utility industry is devoting increased time and talent to dispel personal and local-level resistance to matters that are widely endorsed as generally desirable. One of its most difficult tactical challenges is finding ways to summarize complex issues in twenty- to forty-second messages suitable for the needs of local reporters.

The Utility PR Program

In this overview of the utility and its public, only the highlights in regard to public relations strategies, techniques, and public concerns endemic to utilities can be covered. Additional guidelines appear in Chapters 2 and 18.

Overall strategy in utility public relations should embrace both short-range and long-range plans. Such a program gives direction and stability to all the programs and the proper emphasis and attention to long-range objectives. Although some public relations departments operate without outside counsel, the merits of such assistance should be given great weight. Outside public relations counsel not only brings a more independent perspective to planning and executing public relations programs, but it also can free company people for creative research and planning that will have a beneficial effect on a corporation's community relations.

Virtually nothing in public relations today is locked in concrete. That means possibilities for innovations for the practitioners—innovations that relate more effectively to a society of social change. Innovations that are unconventional today may well be routine practice tomorrow.

Public participation in planning

One such change could be involvement of the public in company decisions affecting public relations through the technique of *negotiation*. Today's economic "lifestyle" results more and more from negotiated compromises—

even in areas, for example, where it has heretofore been illegal to strike.

It is possible that information programs alone will be inadequate in dealing with the "new" public. Effective public relations in some situations may be primarily a matter of give and take. When a company takes a controversial course, it must be prepared to face criticism and, literally, *deal* with its critics. This type of approach calls for more candid information to the public long in advance of the resolution of plans for a new project such as a generating plant. This new approach, in a sense, recognizes the fact that the objectives of the conservationist and the environmentalist have changed and that a company must negotiate with them and the public in regard to future plans.

Regulatory control of the siting and construction process has increased. This has brought utility and critic together in a judicial-type atmosphere as well as in the public forum so commonly used to resolve local issues in the United States. Public relations is closely involved in these activities.

Corporate identity systems

Another relatively new proposition for utilities is the formal "corporate identity system." In the past, according to conventional theory, a corporation achieved an identity with its public or publics through the sum of all of its public relations efforts. There were, however, general objectives. Undoubtedly this practice had considerable success, but the kind of identity the corporation established was arrived at informally. There was no concerted effort within a company to determine just what opinion it wanted the public to have of it as long as the company had reasonably good relations with the public. Today's theory dictates a different and much more formal approach to establishing a corporate identity.

Consequently, intensive research and survey programs related to establishing a more formal corporate identity are receiving considerable attention from utilities today. (*See* Chapters 18 and 49.)

One cannot fault a program that seeks to establish a more viable corporate identity as long as the time and effort devoted to this relatively long-range project do not interfere with the day-to-day stewardship of the public relations program. There is always the danger, however, that an obsession with a long-range objective may damage or even defeat short-range operational needs. A bankrupt firm doesn't need a new enchanting symbol. A new corporate symbol, which usually is one of the products of an intensive identity research program, has no magical message for the consumer if the firm's overall performance in the market is bad.

However, in defense of the corporate identity objective as a public relations system, it may well give everyone a better perspective on the company, involve all levels of management more intensely in promoting the corporate character and goals, and even help eliminate bad corporate performance.

On balance then, it could well be a good discipline for the public relations department and others in the company to do all of the research and study necessary to set up a formal corporate identity system. This type of study that would not neglect ongoing public relations programs and short-range objectives could have long-range benefits.

Checklist of Utility PR Objectives

In looking to activities and programs that should be considered, the following suggestions from Underwood, Jordan Associates are pertinent.

In the area of *community relations* public relations should accomplish the following:

1. Encourage participation by executives and key employees in civic affairs.

2. Provide executive leadership and individual financial support to worthwhile causes—Community Chest and Red Cross campaigns, etc.

3. Give generously in both money and manpower to health and welfare, education, professional and civic fund-raising drives of a community-building nature, in accordance with company policy administered on a uniform basis.

4. Arrange periodic surveys of public opinion, conducted for the company by independent sampling organizations.

5. Maintain a system of routine daily calls on residential customers by trained employee-interviewers.

6. Conduct periodic reviews of customer service and accounting policies and procedures to make sure that they are adequate, understandable, and friendly.

7. Determine the particular "social" needs of the community and then develop specific company-led or company-sponsored programs designed to help meet those needs.

8. Advertise and otherwise publicize the company as "a good place to work," not only to attract job applicants but also to humanize the corporate image.

9. Take a position of genuine leadership in area development by means of industrial expansion efforts.

10. Conduct tours of company facilities for organized local groups and occasional "open houses" for the general public.

11. Maintain (and vigorously promote) a company speakers' bureau.

12. Keep ahead of technological developments affecting the industry, and make sure that the public is aware of the company's investment in time, energy, and money in research and development.

13. Plan, organize, and stage special events, anniversaries, and other company observances in a manner that emphasizes, above all, the identity of interest between the company and the communities and people they serve.

14. Make sure that company properties are so designed, landscaped, and maintained as to provide an example of responsible industrial concern for the environments in the communities in which the company has facilities.

15. Install and properly maintain attractive and uniform identification signs at appropriate company properties.

16. Participate broadly in local exhibitions and fairs of general public interest, thus achieving further identification of the company with the community.

In the area of *public information* public relations should do the following:

1. Plan, prepare, and distribute news releases concerning company and industry developments of public interest or concern.

2. Arrange and conduct individual interviews and collective press conferences between company executives and representatives of press, radio, and television.

3. Maintain a prompt, efficient, uninterrupted press information service that operates around the clock, 365 days a year, to answer inquiries from press and radio-TV people relative to service interruptions and the like as soon as they are received, at any hour of the day or night.

4. Publish institutional advertisements regularly in daily and weekly newspapers and

important regional magazines throughout the company's service area.

5. Plan and process personalized mass mailings, made over the chief executive officer's signature, to newspaper editors, radio and television executives, educators, clergymen, public officials, and other local opinion leaders calling to their attention current developments on the local or national scene that importantly affect the company, the industry, their area, and the public interest.

6. Promptly and fully satisfy requests from public and school libraries throughout the company's service area for factual material concerning the policies, practices, and accomplishments of the company and the industry.

7. Organize series of "Editorial Roundtables" between the company's top management and the editors and publishers of area and regional newspapers, magazines, and radio-TV stations and networks. These "Editorial Roundtables" are not conceived as meetings for the working press. What the company should be looking at them for is knowledge and understanding from the *policy makers* of the news media of the company's position on issues of public concern.

8. Develop and distribute widely (via television, speakers' bureau, and/or commercial theater showings) motion pictures and videotapes portraying the company's operations and highlighting the economic advantages of the company's service areas.

In the area of *customer information* public relations should do as follows:

1. Send "welcome" letters signed by the chief executive officer to customers new to the company's service area, including helpful or desirable information concerning rates, procedures, and service facilities.

2. Prepare an attractive booklet summarizing "what every customer ought to know" about the company, its rates, and facilities.

3. Develop a periodical customer publication to be mailed as an enclosure with each bill or timed for delivery to each customer's home with his bill.

4. Give the company's "contact" employees special public relations training for general guidance in meeting customers and the public.

5. Periodically review the company's collection letters, correspondence forms, and the like, to make sure that they promote a friendly understanding of company policies.

6. Develop brochures and other informative material directed to specific customer segments—women, farm groups, small business proprietors, etc.

7. Prepare special mailings on company and industry problems for transmission over the chief executive officer's signature to customer-stockholders.

In the area of *employee information* public relations should meet the following goals:

1. Make sure the employee publication regularly reviews and reports on major *industry* developments, accomplishments, and problems of critical importance to the company and therefore to its employees.

2. Provide company supervisors with special public relations training to improve their human relations with their employees and to inform them about economic and political issues affecting the industry locally and nationally.

3. Prepare material on major company and industry developments for use at employee meetings or conferences and in conducting the question periods that follow.

4. Mail to employees' homes (and therefore to their families as well) occasional letters

from the company's chief executive officer concerning important changes in personnel policies or administration, or directing attention to major local or national developments that are likely to excite comment or controversy regarding the affairs of the company or the industry.

5. Use bulletin boards in well-lighted employee traffic centers to focus employee attention on current public relations approaches and on current problems of the company and the industry.

6. Develop for use in conjunction with the indoctrination program for new employees, informational materials that properly stress the company's history, business, and problems, an employee manual covering the aims and policies of the company and the industry, as well as the rules and regulations of employment.

7. Provide a sound public relations approach for the company's booklets on safety, medical care, pensions, and other matters of special employee interest.

8. Distribute carefully selected information pieces concerning the company and the industry with employees' pay envelopes or salary checks.

9. Make applicable items among the suggested activities listed above in this section available to retired as well as active employees.

In the area of *stockholder information* public relations should achieve the following:

1. Explain public relations problems and objectives of the company and the industry, in terms of special current developments, in the company's quarterly dividend folders and other stockholder communications.

2. Prepare and send to all stockholders a transcript or highlights of the chief executive officer's remarks at the company's annual meeting.

3. Give special attention to the routine daily informational needs of security analysts and financial editors, and encourage free interchange of information with investor organizations.

4. Conduct special tours of company properties for security analysts and financial editors.

5. Prepare an attractive booklet summarizing the company's history, organization, present status, and future prospects, to be mailed to all current stockholders and sent to new ones with an initial letter of welcome.

6. Make sure that each stockholder inquiry receives a prompt, personalized response, signed by the chief executive officer, the secretary of the company, or the officer to whom the inquiry was directed.

7. Distribute to all stockholders occasional reprints dealing with developments vital to the company and the industry and make other reprints available to interested stockholders on request (the offer normally being made through the quarterly dividend folder).

8. Arrange periodic surveys to ascertain the characteristics and preferences of the company's stockholders and their basic reasons for investing in the company.

35

Public Relations for the Business and Professional Association

J. Carroll Bateman

J. Carroll Bateman was general manager of the Insurance Information Institute from 1960 to 1967 and its president until 1979. The Institute is a public information and education organization supported by several hundred insurance companies in the property and liability field. He was also a public relations consultant and an associate professor of public relations at the College of Communications of the University of Tennessee, Knoxville.

Previously he was a reporter and feature writer for the Baltimore (MD) Evening Sun *and assistant director of public relations for the Baltimore & Ohio Railroad.*

He served the Eastern Railroad Presidents Conference as assistant chairman for public relations and advertising and was public relations director of the Milk Industry Foundation.

Mr. Bateman was an instructor in public relations at Johns Hopkins and the Bernard Baruch School of Business Administration at the City University of New York. He served on the American Council for Education in Journalism, the official accrediting agency for colleges and departments of journalism.

He was national president of the Public Relations Society of America and president of the International Public Relations Association.

After his early nineteenth-century visit to the United States the young Frenchman Alexis de Tocqueville noted in his penetrating analysis of the American system, *Democracy in America*, that Americans are inclined to form associations for virtually any purpose. Over time, this national propensity has, if anything, become even more pronounced. So many associations and societies exist today that it is difficult to obtain an accurate count. Gale's database estimates that the United States is home to 800,000 business leagues, chambers of commerce, trade and professional associations—approximately 23,000 of which are at the national level, the remainder being state and local organizations. Of course many of these organizations are composed of small staffs that do not engage in public relations activities in any organized fashion. On the other hand, thousands of the larger trade and professional organizations operate formal public relations programs, many of them quite extensive in scope.

The American Society of Association Executives defines three distinct types of membership associations in the nonprofit field (distinguished, for example, from a profit-making business service that may use the word *association* in its name):

1. Professional societies or associations—whose membership is made up of individuals, such as doctors, dentists, engineers, and so on

2. Trade or business associations—whose membership is companies in the same business

3. Federations—which are organizations having other associations as their members[1]

Among these three types, the trade association or business-sponsored organization seems to be most common.

The first trade associations in this country date back to the late eighteenth century—before de Tocqueville's visit, of course—but impetus was given to the proliferation of business associations by World War I, the Great Depression of the thirties, World War II, and the vast growth of government since then.[2]

The "countervailing forces" character of American democracy also has encouraged the development of various kinds of individual membership associations in great numbers in recent decades. In addition to the proliferation of professional societies representing doctors, lawyers, engineers, dentists, etc., there have arisen myriad "activist" organizations representing special interests, such as consumers, environmental protectionists, highway safety advocates, civil rights organizations, and others. These activist groups have shown aptitude in public relations, especially in gaining widespread attention on television.

When an individual seeks social, economic, or legislative goals that he or she feels cannot be accomplished alone, he or she looks naturally to an association that can work to such ends—and if the appropriate association does not already exist, he or she sometimes seeks to form a new one.

Thus, each association is made up of individuals or corporate entities that have a mutual interest that draws them together. Almost inevitably, in attempting to achieve their common goals, they utilize—formally or haphazardly, as the case may be—the concepts, functions, and tools of public relations.

---

[1]See *Policies and Procedures of Associations*, American Society of Association Executives, Washington, DC, 1987.

[2]For more information about the history and development of trade associations in the United States see Chapter 1 of *Association Management*, edited by Kenneth G. Hance, Chamber of Commerce of the United States, Washington, DC.

At this very moment, the American scene is overflowing with new challenges to business and professional associations and their members. Activist organizations representing a wide and ever-growing range of issues are in high gear. In recent years, these movements have created a plethora of new laws and regulations affecting businesses and the professions, as well as a number of new government agencies at federal, state, and local levels designed to watch over business activities.

Since the early '80s with the inauguration of the administration of President Ronald Reagan, there has been an effort to cut back government regulation of business to some degree. Nevertheless, many federal agencies charged with such responsibilities will continue to exist and will continue to exert a substantial degree of regulation—among them the Equal Employment Opportunities Commission, the Environmental Protection Agency, the Occupational Safety and Health Administration, the Commission on Consumer Product Safety, the Securities and Exchange Commission, and the Justice Department. Additionally, at the state and local levels there has been a proliferation of consumer protection and environmental agencies over the years.

Despite moves toward deregulation at the federal level, all of these earlier initiatives as well as the continuing pressures from activist groups are placing substantial burdens on the associations representing businesses and professional people. The associations are looked on by their members as appropriate organizations for dealing with government to mold "livable" regulatory policies, to disseminate necessary explanations and instructions to their members, and to influence public opinion if interference by government threatens opportunities for initiative.

The social problems faced by our country seem almost insurmountable: rehabilitation of deteriorated urban centers, renovation of our educational system, racial integration, salvaging the environment, and general improvement of the quality of life. All of these challenges call for new efforts from businesses, from professional groups, federations, and business or trade associations, many of which are being looked to by their members as appropriate mechanisms for dealing with some of these problems.

Recognition of these problems has led to an increased emphasis on public affairs, governmental relations, and programs of social responsibility in many associations. It has also resulted in establishment of some new organizations for grappling with certain of these problems.

In this area, it is worth noting that the Chamber of Commerce of the United States, reacting to the consumer movement, adopted as its official policy a "Basic Business-Consumer Relations Code" that reads as follows:

We reaffirm the responsibility of American Business to:

1. Protect the health and safety of consumers in the design and manufacture of products and the provision of consumer services. This includes action against harmful side effects on the quality of life and the environment arising from technological progress.

2. Utilize advancing technology to produce goods that meet high standards of quality at the lowest reasonable price.

3. Seek out the informed views of consumers and other groups to help assure customer satisfaction from the earliest stages of product planning.

4. Simplify, clarify, and honor product warranties and guarantees.

5. Maximize the quality of product servicing and repairs and encourage their fair pricing.

6. Eliminate frauds and deceptions from the marketplace, setting as our goal not strict legality but honesty in all transactions.

7. Ensure that sales personnel are familiar with product capabilities and limitations and that they fully respond to consumer needs for such information.

8. Provide consumers with objective information about products, services, and the workings of the marketplace by utilizing appropriate channels of communication, including programs of consumer education.

9. Facilitate sound value comparisons across the widest possible range and choice of products.

10. Provide effective channels for receiving and acting on consumer complaints and suggestions, utilizing the resources of associations, chambers of commerce, better business bureaus, recognized consumer groups, individual companies, and other appropriate bodies.

It is interesting to note that Article 10 of this code looks specifically to associations as a mechanism for dealing with consumer relations. Also, Articles 3, 4, 7, 8, 9, and 10 call for the assistance of public relations and communications specialists, if they are to be properly implemented.

One of the unusual responses to the public's demand for greater social responsibility by business is the Center for Corporate Public Involvement, sponsored by associations representing seven hundred life and health insurance companies. The center is designed to encourage, advise, and assist its members in their social responsibility programs. The concept grew out of the effort in social responsibility by insurers when they allocated $2 billion of their investments to urban redevelopment over the years 1967–72. In one year alone, 154 insurance companies reported to the center that they had committed $788 million in investments "which would not otherwise have been made under the companies' customary lending standards, in which social considerations played a substantial part in the investment decision." Stanley G. Karson,

director of the center, claimed that "the life and health insurance business has been the most consistently involved of major businesses in corporate social responsibility programs."

It should be observed that this program grew out of the actions of four trade associations and required the establishment of a new organization for its implementation.

One thing seems certain: the role of associations will not be lessened by consumer relations activities and social problems, or by new government initiatives. Indeed, the likelihood is that the role of associations will be expanded, and their significance will grow in the decades immediately ahead.

Organization of Association Public Relations

Public relations is a significant function of most associations. Many of them employ individuals or complete staffs that specialize in public relations activities. Even where professional public relations people are not employed as staff members, public information and public education activities frequently are conducted under the direction of other staff members or with the assistance of external public relations counsel.

The activities of the trade and professional associations generally are broad, encompassing government relations, technical research, membership education, public relations, sales promotion, and establishment of codes of ethics and industry standards, to name only a few. Some associations are formed expressly to conduct public relations activities on behalf of a particular industry or business. Whatever a particular association's program, public information and public education efforts are more likely than not one of the principal activities. (*See* Figure 35.1.)

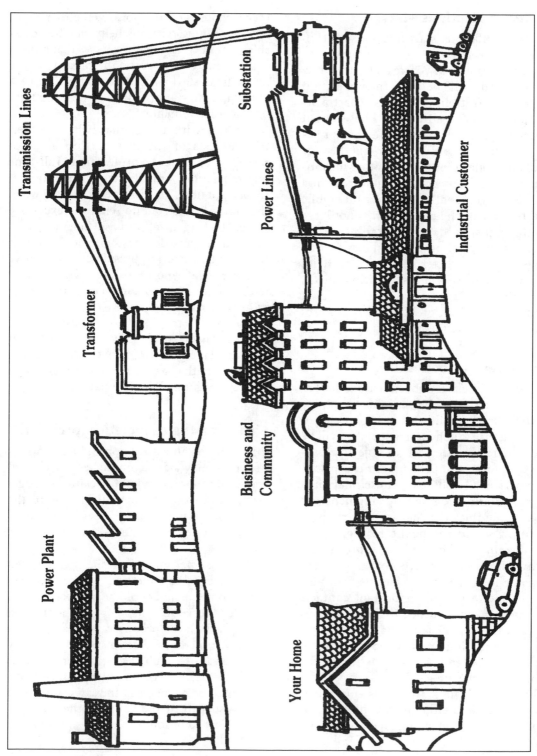

Figure 35.1 Making information about an industry understandable is a challenge to many trade associations. This illustration from the American Public Power Association shows how electricity is routed from the power plant to a home. *Courtesy American Public Power Association, Washington, DC.*

The public relations staff

The public relations staff in an association may range numerically from one person to more than a hundred. Where staffs are large, there naturally will be departmentalization within the staff itself. Often this departmentalization occurs on a functional basis—that is, there may be a department for press relations, another for publications, another for school and college relations, another for motion picture development and production, and so on. More frequently, however, the public relations staff of the association is not large enough to justify departmentalization. In such cases, the staff professional may be well advised to utilize external service agencies that can provide specialists in various fields. Where the public relations staff specialist attempts to be a jack-of-all-trades, output in some areas may be mediocre.

Employment of counsel

Whether the internal public relations staff is large or small, it may be desirable to employ also an external public relations counselor or counseling firm. Such an arrangement will be useful where the need for an objective outside viewpoint is important. An exceptionally experienced and able counsel may provide scope and judgment to augment the staff's. Sometimes the "outside expert" is in a position to aid the public relations staff executive in winning board approval for worthwhile special projects that might otherwise be lost. A public relations firm also may be able to provide important contacts with media people outside the normal contact range of the association staff. Finally, the external counseling firm may be equipped to provide experts in certain areas where the internal staff may be lacking.

The external public relations counseling firm may be hired either on a continuing or temporary basis, depending on the situation.

(*See* Chapter 47.) Temporary employment of external public relations help may be advisable to meet certain contingencies that require a large-scale effort beyond the capacity of the permanent staff—such as celebration of a major industry anniversary or a major fight on a legislative matter.

With or without external help, however, the interests of the membership are best served when there is a professional, full-time public relations practitioner on the staff of the association. This is especially true when the status of the public relations executive within the organization is sufficient to permit him or her to deal firsthand not only with the executive director, president, or executive vice-president who heads the staff, but also with board members, officers, and other industry leaders.

The public relations organization of the association often includes a committee of individual members or member company representatives that serves as an advisory group to the professional public relations staff.

Financing the association program

Financing of an association public relations program may be accomplished in several ways. Commonly, the public relations budget is financed from the general income of the association, which in most cases is composed mainly of dues, assessments, or membership fees.

When some portion of the membership may object to this method (as may happen when some members of the association feel that, for special reasons, they may not benefit as much from the proposed program as certain other members will), a special fund may be set up for the public relations effort. This fund may be based on voluntary assessments, paid by those members of the association who are persuaded of the value of the effort to them. This compromise enables a program to be initiated without the support of all members, the expectation being that eventually more member companies will become convinced of its value and support it.

In some instances, a public relations program for an association may be financed by revenues not coming from members. For example, an association with a magazine that accepts paid advertising may use some of the advertising revenues for public relations purposes. Other associations that sponsor periodic exhibits or trade shows may utilize income from these for financing public relations activities. However, in view of the interest of the Internal Revenue Service regarding the nature of association income, tax problems may arise in such cases. In still other cases, a public relations program for an industry may be supported by levies on related industry trade associations. (For example, the National Dairy Council's efforts in nutrition education and research were paid for, in part, by related organizations of dairy farmers, dairy food processors, and dairy equipment manufacturers.)

Whatever the method of financing, the public relations executive of an association should have an annual budget, so activities can be intelligently planned. He or she is seriously handicapped when each project has to be submitted for board approval and for a special appropriation before it can be undertaken.

Purposes of association programs

The purposes of association public relations programs cover a very wide range. Some typical purposes include the following:

1. Promoting sales through product publicity

2. Creating consumer understanding of how to use the industry's services or products effectively and safely, and of the benefits resulting from their use

3. Overcoming inequities or other problems in the competitive situation in which the industry finds itself, such as may be caused by imports of foreign goods

4. Creating public understanding of the effect of regulation of an industry by government, to assure equitable regulation

5. Combating government interference in or competition with an industry or profession

6. Creating public support for legislative proposals that the association favors or public opposition to legislation it opposes (This can be done effectively only by stressing the public interest in the matter, but this point is often overlooked.)

7. Obtaining public recognition for the social and economic contributions that an industry or profession makes to the nation

8. Forestalling or combating criticism or attacks from outside groups or competitive interests, such as charges that apples are contaminated by pesticides or cereals lack nutritional value

9. Seeing that an industry or profession is accurately represented in the curricula of schools and colleges, and assisting educators in teaching about the industry

10. Recruiting qualified people (especially from among college graduates) for careers in an industry or profession

11. Creating public understanding of an industry's equal employment opportunities policies and of its labor relations

Although many association public relations programs originate in response to attacks on an industry and the initial purpose is to a large extent defensive, a long-range public relations effort must be positive in its approach, and its objectives should be positively stated. A program devoted exclusively to answering attacks on a business is futile over the long term. After years of defensive efforts in public relations, an industry may find itself exactly where it began—or in an even poorer position.

Basic Program Development Steps

Establishing an association public relations program on behalf of a business or industry or a professional group, involves a series of steps that, although subject to some variation in differing situations, generally will include the following:

1. Analysis of the situation
2. Definition of problem areas
3. Identification of pertinent publics
4. Establishment of specific objectives
5. Planning of program
6. Implementation of program
7. Periodic evaluations of progress

Analysis

Analyzing the situation calls for broad study of all aspects of the business that affect the publics. The starting point will be the people in the business or industry (particularly those who are active in the association, such as board members, appropriate committee chairmen and members, and so on) who appear to have an awareness of the public relations situation. The public relations executive newly arrived in an association will begin by interviewing such people; from them he or she will go to people outside the business but in a position to observe it more closely than the average layman (these may include editors of trade publications, officials of chambers of commerce and better business bureaus, government officials concerned with

the regulation of the business or profession— if there are any—and others). Finally, this basic study may approach the general public for additional views. This may be done through an opinion or attitude research study, or market research, conducted by a recognized research firm. Sometimes, this may be done on a more informal basis where the budget will not permit formal research. Such an approach to the general public will be designed to provide a profile of the business as it appears in the public mind. Opinion research is discussed later in this chapter. (*See also* Chapter 18.)

Problem definition

Definition of problem areas flows naturally from these interview and research activities. Comparisons among the views of the public, people in the business, and those who are close observers of the business may reveal some interesting parallels as well as differences and may indicate some cause-and-effect relationships. It should be noted also that ignorance and misconception will not always or necessarily be found only in the public mind. Industry people more often than not will be found to have some misconceptions about the public's viewpoint, too. In such an event, correction of industry thinking will be called for. Sound public relations practice may require changing the attitudes of the client (diplomatically, of course) as much as it involves endeavoring to change the attitudes of certain publics. As a matter of fact, although the public relations person is usually hired to change public attitudes, he or she sometimes performs the most important task in changing the attitude of his client or employer.

In today's climate, the role of the public relations practitioner is enlarging. He or she should be capable of observing and analyzing the social, economic, and political trends and helping his or her management or clients become aware of their significance to the institution. Through such expanded awareness, the manager or clients come to view their business or institution in a new and different perspective.

Identification of publics

A public is a group of people bound together by a specialized interest with reference to a focal point. Thus, employees in the steel mills may constitute one of the publics of a steel industry association's public relations effort; dairy farmers may comprise a special public of the association representing the milk processing industry; automobile dealers may be a special public of the association representing automobile manufacturers; and so on. Customers of a particular business always are a primary public, along with employees, suppliers, dealers, community neighbors, and stockholders.

For an industry association, executives of member companies will be a primary public; for a professional society, the individual members will also be one. Indeed, the association's members must not be overlooked in any public relations effort; their understanding and support are necessary.

Establishing objectives

Once the problem areas are defined, long-range objectives should be established. Usually, these will be outlined in terms of the respective publics involved.

General objectives should be drawn with perspective in order to serve as guides over the long range. If they are drawn only in respect to immediate, short-term problems, they will not serve to provide continuity of direction and they will need constant revision. For example, it would be unwise to draw an overall objective in reference to a specific piece of current legislation that is to be opposed or supported, for once the legislature has adjourned, the objective is meaningless.

Instead, a long-range objective might describe in general terms the nature of legislation that an industry favors.

> To support, in the respective states, legislative efforts that will enable our business to serve the public on a competitive basis in accord with the traditions of a free-market economy, and to oppose legislation that would deny this opportunity.

Any association public relations program must be flexible; obviously it should be modified as time and circumstances may require. But if it is drawn with sufficient perspective, changing day-to-day and month-to-month problems will fit within the framework of its general objectives. Of course, short-range objectives will be developed from time to time. In addition, if sound communications networks have been developed to implement long-range objectives, these networks will facilitate the solution of passing and temporary problems. But common sense demands a long-range plan with specific objectives against which results may be measured.

Program planning

Planning a program involves laying out in detail the various activities and communications that will be employed with reference to the key publics that have been pinpointed in the objectives.

Let us assume, for example, a situation in which an association of home appliance manufacturers finds that the industry has lost standing in the public mind because a substantial number of consumers are dissatisfied with the repair and maintenance services. The industry association identifies, as one of its publics, the retail appliance dealers who are responsible for servicing. The objective with respect to this public is to indoctrinate the dealers in the necessity for providing quality repair services and to provide information to them on the methods by which high-quality servicing may be established.

The program plan will outline the activities to be directed toward gaining the support of dealers for this mutually beneficial purpose. It may, for example, call for the preparation of a "code of good service" and of a manual describing the service functions the dealer is expected to perform. Furthermore, this part of the plan may call specifically for a series of dealer meetings in various communities; for special articles to be prepared for trade publications that are circulated among dealers; for a special periodical to be published by the association especially for the dealer-audience; for paid advertisements in industry publications, addressed to dealers; for conduct of special training schools for the service people employed by the dealers; or for any combination of these and other techniques, some of which may lie outside the field of public relations, strictly defined. But good public relations must, inevitably, be based on good performance, and all of these measures should be designed to improve performance in repair and maintenance.

Program implementation

Program implementation involves carrying out these steps. It calls primarily for hard work by the association's public relations staff or the external counsel. In association work, however, the implementation of a public relations program frequently requires active participation of people in the profession or industry. Indeed, in respect to many objectives, the only path to success is to enroll the people in the business or profession who are located at many points across the country.

No association staff, however large, has sufficient people to perform the grassroots indoctrination task all by itself. Frequently, therefore, means will be devised for recruiting people who are working in the business, but who are not themselves public relations people, to assist in the public relations efforts

of the association. For example, for some years the former Eastern Railroad Presidents' Conference, a regional association of railroads, sponsored "Railroad Community Committees" in major cities throughout its territory. These committees consisted of local representatives from each of the railroads serving a particular city. They maintained speakers' bureaus, engaged in public-service projects, participated in business-education days and in careers days at local high schools, and in other ways demonstrated the interest of the railroad industry in the community's welfare.

For any grassroots efforts by a national, regional, or even a state association, reliance on local representatives of the business, industry, or profession is essential. This is especially important when an attempt is being made to influence legislators, who will be more inclined to listen to their own constituents. Implementation of objectives that focus on relations with individual communities generally involves recruitment, indoctrination, and motivation of volunteers from the profession's or industry's ranks.

Carrying out the program can involve a wide range of functions, always guided by the long-range plan and the association's policies. For example, the program of the Insurance Information Institute includes the following activities:

- Serves as a reliable source to which journalists can turn for prompt and accurate information on insurance

- Works with state and national organizations in conducting public communications campaigns on insurance and related issues

- Conducts conferences, seminars, and public forums on insurance-related public policy issues, such as drunk driving, auto theft, and road safety

- Publishes and distributes books, newsletters, and consumer leaflets on a variety of topics, including accounting and taxation, fire safety, and industry profitability

- Maintains offices in cities throughout the country as links with regional media, agents, consumers, governments, state and local insurer organizations, and other groups
- Conducts a national advertising program on insurance matters
- Maintains an on-line computerized database of information about contemporary insurance issues
- Publishes *Data Base News,* an electronic newsletter with summaries of the day's major insurance news stories five days a week
- Publishes *Data Base Reports,* monthly, in-depth research reports on major subjects affecting the insurance business
- Maintains a library with an extensive collection of books on different lines of property/casualty insurance, studies and reports from the major insurance associations, and nearly one hundred newspapers and periodicals
- Responds promptly to catastrophes by providing on-site information on losses covered by insurance policies, ways to avoid additional losses, and the steps in the claims process
- Monitors legislative, regulatory, and judicial developments at the federal and state levels and informs insurers of these developments
- Provides public relations and communications services to insurance organizations in the fields of property, casualty, fidelity, surety, and marine insurance
- Serves as liaison between the insurance industry and consumer organizations around the country
- Conducts a national speaker program with four hundred local speakers from insurance

companies and agencies speaking to civic and community organizations

- Promotes consumer insurance instruction through the nation's schools
- Publishes *Insurance Review,* a monthly magazine that features news and information of interest to independent agents and brokers, insurance company executives, risk managers, and industry-related readers
- Publishes *The Executive Letter,* a weekly newsletter, which summarizes the latest legislative, regulatory, judicial, economic, and social developments affecting the industry and commentary by authorities on emerging issues
- Trains industry executives to make optimum use of television and radio to get accurate insurance information to the public
- Provides consumers with direct answers to their insurance questions through its hotline: (800) 221-4954.

Periodic evaluations

Evaluations of progress are necessary. Such evaluations should be made on a continuing basis, of course, by the professional public relations staff or public relations counsel or by the association. Progress reports should be made regularly also to the membership and to interested committees and boards of the association.

In many associations, the public relations advisory committee, broadly representative of the association's membership, makes a periodic review of the program and suggests improvements or changes in the effort. To assure continuing top-level support of an association public relations program, it is also wise for the public relations executive or counselor to make a periodic presentation of results to the board of directors. Certainly such a presentation is vital when approval is sought for the succeeding year's public-relations budget.

Association Public Relations Techniques

The techniques utilized by association public relations people are basically the same as those utilized in other public relations fields, and thus most of them need not be discussed in detail here. However, certain techniques perhaps are more pertinent to the association public relations efforts. These include the following:

1. Research on public opinion (*see* Chapter 18) and industry data (as a basis for communications about the industry's progress, problems, and developments)

2. Publicity and personal contacts with media people (*See* Chapters 20–26.)

3. Institutional advertising (*See* Chapter 30.)

4. Production of audiovisuals (motion pictures, videotapes, slide presentations, multimedia presentations, etc.) (*See* Chapter 27.)

5. Speakers' bureaus and speakers' kits (*See* Chapters 31 and 32.)

6. Periodical publications for special audiences (*See* Chapter 31.)

7. Pamphlets (especially statistical yearbooks and handbooks with general background information and consumer-education materials) (*See* Chapter 31.)

The industry association is in a fortunate position as the creator of publicity because its news releases need not contain trade names that often lend an air of commercialism to company publicity. Also, the association frequently will be looked to by the media as a more objective and authoritative source of news about the industry as a whole.

Two kinds of research

Sound public relations planning—in the trade association or anywhere else—begins with two kinds of knowledge:

1. Self-knowledge—the understanding that people in a business or profession should have of themselves and their respective fields of endeavor

2. Knowledge of how the business or profession appears to others with whom it has relationships

In collecting and disseminating such knowledge for a segment of the business or professional world, the association provides a service of major value for its members. The biggest single achievement of a public relations program can be the enlightenment that dawns with this new knowledge. When business executives begin to see themselves and their enterprise in an objective light, they are subtly moved in directions that will tend to improve their public relations. George Eliot once wrote that our deeds tyrannize over us; so also does our knowledge. Truth is the knowledge that makes us better human beings. This kind of knowledge is the basis for sound public relations.

Industry data

To a great extent, the public relations effort revolves around communication in one form or another—communication of facts and ideas to specified audiences in the form of the printed word, the spoken word, or the graphic presentation. Unless it is based on facts, such communication is empty and aimless—and generally not credible. For an association program, such communication must be based on facts even though emotional questions are involved.

Hence one of the first major steps in developing an industry or professional program must be accumulation of facts on an industrywide basis about the activity. It is surprising how little most industries know about themselves. Of course, each company knows what its figures are for such things as employment, payrolls, taxes, gross income, profit, expenditures for materials and supplies, and so on. But frequently, before the beginning of an industry public relations program, no one has bothered to collect and consolidate these figures into national aggregates, unless government regulatory authorities have required it. For some business or professional programs, of course, it may be desirable to have aggregates for various states and major communities, as well.

In many cases the public relations staff must initiate this type of research. Unless such information is available from another authoritative source, the public relations staff of the association has no alternative but to try to compile it.

Opinion research

Opinion research as a public relations tool is perhaps more widely utilized in association public relations than in other areas of public relations practice. However, the probing of public attitudes is not so widely understood and not so broadly utilized as conscientious public relations practice would require it to be.

Opinion research may be described as the attempt to measure, both quantitatively and qualitatively, public attitudes toward a company, industry, profession, or other organization and toward its policies, personnel, services, or products. Where services or products are involved, such research may overlap the area of "Marketing Research."

There are at least four general reasons for the use of opinion research in association public relations:

1. To provide guidance in establishing and developing a public relations program or a specific project. On such occasions, opinion research serves to help crystallize the public relations problem or problems; to help define the crucial issues, to identify significant publics, and to establish objectives. It is, in effect, a navigational tool of the kind that Abraham Lincoln—an expert

in public relations long before it became an organized field of effort—may have had in mind when he said: "If we could first know where we are and whither we are tending, we could better judge what to do and how to do it."

2. To facilitate membership agreement on public relations objectives and courses of action. If, as is so often the case in trade and professional association work (and may be true in corporate life as well), a public relations program is subject to the jurisdiction of a committee or board of directors representing diverse elements, the area of common agreement may be limited. Each member of the group may have his or her own pet ideas as to what ought to be done; arguing these to a conclusion can be a futile and never-ending process. An opinion survey enables the public relations executive to sell the program on the basis of facts that only the most negative and resistant persons should have the temerity to dispute.

3. Where opinion research constitutes a continuing function in the public relations operation, it may uncover incipient problems before they become crises. Thus some major headaches may be forestalled.

4. Opinion research may be utilized to determine the results of public relations efforts —progress toward stated goals. The pitfalls inherent in this utilization are great; hence the reluctance of many public relations practitioners to consider research in this connection. Certainly, changing basic attitudes is a long-range process, and the degree of change, even over a period of several years, may be hardly measurable. Nevertheless, in certain cases such measurement of progress toward goals can be valuable.

In the railroad industry, for example, such measurements were carried out over a period of years to evaluate the proportion of public opinion favoring government ownership of the railroad industry. This was a crucial problem as evidenced by the fact that at the beginning of World War II, 50 percent of the U.S. adult population favored government ownership and operation of the railroads. Effective wartime performance under private ownership and effective reporting to the public on railroad achievements during the war resulted in reducing this sentiment to only 13 percent by 1946, as demonstrated by a continuing public opinion audit. Except for government taking over the money-losing intercity passenger service that is now Amtrak, no serious consideration has been given to government ownership of the railroads since then.

Aim toward action

Opinion research should be developed on an actionable basis. It does little good to ask questions about people's attitudes if the answers do not provide a basis for action—practical, concrete action within the framework of your public relations potential. Sherwood Dodge, former marketing vice-president for Foote, Cone and Belding, has written:

> Make an estimate of the possible outcome of a key question or point. Then ask yourself how this outcome would influence your decision if it proved correct, and how differently you would act if it were incorrect. This is the test of "actionability."
>
> The more the questions take on the form of a hypothesis, related to alternative courses of action, the more research will operate in the field of maximum utility.

An illustration may be found in the Milk Industry Foundation's experience with a nationwide consumer survey designed to provide the basis for its public relations program. There had been considerable pressure from

industry representatives for a communications effort to convince people that the price of milk was low. "Actionable-type" questions in the survey showed that 55 percent of the public thought that the price of milk was "reasonable"—and only 33 percent thought it was "too high." Of the 33 percent, only 8 percent said they had reduced their consumption of milk because of the price. Another question showed that milk ranked above six other important foods, in the public's opinion, as giving the consumer "most value for his money." In view of these responses, it was decided not to give great emphasis to price in the public relations communications for fear of creating a major problem where only a minor one existed.

Marketing values of research

In trade association work it may be easier to sell the idea of a joint marketing and public relations survey than to sell a public relations study alone. Member companies in a trade association are inclined to see more dollars-and-cents value in a study that will give them information they can use in their marketing efforts than in a study that deals with the intangibles of public relations problems only. Combining the two areas of study into one project may be possible, and it may facilitate the appropriation of necessary funds.

Finally, in trade or professional association public relations, it is essential to have a plan for disseminating the results of opinion research to members. In corporate public relations, it may be necessary for only the public relations department and top management to know the results. In an association, research results also should be widely reported to the membership both to demonstrate the value of the study and to encourage the individual members to take appropriate actions of their own.

Bringing together allied forces

Rare is the industry association that does not have a number of allies or potential allies. These allies frequently have their own associations, with related interests. Some successful association public relations programs bring together as many forces as possible to bear on a particular problem. Thus, for example, railroad associations may seek the help of the associations of manufacturers who provide supplies and equipment for the railroad industry; the industry associations representing insurance managements may seek the help of the associations of insurance agents or brokers; associations representing the processors of dairy products may seek the aid of associations representing the dairy farms, and vice versa.

Despite the inevitable differences that occur on some matters between such groups, there are always grounds for cooperation in specified areas. It is unwise to allow admitted differences in limited areas to prevent useful cooperation in other areas. The practical solution, when such a problem exists, is by common agreement to build a fence around the areas of dispute and declare them off-limits insofar as the cooperative effort is concerned. In any event, the mutual benefits from cooperation among associations with allied interests usually will be found to over-balance the advantages (if any) of conflict.

The trade press editor as a friend

In too many instances, the association staff people in the industry or profession are inclined to take the trade press editors for granted. The association public relations staff has no greater ally, generally speaking, than a trade press editor who is convinced of the value and effectiveness of the industry public relations effort.

From an objective perch, the trade press editor can be a powerful force in showing the industry's leaders how the program is progressing. He or she can say things about the program and the industry or profession that the public relations executive can never say. It is important that every association public relations program include continuing efforts to keep trade press editors informed about the progress of the program. Association public relations executives rarely have suffered from taking a trade press editor into their confidence. To the contrary, frequently they gain a great deal.

Association Versus Corporate Public Relations

For the association, the principles and techniques of public relations generally are the same as for the individual corporation. But implementing public relations in the association field has certain marked differences from the corporate practice of public relations.

A major difference involves establishment of public relations policy for the association. In corporate practice policy may be agreed on by a few members of top management after inputs from lower echelons and stakeholders; once established, such policy may be promulgated and enforced through a directive from the chief executive officer of the company. Although much consideration may be devoted to developing the tenets of such corporate policy, the process of policy establishment, promulgation, and enforcement is relatively simple.

In the association, the situation is different. For one thing, the association staff is not in a position to issue directives to the industry. Hence, developing association public relations policy may involve crystallizing and codifying unwritten policies that already exist. This may be accomplished through informal consultation with individual industry leaders, then reducing the resultant knowledge to a simplified statement and submitting this statement for approval to the association's board of directors or to appropriate committees of the association.

Once approved, such policy may be promulgated throughout the industry in a manner designed to encourage its implementation —but it cannot be imposed on association members. Its acceptance must, of course, be voluntary on the part of each member. Obviously, in developing policy the public relations executive of the association is in a position to nudge the membership here and there to correct certain defects or omissions in public policy—but success in this respect demands a degree of diplomatic skill rather than a dictatorial posture.

As Reuel Elton, at one time the general manager of the American Trade Association Executives (now the American Society of Association Executives) said:

> The Trade Association does not order, it advises. It does not coerce, it persuades. It does not issue mandates, or even instructions. It uses only the moving eloquence of a reasoned appeal to the self-interest of its members. It does not tell its members what they must do. It tells them what, if influenced by a decent regard for their own interests, they will be glad to do. It assumes that its members are intelligent men, that they can think about the problems of their business and that if the facts out of which these problems arise are placed fairly before them, and if the significance of the facts is pointed out, a proper and profitable line of action will result.

Relationship to purposes

Association public relations policy necessarily must equate with the broad general objectives of the association (which usually are developed at the time of its establishment and frequently may be found in the association's constitution). But public relations objectives and the general purpose of the organization, except in a few instances, are not necessarily identical.

Although many associations do not have a written public relations policy or written objectives, documenting them provides steady guidance and continuity to a program that may be buffeted off course and led down unprofitable alleys when officers, directors, and committees made up of membership representatives undergo their perennial rotations and changes. Indeed, this is one of the greatest hazards to association programming. As the elected officers change from year to year, there is an inclination on their part to shoot off in new directions, to drop old programs and start new ones, without much evaluation. In the face of this, the public relations executive must endeavor to keep a steady hand on the helm.

Gaining support

Another characteristic that distinguishes association public relations from corporate public relations relates to enlisting and mobilizing the aid of others.

Again, in the corporation this is relatively simple to do. Once the public relations executive has gained approval of top management for a program of action, generally he or she can rely on it to issue instructions to subordinates that will assure cooperation with the public relations plan.

In the association, any attempt to mobilize its professional members or employees of many companies into an effective task force for association public relations purposes must rest on persuasion and voluntary action. Thus, the public relations executive of a trade association needs continuously to woo voluntary help and cooperation. For this reason, he or she should find ways to enable many people to participate in the development of the program—for others will tend to support and assist in implementing a program they feel is at least in part their own. This participation often may be accomplished through the mechanism of committees.

Reports to members

A further necessity in association public relations is a system of reporting—with regularity and frequency—to the membership. The association public relations executive can never assume that the members know what is being done, and why, unless a conscious and continuing effort is made to let them know.

Communication to the membership, thus, is the *sine qua non* of success in association public relations, as indeed it is the key to success for any aspect of association administration.

It is, of course, always desirable for the association public relations executive to be in close liaison not only with the executive secretary or executive director (the principal staff officer of the organization) but also with the elected officers and directors. In the ideal situation, he or she will report periodically and in person to the board, and will personally present the proposed program and budget. Where this is not possible because of the attitude of the executive director, the effectiveness of the public relations executive—and of the whole program—may suffer.

In addition to reporting to the officers and board members, however, means should be established for the reporting to the membership at large on the progress of the public relations effort. This might be done through the association's magazine or newsletter, or with an audiovisual presentation at the annual convention of the association.

Personal qualities of the association public relations executive

The association public relations executive needs all the professional abilities and attributes of counterparts in corporate public relations and counseling—and yet more. He or she must have the diplomatic talents to satisfy the demands of not one executive or several clients, but of scores or hundreds—and sometimes thousands—of corporate officers or individual members of the association. Among countless diverse points of view, the association public relations executive must search out the common ground, establish mutually acceptable objectives, and produce generally satisfactory results. The tasks, in these ways, often are far more demanding than those of the corporate public relations practitioner.

36

PUBLIC RELATIONS FOR FINANCIAL ORGANIZATIONS

RONALD E. RHODY

Ronald E. Rhody, a consultant, was senior vice-president and director of BankAmerica's Corporate Communications and External Affairs Division.

Before joining BankAmerica in 1983, he was corporate vice-president and director of public relations and advertising for Kaiser Aluminum and Chemical Corporation. He served on the corporation's management committee and headed its domestic and international public relations, governmental affairs, advertising, internal communications, community relations, and marketing communications programs.

He has been chairman of Media Analysis Advisory Council of Washington, DC, and is a member of the advisory board of the University of Alabama, College of Communications. He is a member of the board of advisors at the University of Texas School of Journalism and Mass Communications and of the advisory board of the Baruch College, City University of New York, Program in Business and Public Policy.

Financial institutions are unique among profit-making enterprises in their near total dependence on public perceptions and trust for their survival and success. As the CEO of one of the world's largest banks explains, "We live or die on public perceptions." This and other factors make public relations for financial institutions one of the most uniquely challenging communication opportunities.

Financial institutions deal principally—though not exclusively, in a commodity—money—that is as important and personal to most people as is love, safety, or sex. Neither society, nor government, nor institutions can operate without it. Furthermore, it is perhaps the only commodity for which the seller must approve the customer before selling him the goods and that is sold only on the condition that the customer pays it back—with interest.

Accordingly, financial institutions hold the power to affect the life and livelihood of all members of society.

By the same token, they face intense competition among themselves and from a steady stream of new entrants in their field. Yet, virtually no difference exists between the products and services of one financial institution and that of its competitors.

The one trait shared by every financial institution is that they all depend, absolutely, on the trust and confidence of the public for their very existence . . . every day. In this tenuous and competitive environment, sound public relations requires much more than good management. In fact, public relations practices can provide the essential determining factors of the financial organization's success . . . or failure.

Daily headlines and nightly broadcasts confirm the severity of the public relations challenges facing financial institutions, such as the following:

- Bank failures, sparked by the public's lack of confidence in domestic lending practices and the ominous load of Third World debt, reached record levels in the late 1980s.

- Investment firms, rocked by public concern over insider trading scandals and excited by growing opportunities, have been consolidating and restructuring.

- Savings and loans, abandoned by customers with shaken confidence, have had to be propped up by a massive government aid program and nudged toward becoming banks or merging with banks.

- Insurance companies, facing growing discontent over high premiums, have found themselves on the losing end of a damaging ballot referendum in California, and are now fighting that same battle in states throughout the nation.

- The commodity markets, shaken by dozens of indictments, have been forced to reexamine and overhaul their basic operations to restore public confidence.

In addition, the once-familiar lines of demarcation between financial institutions have blurred, with deregulation unleashing a host of new competitors into the field, and existing players expanding into areas from which they have been previously barred. All this is taking place in an environment where perceptions are more important than reality, and change is the only constant.

Underlying and Unique Principles of PR for Financial Institutions

The fundamental considerations involved in planning and implementing a public relations program for a financial organization parallel those of any other type of corporation. As covered in greater detail elsewhere in this handbook, the seven steps in the cycle of public relations functions include the following:

1. Analyzing the general climate of attitudes
2. Determining the attitude of any group toward the company
3. Analyzing the state of opinion
4. Formulating policy
5. Planning means of improving the attitude of the group
6. Carrying out the planned activities
7. Feedback, evaluation, and adjustments, including developing emergency plans for occurrences outside the normal scope of planning and activity and using appropriate communications techniques

Particular needs

In addition to general knowledge of communication practices necessary for success in corporate settings, some specific needs are essential for the practice of public relations in financial institutions.

First is a working knowledge of general economic principles, along with a particular understanding of the financial underpinnings of the specific business or industry you are representing.

Just as a public relations representative for a steel company is expected to know not only the basic process for making steel but also the specifics of the company's line of products, so should spokespeople for a financial institution know where their business fits into the economic scheme and also be able to explain their particular products and services in simple, easy-to-understand terms.

Thus, depending upon your particular financial institution, you should be familiar with how a home equity line of credit works; the differences between whole life, term, and universal life insurance; what a no-load municipal bond fund means; or how hedging financial instruments work. You should understand how your particular line of business fits into the overall financial system, and how your products and services are an essential part of everyday life.

Given this essential background, then, how does a public relations professional approach the business of developing programs that will distinguish and differentiate his or her particular financial institution?

There are a number of attributes that people look for in deciding on the financial institutions they will trust with their money, and successful programs must be tailored to build on those strengths.

Quality of service

The distinction between financial products and services has become blurred as deregulation lowers the barriers that prevented institutions from competing in the past. The regulatory differences between banks, brokerage houses, investment banks, and insurance companies are fading fast, and new players—such as department store chains, automobile manufacturers, and oil companies—are entering the field as well.

Given the fact that most products are essentially the same, the perceived quality of service—whether it is the length of waiting times in lines, the friendliness of the salesperson, the speed of response, or the accuracy of statements—can make the critical difference in how consumers distinguish among all the competing firms. (*See* Figure 36.1.)

As shifting patterns lead to diversification and combinations, what happens in one unit of a multifaceted company—a scandal, a government allegation—can adversely affect people's confidence in every unit.

Internal public relations programs to heighten employee awareness of service quality, to define the attributes the company wishes to convey to its customers, and to recognize and reward high performers can result in a quality of service that will translate into improved sales.

External programs to communicate a company's commitment to quality and to demonstrate its performance in support of those goals can build a perception in the public mind that will distinguish a financial institution from its competition.

Leadership

With so many institutions to choose from in today's marketplace, consumers frequently decide to take their business to a firm that is a perceived leader in the field. Public relations programs dedicated to establishing the basis for that leadership position in the public mind are an important tool for any company that wishes to assure its long-term success.

Leadership in community activities is a traditional way that financial institutions work to achieve this goal. However, it is rarely enough to depend on the activities of senior management to carry the day, particularly when the existence of many branches or sales offices provides the opportunity for leadership at the local community level. (*See* Chapter 8.)

Public relations programs can be constructed to reinforce the leadership activities of local managers and officers of the company at the grassroots level, in concert with the higher-visibility efforts of the chief executive and top managers. This brings the added advantage of building a base of goodwill for those times when a financial institution needs

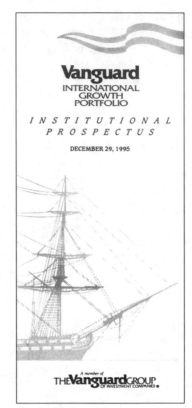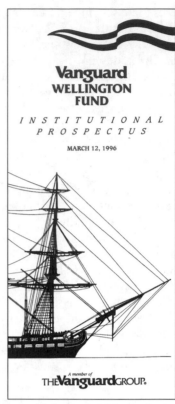

Figure 36.1 Quality of service is reflected in the breadth, scope, and ease of use of the financial institution's communications, including its prospectuses. *Courtesy The Vanguard Group.*

to turn to those grassroots in support of its own position in state and national legislative arenas. (*See* Chapters 5 and 6.)

Still another opportunity to build leadership visibility is through an institution's participation in trade groups and associations. The volunteer activities of a company's executives in these industry-wide groups are not only effective in demonstrating leadership within the industry, but also help guarantee that the policies of those organizations reflect what is best for your firm.

Beyond that, conscious leadership in the development of laws, regulation, and policy at a state and national level is still another way to position senior management as leaders. This is accomplished through testimony in governmental hearings, speeches to major public forums, and op-ed pieces or paid "advertorials" on issues of the day in major media.

Leadership communication is an effective tool for differentiating an individual financial institution from its competitors in a crowded field.

Expertise

Allied with leadership communications in distinguishing a financial institution from its competition are public relations programs designed to demonstrate and support a firm's expertise in the areas in which it operates. The public tends to believe and trust those firms that it perceives to be experts in their fields.

Virtually every institution maintains a research staff of economists, market analysts,

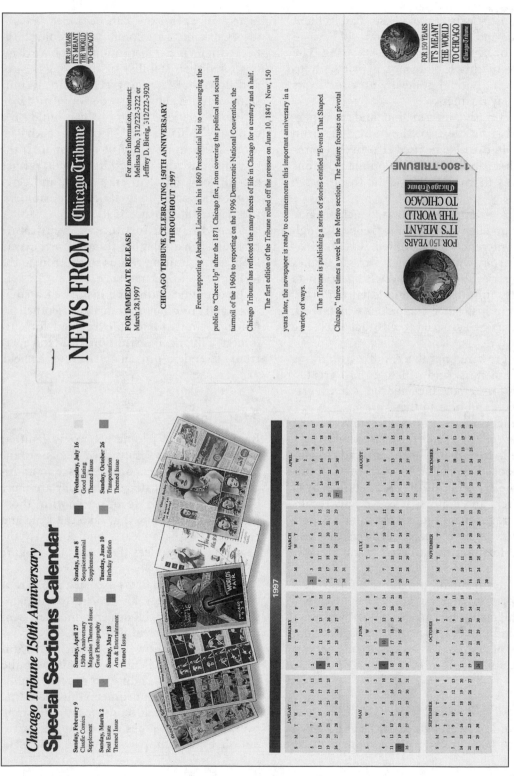

Figure 36.2 To celebrate the 150th anniversary of the *Chicago Tribune*, the Tribune Company drew on its expertise in a range of media. In addition to the many features, series, and supplements that ran in the paper itself, anniversary-related materials were produced by the Tribune's broadcasting, educational, and interactive services arms. *Courtesy Chicago Tribune.*

and industry experts to advise management of trends and developments that will have an impact on their particular businesses. The purpose of this intelligence is primarily to give the individual company an edge in its day-to-day business.

However, this information, and the expertise and reputations of the individuals who develop it, can also be used effectively to create high-visibility, ongoing public relations programs that reach the public through the media.

Typical examples are banks, which provide regular updates on economic trends through press conferences and printed reports; brokerage firms, whose analysts provide studies on industries they track and who participate in media inquiries on individual company plans; and insurance companies which track and report on actuarial trends that affect the industry.

The growing number of TV programs about business and finance has created chances for personable and quotable experts to be seen and heard often.

Excellent opportunities also exist to bring media specialists inside the institution to participate in forums and seminars featuring in-depth looks into major issues of the day, utilizing the expertise of the firm's staff to brief the writers and editors. This not only results in coverage citing your company's expert opinions, but also establishes links that will be used for months and even years after the event.

Long-term media programs built around the expertise that already exists within a financial institution can go a long way in helping an individual company stand apart from the rest of the field as an expert in the eyes of the public.

History

In an industry in which the public must decide to trust a firm with its money, a long history of operations can be a clear advantage. Consumers are comforted by doing business with financial institutions that have demonstrated their stability by surviving the ups and downs of changing economic circumstances over a substantial period of time.

Public relations programs can build on a company's history by focusing activities around the anniversary of its founding, the personalities who shaped its growth, service awards for long-term employees, and ceremonies honoring long-standing customers. (*See* Figure 36.2, page 539.)

Many financial institutions even feature museum-like displays of company artifacts in lobbies and waiting rooms to accentuate the feeling of solid permanence.

By communicating the history of a company, and building programs to accentuate its longevity both for employees and for customers, a financial institution can stand apart from newer, less-proven entries into the field.

Education

Because average people are rarely familiar with all the intricacies involved in many of the major financial decisions they face in an increasingly complicated world, they are more likely to trust, and do business with, those financial institutions that take the time and trouble to explain clearly and concisely the products and services they offer. (*See* Figure 36.3, page 541.)

Thus, successful firms make it a public relations priority to develop brochures and pamphlets explaining in understandable terms what they offer consumers.

Beyond that, however, financial institutions have an excellent opportunity to build trust and understanding among the public through generic consumer education that helps the individual consumer understand overall financial issues and strategies, without pitching a company's specific products.

Figure 36.3 In this issue of its quarterly magazine for employees and customers, the Harris Bank promotes its 115-year history of providing discreet service to the wealthy. *Courtesy Harris Bank, Chicago.*

Thus, programs can be developed to disseminate educational materials that explain how to plan an estate, how to decide on investment goals, how to create a budget, how the stock market operates, how to plan for income taxes, how to design comprehensive insurance coverage, and how to start a small business. These create consumers who are more aware of their options and also more likely to turn to the institution that gave them good advice when they exercise those options.

Public relations programs that provide educational material of value to the consumer are excellent tools for financial institutions building goodwill among the public to distinguish them from their competition.

Openness and responsiveness

Public relations policies that stress willingness to cooperate fully with the media, and that communicate openly and responsively with the public through them, provide another essential ingredient critical to the long-term success of a financial institution. (*See* Chapter 21.)

While this is a solid component of public relations practice in any endeavor, it is particularly important in an industry where public trust and confidence are the basis for doing business.

There are obvious benefits in establishing your institution as one with which the media can be assured of cooperation in dealing with current issues and in obtaining prompt responses to legitimate inquiries for general information. Over time, being open and responsive, and finding knowledgeable spokespersons wherever appropriate, results in stories that cite your institution as an industry leader and a source of expert information.

In times of crisis, however, companies that need to get their messages to the public quickly and accurately will find that the goodwill and trust they have built up with the media are like money in the bank. If you haven't taken the time and the trouble to build solid media relationships as a matter of policy in normal times, you will find it exceedingly difficult to establish the links you need when it becomes imperative to tell your story.

An open and responsive media relations policy is often overlooked as a key ingredient to building a successful public relations program for a financial institution.

Innovation

Finally, when all the appropriate programs are in place, you will still be missing something essential to distinguish and differentiate the financial institution you represent in the marketplace of public opinion.

Innovation in developing public relations programs is the final link in successfully communicating on behalf of your individual firm. This can entail unique responses to the nature of your business, to the particular niche you seek to fill, or to the individual barriers to your company's success. Innovation is essential to fill the needs of your particular institution.

To assure innovation in your public relations performance, you must make sure that you have established programs to cover all the general and specific points listed above, and then you must never be satisfied that those programs are all you need.

Innovation comes from willingness to take the extra step after you've covered all the bases, courage to recognize that being better than most is not good enough, and recognition that a rapidly changing world requires a proactive, not reactive, approach to public relations.

Future Considerations

The fundamental public relations considerations of all financial institutions are similar, but the developments taking place in coming years will result in significant realignments of power and status within the industry.

Who will be the winners and the losers is an open question, at best, but it is obvious that recent trends—deregulation, the blurring of boundaries, new competition, consolidation, worldwide markets—will create a continuing state of flux for financial institutions.

Financial institutions today face a world unlike any they have become accustomed to in the past. It is a time of great danger and a time of great opportunity. The only assurance is that tomorrow will bring change and new challenges at an even faster rate.

Some of the special considerations that will face financial institutions and those who practice public relations for the industry follow.

New loyalties

The true winners in today's deregulated markets are consumers. Their habits and choices in the future will be the determinant of success among financial institutions in the United States.

Consumers have clearly discarded many traditional values of long-term loyalty for better returns on their money.

When money market funds paying interest for deposits were first developed in the late 1970s, deposits flowed out of banks and savings and loans and into these new interest-bearing checking instruments.

As banks and savings and loans were allowed to compete for these funds themselves through the creation of NOW accounts in the early 1980s, price became the determining factor for many consumers.

Deposits were fair game, financial institutions could compete through interest rates, and consumers could shop for the best return on their money.

This competition was not without its price. Financial institutions faced with higher costs to attract funds had to take higher risks in investing their assets to remain profitable.

These higher risks took a toll, with high failure rates among banks in the 1980s. Even more severe structural failure in the savings and loan industry necessitated massive federal bailout.

The financial industry has gone through significant structural changes to accommodate these new loyalties and to compete effectively in the 1990s. The characteristics of these changes will accelerate throughout the current decade.

Global markets

Traditional boundaries that isolated regional world markets in the past have effectively been erased.

Major financial institutions now operate on a global, twenty-four-hour basis, linked to the financial capitals of the world by computers and sophisticated telecommunications. In this increasingly globalized environment, corporate clients rely more on a single institution to handle their financial transactions wherever they do business.

Even within the United States, the legislative and regulatory barriers to interstate banking are being phased out, paving the way for creation of a few "super" financial institutions competing for a national customer base.

Smaller institutions will still be able to compete in selected geographic areas or with specialized services, but the trend will encourage creation of a few national firms offering a variety of financial services to U.S. consumers and competing in world financial markets at the same time.

As this movement accelerates, great benefit will come to those companies that most clearly communicate the multitude of services they offer to consumers, most effectively translate the benefits of their services, and build new loyalties out of a confusing clamor in the marketplace.

The power of information will also develop into one of the deciding factors in this battle for public acceptance.

Successful financial institutions will have increasingly sophisticated databases of information at their disposal. Programs to share this information with customers and enable them to act intelligently in forming their own investment decisions will create an advantage for those firms that can do it most effectively.

Changing demographics

The nature of the consumer market in the United States is changing dramatically, and these changes will also profoundly impact the operation of successful financial institutions.

The "baby boom bubble" of some 76 million people born between 1946 and 1964 is maturing. Now the median age of the baby boomer is about forty.

Between 1970 and 1990, assimilation of this huge population bubble into the economy created high unemployment, high inflation, record levels of personal debt, and extremely low savings rates. Many of these trends are expected to be reversed and many new economic patterns will emerge as the United States population continues to age and mature.

For example, the Federal Reserve has estimated that the current national savings rate of less than 4 percent could easily double to 8 percent as aging baby boomers change their spending and investment habits.

That change alone would translate to as much as $400 billion in new personal savings per year, a tremendous amount of capital for financial institutions to compete for and to invest.

Beyond that, the demographic changes brought on by aging of the population will have many other ramifications that will continue to modify the operational parameters for successful financial institutions. New spending patterns, different investment goals, and altered insurance needs will all require flexibility and innovation in meeting this new population's financial needs.

Impact on Public Relations

As financial organizations shed the tradition of heavy regulation that severely limited the range and scope of their business activities over the past fifty years, the need for public understanding and consent will increase substantially.

It was, after all, abuses of the system in the past that created the wall of regulation that proscribed the operations of various players in the field.

Thus, it will be critical for the wide array of players in today's competition for financial services—both traditional companies with expanded powers and new competitors in previously closed markets—to maintain a favorable climate of opinion in which to operate.

At the heart of successful operations for the new financial institutions—as well as for the entire industry itself—is perceptive, effective, integrated, and innovative public relations planning and programs, executed with excellence.

37

PUBLIC RELATIONS FOR RETAILERS

TERRY MAYER

Terry Mayer has had a diversified career in publicity and public relations for retailers. A native New Yorker and graduate of Long Island University, she began in publicity at Macy's, New York. She then served at Gimbel Brothers, New York, with Bernice FitzGibbon. Later, she became publicity and advertising director for David Crystal, Inc.; fashion director for Amos Parrish, the advisor on fashion merchandising for retailers; and fashion coordinator to JC Penney stores. She established her own publicity firm in New York in 1964.

For eleven years she selected and presented the National Retail Merchants Association's "Top Fashion Promotions of the Year" and for five years the "Top Home Furnishings Promotions."

Miss Mayer has been president of the Publicity Club of New York and headed the Public Relations Committee for New York City's 300th Anniversary.

The continuing turmoil that has racked retailers graphically illustrates the extreme importance of public relations to this industry. In the fallout of these difficult times, Altman's and other venerable firms have disappeared, and many other major retailers were put on the selling block, including Bloomingdale's, Marshall Field's, Saks Fifth Avenue, Sakowitz, and Bonwit Teller. The largest of all retailers, Sears, followed Montgomery Ward's lead in a valiant struggle to redefine itself. Similarly, lesser stores and chains have been merged, sold, or restructured.

Even though Field's and Bloomingdale's probably had the strongest consumer franchises, neither could insulate itself from the internal problems of the conglomerate that had purchased it. For many of the others,

their problems underscored their weak acceptance by the public.

All the elements of public relations discussed elsewhere in this book apply to retail stores. However, retail public relations has one specific primary aim: to give the store *visibility* and *identity*.

The store that gets lost in the crowd loses out. The stores the public regards as "outstanding citizens" are those that never cease to make their marks on the community, the employees, and the manufacturers, as well as on the national scene.

The *Wall Street Journal* quoted former CEO of Montgomery Ward Stephen Pistner as saying that there has been "a polarization of retailing. Any retailer without a clear image is in trouble."

Though inanimate, a store is composed of thinking humans—and *does* have a distinct personality. Employees at all levels of the organization reflect the attitudes at the top, all the way to the president and chief executive officer. If executive management practices effective communications, these capabilities will be mirrored by people throughout the store—to everyone's advantage.

To attain visibility and identity the store must anticipate and plan for the unknown. To fully capitalize on the store's assets, the public relations department must effectively relay its story to the community. This means that the store's public relations personnel must be knowledgeable, well informed, creative, and flexible. Working for a retailer requires the ability "to turn on a dime," as the axiom goes—as well as the capability to see every facet of a project, to analyze its potential, and to develop it to its fullest possibility.

This chapter relates how some stores position themselves to be forever in the public eye with their distinctive personalities, and describes methods that any store can adopt or adapt to gain maximum visibility.

The Unique Nature of Retailing

The people of a store, the advertisements of a store, and the merchandise of a store all bring management into direct contact with the public. To sell merchandise or services, one must know the pulse of the consumer, understand the family budget and know how it is being used, and know the family.

The community's attitude toward the store must be constantly analyzed. When a new boutique for youngsters opens a block away, will your customers be loyal? Will advance merchandising techniques, sales promotion, and special events that make news hold them?

The charm of a freshly sprung boutique is its "personality," reflecting the perspicacity and the taste of the owner, as well as knowledge of what the community wants.

The community's attitude toward a store depends on the attitude of its management toward the community. Many factors contribute to the way in which the public regards the store—among them, the personal magnetism of the top executive or the publicized authority, such as the fashion coordinator or home furnishings coordinator; the respect with which these officials are held; the community's knowledge of them; and how they participate in the community.

Changes in style and public desires affect the retailer more quickly and more acutely than most businesses. Retailers caught with too many of a couturier's styles at the end of a season or after a reasonable period of no-sale, mark them down. Computers that keep track of product movement and inventories help keep the action fluid. Trade periodicals like *Women's Wear Daily*, *HFD Retailing Home Furnishings*, *Apparel Merchandising*, and *Daily News Record* help keep the merchant and retail publicist alert to public opinion and demand. The Sunday *New York Times* often shows how things will be in the United States shortly.

Communication between management and personnel is vital. Large stores have learned the importance of weekly staff meetings and in-department meetings. For instance, in a fashion department the buyer shows the newest styles to her salespeople, with the group getting pointers on fiber, fabric, cut of the garment, and care of the garment. The store's fashion coordinator informs the staff at fashion shows for employees, passing on all the news they can use. The publicity department follows the publications that set consumer tastes and provides analyses for the salespeople so they will talk the customer's language.

Matching the Program to the Store Type

Distinction between various types of retail companies in regard to public relations needs are not so clearly marked as in other fields.

The national chain

The giant operation has its executives working as an integrated team. Each person supports the abilities of others, and their composite skills are passed on in training programs for the whole organization.

Sears has a public relations manual for store executives, who may not have had any public relations training at all. The Sears manual is indexed so a person can get a fairly ready response to almost any problem that may come up.

Major chains believe that the store manager should become involved in the community. The manuals discuss general policy, membership, donations, high school programs, garden club programs, women's club programs, legislative activities, and so on. A national chain's public relations program is highly developed in community participation. Sears, Penney, and Ward are all involved in programs with high schools, with some form of in-store charm school for both boys and girls, with on-the-job training for teenagers, with national organizations like the 4-H group and the Boy Scouts, and so on.

JC Penney supplied store managers with a booklet called *Publicity, How to Get It* that was produced by the company's Media Relations Department.

Penney advises that publicity can do several things for the store: "Create Interest. Build Goodwill, and Attract Customers." The booklet outlines a series of events that can form a basis for publicity and make news. They are fashions, store events, style shows, community projects, personnel promotions, new construction, contest winners, impor-

tant visitors, personal events, big or unusual sales, exhibits, speeches, trips, conventions, humorous incidents.

A page on "Establishing Press Relations" could be a guide to any publicist. It says:

> Sometimes there is fear connected with the idea of approaching the editor of a newspaper. This fear usually is felt only by those who haven't approached an editor.
>
> Most editors are businessmen like yourself and will consider any straightforward proposition just as you would. There is one problem, though, that store managers have that others seeking publicity may not have—you are an advertiser. Because of this it is imperative that as thorough an understanding as possible of newspaper editorial policies should be obtained before meeting with an editor. Some newspapers have firm policies regarding publicity for advertisers, but mention of these policies should be left strictly to the discretion of the editor.
>
> Usually editors will evaluate your story on the basis of its merits alone and if it is a good one, and accepted, he will thank you warmly for bringing it to his attention.
>
> Once you are well acquainted with the newspaper you and the paper will find it expedient to contact the appropriate editor for the story involved. If it's a business page story, see the business editor; see the women's page or fashion editor when you have a story of interest to women.
>
> Many Penney managers, some near you, can give case histories of their excellent relations with the press. Some have established relations to the degree that the editors now ask them for story ideas!

Through help like this, Penney's store management becomes conscious of publicity and its benefits. Managers learn the basics of publicity techniques for store openings and modernizations, special event publicity, what makes a good news picture, and how to write a press release. (*See* Chapters 20–25.)

Penney has various public service programs geared to provide information at the stores. These respond to current events and the needs of their potential customers. Booklets about protection of the home from theft and fire educate the reader while tying in merchandise available in the hardware areas. Some of the Penney stores have special events called Home Security Workshops and give out booklets. The activities are recognized as public service while they feature merchandise.

The local department store

The local department store is often built on the acceptance of the brand names it carries and how it merchandises those names and labels. Carrying nationally advertised brands is a tradition and helps attain consumer acceptance. But it is how the store stage-manages what it has to sell that brings in more customers.

The local department store usually serves as the focal point of the community in meeting most of its shopping needs. Macy's in New York is the largest store in the world, yet it is dependent on the community for its business. Therefore, it is in its own self-interest to benefit the community. More than most stores, it has done a series of "salute" advertisements for cultural organizations.

Knowing that people are tremendously interested in their physical well-being, Macy's featured merchandise that was new in health and beauty products, which made news. Another area that city people are interested in is the crowded housing situation. Macy's put together merchandise ideas, minidryers, miniwashers, wall units, all under the heading of "Space Exploration." This was of interest to the public, and a new way of inviting them to see a collection of merchandise. It provided a "peg" for coverage by the media.

Where Macy's has always served a broad range of customers, other stores can focus on a single type of customer.

The department store must determine what it has to offer that competition doesn't. What unique characteristic can it develop?

To know this, the public relations director must be involved with the merchandise as well as the store, its personnel, and its public. He or she must plan both institutional and product publicity.

At the start the public relations department must set out total objectives for a season to achieve a well-balanced program. There must be continual review of the success of the program.

Dayton's, Minneapolis, from a public relations standpoint, seeks to strike a balance and appeal to all age groups. The store wants to project an image of fashion, excitement, and innovation and at the same time to uphold the store's tradition of quality, integrity, and good citizenship.

Dayton's theory on how to acquire goodwill for the store, internally and externally, is that it is necessary to communicate with:

- employees and managers (current and potential)
- customers
- residents in communities where stores are located
- visitors from out-of-town
- vendors
- "VIP" groups, such as government and community leaders, the academic community, and members of the news media
- corporation shareholders, the financial community, and management personnel of the corporation and other operating companies (handled mostly by Corporate Public Relations office)

Dayton's overall public relations program is a model that can guide many retailers. (*See* Figure 37.1.)

Research

This has included in-depth consumer surveys to pinpoint current attitudes about the store.

Figure 37.1 This ad helped keep customer goodwill during the unexpected closing of Marshall Field's State Street store at the time of the Great Chicago Flood of April 1992. *Courtesy Marshall Field's State Street store, Chicago.*

Community relations

The store works with many civic organizations in staging benefit fashion shows and other events such as an "Orphan Animal Sale" in the store's auditorium for the benefit of the Animal Humane Society.

Other examples include a flower show preview for the benefit of the University of Minnesota Arboretum, and the annual ball of People to People, Inc., held each summer in the store's auditorium.

Institutional advertising

This has included ads emphasizing courtesy, service, and so on; salutes to major league baseball and football teams.

Storewide and department events

These have been planned for various age groups, to bring traffic into the store and to create goodwill. Dayton's large auditorium is utilized throughout the year for events such as bridal shows, flower shows, import fairs, art exhibits, speakers and entertainers, and so on.

Internal communications

These have included the company's monthly publication, the *Daytonian*, published by the Employee Publications Office in cooperation with the Public Relations Department, as well as a weekly newsletter, "This Week at Dayton's."

Other public relations efforts directed toward employees include audiovisual presentations by the Training Department, special programs geared to helping employees advance into better positions ("Operation Upgrade" and a Tuition Refund Program), a suggestion program, special "courtesy" awards, service awards, and so on. Employees are invited to preview major auditorium events.

Sales-support publicity and promotion

Obtaining newspaper, magazine, trade paper, radio, and TV coverage has helped to publicize events, new store openings, new shops and services, other business news, and editorial coverage on merchandise.

Dayton's has sponsored a "Children's Movie of the Month" program, a series of wholesome, quality movies for children, with tickets available in the store. It has a wide variety of special events. Many are of a public service nature like a "Fireworks Spectacular" at one of the city's lakes, a makeup party and fashion show for blind girls, an annual flower show, and an "Empty Nest" symposium for the mature woman. Under the Community Resource Volunteers program, Dayton's provides speakers to the public schools. School tours are also arranged for events of special interest to children.

Dayton's "Events Calendar" lists all events scheduled for the month, with a brief description of each. Many of these do not warrant a complete news release, but the calendar keeps the press aware of what is going on at Dayton's, and results in many inquiries and subsequent news coverage.

Television and radio are used extensively for publicity. Dayton's offers appropriate guests to women's shows, children's shows, radio talk shows, and others.

Dayton's generally has several major press parties each year, to preview major auditorium events. Smaller press parties are occasionally held with an imaginative invitation and theme, for opening of special shops or other special occasions.

Although customer complaints are generally handled by the Customer Service Department, the Public Relations Department answers complaints of a general nature, and works with Customer Service, the Credit Department, and other areas of the store in handling special customer problems.

The specialty shop

The specialty shop arouses interest because of its character and personality. It must make *visual* what it has to sell. The environment of the store sells it. A fur boutique in the Midwest "carpeted," "walled," and "ceilinged" its store in fur. Since it was different and curious, people came in to see, and to touch, and to try on.

In seeking the new and refreshing, some specialty stores use plastics in their displays. They give distinctiveness to the appearance of the store.

It is ideas and selling the distinctive "signature" that feature good public relations in the specialty store. Attention to detail, interesting packaging, color, and concentration on the new theme all are pluses. Adding this to basic public relations techniques makes for a good program. A store has many assets that can make it unique. The task is to find them, then tell.

The discounter

The discounter competes with the luxury of the specialty store by convincing the middle class it can match it at a lower cost. Each discounter, of course, also competes with other discounters. It must lure the public with special events and showmanship; services to the family, like a place to park the children; contests; and community get-togethers.

Adjusting to Current Developments

The retailer must assess the national climate every day. Both community and world events affect the business. For instance, a parade, once a joy because it brought traffic, is now often feared because of activists who have appeared in the community. Stores are considered landmarks and places to make news. They are often singled out by militant groups. In some towns, store owners now lock their doors during the day and admit people on recognizance. A Protection Department should be well briefed in dealing with difficulties and cooperating with local police.

The store is often a mirror of the community. The people of the store are the ones who make it work. Their willingness to participate makes the store a better place.

Defining the Store's Distinctiveness

Stores are constantly analyzing themselves and looking at the type of image they are projecting. Some stores have never found the appropriate image to put them across. People can't recall where they are located in a city full of stores. Others are an experience to be talked about. That is the aim of every sophisticated store today.

Many aim to establish a national image like that of Bergdorf Goodman, Neiman-Marcus, Marshall Field's, and Saks Fifth Avenue. Many contend for that role because the country and the world are becoming smaller as people become more mobile. Also, if a store is well known and has a unique mailing catalog, it will get business from all over and proudly point to its customers in other areas. And vendors will love it and service it first.

A store successful in projecting an image uses repetition in its advertising style. The concept, the tone, and the layout are immediately recognized.

Packaging and visible symbols

Consumer tastes constantly change. To win the customer, you must give her or him "the new."

You also must give the customer the "status bag" if you want her or him to carry it. Various good stores have bags that can be recognized at a distance.

Bloomingdale's discovered a few years ago that they could provide an artistic, colorful bag and leave their name off, and everyone would know that it came from "Bloomies," as they have been nicknamed.

Specialty stores around the country often work with popular artists and paper product producers to participate in chain purchase of shopping bags and cartons. The printer changes the store logo for each order. By working together, the price of the bags and boxes is lower, and a smart look is achieved for all participating stores.

Just as the letterhead is important, since it suggests the attitude of the store, so are the color and quality of the stationery. It is important to review the impression being made and determine the one the individual store should have.

Window Displays as Image Builders

Store windows have long ceased being merely display space for merchandise. Leading retailers recognize their power in establishing a distinctive character for the store. Retailers such as Bloomingdale's and F.A.O. Schwarz in New York, Marshall Field's and Carson Pirie Scott in Chicago, and Neiman-Marcus in Dallas have been venturesome in their window display.

Bloomingdale's attracted national attention by injecting sexual overtones into the choice and positioning of mannequins. Field's—whose windows have always been noted for their distinctiveness and good taste—adds humor and whimsy without sacrificing taste. Carson's uses windows in sequence to tell a story. In one called "Out on the Town," the first window featured several beautifully dressed women before a chrome-and-glass background. The second window showed them at a theater ticket booth. The next had one man and two of the women at a cocktail lounge. The fourth showed them at the theater; the fifth at dinner; the sixth at a discotheque; the seventh outdoors in the moonlight; and the last focused on one of the women at home with an antacid and an ice bag.

The window is the opening of the store to the world, so it says at least as much about the store's personality as a person's facial expression conveys about him or her.

Attracting Youth

Reaching the young buyer and future employees requires special techniques. *Seventeen* magazine often works with store promotion directors, giving them ideas, and helps to put on a fine program.

May D & F substituted a seven-hour marathon television show for the usual fashion shows in the store. It worked fashion for boys and girls into TV variety. It was backed by a high-impact series of newspaper ads. This promotion replaced the usual high school and college fashion shows and boards of college students acting as temporary fashion experts.

Produced on a local television station from Friday at 9:30 P.M. until 5 A.M. Saturday, this seven hour telethon combined fashions, "camp" movies, rock bands, and a teen telephone board seated in bleacher rows on a stage, each with her own telephone.

Many prominent retail firms sponsor and counsel Junior Achievement companies made up of high-school-age youngsters.

J.L. Hudson of Detroit had a car paint-in and a co-ed fashion show, tied in with *Seventeen* magazine as part of a Teen "Out of Sight Week." They staged festivities in their auditorium, and included a chic boutique at one end of it. Four co-ed fashion shows were staged, each running fifteen minutes without commentary. A formal fashion show was held and a big-name band and disk jockey performed.

Many stores have school programs, and many have part-time school employees to give the students a taste of retailing.

The Importance of Employee Communications

Though management policies and the store's posture should be specified in the pages of the company publication, it should not be completely "managed" by management. (*See* Chapter 12.) It is better to have a saleswoman tell her story of the "hardest sale I ever made" to inspire other employees.

Employee clubs

Fayetteville, North Carolina, is the home of the Capitol Department Store, whose employees reach out to do something warm and human for the community. Members of the Capitol Club, composed of employees and executives, each year take on a worthwhile project for the Christmas holidays. Though the Christmas season is hectic the members one year decided to entertain senior citizens, inviting them to join club members and other special guests for a holiday lunch and afternoon of fellowship and entertainment. Club members systematically planned a menu and assigned dishes. Ninety-two employees came on the appointed Sunday, bringing food. A host and hostess were assigned to each table, which had Christmas decorations. Following entertainment, each guest left with a poinsettia and a bag of gifts. The event was treated prominently in the local newspaper.

Hosting Promotions and Events

Neiman-Marcus in Dallas has been known for its Fortnights, celebrating the arts and crafts and products of a particular nation.

Twenty buyers went to France one year for merchandise for the event. Dallas leaders were invited to lunch nine months before the event to get their cooperation. French paintings were exhibited at the Dallas Museum of Fine Arts. French tapestries were shown at the Memorial Auditorium. French films were shown at local theaters, French entertainers were booked into Dallas night clubs, civic clubs heard French speakers. Both *Vogue* and the Dallas *Times-Herald* had advertising supplements. The ambassador from France to the United States and the mayor of Dallas officiated, attending the gala balls and festivities. Air France arranged a charter flight for two hundred French visitors.

This first Fortnight was so successful that before it was over, British interests invited the store to do a fortnight for Great Britain the next year.

In a similar Texas-like fashion, Sakowitz of Houston arranged a Festival of Folkways. Sakowitz adapted the history of Texas to its storewide promotion.

Since patchwork quilted items were in fashion, this fact was exploited. The way America was "stitched together" out of diverse peoples, customs, and countries was demonstrated. A symbol was developed of a patchwork in the shape of a star, and it was colorfully put on posters, shopping bags, program covers, invitations, and other materials. What was at that time the "world's largest patchwork quilt" became the festival banner over Sakowitz's front door.

Inside the store, a large group of old patchwork quilts was on display, and a rare historical collection of clothes and accessories of early America was on view. An American history slide show drew crowds to the first floor; the second floor featured one thousand famous American toys and games; there was a cavalcade of comics and a history-spanning horde of political campaign buttons. The third floor included a roundup of early American farm relics and an exhibit of ethnic confluences in Old New Orleans. Jazz and other music was featured. The fourth floor had an old-fashioned facsimile of America's first drug store, furniture of the folkways, the valentine-strewn history of greeting cards, and a history of American slang. The fifth floor had a Texas-size history of the Lone Star State, a Sky Terrace menu of foods of the folkways, and an old-fashioned American apple-ducking barrel.

It was a store-wide celebration, topped with the launching of Houston's fall social season at a benefit at a hotel with a "Fashions of the Folkways" fashion show. Well-known designers appeared.

These events win publicity because they make news. Newspapers and radio and television stations will cover a happening in which a large part of the community is engaged. The public relations department can set up photographs, arrange interviews, and suggest features coasting on the momentum. Releases, biographies, and speeches can be based on the event. When a store is imaginative enough to attract all age groups it generates publicity in many media.

Direct Mail

Most stores mail statements to their charge customers monthly. Some also enclose chatty newsletters, printed on attractive stationery. Elizabeth Arden beauty salons once sent a letter with the salutation, "Dear, dear Customer" to be just a little friendlier than the stock mailing piece. (*See* Chapter 31.)

Special effort to be original while consistent with the character of the store is called for to make mail communication fully effective.

Communicating with Investors

Information on investor relations in Chapter 11 is applicable to any publicly owned retailer. It is wise to treat this as though the company were a blue chip company on the stock exchange, for any financial statements made must be highly professional. Many stores retain consultants to help them handle this very important and specialized area.

Communicating with the Community

Information on community relations is in Chapter 8. This subject is threaded through this chapter, for it is one of the most important and changing areas of public relations

for a merchant in daily contact with the public.

Community affairs cannot be predicted, and the ability to adapt to new situations is essential.

Gaining support through good citizenship

Symphonies, colleges, charities, and many fund-raising activities give the retailer an opportunity to be a notable corporate citizen. Benefit events that are well produced put a store in a good light and give customers a chance to dress up in clothes they've purchased for the occasion. Notice the attention paid to designer names worn by wives of tycoons. Social notes in many newspapers include references to whose clothes were worn by whom.

An alert store can produce an event that is of such value for its publicity that it becomes an annual occasion.

Many "name" stores have one or more events in honor of a charity or perhaps make their corporate contribution by sponsoring a cultural event on television, as the JC Penney Company had done on public television and at a White House performance of musical stars.

Donating merchandise—one grand prize or souvenirs (often obtained from a cooperating manufacturer)—is another way to attract positive recognition. Some stores keep a notebook on an annual basis, planning in advance for tie-ins of this kind, and including a budget for promotion.

Reaching Minority Groups

Minority group relations ares treated in depth in Chapter 9.

Carson Pirie Scott of Chicago in the 1950s pioneered the employment of African-Americans in visible jobs. But Carson's managers recognized that they had to be more responsive to urban problems after a series of six internal fires broke out in their famous landmark store, which was designed by "Chicago School" architect Louis Sullivan, in 1899.

The management decided to start with a conference on "Urban Racial Crises" for executives. It was later repeated for two additional groups.

Carson's president arranged for the first conferences with the Chicago Business Industrial Project, a nonprofit agency serving as a liaison center among competing groups within and outside Chicago's power structure.

A series of meetings and three-day workshops on race and human relations were held for branch store managers and assistant managers, personnel managers, and first-line supervisors. Topics included a study of preconceived notions about people from other social and ethnic groups, individual attitudes, attitudes of minority groups, and techniques in applying good management and human relations principles.

Carson's contracted the Industrial Relations Center at the University of Chicago to conduct an employee opinion survey and to develop an organizational development program for the 8,500 associates in its retail division. Both feedback and report-back techniques provided information that was relayed to the store's staff. Task forces established programs and projects to help Carson's reach a more adequate ratio of minority-level associates at middle and top-level jobs. Posting of jobs at the State Street store lists job openings. Store tours are conducted for inner-city students to broaden their knowledge of job opportunities in retailing.

Carson's executives act as consultants to black entrepreneurs, providing retail expertness to vendors and suppliers.

Responding to Emergencies

A store's ability to deal with difficulty protects its character in the community.

Emergency procedures for retail stores are often standardized and similar to those of other businesses. (See Chapters 2 and 20 for basic information.) Often, though, a store will be original in handling an unforeseen difficulty and win admiration for its efforts.

Some stores have procedures for dealing with many types of emergency situations or possible negative events. For example, there is a clear-cut procedure to be followed in the event the store has to be closed for severe weather conditions.

Most stores have learned by experience the need for a master book of emergency procedures. The pages are constantly added to, as history is overtaken by current events.

Among the more basic, necessary examples is one developed by Sakowitz of Houston called a Fire Drill and Evacuation Procedure. This is an eleven-page outline of general instructions, including having periodic fire drills in which all employees are required to participate. Fire drills are conducted prior to store opening.

Because of the possibility of in-store demonstrations, retailers are having their executives and staff meet with the public relations people of the police departments to learn the basics of handling emergencies of various kinds.

Though each community has its own problems, many are similar. Local chambers of commerce welcome participation of this nature. The National Retail Merchants Association, 100 W. 31st Street, New York, NY 10001, has procedures that can be of help in many situations.

The Magazine and Movie Connection

An area of store exposure that impresses the customer is the magazine editorial credit. Whether it be home furnishings or fashion (men's, women's, children's), the merchandise the store stocks that appears in a magazine is likely to bring in added business. The store has the opportunity to be acknowledged as head-quarters for this new merchandise, so the publicity department is effective when it gets this coverage for the store.

To become listed, an amicable relationship must be established with the suppliers. Buyers should take the publicity personnel on visits to the leading manufacturers they buy from.

When a manufacturer shows a new line to buyers, the commentator often announces that a certain style will be seen in a certain magazine; the month it will appear is announced.

The route of the magazine tie-in has become the track the wise merchant can take. Those who attend the magazines' semiannual seminars get pace-setting promotion ideas, often supplemented by handsome kits that include newspaper ads, TV material, radio scripts, news releases, display themes, and other materials. The tie-in stores have learned to be performers when the issue hits the sub-scription list and newsstands.

(*See* Chapters 21, 22, and 23 for further information on working in this area.)

Movie tie-ins

As long as there have been a Hollywood and press agents, stores have understood the wisdom of associating their merchandise or visual displays with a new film in town. (*See* Chapter 26.) In the 1940s, windows were given themes to tie in with the names of new films and to show related merchandise. For example, the film *The Big Clock* brought on a display of clocks.

Today, there is great sophistication involved in working with film producers. Stores find it an advantage to make news with a concept from a film, or by touting an institutional tie-in. For instance, retailers in key markets appealed to people's fascination with Batman by tying in with the film.

Promotion people at the film companies help stores carry out their tie-ins. Planning begins about a year in advance of the film's release. *Variety*, the entertainment industry's newspaper, carries the names of contacts at film production companies.

38

PUBLIC RELATIONS FOR THE SMALL TO MID-SIZED COMPANY

PHILIP TAGGART

Philip Taggart, APR, chairman of the Philip Taggart Company, Houston, has represented more than seventy-five corporations in forty different industry groups in the last thirty-five years, principally in the areas of marketing and financial relations. His clients have been headquartered in Rome, London, Paris, Tokyo, Aberdeen, Toronto, and Calgary as well as many U.S. cities. Some have grown from small corporations to industry leaders.

He began his professional career in public relations as staff writer at The Philip Lesly Company in 1955. By 1959, he was one of four vice-presidents and headed an account group that was charged with conducting public relations to Canada, the United States, and Europe.

Churchill Group was founded in 1973 in Houston, specializing in financial relations. About half of its clients are small to mid-sized corporations.

Taggart is an instructor in investor relations at the University of Houston, and a lecturer and author of articles on marketing and financial relations.

Small to mid-sized companies present some of the greatest rewards and challenges to the public relations profession. On one hand they create more than 80 percent of new jobs, many of the most advanced products and services, and the most suspense and excitement in the business world. Yet they have the highest failure rate in American business—nearly nine out of ten fail before their seventh year, primarily due to insufficient capital. The rare few that do take off and soar to the ranks of the *Fortune* 500 within their first five years in business—as Microsoft did—build incredi-ble wealth for their founders, investors, and some of their suppliers.

This chapter focuses on the public relations needs and applicable services for organizations that provide for-profit services and products to customers—whether consumers, business, or industry. (The needs of professional corporations and consulting firms are treated in Chapter 43.)

No true yardstick exists for predicting which company will rise from the mid-size category to "big company" status. Generally speaking, few corporations, regardless of whether they provide products or services, rank as "large" until they exceed one thousand employees. To qualify for *Fortune* 500 status the company usually must reach $500 million in revenues or sales. Companies that fall into the $300–$350-million-per-year revenue or sales bracket are normally considered the upper range of the mid-sized company category.

The public relations activities recommended here also apply to companies with total operating capital of from $100,000 to $50 million. The market capitalization of mid-sized companies is set at up to $100 million.

The first public relations objective of small to mid-sized companies is to identify their strengths and advantages. Then they must use them effectively to facilitate growth by providing better opportunities for their employees, by serving customers better, and by providing better returns for their investors.

Unique Public Relations Needs

The critical difference in public relations activities for these companies stems from the need to gain greater attention while operating from a smaller platform from which to launch the company's messages. Most of the key publics treated elsewhere in this book are of vital interest to the small to mid-sized companies.

Since growing companies are usually cash poor, priority must be given to selecting the publics that are the targets of planned programs. Careful contingencies need to be established for those that may be treated on a reactive basis as events arise.

In some instances, communicating with a key group such as employees may be easier because of the smaller size of the organization. Personal, two-way communication with each individual or small groups of individuals is natural in the smaller corporation, in which the greatest imparting and feedback of information may be gained in the shortest time. These factors contribute to the greatest effectiveness in communication.

Another advantage is that environmental groups and others seeking news-making targets are less apt to attack a small corporation. It is not as well recognized and does not make news as easily as industry leaders. That should not encourage smaller businesses to ignore such areas of responsibility; but if activities in sensitive areas are sound, contingencies for crisis communication can be small.

In most other areas, effective relations with the groups most important to an organization are hampered by small size. Even in direct communication or closely controlled communication, the smaller company usually has less potential to improve the relationship with a key group.

The larger the company, the greater the funds that may be applied to creating better relationships. But size is no substitute for quality. When size meets quality in business services or products, quality wins out most frequently.

Quality starts with a company's ability to discern an audience's perception and expectations. The most neglected element in corporate public relations programs is recognizing the attitudes and opinions of the group addressed and communicating within that mindset, instead of simply sending a message that management wants to be received.

To change a group's attitude or to change opinions most easily, a corporation must first get in step with its audience. It is far more efficient to bend the direction of a group attitude than it is to confront an attitude and attempt to overcome it.

If the small or mid-sized organization cannot find a way to align itself with a group's attitudes without confrontation, that particular group probably should be bypassed if possible. This is particularly applicable to the small to mid-sized corporation that may not be able to bring massive resources to bear on the communication.

Philip Lesly, the editor of this handbook, urges his staff to find out the direction of a given industry trend and to see if that trend fits the goals of a client corporation. If the trend accommodates those goals, Lesly urges that the client take a position at the head of the parade—even if it is only a small factor in the overall industry—and encourages it to act like a leader and talk like a leader and so become that leader, in fact.

While big companies develop distinct perceptions in people's minds, from an outsider's perspective, small companies are lost in the crowd. To compete with other companies on this basis is to put undue stress on the company's special services or lower costs—both of which strain profitability. Accordingly, it is vital for each company to strive for an individualized image.

That can be attained by being seen for something that other companies do not have—such as a colorful or charismatic chief executive, leadership of thought as shown by innovation or brilliant statements, receipt of awards or other recognition, or conducting attention-getting functions or contributions.

At the start, then, every effort should be made to determine what about the company is *distinctive* or *can be made distinctive*. The ability to determine that and to build a program to foster it is a mark of an exceptional public relations person.

Focusing on an issue

Where industry trends are not moving in the direction of the client organization, new issues should be created. One such issue was the "Night Time Driving Accident Problem" for 3M's then fledgling Scotchlite Division. 3M required the division to handle its marketing problems within the constraint of its own cash flow as an almost independent business.

It thus resembled a small business. Though the parent corporation was large, the marketing program for Scotchlite was driven by its own acceptance and the ingenuity of its entrepreneurial management.

The 3M problem was easily identified. States had license plates made for less than 50¢ a plate at prison facilities. The legislative perception was that raising the price above $2.00 to have license plates and traffic control signs reflect light seemed extravagant. The perception began to change when legislators became aware of the number of times "I didn't see . . . the car, the stop sign, the back of the truck" was written in police accident reports. That led to a study at Princeton University on nighttime driving accidents and the efficacy of reflective sheeting as a preventive. Published reports of the results appeared in national publications and an active speaking program was pursued with more than a dozen national organizations, including the Junior Chamber of Commerce, insurance companies, and the Boy Scouts of America.

State legislatures gradually adopted reflective sheeting for signs and license plates. A multimillion-dollar market was created that saves lives and eliminates billions of dollars in property damage.

It is important that legislators recognize their constituents have received the message. The most frequently heard excuse among stage legislators or members of Congress for not supporting an issue is: "I understand the merits of your proposition, but unfortunately the voters in my district do not." In the case of Scotchlite reflective sheeting, hundreds of newspaper clippings and editorials on the benefits of the product from newspapers and broadcasters throughout the state were presented to committees considering adoption of reflective traffic signs and license plates. The sources quoted in the news materials were civic-minded organizations or large insurance companies, providing impeccable sources of persuasion.

Establishing market share in competition with gigantic corporations is most successful when a small niche is recognized that can grow into a wedge at the national or global level. Product cycles—the time required to move a product from recognition of need to actual production—have moved from two years in the early 1980s to eight to ten weeks in many instances. The small company with a breakthrough or simply with a better product that may work faster and more reliably had best move to a global market when the advantage is still on its side.

Three areas of focus

To achieve significance, small corporations must advance on three fronts—lowest cost production, efficient distribution, and obtaining participation of even the lowest-paid employee. Small companies must produce quality; it won't be taken for granted. They must remain focused on their customers' demands. They must be the ones that obsolete their own products. That takes money acquired at the lowest possible rates.

These points must not only be part of the corporate culture, they must be communicated. The way the telephone is answered, the appearance of the letterhead, the appearance of the product itself, or the appearance of the person who delivers the product—all speak more profoundly than a printed message.

Two quick routes to larger market shares are franchising and acquisitions. In both, the company grows either through establishing with the help of others or gaining established operations. But as a small company or even a mid-sized firm, it is much easier to be acquired than to acquire.

Considering these factors and the possible publics, there seem to be three key areas with which even the smallest company cannot afford to do less than its best in managing relations.

The Impact of Employees, Marketing, and Finances

If the employees of any company, large or small, are aligned with its management, it can accomplish great things. Conversely, if employees are against management, it can direct or communicate little that its own employees cannot refute or offset. Employees can guarantee the failure of a company. The history of U.S. business is replete with employee groups that have let companies or plants go out of business rather than accede to management's pressures.

No organization is immune to the destructive forces of a strike. Even the AFL-CIO felt disastrous results when its own clerks went on strike against the union.

Making employees part of the management process is the best way to head off labor-management problems. Chrysler turned to its union and gave its president a seat on its board of directors when the company had its loans guaranteed by the federal government and it was bailing itself out of a debt that threatened to bankrupt it. With 500,000 to 600,000 jobs at stake, counting those of suppliers, it was a case of survival. Labor made many concessions in its own best interest.

To achieve cooperation, management must share with all the workers the company's goals and its global objectives. Technicians must understand the need for teamwork, team leadership, application, and high alertness.

Winning employee support

Such involvement is called "an ownership attitude" and may apply to production methods, financial plans, even story ideas presented to editors. Getting key publics to establish ownership with management is the best way to effect good public relations.

Ownership as used here is an attitude established through shared ideas. While management may lead in developing ideas and providing direction with various publics, it is best to communicate with shorter messages that permit the audience to begin adding thoughts or reacting to suggestions at the earliest possible time. Revealing part of a plan, or part of a story, or part of a procedure provides opportunities to leaders in key publics to offer input, flesh out plans, complete ideas, and provide feedback on the group's participation.

This technique of establishing "ownership" of ideas applies to dealings with a wide range of publics such as media, customers, banks, and employees. It is used most effectively in continuing relationships, where complex ideas involving a number of considerations need to be communicated.

Where active participation exists between employees and management, employees have a sense of satisfaction and ownership. Such employees may participate in profit-sharing plans or employee stock-ownership programs. They may receive performance awards for having contributed to changes in production; or having suggested new advanced equipment to speed responsiveness to customers; or having cut costs by providing shorter production runs and lower inventory levels.

Participation is the principal motivation of the more mentally oriented workforce needed to establish significant market share in today's business climate. Material incentives reinforce, but the appetite of a thinking person is fed by a sense of worthwhile achievement developed through shared decision making.

Value of employee services

Childcare and other family-oriented services were offered, then discontinued by a number of corporations in the early 1980s due to lack of interest, not serving enough of the workforce, being too expensive, and carrying too much potential for liability lawsuits.

Many of these objections have been overcome by corporations through outside suppliers of day care who are near but not on company facilities. It is clear that if corporations wish to have workers consider their jobs a more important part of their lives, the corporation must consider helping the worker care for her or his family.

Such programs involving interaction between workers and corporations communicate a mutuality of concern that attracts the best employees, builds tenure, cuts employee turnover, and thwarts possible union organizing efforts.

Markets

The small to mid-sized business has a number of affordable tools to measure market perceptions. Opinion and attitude surveys may reveal negative or positive factors affecting product acceptance of either new or long-established products or services. (*See* Chapter 18.)

A good place to begin public relations programming in the marketing area is with an audit. This is a review of what has been done and how effective it has been for the company. An analysis tells the company where it is now in reference to competition, customer base, customer satisfaction, product or service quality, delivery times, cooperation with distributors, price acceptance, and share of market. The sum of these factors is the company's marketing profile.

The current definition of that profile should suggest needed activities in the sales force, advertising, publicity, product development, and servicing that will lead to greater revenues, profits, and new market share.

Among findings that can be developed by qualified public relations professionals are the following:

- Share of market held by competitors
- Overall market potential for products and services
- Brand preference ratings

- The reason product acceptance is growing or declining

- Ratings of sales persons, technical abilities, services, manner of presentation

- Effectiveness of advertising programs

- Pricing acceptance versus competition

- Market demands of the future

- Business acquisition surveys that reflect a company's acceptance in its community

The cost of a given tactic compared with the benefit derived from that cost is essential to achieve efficient marketing budgets. There is a trade-off among direct sales efforts, advertising or mass communication, and publicity. All are needed in virtually every program. The correct mix of these disciplines varies from company to company and from situation to situation.

If a product is exceptionally well-known, advertising can be one of the most efficient tools. Publicity may be used to broaden uses of a well-known product, such as has been accomplished in many peripheral uses of Arm & Hammer baking soda.

Publicity

Consumer product publicity is treated in Chapters 14, 22, and 23. Even a smaller company engaged in business-to-business activity has many vehicles available to it that constitute news on its everyday operations in trade publications of its industry and customers' industries among them:

- **Product:** New or new applications; new accessories or improvements; new sizes, capacities, or materials.

- **Collateral material:** Offering of brochures, specification sheets, catalogs, technical reports, internal publications for customers' use, charts, maps, guides, checklists, reprints, speech texts or condensations.

- **Supplies:** Needed for distributors, salespeople, materials, methods.

- **Personnel:** New people with industry reputations; promotions, transfers, awards received and presented to others; recruiting.

- **Technical briefs:** Laboratory procedures, calculator programs, computer programs, field trials, diagrams, hints, patents, tests of resistance to corrosion, bending, breaking and so on.

- **Business gains:** Contracts; new or expanded facilities; better organization for management, sales engineering, distribution, service; joint ventures; mergers; acquisitions; divestitures; price changes; numbers of products shipped, manufactured, sold.

- **Financial data:** Earnings reports, capital expenditures, observations on trends, dividend announcements, indices.

- **Freestanding photos:** Unusual or striking photos that tell a story in themselves. Principal subjects are contrasts in size, areas of unusual design, geometric patterns, assembly or groups of products.

- **Features or case histories:** Reviews of applications that solve a particular problem for a customer or perhaps the result of a study or a technique that has been tested by a third party. Sometimes achieved by placing equipment on memorandum loan with an editor and instructing him or her in its use, with a report on the editor's experience.

- **Participation in round-up stories:** Developed over time, a company may become a source for comments on industry trends and will be included in round-ups as observers on breaking news stories that affect an industry. This is a good way to become recognized as a leader, expert, or authority.

- **How to manage the process:** Select, use, maintain, cut costs, save, reduce rejects, winterize, store, increase yield or output, reduce risk, evaluate, lower maintenance costs, extend service life.

Certain activities or events are expected of leading companies in an industry. At some point in its growth the small to mid-sized corporation will wish to sponsor such events not only for visibility but because it demonstrates leadership in the industry.

In this knowledge-intensive era, many businesses are growing by developing new prototypes. Such radical change in business practice and method creates an enlarged role for public relations in the marketing process.

Philip Kotler, professor of marketing at Northwestern University's Kellogg Graduate School of Business, points out that publicity has more value in market development or in the learning period required for new products and services than either personal sales or advertising. News not only costs less to achieve if the idea or information is there to earn the space, but it has much higher readership and is more credible, hence more persuasive.

But publicity is not a substitute for advertising. Advertising content, placement, and timing may be 100 percent controlled. That, for the smaller company that may try to save dollars by less research into consumer attitudes, is one of its greatest weaknesses. Advertising enables the chief executive officer to project exactly what he or she want to project, even if it is to the company's detriment or if the message has so little interest it falls on blind eyes or deaf ears.

Publicity does not offer 100 percent control of content or timing. But its message tends to be accepted by more readers or viewers because it is perceived to be worthy of publication or broadcast by disinterested media.

The gatekeepers of the media, who will keep the message of the small to mid-sized corporation out of print or off the air unless they perceive it to be news or to have value for readers, listeners, or viewers, do management of the smaller firm a favor. They provide a highly knowledgeable view of their audience's interest and how that audience will react to the message offered for publication.

Market research

In fact, an economical form of market research is an on-line electronic information service. Key words may be input to search through thousands of consumer, business, and technical publications to learn what has appeared on a given product or service and how the media view it. Source, Dialog, and Nexis are three such services.

This is an excellent tool for the small to mid-sized corporation to begin its research. A young company in a new market can determine what information already exists, including market studies.

This information permits the small firm to begin its specific paid research as an add-on to information that already exists instead of "reinventing the wheel" with a lot of needless research expenditures.

It also provides the small company a foundation from which to launch development of its marketing strategy with information on its competitors, competing products, and marketing strategies employed by those competitors.

Combining communication and fact-finding

Communication may proceed in industrial product programs while research and planning are conducted at the same time. This coordinated program does the following:

- Gains new distributor leads

- Furnishes proof of acceptance and product merit to manufacturers' representatives, wholesalers, and retailers

- Pretests media response to get better values when allotting advertising dollars
- Extends communication to markets where advertising dollars are not available
- Tests market response in related industrial areas and achieves initial distribution before entering a new market
- Amplifies the impact of advertising and other sales efforts
- Creates pervasive acceptance and employs new product introductions to reach audiences in the government and financial areas
- Carries special product or service messages to important special-interest groups

The program works efficiently for either new concepts or new uses for old products, for new products, or for modified products. The important consideration in the industrial area is whether the product or concept brings something new to the user. Other companies may have similar products, but they may not use them in the application advanced by your company.

Let's take as an example a product as prosaic as a toilet float. The engineering term for a toilet float is a level control. Level controls may be used to stop flow, to start flow, to sound an alarm, to provide a measurement of a given quantity, to operate remote devices, or to interact with computers. They may be made fire resistant or explosion-proofed for given situations. They may be made to operate magnetically or electrically.

Level controls have applications wherever fluids are used. Liquid Level Lectronics started making level controls in a garage for use in remote tank gauging operations in the oil fields. The concept replaced the old rod man who used to dip the tanks to see how much oil was in each one. The level control could hardly be called new, but remote gauging of the tanks by computer interface was new.

The company needed orders to develop cash flow *now*. It needed representatives to sell and demonstrate its products.

A four-page specification sheet was prepared in two colors that told the story of remote tank gauging and provided specifications, installation, maintenance, and ordering instructions. At the same time, a story reporting that the company was seeking new manufacturing representatives for a new concept in remote tank gauging was released to about twenty publications specializing in oil field equipment, the field of salesmanship, and broadly based news publications such as the *Journal of Commerce*. More than one hundred responses were received covering about seventeen states.

As a second story was being prepared, field representatives were selected and trained, equipped with demonstrators and service parts kits, and sent to the fields.

A new product story and photo on remote tank gauging by the level control system were released to about forty publications. Approximately six hundred inquiries were generated through oil field and tank manufacturing publications. The number of leads from each publication was noted on a columnar pad that set forth all publications to which the news release had been mailed.

Where sales calls were requested, they were passed on to field salespeople.

After six publicity stories, the company was prepared to spend advertising dollars intelligently and selected the four publications that had produced the best return in inquiries as advertising vehicles to sustain the program and develop new leads. The ad themes were derived from input from the sales representatives on those points customers had found most interesting and had chosen as the key reason to act on.

This soon resulted in case history articles to write about the successful application of remote tank gauging. Reprints of those articles were mailed to those who had inquired about but not purchased level controls, and these articles were used as mailers to suggested customers on whom the field representatives were calling.

New level controls and applications for the bottling industry, paper industry, refinery industry, offshore drilling industry, food processing, aviation hydraulic fluid controls, and plant maintenance followed, with essentially the same process used.

Similar programs have been adapted to makers of pianos and organs, springs, tubular goods, disposable medical supplies, architectural elements, plating materials, casters, maintenance services, industrial trash pickup, fountain pens, washing machines, cameras, aircraft engine overhaul, wines, fine furniture, food—about sixty industry categories in all.

This program is an example of an efficient way to research, plan, communicate, and evaluate while getting orders at the same time in a marketing publicity program for products that have no truly "new" or "first time" features.

Financial Considerations

All companies, public and private, have financial relations whether they want them or not. It is simply a question of whether these relations are managed.

Money is so important to the success of any business that even if the source is family and friends, as it is in most start-up situations, some semiformal reporting process should be initiated by the company to the financial source.

Adequate reporting on what has happened to the money is essential to obtain additional funds. Even friends won't give the company more money when management breathlessly declares that it needs more capital because the company is growing so fast. They want to know if the company is making money as well as growing and entering new markets. If it is not making money, they want to know when it expects to start making money.

Explaining how the company makes its money requires explanation of (a) the basic demand for the goods or services of the company; (b) the marketing used to examine and express the fulfillment of that demand; and (c) the operations through which that demand is carried out through research of consumer attitudes; research of the product; manufacturing, distribution, and winning of distributors; consumer and consumer acceptance; after-purchase satisfaction; and even markets for used equipment or second sales.

It is essential that a company's banker or other source of funds understand how the company makes money in order to gain a comfortable feeling that the business can and will repay principal and interest.

Competitive advantages should be openly discussed in a confidential business plan. To demonstrate to the banker the character of its owners, they need to identify the weaknesses and show alternate solutions to how they plan to overcome them.

Bank loans can be paid down with long-term insurance loans if the company has demonstrated staying power. Long-term loans can be paid off with public debt or equity issues. But when a company goes public, it must demonstrate that in its industry group its growth in earnings per share, profit margin, and return on equity—adjusted for the amount of debt the company has incurred to make that return—are comparable with other companies in its industry.

Credibility stems from the company's reporting its plan, then achieving the goals it sets forth. If it has control of its operations and knows what influences cause it to be above and below industry growth trends, it achieves high credibility in financial circles. That opens the door to still further financing.

If, on the other hand, it fails to report future activities and their expected results (this does not refer to making projections of earnings, but rather to reporting where the company is going, how much money is required to get it there, and when those expanded operations can be expected to begin showing a profit), it will find itself with low price-earnings ratios, high interest rates for debt, and many restrictive covenants in its loan agreements. The same will be true if it overestimates performance and errs with unfulfilled promises of future performance, which also can open the company to lawsuits.

Similarly, credibility is completely lost when management does not report the bad news well ahead of its actual occurrence or shrinks from emergencies and crises as they occur.

Most newly public companies find the experience exhilarating. But management also finds that it now has two companies to manage: The operating company that produces the profits and the public company that raises the debt and equity from the public and reports on what profits are being made, builds the trading network for securities, and maintains public confidence.

The reflection of all publics as a whole is not so well summed up in corporate image as it is in the price-earnings ratio and the market-book values of a publicly held company. These figures truly reflect attitudes and opinions on management, its relations with employees, customers, suppliers, investors, the government, community—in short, all who affect the future of the company. Weak relationships with just one of these publics can bring the price of the stock down in relation to the corporation's underlying assets and make the company vulnerable to being acquired against its will.

Other Publics to Consider

The community outside a company's gates, its local taxing authorities and city, county, and state, may become critically important. It is wise to build a reservoir of goodwill with these publics by communicating with them on a continuing basis.

The government through its power to tax and to grant tax abatements can designate which industries, even which companies within a given geographic area, make a profit and which do not. Through laws government can make the costs of doing business selectively high. Or government can award contracts, make research grants, or provide other direct revenue to ensure success. (*See* Chapters 4, 5, and 6.)

If a company is in a regulated industry, what it may charge its customers is under a regulatory commission. Relations with such commissions require many hours of management time and are critical to its ability to survive.

In such circumstances, trade groups, coalitions, and others who have similar interests may offer ways to mount more significant information programs at less cost to the individual company. Even if a company's management is not regarded as an expert in its field, it needs to cultivate relationships with its experts, for in influencing them it may better influence the entire industry and its coalition partners than it can on its own behalf in direct communications.

Among the secondary publics having a high priority are the media. Many banks, investment bankers, securities analysts, and customers will turn to leading trade magazine editors or writers for guidance on how they may regard a specific company. It is wise to be known or to have material on file to permit one to be known in such instances. Under the right circumstances, a personal call to an editor of a key trade publication covering your industry is a wise use of time. Be sure such a call presents useful information to the editor and is not simply a message management wishes to communicate but that has no interest to the editor.

Advance Crisis Preparation

Most corporations with fifty or more employees should have some kind of crisis preparation in place. (*See* Chapters 2 and 12.) This may consist of simply a plastic card given to employees, setting forth what should and should not be said during an emergency. One company spokesman should be designated for control, but other employees will be questioned by the media, especially if the event involves loss of life and injury.

Management should advise its employees to respond first to a concern for those people possibly injured or killed. Other managers and employees must be cautioned not to notify outsiders of names before next of kin are notified and not to speculate but to report only facts they know are true, and then to refer the person presenting the questions to the central source wherever possible.

Second, responses should be framed about when disrupted services to customers or the community can be restored.

Third, concern should be shown for damage to the investor and to the company's ability to continue in business. Guesses should not be made about the extent of damage. Rather, specific information on damage should be gathered from professionals charged with that responsibility, such as fire chiefs and insurance claim agents, and reported accurately.

Until facts are known, what should be reported is "Facts are being gathered." A difficult task in a crisis is to simply report what is actually known and not one thing more. It is not a time for speculation, even though media will ask for assumptions.

For small companies, emergency drills with simulated media interviews for all staff and workforce should be conducted at least once annually.

Mid-sized corporations should conduct a drill with key managers, who in turn will conduct one with their key managers, who in turn will conduct one with employees. It is wise to have such drills at least once a year—twice a year if employee turnover is high and the company is in a particularly sensitive industry.

If the company produces toxic substances, it is required by law to notify police, fire, and medical facilities of the effects of the chemicals in spills, on contact, or in fires and pro-vide information on how they may best be controlled or treated. This mandate may be turned into a positive communication effort with employees and the surrounding community by demonstrating the care and concern of management. Dow Chemical provided such information to its communities for more than twenty years before it was required.

Large corporations have three-inch-thick notebooks filled with crisis preparedness information, message points, and dictates on which managers will be trained as part of their continuing responsibilities to deal with the media. As corporations approach the top of the mid-sized range, they, too, should invest in crisis preparedness. A management that can collect itself in the face of a disaster, reach its people, assess its damage, and report on it in short time frames—with the public interest in the forefront—demonstrates it is in control.

Public Relations Staffing

In the corporation with less than fifteen employees, the chief executive officer is most likely to have direct control of public relations, using a secretary part-time as the public relations staff. His or her attention should be directed to the three primary publics—employees, customers, and financiers.

If the manager of a small company decides to conduct a product news release program, he or she will probably find it advantageous to hire an outside public relations firm. (*See* Chapter 47.)

If the employee range reaches up to 150, the company probably should have a dedicated internal public relations professional, and outside public relations counsel and, possibly, service.

For companies with 150 to 500 employees, the internal staff may consist of a director with managers for employee relations, marketing publicity, and financial relations.

For companies with 500 to 1,000 employees, the internal staff may have a number of specialized managers for key publics and even some assistants.

As companies grow, the rule should be to staff internally where a full-time person is needed and a person qualified to assume that position is available.

Public relations firms are retained to provide services when a full-time person may not be required or may not be available, but the relationship still needs to be well managed. They also are retained to provide objective views of the corporation and its needs; to conduct audits; to provide extra heads, arms, and legs when periods of activity arise above the norm, such as product introductions, analyst meetings, or other activities that may occur only occasionally; to help integrate all communications; or to provide needed experience and expertness that may not be possessed by the internal staff.

If a company is going public, for example, it probably has no one on staff who has been through the exercise before. Outside counsel is mandated and in most instances will be retained for two to two and one-half years, until most financial relations tasks have been conducted on a "first through" basis and internal staff has been acquired, or internal staff has gained experience in gauging the expectations of its financial audience and learning the many guidelines necessary to deal with them.

Some of the initial retainers by newly public companies extend to a decade or more in rapidly growing companies, particularly those growing by acquisition and entering multiple markets. These counsel may be called on again in the event hostile takeover actions are initiated against the company.

Frequently, outside counsel is retained for crisis management to gain the benefit of experience that its professionals may have.

If a company wishes to accelerate its media visibility, it may well retain outside counsel and service. Indeed, in some consumer fields outside specialists are retained as a matter of course because their expertness is much more concentrated and more efficient.

If a company is entering new geographic markets or foreign markets, it probably should retain outside public relations counsel to provide insight into the new areas.

Outside public relations counsel and service is hired, too, when management and internal staff have been unable to solve communication problems or relationships with specific groups. Assignments in this area may mean conducting education campaigns as a precursor to selling efforts or researching and defining problem attitudes and opinions, one of the most frequent causes for unsolved relationships with a particular group.

Managers need to first determine whether to hire an extension of their own staff or additional experience or both. Certainly, experience in the particular area in which the outside counsel and service will serve the company should be a high consideration.

For instance, one would not want to hire public relations counsel and service to prepare and conduct analyst meetings if the account people assigned to the company could not read and interpret income statements and balance sheets and did not have a working knowledge of factors affecting investment decisions.

In the case of unique problems, companies should turn to counsel with a reputation for problem solving. Several hundred practitioners across the country are well qualified for this, having dealt with many "unsolvable" problems. Broad general knowledge, a logical approach, the ability to apply lateral thinking and have creative solutions based on logic, and exceptional writing still are the qualifications.

39

PUBLIC RELATIONS FOR CHARITIES AND OTHER NONPROFIT ORGANIZATIONS

DON BATES

Don Bates is executive vice-president of Sumner Rider & Associates, a public relations firm.

He began his career as a reporter in Massachusetts, then joined the headquarters public relations division of Western Electric Company where he was staff writer and community affairs specialist. From the Bell System he joined the McDonnell Douglas Corporation in California where he was publications manager and promotion specialist in the company's aircraft and space research divisions.

In 1970 he became director of public relations for the 130,000-member National Association of Social Workers, headquartered in Washington, DC, then executive director in 1974 of the National Communication Council, which merged several years later with the Public Relations Society of America. Before starting his own public relations firm, which merged with the Rider organization, he served as vice-president of PRSA and of Planned Parenthood-World Population.

Traditionally, charitable organizations have formed part of the voluntary, nonprofit sector of society. They have also been referred to as "The Third Sector"—in contrast to the business and government sectors. Most recently they have come to be known as "The Independent Sector"—indicative of their independence from the institutional legal and commerce restrictions placed on the other sectors.

The Internal Revenue Service regulates charitable organizations as tax-exempt, not-for-profit organizations. What distinguishes charitable organizations from for-profit organizations are their purposes. To qualify for tax-exempt, nonprofit status under IRS law these organizations must meet one or more of six basic goals:

1. Relief of poverty by assisting the poor, distressed, and underprivileged

2. Advancement of religion

3. Advancement of education and science

4. Performance of government functions and lessening of the burdens of government

5. Promotion of health

6. Promotion of social welfare for the benefit of the community

To maintain their IRS tax-exempt status charitable organizations must operate by rules and regulations decreed by the IRS and the state in which each is incorporated.

Technically, IRS regulations classify charitable organizations as 501(c)(3) groups. This classification means that, unlike other tax-exempt categories, they can raise money from the public—from individuals, foundations, businesses, estates—in the form of tax-deductible contributions. In addition they also receive special not-for-profit bulk postage rates that enable them to use direct mail to raise funds and to communicate with their publics at far less expense. Charitable organizations, like most other nonprofit groups, also get special dispensation from the media, particularly radio and television, by way of nonpaid public service announcements and ads promoting their causes, and occasionally, seeking donations.

The size and scope of charitable organizations range from all-volunteer neighborhood associations to professionally staffed multi-million-dollar national agencies in health and social service. The United States has more than one million tax-exempt organizations—that raise more the $1.1 trillion a year to underwrite their operations.

For more information on charitable organizations and other categories of tax-exempt endeavors, consult *Tax-Exempt Status for Your Organization*, Publication 557 (revised, Oct. '88) available from IRS offices.

Goal of Public Relations

Owing to their purposes, charitable organizations must operate and be managed in the public interest. They must communicate their goals and objectives in order to maintain visibility, credibility, accountability, and growth.

The Expanding Role of Public Relations

Public relations clearly plays a vital role in the management and success of charitable organizations. This is evidenced in press coverage of problems facing the not-for-profit sector. Increasingly, both print and broadcast media pay more attention to why charitable organizations exist and how they function.

Much of the coverage has to do with fund-raising abuses and challenges to the policies and power of federated fund-raising campaigns, but a significant amount also deals with controversies and crises that in the past went uncovered. Some of the allegations involve fiscal mismanagement, racial and sex discrimination, abuses of tax-exempt privileges, misleading public information campaigns, and political chicanery. The coverage involves greater scrutiny of the role of charitable organizations.

No longer are charities "untouchable." Nor are they seen as bastions of Lady Bountifuls or bleeding hearts. Today, charitable organizations are viewed more accurately—and more critically—as publicly supported tax-exempt institutions whose goals and objectives must conform more directly with community needs, not just with the vision and desires of a professional staff or volunteer board.

In almost every opinion poll taken of Americans' attitudes toward charity and philanthropy, the overwhelming consensus is extraordinarily positive. But when their attitudes are probed, that consensus quickly is colored by growing concern with the credibility and accountability of the organizations.

It is precisely in these and related areas that public relations makes its greatest contribution. Applied with the proper balance of research, planning, communications, and evaluation, public relations can spell the difference between success and failure in the marketplace of people and ideas.

Some of the questions that charitable organizations must deal with in their communications with their publics include:

How are they funded? How do they spend their money? Do they do what they say they do? Do they really help? Why don't they do more? Why should we give to them as opposed to other organizations? Are they telling the truth? Why don't they join forces with other organizations in their field? How well are they managed? How qualified are their staffs? Who's on their boards? How many volunteers assist in their work? Do they abide by fundraising standards?

The answers to these questions spell the difference between good and bad public relations.

Importance of Professionalism

Practicing public relations in a not-for-profit organization closely resembles practicing public relations in a profit-making endeavor.

In both instances, you want to gain the support of important publics or constituencies for what you do and how you do it. To that end, you apply the principles of management and communications that have evolved over the centuries from understanding human behavior and human organization.

You also use the same basic tools and techniques to deliver your information and messages: publications, meetings, news releases, press conferences, films, broadcasting, testimony, exhibits, special events—all the time-tested means for reaching people with facts and arguments about your actions or intentions.

Then, you manage with the same four-step process in mind: research, plan, communi-

cate, evaluate. You follow a logical pattern to assure the effectiveness of your efforts.

There's nothing particularly special about the practice in the not-for-profit field that is not found in one form or another in corporations and other organizations. Many people inside and outside of the not-for-profit world have suggested differences where no differences exist. So in addition to what is covered in this chapter, much of what makes up the rest of the handbook applies.

To view public relations as less important or less professional in the not-for-profit sector leads to misleading perceptions about the management and vitality of not-for-profit organizations and limits the use of public relations in support of the very purpose of these organizations—to help people when other institutions with power and influence can't or won't.

Unique Goals and Resources

There are differences, however—most significantly, the goals. By and large, charitable organizations use public relations more to help people, whereas profit-making endeavors use it more to foster their own objectives. In a similar vein, profit-making organizations use public relations more to cultivate customers, government, and stockholders, whereas charitable organizations use it more to attract members, clients, and contributors.

Another difference is the resources available to do the job. Most not-for-profit organizations have smaller public relations staffs and work with fewer public relations consultants. The reason in most cases is lack of money, but frequently it results from lack of managerial concern. Many executives in charitable organizations are social workers, psychologists, or doctors as contrasted with professional managers. Owing to their education and experience, they are unfamiliar with the value of public relations and tend to shy away from its use. Executives in charitable organizations also worry about the wisdom of spending their limited funds on marketing, advertising, and public relations. Often they are biased against these pursuits because of their historic commercial origins. More frequently, however, they are just afraid to spend money on things that aren't directly connected with helping clients or managing internal operations. As modern management practices become more prevalent in the not-for-profit world, more executives learn the value of well-managed communications programs, and their resistance to public relations and related pursuits lessens.

Not-for-profit organizations also lack serious research on which to base their communications programs. Cost is one problem. Another is lack of internal support for planning and evaluating programs and services on the basis of surveys or formal studies of public attitudes or community needs.

Finally, not-for-profit organizations are dependent on volunteers and voluntary support. Without unpaid boards of directors and public contributions, they couldn't survive. They don't have the money or profit-making capability to staff and pay their own way. According to recent studies, more than eighty million Americans volunteer time each year to help not-for-profit organizations. The value of that time has been estimated at well over $150 billion. Americans annually contribute more than $100 billion to charitable enterprises.

For charitable organizations, as opposed to other types of not-for-profits, there are two other distinctions. Public relations in charities usually combines communications with a strong involvement of fund-raising. Indeed, in many charitable organizations, particularly smaller groups, public relations and fund-raising are handled by the same person or department.

Charitable organizations also are more dependent on unpaid time and space in the media to get promotional messages and information to their publics. Few can afford paid advertising except in limited instances. Even if they could, most of them wouldn't because once they paid for advertising, they probably would lose most, if not all, donated space or public service time. (*See* following guidelines on paid and public service advertising.)

Start-Up Plan

The advantages of planning are described in *Communication Resource Handbook*, published by the United Way of America, 701 North Fairfax Street, Alexandria, VA 22314:

- Personally, there is the feeling of being in control of the many continuing and specific responsibilities.

- Professionally, there is the systematic anticipation of what is to be communicated, thereby improving the quality of communication and reducing the chance that some needed communication will "slip through the cracks."

- Planning also has an essential connection with voluntarism. Highly competent, experienced, and influential people are motivated to serve on communication committees and to undertake sizable responsibilities when they know that their contribution of time and expertise will be utilized effectively in a planned communication program.

- A specific and clear plan has the further advantage of facilitating constructive program analysis. When it comes time to account for what has been done and to analyze how communicating can be done better, a communication plan is an immense help in reconstructing the types and sequence of communication activities.

Establishing a Formal Policy

The best public relations programs have support at the highest levels of management. In charitable organizations, the board of directors is where final authority lies. Thus, it makes sense to begin by establishing a board-approved policy statement on public relations. This is usually prepared by staff or by a board committee for final review and approval.

The policy statement of the National Association of Social Workers (NASW) was prepared by the board's public relations committee. Entitled "Communicating for Today and Tomorrow," it begins with a rationale for public relations in "an organization fundamentally dedicated to human well-being" and explains that public relations "will not so much *sell* NASW and social work as it will focus on interpreting and informing the membership and the public about the association's evolving place in the evolving society and the changing needs of people in this context." "In sum," it concludes, "public relations must become the central focus for developing greater innovation in the association and an image of NASW which conveys greater creativity, vigor, and growing societal impact in behalf of human well-being."

The statement details the purposes of public relations within NASW:

- Advocate and interpret the association and its positions, practices, functions, goals, objectives, programs.

- Develop all available communications to improve the association's "image" and acceptance by the profession, the press, legislators, influentials, and others as the "voice" of social work, including newsletters, brochures, news releases, annual report, press conferences, audiovisual materials, exhibits, awards, displays.

- Run an efficient up-to-date program of publicity, promotion, community affairs.

- Keep the profession and the public informed about social work.

- Establish a better understanding of the role of social work in the national life and its contribution to the well-being of people.

- Promote the value and benefits of NASW membership.

- Counsel management on NASW problems and policies and their impact on membership, the profession, and the public.

- Contribute to an improved climate of opinion about the helping professions.

The American Cancer Society's (ACS) policy reads as follows under the heading "The ACS and the Public":

> It is a major policy of the Society to conduct public education and information programs to help save lives from cancer by alerting Americans to cancer's warning signals and by encouraging regular health examinations. These programs and materials, stressing the hopeful aspects of the attack on cancer, are carried out nationally and through the Society's Divisions and Units.

The statement describes activities for the organization's public education and public information divisions. Under "public information" it includes the following entries:

> An annual report, containing a consolidated financial statement of the National Society and the Divisions, shall be published.
>
> The Society follows a policy of candid truthfulness in reporting news, facts, and figures about cancer; there is no acceptance of false or exaggerated claims. All new developments and data are cleared by appropriate medical and scientific authorities before release to newspapers, magazines, radio and television.
>
> Where consistent with truth and accuracy, the Society focuses on the hopeful side of

cancer—that it can be cured—rather than the morbid.

Support is built for the independent educational and fund-raising Crusade, and explanations furnished on how contributed money is spent—locally and nationally.

The NASW and the ACS both use their policy statements to remind staff and volunteers of their obligations in the public relations area; to make a case for paid and voluntary support of public relations activities; and to provide a managerial, philosophical, and ethical framework in which to conduct these activities.

Committee aids planning

A board public relations committee usually is the best vehicle for assuring the continuance and strength of the kinds of public relations programs suggested by these statements. Preferably, the chairperson should be a member of the board so the committee has an advocate with clout and contacts within the organization's power structure. There are three kinds of public relations committees:

1. **Advisory**, the members of which provide counsel to the organization's public relations staff, and help develop an annual communications plan and get it approved by top management and the board.

2. **Operating**, whose members do some or all of the actual public relations work. Such committees are rare. Usually they are composed of public relations professionals who volunteer to serve as unpaid staff.

3. **Ad hoc**, whose members serve for a limited time to execute a plan, perhaps to study a controversial public policy issue, and to recommend appropriate action.

Public relations committees should operate with written statements of purpose and responsibilities. Someone from the organization's staff, the public relations person if one

exists, administers the committee's activities. He or she prepares agendas, reports, budget analyses, policy statements, and other documents that allow the committee to perform productively. The best committees usually involve a mix of volunteers, one or two from the field of public relations, and several who have been active locally and nationally in the organization.

Executive's role

Creation of policy statements and board committees, and the management of a strong public relations program, require the involvement of the organization's chief executive officer. He or she is responsible for administration and usually is the key spokesperson with the public and the media. Following are recommended standards for the executive director's role in public relations:

- Delegates the execution of the public relations program to a consultant or to qualified staff who report directly to him or her

- Meets regularly with this staff or consultant to assure the timely development and smooth administration of the public relations program

- Shares with the staff or consultant all information (including that which is confidential) required to execute the program

- Works with the public relations committee, staff, or consultant to design an annual public relations program and budget for approval by the organization's board of directors

- Schedules annual board review of the public relations program, including a presentation by the appropriate staff, consultant, and committee chairperson

This list and the following lists on staff support are taken from *Using Standards to Strengthen Public Relations*, by Anne L. New and Don Bates, one of six guides in a set on public relations for not-for-profit organizations. (The guides are published by the Institute for Public Relations Research and Education, University of Florida, P.O. Box 11840, Gainesville, FL 32611. Other guides from this series are referred to in this chapter under the sections on planning and evaluation.)

Staff support critical

In most instances the key to a successful public relations program is a good staff to do the work. The range of what this staff has to know or be familiar with is extensive. Although no one can or has to perform all of them all the time, the average public relations specialist in the not-for-profit field is responsible at one time or another for the following activities:

- Assess community opinion and attitudes toward the organization, using among other means, formal and informal opinion surveys, analysis of the news and current sociopolitical trends and issues, interviews with community leaders, discussions with staff and organizational leadership.

- Serve as an advisor to the board and executive director on the public relations implications of organizational policy and program decisions.

- Formulate goals and programs to maintain and strengthen favorable public attitudes toward the organization, and to overcome public criticism.

- Prepare an annual public relations program and budget, keyed to organizational objectives, for review and approval by the executive director and board.

- Utilize print, broadcast, and audiovisual media to disseminate news and other information on the organization's program and goals.

- Handle media requests for information and develop cooperative relations with newspapers, magazines, television and radio stations.

- Prepare and distribute print and audiovisual materials: annual reports, posters, external newsletters, leaflets, speeches, films, filmstrips, audiocassettes, videotapes, radio and television public service announcements, postage meter messages, fact sheets, public statements, and a variety of other publicity and promotion materials.

- Plan and organize special events such as annual meetings, agency tours and open houses, program demonstrations, radio and television shows, exhibits and displays, awards luncheons, campaign dinners, and press conferences or briefings.

- Handle employee and internal communications, which in some instances include development of staff training programs on public relations and related matters.

- Coordinate community relations through liaison with diverse community interests.

- Work with government agencies and officials whose policies and programs affect the organization's operations. Often this means helping prepare legislative testimony. Some organizations employ specialists in government relations and public affairs to handle this responsibility.

- Advise on integration of all policies, functions, and communications.

- Measure and evaluate the effectiveness of the organization's public relations program.

Using this list as a guide, the qualifications for the public relations specialist shape up as follows:

- Graduation from an accredited college or university with a degree in liberal arts or in public relations, communications, journalism, English, or a related field. Equivalent experience, based on a record of competent performance in public relations, advertising, or journalism, may be substituted for this educational requirement.

- Ability to plan and set public relations goals and objectives attuned to the organization's needs and priorities.

- Sensitivity to trends in public opinion and attitudes and to their implications for the organization.

- Knowledge of and ability to work effectively with the media.

- Ability to write and speak clearly, simply, and effectively.

- Knowledge of printing, graphics, and audio-visual techniques.

- Copyediting and proofreading skills.

- General administrative and supervisory ability.

- Membership in public relations societies and continual updating of skills and knowledge through professional literature and professional development programs.

Program Planning

Public relations plans help assure an orderly operation and provide guideposts for evaluating effectiveness.

The best public relations practitioners not only know the value of planning, they use it to make a case for what they can and want to do. In his book, *Communication by Objective*, the late Bob Oaks outlined the major steps required to develop a public relations program in a not-for-profit organization:

- Adopt clearly defined purposes, stated in writing and approved by the governing board.

- Agree on specific long-range and short-range objectives for achieving the organization's purposes.

- Plan at the executive level in consultation with staff a strategy for reaching the organization's objectives.

- Establish deadlines for reporting progress and any difficulties encountered.

- Determine channels for clearing program announcements and other communication, for reporting statistics and their evaluation.

- Provide methods of keeping board members informed of the progress made between meetings.

- Execute communication actions for building understanding of problems and points of view and support for programs with both interested groups and the general public.

- Schedule communication efforts from the center outward—beginning with those who are directly responsible for carrying out programs and including others in accordance with their interest and need to know.

- Break down each communication effort into individual tasks, assigning to each its time frame, essential personnel, and money resources, and choosing media, methods, and message content.

- Assign measurable target results to every communication task. These should be determined by proper goals and reasonable expectations. They will later serve for evaluation.

- Build feedback into every communication program, or arrange for other means of testing public reactions.

- Coordinate all functions for consistency and cumulative effect.

- Assign monitoring responsibilities to determine whether targets are being met as the program proceeds.

- Adjust or augment original communication plans as need is determined. Correct misimpressions or deviations from objectives before a wrong image becomes fixed in people's minds.

Frances A. Koestler says in her *Planning and Setting Objectives*, "The planning process starts with three steps: an inventory of your organization's needs and problems; an assessment of its public relations assets; and a frank acknowledgement of those program liabilities that tend to blur, distort or deface its image." Mrs. Koestler recommends the use of planning charts to get the process on track. She suggests the use of grids, such as those shown in Figure 39.1 from the *Association Public Relations Communications Guide* (Chamber of Commerce of the U.S., 1615 H Street, NW, Washington, DC 20062).

CHARTING PUBLIC OPINION

	What Do They Think Now?	What Do You Want Them to Think?	Specific Projects to Build Better Understanding and Good Will
MEMBERS			
NON-MEMBERS			
ASSOCIATION STAFF			
ALLIED ASSOCIATIONS			
GOVERNMENT REGULATORY AUTHORITIES			
OTHER ASSOCIATIONS			
GENERAL PUBLIC			

USING MEDIA TO REACH TARGET PUBLICS

	Publicity	Advertising	Personal Contact	Radio-TV	Printed Materials	Special Projects
MEMBERS						
NON-MEMBERS						
ASSOCIATION STAFF						
ALLIED ASSOCIATIONS						
GOVERNMENT REGULATORY AUTHORITIES						
OTHER ASSOCIATIONS						
GENERAL PUBLIC						

Figure 39.1 Planning grids, adapted from the *Association Public Relations Communications Guide*, Chamber of Commerce of the United States.

The grids help organize your thinking and build "a picture" of anticipated activities against your knowledge of public perceptions and needs with respect to your organization. In addition to the grids, a good plan usually includes a calendar that shows what you want to do and over what period of time. Besides serving as a ready reference to planned activities it shows how these activities stack up in terms of available time: The calendar can help determine when additional or outside assistance is needed. (The United Way planning calendar, Figure 39.2, is an excellent format.)

Other forms can be used to make a public relations plan more specific (*see* Figure 39.3, pages 580–81).

Evaluation process

Although public relations success is difficult to assess in a scientific manner, evaluation is still one of the most important elements in an annual plan. If you don't evaluate, you run the risk of repeating mistakes, spending money unwisely, and creating credibility problems. At the end of each year, charitable organizations should use the best means available, both objective and subjective, to judge what has been successful and what hasn't. When possible, the executive director, the public relations committee, and the board of directors should be involved. The evaluation process can be strengthened by reporting achievements throughout the year. Progress and success stories can be incorporated in organizational bulletins, internal memoranda, and board reports.

In her guide, *Measuring Potential and Evaluating Results* for public relations programs in charitable organizations, Alice Norton says, "Much of the information you need for evaluation is already on hand within your own organization." This information includes:

- Statistics and other records on the services offered and the persons who use them. A

COMMUNICATION PROGRAM CALENDAR*

	JUL	AUG	SEPT	OCT	NOV	DEC	JAN	FEB	MAR	APR	MAY	JUNE	JUL	AUG	SEPT	OCT	NOV	DEC	JAN	FEB
Organization																				
Activities																				
Materials																				
Analysis																				

Figure 39.2 Planning calendar sample. *Courtesy United Way.*

study of the addresses, ages, occupations, and interests of those your organization serves will tell you whether you are missing geographic areas of your community or failing to reach particular age or occupational groups.

- Phone calls, letters, in-person queries, suggestions, and complaints. Suggestion boxes are often useful.
- Press clippings and records of radio and television announcements and programs.
- Reports (both formal and informal) from agency staff and board members.

Increasingly, however, nonprofit organizations are engaging in professional opinion, attitude, and marketing research to assess their organizations' communications needs. (*See* Chapter 19.)

The Girl Scouts of America (GSA), working with Mojo USA, since merged to become the advertising agency Chiat/Day/Mojo, implemented high-quality research to extend its public relations and marketing outreach. They confirmed that Girl Scouting had to be repositioned so girls and the general public would know that the organization was not just cookies and camping. The recommended strategy was to target Junior Girl Scouts, ages eight to eleven, the group with the highest dropout rate for GSA.

An annual public relations plan also includes affiliate or field support where applicable. This support usually comes in the form of workshops, publications, and counsel by phone and mail. The headquarters for such support becomes the central focus for collecting and disseminating education and information materials that build and sustain public relations as a management function.

Knowing the publics

Public relations planning is greatly enhanced by a working knowledge of the publics you want to reach. A public may be organized, such as the Chamber of Commerce, or unorganized, such as housewives. Publics often are reached through key individuals, sometimes referred to as opinion molders or opinion leaders. They may lead specific groups (the president of the PTA) or hold influence in a field of importance because of their respected roles in the community (a judge or bank president). They provide access to power and authority and they frequently shape the thinking of organizations and constituencies that are important to your future and support.

The following is a list of major publics that charitable organizations deal with:

- **Volunteers**, both leadership and service, without whom charitable organizations couldn't survive
- **Donors** who give the money that allows these organizations to operate
- **Staff** who help to plan and administer what is done with the money raised
- **Clients**, the people the organizations serve in fulfillment of their goals and objectives
- **Members** who, like donors, provide financial and philosophical support
- **Media**, both print and broadcast
- **Foundations** that give big grants that help capitalize and run major activities and initiatives
- **Government agencies**, the conduits of programs and regulations mandated by Congress
- **Legislators**, both local and national, who develop and enact laws that create government agencies, programs, and regulations
- **Community groups** in or near where an organization operates and that help create and sustain a friendly environment
- **Related organizations**, both local and national, with similar or shared interests in the same field

<table>
<tr><td>
United Way
</td><td align="right">**CAMPAIGN COMMUNICATION
PLANNING SHEET**</td></tr>
</table>

	Date to be Completed	Date to be Started

Organization

1. Program guidelines: establish communication needs, activities, materials, and budget.   _____ _____

2. Campaign communication committee: establish objectives, structure, membership, responsibilities, and leadership.   _____ _____

3. Other.   _____ _____

Activities

1. Pre-public campaign: features, interviews, and other orientation publicity in mass and organizational media.   _____ _____

2. Kickoff meeting or event: preparations for the occasion.   _____ _____

3. Kickoff meeting or event: widespread and focused publicity.   _____ _____

4. Report meeting #1: preparations for the occasion.   _____ _____

5. Report meeting #1: widespread and focused publicity: external and internal.   _____ _____

6. Report meeting #2: preparations for the occasion.   _____ _____

7. Report meeting #2: widespread and focused publicity: external and internal.   _____ _____

8. Report meeting #3: preparations for the occasion.   _____ _____

9. Report meeting #3: widespread and focused publicity: external and internal.   _____ _____

10. Agency tours: arrangements.   _____ _____

11. Agency tours: distribution materials for tour participants and United Way displays for agencies.   _____ _____

12. Campaign and solicitation materials: determine types and quantities, and arrange distribution, placement, and communication media utilization.   _____ _____

13. Promotional communications: settings and materials.   _____ _____

14. Speakers: orientation and engagements.   _____ _____

15. Special events: settings and materials.   _____ _____

16. Victory meeting or final report: preparations for the occasion.   _____ _____

17. Victory meeting or final report: widespread and focused publicity: external and internal.   _____ _____

18. Other.   _____ _____

Figure 39.3 First page of a typical campaign communication planning sheet. *Courtesy United Way.*

CAMPAIGN	Date to be Completed	Date to be Started
Materials		
1. Solicitor training: information and materials.	_____	_____
2. Solicitation: materials for individual and group solicitations.	_____	_____
3. Solicitation: materials for mailings and other distribution.	_____	_____
4. News reporting: descriptions, quotes, identifications, photos, etc.	_____	_____
5. Promotional materials: selection, ordering, preparation, and placement.	_____	_____
6. Meetings and special events: graphics, displays, handouts, etc.	_____	_____
7. Agency tours: signage, exhibits, displays, posters, handouts, etc.	_____	_____
8. Recognition materials: selection, ordering, preparation, and placement.	_____	_____
9. Other.		
Analysis		
1. In-process publicity: special content and materials to meet specific solicitation needs or conditions.	_____	_____
2. Publicity: special content and materials for specific types of people ("publics") and solicitation methods.	_____	_____
3. News coverage: identify inaccuracies and misinterpretations which need immediate correcting.	_____	_____
4. News coverage: content and placement results.	_____	_____
5. Audience analysis: pre-campaign analysis of opinion strengths and weaknesses among key contributors and specific community publics which determine selection and uses of content and media	_____	_____
6. Effects analysis: in-process or post-campaign analysis of opinions toward solicitation presentations and campaign publicity.	_____	_____
7. Other.	_____	_____

Figure 39.3 *continued*

- **Headquarters office** for affiliate and field units
- **Affiliate and field offices** for the headquarters

A "target" or "circle" of publics is an excellent way to construct a skeletal view of the people and organized constituencies. It can show the "ripple effect" of communication outward from your organization.

Tools and techniques

The most common tools and techniques for delivering the organization's communications are the following:

- Annual report

- News releases/news announcements

- Leaflets/brochures/fact sheets

- Audiovisuals: audiocassettes, videotapes, films, public service announcements, slide presentations, disks, etc.
- Newsletters/newspapers
- Speeches/speech introductions
- Press conferences/press briefings
- Meetings/conventions
- Opinion polls/attitude surveys
- Exhibits/displays
- Magazines/journals
- Legislative bulletins/legislative testimony
- TV/radio appearances
- Cable/satellite TV broadcasts

- Novelties
- Marches/demonstrations
- Open houses/tours
- Special events

Tools and techniques are the hardware of communication. Understanding their differences helps improve their effectiveness, but their success is largely dependent on software—the information and interpretation they convey. Hard thinking and judgments are needed when selecting and using vehicles of communication. The same is true in designing and presenting messages.

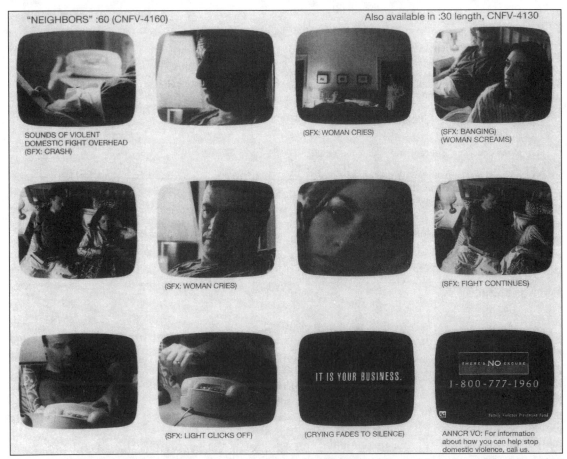

"NEIGHBORS" :60 (CNFV-4160)

Also available in :30 length, CNFV-4130

SOUNDS OF VIOLENT DOMESTIC FIGHT OVERHEAD (SFX: CRASH)

(SFX: WOMAN CRIES)

(SFX: BANGING) (WOMAN SCREAMS)

(SFX: WOMAN CRIES)

(SFX: FIGHT CONTINUES)

(SFX: LIGHT CLICKS OFF)

(CRYING FADES TO SILENCE)

IT IS YOUR BUSINESS.

THERE'S NO EXCUSE
1-800-777-1960
Family Violence Prevention Fund

ANNCR VO: For information about how you can help stop domestic violence, call us.

Figure 39.4 Photo board prepared for a PSA campaign against domestic violence seeking to persuade people to report incidents to the police.

Effective Use of Public Service Announcements

One of the most valuable resources available to charitable organizations is the free air time made available for public service announcements (PSAS) by television and radio stations. It makes possible public information campaigns that would cost thousands, sometimes millions of dollars if they had to be purchased. (*See* Figure 39.4.)

According to the Advertising Council, which develops public service campaigns for U.S. government agencies and national nonprofit organizations, its average campaign generates some $26 million in media time and space for out-of-pocket production costs of $300,000. In total, the Advertising Council's annual campaigns generate more than $1.2 billion in time and space for nonprofit organizations.

In addition, dozens of independent national campaigns are created by major charitable organizations with the pro bono help of advertising agencies. These, too, generate millions of dollars' worth of time and space for a fraction of their production costs. Locally around the country, more than four local PSAS are used by the media for every national PSA they receive. In sum, there may be more than $5 billion in free time and space being contributed by the media to nonprofit public service ads.

Public service time is free but not easy to get. Successful use requires creativity, diligence, and a budget of a few hundred to a few thousand dollars. The following guidelines for handling television and radio PSAS were developed with the assistance of Andrew J. McGowan, a producer of public service films and announcements. (A free guide on how, when, and why to use PSAS is available from Mr. McGowan at Planned Communication Services, 1 Robins Lane, Ridgewood, NJ 07450. The firm also electronically monitors television use.)

The first step is to determine what the public service announcements, known as "spots," are intended to accomplish. This can involve a sort of "give-and-take" process. PSAS can provide an audience with information (e.g., symptoms of cancer), aim to achieve attitude or behavior change (stop smoking), or offer services (free chest X-rays). "Give" spots such as these are generally preferred by public service directors because they allow the station to help both the sponsoring organization and the public. PSAS can also be used to ask the public for assistance to the charities (join our campaign, give blood, volunteer, or send a check). Stations are at least willing to cooperate with "take" campaigns such as these but resist spots requesting contributions; be prepared to submit financial statements and other documents, such as your IRS tax-exempt form.

Asking for money is not necessarily the best way to use PSAS. Since actual contributions are more likely to come from other forms of contact with the public—direct mail, newspaper ads, person-to-person—television and radio spots might be better used to prepare people for those contacts by showing what is done with contributions. Thus, the best kind of "take" spot can be a "give" spot.

PSAS can seek direct response—e.g., writing or calling—but the result will depend on how well the response is motivated and facilitated. Motivation usually comes from some special chord struck in the audiences, convincing them that responding will give them important information or services. (*See* Figure 39.5.) Response can be facilitated by making the address or phone number easy to memorize, write down, or find. "You'll find us in the telephone directory under . . ." is a good way to minimize the need for pencil and paper and to "localize" a spot for a national organization with affiliates. Symbolic words and round or sequential numbers can aid memorization, for example, "Write: Countdown, Box 765, Columbus, OH 43210." De-

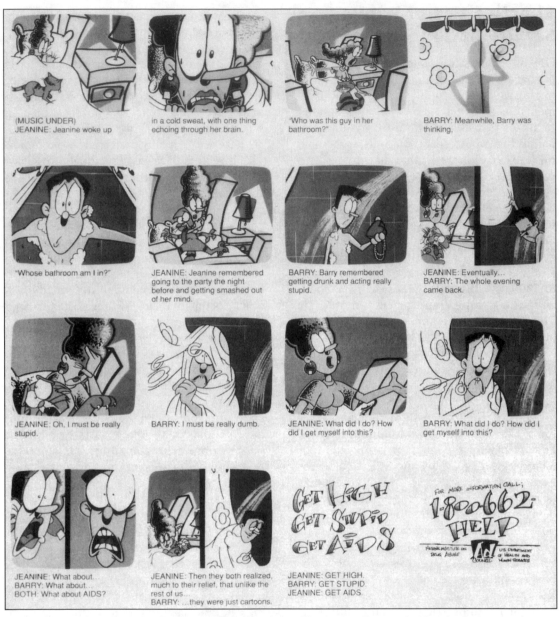

Figure 39.5 A storyboard like this one helps the station public service director decide whether to use the PSA.
Courtesy National Institute on Drug Abuse, NIH, and the Ad Council.

emphasis of elements by abbreviation (OH for Ohio; St. for Street) and deletion (no P.O. before Box) can make essential information stand out.

Writing narration and dialogue for the ear and within the tight time constraints of PSA lengths is different from writing to be read. For example, will the listener know when you mean "write," "right," or "rite"? Check yourself by reading copy aloud and timing it carefully. Figure about 25 words per 10 seconds.

Standard lengths for PSAS are 60, 30, 20, 15, and 10 seconds. However, the 30-second and shorter spots tend to get better placements—larger markets, higher-rated stations, and larger-audience times—in both radio and television.

Public service directors, in addition to overseeing acceptance of PSAS, are often responsible for their stations' community relations and are willing to help develop spots (which may encourage them to use the spots when they are completed). Sometimes stations will produce the spots. A radio station may record a staff announcer or your spokesperson in the studio and perhaps make copies for you to take to other stations.

In producing your own spot, the more professional the production, the greater the chance of acceptance. PSAS are usually placed in the same time slots as paid commercials and must conform to length and technical standards established for those commercials. (*See* Chapter 28.)

Radio, while it lacks a visual element, allows creation, through the listener's imagination, of effects not possible on television. Use of this creative potential can increase acceptance and effectiveness of PSAS.

Placing PSAS on radio and television requires as much care and planning as does their creation. Too often organizations allow the production phase to command so much attention that distribution becomes a last-minute scuffle to "get them out."

Distribution should be planned before or as part of production decision-making because such factors as content and length will influence placement.

Produced television and radio PSAS should be labeled (on their boxes, video "slates," record labels, etc.) with the name of the sponsoring organization, spot subject or title, length and technical characteristics (television tape size, or radio disk, or reel-to-reel tape speed). Accompanying material should be similarly referenced.

Send a transcript for radio spots and a storyboard for television spots, so public service directors can see what they are getting and have a visible record for easy reference; for example, if audience members call to ask for the address in the spot.

Whether you mail or deliver PSAS, enclose a letter covering the following points:

- Purpose of the campaign and how the PSAS serve it.

- If broadcast of the spots should begin or end on particular dates. Also mention any tie-in with national or regional events, but make sure your request is worded to avoid having your spots run only for a limited period (for example, "It would be appropriate to begin broadcast during Eye Safety Month and continue the spots as long as possible.").

- Describe your organization's purpose, its affiliation with larger or better-known agencies, and its nonprofit status. On first contact, especially with small organizations, some stations may ask for an IRS tax-exemption letter, annual report, and other background material.

- The name of a representative of your organization who can be contacted if further information is needed.

The distribution list should be developed according to a sound plan and budget, rather than something vague like "all the stations in the top ten markets." Not all stations air PSAS—for example, some public television stations air no PSAS and most that do reject fund-raising spots. A sound plan is to choose markets according to factors related to the purpose of the spots (for example, ranking of the elderly population or the presence of an affiliate of the organization) and directed to stations according to their record in using previous PSAS.

It is important to consider all appropriate networks. In addition to the four major broadcast television and radio networks, they can include national and state cable television networks, national radio networks such as Mutual, United Stations, and the three black radio networks, and more than a dozen state radio networks.

"Public Service/Cable," operated by Planned Communication Services, puts PSAS from national organizations together on a single tape that is distributed to national and state cable networks and 125 of the largest cable systems. Spreading the cost of dubbing, shipping, and tracking among a dozen or more organizations cuts the cost to about $15 per outlet for two spots. Typically, each spot gets two thousand to four thousand telecasts.

Just as the distribution phase should begin before spots are produced, it should not end when they are delivered. Follow-up to determine where and how often spots were played will help you measure the campaign's success and plan future production and distribution.

Some stations will send a voided bill or check stating the value of time contributed. Others will provide computer printouts of dates and times spots were played. But so few stations provide these documents—perhaps one in a hundred—that even though interesting and often impressive, they're of little value in summarizing the campaign's results. For comprehensive data it's necessary to have a reporting system that applies to all stations.

Here is a very basic system:

1. Keep a list of stations to which spots are sent.

2. Enclose a postcard with the spots for the stations to report acceptance.

3. Mark the original list to indicate acceptance and rejection.

4. Send second cards or follow up with phone calls to stations not responding.

Submitting News Release Tapes

Organizations also can supply regular news material to radio and television.

A video news release (VNR) is, as the name implies, a videotape supplied to television stations for purposes similar to those of a press release to a newspaper. (*See* Chapters 25 and 27.) The VNR usually contains a complete story of one to two minutes that some programs may air unchanged and others may use as an introduction to the subject for producing their own story, perhaps using some or all of the VNR footage. So stations can fit the VNR into their formats, it should have the following:

- No on-camera reporter; no microphone with a station logo

- No identification titles superimposed on spokespeople; instead, put the information in an accompanying transcript so the station can add the title in its own typographic style

- One sound channel with all audio mixed, the other with everything but the narrator so the station can add its own voice-over

- A few minutes of additional scenes after the edited story for stations that edit or expand the story

Three approaches are used to supply a VNR to television outlets:

• Feed it by a satellite service widely available to stations after notifying them by mail or wire what the story is about and how to downlink it. This is usually more effective for late-breaking hard news than for soft feature stories.

• Send a tape unsolicited to stations thought likely to use it.

• Notify a large number of stations about the story, offering to send the tape on request.

The last approach can be very effective for national nonprofit organizations with staff or others in many cities who can serve as spokespeople if a station wants to add a local angle.

Planned Communication Services (*see* section on public service announcements) pioneered a technique incorporating the following steps:

1. A "Newsgram" pitching the story is sent to news and magazine shows all over the country with an offer to supply the tape, background information, and contacts for local shooting.

2. When a station accepts the offer and requests the tape package, a memo is sent with the tape that gives names and phone numbers of specific people (for example, a chapter or affiliate of the national group) or general ideas (such as shooting at a local institution for a story about hospitals or colleges).

Sometimes the station will invite the local spokesperson into the studio and do a long segment or even an entire public affairs show from what began as a two-minute VNR. The two-prong effort usually achieves more coverage than either the national office or affiliate could get alone.

Audio news releases are similar, but the story is produced on audiotape and fed by telephone or satellite. An ANR can be a complete "package"—spokesperson sound-bite with narrator lead and closing, totaling one minute or less—or just one or more sound bites. ANRs are an excellent way for an organization to get national exposure for a press conference, newsworthy meeting, or release of a study or position paper; or to respond quickly to major events or controversies.

Both ANRs and VNRs can be part of a strategy by a national organization to position itself as a leading authority on certain issues.

Planned Communication Services and other producers and distributors offer guides for planning ANR and VNR projects.

Advertising Campaigns

Increasingly, as charitable organizations try to market themselves more strategically, larger, generally better-funded nonprofits have had to look seriously at using paid advertising to reach specific target audiences more precisely than they can with public service announcements.

A decade or so ago, they were subject to prohibitions or restrictions on paid advertising—except for certain kinds of classified advertising such as job listings or estate planning notices in legal publications. Today, leading charitable organizations, such as the United Way and the Boys' & Girls' Clubs of America (formerly the Boys' Clubs), have started using advertising to assure delivery of their messages for particular programs.

Today, they are joining a handful of national organizations, such as Save the Children and Planned Parenthood, who have used paid advertising for many years, as well as voluntary hospitals, most of which use some form of paid advertising to maintain or extend the utilization of their facilities and services.

Before engaging in paid advertising, charitable organizations should consider the implications seriously. Here are a few points to keep in mind:

• Paid advertising is relatively expensive. In addition to production costs, every $1 of airtime costs exactly $1. With PSAs, as shown above in Advertising Council figures, you might obtain as much as $80 in free airtime for every $1 you invest in production. Paid advertising will be targeted more precisely, but can you afford the expense?

• Once you engage in paid advertising, you stand a very good chance of losing most, if not all, of the public service time you have been receiving. This is especially true for media that aren't part of your paid advertising campaign. Why, they reason, should they continue to give you free space when you are willing to pay for it, especially with other media?

If you do engage in paid advertising, you might be able to minimize or protect against the loss of public service time by creating PSAs that are different in content from your paid advertisements. For example, paid ads might be limited to "take" messages; e.g., when you're promoting something that the public has to pay for. PSAs, on the other hand, could be limited to "give" messages; e.g., where you offer something free, such as informational brochures or physical examinations.

U.S. Army advertising is a case in point. Army recruitment ads are paid; ads where the Army announces scholarships to stay in high school run as PSAs.

Fund-Raising Campaigns

When you want to raise money you ask those who have it to give it to the organization. Funds for your activity can come from the four traditional sources of giving: living individuals, bequests, corporations and business firms, and foundations. Individuals usu-

ally offer the best potential because they contribute more than 80 percent of the total U.S. charitable dollar. But depending on your goals, one sizable corporate gift or foundation grant may be all you need.

You can ask for money by using any of several fund-raising techniques: applications for grants from foundations; direct-mail appeals; membership drives; sales of publications; letters to private citizens and to representatives of corporations, business firms, and community service groups; payroll deduction and workplace solicitation campaigns such as those run by the United Way or other community associations; and special events.

In most cases, you get money only when givers know what they're giving for. The more information and understanding they have in advance of an appeal—directly and indirectly—the better. Fund-raising success most often is based on their perception of your organization or program before you arrive with your hand out.

John Price Jones, one of the pioneers in the money-raising business, said, "Fully 50 percent of all the time and effort in the average fund-raising enterprise is in the field of public relations."

But public relations and fund-raising are not the same. Each is a management function that depends on similar communications to succeed, but each has different purposes and responsibilities. Public relations, for example, deals with many aspects of management—analysis, counsel, media relations, employee relations, community relations, etc; fund-raising deals mainly with one aspect—money-raising. Public relations tends to deal more with subtle communication; fund-raising more with hard selling.

Many organizations have the same person or same department handling both public relations and fund-raising. But most management experts prefer a separation between the two individuals or two departments. Only with a division of authority can management—including volunteer leadership—guarantee full attention in each area. All communications efforts, of course, should be integrated.

As Sandra Gordon, vice-president of communications, National Easter Seal Society, explained, "Easter Seals' public relations emphasis is on providing a year-round media presence—through public service announcements, public education, and advocacy programs, as well as traditional media coverage of people served through Easter Seal programs. This is what we do and what donors need to know their gifts are going to. This emphasis on year-round program activities would not be possible if fund-raising and public relations were lumped in the same department. Each requires a very different focus."

Ralph Frede, retired vice-president for public affairs, Baylor College of Medicine, raised more than $300 million during his career. He believes public relations and fund-raising should be more integrated in their support of one another regardless of how they are structured. Each has a major responsibility to "create a mutuality of interest" between their institution and the publics it serves.

The best fund-raising efforts start with a plan of action based on an analysis of what your organization or program does, and which sources of funding might be interested in supporting your endeavors. The fund-raising plan requires a statement of goals, a timetable for action, a budget, a cadre of volunteers, professional staff support when available, informational literature for prospects, good record-keeping, and an evaluation of results.

Like public relations programs, fund-raising efforts should be organized for maximum effect over time and not solely for crisis situations or one-shot appeals. The organizations or program should remain visible and active year-in and year-out so funding sources are constantly reminded of your work.

Once you have contributors, stay in touch with them, thank them for their contribu-

tions, and give them credit where credit is due. Recognize them as part of your ongoing fund-raising activities and they will recognize you as part of their ongoing philanthropy.

A source of in-depth information on the best fund-raising principles and practices is the Foundation Center, 79 Fifth Avenue, New York, NY 10003, (212) 975-1120. The Center has an Associates Program, a fee-based subscription service for not-for-profit organizations. It also maintains several regional libraries for use by phone and mail.

Marketing's Growing Importance

In recent years, probably nothing has altered the practice of public relations in nonprofit organizations more than the adoption of marketing concepts. Once viewed as something applicable only to business, marketing is gaining force as the operational context for much of what nonprofit organizations do and communicate.

Key issues are the appropriateness of marketing as a vehicle of planning and communication in nonprofits, and how to use the tools and techniques that have been so valuable over the years to business without compromising the goals and objectives of charitable enterprise.

Perhaps marketing's greatest value to the nonprofit sector is that it provides a focus for redirecting attention to what has always been the goal of public relations in nonprofits— and of other functions such as fund-raising— but that has been lost sight of for varying reasons—i.e., better planning and management of communications and the organization.

Marketing as a process is an added management tool for nonprofit organizations. It offers a perspective for creating and offering products and services that can make nonprofit organizations more relevant and more successful. The following are a few basics of marketing to consider:

- Marketing is a managerial process involving analysis, planning, implementation, and control. Research is essential to its success.

- Marketing manifests itself in carefully formulated programs to achieve desired responses. Marketing, in the best sense, precedes selling.

- Marketing seeks to bring about "voluntary exchanges" of values. The marketer or organization seeks something of value (purchase, vote, gift, etc.) from another party in exchange for something of equal or greater value to that party—e.g., a product, a job, a piece of legislation, a solution to a community problem such as drug abuse, AIDS, or homelessness. Marketing, in some respects, is the philosophical alternative to force.

- Marketing means the selection of "targeted markets" rather than trying to serve every market and be all things to all people. It means finding out exactly who your organization should be serving and then doing what is required for the satisfaction of all parties.

- Marketing relies on designing the organization's offerings in terms of the target market's needs and desires. Efforts to impose on the market a product, service, or idea that is not matched to the market's needs or wants are likely to fail.

- Marketing utilizes and blends a set of tools called the "marketing mix." Described in different ways, the mix usually means a product or service, somehow designed, somehow priced, somehow packaged, somehow communicated, somehow distributed, somehow promoted to satisfy the needs of target markets.

Conceptually, marketing is a sound idea, but in reality many problems remain in how it is defined and how it is administered in the nonprofit world. Public relations practitioners and departments have a major share of the responsibility for determining the proper "fit."

40

PUBLIC RELATIONS FOR RELIGIONS AND RELIGIOUS GROUPS

MARVIN C. WILBUR

Marvin C. Wilbur was assistant vice-president of the United Presbyterian Foundation and executive secretary of the Religious Public Relations Council, Inc.

Previously, he was director of public information at Union Theological Seminary (New York).

A native of the State of Washington, Dr. Wilbur took his journalism work at Oregon State University where in his senior year he was editor-in-chief of the student newspaper, The Oregon State Daily Barometer. *He served as assistant director of public information for the Oregon State System of Higher Education. He also did graduate work at George Washington University, Washington, DC, and Alma College conferred a Doctor of Divinity degree on him in 1956.*

He is the author of The Every Member Canvass Source Book *and* The Matter of Editing and Publishing a Church Newspaper. *He has received the Outstanding Achievement Award of the National Visual Communication Association and more than a dozen certificates of special merit at annual exhibitions of the New York Employing Printers Association.*

Societal changes have always made a tremendous impact on religion. But never have religious factions had to contend with the incredible rate and breadth of change that they face today. Keeping up with change—especially technology-related changes—comprises one of the major challenges for this generation of religion's public relations people.

It took five years for Johann Gutenberg, the fifteenth-century inventor of movable type printing, to set and print the Bible. With the Linotron high-speed typesetter used by the Government Printing Office, the entire Bible can be set for printing in just 77 minutes—and each copy printed instantly thereafter in any quantity. Today all 1,245 pages of the Bible can be recorded on a film negative no larger than a postage stamp and every one of those pages can be instantly retrieved, blown up, and printed on 8½" × 11" paper.

Even greater than the technological changes in communication have been the sociological changes. Throughout the ages humans have demonstrated their ability to tolerate change—at least at the relatively slow rate of change in past centuries. In our modern world ideas not only change but are exchanged more rapidly and more broadly than ever before. People now must accept or often adapt to more changes in a single month than they did in several years just thirty years ago.

Nowadays we have both greater means of communicating and more necessity to communicate. As humans we undergo a whole cycle, or even several cycles, of changing cultures in one lifetime.

For religion and religious groups this presents significant challenge and opportunity. The public relations problems of today's churches are disheartening and many: alienation, war, poverty, mutiny, moral decay, drugs, civil unrest, reparations, segregation, terrorism, conflict. The opportunity is derived from effectively utilizing the wide range of powerful communications tools to get out the church's message to more people.

The newsletter for Methodist communication leaders, *Community*, featured an article entitled "A Look Toward the Year 2000," which said in part:

> Despite technology and preoccupations with "things," ideas will still be the primary agents of change.
>
> Despite the probe of technology into all the unknowns, people in the year 2000 will still be asking the age-old questions:
> "Who am I?"
> "What is my purpose?"
> "What does it all mean?"
> And in that X factor within man, which prompts those searching questions, lies the only mandate any religion has for existence. Either a religion earns the right of survival by helping man ask ever better questions and discover his own truth, or a religion fails to help man and becomes simply a lingering monument to the past.

Though religion has always needed public relations, it has not always recognized this need. Some years ago Arthur Krock, the famed *New York Times* columnist, wrote:

> Among the anomalies of the American scene is the persistent fact that "public relations" is an art that often is least comprehended by those who must depend on its sound practice. On numerous occasions there have been amazing demonstrations that the ablest personages in industry and government fail to comprehend the simplest principles for establishing a favorable public psychology toward their activities.

Religious institutions, whether headquarters or local church, are not exempt even today from this indictment, but most of them have come a long way in recognizing that they have public relations whether they want to or not. Not long ago, religious public relations was known more for its technique than its policy. There was a time when the department of public relations was in actuality the publicity office, the promotion division, or a radio program. As indicated elsewhere in this handbook, good public relations may be all of these, but it is something more.

Developing Standards

Certainly religion has tooled itself for public relations and communication as never before. In 1970 after five years of planning, a Religious Communication Congress was held in Chicago and attended by more than 450 religious communicators. The Second Religious Communications Congress was held in Nashville in 1980 with more than thirteen hundred religious communicators in attendance. Both events were interfaith in character, sponsored by more than forty organizations, including professionals in public relations, journalism, communications, radio, television, film, research, and publishing.

A group of public relations professionals from all faiths and denominations produced a second edition of the handbook, *Religious*

Public Relations Handbook, that has been widely used. The Contents page (following) gives an inkling of the wide field of religious public relations today:[1]

Public Relations

Media for Your Message

Press Relations

Broadcasting

Advertising

Congregational Publications

Audio Visual Aids

Photography

Displays and Signs

Overlooked PR Opportunities

Community Relations

Direct Mail

Organizing for PR

Other Resources Available

Every public relations professional is familiar with a listing of this type. However, they are included here to indicate that what's good for general public relations is good for religious public relations. Yet many churches feel they are exempt from following the basic public relations rules and from understanding the effective use of all media. They feel that religion is one of the mightiest forces on earth, and people will just understand. Nothing could be further from the truth. A lie repeated often enough over a period of years will be accepted sooner or later as "truth" by a large percentage of hearers. Possession of truth does not guarantee understanding or acceptance. Ideas compete on every hand. If the church and synagogue are to remain vital forces within society, they must know how to interpret their messages convincingly to the community.

[1]*Religious Public Relations Handbook*, Religious Public Relations Council, P.O. Box 315, Gladwyne, PA 19035.

Of course most of the Table of Contents listed above is what other chapters in *Lesly's Handbook of Public Relations and Communications* are all about. Detailed chapters cover most of the subjects as well as many other areas. These chapters are recommended to all of organized religion's public relations professionals and are integral auxiliaries to this chapter.

Special attention, however, is due three aspects of religious public relations:

1. Organizing an effective religious public relations program

2. Financing the religious public relations program

3. Setting up a workable communication center

Program Organization

Since public relations is a two-sided coin—one side being policy, the other technique—it must be represented in the top policy-making group of each religious institution. One of the greatest hindrances to effective religious public relations today is the widespread exclusion of its policy-making function.

This often results because there is no clear-cut organizational structure. The responsibility for the public relations program should lie with the top policy-making body in any religious institution. This body should establish the public relations committee with a well-defined purpose and authority. The chairperson of this committee should be a member—or at least a corresponding member—of the top policy-making body.

Many churches take it for granted that the pastor will be the public relations chairman. He often edits the newspaper, greets the Sunday morning visitors, and sends stories to the local press. There is no doubt as to the image the pastor or rabbi holds in relation to his or her institution, but he or she should not be expected to take over the duties of the public relations committee. These duties can be done effectively by lay people. The pastor or rabbi should, however, participate in the meetings of the committee, and at all times be kept well informed. The pastor or rabbi should see that the public relations committee knows of his or her actions, contacts, speeches, and the like. All functions should be integrated to assure consistency.

Gathering the facts

One of the major duties of the public relations committee will be to set up a research or fact-finding program. This will include the determination of the "publics" within both the congregation and the community, as well as how each "public" might react to theological, sociological, or ethical interpretation.

Jim Suggs, in his chapter on "Organizing for Public Relations" in the *Handbook on Church Public Relations*, says that the public relations committee should know or seek the answers to such questions as the following:

- What do people of the community think of our congregation? Do some segments of the population ("publics") have a better understanding of the church's purposes than other?

- Do members of the congregation think the church's program is balanced and has the right priorities? Do they have a clear understanding of the purposes of the church?

- Where do church members get their information about the plans and activities of the congregation?

- In the minds of various publics—within and outside the church—does the program of the church live up to what it says about itself or to what it preaches to the world?

The public relations committee should have free access to information and authority to have representation on all boards and committees that need assistance. It is often as important to know what not to say as to know what to say.

Finally, in organizing for an effective religious public relations program, a competent staff must be brought together. This is a problem both in national headquarters where, for the most part, budgets are inadequate and at the local institution where volunteer help is the norm.

The following factors should be taken into consideration:

- A book on how to recruit volunteer help should be an available resource.

- Few things can be edited well by a committee.

- Establish guidelines and then give your editor a free hand.

- Expect to pay for most of the services you use.

- Do not take advantage of the talents of your members from which they must make their living.

- Establish a system of cultivating members in the public relations field.

- Get rid of the incompetent volunteer, but don't make any enemies.

Program Financing

There's an old adage that says you have to spend money to make money. Public relations in the church will cost money and should be budgeted. The public relations committee should project its budget in accordance with the budgetary practices of its religious institution. And without apology! Even in lean years!

Remember that in presenting your budget to the Joint Budget Committee you should use the best public relations techniques you know. It should go without saying that "overkill" is not a good technique. You may not get everything you asked for, but remember that you have informed a lot of key people about your program.

Establishing a Communication Center

Timing is one of the most important elements in public relations. The techniques of public relations take space, equipment, storage, servicing, repair, and books. Much of this material may seem expensive. However, if amortized over a number of years, the cost can be reasonable.

A special office should be set up as the communication center with copier, fax, computer, addressing and folding equipment, postage meter, and the like. It should have locked closets for storing projection equipment and screens, easels, tape recorders, display equipment, turnover charts and portable blackboards, CD players, and perhaps even videotape equipment. There could also be many fonts of different size rub-on type for offset printing or posters, as well as other graphic arts equipment. If you are lucky enough to have someone who is a hobbyist in silk screening, equipment for making attractive and inexpensive display posters will be desirable.

Of course, the communication center should have a highly selective library that includes the directives, past minutes, and history of your local church; yearbooks of the national church, the National and World Councils as well as the faith you represent, Bible dictionaries, commentaries and concordances, gazetteers, almanacs, and the like. It also should include selected photographs present and past—all well identified.

Supporting Organizations

There is much assistance available for all groups interested in developing religious public relations. All the major faiths, including most Protestant denominations, have public relations and communication organizations. There are also specialized professional societies and associations whose publications can be excellent sources of assistance. Some of the major areas of assistance are listed here.

Professional associations

The *Religious Public Relations Council*, P.O. Box 296, Wernersville, PA 19565, is an interfaith professional society with five hundred members located in fourteen chapters across the country. Publications include MEDIAKIT, a kit of ideas in communication designed to keep members informed about what's going on in public relations, a quarterly newsletter, *Counselor*, a *Directory*, and the *Religious Public Relations Handbook*. Holds annual convention and monthly chapter meetings.

Associated Church Press, P.O. Box 30215, Phoenix, AZ 85046, is an association of 170 religious publications in the United States and Canada fostering helpfulness among editors and publishers and higher standards of religious journalism. Conducts annual conventions, awards programs. Publishes an annual directory and bimonthly newsletter.

World Association for Christian Communication, 357 Kennington Lane, London SE11 5QY, England. Dr. Hands Florin, Executive Director. A voluntary organization of Christian communicators that gives aid to communication enterprises in many parts of the world. Membership is both personal and corporate.

National Association of Church Business Administration, 7001 Grapevine Highway, Suite 324, Fort Worth, TX 76180. F. Marvin Myers, Executive Director. An international, interfaith association with a membership of approximately fifteen hundred religious institutional administrators, meeting in fifty-five active local chapters and an annual national conference. Publications include the *Ledger*, a quarterly journal containing articles and reports in support of the profession; NACBAGRAM, a monthly report on activities within the association; annual Conference Proceedings; and an annual Membership Roster.

Denominational and faith organizations

The *Catholic Press Association*, with offices at 3555 Veterans Highway, Ronkonkona, NY 11779, publishes monthly *The Catholic Journalist* and annually *The Catholic Press Directory*.

The *Jewish Publication Society*, 1930 Chestnut Street, Philadelphia, PA 19103, publishes materials related to the Jewish faith.

The *Evangelical Press Association*, 485 Panorama Road, Earlysville, VA 22936, is devoted to issues of concern to evangelical denominations.

Baptist Public Relations Association, 1914 Valley Park Road, Nashville, TN 37216, provides assistance to members of its denomination.

Communications Commission, National Council of Churches, 475 Riverside Drive, New York, NY 10115. A cooperating agency of fourteen member denominations and groups who have come together to develop programs and policies of mutual value.

Religion in American Life, Inc. (RIAL), 2 Queenstown Place, Princeton, NJ 08540, is a public relations resource for American churches and synagogues. It utilizes free space and time in the mass media made available through The Advertising Council, including television, radio, newspapers, consumer magazines, business magazines, outdoor posters, transportation posters, and car cards. Materials available include newspaper advertise-

ments, media kits, and resource guides. In addition it operates the Hotel Worship Directory service with display boards with information about local churches and synagogues in many cities.

Broadcasting and films

A number of organizations participate in the broadcasting and films areas including the following:

- *National Religious Broadcasters*, 7889 Ashton Avenue, Manassas, VA 22110
- *Association of Regional Religious Communicators*, 1011 Sandusky Avenue, Perrysburg, OH 43552
- *Office for Films and Broadcasting*, U.S. Catholic Conference, 3211 4th Street, NE, Washington, DC 20017.

Religious periodicals

Every person handling public relations for a religious institution, be it local, state, national, or worldwide, should be familiar not only with denominational or diocesan papers but also at least one or two interdenominational or interfaith periodicals. More than two hundred of these periodicals are listed in the *Yearbook of American and Canadian Churches* (United Methodist Publishing House, 201 Eighth Avenue, S, Nashville, TN 37202. Issued annually.)

The Catholic Press Directory lists more than five hundred Catholic publications. (*See* Catholic Press Association listing earlier.)

Standard Periodical Directory, published by Oxbridge Communications, 150 Fifth Avenue, New York, NY 10011, includes a list of religious media.

Guide to Religious and Inspirational Magazines, published by Writer's Resources, 15 Margaret's Way, Nantucket, MA 02554, is a valuable resource.

See also periodicals and directories available in the Appendix.

Every public relations library should have these indispensable references with their up-to-date statistics and facts on America's major faiths, Protestant, Catholic, Greek Orthodox, and Jewish, and their related organizations.

Religious editors of the secular media

One of the great allies of organized religion's public relations and communication personnel is the interest of secular journalism, both print and broadcasting, in religion today. Few are the churches that could not get some story, or at least announcement, in the local press. Denominations and faith groups set up excellent professional press rooms to accommodate the religion journalists appointed to cover special assemblies and conventions.

One of the most comprehensive sources (and outlets) of religious copy and photos is Religion News Service, 1101 Connecticut Avenue, NW, Washington, DC 20003. RNS is an independently managed organization within the National Conference of Christians and Jews.

The major supplier of news and photos to Catholic publications is the national Catholic News Service, 3211 4th Street, NW, Washington, DC 20017. Richard W. Daw is Director and Editor-in-Chief.

A publication of value to all religion communicators who work in the broadcast media is *If You Want Air Time*, a handbook for publicity chairpersons prepared by the Member Communications Department of the National Association of Broadcasters, 1771 N Street, NW, Washington, DC 20036. Copies of this handbook are available for $3 each.

A complete and detailed listing of all religion editors (they have assorted titles) for newspapers, magazines, wire services, radio, and television appears in the five companion volumes of *The Working Press of the Nation*, published by the National Research Bureau, Inc., 121 Chanlon Road, New Providence, NJ 07974.

The Editor & Publisher International Yearbook, 11 W. 19th Street, New York, NY 10011, lists religion editors among staff people of daily newspapers in the United States and Canada. Its annual Syndicate Directory lists the religion columns of press services and syndicates.

41

PUBLIC RELATIONS FOR EDUCATIONAL INSTITUTIONS

MICHAEL RADOCK

Michael Radock, consultant to and former chief executive officer of the Charles Stewart Mott Foundation, for twenty years was vice-president for university relations and development and professor of journalism at the University of Michigan. He also has been vice-president at the University of Southern California and the Aspen Institute for Humanistic Studies and has taught public relations at five educational institutions. While at Kent State University, he founded the Institute for Public Relations in 1947 to provide professional training for PR executives. He is a past president of the American College Public Relations Association. As manager of educational affairs of Ford Motor Company, he organized the Ford Educational Forum and the Ford National College Seminar Program.

He was a founding trustee of the Council for Advancement and Support of Education and a White House appointee to the Board of Foreign Scholarships, which supervises the Fulbright exchange program. Radock is a graduate of Westminster College and the Medill School of Journalism at Northwestern University and did postgraduate study at Case Western Reserve University.

The role of the public relations officer in the American college and university has undergone dramatic change as the result of several major trends. These public relations officers have moved, figuratively and literally, from the boiler room to the boardroom. The scope of management responsibilities has broadened considerably, both internally and externally. The field's primary national professional organization—the Council for the Advancement and Support of Education (CASE)—was formed through the merger of the American College Public Relations Association and the American Alumni Council, significantly increasing both its size and power. CASE members comprise some 2,900 colleges, universities, two-year colleges, and independent schools, representing more than 14,000 individuals. (The address for CASE is: 11 Dupont Circle, Washington, DC 20036.)

Many recent developments in higher education have exerted enormous pressures on our schools and colleges and have brought considerable change in both the character and structure of U.S. education. The decline in high school graduates that followed a period of growth and expansion provides a source of major concern. Ongoing financial crises continue to threaten the survival of many marginal institutions. The federal government's increased involvement in higher education through government-mandated programs troubles members of the governing boards of learning institutions, educational administrators, and faculty. Other problems have arisen related to the inability of students to find suitable employment to help fund their educations and upon graduation. Internal competition for scarce funds create tensions within and among educational organizations. Other major sources of contention stem from the activism of racial and ethnic minorities, as well as from charges of racism, discrimination, and sexism.

Changing attitudes

The president of the Hewlett Foundation on Education, Roger W. Heyns, noting current tensions, observed:

> Universities have emerged from obscurity to prominence. Now the members of the academic community are involved with the society in many ways. The tensions of the society find expression in the behavior of campus communities and in the reaction of the society to that behavior. It is a matter of greatest moment, not that we cease being sources of discomfort, but that we be uncomfortable for the proper reasons—those that derive naturally from our educational tasks and not those that arise from other characteristics—among them our inability to solve our problems in an orderly way.

New emphasis on public relations

Dr. Derek Bok, former president of Harvard University, believed that when times are bad, the public looks for scapegoats, and education is an attractive candidate for many of the nation's ills. He told members of the Council for Advancement and Support of Higher Education (CAHE):

> Because of increased criticism that is often unfair, colleges around the country are putting new emphasis on public relations to get their stories across and to improve public understanding of what is really going on. Such efforts are useful, and they must continue. But, in my opinion, they will not suffice.
>
> No amount of argument, no amount of positive public relations, is going to fully overcome those critical attitudes. We must remember that we have benefited from too much praise on many occasions in the past, and we will now suffer the opposite.
>
> There are valid reasons for criticizing our performance. Many of our institutions have paid too little attention to teaching, to clarifying their purposes, to the problems of values and ethics, to corruption in athletics. So if we respond only with positive public relations about what we are already doing, we will appear to be even more insensitive and arrogant than many people take us to be at the present time.

Formula for survival

Recognizing the widespread anxiety over survival of colleges and universities, the Carnegie Foundation for the Advancement of Teaching has listed various ingredients for survival:

- Attract all ages rather than only eighteen- to twenty-one-year-olds
- Provide for part-time students
- Have public state support
- Be of an effective size
- Be located in an urban area
- Be an older institution
- Have comparatively low tuition
- Have a national reputation
- Have a stabilized undergraduate enrollment
- Be related to the health professions

The biggest problem in American higher education—as well as in society at large—is learning to accommodate change.

Editorially, the *Public Relations Journal* noted:

> No sector of American society has enjoyed a more sheltered position than higher education. Up to the present, it has been taken for granted by the public as a somewhat esoteric business that is nevertheless good and necessary. An Ivy Curtain has shielded the campus, and few have moved to penetrate it.

But, it added, "the higher education industry is in for major public relations troubles."

Nevertheless, improvement has been made as perceived by a noted English scholar, Sir Eric Ashby, a frequent visitor to American colleges. He declared, "The great American contribution to higher education has been to dismantle the walls around the campus. . . . [It is] one of the rare inventions in the evolution of universities. It is one that has already been vindicated by history. Other nations are beginning to copy the American example."

Forces for change

In 1966 a national poll on confidence in higher education showed that 61 percent of the American people expressed a great deal of confidence in higher education; in 1988 the figure dropped to 34 percent. On many fronts, institutions of higher learning are devoting attention to improving the emotional and social health of the world. Although a wide array of college and university efforts are "relevant," the public is often unaware of the potential impact of the efforts.

Because the structure of higher education is changing, as well as the status and role of both students and faculty members, the problems of managing university communities approach and, in some instances, surpass those of managing cities and corporations.

These are different organisms with peculiar traditions.

From education come the manpower, the ideas, the basic research, the innovation, and the necessary heresies for a dynamic society. All of this spells change. Almost by definition, change is unsettling, be it a new way of thinking or a new demand on resources.

The Public's Invested Interest in Higher Education

One of the most thorough studies of public attitudes on higher education in the United States was conducted by the Council for Advancement and Support of Education (CASE) under the leadership of Dr. Gary H. Quehl, shortly after he assumed the presidency of that organization.

Dr. Quehl spent about two months traveling more than fifty thousand miles to talk with leaders in an on-campus sample of twenty-six college and universities. Using the method of content analysis, he interviewed five principal groups: presidents or chancellors, chief academic officers, institutional advancement officers, representative groups of faculty, and students.

Also interviewed were sixty-six off-campus opinion leaders and representatives: publishers, editors, senior journalists of national and regional news organizations, corporation and foundation executives, governors, national higher education association executives, and senior congressional staffers.

The results of the survey were made available in "A Report to the Campus" by CASE's National Task Force on Higher Education and the Public Interest.

Dr. Quehl quickly determined that a belief that higher education has an "image problem" that can be corrected by furnishing improved information to the American public was completely inaccurate. "The current challenge," he learned, "is not merely a challenge of communication but a challenge of substance."

The CASE interviews determined five public interest areas that require attention:

1. The quality of higher education
2. The price and cost of higher education
3. Opportunity and choice in higher education for all qualified citizens
4. Higher education's relationship with the workplace and economic development
5. Public understanding of the purposes of higher education

Each of the various constituencies expressed differing views on the most critical issues facing higher education.

College and university presidents focused on these concerns:

- The increasing price of higher education
- Understanding the purposes of higher education
- Past promises, future expectations, and the credibility of higher education
- Managing change

Chief academic officers and faculty members reflected a different set of issues:

- Curriculum and the quality of teaching
- The balance between teaching and scholarship
- Time pressures
- Explicit and implicit rewards
- Concerns about the future

Campus interviews revealed that students are serious, single-minded, and have their own list of major concerns:

- The long-term value of their college degree
- The accessibility and interest of faculty
- The impact of drugs and alcohol on campus
- The rising cost of education
- What the future holds

Representatives of news organizations expressed substantial concerns on these issues:

- The public's perception of higher education
- The problem of educating the growing underclass of citizens, primarily minorities and the displaced worker
- The price of higher education
- The need for higher education to take charge of its own house

In its Special Advisory to College Presidents, CASE observed: "Public disillusionment is fed from many quarters—from highly publicized abuses involving the recruiting and paying of intercollegiate athletes, to the falsification of research results by campus scientists; from parental questions about the quality of educational programs, to the mounting costs of obtaining an undergraduate degree. Critics within the Academy and elsewhere worry that institutions of higher learning are not sufficiently involved in helping meet the enormous challenges facing the nation. Others are alarmed by activists' manipulation of course material and the curriculum."

Noting that "evidence is undeniable that public confidence in higher education is continuing to erode," CASE responded that "We believe the damage can be repaired and the public's confidence restored. Not until people begin to understand that initiatives are being taken on campus—and meaningful results are being achieved—will attitudes change."

Athletic scandals

The American college world has been rocked by a series of athletic scandals. The situation has become so serious that one of the nation's wealthiest philanthropic organizations, with roots in newspaper publishing, the Knight Foundation, launched a $2-million, two-year effort to devise a plan to overhaul intercollegiate athletics. The foundation observed that "there is a crisis in college athletics with twenty-two institutions under National Collegiate Athletic Association (NCAA) sanctions; since 1980, more than one hundred campuses have been censured, and basketball and football players are graduated at a low rate, and Congress is beginning to look into the low graduation rates of some college athletes."

The recent high rate of athletes being charged with crimes is another concern. And although new entrance requirements and study standards have had positive effects, they remain targets of minority groups.

In addition, the Association of Governing Boards of Universities and Colleges, acting on the recommendation of its ad hoc committee on intercollegiate athletics, adopted a resolution in support of reforming college athletics.

Basic principles adopted included the following:

1. "Governing boards should see that there are unambiguous policies that state that the athletic program is part of the institution's educational process and the integrity of that primary mission is paramount and must be protected at all times.

2. "Governing boards should assure vigorous oversight of all policies and procedures that govern athletic programs through an appropriate standing committee or subcommittee.

3. "Preferably and ideally, athletic directors should report directly to the president or chancellor.

4. "Colleges and all other athletic staff members should be expected to adhere to all institutional policies and regulations.

5. "Institutional policies should recognize that the primary function of intercollegiate athletics and intramural athletic programs is to ensure broad-based student participation.

6. "Governing boards should protect against abuses related to financing intercollegiate athletic programs and ensure that the activities of booster clubs and other fundraising entities do not control or contradict institutional policies."

Explaining change

Fundamentally, the assignment of the educational public relations person is to explain change occurring in and coming from the college or university and to advise the other leaders of the effect and perceptions of their actions.

Gone is Joe College. Gone is dear old prexy. Gone is the good old absent-minded professor. Gone are the unquestioning alumni. Gone are the indifferent and apathetic students. Gone is the ivory tower. Gone is *in loco parentis*. Gone are the sharp distinctions between the public and the private institutions, the church-related and the secular institutions.

The universe of higher education

The impact of colleges and universities not only upon American society but the world can be measured in one sense by statistics:

- 3,632 colleges and universities
- 14.4 million students, about 5 percent of the U.S. population
- More than 700,000 faculty members
- A $156-billion-a-year enterprise
- A combined physical plant whose total value may be immeasurable

Look at the growth of enrollment in higher education in America (degree-credit enrollment):

1950—2 million

1960—3.5 million

1965—6 million

1970—7.9 million

1975—9.7 million

1980—11.1 million

1989—12.5 million

1994—14.5 million

Identity crisis

While the community and junior colleges appear to have survived a growth period and found their identity, this is not true for the regional universities, including many former state teachers colleges and state colleges. These rapidly developing institutions are now suffering an acute identity crisis, seeking to find their proper niche in the educational spectrum.

Meanwhile, the nation has seen the virtual disappearance of the municipally supported senior institution and the spectacular growth of the large public university, the so-called multiversity or comprehensive university.

Accompanying the growth in numbers has been a trend toward greater coordination and centralized control of public institutions by state boards, super-boards, and similar agencies, and a greater emphasis on planning functions. Meanwhile, private colleges have moved to join in consortia, regional groups, or "cluster college" arrangements.

The nature of a university

A major responsibility of the public relations officer is to convey to the public or publics the nature of the institution so it is not undermined by ignorance, so it is supported through understanding. A university, to continue to meet its responsibilities for education, research, and service, must have resources and freedom.

The public relations departments must try to help educate the public to understand, to appreciate, to tolerate, and to defend the vital necessity of freedom for the student to learn and for the scholar to search for the truth without restriction.

The public must be adequately informed of the true function of a university so it will learn to cherish free inquiry and reckon with pressures, particularly in times of hysteria and tension.

In the public spotlight

It is the business of the public relations counselor to be aware of the vulnerability and the opportunity of the university in the circumstances of the time. More public attention is being focused on education for a number of reasons, among them the age composition of the nation's population, the large percentage of youth seeking college and graduate education, and the consequent demands of education on financial resources.

What is happening in and about and because of, or lack of, education is now more important to more people, whether the issue is admission standards, efficiency, financial needs, interinstitutional cooperation, revision of the curriculum, teaching and/or research, service, and the many tangential responsibilities of higher education.

At the policy level

The public relations officer plays a policy-making role. How large a role depends not so much on the clearly defined responsibilities as on his or her colleagues' appreciation of public relations and their willingness to seek and consider professional counsel.

The basic function of public relations as a part of university administration is to help the institution's people do their job and to make sure the climate is as conducive as possible for them.

The Ongoing Evolution of Educational Relations

Recent studies of public relations programs and activities in American colleges and universities provide substantial evidence of the acceptance of the public relations professional as an integral member of the educational management team in many institutions.

However, the academic community still harbors a deep suspicion of "public relations," associating it with "press agentry" or "propaganda."

"Why should we spend so much money for public relations?" asks the economy-minded administrator.

"Is this an activity that belongs in an educational institution?" asks a faculty member.

"Could not the dollars spent on public relations be used more effectively for faculty salaries and laboratory and other institutional needs? Who needs public relations?"

These and other pointed questions trouble college presidents and administrators.

Because of this climate of distrust and suspicion in the academic environment and because the results of public relations expenditures usually are intangible, the college public relations department may be a target for investigations, audits, and criticism.

Changing faculty attitudes

A chancellor of a large eastern university explained to a national conference of educational public relations officers the reasons for academia's "instinctive reaction" against public relations:

The atmosphere of public relations is uncongenial to the typical academic person, and for some very fundamental reasons. In the first place, academic people are accustomed to having people come to them, not going to people. The student comes to us; the problem comes to us. Ours is not an outgoing kind of reaction to take the product, to take the story, to take the service to the people, to the public. In this sense public relations people are almost diametrically opposed to us, and we're inclined to be analysts and inclined to be concerned about detail. You're concerned about broad impacts. You see things in general terms, as you should; we tend to see them in highly particularistic terms, as indeed we should. Again, we look on things—every problem, every subject—with reservation; you look at it with enthusiasm and from a positive point of view. So once again in discharging your function in a positive sort of way, it's almost inevitable that the academic people feel a little uncomfortable.

Again, we're not comfortable with the media of public relations. The press conference is not in our blood. It's something that the typical academic person shies away from. Promotional literature seems a little unscholarly, and the biographical sketch in a national magazine suggests something less than appropriate academic humility.

Semantic problems

As a result of these circumstances and attitudes, functions broadly categorized under the vaguely suspect term *public relations*, being as necessary in schools and colleges as in business and industry, must be performed under a more acceptable name. Hence, *university relations* has tended to become the academic facade for public relations at many institutions, including the University of Michigan, which as early as 1931 created the position of vice-president for university relations.

Other semantic variations include *public affairs, information services, planning and development, community relations, assistant to the president, news and publications services, public information*, and similar labels.

The Greenbrier Report

The most significant development in the recognition of public relations took place through the efforts of a study committee of the American College Public Relations Association and the American Alumni Council. The major recommendation was a unified organizational approach with a major coordinating officer, reporting directly to the college or university president, responsible for the direction of public relations, alumni relations, and fund-raising. (*See* Figure 41.1.)

The practice of effective public relations in colleges and universities, participants agreed, required certain basic conditions:

1. A clear statement of institutional purposes
2. A "sound product"

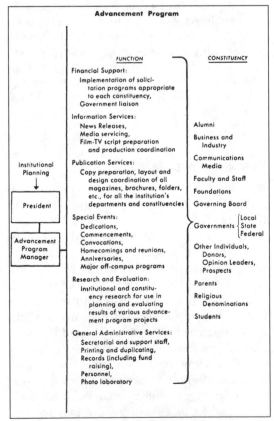

Figure 41.1 Outline of a typical advancement program for an educational institution.

3. An adequate budget
4. Adequate personnel

For educational public relations, the study set forth these basic conclusions that are applicable to a wide variety of institutions:

1. The administrative functions of public relations, alumni relations, and fund-raising should exist on each college campus.
2. Each of these major functions is an essential part of a broadly conceived program of institutional advancement.
3. There must be organizational and administrative coordination of these and other related functions to serve the institution's best interests.
4. No single "ideal" organizational pattern can achieve the necessary coordination.
5. Each institution should determine the most effective organizational structure to serve its special needs and characteristics.

Public relations planning

Kalman B. Druck, a well-known PR counselor, offered his advice on advancement planning to members of the Council for Advancement and Support of Education. "Any institution wants four things," Druck noted, "students, faculty, money, and political support. When you understand that advancement activity should help produce these four things, planning is easy."

He explained that an ideal PR plan would include these two elements:

• A specific statement of objectives
• Your method for achieving those objectives

He emphasized that the plan should consist of four steps:

1. Define your publics.
2. Develop your case.
3. Lay out your program.
4. Evaluate and measure results.

He recommended that PR directors should make greater use of on-campus specialists: "The average institution's faculty can supply most or all the knowledge and skills you need for planning. Meet once in a while with professors and researchers in marketing, journalism, public relations, economics, management, and so on."

Commitment and cooperation

The key administrators should fundamentally agree on the purposes of a program of internal public relations. And they ought to be realistic about expectations. They should understand what is involved in allocation of financial and personnel resources and make the commitment over an extended period. In addition to agreement on purposes and realism about possible accomplishments and commitments to resources, another ingredient must be added: cooperation. While the public relations unit may have the job of carrying out the program, the public relations department cannot do without the continuing cooperation of key administrators. Also, administrators' functions and statements should be integrated with all others' to avoid inconsistencies and confusion. This should be clear before you embark on a program.

Basic organizational structures

A basic principle is that no single organizational structure or pattern applies equally well at all colleges or universities.

A definitive study by the ACPRA showed that certain patterns of organizational structure were best suited to private colleges and universities, and a variation of those structures for public universities.

In this study the term *advancement program* is used to designate the total program devoted to information services, alumni relations, publications, and fund-raising.

Two basic patterns are suggested: A common structure in a state university has a central coordinating officer, usually a vice-president, reporting directly to the president. In some institutions the chief coordinating officer is a director or assistant to the president.

For smaller institutions a common pattern is to have three major functions reporting directly to the president. A frequent variation has two major officers, one for public relations and one for fund-raising, reporting directly to the head of the institution.

Inventory of resources

The standard public relations process of fact-gathering, planning, communication, and evaluation is as essential in educational institutions as in any other area or activity.

A number of the larger institutions have created an Office of Institutional Advancement, combining the functions of public relations, alumni, and development or fund-raising. Typically, the umbrella concept is used to refer to public relations (including information services, publications, community relations, and governmental relations), alumni relations and programs, fund-raising, student recruitment, federal relations, marketing, university press, and printing activities.

One of the leading proponents of the institutional advancement concept, Dr. A. Westley Rowland, former vice-president for university relations at the State University of New York at Buffalo, stresses the importance of establishing goals for the advancement program:

Goals are important because they set directions; they provide a target toward which institutional relations efforts and resources will be directed; they indicate priorities; and they give a real sense of what the institutional relations program is all about, where the program is going, and what, through institutional relations, the college or university wishes to achieve. Thus goals become important operationally because they determine the level of budget needed, the number and type of staff, and the nature of program and activities.

Broadened responsibilities

The principal public affairs responsibility of the central administration of the sixty-four-campus State University of New York (SUNY) system rests with the office of the vice-chancellor for Government and University Relations. The term used in the SUNY system is defined as covering "the service functions of communicating and relating with the internal and external constituencies of the University for their understanding of what the University is, what it is becoming; more specifically, for example, what educational opportunities it offers and will offer, how it views its progress at the moment and for the next decade." The vice-chancellor is given the responsibility "to ensure that every citizen, as a kind of stockholder in this multibillion-dollar enterprise, is kept fully aware of the university's performance for the purpose of making intelligent judgments, not only as to participation but also to provision of support."

The following activities are assigned to the office: relations with the state's executive chamber and the governor's office, the New York state legislature, the SUNY campus presidents and university constituent groups, as well as state and federal legislative groups.

A basic step in any in-depth analysis of the potential for a public relations program is a careful inventory or audit of resources. Here are some of the questions that the public relations director and associates should try to answer:

1. What are the characteristics of your institution? Multiversity? Church-related college? Community college? Urban? Small-town? Activist and liberal? Passive and conservative?

2. What does the administration or governing board believe are your purposes and responsibilities? Are they the same responsibilities you believe you have accepted?

3. What kind of public relations department do you have? Is it basically a news and information service or a comprehensive, multifaceted operation? Are fund-raising considerations more important than student and faculty support?

4. What are the basic operating policies and guidelines that serve as constraints in your daily operation? Must the president, dean, or some other official approve every statement that is issued? At what level of policy making in management do you exist?

5. How is the institution or the department organized?

6. What is the total environment in which you live and work? Reference to environment means it must be described totally: politically, socially, economically, physically, and geographically. Study of these factors helps the public relations officer recognize that the climate in which the institution exists may be favorable, neutral, unfavorable, or downright hostile.

7. What are the strengths and weaknesses of the department and the institution? Is the public relations department understaffed and underbudgeted? Is it strong in the print media and not in the electronic media? Is there any know-how in community relations, or special events, or communication? Does the public relations staff spend all its time on external publics and ignore the faculty, students, and staff?

8. Is the public relations department adapting itself to the changing nature of the institution and the demands of its constituencies? Are there periodic evaluations of its practices and policies?

Profile of Public Relations Staff for Higher Education

Professor or professional—which is most important? Both the colleague relationship with the faculty and the talent and skills for the public relations function are desirable, of course. And particular institutional circumstances make a general rule inappropriate. But if a choice must be made, most colleges choose the professional. Professional trappings do not protect from establishment coloration the teacher who "reluctantly" takes on the administrative task—even if the reluctance is sincere. It is better to have a dedicated professional than a disjointed professor.

What kind of professional?

Is it a journalist by education and/or experience? Is that person an administrator? What about industry and association public relations background? How useful is government background—either administrative or legislative? How important is an understanding of fund-raising? What priority goes to knowledge of alumni relations and acquaintance with the particular institution, region, or state? Is the professional a graduate or nongraduate of the particular institution? These and other considerations need to be weighed against the specific institution's requirements.

Dealing with Internal Publics

By design or by accident, a good share of the job of relating with the internal publics of an educational institution may fall to the public relations unit.

Beyond the fact of skill availability, there is another good reason for linking organizationally internal and external public relations:

one affects the other. Attitudes inside affect actions outside. High morale and enthusiasm developed within an organization radiate beyond the organization. In the same way, low morale and dissatisfaction seep to the outside. That makes coordination essential.

Complex communication

Internal communication in an institution of higher education is more complicated than it may appear to the outsider. The reasons are that (a) the university is not a homogeneous unit, and (b) the university is unlike any other organization.

While it may appear to the outsider (and even a few narrow-visioned insiders) that a college or a university is composed of students and faculty and a few clerks, and that they are similar human types held together by old school ties, that is at best mythology. Even assuming a similarity between a nuclear physicist and a classical scholar, the clerks and assorted other nonacademic types outnumber the teachers on most campuses. Furthermore, ranging from architect to salad-server on the cafeteria line, they may have less in common than the physical scientist and classicist of the faculty. The modern institution of higher education is composed of a greater variety of people—more different types, ranging further to the extremes, probably, than any other organization of comparable size. This complicates the communication job.

Another complication is the nature of the organization—its peculiar structure, relationships, and traditions. A college or university has some attributes of, but is different from, a civil government, a corporation, an army, a church, and an anarchy. For example, faculty members are not employees. Bright students are not orderly soldiers; academic freedom is essential, but so are legislative appropriations and/or private contributions. Profit making is not a purpose, but business methods are necessary. Institutional loyalty is traditional, but the society is mobile and the educational institution is geographically constrained. Stability is expected, but so are social and scientific innovation. A college can be at once a citadel of conservatism and a provenance of radicalism.

Channels of communication

You may be able to influence such formal means of internal communication as staff meetings. You may be able to influence such informal communication channels as conversational exchanges between people about their work situations. You may be able to work with existing faculty or student publications. But your control is marginal at best.

Expectations of accomplishment and the general plan for internal public relations must take into consideration what already exists. In some cases you can work with existing channels of communication, providing material and recommendations. Sometimes you may have to work around the existing channels. And occasionally you may find it necessary to run counter to existing channels. Also to be considered are public news media that reach your internal publics.

Before you develop a plan, determine what you want to accomplish. There are many examples of internal communication programs—some quite elaborate and costly—that have no specific objectives.

Establishing a program of internal communication because it's the thing to do, or because some advisory committee has decried the inadequacy of internal communication, or because the union organizer is signing up members, is not likely to result in a successful effort. There must be objectives and then a plan for reaching them.

Internal communications programs

Purposes for a program of internal communication—though not an inclusive list and not necessarily applicable to all institutions—include the following:

1. Communication of work-related information
2. Development of morale
3. Enlistment of support for and participation in specific institutional objectives
4. Counter-communication

Under the first item may be included things so functional as a faculty and staff directory, or course time and class schedules, or a new employee handbook, or wage and salary regulations, or promotion of safety and efficiency on the job, or the availability of new services, and so on.

The second area—morale—encompasses a broad area. You may want to promote institutional pride or unit loyalty, perhaps competition. You may wish to encourage a "family" spirit. Perhaps you want to develop the status of and trust in *management*, to use an industrial relations term; at the university level it may be a new president or dean or members of the governing board. You may want to promote satisfaction with employment conditions and/or compensation. Simply providing information about "what's going on" so staff members feel more intimately a part of the institution or unit may be a significant contribution to morale. A formal opportunity for feedback or for two-way communication also may be important for morale purposes.

The third purpose in some respects overlaps the development of staff morale. If you have good morale it is much easier to enlist support for and participation in specific institutional objectives; and such involvement itself promotes morale. Examples are alumni relations, fund-raising campaigns, community relations, legislative "lobbying." Faculty and staff support might be enlisted in a broad public relations campaign to publicize the institution's cultural contribution or its economic value or its research impact or its academic status or its faculty prestige. The goal could be as direct as high participation in the United Way.

Communications in crises

The fourth and final purpose, counter-communication, is by all measures the most delicate and difficult and often the reason that a formal program of internal public relations is initiated. Some problem becomes so pointed, some situation becomes so uncomfortable, some crisis appears so imminent, that a program of internal communication seems the answer—or at least, part of the answer.

A formal program of internal public relations, born of crisis, is not likely to suddenly set things right. Crisis communication is most effective as a part of a larger and well-established and credible program of internal public relations. This is treated more fully later in this chapter.

How to combat rumors

Rumor mills operating on or off campus may include a hostile union or business or political group, an unfriendly newspaper or broadcast station, an irresponsible student publication, or an "underground" periodical.

Counter-communication is most delicate and difficult, because you are in a defensive, reactive posture and because you run the risk of sounding like a crybaby or a white-washer. You are in some danger of being forced into an unwise response because of internal pressures to answer some aspersion. On balance, though, the danger of being pushed into a response is less likely than the danger of missing an opportunity to correct or clarify because of executive reluctance and delay.

Counter-communication, by its very nature, places you in opposition. You may find yourself in opposition to an organization or group of considerable credibility. Your counter-communication, if it is to be effective, also must have credibility. This credi-bility must be earned, and earned over a period of time.

Education's internal publics

In developing the plan for a program of internal public relations, the internal publics generally may be categorized as faculty, staff, and students.

It is true that diversity exists within these three categories, and these interests ought to be served. But for a formal program of internal public relations some major groupings must be assumed. The problem is not usually too-precise categorization but overgeneralization—assuming too much community of interest, trying to make one approach broad enough to reach all the audience. Except for very simple, unsophisticated communication—say, bulletin board posters about the blood bank—the all-encompassing approach is not likely to be very effective.

Matching the audience and the message

For more sophisticated messages you need to use styles and methods designed for the audience. A faculty newsletter, if it is effective and useful to the faculty, is not likely to serve the purpose of communication with the maintenance crew. Information about hourly rates and overtime pay, although of considerable interest to some members of the workforce, will not be of much concern to faculty except as supervisors of hourly rated personnel. Those with supervisory responsibilities should receive communications from the personnel office, which you may design and write, as well, but they are specialized for specific purposes.

An argument may be made for trying to design one communication program for teaching both faculty and nonteaching personnel. Of course, the financial outlay tends to be smaller. But the major tenet of the argument is that a single approach tends to unify

INTERNAL COMMUNICATIONS AT THE UNIVERSITY OF MICHIGAN

Objective	Vehicle	Audience	Frequency	Quantity
Provide faculty and staff with an authoritative source of information about activities, programs, goals, and missions of University. Standard items include: University's official announcements, events calendar, job postings, and selected research deadlines. Special focus on campus trends, developments, concerns	University Record	Faculty and staff, state and federal legislators, fund-raising volunteers, U-M retirees	Weekly, Sept. through April; biweekly, May through August	26,000
Immediate communication of facts, highlights, campus developments	News Brief phone lines (audiotape)	Campus community. Available for media taping and general public call-in	2–5 times per week	NA
To inform current and retired University Hospital employees of employee activities and hospital events, including achievements in patient care and medical research	Hospital Star	University Hospital employees including medical students	10 times per year	9.600

(*Note:* Michigan's current internal publication, *The University Record*, was originally established as an official university publication in April 1891, and is believed to be one of the earliest employee-type publications, distributed quarterly and edited by the Faculty Senate. It was revived and revised by University Relations in the "turbulent sixties" in a different format with more frequent publication and wide distribution to faculty, staff, students, and campus visitors.)

Figure 41.2 *Courtesy University of Michigan.*

the workforce. Conversely, separate programs set up class distinctions. This is a danger. But with as broad a spectrum as the university paid staff represents, it seems better to design separate programs if your purposes are more than communication of the most elementary messages. (*See* Figure 41.2.)

You may find that an even more fragmented approach is useful. A highly autonomous unit of the institution, with its own distinct working conditions, may be most effectively served by a separate communica-

tions program that augments the larger design. You also may find that a concentrated effort to communicate a particular message to a segment of the workforce cannot be carried out effectively through the more general communication vehicles. Again, a supplementary program may be needed, although perhaps only temporarily.

Employee communication, in the industrial sense, has become a part of the internal public relations program at some institutions. Chances are this will occur in more and more institutions as unionization of public employees spreads and as these organizations adopt industrial union patterns.

Blue-collar personnel are usually the most likely prospects for unionization. Teaching fellows may organize on some campuses. Those institutions with large research complexes separate from the instructional program of the university may see attempts to organize the technical personnel. Office workers also are targets for unionization. University faculty may be the least likely to join a union.

It is not antiunion to say that if the institution is treating its staff fairly and as adequately as resources permit, a labor union is unnecessary. But the fact must be communicated so an informed judgment may be made about whether unionization would be useful or unnecessary.

The cloistered academic institution is no longer protected from the rigors of what amounts to labor-management relations. (*See* Chapter 13.) Those charged with internal public relations must be prepared to serve the institution in this realm of communication.

Student Body Relations

Students have interests in common with other members of the university community. But students, as a body, also have needs and concerns that require a communication program designed specifically for them. Students are the members of the university community most easily categorized; they are transitory, of a relatively limited age span, and so on.

A development of the past twenty years in higher education has been widespread student participation in decision-making and policy matters. Schools and colleges have made special efforts to open new channels of communication between students, faculty, and administrators and to enable students,

particularly, to participate in and contribute to institutional governance.

Students have been named to governing boards, university-wide administrative councils, faculty senates, and standing committees on curriculum, course evaluation, tenure and promotion, planning, discipline, student affairs, and other areas. Some institutions have given students full voting privileges similar to faculty members' and administrators'.

Communication and consultation with students have been greatly increased through additional devices such as student advisory committees for administrative officers, student membership on presidential-selection committees, president's or regents' "Round Table" groups, alumni boards, special study commissions, and other consultative agencies.

Both students and faculty members have been selected to serve as college or university "ombudsman," a new official position as "people's man," adapted from a similar public watchdog idea common in Sweden. The campus ombudsman receives and investigates complaints and grievances against acts of university officials and faculty and staff members.

Under pressure from students who sought a more responsible role in decisions affecting their lives, many colleges and universities have opened meetings of faculty and administrative groups and governing boards to the public, and have encouraged student participation and dialogue.

Communications devices

The devices and techniques of internal public relations are standard but are enhanced with imagination. The important aspect is judgment in when and how to use them in the environment and with the special as well as more common internal publics.

The most familiar devices probably are the printed media: newspapers, newsletters, magazines, pamphlets, annuals, annual reports, financial reports, pocket guides, speech reprints, brochures, news releases, special publications, and mass-produced letters and memoranda.

Printed material is more than a published record of what one needs to say. Any printed item reflects the competence, professionalism, and stature of the institutional unit that produces it.

What to publish

Any publication should be planned on the basis of answers to four questions:

1. What is the audience for the publication?
2. What do you wish to tell that audience, i.e., what purpose will the publication serve?
3. What action do you wish that audience to take after having read the publication?
4. When must the publication be ready for distribution?

Planning a publication around the answers to these questions will ensure that it achieves an impact and effect that justifies the cost in time and money.

Importance of design

The design of a publication is the first thing that strikes the reader. Well-designed material invites readership and predisposes your audience to attend to your message. A professional designer develops the design in terms of the audience, content, planned distribution methods, and tone of the publication. Use of computer-assisted design and desktop publishing equipment now provides layouts that enable all parties—author, editor, designer, and printer—to visualize the finished publication. (*See* Chapter 33.)

One standard device among the printed media that can be used in unique ways is the clipping collection. If you are trying to show internally what great productivity is achieved by the public relations department externally, the clipping collection will be of all the stories published in all the papers that make your place look good. A more useful service is to collect also items that are critical of the institution—columns and editorial content in particular. Or you may want to clip, reproduce, and distribute articles of concern and interest to the people of your institution, regardless of specific mention of the institution. These methods may be combined.

Other familiar devices include posters, displays, exhibits, buttons, billboards, and bumper stickers. (*See* Chapter 31.)

Exploiting the ordinary

Another broad category includes variations of the conference and mass meeting, oral and video annual reports, welcomes and commencements, open houses, and so on. The important thing to remember here, beyond the needs for content and staging, is full exploitation. For instance, a president's annual address to the faculty on the state of the university ought to be a position paper for quotation and extrapolation the rest of the year. It should be exploited immediately for news release and broadcast, taped for delayed broadcast in full, published in some campus organ, and perhaps reprinted in pamphlet form.

A New Generation in Education PR Techniques

An area not quite so familiar in educational as in industrial circles is formalized upward communication. With increased size and complexity, educational institutions are experiencing some of the same problems of business and industry.

The suggestion box may be appropriate in some parts of the institution. A variation is the advisory committee. Another is a letters column in an internal publication. Fairly closely related is the ombudsman, who provides an outlet for frustrations. The suggestion survey is another device. You must be careful when you solicit suggestions or advice or complaints or attitudes that you make some response—the more promptly the better. If you conduct a survey, do not fail to let those surveyed know the results and what action is intended.

Audiovisuals

The use of audiovisual devices for internal communication depends somewhat on what facilities are available. Where the university dominates the community and is heavily covered in the local news media, the community broadcasting facilities become outlets for internal as well as external public relations. Some institutions have their own radio-TV facilities; some also have student-run campus stations.

Slides and motion pictures can be used effectively for student and new staff orientation. A message you convey to external publics through, say, an ad or a motion picture, may be the same message you would like to reinforce internally. Preview your presentation for the campus.

Changing technology

Tubes, scanners, computers, fax, satellite projection, camcorders, and VTRS continue to change the daily operations of the mass media. You should examine implications of these developments for your particular operation. Hundreds of newspapers have switched first to optical character readers (OCRs), and then to video display terminals (VDTS), computers, and on-line phototypesetters, reducing the number of personnel employed in punching and correcting news copy. Just as news media have saved dollars by "capturing original keystrokes," you may be able to achieve financial savings by a central keyboard. Some campuses have set up Word Processing Centers, with dial dictation equipment designated to accommodate the needs of faculty and administrators. For several years a number of college news offices have taken advantage of modern technology by sending out computerized hometown news. (*See* Chapter 22.) You may also find the computer helpful for direct mail, directories, labels, and management reports.

New uses for telephone

The telephone line has become a means of formal internal public relations. Religious and political groups have used the telephone message for propaganda. It also is being used as a communication tool in industry. The telephone message is particularly useful for emergency communication. Without going into such technicalities as how multiple lines are provided on the same number, fundamentally the system gives a recorded message to the person who calls. The message can be a rewrite of the day's top story from your university news bureau, announcements of events on campus, a message from the president, a situation report on a campus strike, or the latest word on legislative action concerning the institution. It has the advantages of novelty, immediacy, accuracy, and accessibility.

Attainable goals

In planning a program of internal public relations you must take into account the existing channels of both informal and formal communication. You must be clear about what you hope to achieve and be realistic in your expectations. The clarity and realism should be shared by your administrative colleagues. You must have a long-term commitment of adequate resources and cooperation. You must build credibility.

Carefully analyze your internal publics. Design your program to reach the particular audience. Remember that the more sophisticated your message the more elaborate must be your plan, probably involving separate approaches to different segments of the university community.

The generation gap

Recognize, too, that the contemporary institution of higher education is a different place than it was a generation ago and that the positive side of this story needs not only to be told outside but understood inside. The student body—the largest internal public—is different. *In loco parentis* is passé. A bureaucratic attitude is not a good substitute. A professional service-to-client relationship may be the best approach.

Reaching External Publics

A modern college or university requires the services and support of a great variety of people. While its publics are generally above average in intelligence and somewhat parochial in interest, the range is broad and diverse— from discipline-oriented scholar to assembly-line worker, from major donor to a rural legislator, from corporate human resources director to local union president, from the fourth-generation alumni family to the culturally disadvantaged student.

Not only are these audiences numerous; they are prone to "participate" in the operation of the institution. Thus the college public relations person must be deft in balancing a broad spectrum of interests, alert to rapidly changing concerns among various publics, and imaginative and agile in meeting the demands of these special publics.

A continuing program of information and communication is essential to any public relations program. However, broadside communications approaches do not work with all external constituencies of any educational institutions.

Education writers have their own personal perception of academic America. Advising its membership on covering higher education, the Education Writers Association (EWA), in its *Guide to Editors and Writers*, declares:

> For many journalists, colleges and universities are the stepchildren of the education beat. Few reporters write about higher education full-time. And, because higher learning is not required, unlike elementary and secondary education, editors sometimes regard it as more expendable. In truth, the higher education beat is a bit trickier than other kinds of education writing because it is more diffuse. But higher education has a long, rich tradition. . . . With a little digging, it can prove a fertile ground for breaking news, feature stories, and trend and issue pieces.

Major issues on the higher education beat, as seen by EWA, include problems of racism on campus, racial hostility and violence, college remediation courses, costs, student loans, teaching of ethics and morality. Others include drugs and alcohol on campus, athletic scandals, use of graduate students as teachers, and the quality of teacher education courses.

Recognizing that a survey of public attitudes can be helpful in determining the direction of public relations activities, a group of state colleges and universities commissioned a survey research group to study attitudes and interests of a cross section of the adult population in the state.

The survey experts found that they could divide the adult population of the state into five broad classifications, with respect to their knowledge of the institutions and their degree of interest in their educational programs. They are the isolated, the uninterested, the hopefuls, the disaffected, and the influentials.

The isolated

This group, comprising about 20 percent of the population, had less than eight years of education, had never seen a college or actually met anyone they considered to be a college graduate. About half could name one or two of the public institutions in the state.

The uninterested

This group, made up of about 30 percent of the adult population, had between seven and twelve years of education, with some minimum contact with colleges or college-educated people. This group showed more negative attitudes toward colleges and college professors, concluding that, for most of them, the sense of involvement was low, but the job-security threat was real.

The hopefuls

This group, about 30 percent of the adult population, had slightly more formal education than the previous group, but still averaged less than twelve years. Most actually could give names of four or five state institutions, but many were familiar with some aspects of a university's program, particularly medical research and extension courses. This group could be classified as having more favorable attitudes toward higher education, and almost all had high hopes that their sons and daughters would attend college.

The disaffected

This group included about 15 percent of the adult population; all had gone to college but about one-half were what one would term *drop-outs*. Most of the noncontributors to college and university development programs were in this group.

The influentials

This group comprised only 5 percent of the total population but in the study would be classed as most important. They had the most favorable attitudes about the importance of higher education and had considerable knowledge of teaching and service activities of the educational institutions. As a group, these persons wanted more emphasis on the fundamentals of education and favored higher rather than lower admissions standards. These respondents also were very active in civic, educational, and community groups.

The significance of this study is that different means of communication are necessary to reach and appeal to groups with such widely divergent characteristics.

Changing constituencies

Educational public relations and communications officers are developing programs to improve relationships with the "new constituencies" of higher education.

Included in various new clienteles are the following:

- High school students who have advanced beyond the high school level in one or more subject areas
- High school students who have completed all requirements for their diplomas by the end of the eleventh grade
- Transfer students, stop-outs, drop-outs, cop-outs, and flunk-outs who can be retreaded
- Adults making midlife career changes
- Service personnel and persons in occupations that cause them to move around the country
- Veterans
- Professionals in need of continuing education and updating
- Persons in business and industry requiring special training programs
- Women interested in resuming educational programs
- Senior citizens interested in continuing their learning

• Immigrants and racially diverse groups

Another important trend in changing constituencies is the emergence of a new breed of consumers. *U.S. News and World Report* characterized this group as young, more middle class, articulate, mobile, creative, suspicious, impatient, educated, environmentally conscious, and casual.

Garnering Grassroots Support

The problem of declining funding has led a number of colleges and universities to give increased attention to "grassroots" public relations efforts. One of the most comprehensive programs of this nature was developed at the University of Michigan. Officials at the institution, a state-assisted university, noted that public higher education was receiving diminishing state legislative support proportionate to inflation and funding of competing services.

The University of Michigan Board of Regents met extensively with the university's state relations and public relations staff to discuss the problem. A decision was made to take the university's case for higher education into the communities of the state at "grassroots level" to promote citizen caring about funding priorities for the state's colleges and universities.

The program designed was the Michigan Awareness Program. Goals of the program were as follows:

• To organize a systematic program to coordinate institutional resources to enhance public understanding and support for higher education in the State of Michigan, and specifically, for the University of Michigan

• To inform people about the status and needs of higher education, using data that put issues in perspective rather than allowing

decisions to be made on a limited, fragmented basis

• To increase the awareness of selected audiences so that persons and groups choosing to do so could productively participate in the political process and achieve wider support for improved funding

Program planners based their assumptions on the belief that legislators act in the following ways:

• Treat higher education as an area of relatively low political potency because expressed comment from a broad section of the population is missing

• Rely heavily on colleagues they consider to be "experts" or "in a position to know"

• Listen closely to key political leaders

• Often vote on the basis of what they perceive their constituents to want or what they actually hear from their constituents

Targeting Lawmakers

A major target group for the communication campaign was state lawmakers and their advisors. Also identified as target groups were university faculty and staff, alumni, students, families of students, and community leaders.

The Michigan Awareness Program was designed to include seven program elements aimed at facilitating communication with these various groups. The elements included the following:

1. *The Michigan Community Leader Program*, sending regents and university officials to numerous communities across the state.

2. *The Alumni Awareness Program*, asking alumni association clubs to sponsor programs with, and for, their state legislators, business leaders, media, and high school students.

3. *The Internal Awareness Program*, keeping students, faculty, and staff abreast of legislative developments affecting them and informing them of university programs that serve the state through teaching, research, and public service.

4. *The Regents Program*, placing regents in contact with alumni, community leaders, and legislators.

5. *The Parents Program*, keeping parents advised of financial decisions, such as those involving tuition and board, and campus services, such as counseling, housing, and admissions.

6. *The In-State Donors Program*, keeping donors and friends informed about the value of placing both public dollars and private dollars to work for higher education. A newspaper is published four times a year.

7. *The General Public Program*, seeking mass media coverage of the university's problems, needs, and contributions to Michigan and society in general.

The strategy for program delivery incorporated a carefully conceived "communication mix" of person-to-person contact; group interaction through meetings and dinners; specialized communication through newsletters, publications, and direct mail; and mass communication through the news media.

Here are the examples of how information went to audiences through various channels:

• A slide presentation used by the university president in meeting with community leaders and legislators in locations around the state.

• A slide presentation used by university vice-presidents before alumni club audiences.

• Slides, charts, or general speech material used by speakers at service clubs and internal university organizations. One particu-

larly useful graphic was a diagram of the budget request process.

University officials were impressed sufficiently with results of the initial three-year program to fund it on a continuing basis. One of the strengths of the program is the value of having in place a communication system that can be adapted to the present volatile environment.

Crisis Management

As a key member of the educational management team, the public relations officer in a crisis situation often is the key communicator, the interpreter of events, the institutional spokesman, and frequently one of the administrative strategists. The effectiveness of the public relations officer and his staff most often will be measured in terms of the impact of a crisis on a school or college and the relationships of that institution to its diverse publics. Experienced public relations practitioners recognize that the major method of avoiding panic in crisis is through intelligent advance planning. (*See* Chapters 2 and 17, and 21.)

Here are some basic steps to avoid panic-button crisis management:

1. **Premeditate.** Develop plans, understand plans, and revise and update plans. Ask yourself, "Are you prepared to meet an unexpected crisis on your campus?"

2. **Coordinate.** In the event of an emergency or other crisis, does your staff know and understand its assignments? Do you have a special task force for comprehensive news coverage in a crisis situation? Everyone should know who is doing what and when. A simple crisis plan makes provision for several assigned duty officers who cover assignments, notify key officials, and

handle inquiries under a preplanned arrangement.

3. **Communicate.** Beware of that "communications gap" that shows up so often during the campus crisis. Demonstrators, student militants, and other activists quickly publicize their demands. A common complaint among the working press is that educational administrators fail to communicate during times of trouble or delay their responses. This results in an emphasis on the dissidents' point of view. The university community, too, often is ignored in crisis communications and must rely on student newspaper reports that often are highly biased accounts that are issue-oriented. More and more colleges and universities are taking steps to see that views of the administration are quickly made available to students, faculty, staff, community, alumni, and friends, as well as to mass media.

4. **Mediate.** The public relations officer must serve as the mediator between the administrator, trustee, or other officials who are reluctant or unwilling to talk, and the reporter who insists on getting a statement.

5. **Evaluate.** Planning to avoid panic suggests that people should learn from their own or others' mistakes. What did you do wrong the last time? What should College X or University Y have done under the circumstances? Did all the letters the institution received from parents, alumni, taxpayers, or others indicate some constituencies had not been informed? Tomorrow's plans mean an evaluation of yesterday's actions and programs and a revision of today's practices and procedures.

Analytic and Evaluation Components

Close scrutiny is a key part of accountability. It is not surprising that evaluation is in demand. First came student evaluation and teacher evaluation; now program evaluation has moved to practically every section of the university. For people in public relations, program evaluation can be an effective management tool, most valuable if considered not as a one-time project but as a process to be used on a regular basis rather than just in crisis. If you conduct periodic program evaluation and build an operational base of information, you have at hand a set of indicators that you can use as background for decisions and for better projections about the future.

One of the most ambitious evaluations of public relations and development operations in higher education was that developed by COPE (Committee On Program Evaluation) at the University of Michigan. Dr. Harvey Jacobson, who directed the study of operations involving eight units and one hundred fifty persons, maintained that regardless of the size of the institution, the evaluation process tends to embody the same basic characteristics. The manager who wishes to conduct systematic evaluation should consider at least seven steps:

1. **Select the rationale.** What is the guiding philosophy or model? Is the evaluation conducted by internal or external evaluators? Who is the major client?

2. **Specify objectives.** Define and state objectives of the evaluation itself, the objectives of the overall public relations program, and the objectives of the specific units or elements of the program.

3. **Develop measures**. Develop and maintain measures of resources, finances, beneficiary groups, target groups, activities, and outcomes.

4. **Administer the measures and collect the data**. Data can be collected by observation, questionnaire, monthly reports, interview, and other techniques.

5. **Analyze the data**. Allot sufficient time to assure synthesis and interpretation.

6. **Report the results**. Findings should be translated into recommendations and shared with others.

7. **Apply the results to decisions**. If recommendations are expressed in terms of operational statements they are more likely to assure follow-through so the report does not gather dust.

There has been increased emphasis not only on evaluation and strategic planning but also on research. Independent Sector, which was formed in 1980, developed a comprehensive store of knowledge about the sector and identified information sources and gaps. The Greenbrier II Conference in 1985 placed research high on the list of priorities of CASE. CASE appointed a Committee on Research in 1985, which evolved into a National Research Commission in 1988. The Commission stimulates research on institutional advancement, recognizes outstanding research accomplishments, gathers research-based information, and disseminates results to practitioners.

The Future of Education PR

The public relations officer more than other educational administrators must be alert to detect trends, spot danger signals, and be prepared to deal with them. Many changes are under way—changes in political, social, economic, technological, and international scenes.

How do you handle these changes? You have two basic choices: (a) reflex action, the same old response, or (b) plan some new responses to the new demands of a new era. You will be relying on some of each.

In public affairs, the future may see the governmental relations arena as one of conflicting interests. Public cynicism about government is increasing. Lawsuits by individuals or groups who believe their interests have been violated are on the rise. Fragmentation of society is growing as special-interest groups seek not only to protect what they have but to increase their share of national resources.

In educational public relations one can observe the following needs:

- A need for greater professionalism
- A need for career development
- A need for better assessment and evaluation methods
- Better understanding of the principles of modern management
- A need to learn to communicate with audiences that are more likely to be hostile than friendly

Resources for the Educational Practitioner

The following is a list of major organizations that provide resources and professional assistance for the educational public relations practitioner:

American Association for Higher Education
One Dupont Circle, NW, Suite 360
Washington, DC 20036

American Association of Community Colleges
One Dupont Circle, NW, Suite 410
Washington, DC 20036

American Council on Education
One Dupont Circle, NW, Suite 800
Washington, DC 20036

Association of Governing Boards of
Universities and Colleges
One Dupont Circle, NW, Suite 400
Washington, DC 20036

Association of American Colleges and
Universities
1818 R Street, NW
Washington, DC 20009

Education Writers Association
1001 Connecticut Avenue, Suite 310
Washington, DC 20036

Council for Advancement and Support of
Education
11 Dupont Circle, NW, Suite 400
Washington, DC 20036

National Association of State Universities
and Land Grant Colleges
One Dupont Circle, NW, Suite 710
Washington, DC 20036

National Society of Fund Raising
Executives
1101 King Street, Suite 700
Alexandria, VA 22314

National School Public Relations
Association
1501 Lee Highway, Suite 201
Arlington, VA 22209

National Educational Association
1201 16th Street, NW
Washington, DC 20036

42

THE PUBLIC RELATIONS OF GOVERNMENT

WILLIAM I. GREENER JR.
GEORGE J. TANBER

William I. Greener Jr., senior counsel with Fleishman-Hillard, a public relations firm, was previously senior vice-president of public affairs for G. D. Searle. He had primary responsibility for the company's communications, public relations, and governmental affairs activities.

Greener joined Searle as vice-president of corporate relations in 1979. His experience spans two careers—one in the military and the other as a public relations professional. For twenty years, Greener served in the U.S. Air Force, retiring as a lieutenant colonel in 1970. His last assignment was deputy chief to the Public Information Division, U.S. Air Force. During the next seven years he held a number of senior Cabinet and presidential public affairs positions. These included assistant to the IRS commissioner for public affairs; assistant director of the Cost of Living Council for Congressional and Public Affairs; associate director for public affairs, Office of Management and Budget; assistant to the secretary of housing and urban development for public affairs; assistant secretary of defense for public affairs; and deputy White House press secretary. Prior to joining Searle, Greener was senior vice-president and general manager of the Washington, DC, office of Carl Byoir & Associates, a public relations firm.

Greener has an undergraduate degree in economics from the University of Missouri and an M.S. in public relations from Boston University.

George J. Tanber, who aided in preparing this chapter, is a public relations consultant and a freelance journalist and photographer, based in Washington, DC, and Toledo, OH. He has been affiliated with Daniel J. Edelman, Inc.

Every time we read the newspaper, listen to the radio as we drive to work, or watch the evening news on TV, we witness government public relations at work. Yet, we know little about who these people are and what they actually do.

Case in point: An unknown terrorist nabs an American executive who is on a business trip to Egypt. The U.S. Embassy in Cairo relays information about the kidnapping to the State Department in Washington, DC. The public affairs staff there immediately prepares a statement from the secretary and, in conjunction with the White House, calls a news conference. In the meantime the press office at the White House, coordinating with the State Department, also gets busy—preparing a statement that the president reads on his arrival at Andrews Air Force Base and arranges a phone call between the president and the victim's wife. This entire scenario takes place within five hours of the kidnapping.

Case in point: The secretary of the Department of Housing and Urban Development summons his assistant secretary for public affairs to his office to discuss with her the need to announce a forthcoming program to help low-income people buy houses. They decide to arrange a news conference; the secretary asks the assistant secretary to see what she can do to also get them on a few TV talk shows to publicize the housing program. A week later the secretary appears on the *Today* show.

Case in point: Lindsey Walker, a public information specialist with the Food and Drug Administration, receives a phone call from Herb Smith, vice-president of the Acme Drug Co., requesting the FDA's report on Kintrol, a sedative produced by Acme's rival, Doak Pharmaceutical. Required under the Freedom of Information Act to do so, Walker mails the report to Smith the next day.

Case in point: A congressman from Memphis becomes upset when a hometown rival gains favorable press. He instructs his press secretary to call the city editor of the Memphis newspaper to recommend sending a reporter to Washington for a week to put together a series of "a day in the life of a congressman on the Hill" articles. The newspaper takes him up on the suggestion and produces the series, featuring none other than the congressman from Memphis.

All of these seemingly dissimilar and hypothetical events share one thing in common: they demanded the finesse of public relations experts in government.

What constitutes government public relations?

At its most fundamental level—as in the case of the FDA desk officer—it means the dissemination of information. However, its definition expanded considerably within the context practiced by the titled and press secretaries with clout. As with the State Department and White House's handling of the hostage situation, it is crisis management. As with the HUD secretary and his staff, it is image enhancement. Finally, as exercised by the congressman and his secretary, it is publicity.

How much, how many?

Several years ago, Associated Press reporter Harry F. Rosenthal brought up an interesting point about the public relations of government: "The government spends millions of dollars a year and employs thousands of public relations experts who can supply almost any kind of information, except how much it costs to supply that information."[1]

Rosenthal was right. No one in government—not the General Accounting Office (GAO) or even the Office of Budget and Management (OBM)—can put a price tag on its publicity spending.

---

[1]Harry F. Rosenthal, "U.S. Devotes Millions to PR Experts," *The Washington Post*, May 30, 1983.

AP did in 1975, and concluded that government spending and public relations activities in the executive branch alone exceeded $500 million. Added to that were millions spent by members of Congress to promote themselves, plus millions to accommodate the more than four thousand reporters accredited to congressional press galleries and to maintain press facilities elsewhere.

One reason it's difficult for the government to monitor its spending on public information is because of the various ways in which public affairs (the euphemism used by the federal government for public relations, because of legal prohibition on use of the latter term) is defined among the scores of federal agencies. What might be called public affairs at the Department of Transportation can be completely different at the National Labor Relations Board.

Expenses also are obscured when public relations duties are assigned to other departments that have nothing to do with PR. For instance, at the Small Business Administration, speech writing traditionally was the task of its public communications department. In January 1990, the duties were reassigned to the office of advocacy.

Another way in which PR costs are hidden is when agencies retain outside contractors, such as graphic designers, writers, and independent PR firms, for project work they are too busy to handle or do not have the expertise to complete. Often these fees are paid by other departments within the agencies and thus never show up as a PR expense.

The great irony is that, according to law, PR in government doesn't even exist. In 1913 Congress passed legislation that said, in part, "No money appropriated by an Act of Congress shall be used for the compensation of any publicity expert. . . ." Why such a law? One reason was the legislators' inherent mistrust of the executive branch; they didn't want the results of activities to be shaded by professional wordsmiths. Of course, legislators today circumvent the law as much as anyone in government.

For many of the same reasons that it's difficult to put a price tag on government PR spending, it's futile to try to determine how many "public relations" professionals are employed. Even the National Association of Government Communicators doesn't know.

Said former Senator Abraham Ribicoff (D-Conn.) after the release of a less-than-informative GAO report on federal public affairs activities: "So effective have government agencies been in cloaking their PR types in disguises that it is now literally impossible to keep track of them."[2]

Guesstimates range anywhere from 10,000 to 40,000 PR practitioners. In 1987, for example, the Office of Personnel Management listed 2,059 people as GS-1082: writer/editor. There also are specialists in public information, technical writing and editing, editorial assistance, foreign language broadcasting and foreign information, and the press secretaries employed on Capitol Hill.

Yet it's likely just as many people perform public relations duties with job titles completely foreign to that activity. For instance, an attorney heading a recent investigation for the House subcommittee on Science, Space and Technology said he writes his department's news releases and speeches and handles all of its media relations.

Who does what

The duties of government PR practitioners vary little from their counterparts in business. They write press releases and background papers, monitor the media, arrange press conferences, hold press briefings, produce videotapes, answer questions from reporters, and

---

[2]Dom Bonafede, "The Selling of the Executive Branch: Public Information or Promotion," *National Journal,* June 27, 1981.

produce newsletters. They also are required to "make their bosses look good."

(While what is dealt with in this chapter focuses on federal government, for the most part it applies to state, county, and local governments as well.)

Yet there is a very real and fundamental difference between PR in business and in government. Said a practitioner who served in both arenas, "There's no such thing as 'no comment' in government." Simply stated, corporations need answer only to their stockholders, while government has a much larger responsibility—to tell the story to the American people. Of course, in situations involving national security, that is not always possible. Also, as we will discuss, on occasion government spokespersons have deliberately stonewalled, lied to, or misled the media; and in just as many instances, they've not been able to provide information, because they were not included among the inner circle of their superiors.

Demand for information has increased dramatically in recent years, largely because of a burgeoning Washington press corps, which includes many special-interest reporters. New technologies, such as fax machines and satellite dishes, as well as cheaper long-distance telephone rates also have had an impact. An editor in Tacoma thinks nothing of calling the FAA for background on a commuter airline crash, while a TV station in Baton Rouge might send a reporter and film crew to Washington, DC, for a series of profiles on their congressman.

The early days

William Price had no idea what he was starting the day he first waited in front of the White House to interview guests of President Grover Cleveland. The year was 1896 and Price, a reporter with the old *Washington Star*, was doing something no one had ever thought of before—cover the president. His scoops enticed others to follow.

A few years earlier there had been only 127 reporters listed in the *Congressional Directory*; that was the extent of the Washington press corps. After Price's initiative, interest in Washington increased; the president became news. By the turn of the century, Theodore Roosevelt was inviting reporters into the White House, and in 1902 he had a pressroom included in the new west wing. The adventurous Roosevelt knew how to get headlines.

Woodrow Wilson became the first president to hold regular press conferences (1913), and sixteen years later Herbert Hoover was the first to have an official press secretary on his staff. Along with more news-savvy presidents came increasingly imaginative newspaper publishers. New technologies helped their circulations double and redouble; Washington's audience grew.

Government also grew, particularly with Franklin Roosevelt and his New Deal programs. Suddenly Washington became a complicated story. Beat reporters were not prepared to write about collective bargaining and the gold standard. To help, government agencies began hiring people to prepare simplified briefs about their programs so reporters could write stories their readers would understand.

While the executive branch was becoming more sophisticated in its dealings with the press, such was not the case on Capitol Hill, where legislators lagged behind. Yes, they gave interviews to reporters covering the Hill, but their preferred method of promoting themselves was on the stump in their districts or states. President Eisenhower had twelve people on his press staff during the 1950s, for example, whereas only a handful of legislators had press secretaries. The disparity between the two branches in public relations capabilities has continued.

Growth of the media and government PR

From the 1960s through the early 1980s, the number of reporters covering Washington and the number of government PR people hired to provide them with news and information grew massively. In time, Washington became more than the top national story; it became the leading focus of the foreign press as well. Newspapers and broadcasters from abroad scurried to the United States to open bureaus. A soft dollar in the latter part of the 1980s further increased their numbers.

The growth of single-issue newsletters and special-interest magazines during that period gave rise to a new breed of reporter. Savvy specialists began seeking hard-edged information for their sophisticated audiences. That caused government PR people to become more savvy themselves in order to meet these new demands.

Meanwhile, the White House under Presidents Reagan and Bush saw its public relations staff grow to more than sixty people, a five-fold increase from the Eisenhower days. The professionals have become increasingly sophisticated. Many have backgrounds in marketing. They know how to sell the president's policies and how best to present his views.

Legislators on Capitol Hill also have improved the way they promote themselves, though Congress as an institution has not. Rare is the member without a press secretary; most senators now have assistant press secretaries as well. Rather than go on the stump, legislators prefer videotaping messages in their Capitol Hill studios and distributing them to TV stations in their districts and states.

Each of these bodies—federal agencies, the White House, and Congress—handles its PR duties in varying ways. Their success depends, in part, on the skills of the professionals assigned to these tasks—and the measure of access their PR practitioners have to the deci-sion-makers. The most fundamental responsibility of the practitioner is information dissemination, but it can get much more complicated than that. Questions arise. Is the public getting all the information about the federal government it deserves? Do government PR practitioners influence public policy? Let's take a closer look at each of these groups and examine how they implement their public relations duties.

The Workings of PR in Government Departments and Agencies

Only one valid statement applies to the way federal agencies implement their public relations activities: no two do it alike. Each agency is autonomous in structure, titles, salaries, and budgets. The result is a bureaucracy filled with a mishmash of public relations offices that have little in common.

There are fourteen Cabinet departments and a number of independent agencies. Within each department there are scores of offices, agencies, bureaus, and administrations. Many have self-directed public information or media relations offices with individual agendas.

One former assistant administrator for public affairs of the Federal Aviation Administration (FAA) recalled a period during the Ford administration when the Department of Transportation asked FAA to route all of its press releases through DOT. FAA not only refused; its PR people staged their own mini-news conferences to put out the information. There's no easy way for the department's PR officers to control the agency's PR activities, the administrator said, though they have the authority to do so. "It's all a bureaucratic (game)," he said.

Another problem is the sometimes tumultuous relationship between politically appointed officers and the career specialists who work for them. The officers owe their allegiance to the administration that appointed them, while the bureaucrats often are more loyal to their agency. How well the appointees and the career civil servants get along usually determines how successful an agency's PR efforts will be. The appointees, usually talented individuals who may not be familiar with the organization they have joined, often must rely on the expertise of the career PR practitioners until they become familiar with their department.

Conversely, the career PR practitioners, most of whom will remain in their positions long after the appointees have left, are wise to keep on good terms with their bosses, who critique their performance and determine whether they will be promoted.

Eileen Shanahan, former *New York Times* reporter and a veteran of several PR postings in government, recalls the difficulties she faced during her first year as assistant secretary for public affairs at the old Department of Health, Education, and Welfare:

> One of the worst mistakes I made, and I think most new people coming into government do, was thinking, "Oh, that civil service junk. To hell with that, I'll let somebody else do that. It's policy and programs I care about." Well, it took me about a year to realize that meant I had handcuffed myself with (that sort of attitude).[3]

Unlike public relations officers in business, political appointees such as Shanahan rarely stay long. The average stint is two years. Career PR practitioners say that prevents them from developing and implementing effective programs. "Every new appointee wants to go in a different direction, and we have to start all over every time," said a pub-

lic affairs bureaucrat at the Small Business Administration (SBA).

SBA is a good example; the agency had five directors of communications from 1986 through 1989. Compounding the problem, the closer it is to the end of an administration, the harder it is to fill these positions because of their lame duck status.

That the top SBA communications position is appointed is an ominous sign, according to some practitioners who view this as a growing trend among agencies. They see appointees filtering down to positions normally held by career PR people, causing friction among staffs and preventing continuity in their programs.

Career government PR practitioners

While PR officers in government come and go, career specialists often stay for many years. Their tasks require fundamental public relations skills such as media relations, speech writing, monitoring the press, providing briefing documents, video production, and drafting press releases and backgrounders. They also perform internal duties, such as producing in-house newsletters and magazines. Career practitioners rarely interact with agency administrators and thus do not influence policy decision-making. They are, essentially, information disseminators.

The backgrounds of career PR bureaucrats vary, but many have been newspaper reporters, usually for mid-sized and smaller publications. Those who are successful share these abilities:

- They know the inner workings of their agency.
- They know the agency's mission.
- They know how to deal with the media.
- They understand the problems facing political appointees who become their directors.

---

[3]"Public Information in Government: Some Contrasting Views," *Management*, Summer, 1980, pp. 9–14.

- They can mesh their operation with the operation of whoever is in charge.

The power of access

The media expect timely responses from agency press officers. From press secretaries and from high-level agency PR officers they expect something quite different: access to the top. "The media respect power," says Joseph Laitin, who served seventeen years as an executive press officer. "They go to where the power is."

Access is a prerequisite, not a perquisite, of the job. A press officer's rank does not guarantee access. In departmental public affairs, usually only a handful of PR practitioners are part of an administrator's inner circle. It is common for politically appointed public affairs officers to have had no previous relationship with the administrator they will be working with, thus reducing their influence.

When a relationship has been established over time, though, and the public affairs officer is "in the loop," he or she can wield considerable influence within the agency and with the media.

Margaret Tutwiler, the State Department spokesperson under Secretary James Baker, is a good example. Ms. Tutwiler served in the same post under Baker when he was secretary of the treasury in the Reagan administration. She had experience and was known to be an insider. Thus when Tutwiler made a statement reporters were assured that she was speaking for Baker.

For example, in a January 1990 AP story on a proposal by Senate minority leader Bob Dole for the United States to provide new aid to emerging democracies in eastern Europe, it was Ms. Tutwiler who responded on behalf of the State Department, "It's well worth looking at," she said.

Did Ms. Tutwiler have access? Yes. Did she influence policy? That's a larger question that is more difficult to answer, because it is hard to document the specific role politically appointed public affairs officers and press secretaries have in determining policy decisions.

Certainly departmental public affairs officers can influence policy if they are in the administrator's inner circle and if they have the courage to question current practices. For instance, some years ago an assistant commissioner for public affairs at the Internal Revenue Service questioned then-Commissioner John Walters as to why the short filing form was no longer available. "Good question," Walters responded, and asked his deputies to investigate. It turned out that a new computer system unnecessarily eliminated the form, which was more practical for low-income wage earners to use. The short form was reissued.

The big four . . . and the rest

As we have noted, public relations agendas vary considerably from agency to agency. There are four key departments that receive the most attention from the media—State, Defense, Treasury, and Justice. Though State and Defense hold daily news briefings and have media facilities in their buildings, these organizations are considered reactive in their relations with the press. They generally do not seek coverage, particularly Treasury and Justice. State and Defense are prestigious beats for reporters, who must be enterprising in uncovering stories beyond what is given to them in the daily briefings.

A number of the other agencies are more proactive in their media relations; they constantly disseminate information. However, they normally are covered by general assignment reporters who move from agency to agency seeking tidbits of information to file in their daily pieces. Because the information is so readily available to them, these reporters generally are not as enterprising as those covering State and Defense.

Some newspapers editors feel that government PR practitioners at these agencies are making reporters lazy by doing their jobs for them, preventing them from digging for stories. They point to scandals at HUD and at the Federal Home Bank Loan Board as examples of major stories that were missed by the media.

PR at Work in the White House

Public relations methodologies in the White House differ considerably from those practiced in the agencies and in Congress. As we have seen, every agency is autonomous in its PR activities (though there is some control exercised by the White House, which we will discuss). Meanwhile, there are 535 members of Congress, each with his or her own public relations agenda.

The public relations staff at the White House, however, is unified in pursuit of one goal: to promote the policies of the president to the American people and to Congress. Its primary vehicle is the Washington press corps, with TV taking precedence over the print media.

The reporters who cover the White House are different too. They gain more front-page space and air time than other reporters, and they usually make more money. They're also usually the most savvy reporters.

Unlike administrators of government agencies or members of Congress, everything the president says or does is news. Thus more than any other government office, the White House carefully controls what it says to the media. That can make interesting confrontations between enterprising reporters on the White House beat and the president's public relations staff.

David Broder, national political correspondent of the *Washington Post*, writes eloquently on the subject in his book *Behind the Front Page*:

> Almost daily, battles erupt between reporters and presidential spokesmen, as each side attempts to do what it considers its job and objects to the other doing its. The press complains that the president or his agents attempt to manage the news, and the president replies that prying reporters distort or trivialize or simply interfere with important decision making.[4]

Broder continues:

> Unlike Congress. . . the President has political and public relations aides who can lay down rules that work to (his) advantage. They seek to maximize publicity for some of his activities and to keep others secret. They speak volubly at times and attempt to embargo information and comment at other moments. They horde information and disclose or leak it selectively. Reporters attempt to resist all these tactics and, in doing so, often criticize the president and his agents for being manipulative.

Television is the medium of choice for covering the White House. The networks like it because it provides good theater and it's easier to cover than the agencies and Congress. The White House likes it because it's the best way to gain a public forum for its policy briefings.

The key issue is, who controls the stage, the media or the White House? David Gergen, President Reagan's first White House communications director, spoke to that issue in Hedrick Smith's book *The Power Game*:

> We wanted to control what people saw to the extent that we could. We wanted to shape it and not let television shape it. You had to figure out

---

[4]David S. Broder, *Behind the Front Page: A Candid Look at How the News Is Made*, New York: Simon & Schuster, 1987, p. 149.

how to (control) it on your own. I mean, large aspects, the public aspects, of government have become staged, television staged, and there is a real question who is going to control the stage.

Evolution of White House PR

The White House has not always been so sophisticated in its dealing with the press. The new age of the White House public relations dates from the Eisenhower years.

Though Eisenhower used TV effectively in his campaigns against Adlai Stevenson—he was the first presidential candidate to use political ads on TV—his preferred forum was the press conference. He held 193 of them during his two terms in office. Ike was good at handling reporters; he had years of experience while he was the Allied commander during World War II.

Eisenhower went eight years with nary a ruffle. Most people give credit for his success to his press secretary, James C. Hagerty, considered the preeminent practitioner at his profession. Hagerty is credited with developing many of the techniques that other press secretaries and communications directors have copied. One of his most impressive achievements was anticipating the growing technical demands of television. During presidential trips, he made special arrangements for broadcast reporters, and he was a master at developing and releasing news bits to the reporters in the traveling pool.

David Broder describes Hagerty's unique role:

> Hagerty served as *the* press spokesman for the president; reporters who tried to talk to other staff members were routinely sent back to him. But because he was a real White House insider, with full confidence of the president, reporters raised no objection to his role. One measure of his standing—astonishing in retrospect—was the frequency with which Eisenhower conferred with Hagerty and even allowed himself to be

corrected by Hagerty during the presidential press conferences.[5]

James Deaken, author of *Straight Stuff*, says that Hagerty is the father of public relations in the White House as we know it today. "He combined the roles of press officer and public relations expert, and made them one. He served the press—no one ever did it more efficiently—but he served the president. All subsequent press secretaries have accepted Hagerty's order of priorities. The President's image comes first."

John Kennedy had a good relationship with the media during his early years as president, and he had an able press secretary in Pierre Salinger. One difference between Eisenhower and Kennedy was that reporters had access to senior White House staff during the Kennedy years. A number of reporters also formed a close bond with Kennedy.

As Broder says, "Kennedy's reputation was enhanced not only by his own skill in manipulating the press but the willingness of many in the Washington press corps to be manipulated." Hence, details of his private life were never published during his lifetime. Kennedy was brilliant on TV—it's what won him the election; thus it is no surprise that he was the first president to have his news conferences broadcast live on TV.

Lyndon Johnson was a poor TV president; the medium did not serve him well. He also was a secretive president who was not fond of revealing his intended actions, particularly to the media. His strength was in one-on-one meetings with reporters or in small briefing sessions in which his dominating personality served him well. Johnson exhausted three press secretaries during his five years—George Reedy, Bill Moyers, and George Christian.

Nixon, like Johnson, distrusted the media, and he had a stormy relationship with the

---

[5]*Behind the Front Page*, p. 155.

White House press corps even before the Watergate scandal. He was the first president to establish an official office of communications in the White House. His intent was to bypass the hostile White House press corps.

His solution was explained by David Broder in his book: "(The) office of communications, (which was) separate from the press secretary's operation, distributed the administration's message to editors, reporters, and broadcasters outside of Washington, through mailings, briefings and roadshow press conferences, where preference in questioning was given to the local journalists."[6]

Establishing the office of communications was a brilliant stroke. Every president since has expanded the operation to incorporate additional key public relations functions. Nixon's public relations staff was superb at controlling the stage and disseminating information; they were not successful in enhancing the president's image. The White House press secretary, Ron Ziegler, was not included in Nixon's inner circle and was little more than an information disseminator. His lack of access proved frustrating to reporters as the Watergate crisis grew.

One of Watergate's many legacies was its effect on the relationship between the media and the White House press office. Briefings and press conferences became increasingly hostile and aggressive. "In the old days idealistic journalists carried a torch of trust," said Joseph Laitin. "Now they carry a blow torch."[7]

Ford's brief term was notable because his press secretary, Jerald F. terHorst, a widely respected journalist, resigned in protest after only thirty days when Ford pardoned Nixon. As press secretary, terHorst had unique access to Ford, as did his successor, Ron Nessen. Ford was remarkably open and accommo-

dating to the media, yet his image remained that of a clumsy and inarticulate leader.

Both Ford and Jimmy Carter's PR staffs realized that following Nixon they needed to be more open to the media to help restore trust in the office. Carter had an admired press secretary in Jody Powell and a savvy media advisor in Gerald Rafshoon. Powell had complete access to the president, and he was respected by the press corps for his substantive briefings. Carter himself received high marks for his ability to stage press conferences and for his depth of knowledge.

Despite these PR pluses, Carter failed because his policies were counter to the policies of the majority. He also could not handle criticism from the press. These became serious, and eventually fatal, problems during the Iranian hostage crisis when Carter staked his presidency on the fate of the hostages and lost. Powell would later admit that neither his staff nor Carter was as public relations savvy as they should have been, particularly compared with the next president, Ronald Reagan.

The Reagan and Bush years

When nearly three hundred American Marines were killed in Lebanon in 1983, Ronald Reagan suffered little in his approval rating, even though it was his decision to send them in. Meanwhile, Americans were held hostage in Lebanon for nearly half of his tenure. That crisis did little to affect his rating either.

They called Reagan the "Teflon President"; his public relations staff deserves a large share of the credit. In Reagan they had a master communicator. TV would be their key forum, they decided, because of Reagan's formidable skills for that medium, and because they could better control the stage. (It was Reagan, though, who conceived the winning idea of a weekly radio broadcast, which received extensive print coverage.)

The strategy had come from the Nixon White House: Each day a script was built

---

[6]*Behind the Front Page*, pp. 165–66.
[7]Interview with Joseph Laitin, January 21, 1990.

around a key story line, and Reagan's PR people would work to get their line, verbatim, on the evening network news, in headlines, and in the opening paragraph of wire service stories.

"We had a rule in the Nixon operation that before any public event was put on his schedule, you had to know what the headline was going to be, what the picture was going to be, and what the lead paragraph would be," said David Gergen, the communications director, in *The Power Game*. "So you learned to think that a president communicates through the media, through the press, and not directly."

Under Gergen the position of communications director became more influential—and better defined. "Director of propaganda," is how Bill Moyers described the position in a *Newsweek* article.[8] Patrick Buchanan, a conservative columnist who replaced Gergen during Reagan's second term, continued the strategy. Buchanan was fond of quoting Theodore White when asked to explain his mission, "Power in America today is control of the means of communication."[9]

The White House maintained control of the stage at the start of the Bush administration. The president's approval rating of 80 percent was an all-time high. Much of President Clinton's exposure to the media has been dominated by stonewalling, diversions, denials, and control dictions, yet he maintained a high approval rating that led to his reelection.

The question arises: are public relations practitioners in the White House gaining too much influence? Former presidential press secretary George Reedy believes it doesn't matter: "If the policy's wrong, there's ultimately no way to handle it."[10]

The White House versus the agencies

Another trend begun during the Reagan administration was the influence of its PR staff over its Cabinet members and other agency officials with regard to media relations, particularly on issues relating to foreign policy and national security. Administrators were provided daily briefings on what the story line should be on major news stories. The most obvious example of this occurred at the CIA, which at one time held 150 media briefings annually. By the end of the Reagan presidency, the agency no longer held briefings and, finally, its entire public affairs staff was dismissed.

In *The Power Game*, Hedrick Smith relates how Budget Director David Stockman and Secretary of State Alexander Haig became upset with the "public relations obsession of the White House." Smith says, "Haig repeatedly complained that the president's public relations managers ran policy." Later, critics said Clinton let polls—which were slavishly reported by the media—set policy.

Press secretaries, lies, and leaks

Though the communications director appears to have assumed authority among the public relations staffs in recent administrations, it is still the press secretary who is the most visible PR practitioner in government. His effectiveness is based largely on the amount of access he has to the president. Few have managed to be counted among the inner circle.

On occasion, those who have had access have been placed in the uncomfortable position of having to deliberately lie to the press. Jody Powell admitted he fibbed when the Carter administration was planning to rescue the hostages. He was largely forgiven by the media because it was a matter of national security.

On the day the United States invaded Gre-

[8]Jonathan Alter, *Newsweek*, January 15, 1990, p. 29.
[9]*The Power Game*, p. 402.
[10]*Newsweek*, January 15, 1990, p. 29.

nada, the media asked deputy press secretary Larry Speakes if an invasion was under way. "Preposterous," he said.[11] It was not a lie because Speakes was not told the truth by White House officials. Such situations can greatly damage a press secretary's credibility and thus his effectiveness.

Perhaps Pierre Salinger, Kennedy's press secretary, had the best thought on how to handle "hot" information. Prior to the Cuban missile crisis, which he knew about, he simply disappeared for a day.

Though lying is almost always frowned upon, leaking is not. It is a long-practiced art in high-level politicking. Who does it? Jody Powell listed the culprits in one of his syndicated columns. "All administrations pass along to selected reporters information designed to reflect favorably on the administration. White House staffers do it. Cabinet officers do it. Assistant to the deputy assistant secretary for you-name-it does it, and even presidents do it."[12]

Most often leaks are merely trial balloons, to see how the public might react to a certain issue. Other times leaks are "internal administration efforts to influence policy decisions," according to Tom Wicker of the *New York Times*. More often than not, leaks come not from public relations practitioners but from other administration officials.

PR at Work in the Congress

Discussing public relations in Congress deals with three separate issues: Congress as an institution, congressional committees, and the 535 legislators who work on Capitol Hill.

Congress, the institution, has no real mechanism to promote itself. The result was a serious lack of media coverage until the voter up-

heaval of 1994 brought in Newt Gingrich and his fellow government-reducing Republicans. Focus on their "Contract with America" spurred media coverage.

There are more than 4,000 reporters accredited to cover Congress (about one in twenty show up every day). With 535 members and their 14,000 aides churning out reams of information daily, there are plenty of angles for reporters to pursue. Yet most often these stories don't make interesting television, nor do they gain much space in the newspapers, other than the large national dailies. Outside of major legislation stories, such as tax cuts, many of the daily reports found in newspapers are placed into sections called Washington shorts.

Congress has no problem gaining coverage when one of its own is involved in a scandal or when it's investigating a misguided government activity. The cases of Wilbur Mills, Wayne Hayes, and more recently, Jim Wright, Bob Packwood, and Newt Gingrich, played well on the nightly news. Watergate made national figures of members of the House Judiciary Committee, and the Iran-Contra affair also gained widespread national attention.

Though the press has been lax in Capitol Hill coverage, Congress has done little to promote itself. There are no PR practitioners employed by Congress; only individual members have public relations capabilities. Broder suggests its leaders should serve as spokesmen to the public, in addition to their duties as managers of Congress's internal business. Yet the election process of leaders of both House and Senate is a closed-door affair, often resulting in less-than-charismatic legislators gaining these visible positions.

In recent years, the media skills of the congressional leaders have fared poorly compared with those of the president. Thus, they have not done well in the constant battle with the executive branch for control of public policy. Presidential press conferences are elaborately

[11]*Newsweek*, January 15, 1990, p. 29.
[12]Jody Powell, "Leaks: Whys and Wherefores," *The Washington Post*, February 2, 1982.

staged, while briefings given by the congressional leadership are much less sophisticated. Though opposition leaders are given air time for responses following the president's address, they rarely have the same impact. Again, it is a situation they could control better with more public relations skill. J. C. Watts's reply to Clinton's 1997 State of the Union address showed it can be done.

A development that has helped Congress receive more attention has been live TV coverage of its proceedings on the c-span cable network. But, as Broder points out, that has done more to promote the careers of individual members than the institution as a whole.

Members and their PR activities

Individual members of Congress have become expert at utilizing the media for personal gain. Their success is due, in part, to better understanding of how the media work. Also, the overwhelming majority of them now have professional press people on their staffs. In 1970 only 28 percent of all congressional offices had press secretaries. The number jumped to 84 percent by 1984, according to a study carried out by Timothy E. Cook of Williams College, and has increased since.

Generally, representatives have one-person press staffs, while most senators have at least two, a press secretary and an assistant press secretary. (Senate staffs usually are three times the size of a member of Congress's.) Most often, congressmen recruit their press people from their districts or states; frequently they have been reporters for a newspaper that has covered the Hill beat or a press secretary during the election campaign. Many are young, and almost all of them share one important trait: They identify with the ideology of the member they are serving. They perform tasks that are similar to what PR practitioners would do elsewhere in government or in business. They monitor the hometown or home

state media; seek opportunities for their member to comment on events with national implications; write speeches, press releases, editorial page columns, and letters to the editor; send out newsletters to their constituents; and arrange interviews.

They also serve as sounding boards for the members' policy people who write most of the issue papers and want to know: How will this stuff play at home? As in the agencies and in the White House, access is essential for press secretaries to do their job well. Because Hill offices are smaller, press secretaries usually enjoy a more intimate relationship with their employers than their counterparts elsewhere in government. It appears that the role of the press secretary is expanding in many offices, where they increasingly are being asked to participate in policy decisions.[13]

Members are realizing that strategic communications planning and counsel are a critical part of the policy making.

As elsewhere in government, new technologies have aided the PR efforts of legislators. The advent of satellite dishes has enabled members to transmit "video press releases" back home. Both parties maintain TV studios on Capitol Hill that are at the disposal of members and their PR people. Local media usually welcome tapes of their congressman or senator because they don't have the budget—or the capability—to get the information themselves.

Not all members are sold on TV as the best medium to promote themselves. Les Aspin, former chairman of the House Armed Services Committee, was noted for his flair for self-promotion and ability to use the media to publicize his agenda. His favorite means was the press release. Hedrick Smith explains Aspin's reasoning in *The Power Game*, "He prefers press releases over televised press conferences for two reasons: First, his issues are

---

[13]*The Power Game*, pp. 140–41.

complicated, and only print reporters have space to explain them fully; if they get good play in print, TV will follow. Second, with a written release accompanied by a fairly detailed study, Aspin sees greater chance that the story will emerge the way he originally cast it. Press conferences can take unpredictable bounces."

The term of a press secretary on Capitol Hill rarely exceeds four years. Many suffer burnout (as do their counterparts in other areas of government PR) and move on to other jobs, usually for more money. Washington PR firms and corporations with offices in the nation's capital are attracted to ex-congressional press secretaries for two reasons: they have public relations expertise and they understand how Capitol Hill works. Some do move on to grander government offices, such as those who have worked with Jack Kemp and Dan Quayle.

Congressional committees

Staff members of congressional committees play an important role in the public relations of government. Though their task is limited largely to information dissemination, they can help committees gain public support for their legislation.

Most committees do not have professional public relations practitioners on their staffs. Yet staff members are charged with writing press releases based on results of hearings and with preparing statements for members who decide to give press briefings after a hearing. Often committee staffers will work with a member's press secretary to codraft releases and statements. When the issue is national, it is up to the committee's staff members to handle the media relations. If there is a local issue affecting a member's jurisdiction, the member's press office handles the media work. Committee staff members also can serve as spokespeople for the committee on issues they have particular expertise in.

43

Public Relations for the Professional Firm

Richard R. Conarroe
Ronald R. Conarroe

Richard R. Conarroe and Ronald R. Conarroe (father and son) are both highly experienced in serving professional service organizations.

Richard Conarroe founded Walden Public Relations in 1961—a firm specializing in providing public relations services to professional service organizations. Walden merged into Newsome & Company (Boston and New York) in 1979, which was later merged with Hill & Knowlton. A graduate of New York University, Richard Conarroe's books include The Decision Makers *(Prentice-Hall, 1959),* Bravely, Bravely in Business *(Amacom, 1971), and* Executive Search: A Guide for Recruiting Outstanding Executives *(Van Nostrand Reinhold, 1976).*

Ronald R. Conarroe has directed public relations programs for firms specializing in management consulting, executive recruiting, medicine, law, accounting, architecture, engineering, management training, computer software, and other professional areas. He has written articles on direct mail and other public relations techniques and contributed to Advertising and Promoting the Professional Practice *(Hawthorn, 1979). He is a graduate of Bowling Green State University.*

No professional organization today can expect clients to seek them out. Gone forever are the days of, for example, the lawyer launching a practice by hanging out a shingle and, at most, attending meetings of the local Rotary Club.

Now, due in part to an increasingly more service-oriented economy, the competition in virtually every field of professional service has intensified. The number of professionals within a given field has grown faster than the markets they serve. Thus even the highest-quality professional services firm finds it necessary to distinguish itself from the crowd. They must operate from the basic premise that they must influence markets by gaining not only visibility, but also the credibility and endorsement of the media and publications viewed and respected by their potential and existing clients.

Importance of a Creative Approach

Just as competition among professionals has intensified, so has competition for media coverage. A "creative approach" to communicating with target audiences through the media is now required to set a professional firm apart from others in its field. This creative approach almost always requires the professional to provide something of value to the reader or viewers of selected media.

A small accounting firm, for example, offered to explain the impact of the federal government's new economic program on small businesses. The process was time-consuming and demanding. At first, the firm was reluctant to "give away too much." But its public relations counsel encouraged it to provide as much good information as possible.

The media's reaction to the material was overwhelming. Articles were published in several magazines reaching small business owners. These led to speeches and radio appearances—as well as quotations in national publications. The spokesperson for the firm continued to "give away" professional advice. But the payoff was immense in terms of contacts from firms interested in discussing the accounting firm's services.

A well-conceived and well-executed public relations program can be vital in building a practice that is strong and healthy, profitable, and growing. One young firm whose service is counsel on tax-sheltered investments acknowledges that its leadership in its field could not have been achieved—certainly not soon—had it not been for a reputation for professional excellence the firm built in its infancy through a well-planned public relations program.

All the aspects of professional public relations that are dealt with in this handbook apply to some degree to professional organizations. Such organizations also increasingly need skill in judging the trends of public attitudes that may affect their fields as well as the individual firm—pressures for government control, social responsibility, hiring of minority and female personnel, environmental impact, and so on.

For the professional, both accenting good works and avoiding negative impressions are important. That is why so many lawyers, doctors, architects, accountants, and others actively provide their skills to public service organizations; and why they are especially concerned about avoiding charges of malfeasance or other improper practice.

Accordingly, material elsewhere in this book that applies to these and other aspects of public relations for other organizations applies equally to professional organizations. Here we will focus on their special needs—particularly gaining the benefits of prominence and good reputation.

Marketing Strategy Essential

To be successful, every business—whether it is a giant conglomerate selling products or a one-man professional firm selling services—needs a marketing strategy. Increasing numbers of professional firms are discovering that public relations, when used as part of their marketing strategy, is relatively low in cost and high in effectiveness—not necessarily through instantaneous results, although that sometimes happens, but more commonly over the long haul. One management consulting firm, for example, has been conducting an active public relations program for thirty-five years, almost from the day the firm was founded. The firm now has an international reputation and is generally recognized as one of the leaders in the management consulting profession. While the chairman, who founded the firm, says he knows of only two or three clients that have been signed up as a direct result solely of the public relations program, he gives it a significant share of credit for the firm's success. The program has not only reinforced this firm's positions with its existing clients, but has put it in a favorable light with prospective clients who, as a result of the publicity, already know the firm by reputation before any overt sales contact is made.

The best way to build a favorable reputation, of course, is to have satisfied clients recommend the firm to their friends. But building that kind of reputation in a vacuum is slow and hit-or-miss. A public relations program can spread the favorable reputation faster and more broadly, on a more controlled and managed basis.

Ethical considerations

In 1977 the Supreme Court struck down the legal profession's ban on advertising. Accountants, dentist, and others have followed lawyers in producing ad campaigns.

Although tasteful methods of direct solicitation have been used with great success, a stringent standard for professional ethics lingers.

While overt marketing practices may be frowned on, no one can frown on the fact that a third party—a respected professional journal, for example—discusses the results of good work done by an organization or individuals in a professional group. Such third-party endorsement, especially if it is in print or broadcast, usually has far stronger value than the direct sales efforts that are proscribed.

In some professional fields—law and management consulting, for example—ethical restraints continue to disappear. Advertising is becoming acceptable where it was unacceptable before, provided it is done with restraint and dignity. Direct mail is growing in importance in fields where it was not considered good practice. These liberalizing changes in traditional restrictions represent challenges for the professional service organization. As restrictions are being liberalized it is likely that some professional firms are taking full advantage of these changes to strengthen and broaden their strategies for visibility.

Another major ethical consideration involves the interest of the firm's clients. All professional organizations, from medical offices to advertising agencies, are bound to retain as confidential everything they know about a client, as well as everything they do on its behalf, unless the client clearly authorizes exposure of information. For many years management consultants, accountants, and other professionals avoided public discussion of knowledge that even by inference might have been derived from their service to clients. The result was that professionals leaned back so far to avoid possible criticism that they sentenced themselves to virtual anonymity except through activity in professional societies.

The need to maintain the confidentiality of any client's interest remains paramount. However, many clients now agree to have information about their activities reported on, so long as it does not provide undue help to competitors or reveal their weaknesses. Many professionals report on work they do in general terms, without possible identification of the clients involved, when the clients do not want their names used. Just as doctors have for generations been able to report in journals on their findings from serving unnamed patients, now consultants and others often report the knowledge they have derived from solving problems or developing programs for unnamed clients.

A large Midwestern bank willingly identified itself in a feature article discussing its high turnover rate. The story outlined how a small management training firm initiated a program to build the "people skills" of the bank's personnel. The end results—including a drastic lowering of the turnover rate—were truly outstanding. The professional training firm got a valuable endorsement of its services while its client came across as an innovative bank willing to invest in the betterment of its people.

There is yet another point to consider. Every professional services organization faces the critical need to identify its specific service niche in the minds of potential clients. (For the remainder of this chapter, the word *clients* will be used in referring to buyers of professional services, even though in some professional fields the *customer* may be known as a patient or by some other specific designation.) Proliferation of competition in a field, and the likelihood of a cacophony of competitive messages heard by clients, probably causes vagueness in their minds concerning any one firm's service specialty and areas of expertness. Public relations can be helpful in solving this problem, too.

Benefits Derived from Public Relations

The benefits an active public relations program can offer a professional firm are discussed in the text that follows:

Visibility

Public relations—or more specifically, an ethically carried out publicity program—makes the professional organization known to those organizations and individuals who may need or want its services.

Credibility

A book or a play may be excellent, but if those responsible for selling it to readers or audiences don't seek and get reviews and other mentions in the media, the book or play may die in infancy. No matter how good the firm's work is, the word-of-mouth process is too slow and undependable. Using existing communications media—newspapers, magazines, radio, TV, the Internet, or other appropriate

media—the firm can get its story across to many more interested people, and do it in a fraction of the time. Getting endorsement of the media establishes credibility, authority in the field, leadership, and success.

Prestige by association

Just as there is guilt by association, there is also prestige by association. Buyers of professional services certainly know this; often someone will use the services of a physician, an attorney, or an architect, for example, because of the professional's reputation and the prestige that's associated with his name. In the client's mind, some of this prestige of the professional rubs off onto the client itself.

The prestige-by-association phenomenon works both ways. If a firm has prestigious clients and takes proper and ethical steps to see that its name is associated with these clients, some of their prestige rubs off on the organization.

Cost-effectiveness

It would be difficult to find a lower-cost way to communicate positively with clients and prospective clients than through the techniques of publicity. The instruments of communication are there, waiting to be used. Somebody else pays all the costs and handles all the work and problems involved in running the professional journals, newspapers, newsletters, and other available publicity media. The principles of effective publicity discussed in Section 5 can be adapted readily by the professional organization. If considered effective, the publicity material will be welcomed by the media using it to their own advantage but will build the organization's reputation in the process. A well-run publicity program for a professional organization creates a situation in which everybody wins: the professional firm, the media that carry the firm's messages, and the audiences who receive the messages.

Attracting top-caliber personnel

The quality of a professional organization is determined, of course, by the quality of the professionals in it. There will always be too few top-caliber professionals to go around. Sometimes one of the most important—but most overlooked—values of public relations is that it helps an organization attract the best people. Star players like to be associated with teams that are recognized as champions.

First Step: Planning

Probably the most important four words in this chapter are: *Start with a plan.* Without a thoughtfully conceived plan, one will probably waste time and money, get paltry results, and decide that using publicity was a bad idea because it doesn't work. Conversely, with a plan one will most likely get meaningful results, economy of time and dollars, and experience that will make the program increasingly effective.

The plan need not be inspirationally creative or complex. In fact, particularly in the beginning, the simpler the better.

The plan should be committed to writing before action is begun. Although there will probably not be unanimity, it's important to get as much support as possible for the plan from all the key people in the organization.

Preparing a sound public relations plan cannot be done in a vacuum or on a theoretical basis. (*See* Chapter 17.) It will require an analytical look at the entire organization, its present position, its strengths and weaknesses, and its needs for the future. The planning job will probably require researching the public relations plans of others, as well as the unique opportunities available to this organization, the barriers that stand in its way, the distinctive features that give it special personality and uniqueness, the best sources of publicity raw material in the organization, and so on. It's also necessary to determine who has the talent to carry out the program and what time to allot—or which outside services to employ.

The publicity plan should include the following six ingredients.

Goals

What specifically is it that the program should accomplish? The tighter, sharper, and finer the goals are defined, the more effective the program is likely to be. For example, it would be difficult to hang a meaningful program on a goal like this—"to make the principles of our organization better known in the community we serve." A more specific and therefore better goal would be: "During the next twelve months, to attract new clients to our organization that will represent a 15 percent increase in our dollar volume."

It may be decided to aim at only one goal or objective. More typically, there will be two to five specific but closely related goals.

Audiences or markets

The next step is to determine specifically who it is that should be reached to attain your goals. Typically, a key audience consists of the best prospective clients. Are they high-income homeowners? Are they presidents or other senior executives of giant corporations? If your market (audience) consists of companies, you may want to identify them in terms of size, type of business, geographic location, who in the company should be your initial contact, who will make the final buying decision, and so on. If your audience consists of individuals, they may be identified in terms of sex, age, geographic location, income level, occupation, and so on.

Secondary audiences may consist of influential people who are in a position to indirectly endorse the organization or to recommend it to potential clients. In this category might fall bankers, professors, attorneys, heads of professional societies, and so on.

Media

It's a relatively easy matter to identify the media that reach the audiences selected. For example, if the public is insurance executives, obviously the worthwhile and appropriate professional and trade publications in the insurance field should be on the media list. It's a good idea to divide your list into at least primary and secondary targets. Primary media targets will be those enjoying the greatest respect and/or with the highest circulation (commonly the two go hand-in-hand). For example, if your audience is business executives throughout the United States, *Fortune*, *The Wall Street Journal*, and *Business Week* will probably be among the media targets. If the market for services is national, cost-effectiveness can be attained by aiming efforts at national magazines and network TV programs, for example, rather than local newspapers or local radio stations.

Messages

Next, a decision is needed on what information to offer—in terms of news, ideas, or other messages—that will appeal to the media selected (and in turn to their audiences) and will at the same time help accomplish the goals. By looking at the organization as if through the eyes of a journalist or feature writer, it is possible to examine the organization as a reporter might and to write down all the ideas that would probably appeal to him or her. This can provide a "feature ideas inventory" that will serve as excellent raw material.

Each possibility must meet all of these needs: the interests of the organization, the requirements of the media, and the interest of the ultimate audiences.

Special projects

In addition to communicating information that already exists in the organization, it may be wise to create news or other publicity material by special projects. For example, giving a speech or conducting a seminar in one's field of expertness can be a legitimate news event worthy of coverage with photographs in newspapers or appropriate journals. Conducting a survey or other research can serve the same purpose.

One of the common problems of professional organizations is that they don't usually generate much news. However, with a little imagination they can often use special projects to create news where it didn't exist.

Measuring results

The final section of the written plan should specify what will constitute success. For example, after the first year, what should have happened as a result of this effort? Because of the nature of public relations activity and results, it is sometimes difficult to relate results directly to predetermined goals, but this should be done whenever possible and to the degree possible. If no basis is established for measuring the success of the program, little will keep it on track, and there's a far greater chance it will splinter into a number of meaningless segments. With predetermined standards for measuring success—even if it's only in terms of the quantity and quality of publicity sought—the organization is more likely to keep the program focused, narrowed down, disciplined, and aimed at its objectives.

Conducting Periodic Audits

There is another critical requirement: actual performance should be measured against goals and the other aspects of the plan at regular intervals. This should be done at least every six months and probably at shorter intervals during the start-up year. Such a formal review will be invaluable in helping determine which parts of the program are working and which are not, and to revise the program—and perhaps even the goals—accordingly to achieve the greatest possible cost-effectiveness.

Basic Tools of the Function

At this point serious consideration should be given to the available techniques.

Long experience and trial-and-error have shown that of all of the dozens of techniques available, twelve basic techniques work best for professional organizations. It is unnecessary to use all of them, and they can be combined in many ways. But if the program is confined to these twelve techniques, avoiding the temptation to experiment with more esoteric and perhaps even more interesting methods, it provides the best chance of achieving the objectives and getting the maximum return for the time and money invested.

News releases

The workhorse of almost every publicity or public relations effort is the news release. Discussions of news releases and how to use them appear in Chapters 20 and 22. Since professional service firms tend to generate little hard news, news releases will probably be used sparingly. There are exceptions, of course. A research organization may be doing work for its various clients that produces potential news almost every day. If this information is not totally proprietary or confidential, it may be turned into favorable publicity material either jointly with the client or without mentioning the client. Of course, use of any such material must have the client's approval.

A news release should have some real news to report or have a truly fresh and interest-ing idea to express. Expression of an idea without news should be considered only as a substitute.

Quotes, mentions, and short items

A look at newspapers, magazines, and other media of interest to a professional organization's clients will show that most of the material used deals with people—what they are doing and what they have to say. Editors know that their readers' interest can be captured best by stories about people. Stories about tangible things come in second and stories about concepts or theories are a distant third. Professionals can take advantage of this "people interest" of the media by having themselves or other people in the organization quoted in various stories and articles, or mentioned for what they are doing in their professional work. Short written items about the organization and its people can be published—with the advantage that short items in a professional journal, for example, often get far more readership than do longer articles and features.

The way to penetrate a person's consciousness is through spaced repetition. By being mentioned continually and often quoted, a firm's awareness builds up in the minds of its prospective clients.

The easiest way to get these quotes, mentions, and short items published and broadcast is to set up an open, two-way channel of communication between the organization and the media of primary importance to it. For example, opportunities should be created to meet the editors of important publications personally—in their offices, at lunch, at meetings. They should come to know the organization is available as an authoritative source of information in its field. They should be asked what projects they are working on for which helpful information can be provided. Such meetings should be followed with a letter and fact sheet or press kit (*see* the following and Chapters 21 and 22).

Chances are such editors will call back from time to time when they want opinions or specialized information. But it's not necessary to wait to be called. Once you have met the editor, if you have an idea or something you think is worthy of editorial attention you can simply call him or her.

In many successful publicity programs, a major proportion of the coverage results from making the organization a respected source that media people turn to often.

Endorsement articles (or case histories)

Since one of the underlying values of a good program is third-party endorsement of the professional firm, endorsement or case history articles are an ideal technique. They provide a double endorsement—from both the publication that carries the article and from the client who serves as the author or subject of the article. For example, one architectural engineering firm specialized in designing school buildings. After one of the firm's projects was completed with highly favorable reactions from all concerned, the firm asked the chairman of the local school board if he would byline an article in a national education publication, discussing some of the new design ideas used and why they worked so well. The school board chairman agreed, and the firm worked closely with him in getting a favorable article written and placed in a prestigious education publication, where it appeared with attractive photos of the school showing its unique design features. This was a typical situation where everybody benefited. The editor who accepted the article was delighted since it was bylined by the school board chairman and thus could not be construed as merely a puff piece for the architectural firm. The school board chairman and his community were happy, because the article turned the spotlight of favorable publicity on them. The firm, which was prominently

(but not blatantly) mentioned in the article, gained the indirect but strong endorsement that resulted in inquiries from other school boards. Such endorsement articles have the added advantage that they also benefit the clients.

Reprints, brochures, and other direct mail

Certain people are obviously more important to the professional organization than others. No matter how much publicity a firm may get, many of the people in its primary audience will probably miss it. It frequently pays to take the extra step of making reprints of the best publicity material and sending them directly to a mailing list consisting of present clients, prospective clients, business feeders, and others.

The easiest way is simply to photo-reproduce the publicity exactly as it appears. The reprints then can be used as enclosures with letters or other material going out of the office. Alternately, they can be sent specifically to a mailing list with a brief cover letter. The cover letter might simply say, "Recently some of the work of our firm was discussed in the xyz publication. Perhaps you saw the article, but in case you didn't, I'm taking the liberty of sending you this reprint. Incidentally, if our services mentioned here might be of interest to you, I would welcome hearing from you."

Some professional firms make their reprints more elaborate and attractive. There are many ways to do this: adding color and some form of attractive design is perhaps the most obvious. One research company had a feature story about its services in the *New York Times*. Instead of making an unadorned reprint, they reprinted an attractive two-color folder, with the feature story reprinted inside and the cover prominently featuring the logotype of the *New York Times*. Although first printed many years ago, this reprint folder continues to be used year after year as a mailing piece and handout of the firm.

Direct mail is an important aspect of any public relations program since it permits you to rifle-shot your message to the people you want most to reach. As with all mail operations, it is essential to devote attention to keeping mailing lists up-to-date (*see* Chapter 31).

Bylined articles and features

For the professional firm, articles in technical and professional journals, trade publications, and other appropriate periodicals represent one of the most effective ways to obtain valuable publicity. If someone in the firm writes an article dealing with a timely aspect of the field and has the article published in a respected publication, prospective clients are given a visible demonstration of the firm's expert knowledge, experience, and skill.

Before investing time and work in writing bylined articles, check with the editor of the target publication to make sure the article is something he wants and will match his current editorial requirements. It's not uncommon for an author to write an article and submit it for publication only to be told by the editor that although the article is good, a similar article on the same subject has just been accepted. The author then may have to try to place his work in a secondary publication.

Of equal or perhaps even greater importance is a feature article about the firm. In this case, the publication itself may assign its own writer to come in, research the interesting and timely aspects of the work the organization is doing and the personalities involved, then write a story, probably with photographs and other illustrations. Such articles, of course, put the firm directly in the spotlight and offer the advantage of someone else writing what amounts to a review of its work. Presumably, if the writer attempts to produce a balanced story (the best kind from everyone's point of view), everything the article says about the firm will not be totally favorable; but if it is handled carefully it is probable the feature will be generally favorable. Some publications will permit the subject to see the story before it is published in order to verify accuracy of all the facts, but others refuse to do this to prevent efforts to alter other content.

To increase your chances of having a strongly favorable feature article published, it is wise to prepare as much material for the writer as possible in advance and to give him or her as much cooperation as possible.

(For more information on working with the media, *see* Chapters 20–26.)

Research projects

Because professional firms don't generate a great deal of news on their own, they often create news by conducting research, the findings of which will be of timely interest to prospective clients and others important to the firm. The research findings are issued in the form of news releases, bylined or feature articles, speeches, literature, and so on, and clearly identify the firm as the source. It usually helps to include a professional analysis or interpretation of the findings, which further help establish the firm as an authoritative spokesman in its field.

Sometimes research being done on behalf of clients can be used for publicity purposes as well, if the clients approve. Sometimes, however, it is advisable or necessary to create special research projects, the sole purpose of which is publicity for the firm.

It is wise to keep publicity research projects simple, quick, and low-cost. Otherwise the time and money required may outweigh the publicity value. Often such research can be based on a simple survey questionnaire—or even can include library research, for which already existing information is pulled together that shows some trends or other interesting insights that otherwise might not be seen.

For example, one management consulting firm was interested in building its credibility in the eyes of corporation presidents. It did a research study on the backgrounds of presidents of major corporations. The findings showed that over the years during different phases of the economic cycle, corporations tended to choose their presidents with different kinds of backgrounds and experience. This simple study produced a bonanza of nationwide publicity for the management consulting firm in many of the leading business and management periodicals—so much, in fact, that the "Origin of Presidents" study has become a continuing part of the firm's public relations efforts.

Fact sheets and press kits

The quick, easy, low-cost action of preparing a fact sheet about the firm and its services, and putting copies of the fact sheet in the hands of all appropriate editors and other media contacts, has substantial value for a professional services firm. The fact sheet alerts editors to the firm's existence, its areas of expert knowledge, and its availability to provide authoritative material in its field. The result may be telephone calls, for example, from editors who want comments on subjects that the firm is able to provide insights on. Or they may ask for bylined articles, or to come in and do a feature on the firm. In many cases, editors will file the fact sheet so they will have the firm as a regular source of information when they need it, or so they can contact it in the future.

The fact sheet may take a variety of forms. One of the best is a single 8½" × 11" sheet consisting of the following information: name, address, telephone number, and fax number of the firm; a brief description of what it is and what it does; a brief description of what makes the firm unique or spe-

cial; a listing of its areas of expertness; and the names and titles of the key people who can be contacted for more information. Figure 43.1 illustrates a fact sheet that follows this format. It's a good idea to mail an updated copy of the fact sheet with a brief note to the entire media list every six months or yearly.

As the program develops it may be desirable to prepare a more elaborate information package, commonly known as a press kit. Usually a press kit consists of a folder with pockets containing the fact sheet, a brochure on the firm or other such literature, photos of key people and other appropriate subjects, perhaps the history of the firm briefly presented, reprints of articles or other publicity about it, perhaps a list of subjects on which it is prepared to write bylined articles on request, and so on. In other words, the press kit should contain all the pertinent information about the firm that might be of interest or value to editors and other press representatives. It is usually distributed with a cover letter suggesting that the medium may find some immediate use for some of the material in the press kit, but it should also recommend that the material be filed for possible future use or reference. As with fact sheets, press kits should be revised and redistributed at appropriate intervals (see Chapter 22).

Newsletters and brochures

In addition to working with existing publications and other media to carry your publicity material, there are advantages to producing a firm's own publication. For example, a feature article about the firm appearing in a professional journal has the advantages of endorsement of the press and wide distribution on an economical basis. On the other hand, this approach is unlikely to control what the article says and how it is written. Futhermore, the publication may not reach all of the desired audience. On the other hand,

```
                              Consolidated Research Consultants
                              711 Park Avenue West
                              Boston, Massachusetts 01613
                              Telephone:  617/222-3939
                              Fax:  617/222-3944
```

What They Do:

Consolidated Research Consultants is a research and consulting
firm specializing in the design, organization and implementation
of pre-retirement counseling and assistance programs for
employees of corporations and institutions. The firm
serves clients through four offices in the U.S. and one in
Canada.

What Makes Them Unique:

- Founded in 1957, Consolidated Research is the largest
  firm in its field of specialization
- The firm has the most extensive computerized information
  bank on pre-retirement and post-retirement U.S. workers
  (ages 55 through 70)
- At two of its offices, the firm operates "pre-retirement"
  indoctrination schools and courses, run by professional
  psychologists, to help those approaching retirement
  make the transition with a minimum of trauma

Areas of Special Knowledge:

- Financial planning for retirement
- Building a new life in retirement
- Utilizing skills to supplement retirement income
- Planning and managing geographical relocation
- Early retirement vs. running the course -- pros and
  cons based on computerized experience data
- Health and therapeutic aspects of work vs. leisure

Key People:

C. Homer Grant, managing director
Dr. Ralph Esterline, chief psychologist
Harold Kirkpatrick, senior financial consultant

For More Information:

Contact: Edward Parks
Acme Public Relations
1 Broad Street
Waltham, Massachusetts 02173
Telephone: 617/754-1515
Fax: 617/754-1520

Figure 43.1 A typical fact sheet for a (hypothetical) professional organization. Besides answering editors'
questions about the makeup and functions of the firm, it identifies subjects on which it can be consulted as a
spokesperson.

the advantages and disadvantages of publishing one's own newsletter, for example, are probably just the reverse. The organization probably can't get the same kind of broad distribution, since it must carry all the publishing and distribution costs itself, but it can have total control over what the publication says and how it says it, and it can target its newsletter directly at the primary audience.

Many professional services firms use newsletters as communications tools. (Details on the use of newsletters appear in Chapter 32.)

Publication of each issue of a newsletter is in itself an event worth publishing. Some firms merchandise their newsletters to the press by sending out news releases on the contents of each new edition. At least, copies of the newsletter should be sent to the editors of appropriate publications and other media.

In many professional fields, descriptive brochures about the firm and its services are considered essential, and clients and prospective clients expect such brochures to be available. Many professional firms make the mistake of publishing brochures that talk about what interests them rather than what interests their clients or prospective clients. Another mistake is publishing a brochure that looks and sounds like the brochures of other firms in the field. Too many brochures are long-winded, written in professional jargon, poorly designed, and bland. Such brochures usually end up in the wastebasket, unread.

It is good to prepare a brochure about a firm for the nonreader. The recipient is likely to look at the pictures, skim the headlines, read the short blocks of copy, and perhaps the photo captions. It's vital to stress the physical appearance of the brochure and the first impression it makes. Often the biggest value of a brochure is that it establishes the style or personality of the firm—high prestige, down-to-earth, highly technical, expensive, or whatever. Therefore, the design should reflect the true personality of the organization.

Books

The public relations values of writing and publishing a book on the firm's special knowledge are great. Information packaged between the hard covers of a book somehow exudes a special high level of authority. A book gives third-party endorsement of the publisher, who obviously has found the content worthy. A book has long life; whereas a magazine article, for example, may have a life span of only a week or a month, a book's life can extend for years or, with revised editions, even decades. The first edition of this handbook's predecessor was published in 1950. A book also gives the author the distinction of being not only a professional in the field but an authority as well. This distinction usually attracts other publicity opportunities, such as invitations to speak or to write more articles and books. The author of a book published by a respected publisher has one of the chief credentials of a bona fide expert in his or her field.

Books, however, are difficult and time-consuming to write, and because of the competition, difficult to get published. Most professionals who have succeeded in publishing good books find the effort well worth it from a public relations point of view, especially since a successful book will produce royalty income, and thus may represent a self-liquidating publicity effort and may even produce more income than was lost by the time and expenses involved in writing it.

(For other information about books in public relations, *see* Chapter 24.)

Speeches

The special value of speech-making is that it puts one in direct, face-to-face contact with prospective clients or others important to the firm. Another advantage is that the material prepared for a speech can usually be used for other publicity purposes—news releases, bylined articles, book chapters, and so on—if it is planned properly (*see* Chapter 31). Furthermore, unlike a published article, for example, a speech, once prepared, can be reused repeatedly before different audiences, unless it is reprinted fully where the audience is likely to see it.

The best way to get speaking invitations is to give one outstanding speech and let the word get around that you are a good person to have on programs. A more direct approach can also be used: simply writing letters to program chairpersons of appropriate organizations indicating that members of your organization are available to speak. It helps, of course, if a member of the firm is a member of the organizations approached.

Seminars, roundtables, and other sponsored meetings

In many ways, seminars, roundtables, and other meetings the firm sponsors and conducts itself are even better than speeches. The firm has total control over the program, the kind of audience invited, and so on. This does not mean that a seminar, for example, can be made a blatant sales pitch for the organization's services. A successful seminar or other sponsored meeting gives the audience worthwhile, practical, and timely information and knowledge; the effectiveness of the meeting is diminished by making the program self-serving.

Conducting seminars, roundtables, and other meetings requires a lot of work. However, properly planned and organized a seminar program can be a highly effective technique. It may be possible to charge participants a fee, making the project self-liquidating or even profitable. And once the program has been perfected through a few sessions, it becomes easier to do and probably more and more effective.

Regular columns

A doctor at a medical center writes a weekly health column for his local newspaper. A financial consultant writes a regular column on investment strategy in a financial magazine. The head of an advertising agency writes a column on effective advertising techniques in a marketing publication. All of these and many like them are examples of a proven publicity technique that has many special advantages. First of all, if you sell an editor on publishing a bylined article, for example, you've made only one sale. But if you sell him on running a column regularly with the same sales effort you get an ongoing flow of regular publicity.

Furthermore, being a regular columnist on subjects related to one's services affords an extra level of prestige and credibility.

It is sometimes relatively easy to get a column writing assignment from a good publication. It may be as easy as preparing three or four sample columns, sending them or taking them to the editor, and asking if she would like to have such a feature regularly. Preparing sound material in your sample columns, you have a good chance of succeeding with your objective. In some cases—but certainly not all—there may even be a token writing fee for the author.

Flexibility and diversity

A properly designed program must be flexible—so that a firm can capitalize on a "golden opportunity" that might come along once a year.

Because the use of public relations by professionals has expanded, applications of the twelve basic tools have diversified. Each tool—news releases, research projects, direct mail, etc.—can represent a working program by itself or in combination with other tools. All activities should be integrated to assure consistency and the synergy of multiple impact.

Each component has limitless applications. A leading Washington law firm, for example, uses direct mail to tell high-tech companies about its services. But they do more than send out sales letters. The firm sends a survey questionnaire to company presidents. The questions are designed to suggest the kind of services the querying firm provides—and the high level of professionalism with which they are provided.

A survey like this gives the professional an opportunity for multiple contacts with new business targets. For example, a survey might allow for contact in the following ways:

1. **An announcement letter** indicating that the questionnaire is forthcoming

2. **Survey questionnaire**

3. **Thank-you letter** to respondents

4. **Report on results**

5. **News release** based on results

6. **Article reprints** connected with findings of survey

7. **Request for meeting** to discuss how the responding company might use the firm's professional services

In this example, the "direct-mail" effort of the law firm produced a considerable amount of news value that was converted into national publicity.

Practical Tips

Almost all of these twelve basic techniques involve dealing with editors, program directors, or others in a position to accept or reject ideas or material. Many people inexperienced in public relations techniques are awed by this seemingly high hurdle. "Why should an important, busy editor be willing to talk to me?" they ask themselves. "I'm handicapped because I don't have any special 'in' with the editor."

The fact is that you don't need an "in," and you don't need to feel self-conscious about directly approaching editors, even the most important. All editors are constantly seeking to upgrade the quality and value of the material they use. If you have material that will help them accomplish that and if you present it to them in a clear, concise, understandable way, you will be welcomed, not fended off. For some editors it's best to make contact in writing, by letter. For others it makes sense to pick up the phone, introduce yourself, and present your idea. Circumstances and a little trial and effort will determine the best approach to use in each case.

Don't hesitate to make personal contact with appropriate editors, visit them in their offices, take them to lunch, invite them to see the firm's facilities. When you make such introductory contacts, it is best to have some specific ideas in which the editor may be immediately interested but your underlying purpose can be to establish a good, continuing personal relationship that will work to your mutual interests.

The firm may find that the public relations job is too big to be handled as a supplementary, as-time-permits function by someone in the firm. It may be wise to appoint someone to pursue this function full-time. If the function is to be handled internally, it should be handled by someone with stature and influence in the organization.

Often there are value and economy in calling on outside public relations experts and services. Just as the organization can conduct its professional services for its clients better than they can themselves, a public relations expert can often handle a public relations program better than the firm can itself. It's important that the selected public relations firm understands the subtleties involved in professional services and is aware of the taboos and ethical standards involved, as well as the judgment, experience, and skills detailed here.

44

PUBLIC RELATIONS FOR POLITICAL CANDIDATES

JOHN F. KRAFT
MORRIS V. ROSENBLOOM
DIANE HENDRICKS

John F. Kraft, as president of John F. Kraft, Inc., of New York and Washington, DC, was a major factor in hundreds of election campaigns. Some thirty United States senators were among the officeholders who drew on Kraft research and advice in their campaigns.

Morris V. Rosenbloom is president of American Surveys, which he founded in 1939 as a public relations, opinion survey, publishing, and economic research firm serving international, national, and local clients.

During emergency mobilization periods, he has been an executive with the War Production Board, the National Security Resources Board, the Defense Production Administration, and the Office of Defense Mobilization. In 1951–52, he organized and served as executive director of the Institute on Economics of Defense Mobilization cosponsored by the American University and the Office of Defense Mobilization.

Diane Hendricks, a Washington lobbyist, contributed to this chapter.

A good political campaign epitomizes public relations. How good the campaign, or the public relations, is becomes clear at the final moment when the relationship gels—and the votes are cast and tallied. It is the public alone that decides the outcome in this measurable competition between a single winner and one or more losers. Hence, in this environment—wherein the candidate and party direct all appeals toward the public, and the public serves as the jury—whatever causes the candidate to win or lose is a matter of public relations.

The challenge then, in oversimplistic terms, becomes how to win with what you have.

Of course there are guidelines to help bring about the desired vote, some of which are given in this chapter. But it should be reiterated that they are guidelines, not a guarantee. No step-by-step formula exists that can be broadly applied to any given campaign; no surefire answers exist for all the questions and challenges. To borrow the favorite watchword of the late Thomas Watson of IBM, the guiding principle for political campaign public relations is: THINK.

For example:

• Design a beautiful billboard in yellow and black because the colors are visible. But don't do it against a Western autumn background, where it gets lost with the golden fields and black earth.

- Come up with a slogan that says it for your candidate: "In your heart you know he's right." But you'd better think first of the opponent's possible counter that says "Yes, he's very *far* right."

Good politicians, whether they be candidates or the people who know how to help elect them, are all public relations practitioners. They don't need PRSA confirmation of the role. This refers to people who either can, or think they can, measure public reaction to a specific political action.

The public relations practitioner involved for the first time in a political campaign must, therefore, reconcile himself to a fact of life: however expert in public relations, he or she is dealing with people who consider themselves expert, too, and in the very sensitive area of politics.

Actually, much political or public relations sense is acquired by soaking up every experience, be it written, visual, spoken, or overheard, from the old pros or fledglings. Anyone whose vocation or avocation is politics will glean as much information from as many different sources about it as possible. This means that the public relations firm or staff must be sharp to stay ahead of the campaign team.

The political team's wisdom can be put to a speedy test by noting the date it first checks in with a public relations firm or advertising agency.

The wise politicians retain firms early enough to jump the gun on the opposition. Even if it turns out that it isn't needed for six months—or needed at all—the foresighted politician is not left searching for a firm at the last minute. The smart candidate will give the retainer contract to the firm that can prove that, regardless of office, he or she will get special care and not get lost beneath bigger accounts.

In ideal circumstances, the candidate or manager should decide at least a year ahead of election day whom he wants as public relations advisors, and inform them. Even if there is no immediate need for counsel (or inability to pay, because funds won't really roll in until the last months), the advisors will consciously or unconsciously begin thinking and reading about "their candidate," and the value of subsequent counsel will inevitably be increased. The same argument for early selection applies in many cases to the advertising agency. It can also be important for the public relations firm to know and establish early rapport with the research firm to be employed.

The campaign organization

The reason for such advance planning is that the candidate and team must gear up for the final three hectic months of campaigning and they want no last minute extraneousness interfering with the intensity of their efforts.

Particularly during the last three months before the one-day sale of the political product, the candidate—whether aspiring mayor or U.S. senator—must vie intensively for the attention of the voter. He or she will be in blood-and-guts competition for that attention with every other politician of the season.

Focusing interest on the candidate

The major question becomes, how do you get the voter's attention to *your* candidate rather than to the dozen others? Of course, while the political competition for attention is in progress, there will also be competition from campus disorders or mass murders prominently featured in the news, the demands on the consumer-voters to buy, the suggestions that they subscribe, that they read this or that, and that they listen to the requests of their families.

The competitive situation calls for raising the candidate's voice effectively enough to be heard by a sufficient number of people by election day. This means in those last three months of concentrated effort, the candidate must be seen, heard, and listened to by the majority of voters. And the message espoused must appeal to them to support him or her. The reason generally given when asked why a vote was cast a certain way, is that the voter was encouraged to do so by one of three sources: the candidate, a party worker, or a friend. It might be said that *the whole business of a political campaign is to ask people to vote for you.*

Reaching the voter

The ways to reach voters are numerous: speeches and rallies by candidates and supporters, party organization workers ringing doorbells and asking for support of the slate, and the candidate's personal organization asking workers to go out in the candidate's behalf. The candidate can reinforce these efforts by personal letters, advertising, radio spots, and television time.

In any of these ways, the candidate is basically asking for the vote. To persuade people to be his or her followers, he must appeal to all sorts of them. There's no right or wrong way to go about this. However, certain factors apply to making the decision about the way the candidate states his appeal. For example:

- **Television** is undoubtedly an excellent tool if the candidate is running for mayor in Salt Lake, Atlanta, or Boston. But in Jersey City? Virtually all of the audience votes in New York City and its suburbs.
- **Radio** is a good buy—particularly at 4:30 in the morning in North Dakota when the farmers begin the milking by turning on

the radio in the barn. But who would buy the same time in San Francisco?

Appeals for the voter's attention should be tailored as nearly as possible to the kind of voter and the person he or she is. *The voter can be reached only in a way that interests him or her.* Is it best to communicate on the voter's way to or from work via a car, through a friend, at the shopping center, or at a union meeting? A reprint of a magazine article, brochures or buttons, balloons or girls in sashes, sound trucks or banners, endorsements or debates? In certain areas, voter appeals must be specialized by using the telephone, direct mail, or personal visits.

For instance, direct mail sent to residents of New York's Silk Stocking 17th Congressional District stands to have much less impact than direct mail to poor white families in Appalachia. The 17th District is deluged with mail—so much so that often letters get thrown away after a glance at the envelopes.

At campaign time voters are swamped with political-type mail. So unless it's exceptional, political mail is often thrown out and forgotten.

The trick of sending mail personalized with individual address labels via computer is losing its charm, but this is much better than shotgun efforts addressed to "Occupant."

However, if computer programs are available and can be afforded, it is possible to send out more than one message to many different groups of voters or different messages to houses on opposite sides of the street. A series of letters can be sent to persons of different levels of education, occupation, and income.

The techniques a candidate uses in asking for the vote will vary from place to place depending on circumstances. Consideration should be given to the cost and numbers involved, quality, and the possible effect on the recipient. Common sense will determine how the appeal is made in light of the four major components of each political campaign: *money*, *the candidate*, *the political organization*, and *the issues*. Public relations plays a keen part in fulfilling each of these components.

The Impact of Funding Laws on PR

What do funding laws have to do with public relations? A great deal. Besides the obvious question of how much is available to publicize the candidates' abilities and political programs, there is considerable interest in where the money and support are coming from. *Time* magazine ran a cover story titled "Pac Men Turning Cash into Votes," and *U.S. News & World Report* featured a cover, "Is Congress For Sale?" Methods used by President Clinton in 1996 created a furor after his reelection.

With this kind of publicity, a candidate cannot afford even the perception that his or her financial house is not in order. What a shame it would be to lose an election because the campaign staff did not know the law and that became the story that dominated the morning news!

The rules for raising funds by the major national parties and candidates for the president, vice-president, and Congress have changed drastically in recent years. The effect has been to change the entire nature of national party politics and the campaigns for the top offices of the nation.

While the federal election campaign laws do not apply to local campaigns, almost half of the states (twenty-three and the District of Columbia) limit the role of special interests by restricting the amount that their Political Action Committees (PACs) may contribute to candidates in federal elections. These in-

clude Alaska, Arizona, Arkansas, Connecticut, Delaware, Florida, Hawaii, Kansas, Kentucky, Maine, Michigan, Minnesota, Montana, New Hampshire, New Jersey, New York, North Carolina, Oklahoma, Texas, Vermont, Washington, West Virginia, Wisconsin, and Washington, DC.

With all the rules, regulations, and potential changes in campaign finance, it is essential for any political candidate to work closely with the Federal Election Commission (FEC). It is important that the legal counsel check and recheck what is being done in the candidate's name. Reforms are proposed often. Election funding laws must be checked to be sure changes are known and followed. Besides the potential of being on the receiving end of a strong media attack whereby an election could be lost, there are severe penalties for violations.

Despite attempts to control contributions by PACs and their undue influence on elections, the *Final Report* by the Federal Election Commission (FEC) shows that 74.2 percent of all PAC money went to incumbents in 1988.

Summarized below are some other major provisions of new laws dealing with the funding for national races.

Disclosure

Detailed records of a campaign's financial dealings must be kept and reported to the FEC in Washington. The name and address of every person giving in excess of $200 (in the aggregate) within a year must be reported.

Contribution limits

Individuals (except candidates contributing to their own campaigns) may give no more than $1,000 per election to one candidate or candidate committee. Individuals may give no more than $25,000 in total per year. Multicandidate committees, such as House and

Senate campaign committees, may give up to $5,000 per election but there is no limit on the total number of dollars a committee may give per candidate per year.

Independent expenditures

Individuals may make expenditures (such as for advertising) to a candidate, without these amounts being counted toward contribution limits, if the outlay is an independent one that is not made in collaboration with the candidate or his/her committee or agents. Should all such outlays exceed $250 in a calendar year, all must be reported to the Federal Election Commission. If there were not a category such as independent expenditures, campaigns would have to raise more money. Two-thirds of the independent expenditures generally are focused on presidential candidates, with 33 percent in connection with congressional races.

Federal money for presidential races

Presidential candidates in a primary who raise enough money to qualify for matching funds from the Treasury must agree to a spending limit in the primary election. By accepting public funds for the general election, however, the candidates have to give up the right to accept private donations.

Federal money for national conventions

In 1984 Congress increased the public funding entitlement and spending limit for national nominating conventions. This money is collected from voluntary taxpayers' funds to conduct their nominating conventions.

One of the reasons there is always current legislation regarding funding is the enormous amount it takes to run a modern campaign. The public and then Congress react to the pendulum of facts and opinions of the day. As soon as one set of laws is enacted, some-

one or some group finds a way around the law and the cycle starts again. Forthcoming legislation will undoubtedly try to eliminate PACS, to lower contribution limits, to prohibit "bundling" except by political parties, to prohibit candidates from rolling over excess campaign funds to the next election cycle, to require full disclosure of soft money (not directly attributed to a specific candidate), and to increase the role of political parties, and many other restrictions.

Effects on dealing with politicians

Office seekers are likely to deal more cautiously with potential campaign contributors than ever before. To fail to comply with some provision of the complex new laws—however inadvertently—can bring swift accusation from an opponent, with serious damage to the chances for election.

Even in nonelection years among incumbents secure in office, lobbyists, trade associations, and constituents may encounter increased caution and a tendency to put "everything on the record." In part, this can be attributed to scandals under the loose headings of "Watergate," the Savings and Loan debacle, and Clinton's multiple slipups. There is also pressure on Congress to open up its own proceedings—to make the *Congressional Record* more truly reflect what actually was said in Congress, and to further publicize government payrolls, among other things.

Effort to reform lobbying is a continuing process that calls for close attention to what is permissible. A former chairman of the House Judiciary Committee defined lobbying as the

total of all communicated influences upon legislators, pointing out that the distinction between good and bad lobbying is "not whether the objectives of persuasion are selfish or altruistic, liberal or conservative, pro-labor or pro-business, but solely and simply whether the message conveyed is intelligible, accurate, and informative, or cryptic, deceptive, and obscure."

Pressure for elections and lobbying "reforms" is placed on Congress continuously. In view of changing developments in political operations and opportunities, candidates will lean heavily on their attorneys and their campaign treasurers. Public relations advisors assisting candidates (whether as staff members or under contract) must follow every development in the field of campaign law and ethics. (*See* Chapters 5, 6, 8, and 48.)

Raising Funds/ Generating Capital

In all other campaigns the importance of raising money remains crucial.

People do not want to throw away their money; they want to go with the winner. The finance committee's success is dependent on its convincing people that the candidate has a chance of winning. If the candidate says things the people want to hear, it can be an additional boost to fund-raising, but the candidate's words must be publicized or no one will reach for the checkbook.

While contributors must be convinced that the candidate is on top, they also need reassurance that each contribution is vital for the candidate to win.

In actuality, it is not so important what the contributor gives so long as he or she gives something. Anyone who gives $1 or $5 has a vested interest and will probably talk about and vote for the candidate.

Money is the name of the game. Regardless of money's abundance or absence, the most effective campaign involves developing a budget well in advance and deciding on an advertising and public relations plan that is feasible enough to stick to. Careful advance planning will save shredded shirts during the heat of the political battle when time

can be spent better than on debates over postcard purchases. A smoothly running campaign headquarters presents a solid impression, whereas one where people are haggling over prices and expenditures presents a picture of obvious lack of organization.

Some political campaigners think it's best to ask the big givers first for help to set a high collection pace or average gift for the campaign. Others think big gifts should be paced to keep morale levels high throughout the campaign.

No matter what money-raising theory is followed, the quickest way to lose or lower the size of a gift is not to know the answers to people's questions about where the money is going. Canvassers should be schooled in how to answer the most frequently asked questions and how to handle objections. They should have a direct answer ready when people ask how the money will be used.

Of course, if time and money are available, professional fund-raisers can advertise the money drive effectively and give the public relations chairman pointers that few amateurs are aware of. Regardless of the degree of professionalism, it will take organization, a timetable, and training.

Knowing the Candidate

Part of the public relations of dealing with any candidate is an appraisal of that candidate. Is he or she free of serious flaws that can be used to attack? Will he or she stand up under pressure?

No matter how you have to find the answers to these questions, do it. If you don't know the candidate's weaknesses, you don't know and won't be prepared for what the opposition might come up with. You also have to know how your candidate and the opposition behaved if either was ever in office previous to the present election.

Victory depends on the most effective projection of the candidate and the issues—and avoiding unfavorable exposures.

Is the candidate healthy? Can he or she stand the pace of a strenuous schedule the last three imperative months? Does he have the stamina to complete a 16-hour day, day after day after day? How avidly does she want to win? Does he have the drive? Can he communicate his desire and drive to the voter?

The candidate should be measured by appraising his or her assets and deficits in hard reality. Is the candidate attractive and articulate? He may be intelligent, but what does his voice sound like when he talks? What are the spouse and children like? Is she from a segment of the community where she stands strong vis-à-vis the power structure? Is he or she happy in a crowd? Is he more popular with members of the opposite sex? These are some of the many things involved in an appraisal of the candidate. In some way or another, each element of the appraisal determines the methods the candidate will use to get the attention of the voter.

Deciding the candidate's approach

It must be determined whether the candidate can benefit from high visibility or if he or she should be prevented from surfacing. If the candidate is not effective on television, keep him off camera; if his voice is poor, keep him off the air. If someone else's voice can tell the candidate's story better than the candidate, use it. Or if a touched-up photo behaves better on television than the candidate, but the voice is no problem, use the still and the candidate's voice. Your appraisal of the candidate will indicate the right combination and determine whether she should be exposed to public view over a long period of time. Remember, how well she will do as a public servant is not closely related to the charisma she shows or lacks in running for office.

By maximizing the candidate's strength through insights provided by analysis, you afford a better chance of winning. However, he must be advised not to overstep his natural bounds or territory if he is to maintain a campaign strong on the offense rather than being put on the defensive.

Of course analysis works two ways. The candidate will no doubt ask similar questions and make similar decisions about the background of the manager and the public relations executive. So in either case, when sizing up the personal traits that indicate ability and character of the would-be clients, check these items.

- **Trustworthiness**—through reputation or association
- **Compatibility**—to hold up between the candidate and staff executives during the strain and closeness of the campaign
- **Experience**—the more, the better
- **Objectivity**—ability to face reality
- **Administrative ability**—ease in delegating, supervising, following up, and relating
- **Energy**—stamina
- **Good judgment**—thorough thinking
- **Unflappability**—remaining cool under pressure
- **Character**—remember Gary Hart and Dick Morris

The virtues of either the campaign manager or candidate may be much the same, but the degree of trait development may differ. For instance, it's more important for the manager than the candidate to possess the highest degree of administrative ability.

Categories of candidate

It's imperative to examine the candidate's potential in realistic terms of position in the political arena. For the sake of simplification, there are two categories of candidates.

- **Category One** is the incumbent—sitting behind the officeholder's desk with full staff, a robot machine, privileges, and status—and the person who should have moved into gear for the next campaign the day after the last election.

- **Category Two** is the nonincumbent—most often the novice, the loser, or the rising candidate—fighting for identity or seeking a new look that will make this campaign a winner, or trying to get ahead by convincing people that he or she is good enough for a heftier job. In any case, he is faced with different types of problems and circumstances than the incumbent. (Old pros sometimes come out of retirement and back into this category as strong but nevertheless Category Two candidates.)

Knowledgeability is the weapon that can most readily close the gap between the incumbent with a record of active service to constituents and materials and facilities, and the Category Two candidate clamoring for volunteers, a budget, a record, and some prestige.

TV Opportunities for the Candidates

One of the main objectives of a good public relations plan for a candidate is to raise voter identification. There is no better way to do this than by the use of TV. Since TV is very expensive, it is important to orchestrate as much free TV exposure as possible. The candidate should get on every favorable TV program he or she can. The best way is to have him or her known for something distinctive. A strongly opinionated person usually adds drama to a media event and many times the media will request a story or free TV time. It is far better to be known for a particular point of view than not to be known at all. The one caution is to make sure he or she does not

change positions once they are stated, except in extreme circumstances.

Good advertising is important—and sometimes so is negative advertising. It is important that the advertising be carefully worded and presented, and consideration be given to whether a backlash may result. While the "game of politics" has always been considered "dirty," today there is more accountability associated with media attacks. Since the 1988 presidential campaigns, there have been several legislative proposals that attempt to bring more fairness, especially to TV advertising. It is unfortunate that negative campaigns often work, though frequently they are the only way to disclose an opponent's disqualification for office. It is hoped that the general public will "turn" on extremely unfair campaign tactics and reject the candidates who use them.

Incumbents have additional opportunities for TV coverage. An unintended effect of TV is that incumbents can be shown doing the job they are elected to do. They can do this by being well prepared for events, hearings, and floor debates. It is very hard for an outsider to compete against someone whom the public already identifies as their active and well-informed officeholder.

The lesson for political candidates is that TV must be used to his or her advantage. If a person is an incumbent, TV should be used as much as possible. If a person is a challenger, the opponent should be watched often to help plan and implement the attack.

The Impact of Party Structure

The importance of the party structure varies a great deal. If it is weak, fragmented, or there is no party structure at all, the candidate and manager may have to go it alone.

When an organized party actually exists, it is important to work on the basis that the party structure or organization is imperfect at best. That's not enough reason to ignore or slight it. If you do, the party machinery—well-oiled or not—will trash the candidate. It's important to get along with the party and to show that you want to.

The candidate and the campaign manager should check with the organization leaders on a regular basis at least once a week. A developing and continuing liaison of this kind prevents any misunderstanding that the candidate is running his or her own show. Similar efforts must be taken to keep the candidate in good graces with other members of the ticket, the political offices, and the workers. This doesn't mean a lot of yes-mamming and kowtowing, but just simply party etiquette or preventive medicine for a fatal disease known as political backstabbing.

Working with the party organization

Regardless of the structure, the party or following must be more than acknowledged because it can be helpful to the candidate—and in some cases can decide the election. Party organization can help the candidate educate the voter on how to register and how to vote using a machine, and in distributing other candidate-selling information.

Established organizations most often maintain files of community leaders, good speakers, and community information that can provide great insight when shared with the candidate trying to build up lists of workers, fund-raisers, friends, and even foes. Coordination of plans means strength, but watch out for signs that someone or some group may be trying to use another politically.

Motivating supporters

The organization can be helpful, but because of natural party structures the candidate must develop his or her own organization auxiliary to the party's. He or she will need candidate support committees, such as Teachers for Jones, Doctors for Jones, and so on, as well as a personal group of supporters. He must deal with his auxiliaries on a personal level because most of the volunteers he enlists will be working out of love. How does he keep them happy?

One way is to thank them a lot. This means meeting with key volunteer leaders at least once a week to tell them what a good job they are doing and will do. If they add names and addresses to the computerized mailing list, make them feel that they are the key to whether a letter reaches its destination.

In return for showing personal interest, the candidate and manager will generate an alert following that will demand as much as it receives. It will of course demand that all meetings be worth attending. Otherwise volunteers, party organization members, and other followers will consider meetings a waste of time or feel their absence won't really matter.

Another way to keep the followers happy is through a special newsletter marked "Confidential" that goes on a regular basis to each volunteer. By getting personal political tidbits from the candidate the volunteer feels like the insider that he or she is, but more importantly like a member of the team.

To keep team members happiest the candidate should never be put in the position of saying "no" to their requests. The candidate must be protected from requests for a job or demands on his or her time by referring them to the secretary or manager—after acknowledging interest in the request. It's passing the buck, but it keeps the money in circulation longer and the candidate can concentrate time and energy where the campaign plan requires.

Identifying the Issues

Communicating with the right voters at the right time, in the right place, with the right message is the essence of the campaign. And they must all be tied together. Without this kind of expertness the candidate and manager are flying blind.

It used to be enough for the candidate to know the district or state by extensive traveling through it and by listening to counsel of friends who felt they knew what this group or that group of voters were concerned about. But changes have occurred and continue to occur: 20 percent of the population now moves each year; the average voting age is younger; and more and more people who were previously unregistered are getting onto the election rolls.

Use of surveys

There has been a steady growth in the use of "voter attitude studies," or "surveys," or "polls," depending on one's choice of definitions, designed to find out what messages a candidate should attempt to convey to various voting publics. (*See* Chapter 18.) Other studies develop precinct profiles and other sophisticated guides developed with the aid of computers.

A well-done survey, used widely by clever campaign management, should add 2 or 3 percent to a candidate's strength—at a very conservative minimum.

A candidate who has had no prior exposure to surveys wants to know what he's buying, and usually begins with two basic questions:

1. "How is a survey done?"
2. "What do I get out of it, or what can I learn?"

A succinct answer to the first question from a professional pollster would be something like this:

First, we try to learn as much as we can about you, your assets and liabilities, and those of your opponent, and what you feel the issues may be. We then construct a questionnaire that will be used by professional interviewers who will conduct in-person interviews in the homes of the voters. The people who are interviewed will be predesignated by a plan drawn up by our statistician in such a fashion as to ensure that it will represent a cross section, or microcosm, of your entire electorate. The interviews are returned, processed, and the computer printout is analyzed, resulting in a written analysis of the results. Discussion should follow to permit us to offer suggestions and recommendations. The end product of the research should be thought of as a campaign tool to guide strategy and campaign tactics.

The benefits of research

This leads into, and anticipates, the answer to the second question. Former National Democratic Committee Chairman Lawrence O'Brien made these comments about the value of poll-taking in his *Democratic Congressional Campaign Manual.*

What can be learned by polling?

- The issues people are concerned about, and how they feel about those issues
- Voter reaction toward specific proposals or programs advanced or under consideration by the candidate
- Voter attitudes toward a candidate and the opponent
- Areas of strength and weakness for a candidate and opponent (These may be classified by race, religion, income, amount of schooling, sex, age, national ancestry, region, or any other pertinent factor.)
- Voter evaluation of various officeholders and the job they are doing
- Priority ratings that exist in the minds of voters on various issues or proposals
- Relative standing of the candidates at the time the poll was taken

There are other uses of this same kind of research, of course. In a midwestern state a few years ago the incumbent was considered unbeatable, and his opponent's fund-raising efforts were producing negligible results. Then a survey showed that he had an excellent chance of unseating the incumbent and the money started flowing. That opponent became a senator.

In an eastern state a survey analysis demonstrated that the gubernatorial candidate could win only if the voters could be persuaded the election really was important. The lassitude on the part of the voters was overcome, just enough, when the president was persuaded by the survey results to make a special trip to the state and stress the importance of the election of that candidate. It has been suggested that the presidential endorsement may have resulted in getting another 100,000 voters to the polls. The candidate won by a few tenths of one percent of the total vote.

Aside from the basic purpose for conducting surveys, they have been used to

1. raise funds or discourage fund-raising

2. buoy up the spirits of the campaign workers, or discourage the workers for the opposition

3. get important support from people in higher office, even if it means no more than one percent of the vote

But these are ancillary uses of research. The use of opinion research is on the rise for many reasons. Research efforts in a sensibly conducted campaign should be guided by these "do's and don'ts":

Do:

- **Start** research early. Some gubernatorial and senatorial candidates conduct voter attitude research all through their terms of office. Many others, if not most incumbents, start pulse-taking two years or more prior to election day. The trend in this direction of earlier, more-intensive use is on the rise.

- **Investigate** the background of your research firm. What do its former clients think of it?

- **Ask** who the candidate will be dealing with in the firm.

- **Confine** the reporting of research results to no more than one or two key campaign decision-makers.

- **Give** the researcher a thorough backgrounding regarding the needs, candidates, and issues.

- **Expect** a full discussion of the written research results. Insist on complete interpretation.

Don't:

- **Haggle** with the research firm about price, once you've established that the firm is respected and to be trusted.

- **Buy statistics** and a bunch of tabulations without explanation.

- **Buy research** on the assumption that it is a prediction of whether your candidate will win. The real value of research is not to predict the election results, but to help you affect the outcome.

- **Keep the researchers** in the dark. Hiding information prevents the firm from full interpretation of the data produced.

Implementation Tools

After culling all of this information, it takes public relations tools to make the knowledge work for the candidate. The obvious tools are advertising, television, radio, newspapers, magazines, direct mail, billboards, car cards, posters, and bumper stickers.

Each of the tools must be considered carefully. For instance, when it comes to advertising it is usually best done by an agency. It can buy time, book space, lay out ads, and for forth. It should help decide *how* and *when* things should be said, but not *what* should be said. If this decision is left up to the agency, there is risk that the messages will reflect the professional ad man and not the candidate's sense of his or her constituency.

All activities and communications must be integrated to avoid contradictions or inconsistencies and to give every effort a synergistic effect.

One more caution: the agency, not surprisingly, tends to be somewhat heavy in advocating use of commissionable media. It's likely to be less than enthusiastic about using anything else. Take advice from the baseball shortstop by making sure you play the ball and that you not let the ball play you.

Choosing an advertising agency

Selecting an agency involves much of the same appraisal involved in sizing up the candidate. What is the agency's background? Has it worked for political candidates before? If it hasn't, the candidate may stand to lose in the hottest of all campaign moments. There's a good deal of difference between marketing the political product and marketing a bar of soap. The agency without perspective concerning that difference might try to wrap the candidate in too fancy a foil for the voters.

Other determinants include the agency's ability to work quickly and on-call, and its talent for delivering good art and layout.

The agency, like everything else the candidate touches, must be respected and accepted by the media with which it deals. Again, much of the decision should be based on how high a priority the agency will give the candidate's account.

Of course, the advertising must be closely supervised by the campaign manager. He or she should do the directing, implementing all efforts of the advertising agency and publicity director. With his coordination, the efforts

come together into sharp focus, making direct appeal to the populace.

Public relations in the campaign

The public relations substance for a campaign comes in from a variety of sources: research, finance, opinion makers, publicity and advertising, speakers' bureau and scheduling, party organization, and volunteers.

These sources must all be under the command of the manager. It cannot be stressed too strongly that *everything* must be cleared through him. Otherwise the most important campaign element—theme—will be forgotten and there will be a lot of loose ends and a lot of lost votes on election day.

Importance of theme

Theme gives unity to the entire campaign. It is the central idea that binds all the single cords into a solid rope. It must be clear enough to describe the campaign in less than twenty words.

Eisenhower took "Peace, Progress and Prosperity" and from it came up with the combined slogan "Time for a change—I like Ike." Every issue brought the theme and the slogan home to the voter.

The next candidate, John Kennedy, couldn't argue with peace and prosperity, so he took progress and had the theme, "Let's get the country moving again!" Bush said, "Read my lips: No new taxes," and Clinton talked of "building a bridge to the 21st century."

In picking a theme, it is important to use a broad brush and to paint the words in bright poster colors instead of pastels. To do this, every aspect of the campaign, from direct mail to where the candidate will speak, must add up to saying the same thing. It must be the focal point. Otherwise the voter sees a blurred kaleidoscope. The point of "theme" is to magnify the focus. And the theme is needed before the first fund-raiser.

Avoiding shackles

Staying fluid is sometimes difficult to do—particularly when a candidate gets locked into the notion that he or she must have certain things in the public relations aspects of the campaign. Those certain things may be anything from a half-hour documentary to billboards. Candidates or their managers tend to get locked in much the same way they pick up good plans: from their own vanities or from someone who stands to make a buck off the placement of the half-hour documentary. Needless to say, neither source is completely objective.

Another way to get locked in or bogged down is through the candidate's friend. The candidate usually has some friend who runs a local advertising agency or who is a printer, who purports to be a designer, or whatever, but only occasionally is there any evidence of this friend's professionalism in the production of the brochures or even bumper stickers.

Perhaps the most landlocked of all is the candidate whose campaign strategists consist of relatives—the administrative assistant and an appointments secretary. These people immediately become self-appointed experts in the fields of advertising, media research, precinct organization, public relations, and many other vital areas.

A candidate is often better than the campaign and, as has been well established, the campaign is sometimes much better than the candidate. Those who make the decision to get involved in a campaign, and to be honest with themselves and the candidate, will commit themselves to the fact that the idea is to win, and that the Judgment Day comes when the voter pulls the lever down.

Unlike the commercial world, the only "share of market" a political candidate can care about is "50 percent-plus-one."

45

INTERNATIONAL PUBLIC RELATIONS

ROBERT S. LEAF

Robert S. Leaf is chairman of Burson-Marsteller International. He joined Burson-Marsteller in 1957 as the company's first trainee. He became vice-president in 1961, executive vice-president of international operations in 1965 when he moved to Europe, president in 1968, and chairman in 1985. He was responsible for setting up offices in Latin America, Europe, Australia, the Middle East, and Asia (including China). He is presently headquartered in London.

He graduated from the University of Missouri. He has written and lectured extensively on public relations and marketing subjects. He has given speeches before management and marketing groups throughout the United States, Western Europe, Eastern Europe (including Russia), South America, Asia, and Australia.

He is listed in Who's Who in America, Who's Who in the World, Who's Who in International Business, *and* Who's Who in Public Relations.

Beginning in the early 1980s public relations began to make great strides throughout the world. Where it was once effectively used primarily in the United States and in certain European countries and Australia, it has quickly spread to virtually all corners of the globe. Most countries now host competent public relations consultancies. Professional organizations, such as the International Public Relations Association, have grown in numbers and importance. Public relations is now taught in schools around the globe—Hong Kong, Ghana, Malaysia, Nigeria, and elsewhere. Significantly, corporations and their executive management have been placing ever greater importance on public relations and allotting more responsibility to their public

relations departments. Today, public relations practitioners on the international front increasingly support not only the marketing process but also the corporate strategy.

At the same time, governments and government departments, such as export, industrial development, and tourism, have recognized the need for expanded PR programs. For example, the Industrial Development Board of Northern Ireland had to contend with and address the fact that the media found stories that reflected negatively on Ireland to be more exciting for their readers. Accordingly they launched a public relations campaign to counter this negative image by presenting the situation in an appropriate perspective to potential investors from leading industrial nations. This effective campaign resulted in a significant increase in investment. By the same token, countries whose tourism was threatened by the aftermath of hurricanes, pollution, or other natural or unnatural disasters have had to make sure the message spread to the major tourist markets that their situations had improved and things were "back to normal."

Then in the 1990s, the whole issue of crisis management—with its multitude of public relations manifestations—came full-force to the forefront. Perhaps the single greatest development impacting public relations so far this decade has been the increased cross-border activity of many corporations. Many U.S. firms ventured into what were for them previously uncharted territory, such as the Pacific Rim, China, Russia, and Eastern Europe. They began to acquire more subsidiaries outside their country's borders, creating the need for increased communications with governments, employees, and local communities. They also began to borrow more heavily abroad and to list on more foreign stock exchanges, requiring expanded financial public relations service.

In this whirlwind of new and increased activities, the qualifications profile of the average public relations executive needed worldwide has changed dramatically. No longer can corporations and PR consultants look primarily to the journalist as the key source of the talent needed to spearhead an international public relations program. In several countries public relations has risen to a status that makes it acceptable for lawyers, bankers, merger and acquisition specialists, government officials, marketing executives, and other respected and valued professionals to become public relations consultants.

Understanding Global Publics

The greatest need of an individual or company dealing internationally is understanding the local culture and having the ability to use that understanding effectively. In the Middle East, for example, many key purchasing influences place greater importance on personal relationships than on price. This is often hard for many Western business people to understand. But with Bedouins, friendship and trust take precedence over the normal give and take of the capitalistic marketplace.

Japan can be frustrating, because decision-making is normally a committee function rather than an individual action. That means everything takes more time and involves complex audiences. But employee relations are far easier in Japan than in the West, because staff loyalty is more built-in. This is beginning to modify slightly. Japanese employees are starting to change jobs, something once very rare. In previous years it was expected that a Japanese employee joined a company for life. In fact, many Japanese meeting one another for the first time mentioned their company before they mentioned their name when introducing themselves.

Some Western companies following the Japanese approach are beginning to make more effective use of their employees in groups such as quality circles, whereby working on the production line becomes a greater part of the manufacturing planning process.

Even in Japan employee relations cannot be overlooked. In many cases, far more important than the pay scale is what the Japanese refer to as the *wa* (harmony). If that is disturbed, the whole working relationship can be upset. The *wa* can be disturbed by the introduction of one wrong person into an operation. It can be disturbed in the case of multinationals by having in authority a *gaijin* (foreigner) who does not understand the importance of local attitudes.

Overseas, even an understanding of body language can have an impact. Taking your thumb and second finger and forming it into a circle means "A OK" in the United States, but in France it means "zero," in Japan it means "money," and in Tunisia it means "I'll kill you."

Dealing in multiracial societies requires a special understanding. No one should operate in Malaysia without understanding the government's desire to increase local participation in operating companies and the role of Bumiputras (sons of the soil), as the ethnic Malays are called. Even though the desire to increase investment has lessened the more xenophobic aspects of the policy, it still lies below the surface and must be taken into account when practicing public relations. Even recently, both local and national governments have fallen due to the clash between the two communities.

It is not only in the East that such problems exist. Belgium, with its continuing conflict between the Walloons (French-speaking) and Flemish (Dutch-speaking) sections of the population creates a never-ending public relations difficulty. When I lived in Brussels, we originally planned to send out invitations to a major plant opening only in French or Flemish. But in some cases it was unclear by the name of the invitee whether he was French or Flemish, and we were strongly advised to send the invitations out in English rather than risk creating ill will.

The focus on Russia and Eastern Europe will continue to accelerate, meaning new opportunity. In 1989 we established an office within Moscow run by the first full-time Western public relations man in Russia. Things had changed dramatically from my previous visits to the USSR when it was mandatory that a speech I gave be sent well in advance to be translated by the local organization sponsoring my visit, lest my words contradict local dogma. Relations with the press are now easier, and what you say does not

have to be as circumscribed. Interest in public relations has increased in Russia, especially about how to use it to sell products. Three of our first clients were Russian organizations wanting to increase sales to the West.

The need for realism still exists, however. Ethnic considerations, if anything, are greater. That means public relations programs cannot be aimed just at the Russians but must take into account other nationalities. Even with goodwill, things cannot change immediately. As Russia and Eastern Europe move toward becoming societies of open information and communication, those firms operating there will still face a constantly evolving political situation. That makes it especially important for companies operating in these countries to continually monitor changes in key people and attitudes, especially if they plan to expand. Public relations practitioners often can help provide the necessary information to make proper decisions.

Respecting Local Customs

When you do business in foreign countries, the key to your success can be how quickly you become a part of that market. That often depends on your acceptance of local customs. That is sometimes difficult for Americans, who by nature are more relaxed and informal about relationships.

In Japan, China, most of Scandinavia and Germany, and many other parts of the world, you still do not use first names, even after you have met a person a few times. In many parts of the world, you do not include the wives for dinner. This is not purely a "macho" outlook; in most cases the wives would feel more uncomfortable than their husbands.

Some customs might make you swallow hard; when, for example, as a guest of honor at a Middle Eastern banquet you must swallow the sheep's eye. What you might feel is superstition is often of great importance to the local staff and company. In Malaysia a leading electronics company could not get its female staff to return to work until the local *Bomoh* (holy man) exorcised an evil spirit from the ladies' room.

In Hong Kong the expert in *Feng Shui* (wind and water) is a necessity even for the largest firms when it comes to acceptable office design or renovation. Every time we laid out an office, it was in part dictated by the Feng Shui man. It was of great importance to our staff—and in public relations all we have as a commodity is people.

In China understanding local customs becomes even more important, since the country remains a great enigma to the West. Without proper guidance, how many Western executives would know that formal thank-you notes are never written and that you should always leave something on your plate—otherwise, the host may think he has not served enough? You should not linger after the meal (once fruit is served and it is about 8:30, the banquet is usually over). There is no taboo about being a noisy eater (your host can and will talk through a mouthful of food, slurp his soup, sneeze or cough while continuing to eat). In various cultures, bad manners differ and what you might consider correct might actually be offensive and vice versa.

Position of the Multinational

In the '60s and early '70s, many people in Europe feared the influence of the multinational. Jean-Jacques Servan-Schreiber in his oft-quoted book *The American Challenge* stated that the power of the multinationals was so great that they were creating states within states and were, in reality, weakening local political structures. That coincided with the trend of more American firms and other multinationals to invest heavily in Europe. So

it was not only influentials, such as Servan-Schreiber, but also local manufacturers who feared being swamped and were vocal in their condemnations.

But economic conditions changed in the '80s. In some countries more foreign companies closed plants than opened them, and countries throughout the world sought more investment to cut unemployment. At the same time, many multinationals, appreciating that they were suspect, strove to be good local corporate citizens. Companies like Levi Strauss established social action plans in many countries without great fanfare but in the belief it was part of their corporate responsibility.

Corporations such as IBM, while recognizable as foreign ventures, have become acceptable parts of local cultures. Others were able to fade into the local landscape. Many Americans are unaware that Nescafé is not an American product but Swiss, or that Electrolux is not American but Swedish, or that Lever Brothers is Anglo-Dutch.

As companies became more greatly entrenched outside their borders, they began to give increased authority to local nationals. Europeans became more prevalent on American boards. European companies began to select more board members from outside their countries. As the '90s started, the Japanese were still the most closely controlled, but even there cracks appeared and a few Japanese firms even moved some controls from Tokyo.

Service organizations led the way in having local staff manage their overseas offices. Twenty-six of our overseas offices are run by nationals of those countries.

The more a part of the community the company becomes, the more actively it can take part in local politics without causing offense. A strong national staff with the help of outside counsel can advise the parent company what is most likely to happen in that country over the short and long term and what their possible options are.

Intricacies of International PR Program Management

Certain concepts are always valid in managing an international public relations program. These programs are typically used in addition to local PR activities geared specifically toward individual markets, which adhere to guidelines valid only for those markets. Let us use an American multinational as an example, though the same rules would hold for German, Swedish, French, or Japanese multinationals, as well as for government bureaus or other organizations.

The company has two major divisions that manufacture industrial products. They operate in most countries throughout the world with a strong local presence. Their products are known and respected, so there is no need for them to do a missionary communications job. They have been in the international business for many years and have built up a competent local management in most countries. In some countries they are considered good local corporate citizens, while in others they are tarred with the same brush as many other multinationals.

First we must differentiate between two different kinds of program—corporate and product. Tighter control is necessary with corporate programs, because an error can be more damaging.

In both cases a written program is needed. Each foreign operation should be asked to contribute to its preparation. Except where strict confidentiality is required all those involved in preparing the program should be shown the final result.

In the case of a marketing-oriented program, most of the input should come from local organizations, because they are close to the market. Public relations programs aimed at selling goods and services are usually the responsibility of the local sales or marketing manager. They must be closely coordinated with other forms of communications directed at the customer public, such as advertising. A distinct trend has emerged throughout the world for advertising agencies and public relations firms to work together in preparing an integrated communications program, with each of the disciplines having a different role.

An important reason for maintaining a centralized source is that ideas that result from a local program in one country can be transferred to another: ideas cross borders. That is nearly always true when dealing with industrial products, because what motivates an engineer in one country will motivate an engineer in another. The same is true with pharmaceutical products, because doctors throughout the world look for exactly the same information. In pharmaceuticals, though, one must take into account local legislation regarding drug promotion.

Even consumer promotion ideas cross borders. The public relations support that was given to Coca-Cola has been successful with worldwide promotions, because the product's appeal is universal.

If the audience profile is the same and the product fills the same need, public relations support can be the same. That is why food companies' recipe programs aimed at women's pages can succeed. If you are promoting Spanish olives and prepare a recipe for a dish called "steamed fish and olives," it would be necessary to change the recipe only to include the local fish that goes best with the flavor of olives—being sure to test the recipe with the actual item.

In the case of product-oriented programs, the parent company should always be aware of what is being done so it can lend support. Often material is already available that can be used to back up similar efforts in markets elsewhere. Also, the parent can provide guidance on proper use of trademarks or check product claims that the legal department might feel are questionable.

Another important reason for close coordination is that the parent company can provide information and background when a health scare starts in one country. These scares move quickly from country to country, and no one knows when this will arise—as the producers of apples, sugar, baby formula, pâté, and cheese have learned.

One must be wary of the local argument "it cannot work here" just because the concept came from another country. A program developed in England for a major brand of an international food company was used with suitable changes to sell the brand in France, Japan, Australia, and Canada. When Avon developed a marathon for women in Tokyo, an approach that Avon had used successfully in other countries, many Japanese said it was doomed to failure because Japanese women would not run in a public marathon. Not only did Japanese women run, but the Tokyo Marathon became Avon's most successful marathon at that time. Not only did Japanese women run in Tokyo, they ran in marathons throughout Japan, including areas that are considered much more traditional. This success led to Avon's starting women's relays in Japan, including one in which the racecourse was around the national palace. Avon achieved its main aim—greater identification with Japanese women—and had the added fillip of extensive coverage by all media, including television.

Promoting the Corporation Abroad

The parent company must be kept informed of all international efforts and activities to promote the corporation that may affect it, whether negatively or positively. A statement made about a company abroad can affect the stock in the United States, for instance, if it indicates that a major subsidiary is in serious financial trouble. The wrong statement abroad might endanger negotiations by the parent company to purchase or sell an overseas company. It could also get a company into trouble with the U.S. government if the statement relates to government policy on issues such as the Arab boycott of companies doing business with Israel or sensitive payments to foreign officials.

This does not suggest that all statements must come from the parent company. Rather, it means that corporations should prepare clear guidelines on which subjects local management can discuss without clearance and which subjects need clearance. Also, the guidelines should outline specific company policy on sensitive issues. For example, who is responsible within an oil company for comments in the event of an oil spill, a fire in a refinery, or a threatened takeover by the government of a foreign country?

While the parent company has the right to control dissemination of information on sensitive issues, it must realize that it has an equal responsibility to its subsidiaries. What is said at headquarters can have great effect in local countries. This effect can be serious because or the instantaneous transmission of news. For example, one company chairman commented in a financial release that the company was in excellent shape and the coming year should be a good one. At the same time its French subsidiary, which was losing money, was negotiating with militant unions. The unions used the parent company's statement, which was carried in the French press, to become more intransigent. The facts should not be tampered with, and there are U.S. regulations on release of information about company earnings. Had the French company been warned that such statements were a possibility, it could have factored that into its thinking about how to negotiate.

In another case, as an aside in an interview a U.S. company executive announced the closing of some overseas facilities before the local company had discussed it with local unions as required under local law. The company had a much more difficult time reaching terms with the local employees, and closing costs were considerably higher than necessary.

Even a statement by the president of the company supporting the position of the U.S. government can create difficulties with staff in a local country if they are emotionally in disagreement with the U.S. policy.

Some problems can be avoided through use of public relations departments in the local companies. There should be company-wide public relations meetings at least annually so views can be exchanged, positions integrated, and warnings sounded about sensitive areas.

Foreign Government Relations

Government relations are very sensitive and vary from country to country. The lobbying laws in the United States are probably the strictest. People representing foreign interests that are trying to affect legislation in any way must register with the U.S. government and spell out their involvement.

That is not necessary overseas. Also, conflict-of-interest laws are different, even in countries with similar types of government, such as England. A member of Parliament in England can be a director of a public relations firm or represent a trade union or a corporation and still be on their payroll. He has only to declare his interests.

Americans working on behalf of a foreign government or a foreign corporation as lobbyists must register. We, as a company, never accept a foreign government account without checking with the State Department to see if handling the account would undermine government policy. This, while not binding, is the same as informal clearance. The country

desk in the State Department is always cooperative in answering this type of request. Also, we do not have any overseas offices handle accounts that would be adverse to the interests of the government in which the office is located.

Government relations is a specialized skill and calls for special expertise in each country within which a firm operates. To lobby effectively in the United States, you must understand exactly how the Senate and the House of Representatives operate, something many foreigners do not. In England, you would have to understand the workings of the Civil Service, which has a great deal to say about legislation.

In some countries the key can be certain government departments; in others, a few individuals can make the difference. As both individual and group power bases continually change, the public relations professional must keep up with these changes.

It is not just the government that counts when you are concerned with legislation. Numbers of activist groups can provide support or opposition. Who would have thought a decade ago of the strength of environmentalists throughout the world? How many predicted the growing political clout of senior citizens? Noting that the American Association of Retired Persons (AARP) became the second largest group in the United States (next to the Catholic Church), a similar group —the Association of Retired Persons (ARP)— was formed in England and a group with similar aims began in Germany.

The increase in the number of groups taking a more active position has led to increased use of coalition building. Coalition building is the linkage of groups, at times seemingly disparate, working together to accomplish one objective. Sometimes these groups come together spontaneously. The amazing changes that took place in Eastern Europe during the very end of the 1980s in many cases had their impetus first among intellectuals, then students, then workers. It is for the skilled public relations executive to determine which groups he or she can help bring together to achieve a common objective.

Sometimes these similar interest groups come from outside the country, as shown by the number of industries from various countries pressuring Japan to open her borders to more imports; or the numerous pressure groups from many lands that fought—successfully—to get South Africa to change its policy on apartheid.

Since 1980 more and more governments and government departments have turned to greater use of public relations to get their messages across. Some government departments such as tourism and industrial development had done so for many years. Others followed their leads. In Germany one of the largest government campaigns was an AIDS education program. In England each new government privatization program was accompanied by strong public relations input and activity. In the United States the Army and the Postal Service both expanded their communications programs.

Countries also backed up their normal lobbying efforts by hiring outside counsel. The Sultan of Brunei launched a major program to present himself and his country in a more favorable light. The government of Turkey looked outside for guidance and support to get admittance to the Common Market. Japan, traditionally very conservative in public relations, expanded activities in the United States and Europe to present its side in the question of trade disputes.

In addition to countries, many cities, states, and regions spread their messages throughout the world, backing up their government efforts to bring in tourism and investment. A notable success was Lillehammer, Norway, whose effective public relations campaign was a major factor in its being selected as the site for the winter Olympics in 1994.

Governmental groups that had been traditional users became more sophisticated. One tourism organization zeroed in on American doctors and dentists because their research showed these groups vacationed more than average and had money to spend. Industrial development departments targeted the exact industries most likely to be attracted and held seminars, wrote newsletters, planned visits, and geared most of their publicity toward these groups.

Watchpost for Early Warning Signals

With increasing legislation aimed at companies or products, many companies are using public relations consultancies as an early warning system. This is especially true in Washington because of the size of the United States and in Brussels where Common Market legislation can affect a product's chance of success within the entire European community.

The watchpost assignment is also increasing in Japan, because Japan will have to continue to open its borders to an increasing number of foreign products. Without local assistance it is difficult to understand the nuances of Japanese law and custom and to make a proper judgment about trying to crack the Japanese market.

International Investor Relations

More companies are undertaking investor relations programs abroad, especially in Europe and Japan. Foreign investors are second only to U.S. pension funds in the net purchases of U.S. equities.

The most obvious financial objectives of an investor relations program overseas are the same as in the United States: keeping existing shareholders informed and loyal, gaining additional support for the stock, widening the shareholder base, and facilitating financing. (*See* Chapter 11.)

In order of importance, the key European financial markets are the United Kingdom, Germany, France, and Switzerland.

The investment communities are different from the United States and differ from one country to the other. In Switzerland virtually all of the investment management lies in the hands of the banks, ranging from the "Big Three" (Swiss Bank Corporation, The United Bank, and Credit Suisse) to small private banks. In the United Kingdom, on the other hand, there is great variety, with investment professionals scattered among investment banks (known as merchant banks), commercial banks (clearing banks), mutual funds (unit trusts), brokers, specialized investment management companies, insurance companies, and pension funds.

In Germany banks handle private customers, while for institutional portfolios the larger banks have created two types of investment management companies, one for publicly sold funds and the other for pension and other institutional funds. In France, too, banks dominate the investment scene, but many private customers give their business to French brokers. The large insurance companies and publicly sold funds (so-called Sicav's) manage their own portfolios.

These varied audiences have one common trait: They include few industry specialists. Those investment professionals whose duty is to follow U.S. securities do so as generalists. This is the key difference between investor relations in the United States and in Europe. Managers of American corporations are accustomed to addressing American analysts who understand their industry in considerable depth, its terms of reference, and special jargon. Not so overseas. The chief executive officer on a European tour must learn to address foreign analysts as he would a lay audience, albeit a highly intelligent one. What is more, for audiences on the Continent, English is not their first language, so what the CEO has to say must also be linguistically precise and easy to understand. While most European tours by top management include London, Paris, Frankfurt, and Zurich, Edinburgh is growing in importance, and Amsterdam and sometimes Brussels are included.

It is even more difficult in Japan where, in many cases, a translator is involved—sometimes following the English and sometimes translating simultaneously. The translator obviously is not normally aware of the specialist terms within the industry and so a day should be put aside to brief the translator carefully in advance.

The most sophisticated U.S. corporations have discovered that investor relations functions abroad can provide convenient platforms for other corporate communications: to put the company into focus for target audiences other than investors, to publicize expansion or acquisition plans in Europe, and to support marketing efforts. Also, a company facing a controversial issue in a particular country can use an investor relations function as a neutral platform to state its position. Thus it often pays to plan a European investor relations program within a wider frame of reference.

There are non-financial reasons for listing on certain exchanges even though trading will be limited. These primarily relate to corporate visibility. Frequently, even very large U.S. corporations have facilities in Europe whose size is quite modest. A listing on the national stock exchange and the attendant and ongoing publicity may be important to the European general managers in their dealings with the authorities, banks, and other organizations. A listing means closer identification with the host country and is a goodwill gesture toward the local financial and business communities. Listing in the company's key markets also ensures better coverage of company news by the press, supports marketing efforts, and creates potential financing advantages on the local market.

More than in the United States, investor relations in Europe are closely linked with other forms of public relations. Handling a European financial relations program successfully thus requires close cooperation between communications and financial functions.

One complaint that institutions have overseas is that top managements come to make presentations once a year or once very two years, but between those visits they learn little about the company. To be effective, a financial relations program must be ongoing and key influencers provided with a continuing flow of information.

This can be thorough follow-up visits, corporate advertising, publicity, and direct mail.

Global markets require global and simultaneous access to information. That has led to the emergence of satellite teleconferencing as the best method for presenting news to multiple audiences at the same time or directly to foreign audiences. For example, Glaxo, the UK's largest pharmaceutical company, was able to use a satellite from London for a presentation and question-and-answer period to leading members of the Japanese financial community in Tokyo. As international communication costs continue to drop, this will increasingly become the norm.

The Worldwide Webs of the Internet are also being used more frequently.

Relations with International Employees

Many countries face a demographic pattern of an aging society. The percentage of people in the active workforce is due to decline. That means increased competition for staff at all levels and a greater need to adapt employee practices to help tie the individual to the firm. Salary packages alone often are not enough. Communications can be a major factor in keeping employees. It must run two ways. The employee needs the opportunity to communicate ideas upward and have them listened to. More and more information must permeate throughout the organization so all levels are kept informed.

As noted previously, it is important when starting in another country to take into account the local culture. But that doesn't mean you can't inject some of your own. As Japanese automotive manufacturers moved into the United States, they followed many American concepts but included their policy of making the workers much more of the overall team; in general, the result was a record of labor harmony. When Nissan opened the first one-union automotive plant in the United Kingdom in an area that had a long tradition of multiunion operations, they were careful to seek the workers' opinion. And they agreed that the workers did not have to sing the company song.

As companies spread their wings throughout the world, they will have to establish systems by which staff at all levels can communicate. There has always been the suggestion box, which has been effective. But more organizations are sending out employee questionnaires and conducting focus groups, not only to find out what the employee is thinking but to learn ways the company might improve.

Any employee relations program should be continuous and become a fabric of the operation. In some areas where the political situation is unstable, governments can change frequently, and both the position and acceptability of foreign concerns also change. Those companies with a history of good employee relations often receive more favorable treatment.

Many employees of foreign companies know little about the parent company. Often managers report they learn most about the parent company from what they read in the American business press or even their local papers.

Companies should have a basic brochure about the company that is given to all employees in the local language. It should describe the history of the company, how it has developed, where the company operates, and the products it makes. The more the employee knows about the company he or she works for, the greater the sense of involvement and the more favorable will be his or her attitude and comments within the local community. There is no better person to tell the company story in a foreign country than the local employee.

The Differences and Importance of Foreign Media

International media relations as a proportion of the activity undertaken by public relations practitioners in the United States has steadily decreased. The proportion of journalists being employed by consultancies has also declined. Investor relations, government relations, employee relations, corporate positioning, crisis management, and marketing public relations have expanded in significance, calling for different backgrounds and skills. While that is basically true overseas, in many countries these newer activities have not reached the same level of acceptance as in the United States. So international media relations remains of primary importance.

The types of media are the same throughout most of the world. Instead of the *Wall Street Journal* there is the *Financial Times* in England, *Handelsblatt* in Germany, *Nihon Keizai Shimbun* in Japan, *Neue Zürcher Zeitung* in Switzerland, *Corriere della Sera* in Italy, the *Australian Financial Review*, etc. Instead of AP and UPI, there are the Hsinhua News Agency, Tass, Reuters, Agence France Presse, Deutsche Press Agentur, New Zealand Associated Press, the Middle East News Agency, etc.

There are newspapers of all political persuasions, women's magazines, men's magazines, news magazines, sports magazines, entertainment magazines, and so on. The numbers depend on the size of the country and its interests.

In many countries, there is also a well-developed trade press interested in the latest technical developments regardless of where they originate. Most European countries have a wide range of technical magazines that reach nearly all opinion formers. These publications are on the lookout for technical articles, because they do not receive the constant flow of material their Western counterparts do.

In most countries, you would apply the same criterion to whether a story is good for a newspaper, wire service, or a trade magazine: Is it news and and is it news that would interest their readers?

The biggest change and growth of opportunity is electronic media. Throughout the world, an increasing number of radio and TV stations have been licensed. They are constantly on the lookout for material. Cable TV and satellites have also increased the possibilities. Cable Network News (CNN) has made a major impact and is continuing to grow rapidly. In Europe, Sky TV has made an impact.

Many countries that previously had only government TV have added commercial channels; and there has been a great expansion of regional channels. Regional and national radio have expanded both in number of stations and type of material they broadcast. When you have an important executive visiting abroad, it often creates a great opportunity for an interview with a news or business program.

Translation Requirements

Even in the 1980s some companies still sent press material to foreign publications in English. The result is that it got the same attention a press release in Japanese would get at the *New York Times*.

All material to newspapers, wire services, and news magazines must be in the language of the country. The only exception is technical magazines. Sometimes they prefer to receive bylined stories in English so they can arrange the translation and be assured that the proper translations are made of difficult technical terms. It is wise when placing a technical article that has been translated to send the original English along so the editor can judge whether the translation has been perfect.

Proper translations are always a problem because new technical terms are constantly being introduced and idioms sometimes vital to the sense of the original release are difficult to translate. For those working on stories that are to be translated into a variety of languages, the rule is to avoid idioms and humor, and to write with an eye to an easy translation.

Numerous stories exist of the results of improper translations. One translation of a technical story had the phrase *water goat*— the original English was *hydraulic ram*. A translated financial release in Italy, when referring to the market, used a word relating to a supermarket rather than a stock market as an ideal place to float shares.

In general, translation should be done in the country involved if possible, and no translation should ever be sent out without being checked by someone from the company organization fluent in the language involved.

Proper Timing of Worldwide Releases

A difficult problem to resolve is how to send out stories simultaneously in many parts of the world. To deserve this treatment a story has to be of major importance, such as a scientific or technological breakthrough, an announcement of a major new drug, or a significant announcement from a company that has world stature about acquisition or a major retrenchment or expansion.

Of special importance is how to disseminate a financial release such as year-end earnings or quarterly statements. The stock exchanges have specific rules about publishing financial information. You cannot send confidential financial data overseas days in advance for translation, lest you run the risk of too many people being able to act on "insider information." So you must alert the people in the overseas country that it will come at a specific time and to have a translator available so it can be translated, approved, and disseminated. Time is lost but there is no alternative.

Too many companies send out a financial release in the United States, then send it abroad later as somewhat of an afterthought. By the time it is translated and mailed out, at least a day has elapsed. If the story was significant, it was already transmitted by the wire services and the local paper, if interested, would have printed it.

One unique system involves Japan, where there are about forty press clubs, all attached to government ministries or major nonprofit business organizations. Each includes members of key national media and is their "beat." Each press club has two or three *Kanji* (chairmen), and the chairmanship usually rotates every two months among member publications. They arrange members' attendance at press conferences, distribute press releases to members, and are virtually all-powerful during their time. So when a press conference is to be held or a release sent to a specific club, the press officer in Tokyo informs the Kanji at least one day in advance and gets permission.

The Kanji, if he desires, can ensure that press conferences are boycotted or refuse press release distribution. He does so when he feels the press release does not carry enough information, has wrong information, is exaggerated, or is not newsworthy. While to many Westerners it might appear to be a barrier to the free flow of information, it is in keeping with the cultural norm in Japan. It underlines the need to understand the nuances of the country to run a successful public relations program.

Other countries have their own peculiarities and some touch a Western nerve. One is payment to journalists. In one Far Eastern country it was, and sometimes still is, a custom to send the journalist a small fee to cover a press conference. This was not considered a bribe (and could be as little as 15¢), but it was to pay for the journalist's transportation to and from the press conference location, since in this country expense allowances were very low.

Some newspapers make it clear that certain types of information, such as personnel releases, are charged for at a specific rate if they are to be printed. The Middle East is an area where payment for editorial space is most predominant. Some newspapers quote editorial rates. It is culturally acceptable that stories that might be of interest but are marginal should be paid for.

Critical Role of Backgrounders and Corporate Interviews

Key publications abroad want to cover business activities in the United States, but even some of the larger publications do not have adequate budgets and staff to cover all key American industries and companies. So they are pleased to interview top executives or other members of management with specific expertise (research, overseas sales, etc.).

When setting up an interview for an American executive abroad, it's important to remember that companies that are a household word in the United States are relatively unknown in many parts of the world. It is advisable to provide the prospective interviewer with detailed background on the company and the topics the executive will discuss, and if the executive is senior you should provide a photograph. Newspaper reporters throughout the world do not want to meet executives just to exchange pleasantries; they want to talk about things that are hard news. Also, they want a local angle; they are usually not interested in a plant expansion in Pittsburgh or Houston.

Executive interviews do more than result in an immediate story. They personalize the company with the paper. There is a dramatic increase in news that subsequently appears about a company after one of its top executives has been interviewed.

Often an executive traveling abroad can get major coverage in the United States by giving an interview overseas to a local bureau. Material filed from the London bureau of the *Wall Street Journal* has a good chance of appearing in print. Often the local reporter and the executive have the time for a more in-depth story than would be the case in the United States.

Not only when an executive is going to be

interviewed is it advisable to send a back-grounder to the media. If a company plans to disseminate material about the company on a continuing basis in a country, it is wise to provide a background in the language of the country to key media. That will help them flesh out a piece and help get the company included in round-up stories the publication prepares.

Coordinating Press Visits to the U.S. and Abroad

International public relations is a two-way street so far as press relations are concerned.

It is sometimes advisable to invite the American press to see a company's overseas operation to provide a total picture of the corporation's activities. Some publications, such as the *Wall Street Journal* and *Business Week*, insist on paying for their transporta-tion, so the story must be meaningful for them to send someone. Also, it's important that they have access to the top management abroad.

There is an increasing trend to bring for-eign journalists to the United States to inter-view U.S. management and to see production or research facilities. Such trips must be care-fully thought out and coordinated. There must be proper briefings before the journal-ists leave their own country. Because the jour-nalist will be away from the desk for so long a time, the company must provide the amount of time and information needed for a worth-while story. Overseas travel is exhausting, so time should also be allotted for leisure, most of it planned (theater, concerts, dinners, etc.) because usually the journalist is unfamiliar with the country. There should always be an afternoon or evening where the journalist can select his or her own form of amusement.

It is important to know the degree of flu-ency of the visiting journalists. Most jour-nalists coming on such a trip will be relatively fluent in English, but any speeches to them should avoid idioms and colloquialisms.

Sometimes if the story is of interest but not significant enough to have a major publica-tions send someone thousands of miles, it is advisable to make your story part of a larger one. That can be done arranging for the jour-nalist to see someone noncompetitive in your industry or someone from another industry who has a similar story to tell.

If you are bringing a group of journalists, it is important they know if a competitive publication is also being invited. The same is true if you are inviting U.S. journalists abroad. Often *Business Week* would not be interested if you are offering the same story to *Fortune*.

Global Crisis Management and Risk Analysis

As worldwide communications channels broadened, so did the need for crisis man-agement. (*See* Chapters 2 and 20.) There were very few people who did not know about Thalidomide, Bhopal, Chernobyl, or the Alaska oil spill. What happened to a corpo-ration in one country often had major impact in many others. In most cases, though unfor-tunately not all, there was an attempt to man-age the crisis. At Chernobyl the Russians for the first time admitted a crisis, admitted neg-ligence, and tried to let the world know they were trying to handle it as effectively as pos-sible. Johnson & Johnson became the text-book case for proper procedure for its han-dling of the Tylenol case after people died in Chicago when some capsules were laced with cyanide by an unknown perpetrator.

Now crisis management is no longer enough, because of the growing international ramifications of potential problems. Crisis preparedness became the new byword. Multinational companies decided not to wait for the crisis to happen. Just as airlines always knew that someday they faced the problem of a crash, many food companies knew a salmonella outbreak could happen as occurred with Belgian pâté exported to England. Companies now run crisis preparedness seminars for staff and prepare instruction manuals in different languages saying what to do and how they are to communicate in a crisis.

Companies are now moving one step further—to risk analysis. No longer is it enough to know what to do when a crisis occurs. What is important is to study the business in various markets and decide which risks are most likely to occur. Then you are able to establish in more detail sensible approaches to various significant publics should the risk turn into reality.

James Lindheim, our European-based authority on the subject, reports that rationality and facts do not usually control perceptions of risk, so corporations must not assume that facts, no matter how compelling, will carry the day. This was certainly found to be true by the nuclear energy industry throughout many parts of Europe. Also, the source of information about a risk can be crucial. Developing medical, community, and government leaders as spokespeople within your markets is far more important than direct communication from your management.

In addition, you can create trust by emphasizing in advance what corporate actions have been to monitor, manage, and reduce risk. A chemical company moving into the Far East should from the very beginning not only stress the advantages of the products it produces but also what it is doing to minimize risk. It is important to build support and understanding among employees, especially when you are a foreign company, because they have greater believability in the individual marketplace than American spokespeople.

As more and more activist groups arise, even in parts of the world previously known for a strong laissez-faire attitude such as Asia, and issues from animal testing to water pollution move more deeply into the public psyche, the PR practitioner will be pressed to provide answers quickly and effectively. As noted earlier, the shift will move even faster from those with journalistic backgrounds, to sociologists, psychologists, and others with specialized knowledge.

Speaker Preparation

While speaker training for executives before they talk to the press, security analysts, government committees, and action groups has been prevalent in the United States for many years, it is even more vital in the international arena. Language differences make it important to enunciate the key messages clearly. It is important to train local spokespeople in various parts of the world. This is by far most difficult in Japan. For cultural reasons the Japanese do not like to appear as spokespeople. They believe strongly in consensus, not individual action; and they are uncomfortable with any type of unfriendly questioning.

When an American spokesperson is going to talk abroad, it is vital that he or she be trained in the key issues facing that country and not only on what he or she feels is important. Issues and their significance often change, so there should be an update-training session every year. Some executives perform better before foreign groups than others. In Asia a dynamic, forceful chairman or president might not be as effective as a more soft-spoken vice-president of research.

Event Promotion

In the world of international communications the role of event marketing is taking on increasing importance. Events, whether based on sports, art, or entertainment, easily cross borders. People throughout Europe understand European football (soccer) and are learning a great deal more about American football, which has started a league in Europe. Rock groups draw throughout the world, providing great opportunities for the companies sponsoring them. Art exhibitions and symphony orchestras appeal on a universal plane.

Companies have rushed to sponsor sporting events and stars. Companies increasingly sponsor art exhibitions and orchestras. They saw the opportunity to reach specific up-market audiences with high spending power. Entertainment sponsorship is also expanding dramatically. After Frank Sinatra, Sammy Davis Jr., and Liza Minnelli had a major success touring the United States under the sponsorship of American Express they had similar success throughout Europe. Entertainment sponsorship can work for a region or a country. When Levi Strauss wanted to increase the appeal of their jeans to the youth market of Germany, it sponsored a series of concerts of German rock and roll artists.

In addition to sponsorships, there are major events that occur on a regular basis wherein companies can take an active part such as the Olympics, World Fairs, industrial trade shows, or ones that are really special such as the U.S. Bicentennial or the French Bicentennial.

It is important to carefully select the event according to marketing needs and not to choose it just because it is available. After the initial outlay, the key to success is how you merchandise it to various audiences in each country, such as customers, staff, and local and federal government officials. Many companies spend large sums to acquire the rights to use athletes or entertainers and don't spend the relatively small amounts necessary to make sure the event they are sponsoring achieves maximum effectiveness. Burson-Marsteller's scope (Sports Capability Profile) helps companies systematically match their product or service category with an appro-

priate sports vehicle. RVA (Relative Value Assessment) enables companies to objectively evaluate event sponsorship opportunities.

Utilizing Public Relations Consultancies Abroad

The public relations consultancy business has grown dramatically around the world. Few countries do not have a number of capable consultancies. They vary from local offices of large multinational organizations to small one- or two-person shops.

Even the large multinational consultancies differ in their approach. Some, such as Burson-Marsteller, have wholly owned offices. Others have tie-ups with local organizations that work together under one umbrella, sharing mutual clients.

Whether to pick a multinational or local consultancy depends on the job to be done and the funds available. In nearly all cases, the majority of the employees of a multioffice firm are local, with the same knowledge as employees at the local agencies. But the degree of expertise a multinational firm can offer differs from country to country. The key, just as in the United States, is who will work on the project and what are their backgrounds.

Before selecting a public relations firm abroad, it's wise to do some basic research. In some countries, such as England or France, local consultancy associations can provide a list of their members by particular areas of expertness. For names of practitioners in developing countries, the International Public lic Relations Association, headquartered in London, is a good source. (*See* Appendix.)

Checks can also be made with people in local media, companies in the same industry, and people in aligned communications industries, such as advertising or marketing. Check to see how long an international public relations firm has been active in the market or markets being considered. If the assignment is regional, find out how often they have handled accounts in the countries involved.

Considering the relatively small size of the markets, public relations is more expensive abroad. In Belgium you have to work in three languages (English, French, and Flemish); in Switzerland sometimes four (English, French, German, and Italian); and in Malaysia sometimes four (English, Chinese, Malay, and Tamil). The use of time is different in many countries. In Japan the local culture calls for a series of meetings and discussions, each taking numerous hours, and since the only marketable product a public relations firm has is hours, that is expensive.

Because you pay for hours, help the consultancy make those hours effective. Provide them with as much background as possible, shortening the learning curve. Try not to change direction often. Establish contact for them with your local executives, licensees, or distributors. Make clear exactly what their assignment and areas of responsibility are. Make sure that directions are funneled from only one source. And realize that there might

not be the same reaction times in countries where public relations is relatively new.

It is necessary to insist on a businesslike approach to a consultancy-client relationship. Insist on a written program. Insist on receiving continuing contact reports and status reports. Insist that bills be itemized for out-of-pocket expenses.

No consultancy replaces the need for internal public relations competence. To function effectively, the public relations firm must deal with a professional internal public relations staff. This is especially true when the consultancy is abroad and the client is in the United States, because distance and cultural differences can lead to confusion and misunderstanding. Because of cost and distance, an outside consultancy should not be employed to do what the company itself can do. They should be used only to add competence, not duplication of effort. Also, termination procedures must be clear and fair. If the consultancy has had to add staff to handle the account, in many countries, such as Japan, Italy, Spain, and Belgium, it is very difficult to let staff go and, where it is possible, it is costly.

Section 6

THE PRACTICE OF PUBLIC RELATIONS

46

ORGANIZATION AND FUNCTION OF THE CORPORATE PUBLIC RELATIONS DEPARTMENT

CHARLES H. PROUT

Charles H. Prout headed the public relations functions at three major American companies and is a well-known writer on public relations.

Now retired, he was vice-president, communications, of Eaton Corporation, where he directed a multimillion-dollar program encompassing all internal and external communications worldwide. Previously he was vice-president, corporate relations and corporate secretary for Cutler-Hammer, Inc., electrical/electronics manufacturing. He organized and had full responsibility for the public relations function, and served as chairman of the company's Public Policy Committee and president of the Cutler-Hammer Foundation. For nine years prior to joining Cutler-Hammer in 1963, he had been director of public relations at Mead Johnson & Company, pharmaceutical and nutritional products manufacturer.

He founded and edited PR Reporter, *a professional newsletter, which became one of the leading professional periodicals in the public relations field.*

Though certainly not the first socioeconomic sector in the United States to recognize the need for or the value of organized public relations, business has since fully embraced the profession and incorporated it into its very fiber. Several recent studies show that virtually every medium-sized to large company, as well as hundreds of smaller ones, now operate formal functions described as public relations, public affairs, and/or communications.

This widespread acceptance results, in part, from the increased and urgent public pressures facing our tumultuous society today. It also stems from corporate management's growing recognition of and respect for the myriad positive contributions that good public relations can bring to corporate growth and progress.

The Pivotal Corporate Role of Public Relations

The first sixteen chapters of this book focus on the principles of public relations in a business organization. This chapter outlines the functional responsibilities for planning and coordinating the company's interface with its publics. In other words, public relations is that function within the company responsible for ensuring corporate goodwill—by protecting the goodwill the company has already gained, by building additional stores of it for the future, and by using it to safeguard and facilitate the company's public affairs position.

Public relations, in essence, builds acceptance for the corporation as a whole much as marketing departments build acceptance for individual products.

To accomplish its role public relations often has to take two different postures: defensive in the face of attack; positive in the effort to enhance goodwill. But in all cases it must be based on coordinating corporate performance with the public interest while simultaneously assuring public awareness and understanding of that performance. As has often been stated in public relations circles, "No organization can be made to look better than it actually is." Public relations cannot be fancy window dressing for a company whose policies and actions are unworthy of public scrutiny and acclaim. So, essentially, good corporate public relations begins at the top management level with establishment of company policies and practices that are ethical, honest, and in keeping with the public interest. Then the public relations staff function can take those policies and practices to the public for acclaim, understanding, and, if need be, for use as defense against attack.

Two things corporate public relations should not be—but often is misinterpreted as—is a willy-nilly "do gooder" function or a purely publicity operation.

Publicity is a tool of public relations and, as such, is widely and effectively used. But publicity does not constitute a public relations program any more than an employment office represents a personnel program or a bookkeeper represents a financial division. Only insofar as a management recognizes this difference can it hope to make effective use of public relations.

"Doing good" is a logical part of a sound public relations program because such action helps keep corporate actions aligned with the public interest. But public relations cannot be an effective part of the management team if it is not contributing toward corporate progress. Tangential, inconsequential activities designed to do good with no discernible benefit to the corporation can become wasteful and noncontributory.

T. J. Ross, one of the early leaders of the profession, lent emphasis to the point when he said:

> A public relations man is not worth his salt if he succumbs to "pie-in-the-sky" thinking divorced from the realities of his business. And he will not stay long on the management team if he does. In his zeal to place his corporation in the most favorable public light, he must not forget that a business is first and foremost a profit-making enterprise, not an eleemosynary institution. In the relationships he seeks to create between the corporation and its publics, he may be softhearted, but he must not be softheaded.

Functional Scope of Public Relations

In actual practice, the role of public relations in corporations varies widely with the type and size of company, management's understanding of the proper uses of public relations, and the caliber of the internal public relations staff and/or external public relations counsel.

This is not surprising since public relations is still such a new facet of business life; concepts for its proper use have not fully permeated the business community. In truth, even many long-established business functions, such as advertising, human resources, and finance, still tend to vary considerably in their application in different companies.

However, the preferred and most productive role for public relations in the modern corporation has been clearly defined and demonstrated in many companies that have had long experience in the field.

Public relations properly practiced at the corporate level should be an integral part of the top management team, serving alongside such other staff functions as finance, human resources, legal, and long-range planning, to provide guidance and counsel on the corporation's basic decision processes. At the same time, it must be geared to provide professional communications planning and service to both the corporation as a whole and the various operating units on a broad range of subjects from management communications to financial disclosure to marketing publicity.

To achieve these objectives, the public relations staff must be prepared to function in five basic service areas:

1. Advice
2. Communications service
3. Public issues research and analysis
4. Public relations action programs
5. Integration of all communications functions

Advice on public relations-connected subjects is provided to both corporate management and the management of other departments and divisions. Since public relations is a staff function, it customarily does not establish policies or make basic operating deci-

sions. But it bears a direct responsibility to seek, identify, and recommend to management appropriate corporate decisions and policies to assure maintenance of an even public relations keel.

Ideally, the top corporate public relations executive does this by sitting as a member of the corporate management committee and in personal discussion with line management executives. However, lacking such a position in the organization, he or she still has the responsibility to make recommendations through whatever oral or written channels are available within the structure of the company.

These recommendations may range from advising on the best way a public announcement of a corporate action might be made, to recommending a change in a basic corporate policy or proposed activity to bring it closer into line with the public interest; and from analyzing and interpreting the impact on the company of pending governmental policies or regulations, to producing a corporate information program designed to help the company advance toward its goals or to cope with problems.

The Public Relations Society of America's task force *Report on the Stature and Role of Public Relations* (the "Lesly Report") said the success of the public relations professional's performance of this function determines the ultimate success of the entire program.

Communications service is the role most frequently associated with public relations. It includes the outward communication of information about the company and its activities to all publics of interest to the company via whatever communications media are appropriate.

It is far broader than mere issuance of news releases. Communications service encompasses the total process of projecting the corporate image, whether via news media, setting a corporate citizenship example, or disseminating information about the company's

688 The Practice of Public Relations

actions and motives in booklets, speeches, or advertisements. It includes assuring compliance with requirements for appropriate public disclosure of financial, environmental protection, and product safety information. It also includes communicating the company's views on pending legislative and regulatory issues to leaders of government, as well as to employees, shareholders, and other interested publics. In essence, it is the function of "letting the public know" by whatever means are appropriate to the individual situation.

Public issues research and analysis is a less widely known activity but has been one of the fastest growing and most significant facet of the development of corporate public relations. (*See* Chapter 2.) While communications service implies outward dissemination of information, public issues research and analysis means the identification, evaluation, and communication inward to the company of information of the outside world that may be of value to the company in managing its affairs—the business equivalent of military intelligence.

While deeply engaged in the day-to-day operations of a business, management often has neither the opportunity nor the inclination to stay fully abreast of outside developments of interest to the company. Through close association with public agencies and publications and through professional journals, clipping services, and opinion surveys, the public relations department can often detect trends or anticipate events of pertinence to the company. Or it may seek out and measure tides of public opinion that may affect the company's operations. This is particularly true in the case of government regulation and legislation but also applies, on occasion, to many other forms of sociopolitical pressure and/or expectation. When broad or specific evaluation of a climate of opinion is desired, an opinion survey may be called for. (*See* Chapter 18.)

Public relations action programs encompass a variety of programs designed specifically to build acceptance for the company among its various publics—customers, plant communities, stockholders, and so on—or to further the company's views on current issues.

Though all public relations activities are intended to produce goodwill to one degree or another, some of them are neutral or defensive—designed to maintain goodwill or protect it against attack. On the other hand, public relations action programs are usually more comprehensive, more positive, and more creative. They are designed to generate new goodwill or enhance that which already exists—to increase company acceptance with customers as a means of indirectly stimulating sales (*see* Chapters 14 and 15), with government agencies to avert restrictive rulings (*see* Chapters 4–6), with the local community to reduce friction over industrial annoyances (*see* Chapter 8), to attract more and better employees.

In some instances, corporate public relations programs may encompass noncommercial services provided to customers or other publics. By thus helping the publics with some of their own problems, acceptance and goodwill are engendered for the sponsor that presumably may be converted to increased sales or cooperation at a later date when the company's need is great. However, *Fortune* points out that such giving is clearly designed, for the most part, to benefit the corporation's own long-term interests—or at least what is perceived as their own long-term interests.

In another area, the public relations operation may provide product publicity to marketing divisions. Often through other programs, encompassing the use of publicity in the editorial channels of the public and trade media plus other means of exposure in influence-molding locations and situations, acceptance for a company or product can be achieved that would be almost impossible through direct advertising and promotion alone.

Such acceptance often takes the form of a ground swell of public awareness and use of a product or adoption of a corporate concept. As a consequence, such promotion is most effective when the product or concept is new, although promotional publicity can be used successfully to support continuing programs.

Because it is usually quite difficult to fully separate such promotional publicity and corporate publicity, this type of activity is often centered in the central public relations department, even while other purely product promotion is concentrated within the separate marketing units. Of equal importance is the fact that product publicity involves specialized personnel and techniques that are most economically provided on a service basis to all marketing divisions from a central department, as needed.

Integration of everything that affects public attitudes or opinion is essential to avert inconsistencies and to enhance synergy.

Functional Responsibilities of the PR Department

The list of functions performed by corporate public relations departments to accomplish the role just described varies from company to company, but certain standard functions have emerged as common in most balanced departments. They are listed in approximate order of prevalence.

- **Public relations policy**—Develop and recommend corporate public relations policies, contribute public relations viewpoint in formulation of corporate decisions, help define and establish the corporation's public relations "posture." Provided mainly to top management but also to other departments and divisions.

- **Corporate statements**—Preparation of speeches and other statements by corporate executives not only projects the judgments and influence of the company. In developing these statements, public relations people often participate strongly in developing and articulating policies.

- **Corporate publicity**—Development and issuance of announcements of company activities to external communications media, handling inquiries from the press, and development and placement of promotional publicity about the corporation as a whole or any of its units.

- **Product publicity**—Announcement of new products through editorial channels of communications media and development and execution of promotional product publicity campaigns.

- **Government relations**—Maintain liaison with appropriate governmental units at local, state, and national levels; report trends in government affecting the company; advise action as needed; help prepare for and direct corporate appearances before investigating bodies or legislative hearings; direct programs designed to promote the company's point of view in legislative or regulatory matters.

- **Community relations**—Plant community contacts; performance and/or coordination of corporate "good neighbor" activities, including compliance with environmental protection standards, fostering equal employment opportunity, and cooperating in urban improvement programs; development of community understanding of company's problems and needs.

- **Inventory relations**—Communications between company and shareholders, as well as between company and the investment community in general; development of acceptance of company among investors via broadening exposure of company's policies and financial results in the investment community; preparation of annual report, quarterly reports, dividend check inserts, etc.; planning and staging annual meetings of stockholders and appearances before meetings of security analysts.

- **Institutional promotion**—Programs designed to build corporate acceptance among key publics: including institutional advertising, public relations literature, and special events.
- **Corporate donations**—Develop policy for company contributions, process donations requests; administer company's foundation, and conduct employee solicitations for approved drives.
- **Employee publications**—Prepare and publish employee magazine, newspaper, bulletins, management communications, etc.
- **Guest relations**—Plant tours, new plant and/or building dedications, and guest reception activities.
- **Coordinating and integrating**
- **Miscellaneous**—Speakers' bureau; education relations.

Probably the broadest study ever made of corporate departments' functions, conducted by Neomathics for AT&T Communications, revealed the following:

- Thirty percent of time (after policy functions and administration and not counting investor relations) is spent communicating with media, 24 percent with employees, 21 percent with communities, 16 percent with mass audiences, and 7 percent with government.
- Of time spent on financial communication, 46 percent is devoted to annual and quarterly reports; 31 percent to communicating with analysts, brokers, etc.; 10 percent to annual and quarterly meetings; 8 percent to written and phone responses to queries.

- In media relations, 45 percent of time is spent handling inquiries, 42 percent preparing and issuing news releases, and only 4 percent on news conferences.
- The mean number of releases issued per year is 108. They are sent to an average of 287 recipients. The average release is two pages.
- The mean number of media inquiries received per month is 80.

The Position of Public Relations in the Corporate Structure

To operate effectively, the function must fit into the corporate organization structure directly under top management. This reporting relationship to top management has emerged strongly over the years, as experience has demonstrated its necessity.

This is easy to understand in light of our outline of the role and functions of the public relations department. Most of the functions listed are of direct concern to top management—and are of only indirect or partial concern to any one of the operating divisions or departments of a company.

The specific person to whom public relations reports in top management varies with the company's overall organizational structure. Most frequently that person is the president. Others may include the chairman of the board, the board of directors itself, or an executive vice-president who includes other people-related functions in his or her responsibilities.

Departmental Organization

The designation under which the public relations department or its top executive is known is most often *public relations*. However, in recent years the tendency in a number of companies has been to move to other designations deemed to more fully encompass the range of responsibilities or to avoid negative connotations that have become attached to the term *public relations* in some people's minds.

The choice of alternate designation seems to vary with the size of the company. In a Conference Board study of 141 medium- and large-sized corporations, the split was almost even between *public relations* and *public affairs*, with names such as *corporate communications* and *corporate relations* following at a distance. Other assorted designations trailed even further behind.

The trend toward other terms is noticed primarily among large corporations. As pointed out in the report of the Special Committee on Terminology of the Public Relations Society of America, written by Philip Lesly, almost all organizations in the field throughout the world use *public relations* in their titles. Almost all publications and books also carry that term.

Since *public relations* is by all standards the most commonly accepted designation—and as this book indicates, *public affairs* is encompassed within it—it is used throughout this chapter to encompass all of the aforementioned titles. The reader may make such mental substitutions in the semantics of nomenclature as seem desirable—the substance will remain the same.

The size and organization of the public relations department naturally varies with the size of the company and the scope of the public relations program. Departments range from one-man operations in smaller corporations to organizations of more than 200 persons in some giant companies.

Surveys by *PR Reporter*, a leading professional newsletter, and by the Conference Board have determined that among many large corporations in the United States, the average public relations department has between five and twenty professional staff members. By contrast, smaller organizations (including businesses, associations, and institutions) usually have public relations staffs of three to ten persons.

In addition, of course, many of these companies also retain public relations firms or counsel.

The corporate public relations department usually is headed by a person bearing the title of vice-president or director of public relations. However, designations such as senior vice-president or executive vice-president also are used in some large companies as the breadth of the public relations function grows. In some smaller firms or in those where public relations has not achieved full management recognition and confidence, public relations manager is the title applied.

The vice-presidential designation is rapidly growing in use both because management has recognized the significance of the contribution to corporate affairs made by the public relations function and because the title facilitates the public relations department's dealings with other departments and divisions of the company, as well as with outside groups.

Obviously, the allocation of functions among staff members of the public relations department varies widely from company to company, according to the needs of the organization and the abilities of the individuals. There is no absolutely right or wrong. The first staff member to be added usually is assigned responsibility for press relations and publicity, since that is the single heaviest area of workload. The department head personally handles all other duties. Later staff additions normally are assigned such responsibilities as community relations, stockholder relations, institutional promotion, government relations, employee communications, and so on, according to the needs of the particular company.

In larger, multiplant companies members

of the public relations department often are assigned to detached service at various regional plant locations. In such instances, the staff member may have a dual reporting relationship: a direct staff responsibility to the regional vice-president or the plant manager and a dotted-line policy relationship to the central public relations department.

Similarly, in larger, multidivision corporations with independent divisional marketing functions, members of the central public relations department often are assigned on detached service with each division or at least to all that are large enough to require such service. These persons normally devote most of their time to promotional product publicity for the divisions concerned, whereas the central public relations department carries on all other corporate public relations functions and provides product publicity service to those divisions not large enough to support a full-time staff member.

In particularly large and decentralized companies, each divisional public relations office takes on a more autonomous role and performs a complete range of public relations functions. As in the case of the public relations staff on plant duty, these divisional public relations personnel usually report directly to the division head but maintain a dotted-line responsibility to the central public relations department for corporate coordination and policy compliance. They also draw on the central department for advice and staff support in times of heavy workload.

Figures 46.1, 46.2, and 46.3 (page 694) illustrate representative organization charts for typical small, medium, and large public relations departments.

Compensation

Corporate public relations budgets are determined mainly by three factors:

1. The scope of the public relations function
2. How much of the cost of public relations programs is charged to the public relations budget and how much is charged to the operating divisions being benefited
3. The size of the company

Thus it is difficult to give meaningful comparisons or suggestions, other than to indicate that it would be difficult to have a significant program in a small to medium-sized company for less than $200,000 to $300,000 a year. In larger firms, budgets ranging from $1 million to $10 million are common, even after recent downsizing.

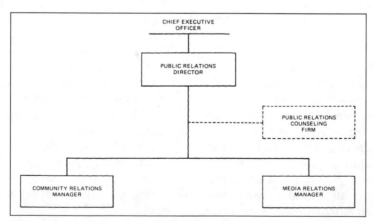

Figure 46.1 Typical small public relations department.

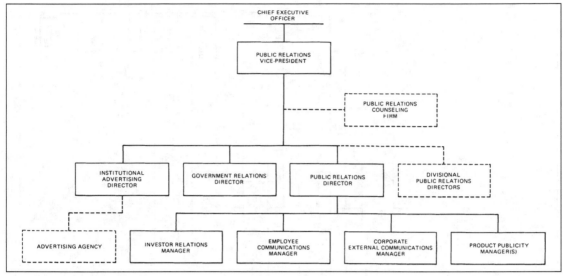

Figure 46.2 Typical medium-sized public relations department.

However, salaries can be compared in a meaningful way and provide a good insight into budgets, since salaries are the major factor in the expenses of most public relations departments.

Salaries in corporate public relations tend to follow fairly consistent patterns and have been clearly defined in salary surveys over the years.

Corporate salaries and those in public relations counseling firms tend to run rather parallel to each other, with a slight edge enjoyed by the counseling firms. Other types of organizations (colleges, universities, trade associations, and so on) lag significantly on salary levels.

Many larger corporations pay salaries in the $75,000-and-up range to their top public relations executive, with individual instances running into the $100,000 to $350,000 bracket. This reflects the growing importance of the public relations function in business life and the broad range of capabilities and experience required.

Participation of the Board of Directors

In recent years, as public demands and expectations for closer board of directors attention to the ethical, moral, and legal conduct of business have grown, board involvement in the public relations function has increased. This is a welcome development for the public relations staff since it evidences top corporate attention to public relations as well as assuring serious and attentive consideration of public policy issues through all levels of the organization.

Since the directors cannot and should not become involved in the day-to-day public relations activities of the company any more than they can or should be involved in other day-to-day operating functions, their principal public relations involvement usually comes through an overview—audits of corporate ethical practice and/or establishment of policy standards for the guidance of management.

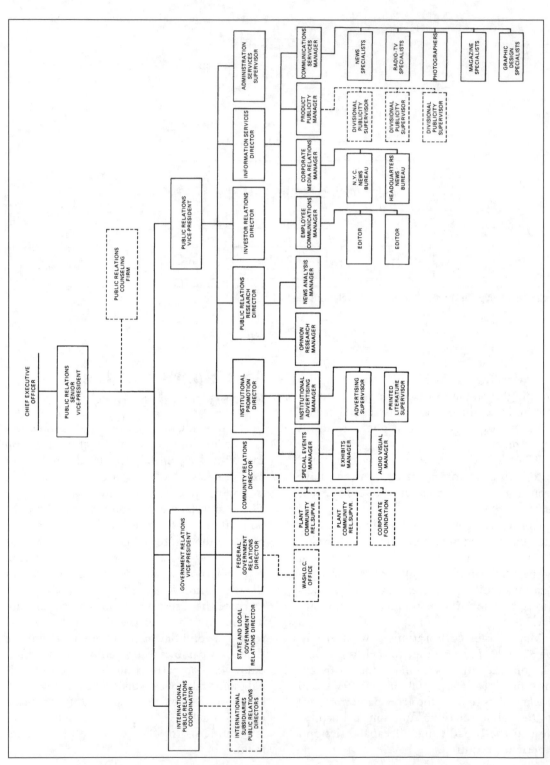

Figure 46.3 Typical large public relations department

Most frequently, a public policy committee of the board is established to perform these functions. Participation may be solely by directors or by a combination of directors and nondirectors representing operating management and respected outsiders. The top public relations officer is a key member in the latter instance, or a close staff associate in the former.

The Public Relations Firm's Involvement

Outside public relations counsel plays an essential role in corporate public relations, whether or not an internal department exists. This is amply evidenced in a Conference Board survey of medium- and large-size companies that found that most of the corporations used one or several consulting firms, often retaining one full time and bringing in additional ones from time to time for special assignments.

In the case where no internal public relations function operates, outside counsel usually is retained by management to do one of three things:

- Provide the internal management with continuing input, creative stimulation, special skills, and an objective review of activities, as well as an intelligent sounding board for ideas and plans

- Advise the company on public relations problems and act as the public relations service function

- Assist the company in establishing an internal public relations department, including the formulation of policy and recruitment of personnel

In companies where internal public relations departments already exist, the role of the outside firm is usually a combination of advising and counseling the internal staff on basic problems and serving as a staff extension of the internal department in handling peak workloads or specialized projects, and in providing creative services and facilities.

Since public relations is a diverse field with a variety of facets, new and unexpected problems frequently present themselves. In such instances the public relations staff, as well as top management, can benefit from the cumulative experience and wide range of contacts of the outside counsel as gained from working with a good many other clients.

By the same token, an outside counseling firm with its multiple clients can maintain a staff of creative specialists that it is not economically feasible to maintain in an internal public relations department where only sporadic use would create an undesirable overhead problem. Hence, such an outside agency serves as a ready pool of extra talent to be called on for specialized tasks as needed by the internal department.

47

THE PLACE AND FUNCTION OF THE PUBLIC RELATIONS COUNSEL

PHILIP LESLY

The executive responsible for an organization's public relations activities must have complete understanding of the functions, benefits, and practices of those specialists whose services he or she may call on. Consideration of the professional consultant's participation in the organization's public relations program necessarily begins with both the meaning of the term *public relations counsel* and its implications, broadly and strictly speaking.

The Nature of Public Relations Counsel

Since public relations has fast become a profession lacking standards of acceptance, the term has been conveniently adopted by a wide range of practitioners of any activity involving contact with people—which, obviously, covers an extensive area. There are many people who call themselves "public relations counsel" who, though their responsibilities may involve some limited counseling on public relations matters, are essentially and foremost press agents, lobbyists, "fixers," publicity representatives, union negotiators, personnel specialists, or ghostwriters. As such, these people do not comply with the require-

ments and functionality of public relations counsel as it is widely accepted today. Therefore, they are not considered in that context for the purposes of this chapter.

The true public relations counsel is a professional who functions independently on a fee or retainer basis for one or more clients. Advice and service offered cover virtually all aspects of public relations considered in this book. He or she functions on the executive level of the client's management, rather than with subordinates, in most cases.

Actually, relatively few people are strictly public relations counsel in the United States today, compared with the large number of workers in the various phases of public relations, such as publicity, labor relations, government relations, financial community relations, and company publications.

The public relations counsel is often the face an organization puts before its most important publics: the press and broadcasters, important organizations, schools, and communities, all of whom the counsel deals with on behalf of the client. For this reason, the counsel an organization chooses is important to its own "image." The organization frequently can rise no higher in esteem than the caliber of counsel it retains, no matter how good a program may be conceived and executed. For this reason, the caliber of a counsel's stature and clientele is one of the most important measures to be applied by a prospective client. A client concerned about its esteem and prestige is more likely to advance it with a counsel who is esteemed than with one known for lesser characteristics.

In a real sense, clients and counsel tend to find each other on the basis of characteristics they have in common.

The counsel's background

Because of the broad scope of his or her activities, the counsel must necessarily be a person who has had extensive training in many fields, as well as the abilities called for in serving the clients.

- Judgment
- Ability to think in sharp, logical patterns
- Ability to express oneself clearly, both orally and in writing
- Ability to plan on a broad scale—to go below the surface, far beyond the immediate horizon
- Executive ability—to direct extensive operations involving much detail and many abstract elements
- Sales ability—to know how to put over an idea, a product, or a cause
- Constant objectivity—to keep oneself in the background, able to evaluate any situation from the outsider's viewpoint
- Open-mindedness—even after *almost* all the facts seem to lead to one conclusion
- Humility—to be able to acknowledge that one's judgment may be wrong
- Courage—to be willing to lose a client if continuing could require compromising one's convictions and judgment
- Ability to put just as much stress on details as on vast plans
- Interest in people—in their ideas, in why they do things

- Lively imagination, tempered by good judgment

In almost all cases, the professional public relations counsel is a principal or an executive in a firm of counselors, or in an advertising agency. This makes him or her a business person, who deals with problems of rent, personnel, taxes, overhead, and other matters that do not directly involve clients but are essential to one's ability to serve the clients effectively. We shall consider these business aspects later. The counsel's functions on behalf of clients receive first attention.

Working with a PR Counsel

A counsel or a public relations firm as a whole is retained by a corporation, trade association, nonprofit organization, individual, institution, or other group on any of several bases:

1. Retained only to counsel the management and public relations personnel of the client organization on matters that will affect public opinion toward the client. Services may include analysis, planning, programming, key writing and other creative services, critiquing materials prepared by the client, and coordinating all communications.

2. Provides all the public relations services utilized by the client—counsel, research, planning, publicity, preparation of institutional literature, and other functions—either with or without direction by an internal public relations executive.

3. Provides the counsel and services, with a director of public relations acting as a liaison and agent of the management within the organization.

4. Counsels the management and guides the public relations activities, which are carried out by the director of public relations and his staff.

5. Provides counsel and conducts specified public relations activities, while the director of public relations and staff coordinate on behalf of management and conduct other specified activities.

6. May be called in by a firm that has its own staff, when advice is sought or when special abilities, experience, and facilities may be required. Sometimes this type of assignment is a publicity project, such as an anniversary observance. More often it is a continuing relationship of indefinite duration.

7. Called on to study the client's situation, to make recommendations, and perhaps to supervise installation of what he or she recommends. This may involve any or all of the following activities:

   • Analyze the conditions in which the client is likely to have to function

   • Assess its present policies and personnel in light of anticipated needs

   • Develop a proposed program and timetable

   • Specify personnel needed or reassignments of present personnel, general compensation patterns, and organization

   • Find candidates for new positions

   • Make recommendations on outside services to be employed

   • Help guide the staff and management through the transition stage

   • Provide judgment and ideas as the program proceeds

The trend in recent years has been toward combining the services of the counseling firm and the internal staff. Most frequently the counseling firm affords specific services, as well as advice and creativity, while the public relations department carries out most activities. In a few cases, the counsel selects the person who is placed on the organization's staff as its public relations director. Not only is the counsel's knowledge of public relations invaluable in judging the person's fitness for the job and in creating the setup in which he or she will function, but the counsel is able to select the person for qualities that will enable him or her to coordinate effectively with the counsel's operations.

The Value of Using Counsel

With this wide variety of patterns in which the counsel may be employed, it is important to evaluate what he or she affords the client that cannot be obtained any other way. The advantages that a counsel affords include the following:

1. Because there is always a shortage of exceptionally capable people in the field, a counsel serving a number of clients can make his or her talents available to all of them. Since there is a tendency for exceptional people to function as professional counsel because of the greater income and other advantages, it is difficult for any organization to employ an entire staff of unusual ability. The good counsel, then, often makes available the highest degree of skill the client can retain to augment its public relations aides.

2. Similarly, the counsel's staff can be made up of people with more than average ability, since the flexibility of the counsel's agency—serving a number of clients— permits them to use their skills intensively.

3. In serving a number of clients, the counsel's organization can be made up of a number of capable people who are experienced in many phases of public relations. To get the same variety of skills, any single organization's staff will have to employ full-time the same number of people, at far greater cost.

4. The counseling firm is flexible. When one client has an emergency, a seasonal need, or an important event, a number of people can be assigned to it until the need has been met. The organization with its own set staff has no such flexibility—the personnel available for emergencies are the same as are on hand during routine periods.

5. Similarly, the facilities of the counsel's firm are available to all the clients. The contacts and mailing lists, for instance, are maintained constantly and are accessible for every client. If each client maintained its own staff operation, each would have to keep up its mailing lists, its addressing function, its mailing staff, and so on.

6. By carrying on a great variety of public relations activities, the counsel develops a wide range of experience, broad judgment, and extensive contacts. The employed staff of an organization, on the other hand, works year after year on one subject, in one area.

   Ideally, the counsel provides the strong trunk of the client organization with an instant transplant of wide knowledge and years of diverse experience. As in other forms of transplanting, the resultant organism becomes far more than if it grew strictly on its own.

7. The counsel's reputation accrues to the client. When an agency has been issuing publicity releases for a number of organizations, for instance, the firm becomes recognized among the media. If its work is good and reliable, the press and broadcast editors come to accept it. This immediate acceptance is available to each new client of the counsel, whereas if the client organization sent out its own material, it would have to develop its own acceptance—often after a period of ineffectiveness or harmful mistakes.

8. The counsel is more independent. First, he or she is a professional, able to meet top executives on their own level. Second, he has a number of sources of income and is not wholly dependent on any one client. Third, when his contact within the client organization is established, he is reasonably free of the internal political problems that beset the paid employee. Independence in a public relations person is essential if he or she is to provide proper policy guidance and effectively handle activities.

9. In the same way, the counsel is objective. He or she is not directly involved in the operations and machinations of the client organization. She does not spend all of her time dealing with a particular cause. She is able to retain the point of view of the outsider, the type of person who is the object of the public relations program. The fact that she is also representing a number of other organizations, in different fields, also gives her a broader perspective.

   Donald W. MacKinnon of the Institute of Personality Assessment and Research at the University of California, Berkeley, reported to a PRSA conference that studies in the field brought this judgment:

   > If, as compared with the public relations officer in a company, the public relations counselor is at a disadvantage as regards the manner in which problems are presented to him, he has the distinct advantage of being able to look at them with a fresh eye unclouded by long and intimate association with the firm. He is thus in the fortunate position, if he has any creative potential at all, of more easily restructuring and reformulating the problem, reconciling his general expertise in the field of public relations with a fresh, unhampered perception of the specific situation which now confronts him . . .
   >
   > One must have the relevant and necessary information if the problem is to be solved. But . . . too much information can interfere

with the attainment of a creative solution. . . . Most of the major inventions have been made by persons who have not been experts in the field of their innovation.

10. In many cases, the counsel's services are more economical. The centralized facilities, the flexibility of manpower, the opportunity for the counsel to serve more than one client when making business trips and in other ways all provide economies. Of course, nowhere is it more true than in public relations that no service is worth what it costs except good service—"cheap" service is often extremely expensive, whereas excellent service always more than repays the cost.

11. On frequent occasions the counsel can benefit several clients at one time. For instance, when a publication is developing a complete story on business conditions, he or she may provide the point of view of several of his or her corporate clients.

12. The organization of the counsel's business often affords the client the service it needs wherever and whenever it may want it. Large public relations organizations have branch offices in various places, on whom they can call for help in these localities on an instant's notice.

13. By handling a variety of public relations assignments, the counsel and its organization gain experience that is valuable to each client. The know-how, the groundwork, and the techniques involved in each given situation can most effectively be applied by those who have themselves applied them effectively in other cases.

14. The counsel can be a focal point on whom the diverse and sometimes conflicting elements in an organization—the members of an organization, the department heads in a corporation—can agree and turn to for advice.

Professional Counsel's Limitations

At the same time, it must be recognized that in some cases the counseling firm, serving alone, has limitations. These drawbacks are among the reasons for the trend toward a combination of internal departments and outside counsel. Some of the limitations that have been cited are the following:

1. Because he or she is not spending full time and concentration on the one organization's problems, the counsel cannot become so familiar with all aspects of its operations. In providing objectivity and a great variety of experience, the counsel sacrifices having a complete knowledge of any client.

2. Because he or she sometime deals with top management executives, the counsel is sometimes exposed to the jealousy of lower officials who would be superior to the public relations director if he or she were a staff employee. The desirability of policy-level consideration of public relations thus has its disadvantage. This occasionally creates friction within the organization, sometimes resulting in lack of cooperation on public relations matters.

3. On the surface, it is sometimes more economical to carry on public relations activities within the client organization. Existing office space, telephone service, reproduction and mailing facilities, and secretarial personnel can be used, instead of having to pay for these when they are used by the counsel. Actually, of course, on a strict accounting basis, these functions must be charged to public relations anyway and seldom represent a true saving.

4. Internal public relations executives sometimes are negative to outside counsel. Some counselors have been known to undermine the status of the staff executive for their

own aggrandizement, though that is rare. Seeking to gain the acceptance of management, staff executives sometimes see the outsider who has this acceptance as a barrier rather than an aid to their progress. In some cases, where the counsel is selected by management, internal executives resist cooperating in the hope they will discredit the counsel by forestalling ability to function. The more inexperienced and insecure the internal executive, the more likely he or she is to prefer an outside firm he is sure he can dominate, rather than one best able to provide professional skill and judgment. Thus, the more respected the outside counsel, the more likely it is that the public relations director is a sound and conscientious executive. In many instances, strong public relations officers and strong counselors work harmoniously together, with the result that the status of both is greatly enhanced with the managements.

5. In medium- and large-sized counseling firms, the caliber of judgment and skills will vary greatly, depending on which personnel happen to be assigned to the account. Often the principals devote their main efforts to obtaining new clients and to administering the business, rather than to serving clients. Though the organization is large, staff people often work in virtual isolation from each other. It is thus necessary to the success of the relationship for the client to ascertain at the start which personnel will provide counsel, skills, production of materials, and other services; and how the firm plans to service the client—to what extent its full resources will be provided or whether the account will be "pigeonholed" with limited personnel.

Payment Arrangements

Because public relations involves such a wide variety of possible functions for clients, there is a wide range in methods of charging for services. There is also a wide variance in the rates charged, just as there is in other professions. Rates generally depend on the reputation and caliber of the counsel's organization, but do not necessarily reflect the quality of the service to be provided. It is important for every prospective client of a public relations organization to analyze the operating methods of the various firms and the components included in various budget items at the same time the prices quoted are evaluated. Otherwise, it may find that public relations service is a "blind" item.

The most common systems of charges follow:

1. A retainer fee for counseling only. This method applies whenever the counsel's guidance and attention are all that are desired, and is similar to the retainer of an attorney on an annual basis. This fee may be a fixed annual amount, or it may vary with the rate of activity, as in items 6 or 9 following.

2. Sometimes a counsel is retained to analyze an organization's public relations operations, problems, and needs, and make a report and recommendation. This is charged on either a *per diem* basis or at a flat fee with expenses added.

3. Some counseling firms establish a breakdown of charges to apply to every client, regardless of the size of the project involved or the scope of the services required:

   a. A set fee for the counsel

   b. The total cost of all personnel required, on an hourly basis that allows for all costs of the counsel's firm and allows for a profit (*see* Figure 47.1, page 704)

c. A proportionate share of the firm's total overhead, including rent, light, telephone, depreciation on equipment, taxes, supplies

d. All expenses entailed in serving the client—so-called mechanical expenses, such as travel, photography, mailing costs, clippings, stationery, long-distance telephone and fax, and so on

e. A fixed percentage of override on items b, c, and d—usually 17.65 percent

4. The most common system breaks the budget down into two items:

a. Fee, covering the entire services of the counsel's organization, including personnel, overhead, his own services

b. Mechanical expenses

As in all the methods discussed here, some firms charge the mechanical expenses at actual cost, while others add a percentage to cover "cost of handling." This relieves the firm of the incentive to hold down expenses (and, in fact, often rewards swollen expenditures). If the client is fully aware of these factors in advance and exerts control over them, it seems to make little difference which method is used; but, since this "cost of handling" charge is absorbed in the fee of firms that do not bill the client for it, its presence or absence has an important determination on any comparison of fees.

5. Another common method breaks the charges down into three categories:

a. Fee, covering all the firm's costs except the salaries of personnel required on the account

b. Personnel costs—either charged at a specific hourly rate for each caliber of employee, or at the actual weekly or monthly salary, when all or almost all the employees' time is spent on the account

c. Mechanical expenses

6. Where the demand on the counsel's services is irregular or unpredictable, charges are sometimes made on an hourly basis for the firm as a whole. The counsel sets the rate per hour to suit his or her own needs and the requirements of the account. Since this system makes it very difficult for the counsel to plan his staff schedule or predict his own costs, it is rarely accepted by an established firm unless there is also a retainer fee, as in item 3, or a monthly minimum, as in item 9.

7. Where a client wants to retain the counsel for a specific assignment—such as meeting a problem that arises suddenly, or augmenting its own staff to plan observance of an anniversary—a flat charge arrangement, plus expenses, is usually made. The counsel estimates the costs of personnel, overhead, his own time, a margin of safety, and profit, and sets a fee for the assignment. Mechanical expenses are billed either at cost or with an "override," as agreed with the client.

8. Sometimes the retainer fee and the assignment budget are combined. The counsel may accept an annual fee for normal service, and quote a figure for each special project that may come up during the year. These special budgets are agreed on before the project planning begins.

9. Where there is to be continuing service but the level of needs will vary considerably, a minimum guaranteed fee may be set. Thus there may be a basic payment of perhaps $4,000 a month. In those months where time charges exceed $4,000, the total accrued is billed. This permits assigning the attention of skilled executives and staff, and adjusting payments to needs, as basic levels are exceeded.

In most cases where the counsel is on a continuous basis, the budget is set annually and

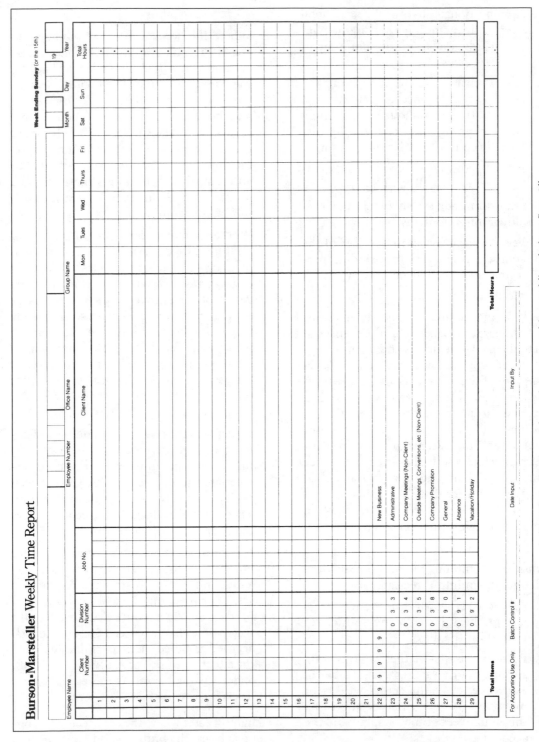

Figure 47.1 Example of a time record sheet for executive and creative personnel in a public relations firm. All business time, including overtime, is accounted for.

the agreement runs for one-year periods. Sometimes the agreement is bound in a strictly legal contract; more often there is a covering letter citing the terms of the agreement, accepted by both parties; sometimes there is merely a gentleman's agreement. Because of the confidential and intimate nature of this profession, disagreements over terms of payments are incompatible with good service, and it is widely considered that a gentleman's agreement is really the basis for every arrangement, whether there is a legal contract or not.

Because the client will be the source of information involved in the program and will have final approval of materials, it is customary for the letter of agreement to contain a clause that protects the counsel from lawsuits. This "hold harmless" clause may read as follows:

> You agree to indemnify and hold harmless XXX Associates from and against all losses, claims, damages, expenses, or liabilities that we may incur based on information, representation, reports, or data you furnish us, to the extent that such material is furnished, prepared, approved, and/or used by us.

Liability may involve more than written materials or other communications. The counsel may be brought into disputes by activist groups or others. To deal with this, some counseling firms buy professional liability insurance. A firm that provides such insurance for public relations firms is Frankel & Company, 23 William Street, New York, NY 10038, (212) 267-2200.

The annual budget is usually broken down into monthly installments. If the fee is $48,000 and the established expenses are $24,000, for instance, the budget would call for $4,000 and $2,000 a month, respectively. Though the monthly budget for expenses should be watched as a guide to the pace of activity and the balance of the program, it is not wise to set it so rigidly that it prevents exceeding it when

necessary. Monthly expense costs vary widely in many cases, and in the example, the $2,000 should be taken as an average. Where the billing method also varies costs for personnel and other things from month to month, it is more difficult to make the annual budget come out even and the possibility of its being spent too soon is greater; but careful management by the counsel and supervision by the client will control it.

Variations in charges

Even aside from this variety of billing methods, there are other differences that affect the cost to the client.

As in every human activity, the demand for the counsel's services—as reflected in the compensation received—inevitably affects the fees charged. This explains why, when several counsel are asked to submit bids for an account, their charges may differ by 300 to 400 percent. By setting a price on their services that they feel is justified, successful public relations counsel automatically are being selective of prospective clients; they are eliminating those that cannot or will not pay this standard. It is possible by looking at a counsel's lists of clients to evaluate the comparative selectiveness (by fees) of different counsel.

Aside from the counsel's own compensation, there are variations in the other factors of charges: personnel, overhead, and billing methods.

Personnel

Salaries usually reflect the caliber of the men and women employed. It is important to remember, however, that charges made on an hourly basis (and sometimes on a monthly salary basis) do not necessarily reflect the salaries actually paid to the employees. They may be a working scale devised on a theoretical system, or they may be developed on the basis of what the traffic will bear.

Overhead

Some firms believe that distinguished-looking offices in the finest available building are necessary for their prestige and standing. Others prefer to settle for utilitarian working space that is as inexpensive as possible. Most are moderately between these extremes. Sales efforts, stationery, equipment, and other items are also variable. It is up to the client to decide whether it benefits from the cost of the counsel's overhead, or whether it is important enough to make any difference.

Billing methods

Some firms prepare bills in minute detail—listing every single item, wherever possible, and attaching invoices for all billed items. Others give only a broad outline of expenses incurred. The first system involves much more bookkeeping expense than does the second. Indirectly or directly, the client pays for the cost of the system. Usually the carefully detailed billing system is preferred because it can be demonstrated to be authentic.

Advance Preparations

Before an effective working plan can be established, the counsel should take several steps:

1. Make sure there is a clear-cut definition of the goals and purposes of the function. Fundamental as this may seem, it is needed to prevent serious difficulties due to the client and the counsel coming to the relationship with entirely different backgrounds about public relations and having different impressions of what the function is to be.

   This is not taken care of by vague generalities, such as: "Improve the company's image," or "Help increase effectiveness of

the entire marketing mix," or "Make certain the financial community fully appreciates the merits of the company and its stock."

The definitions should be incisive. Examples follow:

- "Establish the changing character of the company—from a specialized industrial producer to a research-oriented, diversified, highly technical firm in the forefront of fast-growing industrial and consumer markets."

- "Convince the public by demonstration that the company is a good citizen of its plant communities: supporting desirable community efforts, unrestricted in its employment policies except on the basis of merit."

- "Convey the 'difference' behind the company's products from those of its competitors by conveying the exceptional character of its management and principles."

2. Management executives should be involved in public relations up to the highest level at which it realistically may be a factor in that organization. This will usually be the president or the executive vice-president, and should include the chairman of the board. Their thinking should be obtained at the start of what they see the public relations needs of the organization to be and their reasons of having the function. The counsel should determine—on the basis of what they say and judgment based on experience with various other management executives—how far they will go to participate in the functions of public relations. He or she should assess how they will act in dealing with the press, security analysts, or other publics, as well as how they project in a public meeting. What may be unsound for one organization's top executive may be ideal for another.

3. Interview editors of publications in the client's field of interest, others in that field, staff personnel, and former employees or members—with the client's permission in advance—to get an objective analysis of the organization's characteristics, how it functions, and what can realistically be expected in response to innovative suggestions or to unexpected developments.

4. Analyze the organization's public relations staff personnel to assure rapport with them. Some staff people, by experience and personality, are more aggressive or venturesome than others; some lean to traditionalism more than others.

5. If the role for which the counsel has been retained is not clearly defined, determine where he or she will be needed most: providing ideas; guiding internal staff; creative work; review of staff-produced materials; contacts with various publicity media, security analysts, or other outlets for communication; setting up and handling events; getting out publications; producing literature or films; acting as a listening post to feed back information about the client derived from various sources.

Client Education and the PR Counsel

In many ways, the most difficult phase of any public relations account is developing full understanding among the client's executives and personnel about the nature, scope, and functions of public relations; the techniques, problems, ethics, and standards of the counsel; and the means of using and judging the counsel's services.

Difficulties that most often arise include the following:

1. The client misunderstands practices of the profession. It wants to use advertising pressure on newspapers to print stories. It thinks every news release should be printed verbatim in every newspaper to which it is sent. It thinks the management's point of view should be forced on employees and that the only measure of success is how well this point of view is accepted. It wants to withhold some facts from the public, and blames the counsel when the watered-down story is not accepted, or the full story comes out with an unfavorable slant. These are just a few examples.

2. It has a narrow knowledge of public relations. It may recognize that the counsel is involved in publicity functions, but neglect to call on him or her in connection with issues or opportunities, employee relations matters, stockholder relations, or any other phase of the field.

3. It may try to restrict the counsel's part in functions that are necessary. It may ask that the president's statement be written for the annual report, but refuse or neglect to have the counsel guide the planning of the report itself, or its distribution.

4. Most commonly, it may misevaluate results. It may put great emphasis upon newspaper clippings and fail to see the intangible benefits in problems averted, improved employee morale, prevention of customer complaints, and other successes. Because most executives are accustomed to dealing with tangibles and "black and white," they have difficulty in appreciating the value of intangibles.

5. It may bypass the counsel inadvertently or by failing to consider him or her an integral cog in its own operation. This reflects itself in formation of policies having great influence on attitudes toward the company without consulting the counsel, or dealing directly with the press, without the counsel's knowledge and sometimes opposite to the counsel's own commitments and plans.

These problems of the counsel must be resolved by educating the client. The client, in turn, is wise to seek a clear understanding on such matters as soon as possible in its relationship with the counsel.

Establishing a working pattern

At the beginning of the relationship with the client, the counsel must set up a plan of procedure. This plan should include the following:

1. Arranging to be called on as soon as anything involving public notice—particularly publicity and media relations—occurs.

2. Arranging for participation in all meetings that affect the organization's policy—with the possible exception of board of directors' meetings, but ideally including these.

3. Arranging for periodic (preferably monthly) meetings between officials of the client organization who guide the public relations program and the staff members of the counsel's firm who carry out the program. At these meetings the events, accomplishments, and problems encountered since the previous meeting should be discussed; all matters affecting public relations should be evaluated and worked into the program; and plans for future activity should be made.

4. Setting methods for judging the results of the work. If periodic reports are to be made to the client, what form should they be in, how often should they be made, what aspects of the effort should be emphasized? If clippings and broadcast time are to be important, methods of obtaining and evaluating them should be agreed on.

5. Setting up channels for getting information before any activity is begun. Someone within the client organization should be specified as the liaison for information, or one person should be named as source of information on each phase of the organization's operation.

6. Establishing clear understanding that all material and stories must be approved before publication, use, or release. It must be established that once an item has been approved by the authorized person, it has the official blessing of the client, and except where a crisis is involved must be backed up by the client.

7. Arranging for periodic checking by the counsel of all pertinent phases of the client's operations.

8. Establishing communication between the counsel and the client. Should the counsel send the client copies of all correspondence handled on the account, or only on specified subjects or in specified connections? Should the counsel prepare a written report on each meeting with client personnel, for circulation to all concerned within the client organization and the counseling firm?

Confidentiality

It should go without saying that everything the counsel knows about each client and everything done for it is held in strict confidence, unless it is used as public information or the client agrees to have it revealed. This not only applies to what the counsel says to the press or to competitors, but also to other clients. A leak is serious, whether it occurs in an interview with a reporter for the Associated Press or across the desk from the president of a company in an entirely different line of business. Corporation presidents are human enough to pass on what they hear.

This secrecy requirement is the basis for many counsels' opinion that it is permissible to represent two organizations that may in whole or in part be competitors. Since there is no transfer of information or conflict of interest, they feel there is nothing to prevent their doing an objectively honest job for both. In this respect, they say, they differ from advertising agencies, which because of the nature of their operations cannot establish such objectivity between accounts and, therefore, generally will not represent competitors. In general, however, most counsel will not represent organizations that compete broadly with each other. (*See* Figure 47.2.)

STRICTLY CONFIDENTIAL

Maintenance of absolute confidence is an inherent necessity for effective public relations. Information regarding any of our accounts; any prospective accounts on which we may be working; and any company activities, techniques, or policies should not be mentioned outside the office even when with our own staff members. Such mention can lead to very serious consequences in relations with clients or in our ability to obtain new clients, thereby being harmful to all of us. It is all right to talk enthusiastically about how well we do on certain situations, but we should give no information on specifics.

It is also a good policy for individual staff members to maintain confidence concerning their salaries, bonuses, and fees. Executives working on an account may have information about its budget, but this must not be disseminated to others. This is important in protecting us from efforts of competitors to determine our fees.

CONTRACTS AND RELEASES

Each member of the executive and creative staff is asked, as a condition of employment, to sign a contract agreeing to maintain the company's standards of practice and to forego employment or other association with any client of this firm for a reasonable period after he may leave its employ.

Model releases should be signed immediately on shooting of photos in which one or more persons are identifiable. A release is necessary for each individual.

Photographs that contain an identifiable likeness of an individual should not be used in connection with public relations material you may prepare and distribute unless the written consent of such individual is obtained.

All contracts or commitments should be made subject to approval of the account supervisor to whom you report.

OUTSIDE ACTIVITIES

Outside activity that might in any way reflect on the company or affect anything the company does should be checked with the president. This might include volunteer publicity service for a non-profit organization; participation in group activities that might identify the person with the company in print or otherwise; writing on subjects that directly or indirectly might affect our connection with a client or a publication or other medium—in other words, those things which good judgment would indicate ought to be reviewed because they can have an effect on the company's position, reputation, or activities. This is especially true if in any way the work involved might require contact at the office or activities in conjunction with office activities.

Figure 47.2 Page from a manual of policies and procedures of a public relations firm.

Open-book policy

While keeping the affairs of clients confidential, the counsel should maintain the most open policy about his or her own affairs. In this respect, it is practicing what one preaches to let interested parties know the truth about the firm. The profession has always had a strong tendency to either refuse information about the number of accounts represented and the number of persons in the firm, or to distort these figures grossly. Lack of a central ethical society to which reports on these matters must be made has permitted falsification to go largely unchallenged.

O'Dwyer's Directory of Public Relations Firms (271 Madison Avenue, New York, NY 10016) requires audited financial information from the largest firms listed. It does not, however, verify the extent of a counseling firm's relationship with any client it lists, or whether that relationship or the number of employees listed is current at the time of publication; and it does not audit the information provided by smaller firms.

Accordingly, it is wise for the prospective client to ask for detailed and verified information about any firm it is interested in retaining, and to check the information given.

Frankness in dealing with clients, the press, and everyone else is also a necessity for the counsel. He or she must immediately acknowledge errors or failures to ensure that the client has the facts necessary to guide its judgment on everything affecting public relations. Of course, there should never be any attempt to distort information to the media, to mislead a reporter, to withhold information desired in favor of other media, or to do anything else that will cause any medium to feel it has not been treated with complete fairness. (*See* Chapter 21.)

The Business of the Public Relations Counsel

Organizing the staff

In the well-rounded public relations firm, regardless of size, certain basic abilities and the following talents are required:

1. Writing skill—versatile, prolific, distinctive, clear

2. Broad knowledge of business affairs and good judgment

3. Ability to make intangibles and abstractions attractive to great numbers of people—to "sell ideas"

4. Sensitivity to the mass mind, or the feelings and reactions of people

5. Knowledge of the production processes involved in printing, photography, and other techniques employed in public relations

6. Knowledge of media—newspapers, magazines, radio, television, movies, books, speeches, special events, and the like

7. Organizing and planning ability—to develop broad, long-term operations as well as organize masses of details

8. Intimate knowledge of the specialties involved in the firm's accounts—technical information, women's interests, financial affairs, and so on

The firm combines these qualities in its personnel and, at the same time, ensures the right kind and the right amount of manpower available to meet the needs of its clients at any time.

This almost inevitably demands great versatility in the persons employed. The only alternatives are departmentalization that is almost certain to be wasteful and, therefore, expensive; or specialization, whereby the counsel or the firm limits the scope of what it offers to provide to clients.

For this reason, most public relations organizations are largely nondepartmentalized. Although persons with special experience and skill are called on when needed, most persons are also called on to fill other needs.

Branch operations

Public relations firms have three methods of carrying on their activities in cities outside their headquarters city: branch offices, reciprocal arrangements, and correspondents.

Branch offices

These require either one very large account that can support the cost of an office to augment the headquarters' services, several accounts needing consistent service there, or several accounts in the region.

Reciprocal arrangements

For example, one counsel in New York will agree to handle assignments from another in Washington, in return for similar consideration when needed. Either each charges the other at a specified rate or an effort is made to keep mutual favors balanced without exchange of money.

Correspondents

A firm in Chicago may assign a person or a firm in Houston to carry out a project, at a mutually satisfactory rate. This may involve the one assignment, or may be a permanent arrangement. The so-called field networks are essentially made up of lists of such correspondents.

Specialization

Because the scope of public relations is so broad and the needs of various clients vary so greatly, there is a tendency for some counsel to specialize. Some represent only non-profit organizations; others handle only industrial relations matters; still others have a clientele composed entirely of trade associations. Major areas of specialization are investor relations, public affairs, and product publicity.

At the other pole from specialists is the counsel who has developed a very broad scope of experience, judgment, and creativity. All these traits are scarce, and such a counsel can benefit almost any organization without attempting to provide services that are readily available through staff personnel or standard outside firms.

Specialization seems to have merits and weaknesses. Because public relations is such a broad field, the counsel who narrows his or her interest and activities is cutting off wide areas of experience and contact that are helpful in serving any client. Also, the specialist has an inflexible type of business and is more vulnerable to changes in economic and social conditions.

At the same time, it is true that a specialist in such fields as financial public relations, nonprofit corporations, and industrial relations is able to learn these fields thoroughly, which a general counsel might not be able to do.

This seems to be one question in the profession that shows no signs of being resolved soon. While some counsel are turning toward specialization, others are very successful in handling a wide variety of accounts and are sought out by all types of clients because they have proved their overall ability in public relations.

The size of the organization

Another question on which there are divergent views is the limitation of the counseling organization's clientele. Some claim that it is primarily the ability of the head of the firm that is employed by clients, and that he or she

is able to effectively serve only a few accounts by devoting personal attention to them. Whether "few" means six accounts or nine often depends on whether the counsel advocating this policy has six accounts or nine. At the same time, where a firm is established to chiefly provide the benefits of one mind, it is undoubtedly true that a low limit must be set on the clientele.

Few people can know all the aspects of public relations, can embody all the necessary skills, or can provide the many types of thinking that are called for in public relations work. But the thoroughly experienced counsel is versatile and has had opportunity to work in all important areas. Also, broad judgment enables him or her to select those special skills needed and to find sources of special information.

On the other hand, much can be said for large firms. No one any longer questions the ability of a large advertising agency, for example, to do an excellent job even though its principals do not write all the copy, plan all the campaigns, devise all the themes, or make all the layouts.

Good public relations organizations in which there is more than one trained executive typically hold conferences about major matters involving any client. The ability, skill, and imagination of everyone are brought into play for each problem. The interplay of minds sometimes comes up with a result beyond the capacity of any one of the minds.

The conclusion seems to be that, for a client who prefers constant personal attention from one person in whom it has great faith, there is need for the counsel with a limited number of clients. For other counsel, the size of the clientele depends on their ability to build a sound, efficient, and intelligent organization that works well together.

Related to this question is the problem of whether a firm should concentrate full authority and last judgment in one person, or should have two or more principals who are equally fitted to represent the firm with clients, the press, or others.

In instances where the firm has been built up by one person, and his or her reputation has become the cornerstone of the business, it is probable that person will always be looked upon as the one head of the firm.

When the founder of the company is not such an outstanding figure, partners who work compatibly together can help each other. In either case, it is essential for the client that one person be in a position to make definite decisions and take direct action without delay.

Control by advertising agencies

Several large public relations firms have been taken over by holding companies dominated by advertising agencies. That has focused attention on the role of public relations counseling services when they are dominated by another field.

While the public relations wing of the organization can draw on resources of the parent organization—charged to the client— it is also subject to that organization's management domination and superior billing volume. The client should explore whether judgment is truly independent if the firm's profit might be adversely affected; whether the extra layers of management and overhead are worth the cost or whether they discourage the best people from choosing to work for that firm; and whether the narrow concentration of attention to marketing inherent in advertising thinking can permit the broad gauged thinking that marks the best public relations minds. Also, the large number of clients represented by the joint operations creates more possibilities of client conflicts.

Sales activities

Whether public relations is a business or a profession, it is faced with the business necessity of attracting clients. Because it tends toward being a profession, the means of gaining a clientele are limited by propriety and good taste. It is generally considered unethical to sell judgment and counsel through salespeople, pressure promotion, or other devices used to push merchandise. At the same time, the need for public relations is not yet so well established in the minds of the public that many counsel can afford to wait for businessmen to seek them out as patients seek out doctors. It is necessary to find a middle ground between hopeful waiting and brazen chasing.

In general, firms in the public relations field tend to be either "selling oriented" or "service oriented." The first type concentrates primarily on seeking new clients, devoting a major share of the principals' time and talents, as well as resources, to this function. Serving the clients then becomes a follow-up requirement.

The firm that is oriented to serving its clients, on the other hand, counts on the caliber of its service to build its reputation and help attract clients. Seeking new clients is confined to available time and attention.

The marks of the selling-oriented firm include frequent mass sales contacts or broad mailings soliciting business and, usually, a high turnover rate of clients.

For counsel who are established and have built a good reputation, new accounts usually come through recommendations of present clients, word of mouth in business circles, or tips from friends. This, of course, is the ideal way to get new business. Because of its irregularity and unpredictability, however, it usually cannot be the only source of accounts. When a counsel has resigned an account, for instance, or has completed an assignment, it may be necessary to add business to retain a margin of profit.

The following methods of selling are generally accepted as ethical within the profession:

1. Personal inquiries made of prospects at clubs, business meetings, or conventions.

2. Letters or calls prompted by reports that the recipient is contemplating employing counsel.

3. Mediation of mutual acquaintances who feel that the counsel and the prospect can benefit each other.

4. Distribution of institutional literature on public relations or phases of it, in which low-key description of the counsel's organization and services may be included.

5. Mailings containing specific information about a specific type of business, with distribution confined to that business (such as newsletters, folders on activities conducted in that field, and the like).

6. Third parties who inform the counsel of "tips" to follow. It is considered ethical to pay "finder's fees" or commissions, not to be added to the fee charged the client, for such leads.

The following are considered acceptable by most practitioners:

1. Institutional advertising, including mailing of information about the firm, inviting inquiries

2. Brochures about the counseling firm itself or about its principals openly intended to be sales devices

3. Offering commissions to advertising agencies, management consulting firms, and others who can direct public relations accounts

4. "Cold calls" in letters, in person, or by telephone

These methods are generally considered improper:

1. Employed salespersons who make the rounds of possible clients and then are paid out of the fees received from the accounts brought in

2. Solicitation of accounts already held by other counsel when sales methods involve criticizing the services, undercutting the fees, or offering favors

Presentations and proposals

Public relations is not yet well enough understood among businesspeople and the means of measuring counsel are not well enough defined to enable most organizations to choose a counsel on reputation only, as doctors and lawyers are chosen. It is usually necessary for the counsel to demonstrate what he or she feels can be done for the prospective client and, in many cases, to also define the ways in which public relations itself will function.

This means that counsel are faced with the necessity of preparing a presentation or proposal before being retained. The term *presentation* generally means a rather elaborate accumulation of facts, ideas, graphic devices, sales talk, and budget. A "proposal" may consist of only a brief analysis of the services required and the terms of the counsel for performing them.

Because of the variety of public relations problems and techniques, it is hardly possible to develop one presentation that can be adapted for almost every prospect, as many advertising agency presentations can be. They must be made to order and, as a result, their preparation can become a major problem for the counsel. The trend is for organizations, particularly trade associations, to invite eight to twelve counsel to make presentations for an account. To compete favorably each must go to considerable trouble and expense for what is, at best, a long-shot possibility. As a result, there has been discussion within the field of an agreement to limit the type of presentation that a counsel may be called on to prepare for such a process of selection.

Another suggested remedy is that the prospective client agree to pay the costs of a presentation. Rather than making this a financial burden, it is expected to discourage wholesale interviewing and lead the prospect to narrow its field to two counsel before calling for presentations.

How much to put into a presentation or proposal is also a matter of debate. Many counsel say that since the chief stock-in-trade of a public relations person is ideas, it is a mistake to fill the presentation with the ideas that are to be the basis for the fees expected. Although they are rare, there have been instances of organizations culling ideas from a number of counsel's presentations and utilizing them without compensation.

Until such time as public relations counsel are retained on their reputation alone, it will probably be the problem of each one individually to determine how to proceed in dealing with each prospective client's demand for proof of competence and what can be accomplished.

Resigning an account

The value of a public relations counsel to a client is based on common understanding and respect, complete cooperation and confidence, and mutual willingness to help the other in the common cause. When any of these elements is lacking, the ability of the counsel to perform the function for which he or she is retained decreases. When he feels that this ability is so much affected that he is not serving effectively, he should feel justified in resigning the account. It has become a common saying in the field that the true public relations counsel must be continually prepared to lose the job or the client. No stigma is attached today to such resignations.

The counsel is equally justified in breaking off relations with a client when demands for service make the account unprofitable or when the client's policies force the counsel to put his or her name on releases or reports he or she cannot believe in.

It is difficult to give up an account, especially when it is profitable. But it is often wise to protect one's reputation and feeling of integrity, even at the cost of momentary financial loss.

Internal functions of the firm

In general, operation of the counsel's office is similar to the functioning of any general business office. Bookkeeping, for example, follows normal patterns and the specific techniques depend largely on the methods of billing discussed earlier in this chapter.

There are a few procedures, however, that are peculiar to the business: developing mailing lists and contacts, preparing clippings, contacting clients, and presenting and reviewing progress reports.

Mailing lists and contacts

The discussion of lists in Chapters 20 and 22 makes clear how important and extensive is the job of building and maintaining lists. Since almost all the contacts the counsel's clients have with their publics depend on the use of these lists, they are a cornerstone of the firm's procedure.

Clippings

Recording, sorting, collecting, analyzing, and preparing clippings and other reports of results for presentation to the client frequently require major consideration, particularly during publicity campaigns for a client.

Contacts with the client

Usually all meetings and discussions with a client that are more than routine checks or seeking of information are handled by a principal of the firm or an executive assigned to the account. The contact between the client and the firm not only establishes policies and sets plans, but serves as the crucial point at which the counsel and associates serve as liaison between the client and its publics. Because it is so important, it demands the best skills and experience of the firm.

Reports

When monthly roundtable meetings are held with the client, a progress report and an outline of proposed new activities are required as the agenda for the meeting. Meeting reports should be drafted and sent to all concerned. In other cases, periodic reports are desirable even where the client does not request them. They serve to keep visible what is being done and the up-to-date status of the program. Memories of busy people are short unless they are prompted.

48

CONSIDERATIONS OF LAW IN PUBLIC RELATIONS

FRANK WALSH

Frank Walsh combines expertness in law and public relations. He is an attorney who specializes in communications law and operates Walsh Public Relations and Research, a counseling firm in Austin, Texas. He also conducts seminars on public relations law. Besides his law degree, he holds bachelor's degrees in journalism/English and political science/ history.

Legal, judicial, and legislative additions defining, regulating, and in some cases, limiting the communications role of public relations have fallen somewhat behind the growth of the public relations field in general. The law pertaining to public relations activities is in a continual state of development, challenging the practitioner to keep abreast of the laws affecting his or her role as a communications manager.

The most important broad step today's public relations professional or department can take is to establish a solid working relationship with a reputable attorney experienced in public relations–related law. When doing so, it is important to keep in mind these two guiding principles:

1. Don't assume your department does not need legal representation simply because it is small or a nonprofit organization. Insist that public relations be given the same access to legal counsel as finance, human resources, legislative, or any other function.

2. Just as important as access to legal counsel is the nature of the relationship between that counsel and the public relations practitioner(s). The legal counsel must be or become sufficiently familiar with ever-changing communication law to serve as your advocate—rather than merely playing the all-too-familiar and often ineffective role of "Let's don't and just be safe" attorney. In most cases the question is not whether communication should or should not be done, but instead, how the communications should be administered to meet all legal requirements. In order for the PR person and the attorney to work as a team, each must first understand the other's role. Establishing that kind of understanding takes time and effort and usually will not assume a positive note if developed under duress during a time of crisis.

The public relations practitioner who fails to familiarize himself or herself with public relations laws and to practice accordingly places himself, as well as his organization, at great financial risk. Obviously it also holds the risk of seriously undermining the professional and ethical reputation of the practitioner.

It is imperative, therefore, that public relations practitioners gain a working knowledge of those areas of law affecting public relations. Only then can they understand the basic guidelines of communications law, identify potential problems, and know when to seek legal counsel.

This chapter provides an overview of many of the communications areas in which the practitioner should be aware of the law. It also covers in more depth some of the communications areas that have the most frequent applications to public relations. A more in-depth explanation of these areas is covered in *Public Relations and the Law*, by Frank Walsh, published by the Public Relations Institute, 310 Madison Avenue, New York, NY 10017.

The legal areas of concern to the public relations practitioner that are covered in this chapter are as follows:

- Privacy
- Copyright
- Advertising and corporate free speech
- Defamation
- Investor relations
- Lobbying
- Representing foreign interests
- Broadcasting fairness rule
- Rights to creative materials
- Trademarks
- Access to federal information
- Communication by management with labor

Public relations practitioners should take advantage of professional seminars and public relations publications to update themselves on additional legal areas of law not covered in this chapter, including the following:

- Potential liability of the public relations practitioner
- Federal Trade Commission
- U.S. Postal Service regulations

Protecting the Right to Privacy

Commonly, and in its most general terms, privacy is "the right to be left alone." More specifically, privacy "defends those intangible attributes of the human personality that exist apart from his physical person and his worldly assets."

Four distinct legal concepts create the privacy umbrella: appropriation, intrusion on the plaintiff's physical solitude, publication of private matters violating the ordinary decencies, and putting the plaintiff in a false position in the public eye. Only one of these, appropriation, has a significant impact on the practice of public relations.

Appropriation is the taking of a person's name or likeness for "advertising purposes" or "purposes of trade." Except for identical twins, a person's face is unique and, therefore, the value of an image or likeness can be easily traced to a particular individual. The use of a name by itself, on the other hand, is not enough to successfully bring an appropriation lawsuit; many persons have the same name. It is a name plus the personality or experience of a particular individual that makes that one name among several more identifiable and valuable. One Tom Jones among the many can be set aside as unique because of his experience or personality.

While most cases of appropriation involving advertising present the public relations practitioner with a clear black-and-white guideline of when consent is necessary, cases involving "purposes of trade" are exceptionally gray. When a person's name or likeness appears in an advertisement, consent is needed. Where the common-law right of privacy is recognized, financial gain is not the only standard of whether a person's name or likeness has been appropriated. The following short factual situations provide the practitioner incidences in which there was no financial gain, but the court found appropriation: plaintiff's name signed to a telegram to governor urging him to veto a bill; use of a person's name as a candidate for office by a political party; using the name of a person as the father of a child on a birth certificate; use of a name in title of a corporation; impersonation to obtain secret information; or the use of a photograph of plaintiff entering and leaving streetcar to teach other passengers how to do it. Consent is needed for such activities.

However, New York, Oklahoma, Virginia, Utah, and California have privacy statutes requiring proof of monetary advantage gained by the publication before a suit may be successful.

Also, the "purposes of trade" concept does not apply to publication of news. The courts, in defense of press freedom, have repeatedly held that even though a newspaper, magazine, or broadcast station makes a profit, that does not mean that everything published is "for purposes of trade."

Contrary to the general rule of not being able to use a person's likeness in an advertisement without consent, the reverse is true when the likeness constitutes only incidental use. A legal researcher suggests for such cases: "The general rule is that a photograph reasonably related to an article or book on a matter of public interest will not be actionable."

Privacy and employee publications

One of the primary responsibilities of the public relations practitioner is informing employees. Most organizations have employee publications—bulletins, newspapers, or various forms of audio or videotapes. Invasion of an employee's privacy by appropriation is as important a consideration in this area as in other areas of privacy. Unfortunately, the legal guidelines are unclear and the public relations practitioner operates in an extremely gray area.

What is the "primary purpose" of a publication or a particular article? The law of privacy turns on this "primary purpose" concept. Generally, employee publications can be divided into three broad categories: internal, external, and internal-external. (*See* Chapters 12 and 31.)

The legal exposure for invasion of privacy by appropriation increases from completely internal to totally external publications. It should not be assumed that a person's status as an employee waives his or her right of privacy. However, there are circumstances in which the employment relationship may provide an implied consent or waiver sufficient to invalidate an invasion of privacy suit.

For example, if the practitioner publishes a factual item as a "personal" in an internal publication, it most likely will be treated as newsworthy to employees reading it. The publication and the particular article receive the same protection given to the public press and no consent is needed. Close association of the employee with the organization, his or her work, or the organization's activities (contribution to a new product, company-sponsored softball team, a promotion) tends to focus on the organization and away from the employee. With more organization and less employee emphasis, there is less opportunity to invade the individual's privacy.

Even with implied or written consent, no material should be used once the employee leaves the organization. The courts see a difference between consent of employer and employee and consent between an organization and an independent person.

Intrusion is invading a person's solitude, including the use of cameras or microphones.

In its simplest terms, privacy protects the physical space around a person. In his or her home it is greatest; on a public street or other public place it is least protected.

The general rule is that if you can see something of public interest in a public place, you can photograph it. However, protection does not extend to cases in which the photograph opens the individual to more than general observation. Such was the case in which a woman was photographed in a "Fun House" with her dress blown up over her head and for a football player when a photograph showed him with his fly zipper open. The courts found an invasion of privacy by intrusion.

The intrusion tort also includes information obtained by illegal entry to a house, or to office files, or by surreptitious tape recording of information.

Telephone company tariffs forbid recording two-way telephone conversations without a beep tone or prior consent or notice to the parties. Some practitioners like to tape telephone conversations with media representatives as protection against being misquoted. Media representatives also like to record conversations for accuracy and perhaps to have a record of "off the record" comments. While federal law does not prohibit taping telephone conversations as long as the recording is done by one of the parties, local telephone company tariffs forbid such taping. The penalty, however, is for the phone company to cut off service, which is unlikely.

Publication of private matters involves the right to be free from unwanted publicity about private affairs which, although true, would be offensive to a person of ordinary sensibilities.

Most of the cases in this area apply to the news media. However, a couple of the more prominent cases might well apply to public relations. The first case involves a bank's community relations effort in publishing a history of its community. The history included a short summary of the first-degree murder trial and conviction of the plaintiff for the shooting death of a policeman. The history was published in 1980; the death occurred in 1952. The plaintiff pleaded that he was no longer newsworthy and that the history invaded his privacy. The second case involves a "Page from Our Past" feature of a weekly newspaper about the cattle-theft trial of three brothers four years earlier. While this was in a newspaper, many public relations campaigns use similar "looks back into the past" to highlight some aspect of a person or organization.

In both cases the court found for the defendant, because the information was part of public record. Still, the courts may take a different view of its use if the public relations program used paid space to disseminate the information. At the core of a defense in such cases is the public interest as determined by newsworthiness.

False light is placing an individual in an objectionable false light in the public eye.

While most of these involve the use of photographs, false light can involve written material in the form of a story or a caption. For the public relations practitioner, the use of stock photographs a second or third time for different purposes increases the chances of a false light case, as some of the following illustrate: The picture of a child hurt in an automobile accident, later used to illustrate an article, "They Ask to Be Killed"; the picture of an honest taxi driver illustrating an article on the cheating propensities of taxi drivers; and a photograph of an embracing couple illustrating an article on the "wrong kind of love."

News and Consent Privacy Defenses

News as a defense

Newsworthiness is a defense to an invasion of privacy. In general, the defense applies much more to the mass media than to public relations efforts, though public relations practitioners will cite examples in which newspapers and radio and television stations are not the only organizations that distribute news to the general public or to specific publics. Examples would be when a health organization goes directly to the public with important health information, or a corporation sponsors a community event and uses direct mail to inform the public.

If news is to be a defense to an invasion of privacy, the answer to the question, "What is news?" is important. Just calling something news does not necessarily make it news. For a long time and in many jurisdictions, courts tended to accept whatever journalists defined as news. However, one circuit court and the highly respected *Restatement of Torts* suggest that courts—meaning the jury—should set standards of newsworthiness. There would be a "community standard" applying to privacy cases that juries would use to determine that something is "highly offensive to a reasonable person" and whether it is "of legitimate concern to the public."

Taste and good judgment should eliminate any problem with distribution of material. One guideline of whether something is of legitimate concern to the public is whether the subject matter has appeared in the mass media and how it has been treated. Certainly courts that allow news to be determined by journalists would allow this approach. There is an important caveat here: the courts draw an important distinction between mass media organizations and all other organizations. Although mass media organizations make a profit by the dissemination of information (news), the courts do not interpret this as "purposes of trade." The courts may well see similar dissemination of information by another organization as being done for "purposes of trade," thus removing the defense of newsworthiness.

Consent as a defense

If other areas of privacy are gray, consent is refreshingly clear and straightforward. Despite this and the significant dangers of not obtaining consent, a surprising number of practitioners either do not use consent releases or use weak ones.

In states that have privacy statutes—California, New York, Oklahoma, Utah, Wisconsin, and Virginia—prior written consent is the only way an organization will not be liable for invasion of privacy. In common law states, those states not having privacy statutes, implied or oral consent may mitigate or reduce damages. However, it doesn't seem prudent for the public relations practitioner to expose his or her organization to the dangers of a privacy suit by not using a well-written, enforceable consent release.

Consent releases need to cover a variety of circumstances. Below are several of the more important elements that may be included to make a consent release protect both the public relations practitioner and his or her organization. A typical release is shown in Figure 48.1 (page 722) to provide examples of wording that includes each of these elements.

Written

Consent releases must be written to be recognized in states that have privacy statutes. In states that do not have statutes, implied consent is far too weak a defense on which to depend, particularly when legal suits can cost an organization several hundreds of thousands of dollars in damages. The only area in which the public relations practitioner can safely rely on implied consent is in the use of

MODEL CONSENT RELEASE*

In consideration of the sum of (amount) dollar(s) and other valuable
consideration, the receipt of which is hereby acknowledged, I certify to
being over twenty-one years of age and hereby give (organization's name),
its successors and assigns and those acting under its permission or upon its
authority, the unqualified right and permission to reproduce, copyright,
publish, circulate or otherwise use photographic reproductions or likenesses
of me and/or my name. This authorization and release covers the use of said
material in any published form, and any medium of advertising, publicity, or
trade in any part of the world for ten years from date of this release or as
long as I am an employee of said organization.

Furthermore, for the consideration above mentioned, I, for myself, my
heirs, executors, administrators or assigns, sell, assign and transfer to
the organization, its successors and assigns, all my rights, title, and
interests in and to all reproductions taken of me by representatives of the
organization. This agreement fully represents all terms and considerations
and no other inducements, statements or promises have been made to me.

_____   _____

Signature of Employee   Date

_____   _____

Signature of Organization Representative Date

*While this model consent is suggested as providing most of the requirements
of a valid release form each person and organization should consider circumstances special to the particular organization before designing a consent
form. As written, this model release may or may not provide adequate protection.

Figure 48.1 A prototype release form.

an employee's name or likeness in a strictly internal employee publication.

Proper parties

This is one of the areas in which a consent release may differ. *Proper parties* for the vast majority of consent releases means the name(s) of the organizations' representatives and the person(s) whose name, photograph, or other information will be used.

A release signed by a minor (someone under age twenty-one) is not sufficient protection for the organization. The release should by signed not only by the minor, but also by parents, guardian, or the person *in loco parentis*. A consent release signed by a minor is not void, but it is voidable when the minor reaches majority.

Consideration

Legally, consideration is value given for something received. If an organization uses a person's name or likeness and wants to make such use irrevocable, the organization has a legal obligation to give the person something of value in return. If value is not exchanged, the release is not illegal, but the person can revoke consent at any time and require the organization to stop using his or her name or likeness. This can be a significant expense if the material is used in an annual report, videotape, or other expensive communication medium. It has also been held that revocation takes place "automatically" if the relationship at the time consent was initially implied or granted has ended.

It is not unusual that the consideration is only $1. Consideration may be much larger in the case of a model or celebrity who earns his or her living with name and likeness. The consideration may be a direct payment or part of a larger agreement. An example would be the appearance of a sports figure or an employment contract.

Scope

The scope of a consent release should be as broad as possible. For example:

- It should cover the different kinds of communication, such as advertising, publicity, etc.

- It should say who can use the information. Not only should the organization signing the release be able to use the information, but it should be able to give permission without having to go back to the other party involved.

- Just for safe measure, the release should cover where the information might be used. This means the practitioner might include the state, states, or even the world as possibilities.

Creative use of photographs may call for the photograph to be altered. This may cause some danger for the public relations practitioner.

Duration

The prudent public relations practitioner should include a time element, which may be five, ten, twenty, or even fifty years. Include a time element so the subject will know definitely when he or she signs the consent the extent of the permission and will have the opportunity to object.

Words binding on personal representatives

Such words bind the heirs of the subject consenting to use of his or her name or likeness, as well as any other person who may succeed to the rights of the subject. Though such words would not apply to an employee, since consent ends when employment ends, the prudent public relations practitioner always will include them in a consent release.

Tie the release to a broader agreement

Consent may be included in an agreement that has a purpose much broader than consent. The following are just a few examples to give the public relations practitioner a feel of how this might be done:

- A patient's consent to be treated by a physician may also include consent to use information about the patient, including photographs, if the treatment might be used as part of a research report.
- The employee's work contract if the public relations practitioner foresees possibly using the employee's name or likeness in publications that are distributed outside the organization.
- An athlete or celebrity is making an appearance for your organization and you need to use his or her name and likeness to promote the event.

No other inducement

This is important should your consent release reach the courts for interpretation. In effect, include words that specifically state everything agreed to is in the consent release and if it's not in the release, it's not part of the agreement. Courts like to see this so they are not put in a position of believing one side or the other about what really was included in the agreement.

It is important to tie together the various elements of the consent so consent is irrevocable—making sure some exchange of value is provided.

Use or purchase of photographs acquired from a secondary source raises the same privacy questions. It's common for one practitioner to give permission to another to use a photograph or for the practitioner to buy the use of the photos from a stock-photo house. It is common that the supplier of the photo will stamp the back of the print with "Model Release" or even a more complete release. The challenge for the practitioner is to determine what, if any, limitations exist in the release. In some instances, the supplier of the photograph may not have releases or, perhaps, releases of a scope sufficient to protect the purchaser.

Copyright Law

Few areas of the law apply so directly and frequently to the practice of public relations as the law of copyright. The practitioner produces information and in the process uses information from a variety of sources. Producing information raises the question of how a practitioner gains protection for his or her or the organization's work. The use of information raises the question of what information can be used by the practitioner without infringing the copyright protection of another person or organization.

New federal law eliminates all state copyright statutes and the dual system of common law copyright protection for unpublished works and statutory protection for published works.

Practitioners should not confuse copyright law with the law of patent. Patent is the legal protection covering a process or method rather than something in a fixed form, which is a requirement of copyright. Copyright also is different from trademark. Trademark may be a "word, symbol, design or combination word and design, a slogan or even a distinctive sound which identifies and distinguishes the goods or services of one party from those of another." Also, unlike a copyright or patent, trademark rights can last indefinitely if the mark continues to perform a source-indicating function.

Copyright is also different from plagiarism. Copyright is a legal concept enforceable by law; plagiarism is an ethical concept enforceable only with the organization by its own ethical standards. If a piece of information is in public domain, that is, the information either never had copyright protection or copyright protection has ended, the practitioner has the legal right to use the information without asking permission of the author. However, the practitioner still has an ethical responsibility to attribute the information to the author. If the information is not attributed to the author, readers may assume the practitioner wrote the material; this then becomes plagiarism.

Copyright protection

Copyright's foundation is the concept that the material must be in a fixed form. Ideas, procedures, processes, systems, method of operation, concept, principle, or discovery cannot be copyrighted; what may be copyrighted is the form in which facts and ideas are presented. For example, the idea of a sunset cannot be copyrighted, but the words and sentences describing a sunset in a fixed form can be. A photograph of the Statue of Liberty may be copyrighted, but that does not prevent anyone else from taking photos of this landmark. Protection is provided only to that one photographic illustration.

What can be copyrighted includes a broad spectrum of material. Specifically the statute provides: "Works of authorship fixed in any tangible medium of expression, now known or later developed, from which they can be perceived, reproduced, or otherwise communicated, either directly or with the aid of a machine or device."

Material produced by the U.S. government is not protected by the new law. All material produced by the federal government is in the public domain and available for use by any of its citizens.

Copyright protection begins "when it is fixed in a copy or phonorecord for the first time." That means when photographic film is exposed, words are printed on paper, and

images are recorded on videotape, they have copyright protection. As will be stated later, additional requirements are necessary to enforce this protection. The section goes on to say that when a work "is prepared over a period of time, the portion of it that has been fixed at any particular time constitutes the work as of that time, and where the work has been prepared in different versions, each version constitutes a separate work."

In general, copyright protection "endures for a term consisting of the life of the author and 50 years after the author's death." The life-plus-50 rule is different for organizations. Under the provision for works made for hire, the law states that "the copyright endures for a term of 75 years from the year of its first publication, or a term of 100 years from the year of its creation, whichever expires first."

While death of the author starts the clock running in terms of individual authorship, publication starts the clock running for an organization. Because publication can take many forms, the law goes to some length to provide guidelines:

- Publication means distribution of copies or phonorecords of a work to the public by sale or other transfer of ownership, or by rental, lease, or lending.

- Offering to distribute copies or phonorecords to a group of persons for purposes of further distribution, public performance, or public display constitutes publication.

- A public performance or display of a work does not of itself constitute publication.

The element of notice is the first step for formal copyright protection. Its purpose is to give notice to users that the material belongs to the person named in the notice. The notice must appear in a place sufficiently obvious to give reasonable notice to a user that the material is copyrighted. There are three subelements:

1. The symbol "c" in a circle (©), or the word "Copyright," or the abbreviation "Copr."

2. The year of first publication of the work

3. The name of the owner of copyright in the work, or an abbreviation by which the name can be recognized, or a generally known alternative designation of the owner.

The owner of a published copyrighted work with notice must deposit two copies of the material with the Copyright Office, Library of Congress, Washington, DC 20559, within three months of publication, accompanied with an application for registration for copyright. This is a simple four-page form that can be obtained from the Copyright Office, 101 Independence Avenue, Washington, DC 20559. A copyright hotline is available to answer questions between 8:30 A.M. and 5 P.M. during the week. The number is (202) 707-3000.

Fair use versus infringement

The statute provides exceptions to general copyright protection when protected material may be used without fear of an infringement action. "Fair use" includes that the use "of a copyrighted work, including such use by reproduction in copies or phonorecords . . . , for purposes such as criticisms, comment, news reporting, teaching, is not an infringement of copyright."

As factors to consider in determining whether the use made of a copyrighted work constitutes "fair use," the statute suggests looking at the following:

1. The purpose and character of the use, including whether such use is of a commercial nature or is for nonprofit educational purposes

2. The nature of the copyrighted work

3. The amount and substantiality of the portion used in relation to the copyright work as a whole

4. The effect of the use on the potential market for or value of the copyright work

For the public relations practitioner, the most important of these guidelines is any impact on the potential market for or value of the work. Infringement in this area is more apt to raise problems than the other guidelines. Another hard question is whether an author makes use of another's work without doing substantial independent work. Obviously, wholesale copying is not fair use.

If the practitioner wants to use all or part of a copyrighted work, the Copyright Office will have the full name and address of the owner. A letter to the owner detailing the part to be used, the intended use of the material, and the identity of the organization to be using the material is sufficient to gain permission. The owner may well respond with restriction on the use, the length of time it may be used, any income that might be obtained in the use, and how a credit line recognizing the copyright owner would be given. It may also be important to indicate whether the organization requesting permission is profit or nonprofit.

The statute defines infringement of copyright as "anyone who violates any of the exclusive rights of the copyright owner . . . or who imports copies or phonorecords into the United States. . . ." The courts have the power to issue injunctions, impound and dispose of infringement articles, and award monetary damages as means of enforcement of the statute. The plaintiff may recover actual damages caused by an infringement or ask for statutory damages that can run as high as $10,000. If the copyright owner sustains the burden of proving copyright infringement and the court finds the infringement was willful, the damages may go as high as $50,000. Criminal penalties may include fines of up to

$50,000 and two years in prison. Both civil and criminal actions for infringement must start within three years after the infringement began or any legal action is lost.

In 1964, the Supreme Court extended First Amendment constitutional protection to ideas of public interest conveyed in advertising. More and more public relations practitioners are taking advantage of the control offered by advertising to communicate important messages.

The changes that have taken place in this area of law offer an excellent example of legal evolution. In more than forty years, the Supreme Court has gradually changed its position. More than likely, the law will change again, making it necessary for the practitioner to keep up-to-date.

The *New York Times* case in 1964 granted constitutional protection for advertisements that deal with important or social matters.

Later it ruled that the relationship of speech to the marketplace of products or services does not make it valueless in the marketplace of ideas. The court has ruled that a state cannot ". . . completely suppress the dissemination of concededly truthful information about entirely lawful activity, fearful of the information's effect upon its disseminators and its recipients."

With First Amendment protection extended to products and services of interest to citizens, the court ruled that corporate political speech is entitled to First Amendment protection saying such activity "is at the heart of the First Amendment protection . . . the First Amendment goes beyond protection of the press and the self-expression of individuals to prohibit government from limiting the stock of information from which members of the public may draw."

Understanding Defamation

Defamation presents perhaps the most complex and confusing rules for everyday tools of the profession. Consider the following:

1. For the most part, defamation deals with the reputation of a person, corporation, or organization. The definition of reputation is intangible—it changes from one person to another, from one area of the nation to another, from one profession to another, and from one jury to another.

2. Words that defame can be contained in almost all communication tools available to the public relations practitioner.

3. The damages awarded for defamatory words reach millions of dollars and the legal fees of a defense for a defamatory suit can also be huge. Also, an organization found liable for defamatory words often suffers embarrassment within its industry and among its supporters.

4. Legal opinions on government defamation differ by degree from state to state and from one federal district to another, leaving the public relations practitioner looking for local application of important restraints on government communication.

Morton J. Simon, in his *Public Relations Law,* summarizes it well, "Much of the law of defamation may seem erratic and even ridiculous to both lawyer and layman."

Defamation also has an ethical side. As one example of this, Article 10 of the PRSA Code of Professional Standards states: "A member shall not intentionally injure the professional reputation or practice of another practitioner." Obviously, if a person violates the ethical side of this issue, he or she also may be open to legal redress.

No one definition of defamation appears to be accepted by all courts. It has evolved, and the modern definition states defamation is a communication that tends to "diminish the respect, goodwill, confidence, or esteem in which he is held, or to excite adverse or unpleasant feelings about him."

As the definition of defamation has evolved, the historical definitions of its two major components—libel and slander—also have changed. At one time, libel was defined as written defamation; slander as oral. Today, libel is the principal branch of defamation. In general, libel is derogatory statements that are printed or otherwise permanent; slander is transitory and usually consists of spoken words or insulting gestures. For the public relations practitioner, slander has little importance compared with libel.

The status of libel took on particular importance with the modern concept of "defamacast," suggesting that radio and television have the potential for damaging a reputation that was more akin to print than to oral expression.

Most often we think of an individual as the subject of defamatory comments, but the application of defamation is much broader.

Any living person, including children, may be the subject of defamation. Ordinarily a dead person may not be defamed. However, living persons may be mentioned in connection with stories of deceased persons and, if the references to the living are defamatory, the living may recover damages. A curious note to this area is that a person may be so notorious as a criminal that he or she becomes "libel-proof" and the courts will not accept a libel action.

More important to the public relations practitioner is application of defamation to a corporation, nonprofit organization, partnership, association, or union, where the comments cast aspersion on its honesty, credit, efficiency, or other business character. However, the courts have held that a government entity, such as a city, cannot bring a civil libel action.

Generally, large groups cannot sue for libel. Examples would be businessmen, lawyers, members of a political party, or members of an ethnic group. "Where the group or class libeled is small, and each and every member of the group or class is referred to, then any individual member can sue." How small is small? Twenty-five has been suggested.

Every communication tool used by the public relations practitioner has the potential to carry defamatory messages. That includes news releases, employee publications, posters, brochures, slide shows, videotapes, speeches, and reports. Headlines and tag lines, in some states, may be defamatory. The same is true of cartoons and caricatures. Photographs standing alone rarely pose defamatory danger, but with some ill-placed words a photo can open the door for recovery. The general rule is that a publication must be considered in its entirety, both the picture and the story which it illustrates. Mistake or poor judgment doesn't excuse these facts, as court rulings illustrate. A model was photographed in a Camel cigarette advertisement. Due to a photographic quirk, a portion of the saddle held by the model appeared to be attached to his body, making him appear guilty of indecent exposure. The court said the photograph, though not intentional, was actionable as a libel.

It is well established that defamatory copy in an advertisement leaves the publisher guilty along with the merchant or agency that furnishes it. More extreme, but still illustrating the fact that defamation can take almost any form, a court has found that statues and other three-dimensional forms, such as hanging a person in effigy, constitute publication.

There are two categories of defamatory defenses. The first deals with defamation as applied to "private individuals," and the second additional defense as applied to "public figures or officials." When private individuals are plaintiffs, they need only to show ordinary negligence on the part of the defendant. Public officials or public figures must prove "actual malice." (See discussion of actual malice later in this chapter.)

The defenses for private individuals are truth, privilege, and fair comment. The additional defense for public officials or figures is the "malice rule" coming out of the 1964 *New York Times* case.

Truth

According to some courts, truth alone is a complete defense, regardless of the motives behind its publication. The same is true with most state statutes. A few states still provide truth as a defense if it is published "with good motives and justifiable ends." The defense must be proven as "substantially" true by the defendant, that is, the practitioner. Proof of partial truth is insufficient as is proof of similarity to other facts.

Truth may not be easy to show. Reputation is intangible. Different persons may have different ideas of what ordinary words mean, especially if the defamatory statement is in the area of such loosely used words or phrases as "near bankruptcy," or "is close to a nervous breakdown." Also, truth is not the same as accuracy. The communicator may accurately quote a source. If the statement is legally defamatory, the accuracy of the quote does not relieve the communicator. Often the public relations practitioner and the source, such as a newspaper or broadcast station, become joint defendants.

Privilege

In its most general terms, privilege means communicating in the public interest. Members of the general public, including public relations writers and reporters, all have the defense of qualified privilege. Privilege involves the concept that certain day-to-day activities of individuals and business are important enough for at least some members of the public to know about. When these circumstances occur, the communication of defamatory information is protected.

Absolute privilege against defamatory liability is, in some instances, afforded communicators. This is ordinarily limited to such persons or situations as judges and judicial proceedings, counsel, litigating parties and witnesses, legislative proceedings and legislators (federal and state), and members of the executive branch.

Qualified privilege is a defense for persons covering an absolute privilege circumstance with substantial accuracy and without malice.

When the practitioner is reporting government affairs, qualified privilege applies to the communication. This kind of communication is becoming more frequent as government involvement with business increases. Often testimony, court orders or decrees, bills, and resolutions are stated in legal jargon and are not easily understood. If this is the case, the practitioner has the responsibility to seek clarification of the material before publishing the story.

The defense of qualified privilege depends on fair, accurate reporting. Errors destroy the defense. Opinion and extraneous material will also destroy the defense. To keep the defense of qualified privilege, all the information in an article must come from privileged sources.

The last defense for defamation that applies to a private individual is "consent." If a person approves an article about him, he or she cannot later claim he or she has been libeled in the article. A person, company, or trade group cannot deliberately invite investigation, then sue for defamation as a result of the investigation and the publication of the results.

The standard of negligence increases to "actual malice" with the 1964 *New York Times v. Sullivan* case. The Supreme Court said that

(the First Amendment) prohibits a public official from recovering for a defamatory falsehood relating to his official conduct unless he proves that the statement was made with "actual malice"—that is, with knowledge that it was false or with reckless disregard of whether it was false or not.

The application of this rule raises two important questions: Which persons are contained in the "public official" or "public figure" category? And what constitutes "actual malice"?

Since the *Times* case the courts have been unable to specifically define individuals who fit the "public official" or "public figure" categories. The trouble is not with defining *public official*. It includes persons elected or appointed to public office such as state legislators, a former mayor, a deputy sheriff, a school board member, an appointed city tax assessor, and a police sergeant. The public figure rule also can apply to businesses such as a credit union corporation chartered under law, in whose financial condition the general public has "a vital interest," and an insurance company which, in view of the insurance business' power and influence, invites attention and comment from the media.

Close to the practice of public relations is the question: When will the corporate or organization executive be judged a public figure? Some executives will be and others will not.

The courts continue to define what constitutes *actual malice*. In a case four years after the *Times* case, the Supreme Court reviewed the concept and said:

> These cases are clear that reckless conduct is not measured by whether a reasonably prudent man would have published, or would have investigated before publishing. There must be sufficient evidence to permit the conclusion that the defendant in fact entertained serious doubts as to the truth of his publication. Publishing with such doubts shows reckless disregard for truth or falsity and demonstrates actual malice.

Basic reporting standards, such as checking for accuracy and making sure of sources, help communicators stay away from the actual malice problem. The following are a few instances in which the court found actual malice: A reporter did not make personal contact with anyone involved in the event before writing about it; a publication relied on an obviously biased source, was advised of the falsity of information, and published it with no further investigation of the story; and the publication printed it although the story was inherently improbable.

Legal Considerations in Investor Relations

Investor relations is a significant and changing area of the law. Attorneys devote entire careers learning, interpreting, and practicing in this area. There is a great deal for the public relations practitioner to know, but perhaps the most important is when to turn to an attorney. In no other area of public relations law does the attorney play such a leading role in setting the tone and direction of financial activity. The role of the public relations practitioner is to fulfill the dissemination requirements stated in the various laws and regulations.

(A summary of what the practitioner involved with financial relations needs to know appears in Chapter 11.)

It used to be an interesting debate whether the public relations practitioner could be an "insider." Today the critical role played by the practitioner in corporate financial relations leaves no doubt. One definition of an *insider* is "all persons who come into possession of material inside information, before its public release, are considered insiders." The definition goes on to specifically name public relations advisors and advertising agencies as examples.

The cases and regulations also expand the definition to include husbands, wives, immediate families, and those under the control of insiders. For lack of a better term, also included are *tippees*, those who receive the information.

A case of the SEC should put the practitioner on notice that his or her activities in this area are being watched. The corporation involved issued a projection of earnings of $3.25 a share and $300 million in sales for the year (material information). Somewhat later the public relations executive representing the corporation learned that the projections were inaccurate. The practitioner passed the new information on to a stockbroker who in turn passed it to another stockholder. The two stockbrokers are said to have sold or advised the sale of more than $2 million in the corporation's stock before the public announcement was made. In this situation the practitioner became an insider and violated SEC regulations, but the stockbrokers were "tippees" and therefore insiders also.

Once an individual qualifies as an insider, he or she is prohibited from buying or selling the corporation's stock, as well as making the purchase or selling puts, calls, or other options in the corporation's stock. Insiders are released from this prohibition after the information has been made public and the investing public "readily understands" the information. The exchanges indicate that the time frame for when an insider may deal in the stock may change depending on the material. Some corporations and public relations agencies simply make it a policy to prohibit employees dealing with insider information from buying or selling the stock.

The PRSA Code of Professional Standards as it applies to financial relations appears in the Appendix.

Additional Considerations

Lobbying

Federal law requires that any person whose main purpose is to influence legislation through direct communication with members of Congress on pending or proposed federal legislation must register as a lobbyist. This includes direct influence on congressmen but not public relations programs that attempt to build up community support about issues, testimony before Congress, or publications that, as part of their normal operations, carry news and editorials urging the passage or defeat of legislation. It also does not include contacts with members of the executive branch, including various agencies, who then deal with members of Congress. (*See* Chapters 5 and 6.)

States and many cities also require registration of people who engage in lobbying.

Representing foreign interests

The Foreign Agents Registration Act requires anyone working as an agent of a foreign government, company, or political party to register within ten days with the U.S. Attorney General. Reports are required every six months on the names of foreigners served, activities conducted, and where and how funds were spent.

Broadcasting fairness rule

The personal attack rule of the Federal Communications Commission requires a station to provide time for reply to a person or group whose honesty or integrity is attacked during a discussion of a controversial issue. An editorial endorsement rule requires a station to provide time for reply to a candidate who is not endorsed in a station's commentaries. The person or candidate attacked must be notified, be given a transcript of the critical passage, and be provided with free time for a response if unable or unwilling to pay the station's rates.

Rights to creative materials

The work of a public relations practitioner in preparing written material or illustrations in the normal course of work creates "works made for hire" that belong exclusively to the employer or client. Work performed during off-hours or by outside freelancers and contractors calls for written contracts to define the rights of the employer and the creative person. A freelancer who sells work without a contract is giving up only the rights to first use.

Trademarks

The right to a trademark is established through usage in trade. Such rights are protected under common law. However, for protection it is wise to register a trademark with the U.S. Patent and Trademark Office any time after the product involved has been offered for sale. Registration lasts for twenty years but can be renewed as long as it is used actively. To prevent a trademark from being lost by becoming a generic term, such as cellophane or vaseline, many companies mark the name with a trademark symbol every time that it appears.

Access to federal information

The Freedom of Information Act gives "any person" (including corporations) access to all records of federal agencies unless those records are specifically exempted. Agencies need not release information that would jeopardize national security, reveal business trade secrets, invade an individual's privacy, or interfere with a law enforcement investigation. Internal agency memoranda and information specified by federal statutes are also exempted from disclosure. The government has ten days to respond to a request and twenty days to respond to an appeal if records are denied. However, long delays often occur.

Communication by management with labor

The Supreme Court has ruled that an employer is free "to take any side it may choose" on a labor issue so long as the employer does not restrain or coerce the employees. It is the company's course of conduct, not any individual statement, that can be considered coercive. (*See* Chapter 13.)

The Taft-Hartley Act, Section 8(c), says that no view, argument, or opinion of management is unfair labor practice if the expression contains "no threat of reprisal or force or promise of benefit."

Influencing potential jurors in lawsuits

Juries are often preconditioned to be negative about corporations being sued in liability cases. Plaintiffs' lawyers gain one-sided publicity about the alleged damage done, such as effects of gas leaks or implanted silicone breasts. To counteract this, some defendants have run advertisements in advance of jury selection to neutralize this preconditioning. Usually the ads do not directly refer to the issue in the case, to avoid charges of jury tampering (even though no jury has yet been selected). Instead, they deal with the good works and character of the company, the benefits of the product being attacked, and other positive factors.

Plaintiffs' lawyers have attacked this practice. Defendants cite their right to communicate under the First Amendment. As of March, 1997, the issue had not been resolved by the courts.

49

OTHER FUNCTIONS, PRINCIPLES, AND TRENDS

PHILIP LESLY

The pace of scientific advancement is usually greater than humanity's ability to understand and cope with humankind. Yet the great need to achieve the same degree of order in human relationships as that attained in the physical world is a common belief shared by social scientists, religious leaders, psychologists, historians, and others. Justifiably, these leaders of society fear that the rush of scientific knowledge is outpacing our ability to adapt to the rapid-fire changes taking place at the human level of our world.

The evolving principles now known about group attitudes—how they develop and how we consequently deal with them—comprise some of the most significant developments of the twentieth century. Of course, these have been paid only moderate attention, primarily because they lacked the dramatic flair of a spectacular explosion, man's propulsion into outer space, the conquering of a deadly disease, or the alleviation of invidious labor. In fact, some circles still ignore or regard with skepticism the advancement of techniques to influence group attitudes, as though they were not quite respectable.

However, given the relatively short period of time with which this evolution of public relations principles has transpired—indeed, well within the lifetime of many who remain active members of society—the high rate of its development and acceptance pays witness to its importance relative to all aspects and locales of life in a rapidly changing world.

Complexity of Group Attitudes

Public relations is one of the youngest of the basic disciplines. As a result, too little recognition is given to the great complexity in achieving any accurate knowledge, let alone control, of the attitudes of large masses of people. Any one person defies full understanding, or even knowledge, of the source of life itself, the forces that motivate it, or the drives that carry it through the myriad thoughts and emotions of a single day. Just one person is a puzzle far greater to humanity's understanding than any inanimate challenge it has conquered. And not only is a large group of such individuals infinitely more complex than one person, but as has been recognized since the explorations in Gustave LeBon's famous *The Crowd*, published in 1895, the sum of complexity of a large group is greater than the multiplication of individuals involved.

Achieving knowledge of how a virus causes a disease and finding an agent to destroy that virus is a miracle of man's capacity for creative and brilliant thought. But the virus is incomparably simpler a mechanism than the simplest of human beings, and the human being is infinitely simpler than the psychological group to which it belongs, in any given context.

It is encouraging that so much progress toward understanding what is involved in enabling groups to understand and cope with each other has been made in so short a time. It is even more encouraging that on the horizon can be seen promise of greater understanding in many areas of group psychology and communication. A few of those areas not otherwise treated in depth in this volume can be cited to indicate the direction in which thought is leading and to offer stimulus to further understanding and exploration.

Dealing with Intangibles in a Tangible World

Emphasis in management of all kinds of organizations is increasingly on evaluating, measuring, and predicting. The growing complexity of all aspects of life has come into confluence with the computer, quantitative analysis, and other tools for coping with complexity.

But the major problems facing business today are mostly intangible, immeasurable, and not subject to factual analysis. This applies also to governments, institutions, and other organizations.

- The main problem in manufacturing is no longer increasing the efficiency of our plants but affecting the attitudes of the people whose jobs are to be changed or eliminated by more efficient methods.

- The principal obstacle to planning for growth, increasing employment, and meeting the expectations of the public is not the availability of resources but the attitudes of conservationists, community organizations, and others who resist construction and technological innovation.

- The principal problem of growth through innovation is not organizing and administering development programs, but the reactions of the intended customers and dealers to the products.

- The personnel problem is not projecting a firm's manpower needs and standards, but persuading the best people to work for the company—then to stay and do their best work.

- The financing problem is not financial planning for the company's funding but the attitude of the stock market or other investors.

- The problem in advertising is not minutely analyzing the media, the timing, and the costs but how to reach the minds and hearts of the audience.

- The problem of business acceptance is not only demonstrating that it operates in the public interest but getting people to understand that its cornucopia works better when it is not unduly hampered by restraints.

All of these problems, and others, are in the minds of people—the most intangible, immeasurable, and unpredictable of all elements affecting a business.

Resistance of attitudes

Many of the recommendations that come out of hard-headed analysis of the "facts" are frustrated by existing attitudes. Not only are the analyses likely to be distorted by the lack of input about attitudes, but the "answers" cannot be executed.

- When the facts add up to moving a plant or headquarters, the move is often blocked by opposition of employees.

- Efforts to meet threats of new competition are hobbled by resistance of employees—for example, department stores' night and Sunday hours, refusal to accept partial cost of health care.

- The need to follow changing social patterns is blocked by lingering prejudices from past problems; efforts of major banks to follow population trends are balked by the laws limiting branch banking.

- Meeting competition: the public's readiness to have tax laws favor cooperatives and credit unions over their profit-making competitors.

- Technological innovation: delayed use of new materials and techniques because unions and activist groups block new methods or installation.

- Building excellence into the staff: employee and community sympathy for the weak but veteran employee; objection of career employees to bringing in outsiders rather than promoting from within.

Two electronic revolutions collide

The isolation of executives from the rest of society is abetted by the impact of electronic data processing and automation.

The size and function of complex institutions demand that their managers organize for their goals, eliminate unplanned variables, and systematize their decision-making process. They must have "smooth operations" and "scientific management." This science of management is geared to data processing and automation—an electronic revolution.

On the other hand, a generation whose development has been dominated by the electronic revolution of television and films assumes an activist role on behalf of the "human feelings" of social objectives. They pit "human feelings" against the "inhumanity" of mechanisms and institutions. They get high visibility through instant and widespread picturing of emotional "human interest events." This force is attuned to the picture tube and movie camera—another electronic revolution.

The anomaly existing between those opposing products of an electronic age and those who demand the benefits that are made possible only by electronic facilities constitutes a major problem. Communication between the two forces is vital, as is each one's understanding of the nature of today's communications.

The End of an Era of Oversimplification

In the developing maturity of public relations, a succession of concepts for a time evoked enthusiasm because they appeared to offer a simple means toward influencing desired audiences. A sign that the field is approaching true maturity is that these oversimplified panaceas are losing support and new ones are being met with considerable skepticism as they appear.

Some of those that have risen to attention and been found to lack sufficient scope to present answers include the following:

1. The concept of the "image" as the means toward recognition and acceptance. The idea that a "corporate image" can be developed to such a graphic state that the great majority of people the company is interested in will visualize it has faltered of its own inadequacies. It has been demonstrated that even the strongest corporate images are envisaged similarly by only a small fraction of any organization's public.

   However, the effectiveness of sharply defining the traits and characteristics of an organization so that it can be more readily understood by its various publics continues to be important. Development and projections of these characteristics represent much of the functioning of a sound public relations program.

   The most extreme efforts toward oversimplification of the image concept were found in organizations that sought to derive a visual symbol as if it alone were the corporate image. The *visual* elements of what a company represents are important, but they are not total.

2. The oversimplified belief that sufficient exposure of an idea is an assured means of driving it into the public's consciousness, then into acceptance.

3. What might be called the "bulldozer technique" in public relations. This is the belief

that if you spend enough money and have enough people on the payroll, you will accomplish your objectives. Actually, there are innumerable instances in which a small group of talented people with limited budgets but with creativeness and dedication have greatly outperformed monolithic masses of people and funds.

4. Various techniques of communication have become highly popular, taking on almost the essence of business fads, only to prove incapable of serving as cure-alls. They are gradually leveling off to a proper proportionate value in the list of resources available to the public relations person. At one time the open house was "the thing to do" for any company that felt it was enlightened about its public and community relations. Open houses became more and more elaborate, more and more common, and less and less effective, because they were not carefully selected and set up to meet a specified need. Today the open house is used selectively. The elaborate annual report was another technique that went through the overdevelopment stage and then leveled off as one tool in the communications kit.

Acknowledging the Fallacies of Communication

Recently there has been increased recognition of the limitations of many long-held beliefs about communication.

Many programs of communication are designed to "educate" the publics involved. In this sense, education is meant as the transfer of information from a knowing source into the minds of an unaware group. It is based on a faith that once people know the facts they will respond in precisely the way the source wants them to; that "they shall know the truth and the truth shall make them free." Faith in this type of "education" is expressed in the famous dictum of H. G. Wells: "Human history becomes more and more a race between education and catastrophe."

The actualities demonstrate the fallaciousness of this faith. Drug education programs that inform people of the dangers have reached billions of people many times—yet many of them have become addicted. A nine-month saturation campaign to persuade people to use auto seatbelts, conducted by the Insurance Institute for Highway Safety in a medium-sized city, had "no effect whatsoever." In fact, many people paid to have their seatbelt buzzers disconnected or to have the belts removed entirely. There is a high public awareness of the penalties of smoking, but the number of people who start smoking continues to be high.

It is evident that education can take place only when the intended recipient is inclined to accept it and takes the trouble necessary to respond. Yet as more people go through the formal education process, the faith in "education" as a cure for ills continues to grow, in the face of evidence that it usually fails or causes more problems. Many social-engineering efforts, as well as campaigns by private organizations, are based on faith that somehow a formula will be found for transmitting the facts into the minds and hearts of the audience.

Faith in interchange

It has been widely believed that friction between groups of people is the result of separateness; that if only they could be brought together and "get to know each other" they would develop mutual respect and understanding. That is the principle behind "involvement" and "sitting down together," both of which have been propounded as means to resolve conflicts.

However, like many rules, this one is often

untrue. Few groups are more "involved" with each other or understand each other so well as the Protestants and Catholics in Northern Ireland, the Turks and Greeks on Cyprus, the Jews and Arabs in the Middle East, and millions of husbands and wives everywhere.

Close involvement often emphasizes differences more than similarities. Especially, *forced* interchange that can lead to explosive opposition.

Interchange as a means of achieving understanding between groups is an important factor to consider; but the chances for making real progress must be assessed soberly and realistically. Where the groups have wide differences that their very nature prevents them from ceding, a realistic awareness of the impasse may be the only course of wisdom.

Discommunication[1]

Communication that's intended to get somebody's support for ideas is like courtship. We want to win that person over with labor, ardor, charm, and persuasion.

Yet millions of people who think they are communicating are really repelling the objects of their intention. There are eight ways that people discommunicate when they think they are communicating.

1. **The snobbery of jargon.** When we try to make others recognize we are in a different class, we use the language of our special field. We say things like *motivational deprivation* when we mean laziness. Language is supposed to be a bridge between people. Jargon instead digs chasms.

2. **No-name names.** There is a proliferation of company names that look and sound alike or like nothing at all—acronyms such as AMF, ACF, and ARA; coined names such as Ampco, Amrep, Amstar, and Amfac.

___
[1]From *How We Discommunicate*, Philip Lesly, AMACOM, N.Y., 1979.

3. **The lost art of expression.** Today most people have trouble expressing themselves, because they never really learned how to write and how to read. Good use of language is one of the greatest achievements of civilization. Most people use language like underwear, merely to cover the subject; only a few use it like lingerie, to show it at its best. They are the ones who beguile their audiences.

4. **Putting art ahead of meaning.** Illustration and design are supposed to help get a message across; but often the design is put ahead of the message, instead of being a vehicle for it. So we find corporate signatures that cannot be read, signs that don't direct, and color combinations that lose the printing. (*See* Chapter 3.)

5. **Deliberate destruction of communication.** Commercials blare, "Mc and my RC . . . 'cause what's good enough for other folks ain't good enough for me." Suave actors talk of "prespiration." Punctuation, such as apostrophes, wanders in and out of likely and unlikely places. The attitude is growing that language that's almost right is okay; but "almost right" communication can be as ineffectual as an almost right 23-foot leap over a 25-foot chasm.

6. **The temptation of "controlled communication."** Managers are inherently geared to seeing tangible things and to having control of what happens. They tend to be uneasy with communications that are invisible and that depend on how others use them, such as the press and broadcast outlets. So they are inclined to choose "controlled communication" to get across their ideas: ads they can see and approve in advance (*see* Chapter 30), company publications (*see* Chapter 12), bulletin board notices. Such overt messages can be effective in conveying information but are likely to be less effective in changing attitudes. They visibly tell the audience that

these are efforts to impose opinions on them.

7. *Euphemisms.* Many young people pride themselves on the forthrightness of their language. These same people are asked by many organizations to accept such terms as *deaccession* for unloading a losing division, *early retirement* for discharge with reduced pay, *discontinued* or *laid off* for fired, *misappropriated* for stolen. Efforts to mislead through euphemisms not only fail in the long run; the oral or written insincerity repels today's cynical, suspicious, educated audience.

8. **Condescension.** When a communicator is eager to exhibit his or her own stature and superior intellect, he shows he is manipulating the audience, rather than serving it; he condescends to his readers or viewers. He shows off the big words he knows, uses foreign phrases without translations, or wallows in gobbledygook to avoid simple, clear statements.

The biggest cause of these sins of discommunication is thinking about oneself instead of the audience. Ego is singular, likely to be massaged in solitude. Communication is plural, involving interaction with others, and makes it possible to win over multitudes. Ego is the enemy of good communication.

Media's Changing Role

For a whole network of reasons, the nature of the communications media has changed in the past generation—not only technologically, but in orientation and effect. The change is both the result and the cause of ferments in our society; and how it is accommodated will have much to do with the future nature of society.

In many ways, mass communication has progressed and improved more than any other aspect of modern living. Its impact, therefore, has been vastly increased and is now dominant in determining what course events shall take. Accordingly, it calls for constant review and evaluation. Public relations people must keep abreast of the media patterns constantly.

When there were only a few thought leaders and a few media, the individual medium tended to be highly personal. It was strongly marked with the personality of its moving force—a Greeley, a Hearst, a Pulitzer, a McCormick, a McClure, a Lorimer. Publishing a newspaper was possible and attractive for many people, so most people had a wide choice of papers and magazines.

Today, the major media are institutions. Few of them are organs of a leader's personality. What goes into the press and over the air is now largely determined by the bent of the creative staffs. Creative people are, by definition, sensitive—and this often means they are critical of all about them. They see a world that puts greater store on solid (they would say, stolid) virtues and achievements than on their valued intangibles.

Dr. Donald W. MacKinnon of the Institute of Personality Assessment and Research at the University of California, Berkeley, has said:

> There is the necessity in a creative person for a certain amount of what the poets have called "divine discontent."

Where the "media baron" who controlled voices of opinion in the past tended to be biased in favor of the *status quo*, many of the creative staffs of media today automatically favor anything that attacks it.

New competitive forces

First radio and then television heated up the competitive pressure among the media. Competition for audiences and, even more, for advertising support becomes more fierce constantly. Mass magazines find it hard to demonstrate their reasons for existence in a world of color television. Newspapers—even where there is a monopoly in a given city—find it harder to hold readers' attention and to keep advertising dollars ahead of rising costs. Costs of TV demand that audiences be vast so ad rates can be vaster. The pressure to grasp for attention—to sensationalize—intensifies.

In this climate, the reporter who produces a sensation is rewarded. The one who comes in with a solid but unspectacular report may find it hard to be appreciated.

The forces at work are augmented by the rapidly rising education and awareness of the public. An officeholder's embezzlement pales in interest when thousands are rioting or crowds shout for revolution. In other areas, such as science, the straight facts no longer are enough. Part of the reader's need is interpretation of the news. Especially in the print media, where space and time are available, it is the sensibility and sensitivity of the interpretation that mark the effective report.

Media as creators of news

All the factors mentioned combine to alter greatly the role of communications media. While Hearst's ability to produce a war in 1898 was so exceptional it marked the history books, today the media are creating events at every turn. TV broadcasters especially, apparently unaware of the great potency of their own medium, find it hard to recognize the impact of what they carry and are shocked when others question the consequences of treating equally such events as St. Patrick's Day parades and riots as spectacles.

The selection process, egged on by the hunger for sensation, creates "leaders" out of criminals who have minuscule followings—until the media anoint them.

This ability of the media to create "leaders" and "issues" by succumbing to the most unrestrained publicity hounds was noted as long ago as 1948 by Dr. Paul Lazarsfeld and Dr. Robert Merton of Columbia University in their paper "Mass Communication, Popular Taste and Organized Social Action":

> The mass media *confer* status on public issues, persons, organization and social movements. . . . Enhanced status accrues to those who merely receive attention in the media, quite apart from any editorial support. The mass media bestow prestige and enhance the authority of individuals and groups by *legitimatizing their status*. Recognition by the press or radio or newsreels testifies that one has arrived . . . that one's behavior or opinions are significant enough to require public notice. . . . The audiences of mass media apparently subscribe to the circular belief: "If you really matter, you will be the focus of mass attention, and if you *are* at the focus of mass attention, then surely you must really matter."

Now this process is accelerating in the area of issues and ideas.

Focusing attention on the media

While much that is remarkable and constructive has resulted from the media revolution, the force and importance of what has been happening inevitably has led to widespread concern. New looks at the role of media have been called for from all elements of society. The ownership of many media by one organization, either locally or nationally; the right to renewal of broadcast licenses regardless of the caliber or type of programming offered; the question of balance in presentation of differing viewpoints; the widespread efforts to "recreate" or otherwise alter events; the nature and influence of some types of advertising—these and other matters are being questioned with increasing urgency. Inquiry is healthy, but there is always danger of suppression, of government influence on a free press, or of other aberrations.

New shifts in the media mix

The complexity in the media situation is further accentuated by trends that seem to reverse some of the patterns cited: the difficulties of the mass magazines; the pressures from new competition to weaken large media combines and disperse influences of public opinion; the growing influence of publications reaching special-interest segments of the populace; and the growing prominence of the Internet and other new forms of media created by technology.

These trends lead to many more media units—local cable TV stations, videotapes for rental or purchase, more media voices in many localities, expanded public broadcasting, more magazines, the Internet, and newsletters devoted to specific interests. They may bring a partial return of the personal, involved media owner who is close to the audience, sensitive to it, and influential with it.

It is clear that as great as the change has been in mass communications in just a few years, much more change is ahead. Old methods of dealing with them, based on the press release and the quiet event, are obsolete. Today's methods probably will also be obsolete before long. It will be one of public relations' greatest challenges to keep abreast of this multifaceted pattern.

The Name's Impact on Image

The importance of concentrating on instilling readily identifiable characteristics of an organization into the minds of its publics is properly gaining the recognition of management leaders. It is difficult enough to get across the image of an organization without having it handicapped by a name that is inappropriate in any one of many ways.

That led to a pell-mell, faddist rush toward "simplification" that really bred confusion and difficulty. In an effort to derive names that are not at all misnomers, some companies adopted names that are not names at all.

A random look at a list of companies big enough to be listed on the New York Stock Exchange reveals more than fifty with initials or coined names based on esoteric syllables. There are many others among smaller companies. Many of them are recognizable only by their own employees and a few other people. After years of trying, only a few companies with such coined names have succeeded in attaining distinctiveness in the minds of even sophisticated businessmen and financial specialists.

One of the basic principles of names is that the right degree of distinctiveness—not too difficult, but not commonplace or meaningless—is important if the owner of the name is to make a lasting impression.

It is easier to remember Martin Morrison than it is 384-1093. Henry Josephson is remembered more easily than John Johnson. It is easier to distinguish between Annotated Notes Company and Amplified Notions Systems than it is between ANC and ANS.

The loss of identity that can result from this lack of recognition can be costly. The name is the distillation of what the company is and stands for in people's minds. It is much more its "image" than any emblem or logotype. The recognition it creates affects its impression among prospective employees, potential investors, dealers, customers, and others.

Factors in choosing a name

While there are many approaches to the selection of a new name, each of which has its proponents, it is important that the basic elements involved in the choice of a name be kept in mind during considerations. These include the following:

1. It must be *euphonious*—pleasant to the ear, easy to say, not subject to such mispronunciation as is common with Uslife and Tesoto.

2. It must be *memorable*—avoiding names that are too commonplace, such as "Smith," "National," "Universal," etc.—and easy to remember.

3. It should create a feeling of *friendliness and warmth*, if possible; a good name of a person would be preferable to an institutional name like "Standard" or "Empire." The word *Corporation* is likely to create more resistance than *Company*.

4. It should be *timeless*. It must not only be effective and suitable for the present, but safe from any conceivable developments of the future. It should not be associated with any techniques, product type, or other factor that could be outdated or limited by future events.

   It is possible, for instance, that companies now using the name "National" will be embarrassed in their efforts to exploit worldwide markets; and, going further into the future, should these companies adopt "International," they may have to change later to "Interplanetary."

5. The name should be *all-inclusive*, so it in no way limits future possibilities. For example, Frigidaire is good for a refrigerator but not a range. It is hardly possible now to predict what any company may be identified with thirty years in the future.

6. It must be *unduplicated*—not only in its own business but, if possible, in any area of business. This is not only important in preventing confusion and legal complication. It can be devastating if a company in any line, having a similar name, should run into very unfavorable publicity.

7. Similarly, the name must have *good associations* in the minds of all groups of people. It should not bring up unpleasant connotations or prejudices.

8. It should be *conducive to use*, in a logotype, on labels, and in other printed forms. Some combinations of letters are hard to distinguish at a glance or a distance, such as COATES, in which the capital "C" and capital "O" look so much alike.

9. It should be *registerable* in all countries.

10. It should have *quick acceptability*—not requiring a slow memorization or recognition process.

Despite the great attention being given to the name as an important image factor, there is no agreement on its role in marketing.

Exceptionally successful companies, such as General Electric and IBM, identify all products with the corporate name, feeling that its penetration fosters acceptance of each product. Equally successful companies, such as Procter & Gamble and American Home Products, subdue the corporate name and let each product develop acceptance under its own name.

The "umbrella-name" advocates point out that impressions much more massive than is possible for separate names accrue from total identification in advertising, publicity, cartons, truck signs, and other exposures.

The product-name advocates feel that the lack of success of one product or an unfavorable experience can too readily damage other products under the same corporate name. Products can be phased in and out of the market readily without affecting attitudes toward other products or the company. And a company can market products that compete with each other when they are named and marketed as competitors rather than as members of the same family.

Distinctive Corporate Identity and Other Symbols

Visibility is a major factor in the impression people have of any organization. The primacy of TV and film as the sources of most people's impressions has made how something looks almost as important as what it is or does. That has led to awareness that how the organization is identified is vital to creating the desired perception.

As a result, the art and science of corporate visual identity has become a prominent service used by public relations executives. Many companies have had new logotypes and name identification programs carried out to convey what they feel is their present-day impression. The program of the Pacific Gas & Electric Company is a good example.

Richard A. Clarke, president, explained: "A good corporate identity accurately reflects the mission, values and culture of a company. Research determined that the beige and brown PG&E logo detracts, *significantly* detracts, from an otherwise quite favorable perception of the company. That is, if they don't *see* the present logo, the customers think quite highly of PG&E. When they *do* see the logo, they think less highly of the company—even to the point of thinking the company to be old-fashioned, dull, and out of date."

When the new logo was introduced he was able to say, "The new visual identity is a *symbol* of change and an *agent* of change."

The PG&E program embodied the following representative schedule of activities:

1. Research, evaluation, and recommendations for identity strategy, including exploring the "corporate culture," interviewing company executives, and surveying employees, customers and opinion leaders

2. Exploring possible name modification

3. Developing objectives and design concepts

4. Refining the design concept chosen

5. Evaluating the proposed new design and researching its acceptance

6. Making any modifications needed and developing applications systems

7. Implementing the installation of the new visual system, educating company personnel and suppliers, and developing an Identity Standards Manual

Figure 49.1 shows the change from various old logos in use to the new one, which has been applied to all materials that identify the company, including checks, news release forms, advertising, posters and displays, trucks, publications, flag, pins and mementos, bill forms, stationery, all printed materials, uniforms and hard hats, signs, and awards.

Buildings as visual symbols

Although Americans have been in love with large or distinctive buildings for generations, it was not until recently that the great value of the symbolic building to a corporation's image has been widely recognized.

Early in the twentieth century, the Woolworth Building in New York became known throughout the world and helped make the company name distinctive. The Wrigley Building in Chicago was one of the few others that were overtly developed to focus distinction on their occupants. But the great majority of landmark buildings were, like the Flatiron in New York, not identified with any one firm. Even the major tenants in Rockefeller Center, such as RCA, were subdued in the identity of the whole development.

After World War II, the erection of Lever House in New York and a series of distinctive regional headquarters offices of the Prudential Insurance Company awakened corporate managements to the possibilities. While many firms erected buildings bearing their names, only a few achieved the distinctiveness and admiration that made their buildings stand out as widely recognized symbols. The Seagram Building in New York, the Deere headquarters in Moline, Illinois; the Connecticut General Life Insurance Company office in Hartford, Connecticut; the General Motors Research Center in Michigan; and the

Figure 49.1 Pacific Gas & Elecric Company had a variety of logotypes in various designs and colors, such as the two at the top. Its new logo is the one on the bottom. *Courtesy Pacific Gas and Electric Company.*

Sears building in Chicago have been among those that have achieved this symbolism.

Strong public interest in the total environment and the need for extensive facilities are moving companies toward complexes, rather than just buildings. The First Chicago/NBD has developed an 850-foot sloping tower as its headquarters, a thirty-two-story office building across the street, another skyscraper nearby, a two-story landscaped plaza with a four-sided mural by Chagall, and a huge fountain. The total complex is influencing the core of the city it is dependent on.

The next step may be toward whole environments, in which the company offices and facilities are the focus of a new community—inspired and motivated by the company, but not dependent on its paternalism.

Some companies have found pitfalls in their approaches to edifices. Architecture that sharply clashes with the character of the area and buildings that threaten to accent pollution or congestion have made their sponsors the objects of sharp attacks and boycotts. As in all other matters, sensitivity to the situation and attitudes involved is an essential ingredient of planning.

Techniques for Preempting Leadership

Introducing a new product or concept is becoming increasingly difficult. Entrenched large companies and institutions have the money, position, and following to dominate their positions. The costs involved in making an impact are becoming ever higher. Getting the public's attention and recognition is increasingly hard; avenues to the public's eyes and ears are multitudinous and scattered.

So how does an organization not only break through with something new, but get it recognized quickly as the leader so it can sustain massive counterattacks by established products or concepts?

Here are some examples:

- Softsoap, which invaded near-monopolies of Colgate and Procter & Gamble

- Sensodyne, which remains viable against inroads by the same big companies

- Gatorade, which took on Coke and Pepsi and so far withstands their catch-up efforts

This is a highly complex subject, with many facets to consider, and each instance is unique so only general principles can be followed, such as:

1. **Start with a distinctive identity**—and a distinctive name.

2. **Push that identity**—at least as much as the product or concept—from the start.

3. **Assume the position of leader**—even if you're small in the industry. Talk like a leader and take leadership positions. (Be quoted on industry-related matters, make predictions, answer criticisms of the whole industry, etc.)

4. **Treat others who follow your initiative as copycats**—confidently, not arrogantly or in a gloating manner.

5. **Maintain aggressive development**—even if that means obsoleting your original product or feature. IBM's refusal to shift emphasis from mainframes to PCs helped Apple, Compaq, and others get established. Apple, in turn, lost its leadership when it failed to move toward new trends.

In general, these principles can also be applied for politicians' ideas, causes, etc.

Emerging Trends and Requirements

Increasingly, it is important for the public relations person to help his or her organization anticipate and deal with future trends and developments, as well as to present conditions. Sensitivity to what people are concerned with, research experience, and judgment combine to make the qualified public relations person better able to anticipate trends and to advise on courses of action than most other people.

For the intelligent and experienced person, the body lives in the present but the mind needs to live in the future. What we do today is likely to have been largely determined by the time we do it—determined by our heritage, our training, our position, our outlook on the world. What we do in the future will be largely determined by whether we let the future roll upon us, or whether we think about it and prepare ourselves for the shape it is likely to have.

Scarcely anywhere is this more true than in public relations. The greatest value of the public relations professional is in anticipating and shaping what is developing, not in reporting or coping with what has already been determined. By the time an organization is confronted with attitudes of its publics it is usually too late for public relations thinking to have much effect on them. Dealing with existing attitudes is important, but helping to shape and direct future attitudes is far more valuable.

In an era of widespread uncertainty, iconoclasm, and transformation, how can points of reference be found to serve as the foundation from which to detect the shape of the future?[2]

Here are five basics that can probably be counted on:

---

[2]"The Problems in Our Future," *ibid.*, p.10.

1. In every human society, no matter what else may wither or alter, the attitude of the people will determine what can and cannot be done. That has long been believed of Western democratic societies, but current events demonstrate its validity in such undemocratic societies as China, Russia, Cuba, and Iraq. We now know, from revelations about the Underground in Nazi Germany during World War II, that even that most ruthless of controlled societies was permeated with dissent during the nation's life struggle. Stalin repeatedly felt the need to remove pockets of opposing attitudes. So whatever course our society may take, we can be sure the human climate will determine how it fares.

2. In human affairs, all excesses create their own demise. Nature hates untenable extremes as much as vacuums. The "1,000-year Reich" lasted 12 years because its excesses destroyed the stability necessary for any social system to continue. So extremism in the interest of any doctrine or dogma or discipline is likely to bring on its dissolution. The absolute authoritarianisms in Russia—first the czars and then the Soviets—were broken by their own excesses.

3. There will constantly be changes that create new challenges for those who must understand and deal with human attitudes. In today's volatile world there will be changes in technology, nature, demographics, ideas, tastes—all having impact on many aspects of our social structure and on each other. All these changes will create problems, needs, or opportunities for the organizations that employ or need skilled public relations people.

4. Excellence in mind and attitude ultimately will prevail over poor standards and destructive attitudes. If they should fail to prevail in the United States, then those who have such standards and attitudes will surpass or conquer us.

5. Reality will prevail over wishfulness. It is still true that some people are smarter than others. There are limits to the resources that can be apportioned among people. Despite the ultimate expression of wishfulness—Alan Harrington's "Death is an imposition on the human race, and no longer acceptable"—mankind is mortal and still is subject to the consequences of its own neglect, its own delusions, and the ravages of time.

These verities provide some foundation for our speculations. We must constantly ensure that what we dream or plan remains in touch with these points, lest we build our castles on illusory horizons. Beyond these bases, there seems to be little else that can be assumed. The expectations of futurologists have repeatedly been shattered by actual events—often while the binderies were still getting their prognostic volumes ready for distribution.

Evaluating the Effects of Public Relations

Sophisticated companies and organizations are basing their selection of public relations personnel or agencies on penetrating analyses of their skills as demonstrated in meeting challenging assignments, rather than on their persuasive oratory, graphic promises of results, and other irrelevant sales techniques.

Measurability

With business and other organizations moving precipitately toward using computers and other quantifying techniques to "get answers" and "organize" efficiently, there has been growing pressure to apply the same methods to public relations. Since this field deals with the most intangible factors with which managers must cope—human attitudes—the discomfort it can evoke in a person trained to be entirely practical and fact-oriented is understandable.

However, the danger exists that the more effort that is made to apply standards of prediction and measurement to public relations, the more emphasis will be placed on the superficial and the more difficult it will be to make progress against the real problems.

There are several reasons for this.

1. The greatest resource of public relations is human intellect and creativeness. The very ability to perceive why people do not follow the expected patterns and how they might be reached with messages not projected previously is the greatest value a client can receive.

    To the degree that direct measurements are attempted against these attributes, there is danger that the unremarkable and the undistinguished—what has been done before and therefore can be measured—will be emphasized at the expense of the unique and the excellent. If managements expect to be able to predict and measure quantitatively in public relations, public relations people will be inclined to confine themselves to things that are predictable and measurable, and the best thinking and creativity will be lost.

2. Public relations must deal with *changes* in attitude. It must lead its target, not follow it. The greatest source of problems and needs is *change*. If too much weight is given to what surveys and computer readouts show attitudes *were*, it is less likely that the public relations program will have an effect on what they *will be*.

3. In obtaining data for quantified judgments, it is necessary to probe into the minds of people. The human mind is murky and its ramifications multitudinous. All the mental resources of the person are arrayed in defense of private thoughts and feelings. It is not sound to assume that effective

measurements of some attitudes indicate the possibility of accurately measuring all others. In any survey, interviewees' reactions are meaningful only when the subject is really meaningful to them: a major election, for instance. When queried about something less meaningful—such as acceptable profit margins of aluminum companies—they may answer, but the validity and stability of their answers—especially numerically and over a period of time—are dubious.

Measuring effectiveness

Public relations faces problems created by its strengths. It covers such a wide range, it's difficult to measure and evaluate. Yet it is necessary to meet the natural demand of management that all functions be evaluated.

Most other disciplines are complex, but their functions are cohesive and clearly definable: finance, production, marketing, advertising, research, personnel, and so on. Public relations is diverse and seems even more diffuse because most of its elements are intangibles.

The growing importance of public relations, its bearing on all phases of the organization, and its growing budgets add to the demand for accountability. There are sound ways to meet that desire and still recognize the differences and diffusion of public relations.

Measurements should fit the function; and since there are many types of function, there are at least six levels of measurability.

Specific measurement

Functions involving a specific activity and a specific goal can be measured quantitatively. They include the following:

- Product publicity. How many media carried it, what was the circulation, what was the penetration of awareness, how many inquiries resulted?

- Financial news, personnel announcements, etc. How many and what type of media covered it, how prominently?
- Starting or pushing a trend.
- Coverage of an event. How heavy was the media coverage? What was attendance? Were reports favorable?

Even here, it's vital to ask: What *happened* because of these results?

Semispecific measurement

Experienced professionals can get a reading of effectiveness that lacks numerical or other measurement.

- Dealing with an issue or crisis. If an environmental group attacked the organization, what was the balance of treatment in the media?
- What was the reaction to a presentation before a Senate committee or to an officer's speech?
- What has been the trend of stockholder numbers (or membership), related to the effect of public relations efforts?
- Has a new product been successful partly because of publicity (as well as advertising, marketing, sales effort, etc.)?
- Do employee surveys show a favorable trend in understanding and rapport?
- Do government actions seem to reflect the influence of public relations efforts?
- Does the tendency of workers to strike seem to be affected by public relations efforts?

Acceptance on basis of judgment

Tangible measurements are not possible, but management believes the following efforts have been valuable:

- Work with minorities, communities, church groups, etc.
- Conveying ideas (for example, value of the organization's work to society)

- Winning public opinion (fostering a concept such as tax reform)
- Informing Congress, legislators, agencies about the organization's activities and interests

Recognizing value of input

Have public relations' concepts led to marketing themes that have captured buyers' enthusiasm? Has posture of the organization recommended by public relations proved congenial with its publics?

Prevention

What *doesn't happen* as a result of public relations advice may be by far the most valuable service. Special evaluations are necessary for issues that were blunted before they arose, emergencies that didn't arise, improved relations with media because of trained executives, statements that calmed the waters instead of stirring them.

Guidance

The best "public relations program" may be like a car—operating so quietly that no one is concerned with it. Many functions may be performed, but the absence of issues, alarms, and calls for "accountability" may be testimonials to efficiency.

The best public relations people perform all of these. They know how to plan and evaluate them, to keep perspective and not be stampeded into pushing "visible" functions merely to have tangible things to show.

Of these, the first three basically involve communication functions. The last three may not, yet they are at the highest level of public relations service.

Evaluating noncommunication functions

Most evaluation is done using the first three measures above. The others are valued in terms of *judgment* by those involved and by the *appreciation* of management. Looking at these first, the following are bases for evaluating the judgment, strategy, creativity, and effectiveness of *input, prevention,* and *guidance*:

Degree of participation

Has the public relations person or staff been integral in formulating policy, deciding on actions to be taken, selecting responses to initiatives by others, recommending for or against various courses of action, drawing up statements? If so, in most cases the management will be aware of it.

Offering inputs and insights

Has public relations made suggestions or presented observations that helped steer the course of policy making and program setting?

Support of other departments and individuals

Do those outside the immediate interchange between public relations and management appreciate the value of what is suggested, guided, and carried out? Public relations people should make sure these others know about their work and voice their support in dealings with top management.

Frequent reporting and positioning

Especially at meetings of the board, executive committee, or other decision-making groups, there should be inputs about the benefits of public relations service.

Evaluating communications-related functions

In campaigns and programs based on informing and/or influencing publics, benchmarks are needed at the start. These may be research studies, sales levels at various points, or agreement by those concerned about the level of awareness and public attitudes. If at the start

the public in unaware of the subject, that is the benchmark. Then it is possible to measure what happens as a result.

It is important to note that changing public opinion does not mean transforming the viewpoint of the entire public. It doesn't even mean transforming the viewpoint of a majority. It can be brought about by getting a comparatively small number of aware but passive people to reflect on the subject and form an opinion they haven't had. (*See* Chapter 2.)

In weighing the results of publicity and other communications, the four levels of impact must be kept in mind.

1. The number of people reached with messages.

2. The number who were influenced—who became aware of the subject, who became interested in the product, and so on.

3. The number who changed their attitudes—which go beyond just being aware or even of forming an opinion.

4. The number who act as a result. In most cases this is the only important fact. Reports that treat only the number of clippings and broadcast reports, that total only circulation, or that report people lean toward the organization's point of view are not conclusive. To tell an employer or client that they are is unsound. The only true measurement is: Has the goal been achieved?

It is also important to recognize that "winning" does not have to mean conquering the opposition or putting its cause to rout. (*See* Chapter 2.) Most people are intellectually apathetic. Neutralizing public opinion on a subject that is threatening or disruptive can have the desired effect.

Accordingly, numerical measurements in many surveys can be misleading.

It is not numbers that count, but what happens as a result of public relations activity. That is the underlying essential fact in all evaluations.

Progress Toward Professionalism

Five major factors have retarded the maturity of public relations as a profession:

1. It has grown very rapidly in response to needs. With effective sources of training developing much more slowly, many unqualified persons—often with unsound motives—have called themselves public relations specialists and offered their services. In many cases, they have been able to prosper, though damaging confidence in the field and its practices among many of those they have dealt with.

2. It covers an exceedingly wide scope. People with skills in arranging special events or in editing a company publication, for instance, are public relations practitioners. People who encounter such specialists, however, often do not understand the difference between a special range of experience and skill and the entire field. There is considerable difference between an ophthalmologist and a psychiatrist—both of whom must have M.D. degrees—and often there is an equal difference between persons who have concentrated on separate aspects of public relations.

3. Forces within the field and outside have created misunderstanding. Because journalists tend to interpret anything dealing with communication as a form of journalism, many writers have had a narrow view of public relations. Many articles have been based on the preconceived premise that *public relations* is a pseudo-journalist's snobbish term for trying to "use" the press. As public relations has developed and many of its practitioners have prospered, this prejudice has sometimes been tinged with envy. While treatment of public relations has tended to improve gradually, it is still among the most stubbornly distorted subjects covered by the media in general.

Some practitioners, in turn, have tended to create an aura of mystery about the field, to aggrandize their stature and to glorify talents supposedly only they can provide. This has included sweeping promises to make any business tycoon an international personage; assurances that social and economic tides can be reversed merely through propaganda "magic"; and claims of solving a great industry's problems by forming a committee and holding a conference. Propounding of terms like *engineering of consent* to describe a public relations person's functions, that imply both omnipotence and manipulation of the public, has aroused fears of intellectuals and public officials.

4. The fact that the best public relations service is often intangible and comparatively immeasurable has often made it easier for the charlatan to obtain an assignment than the sound practitioner. The man or organization that spells out specific promises where none can be made; who finds out what the prospect will buy and then develops his presentation accordingly, rather than on what sound judgment calls for; the periodic report that stresses visible items—selected press clippings and circulation figures, regardless of their relations to the problem and objective—these often appeal to the practical-minded management executive who is not trained to understand the nuances of public relations.

5. Until recently there has been little enforcement of any standards that practitioners are expected to meet.

Because of such problems, from time to time a simplistic suggestion is made that the field have state licensing imposed on it. A flurry of such interest arose in 1986; but after a report for the Public Relations Society of America by this author cited nineteen compelling reasons why licensure would damage society and the field, the notion withered again.

Sources of criticism

Practices depleting respect for public relations have been of two general types: those that result in widespread attention to malpractices and those that are not exposed but still undermine confidence in the field. This may be said of any field of endeavor, from law and college teaching to operating subways. In the case of public relations, the first group has been far less numerous than the second, but the publicized exposes have been deeply impressed on the minds of many people.

They have included investigations of the Securities and Exchange Commission into stock promotion practices; investigations by the U.S. Senate into efforts of a few practitioners to foster foreign interests in the United States without listing themselves with the State Department, as required by law; and the monumentally publicized habit of the Watergate gang of using *public relations* and *PR* as terms for their dirty tricks and efforts to delude the public. None of the gang was truly a public relations person, and none of the practices they attributed the terms to was acceptable among professionals in this field.

The fact that these three scandals involved less than twenty individuals—some of whom were exonerated—does not lessen their impact on the many thousands of sound and ethical practitioners.

More numerous are the lesser and less-visible abuses: attempting to suborn writers or broadcasters to carry publicity material or suppress unfavorable news, misleading prospective clients in sales presentations with almost-promises of results that cannot be obtained or predicted, seeking to get a client by calumniating a competitor, misrepresenting the size of the firm's staff or the clients it serves, falsifying or distorting reports to clients, and others.

As in almost all fields, the most common failing of practitioners is assuming assignments they are not qualified to perform. For this and all other reasons, the leaders in the field have long sought means of educating potential clients and employers so they will be inoculated against deception, and an enforceable set of standards and ethics to be applied to anyone seeking to function in this field.

Values to the public

The milestone report of the Task Force on the Stature and Role of Public Relations, headed by this author, focused for the first time on the values derived from public relations by the public. It pointed out that these are the basis on which the field can hope to achieve widespread respect and overcome criticisms.

The efforts of the field have been self-consciously directed toward itself, rather than toward the interests of the publics. There has been much attention to explaining public relations, talking about it, and responding to criticism. But no systematic effort has been made to get the publics to recognize the values *to them* of public relations. These values include the following:

- Public relations is a means for the public to have its desires and interests felt by the institutions in our society. It interprets and speaks for the public to otherwise unresponsive organizations, as well as speaking for those organizations to the public.

- Public relations is a means to achieve mutual adjustment between institutions and groups, establishing smoother relationships that benefit the public.

- Public relations is a safety valve for freedom. By providing a means to work out accommodations, it makes arbitrary action or coercion less likely.

- Public relations is an essential element in the communications system that enables individuals to be informed on many aspects of subjects that affect their lives.

- Public relations personnel can help activate the organization's social conscience.

• Public relations (either systematic or unconscious) is a universal activity. It functions in all aspects of life. Each member of the public practices principles of public relations in seeking the acceptance, cooperation, or affection of others. Public relations professionals only practice it in a more professional manner.

Ethics and standards

As part of a growing concern for the moral and ethical standards of society as a whole, increasing attention has been paid to ethics in public relations.

The pressures that create ethical dilemmas in government, business, universities, family relations, and all other spheres also bear on this field: emphasis on immediate and extreme monetary benefits; lowering of all standards resulting from overzealous desires to benefit the underclass; and emphasis on hedonism and self-gratification. Another factor is the doctrine of management by objective, which makes the end result the overwhelming consideration in making all decisions.

A particularly strong factor is growing bureaucratization in all organizations, with the tone set by government but strongly evident in business, universities, nonprofit organizations, and other institutions. "Bureaucracies . . . erode all standards of morality but their own," says Robert Jackall of Williams College. "In this sense, bureaucracies may be thought of as vast systems of organized irresponsibility."

It should be borne in mind that ethics and principles are variables, caught up in the human climate of the time. Sex before marriage was evil throughout most times in history. The Rothschilds became fabulously wealthy by using ways to get inside information first; Ivan Boesky and others were sent to prison for using inside information in 1986. Capital punishment was an unquestioned part of the protection of society for millennia.

Employers had the unquestioned right to hire or not hire whomever they pleased until a few years ago.

All considerations must be taken in the context of the universe the organization is in—and over a long period. That also applies to the individual working within the organization.

Here are some principles to apply when considering questions of ethics or principles:[3]

1. Each case is separate. No formulas should be relied on; no copies of others' programs.

2. Experience, judgment, and objectivity are vital to weigh *all* considerations, consequences, and time periods.

3. Sober judgments must be made—not based on emotion or panic.

4. *Long-term* consequences must be perceived and weighed.

5. The purpose of the action taken must be clear, and consistent with the organization's total posture.

6. The reasons for the decision must be communicated effectively—in many ways—to all publics concerned.

7. The issue must not be considered finished when things have been done in response, but must be reviewed constantly in light of new developments and trends.

Practical aspects of ethics in the practice of public relations are treated throughout this book, in each phase of the subject. (Legal aspects are treated in Chapter 48.)

In 1954 the Public Relations Society of America adopted a mild code of professional standards for its members. This was strengthened in 1959 and amended in 1963 and 1977. The text of this code appears in the Appendix.

In 1963, following extensive exposures of practices by a few public relations men in

---

[3]From *Managing the Human Climate*, Philip Lesly, #105, July-August, 1987.

efforts to boost the market prices of clients' stocks, PRSA named a committee to work out with the Securities and Exchange Commission a specific code applying to investor public relations. The text of this code also appears in the Appendix. Various associations in public relations have established programs for accrediting members who meet basic standards. Those who qualify are permitted to use a designation, such as Public Relations Accredited, by the Public Relations Society of America.

While public relations goes through its process of maturing, the best means of raising standards and protecting the public interest will continue to be educating users of the service, the press, and the public on the true nature of the field. The reputation of the practitioner among clients and the best of his or her contemporaries is the surest measure of stature and integrity.

Broadening the Scope of Public Relations

For a time it appeared that the trend in the public relations field might be similar to that in other increasingly complex disciplines, toward development of specialists in the various phases. A number of such specialties were charted by enterprising workers in the field, such as investor relations, government relations, and public affairs.

However, the indivisibility of a company's impression on the people it deals with; the fact that communications do not stop at imaginary lines between publics but inevitably overlap; and the practical advantage of dealing with all elements involved in an organization's nonselling communications have increased the need for full-scope public relations people as well as the specialists.

Adding increasingly to the requirements is the international scope of many organizations' relationships, carrying the need for a breadth well beyond the borderlines of the United States.

As a result, many intensified and specialized talents are needed, but they must be coordinated and integrated so they work effectively together and meet all the requirements of the client organizations. This calls for either a large and expensive internal staff, including a good many specialists, some of whose talents will be required only part of the time; a broad public relations organization that can provide the talents and skills in all the necessary areas; or an internal staff augmented by the broad experience, judgment, and skills of an exceptional counsel. In many cases, a combination of the internal staff and the external organization most effectively meets the needs.

Accordingly, the opportunities in public relations are growing in both intensified specialization and broad overall knowledge and talent. The path to future success for the individual can come from either direction.

In a world that at times seems to be tenuously held together by too-little-understood principles of group attitudes, the challenge and opportunities for the field that specializes in understanding and developing group attitudes still appear to be in their infancy.

APPENDIXES

SOURCES OF INFORMATION

I. Media Directors

The first principle in using any media list is: *update the list every time it is to be used in a campaign.*

The following are reliable sources of lists:

Editor and Publisher International Year Book[1] includes every daily newspaper published in the United States and Canada, and many published in Latin America and Europe. It lists the major editorial executives of each news-paper. It also gives separate lists of syndicates, feature services, advertising agencies, sports editors, women's editors, other department editors, foreign-language dailies of the United States, and leading black publications. *Editor and Publisher International Year Book* is the most valuable reference work on newspapers in the United States and many other countries.

Bacon's Directories (annual) are indispensable guides to all major magazines and newspapers published in the United States and Canada. *Bacon's* classifies them by subject interest; cites circulation, frequency of publication, name of editor, address, and telephone number; and includes a code that indicates the types of publicity material each is interested in receiving. Periodic correction sheets help keep the listings up-to-date.

Bacon's Radio/TV Cable Directory[2] (annual). Covers the broadcast media in a manner similar to the print media directories above.

Bacon's International Publicity Checker—European Edition[2] (annual) lists trade, technical, and business publications in Western Europe that accept publicity releases.

Directory of the American Society of Journalists and Authors[3] includes names, addresses, areas of interest, and publications served regularly of many of the most successful nonfiction writers in America. Many of these writers, in addition to preparing articles on assignment for the magazines or on their own speculation, will accept writing assignments from publicity people. In this case, however, it is clearly understood that the writer is working for the publicity office, and editors to

---

[1]11 W. 19th Street, New York, NY 10011.

[2]332 S. Michigan Avenue, Chicago, IL 60604.

[3]1501 Broadway, New York, NY 10036.

whom the manuscript is submitted are informed of the sponsor's interest.

Standard Rate and Data Service,[4] the *American Society of Media Photographers Directory*,[5] *Broadcasting & Cable Yearbook*,[6] *Television & Cable Factbook*,[7] and many writers' publications publish valuable lists and tips for publicists.

Ulrich's International Periodicals Directory,[8] a listing of all major periodicals in the world by categories; *The Working Press of the Nation*,[9] a directory of key personnel under more than 100 different news classifications for newspapers, magazines, internal publications, feature writers and photographers, radio and television stations; *The Standard Periodical Directory*,[10] *Directory of Ethnic Periodicals*,[10] *College Newspaper Directory*,[11] and *Newsletters in Print*[12] are all useful sources of lists for distribution of publicity material.

Very helpful, too, are *Educational Press Directory*;[13] the *U.S. Government Organizations Manual*,[14] which includes names of public information people in all divisions of government and their addresses; and the *Catholic Press Directory*,[15] which lists Catholic publications and their publication dates.

---

[4] 3004 Glenview Road, Wilmette, IL 60091.
[5] 14 Washington Road, Princeton Junction, NJ 08550.
[6] Broadcast Publications, 121 Chanlon Road, New Providence, NJ 07974.
[7] Television Digest, Inc., 2115 Ward Street, NW, Washington, DC 20037.
[8] R. R. Bowker Co., 121 Chanlon Road, New Providence, NJ 07974.
[9] R. R. Bowker Co., 121 Chanlon Road, New Providence, NJ 07974.
[10] 215 W. Harrison, Seattle, WA 98119.
[11] John Wiley & Co., 605 Third Ave., New York, NY 10158.
[12] Gale Research Co., 835 Penobscot Building, Detroit, MI 48226.
[13] Rowan College, Glassboro, NJ 08028.
[14] Superintendent of Documents, Government Printing Office, Washington, DC 20402.
[15] Catholic Press Association, 3555 Veterans Highway, Ronkon Homa, NY 11779.

The Department of Commerce publishes state-by-state lists of trade associations, with separate lists for New York City and Chicago. In addition, it has a special list of national trade associations. *The Encyclopedia of Associations*[16] is another source.

The United States Chamber of Commerce[17] has a list of chambers of commerce.

Other good source references for lists include newspaper publishers' associations, radio and TV broadcasters' associations, various trade groups, competent publicity clubs and public relations groups, classified telephone directories, advertising agencies, many individual organizations, direct-mail houses, clipping services, and, in some cases, list brokers.

Editor and Publisher issues a *Directory of Syndicated Services* carrying listings of syndicates and names and features handled and their authors.

Print Media Editorial Calendars, Standard Rate and Data Service, 3004 Glenview Road, Wilmette, IL 60091.

The Oxbridge Directory of Newsletters, 150 Fifth Avenue, New York, NY 10011, is useful in reaching newsletters not appearing in many other directories.

American Newspaper Representatives, 100 Shelard Pkwy., Minneapolis, MN 55426, publishes an annual *National Directory of Newspapers*.

Across the Dial, Broadcasting Plus, 1705 De Sales, Washington, DC 20036.

Benn's Media (International), Nichals Publishing, 155 W. 72nd Street, New York, NY 10023.

Broadcasting Cable Yearbook, 121 Chanlon Road, New Providence, NJ 07974.

Business and Financial News Media, Larriston Communications, P.O. Box 20229, New York, NY 10025.

---

[16] Gale Research Co., 835 Penobscot Building, Detroit, MI 48226.
[17] U.S. Chamber of Commerce, 1615 H Street, NW, Washington, DC 20062.

Cable & Station Coverage Atlas, 2115 Ward Court, NW, Washington, DC 20037.

Data Base Directory, 701 Westchester Avenue, White Plains, NY 10604.

Directory of Women's Media, 530 Broadway, New York, NY 10012.

Electronic Media, 965 E. Jefferson Avenue, Detroit, MI 48207.

Feature News Publicity Outlets (family interest), 800 Masons Mill Business Park, 1800 Byberry Road, Huntingdone Valley, PA 19006.

FYI Directory of News Sources and Information, JSC Group, 2 Evergreen Road, Severna Park, MD 21146.

Freelancers of North America: Marketplace, Author Aid/Research Associates, 340 E. 52nd Street, New York, NY 10022.

Gale Directory of Databases, 835 Penobscot Building, Detroit, MI 48226.

Gale Directory of Publications and Broadcast Media, 835 Penobscot Building, Detroit, MI 48226.

Gebbie Press All-in-One Directory, Gebbie Press, Box 1000, New Paltz, NY 12561. List of most outlets for publicity in the United States. Also available on disks.

Hispanic Media and Market Source, 3004 Glenview Road, Wilmette, IL 60091.

Hollis Press & Public Relations Annual, Hollis Directories, Contact House, Lower Hampton Road, Sunbury-On-Thames, Middlesex TW16 5BR, England. United Kingdom listings of media services, consultants, sources.

Hudson's State Capitals News Media Contacts Directory, 44 W. Market Street, P.O. Box 311, Rhinebeck, NY 12572.

Hudson's Washington New Media Contacts Directory, edited by Howard Penn Hudson. Hudson's Directory, 44 W. Market Street, P.O. Box 311, Rhinebeck, NY 12572 (annual).

International Directory of Little Magazines and Small Presses, Dustbooks, Paradise, CA 95967 (annual).

International Literary Marketplace, R. R. Bowker Co., 121 Chanlon Road, New Providence, NJ 07974.

International Media Guide, International Media Guide Enterprises, 85 Perimeter Road, Nashua NH 03063.

International Media Guides: Consumer Magazines Worldwide; Newspapers Worldwide; Business/Professional: The Americas; Business/Professional: Asia/Pacific Middle East/Africa; Business/Professional: Europe. Phillips Business Information, 7811 Montrose Road, Potomac, MD 20854.

The Internet Media Directory, Ragan Communications, 212 W. Superior Street, Chicago, IL 60611.

LMP: Literary Marketplace, 121 Chanlon Road, New Providence, NJ 07974.

Madison Avenue Handbook: The Image Makers' Source, 42 W. 38th Street, New York, NY 10018.

Marketing Made Easier: Guide to Product Publicity, 18 N. Greenbush Road, West Nyack, NY 10994.

The National Directory of Magazines, Oxbridge Communications, Inc., 150 Fifth Avenue, New York, NY 10011.

National PR Pitchbooks, 1250 45th Street, Ste. 200, Emeryville, CA 94608.

National Publicity Database, Ad-Lib Publications, 51 N. 5th, Fairfield, IA 52556.

National Radio Publicity Outlets, 800 Masons Mill Business Park, 1800 Byberry Road, Huntingdon Valley, PA 19006.

National Directory of Newspaper Op-Ed Pages, Communications Creativity, P.O. Box 909, DIP, Buena Vista, CO 81211.

Newsletters in Print, 835 Penobscot Building, Detroit, MI 48226.

Newspapers Directory, 5711 S. 86th Circle, Omaha, NE 68127.

O'Dwyer's Directories: Corporate Communications; Public Relations Executives; Media

Placement Guide (and weekly supplement); and *Public Relations Firms*, 271 Madison Avenue, New York, NY 10016.

Radio Programming Profile, BF/Communication, 66 Chestnut Lane, Woodbury, NY 11797.

Radio Talk Shows & Hosts in Radio, 806 Oakwood Boulevard, Dearborn, MI 49124.

Radio Talk Shows Need Guests, P.O. Box 101330, Denver, CO 80254.

Radio TV Contact Service, Media News Keys, 40-29 27th Street, Long Island City, NY 11101.

Reed's Worldwide Directory of Public Relations Organizations, Pigafetta Press, P.O. Box 39244, Washington, DC 20016.

Senior Media Directory, 250 E. Riverview Circle, Reno, NV 85909.

Talk Show Selects, Broadcast Interview Source, 2233 Wisconsin Avenue, NW, Washington, DC 20007.

Television & Cable Factbook, Warren Publishing Co., 2115 Ward Court, NW, Washington, DC 20037.

The Working Press of the Nation, five volumes: Newspapers, magazines, TV and radio, feature writers and photographers, internal publications. 121 Chanlon Road, New Providence, NJ 07974.

World Radio/TV Handbook, BPI, 1515 Broadway, New York, NY 10036.

II. Media

General magazines

Leading magazines in this field are:

Grit, 1503 S.W. 42nd Street, Topeka, KS 66609-1265.

Money, Time & Life Building, Rockefeller Center, New York, NY 10020.

Moneysworth, 1780 Broadway #811, New York, NY 10019.

National Enquirer, 700 S.E. Coast Avenue, Lantana, FL 33464.

National Geographic Magazine, 17th & M Streets, NW, Washington, DC 20036.

New York, 755 Second Avenue, New York, NY 10017.

The New Yorker, 25 W. 43rd Street, New York, NY 10036.

Omni, 1965 Broadway, New York, NY 10023.

People, Time & Life Building, New York, NY 10020-1300.

Psychology Today, 80 Fifth Avenue, New York, NY 10011.

The Saturday Evening Post, 1100 Waterway Boulevard, Indianapolis, IN 46202.

News and illustrated magazines

News magazines

Newsweek, 251 W. 57th Street, New York, NY 10019.

Time, Time & Life Building, New York, NY 10020.

U.S. News & World Report, 2400 N Street, NW, Washington, DC 20037-1196.

Canadian

MacLean's News Magazine, 777 Bay Street, Toronto, Ontario, M5W 1A7 Canada.

Illustrated magazines

Ebony, 820 S. Michigan Avenue, Chicago, IL 60605.

Life, Time & Life Building, Rockefeller Center, New York, NY 10020.

People, Time & Life Building, Rockefeller Center, New York, NY 10020.

US, 1290 Avenue of the Americas, New York, NY 10104.

Class magazines

Harper's Bazaar, 1700 Broadway, New York, NY 10019.

Town & Country, 1700 Broadway, New York, NY 10019.

Vanity Fair, 350 Madison Avenue, New York, NY 10017.

Vogue, 350 Madison Avenue, New York, NY 10017.

Women's and home magazines

American Baby, 249 W. 17th Street, New York, NY 10011.

Baby Talk, 25 W. 439th Street, New York, NY 10036.

Better Homes and Gardens, 1716 Locust Street, Des Moines, IA 50309.

Bon Appetit, 6300 Wilshire Boulevard, Los Angeles, CA 90080.

Bride's and Your New Home, 140 E. 45th Street, New York, NY 10017.

Cooking Light, P.O. Box 1748, Birmingham, AL 35201.

Cosmopolitan, 224 W. 57th Street, New York, NY 10019.

Essence Magazine, 1500 Broadway, New York, NY 10036.

Family Circle, 110 Fifth Avenue, New York, NY 10011.

Family Safety & Health, 1121 Spring Lake Drive, Itasca, IL 60143.

Glamour, 350 Madison Avenue, New York, NY 10017.

Good Housekeeping, 959 Eighth Avenue, New York, NY 10017.

Gourmet, 560 Lexington Avenue, New York, NY 10022.

House Beautiful, 1700 Broadway, New York, NY 10019.

Ladies Home Journal, 100 Park Avenue, New York, NY 10017.

Lady's Circle, 152 Madison Avenue, New York, NY 10016.

Mademoiselle, 350 Madison Avenue, New York, NY 10017.

McCall's Magazine, 110 Fifth Avenue, New York, NY 10011.

Metropolitan Home, 750 Third Avenue, New York, NY 10017.

Mirabella, 200 Madison Avenue, New York, NY 10016.

Modern Bride, 245-249 W. 17th Street, New York, NY 10011.

Ms., 620 Park Avenue, New York, NY 10169.

National Business Woman, 2012 Massachusetts Avenue, NW, Washington, DC 20036.

New Woman, 215 Lexington Avenue, New York, NY 10016.

Parents' Magazine, 685 3rd Avenue, New York, NY 10017.

Playgirl, 801 Second Avenue, New York, NY 10017.

Redbook, 224 W. 57th Street, New York, NY 10019.

Self, 350 Madison Avenue, New York, NY 10017.

Seventeen, 850 Third Avenue, New York, NY 10022.

Sunset Magazine, 80 Willow Road, Menlo Park, CA 94025.

W, 7 W. 34th Street, New York, NY 10001.

Woman's Day, 1633 Broadway, New York, NY 10019.

Woman's World, 270 Sylvan Avenue, Englewood, NJ 07632.

Workbasket, 700 W. 47th Street, Kansas City, MO 64112.

Working Woman, 230 Park Avenue, New York, NY 10169.

Canadian

Chatelaine Magazine, 777 Bay Street, Toronto, Ontario MSW 1A7 Canada.

Homemaker's Magazine, 25 Sheppard Avenue, W, #100 North York, Ontario M2N 657 Canada.

Men's magazines

Esquire, 250 W. 55th Street, New York, NY 10019.

GQ: Gentlemen's Quarterly, 350 Madison Avenue, New York, NY 10017.

Oui, 28 W. 25th Street, New York, NY 10010.

Penthouse, 1965 Broadway, New York, NY 10023.

Playboy, 680 N. Lake Shore Drive, Chicago, IL 60611.

Swank, Zip Route 4 East, #401, Paramus, NJ 07652.

Juvenile magazines

American Girl, 8400 Fairway Place, Middleton, WI 53562.

Boy's Life, 1325 Walnut Hill Lane, P.O. Box 152079, Irving, TX 75015.

Barbie, 300 Madison Avenue, New York, NY 10017.

Crayola Kids, 1912 Grand Avenue, Des Moines, IA 50309.

Highlights for Children, 803 Church Street, Honesdale, PA 18431.

IN 2 IT, 141 N.W. Point Boulevard, Elk Grove, IL 60009.

Jack and Jill, 1100 Waterway Boulevard, Indianapolis, IN 46202.

Kids Discover, 170 Fifth Avenue, 6th Floor, New York, NY 10010.

Mickey Mouse Magazine, 300 Madison Avenue, New York, NY 10017.

National Geographic World, 1145 17th Street, NW, Washington, DC 20036.

Nickelodeon, 1515 Broadway, New York, NY 10036.

Quake, 300 Madison Avenue, New York, NY 10017.

Ranger Rick, 8925 Leesburg Pike, Vienna, VA 22184.

Scholastic Choices, 555 Broadway, New York, NY 10012.

Scholastic Scope, 555 Broadway, New York, NY 10012.

Scouting, 1325 Walnut Hill Lane, P.O. Box 152079, Irving, TX 75015.

Sports Illustrated for Kids, 1271 Avenue of the Americas, New York, NY 10020.

'Teen, 6420 Wilshire Boulevard, Los Angeles, CA 90048.

Teen Machine, 233 Park Avenue South, New York, NY 10003.

Zillions, 101 Truman Avenue, Yonkers, NY 10703.

Senior citizen magazines

AARP Bulletin, 601 E Street, NW, Washington, DC 20049.

Mature Outlook, 1912 Grand Avenue, Des Moines, IA 50309.

McCall's Extra Edition, 110 Fifth Avenue, New York, NY 10011.

Modern Maturity, 3200 E. Carson Street, Lakewood, CA 90712.

New Choices for Retirement Living, 26 W. 23rd Street, New York, NY 10010.

Retirement Life, 1533 New Hampshire Avenue, NW, Washington, DC 20036.

Senior Citizen News, 1331 F Street, NW, Washington, DC 20004.

Senior World News Magazine, 1000 Pioneer Way, El Cajon, CA 92020.

Vantage, 200 N. Martingdale Road, Schaumburg, IL 60173.

Intellectual magazines

American Scholar, 1811 Q Street, NW, Washington, DC 20009.

The American Spectator, P.O. Box 549, Arlington, VA 22216.

The Atlantic Monthly, 745 Boylston Street, Boston, MA 02116.

Commentary, 165 E. 56th Street, New York, NY 10022.

Harper's Magazine, 666 Broadway, New York, NY 10012.

The Mother Earth News, 80 Fifth Avenue, New York, NY 10011.

Mother Jones, 731 Market Street, San Francisco, CA 94103.

The Nation, 72 5th Avenue, New York, NY 10011.

National Review, 150 E. 35th Street, New York, NY 10016.

The New Republic, 1220 19th Street, NW, Washington, DC 20036.

Smithsonian, 900 Jefferson Drive, SW, Washington, DC 20560.

The Utne Reader, 1624 Harmon Place, Minneapolis, MN 55403.

Vital Speeches, P.O. Box 1247, Mt. Pleasant, SC 29464.

The Weekly Standard, 1150 17th Street, NW, Washington, DC 20036.

Digest magazines

Catholic Digest, P.O. Box 64090, St. Paul, MN 55164.

Farmer's Digest, Box 624, Brookfield, WI 53008.

Reader's Digest, Pleasantville, NY 10570.

Sport and hobby magazines

American Hunter, 11250 Waples Hill Road, Fairfax, VA 22030.

American Photo, 1633 Broadway, New York, NY 10019.

Arizona Highways, 2039 W. Lewis, Phoenix, AZ 85009.

Backpacker, 33 E. Minor Street, Emmaus, PA 18098.

Baseball Digest, 990 Grove Street, Evanston, IL 60201.

Basketball Digest, 990 Grove Street, Evanston, IL 60201.

Basketball Weekly, 8033 W. 36th Street, Miami, FL 33166.

Boating, 1633 Broadway, New York, NY 10019.

Bowling Magazine, 5301 S. 76th Street, Greendale, WI 53129.

Car & Driver, 2002 Hogback Road, Ann Arbor, MI 48105.

Conde Nast Traveler, 360 Madison Avenue, New York, NY 10017.

Field & Stream, 2 Park Avenue, New York, NY 10016.

Fishing & Hunting News, 511 Eastlake Avenue E., P.O. Box C-19000, Seattle, WA 98109.

Football Digest, 990 Grove Street, Evanston, IL 60201.

Golf Digest, 5520 Park Avenue, Trumbull, CT 06611.

Golf Magazine, 2 Park Avenue, New York, NY 10016.

Inside Sports, 990 Grove Street, Evanston, IL 60201.

Motor Boating & Sailing, 2550 W. 55th Street, New York, NY 10019.

Motor Trend, 6420 Wilshire Boulevard, Los Angeles, CA 90048.

National Geographic Traveler, 17th and M Streets, NW, Washington, DC 20036.

Odyssey, 131 Stoney Circle, Santa Rosa, CA 95401.

Outdoor Life, 2 Park Avenue, New York, NY 10016.

Petersen's Hunting, 6420 Wilshire Boulevard, Los Angeles, CA 90048.

Petersen's Photographic Magazine, 6420 Wilshire Boulevard, Los Angeles, CA 90048.

Popular Photography, 1633 Broadway, New York, NY 10019.

Runner's World, 33 E. Minor, Emmaus, PA 18098.

Sail, 275 Washington Street, Newton, MA 02158.

Shooting Times, News Plaza, P.O. Box 1790, Peoria, IL 61656.

Ski America, P.O. Box 1140, Pittsfield, MA 01202.

Skin Diver Magazine, 8490 Sunset Boulevard, Los Angeles, CA 90069.

Snowmobile, 601 Lakeshore Parkway, Minnetonka, MN 55305.

Sport Magazine, 6420 Wilshire Boulevard, Los Angeles, CA 90048.

The Sporting News, 1212 N. Lindbergh Boulevard, St. Louis, MO 63132.

Sports Afield Magazine, 250 W. 55th Street, New York, NY 10019.

Sports Illustrated, 1271 Avenue of the Americas, New York, NY 10020.

Surfer, 33046 Calle Aviador, San Juan Capistrano, CA 92675.

Tennis, 5520 Park Avenue, P.O. Box 0395, Trumbull, CT 06611.

Travel America, 990 Grove Street, Evanston, IL 60201.

Travel and Leisure, 1120 Avenue of the Americas, New York, NY 10036.

Travel/Holiday, 28 W. 23rd, New York, NY 10010.

Vista USA, 30400 Van Dyke Avenue, Warren, MI 48093.

Western Outdoors, P.O. Box 2027, Newport Beach, CA 92658.

Women's Sports and Fitness, 2025 Pearl Street, Boulder, CO 80302.

Yachting, 2 Park Avenue, New York, NY 10016.

Institutional magazines

An institutional magazine is the official organ of some specific organization of people united in their interests, occupations, ideas, religion, or social life. Institutional magazines include religious, fraternal, university, lodge, and organization publications.

The American Legion, P.O. Box 1055, Indianapolis, IN 46206.

Columbia (Knights of Columbus), One Columbus Plaza, P.O. Drawer 1670, New Haven, CT 06507.

Eagle Magazine, 12660 W. Capitol Drive, P.O. Box 25916, Milwaukee, WI 53225.

The Elks Magazine, 425 Diversey Parkway, Chicago, IL 60614.

Kiwanis Magazine, 3636 Woodview Trace, Indianapolis, IN 46268.

The Lion, 300 22nd Street, Oak Brook, IL 60570.

Moose Magazine, Supreme Lodge Building, Mooseheart, IL 60539.

The Rotarian, 1650 Sherman Avenue, One Rotary Center, Evanston, IL 60201.

V.F.W. Magazine, 406 W. 34th Street, Kansas City, MO 64111.

Woodman, 1700 Franam Street, Omaha, NB 68102.

City and state magazines

Alaska, 808 E Street, Anchorage, AK 99501.

Aloha, P.O. Box 3260, Honolulu, HI 96811.

Avenue, 950 3rd Avenue, New York, NY 10022.

Baltimore Magazine, 16 S. Calvert Street, Baltimore, MD 21202.

Boston Magazine, 300 Massachusetts Avenue, Boston, MA 02115.

Chicago, 414 N. Orleans, Chicago, IL 60610.

Cincinnati, 409 Broadway, Cincinnati, OH 45202.

Cleveland Magazine, 1422 Euclid Avenue, Cleveland, OH 55114.

Detroit Monthly, 1400 Woodbridge, Detroit, MI 48207.

Houston Life, 5615 Kitby Drive, Houston, TX 77005.

Kansas City Magazine, 7007 College Boulevard, Overland Park, KS 66211.

The L.A. Weekly, 6715 Sunset Boulevard, Los Angeles, CA 90028.

Los Angeles Magazine, 1888 Century Park E., #920, Los Angeles, CA 90067.

Louisville, One Riverfront Plaza, #604, Louisville, KY 40202.

Memphis, P.O. Box 256, Memphis, TN 38101.

Miami Today, 840 Biscayne Boulevard, P.O. Box 1368, Miami, FL 33101.

Mpls.–St. Paul Magazine, 220 6th Street, Minneapolis, MN 55402.

Nevada Magazine, 1800 Highway 50 E., Carson City, NV 89710.

New Jersey Monthly, 55 Park, P.O. Box 920, Morristown, NJ 07963.

New Mexico Magazine, 495 Old Santa Fe Trail, Santa Fe, NM 87503.

New Orleans, 111 Veterans Boulevard, #1810, New Orleans, LA 70005.

New York, 755 Second Avenue, New York, NY 10017.

The New Yorker, 20 W. 43rd Street, New York, NY 10036.

Ohio Magazine, 62 E. Broad Street, Columbus, OH 53215.

Orange Coast, 245-D Fischer, #8, Costa Mesa, CA 92626.

Philadelphia Magazine, 1818 Market Street, Philadelphia, PA 19103.

Phoenix Magazine, 5555 N. 7th Avenue, Phoenix, AZ 85014.

Pittsburgh, 4802 Fifth Avenue, Pittsburgh, PA 15213.

San Diego Magazine, 4206 West Point Loma Boulevard, San Diego, CA 92110.

San Francisco Focus, 2601 Mariposa, San Francisco, CA 94110.

Southern Living, 2100 Lake Shore Drive, Birmingham, AL 35209.

Texas Monthly, 701 Brazos, Austin, TX 78701.

The Washingtonian, 1828 L Street, NW, Washington, DC 20036.

Agricultural magazines

Farm Journal, 230 W. Washington Square, Philadelphia, PA 19105.

Prairie Farmer, P.O. Box 3217, Decatur, IL 62524.

Progressive Farmer, 2100 Lakeshore Drive, Birmingham, AL 35209.

Successful Farming, 1716 Locust Street, Des Moines, IA 50336.

Wallace's Farmer, 6200 Aurora Avenue, Urbandale, IA 50722.

Financial and business publications

American Banker, One State Street Plaza, New York, NY 10004.

Barron's National Business and Financial Weekly, 200 Liberty Street, New York, NY 10281.

Better Investing, 1515 Eleven Mile Road, P.O. Box 220, Royal Oak, MI 48060.

Business Conditions, Federal Reserve Bank of Chicago, Publications Section, Research Dept., Box 834, Chicago, IL 60690.

Business Week, 1221 Avenue of the Americas, New York, NY 10020.

Financial World, 1328 Broadway, New York, NY 10001.

Forbes, 60 Fifth Avenue, New York, NY 10011.

Fortune, Time & Life Building, Rockefeller Center, New York, NY 10020.

INC., 38 Commercial Wharf, Boston, MA 02110.

Industry Week, 1100 Superior Avenue, Cleveland, OH 44114.

Institutional Investor, 488 Madison Avenue, New York, NY 10022.

Investment Dealer's Digest, 2 World Trade Center, #18, New York, NY 10048.

Investors' Business Daily, 12655 Beatrice Street, Los Angeles, CA 90066.

Journal of Commerce, 2 World Trade Center, New York, NY 10048.

U.S. Banker, 11 Penn Plaza, New York, NY 10001.

The Wall Street Journal, 200 Liberty Street, New York, NY 10281.

The Wall Street Transcript, 100 Wall Street, New York, NY 10005.

Computer communicating publications

Information Today, 143 Old Marlton Road, Medford, NJ 08055.

Interactive Public Relations, 212 W. Superior Street, Chicago, IL 60610.

Link Up, 2222 River Drive, King George, VA 22485.

Micro Processing News, 21150 Hawthorne Boulevard, Torrance, CA 90503

Online Access, 900 N. Franklin Street, Chicago, IL 60610.

The Online Manual, 64 Depot Road, Colchester, VT 05446 (databases).

Feature syndicates

AP Newsfeatures, 50 Rockefeller Plaza, New York, NY 10020.

Associated Press, 50 Rockefeller Plaza, New York, NY 10020.

Bloomberg Business News, 100 Business Park Drive, Princeton, NJ 08542.

Chronicle Features Syndicate, 870 Market Street, San Francisco, CA 94102.

Copley News Service, P.O. Box 190, San Diego, CA 92112.

Gannett News Service, 1000 Wilson Boulevard, Arlington, VA 22229.

Hearst Newspapers, 959 Eighth Avenue, New York, NY 10019.

King Features Syndicate, 216 E. 45th Street, New York, NY 10017.

Knight-Ridder Financial News, 2020 W. 89th Street, Leawood, KS 66206.

Los Angeles Times-Washington Post News Service, 1150 15th Street, N.W., Washington, DC 20071.

Los Angeles Times Syndicate, Times Mirror Square, Los Angeles, CA 90053.

McClatchy News Service, P.O. Box 15779, Sacramento, CA 95852.

New York Times News Service, 229 W. 43rd Street, New York, NY 10036.

Religious News Service, 1101 Connecticut Avenue, Washington, DC 20026.

Reuters America, 1333 N Street, NW, Washington, DC 20005.

Scripps-Howard News Service, 1090 Vermont Avenue, NW, Washington, DC 20005.

Tribune Media Services, 435 N. Michigan Avenue, Chicago, IL 60611.

United Feature Syndicate, 200 Park Avenue, New York, NY 10166.

United Press International, 1400 I Street, NW, Washington, DC 20005.

Universal Press Syndicate, 4900 Main Street, Kansas City, MO 64112.

Washington Post Writers Group, 1150 Fifteenth Street, NW, Washington, DC 20071.

Syndicated financial columns

King Features Syndicate, 216 East 45th Street, New York, NY 10017, (212) 455-4000.

Los Angeles Times Syndicate, Times Mirror Square, Los Angeles, CA 90053, (800) 421-8266.

United Feature Syndicate, 200 Park Avenue, New York, NY 10166, (212) 692-3700.

Washington Post Writers Group, 1150 Fifteenth Street, NW, Washington, DC 20071.

Financial broadcast outlets

Wall Street Week, featuring discussions with security analysts and other experts on the financial markets, is broadcast weekly on many stations on a syndicated basis. Its address is:

Pbs Television Network, 1320 Braddock Place, Alexandria, VA 22314.

Cnbc, 2200 Fletcher Avenue, Fort Lee, NJ 07024. A service of the National Broadcasting Company that features shows on business and finance.

National television and radio networks

Abc Radio Network, 125 West End Avenue, 7th Floor, New York, NY 10023.

Abc Television Network, 77 W. 66th Street, New York, NY 10023.

AP Broadcast News, 1825 K Street, N.W., Washington, DC 20006.

cbs Radio Network, 524 W. 57th Street, New York, NY 10019.

cbs Television Network, 524 W. 57th Street, New York, NY 10019.

cnn, P.O. Box 105366, Atlanta, GA 30348.

Fox Broadcasting Company, 10201 W. Pico, Los Angeles, CA 90035.

nbc Radio Network, 1755 Jefferson Davis Highway, Arlington, VA 22202.

nbc Television Network, 30 Rockefeller Plaza, New York, NY 10112.

npr/National Public Radio, 635 Massachusetts Avenue, N.W., Washington, DC 20001.

These directories list specific shows available to publicity people.

Bacon's Radio and TV/Cable Directories, 332 S. Michigan Avenue, Chicago, IL 60607.

Broadcasting & Cable Yearbook, Broadcasting Publications, Inc., 1705 DeSales Street, NW, Washington, DC 20036.

Television & Cable Factbook, Television Digest, Inc., 1836 Jefferson Place, NW, Washington, DC 20036.

III. Press Clipping Bureaus

U.S. Bureaus

ALLEN'S PRESS CLIPPING BUREAU
657 Mission Street
San Francisco, CA 94105
Phone: (415) 392-2353
Fax: (415) 362-6208
Contact: Mr. John N. McCombs

BACON'S CLIPPING BUREAU
332 S. Michigan Avenue
Chicago, IL 60604
Phone: (312) 922-2400
Fax: (312) 922-3127
Contact: Mr. R. Stephen Newsman

BURRELLE'S INFORMATION SERVICES
75 E. Northfield Road
Livingston, NJ 07039
Phone: (201) 992-6600
Fax: (201) 992-0407
Contact: Mr. R. C. Waggoner

LUCE PRESS CLIPPINGS, INC.
420 Lexington Avenue
New York City, NY 10170
Phone: (212) 889-6711
Fax: (212) 481-0105
Contact: Mr. W. H. French

MAGNOLIA CLIPPING SERVICE
P.O. Box 12463
Jackson, MS 39236-2463
Phone: (601) 956-4221
Fax: (601) 956-6700
Contact: Mr. Dred P. Porter

MIDWEST NEWSCLIPS
363 W. Erie Street
Chicago, IL 60610
(312) 751-7300

NEW ENGLAND NEWS CLIPS
P.O. Box 9128
Framingham, MA 01701
(508) 879-4460

OHIO NEWS BUREAU COMPANY
1900 Euclid Avenue, Room 608
Cleveland, OH 44115
Phone: (216) 241-0675
Fax: (216) 241-0678
Contact: Mrs. Frances Tratnik

International Bureaus

Australia

MARKETRAK PTY LTD
19 Franci Street
Sydney NSW 2010
Phone: 61 (2) 360 2791
Fax: 61 (2) 331 1106

MEDIA MONITORS AUSTRALIA Pty Ltd
303 Cleveland Street, Surry Hills
P.O. Box 2110 Strawberry Hills NSW 2012

Phone: 61 (2) 310 3155
Fax: 61 (2) 319 0616

MONITORING PERTH MEDIA
511 Fitzgerald Street/Box 42
North Perth WA 6006
Phone: 61 (9) 328 9915
Fax: 61 (9) 227 8587

Austria

OBSERVER Ges. m.b.H
Lessinggasse 21
1020 Wien
Phone: 43 (1) 213 22 42
Fax: 43 (1) 213 22 15
Telex: 01-31742 obser a

Belgium

AUXIPRESS SA
Quai aux Pierres de Taille 37–39
1000 Bruxelles
Phone: 32 (2) 217 43 02
Fax: 32 (2) 219 13 29

CLIPCO—PRESS/RD/TV-MONITORING
Brusselsesteenweg 297
B-3020 Herent/Veltem
Phone: 32 (16) 49 02 41
Fax: 32 (16) 48 14 72

EURO-ARGUS SA
Quai aux Pierres de Taille 37–39
1000 Bruxelles
Phone: 32 (2) 218 34 67
Fax: 32 (2) 218 45 01

Canada

MH MEDIA MONITORING LIMITED
2206 Eglinton Avenue E., Suite 190
Scarborough, ONT M1L 4T5
Phone: (416) 750-2220
Fax: (416) 750-2233

CLIP INC.
1111, rue St. Urbain
Montréal, QUE H2Z 1Y6
Phone: (514) 871-1455

Fax: (514) 871-9864

MEDIASCAN CANADA INC.
550 rue Sherbrooke Ouest/Bureau 2050
Montréal, QUE H3A 1B9
Phone: (514) 842-3792
Fax: (514) 842-6680

Cyprus

BLADE INFORMATION & CLIPPING
P.O. Box 323
Nicosia
Phone: 357 2 311 553

Denmark

ARGUE DANMARK
    MEDIEOVERVAGNING A'JOUR KLIP
    UDKLIPSBUREAU
Ravnsborggade 12–14
2200 Copenhagen N
Phone: 45 3139 1300
Fax: 45 3139 1339

PRESSEKLIP A/S
Glentevej 61–65
2400 Copenhagen NV.
Phone: 45 31 19 34 00
Fax: 45 31 19 93 51

Finland

SANOMALEHTIEN ILMOITUSTOIMISTO
    OY (SITA)
Strombergintie 4
FIN-00380 Helsinki
Phone: 358 0 561 1011
Fax: 358 0 561 1092
358 0 561 1010/Press
358 0 561 1061/Radio and TV

France

AGENCE FRANCAISE D'EXTRAITS DE
    PRESSE
13, avenue de l'Opera
75001 Paris
Phone: 33 (1) 40 15 17 89
Fax: 33 (1) 40 15 17 15

ARGUS DE LA PRESSE
130, rue du Mont-Cenis
75018 Paris
Phone: 33 (1) 49 25 70 00
Fax: 33 (1) 49 25 70 01

LE NOUVEAU COURRIER DE LA PRESSE
LIT TOUT + MEDIA SCAN SERVICES
15, rue Colonel Driant
75001 Paris
Phone: 33 (1) 42 61 52 15
Fax: 33 (1) 49 27 07 10

PRESSE-CLEARING
1, rue Mirabeau
75016 Paris
Phone: 33 (1) 42 24 13 56 / 45 20 76 52
Fax: 33 (1) 45 20 14 54

Germany

ARGUS MEDIA GmbH
Hohenstrasse 16
D—70736 Fellbach
Postal Address: Argus Media GmbH
D-7073 Fellbach
Phone: 49 (711) 57 531 0
Fax: 49 (711) 57 531 11

DER AUSSCHNITT
ACHTERBERG GmbH & Co.
Gneisenaustrasse 66
D—10961 Berlin
Phone: 49 (30) 695 91 40
Fax: 49 (30) 694 11 66

METROPOL-GESELLSCHAFT E. Matthes
    & Co.
Uhlandstrasse 184
D—10623 Berlin
Phone: 49 (30) 881 68 31 + 882 57 89
Fax: 49 (30) 882 56 29

PRESSE-ARCHIV
Zeitungsausschnittdienst GmbH
Tulpenweg 7
D—64319 Pfungstadt
Phone: 49 (61) 57 20 91
Fax: 49 (61) 57 20 92

Great Britain

CLIPABILITY
39–41 Carrholm Road
Leeds LS7 2NQ
Phone: 44 (532) 693 290
Fax: 44 (532) 687 981

DURRANT'S PRESS CUTTING LIMITED
103 Whitecross Street
London EC1Y 8QT
Phone: 44 (171) 588 3671
Fax: 44 (171) 374 8171

INTERNATIONAL PRESS CUTTING
  BUREAU
224–236 Walworth Road
London SE17 21JE
Phone: 44 (171) 708 2113
Fax: 44 (171) 701 4489

LINCOLN HANNAH LTD
89½ Worship Street
London EC2A 2BE
Phone: 44 (71) 377 1742
Fax: 44 (71) 377 6103

ROMEIKE & CURTICE LIMITED
Hale House
290–296 Green Lanes
London NI3 5TP
Phone: 44 (181) 882 0155
Fax: 44 (181) 882 6716

PREMIUM PRESS MONITORING
193 Tooley Street
London SEI 2HZ
Phone: 44 (71) 403 6033
Fax: 44 (71) 407 5857

Greece

PRESS CLIPPING SERVICE
STATHIS KALLOS
Trapezountos 28
171.24 N. Smirni
Phone: 30 (1) 9333 523
Fax: 30 (1) 9359 917
Telex: 22-5041 ECAL

Hong Kong

NEWSCLIP MEDIA MONITOR SERVICE
(A member of Newscan Company Ltd.)
19/F., Sing Pao Building
101 King's Road, North Point
Hong Kong
Phone: 852 566 1311
Fax: 852 510 8199

Hungary

MAHIR OBSERVER
Ulloi ut 51
1091 Budapest
Phone: 36 (1) 33 4713 / 114-3421
Fax: 36 (1) 13 0688

India

INDIAN PRESS SERVICE
16-A, Friends Colony
New Dehli - 110 065
Phone: 91 (11) 6831 995
Fax: 91 (11) 6831 874
Telex: 031 - 75496

Iceland

MIDLUN
Aegisgata 7/ P.O. Box 155
121 Reykjavik
Phone: 354 562 22 88
Fax: 354 552 69 94

Ireland

NEWS EXTRACTS
7 Ely Place
Dublin 2
Phone: 353 (1) 66 16 966
Fax: 353 (1) 66 15 361

Israel

IFAT MEDIA INFORMATION CENTER
PRESS CLIPPINGS T.V. & RADIO
  MONITORING
96 Derech Petah-Tikva Street
Tel-Aviv 67138
Phone: 972 (3) 563 50 50
Fax: 972 (3) 561 71 66

Italy

ECOSTAMPA MEDIA MONITOR srl
L'ECO DELLA STAMPA (Trade Mark)
Via G. Compagnoni 28, P.O. Box 12094
I - 20129 Milano
Phone: 39 (2) 7611 0307
Fax: 39 (2) 7611 0346

PRESS SERVICE
SERVIZIO RITAGLI STAMPA
Via Cassidoro 1 a
00193 Roma
Phone: 39 (6) 687 8215
Fax: 39 (6) 654 4545

Japan

JAPAN INFORMATION SERVICE
Taisei Building 4-10
Kayabacho 2-chome
Nihonbashi Chuo-ku
Tokyo 103 Japan
Phone: 81 (3) 3667 4811
Fax: 81 (3) 3667 9237

NAIGAI PRESSCLIPPING BUREAU LTD.
14-4 Okubo 3-Chome
Shinjuku-ku
Tokyo 160
Phone: 81 (3) 3208 5134
Fax: 81 (3) 3208 5199

PRESS RESEARCH INTERNATIONAL
3FL.RJ-Plaza
2-30-20, Nishi-Ikebukuro
Toshima-ku, Tokyo
Phone: 81 (3) 3980 6251
Fax: 81 (3) 3980 8201

The Netherlands

ANTAL CLIPPING B.V.
Press - RD - TV monitoring
De Gaarde 35/51, Postbus 40264
2504 LG Den Haag
Phone: 31 (70) 367 10 06
Fax: 31 (70) 367 78 46

KNIPSEL INFO SERVICE
Randstad 21/71
1314 BJ Almere
Phone: 31 (36) 534 35 70
Fax: 31 (36) 534 31 54

EUROCLIP
High Tech Center
Radarweg 529
Postbus 1776
1000 BT Amsterdam
Phone: 31 (20) 6815 815
Fax: 31 (20) 6817 477

New Zealand

CHONG PRESS CLIPPING BUREAU
17, Spring Str, Onehunga
P.O. Box 13-330
Auckland
Phone: 64 (9) 634 0463
Fax: 64 (9) 636 7607

Norway

NORSKE ARGUS A/S
Storgt. 25
0184 Oslo
Phone: 47 22 20 46 75
Fax: 47 22 33 34 95

Pakistan

PAN ASIA NEWS (Pvt) LTD
Ebrahim Building, West Wharf Road
P.O. Box 5486
Karachi 74000
Phone: 92 (21) 202 155
92 (21) 493 4012 (Home)
Fax: 92 (21) 241 8460
Telex: 23715 HAEGS PK

Poland

AGENCJA PRASOWO-INFORMACYJNA
  "GLOB"
Al. Stanów Zjednoczonych 53
04-028 Warszawa
Phone: 48 (22) 13 42 34 / 13 44 95
Fax: 48 (22) 13 44 95

Portugal

MEMORANDUM-PRESS CLIPPING
    SERVICE
Rua Carlos Seixas, 158, Apartado 4003
3030 Coimbra
Phone: 351 (39) 713 548 / 701 989
Fax: 351 (39) 701 396 / 701 105

RECORTE
Avª·Almirante Reis 19-2.Esq.
Apartado no. 2571
1114 Lisboa Codex
Phone: 351 (1) 885 03 01 / 885 00 39
Fax: 351 (1) 883 30 04

Singapore

PEACE TRANSLATION & CLIPPING
    SERVICES
PRIVATE LIMITED
2 Finlayson Green #13-06
Asia Insurance Building
Singapore 0104
Phone: 65 227 7665
Fax: 75 227 0837

Slovenia

PRESS CLIPPING
Tatjana Novak & Co., D.N.O.
Gregorciceva 37
62000 Maribor
Phone: 386 (62) 223 219
Fax: 386 (62) 226 491

South Africa

NEWSCLIP
1st Floor, East Wing
Petrob House
343 Surrey Avenue
Ferndale Randburg
2194 Transvaal
Postal address:
Private Bag XI, Fontainebleau
2032, Transvaal
Phone: 27 (11) 787 9622
Fax: 27 (11) 886 8353

S.A. PRESS CUTTING AGENCY PTY. LTD.
22/23 Westcliffe
127 West Street
Durban 4001
Phone: 27 (31) 370 403
Fax: 27 (31) 374 307

Spain

AGENCIA INTERNACIONAL
    CAMARASA, S.L.
Plaza Reyes Magos No. 12
28007 Madrid
Phone: 34 (1) 551 49 46 / 551 53 12
Fax: 34 (1) 501 30 03

D+A DOCUMENTACION Y ANALISIS SA
Montera, 48.4ª planta
28013 Madrid
Phone: 34 (1) 523 02 46
Fax: 34 (1) 523 08 71

Sweden

AB PRESSURKLIPP
P.O. Box 1510
17129 Solna
Phone: 46 (8) 705 12 00
Fax: 46 (8) 83 99 40

IMEDIA AB
P.O. Box 4404
102 68 Stockholm
Phone: 46 (8) 702 53 00
Fax: 46 (8) 714 86 24

PRESSE UND MEDIENARCHIV AG
Muhlebachstrasse 42
8008 Zurich
Phone: 41 (1) 261 70 70
Fax: 41 (1) 261 79 69
Telex: 81 63 63

Switzerland

ARGUS DER PRESSE AG
Streulistrasse 19
8030 Zurich
Phone: 41 (1) 388 82 00
Fax: 41 (1) 388 82 01

Turkey

AJANS PRESS A.S.
Hudavendigar Cad. No: 10 Kat: 3/4
34420 Sirkeci / Istanbul
Phone: 90 (212) 526 37 55 / 526 11 62 / 513
     54 96 / 526 40 33 / 526 40 36
Fax: 90 (212) 512 30 69 / 527 53 05

PUBLIC RELATIONS ORGANIZATIONS

Associations in U.S. and Canada

Agricultural Relations Council
1629 K Street, NW, Suite 1100
Washington, DC 20006
(202) 785-6710

American Jewish Public Relations Society
234 Fifth Avenue
New York, NY 10001
(212) 697-5895

American Society for Health Care
  Marketing and Public Relations
1 N. Franklin Street
Chicago, Illinois 60606
(312) 422-3737

Bank Marketing Association
1120 Connecticut Avenue, NW
Washington, DC 20036

Baptist Public Relations Association
c/o Southwest Baptist University
1600 University Avenue
Bolivor, MO 65613
(417) 326-1503

Canadian Public Relations Society
22 Laurier Avenue West, Suite 720
Ottawa, ONT K1P 529

Council for Advancement and Support of
  Education (CASE)
11 Dupont Circle, NW, Suite 400
Washington, DC 20036
(202) 328-5900

Florida Public Relations Association
P.O. Drawer 7411
Winter Haven, FL 33883
(813) 294-5366

Institute for Public Relations Research &
  Education
University of Florida
P.O. Box 118400
Gainesville, FL 32611

International Association of Business
  Communicators
One Hallidie Plaza, #600
San Francisco, CA 94102
(415) 433-3400

National Association of Government
  Communicators
669 S. Washington Street
Alexandria, VA 22314
(703) 823-4821

National Investor Relations Institute
8045 Leesburg Pike
Vienna, VA 22182

National School Public Relations
  Association
1501 Lee Highway, Suite 201
Arlington, VA 22209
(703) 528-5840

New York Financial Writers' Association
P.O. Box 21
Syosset, NY 11791
(516) 921-7766

Arthur W. Page Society
1301 Avenue of the Americas, #3100
New York, NY 10019
(212) 841-4674

Public Affairs Council
1019 19th Street, NW, Suite 200
Washington, DC 20036
(202) 872-1790

Publicity Club of Chicago
200 N. Michigan Avenue
Chicago, IL 60601
(312) 541-1747

Public Relations Seminar
(address changes annually)

Public Relations Society of America
33 Irving Place, 3rd Floor
New York, NY 10003
(212) 995-2230

Religious Public Relations Council
P.O. Box 296
Weonesoville, PA 19565
(610) 373-1067

South Public Relations Federation
479 Corby Drive
Baton Rouge, LA 70810
(504) 766-3111

Utility Communicators International
5316 E. Kings Avenue
Scottsdale, AZ 85254
(602) 971-1989

Women Executives in Public Relations
P.O. Box 609
Westport, CT 06881
(203) 226-4947

Women in Communications, Inc.
3717 Columbia Pike, #310
Arlington, VA 22204
(703) 920-5555

International Public Relations Organizations

A list is available in Reed's Worldwide Directory of Public Relations Firms, 121 Chanlon Road, New Providence, NJ 07974, (800) 521-8110.

CODE OF PROFESSIONAL STANDARDS FOR THE PRACTICE OF PUBLIC RELATIONS[1]

Declaration of Principles

Members of the Public Relations Society of America base their professional principles on the fundamental value and dignity of the individual, holding that the free exercise of human rights, especially freedom of speech, freedom of assembly, and freedom of the press, is essential to the practice of public relations.

In serving the interests of clients and employers, we dedicate ourselves to the goals of better communication, understanding, and cooperation among the diverse individuals, groups, and institutions of society, and of equal opportunity of employment in the public relations profession.

We pledge:

To conduct ourselves professionally, with truth, accuracy, fairness, and responsibility to the public;

To improve our individual competence and advance the knowledge and proficiency of the profession through continuing research and education;

And to adhere to the articles of the Code of Professional Standards for the Practice of Public Relations as adopted by the governing Assembly of the Society.

Code of Professional Standards for the Practice of Public Relations

These articles have been adopted by the Public Relations Society of America to promote and maintain high standards of public service and ethical conduct among its members.

1. A member shall conduct his or her professional life in accord with **public interest**.

2. A member shall exemplify high standards of **honesty and integrity** while carrying out dual obligations to a client or employer and to the democratic process.

3. A member shall **deal fairly** with the public, with past or present clients or employers, and with fellow practitioners, giving due respect to the ideal of free inquiry and to the opinions of others.

4. A member shall adhere to the highest standards of **accuracy and truth**, avoiding extravagant claims or unfair comparisons and giving credit for ideas and words borrowed from others.

5. A member shall not knowingly disseminate **false or misleading information** and

---

[1]This Code was adopted by the Public Relations Society of America Assembly in 1988. It replaces a Code of Ethics in force since 1950 and revised in 1954, 1959, 1963, 1977, and 1983.

shall act promptly to correct erroneous communications for which he or she is responsible.

6. A member shall not engage in any practice which has the purpose of **corrupting** the integrity of channels of communications or the processes of government.

7. A member shall be prepared to **identify publicly** the name of the client or employer on whose behalf any public communication is made.

8. A member shall not use any individual or organization professing to serve or represent an announced cause, or professing to be independent or unbiased, but actually serving another or **undisclosed interest**.

9. A member shall not **guarantee the achievement** of specified results beyond the member's direct control.

10. A member shall **not represent conflicting** or competing interests without the express consent of those concerned, given after a full disclosure of the facts.

11. A member shall not place himself or herself in a position where the member's **personal interest is or may be in conflict** with an obligation to an employer or client, or others, without full disclosure of such interests to all involved.

12. A member shall **not accept fees, commissions, gifts, or any other consideration** from anyone except clients or employers for whom services are performed without their express consent, given after full disclosure of the facts.

13. A member scrupulously safeguard the **confidences and privacy of rights** of present, former, and prospective clients or employers.

14. A member shall not intentionally **damage the professional reputation** or practice of another practitioner.

15. If a member has evidence that another member has been guilty of unethical, illegal, or unfair practices, including those in violation of this Code, the member is obligated to present the information promptly to the proper authorities of the Society for action in accordance with the procedure set forth in Article 12 of the Bylaws.

16. A member called as a witness in a proceeding for enforcement of this Code is obligated to appear, unless excused for sufficient reason by the judicial panel.

17. A member shall, as soon as possible, sever relations with any organization or individual if such relationship requires conduct contrary to the articles of this Code.

Official Interpretations of the Code

Interpretation of Code Paragraph 1, which reads, "A member shall conduct his or her professional life in accord with the public interest."

> The public interest is here defined primarily as comprising respect for and enforcement of the rights guaranteed by the Constitution of the United States of America.

Interpretation of Code Paragraph 6, which reads, "A member shall not engage in any practice which has the purpose of corrupting the integrity of channels or communication or the processes of government."

1. Among the practices prohibited by this paragraph are those that tend to place representatives of media or government under any obligation to the member, or the member's employer or client, which is in conflict with their obligations to media or government, such as:

a. the giving of gifts of more than nominal value;

b. any form of payment or compensation to a member of the media in order to obtain preferential or guaranteed news or editorial coverage in the medium;

c. any retainer or fee to a media employee or use of such employee if retained by a client or employer, where the circumstances are not fully disclosed to and accepted by the media employer;

d. providing trips, for media representatives, that are unrelated to legitimate news interest;

e. the use by a member of an investment or loan or advertising commitment made by the member, or the member's client or employer, to obtain preferential or guaranteed coverage in the medium.

2. This Code paragraph does not prohibit hosting media or government representatives at meals, cocktails, or news functions and special events that are occasions for the exchange of news information or views, or the furtherance of understanding, which is part of the public relations function. Nor does it prohibit the bona fide press event or tour when media or government representatives are given the opportunity for an on-the-spot viewing of a newsworthy product, process, or event in which the media or government representatives have a legitimate interest. What is customary or reasonable hospitality has to be a matter of particular judgment in specific situations. In all of these cases, however, it is, or should be, understood that no preferential treatment or guarantees are expected or implied and that complete independence always is left to the media or government representative.

3. This paragraph does not prohibit the reasonable giving or lending of sample products or services to media representatives who have a legitimate interest in the products or services.

4. It is permissible, under Article 6 of the Code, to offer complimentary or discount rates to the media (travel writers, for example) if the rate is for business use and is made available to all writers. Considerable question exists as to the propriety of extending such rates for personal use.

Interpretation of Code Paragraph 9, which reads, "A member shall not guarantee the achievement of specified results beyond the member's direct control."

This Code paragraph, in effect, prohibits misleading a client or employer as to what professional public relations can accomplish. It does not prohibit guarantees of quality or service. But it does prohibit guaranteeing specific results which, by their very nature, cannot be guaranteed because they are not subject to the member's control. As an example, a guarantee that a news release will appear specifically in a particular publication would be prohibited. This paragraph should not be interpreted as prohibiting contingent fees.

Interpretation of Code Paragraph 13, which reads, "A member shall scrupulously safeguard the confidences and privacy rights of present, former, and prospective clients or employers."

1. This article does not prohibit a member who has knowledge of client or employer activities that are illegal from making such disclosures to the proper authorities as he or she believes are legally required.

2. Communications between a practitioner and client/employer are deemed to be confidential under Article 13 of the Code of Professional Standards. However, although practitioner/client/employer communications are considered confidential between the parties, such communications are not

privileged against disclosure in a court of law.

3. In the absence of any contractual arrangement, the client or employer legally owns the rights to papers or materials created for him.

Interpretation of Code Paragraph 14, which reads, "A member shall not intentionally damage the professional reputation or practice of another practitioner." Blind solicitation, on its face, is not prohibited by the Code. However, if the customer list were improperly obtained, or if the solicitation contained references reflecting adversely on the quality of current services, a complaint might be justified.

An Official Interpretation of the Code as It Applies to Political Public Relations

Preamble

In the practice of political public relations, a PRSA member must have professional capabilities to offer an employer or client quite apart from any political relationships of value, and members may serve their employer or client without necessarily having attributed to them the character, reputation, or beliefs of those they serve. It is understood that members may choose to serve only those interests with whose political philosophy they are personally comfortable.

Definition

"Political Public Relations" is defined as those areas of public relations that relate to:

a. the counseling of political organizations, committees, candidates, or potential candidates for public office; and groups constituted for the purpose of influencing the vote on any ballot issue.

b. the counseling of holders of public office;

c. the management, or direction, of a political campaign for or against a candidate for political office; or for or against a ballot issue to be determined by voter approval or rejection;

d. the practice of public relations on behalf of a client or an employer in connection with that client's or employer's relationships with any candidates or holders of public office, with the purpose of influencing legislation or government regulation or treatment of a client or employer, regardless of whether the PRSA member is a recognized lobbyist;

e. the counseling of government bodies, or segments thereof, either domestic or foreign.

Precepts

1. It is the responsibility of PRSA members practicing political public relations, as defined above, to be conversant with the various statutes, local, state, and federal, governing such activities and to adhere to them strictly. This includes, but is not limited to, the various local, state, and federal laws, court decisions, and official interpretations governing lobbying, political contributions, disclosure, elections, libel, slander, and the like. In carrying out this responsibility, members shall seek appropriate counseling whenever necessary.

2. It is also the responsibility of members to abide by PRSA's Code of Professional Standards.

3. Members shall represent clients or employers in good faith, and while partisan advocacy on behalf of a candidate or public issue may be expected, members shall act

in accord with the public interests and adhere to truth and accuracy and to generally accepted standards of good taste.

4. Members shall not issue descriptive material or any advertising or publicity information or participate in the preparation or use thereof that is not signed by responsible persons or is false, misleading, or unlabeled as to its source, and are obligated to use care to avoid dissemination of any such material.

5. Members have an obligation to clients to disclose what remuneration beyond their fees they expect to receive as a result of their relationship, such as commissions for media advertising, printing, and the like, and should not accept such extra payment without their client's consent.

6. Members shall not improperly use their positions to encourage additional future employment or compensation. It is understood that successful campaign directors or managers, because of the performance of their duties and the working relationship that develops, may well continue to assist and counsel, for pay, the successful candidate.

7. Members shall voluntarily disclose to employers or clients the identity of other employers or clients with whom they are currently associated, and whose interests might be affected favorably or unfavorably by their political representation.

8. Members shall respect the confidentiality of information pertaining to employers or clients past, present, and potential, even after relationships cease, avoiding future associations wherein insider information is sought that would give a desired advantage over a member's previous clients.

9. In avoiding practices that might tend to corrupt the processes of government, members shall not make undisclosed gifts of cash or other valuable considerations

that are designed to influence specific decisions of voters, legislators, or public officials on public matters. A business lunch or dinner, or other comparable expenditure made in the course of communicating a point of view or public position, would not constitute such a violation. Nor, for example, would a plant visit designed and financed to provide useful background information to an interested legislator or candidate.

10. Nothing herein should be construed as prohibiting members from making legal, properly disclosed contributions to the candidates, party, or referenda issues of their choice.

11. Members shall not, through use of information known to be false or misleading, conveyed directly or through a third party, intentionally injure the public reputation of an opposing interest.

An Official Interpretation of the Code as It Applies to Financial Public Relations

This interpretation of the Society Code as it applies to financial public relations was originally adopted in 1963 and amended in 1972, 1977, 1983, and 1988 by action of the PRSA Board of Directors. "Financial public relations" is defined as "that area of public relations which relates to the dissemination of information that affects the understanding of stockholders and investors generally concerning the financial position and prospects of a company, and includes among its objectives the improvement of relations between corporations and their stockholders." The interpretation was prepared in 1963 by the Society's Financial Relations Committee, working with the Securities and Exchange Commission and with the advice of the Society's legal counsel. It is rooted directly in the Code with the full force of the Code behind it, and a violation of any of the following paragraphs is subject to the same procedures and penalties as violation of the Code:

1. It is the responsibility of PRSA members who practice financial public relations to be thoroughly familiar with and understand the rules and regulations of the SEC and the laws it administers, as well as other laws, rules, and regulations affecting financial public relations, and to act in accordance with their letter and spirit. In carrying out this responsibility, members shall also seek legal counsel, when appropriate, on matters concerning financial public relations.

2. Members shall adhere to the general policy of making full and timely disclosure of corporate information on behalf of clients or employers. The information disclosed shall be accurate, clear, and understandable. The purpose of such disclosure is to provide the investing public with all material information affecting security values or influencing investment decisions. In complying with the duty of full and timely disclosure, members shall present all material facts, including those adverse to the company. They shall exercise care to ascertain the facts and to disseminate only information they believe to be accurate. They shall not knowingly omit information, the omission of which might make a release false or misleading. Under no circumstances shall members participate in any activity designed to mislead or manipulate the price of a company's securities.

3. Members shall publicly disclose or release information promptly so as to avoid the possibility of any use of the information by any insider or third party. To that end, members shall make every effort to comply with the spirit and intent of the timely disclosure policies of the stock exchanges,

NASD, and the SEC. Material information shall be made available on an equal basis.

4. Members shall not disclose confidential information the disclosure of which might be adverse to a valid corporate purpose or interest and whose disclosure is not required by the timely disclosure provisions of the law. During any such period of nondisclosure members shall not directly or indirectly (a) communicate the confidential information to any other person or (b) buy or sell or in any other way deal in the company's securities where the confidential information may materially affect the market for the security when disclosed. Material information shall be disclosed publicly as soon as its confidential status has terminated or the requirement of timely disclosure takes effect.

5. During the registration period, members shall not engage in practices designed to precondition the market for such securities. During registration, the issuance of forecasts, projections, predictions about sales and earnings, or opinions concerning security values or other aspects of the future performance of the company, shall be in accordance with current SEC regulations and statements of policy. In the case of companies whose securities are publicly held, the normal flow of factual information to shareholders and the investing public shall continue during the registration period.

6. Where members have any reason to doubt that projections have an adequate basis in fact, they shall satisfy themselves as to the adequacy of the projections prior to disseminating them.

7. Acting in concert with clients or employers, members shall act promptly to correct false or misleading information or rumors concerning clients' or employers' securities or business whenever they have reason to

believe such information or rumors are materially affecting investor attitudes.

8. Members shall not issue descriptive materials designed or written in such a fashion as to appear to be, contrary to fact, an independent third-party endorsement or recommendation of a company or a security. Whenever members issue material for clients or employers, either in their own names or in the name of someone other than the clients or employers, they shall disclose in large type and in a prominent position on the face of the material the source of such material and the existence of the issuer's client or employer relationship.

9. Members shall not use inside information for personal gain. However, this is not intended to prohibit members from making bona fide investments in their company's or client's securities insofar as they can make such investments without the benefit of material inside information.

10. Members shall not accept compensation that would place them in a position of conflict with their duty to a client, employer, or the investing public. Members shall not accept stock options from clients or employers nor accept securities as compensation at a price below market price except as part of an overall plan for corporate employees.

11. Members shall act so as to maintain the integrity of channels of public communication. They shall not pay or permit to be paid to any publication or other communications medium any consideration in exchange for publicizing a company, except through clearly recognizable paid advertising.

12. Members shall in general be guided by the PRSA Declaration of Principles and the Code of Professional Standards for the Practice of Public Relations of which this is an official interpretation.

GLOSSARY

Access. The means of getting into an online system.

Address. Where mail or files can be sent to you at an online site.

Advertising. Persuasive material that is presented to the public as the acknowledged appeal of an identified party. It is almost always paid for, and therefore fully controlled in context, presentation, medium, and time by the appealing party. In some instances, an item may be called either advertising or publicity, such as posters, brochures, and industrial motion pictures.

Agate. A type size, 5½ points. There are 14 agate lines to an inch. The agate line is the standard unit of measurement for advertising space.

Air Brush. An art process widely used for retouching photographs, applied with aid of compressed air and an air brush. Also used by many illustrators to obtain interesting tone effects.

Air Check. Tape made of a TV or radio program.

Alignment. Arrangement of type so that the bottoms of the characters are in a straight line. May also be applied to positioning type and illustrations for pleasing effect.

Angle. Particular emphasis of a story or broadcast; also called "slant."

Annual Report. A financial statement by management, required by the Securities and Exchange Commission. Frequently summarized and translated into layman's language for distribution to stockholders and interested media.

Answer Print. Print of a motion picture film used to check quality before final printing.

Antique-Finish Paper. A stock with a soft, fluffy surface used primarily for type matter. Will take wood cuts and line illustrations but not half-tones, except in the very highest grades. This stock varies widely in grade.

Art. All types of illustration in any medium.

Attitude. The composition of a person's bent on any issue or question, made up from all the influences that have built up throughout his lifetime. Usually unexpressed.

Audience. Denotes the group or groups to whom the public relations program, or any part thereof, is directed.

Backgrounder. A document prepared to provide the facts and significance underlying a subject, as a means of "backgrounding" an editor or writer.

Baud (or bauds per second or bps). Rate at which information travels from computer to computer.

Bbs. Bulletin board system, an electronic version of old bulletin boards on which people attach notices.

Beat. (1) An area or subject that a medium assigns to a given reporter or department, such as the criminal courts or boating. (2) An exclusive story; a "scoop."

Beeper. Device attached to a telephone that "beeps" every 14 seconds, as required by FCC, to indicate conversation is recorded. Also, recorded telephone interview on TV or radio.

Behavior Pattern. A recurrent way of acting toward a given object or in a given situation.

Ben Day. A process, named after its originator, that enables photoengravers to produce a variety of shadings in line plates. This process reduces the amount of artwork necessary to obtain the effects desired and makes it possible for the engraver to prepare a line cut rather than the more expensive halftone.

Blow Up. Increase the size of any visual item by photographic reproduction.

Blurb. Short description of story or article, usually used to promote it.

Body Type. As distinguished from display type used in headlines, body type is that used for the text. Rarely is body type larger than 14 points in size; rarely should it be in less than 8-point size for readability in public relations work.

Boiler Plate. Case-metal reproductions of newspaper stories and illustrations, sent by syndicates to small newspapers that have limited facilities for typesetting. Often full pages of boiler plate are used by small country papers to fill in the space not occupied by local items or advertisements.

Boldface Type. A blacker, heavier type than its regular or medium counterpart in any given typeface. The elements are made thicker for boldface than the normal width for the regular face, to make the matter stand out from the surrounding copy.

Bond Paper. Paper ranging in grade from a low-grade sulphite to 100 percent rag content. Used mainly for office stationery.

Booklet. A printed piece of six or more pages, with a paper cover and prepared as a bound unit, usually by stapling. (*See* **Brochure**.)

Boomerang Effect. In propaganda, when the affected individual reacts in the opposite from the expected way.

Box. A newspaper item enclosed within printed borders.

Bridge. Phrase or sentence connecting two stories or segments of a telecast.

Broadside. A printed piece intended for quick reading and motivation to quick action. Printed on one side of a single sheet.

Brochure. A printed piece containing six or more pages. More elaborate than a booklet.

Browser. Software designed to view documents created specifically for the Internet's World Wide Web.

Business Publications. Periodicals directed primarily to business and financial groups.

Byline. Signature of the author on a newspaper or magazine story.

Campaign. An organized effort to poll, formulate, or alter the opinion of any groups on a selected subject.

Candids. Unposed but effective photographs.

Caps. Capital letters.

Caption. Descriptive matter accompanying an illustration. Also referred to as a **cutline**.

CCTV. Closed-circuit television, wherein the signal is transmitted by wire to a limited number of receivers.

Center Spread. The two facing center pages of a publication appearing on a continuous sheet.

CEO, CFO. Chief executive officer, chief financial officer, usually of a corporation.

Channel. A place on the television dial where a station can be received. Also, in communication, one of the avenues for reaching an audience.

Character. A single unit of type, such as a letter, number, or punctuation mark.

Chat. Real-time online conversation in which two or more people type to one another.

Cheesecake. Photographs depending for their appeal on display of feminine sex appeal. "Leg art."

Chroma Key. A process for incorporating artwork in TV commercials.

Circular. A mailing piece or free-distribution item, usually one sheet. An item intended for widespread, inexpensive distribution.

Circulation. For print media, number of copies put into the hands of readers; often substantially less than readership because of multiple use of each copy. In broadcasting, number of people who regularly or often view or listen to a station.

Class Publications. Periodicals designed to appeal to particular, well-defined groups interested in certain limited subjects.

Cap/lc. In typesetting, capital and lower-case letters.

Client. Organization or individual employing public relations counsel or other service.

Clip. In broadcasting, a short segment taken from the whole or to be spliced in. In print media, a clipping.

Clipping Returns. Clippings of stories or other published material mentioning a specific subject, taken from newspapers, magazines, trade journals, specialized publications, and/or house organs. Most frequently these are obtained from commercial clipping services that supply clippings from numerous publications for a flat rate per clipping.

Clipsheet. A printed page of stories and/or illustrations, sent to publications so they may clip out any item they may wish to use. Combines a number of releases into one mailing and provides editors with a quick means of judging story value and length.

Color. (1) To exaggerate or distort. (2) Background or mood material to accompany factual report. (3) Colored art or printing.

Column Rule. Printed vertical line between columns of type.

Combination Publication. A publication distributed both to an organization's own employees or members and to outside groups or individuals.

Comic Book. A leaflet or magazine using the comic strip method to tell its purpose.

Commercial Online Service. An online bulletin board–like service that provides services for a fee.

Communication. The transaction of conveying thought from one party or group to another. Also, the thought so conveyed.

Community. The adjacent geographical area influenced and affected by company policy and production.

Composition. Setting type. Also arrangements of the elements in a paragraph or a photograph.

Condensed. Type with a narrower face than the regular face.

Conference Report. A summary of the points discussed, actions taken, and assignments made at a conference among various members of an organization, or between members of the organization and its counsel.

Conservation. Support of the public's existing opinion and preventing it from changing.

Consumerism. The composite of movements and causes purporting to protect the consumer in the purchase of goods and services, product safety, and other matters.

Control Group. Group in which the members are chosen for their characteristics or opinions. Often, a group not exposed to a test that is used as a comparison to a test group in equating results.

Conversion. To sway public opinion from one side of an issue to another.

Copy. Written material, such as press releases, the text of booklets, broadcast material, or a magazine article.

Copy Desk. Editors' center at a newspaper, magazine, TV, or radio station where copy is edited and headlines written.

Copyreader. Editor who reads and corrects copy and usually writes headlines.

Correspondent. Out-of-town or traveling reporter.

Coverage. Extent of distribution of publicity or opinion-affecting material.

Cover Stock. Sturdy papers used for pamphlet and booklet covers, posters, memo cards, announcement cards, and similar purposes.

Cropping. Changing the proportions or size of an illustration to eliminate unnecessary or undesirable background or to enable the reproduction to fit into a specific space.

Crystallization. Bringing into public consciousness previously vague or subconscious attitudes.

Cut. A term used for an engraving of an illustration, either line or screened, to be used in letterpress printing. A cut can be made of metal, wood as in wood engravings, or a plate with a raised printing surface made from a matrix, etc.

Cutline. Photo caption.

Cyberspace. "World" in which information passes between computers.

Cylinder Press. A press with a cylinder around which paper travels as it is pressed against the printing form.

Dateline. Line at start of a story giving point of origin and date.

Deadline. Time when story must be completed.

Dealer Imprint. Name and address of dealer printed on leaflet, pamphlet, poster, or similar matter, usually in space set aside for this purpose.

Debrief. Originally, to interrogate a serviceman after returning from a combat area. Now includes interviewing members of an organization on their readings of public attitudes.

Demographics. Various characteristics of an audience—age, sex, size of family, economic status, etc.

Desktop Publishing. Use of special computers and related equipment to produce publications in the office without use of commercial printers.

Dish. Slang for "earth station," the umbrella-shaped antenna that sends or receives satellite signals.

Display Face. Type or hand lettering, normally larger than 14 points, used for headlines.

Documentary. Informational film or television show with a unified subject or purpose.

Double Truck. Same as center spread when two pages are in chapter of publication and on same sheet. Otherwise, two full facing pages.

Downlink. Industry jargon for a satellite receiving dish, or for the process of beaming signals from satellites down to earth stations.

Download. Move files from a remote computer to your own.

Dub. To transcribe one medium onto another, such as sound from a tape onto a soundtrack of a film or videotape.

Dummy. Sheets of paper cut and folded to the size of a proposed printing job. Layouts can be drawn on the dummy and a finished dummy may be made from proofs to portray how the finished job will appear.

Earth Station. An antenna that sends or receives satellite signals.

Editorialize. Inject opinion into a news story.

Electronic Newsletter. A newsletter distributed digitally from one computer to many other computers.

E-Mail. Short for electronic mail. A message passed from one person to one or more other people via computer.

Exclusive. Article, story, or broadcast show limited to one medium or network.

Extended or Expanded. Extra wide typeface.

External Publication. A publication issued by an organization to people outside its own employee or membership groups, such as to customers, the local community, the financial world, etc.

Extra Condensed. Especially compressed typeface.

Face. The uppermost part of a piece of type. The printing surface. Also used to differentiate one style of type from another.

Facsimile. An exact copy or reproduction of something, usually produced by a mechanical or photographic process from the original. Also the electronic process of transmitting exact copies of printed or photographic material over long distances, also called fax.

Fact Sheet. A document containing essential facts, usually in non-narrative form, on a given subject.

False Front. An organization created to give the appearance of support for a cause from a segment of the populace it does not represent.

FAQ. Frequently Asked Questions, lists of questions about a particular Usenet newsgroup and its particular topic.

Feature. (1) A story based more on interest or background than on news. (2) The main topic of interest in a story.

Feed. Electronic signal sent from the source to other outlets.

Fiber Optics. A technology that transmits voice, video, and data by sending digital pulses of light through hair-thin strands of flexible glass.

File. A single archive of information recognized as an information unit by a computer. Also, to send a story by wire or electronic means.

Filler. A short bit of copy used in making up the pages of a publication to fill small spaces.

Fill-In Stories. Press releases drafted at a central point for filling in of specific information locally or on a great many separate individuals. Local dealers may be quoted and their stores cited; or promotions of members of the armed forces may be processed for hometown papers.

Financial Analyst. A specialist in studying and evaluating securities. May be with a brokerage house, bank, institutional investor, or investment counselor.

"Flack." A press agent. Standard in entertainment business, usually derogatory elsewhere.

Flagship Station. The major, usually program-originating, station of a broadcasting network.

Flame. Angry response to a posting, typed in all capital letters, usually in a newsgroup.

Floppy Disk. A pliable disk on which information is stored for use with a computer or word processor.

Flyer. A mailing piece prepared to announce or promote new merchandise, a sale, a special offer, or an event.

FM. Frequency modulation; broadcasting in higher frequency bands that are freer from distortions and static than AM (amplitude modulation).

Folder. A printed piece of four pages. Also a four-page heavy-paper container for other printed materials.

Follow-Up. A broadcast or story that follows a news report; also known as second- or third-day story.

Font. An assortment of typefaces in one size.

Format. Size, shape, and general makeup of a publication.

Four-Color Process. Reproduction of full-color illustrations by the combination of plates for yellow, blue, red, and black ink. All color illustrations are separated photographically into these four primary colors. The four-color process is applicable to the letterpress, offset, and gravure processes.

Frame. (1) Single picture in film footage. (2) $\frac{1}{30}$ of a second in TV, $\frac{1}{24}$ of a second in film. (3) A single illustration on a storyboard.

Franchise-Building Services. Activities aimed at firmly establishing an organization's purposes in the minds of various publics— building a "franchise" with them for carrying on its functions.

Freelance. An unaffiliated writer, photographer, cameraman, artist, or other person who is available on assignment or contract basis.

FTP. File transfer protocol, a principal means for retrieving files from the Internet.

Gag. A created event, sometimes fictitious, developed by a press agent to seek media coverage.

Galley Proofs. Proofs not made up in page form, but drawn from the type as it stands in galley trays following composition, or as it is reproduced from cold (computer-generated) type.

Ghostwriter. One who writes speeches, articles, or other manuscripts that will be presented as the work of the employer or client.

Glossy Print. A smooth, shiny-surfaced photograph. Most suitable form for reproduction. Also called "glossy."

Goodwill. The favorable attitude of other persons or groups toward any person, institution, or group.

Gopher. Means of finding information on the Internet.

Grapevine. Informal word-of-mouth process of disseminating information or rumors.

Graphics. Illustrative material in all media.

Grassroots. The dispersed membership or constituency of an organization throughout a geographical area, such as a country or a region. The anonymous, scattered holds of opinions or attitudes.

Gravure. A form of intaglio printing.

Halftone. A screened reproduction of a photograph, painting, or drawing.

Handout. Publicity release, especially when it is widely distributed rather than given as an exclusive.

Hard Sell. Overt, forceful effort to persuade, such as advertising about a product's merits or a direct argument on behalf of an idea.

Head. Headline or title of a story.

Headnote. Short text before beginning of an article, usually featuring its highlights and information about the author.

High-tech. A condition involving extensive use of sophisticated technology.

Hold. Refrain from publishing or broadcasting until authorization is given.

Hold for Release. Material not to be printed or broadcast until a designated time or under specific conditions.

Home Page. Entry point to a World Wide Web site.

Hometown Stories. Stories, prepared for the local newspapers, of individuals who are participating in an event or activity.

House Magazine. Internal publication.

Human Interest. Feature material appealing to emotions, such as humor, sympathy, or passion.

Hypertext. Text that has links within it, to allow users to jump from section to section in a document.

Image. The subconscious impression a person has of an organization, institution, or person. Based on the interaction of all exposures he has had to the subject of the image. A "corporate image" is the supposed impression toward a company held in common by a whole public.

Input. Information fed into a data processing system. By extension, information obtained in the process of human considerations.

Insert. Printed matter prepared for enclosure with letters. Also, new material inserted into a story already written.

Institutional Investors. Nonpersonal holders of blocks of securities: mutual funds, insurance companies, pension funds, banks, universities, etc.

Interactive. Television technologies that permit viewer participation, such as two-way cable, videotex, or the optical video disc.

Interface. Association between two organizations, individuals, or forces.

Internal Communications. Communications with personnel or membership of a company or organization.

Internal Publication. A publication directed to the personnel or membership of a company or organization.

Internet. Network of connected computer networks that allow computers in one part of the world to instantly access computers in another.

Interviewer. A person who asks respondents the questions specified on a questionnaire in an opinion or market survey. Also, a person who seeks information for media use—a newspaper reporter, a television or radio panel show moderator, etc.

Issue. A matter that causes concern to an organization.

Issue and Opportunity Management. Analyses, plans, and activities aimed at dealing in a systematic manner with the issues and opportunities faced by an organization.

Jump and Jump Head. Continuation of a story on a later page in a publication, and the head put on the continuation.

Junket. A trip for press people at the expense of the organization seeking publicity. Usually based on a need to see what is distant from press centers, such as a new plant, a new resort, or a convention. Many media will not accept payment of expenses for such trips.

Kicker. A short line over the headline.

Kill. To eliminate part or all of a story or to discontinue a program or broadcast.

LAN. Local area network, a small system of computers that are linked together by a "server."

Lc. Lower-case letters. The small letters in the alphabet.

Laser Printing. A process of reproducing complete filled-in forms or other documents rapidly, in single electronic actions.

Layout. An outline for presentation of material for publication or reproduction within the confines of the previously designated format.

Lead (pronounced "leed"). The beginning of a newspaper story. Also, a tip on a potential story.

Leaflet. A printed piece, usually of four pages.

Letterpress. A printing process in which the ink is applied to raised type and plates and then applied to the paper by direct pressure.

Letterspacing. Placing thin spaces between letters.

Light Pen. Tube with photocell used to edit or revise text stored in computer and displayed on cathode ray tube.

Line Function. In a large organization the "line" structure is the operating force, such as managers and personnel of manufacturing plants or officers of combat units in the armed forces. A function of this line is something to be executed, rather than basic planning.

Lineprinter. Computer-related device for printing out complete lines of copy from the memory bank.

Linotype. Machine that sets full lines of type in metal.

Listserve. A program that permits maintaining an E-mail mailing list.

Lithographic Printing. Transferring an inked image from a smooth surface to paper by a chemical (mutual repulsion of grease and water) process. Kinds of lithographic printing: Planography, offset lithography, offset printing, photo-offset.

Live. Performed or reported now; also, not recorded.

Localize. Make specific references to a locality in a mass-distributed story or broadcast.

Logotype. Emblem or mark used to identify a given company.

Long Shot (LS). Photo or film shot from a distance.

Low-Power TV. Television of low wattage, intended for narrow community coverage.

Management. Those persons charged with the responsibilities of determining company or organization policy and planning and directing operations.

Management Chart. A diagram that illustrates the lines of responsibility and authority within an organization.

Manual. A compilation of directions and instructions in book or booklet form.

Mass Publications. Periodicals having a wide variety of appeal and a large, general circulation.

Masthead. Name of publication and staff, usually boxed and appearing in each issue.

Mat or Matrix. A papier-mâché impression of a printing plate, from which a lead casting can be made to reproduce the material on the original plate.

Matte. Dull finish on illustrations. Needed to prevent glare from stills on television.

Media. Avenues through which public relations messages are transmitted. Common media (singular is "medium") include newspapers, magazines, radio, books, music, paintings, cartoons, posters, leaflets, brochures, speeches, window displays, bumper stickers, trade or business papers, envelope stuffers, calendars, house publications, motion pictures, slide films, television.

Merchandising. Promotion of a product or idea by making it attractive, easier to buy, and/or more desirable.

Microwave. A high-frequency radio wave (above 500 megahertz) that can be used for the transmission of TV signals. Microwaves are easily disturbed by trees or buildings in their path.

Microwave Relay. Sending broadcasts from one point to another by ultrahigh frequency signals.

Mock-Up. A scale model used for study, testing, or instruction.

Model. (1) A person employed to pose in photographs, style shows, or other activities. (2) A representation of a large entity, to provide a smaller, inexpensive means of visualizing it. A model of a new skyscraper, for instance, may be shown in a company's lobby or used in photography to approximate the appearance of the building.

Model Release. A document signed by a model allowing use of pictures of the model.

Monitor. (1) TV receiver used to watch broadcasts or closed-circuit signals. (2) To review a broadcast station's content.

Morgue. The department of a publication that contains clippings, reference materials, illustrations, and other source materials. It sometimes incorporates the traditional library of reference works.

Multiple-Channel Approach. Impressing an idea or subject on an audience by utilizing many types of media and communications, to "surround" them with it.

Multiplier Effect. Using a communications device that stimulates many others to disseminate the same information. For example, a folder of press stories that members of an organization in many areas use with local media.

Narrowcasting. Broadcasting to a small segment of the total populace, usually on the basis of interest in the subject.

Network. Linkup of two or more broadcast stations to carry the same material. Also, two or more linked computers.

Newsletter. A publication in letter-size format, usually issued periodically.

Newsprint. The paper on which most newspapers are printed. Also used for inexpensive printed material.

Online. Any situation when two computers are talking to each other.

Op Ed. Opposite editorial. The page facing the editorial page in newspapers. Some are now devoted to statements of views from non-staff sources.

Open End. Broadcast material in which time is left at the beginning or end for addition of material by the station.

Open House. An event in which a company invites its employees, dealers, suppliers, and/or community to visit it and see how it operates. A device of employee, stockholder, supplier, dealer, and/or community relations.

Opinion. A person's view on an issue or subject as he or she articulates it. More conscious than an attitude.

Optical Center. A point equidistant from the left and right sides of a sheet of paper and five-eighths of the way from the bottom.

Optical Reader. Electronic reader (or "scanner") of printed material.

Outline. The skeleton or gist of an article or a program.

Outtake. Filmed or taped material not used in the final program.

Over the Counter. Stocks not sold on a registered exchange.

Over the Transom. Pertaining to material submitted to a medium without its request. Unsolicited offerings.

Overline. *See* **Kicker.**

Page Proof. Proof of the type and engraved matter as it will appear in final page form.

Pamphlet. A printed piece of a few pages, with a paper cover. Often interchangeable with "leaflet," except that a pamphlet may contain more pages than the word "leaflet" will permit.

Panel. An area of type different in size, weight, or design from the text and usually wholly or partially surrounded by text. Also, a group of persons used in research to provide information repeatedly. Also, a group sharing discussion on a subject at a meeting.

Pasteup. A dummy.

Photo Composition. A method of setting type photographically to produce proofs on paper or film without the need for handling and inking metal types.

Photo Montage. A layout of photographs in which the pictures blend into each other to give the effect of unity.

Picturephone. Telephone service providing simultaneous transmission of voice and picture.

Pitch. The idea that the source wants to get across to the audience. To "make your pitch" is to present your argument.

Pix. Photographs.

Planting. Placing publicity material with the media.

Plug. A free and favorable reference.

Point and Pica. The standard unit of measure used by printers is the point. It is 0.1384 inch. For most purposes consider that 72 points equal one inch. The pica is exactly 12 points, thus there are 6 picas to the inch. Lengths of type lines are specified in picas. Half picas can be used, never quarters or thirds of a pica. Sizes of type and amounts of leading are specified in points.

Policy. The basic tenets of an organization that determine the pattern of its attitudes and activities.

Poll. A survey of the attitudes, opinions, and/or desires of a specified group of people.

Pose. Compose a message and send it to a listserve or Usenet group.

Position Paper. A document that presents an organized exposition of an organization's position on a given issue. It may be used with the media, with government bodies, or in other ways.

Posture of Receptivity. Readiness of a person to receive and respond to communications from a given source.

Precinct Principle. Organization of a campaign through delegation of local responsibilities to chosen leaders in each community, as in the precincts of a city in a political campaign.

Presentation. Offering of a program or services at a meeting. May involve written materials, graphic displays, films, or other materials.

Press Agentry. Seeking publicity by creating news of a flighty or dubious sort.

Press Conference. A meeting called to inform members of the press about an event or news subject, and to provide them an opportunity to ask questions and explore their areas of interest in the subject.

Prestige. The reputation and standing of a person, institution, or group.

Pretesting. Sampling techniques in a survey to be confident they are right before setting up the complete survey pattern.

Price-Earnings Level or Ratio. Multiple of the stock market price of a security on the basis of its current earnings per share. For example, a stock selling at $100 and having current after-tax earnings of $10 a year would be at a 10-to-1 price-earnings level.

Prime Time. Broadcast hours when the potential audience is largest—usually weekday evenings.

Program. The planned outline of activities for a campaign.

Promotion. Special activities designed and intended to create and stimulate interest in a person, product, organization, or cause.

Proof. Inked impression of type and engraved matter. The process of taking the impression is called "pulling a proof."

Propaganda. An effort to influence the opinion of others.

Proposal. Materials organized to offer plans for a program or services. A proposal may be used at a presentation or submitted by mail or hand delivery.

Provider. An entity (university, association, corporation, or private business) that provides Internet access.

Proxy. Written authorization given by a stockholder to someone else to vote his or her stock.

Proxy Fight. Combative effort by a stockholder or group to win the voting support of stockholders holding the controlling number of shares.

Proxy Statement. Document required by government regulation and stock exchanges, detailing for stockholders all information pertinent to a request for their vote or proxy on any question or group of questions to be acted on at a meeting of stockholders.

Public (plural, publics). Any group of individuals that a public relations program seeks to influence. A committee of three may be a public; so may a firm's stockholders, its employees, its customers, its community; so may a legislative body, the entire nation, or the world.

Public Relations. All activities and attitudes intended to judge, adjust to, influence, and direct the opinion of any group or groups of persons in the interest of any individual, group, organization, public or private institution, or business. Also, helping an organization and its publics accommodate to each other.

Publicity. A technique of public relations. A message purposefully planned, executed, and distributed through selected media to further the particular interest of the client without specific payment to media.

Puffery. Exaggeration or unsubstantiated material appearing in publicity.

Punch. Emphasis or vigor in story or broadcast material.

Put in Play. Make a bid for a company that attracts other bidders and so creates an active market.

Quality Circle. A group within a workplace devoted to seeking improved methods of operating.

Quarterly Report. Statement of a company's sales and earning experience for three months. Issued for the first, second, and third quarters of the year. Often contains information on other developments in the quarter reported.

Query. Written inquiry to an editor or broadcaster outlining a proposed story or treatment.

Questionnaire. The body of questions asked of persons interviewed in a survey of attitudes, opinions, intentions, desires, activities.

Quote. (1) A quotation used in a story. (2) Quotation mark. (3) A price estimate.

Rear Screen Projection. Projection of transparencies behind a speaker or newscaster so they will be seen as background.

Recap. Recapitulation of subject matter, series, or program.

Reduce. Decrease the size of any visual item in reproducing it.

Registrar. An agent or officer of a corporation appointed to keep a record of its securities and to certify that the name on each certificate issued is that of the owner of record. Often a bank or trust company.

Release. *n.* A manuscript prepared for issuance to the press or broadcast media. *v.* To issue material to the press or broadcast media.

Release Date. The time and day on which information issued to the press and broadcast media is to be exposed to public view. A release date is justified when it coincides with an occurrence that has not yet taken place, such as a speech.

Reprint. A second or new impression of a print work (book, magazine or newspaper article; chart or graph; picture or map; and the like). If a photographic process is used, the subject may be enlarged ("blown up") for framing, window display, or poster; or reduced. Additions or deletions can readily be made before reprinting.

Respondent. The person of whom questions are asked in a survey.

Retouch. To improve by artwork the definition of photographs for halftone reproduction.

Reverse. To run printed material (especially cuts) with white type on a dark background. Also, in making a cut from a picture, to turn over the negative so that everything falls in the opposite direction.

Review. Commentary on event, art, or performance.

Roman Type. Most commonly used kind of type as distinguished from Text, Script, and Gothic. Roman type, distinguished by serifs, comes in modern and old-style groups.

Rough. Preliminary draft of manuscript or visualization of graphic.

Rough Cut. First editing of film before effects, titles, and sound have been added.

Roundup. Story prepared from material derived from various sources.

Sample. The portion of the total population involved in a survey, of whom questions are asked. The sample is intended to be representative of the population involved.

Sans Serif. Letters without serifs.

Satellite. An electronics-equipped space object used to receive and direct broadcast signals.

Scaling. Measuring and marking illustrations for engravings.

Security Analyst. Financial analyst.

Segue (say'-gway). An uninterrupted transition, as when one scene moves directly into another in a motion picture.

Selective Attention. Singling out particular objects from among many for concentration of the mind.

Selective Reinforcement. Tendency to pick out of many ideas or messages those that confirm an opinion or attitude already held.

Self-Cover. Printed matter in booklet form without a protective cover.

Self-Mailer. Printed folder prepared for mailing without an envelope.

Serifs. Small decorative lines at the ends of elements on letters. The most distinguished feature of some faces.

Sidebar. A secondary story that accompanies a main news story or feature article, sometimes in a box set into the larger story.

Signal. The detectable impulse by which sound, images, and date are conveyed electronically or optically, either through the air or by wire.

Silver Print. Proof, taken on sensitized paper, of negative for offset plate. Used as final proof before plates are made. Sometimes referred to as a Vandyke, or simply "blues."

Simulcast. Simultaneous transmission over television and radio.

Slant. Emphasis given in a story or program.

Slick. A publication published on coated, smooth paper.

Slides. Individual film frames that are projected onto a screen to serve as visual accompaniment to an oral presentation.

Slug Lines. Words placed at the upper left of a page to identify the story during typesetting and makeup of a publication.

Soft News. Feature news or news that has no immediate timeliness.

Soft-Sell. Indirect, subtle effort to persuade without overt presentation of arguments on the issue. Motivation by indirect techniques.

Software. Programs used in computers and word processors containing the information to be processed or the instructions for processing.

Spike. To kill copy.

Split Play. Treatment of a news event in which one side of an issue is presented prominently first, and the other side not until later. Often results from second party being unprepared or late in issuing its information.

Split Run. Publication in part of the total circulation of a newspaper or magazine.

Split Screen. Two or more images shown simultaneously in a TV transmission.

Spread. An advertisement, group of related photographs, or copy that occupies two facing pages in a publication, usually without separation by "gutters," and usually printed from a single plate.

Squib. A short story in a newspaper or magazine. Sometimes, a short second heading that tells more about a long story.

Staff Function. Analysis, planning, or communications by an organization's headquarters, as opposed to the execution of tasks by the line or divisional forces.

Stet. Proofreader's designation to let copy stand—to disregard change marked previously.

Stock Letters (or stories, etc.). Letters prepared at a central office that are provided to members or others in various areas for their dissemination.

Story Angle or Peg. The distinctive interest element that makes a story notable or newsworthy.

Storyboard. Sequence of roughs, depicting the continuity of a television program or commercial.

Street Name. Securities that are held for the investor by his broker, and not identified with him, are listed on the stock registrations in the broker's name. Street names may be a shield of secrecy for buying up blocks in seeking to gain control of the company.

Stringer. A reporter in a given area who is available on call to cover stories for a medium headquartered elsewhere.

Stuffer. A printed piece intended for insertion into something else being sent—pay envelopes, packages delivered to customers, with bills and receipts, or any other item that provides a medium of delivery.

Stunt. A created event developed by a press agent to evoke publicity.

Style Book. Manual setting up standards for handling copy—i.e., spelling, capitalization, abbreviations, word usages, and so on.

Subhead. Small heading within a news story or article to break up solid type mass and catch reader's eye.

Survey. An analysis of a market or state of opinion among a specified group of persons, groups, or institutions.

Tabloid. A newspaper format, smaller than standard size, and usually having five columns per page, each page being slightly more than half the size of a standard paper.

Takeover Bid. An effort to assume control of a publicly held company without the approval of the management. This may be through election by stockholders of a controlling number of directors, or through purchase of a controlling proportion of the shares.

Talent. Actors, performers, musicians, models—usually in television or motion pictures.

Tally Light. Red light on TV camera indicating its picture is being transmitted.

Teaser. Material that stimulates interest in forthcoming media content without providing specifics.

Telecommunications. Long-distance transmission of signals.

Teleconference. A conference involving two or more locations, conducted by transmitting pictures and sound by cable or satellite.

Teletex. The process of sending letters and manuscripts from one's word processor or computer to someone else's.

Teletext. Information received on the home TV screen in written form, such as shopping notes, stock market reports, news bulletins, weather news, etc.

Teletype. An electronic system of transmitting information in typewritten form. Used in the operation of the various public relations newswires, as well as by the Associated Press and United Press International.

Teletypesetting. Setting type from punched tape, enabling one source to provide exact typeset material to many linotype locations.

Tender Offer. Offer to purchase a designated number of shares of a corporation at a specified price by a specified date. This is often, but not always, intended to acquire enough shares to control the corporation.

Terminal. A place in a communication system where information can either leave or enter.

Test Group. A group selected for reaction to or use of a product or an idea.

Testing. To sample the opinion of acceptance of a carefully selected and well-defined area or group on any particular product, event, or question. Tabulated results frequently serve as the basis for determining the direction of a larger campaign.

Text. The body of any written material—the copy.

Threshold of Consciousness. The point at which a given subject passes out of the mass of unperceived subjects into the awareness of the individual.

Tie-In. A promotional technique used to describe the joint (or combined) activities of two or more organizations on one project.

Tipping-In. In producing printed materials, a process used to insert or attach extra pages or other items. Example: pages 5 and 6 of a 10-page booklet are tipped-in; a swatch in a textile catalog is also tipped-in.

Trade Publications. Periodicals dealing with matters of interest to a particular trade or industry.

Transfer Agent. An office, usually a bank or trust company, that acts for a corporation in transferring stock from one owner to another.

Transparency. A plastic or film reproduction, through which light can be projected to show its full contents on a screen. Color transparencies are commonly used in making color plates for printing.

Trim. (1) In publications, reducing the length of copy. (2) In printing, cutting pages to final size.

Trim size. The dimensions the final printed item will be after being cut and/or folded.

Type Page. The printed area on a page. The area around the type page is the margins. Inside margins, adjacent to the fold, are called gutters.

Typo. Typographical error.

UHF (ultrahigh frequency). The added band of television broadcast channels in the U.S., added to the 2-to-12 group to provide added outlets.

U/lc. Upper and lower case; capitals and small letters.

Update. Bring the information in a story up-to-date.

Uplink. The beaming of signals from the earth to a satellite.

Upload. Send a file from one computer to a remote system.

Upper Case. Another term for capital letters, small letters being "lower case."

Usenet. An international meeting place where people gather to communicate via computer.

Vandyke. *See* **Silver Print**.

VHF (very high frequency). The original band of television broadcast channels in the U.S., 2 though 12.

Video. The visual television signal.

Videoconference. A temporary private TV network in which large-screen TV sets, cameras, and satellite uplinks and downlinks are used to join numerous remote locations for anything from a business meeting to an entertainment event.

Videophone. Combined telephone and television transmission by which voice and sight of the two parties are received at each end.

Videotape. A recording of the video and sound of television subject matter.

Vignette. Feature, usually a sidebar, providing a humorous, poignant, etc., look at a subject.

Visual Display Terminal (VDT). Displays copy selected from computer memory and allows editing.

VCR. Videocassette recorder.

White Paper. A document prepared as an argument in behalf of an organization on a given issue. It may be more argumentative than a position paper.

Work Print. Print of a film used for first editing.

World Wide Web. A hypertext-based, distributed information system. Users may create, edit, and browse hypertext documents.

Wrong Font (w.f.). Letter from one font of type mixed with another.

Zinc Etching. A line engraving etched in zinc.

BIBLIOGRAPHY

Public relations

Black, Sam and Melvin L. Sharpe. *Practical Public Relations*. Prentice-Hall, 1983.

Brody, E. W. *The Business of Public Relations*. Praeger, 1987.

Brody, E. W. *Public Relations Programming and Production*. Praeger, 1988.

Budd, John. *Street Smart Public Relations*. Turtle, 1992.

Cantor, Bill (Chester Burger, ed.). *Experts In Action: Inside Public Relations*, 2nd ed. Longman, 1989.

Cohen, Paul. *A Public Relations Primer: Thinking and Writing in Context*. Prentice-Hall, 1987.

Cutlip, Scott. *Public Relations History: From the Seventeenth to the Twentieth Century*. L. Erlbaum, 1995.

Cutlip, Scott. *The Unseen Power: Public Relations. A History*. L. Erlbaum, 1994.

Cutlip, Scott M., Allen H. Center Broom. *Effective Public Relations*, 7th ed. Prentice-Hall, 1994.

Dozier, David and James & Larissa Grunig. *Manager's Guide to Excellence in Public Relations & Communication Management*. L. Erlbaum, 1995.

Grunig, James E. *Excellence in Public Relations and Communication Management*. L. Erlbaum, 1992.

Haberman, David A. and Harry A. Dolphin. *Public Relations: The Necessary Art*. Iowa State U Press, 2121 S. State Ave., Ames, IA 50010, 1988.

Harris, Thomas. *Choosing & Working with Your Public Relations Firm*. NTC Business, 1992.

Harris, Thomas L. *The Marketer's Guide to Public Relations*. John Wiley, 1993.

Hendrix, Jerry A. *Public Relations Cases*. Wadsworth, 1988.

Hiebert, Ray E. *Courtier to the Crowd* (story of Ivey Lee). Iowa State U Press, Ames, IA, 1966.

Hiebert, Ray Eldon, ed. *Precision Public Relations*. Longman, 1988.

Jefkins, Frank. *Public Relations Techniques*, 2nd ed. Butterworth-Heinemann, 1994.

Kendall, Robert. *Public Relations Campaign Strategies: Planning for Implementation*. Harper Collins, 1991.

Lesly, Philip. *Bonanzas and Fool's Gold: Treasures and Dross from the Nuggetizing of Our Lives*. Philip Lesly Co., 1987.

Lesly, Philip. *Selections from Managing the Human Climate*. Philip Lesly Co., 1979.

Moss, Danny. *Public Relations in Practice: A Casebook*. Routledge, 1991.

Nager, Norman R. and T. Harrell Allen. *Public Relations: Management by Objectives*. University Press of America, 1991.

Nager, Norman and Richard Truitt. *Strategic Public Relations Counseling*. University Press of America, 1991.

New Technology and Public Relations. Institute for PR Research and Education, 1988.

Newsom, Doug and Alan Scot. *This Is PR: Realities of Public Relations*, 5th ed. Wadsworth, Belmont, CA, 1993.

Phillips, David. *Evaluating Press Coverage: A Practical Guide to Measurement and Cost Effectiveness*. Kogan Page, 1992.

Report and Recommendations: 2d Task Force on Stature and Role of Public Relations. (Philip Lesly, Chairman). Public Relations Society of America, 1994.

Seitel, Fraser. *The Practice of Public Relations*, 6th ed. Prentice-Hall, 1995.

Wilcox, Dennis, et al. *Public Relations: Strategies & Tactics*, 4th ed. Harper College, 1995.

Public relations periodicals

Broadcasting. 1735 DeSales Street, NW, Washington, DC 20036. Weekly.

Bulldog Reporter. 2115 Fourth Street, Berkeley, CA 94710. Semi-monthly.

Currents. Case. Monthly.

Channels. PR Publishing, POB 600, Exeter, NH 03833-0600. (603) 778-0514. Monthly.

Communication Briefings. 140 S. Broadway, Pittman, NJ 08071. Monthly.

Community Relations Report. POB 924, Bartlesville, OK 74005. (918) 336-2267. Monthly.

Corporate Annual Report Newsletter. Ragan Communications, 212 W. Superior Street, #200, Chicago, IL 60605. (312) 922-3336. Monthly.

Corporate Public Issues & Their Management. 207 Loundoun Street, SE, Leesburg, VA 22075. (703) 777-8450. Semi-monthly.

Investor Relations Newsletter. 350 W. Hubbard Street, Suite 440, Chicago, IL 60610. (312) 464-0300. Monthly.

Jack O'Dwyer's PR Newsletter. 271 Madison Avenue, New York, NY 10016. (212) 679-2471. Weekly.

Managing the Human Climate. Philip Lesly Co., 155 N. Harbor Drive, #5311, Chicago, IL. Bimonthly.

Newsletter on Newsletters. 44 W. Market Street, POB 311, Rhinebeck, NY 12572.

O'Dwyer's PR Marketplace. 271 Madison Avenue, New York, NY 10016. (212) 679-2471. Biweekly.

O'Dwyer's PR Services Report. See above. Monthly.

O'Dwyer's Washington Report. See above. Biweekly.

Party Line. 35 Sutton Place, New York, NY 10022. (212) 755-3487. Weekly.

PR Clock. 25 W. 39th Street, New York, NY 10018. Biweekly.

PR Reporter. Box 600, Dudley House, Exeter, NH 03833. Weekly.

PR Watch. 3318 Gregory Street, Madison, WI 53711. Quarterly.

Public Relations Tactics. Prsa. Monthly.

Public Relations News. 1201 Seven Locks Road, Potomac, MD 20854-3394. Weekly.

Public Relations Quarterly. 44 W. Market Street, POB 311, Rhinebeck, NY 12572.

Public Relations Review. 55 Old Post Road, #2, Greenwich, CT 06836-6200.

Ragan Report. 212 W. Superior Street, #200, Chicago, IL 60605. Weekly.

Special Events Report. 213 W. Institute Place, Chicago, IL 60610. (312) 944-1727. Biweekly.

Speechwriter's Newsletter. 212 W. Superior Street, #200, Chicago, IL 60605. (312) 922-9245. Weekly.

Public affairs

Dennis, Lloyd B., ed. *Practical Public Affairs in an Era of Change.* University Press of America. Available from Public Relations Society of America, New York, 1995.

Foundation for Public Affairs. *Public Interest Profiles.* Congressional Quarterly, 1991.

Leveraging State Government Relations. Public Affairs Council, Washington, DC, 1990.

Passarelli, Anne B. *Public Relations in Business, Government and Society: Bibliographic Guide.* Libraries Unlimited, 1989.

Post/Mahon. *Corporate Public Affairs.* Ballinger, 1989.

Remmes, Harold. *Lobbying for Your Cause.* Pilot Books, 103 Cooper Street, Babylon, NY 11702.

Shafer, Peter. *Adding Value to the Public Affairs Function: Using Quality to Improve Performance.* Public Affairs Council, 1994.

Trent, Judith and Robert Friedenburg. *Political Campaign Communication: Principles and Practices,* 2nd ed. Greenwood, 1991.

Winning at Grassroots. Public Affairs Council, 1019 19th Street, NW, Washington, DC 20036.

Wittenberg, Ernest and Elisabeth Wittenberg. *How to Win in Washington.* Basil Blackwell, 1994.

Publicity

Barhydt, James D. *Complete Book of Product Publicity.* AMACOM, 1987.

Bly, Robert. *Targeted Public Relations: How to Get Thousands of Dollars of Free Publicity for Your Product.* Seaver Books, 1994.

Ellmore, R. Terry. *NTC's Mass Media Dictionary.* NTC Business, 1991.

Goff, Christine Friesleben, ed. *The Publicity Process,* 3rd ed. Iowa State University Press, 2121 S. State Avenue, Ames, IA 50010, 1989.

Hilton, Jack. *How to Meet the Press: A Survival Guide.* Dodd, Mead & Co., 1987.

Howard, Carole and Wilma Mathews. *On Deadline: Managing Media Relations,* 2nd ed. Waveland, 1994.

Levine, Michael. *Guerilla PR: How to Wage an Effective Publicity Campaign—Without Going Broke.* Harper Business, 1994.

Lukaszewski, James. *Executive Action Emergency Media Relations Guide.* Lukaszewski, 1993.

Quinlan, Joseph. *Industrial Publicity.* Van Nostrand, 1983.

Yale, David. *The Publicity Handbook.* NTC Business, 1991.

Investor relations

A.R.3: The Corporate Annual Report & Corporate Image Planning Book. Marquis Who's Who, 1988.

Arfin, F. N. *Financial Public Relations.* Trans-Atlantic, 1994.

Bowman, Pat. *Handbook of Financial Public Relations.* Butterworth-Heinemann, 1993.

Rosenbaum, Michael. *Selling Your Story to Wall Street: The Art & Science of Investor Relations.* Probus, 1994.

Taggart, Philip W. *Taking Your Company Public.* AMACOM, 1990.

Public opinion and polling

Barzun, Jacques and Henry F. Graff. *The Modern Researcher*, 5th ed. HBJ College, 1992.

Bradburn, N. M. *Polls and Surveys.* Jossey-Bass, 1988.

Brody, William and Gerald Stone. *Public Relations Research.* Praeger, 1989.

Broom, Glen and David Dozier. *Using Research in Public Relations.* Prentice-Hall, 1989.

Pavlik, John V. *Public Relations: What Research Tells Us.* Sage, 1987.

Stempel, Guido and Bruce Westley. *Research Methods in Mass Communication*, 2nd ed. Prentice-Hall, 1989.

Communications and persuasion

Agee, Warren K. and others. *Introduction to Mass Communications*, 9th ed. Harper & Row, 1988.

Aronson, Elliot. *Age of Propaganda: The Everyday Use & Abuse of Persuasion.* W.H. Freeman, 1991.

Bateman, David and Norman Sigband. *Communicating in Business*, 3rd ed. Harper College, 1988.

Becker, Samual and Churchill Roberts. *Discovering Mass Communication*, 3rd ed. Harper Collins, 1992.

Berelson, Bernard and Gary Steiner. *Human Behavior.* Harcourt, Brace & World, NY, 1967.

Bittner, John R. *Mass Communication*, 4th ed. Prentice-Hall, 1986.

Boettinger, Henry. *Moving Mountains.* Macmillan, 1975.

Brody, E. W. *Communication Tomorrow: New Audiences, New Technologies, New Media.* Praeger, 1990; Greenwood, 1990.

Brody, E. W. *Managing Communication Processes: From Planning to Crisis Response.* Greenwood, 1991.

Creedon, Pamela J. *Women in Mass Communications*, 2nd ed. Sage, 1993.

Lebon, Gustave. *The Crowd.* Macmillan, New York, 1925; E. Benn, London, 1952.

Lesly, Philip. *How We Discommunicate.* AMACOM, NY, 1979.

Lesly, Philip. *Selections from Managing the Human Climate.* Philip Lesly. Co., 155 N. Harbor Drive, Suite 5311, Chicago, IL 60601, 1979.

Lippmann, Walter. *Public Opinion.* Macmillan, NY, 1965.

McLuhan, Marshall. *Understanding Media.* McGraw-Hill, NY, 1964.

Redding, W. Charles. *Corporate Manager's Guide to Better Communication.* Scott-Foresman, 1984.

Winett, Richard. *Information & Behavior: Systems of Influence.* Erlbaum, 1986.

Crises, emergencies, and issues

Bernstein, Alan. *Emergency Public Relations Manual*, 3rd ed. PASE, P.O. Box 1299, Highland Park, NJ 08904, 1988.

Dougherty, Devon. *Crisis Communications: What Every Executive Needs to Know.* Walker & Co., 1992.

Ewing, Raymond P. *Managing the New Bottom Line: Issues Management for Senior Executives.* Dow Jones Irwin, 1987.

Gottschalk, Jack. *Crisis Response: Inside Stories on Managing Image Under Siege.* Gale, 1993.

Heath, Nelson. *Issues Management.* Sage Inc., 1985.

Irvine, Robert B. *When You Are the Headline: Managing A Major News Story*. Dow Jones-Irwin, 1987.

Lesly, Philip. *Overcoming Opposition*. Prentice-Hall, 1984. Available from Philip Lesly Company.

Lukaszewski, James. *Executive Action Crisis Management Workbook*. Lukaszewski, 1993.

Lukaszewski, James. *Executive Action: Managing Litigation Visibility*. Lukaszewski, 1993.

Mitroff, Ian and Christine Pearson. *Crisis Management: A Diagnostic Guide for Improving Your Organization's Crisis-Preparedness*. Jossey Bass, 1993.

Pinsdorf, Marion. *Communicating When Your Company Is Under Siege*. Lexington Books, 1986.

Special events

Chase's Calendar of Events. Contemporary Books, 1998.

Ernst & Young Staff. *The Complete Guide to Special Events Management*. John Wiley, 1992.

Geiet, Ted. *Make Your Events Special*. Folkworks, 39 W. 14th Street, New York, NY 10011, 1986.

Management and policy

Budd, John. *CEO Credibility: The Management of Reputation*. Turtle Publishing, 1993.

Carter, David E. *American Corporate Identity No. 10*. Art Direction, 1995.

Deal/Kennedy. *Corporate Cultures*. Addison-Wesley, 1984.

Garbett, Thomas F. *How to Build a Corporation's Identity and Project Its Image*. Lexington Books, 1988.

Graham, John and Wendy Havlick. *Mission Statements: A Guide to the Corporate and Non-Profit Sectors*. Garland, 1994.

Gray, James G., Jr. *Managing the Corporate Image: The Key to Public Trust*. Greenwood, 1986.

Green, Peter. *Reputation Is Everything: How to Safeguard Your Company's Image*. Irwin, 1994.

Gregory, James R., Weichmann, Jack G., et al. *Marketing Corporate Image; The Company as Your Number 1 Product*. NTC Business, 1993.

Hart, Norman. *Effective Corporate Relations: Applying Public Relations in Business and Industry*. McGraw-Hill, 1987.

Haywood, Roger. *Managing Your Reputation: How to Plan & Run Communications Programs That Win Friends & Build Success*. McGraw-Hill, 1994.

Heath, Robert. *Management of Corporate Communications*. L. Erlbaum, 1994.

LaBorde, Allyson. *Corporate Image: Communicating Visions and Values*. Conference Board, No. 1038, 1993.

Leavitt, Harold J. *Managerial Psychology*. U. of Chicago Press, Chicago, IL, 1978.

Lesly, Philip. *Bonanzas and Fool's Gold: Treasures and Dross from the Nuggetizing of Our Lives*. Philip Lesly Company, Chicago, IL, 1987.

Lesly, Philip. *The People Factor: Managing the Human Climate*. Dow Jones-Irwin, Homewood, IL, 1974.

Olins, Wally. *Corporate Identity*. Harvard Business School Press, 1990, 1992.

Sauerhaft, Stan and Chris Atkins. *Image Wars: Protecting Your Company When There Is No Place to Hide*. John Wiley, 1989.

Sobel, Marion. *Shaping the Corporate Image: An Analytical Guide for Executive Decision Makers*. Greenwood, 1992.

Wiener, Valerie. *Power Communications: Positioning Yourself for High Visibility*. NYU Press, 1994.

Cultural diversity

Cox, Taylor, Jr. *Cultural Diversity in Organizations: Theory, Research and Practice.* Berrett-Koehler, 1993.

Henderson, George. *Cultural Diversity in the Workplace: Issues and Strategies.* Quorum, 1994.

Sims, Ronald and Robert Dennehy. *Diversity and Differences in Organizations: An Agenda for Answers and Questions.* Greenwood, 1993.

Trompenaars, Fons. *Riding the Waves of Culture: Understanding Cultural Diversity in Business.* Irwin, 1994.

Political public relations

Armstrong, Richard. *The Next Hurrah: The Communications Revolution in American Politics.* Morrow, 1988.

Cook, Fred J. *Lobbying in American Politics.* Watts, NY, 1976.

Government/Press Connection: Press Officers and Their Offices. Brookings Institution, 1775 Massachusetts Ave. NW, Washington, DC 20036, 1984.

Morrison, Catherine. *Managing Corporate Political Action Committees.* The Conference Board, 1986.

Sabato, Larry J. *The Rise of Political Consultants: New Ways of Winning Elections.* Basic Books, NY, 1981.

Trent/Friedenburg. *Political Campaign Communication: Principles and Practices.* Praeger, 1983.

Yorke, Harvey and Liz Doherty. *The Candidate's Handbook for Winning Local Elections.* Box 252, Novato, CA 94948, 1982.

Community relations

Kruckeberg/Stark. *Public Relations and Community: A Reconstructed Theory.* Praeger, 1988.

Making Community Relations Pay Off. Public Affairs Council, 1987.

Yarrington, Roger. *Community Relations Handbook.* Longman, 1983.

Journalistic writing

Aronson, Merry and Donald Spetner. *The Public Relations Writer's Handbook.* Free Press, 1993.

Bivins, Thomas. *Handbook for Public Relations Writing.* NTC Business, 1991.

Gompertz, Rolf. *Publicity Writing for Television and Film.* Word Doctor, 1992.

Hough, George A. *News Writing.* Houghton Mifflin, NY, 1981.

Jacobi, Peter. *Writing with Style: The News Story and the Feature.* Ragan Communications, 1982.

Maloney, Martin and P. M. Rubenstein. *Writing for the Media.* Prentice-Hall, 1981.

McNaughton, Harry H. *Proofreading & Copyediting.* Hastings House, Philadelphia, 1973.

Editors of UPI Broadcast Services. *United Press International Broadcast Stylebook.* UPI, New York.

Television and radio

Blythin/Samovar. *Communicating Effectively on Television.* Wadsworth, 1985.

Chambers/Asher. *TV PR: How to Promote Yourself, Your Product/Service or Your Organization on TV.* Prima, P.O. Box 1260 TV, Rocklin, CA 95677, 1987.

Getting Your Public Relations Story on TV/Radio. Pilot Books, 103 Cooper, Babylon, NY 11702, 1986.

If You Want Air Time: A Handbook for Publicity Chairmen. National Association of Broadcasters, Washington, DC (Pamphlet).

Klepper, Michael. *Getting Your Message Out.* Prentice-Hall, 1984.

Radio Interview Guide. Book Promotions, 26 E. 33rd St., New York, 10016, 1988.

Schwartz, Tony. *The Responsive Chord.* Anchor Press-Doubleday, Garden City, NY, 1974.

Employee relations and internal communications

Arnold, Edmund. *Editing the Organizational Publication.* Ragan Communications, 1982.

Beach, Mark. *Editing Your Newsletters*, 3rd ed. Coast to Coast Books, 1988.

Bivins, Thomas and William E. Ryan. *How to Produce Creative Publications: Traditional Techniques and Computer Applications.* NTC Business, 1992.

Corrado, Frank. *Communicating With Employees.* Crisp Publishing, 1994.

Employee Opinion Surveys: Guide to Measuring Employee Attitudes. Anderson Press, Box 774, Madison Square Station, NY.

Fallon, William. *Effective Communication on the Job.* AMACOM, NY, 1981.

How to Prepare and Write Your Employee Handbook. AMACOM, 1984.

Larkin, T. J. and Sandar Larkin. *Communicating Change . . . Winning Employee Support for Business Goals.* McGraw-Hill, 1994.

Reuss, Carol and Donn Silvis. *Inside Organizational Communication*, 2nd ed. Longman, NY, 1984.

Williams, Patrick. *Employee Annual Report.* Lawrence Ragan Communications Inc., Chicago, IL, 1986.

Graphic arts, printing, and production

Baird, Russell, et al. *The Graphics of Communication/Typography, Layout, Design, Production,* 5th ed. Holt, Rinehart, Winston, 1987.

Beach, Mark. *Editing Your Newsletter*, 3rd ed. Coast to Coast Books, 2934 NE 16th Avenue, Portland, OR 97212, 1988.

Beach, Mark, et al. *Getting It Printed: How to Work with Printers/Graphic Arts Services.* North Light Books, 1993.

Bivins, Thomas. *Fundamentals of Successful Newsletters.* NTC, 1994.

The Complete Guide to Creating Successful Brochures. Asher-Gallent Press, 131 Heartland Boulevard, Brentwood, NY 11717, 1988.

Conover, Theodore. *Graphic Communications Today.* West Co., 1985.

Crow, Wendell. *Communication Graphics.* Prentice-Hall, 1986.

Douglis, Philip. *Pictures for Organizations: How and Why They Work as Communication.* Lawrence Ragan Communications Inc., 1982.

Downs, Matthews. *How to Manage Employee Publications.* Joe Williams Communications, Inc., P.O. Box 924, Bartlesville, OK 74005, 1988.

Ganim, Barbara. *The Designer's Commonsense Business Book.* NTC, 1993.

Hudson, Howard Penn. *Publishing Newsletters.* Scribner's, 1988.

Lefferts, Robert. *Elements of Graphics: How to Prepare Charts/Graphics for Effective Reports.* Harper & Row, 1981.

Marsh, Patrick. *Messages That Work: Guide to Communication Design.* Educ. Tech. Publications, 1983.

Napoles, Veronica. *Corporate Identity Design.* Von Nostrand Reinhold, 1988.

Production Yearbook. Colton Press, NY, annual.

Skillin/Gay. *Words Into Type.* Prentice-Hall, 1974.

Speeches and writing

Cotmier, Robin. *Error-Free Writing*. Prentice-Hall, 1995.

Detz, Joan. *How to Write and Give a Speech*, rev. ed. St. Martin's Press, 1992.

Klepper, Michael and Robert Gunther. *I'd Rather Die Than Give a Speech!* Irwin, 1993.

Newsom, Doug and Bob Carrell. *Public Relations Writing: Forms and Style*, 4th ed. Probus, 1995.

Starr, Douglas. *How to Handle Speechwriting Assignments*. Pilot Books, 1994.

Tucker, Kerry. *Public Relations Writing: An Issue Driven Behavioral Approach*, 2nd ed. Prentice-Hall, 1994.

Wilcox, Dennis L. and Lawrence W. Nolte. *Public Relations Writing and Media Techniques*, 2nd ed. Harper College, 1994.

Semantics and usage

Flesch, Rudolf. *The Art of Readable Writing*. Harper & Row, NY, 1974.

Follett, Wilson. *Modern American Usage*. Hill & Wang, NY, 1968.

Guidelines for Equal Treatment of the Sexes in McGraw-Hill Publications. McGraw-Hill.

Miller, Casey and Kate Swift. *The Handbook of Nonsexist Writing*. Barnes & Noble, NY, 1980.

Morris, William and Mary Morris. *Harper Dictionary of Contemporary Usage*. Harper & Row, NY and Evanston, 1975.

New York Times. *Manual of Style*. NY.

Stoughton, Mary. *Substance & Style: Instruction and Practice in Copyediting*. Editorial Experts, Alexandria, VA, 1989.

Strunk, William, Jr. and E. B. White. *The Elements of Style*. Macmillan, NY, 1979.

University of Chicago. *Manual of Style*. University of Chicago Press, Chicago.

Wentworth, Harold and Stuart Berg Flexner. *Dictionary of American Slang*. Crowell, NY.

Winkler, G. P. *The Associated Press Stylebook*. The Associated Press, NY.

Advertising

Burton, Philip W. and William Ryan. *Advertising Fundamentals*, 3rd ed. Publishing Horizons, Columbus, OH, 1981.

Controversy Advertising (Group Authorship). Hastings House, NY, 1977.

Garbett, Thomas F. *Corporate Advertising*. McGraw-Hill, NY, 1981.

Sethi, S. Prakash. *Handbook of Advocacy Advertising Concepts, Strategies, and Applications*. Ballinger, 1987.

Nonprofit organizations and fund-raising

Bates, Don. *Communicating and Moneymaking*. Heladon, Box 2827 Gcs, NY, 1979.

Broce, Thomas E. *Fund Raising*. University of Oklahoma Press, Norman, OK, 1986.

Connors, Tracy. *Nonprofit Organization Handbook*, 2nd ed. McGraw-Hill, 1988.

Gaby, Patricia V. and D. M. Gaby. *Nonprofit Organization Handbook: A Guide to Fundraising, Grants, Lobbying, Membership Building, Publicity and Public Relations*. Prentice-Hall, 1979.

Hauman, David J. *The Capital Campaign Handbook: How to Maximize Your Fund-Raising Campaign*. The Taft Group, 5130 MacArthur Boulevard, NW, Washington, DC 20016, 1987.

Riggs, Frank L. *The Health Care Facility's Public Relations Handbook*. Aspen, 1982.

Smith, W. J. *The Art of Raising Money*. AMACOM, 1985.

Careers in public relations

Careers in Public Relations. Public Relations Society of America, NY.

Field, Shelly. *Career Opportunities in Advertising & Public Relations*. Facts on File, 1990.

Morgan, Bradley. *Public Relations Career Directory*. 5th ed. Gale Research, 1993.

Rotman, Morris. *Opportunities in Public Relations Careers*. NTC Business, 1988.

Rudman, Jack. *Director of Public Information*. National Learning, 1991.

Rudman, Jack. *Public Relations Assistant*. National Learning, 1991.

Rudman, Jack. *Public Relations Director*. National Learning, 1991.

Rudman, Jack. *Public Relations Specialist*. National Learning, 1991.

Religion

Craig, Floyd. *Christian Communicators Handbook*. Broadman Press, Nashville.

Reagen, Michael and Doris Chertow. *The Challenge of Modern Church Public Relations*. Syracuse University, 1972.

Religious Public Relations Handbook for Local Congregations. Religious PR Council, 1988.

Selling Your Church in the Nineties. Religious PR Council, 1992.

Stevens, Robert E. and David Loudon. *Marketing for Churches and Ministries*. Haworth Press, 1992.

Small business

Bellavance, Diane. *Advertising and PR for a Small Business*, 5th ed. D. Bellavance Agency, 1991.

Carlson, Linda. *Publicity/Promotion Handbook: Complete Guide for Small Business*. Van Nostrand Reinhold, 1982.

Real estate

Guide to Effective Public Relations. National Association of Realtors.

Home Builders Publicity Manual. NAHB, 15th & M Streets, NW, Washington, DC 20005, 1984.

Marcus, Bruce. *Marketing Professional Services in Real Estate*. National Association of Realtors, 430 N. Michigan Avenue, Chicago, IL 60611, 1981.

Legal

Middleton, Kent and Bill Chamberlin. *Law of Public Communication*. 3rd ed. Longman, 1994.

Roschwalb, S. and B. Stark. *Litigation Public Relations: Courting Public Opinion*. Fred B. Rothman, NY.

Walsh, Frank. *Public Relations & The Law*. Books on Demand.

INDEX